PENGUIN BOOKS

THE COMPLETE BOOK OF THE OLYMPICS

David Wallechinsky is the coauthor of several books, including *The People's Almanac*, *The Book of Lists*, *What Really Happened to the Class of '65?*, and, most recently, *Significa*. He was first introduced to the joys of the Olympics by his father, Irving Wallace, who took him to the Summer Games at Rome in 1960. Mr. Wallechinsky lives in Santa Monica, California, with his wife, Flora Chavez, and their son, Elijah.

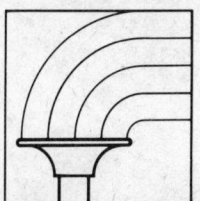

THE COMPLETE BOOK OF THE OLYMPICS

by DAVID WALLECHINSKY

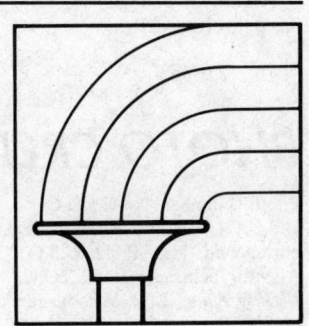

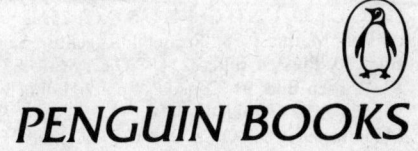

PENGUIN BOOKS

TO ELIJAH, A CHAMPION ALREADY

Penguin Books Ltd, Harmondsworth,
Middlesex, England
Penguin Books, 40 West 23rd Street,
New York, New York 10010, U.S.A.
Penguin Books Australia Ltd, Ringwood,
Victoria, Australia
Penguin Books Canada Limited, 2801 John Street,
Markham, Ontario, Canada L3R 1B4
Penguin Books (N.Z.) Ltd, 182–190 Wairau Road,
Auckland 10, New Zealand

First published in the United States of America
in simultaneous hardcover and paperback editions
by The Viking Press and Penguin Books 1984

Copyright © David Wallechinsky, 1984
Pictograms by Anita Giraldo copyright
© Anita Giraldo 1984
All rights reserved

Printed in the United States of America by
R.R. Donnelley & Sons Company,
Crawfordsville, Indiana
Set in Spectra Light and Times Roman
Designed by Beth Tondreau

PHOTO CREDITS

Photo Number 1, U.S.O.C.; 3, U.S.O.C.; 4, Popperfoto; 6, U.S.O.C.; 7, Brown Brothers; 8, U.S.O.C.; 9, Popperfoto; 10 Reportagebild; 11, AP; 12, U.S.O.C.; 13, U.S.O.C.; 14, Pressebild–Agentur Schirner; 15, U.S.O.C.; 17, U.S.O.C.; 18, *Herald and Weekly Times*, Ltd., Melbourne picture; 19, AP; 20, AP; 21, Popperfoto; 22, U.S.O.C.; 23, U.S.O.C.; 24, U.S.O.C.; 25, Popperfoto; 27, U.S.O.C.; 29, UPI; 31, Missouri Historical Society; 32, Missouri Historical Society; 33, Missouri Historical Society; 35, U.S.O.C.; 37, Mark Shearman; 39, UPI; 41, U.S.O.C.; 42, U.S.O.C.; 43, Popperfoto; 44, Pelham Books; 45, Popperfoto; 46, Reportagebild; 47, Reportagebild; 48, Pressen Bild; 49, Pressen Bild; 50, Pressen Bild; 51, U.S.O.C.; 52, U.S.O.C.; 53, J. Fairfax & Sons, Ltd.; 56, Pelham Books; 57, Toni Nett; 58, Toni Nett; 59, Toni Nett; 60, Toni Nett; 61, U.S.O.C.; 62, Reportagebild; 63, University of Michigan Archives; 65, UPI; 66, U.S.O.C.; 67, Courtesy of Erich Kamper; 68, Progress Publishers, Moscow; 69, U.S.O.C.; 70, U.S.O.C.; 74, U.S.O.C.; 75, U.S.O.C.; 76, Courtesy of Bob Mathias; 78, Pressebild–Agentur Schirner; 79, Pressen Bild; 80, Pressen Bild; 82, U.S.O.C.; 86, U.S.O.C.; 87, U.S.O.C.; 89, Pressen Bild; 91, Canada's Sports Hall of Fame; 92, U.S.O.C.; 93, Courtesy of Iolanda Balas; 94, U.S.O.C.; 95, Courtesy of Lia Manoliu; 96, U.S.O.C.; 97, U.S.O.C.; 98, Frederick Fliegner, Publ.; 100, U.S.O.C.; 101, Olympische Sports Bibliotek; 102, U.S.O.C.; 103, AP; 104, U.S.O.C.; 106, Hungarian Olympic Committee; 108, AP; 109, U.S.O.C.; 110, U.S.O.C.; 111, Reportagebild; 113, Erik Betting/Pressehusel; 115, Melbourne *Herald and Weekly Times*; 117, Popperfoto, 118, Novosti Press Agency; 119, Proteus Books, Ltd.; 120, U.S.O.C.; 122, Canada's Sports Hall of Fame; 124, The Academy of Motion Picture Arts and Sciences; 125, UPI; 127, U.S.O.C.; 128, Hungarian Olympic Committee; 129, Fizkultura Isdalesvo, Moscow; 130, Pressen Bild; 131, Reprinted by permission of Coward, McCann & Geoghegan, Inc., from *The Miracle Machine*, by Doug Gilbert, copyright © 1980 by P.L.T. Consultants, Ltd.; 132, U.S.O.C.; 135, from the David Webster Collection; 137, U.S.O.C.; 139, from the David Webster Collection; 140, Progress Publishers; 141, Frederick Fliegner; 145, Gerry Cranham of Sporting Colour Library; 149, U.S.O.C.; 150, Barton Silverman/*The New York Times*; 152, U.S.O.C.; 153, Pressen Bild; 154, U.S.O.C.; 157, U.S.O.C.; 159, AP; 161, Frederick Fliegner; 163, U.S.O.C.; 166, U.S.O.C.; 167, U.S.O.C.; 168, U.S.O.C.; 169, Keystone Press Agency; 170, U.S.O.C.; 172, U.S.O.C.; 173, Bill Hickey, reprinted with permission from the book *The Rings of Destiny*, © 1968, published by David McKay Co. Inc.; 175, Pressen Bild; 177, U.S.O.C.; 178, Pressebild–Agentur Schirner; 179, Pressen Bild.

CONTENTS

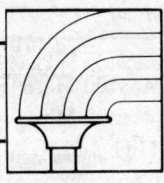

SUMMER GAMES

Photographs follow pages 120, 290, 428, and 552

THE OLYMPIC GAMES

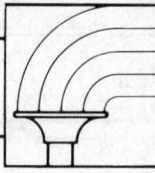

SUMMER

| | | | | COMPETITORS | | NATIONS |
				Men	Women	REPRESENTED
I	1896	ATHENS, GREECE	April 6–15	311	0	13
II	1900	PARIS, FRANCE	May 20–October 28	1319	11	22
III	1904	ST. LOUIS, U.S.A.	July 1–November 23	681	6	12
—	1906	ATHENS, GREECE	April 22–May 2	877	7	20
IV	1908	LONDON, GREAT BRITAIN	April 27–October 31	1999	36	23
V	1912	STOCKHOLM, SWEDEN	May 5–July 22	2490	57	28
VI	1916	BERLIN, GERMANY	Cancelled because of war	—	—	—
VII	1920	ANTWERP, BELGIUM	April 20–September 12	2543	64	29
VIII	1924	PARIS, FRANCE	May 4–July 27	2956	136	44
IX	1928	AMSTERDAM, HOLLAND	May 17–August 12	2724	290	46
X	1932	LOS ANGELES, U.S.A.	July 30–August 14	1281	127	37
XI	1936	BERLIN, GERMANY	August 1–16	3738	328	49
XII	1940	TOKYO, JAPAN; HELSINKI, FINLAND	Cancelled because of war	—	—	—
XIII	1944	LONDON, GREAT BRITAIN	Cancelled because of war	—	—	—
XIV	1948	LONDON, GREAT BRITAIN	July 29–August 14	3714	385	59
XV	1952	HELSINKI, FINLAND	July 19–August 3	4407	518	69
XVI	1956	MELBOURNE, AUSTRALIA*	November 22–December 8	2958	384	67
XVII	1960	ROME, ITALY	August 25–September 11	4738	610	83
XVIII	1964	TOKYO, JAPAN	October 10–24	4457	683	93
XIX	1968	MEXICO CITY, MEXICO	October 12–27	4750	781	112
XX	1972	MUNICH, GERMANY	August 26–September 10	5848	1299	122
XXI	1976	MONTREAL, CANADA	July 17–August 1	4834	1251	92†
XXII	1980	MOSCOW, U.S.S.R.	July 19–August 3	4265	1088	81
XXIII	1984	LOS ANGELES, U.S.A.	July 28–August 12			

*The equestrian events were held in Stockholm, Sweden, June 10–17, 1956.
†Most sources list this figure as 88. Cameroon, Egypt, Morocco, and Tunisia all boycotted the 1976 Olympics; however, athletes from each of these countries had already competed before the boycott was officially announced.

WINTER

				COMPETITORS		NATIONS
				Men	Women	REPRESENTED
I	1924	CHAMONIX, FRANCE	January 25–February 4	281	13	16
II	1928	ST. MORITZ, SWITZERLAND	February 11–19	468	27	25
III	1932	LAKE PLACID, U.S.A.	February 4–15	274	32	17
IV	1936	GARMISCH-PARTENKIRCHEN, GERMANY	February 6–16	675	80	28
—	1940	SAPPORO, JAPAN; ST. MORITZ, SWITZERLAND; GARMISCH-PARTENKIRCHEN, GERMANY	Cancelled because of war	—	—	—
—	1944	CORTINA D'AMPEZZO, ITALY	Cancelled because of war	—	—	—
V	1948	ST. MORITZ, SWITZERLAND	January 30–February 8	636	77	28
VI	1952	OSLO, NORWAY	February 14–25	623	109	30
VII	1956	CORTINA D'AMPEZZO, ITALY	January 26–February 5	686	132	32
VIII	1960	SQUAW VALLEY, U.S.A.	February 18–28	521	144	30
IX	1964	INNSBRUCK, AUSTRIA	January 29–February 9	986	200	36
X	1968	GRENOBLE, FRANCE	February 6–18	1081	212	37
XI	1972	SAPPORO, JAPAN	February 3–13	1015	217	35
XII	1976	INNSBRUCK, AUSTRIA	February 4–15	900	228	37
XIII	1980	LAKE PLACID, U.S.A.	February 14–23	833	234	37
XIV	1984	SAREJEVO, YUGOSLAVIA	February 7–19			

NATIONAL MEDAL TOTALS IN EACH OLYMPICS

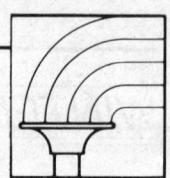

SUMMER

1896 Athens

	G	S	B*
USA	11	6	2
GRE	10	19	18
GER	7	5	3
FRA	5	4	2
GBR	3	3	1
HUN	2	1	3
AUT	2	0	3
AUS	2	0	0
DEN	1	2	4
SWI	1	2	0

1900 Paris

	G	S	B
FRA	29	41	32
USA	20	14	19
GBR	17	8	10
BEL	8	7	5
SWI	6	2	1
AUS	4	0	4
GER	3	2	2
DEN	2	3	2
ITA	2	2	0
HUN	1	3	2
HOL	1	1	3
CUB	1	1	0
SWE	1	0	1
CAN	1	0	1
AUT	0	3	3
NOR	0	2	3

IND	0	2	0
SPA	0	1	0

1904 St. Louis

	G	S	B
USA	80	86	72
GER	5	4	6
CUB	5	3	3
CAN	4	1	1
HUN	2	1	1
AUT	1	1	1
GRE	1	0	1
SWI	1	0	1
IRL	1	0	0
GBR	0	1	1

1906 Athens

	G	S	B
FRA	15	9	16
USA	12	6	5
GRE	8	13	13
GBR	8	11	6
ITA	7	6	3
SWI	5	4	2
GER	4	6	4
NOR	4	1	0
AUT	3	3	2
SWE	2	5	7
HUN	2	5	3
BEL	2	2	3
DEN	2	2	1
FIN	2	0	1
CAN	1	1	0
HOL	0	1	2
AUS	0	0	3
CZE	0	0	2
SAF	0	0	1

1908 London

	G	S	B
GBR	56	50	39
USA	23	12	12
SWE	8	6	11
FRA	5	5	9
GER	3	5	5
HUN	3	4	2
CAN	3	3	10
NOR	2	3	3
ITA	2	2	0
BEL	1	5	2
AUS	1	2	2
RUS	1	2	0
FIN	1	1	3
SAF	1	1	0
GRE	0	3	1
DEN	0	2	3
BOH	0	0	2
HOL	0	0	2
AUT	0	0	1

1912 Stockholm

	G	S	B
SWE	24	24	17
USA	23	19	19
GBR	10	15	16
FIN	9	8	9
FRA	7	4	3
GER	5	13	7
SAF	4	2	0
NOR	4	1	5
CAN	3	2	3
HUN	3	2	3
ITA	3	1	2
AUS	2	2	3

BEL	2	1	3
DEN	1	6	5
GRE	1	0	1
RUS	0	2	3
AUT	0	2	2
HOL	0	0	3

1920 Antwerp

	G	S	B
USA	41	27	28
SWE	19	20	24
GBR	15	15	13
FIN	15	10	9
BEL	14	11	10
NOR	13	7	8
ITA	13	5	5
FRA	9	19	13
HOL	4	2	5
DEN	3	9	1
SAF	3	4	3
CAN	3	3	3
SWI	2	2	7
EST	1	2	0
BRA	1	1	1
AUS	0	2	1
JAP	0	2	0
SPA	0	2	0
GRE	0	1	0
LUX	0	1	0
CZE	0	0	2
NZE	0	0	1

1924 Paris

	G	S	B
USA	45	27	27
FIN	14	13	10

	G	S	B
FRA	13	15	10
GBR	9	13	12
ITA	9	3	5
SWI	7	8	10
NOR	5	2	3
SWE	4	13	12
HOL	4	1	5
AUS	3	1	2
DEN	2	5	2
HUN	2	3	4
YUG	2	0	0
CZE	1	4	5
ARG	1	3	2
EST	1	1	4
SAF	1	1	1
URU	1	0	0
CAN	0	3	1
AUT	0	3	1
POL	0	1	1
JAP	0	0	1
ROM	0	0	1
NZE	0	0	1
POR	0	0	1
HAI	0	0	1

1928 Amsterdam

	G	S	B
USA	22	18	16
GER	10	7	14
FIN	8	8	9
SWE	7	6	12
ITA	7	5	7
SWI	7	4	4
FRA	6	10	5
HOL	6	9	4
HUN	4	5	0
CAN	4	4	7
GBR	3	10	7
ARG	3	3	1
DEN	3	1	2
CZE	2	5	2
JAP	2	2	1
EST	2	1	2
EGY	2	1	1
AUT	2	0	1
AUS	1	2	1
NOR	1	2	1
POL	1	1	3
YUG	1	1	3
SAF	1	0	2
IND	1	0	0
IRL	1	0	0
NZE	1	0	0
SPA	1	0	0
URU	1	0	0
BEL	0	1	2
CHI	0	1	0
HAI	0	1	0
PHI	0	0	1
POR	0	0	1

1932 Los Angeles

	G	S	B
USA	41	32	31
ITA	12	12	12
FRA	10	5	4
SWE	9	5	9
JAP	7	7	4
HUN	6	4	5
FIN	5	8	12
GER	4	12	5
GBR	4	7	5
AUS	3	1	1
ARG	3	1	0
CAN	2	5	8
HOL	2	5	0
POL	2	1	4
SAF	2	0	3
IRL	2	0	0
CZE	1	2	1
AUT	1	1	3
IND	1	0	0
DEN	0	3	3
MEX	0	2	0
SWI	0	1	0
NZE	0	1	0
LAT	0	1	0
PHI	0	0	3
SPA	0	0	1
URU	0	0	1

1936 Berlin

	G	S	B
GER	33	26	30
USA	24	20	12
HUN	10	1	5
ITA	8	9	5
FIN	7	6	6
FRA	7	6	6
SWE	6	5	9
JAP	6	4	8
HOL	6	4	7
GBR	4	7	3
AUT	4	6	3
CZE	3	5	0
ARG	2	2	3
EST	2	2	3
EGY	2	1	2
SWI	1	9	5
CAN	1	3	5
NOR	1	3	2
TUR	1	0	1
IND	1	0	0
NZE	1	0	0
POL	0	3	3
DEN	0	2	3
LAT	0	1	1
SAF	0	1	0
ROM	0	1	0
YUG	0	1	0
MEX	0	0	3
BEL	0	0	2
AUS	0	0	1
PHI	0	0	1
POR	0	0	1

1948 London

	G	S	B
USA	38	27	19
SWE	16	11	17
FRA	10	6	13
HUN	10	5	12
ITA	8	12	9
FIN	8	7	5
TUR	6	4	2
CZE	6	2	3
SWI	5	10	5
DEN	5	7	8
HOL	5	2	9
GBR	3	14	6
ARG	3	3	1
AUS	2	6	5
BEL	2	2	3
EGY	2	2	1
MEX	2	1	2
SAF	2	1	1
NOR	1	3	3
JAM	1	2	0
AUT	1	0	3
IND	1	0	0
PER	1	0	0
YUG	0	2	0
CAN	0	1	2
URU	0	1	1
POR	0	1	1
CUB	0	1	0
SPA	0	1	0
TRI	0	1	0
SRL	0	1	0
KOR	0	0	2
PAN	0	0	2
POL	0	0	1
PUR	0	0	1
IRN	0	0	1
BRA	0	0	1

1952 Helsinki

	G	S	B
USA	40	19	17
SOV	22	30	19
HUN	16	10	16
SWE	12	13	10
ITA	8	9	4
CZE	7	3	3
FRA	6	6	6
FIN	6	3	13
AUS	6	2	3
NOR	3	2	0
SWI	2	6	6
SAF	2	4	4
JAM	2	3	0
BEL	2	2	0
DEN	2	1	3
TUR	2	0	1
JAP	1	6	2
GBR	1	2	8
ARG	1	2	2

	G	S	B
POL	1	2	1
CAN	1	2	0
YUG	1	2	0
ROM	1	1	2
BRA	1	0	2
NZE	1	0	2
IND	1	0	1
LUX	1	0	0
GER	0	7	17
HOL	0	5	0
IRN	0	3	4
CHI	0	2	0
LEB	0	1	1
AUT	0	1	1
SPA	0	1	0
IRL	0	1	0
MEX	0	1	0
URU	0	0	2
TRI	0	0	2
KOR	0	0	2
POR	0	0	1
VEN	0	0	1
BUL	0	0	1
EGY	0	0	1

1956 Melbourne

	G	S	B
SOV	37	29	32
USA	32	25	17
AUS	13	8	14
HUN	9	10	7
ITA	8	8	9
SWE	8	5	6
GBR	6	7	11
GER	5	9	6
ROM	5	3	5
JAP	4	10	5
FRA	4	4	6
TUR	3	2	2
FIN	3	1	11
IRN	2	2	1
CAN	2	1	3
NZE	2	0	0
POL	1	4	4
GDR	1	4	2
CZE	1	4	1

BUL	1	3	1
DEN	1	2	1
IRL	1	1	3
NOR	1	0	2
MEX	1	0	1
BRA	1	0	0
IND	1	0	0
YUG	0	3	0
CHI	0	2	2
BEL	0	2	0
KOR	0	1	1
ARG	0	1	1
ICE	0	1	0
PAK	0	1	0
SAF	0	0	4
AUT	0	0	2
URU	0	0	1
SWI	0	0	1
GRE	0	0	1
BAH	0	0	1

1960 Rome

	G	S	B
SOV	43	29	31
USA	34	21	16
ITA	13	10	13
GER	10	10	6
AUS	8	8	6
TUR	7	2	0
HUN	6	8	7
JAP	4	7	7
POL	4	6	11
GDR	3	9	7
CZE	3	2	3
ROM	3	1	6
GBR	2	6	12
DEN	2	3	1
NZE	2	0	1
BUL	1	3	3
SWE	1	2	3
FIN	1	1	3
YUG	1	1	0
AUT	1	1	0
PAK	1	0	1
ETH	1	0	0
GRE	1	0	0
NOR	1	0	0
SWI	0	3	3

FRA	0	2	3
BEL	0	2	2
IRN	0	1	3
HOL	0	1	2
SAF	0	1	2
UAR	0	1	1
ARG	0	1	1
GHA	0	1	0
IND	0	1	0
CAN	0	1	0
MOR	0	1	0
POR	0	1	0
SIN	0	1	0
TAI	0	1	0
BWI	0	0	2
BRA	0	0	2
IRQ	0	0	1
MEX	0	0	1
SPA	0	0	1
VEN	0	0	1

1964 Tokyo

	G	S	B
USA	36	26	28
SOV	30	31	25
JAP	16	5	8
ITA	10	10	7
HUN	10	7	5
GER	7	14	14
POL	7	6	10
AUS	6	2	10
CZE	5	6	3
GBR	4	12	2
GDR	3	11	5
BUL	3	5	2
FIN	3	0	2
NZE	3	0	2
ROM	2	4	6
HOL	2	4	4
TUR	2	3	1
SWE	2	2	4
DEN	2	1	3
YUG	2	1	2
BEL	2	0	1
FRA	1	8	6
CAN	1	2	1
SWI	1	2	1
ETH	1	0	0

BAH	1	0	0
IND	1	0	0
KOR	0	2	1
TRI	0	1	2
TUN	0	1	1
ARG	0	1	0
CUB	0	1	0
PAK	0	1	0
PHI	0	1	0
IRN	0	0	2
BRA	0	0	1
GHA	0	0	1
IRL	0	0	1
KEN	0	0	1
MEX	0	0	1
NGR	0	0	1
URU	0	0	1

1968 Mexico City

	G	S	B
USA	45	28	34
SOV	29	32	30
JAP	11	7	7
HUN	10	10	12
GDR	9	9	7
FRA	7	3	5
CZE	7	2	4
GER	5	11	10
AUS	5	7	5
GBR	5	5	3
POL	5	2	11
ROM	4	6	5
ITA	3	4	9
KEN	3	4	2
MEX	3	3	3
YUG	3	3	2
HOL	3	3	1
BUL	2	4	3
IRN	2	1	2
SWE	2	1	1
TUR	2	0	0
DEN	1	4	3
CAN	1	3	1
FIN	1	2	1
ETH	1	1	0
NOR	1	1	0
NZE	1	0	2

	G	S	B
TUN	1	0	1
PAK	1	0	0
VEN	1	0	0
CUB	0	4	0
AUT	0	2	2
SWI	0	1	4
MON	0	1	3
BRA	0	1	2
KOR	0	1	1
UGA	0	1	1
JAM	0	1	0
CAM	0	1	0
ARG	0	0	2
GRE	0	0	1
IND	0	0	1
TAI	0	0	1

1972 Munich

	G	S	B
SOV	50	27	22
USA	33	31	30
GDR	20	23	23
GER	13	11	16
JAP	13	8	8
AUS	8	7	2
POL	7	5	9
HUN	6	13	16
BUL	6	10	5
ITA	5	3	10
SWE	4	6	6
GBR	4	5	9
ROM	3	6	7
FIN	3	1	4
CUB	3	1	4
HOL	3	1	1
FRA	2	4	7
CZE	2	4	2
KEN	2	3	4
YUG	2	1	2
NOR	2	1	1
PRK	1	1	3
NZE	1	1	1
UGA	1	1	0
DEN	1	0	0
SWI	0	3	0
CAN	0	2	3

IRN	0	2	1
BEL	0	2	0
GRE	0	2	0
COL	0	1	2
AUT	0	1	2
ARG	0	1	0
KOR	0	1	0
LEB	0	1	0
MEX	0	1	0
MON	0	1	0
PAK	0	1	0
TUR	0	1	0
TUN	0	1	0
ETH	0	0	2
BRA	0	0	2
GHA	0	0	1
IND	0	0	1
JAM	0	0	1
NIG	0	0	1
NGR	0	0	1
SPA	0	0	1

1976 Montreal

	G	S	B
SOV	49	41	35
GDR	40	25	25
USA	34	35	25
GER	10	12	17
JAP	9	6	10
POL	7	6	13
BUL	6	9	7
CUB	6	4	3
ROM	4	9	14
HUN	4	5	13
FIN	4	2	0
SWE	4	1	0
GBR	3	5	5
ITA	2	7	4
FRA	2	3	4
YUG	2	3	3
CZE	2	2	4
NZE	2	1	1
KOR	1	1	4
SWI	1	1	2
NOR	1	1	0
PRK	1	1	0
JAM	1	1	0
DEN	1	0	2

MEX	1	0	1
TRI	1	0	0
CAN	0	5	6
BEL	0	3	3
HOL	0	2	3
SPA	0	2	0
POR	0	2	0
AUS	0	1	4
IRN	0	1	1
MON	0	1	0
VEN	0	1	0
BRA	0	0	2
AUT	0	0	1
PUR	0	0	1
BER	0	0	1
PAK	0	0	1
THA	0	0	1

1980 Moscow

	G	S	B
SOV	80	69	46
GDR	47	37	42
BUL	8	16	17
CUB	8	7	5
ITA	8	3	4
HUN	7	10	15
ROM	6	6	13
FRA	6	5	3
GBR	5	7	9
POL	3	14	15
SWE	3	3	6
FIN	3	1	4
CZE	2	3	9
YUG	2	3	4
AUS	2	2	5
DEN	2	1	2
BRA	2	0	2
ETH	2	0	2
SWI	2	0	0
SPA	1	3	2
AUT	1	2	1
GRE	1	0	2
IND	1	0	0
BEL	1	0	0
ZIM	1	0	0
PRK	0	3	2
MON	0	2	2
TAN	0	2	0

MEX	0	1	3
HOL	0	1	2
IRL	0	1	1
UGA	0	1	0
VEN	0	1	0
JAM	0	0	3
GUY	0	0	1
LEB	0	0	1

WINTER

1924 Chamonix

	G	S	B
NOR	4	7	6
FIN	4	3	3
AUT	2	1	0
USA	1	2	1
SWI	1	0	1
CAN	1	0	0
SWE	1	0	0
GBR	0	1	2
BEL	0	0	1
FRA	0	0	1

1928 St. Moritz

	G	S	B
NOR	6	4	5
USA	2	2	2
SWE	2	2	1
FIN	2	1	1
FRA	1	0	0
CAN	1	0	0
AUT	0	3	1
CZE	0	0	1
SWI	0	0	1
BEL	0	0	1
GER	0	0	1
GBR	0	0	1

1932 Lake Placid

	G	S	B
USA	6	4	2
NOR	3	4	3
SWE	1	2	0
CAN	1	1	5
FIN	1	1	1
AUT	1	1	0

	G	S	B
FRA	1	0	0
SWI	0	1	0
GER	0	0	2
HUN	0	0	1

1936 Garmisch-Partenkirchen

	G	S	B
NOR	7	5	3
GER	3	3	0
SWE	2	2	3
FIN	1	2	3
SWI	1	2	0
GBR	1	1	1
USA	1	0	3
CAN	0	1	0
FRA	0	0	1
HUN	0	0	1

1948 St. Moritz

	G	S	B
SWE	4	3	3
NOR	4	3	3
SWI	3	4	3
USA	3	4	2
FRA	2	1	2
CAN	2	0	1
AUT	1	3	4
FIN	1	3	2
BEL	1	1	0
ITA	1	0	0
CZE	0	1	0
HUN	0	1	0
GBR	0	0	2

1952 Oslo

	G	S	B
NOR	7	3	6
USA	4	6	1
FIN	3	4	2
GER	3	2	2
AUT	2	4	2
ITA	1	0	1
CAN	1	0	1
GBR	1	0	0
HOL	0	3	0

	G	S	B
SWE	0	0	4
SWI	0	0	2
FRA	0	0	1
HUN	0	0	1

1956 Cortina d'Ampezzo

	G	S	B
SOV	7	3	6
AUT	4	3	4
FIN	3	3	1
SWI	3	2	1
SWE	2	4	4
USA	2	3	2
NOR	2	1	1
ITA	1	2	0
GER	1	0	0
CAN	0	1	2
JAP	0	1	0
GDR	0	0	1
POL	0	0	1
HUN	0	0	1

1960 Squaw Valley

	G	S	B
SOV	7	5	9
USA	3	4	3
NOR	3	3	0
SWE	3	2	2
FIN	2	3	3
GER	2	2	1
CAN	2	1	1
GDR	2	1	0
SWI	2	0	0
AUT	1	2	3
FRA	1	0	2
HOL	0	1	1
POL	0	1	1
CZE	0	1	0
ITA	0	0	1

1964 Innsbruck

	G	S	B
SOV	11	8	6
AUT	4	5	3
NOR	3	6	6
FIN	3	4	3
FRA	3	4	0
SWE	3	3	1
GDR	2	2	0
USA	1	2	3
HOL	1	1	0
GER	1	0	3
CAN	1	0	2
GBR	1	0	0
ITA	0	1	3
PRK	0	1	0
CZE	0	0	1

1968 Grenoble

	G	S	B
NOR	6	6	2
SOV	5	5	3
FRA	4	3	2
ITA	4	0	0
AUT	3	4	4
HOL	3	3	3
SWE	3	2	3
GER	2	2	3
USA	1	5	1
GDR	1	2	2
FIN	1	2	2
CZE	1	2	1
CAN	1	1	1
SWI	0	2	4
ROM	0	0	1

1972 Sapporo

	G	S	B
SOV	8	5	3
GDR	4	3	7
SWI	4	3	3
HOL	4	3	2
USA	3	2	3
GER	3	1	1
NOR	2	5	5
ITA	2	2	1
AUT	1	2	2
SWE	1	1	2
JAP	1	1	1
CZE	1	0	2
POL	1	0	0
SPA	1	0	0
FIN	0	4	1

1976 Innsbruck

	G	S	B
SOV	13	6	8
GDR	7	5	7
USA	3	3	4
NOR	3	3	1
GER	2	5	3
FIN	2	4	1
AUT	2	2	2
SWI	1	3	1
HOL	1	2	3
ITA	1	2	1
CAN	1	1	1
GBR	1	0	0
CZE	0	1	0
SWE	0	0	2
LIE	0	0	2
FRA	0	0	1

1980 Lake Placid

	G	S	B
SOV	10	6	6
GDR	9	7	7
USA	6	4	2
AUT	3	2	2
SWE	3	0	1
LIE	2	2	0
FIN	1	5	3
NOR	1	3	6
HOL	1	2	1
SWI	1	1	3
GBR	1	0	0
GER	0	2	3
ITA	0	2	0
CAN	0	1	1
JAP	0	1	0
HUN	0	1	0
CZE	0	0	1
FRA	0	0	1
BUL	0	0	1

A BRIEF HISTORY OF THE MODERN OLYMPICS

The ancient Olympic games were held in Olympia, Greece, every four years from at least 776 B.C., until they were banned by Emperor Theodosius in 393 A.D. Originally there was only one race, a sprint, and the prize for the winner was an olive wreath. As time went on, other races were added, as were other sports, including boxing and wrestling. Prizes became more elaborate, and there were even cases of bribery and corruption.

Inspired by the original, uncorrupted Olympics, Baron Pierre de Coubertin of France conceived the modern Olympic Games. He proposed the idea publicly for the first time in 1892 and then spent the next three and a half years drumming up support. Interest was strongest in Greece, so it was decided to hold the first Olympics in Athens.

The **1896** Athens Games were funded by a gift from wealthy architect Georgios Averoff of one million drachma, and by the sale of souvenir stamps and medals. Although the quality of the athletes' performances was only mediocre, the Games were a huge success. The enthusiasm and good sportsmanship of the Greek spectators were rewarded when the highlight event, the marathon, was won by a Greek peasant, Spiridon Louis.

The second Olympic Games were held in de Coubertin's hometown of Paris in **1900**, but they turned out to be a failure. Reduced to a mere appendage to the World Exhibition of that year, the events of the Olympics were spread out over five months. Poor organization and poor attendance made things worse; some of the athletes were actually unaware that the meet they had taken part in was the Olympics.

De Coubertin had high hopes for the **1904** Games, which were scheduled for Chicago because Americans had shown great enthusiasm for the first two Olympics. However a dispute broke out between Chicago and St. Louis, which wanted the Games to be held as part of the Louisiana Purchase Exhibition. President Theodore Roosevelt eventually sided with St. Louis, and the Games were moved. This change proved to be an awful mistake, as the St. Louis organizers turned out to be even less competent than the Paris organizers. Most European nations skipped the Games, and not even Baron de Coubertin bothered to attend. Events were spread out over four and a half months, and some included only U.S. athletes.

After two straight disasters the Olympic movement might have died had it not been for the Intercalated (or Interim) Games of **1906**. After the success of the 1896 Games, the Greeks had hoped to hold their own international games every four years between Olympics. However the proposed Games of 1898 had to be cancelled because of political and economic upheaval, and the 1902 Games weren't even considered. By 1906, though, the Greeks were ready to try again. Although de Coubertin opposed the Intercalated Games, they were quite successful and actually helped save the Olympic movement. These Games are considered unofficial by the International Olympic Committee (I.O.C.).

The **1908** Games had been planned for Rome, but the Italians backed out for financial reasons, and the Games were then awarded to London. Most of the events were held in Shepherd's Bush Stadium, which included a cycle track, a running track, a soccer field, a swimming pool, and a platform for wrestling and gymnastics. The London Games were basically well organized and produced the first comprehensive Official Report. There were, however, numerous disputes. The Russians tried to prevent the Finns from displaying the Finnish flag, and the English did the same to the Irish. The competitions were run entirely by the British, which led to protests over the rules by representatives of France, Canada, Italy, Sweden, and, especially, the United States. The bickering between Great Britain and its cheeky former colony was so acute that it almost put an end to the Olympics.

Fortunately, the **1912** Olympics were held in Stockholm. Well-organized, the Stockholm Games saw the first use of electric timing devices and a public address system. The Swedes refused to allow boxing matches to be held in their country, which led the I.O.C. to pass a rule limiting the power of local organizing committees in future Olympics. The success of the 1912 Games helped the Olympic movement survive the interruption that came to be known as World War I. In ancient times, all wars were suspended during the period of the Olympics. In modern times, the reverse has been true. Scheduled for Berlin, the **1916** Olympics were cancelled.

The **1920** Games were awarded to Antwerp, Belgium, as compensation for all the grief that had been inflicted on the

Belgians during the war. The losers of World War I, Austria, Bulgaria, Germany, Hungary, and Turkey, were not allowed to participate. With little money available to run the Games, the 1920 Olympics were not very impressive and were not well documented. An Official Report does not exist for 1920—only a typed manuscript containing an incomplete listing of the results.

Much to the delight of Baron de Coubertin, Paris was given a second chance to host the Olympics in **1924**, which also saw the staging of the first Winter Olympics in Chamonix, France. The second Paris Games were well attended, with athletes from 44 nations taking part, as opposed to the previous record of 29. Competition was of a very high standard. However, the fanaticism of Parisian sports fans led to several outrages, including booing during the playing of national anthems of other countries and numerous incidents during the boxing and fencing tournaments. The French, who never had a very high opinion of their neighbors, were particularly irritated by the Americans, since the U.S. government had only recently criticized the French occupation of the Rühr. During a rugby match between France and the United States, an American art student was severely caned by an incensed French spectator who had become annoyed by the loud U.S. "rooting."

In Europe and North America countless editorials were written calling for an end to the Olympics, but the next Games were held on schedule in Amsterdam in **1928**, with Germany taking part for the first time since 1912. The boxing tournament was once again disrupted by protests, but for the most part, the Amsterdam Games were a success. For the first time track and field events for women were included in the program, although women had previously taken part in tennis, golf, archery, figure skating, yachting, swimming, and fencing.

The **1932** Los Angeles Olympics faced two major obstacles: the Depression and the geographical isolation of California. Participation was the lowest since 1906, although the level of competition was excellent. Only three teams took part in the field hockey tournament, and football (soccer) had to be dropped completely. All of the male athletes lived in a makeshift Olympic Village in Baldwin Hills, while the women stayed in a hotel on Wilshire Boulevard. Although the United States was in the midst of Prohibition, an exception was made for the French, who claimed that wine was an essential component of their diet. The 1932 Olympics saw the introduction of automatic timing and the photo-finish camera.

In 1931, when Berlin had been chosen as the site for the **1936** Olympics, few people suspected that a mere five years would see the rise to power of Adolf Hitler and the Nazi Party. Jews in various countries asked for a boycott of the Berlin Olympics, and in the United States, a boycott proposal was only narrowly defeated. An alternative People's Olympics was scheduled to take place in Barcelona, Spain, but it was cancelled at the last minute when the Spanish Civil War broke out the day before competition was set to begin. The 1936 Olympics are best remembered by Hitler's failed attempt to use them to prove his theories of Aryan superiority, but they are also noteworthy because they saw the introduction of the torch relay, in which a lighted torch is carried from Olympia to the site of the current Games. The 1936 Olympics were also the first to be shown on television. Twenty-five large TV screens were set up in theaters throughout Berlin, allowing locals to see the Games for free.

The **1940** Olympics were awarded to Japan—the Winter Games to Sapporo and the Summer Games to Tokyo—but when Japan invaded China and became caught up in a major war, the Olympics were taken away from the Japanese. The Winter Games, rescheduled for Garmisch-Partenkirchen, site of the 1936 Games, were cancelled less than five months before the planned starting date, when Germany invaded Poland to kick off World War II. The Summer Games, reawarded to Helsinki, were cancelled when Soviet troops invaded Finland.

After the war ended London took on the unenviable task of staging the **1948** Olympics, the first in 12 years. There was much grumbling in England that the project was a waste of money, considering that Britain was still recovering from the war. However, the Games went off well, and interest among Londoners increased rapidly as the competitions progressed. Following the precedent set after World War I, the World War II losers, Germany and Japan, were not invited to participate. A minor incident developed when two swimmers from Northern Ireland were refused permission to compete for the team from Eire (Ireland). The 1948 Olympics also saw the first participation by Communist countries and, with this, the first defections of athletes.

The U.S.S.R. joined the Olympics for the first time in Helsinki in **1952**. In the United Nations, the Ukraine and Byelorussia are both treated as independent nations, with full voting privileges. In the Olympics, on the other hand, the Ukraine and Byelorussia are considered part of the U.S.S.R., and Ukrainian and Byelorussian athletes were forced to represent the Soviet Union. Despite fears of a Cold War showdown, Soviet and American athletes in Helsinki were on their best behavior and actually got along quite well. In fact, the 1952 Games were so well run that some observers suggested the Olympics be held permanently in Scandinavia.

In **1956** the Olympics were staged in the southern hemisphere for the first and only time. Melbourne, Australia, was so remote from most parts of the world that the number of competitors was the smallest since 1932. Australian quarantine laws caused the equestrian events to be held separately, in Stockholm. The Melbourne Games were stung by two boycotts. Egypt, Iraq, and Lebanon withdrew to protest the Israeli-led takeover of the Suez Canal, and Holland, Spain, and Switzerland boycotted to protest the Soviet invasion of Hungary. Actually, public pressure in Switzerland was so great that the Swiss Olympic Committee changed its mind and voted to participate after all, but by then it was too late to get the entire Swiss team to Australia in time. On the brighter side, the I.O.C. scored a major political coup by convincing West and East Germany to enter a combined team. This practice continued for the next two Olympics, but since 1968 the two German nations have sent separate teams. The 1956 Olympics were also highlighted by an innovation in the closing ceremonies. Following a suggestion by a 17-year-old Chinese boy, it was decided to let all the athletes march together instead of by nation, as a symbol of global unity.

The **1960** Olympics, held beneath the blazing summer sun of Rome, went off without major incident. Like Londoners in 1948, the Romans were fairly blasé at first, but got caught up in the excitement once the games got going. Even the Pope became a spectator, as he watched the canoeing semifinals from a window of his summer residence. The Rome Olympics were the last in which South Africa was allowed to take part, as the I.O.C. bowed to international pressure to punish the South African government for its racist policies.

In 1963 Indonesia staged the Games of the New Emerging Forces (GANEFO) in Jakarta. When the Indonesians refused to allow athletes from Israel and Taiwan to take part, the I.O.C. put its foot down and announced that any athletes who competed at GANEFO would be banned from the **1964** Tokyo Olympics. The I.O.C. enforced this ruling the following year, leading Indonesia and North Korea to withdraw their entire teams just before the Tokyo Games began. With that problem out of the way, the 1964 Olympics proceeded smoothly and efficiently, something that has never happened since.

The **1968** Mexico City Olympics are best known for the Black Power protests of the U.S. runners, which are discussed at greater length later in the following section, "Issues: Olympic Politics." Two other controversies of 1968 were the introduction of sex tests for women athletes (first used at the Winter Games in Grenoble) and the altitude of Mexico City (7347 feet). The rarefied air led to numerous world records in races of short distances, but was disastrous to competitors engaged in endurance events, except those who had trained at high altitudes.

In **1972** the West Germans, hoping to erase embarrassing memories of the Nazi Games of 1936, staged the biggest Olympics yet in Munich. However the Olympic movement was permanently scarred on the morning of September 5, when eight Palestinian terrorists broke into the Olympic Village and made their way to the dormitory of the Israeli team. Two Israelis were killed immediately and another nine were taken hostage. The terrorists demanded the release of 200 prisoners from Israeli jails and safe passage for themselves out of Germany. They got as far as the airport, where West German sharpshooters killed three of the terrorists. The battle that ensued left all nine Israeli hostages dead, as well as two more terrorists and one policeman. The Olympics were suspended for 34 hours, and a memorial service was held in the main stadium. Although the Games continued, many athletes found that they had lost their desire to compete.

The **1976** Olympics, held in Montreal, were hit by a boycott of African nations led by Tanzania. The Africans had demanded expulsion of New Zealand because a rugby team from that nation had made a tour of South Africa. The I.O.C. claimed that controlling the travel of rugby teams was outside its authority since rugby isn't an Olympic sport, but the Africans, joined by Iraq and Guyana, held firm. Of the boycotting nations, only Tanzania stayed home completely, while the others traveled to Canada and didn't make their final decision until the last minute. Despite the absence of the Africans, the 1976 Olympics were filled with excellent competitions. However, poor planning and corruption caused the city of Montreal to suffer a major financial loss.

The **1980** Moscow Olympics were disrupted by another boycott, this one led by U.S. President Jimmy Carter, who was unable to come up with any other way to protest the Soviet invasion of Afghanistan. With his eyes on the upcoming presidential election and his pride on the line, Carter engaged in extensive arm-twisting to get other nations to support the boycott. Some governments, such as those of Great Britain and Australia, supported the boycott, but allowed the athletes to decide for themselves if they wanted to go to Moscow. No such freedom of choice was allowed U.S. athletes, as Carter threatened to revoke the passport of any athlete who tried to travel to the U.S.S.R.

Certain sports, such as yachting, equestrian events, field hockey, and men's swimming were hit particularly hard by the boycott. Yet the Games proceeded with much pomp and more world records than had been set in 1976. Security precautions were paranoiacally thorough, with track and field winners physically prevented from taking victory laps. Meanwhile, the Soviet spectators gave the worst impression of any host city since the Paris Olympics of 1924. With the traditional Olympic powers West Germany, Japan, and the United States missing, the Soviets took out their aggressions by booing and heckling the Poles and East Germans.

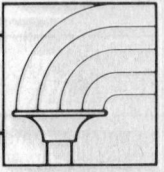

OLYMPIC POLITICS

There are only two places today where people from all parts of the world gather: the United Nations and the Olympics. The trouble with the United Nations is that two-thirds of the governments represented are ruled by dictators, royal families, and single parties that permit no opposition. Consequently, the people who represent these countries at the United Nations, far from being typical citizens, are generally the worst the country has to offer. Even those nations that aspire to democracy are represented by a most unrepresentative group: wealthy men and women, mostly men, who have gone to the right schools and know the right people.

Unlike U.N. delegates, Olympic athletes represent an almost complete economic cross-section of the world's population. In this book you will meet carpenters, farmers, housewives, teachers, psychiatrists, accountants, nurses, secretaries, and cartoonists, as well as the usual hordes of students, soldiers, and state-supported athletes. Some Olympians have been unemployed. Others came from families of sharecroppers, or from no families at all. Even lawyers, businessmen, and royalty have taken part in the Olympics.

This is not to say that the Olympics are any less political than the United Nations. However, contrary to popular belief, the politicization of the Olympics is not a recent phenomenon. From the very beginning the Olympics were exploited by the ruling classes of the nations in which they were held. In 1896 and 1906 the Greek royal family was highly visible at the Games, placing its box at the finish line and inserting itself into the festivities at the most exciting parts—the moment of victory and the award ceremonies. The British royal family did the same thing in 1908. In 1912 awards were handed out not only by King Gustav of Sweden, but by Czar Nicholas of Russia as well. The 1920 Olympics were officially declared open by King Albert of Belgium, and the 1928 games by Prince Henry of the Netherlands.

Staging the Olympics also helped the ruling classes by providing a distraction from serious political and economic problems. During the 1906 Intercalated Games in Athens, British and American tourists were shocked when a riot broke out in front of their hotel. Government troops attacked a political demonstration, killing three people and injuring 57. Meanwhile the Greek royal family was busy entertaining the English royal family at Olympic-related functions, including the competitions themselves.

Despite this history, it is often stated that the "intrusion" of politics into the Olympics began in a serious manner with the black-gloved, clenched-fist salutes of U.S. sprinters Tommie Smith and John Carlos in Mexico City in 1968. Smith and Carlos staged their Black Power protest while "The Star-Spangled Banner" was being played during the medal ceremony for the 200-meter dash. They were immediately suspended by the I.O.C. and ordered to leave the country by the U.S.O.C. Yet they were hardly the first to make political gestures on the victory platform. During the 1936 Berlin Games, all German winners and several foreigners as well raised their right arms in the Nazi salute. Countless American athletes have placed their right hands over their hearts during the playing of their national anthem. Needless to say, none of these athletes was punished the way Smith and Carlos were.

The question then arises: If it was acceptable in 1936 to raise your right arm in the air with the open palm face down, and today it is acceptable to put your right hand over your heart, why was it *not* acceptable in 1968 to bow your head and raise your arm into the air with your gloved fist closed?

From the point of view of the I.O.C., the "crime" committed by Smith and Carlos was not that they had made a political statement, but that they had made the *wrong* political statement. Although Olympic *athletes* may be a representative group, I.O.C. members and other Olympic leaders are not. They are, in fact, very much like U.N. delegates. They have definite political beliefs. They support nationalism, and they support the ruling elites of the various nations of the world, no matter if they are Communist or capitalist. Thus it was perfectly all right in 1936 for German athletes to give the Nazi salute, because that salute was approved by the German government. And it is quite within the rules for U.S. athletes to put their hands over their hearts because that is a patriotic gesture which shows support for nationalism and the status quo.

It was *not* acceptable to the I.O.C. to have Smith and

Carlos raise clenched fists because their gesture, rather than showing support for a recognized nation-state, showed support for an unrecognized political entity—black Americans.

The year 1968 was a highly politicized one. China was in the throes of the Cultural Revolution, Czechoslovakia's burst of freedom was crushed by Soviet troops, the government of France was almost overthrown by student-led demonstrations, and civil rights and antiwar demonstrations were spreading across the United States. Mexico was by no means immune to such revolutionary activity. As the Olympics approached, 300,000 Mexican students and teachers were on strike. Ten days before the Olympics were scheduled to begin, government troops opened fire on several thousand unarmed students holding a rally in the Plaza de las Tres Culturas. Hundreds of young people were killed. The I.O.C. refused to take a stand on this, declaring that the incident was "an internal affair" which was "under control." Yet exactly two weeks later, when two black men made a silent, nonviolent protest, the I.O.C. was up in arms, condemning Smith and Carlos for their shocking, disrespectful behavior.

The Olympics have always reflected the politics of the world, from which they provide a temporary respite, and they always will. As long as the International Olympic Committee insists on emphasizing national divisions through the wearing of national uniforms, the playing of national anthems, and the housing of athletes by nation instead of by sport, it will continue to face an extra layer of problems beyond the natural ones faced in running any large-scale enterprise.

AMATEURISM

Contrary to popular belief, the Ancient Greek athletes were not amateurs. Not only were they fully supported for almost a year prior to the Olympics, but even though a winner received only an olive wreath at the Games, back home he was amply rewarded and could become quite rich.

The concept of amateurism actually developed in nineteenth-century England as a means of preventing the working classes from competing against the aristocracy. The wealthy could take part in sports without worrying about having to make a living, and thus could pursue the ideal of amateurism. Everyone else had to give up training time in order to earn a living, or else take money for sports performances and become a professional, ineligible for competitions such as the Olympics.

Baron de Coubertin, although a member of the French aristocracy, was well aware of the inequities of the amateur system. His solution was to have wealthy people come forward as "patrons" to support worthy working-class athletes.

The qualifications for being an amateur have varied from decade to decade and from sport to sport. In the 1920s British sportsmen accused the Americans of circumventing the rules of amateurism by the awarding of athletic scholarships to universities (although even the ancient Greek medical colleges recruited athletes). As late as the 1930s physical education teachers and recreation directors were considered professional athletes and thus ineligible for the Olympics.

These restrictions seem archaic today, but don't be surprised a few decades from now if our present-day restrictions seem just as silly. I believe that the code of amateurism will eventually be discarded and that the Olympics will be declared open to all qualified athletes. If the constant bickering over the definition of amateurism doesn't bring about the change, then the absurd advantage given to Communist countries will. Because the Communist nations claim that they have no professional athletes, they are able to field the best possible teams in every sport. Non-Communist countries are handicapped in any sport popular enough to support professionals, such as basketball, boxing, cycling, and football (soccer). The situation in football is particularly ridiculous, as the Communist teams constantly dominate the Olympic tournament even though they never do well in the World Cup.

I appreciate the arguments of those who believe the Olympics would be made gaudy and commercial if they were opened to professionals, but I believe it is more important to eliminate the unfair advantages that the rules of amateurism provide for the rich and the Communists.

ACKNOWLEDGMENTS

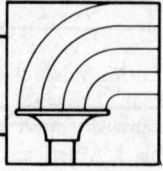

First of all I would like to thank my father, Irving Wallace, who introduced me to the world of the Olympics. In the course of my research I encountered numerous people who graciously helped me on my way, starting with C. Robert Paul, who made available to me the archives of the United States Olympic Committee, including the Official Reports of the Organizing Committees of the various Olympic Games, which form the basis of the statistics in this book. Mr. Paul was also kind enough to review my manuscript in light of his long experience with the Olympic movement. I would also like to acknowledge the aid of David Kelly at the Library of Congress, Jan Foulstich and other members of the staff of Representative Anthony Beilenson, the staff of the Library of Notre Dame University, Maynard Brichford and others at the University of Illinois, Champaign-Urbana, which houses the Avery Brundage Collection, and Sandy Duncan and Bob Wight of the British Olympic Association.

I am indebted to John Lucas, Bill Mallin, Harvey Abrams, and Peter Diamond, who allowed me to enjoy and make use of their personal libraries. I would also like to thank the following people for their help in the research process: Aleen Stein, Anita Taylor, Helen Ginsburg, Atsuo Inoue, Kenjo Yoshida, Wolf Lyberg, David Guiney, Joanne Lander, and Miguel Garcia, as well as the numerous people at the various National Olympic Committees, International Sports Federations, and other sports organizations who responded to my pleas for information.

The research materials I gathered were clipped, marked, and sorted into 2972 files, one for each event held in each Olympic Games. From these files I wrote the stories that accompany the statistics. The statistics and stories were then entered into a computer. Many people helped me in various stages of this process. I would particularly like to thank Jeff Lewinter, Hilarie Kelly, Patrice Bivins, Morris Levenspiel, Wes Samuels, Carlos Chavez, Winnie Van DerWorde, Jennifer Frank, Kristine Johnson, and Vicki Scott.

I would also like to thank Carol Gershfield and John MacClancy for helping in the acquisition of the photographs used in this book.

Special acknowledgments are due to my wife, Flora Chavez, who helped when I needed it most; to my agent, Ed Victor, for his support and encouragement; and to my editor, Charles Verrill, and to many other people at Viking Penguin, for their patience. While on the subject of patience, I would like to thank my friends and relatives who allowed me to suspend my social life for the duration of this project. And I would like to apologize to all the people who wrote to me during the final 11 months of intense work. I hope by the time you read this you will have received a reply.

The author of this book may be reached by writing to:

Olympics
P.O. Box 49328
Los Angeles, California 90049

I would particularly appreciate hearing from former Olympians willing to share their recollections.

THE CHARTS

SOURCES

Although the primary sources for the information included in the charts are the Official Reports of the various Olympics, these reports are often incomplete or incorrect. The man who has done the most to correct these inadequacies is Erich Kamper of Austria, author of *Enzyklopädie der Olympischen Spiele*, which lists the top six places in each event of the Summer Games from 1896 to 1968, and *Lexikon der 14,000 Olympioniken*, which gives basic biographical information for all medal winners. My search for correct spellings and accent marks also led me to *Die Olympischen Spiele von 1896 bis 1980* by Volker Kluge of East Germany; *Starozytme i Nowozytne Igrazyska Olimpyskie* by Zbigniew Porada of Poland; *Meet the Bulgarian Olympians* by Kostadinov, Georgiev, and Kambourov; *Az Olimpiajátékokon Indult Magyar Versenyzök Névsora 1896–1980; Die Deutschen Sportier der Olympische 1896 bis 1968*; and *Sveriges Deltagare i de Olumpiska Spelen 1896–1952*. For the early games (1896–1904) I am particularly indebted to Bill Mallon of the United States, author of *A Statistical Summary of the 1904 Olympic Games*.

While I was in the final stages of proofreading my own book, the *Official Report of the 1906 Intercalated Games* suddenly appeared in the world of Olympic historians after being missing for 77 years. Through sheer luck I am now able to present these official results to the public for the first time.

Track and field fans are advised to subscribe to the excellent monthly periodical *Track and Field News* (P.O. Box 296, Los Altos, California 94022).

HOW TO READ THEM

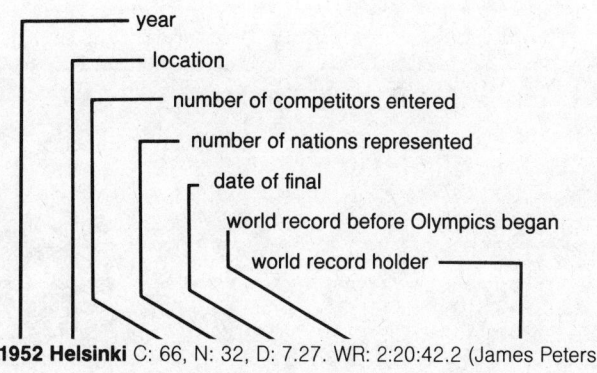

Numbers in the charts indicate times unless otherwise noted. A dash symbol in the numbers column means that the information was not taken or is otherwise unavailable.

Whenever possible I have included an athlete's first and last names. If the first name was unavailable, I have included the first initial. If that was unavailable I just included the surname. If a female athlete competed under her maiden name, then got married and took part in a second Olympics using her married name, I have included her maiden name in parentheses.

The 1906 Intercalated Games are considered unofficial by the I.O.C., but I have included them because of their historical importance.

In 1956, 1960, and 1964, West Germany (GER) and East Germany (GDR) entered combined teams. Nevertheless I have indicated which athletes were actually from each country because I thought it was interesting.

KEY TO ABBREVIATIONS

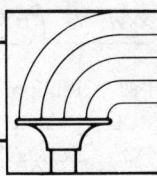

NATIONS

AFG	Afghanistan
ALG	Algeria
ARG	Argentina
AUS	Australia
AUT	Austria
BAH	Bahamas
BEL	Belgium
BER	Bermuda
BOH	Bohemia
BRA	Brazil
BUL	Bulgaria
BUR	Burma
BWI	British West Indies (Jamaica and Trinidad)
CAM	Cameroon
CHI	Chile
CAN	Canada
COL	Colombia
CON	Congo
COS	Costa Rica
CUB	Cuba
CZE	Czechoslovakia
DEN	Denmark
EGY	Egypt
EST	Estonia
ETH	Ethiopia
FIN	Finland
FRA	France
GBR	Great Britain and Northern Ireland
GDR	East Germany (German Democratic Republic)
GER	Germany (1896–1936), West Germany (Federal Republic of Germany, 1952–1980)
GHA	Ghana
GRE	Greece
GUA	Guatemala
GUY	Guyana
HAI	Haiti
HOL	Holland (Netherlands)
HUN	Hungary
ICE	Iceland
IND	India
INO	Indonesia
INT	International team
IRL	Ireland (Eire)
IRN	Iran
IRQ	Iraq
ISR	Israel
ITA	Italy
IVC	Ivory Coast
JAM	Jamaica
JAP	Japan
KEN	Kenya
KOR	South Korea
KUW	Kuwait
LAT	Latvia
LEB	Lebanon
LIE	Liechtenstein
LIT	Lithuania
LUX	Luxembourg
MAD	Madagascar
MAL	Malaysia
MEX	Mexico
MON	Mongolia
MOR	Morocco
NGR	Nigeria
NIG	Niger
NOR	Norway
NZE	New Zealand
PAK	Pakistan
PAN	Panama
PER	Peru

PHI	Philippines	DNC	Did not compete in final
POL	Poland	DNF	Did not finish
POR	Portugal	DNS	Did not start in final
PRK	North Korea (People's Republic of Korea)	e	Estimated
PUR	Puerto Rico	EOR	Equaled Olympic record
ROM	Romania	EWR	Equaled world record
RUS	Russia (1908–1912)	F.I.N.A.	International Amateur Swimming Federation
SAA	Saar	FT.	Feet
SAF	South Africa	GA	Goals against
SEN	Senegal	GF	Goals for
SIN	Singapore	H	Hurdles
SOV	Soviet Union	HAM	Hammer throw
SPA	Spain	HJ	High jump
SRL	Sri Lanka (Ceylon)	I.A.A.F.	International Amateur Athletic Federation
SWE	Sweden	IN.	Inches
SWI	Switzerland	I.O.C.	International Olympic Committee
SYR	Syria	JAV	Javelin throw
TAI	Taiwan	kg	Kilograms
TAN	Tanzania	km	Kilometers
THA	Thailand	KO	Knockout
TOG	Togo	L	Lost
TRI	Trinidad and Tobago	LBS.	Pounds
TUN	Tunisia	LJ	Long jump (broad jump)
TUR	Turkey	M	Meters
UAR	United Arab Republic (Egypt and Syria)	m.p.s.	Meters per second
UGA	Uganda	N:	Number of nations represented
URU	Uruguay	OR	Olympic record
USA	United States of America	PA	Points against
VEN	Venezuela	PF	Points for
YUG	Yugoslavia	PTS.	Points
ZAM	Zambia	PV	Pole vault
ZIM	Zimbabwe	RSC	Referee stopped contest
		SP	Shot put

TERMS

A.A.A.	Amateur Athletic Association	T:	Number of teams entered
A.A.U.	Amateur Athletic Union	T	Tied
AC	Also competed	TG	Touches given
C:	Number of competitors entered	TR	Touches received
D:	Date of final	W	Won
Dec.	Won by judges' decision	w	Wind-aided
DISC	Discus throw	WB	World best
DISQ	Disqualified	WO	Walkover
		WR	World record
		YDS.	Yards

SUMMER GAMES

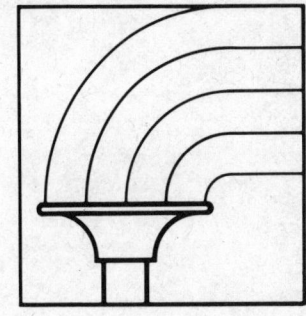

TRACK AND FIELD

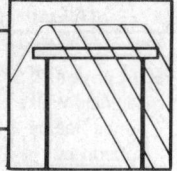

MEN

100 METERS

1896 Athens C: 17, N: 9, D: 4.10. WR: 10.8 (Luther Cary)
1. Thomas Burke   USA   12.0
2. Fritz Hofmann   GER   12.2e
3. Alajos Szokolyi   HUN   12.6e
4. Francis Lane   USA   12.6e
5. Alexandros Chalkokondilis   GRE   12.6e
DNS: Thomas Curtis (USA)

The very first race of the modern Olympics was the open-ing heat of the 100-meter dash. It was won by Francis Lane of Princeton in the time of 12⅕ seconds. The Europe-an crowd was fascinated by the "crouch" start of the Americans, as Thomas Curtis and Thomas Burke, both of Boston, won the other two qualifying heats. The first two finishers in each of the heats qualified for the final four days later, but Curtis chose not to start, preferring to save himself for the 110-meter hurdles, which was the next race. Burke, who had registered the fastest time (12.0) in the heats, equaled his time in the final and defeated Hofmann by two meters. The other runners were bunched four me-ters further back. Although Hofmann was a champion sprinter, his athletic specialty was actually rope climbing. Thomas Burke, the first Olympic 100 meters champion, later became a lawyer and also wrote part-time for the *Boston Journal*. He died on Valentine's Day, 1929, at the age of 53.

1900 Paris C: 20, N: 9, D: 7.14. WR: 10.8 (Luther Cary)
1. Frank Jarvis   USA   11.0
2. John Walter Tewksbury   USA   11.1
3. Stanley Rowley   AUS   11.2
DNF: Arthur Duffey (USA)

The American runners had never competed before on a grass track, however this didn't prevent Jarvis of Princeton and Tewksbury of Pennsylvania from equaling the world record of 10.8 in the heats and semifinals, respectively. De-spite these performances, the clear favorite was 5-foot 7-inch Arthur Duffey of Georgetown University, who had defeated both Jarvis and Tewksbury in London the previ-ous week. As expected, Duffey burst into the lead and seemed well on his way to victory when he suddenly began to wobble and fell to the ground at the 50-meter mark, the victim of a strained tendon in his left leg. Jarvis went on to win by about two feet. Duffey later told the press, "I do not know why my leg gave way. I felt a peculiar twitching after going twenty yards. I then seemed to lose control of it, and suddenly it gave out, throwing me on my face. But that is one of the fortunes of sport, and I cannot com-plain." In 1902 Duffey ran 100 yards in 9.6 seconds, set-ting a world record which stayed in the books for 24 years. Later he became a columnist for the *Boston Post*.

1904 St. Louis C: 13, N: 2, D: 9.3. WR: 10.8 (Luther Cary, Frank Jarvis, John Walter Tewksbury)
1. Archibald Hahn   USA   11.0
2. Nathaniel Cartmell   USA   11.2
3. William Hogenson   USA   11.2
4. Fay Moulton   USA   —
5. Frederick Heckwolf   USA   —
6. Lawson Robertson   USA   —

Archie Hahn, "The Milwaukee Meteor," had already won the 60-meter and 200-meter dashes when he settled down for the final of the 100. Running into a heavy wind, he shot out to a fast start, had a one yard lead by the 20-meter mark, and held off the fast-finishing Louisville sprinter Nate Cartmell to win by almost two yards.

1906 Athens C: 42, N: 13, D: 4.27. WR: 10.8 (Luther Cary, Frank Jarvis, John Walter Tewksbury)
1. Archibald Hahn   USA   11.2
2. Fay Moulton   USA   11.3
3. Nigel Barker   AUS   11.3
4. William Eaton   USA   —
5. Lawson Robertson   USA   —
6. Knut Lindberg   SWE   —

William Eaton of Boston recorded the fastest time in the semifinals (11.2), but in the final Hahn, with a quick start, led the whole way and won by a yard. Back in the United States, Hahn studied law at Michigan, but never practiced his profession. Instead he devoted his life to coaching younger runners. His book *How to Sprint* is still considered a classic text.

1908 London C: 57, N: 16, D: 7.22. WR: 10.6 (Knut Lindberg)

1. Reginald Walker	SAF	10.8 OR
2. James Rector	USA	10.9
3. Robert Kerr	CAN	11.0
4. Nathaniel Cartmell	USA	11.2

In 1908 the excitement surrounding the 100-meter race rivaled that of the marathon. The tension was heightened by the fact that only the winner of each heat advanced to the next round. The favorites, James Rector, a University of Virginia student from Hot Springs, Arkansas, and Bobbie Kerr, the Irish-born Canadian champion, did not disappoint their supporters in the opening heats. Rector was particularly impressive, tying the Olympic record of 10.8 seconds. He equaled this time in the semifinals, but so did Reggie Walker, a 19-year-old clerk from Durban. Walker had not been chosen for the South African team, but was sent to London as an afterthought by his fans in Natal. Arriving three weeks before the Olympics, he lost to Kerr in the final of the British A.A.A. Championship. Nevertheless he caught the eye of the famous coach Sam Mussabini, who took the young man under his wing and spent the next couple of weeks working with him on his start. This last-minute training worked wonders. Running on the inside lane, Walker stormed into an early lead, gave way to Rector at the halfway point, and then was able to pull ahead once again to win by a "long yard," with Rector holding on to second by mere inches. The 5-foot 7-inch, 130-pound Walker, who had been previously unknown to the general public, became an instant hero, as the crowd of 49,000 cheered wildly and threw their hats and programs into the air, while friends and officials competed for the right to carry him on their shoulders. In the words of one U.S. newspaper, "The Englishmen were gratified to see the monotonous succession of American victories broken by a Britisher, even if he was a colonist."

1912 Stockholm C: 68, N: 22, D: 7.7. WR: 10.5 (Richard Rau)

1. Ralph Craig	USA	10.8
2. Alvah Meyer	USA	10.9
3. Donald Lippincott	USA	10.9
4. George Patching	SAF	11.0
5. Frank Beloit	USA	—

DNS: Howard Drew (USA)

Ralph Craig of the University of Michigan was considered the pre-Olympic favorite until he was beaten in the U.S. trials by Howard Drew, a strong black student from Springfield, Massachusetts. In the first round in Stockholm, Donald Lippincott, the star of the University of Pennsylvania track team, set an Olympic record by winning his heat in 10.6 seconds. The semifinals were run with only the winner of each race advancing to the final. The Americans showed their strength by winning all five of the heats in which they were entered. Unfortunately, Drew strained a tendon just before the finish of his heat and, despite qualifying, was unable to start in the final.

The final was marred by seven false starts, the first three by Craig. At the eighth try a clean break was made, with Patching taking the early lead. Craig caught him at the 60-meter mark and went on to win by two feet. Thirty-six years later, Craig, by then a wealthy 59-year-old industrial engineer, reappeared at the London Olympics as an alternate on the U.S. yachting team.

1920 Antwerp C: 59, N: 23, D: 8.16. WR: 10.5 (Richard Rau)

1. Charles Paddock	USA	10.8
2. Morris Kirksey	USA	10.8
3. Harry Edward	GBR	11.0
4. Jackson Scholz	USA	11.0
5. Emile Ali Khan	FRA	11.1
6. Loren Murchison	USA	—

Charley Paddock was born in Gainesville, Texas, on August 11, 1900. A sickly child, he weighed only 7½ pounds at the age of 7 months. His parents moved to Southern California for his health, eventually settling in Pasadena. The change of climate must have done the trick, because by age 15, Charley was a barrel-chested 170-pounder with big strong legs and a sprinter's body. He loved to run long distances, but his father convinced him to concentrate on the 100 yards and the 220 yards. Paddock came to international attention in 1919 when he won both metric sprints at the Inter-Allied Games in Paris, with times of 10.8 and 21.6. Charley was a great crowd-pleaser, who delighted photographers with a flying finish in which he would leap at the tape from about 12 feet out, with his arms flung wide.

The semifinals of the Olympic championship were held in the early morning on Monday, August 16. The first heat was won by Guyanese-born Harry Edward and the second by Charley Paddock, both in 10.8. Scholz and Murchison had also run 10.8 in the earlier rounds. All four Americans qualified for the final and spent the next few hours together, waiting anxiously for their late afternoon race. The blond-haired Murchison kept muttering, half to himself, "I'm going to win. I've known it all along. . . . I can trim any sprinter who ever lived." The others tried to ignore him. Just before it was time to take the field, the four runners were approached by coach Lawson Robertson, who said, "What you fellows need to warm up is a glass of sherry and a raw egg." Murchison, Scholz, and Paddock were horrified by the suggestion, but when Stanford's Morris Kirksey agreed to try the drink, the others feared it would give him a psychological advantage to be the only one to follow the coach's advice, so they guzzled down the strange concoction as well.

Like many athletes, Charley Paddock followed a set of good luck rituals. On the way to the starting line he would knock on "a friendly piece of wood." When called to his mark, he would put his hands far across the starting line and then draw them slowly back before the second call of "get set." Paddock was the last to stoop to his mark at the starting line of the 1920 100-meter final. The assistant starter, unaware of Charley's ritual, ordered him in French to pull back his hands, which he was actually already in the process of doing. The starter then called out *"prêt,"* the French equivalent of "get set." Murchison misinterpreted the exchange and thought the runners had been ordered to stand up, so he was just beginning to relax and rise when the gun went off. He was left 10 yards behind. Kirksey took the early lead, but at the halfway mark Scholz had a two-foot advantage, with Edward in second. Then Kirksey surged ahead again, with Paddock at his shoulder. In the words of Charley Paddock: "Then I saw the thin white string stretched to the breaking point in front of me. I drove my spikes into the soft cinders and felt my foot give way as I sprang forward in a final jump for the tape. . . . There was nothing more I could do. My eyes closed as my chest hit the string and when I opened them, my feet were on the ground again and I was yards ahead of the field. I did not know if I had been in front when the string was broken. I dared not ask." In fact, Charley Paddock had won the race by 12 inches. "My dream had come true," he later wrote, "and I thrilled to the greatest moment I felt that I should ever know. . . . The real pleasure had been in the anticipation and in that single moment of glorious realization."

1924 Paris C: 82, N: 34, D: 7.7. WR: 10.2 (Charles Paddock)

1.	Harold Abrahams	GBR	10.6 OR
2.	Jackson Scholz	USA	10.7
3.	Arthur Porritt	NZE	10.8
4.	Chester Bowman	USA	10.9
5.	Charles Paddock	USA	10.9
6.	Loren Murchison	USA	11.0

The story of Harold Abrahams' victory in Paris in 1924 is well told in the beautiful film *Chariots of Fire*. Unfortunately, despite its claim of being "A true story," the film contains several factual distortions. Abrahams did not race around the great courtyard of Trinity College at Cambridge. (It was Lord Burghley who did that.) He did not look at the 100-meter contest as a chance to redeem himself after his failure in the 200, since the running of the 100 actually preceded the 200 in real life. Although Abrahams did feel himself an outsider because he was Jewish, a much more important motivating factor in his quest for victory was a desire to do better than his two older brothers, both of whom were well-known athletes and one of whom had represented Great Britain at the 1912 Olympics in Stockholm. Abrahams himself had competed in the 100 and 200 meters in Antwerp in 1920, but had been eliminated in the quarterfinals. In the year preceding the Paris Olympics, Abrahams came under the direction of Sam Mussabini, who had successfully coached Reggie Walker to victory in 1908. Among other things, Mussabini stressed to Abrahams the importance of the length and number of his strides. During practice sessions Abrahams would place pieces of paper on the track, to indicate where each stride should end. Then he would try to pick them up on his spikes as he ran. He always carried with him a piece of string the length of his first stride. Before a race he would

pull out the string, measure forward from the starting line, and make a mark on the track where his first step should land.

Abrahams was also a proficient long-jumper. One month before the Olympics he leaped 24 feet 2½ inches (7.38 meters) to set an English record which lasted until 1956. For this reason he was chosen to represent Great Britain in the long jump as well as the 100, 200 and 4 × 100 relay. When an anonymous letter appeared in the *Daily Express*, criticizing the decision to enter Abrahams in the long jump, few people knew that the letter had been written by Harold Abrahams himself. He made his point and was excused from that event.

Despite his great feats, the 6-foot ½-inch 175-pound Abrahams was considered a long shot in comparison to the U.S. team, which included defending champion Charley Paddock as well as Antwerp finalists Jackson Scholz and Loren Murchison. On June 18, 1921, Paddock had stunned the track world by running 110 yards (which is actually longer than 100 meters) in the unheard-of time of 10.2 seconds, a record that remained unbeaten for 29 years. Although the Americans were the favorites, it was Harold Abrahams, running faster than he had ever run before, who registered the fastest times in the early heats, tying the Olympic record (10.6) twice, in the quarterfinals and the semifinals, where he overcame an awful start. For the first time Abrahams realized that he had a chance to win the Olympic gold, and for the first time he lost his carefree attitude and began to feel the pressure. For the next 3¾ hours, as he waited for the final, he "felt like a condemned man feels just before going to the scaffold." As he went to his mark at 7:05 p.m. on July 7, Abrahams recalled Sam Mussabini's final words of advice: "Only think of two things—the report of the pistol and the tape. When you hear the one, just run like hell till you break the other." After a perfect start, the runners ran almost even for the first 40 or 50 meters, but then Abrahams began to move ahead, gaining with each stride until he crossed the tape with a two-foot victory.

Harold Abrahams is a perfect example of an athlete who peaks at exactly the right moment. After that day at the Stade Colombes in Paris, he never raced well again. The following year he injured his thigh while long-jumping and retired from competition forever. He once wrote, "I wonder if, in a sense, that was not another piece of good bad-luck. How many people find it almost impossible to retire at the right time. Would I have gone downhill, and tried to go on? That was the decision I never had to make; it was made for me. Rather painfully, but it was made." Abrahams went on to great success as a radio commentator, lawyer, writer, statistician and as president of the British Amateur Athletic Association. Arthur Porritt, who took the bronze medal even though he failed to win a single heat, had an even more distinguished career, culminating in a five-year term as Governor-General of New Zealand. As for Charley Paddock, he died in 1943 while a captain in the U.S. Marine Corps and had a ship named after him.

1928 Amsterdam C: 81, N: 33, D: 7.30. WR: 10.2 (Charles Paddock)

1. Percy Williams	CAN	10.8
2. Jack London	GBR	10.9
3. Georg Lammers	GER	10.9
4. Frank Wykoff	USA	11.0
5. Wilfred Legg	SAF	11.0
6. Robert McAllister	USA	11.0

Percy Williams was one of the most popular winners of the Amsterdam Games. Not considered a serious threat by the experts, the slim, almost frail-looking 20-year-old from Vancouver, British Columbia, caught the fancy of the crowd in the second round, when he tied the Olympic record of 10.6. This time was matched in both semifinals, first by Bob McAllister, "The Flying Cop" of New York City, who barely held off a slow-starting Williams, and then by Jack London, a Guyanese-born university student who was the first Briton to use starting blocks. As the six finalists lined up for the deciding race, the 126-pound Williams seemed an unlikely bet to become Olympic champion, particularly as he was standing beside the muscular 6-foot 2-inch, 200-pound London. After two false starts, by Legg and Wykoff (who had gained 10 pounds on the boat ride from the United States), the runners were off. Williams took the lead immediately and kept it the entire way, holding off late rushes by London and Lammers to win by two feet. McAllister pulled a tendon 20 meters from the tape and finished last.

Upon his return to Canada, Williams, who also won the 200 meters, was greeted with an enthusiasm reminiscent of the ancient Greek Olympics. Crossing the continent by train with his mother, he stopped in Montreal, where he was presented with a gold watch. In Hamilton he received a silver tea service and in Winnipeg a bronze statue and a silver cup. When he finally reached Vancouver, he was met by tens of thousands of cheering fans and was given a blue Graham-Paige sports car as well as $14,000 for his education.

1932 Los Angeles C: 32, N: 17, D: 8.1. WR: 10.2 (Charles Paddock, Ralph Metcalfe)

1. Thomas "Eddie" Tolan	USA	10.3 OR
2. Ralph Metcalfe	USA	10.3
3. Arthur Jonath	GER	10.4
4. George Simpson	USA	10.5
5. Daniel Joubert	SAF	10.6
6. Takayoshi Yoshioka	JAP	10.8

Eddie Tolan was the third University of Michigan athlete to win the Olympic 100 meters gold medal, following in the tradition of Archie Hahn and Ralph Craig. The 5-foot 7-inch Tolan dominated U.S. sprinting from 1929 to 1931, but he was dethroned by Ralph Metcalfe of Marquette University in Milwaukee, who breezed undefeated through the 1932 season. At the U.S. Olympic trials Metcalfe beat Tolan in both sprints and went to Los Angeles as the favorite. But in the second round it was Tolan who set an

Olympic record of 10.4. In the final Yoshioka, an excellent starter, took the lead from the first step and held it for 40 meters, when he was caught by Tolan. Yoshioka faded at 60 meters, while Metcalfe began his famous finishing spurt. He pulled even with Tolan at 80 meters and the two ran neck and neck for the rest of the race, crossing the finish line in a near dead heat. Most of the spectators felt that there had been a tie or that Metcalfe had won. Several hours later, seven judges viewed a film of the race and determined that Tolan had *crossed* the line two inches ahead of Metcalfe. Current rules state that the first runner to *reach* the finish line is the winner. So close was the race that if the current rules had been in effect in 1932, Metcalfe would have been the winner.

After the games Tolan tried his hand at the vaudeville circuit, joining forces with the famous dancer Bill "Bojangles" Robinson. He was more successful as a professional runner, and was especially popular in Australia. Two of the also-rans in 1932 provoked almost as much interest as the winners. The first was Daniel Joubert, a white South African who spoke seven African dialects. Joubert arrived in Los Angeles in a somewhat weakened condition, having traveled 38 days to get there. Considering his ordeal, it was quite an achievement that he even made the final. Even more popular was Cheng-Chun Liu who marched in the opening day ceremony as the one and only representative of the 400,000,000 people of China. Cheng finished last in his first round heat in both the 100 and 200. He also competed in both events at the Berlin Olympics four years later.

1936 Berlin C: 63, N: 30, D: 8.3. WR: 10.2 (Charles Paddock, Ralph Metcalfe, Jesse Owens)

1. Jesse Owens	USA	10.3
2. Ralph Metcalfe	USA	10.4
3. Martinus Osendarp	HOL	10.5
4. Frank Wykoff	USA	10.6
5. Erich Borchmeyer	GER	10.7
6. Lennart Strandberg	SWE	10.9

Jesse Owens assured himself a permanent place in sports history on May 25, 1935, when, while competing at the Big Ten championships at Ann Arbor, Michigan, he broke five world records and equaled a sixth in the space of 45 minutes. At 3:15 p.m. he won the 100-yard dash by five yards in 9.4 seconds to tie the world record. At 3:25 he long-jumped 26 feet 8¼ inches, breaking the existing world record by six inches. It was his only jump of the day, but it wasn't beaten for 25 years. At 3:45 he scored a ten-yard victory in the 220-yard dash, clocking 20.3 seconds and bettering the listed record by three-tenths of a second. He was also given credit for lowering the world record in the shorter 200-meter dash. At 4:00 p.m. he flew over the 220-yard low hurdles in 22.6, the first man to beat 23 seconds. En route he also established a record for the 200-meter hurdles. Despite these and other sensational performances, in the following year Owens lost three times to the great Alabama-born sprinter Eulace Peacock. And it wasn't until one week before the Olympic trials that Jesse was able to defeat Ralph Metcalfe. But he peaked when he needed to, winning the 100, 200, and long jump at the trials, and he went to Berlin as the favorite in all three events.

Owens had little trouble living up to expectations. In the first round of the 100 meters he tied the Olympic record of 10.3. In the second round he ran a wind-aided 10.2. Jesse took it easy in the semifinals, winning his heat in 10.4 while Metcalfe won the other in 10.5. The final saw Owens take the lead from the first stride and pull out to a five-foot lead by the halfway mark. As usual Metcalfe started slowly and came on strong in the last 25 meters. He closed the gap, but was still a yard back when Owens broke the tape. Metcalfe, who was elected to the U.S. Congress 34 years later, picked up his second straight 100 meters silver medal, while Osendarp became the first Dutchman to win an individual track and field medal. Strandberg appeared to be a sure medalist, but he strained a tendon at the 80-meter mark and limped home in last place. Before the week was out, Jesse Owens had earned three more gold medals.

Nazi propaganda had portrayed Negroes as inferior, taunting the United States for relying on "black auxiliaries." Evidently, though, the message had little effect on the German masses, who considered Owens the hero of Berlin. Everywhere he went around town he was mobbed by fans seeking his autograph or photograph. They even shoved autograph books through his bedroom window in the Olympic Village while he tried to sleep.

Jesse Owens was born September 12, 1913, in Danville, Alabama, the son of sharecroppers and the grandson of slaves. By the age of 7 he was expected to pick 100 pounds of cotton a day. When he was 9 his family moved north to Cleveland, where Jesse pumped gas and delivered groceries. After he set national high school records in the broad jump, the 100-yard dash, and the 220, he was recruited by 28 colleges, but chose to stay close to home at Ohio State. While a student there he worked as an elevator operator and, later, as a page in the state legislature. There is a famous myth that after Jesse won the 100 meters in Berlin he was snubbed by Adolf Hitler, who refused to meet Owens after he had personally congratulated three earlier gold medal winners. Actually, if such a snub did occur, the recipient was not Jesse Owens, but Cornelius Johnson and David Albritton, black Americans who had finished one-two in the high jump the previous day.

Owens *was* snubbed by a different world leader—Franklin Delano Roosevelt. Although Jesse received tickertape parades in New York City and Cleveland, the President not only failed to invite him to the White House, he never even sent a letter of congratulations. Owens was also snubbed by the Amateur Athletic Union, which suspended him for refusing to run in a Swedish meet which he had never agreed to enter. The A.A.U. also bypassed him for the Sullivan award, which was presented to the best U.S.

amateur athlete of the year. In 1935, the year that Jesse Owens set six world records, the award was given to a golfer named Lawson Little. In 1936, the year of Owens' four gold medals, the award went to Glenn Morris, the Olympic decathlon champion.

After the Olympics Jesse worked as a paid campaigner for presidential candidate Alf Landon. When Landon lost to Roosevelt in a landslide, Jesse took a $130 a month job as a playground instructor in Cleveland. In an attempt to make ends meet, the hero of Berlin, "The Ebony Antelope," allowed promoters to stage exhibitions in which he raced against horses, dogs, and motorcycles. Tiring of this, he returned to his job as a playground instructor. Then he lent his name to a chain of cleaning stores which went bankrupt, leaving Jesse $114,000 in debt. In the 1950s he finally achieved financial security when he opened a public relations firm and became a public speaker on behalf of various corporate sponsors. He developed a repertoire of five basic speeches including ones on religion, patriotism, and marketing for salesmen. In the words of writer William Oscar Johnson, Jesse Owens had become "a professional good example."

In 1968 Owens took the side of the U.S. Olympic Committee in its struggle with militant black athletes and two years later he wrote a book called *Blackthink,* which criticized racial militancy. However in 1972 he published another book, *I Have Changed*, retracting his earlier criticisms. After 35 years of pack-a-day cigarette smoking, Jesse Owens died of lung cancer in Tucson, Arizona, on March 31, 1980. Would-be Olympic sprint champions might be interested to know the secret of his success. In 1936 he told one London reporter, "I let my feet spend as little time on the ground as possible. From the air, fast down, and from the ground, fast up. My foot is only a fraction of the time on the track."

1948 London C: 66, N: 34, D: 7.31. WR: 10.2 (Charles Paddock, Ralph Metcalfe, Jesse Owens, Harold Davis, Lloyd LaBeach, H. Norwood "Barney" Ewell)

1. Harrison Dillard	USA	10.3 EOR
2. H. Norwood "Barney" Ewell	USA	10.4
3. Lloyd LaBeach	PAN	10.4
4. Alistair McCorquodale	GBR	10.4
5. Melvin Patton	USA	10.5
6. Emmanuel McDonald Bailey	GBR	10.6

Harrison Dillard was a 13-year-old schoolboy in Cleveland when he attended the huge parade in 1936 in honor of Jesse Owens. Later he met Owens, who took a liking to the young man and presented him with the running shoes he had used to win his gold medals. Dillard did an outstanding job of literally filling those shoes. By 1952 he had matched his hero's total of four Olympic victories. From May 31, 1947, through June 26, 1948, "Bones" Dillard, running mostly the hurdles, ran up an unprecedented string of 82 consecutive victories. The streak finally came to an end at the A.A.U. meet in Milwaukee when he tried to run four races in 67 minutes. First he lost the 100 meters to Barney Ewell and then he lost the 110-meter hurdles to Bill Porter. Nevertheless, when the Olympics trials were held the following week in Evanston, Illinois, there seemed no surer gold medal bet than Harrison Dillard, the world record holder in the 110-meters hurdles. However, in the final he uncharacteristically hit the first hurdle, lost his stride, hit two more hurdles, and stopped at the seventh hurdle as the others raced ahead. Dillard's Olympic hopes seemed over. Fortunately he had qualified the day before as third man in the 100 meters. But Dillard would face stiff competition in London. First there was the prerace favorite, U.S.C.'s Mel Patton, who held the world record of 9.3 in the 100 yards. Then there was 30-year-old Barney Ewell, who had beaten Patton at the U.S. trials in the world record time of 10.2. And there was Patton's arch rival from U.C.L.A., Lloyd LaBeach, who had also run 100 meters in 10.2 and who went to London as the sole representative of his native country, Panama.

The three favorites and Dillard were joined in the Olympic final by two representatives of Great Britain, Mac Bailey of Trinidad who, like Dillard, had been inspired by the feats of Jesse Owens, and Alistair McCorquodale, a burly Scot who had taken up running only a year earlier and who actually preferred rugby and cricket to track. After one false start, Dillard flashed into the lead and held it the entire way. Ewell caught him at the tape and, thinking he had won, danced around the field joyfully and embraced his opponents. When the photo-finish had been studied and it was announced that Dillard had won, Ewell happily congratulated him on his good fortune, greatly impressing the crowd of 82,000 with his sportsmanship. LaBeach is the only Panamanian ever to have won an Olympic medal.

1952 Helsinki C: 72, N: 33, D: 7.21. WR: 10.1 (Lloyd LaBeach)

1. Lindy Remigino	USA	10.4
2. Herbert McKenley	JAM	10.4
3. Emmanuel McDonald Bailey	GBR	10.4
4. F. Dean Smith	USA	10.4
5. Vladimir Sukharyev	SOV	10.5
6. John Treloar	AUS	10.5

The 1952 100-meter final produced the closest finish in Olympic history and also one of the biggest sprint upsets. The title seemed pretty much up for grabs, particularly after the U.S. college champion, Jim Golliday, was injured and unable to participate in the Olympics. The position of favorite shifted to 31-year-old Mac Bailey and Arthur Bragg of Morgan State College. But Bragg pulled a muscle in the semifinals, which were won by Bailey and 30-year-old Herb McKenley, the 400-meter world record holder who stepped down to the 100 when he saw that there was an open field. The surviving U.S. representatives were Texan Dean Smith, who later became a stuntman in hundreds of television shows and films including *Stagecoach* and *True Grit*, and Lindy Remigino, a modest Manhattan College student from Hartford, Connecticut. Remigino must have been amazed to find himself a finalist in the Olym-

pics. He had barely qualified for the U.S. Olympic tryouts by finishing fifth in the N.C.A.A. championship and then barely made the team thanks to a photo-finish. Smith showed in front first, but Remigino had a clear lead at the halfway mark. He held on gamely for 90 meters, but was passed by McKenley just as they reached the tape.

"I was sure I had lost the race," said Remigino afterward. "I started my lean too early . . . and I saw Herb McKenley shoot past me. I was heartsick. I figured I had blown it." Lindy walked over to the delighted Jamaican and offered his congratulations. But a photo-finish showed that Remigino's right shoulder had reached the finish line an inch ahead of McKenley's chest, and the judges ruled him the winner. When someone told Remigino the results before they had been flashed on the scoreboard, he was incredulous and was sure there had been a mistake. Finally he turned to McKenley and is reputed to have said, "Gosh, Herb, it looks as though I won the darn thing." The closeness of the finish is shown by the fact that Dean Smith was only 14 inches behind the winner, yet placed only fourth.

1956 Melbourne C: 65, N: 31, D: 11.24. WR: 10.1 (Lloyd LaBeach, Willie Williams, Ira Murchison, Leamon King)

1. Robert Morrow	USA	10.5
2. W. Thane Baker	USA	10.5
3. Hector Hogan	AUS	10.6
4. Ira Murchison	USA	10.6
5. Manfred Germar	GER	10.7
6. Michael Agostini	TRI	10.7

The Olympic record was tied in the second round by the favorites, 6-foot 1½-inch Bobby Morrow and 5-foot 4½-inch Ira Murchison. The same pair won the two semifinal heats with Morrow again running 10.3. The final was run into a 9 m.p.h. wind, which accounts for the slow times. Hec Hogan, the five-time Australian 100-yard champion from Queensland, took the early lead, but Morrow passed him after 50 meters and stormed to a decisive victory. Baker and Murchison caught Hogan with 25 yards to go, but Hogan churned out a final burst, and only a desperate lunge by Baker kept the Aussie from a silver medal. Morrow, a devout Christian from Harlingen, Texas, never tried to anticipate the starters' gun with a rolling start because he considered it unsportsmanlike. A cotton and carrot farmer, he relied on getting 11 hours sleep a night to keep up his strength. "Whatever success I have had," he said, "is due to being so perfectly relaxed that I can feel my jaw muscles wiggle." Bronze medalist Hogan died of leukemia at the age of 29 on September 2, 1960, the day after the 100-meter final at Rome.

1960 Rome C: 61, N: 45, D: 9.1. WR: 10.0 (Armin Hary, Harry Jerome)

1. Armin Hary	GER	10.2 OR
2. David Sime	USA	10.2
3. Peter Radford	GBR	10.3

4. Enrique Figuerola Camue   CUB   10.3
5. Francis "Frank" Budd   USA   10.3
6. O. Ray Norton   USA   10.4

On June 21, 1960, Armin Hary, a controversial, self-coached office worker from Frankfurt, became the first man to be credited with 10.0 in the 100 meters. Running in Zurich, this fast-starting son of a coal miner in Quierschied, Saarland, actually achieved the time twice in one day. On the first occasion he was accused of "taking a flyer," or beating the gun, a tactic for which he was notorious. When the starter ordered the race rerun, Hary protested, but went ahead and ran another 10.0. Three and a half weeks later, on July 15, the son of a Pullman coach attendant, 19-year-old Harry Jerome of Vancouver, recorded the second official 10.0 at the Canadian Olympic trials in Saskatoon.

Despite the achievements of Hary and Jerome, most track aficionados were predicting victory for Ray Norton, who had swept both sprints at the U.S.A.–U.S.S.R. meet, the 1959 Pan American Games, and the 1960 U.S. Olympic trials. Another contender was Dave Sime, a medical student from Fair Lawn, New Jersey. Sime set a rather unusual world record when he ran 100 yards in 9.8 seconds while dressed in a baseball uniform. The previous record had been set by Jesse Owens in 1936.

In the second round in Rome, Armin Hary beat Dave Sime by a yard and set an Olympic record of 10.2. The first semifinal was won by Peter Radford, a Walsall schoolteacher who had spent three childhood years in a wheelchair because of a kidney disease. Harry Jerome had been in the lead when he pulled a muscle and couldn't finish. The second semi saw Armin Hary beat both Sime and Norton, who was running unusually tightly.

The start of the final was a tense affair. First Hary and Sime broke without a gun, but neither was penalized. The next try for a start was halted when Figuerola needed his starting block repaired. Then Hary beat the gun and was penalized. One more false start and he would be disqualified. But the usually volatile Hary kept his poise and at the next attempt got off to a fair and perfect start. By the end of the first stride he was already in the lead, and at the five-meter mark he led by a full meter. In the second half of the race, Sime stormed back from last place to make up over three meters, but Hary held on to win by a "long foot." Not only was Armin Hary the first winner of the Olympic 100 meters to come from a non-English-speaking country, he was also the first German male to win an Olympic gold medal in a track event.

In the end Hary proved that his amazing "blitz start" was legitimate. He contended, however, that there was more to it than quick reflexes. "More important to me," he said, "is the fact that I have learned, through relaxation, how to achieve full stride and smooth forward action very early in the race." Hary's competitive career came to an abrupt halt shortly after the Olympics, when his knee was severely injured in an auto accident.

1964 Tokyo C: 73, N: 49, D: 10.15. WR: 10.0 (Armin Hary, Harry Jerome, Horacio Estevez)

1. Robert Hayes   USA   10.0 EWR
2. Enrique Figuerola Camue CUB   10.2
3. Harry Jerome   CAN   10.2
4. Wieslaw Maniak   POL   10.4
5. Heinz Schumann   GER   10.4
6. Gaoussou Kone   IVC   10.4
6. Melvin Pender   USA   10.4
8. Thomas Robinson   BAH   10.5

This was one 100-meter final that was run exactly to form. Any doubts that Hayes had not recovered from a June leg injury were quickly dispelled when the burly, pigeon-toed Florida speedster demolished the field in the first semifinal in a wind-aided 9.9. Harry Jerome won the second semi, ahead of Kone, Figuerola, and Pender. Pender led most of the way but tore a rib muscle and had to be carried off the field on a stretcher. Advised by doctors to withdraw from the final, he ran anyway and spent the next three days in the hospital as a result. Hayes, who was the first person to run 100 yards in 9.1 and the first person to break 6.0 for 60 yards, entered the Olympics with a record of 48 straight finals victories at 100 yards and 100 meters. The start was delayed 10 minutes while the curb lane, Hayes' lane, was raked after having been chewed up by the start of the 20-kilometer walk. The big three, Hayes, Figuerola and Jerome, had pulled away from the others by the 10-meter mark. Then Hayes unleashed his power, took a one-meter lead halfway, and pulled away to an awesome seven-foot victory—the widest in Olympic history. Both Figuerola, who became the first Cuban to win an Olympic track and field medal, and Jerome called it the best race they had run all year and had nothing but praise for the winner. After the Olympics, Bob Hayes became a professional football player and was twice chosen All-Pro as a wide receiver for the Dallas Cowboys.

1968 Mexico City C: 64, N: 42, D: 10.14. WR: 9.9 (James Hines, Ronnie Ray Smith, Charles Greene)

1. James Hines   USA   9.95 WR
2. Lennox Miller   JAM   10.0
3. Charles Greene   USA   10.0
4. Pablo Montes   CUB   10.1
5. Roger Bambuck   FRA   10.1
6. Melvin Pender   USA   10.1
7. Harry Jerome   CAN   10.1
8. Jean-Louis Ravelomanatsoa MAD 10.2

The first accredited time of 9.9 seconds for 100 meters was registered at the A.A.U. Championships in Sacramento, California, on June 20, 1968, by Jim Hines, the son of an Oakland construction worker. Hines had run a wind-aided 9.8 in a heat, then followed with his history-making run in the semifinal. However, in the final he was beaten by Charlie Greene, a graduate of the University of Nebraska. Previous to the Olympics, Hines and Greene had met in 12 finals, with Greene winning eight of them. However two of

Hines' four victories had been the last two times they met, at the U.S. Olympic trials.

Competition was stiff in Mexico City. In the second round Heinz Erbstösser of East Germany had the distinction of being the first person to run 10.2 and not qualify for the semifinals. Greene clocked 10.0 in his first two heats, while Hines matched the time in the semis. Hermes Ramirez of Cuba also ran 10.0 in the second round, but was eliminated in the semis. The 1968 100 meters saw the first all-black final in Olympic history. Hines got off to what he later said was the best start of his career. However it was U.S. Army captain Mel Pender, now 30, who took the early lead. By 50 meters Hines and Greene had pulled even, and at 70 meters Hines shifted gears and pulled away to win by a meter. Greene, discouraged and suffering a cramp, was nipped at the tape by Lennox Miller, who represented U.S.C. in U.S. collegiate competition. Hines' electronically timed 9.95 was considered faster than the hand-timed world record of 9.9. Four days after his Olympic victory, Hines signed a contract with the Miami Dolphins football team. Another man who went into professional sports was Japan's Hideo Iijima, who made it to the semifinals in 1964 and 1968. As the fastest sprinter in Japanese history, Iijima attracted the attention of the Lotte Orions baseball team, who hired him to become a pinch-runner and base-stealer. The club insured Iijima's legs for 50 million yen. Unfortunately Iijima, though fast, hadn't played baseball since he was 12 and had no aptitude for getting a jump on a pitch or for sliding. After two years, during which he was caught stealing 17 of 40 times, he was finally dropped from the team.

1972 Munich C: 84, N: 55, D: 9.1. WR: 9.95 (James Hines)

1.	Valery Borzov	SOV	10.14
2.	Robert Taylor	USA	10.24
3.	Lennox Miller	JAM	10.33
4.	Aleksandr Kornelyuk	SOV	10.36
5.	Michael Fray	JAM	10.40
6.	Jobst Hirscht	GER	10.40
7.	Zenon Nowosz	POL	10.46

DNF: Hasely Crawford (TRI)

Valery Borzov was the clear favorite in 1972. The blond-haired, blue-eyed Ukrainian was extremely consistent and had not been beaten in almost two years. However Eddie Hart of Pittsburg, California, and Rey Robinson of Lakeland, Florida, had both been timed at 9.9 in the U.S. Olympic trials. Hart was considered the number-one threat to Borzov. The first round of 12 heats began at 11:09 a.m. on August 31. Borzov, Hart, and Robinson each won their heats. Vassilios Papageorgopoulous of Greece recorded the fastest time of the round, 10.24, a time that might have earned him a silver medal had he not suffered a groin injury that forced him to withdraw from the semifinals. The second round, the quarterfinal, was scheduled to commence at 4:15 p.m. As that time drew nearer, 1968 400-meter gold medalist Lee Evans noticed that Hart, Robinson and the third U.S. sprinter, Robert Taylor, had

not yet arrived at the stadium. When he couldn't find them at the warm-up track, Evans began to worry. Scheduled to run in the 4 × 400-meter relay later in the week, he raced at top speed from the stadium to the Olympic Village three quarters of a mile away in search of the missing Americans. But it was too late.

Two minutes earlier, Hart, Robinson, and Taylor, thinking the quarterfinals didn't begin until 7 p.m., had casually left their quarters to return to the stadium. Accompanied by their coach, Stan Wright, who had been working from an outdated 18-month-old preliminary schedule, the trio made their way to the bus stop at the Village gate. While waiting for the track stadium bus, they wandered into the doorway of the ABC-TV headquarters and began watching the television monitor. What they saw on the screen was several 100-meter runners lining up at the starting line. Robinson asked if this was a rerun of the first round. Told that it was a live transmission, Robinson realized with horror that he was watching the very heat in which he had been scheduled to run. Hart was entered in the second heat and Taylor in the third. The three athletes and their coach were pushed into a car and driven at breakneck speed to the stadium by ABC employee Bill Norris. It was too late for Robinson and Hart, but Taylor who, like Jim Hines, had studied at Texas Southern, arrived just in time to slip off his sweats, put on his shoes, do a couple knee-bends, and settle into the starting blocks. He finished second in the heat, a yard behind Borzov, which is exactly where he ended up 25 hours later, in the final. In that race, Borzov took the lead after 30 meters and was never headed. He even eased up at the end, throwing his arms wide in exultation five meters from the finish. A last-chance dive gained dental student Lennox Miller third place over Aleksandr Kornelyuk, the 5-foot 5-inch surprise from Azerbaijan.

Following the race, Borzov told reporters (in English) that he owed his success, "First and foremost to my country, secondly to my coach, Valentin Petrovsky, thirdly to all the people who helped me develop, and fourthly to myself." Borzov wasn't just toeing the party line. Listen to Petrovsky explain what went on at the Kiev Institute of Physical Culture, where Borzov was a graduate student: "We began with a search for the most up-to-date model of sprinting. We studied slow-motion films of leading world sprinters of past and present, figured out the push-off angle and the body incline at the breakaway and went deeply into a whole number of minor details. . . . For Borzov to be able to clock 10 seconds flat over 100 meters, a whole team of scientists conducted research resembling the work of, say, car or aircraft designers. . . . When the mathematical equivalent of a runner was worked out and given a scientific basis, we began testing our calculations in practice. It was subtle work, which could be compared to the training of a ballerina." Such statements give the impression that Borzov was just a machine, but he was quite human. He once said, "I very often have the following urge: I suddenly feel on the street that I have to run. I absolutely have to run, dressed in a suit, wearing my hat and tie, not paying any attention to the passers-by. . . . Then convention gets the upper hand and I restrain myself." Borzov eventually married the famous gymnast Lyudmila Turischeva, who won even more gold medals than he did.

1976 Montreal C: 63, N: 40, D: 7.24. WR: 9.95 (James Hines)

1. Hasely Crawford	TRI	10.06
2. Donald Quarrie	JAM	10.08
3. Valery Borzov	SOV	10.14
4. Harvey Glance	USA	10.19
5. Guy Abrahams	PAN	10.25
6. John Jones	USA	10.27
7. Klaus-Dieter Kurrat	GDR	10.31
8. Peter Petrov	BUL	10.35

Several runners were given a strong chance to win, but the leading choices of track experts were Donald Quarrie, Silvio Leonard of Cienfuegos, Cuba, and Valery Borzov, who was aiming to become the first man to win two 100 meters gold medals (not counting Archie Hahn, whose second victory was in the Intercalated Games of 1906). In fact, Borzov was the first gold medalist even to attempt the feat since Percy Williams had been eliminated in the semifinals in 1932. The first of the leading contenders to fall by the wayside was the accident-prone Cuban Silvio Leonard. Leonard had won the 100 meters at the 1975 Pan American Games in Mexico City, but had pulled a muscle as he crossed the finish line. Hobbling forward in pain, he was unable to stop himself and fell into the 10-foot moat that surrounded the track. Seriously injured, Leonard nonetheless regained his form in time for the Olympics. Ten days before the Games, however, he stepped on a cologne bottle during a bit of horseplay and cut his foot. He was eliminated in the quarterfinals.

Meanwhile, 6-foot 2¾-inch Hasely Crawford, a gear machinist from San Fernando, Trinidad, was breezing through his heats. In the quarterfinals he beat Borzov, and in the semis he defeated Quarrie. Crawford had been a finalist in Munich four years earlier but had stopped running after four or five strides, the victim of a hamstring pull and nervousness. He was still fighting his nerves in Montreal, but he wasn't the only one. In the staging room before the final he looked over at Glance and Jones, who were only 19 and 18 respectively, and their "eyes showed they were already defeated." Crawford later told reporters, "At the line I knew I could beat Borzov. I feared Don Quarrie." At the starting line, Crawford "shook a little bit," but got a good start anyway. Glance took the early lead. Quarrie caught him after 60 meters and passed him at 75 meters. Then Crawford flew past on the curb lane. He stumbled just before the finish, but held off the lunging Quarrie to win. Crawford kept running for another 150 meters, then stopped suddenly, as if the realization of his accomplishment had just hit him.

1980 Moscow C: 65, N: 40, D: 7.25. WR: 9.95 (James Hines)

1. Allan Wells	GBR	10.25
2. Silvio Leonard Tartabull	CUB	10.25
3. Peter Petrov	BUL	10.39
4. Aleksandr Aksinin	SOV	10.42
5. Osvaldo Lara Cañizares	CUB	10.43
6. Vladimir Muravyov	SOV	10.44
7. Marian Woronin	POL	10.46
8. Hermann Panzo	FRA	10.49

Stanley Floyd of Albany, Georgia, won the U.S. Olympic trials and also recorded the best time of the year (10.07). But with U.S. athletes boycotted out of the Olympics the mantle of favorite fell to Silvio Leonard, who had successfully managed to steer clear of moats and cologne bottles. His most serious challengers were considered to be Marian Woronin, who predicted that he would win the gold medal in a time of 10.10, and Eugen Ray of East Germany. Aleksandr Aksinin recorded the fastest time of the first round—10.26. When the draw was announced for the second round, many eyebrows were raised. Of the nine first-round winners, four were thrown into the first heat, as was defending champion Hasely Crawford. On the other hand, heat number three saw Aksinin unburdened by competition from other first-round winners. Aksinin won that heat in 10.29, a time which would have placed him seventh in the first heat. Heat number one was won by Allan Wells, a marine engineer from Edinburgh. His time of 10.11 pushed him up to cofavorite with Leonard.

The final took place during the last round of the triple jump, an event of great interest to the Soviet crowd. Just as the starter called "set," a great roar went up for a jump made by local favorite Viktor Saneyev. The starter held the runners in their crouch, then shot the gun. Aksinin and Lara were off the fastest, with Leonard and Wells close behind. By 60 meters Lara had faded, and by 80 meters the race was between Leonard on the inside and Wells on the outside. Wells edged ahead, but Leonard drew even again. With seven meters to go the stocky Scot began an extreme lean which allowed his shoulder to cross the finish line two or three inches before Leonard's chest. Allan Wells had become Great Britain's first 100 meters winner since Harold Abrahams and Scotland's first track gold medalist since Eric Liddell. At 28 he was also the oldest winner of the 100 meters in Olympic history. As a youngster Wells had enrolled in a Charles Atlas correspondence course in bodybuilding. His father was a blacksmith and his mother sewed nets for fishermen and worked as a hospital cleaner. Coached by his wife, Wells did not use starting blocks until 1980, when the International Amateur Athletic Federation (I.A.A.F.) required their use in international competitions.

200 METERS

1896 not held

1900 Paris C: 15?, N: 7?, D: 7.22. WR(220 yards): 21.2 (Bernie Wefers)

1. John Walter Tewksbury	USA	22.2
2. Norman Pritchard	IND	22.8
3. Stanley Rowley	AUS	22.9
4. William Joseph	USA	—

With this victory Tewksbury earned his fifth medal of the games. He had already won the 400-meter hurdles, finished second in the 60-meter and 100-meter sprints, and third in the 200-meter hurdles.

1904 St. Louis C: 7, L: 2, D: 8.31. WR(220 yards): 21.2 (Bernie Wefers)
1. Archie Hahn   USA   21.6 OR
2. Nathaniel Cartmell   USA   21.9
3. William Hogenson   USA   —
4. Fay Moulton   USA   —

Cartmell, Hogenson, and Moulton each false started once which, according to the rules at that time, resulted in their being penalized two yards. Hahn took good advantage of his head start and led the entire way. Cartmell closed within one yard, but Hahn pulled away again and won by three yards. Commented Cartmell, "He's little, but he certainly can run."

1906 not held

1908 London C: 43, N: 14, D: 7.23. WR(220 yards): 21.2 (Bernie Wefers, Dan Kelly)
1. Robert Kerr   CAN   22.6
2. Robert Cloughen   USA   22.6
3. Nathaniel Cartmell   USA   22.7
4. George Hawkins   GBR   —

Bobby Kerr was born in Enniskillen, Ireland. When he was 7 years old his family moved to Canada, settling in Hamilton, Ontario. As a teenager Kerr joined the International Harvester Fire Brigade, which prided itself on the speed of its members. Kerr represented Canada at the St. Louis Olympics in 1904 and had hoped to compete at Athens in 1906, but not enough money could be raised to pay his passage. He did make it to London, where, ten days before the Olympics, he swept both sprints at the British A.A.A. championships. At the 1908 Olympics he rebounded from the disappointment of finishing third in the 100 meters to win the 200 meters by less than a foot. The following year Kerr returned to Ireland and fulfilled his dream of representing the nation of his birth in an international meet. In 1928 he was the captain of the Canadian Olympic team, and in 1932 he was manager of the track and field division. Cloughen, the silver medalist, did not qualify for the U.S. team and was only able to compete because his parents paid his way.

1912 Stockholm C: 60, N: 19, D: 7.11. WR(220 yards): 21.2 (Bernie Wefers, Dan Kelly, Ralph Craig)
1. Ralph Craig   USA   21.7
2. Donald Lippincott   USA   21.8
3. William Applegarth   GBR   22.0
4. Richard Rau   GER   22.2

5. Charles Reidpath   USA   22.3
6. Donnell Young   USA   22.3

1920 Antwerp C: 45, D: 17, D: 8.20. WR(220 yards): 21.2 (Bernie Wefers, Dan Kelly, Ralph Craig, Howard Drew, William Applegarth)
1. Allen Woodring   USA   22.0
2. Charles Paddock   USA   22.1
3. Harry Edward   GBR   22.2
4. Loren Murchison   USA   —
5. George Davidson   NZE   —
6. Jack Oosterlaak   SAF   —

Allen Woodring of Syracuse University had qualified for the U.S. team only as an alternate, but when George Massengale of Missouri was stiffened by an attack of rheumatism, Woodring was allowed to compete. In the final Paddock led from the start, but Woodring caught him at the 180-meter mark. Just as Paddock began the takeoff of his flying finish, Woodring flashed by him to steal the victory. The young New Yorker couldn't believe he had won and was sure that Paddock had graciously allowed him to finish first. Paddock finally convinced him that he had given his all and that the victory was legitimate.

1924 Paris C: 62, N: 32, D: 7.9. WR: 21.0 (Charles Paddock)
1. Jackson Scholz   USA   21.6
2. Charles Paddock   USA   21.7
3. Eric Liddell   GBR   21.9
4. George Hill   USA   22.0
5. Bayes Norton   USA   22.0
6. Harold Abrahams   GBR   22.3

The day before the semifinals and final, Charley Paddock was convinced that he was over the hill and could never succeed the following day. His friend Douglas Fairbanks took him home, and together they dined and joked with Mary Pickford and Maurice Chevalier, who entertained them with imitations of Paavo Nurmi and Harold Abrahams, who had already won the 100 meters and who had beaten Charley in the first round of the 200 earlier that day. After dinner Fairbanks and Chevalier went for a walk while Mary Pickford gave Paddock an inspirational pep talk. She told him that his fate rested in his own hands. "If you believe in yourself," she said, "you will win tomorrow."

Paddock took her advice to heart, slept well, and awoke the next day refreshed and relaxed. He won his semifinal heat with ease, with Scholz winning the other semi. In the final Abrahams fell behind quickly while the others ran almost evenly. By the 120-meter mark Paddock had opened up a two-foot lead, but Scholz came on strong, reaching Paddock's shoulder with ten yards to go. In the final stride he moved ahead and won by less than a foot. Paddock pulled a ligament in his thigh in his final leap and collapsed to the ground beyond the finish line.

Scholz, who was born in St. Louis, later made his living

as an author of "pulp" fiction, publishing 31 sports novels. Interest in Scholz was renewed with the release of the film *Chariots of Fire,* which took great liberties in its portrayal of him. There is one scene in the film in which Scholz, just before the start of the 400 meters, approaches Eric Liddell and hands him a piece of paper inscribed with a religious message. Scholz actually did no such thing—he wasn't even religious. This put him in a difficult situation. When *Chariots of Fire* became a hit, the 84-year-old Scholz, now living in Delray Beach, Florida, was inundated with mail from people requesting spiritual inspiration. "I'm afraid," he told reporters, "that my religious background was rather casual."

1928 Amsterdam C: 62, N: 30, D: 8.1. WR: 20.6 (Roland Locke)
1. Percy Williams   CAN   21.8
2. Walter Rangeley   GBR   21.9
3. Helmuth Körnig   GER   21.9
4. Jackson Scholz   USA   21.9
5. John Fitzpatrick   CAN   22.1
6. Jakob Schüller   GER   22.2

The early rounds saw unusually stiff competition. In the quarterfinals Helmuth Körnig, pressed by Walter Rangeley of Salford, Lancashire, and Charlie Borah, the U.S. champion, equaled the Olympic record of 21.6. Since only two from each heat advanced to the semifinals, Borah was eliminated. The first semi saw the fall of Charley Paddock, who finished fifth behind Williams and Rangeley. The second semi was won by Körnig, with defending champion Scholz second. In the final Körnig led coming out of the turn, but with 50 meters to go he was passed by Williams and Rangeley. Williams, running his eighth race in four days, pulled away and won by almost a yard. A dead heat was declared for third place between Körnig and Scholz, and a rerun between the two was ordered. However, by the time this decision had been reached, Scholz had already broken training, so he forfeited the runoff. Subsequent examination of the photo-finish revealed that Kornig had actually won third place anyway.

1932 Los Angeles C: 25, N: 13, D: 8.3. WR: 20.3 (Ralph Metcalfe)
1. Thomas "Eddie" Tolan   USA   21.2 OR
2. George Simpson   USA   21.4
3. Ralph Metcalfe   USA   21.5
4. Arthur Jonath   GER   21.6
5. Carlos Bianchi Luti   ARG   21.7
6. William Walters   SAF   21.9

One man who did not compete in the 1932 Olympics was James Carlton of Lismore, New South Wales, who had beaten George Simpson twice. On January 16, 1932, Carlton shocked the world by winning the Australian 220-yard championship in 20.6, around the curve of an oval track. Speculation on Carlton's chance for an Olympic gold medal was cut short when the 24-year-old became a monk and retired to a monastery. In the quarterfinals at Los Angeles the Olympic record of 21.6, which had first been set by Archie Hahn back in 1904, was broken in each of the four heats. In the first two heats it was lowered to 21.5 by Metcalfe, who had won the U.S. trials, and by Tolan, who had edged Metcalfe to win the 100 meters gold medal the day before. In the third heat Luti broke the record again, at 21.4, and in the fourth heat his time was matched by sportswriter Arthur Jonath. The following day the first heat of the semifinals was won by Metcalfe, with Simpson beside him. In the second semi, won by Jonath, Tolan was almost eliminated. Content to qualify for the final with a third-place finish, Tolan almost failed to notice the closing rush of Canadian Harold Wright, who closed within a foot but fell short.

Luti had the quickest start in the final, but as they came out of the turn Simpson of Ohio State was leading by almost a yard. Tolan, who chewed gum while he ran, surged ahead with 50 meters to go, stumbled just before the finish, and held on to win by five or six feet. Tolan's time of 21.2 was declared an official world's record for 200 meters around a curve. When films of the race were viewed, it was discovered that Metcalfe had inadvertently been forced to dig his starting holes three or four feet behind the spot where they should have been, which deprived him of a silver medal. Metcalfe was offered a rerun by race officials, but he didn't want to jeopardize the U.S. medal sweep and so declined. There is a counter theory that the gap was actually an optical illusion caused by the fact that Metcalfe, in Lane 2, dug his holes on the inside of the lane, while Simpson, in Lane 3, dug his holes on the outside of his lane.

1936 Berlin C: 44, N: 22, D: 8.5. WR: 20.3 (Ralph Metcalfe, Jesse Owens)
1. Jesse Owens   USA   20.7 OR
2. Matthew "Mack" Robinson   USA   21.1
3. Martinus Osendarp   HOL   21.3
4. Paul Hänni   SWI   21.6
5. Lee Orr   CAN   21.6
6. Wijnand van Beveren   HOL   21.9

In the first round Jesse Owens set an Olympic record of 21.1 seconds, a time that he repeated in the second round and which was matched by Mack Robinson of Pasadena, California in the semifinals. The final was run in a light rain, but this didn't prevent Owens from sprinting away from the field in record time. He led by almost two yards entering the straightaway and won by four yards to gain his third gold medal of the Berlin games. His time of 20.7 set a world record for 200 meters around a curve. Silver medalist Robinson was something of a surprise. In high school the coaches did not consider him athletic material and made his mother sign a statement absolving them of blame if his heart was damaged. Local businessmen paid his way to the U.S. Olympic trials. His younger brother,

Jackie Robinson, gained fame with the Brooklyn Dodgers as the first black major league player in modern baseball history.

1948 London C: 50 N: 26, D: 8.3. WR: 20.3 (Ralph Metcalfe, Jesse Owens)

1. Melvin Patton	USA	21.1
2. H. Norwood "Barney" Ewell	USA	21.1
3. Lloyd LaBeach	PAN	21.2
4. Herbert McKenley	JAM	—
5. Clifford Bourland	USA	—
6. Leslie Laing	JAM	—

McKenley and Bourland looked strongest in the preliminaries, both of them clocking 21.3 in each of the first two rounds. They also won their respective semifinal heats. In the final, however, it was the favorites who came through fastest. Patton, intent on making up for his disappointing fifth place finish in the 100, pulled away coming out of the turn and led by almost two meters. Ewell closed fast, but Patton held him off with a final spurt to win by two feet.

1952 Helsinki C: 71, N: 35, D: 7.23. WR: 20.2 (Melvin Patton)

1. Andrew Stanfield	USA	20.7
2. W. Thane Baker	USA	20.8
3. James Gathers	USA	20.8
4. Emmanuel McDonald Bailey	GBR	21.0
5. Leslie Laing	JAM	21.2
6. Gerardo Bönnhoff	ARG	21.3

Stanfield, a 6-foot 1-inch 24-year-old from Jersey City, New Jersey, was the unanimous favorite. As expected, he and Mac Bailey won the semifinals. Bailey ran well on the turn in the final, and as they hit the staightaway he was almost even with Stanfield, but Stanfield pulled away with ease and won by a yard and a half. The official times appear to be incorrect, since Bailey actually finished quite close to Gathers. The electronic times for the first four were 20.81, 20.97, 21.08, and 21.14.

1956 Melbourne C: 67, N: 32, D: 11.27. WR: 20.0 (David Sime)

1. Robert Morrow	USA	20.6 OR
2. Andrew Stanfield	USA	20.7
3. W. Thane Baker	USA	20.9
4. Michael Agostini	TRI	21.1
5. Boris Tokaryev	SOV	21.2
6. José Telles da Conceição	BRA	21.3

Bobby Morrow, the winner of the 100, was the favorite to win the 200 and become the first man since Jesse Owens to achieve a double in the Olympic sprints. He appeared for the first round with his left thigh bandaged, having suffered a slight groin pull in the final of the 100. Fortunately he was able to breeze through the early heats with little competition while allowing his muscle to heal. Abdul Khaliq of Pakistan ran 21.1 in both of the first two rounds, but tired himself out and was eliminated in the semifinals,

which were won by Baker (21.1) and Stanfield (21.2). One unexpected finalist was Telles da Conceição, who had won the bronze medal in the high jump at Helsinki four years earlier. Baker was so upset at receiving the outside lane in the final, just as he had at Helsinki, that he put his starting blocks in backwards, necessitating a delay while he readjusted them. At the halfway mark Stanfield led Morrow by a foot, but 20 meters later Morrow swept past the defending champion and won going away, with Stanfield and Baker completing the second straight sweep of the 200 for the United States. Of the 15 medals awarded between 1932 and 1956, 13 were won by the United States, which took the first two places in five straight Olympics.

1960 Rome C: 62, N: 47, D: 9.3. WR(track with curve): 20.5 (Peter Radford, Stonewall Johnson, O. Ray Norton)

1. Livio Berruti	ITA	20.5 EWR
2. Lester Carney	USA	20.6
3. Abdoulaye Seye	FRA	20.7
4. Marian Foik	POL	20.8
5. Stonewall Johnson	USA	20.8
6. O. Ray Norton	USA	20.9

On May 28, 1960, Peter Radford set a world record of 20.5 around a turn. His record was matched five weeks later at the U.S. Olympic trials in Los Angeles by Stone Johnson of Dallas, Texas, and Ray Norton. In Rome, the first semifinal was won by Seye in 20.8. The second semi saw some bad seeding as the three world record holders were thrown together with local favorite Livio Berruti, with only three to qualify for the final. It was Radford who was left out, with Berruti, a chemistry student at the University of Padua, finishing first in the world record time of 20.5. The second semi was so hotly contested that last-place finisher, Paul Genevay of France, ran 21.0, good enough to take second place in the first semi.

The final saw one false start by Berruti and Johnson, although neither was charged. Berruti, always strong on the curve, hit the straight with a one-yard lead, which he held until the finish. Norton was placed second with 80 meters to go, but he faded. After crossing the line, both Berruti, who ran with dark glasses, and Carney (of Akron, Ohio) fell to the ground. Berruti's victory was met with enthusiastic cheering that went on for five minutes, and after the medal ceremony he was led to the V.I.P. box, where each Italian dignitary kissed him on both cheeks. Berruti was the first non-North American to win the 200 meters.

1964 Tokyo C: 57, N: 42, D: 10.17. WR: 20.2 (Henry Carr)

1. Henry Carr	USA	20.3 OR
2. O. Paul Drayton	USA	20.5
3. Edwin Roberts	TRI	20.6
4. Harry Jerome	CAN	20.8
5. Livio Berruti	ITA	20.8
6. Marian Foik	POL	20.8
7. Richard Stebbins	USA	20.8
8. Sergio Ottolina	ITA	20.9

This event went according to form. Drayton, a 25-year-old Army private, recorded the best series in the preliminaries (20.7, 20.9, and 20.5), but Carr, the world record holder, had paced himself well and turned it on in the final. Carr overtook Drayton quickly, led by a yard entering the stretch, and was able to extend his lead to win by over four feet.

1968 Mexico City C: 49, N: 36, D: 10.16. WR: 19.92 (John Carlos)

1. Tommie Smith	USA	19.8 WR
2. Peter Norman	AUS	20.0
3. John Carlos	USA	20.0
4. Edwin Roberts	TRI	20.3
5. Roger Bambuck	FRA	20.5
6. Larry Questad	USA	20.6
7. Michael Fray	JAM	20.6
8. Joachim Eigenherr	GER	20.6

There seemed little question that the battle for the gold medal would be between Tommie Smith and John Carlos, both students at San Jose State College in California and both members of the Olympic Project for Human Rights, a group of athletes organized to protest the treatment of blacks in the United States. The 6-foot 3-inch, 180-pound Smith was an extraordinary runner who held 11 world records indoors and outdoors at distances up to 440 yards. He had also long-jumped 25 feet 11 inches (7.90 meters). Carlos, who grew up in Harlem, beat Smith for the first time (by three yards) at the U.S. Olympic trials and clocked a world record time of 19.7 seconds. His record was never officially recognized because he was wearing multipronged "brush spike" shoes which, at the time, were considered illegal. At 6 feet 4 inches and 198 pounds, Carlos was the largest competitor in the 1968 200 meters, 90 pounds heavier than José Astacio, who represented El Salvador.

In Mexico City Smith set the stage in the first round by tying the Olympic record of 20.3. But four heats later a surprise occurred when Peter Norman ran 20.2 to break the Olympic record. Norman, a 26-year-old physical education teacher and Salvation Army officer, had never beaten 20.5 until he arrived in Mexico. In the first heat of the second round Carlos slipped on the bend, but he regained his balance and won in 20.6. In the third heat Smith equaled Norman's earlier mark of 20.2. The semis were won by Carlos and Smith in 20.1, but Smith pulled an abductor muscle in his groin and limped off the field. "I was 80 percent certain I was out," he said, but he made it to the starting line of the final anyway. Coming out of the turn Carlos led by 1½ yards, but then Smith turned on his "Tommie-jets," in a stunning display of speed reminiscent of Bob Hayes' 4 × 100-meter relay anchor leg in Tokyo. He passed his teammate with 60 meters to go and won so decisively that he was able to raise his arms in victory 10 yards from the tape and smile and wave as he crossed the finish line. Carlos turned his head to watch Smith go by, allowing Norman, who had been in only sixth place entering the straight, to slip by on the other side and take the silver medal with a final lunge.

Smith's victory caused a sensation, but it was nothing compared to the sensation that he and Carlos caused at the victory ceremony. Mounting the dais barefooted, they wore civil rights buttons, as did Norman. When "The Star-Spangled Banner" was played, Smith and Carlos bowed their heads and each raised one black-gloved hand in the black-power salute. They later explained that their clenched fists symbolized black strength and unity and that their bare feet were a reminder of black poverty in the United States. They bowed their heads to express their belief that the words of freedom in the U.S. national anthem only applied to Americans with white skin. Carlos told reporters, "White America will only give us credit for an Olympic victory. They'll say I'm an American, but if I did something bad, they'd say I was a Negro." Olympic officials were outraged. The International Olympic Committee made it known that Smith and Carlos should be punished, and the U.S. Olympic Committee responded quickly, suspending the two athletes and ordering them to leave Mexico within 48 hours.

The international response to the demonstration by Smith and Carlos was generally sympathetic, but back in the United States they were not so well received. Chicago sports columnist Brent Musburger spoke for the Establishment when he called them "black-skinned storm troopers." The two Olympic medalists found it difficult to make a living, and both their marriages broke up. In 1972 Smith finally got a position as track coach at Oberlin College in Ohio. Six years later he moved to Santa Monica College in California. Carlos had an even tougher time—hustling, gambling, taking menial jobs. In 1977 he founded the John Carlos Youth Development Program in Los Angeles, which encourages ghetto youth to become well educated. In February 1982, Carlos' Olympic experiences came full circle when he was hired by the Los Angeles Olympic Organizing Committee to promote the 1984 games and act as liaison with the black ghetto.

In retrospect, Smith and Carlos' gestures on the victory platform in Mexico City appear as eloquent expressions of nonviolent protest, while the reactions of the I.O.C. and the U.S.O.C. come off as knee-jerk traditionalism. Smith and Carlos made their point without interfering with anyone's free will. The same cannot be said of Jimmy Carter's arm-twisting boycott, with its threats of passport revocations, or of the Black September guerrillas, whose attempt to stop the games was accompanied by murder. John Carlos responded to criticisms that his political protest had tainted the games by pointing out that the Olympic movement was already highly political. "Why do you have to wear the uniform of your country?" he asked. "Why do they play national anthems? Why do we have to beat the Russians? Why do the East Germans want to beat the West Germans? Why can't everyone wear the same colors but wear numbers to tell them apart? What happened to the Olympic ideal of man against man?"

1972 Munich C: 57, N: 42, D: 9.4. WR: 19.83 (Tommie Smith)

1. Valery Borzov	SOV	20.00
2. Larry Black	USA	20.19
3. Pietro Mennea	ITA	20.30
4. Lawrence Burton	USA	20.37
5. Charles Smith	USA	20.55
6. Siegfried Schenke	GDR	20.56
7. Martin Jellinghaus	GER	20.65
8. Hans-Joachim Zenk	GDR	21.05

Borzov completely dominated the opposition to become the first non-North American to win the Olympic sprint double. He won his first two heats in 20.64 and 20.30 despite the fact that he turned around several times to check the position of the other runners. In the first heat of the semifinals he turned and spoke to Larry Burton as he passed him with 50 meters to go. Burton was a 6-foot 2-inch Purdue football player who had run in his first track meet only eight months earlier, and had competed in his first 220-yard race a mere four and a half months before the Olympics. The winner of the second semi was Larry Black, a Florida-born student of North Carolina Central. In the final, Black came out of the turn with a slight lead, but with 70 meters to go Borzov appeared to shift into overdrive, rocketing ahead to a clear two-meter lead. With five meters left, Borzov turned back for a final look at Black and the others, then crossed the line with arms flung high. Mennea edged past Burton at the 175-meter mark to take third. During the second round Mennea had entertained the crowd by stripping down to his jock strap while changing into his running shorts. Borzov refused to participate in the postrace interview, stating, with some justification, that he had been treated in an insulting manner by U.S. journalists after his victory in the 100.

1976 Montreal C: 45, N: 33, D: 7.26. WR: 19.83 (Tommie Smith)

1. Donald Quarrie	JAM	20.23
2. Millard Hampton	USA	20.29
3. Dwayne Evans	USA	20.43
4. Pietro Mennea	ITA	20.54
5. Ruy da Silva	BRA	20.84
6. Bogdan Grzejszczak	POL	20.91
7. Colin Bradford	JAM	21.17
8. Hasely Crawford	TRI	1:19.60

Donald Quarrie's Olympic career began back in 1968 when he was 17 years old. He made it to Mexico City but injured himself during training and was unable to compete. In 1971 he won the Pan American Games in 19.86, the second fastest electronically timed 200 on record, but at the Olympics in Munich he pulled a hamstring muscle in the semifinals and had to be carried off the field on a stretcher. At Montreal he had already finished second to Crawford in the 100 and was now the odds-on favorite to take the gold in the 200.

His challengers included one man who wanted to run but wasn't allowed to and another who didn't want to run but was forced to. James Gilkes of Guyana was the victor in the 1975 Pan American Games, but his government decided to boycott the Olympics. Gilkes appealed to the I.O.C. to let him compete under the Olympic flag, but his request was denied. Pietro Mennea, on the other hand, was so disappointed with his performance at the Italian championships in July that he decided not to compete in Montreal. Public reaction to his decision was so strong that he changed his mind. Also in the running were Millard Hampton of San Jose and 17-year-old Dwayne Evans of Phoenix, the first high school student to represent the United States in an Olympic running event since 1964.

Quarrie had the lead coming out of the turn. Hampton made a run at him, but Quarrie held on to win by two feet. His long quest for an Olympic gold medal finally achieved, Don Quarrie is now honored by a statue in his hometown of Kingston, Jamaica.

The three medalists took the slowest victory lap on record. Forced to stop when they encountered the victory ceremony for the javelin, it was ten minutes before they completed their circuit of the track.

Hasely Crawford, whom the official report lists as not finishing, suffered a cramp after 50 meters and ended up on the ground, but a California track fan named Pitch Johnson noted that Crawford never actually left his lane until after he had jogged past the finish line, so he did finish the race, albeit in a rather unusual time.

1980 Moscow C: 57, N: 37, D: 7.28. WR: 19.72 (Pietro Mennea)

1. Pietro Mennea	ITA	20.19
2. Allan Wells	GBR	20.21
3. Donald Quarrie	JAM	20.29
4. Silvio Leonard Tartabull	CUB	20.30
5. Bernhard Hoff	GDR	20.50
6. Leszek Dunecki	POL	20.68
7. Marian Woronin	POL	20.81
8. Osvaldo Lara Cañizares	CUB	21.19

Like Donald Quarrie before him, Pietro Mennea of Barletta, Italy, had to wait until his third try to gain an Olympic gold medal. In 1979 at the World Student Games in Mexico City, Mennea had run 19.72 to break Tommie Smith's 11-year-old world record. But that same year, before a hometown crowd at the European Cup in Torino, Mennea had lost to Allan Wells. For this insult, the otherwise blameless Wells had become known as "The Beast" in Mennea's household. For the final of the 1980 Olympics, Mennea drew the outside lane, with "The Beast" just behind him in Lane 7. At the sound of the gun Wells tore out of the blocks at full speed and had made up the stagger after only 50 meters. Coming out of the turn he had a two-meter lead over Leonard, with Quarrie and Mennea close behind. But Mennea, as usual, shifted gears in the straight, closing the gap with each stride until he moved ahead of Wells with less than ten meters to go. At the last moment Wells attempted the same final dip which had brought him victory in the 100, but this time he fell short. Quarrie's third-place finish, impressive as it was, was all the more remarkable considering he had been injured in an auto accident the previous year. Mennea, employed by the public relations department of Fiat, had received his doctorate in political science two weeks before the Olympics. He had been a candidate for local office for the Social Democratic Party, which supported the Moscow boycott, but 15 years of training and his belief in the Olympic ideal proved more important than the party line, and he decided to enter anyway.

400 METERS

1896 Athens C: 11, N: 6, D: 4.7. WR(440 yards): 48.5 (H.C. Lennox Tindall, Edgar Bredin)
1. Thomas Burke   USA   54.2
2. Herbert Jamison   USA   —
3. Charles Gmelin   GBR   —
4. Fritz Hofmann   GER   —

The slow time was a result of the quality of the track rather than the quality of the contestants. The turns were so sharp that the runners had to slow down drastically to keep from falling. Burke, who won by over 13 meters, had previously beaten the world record holder Edgar Bredin. In 1896 Bredin, in the words of former 440 champion Montague Shearman, "voluntarily joined the professional ranks, a step which was received with great surprise, as he was a gentleman by birth and education."

1900 Paris C: 16, N: 7, D: 7.15. WR(440 yards): 48.5 (H. C. Lennox Tindall, Edgar Bredin)
1. Maxwell "Maxey" Long   USA   49.4 OR
2. William Holland   USA   49.6
3. Ernst Schultz   DEN   —
DNS: Dixon Boardman (USA), Harry Lee (USA), William Moloney (USA)

Long was cheered heartily by the French spectators, who mistook his light-blue-and-white Columbia University uniform for that of the Racing Club of France. Boardman, Lee, and Moloney refused to compete in the final for religious reasons, since the race was run on a Sunday.

1904 St. Louis C: 13, N: 3, D: 8.29. WR(440 yards): 47.8 (Maxwell "Maxey" Long)
1. Harry Hillman   USA   49.2 OR
2. Frank Waller   USA   49.9
3. Herman Groman   USA   50.0
4. Joseph Fleming   USA   —
5. Meyer Prinstein   USA   —
6. George Poage   USA   —

One can only imagine the chaos of this race, which the 13 entrants ran without lanes even though the course was only 1¼ laps long. Poage of Milwaukee was one of the first two blacks to compete in the Olympics.

1906 Athens C: 25, N: 8, D: 4.29. WR(440 yards): 47.8 (Maxwell "Maxey" Long)
1. Paul Pilgrim   USA   53.2
2. Wyndham Halswelle   GBR   53.8

3. Nigel Barker   AUS   54.1
4. Harry Hillman   USA   —
5. Charles Bacon   USA   —
6. Fay Moulton   USA   —
7. W.D. Anderson   GBR   —
8. M. Bellin du Coteau   FRA   —

The victory of Pilgrim came as a complete surprise. This was the first time that the United States sent an official team. Pilgrim, a member of the New York Athletic Club, didn't make the team, but he paid his own way to Athens and was allowed to compete.

1908 London C: 36, N: 11, D: 7.25. WR(440 yards): 47.8 (Maxwell "Maxey" Long)
1. Wyndham Halswelle   GBR   50.0
DNS: W.C. Robbins (USA), John Taylor (USA)
DISQ: J.C. Carpenter (USA)

Few events in Olympic history have caused as much controversy as the final of the 1908 400 meters in London. The favorite was Lieutenant Wyndham Halswelle, a 26-year-old London-born Scot who had served in the Boer War. Halswelle was joined in the final by three Americans—John Taylor, W.C. Robbins, and J.C. Carpenter of Cornell. The British, afraid that the Americans would use team tactics, stationed officials every 20 yards around the track. Robbins charged to the front and built up a 12-yard lead by the halfway mark. Coming into the homestretch he was passed by Carpenter and Halswelle. Halswelle then attempted to go by Carpenter on the outside, but the American ran wide and kept Halswelle from taking the lead. British officials yelled "foul" and "no race" and broke the tape before Carpenter reached it. Taylor was physically pulled off the track by officials. British and American partisans argued and yelled at each other for a half hour before the track could be cleared. Carpenter was disqualified and the race was ordered rerun without him two days later, this time with strings laid out to divide the lanes. Robbins and Taylor refused to participate, however, and Halswelle was left to run the race alone.

1912 Stockholm C: 49, N: 16, D: 7.13. WR(440 yards): 47.8 (Maxwell "Maxey" Long)
1. Charles Reidpath   USA   48.2 OR
2. Hanns Braun   GER   48.3
3. Edward Lindberg   USA   48.4
4. James "Ted" Meredith   USA   49.2
5. Carroll Haff   USA   49.5

The 400 meters was again the subject of controversy, this time occasioned by an incident at the beginning of the last heat of the semifinal round. Donnell Young of the United States jumped into the lead, but before the first curve the German champion, Hanns Braun, tried to cut in front of him. Young refused to allow this and rammed into Braun, throwing him to the outside. Young went on to win, but was disqualified. Young deserved to be disqualified; however, Braun's move was uncalled for and might have resulted in *his* disqualification had not Young responded so violently. The Swedish officials wisely decided that the final should be run in lanes. Braun took the lead at the half-way mark, but Charlie Reidpath of Syracuse passed him with 15 meters to go and won by two feet.

1920 Antwerp C: 37, N: 14, D: 8.20. WR(440 yards): 47.4 (James "Ted" Meredith, Jesse Binga Dismond)
1. Bevil Rudd	SAF	49.6
2. Guy Butler	GBR	49.9
3. Nils Engdahl	SWE	50.0
4. Frank Shea	USA	—
5. E. John Ainsworth-Davis	GBR	—
6. Harry Davel	SAF	—

Born in South Africa and educated at Oxford, Bevil Gordon D'Urban Rudd was an extremely popular winner who looked at running as a joyful experience. He was often seen smoking a pipe and drinking beer while watching the other athletes go through their strenuous exercises.

1924 Paris C: 60, N: 27, D: 7.11. WR(440 yards): 47.4 (James "Ted" Meredith, Jesse Binga Dismond)
1. Eric Liddell	GBR	47.6 OR
2. Horatio Fitch	USA	48.4
3. Guy Butler	GBR	48.6
4. David Johnston	CAN	48.8
5. John Coard Taylor	USA	—
DNF: Josef Imbach (SWI)		

Eric Liddell was born on January 16, 1902, in Tientsin, China, where his father was a missionary. He grew up in Scotland from the age of 5. His favorite sport was rugby, but he gave up a promising career in it in order to concentrate on running. He gained national attention in 1923 when he won both sprints at the A.A.A. championships. The following week his reputation was enhanced when he was knocked to the ground during a 440-yard race against England and Ireland. By the time he had regained his feet, Liddell was 20 yards behind the field. Yet he was able to overtake every runner and win the race. Afterward he repeated his oft-spoken dictum, "I do not like to be beaten."

In the film *Chariots of Fire* Eric Liddell is portrayed as a devout Christian who learns, as he is boarding a ship en route to the Paris Olympics, that the heats of the 100-meter dash, his specialty, will be run on a Sunday. Because of his respect for the Sabbath, he refuses to run. Finally another member of the British team, a cinematic version of Lord Burghley, offers Liddell his spot in the 400 meters. This highly dramatized rendition of Liddell's Olympic experience bears only a slight resemblance to reality.

Liddell was in fact a devout Christian, and it is true that he withdrew from the 100 because he wouldn't run on a Sunday. He dropped out of the relays for the same reason. However, he did *not* find out the Olympic schedule at the last minute. In real life Liddell learned the schedule over six months in advance and, once he had made his decision not to enter the 100, he was able to concentrate his training

on the 200 and 400. As for Lord Burghley, he wasn't even a member of the 1924 Olympic team. Liddell did spend the Sunday of the 100-meter heats giving a sermon at a Scottish church in Paris, but he had doubts about his decision right up to the end, particularly as a result of criticism he received from certain quarters that he was being unpatriotic, since Scotland had few opportunities to win Olympic championships.

On July 9, Liddell finished third in the 200 meters, behind Jackson Scholz and Charley Paddock. The first two rounds of the 400 were held the next day, and Liddell qualified in respectable, but unspectacular times. The fastest race of the day was won by Imbach in 48.0. The first semifinal, held the morning of July 11, was won by Fitch in 47.8 and the second by Liddell in 48.2, an impressive performance by the "Flying Scot" considering that he had never before beaten the 49-second mark. The final, contested later in the day, was won by Liddell in an unorthodox and electrifying manner. Racing in the outside lane, Liddell took off as if he were running a short dash and passed the halfway mark in an extraordinary 22.2 seconds, only 0.3 seconds slower than he had run in the 200-meter final. Track experts considered this to be tactical foolishness, but Liddell was a man inspired. He actually increased his lead during the second half of the race and won by over five meters. His pace was so fast that two of his opponents, Imbach and Taylor, fell while trying to keep up. Taylor crawled and scrambled the last few yards to the finish line.

Eric Liddell returned to Scotland a hero of heroes and was paraded through the streets of Edinburgh. A year after his Olympic triumph, he returned to China to join his father in missionary work. Liddell made two more trips to Scotland, but he was back in China during World War II. He died of a brain tumor in a Japanese internment camp, on February 21, 1945.

1928 Amsterdam C: 51, N: 20, D: 8.3. WR: 47.0 (Emerson Spencer)
1. Raymond Barbuti	USA	47.8
2. James Ball	CAN	48.0
3. Joachim Büchner	GER	48.2
4. John Rinkel	GBR	48.4
5. Werner "Harry" Storz	GER	48.8
6. Herman Phillips	USA	49.0

On May 12, 1928, Emerson Spencer set a world record of 47.0. But he failed to qualify for the Olympics except as a member of the relay team, because of a major misunderstanding at the U.S. Final Olympic Tryouts. Thinking he was running in a heat, he finished only fast enough to qualify for what he thought was the next round. Actually the race had been to decide the final places on the U.S. team and Spencer lost out.

The semifinals in Amsterdam were won by Ball and Buchner in 48.6. In the final Barbuti, a former captain of the Syracuse football team, started his finishing kick at the 300-meter mark even though he had been instructed to wait an extra 30 meters. Fortunately for Barbuti, James Ball of Winnipeg made the opposite mistake. Unaccustomed to running in lanes, Ball misjudged his position until the final straightaway and then unleashed a great finishing kick. As they approached the finish line, Ball had closed within a foot of Barbuti, but he turned to see where his opponent was just as Barbuti lunged for the tape. The plucky New Yorker fell to the ground, scraping his arm, leg, and side, but he had gained the victory. Afterward he told reporters, "I never noticed the other runners after the start. I heard them, but all I kept thinking was 'run, kid, run.' I don't remember anything of the last 100 meters except a mad desire to get to that tape."

1932 Los Angeles C: 27, N: 15, D: 8.5. WR(440 yards): 46.4 (Benjamin Eastman)

1. William Carr	USA	46.2	WR
2. Benjamin Eastman	USA	46.4	
3. Alexander Wilson	CAN	47.4	
4. William Walters	SAF	48.2	
5. James Gordon	USA	48.2	
6. George Golding	AUS	48.8	

Ben Eastman of Stanford University was considered king of the world at 400 and 800 meters, particularly after March 26, 1932, when he lowered his own world record at 440 yards (402.3 meters) by a full second in running the extraordinary time of 46.4. He ran 46.5 two months later and appeared to be a sure bet to win either the 400 or 800 at the Los Angeles Olympics. Then, seemingly from out of nowhere, came a new contender, University of Pennsylvania Junior Bill Carr of Pine Bluff, Arkansas. At the U.S. intercollegiate championships at Berkeley on July 2, Carr came from behind to gain a shocking 440 victory over Eastman, 47.0 to 47.2. Two weeks later at the U.S. Olympic tryouts on Eastman's home track in Palo Alto, California, Carr again came from behind to defeat Eastman, 46.9 to 47.1.

Unfortunately, Eastman got caught up in a rivalry between his own coach, Dink Templeton of Stanford, and Carr's coach, Lawson Robertson of Pennsylvania, who had been chosen to coach the U.S. Olympic team. Obsessed with beating Robertson, Templeton convinced Eastman to skip the Olympic 800 meters, which was actually his best event, and concentrate on beating Carr at 400 meters.

At the 1932 Olympics Carr posted the fastest time in each of the first two rounds. Then he won the first semifinal in 47.2. Eastman won the second in 47.6. In the final Eastman held a slight edge through most of the race. Carr drew even with 80 meters to go and gradually pulled away to win by two yards. Whatever Dink Templeton thought of the race, Ben Eastman himself was an amiable loser. "Bill's just too fast for me," he said. "You don't need to sympathize. I know when I'm licked by a better runner." Unfortunately, Bill Carr's running career came to an abrupt halt in March 1933, when he fractured his pelvis in an automobile accident.

1936 Berlin C: 42, N: 25, D: 8.7. WR: 46.1 (Archie Williams)

1. Archie Williams	USA	46.5
2. Arthur Godfrey Brown	GBR	46.7
3. James LuValle	USA	46.8
4. William Roberts	GBR	46.8
5. William Fritz	CAN	47.8
6. John Loaring	CAN	48.2

Prior to the 1936 season, Archie Williams of Oakland, California had never run a quarter-mile faster than 49 seconds. However, in April, 1936, he ran 47.4, in May 46.8, and on June 19, at the N.C.A.A. championships in Chicago, he clocked 46.5 for 440 yards around one turn, passing the 400-meter mark in 46.1 to break Bill Carr's world record. In the Olympic final Williams and fellow Californian James LuValle led the field entering the homestretch. But Godfrey Brown, three yards behind with 100 meters to go, staged a thrilling stretch drive, passed LuValle 40 meters from the tape, and closed in on the exhausted Williams. Brown had pulled within inches and was still coming strong when Williams breasted the tape before Brown could get any closer. The official times appear to have been inaccurate; the photo-finish camera yielded the following, more reliable results: Williams 46.66, Brown 46.68, LuValle 46.84, and Roberts 46.87. The day after Godfrey Brown won the 400 meters silver medal, his sister Audrey earned a silver medal of her own in the women's 4 × 100-meter relay. Godfrey added a gold medal to the family haul in the men's 4 × 400-meter relay.

1948 London C: 53, N: 28, D: 8.5. WR: 45.9 (Herbert McKenley) WR(440 yards): 46.0 (Rudolf Harbig, Grover Klemmer, Herbert McKenley)

1. Arthur Wint	JAM	46.2
2. Herbert McKenley	JAM	46.4
3. Malvin Whitfield	USA	46.9
4. David Bolen	USA	47.2
5. Morris Curotta	AUS	47.9
6. George Guida	USA	50.2

Jesse Abramson of the New York *Herald Tribune* had called Herb McKenley "the surest sure thing of the Games," but whenever anyone asked McKenley about it, he told them that his older teammate, 6-foot 4½-inch Arthur Wint, was really the man to beat. McKenley may not have actually believed that himself at the time, but it turned out that he was absolutely correct. Wint, a minister's son whose mother was a Scot, had joined the Royal Air Force during World War II. Staying on in England after the war, Wint was a 28-year-old medical student at the University of London at the time of the 1948 Olympics. Consequently, he was quite a local favorite among London sports fans.

Disappointed at having lost to Mal Whitfield at 800 meters, Wint was determined to finish ahead of the American at 400 meters. Although Wint had never lost to McKenley at 400 meters, he was prepared to settle for a silver medal behind his friend and rival, who seemed to be in prime condition. McKenley's usual tactics, or lack of them, consisted of running as fast as he could as soon as the starter's gun went off. Normally he could keep up his all-out pace for 350 meters and then coast through the final 50 meters.

True to form, McKenley went away at breakneck speed in the London final. Coming out of the final curve he was four yards ahead of Whitfield. But, McKenley, uncharacteristically, broke stride about 25 meters early and began to fade. Noticing the plight of his fellow Jamaican, Wint took off after him, closed the gap, caught McKenley with about 20 yards to go, and went on to win by two and a half yards.

Dave Bolen, who finished fourth, was later appointed U.S. ambassador to Botswana, Lesotho, and Swaziland.

1952 Helsinki C: 71, N: 35, D: 7.25. WR: 45.8 (V. George Rhoden)

1. V. George Rhoden	JAM	45.9	OR
2. Herbert McKenley	JAM	45.9	
3. Ollie Matson	USA	46.8	
4. Karl-Friedrich Haas	GER	47.0	
5. Arthur Wint	JAM	47.0	
6. Malvin Whitfield	USA	47.1	

In 1952 the track world had different expectations of Herb McKenley. The 30-year-old McKenley was considered a sure finalist but an unlikely medal winner. The favorite was George Rhoden, a 25-year-old from Kingston who had just graduated from Morgan State College in Baltimore. In the 1948 Olympics he had been eliminated in the semifinals, but by August of 1950 he had broken the 400-meter world record in 45.8.

Rhoden and McKenley were joined in the 1952 final by fellow Olympic veterans Arthur Wint and Mal Whitfield, who had already won the 800 meters, but was now fighting off a cold with benzedrine. The other starters were University of San Francisco football star Ollie Matson, who later achieved success as a five-time All-Pro back in the National Football League, and Kaaro Haas, the only white finalist. McKenley had the sympathy of much of the crowd as a result of his photo-finish loss in the 100-meter final four days earlier.

The amazing thing about the 1952 400-meter final was that Wint and McKenley completely reversed the tactics that they had used in the 1948 final. McKenley, having learned from his experience four years earlier, began cautiously and saved his strength for the finish. Wint, on the other hand, for some reason unknown even to himself, took off at full speed and led by three yards at the 200-meter mark in 21.7—0.2 seconds faster than he had ever run the distance. Not surprisingly, Wint ran out of steam early and was passed by Rhoden, who entered the long final straightaway with a four-yard lead over McKenley. But then McKenley began to close the gap, pulling closer with every stride until he almost drew even. Rhoden recalled the moment after the race: "About 20 meters from home I heard the roar of the crowd and with split vision saw some-

one coming up. From someplace I summoned the necessary strength and held him off. I surely was glad to see that tape." Rhoden's margin of victory was about 18 inches.

1956 Melbourne C: 42, N: 23, D: 11.29. WR: 45.2 (Louis Jones)

1. Charles Jenkins	USA	46.7
2. Karl-Friedrich Haas	GER	46.8
3. Voitto Hellsten	FIN	47.0
3. Ardalion Ignatyev	SOV	47.0
5. Louis Jones	USA	48.1
6. Malcolm Spence	SAF	48.3

Lou Jones set a world record of 45.2 at the U.S. Olympic tryouts and went to Melbourne as the clear favorite. Ignatyev won the first semifinal in 46.8, with Jones coasting in third place to qualify for the final. The second semi was a hard-fought affair, won by the third-string U.S. runner, Charley Jenkins of Cambridge, Massachusetts. Jenkins had barely made the semifinal round by finishing third in his first- and second-round heats. The second semifinal was so fast that Kevan Gosper of Australia was eliminated even though he finished in 46.2 seconds.

Jones led the final for the first 300 meters. Coming out of the final turn he had expected to have a three- or four-meter lead and was psychologically unprepared when he realized that Ignatyev was right behind him. The Soviet runner took the lead with 60 yards to go, but then Jenkins launched a finishing kick, passed Ignatyev 25 yards from the finish, and broke the tape just ahead of Haas, who came from last place to second in the final 100 meters. The photo-finish was unable to separate Hellsten and Ignatyev, so they were both awarded third place. After the race Jenkins modestly told reporters, "Jones is still the champ. That 45.2 is it."

1960 Rome C: 54, N: 41, D: 9.6. WR: 45.2 (Louis Jones)

1. Otis Davis	USA	44.9	WR
2. Carl Kaufmann	GER	44.9	WR
3. Malcolm Spence	SAF	45.5	
4. Milkha Singh	IND	45.6	
5. Manfred Kinder	GER	45.9	
6. Earl Young	USA	45.9	

This was the first time since 1912 that the final was held on a different day than the semifinals. The improvement in times spoke well for the new procedure. Spence took the early lead and was still in front at 200 meters, followed by Kaufmann, Milkha Singh, and Davis. Then Davis accelerated dramatically, covering the next 100 meters in 10.8 seconds and entering the final straight with a four-yard lead over Brooklyn-born Carl Kaufmann. Next it was Kaufmann's turn to stage a sensational sprint. He almost caught Davis, but the American leaned forward just in time, crossing the finish line ahead of the flying Kaufmann, who ended up sprawled on the track from exhaustion. The electronic timer gave Davis a victory of .02 seconds, both men being credited with a new world record.

Otis Davis was born in Tuscaloosa, Alabama. A basketball player at the University of Oregon, he didn't start running until he was 26 years old, two years before the Olympics. Like Charley Jenkins before him, Davis finished only third at the U.S. Olympic tryouts.

1964 Tokyo C: 50, N: 33, D: 10.19. WR: 44.9 (Otis Davis, Carl Kaufmann, Adolph Plummer, Michael Larrabee)

1. Michael Larrabee	USA	45.1
2. Wendell Mottley	TRI	45.2
3. Andrzej Badeński	POL	45.6
4. Robbie Brightwell	GBR	45.7
5. Ulis Williams	USA	46.0
6. Timothy Graham	GBR	46.0
7. Peter Vassella	AUS	46.3
8. Edwin Skinner	TRI	46.8

His students laughed when Los Angeles high school mathematics teacher Mike Larrabee told them he was going to try out for the Olympics, but their laughter turned to excitement when they saw the times he was producing on the school track and at local meets. Larrabee had been a major contender in 1960, until he injured a tendon. Most observers thought Larrabee's track career was finished, but he returned in 1964 and qualified for the U.S. team at the age of 30. Sixth at the halfway mark of the final and fifth coming out of the final curve, Larrabee unleashed his patented finishing kick and churned past one runner after another. At last he caught Wendell Mottley of Yale ten meters from the finish and won by two feet. During a record-setting two-hour press conference following his victory, Larrabee told reporters, "I kept a copy of one story written about me that said I was too old. It's still on my wall. I think I'll take it down now." Larrabee was the first white winner of the 400 meters in 32 years.

1968 Mexico City C: 54, N: 35, D: 10.18. WR: 44.0 (Lee Evans)

1. Lee Evans	USA	43.8	WR
2. Larry James	USA	43.9	
3. Ronald Freeman	USA	44.4	
4. Amadou Gakou	SEN	45.0	
5. Martin Jellinghaus	GER	45.3	
6. Tegegne Bezabeh	ETH	45.4	
7. Andrzej Badeński	POL	45.4	
8. Amos Omolo	UGA	47.6	

A U.S. sweep seemed inevitable, considering that the top 12 400-meter runners in the world were all Americans. With each nation limited to only three entrants per event, several first-class U.S. runners had to be left behind. The big surprise was the success of the Africans, particularly Amadou Gakou of Senegal, who lowered his personal best from 46.7 to 45.0 and became the first black to hold the African 400-meter record. The first seven finishers all bettered their pre-Olympic best times. When asked his theory as to why U.S. blacks were such good runners, Evans replied, "Maybe a white boy can get an education because his parents can pay for it, but I wouldn't be going to school right now if I hadn't got an athletic scholarship. That's my theory—others may have a different one." However Evans was quick to thank his white friends as well as his black friends for all the help they had given him. His winning time was recorded as 43.86 by electronic timing.

1972 Munich C: 64, N: 49, D: 9.7. WR: 43.86 (Lee Evans)

1. Vincent Matthews	USA	44.66
2. Wayne Collett	USA	44.80
3. Julius Sang	KEN	44.92
4. Charles Asati	KEN	45.13
5. Horst-Rüdiger Schlöske	GER	45.31
6. Markku Kukkoaho	FIN	45.59
7. Karl Honz	GER	45.68

DNF: John Smith (USA)

Another U.S. sweep seemed to be a distinct possibility even though defending champion Lee Evans, hampered by a hamstring pull, had finished fourth at the U.S. Olympics trials and only qualified as a member of the 4 × 400 relay team. In his place was Vince Matthews, a New York City social worker who had just missed making the U.S. entry in 1968. U.S. officials and coaches were clearly disappointed that Evans hadn't qualified for the 400, and made Matthews feel extremely unwanted. The pre-Olympics favorites were Californians John Smith and Wayne Collett. In the final, Smith, running with an injured leg, pulled up lame after only 80 meters, but Collett and Matthews drove on. Matthews was somewhat shocked to find himself in the lead entering the final straight and still feeling strong. He held off Collett the rest of the way and won by four feet.

At the medal ceremony, Matthews and Collett showed little respect for the proceedings, talking and fidgeting during the playing of "The Star-Spangled Banner" rather than standing quietly at attention. The West German crowd booed them, and the International Olympic Committee, ignoring the U.S. Olympic Committee, banned the two runners from further competition. Matthews and Collett denied that their actions had constituted an organized protest. "If we did have any ideas about a demonstration," Matthews said, "we could have done a better job than that." Collett added, "I couldn't stand there and sing the words [to the national anthem] because I don't believe they're true. I wish they were. I think we have the potential to have a beautiful country, but I don't think we do."

Stepping down from the victory platform, Matthews had taken off his gold medal and twirled it around his finger, leading some people to believe that the medal meant little to him. In an article in *The New York Times*, Matthews responded to this criticism: "I took it off to tell them this was my medal. A lot of people had forgotten about me and given up on me. . . . Twenty years from now, I can look at this medal and say, 'I was the best quarter-miler in the world that day.' If you don't think that's important, you don't know what's inside an athlete's soul."

1976 Montreal C: 44, N: 29, D: 7.29. WR: 43.86 (Lee Evans)
1. Alberto Juantorena Danger CUB 44.26
2. Frederick Newhouse USA 44.40
3. Herman Frazier USA 44.95
4. Alfons Brijdenbach BEL 45.04
5. Maxie Parks USA 45.24
6. Richard Mitchell AUS 45.40
7. David Jenkins GBR 45.57
8. Jan Werner POL 45.63

In 1972 Alberto Juantorena had been narrowly eliminated in the Olympic semifinals. He was unbeaten in 1973 and 1974, but before the 1975 season he underwent two operations on his foot. By the time of the Montreal Olympics he had emerged as the clear favorite at 400 meters. When he scored a surprising victory at 800 meters, it appeared that he had an excellent chance to become the first runner to score a 400/800 double since Paul Pilgrim in the Intercalated Games of 1906. Juantorena waltzed through the first two rounds, content to qualify without extending himself. After finishing his second-round heat, he kept on running, continuing through the tunnel and into the locker room without stopping. In the semifinals, Juantorena started poorly, then accelerated into first place and jogged home in 45.10, looking back at the other runners seven times on his way to the tape. Fred Newhouse, winner of the second semifinal in 44.89, sprinted into the lead in the final and was sure he was about to win the gold medal when Juantorena, the man with the nine-foot stride, appeared at his shoulder with 20 meters to go and moved right by him. Juantorena's winning time was a half-second faster than he had ever run before. The 6-foot 2-inch Cuban hero became the first man from a non-English speaking country to win the 400 meters, although Juantorena himself actually spoke English quite well. Before the 1976 Olympics were over, Alberto Juantorena had run nine races and lost 11 pounds.

1980 Moscow C: 50, N: 32, D: 7.30. WR: 43.86 (Lee Evans)
1. Viktor Markin SOV 44.60
2. Richard Mitchell AUS 44.84
3. Frank Schaffer GDR 44.87
4. Alberto Juantorena Danger CUB 45.09
5. Alfons Brijdenbach BEL 45.10
6. Michael Solomon TRI 45.55
7. David Jenkins GBR 45.56
8. Joseph Coombs TRI 46.33

For the third straight time the 400 meters was won by the runner in Lane 2. This time, though, the man in Lane 2 was a complete outsider: a 23-year-old Siberian-born medical student named Viktor Markin, who wasn't even listed in the 300-page U.S.S.R. Olympic Candidate book. Markin gained the lead from Schaffer with 80 meters to go. Mitchell also finished strongly, moving from last to second in the final 100 meters. Although Juantorena was only a shadow of his former self, his fourth-place finish was actually quite an achievement considering that he was still recovering from an Achilles tendon operation. Markin's time, 0.73

seconds faster than his previous best, was the fastest 400 meters to be run in over two years. "I don't know my own limits," he said afterward. "Everything came to me so quickly in the final. . . . I finished like I was in a dream."

800 METERS

1896 Athens C: 9, N: 5, D: 4.9. WR(880 yards): 1:53.4 (Charles Kirkpatrick)
1. Edwin Flack AUS 2:11.0
2. Nándor Dáni HUN 2:11.8e
3. Demitrios Golemis GRE —
DNS: Albin Lermusiaux (FRA)

Teddy Flack was a 22-year-old accountant who took a month's holiday from his job with Price, Waterhouse and Company in London to travel to Athens and take part in the Olympics.

1900 Paris C: 18, N: 8, D: 7.16. WR(880 yards): 1:53.4 (Charles Kirkpatrick)
1. Alfred Tysoe GBR 2:01.2
2. John Cregan USA 2:03.0
3. David Hall USA —
4. Henri Deloge FRA —
5. Zoltán Speidl HUN —
6. John Bray USA —

David Hall won the first qualifying heat in 1:59.0, but was unable to repeat his time in the final, which was won by Tysoe, who ran the last lap in 56.2 seconds.

1904 St. Louis C: 13, N: 3, D: 9.1. WR(880 yards): 1:53.4 (Charles Kirkpatrick)
1. James Lightbody USA 1:56.0 OR
2. Howard Valentine USA 1:56.3
3. Emil Breitkreutz USA 1:56.4
4. George Underwood USA —
5. Johannes Runge GER —
6. William Frank Verner USA —

Lightbody ran most of the race in fifth place, then moved to the outside and passed the leaders to win by one and a half yards.

1906 Athens C: 23, N: 7, D: 4.30. WR(880 yards): 1:53.4 (Charles Kirkpatrick)
1. Paul Pilgrim USA 2:01.5
2. James Lightbody USA 2:01.6
3. Wyndham Halswelle GBR 2:03.0
4. Reginald Percy Crabbe GBR —
5. Kristian Hellström SWE —
6. Charles Bacon USA —
7. Eli Burton Parsons USA —
DNF: Johannes Runge (GER)

Coming down the homestretch, Lightbody looked over his left shoulder to check the position of the other runners. Just then, Paul Pilgrim, the upset winner of the 400 meters the previous day, sped past him on the right to win by about two feet. Pilgrim never won a major race before or after the 1906 Games.

1908 London C: 39, N: 10, D: 7.21. WR(880 yards): 1:53.4 (Charles Kirkpatrick)
1. Melvin Sheppard   USA   1:52.8 WR
2. Emilio Lunghi   ITA   1:54.2
3. Hanns Braun   GER   1:55.2
4. Ödön Bodor   HUN   1:55.4
5. Theodore Just   GBR   —
6. John Halstead   USA   —
DNF: C.B. Beard (USA); Ian Fairbairn-Crawford (GBR)

Fairbairn-Crawford raced into the lead and set a blistering pace, in the hope of wearing out 1500-meter winner Mel Sheppard for the benefit of Britain's number-one runner, Theodore Just. Fairbairn-Crawford opened a 15-yard gap after 200 meters and finished the first lap in 53 seconds. The British strategy failed, as Sheppard kept to his own pace, moved into the lead after 500 meters, and won by ten yards over the surprising Emilio Lunghi. A second tape had been set up 5.6 yards after the finish so that the winner's time could be measured at 880 yards. Sheppard slowed down so much that he needed 2.2 seconds to cover the extra distance, and thus missed breaking Kirkpatrick's 13-year-old half-mile world record.

1912 Stockholm C: 48, N: 15, D: 7.8. WR: 1:52.8 (Melvin Sheppard)
1. James "Ted" Meredith   USA   1:51.9 WR
2. Melvin Sheppard   USA   1:52.0
3. Ira Davenport   USA   1:52.0
4. Melville Brock   CAN   1:52.7
5. Daniel Caldwell   USA   1:52.8
6. Hanns Braun   GER   1:53.1
7. Clarence Edmundson   USA   —
8. Herbert Putnam   USA   —

Sheppard led from the start, passing the halfway mark in 52.5. Ted Meredith edged ahead in the final straightaway and won by about 18 inches, with the first four runners all breaking the world record. Meredith continued on to set a new 880-yard record of 1:52.5. According to *The New York Times,* "The excitement during the race was terrific, and was made more so by the terrible noise caused by thousands of throats yelling injunctions in every language to those in front to 'sit down.'"

1920 Antwerp C: 39, N: 18, D: 8.17 WR: 1:51.9 (James "Ted" Meredith)
1. Albert Hill   GBR   1:53.4 WR
2. Earl Eby   USA   1:53.6 WR
3. Bevil Rudd   SAF   1:54.0
4. Edgar Mountain   GBR   —
5. Donald Scott   USA   —
6. Albert Sprott   USA   —
7. — Esparbès   FRA   —
8. Adriaan Paulen   HOL   1:56.4

Albert Hill, a 31-year-old World War I veteran, won an exciting race in which the lead changed hands numerous times. A notable instance of gentlemanly good sportsmanship was related by bronze medalist Bevil Rudd. When one of the American runners accidently bumped into Rudd in the midst of the race, he turned to the South African and said, "Sorry, Bevil."

1924 Paris C: 41, N: 21, D: 8.7. WR: 1:51.9 (James "Ted" Meredith)
1. Douglas Lowe   GBR   1:52.4
2. Paul Martin   SWI   1:52.6 WR
3. Schuyler Enck   USA   1:53.0
4. Henry Stallard   GBR   1:53.0
5. William Richardson   USA   1:53.8
6. Ray Dodge   USA   1:54.2
7. John Watters   USA   —
8. Charles Hoff   NOR   —

The favorite, Henry Stallard, was suffering from an injured foot, but this didn't stop him from giving his all in the final and leading for the first 700 meters. Finally he was passed by Lowe and Martin, who engaged in a frantic battle, which Lowe won by about a yard. The final took place on Lowe's 22nd birthday. Charles Hoff, who finished in eighth place, was the reigning world record holder in the pole vault.

1928 Amsterdam C: 54, N: 26, D: 7.31. WR: 1:50.6 (Séraphin Martin)
1. Douglas Lowe   GBR   1:51.8 OR
2. Erik Byléhn   SWE   1:52.8
3. Hermann Engelhard   GER   1:53.2
4. Philip Edwards   CAN   1:54.0
5. Lloyd Hahn   USA   1:54.2
6. Séraphin Martin   FRA   1:54.6
7. Earl Fuller   USA   1:55.0
8. Jean Keller   FRA   —

The 1928 800 meters was an anxiously awaited contest among Germany's Dr. Otto Peltzer, who had broken Ted Meredith's 14-year-old world record in a classic showdown with Douglas Lowe in 1926, Lloyd Hahn, who had broken Peltzer's record, and Séra Martin, who had broken Hahn's record. Unfortunately, Peltzer became ill and was eliminated in the semifinals. As it turned out, the big confrontation was actually a rout, as defending champion Douglas Lowe swept past Hahn in the final curve and won by about eight yards.

1932 Los Angeles C: 19, N: 10, D: 8.2. WR: 1:50.6 (Séraphin Martin)
1. Thomas Hampson   GBR   1:49.7 WR
2. Alexander Wilson   CAN   1:49.9
3. Philip Edwards   CAN   1:51.5
4. Edwin Genung   USA   1:51.7
5. Edwin Turner   USA   1:52.5
6. Charles Hornbostel   USA   1:52.7
7. John Powell   GBR   1:53.0
8. Séraphin Martin   FRA   1:53.6

Missing from the competition was Ben Eastman, who had recorded 1:50.0 for 800 meters earlier in the year on his way to a time of 1:50.9 for 880 yards. Eastman had decided to concentrate on the 400 meters. Guyanese-born medical student Phil Edwards sprinted into the lead, covering the first lap in 52.8 seconds. Inevitably, he faded and was passed, first by Alex Wilson and then by 24-year-old schoolteacher Tommy Hampson, who had never before run faster than 1:52.4. Wilson and Hampson dueled stride for stride over the last 50, yards with Hampson just edging ahead to win by a foot.

1936 Berlin C: 43, N: 24, D: 8.4. WR: 1:49.7 (Thomas Hampson)
1. John Woodruff   USA   1:52.9
2. Mario Lanzi   ITA   1:53.3
3. Philip Edwards   CAN   1:53.6
4. Kazimierz Kucharski   POL   1:53.8
5. Charles Hornbostel   USA   1:54.6
6. Harry Williamson   USA   1:55.8
AC: J.C. Anderson (ARG), G.I.D. Backhouse (AUS), B.F. McCabe (GBR)

John Woodruff was a 21-year-old University of Pittsburgh freshman who came from a poor black family in Connellsville, Pennsylvania. His time of 1:52.7 was the fastest of the qualifying rounds. As usual, Phil Edwards, now a doctor, stormed into the lead and led the field around the first lap. Meanwhile Woodruff was executing one of the most unusual tactics ever seen in the Olympics. Finding himself boxed in after 300 meters, Woodruff slowed down to the pace of a brisk walk and let all the other runners pass him. Then he moved way to the outside and sprinted past his opponents one by one until he found himself in the lead with one lap to go. Some observers felt that he had run as much as 50 extra meters. Edwards regained the lead on the backstretch, but Woodruff took over again in the last curve. Mario Lanzi staged a great finishing drive, but Woodruff used his loping ten-foot stride to stave off the challenge and win by two yards. Woodruff was the first winner of the Olympic 800 meters to run the second lap faster than the first. Phil Edwards won his fifth Olympic bronze medal.

1948 London C: 41, N: 24, D: 8.2. WR: 1:46.6 (Rudolf Harbig)
1. Malvin Whitfield   USA   1:49.2 OR
2. Arthur Wint   JAM   1:49.5
3. Marcel Hansenne   FRA   1:49.8
4. Herbert Barten   USA   1:50.1
5. Ingvar Bengtsson   SWE   1:50.5
6. Robert Chambers   USA   1:52.1
7. Robert Chef d'Hôtel   FRA   1:53.0
8. Niels Holst-Sörensen   DEN   1:53.4

Chef d'Hôtel held the early lead, but at the end of the first lap 23-year-old Air Force sergeant Mal Whitfield jumped the field and pulled away. Arthur Wint made a late charge, but Whitfield held on to win by three yards. Between 1948 and 1954 Whitfield won 66 of 69 half-mile races.

1952 Helsinki C: 50, N: 32, D: 7.22. WR: 1:46.6 (Rudolf Harbig)
1. Malvin Whitfield   USA   1:49.2
2. Arthur Wint   JAM   1:49.4
3. Heinz Ulzheimer   GER   1:49.7
4. Gunnar Nielsen   DEN   1:49.7
5. Albert Webster   GBR   1:50.2
6. Günter Steines   GER   1:50.6
7. Reginald Pearman   USA   1:52.1
8. Lars-Eric Wolfbrandt   SWE   1:52.1

Between Olympics Mal Whitfield had worked as a tailgunner during the Korean War. But on July 22, 1952, he was back in the final of the Olympic 800 meters run, once again facing the challenge of Arthur Wint. The 32-year-old Wint led the field around the first lap, reaching 400 meters with Ulzheimer second and Whitfield third. On the backstretch, with 250 meters to go, Whitfield made his move and entered the final curve in first place. Coming into the homestretch, Wint made a move of his own and gradually drew up to Whitfield's shoulder. But Whitfield had kept some extra strength in reserve and was able to pull away to a two-yard victory. Whitfield's time was exactly what it had been four years earlier, but Wint finished one yard closer.

1956 Melbourne C: 38, N: 24, D: 11.26. WR: 1:45.7 (Roger Moens)
1. Thomas Courtney   USA   1:47.7 OR
2. Derek Johnson   GBR   1:47.8
3. Audun Boysen   NOR   1:48.1
4. Arnold Sowell   USA   1:48.3
5. Michael Farell   GBR   1:49.2
6. Lonnie Spurrier   USA   1:49.3
7. Emile Leva   BEL   1:51.8
8. Bill Butchart   AUS   —

On August 3, 1955, Roger Moens of Belgium ran 1:45.7 to break finally Rudolf Harbig's 1939 world record. Unfortunately, Moens sustained a leg injury late in the 1956 season and was unable to compete in the Olympics. Nevertheless, the 800 meters final turned out to be the most dramatic race of the Melbourne Olympics. With Moens gone, the race shaped up to be the climactic chapter in the ongoing rivalry between Arnie Sowell of Pittsburgh and Tom Courtney of Livingston, New Jersey.

Sure enough, Courtney took the early lead, but Sowell quickly passed him and led the pack through the first lap and into the second. Toward the end of the backstretch, Courtney tried to pass Sowell, and the two ran shoulder to shoulder around the final curve. Emerging into the homestretch, the runners found themselves confronted by a stiff wind. Courtney moved ahead and then shifted to the third lane in order to avoid the chewed up inner lane. Noticing the sudden opening between the two Americans, Derek Johnson dashed between them and, with 60 yards to go, pushed into first place. It looked like a major upset in the making, but Courtney was not about to give up. Courtney later recalled, "I looked at the tape just 40 yards away and realized this was the only chance I would ever have to win the Olympics." Ignoring the pain throughout his body, Courtney fashioned one last sprint out of nothing but determination. Step by step he gained on Johnson and lunged across the finish line. In a delirium, he turned to Johnson and asked who had won. "Why you did, Tom," came the reply.

"It was a new kind of agony for me," Courtney recalled. "I had never run myself into such a state. My head was exploding, my stomach ripping and even the tips of my fingers ached. The only thing I could think was, 'If I live, I will never run again!'" The victory ceremony had to be delayed for an hour until he recovered. Twenty years later, Tom Courtney wrote about his years of competitive running: "It is a world that is gone now, but I still enjoy going out to a local track and taking a run and, with a half lap to go, I kind of savor the idea that I am re-running the last half lap of the best part of my life."

1960 Rome C: 51, N: 35, D: 9.2. WR: 1:45.7 (Roger Moens)

1. Peter Snell	NZE	1:46.3 OR
2. Roger Moens	BEL	1:46.5
3. George Kerr	JAM	1:47.1
4. Paul Schmidt	GER	1:47.6
5. Christian Wägli	SWI	1:48.1
6. Manfred Matuschewski	GDR	1:52.0

The 1960 800 meters was expected to be a great duel between 30-year-old world record holder Roger Moens and George Kerr of Jamaica. Kerr won the first semifinal, but the second semi produced a surprise when Moens was beaten by a little-known New Zealander named Peter Snell, whose pre-Olympic best had been 1:49.2 for 880 yards. However Moens had not really extended himself, so Snell was still not taken seriously. As expected, Christian Wägli took the lead in the final and held on for 700 meters, at which point Moens moved ahead. In the homestretch he looked back three times to check the position of the other runners, particularly George Kerr. Moens was still ahead 25 yards from the tape when Snell, realizing for the first time that he actually had a chance to win, charged ahead on the inside. "All I remember from that point is hurling every ounce of effort into the finish, and flinging myself forward," Snell wrote in his autobiography, *No Bugles, No Drums*. Like Tom Courtney four years earlier, Peter Snell had no idea in which place he had finished. Then a dejected Roger Moens approached him with congratulations. "Who won?" asked Snell. "You did," replied Moens.

"It was a strange moment," Snell recalled. "What should I do now? Flashingly, I recalled films of past Olympics, and of champions who cavorted round the track, presumably letting their happy emotions run riot. But I felt in a semi-daze, partly from fatigue, partly from disbelief that this had actually happened to me." Snell did not take a victory lap. Instead he channeled his emotions into rooting for fellow New Zealander Murray Halberg, who won the next race on the schedule, the 5000 meters.

A word about one runner who never even made it to the starting line. Wym Essajas was the first person to represent the South American nation of Surinam at the Olympics. Unfortunately he was mistakenly told that the 800-meter heats would be held in the afternoon, so he spent the morning resting. When Essajas arrived at the stadium the heats were over, and he was forced to return to Surinam without having competed. It was eight years before Surinam sent another athlete to the Olympics.

1964 Tokyo C: 47, N: 32, D: 10.16. WR: 1:44.3 (Peter Snell)

1. Peter Snell	NZE	1:45.1 OR
2. William Crothers	CAN	1:45.6
3. Wilson Kiprugut Chuma	KEN	1:45.9
4. George Kerr	JAM	1:45.9
5. Thomas Farrell	USA	1:46.6
6. Jerome Siebert	USA	1:47.0
7. Dieter Bogatzki	GER	1:47.2
8. Jacques Pennewaert	BEL	1:50.5

When Peter Snell arrived in Rome in 1960, no one had paid any attention, but four years later in Tokyo it was a completely different story. In one week in 1962 Snell had set world records of 3:54.4 for the mile and 1:44.3 for 800 meters. Now he was the favorite in both the 800 and 1500, although he didn't make his final decision to enter the 800 until the last minute. In the first round, Francis Chatelet of France had the unfortunate experience of recording the fifth fastest time of the round, and yet being eliminated because he finished fifth in his heat, with only the top four from each heat advancing to the semifinals. The final saw stocky Wilson Kiprugut lead the field for 550 meters. Then Snell swung outside, stormed around the leaders into first place, and pulled away to win by four yards. Kiprugut tripped on George Kerr's heel 50 yards from the finish, but still managed to gain a bronze medal, the first Olympic medal ever won by a Kenyan. Snell's winning time was the best on record since his own world record performance.

1968 Mexico City C: 41, N: 31, D: 10.15. WR: 1:44.3 (Peter Snell)

1. Ralph Doubell	AUS	1:44.3 EWR
2. Wilson Kiprugut Chuma	KEN	1:44.5
3. Thomas Farrell	USA	1:45.4
4. Walter Adams	GER	1:45.8
5. Josef Plachy	CZE	1:45.9
6. Dieter Fromm	GDR	1:46.2
7. Thomas Saisi	KEN	1:47.5
8. Benedict Cayenne	TRI	1:54.3

Following the usual Kenyan tactics, Kiprugut led the field from the start and still had a six-yard lead after 600 meters. Unheralded Ralph Doubell, who had nipped Kiprugut in the second semifinal, repeated his come-from-behind performance in the final. He passed Kiprugut 50 yards from the finish and won by a long yard.

1972 Munich C: 61, N: 46, D: 9.2. WR: 1:44.3 (Peter Snell, Ralph Doubell, David Wottle)

1. David Wottle	USA	1:45.9
2. Yevgeny Arzhanov	SOV	1:45.9
3. Michael Boit	KEN	1:46.0
4. Franz-Josef Kemper	GER	1:46.5
5. Robert Ouko	KEN	1:46.5
6. Andrew Carter	GBR	1:46.6
7. Andrzej Kupczyk	POL	1:47.1
8. Dieter Fromm	GDR	1:48.0

At the U.S. Olympic tryouts, Dave Wottle of Canton, Ohio, had equaled the world record of 1:44.3, three seconds faster than he had ever run before. However, because of his lack of international experience and because he had suffered a recent attack of tendinitis, Wottle was not the favorite in Munich. This role fell rather naturally to Yevgeny Arzhanov, who had not lost an 800-meter final in four years. As expected, the two Kenyans, Ouko and Boit, rushed into the early lead in the Olympic final, while Wottle ran in sixth place. Coming into the homestretch it looked like Arzhanov's race, and even Wottle, who had now begun his finishing kick, was only hoping for a medal. As the Kenyans faded, Wottle, who always wore an old golf cap while he ran, saw his chance for second place. Then, 20 yards from the finish, he realized that Arzhanov had run out of steam and that the gold medal was still a possibility. Drawing on his last reserve of energy, Wottle caught and passed Arzhanov, who stumbled two meters short of the tape and fell onto the synthetic track. "It is very disappointing," Arzhanov later told the press, "to lose in the very last stride by the length of your nose."

Wottle was so shocked by his victory that he forgot to take off his cap during the playing of "The Star-Spangled Banner" at the medal ceremony. He didn't realize what he had done until a reporter asked him if he had been staging a protest. Although nobody back in the United States actually held it against him, Wottle, a member of the Air Force ROTC at Bowling Green University, was embarrassed to the point of tears and felt obliged to make a formal apology to the American people.

1976 Montreal C: 42, N: 31, D: 7.25. WR: 1:43.7 (Marcello Fiasconaro)

1. Alberto Juantorena Danger	CUB	1:43.50 WR
2. Ivo van Damme	BEL	1:43.86
3. Richard Wohlhuter	USA	1:44.12
4. Willi Wülbeck	GER	1:45.26
5. Steven Ovett	GBR	1:45.44
6. Luciano Susanj	YUG	1:45.75
7. Sriram Singh	IND	1:45.77
8. Carlo Grippo	ITA	1:48.39

Alberto Juantorena went to the Montreal Olympics as the favorite at 400 meters, but somewhat of an unknown quantity at 800 meters. Although he had recorded 1:44.9 in April, the second fastest time of the year (to Rick Wohl-huter's 1:44.8), Juantorena had very little experience at the distance. Wohlhuter himself dismissed the Cuban as a non-contender, assuming that he would not have the stamina to make it through three rounds of metric half-mile races. Wohlhuter could not have been more wrong. In the final, Juantorena moved ahead as the runners broke to the inside after running the first 300 meters in lanes. He passed the halfway mark in 50.9 seconds. Sriram Singh took the lead briefly, but Juantorena fought him off, easily beat back a challenge from Wohlhuter, and won decisively, to become the first 800 meters gold medalist from a non-English-speaking country. Conspicuously missing from the competition was Mike Boit of Kenya, who was forced to watch the meet from the stands after his nation's government joined the African boycott. Four weeks later Boit ran 1:43.90 and 1:43.57, leaving track fans to wonder what might have been. Silver medalist Ivo van Damme died in a car crash on December 29, 1976. He was only 22 years old.

Olympic history, of course, is not just made up of medalists, and some mention should be made of Wilnor Joseph of the notorious Haitian track and field team. Joseph finished the second heat of the first round in 2:15.26, a time so slow that it would not have qualified him for the 800 meters final in 1900, much less 1976.

1980 Moscow C: 41, N: 28, D: 7.26. WR: 1:42.33 (Sebastian Coe)

1. Steven Ovett	GBR	1:45.4
2. Sebastian Coe	GBR	1:45.9
3. Nikolai Kirov	SOV	1:46.0
4. Agberto Conceição Guimaraes	BRA	1:46.2
5. Andreas Busse	GDR	1:46.9
6. Detlef Wagenknecht	GDR	1:47.0
7. Jose Marajo	FRA	1:47.3
8. David Warren	GBR	1:49.3

The final of the 1980 800 meters race was one of the most eagerly anticipated confrontations in Olympic history. Although there were six other runners in the race, the entire focus of sports fans around the world was on the two English world record holders, Sebastian Coe and Steve Ovett. The last time the two had met was at the 1978 European championships, where Ovett had beaten Coe at 800 meters, but both had lost to Olaf Beyer of East Germany. Since then Ovett and Coe had avoided each other like the plague, preferring to heat up their rivalry with increasingly faster times.

In 1979 Coe set the track world on its heels by breaking three world records in 41 days. On July 5 he ran 800 meters in 1:42.33 to lower Alberto Juantorena's world record by a full second. On July 17 Coe became the first person since Peter Snell to hold the records for both the 800 and the mile, when he ran the classic distance in 3:48.95. Then, on August 15, he covered 1500 meters in 3:32.03, to break Filbert Bayi's five-year-old mark.

The following year it was Steve Ovett's turn to enter the record books. On July 1, 1980, less than an hour after Coe set a new record for 1000 meters, Ovett gained great satisfaction by running a 3:48.8 mile to snatch the world record away from his rival. On July 15, nine days before the heats of the Olympic 800, Ovett beat a distinguished field of Olympic boycotters to win a 1500-meter race in 3:32.09, a time that rounded up to 3:32.1, the same as Coe's 3:32.03. The stage was definitely set for fireworks in the Olympics.

When Coe arrived in Moscow with the rest of the British team, he was met by an army of no less than 400 journalists, who assaulted him with a barrage of inane questions, such as, "Do you think you will win?" "How do you feel as a human being?" (this one from the representative of Tass, the Soviet news agency), and "How do you like Moscow?" (he had been there only a few hours). Ovett, on the other hand, slipped in two days before he was due to run and, following his usual procedure, refused to talk to the press, a wise decision considering Coe's experience.

The consensus of track experts was that Coe was the favorite at 800 meters, but that the 1500 was a toss-up. Ovett, on the other hand, had issued a public statement that the 800 was a toss-up, but that he was 90 percent sure he would win the 1500. The two did not meet in the heats and semifinals of the 800 meters, the first middle-distance race to be contested.

The first round was run without incident, but the semifinals saw the surprise elimination of Olaf Beyer. The three semifinal heats were won by Ovett, Nikolai Kirov, and Coe.

The final, run at 7:25 p.m. on July 26, turned out to be a strange, almost sluggish affair. The first lap was covered in the unusually slow time of 54.3 with Guimaraes in the lead, Ovett badly boxed in, in sixth place, and Coe running last. Dave Warren jumped into the lead, but in the backstretch Kirov moved in front by three meters, while Ovett pushed his way into second place, throwing so many elbows that he verged on disqualification. Meanwhile Coe was floundering, wasting his time in outside lanes and evidently unsure of what tactics to follow. By the time he finally made his move, it was too late. Ovett shot past Kirov 70 meters from the finish and won by over three meters. Ironically, Ovett's winning time was exactly the same as his fifth-place time in Montreal four years earlier. Coe outsprinted Kirov for the silver medal, a prize that would earn a place of honor in most homes, but which for Sebastian Coe was a symbol of failure.

As usual, Ovett declined to attend the postrace press conference. However Coe did not. Sorrowfully, he told the world, "I chose this day of all days to run the worst race of my life. I cannot even explain why. I suppose I must have compounded more cardinal sins of middle-distance running in 1½ minutes than I've done in a lifetime. What a race to choose." Fortunately for Coe, he still had a chance to redeem himself six days later. "I've got to come back and climb the mountain again," he said. "The 1500 was going to be a hard event anyway, but now it's going to be the big race of my life. I must win it."

1500 METERS

1896 Athens C: 8, N: 5, D: 4.7. WR(1 mile): 4:12.8 (Walter George)
1. Edwin Flack   AUS   4:33.2
2. Arthur Blake   USA   4:34.0e
3. Albin Lermusiaux   FRA   4.36.0e
4. Karl Galle   GER   4.39.0e
5. Angelos Phetsis   GRE   —
6. Demitrios Golemis   GRE   —

Flack outsprinted Blake in the final straightaway to win by about five yards. Two days later Flack also won the 800 meters race.

1900 Paris C: 9, N: 6, D: 7.15. WR: 4:10.4 (Albin Lermusiaux)
1. Charles Bennett   GBR   4:06.2 WR
2. Henri Deloge   FRA   4:06.6
3. John Bray   USA   4:07.2
4. Christian Christensen DEN   —
5. David Hall   USA   —
6. Hermann Wraschtil   AUT   —

Two of the leading contenders, John Cregan and Alex Grant of the United States, withdrew because the race was held on a Sunday.

1904 St. Louis C: 9, N: 3, D: 9.3. WR: 4:06.2 (Charles Bennett)
1. James Lightbody   USA   4:05.4 WR
2. William Frank Verner USA   4:06.8
3. Lacey Hearn   USA   —
4. David Munson   USA   —
5. Johannes Runge   GER   —
6. Peter Deer   CAN   —
7. Howard Valentine   USA   —
8. Harvey Cohn   USA   —

Lightbody moved into the lead at the end of the backstretch and won by six yards. The first three finishers were all members of the Chicago Athletic Association.

1906 Athens C: 20, N: 8, D: 4.30. WR: 4:05.4 (James Lightbody)
1. James Lightbody   USA   4:12.0
2. John McGough   GBR/IRL 4:12.6
3. Kristian Hellström SWE   4:13.4
4. George Wheatley   AUS   —
5. James Sullivan   USA   —
6. George Bonhag   USA   —
AC: Reginald Percy Crabbe (GBR), Harvey Cohn (USA)

1908 London C: 43, N: 15, D: 7.14. WR: 3:59.8 (Harold Wilson)
1. Melvin Sheppard   USA   4:03.4 OR
2. Harold Wilson   GBR   4:03.6
3. Norman Hallows   GBR   4:04.0
4. John Tait   CAN   —
5. Ian Fairbairn-Crawford GBR —
6. Joseph Deakin   GBR   —
AC: James Sullivan (USA), E.V. Loney (GBR)

Unfortunately, British officials decided to divide the 43 entrants into eight heats and allow only the winner of each heat to advance to the final. Because the runners were not seeded, this caused the elimination of several major contenders, particularly Emilio Lunghi, who clocked the second fastest time (4:03.8), but lost his heat to Norman Hallows, who ran 4:03.4. The final looked like a victory for the 5-foot 4-inch, 115-pound world record holder, Harold Wilson, until Mel Sheppard launched a sprint 100 yards from the tape, passed Wilson with 15 yards to go, and won by a yard and a half. For Sheppard, it was the first of his four Olympic gold medals. Ironically, Sheppard had applied to become a New York City policeman, but was rejected because he had a "weak heart."

1912 Stockholm C: 46, N: 14, D: 7.10. WR: 3:55.8 (Abel Kiviat)
1. Arnold Jackson   GBR   3:56.8 OR
2. Abel Kiviat   USA   3:56.9
3. Norman Taber   USA   3:56.9
4. John Paul Jones   USA   3:57.2
5. Ernst Wide   SWE   3:57.6
6. Philip Baker   GBR   4:01.0e
7. John Zander   SWE   4:02.0e
8. Henri Arnaud   FRA   4:02.2e

The United States entered a powerful team, including defending champion Mel Sheppard, 1500-meter world record holder Abel Kiviat, and mile world record holder John Paul Jones. Kiviat took the lead entering the final lap, followed by Taber and Jones, with Jackson and Sheppard close behind. Sheppard faded first. Entering the final straight it still looked like an American sweep, as Kiviat, Taber and Jones raced almost shoulder to shoulder. Thirty meters from the finish Kiviat seemed assured of victory, when suddenly Arnold Jackson of Great Britain burst by on the outside and won by two yards. The winner later gained greater fame as Arnold Nugent Strode-Jackson following his participation in World War I, during which he was wounded three times. In 1918, at the age of 27, he became the youngest acting brigadier general in the British army. As an athlete, Jackson was rather casual in his training, prefering golf, walking, and massages to the more vigorous and acceptable techniques of keeping in shape.

1920 Antwerp C: 26, N: 11, D: 8.19. WR: 3:54.7 (John Zander)
1. Albert Hill   GBR   4:01.8
2. Philip Baker   GBR   4:02.4
3. Lawrence Shields   USA   4:03.1
4. Václav Vohralik   CZE   —
5. Sven Lundgren   SWE   —
6. André Audinet   FRA   —
7. Arturo Porro   ITA   —
8. Joie Ray   USA   —

The 36-year-old Hill completed his 800/1500 double with the help of Baker, who ran beside him for most of the final

lap in order to "protect him from attacks." Baker later adopted his wife's maiden name and changed his name to Philip Noel-Baker. He served as a member of Parliament for 36 years and was awarded the 1959 Nobel Peace Prize in honor of his work in the pursuit of disarmament.

1924 Paris C: 40, N: 22, D: 7.10. WR: 3:52.6 (Paavo Nurmi)
1. Paavo Nurmi   FIN   3:53.6 OR
2. Wilhelm Schärer   SWI   3:55.0
3. Henry Stallard   GBR   3:55.6
4. Douglas Lowe   GBR   3:57.0
5. Raymond Buker   USA   3:58.6
6. Lloyd Hahn   USA   3:59.0
7. Raymond Watson   USA   4:00.0
8. T. Liewendahl   FIN   4:00.4

The crowd at the Stade Colombes Stadium rose to their feet to watch the thrilling race to the finish line, as Willy Schärer moved ahead in the last few strides to defeat the desperately struggling Henry Stallard, who collapsed to the ground and remained unconscious for a half hour. It had been an exciting battle—for second place. The race for first place had been no race at all, due to the presence of "The Phantom Finn," Paavo Nurmi.

Finnish Olympic officials had been extremely upset when the track and field schedule was announced and they learned that the final of the 1500 meters and the final of the 5000 meters would be separated by only a half hour, giving negligible time for recuperation to Nurmi, their star entrant in both events. A protest was filed, and the French organizers grudgingly agreed to expand the interval to 55 minutes. It still seemed an impossible feat to attempt, particularly after Nurmi injured both legs in training. But the challenge simply made Nurmi more determined to succeed. On June 19, three weeks before the day of the two Olympic finals, Nurmi decided to simulate the task ahead of him. First he ran a 1500-meter race, setting a world record of 3:52.6. After a one-hour rest he returned to the track and ran 5000 meters, setting another world record of 14:28.2.

Needless to say, when the other runners lined up for the start of the Olympic 1500 final in Paris, they had little hope for the gold medal. Nurmi took off, stopwatch in hand, as usual, covering the first 400 meters in a blistering 58.0 designed to kill off the opposition. Ray Watson made the mistake of trying to keep up with the Finnish running machine, and paid for his folly by fading to a disappointing seventh place. As soon as Watson had dropped away, Nurmi consulted his stopwatch one last time, tossed it onto the infield, and sprinted away to a 40-meter lead. In order to save his strength for the 5000, he coasted the final 300 meters, picking up speed briefly just before the end to make sure the others didn't catch up. After he crossed the finish line, he ignored the cheers of the crowd, picked up his sweater, and disappeared into the dressing room to rest up for his next race.

1928 Amsterdam C: 54, N: 26, D: 8.2. WR: 3:51.0 (Otto Peltzer)

1. Harry Larva	FIN	3:53.2 OR
2. Jules Ladoumégue	FRA	3:53.8
3. Eino Purje-Borg	FIN	3:56.4
4. Hans-Georg Wichmann	GER	3:56.8
5. Cyril Ellis	GBR	3:57.6
6. Paul Martin	SWI	3:58.4
7. Helmut Krause	GER	3:59.0
8. W. Whyte	AUS	4:00.0

Two hundred meters from the finish, Ladoumegue took the lead from Purje and appeared to be headed for victory. However he was passed 20 meters from the tape by "Harri" Larva, a goldsmith's engraver, who won by four yards. Larva was born to Swedish parents who lived in Turku, the hometown of Paavo Nurmi. He began training as a runner in 1924 after attending a post-Olympic race between Nurmi and Ritola.

1932 Los Angeles C: 27, N: 15, D: 8.4. WR: 3:49.2 (Jules Ladoumégue)

1. Luigi Beccali	ITA	3:51.2 OR
2. John Cornes	GBR	3:52.6
3. Philip Edwards	CAN	3:52.8
4. Glenn Cunningham	USA	3:53.4
5. Eric Ny	SWE	3:54.6
6. Norwood Hallowell	USA	3:55.0
7. John Lovelock	NZE	3:57.8
8. Frank Crowley	USA	—

World record holder Jules Ladoumégue was banned from competition by the French Federation after being charged with accepting pay for running in certain meets. The heated protests of French sports fans were to no avail. Still, the 1932 Olympic final was packed with splendid runners. The lead changed hands several times in the early going. Then, as the second lap came to a close, Glenn Cunningham, who was suffering a bad case of tonsilitis, burst ahead, followed by Phil Edwards. By the time the bell had rung to signal the final lap, Cunningham and Edwards had opened a 20-meter gap over the rest of the field. With 300 meters to go, John Cornes and 5-foot 6½-inch Luigi Beccali gave chase. In the backstretch Edwards passed Cunningham and took a five-yard lead. Beccali caught Cunningham at the head of the homestretch and then passed Edwards 100 yards from the finish. The young man from Milan won by six yards, breaking the tape by grabbing it in his hands and tearing it apart. At the medal ceremony Beccali gave the Fascist salute and became a national hero overnight. As a matter of fact, when he emerged from his cottage in the Olympic Village the next morning, he discovered that his Italian teammates had covered the walk from his bungalow with rugs from their own rooms and lined the path with wicker chairs adorned with flowers. Standing behind the chairs were his teammates, chanting, "Luigi, Luigi, Luigi." Beccali, choked with emotion, was speechless. He later emigrated to New York and went into the wine business.

1936 Berlin C: 44, N: 27, D: 8.6. WR: 3:48.8 (William Bonthron)

1. John Lovelock	NZE	3:47.8 WR
2. Glenn Cunningham	USA	3:48.4
3. Luigi Beccali	ITA	3:49.2
4. Archie San Romani	USA	3:50.0
5. Philip Edwards	CAN	3:50.4
6. John Cornes	GBR	3:51.4
7. Miklós Szabó	HUN	3:53.0
8. Robert Goix	FRA	3:53.8

The 1936 1500-meter final promised to be one of the great races of all time and, unlike many athletic contests with great expectations, it lived up to its advance billing. Among the starters were six of the top seven finishers from the 1932 Olympics. The favorites were defending champion Luigi Beccali, one mile world record holder Glenn Cunningham of Elkhart, Kansas, whose leg had been severely burned in a fire when he was 8 years old, and Jack Lovelock of New Zealand, who had beaten Cunningham in "The Mile of the Century" at Princeton in 1935. Lovelock, a former Rhodes scholar at Oxford, was now a medical student who ran numerous tests on himself in order to determine the conditions necessary to achieve an optimum performance. He was particularly interested in learning how long he could sustain a final sprint, and this led to his development of a secret strategy to win at the Berlin Olympics.

When the great race finally began at 4:18 p.m., there was a good deal of jockeying for position. Cunningham took the lead at 400 meters, followed by Lovelock, who later dropped back to fourth place. Just before the bell, Eric Ny passed Cunningham. Then, 300 yards from the tape, Lovelock passed Cunningham and reached Ny's shoulder. Cunningham followed him. But then Lovelock paused and so did Cunningham, thinking the move had been a false alarm. But one second later Lovelock was off again, beginning the unusually long sprint that he had planned so carefully. Cunningham raced after him, but Lovelock was able to open up a lead of six yards. Cunningham tried to close the gap, but he could get no closer than four yards. Lovelock ran the final 400 meters in 56.8 seconds and the last 200 meters in 27.2, even though he slowed up in the last 20 yards, realizing that his victory was assured. Lovelock didn't believe in setting records, only in winning, but he broke the world record by a full second because that was what was required to defeat Cunningham.

In 1940 Jack Lovelock was thrown from a horse during a hunt and lay unconscious for an hour before he was discovered. He recovered, but suffered double vision and occasional dizziness for the rest of his life. He and his wife moved to New York, where Lovelock obtained a position as assistant director of physical medicine at the Hospital for Special Surgery. On December 28, 1949, eight days before his 40th birthday, Lovelock began having dizzy spells and telephoned his wife that he would be coming home early. He was standing on the southbound platform of the Church Street subway station in Brooklyn when he suddenly became woozy and pitched forward onto the tracks. He was struck by an oncoming train and died instantly.

1948 London C: 37, N: 22, D: 8.6. WR: 3:43.0 (Günder Hagg, Lennart Strand)

1. Henry Eriksson	SWE	3:49.8
2. Lennart Strand	SWE	3:50.4
3. Willem Slijkhuis	HOL	3:50.4
4. Václav Čevona	CZE	3:51.2
5. Gösta Bergkvist	SWE	3:52.2
6. William Nankeville	GBR	3:52.6
7. Sándor Garay	HUN	3:52.8
8. Erik Jörgensen	DEN	—

The 1948 final was run on a rain-soaked track in the middle of a downpour. The two great Swedish runners Günder Hagg and Arne Andersson had been banned as professionals, but the Swedes still fielded the strongest team in Lennart Strand, Henry Eriksson, and Gösta Bergkvist. Marcel Hansenne of France led for 1000 meters, at which point the three Swedes, led by Eriksson, made their move. Coming out of the final turn, Eriksson, who had never beaten Strand, held a three-yard lead. Strand closed up to his shoulder and ran even for another 20 yards, but with 50 yards to go he realized that he couldn't pass his teammate. Looking behind him he saw Slijkhuis coming with a great rush on the inside. Determined to preserve second place, Strand veered to his left and bumped the Dutch runner off the track long enough to prevent him from passing. Eriksson was a fireman, Strand a linotype operator and pianist.

1952 Helsinki C: 52, N: 26, D: 7.26. WR: 3:43.0 (Günder Hagg, Lennart Strand, Werner Lueg)

1. Josef "Josy" Barthel	LUX	3:45.1 OR
2. Robert McMillen	USA	3:45.2
3. Werner Lueg	GER	3:45.4
4. Roger Bannister	GBR	3:46.0
5. Patrick El Mabrouk	FRA	3:46.0
6. Rolf Lamers	GER	3:46.8
7. Olle Åberg	SWE	3:47.0
8. Ingvar Ericsson	SWE	3:47.6

The 1952 1500 meters was up for grabs. If there were favorites they were probably Werner Lueg, who had tied the world record at the German championships on June 29, and Roger Bannister, whose greatest fame was yet to come. Bannister, a medical intern, had prepared himself very carefully for a competition that would include a heat and then a final two days later. Unfortunately, I.A.A.F. officials decided to add a semifinal round, which meant that the finalists would run three races in three days. This change of schedule greatly upset Bannister's plans. The semifinals were won by local favorite Denis Johansson in 3:49.8 and lightly regarded Josy Barthel, a small man from the small nation of Luxembourg, who finished in 3:50.4.

Audun Boysen of Norway was the first in front in the final, but he was soon passed by Rolf Lamers, who held the lead until the third lap, when he surrendered it to his teammate Werner Lueg. Coming into the backstretch, the ac-

tion became frantic. Lueg fought off challenges from Olle Åberg, Patrick El Mabrouk, and Bannister. Lueg opened up a three-yard lead and held it around the final turn. However, almost unnoticed, two outsiders, Josy Barthel and Bob McMillen, had sprinted up from the very back of the field to within striking distance.

Fifty yards from the finish, Lueg began to tie up. With the crowd screaming wildly, first Barthel and then McMillen passed the German. Barthel could feel McMillen literally breathing down his back as the American inched closer with every stride until he was only one and a half feet behind. Let Josy Barthel tell the rest of the story: "Five meters to run, the victory is mine, and, just as I had always dreamed in secret, I raised my arms, I smiled and I crossed the finish line.

"Afterward, I didn't appreciate right away that I had won. For me, as for the public, it was a surprise. I sat down, without being excited, on a bench in the middle of the infield. Then, no longer able to contain my joy, I cried. My friend Audun Boysen asked me, '*Eh bien,* Josy, why are you crying? Are you ill?' It was only then that I truly understood. 'No,' I replied, 'I am crying because I won.'"

Six of the 12 finalists had run their best time ever, including Barthel, whose previous best had been 3:48.4, and McMillen, who had never bettered 3:49.3. On the victory platform, as he listened to the national anthem of Luxembourg being played for the first and only time in Olympic history, Josy Barthel cried again. Roger Bannister recalled, "He raised his hand to wipe away a tear. His great strength was overcome by the tide of joy. Then he turned the movement into a wave of gratitude to the crowd. . . . In the great joy of that single moment the agony of the previous week was quite forgotten. I had found new meaning in the Olympic words that the important thing was not the winning but the taking part—not the conquering but the fighting well."

1956 Melbourne C: 37, N: 22, D: 12.1. WR: 3:40.6 (István Rózsavölgyi)

1. Ron Delany	IRL	3:41.2 OR
2. Klaus Richtzenhain	GDR	3:42.0
3. John Landy	AUS	3:42.0
4. László Tábori	HUN	3:42.4
5. Brian Hewson	GBR	3:42.6
6. Stanislav Jungwirth	CZE	3:42.6
7. Neville Scott	NZE	3:42.8
8. Ian Boyd	GBR	3:43.0

May 6, 1954, stands as probably the greatest day in track and field history. Running in Oxford with the help of pacesetters Chris Brasher and Chris Chataway, Roger Bannister attempted to break the barrier of barriers—the four-minute mile. In his autobiography, appropriately entitled *The Four-Minute Mile,* Bannister recalled the final lap of that race: "I felt that the moment of a lifetime had come. . . . The world seemed to stand still, or did not exist. The only reality was the next two hundred yards of track under my feet. . . .

"I felt at that moment that it was my chance to do one thing supremely well. I drove on, impelled by a combination of fear and pride. The air I breathed filled me with the spirit of the track where I had run my first race. The noise in my ears was that of the faithful Oxford crowd. Their hope and encouragement gave me greater strength. I had now turned the last bend and there were only fifty yards more. . . .

"Those last few seconds seemed never-ending. The faint line of the finishing tape stood ahead as a haven of peace, after the struggle. The arms of the world were waiting to receive me if only I reached the tape without slackening my speed. If I faltered, there would be no arms to hold me and the world would be a cold, forbidding place, because I had been so close. I leapt at the tape like a man taking his last spring to save himself from the chasm that threatens to engulf him."

The track announcer that day was none other than Norris McWhirter, who later became world famous as the compiler, along with his brother Ross, of *The Guinness Book of World Records*. McWhirter milked the dramatic moment for all it was worth. "Ladies and gentlemen," he began, "here is the result of event number nine, the one mile. First, number forty-one, R.G. Bannister of the Amateur Athletic Association and formerly of Exeter and Merton Colleges, with a time which is a new meeting and track record and which, subject to ratification, will be a new English Native, British National, British All-Comers', European, British Empire and World's record. The time is THREE. . ." The rest of the announcement was lost in the roar of the crowd. In fact, Bannister's time was 3:59.4.

In the two and a half years between that day in Oxford and the Melbourne Olympics, Bannister had retired from competition, but nine other runners had broken the four-minute barrier. All ten were present in Melbourne for the running of the 1500 meters—six on the track (John Landy, Brian Hewson, Laszlo Tabori, Ron Delany, Gunnar Nielsen, and István Rózsavölgyi) and four in the stands (Bannister, Jim Bailey, Chris Chataway, and Derek Ibbotson). Bannister presented to each of his successors a black silk tie with a monogram of a silver "4" and two gold "M"s within a gold laurel wreath.

The very first heat saw the elimination of several great runners, including Josy Barthel, István Rózsavölgyi, who had broken training during the Hungarian uprising against the U.S.S.R., Michel Jazy, who was to win a silver medal four years later in Rome, and an obscure Ethiopian named Mamo Wolde, who would gain fame *12* years later when he won the 1968 Olympic marathon.

The final turned out to be just as great a contest as had been expected. Before the race, the great sportsman John Landy, who once stopped in the middle of a race to help a fallen runner, gave a pep talk to Ron Delany, the youngest of the four-minute milers, and told him, "I think you can win this one, Ron." The twelve finalists were so well matched that when they began the final lap, less than eight yards separated the leader from the man in last place. The

official in charge of signaling the beginning of the final lap was so excited that he forgot to ring the bell. Hewson and Merv Lincoln of Australia were in the lead, but Lincoln, feeling a pain in his leg, began to fall back quickly. Meanwhile, Ron Delany was boxed in at tenth place. His coach at Villanova University, Jumbo Elliott, had always told him that if he was ever in a box just to relax. So Delany relaxed, even though there were only 300 yards left in the race.

Just then the runner in front of Delany, Gunnar Nielsen, realizing that he himself couldn't win the race, turned around and motioned Delany to pass him on the inside. Gradually Delany moved up; then, 120 meters from the finish, he burst out with all he had. The power of his sprint demoralized the other runners, and he was home free. He ran the last lap in 53.8, the last 200 meters in 25.6, and the final 100 meters in 12.9. He flew past the tiring Hewson and won by almost six yards, breasting the tape with his arms spread wide and a huge grin on his face. After crossing the finish, Delany fell to his knees. John Landy, thinking Delany was ill or injured, rushed up to help him, only to discover that the new Olympic champion was actually deep in prayer.

1960 Rome C:39, N: 25, D: 9.6. WR: 3:36.0 (Herbert Elliot)

1. Herbert Elliott	AUS	3:35.6 WR
2. Michel Jazy	FRA	3:38.4
3. István Rózsavölgyi	HUN	3:39.2
4. Dan Waern	SWE	3:40.0
5. Zoltan Vamoş	ROM	3:40.8
6. Dyrol Burleson	USA	3:40.9
7. Michel Bernard	FRA	3:41.5
8. James Grelle	USA	3:45.0

World record holder Herb Elliott of Perth was the clear favorite in 1960. After 950 meters he passed Michel Bernard and took off like a "scared bunny." To his opponents and to the 90,000 people in the stadium, Elliott appeared to be a sure winner, but Elliott himself refused to look behind him. Unaware that he had opened up an insurmountable 20-yard lead, he was sure that someone was close on his heels. When he reached the backstretch he saw his coach, Percy Cerutty, standing by the side of the track waving a white towel, which meant that a world record was achievable and that Elliott should give it all he had. Actually, the 66-year-old Cerutty had raced out of the stands and dashed across the protective moat that surrounded the track in order to signal his pupil. He was quickly grabbed by the police and hauled away, but his effort had been worth it. Elliott, still refusing to turn around and still thinking he might lose the gold medal, strained to the finish line and won by the amazing margin of 20 yards. His time of 3:35.6 was a new world record. Elliott, whose diet usually consisted of raw, natural foods, celebrated by going out drinking. His most difficult concern for the remainder of the Olympics was protecting his kangaroo-hide track shoes, which were almost stolen on three separate occasions. Between 1954 and 1960, Herb Elliott won 44 consecutive races at 1500 meters or one mile before retiring from competition at that distance.

1964 Tokyo C: 43, N: 34, D: 10.21. WR: 3:35.6 (Herbert Elliott)

1. Peter Snell	NZE	3:38.1
2. Josef Odložil	CZE	3:39.6
3. John Davies	NZE	3:39.6
4. Alan Simpson	GBR	3:39.7
5. Dyrol Burleson	USA	3:40.0
6. Witold Baran	POL	3:40.3
7. Michel Bernard	FRA	3:41.2
8. John Whetton	GBR	3:42.4

Before the Tokyo Olympics, Peter Snell had never run a race at 1500 meters, although he had competed in many one-mile contests. Running his sixth race in eight days, Snell ran away from the field in the backstretch and won by 12 yards, to gain his third Olympic gold medal.

1968 Mexico City C: 54, N: 37, D: 10.20. WR: 3:33.1 (James Ryun)

1. H. Kipchoge Keino	KEN	3:34.9 OR
2. James Ryun	USA	3:37.8
3. Bodo Tümmler	GER	3:39.0
4. Harald Norpoth	GER	3:42.5
5. John Whetton	GBR	3:43.8
6. Jacques Boxberger	FRA	3:46.6
7. Henryk Szordykowski	POL	3:46.6
8. Josef Odložil	CZE	3:48.6

Jim Ryun of Wichita, Kansas, went to the 1968 Olympics as the world record holder at 880 yards, 1500 meters, and the mile. He had not been beaten at 1500 or the mile in over three years. Yet his status as favorite was threatened by an attack of mononucleosis in June and by the fact that the Olympics were being held in the high altitude of Mexico City. For this reason, 28-year-old Kip Keino, an uncoached Nandi tribesman who had never defeated Ryun, was considered a serious contender. However Keino was having problems of his own. Recently he had been suffering violent stomach pains, which later turned out to be the result of a severe gall bladder infection. Ignoring the advice of doctors, Keino went ahead and entered not only the 1500, but also the 5000 and the 10,000. The 10,000 came first and Keino was running with the leaders with only two laps to go, when he suddenly doubled up in pain and fell onto the infield. When the stretcher-bearers came to get him, he jumped back onto the track and, even though he had been disqualified, he finished the race. Four days later he took second place in the 5000 meters.

As if he hadn't run enough already, the day of the 1500 meters final he got caught in a traffic jam and jogged the last mile to the stadium. Keino was well aware that Jim Ryun possessed a devastating finishing kick, so he decided to try a dangerous gamble, hoping to neutralize Ryun's sprint by building up a huge lead. After fellow Kenyan Ben Jipcho set a torrid pace of 56.0 for the first 400 meters, Keino took over and pulled away from the pack, passing

the 800-meter mark in a seemingly suicidal 1:55.3. Everyone waited for Keino to run out of steam, but, remarkably, he never did. Ryun's famous kick was impressive, but he was unable to close within 12 yards of Keino and finally eased up in pain, as the Kenyan went on to win by 20 meters, the largest margin of victory in Olympic 1500 meters history. Keino improved his personal best by 1.8 seconds and lowered his own high-altitude world record by a phenomenal five seconds. That same day, back in Kenya, Kip Keino's wife gave birth to their third daughter, who was named Milka Olympia Chelagat in honor of her father's achievement.

1972 Munich C: 66, N: 46, D: 9.10. WR:3:33.1 (James Ryun)

1. Pekka Vasala	FIN	3:36.3
2. H. Kipchoge Keino	KEN	3:36.8
3. Rodney Dixon	NZE	3:37.5
4. Michael Boit	KEN	3:38.4
5. Brendan Foster	GBR	3:39.0
6. Herman Mignon	BEL	3:39.1
7. Paul-Heinz Wellmann	GER	3:40.1
8. Vladimir Pantelei	SOV	3:40.2

Track aficionados awaited another showdown between defending champion Kip Keino and Jim Ryun, who had retired, returned to competition, had his ups and downs, and was now in top form once again. What no one expected was that their last confrontation as amateurs would come not in the Olympic final, but in the opening round. Entrants in the Olympics are seeded according to their previous times, so that leading contenders are separated in the opening heats. U.S. officials had submitted Ryun's superb time of 3:52.8 for the mile. However, somewhere along the line, this time was interpreted as being for 1500 meters, so the computer in charge of seeding treated Ryun as just another mediocre runner. Consequently, Ryun was thrown into the same first round heat as top-seeded Kip Keino.

The fateful fourth heat, won easily by Keino, was to prove the end of Jim Ryun's amateur career. Caught in a box 550 meters from the finish, Ryun tried to squeeze his way between runners rather than pass on the outside. As early leader Mohamed Younis of Pakistan faded on the inside lane, Vitus Ashaba of Uganda stepped to the outside to avoid him, and moved right into the space that Ryun was trying to fill. Ryun tripped on Ashaba's heel and fell back on Billy Fordjour of Ghana, sending both of them crashing to the ground. Ryun landed on the curb and Fordjour landed on Ryun, who came away with a bruised hip, a scraped knee, a sprained left ankle, and a concussion to his Adam's apple. Stunned, Ryun lay on the track for eight seconds before he got up and began chasing after the field. The sympathetic German crowd rooted him on, but he had lost at least 75 meters and it proved impossible for him to catch up. Ryun was in shock. "All I know is everything was going well," he said, "and I felt good, and the next thing I knew I was trying to figure out what happened."

Two days later, in the final, Kip Keino faced the challenge of Pekka Vasala, by no means an outsider, even though he was known in Finland as "Mr. Unpredictable." Vasala had competed in the Mexico City Games, but, struck down by "Montezumas's Revenge," he had finished last in his heat. Nevertheless, he had been quite moved by the opening ceremonies and vowed to himself that "someday, somewhere, I would accomplish something great."

In Munich, Keino made his move after 600 meters and Vasala followed close behind, dogging the former goat-herder all the way until the homestretch, when he moved ahead to win by about three meters. Vasala had run the last 800 meters in the amazing time of 1:49.0. The surprise bronze medalist was Rod Dixon of New Zealand, who began sobbing when he realized that his dream of an Olympic medal had come true. Still weeping, he was ushered backstage for the urine test. After producing a meager sample, Dixon sheepishly asked the German official if it was enough. "For the gold medal, no," was the reply, "but for the bronze medal, it will do."

Dixon was not the only one to be moved to tears. Pekka Vasala recalled, "When I walked into the dressing room after the race. . . I realized in a second I had won. Somehow I had not fully understood it on the track. All became misty and I was crying uncontrollably. I had completely lost control of myself. I was still confused on the victory stand. It was not until I put the gold medal into my pocket and grabbed it in my fingers that I finally woke up."

1976 Montreal C: 42, N: 28, D: 7.31. WR: 3:32.2 (Filbert Bayi)

1.	John Walker	NZE	3:39.17
2.	Ivo van Damme	BEL	3:39.27
3.	Paul-Heinz Wellmann	GER	3:39.33
4.	Eamonn Coghlan	IRL	3:39.51
5.	Frank Clement	GBR	3:39.65
6.	Richard Wohlhuter	USA	3:40.64
7.	David Moorcroft	GBR	3:40.94
8.	Graham Crouch	AUS	3:41.80

In 1976, black African nations boycotted the Olympics because a rugby team from New Zealand had played a team from South Africa. Ironically, this prevented Tanzanian world record holder Filbert Bayi from competing, and handed over an almost sure gold medal to New Zealand, which was represented by John Walker, who held the world record for the mile. It was Walker who had pushed Bayi to his 1500 meters record at the 1974 Commonwealth Games, and the two friends had been looking forward to their Olympics showdown ever since. Without Bayi and Kenyan Mike Boit to set the pace, the Olympic final was a slow, almost dull affair that came down to the final sprint. Walker passed Eamonn Coghlan in the backstretch and won by a meter. His winning time was the slowest in 20 years. When asked why he hadn't tried for a record even with Bayi missing, Walker replied, "Every record set in Montreal will eventually be broken and forgotten. The gold medal is the thing they can never take away from you."

1980 Moscow C: 40, N: 29, D: 8.1. WR: 3:32.1 (Sebastian Coe, Steven Ovett)

1.	Sebastian Coe	GBR	3:38.4
2.	Jürgen Straub	GDR	3:38.8
3.	Steven Ovett	GBR	3:39.0
4.	Andreas Busse	GDR	3:40.2
5.	Vittorio Fontanella	ITA	3:40.4
6.	Josef Plachy	CZE	3:40.7
7.	José Marajo	FRA	3:41.5
8.	Stephen Cram	GBR	3:42.0

It certainly seemed to most observers that Steve Ovett entered the 1500 meters final with a tremendous advantage. Not only had he defeated Sebastian Coe at Coe's best distance, the 800, but Ovett had won 45 consecutive races at 1500 meters and one mile, gong back to May 1977. In the semifinals Ovett had been so relaxed and in control that he actually gave a victory wave to the crowd before he had even taken the lead. Coe, on the other hand, had struggled through his first round heat and had been hounded and mercilessly criticized by the British press during the six days since the 800 meters final. As it turned out, however, Ovett's gold medal had taken away his competitive edge ever so slightly, while Coe had conquered his disappointment and depression, and couldn't wait to get out on the track to prove that he was a winner and not just a record-setter.

The withdrawal of Filbert Bayi, who had decided to concentrate on the 3000 meters steeplechase, left the race without a pace-setter, but before the first lap had ended it became clear that this was not going to be just a two-man race. Jürgen Straub took the lead at 400 meters, followed by Coe, who was determined to stay near the front and avoid the tactical errors he had committed in the 800. With 780 meters to go, Straub stepped up the pace, with Coe and Ovett close behind. It was just what Coe had hoped for: a long, open run to the finish.

With 200 meters to go, Straub was four meters ahead of Coe and six meters ahead of Ovett. Coming into the final curve, Coe unleashed his finishing kick, unaware that Ovett had chosen the exact same moment to make *his* move. Straub was not about to give in, but by the time they had hit the homestretch, Coe had taken the lead. A quick glance to each side to check the position of his opponents, and then, 80 meters from the finish line, Coe increased his speed again, crossing the finish line with a look of ecstatic relief that spoke far more than a thousand words. Straub, four meters back, held off Ovett, who finished with a peaceful, almost spiritual, smile on his face. Coe dropped to his knees and touched his forehead to the ground, seemingly unaware of the hearty congratulations being offered by Straub and Ovett. Coe had run the last lap in 52.2 seconds and the final 100 meters in 12.1.

Afterward, Coe and Ovett, who had been constantly portrayed by the press as bitter rivals, discussed the relief that they both felt and agreed to have a couple drinks together. Ovett let it be known that he was just as proud of his bronze medal as he was of his gold, because he had given his best. On the victory stand, Coe looked up to the sky. When asked why he had done this, Coe replied, "Perhaps somebody, somewhere, loves me after all."

5000 METERS

1896-1908 not held

1912 Stockholm C: 31, N: 11, D: 7.10. WR: 15:01.2
1. Johannes Kolehmainen	FIN	14:36.6 WR
2. Jean Bouin	FRA	14:36.7
3. George Hutson	GBR	15:07.6
4. George Bonhag	USA	15:09.8
5. Tel Berna	USA	15:10.0
6. Mauritz Karlsson	SWE	15:18.6

Hannes Kolehmainen, a vegetarian bricklayer from a running family, had already won the 10,000 meters two days earlier, and was taking part in his fourth long-distance race in four days. He and Jean Bouin pulled away from the other eight finalists after a couple of laps and ran the rest of the race with Bouin in front and Kolehmainen right behind him. Every time Kolehmainen tried to pass, Bouin would resist his challenge. On the final curve of the final lap, Kolehmainen tried again. Bouin swung wide, forcing the Finn back in line. When they reached the homestretch, Kolehmainen tried once more, finally reaching Bouin's shoulder 20 meters from the tape. Bouin veered into Kolehmainen, but his legs began to buckle, and "Hannes the Mighty," as he became known, was able to win by a yard. Silver medalist Bouin and bronze medalist George Hutson were both killed in action in 1914. Kolehmainen, on the other hand, moved to the United States and reappeared in Antwerp to win the 1920 marathon.

1920 Antwerp C: 31, N: 11, D: 8.17. WR:14:36.6 (Johannes Kolehmainen)
1. Joseph Guillemot	FRA	14:55.6
2. Paavo Nurmi	FIN	15:00.0
3. Erik Backman	SWE	15:13.0
4. Teudor Koskenniemi	FIN	15:17.0
5. Charles Blewitt	GBR	—
6. William Seagrove	GBR	—
7. Carlo Speroni	ITA	—
8. Alfred Nichols	GBR	—

This race, the first Olympic appearance by Paavo Nurmi, proved to be sweet, though temporary, revenge by the French for Kolehmainen's defeat of Bouin eight years earlier. Nurmi took the lead during the third lap and the 5-foot 3-inch Guillemot, whose heart was on the right side of his chest, followed him around until the final straightaway, at which point Guillemot sprinted away to win by 30 yards.

1924 Paris C: 39, N: 22, D: 7.10. WR:14: 28.2 (Paavo Nurmi)
1. Paavo Nurmi	FIN	14:31.2 OR
2. Vilho "Ville" Ritola	FIN	14:31.4

3. Edvin Wide	SWE	15:01.8
4. John Romig	USA	15:12.4
5. Eino Seppälä	FIN	15:18.4
6. Charles Clibbon	GBR	15:29.0
7. L.L. Dolques	FRA	15:33.0
8. Axel Eriksson	SWE	15:38.0

Paavo Nurmi had hoped to defend his 10,000 meters championship in Paris and was very resentful when Ville Ritola returned from four years in the United States to break Nurmi's world record and bump him from the Finnish 10,000 meters entry. On July 6, Ritola had proved his worth by winning the 10,000 in world record time. Nurmi got his chance to face Ritola 4 days later in the 5000, a race that began less than an hour after Nurmi had won the 1500 meters. Taking advantage of Paavo's lack of rest, his opponents set a torrid pace, passing the 1000-meter mark in 2:46.4, the same pace as the 1972 Olympic final 48 years later. Unruffled, Nurmi stayed close and then took the lead at the halfway mark, followed by Ritola. For the last eight laps, Nurmi, refusing to look behind him, stayed two yards ahead of his rival. With 500 meters to go he checked his watch for the last time, threw it to the grass, and picked up the pace. Twenty yards from the tape Ritola tried to pass, but Nurmi increased his speed and won—by two yards.

1928 Amsterdam C: 36, N: 17, D: 8.3. WR: 14:28.2 (Paavo Nurmi)
1. Vilho "Ville" Ritola	FIN	14:38.0
2. Paavo Nurmi	FIN	14:40.0
3. Edvin Wide	SWE	14:41.2
4. Leo Lermond	USA	14:50.0
5. Ragnar Magnusson	SWE	14:59.6
6. Armas Kinnunen	FIN	15:02.0

By 1928 it was a familiar sight to see Nurmi and Ritola pull away from the field, with only Edvin Wide able to keep close. This time Ritola drew clear of Nurmi in the final curve and won by over 12 yards. Wide picked up his fourth bronze medal to go with his one silver. Ritola finished his Olympic career with five gold medals and three silver medals.

1932 Los Angeles C: 19, N: 12, D: 8.5. WR: 14:17.0 (Lauri Lehtinen)
1. Lauri Lehtinen	FIN	14:30.0 OR
2. Ralph Hill	USA	14:30.0
3. Lauri Virtanen	FIN	14:44.0
4. John Savidan	NZE	14:49.6
5. Jean-Gunnar Lindgren	SWE	14:54.8
6. Max Syring	GER	14:59.0
7. James Burns	GBR	—
8. Erik Pettersson	SWE	15:13.4

This race produced the ugliest incident of the 1932 Olympics. Running in last place for the first mile, Ralph Hill of Oregon gradually moved his way up to third place behind the Finnish favorites, Lehtinen and Virtanen. Then, with the surprised American crowd wild with excitement, Hill passed Virtanen, who faded back. Over the last two laps Lehtinen tried desperately to shake the pesky Hill, but couldn't. Fifty yards from the finish, Hill moved to pass Lehtinen on the outside, but the world record holder swerved out to the third lane and blocked his path. Hill broke stride, dropped back, and attempted to pass on the inside. Lehtinen swerved back into lane one, again impeding Hill's progress. Forced to break stride again, Hill made one more move, but Lehtinen was able to beat him to the tape by about three inches. After a moment of stunned silence, the audience broke into a loud chorus of boos, which didn't end until announcer Bill Henry got on the public address system and said, "Please remember, folks, that these people are our guests." Although films of the race clearly showed that Lehtinen had interfered with Hill, U.S. officials declined to lodge a protest. At the victory ceremony, a chagrined Lehtinen attempted to lift Hill onto the first-place platform, but Hill refused.

1936 Berlin C: 41, N: 23, D: 8.7. WR: 14:17.0 (Lauri Lehtinen)
1. Gunnar Höckert   FIN   14:22.2 OR
2. Lauri Lehtinen   FIN   14:25.8
3. Henry Jonsson   SWE   14:29.0
4. Kohei Murakoso   JAP   14:30.0
5. József Noji   POL   14:33.4
6. Ilmari Salminen   FIN   14:39.8
7. Umberto Cerati   ITA   14:44.4
8. Louis Zamperini   USA   14:46.8

The 10,000 meters champion, Ilmari Salminen, lost his chance for a second medal when he tripped on Lehtinen with two laps to go and fell. At the same moment, Höckert made his move into the lead. Ahead by two yards at the bell, he sprinted away and won by 20 yards.

1948 London C: 33, N: 20, D: 8.2. WR: 13:58.2 (Günder Hagg)
1. Gaston Reiff   BEL   14:17.6 OR
2. Emil Zátopek   CZE   14:17.8
3. Willem Slijkhuis   HOL   14:26.8
4. Erik Ahldén   SWE   14:28.6
5. Bertil Albertsson   SWE   14:39.0
6. Curtis Stone   USA   14:39.4
7. Vaino Koskela   FIN   14:41.0
8. Vaino Makela   FIN   14:43.0

Zátopek was perhaps a bit too tired from winning the 10,000 meters three days earlier, particularly after he had unneccessarily sprinted at the end of his 5000 heat. Trailing Reiff by 50 meters at the bell in the final, Zátopek thrilled the crowd by sprinting around the rain-soaked track and pulling closer and closer. Reiff thought that the applause he heard was for him, until someone on the infield called his attention to Zátopek's unexpected spurt. Reiff was able to pick up his own speed just enough to reach the finish one and a half meters ahead of the charging Czech. Reiff was the first Belgian to win a track and field gold medal.

1952 Helsinki C: 45, N: 24, D: 7.24. WR: 13:58.2 (Günder Hagg)
1. Emil Zátopek   CZE   14:06.6 OR
2. Alain Mimoun O'Kacha   FRA   14:07.4
3. Herbert Schade   GER   14:08.6
4. Gordon Pirie   GBR   14:18.0
5. Christopher Chataway   GBR   14:18.0
6. Leslie Perry   AUS   14:23.6
7. Ernő Béres   HUN   14:24.8
8. Åke Andersson   SWE   14:26.0

After he had won the 10,000 meters for the second time, Emil Zátopek was asked if it was true that he would also contest the 5000. "The marathon contest won't be for a long time yet, so I simply must do something until then," he replied. With five runners in each of the three heats qualifying for the final, Zátopek decided to enjoy himself during his heat. As the laps piled up, the multilingual Czech chatted amiably with the other runners, particularly after it had become clear who the five qualifiers would be. As they approached the bell lap, Zátopek, in the lead, slowed down, waited for Aleksandr Anoufriev of the U.S.S.R., and motioned for him to pass, acting like a traffic cop clearing an intersection. As he rounded the final turn, Zátopek noticed Bertil Albertsson of Sweden sprinting for the finish. Slowing down again, he hailed Albertsson as if he were hitching a ride and engaged him in conversation. The two ran the last straight together, with Zátopek giving way just before the finish. He also took a liking to fourth-place finisher Les Perry of Australia and later presented him with a gift of his training suit.

The final was, of course, a more serious affair. Yet Zátopek still took the time to speak to Herbert Schade before the start, advising him to hold back for the first 2000 meters and not waste his energy setting the pace. Schade ignored this advice and paid the price. The race itself was full of action, with the lead changing hands numerous times. As the laps wound down, it appeared that any of five runners could win: Zátopek, Schade, Mimoun, Chataway, or Pirie. At the bell, Zátopek was in first place, hard-pressed by Schade. In the backstretch, Chris Chataway, who later paced Roger Bannister and John Landy to the first two sub-four-minute miles, dashed into the lead, followed by Mimoun and Schade, leaving Zátopek in fourth place. Entering the final curve, Zátopek made his move, swinging wide into Lane 3. Halfway through the bend, he was already in front again and pulling away. Entering the home straightaway, Chataway, exhausted, stepped on the curb and fell. He was able to regain his feet and stagger home, but by that time Zátopek had already gained a five-yard victory over Mimoun, who finished second to Zátopek for the third time in an Olympic final and improved his personal best by over 14 seconds.

Later in the afternoon, Emil Zátopek learned that his wife, Dana, had won a gold medal in the javelin throw. When asked if it was true that he was going to try for another win in the marathon, Zátopek replied, "At present, the score of the contest in the Zátopek family is 2–1. This result is too close. To restore some prestige I will try to improve on it—in the marathon race."

1956 Melbourne C: 23, N: 13, D: 11.28. WR: 13:36.8 (Gordon Pirie)

1. Vladimir Kuts	SOV	13:39.6 OR
2. Gordon Pirie	GBR	13:50.6
3. Derek Ibbotson	GBR	13:54.4
4. Miklos Szabo II	HUN	14:03.4
5. Albert Thomas	AUS	14:04.6
6. László Tábori	HUN	14:09.8
7. Maiyoro Nyandika	KEN	14:19.0
8. Thyge Tögersen	DEN	14:21.0

After Kuts' decisive victory in the 10,000 five days earlier, it seemed a long shot that anyone would beat him in the 5000, although Gordon Pirie had defeated Kuts at this distance in world record time on June 9. In the Olympic final, Kuts went to the front immediately and was never headed, finishing 75 yards in front of Pirie and Ibbotson. Unfortunately for Kuts, the experimental training program which the Soviet coaches had imposed on him took its toll. By 1960 he had suffered his first heart attack. His fourth heart attack killed him, on August 17, 1975, at the age of 48.

1960 Rome C: 48, N: 31, D: 9.2. WR: 13:35.0 (Vladimir Kuts)

1. Murray Halberg	NZE	13:43.4
2. Hans Grodotzki	GDR	13:44.6
3. Kazimierz Zimny	POL	13:44.8
4. Friedrich Janke	GDR	13:46.8
5. David Power	AUS	13:51.8
6. Maiyoro Nyandika	KEN	13:52.8
7. Michel Bernard	FRA	14:04.2
8. Horst Flossbach	GER	14:06.6

When he was 17 years old, Murray Halberg was hit from behind in a crash tackle during a rugby match. He was left with a dislocated shoulder, ruptured veins and arteries, blood clots, and a paralyzed left arm. After two months in the hospital and two operations, he was released with a withered arm and shoulder. He had to relearn how to walk, run, dress himself, and feed himself. Prevented from competing in contact sports, Halberg concentrated on running. Six years after his accident, he represented New Zealand at the Melbourne Olympics and two years after that he broke the four-minute mile.

Back in the Olympics in 1960, Halberg and his coach, Arthur Lydiard, devised a radical strategy to win the 5000 meters. With three laps to go, at the stage in the race when runners usually gather their strength for the last lap sprint, Halberg suddenly pushed to the front of the pack and then darted away as if the finish line was just around the next curve. The tactic worked perfectly. His startled opponents were confused, and before Grodotzki was able to respond, Halberg had covered the tenth lap in 61.1 seconds and opened up a lead of 25 yards. He also ran the next lap as fast as he could, preventing Grodotzki from closing any ground. Then Halberg faced the grim task of completing

the final lap even though he was totally exhausted. Checking behind himself frequently, he watched as Grodotzki gradually whittled his lead down to 15 yards, 12 yards, 10 yards. But then Halberg reached the finish line with eight yards to spare. He collapsed on his back on the infield, still holding the tape between his fingers. In his autobiography, *A Clean Pair Of Heels,* Halberg recalled, "I had always imagined an Olympic champion was something more than a mere mortal, in fact, a god. Now I knew he was just a human being."

1964 Tokyo C: 48, N: 29, D: 10.18. WR: 13:35.0 (Vladimir Kuts)

1. Robert Schul	USA	13:48.8
2. Harald Norpoth	GER	13:49.6
3. William Dellinger	USA	13:49.8
4. Michel Jazy	FRA	13:49.8
5. H. Kipchoge Keino	KEN	13:50.4
6. William Baillie	NZE	13:51.0
7. Nikolai Dutov	SOV	13:53.8
8. Thor Helland	NOR	13:57.0

Ron Clarke of Australia led the way for most of the race, but gave up the lead to Michel Jazy shortly before the 4000-meter mark. With one and a half laps to go, Bill Dellinger moved ahead, but just after the bell Jazy regained the lead and pulled ahead by ten yards, with Norpoth second and the favorite, Bob Schul, third. Schul, known for his finishing kick, began sprinting in the backstretch. By the final curve he had cut Jazy's lead to five yards. Coming out of the turn, Schul saw Jazy look back and noticed his shoulders tighten. "I smiled inwardly," said Schul. "I knew I had him." He passed the discouraged Frenchman 50 meters from the tape. Schul had run the last 300 meters in 38.7 seconds. Jazy was so disappointed that he wasn't even able to hold on to third place.

1968 Mexico City C: 37, N: 25, D: 10.17. WR: 13:16.6 (Ronald Clarke)

1. Mohamed Gammoudi	TUN	14:05.0
2. H. Kipchoge Keino	KEN	14:05.2
3. Naftali Temu	KEN	14:06.4
4. Juan Martinez	MEX	14:10.8
5. Ronald Clarke	AUS	14:12.4
6. Wohib Masresha	ETH	14:17.6
7. Nikolai Sviridov	SOV	14:18.4
8. Fikru Deguefu	ETH	14:19.0

Mohamed Gammoudi, a 29-year-old soldier, moved in front with two laps to go and, with great grit and determination, held off alternating challenges from Keino and Temu, finally winning by about four feet after running the last lap in 54.8 seconds. A Tunisian biography of Gammoudi claimed that a typical day's diet for the Olympic champion consisted of five yogurts, ten pieces of fruit, four cups of tea, two coffees, two pastries, large quantities of meat, fish, milk, and cheese, and as much parsley as he could eat. Gammoudi weighed 135 pounds.

1972 Munich C: 61, N: 35, D: 9.10. WR: 13:16.6 (Ronald Clarke)

1. Lasse Viren	FIN	13:26.4 OR
2. Mohamed Gammoudi	TUN	13:27.4
3. Ian Stewart	GBR	13:27.6
4. Stephen Prefontaine	USA	13:28.4
5. Emiel Puttemans	BEL	13:30.8
6. Harald Norpoth	GER	13:32.6
7. Per Halle	NOR	13:34.4
8. Nikolai Sviridov	SOV	13:39.4

Before the competition, Steve Prefontaine had boldly warned that he would run the final mile in less than four minutes. Right on cue, Prefontaine took the lead with four laps to go and picked up the pace. Most of the field fell behind, but Viren and Gammoudi would not be shaken and were still shooting for the gold medal when the bell rang to signal the final lap. Viren led the way into the backstretch, was headed briefly by Gammoudi, but was back in the lead before the homestretch and couldn't be caught. Prefontaine faded and lost the bronze medal to the fast-finishing Ian Stewart. The last mile had been run in 4:01.2. Lasse Viren became the fourth runner to achieve a 5000/10,000 double, joining the ranks of Hannes Kolehmainen, Emil Zátopek, and Vladimir Kuts. On May 30, 1975, Steve Prefontaine lost control of his sports car and was killed in a crash, at the age of 24.

1976 Montreal C: 36, N: 23, D: 7.30. WR: 13:13.0 (Emiel Puttemans)

1. Lasse Viren	FIN	13:24.76
2. Dick Quax	NZE	13:25.16
3. Klaus-Peter Hildenbrand	GER	13:25.38
4. Rodney Dixon	NZE	13:25.50
5. Brendan Foster	GBR	13:26.19
6. Willy Polleunis	BEL	13:26.99
7. Ian Stewart	GBR	13:27.65
8. Aniceto Silva Simoes	POR	13:29.38

Following his victory in the 10,000 meters, Lasse Viren was subjected to a double inquisition. First, members of the press grilled him about the practice of blood boosting. This unnatural, but not illegal, procedure involves the extraction of a quart or more of blood from a runner before a major competition. This blood is frozen, while the runner's body rebuilds its blood to a normal level. Then, just before the race, the extracted blood is unfrozen and reinjected into the runner, increasing the body's hemoglobin level and oxygen-carrying capability, and thus providing the runner with greater endurance. Viren was accused of blood boosting because the procedure was first experimented with in Scandinavia, and because Viren only recorded his best performances in major competitions, particularly the Olympics. Viren always denied that he engaged in blood boosting and claimed that his training schedule was organized to peak at the Olympics, because only the Olympics really mattered to him.

The day before the 5000 meters final, Viren was called before the Technical Committee of the International

Olympic Committee and asked to explain why he had carried his running shoes aloft while taking his victory lap following the 10,000 meters final. Accused of commercialism, the soft-spoken policeman said that he had removed his shoes because he had a blister. This seemed to satisfy the committee, which allowed him to continue competing.

The most notable performers in the 5000 heats were Brendan Foster, who set an Olympic record of 13:20.34 and Dieudone Lamothe of Haiti, who led after the first lap, but finished five minutes after the other runners in his heat. His time, 18:50.07, was the slowest ever recorded in the Olympics.

In the final, most of the pace-setting was done by Viren and Foster, although the fourth kilometer saw Quax and Hildenbrand take their turns in front. With three laps to go, Viren picked up the pace, but at the start of the final lap there were still only five meters separating the first six runners. "At the bell," said Viren later, "I gave just one quick glance behind me and took in the situation in all its ghastliness. The wall at my heels was thick. . . . I had put in a couple of sixty-second laps and almost everybody was still chasing me, damn it! I was the fugitive now, and I realized I had to flee as if my life depended on it. . . . In the far turn I had the most frightening experience of my career. Some guy in black was forcing himself past me. It was Quax, whom I really hadn't reckoned very seriously. . . . I found my last gear, and it was just enough. The black shadow glided away from my eyes. The holy sanctuary of the finish line engulfed me—I had won!" Lasse Viren had earned his fourth gold medal and had became the first repeat winner of the 5000.

1980 Moscow C: 35, N: 22, D: 9.1. WR:13:08.4 (Henry Rono)

1. Miruts Yifter	ETH	13:21.0
2. Suleiman Nyambui	TAN	13:21.6
3. Kaarlo Maaninka	FIN	13:22.0
4. Eamonn Coughlan	IRL	13:22.8
5. Markus Ryffel	SWI	13:23.1
6. Dietmar Millonig	AUT	13:23.3
7. John Treacy	IRL	13:23.7
8. Aleksandr Fedotkin	SOV	13:24.1

Miruts Yifter's quest for a gold medal at 5000 meters is a frustrating eight-year saga with a happy ending. Yifter first gained international attention in 1971 at a U.S.–Africa meet in North Carolina, when he sprinted to an apparent victory over Steve Prefontaine in the 5000 meters race, only to discover that he had miscounted the laps and quit running one lap too soon. The next day he made up for his mistake by defeating Frank Shorter at 10,000 meters. At the Munich Olympics in 1972, Yifter gained a bronze medal at 10,000 meters, but missed the start of his heat in the 5000 meters race. Typical of the mystery surrounding Yifter is the fact that there are three explanations for his failure to appear at the starting line. The first is that he was directed to the wrong check-in gate at the stadium and was refused admittance by German guards. The second is that he spent too long in the toilet before the race, and the third is that he left the bathroom in time but got lost on the way to the track. In 1976 he was prevented from competing when Ethiopia boycotted the Olympics.

In Moscow, the 5-foot 4-inch, 117-pound father of six faced no such problems. For some strange reason, a semifinal round was added to the 5000 meters competition, despite the fact that the field of 35 was the smallest in 24 years. This didn't bother Yifter, who won his opening heat and finished second to teammate Yohannes Mohammed in the semifinals.

After 4000 meters of the final, the 12 finalists were still bunched within 12 meters. Ninety-nine pound Mohammed Kedir led at the bell, as everyone waited for the infamous Yifter kick that had already brought victory in the 10,000 meters. However, in the backstretch Yifter was completely caught in a box, with Kedir in front of him, Eamonn Coughlan beside Kedir, and the pack behind him. Then, with less than 300 meters to go, Kedir turned around and asked Yifter if he was ready. A wave of the hand from the master and the selfless Kedir stepped aside. Yifter shot through on the inside as Coughlan watched in amazement. The rest was academic. Yifter ran the last 200 meters in 27.2 seconds to gain his long-awaited 5000 meters gold medal. Kedir got tripped up by the pack, lost his shoe, and finished last. Coughlan lost the bronze medal to Kaarlo Maaninka, who came from a family of 23 children in Lapland.

Part of the mystery of Miruts Yifter is the question of his age, which was variously reported as 33, 35, 36, 37, or 42. When asked for a definitive answer, Yifter would only reply, "I don't count the years. Men may steal my chickens, men may steal my sheep. But no man can steal my age."

10,000 METERS

1896–1908 not held

1912 Stockholm C: 30, N: 13, D: 7.8. WR:30:58.8 (Jean Bouin)
1. Johannes Kolehmainen	FIN	31:20.8
2. Louis Tewanima	USA	32:06.6
3. Albin Stenroos	FIN	32:21.8
4. Joseph Keeper	CAN	32:36.2
5. Alfonso Orlando	ITA	33:31.2

Fifteen men qualified for the final but only 11 started. The hot sun and hard pace cut the field down further and only five finished. Twenty-two-year-old Hannes Kolehmainen took the lead in the first lap and won the first of his four Olympic gold medals without being challenged. Silver medalist Louis Tewanima was a Hopi Indian.

1920 Antwerp C: 37, N: 17, D: 8.20. WR:30:58.8 (Jean Bouin)
1. Paavo Nurmi	FIN	31:45.8
2. Joseph Guillemot	FRA	31:47.2
3. James Wilson	GBR	31:50.8
4. Augusto Maccario	ITA	—
5. James Hatton	GBR	—
6. Jean Manhès	FRA	—
7. Heikki Liimatainen	FIN	—
8. Frederick Faller	USA	—

Paavo Nurmi was born in Turku, Finland, on June 13, 1897, the son of a carpenter who died when Paavo was 12. He first gained athletic renown in Finland while serving in the army in the early summer of 1919. He entered a 20-kilometer march with full equipment. Running was allowed, so Nurmi ran the entire distance. Carrying a rifle, a cartridge belt, and an 11-pound sack of sand, he finished the course so quickly that some officials thought he must have discovered a shortcut.

In Antwerp Nurmi lost his first final, the 5000 meters, to Joseph Guillemot, but sought revenge three days later in the 10,000. This time he let James Wilson of Scotland do most of the pace-setting. Nurmi took the lead with two laps to go. Guillemot passed him in the backstretch of the final lap, but Nurmi sprinted back into the lead almost immediately and won by eight yards.

Although Paavo Nurmi's first Olympic victory was not his most difficult, it *was* his most unpleasant, since Guillemot vomited on him as soon as he crossed the finish line. The source of Guillemot's distress was a last-minute change in the starting time of the race. Guillemot had just finished a large lunch when he was informed that the race had been moved up from 5 p.m. to 1:45 p.m. at the request of the king of Belgium, leaving the Frenchman no time to digest the food.

1924 Paris C: 43, N: 17, D: 7.6. WR: 30:35.4 (Vilho ''Ville'' Ritola)
1. Vilho ''Ville'' Ritola	FIN	30:23.2 WR
2. Edvin Wide	SWE	30:55.2
3. Eero Berg	FIN	31:43.0
4. Väinö Sipilä	FIN	31:50.2
5. Ernest Harper	GBR	—
6. Halland Britton	GBR	—
7. G. Tell	FRA	32:12.0
8. Earl Johnson	USA	—

For the first time, the 10,000 meters was run without heats. Ritola and Wide pulled away from the other 41 contestants after only two laps, but even Wide couldn't keep up with Ritola, who won by a half lap and broke his own world record by over 12 seconds. He continued on for another quarter lap before the officials were able to convince him that the race was over. Paavo Nurmi had been prevented from entering this race by Finnish officials, who felt he was entering too many events. Back in Finland after the games, Nurmi made his point by setting a world record of 30:06.2 that was to last for almost 13 years.

1928 Amsterdam C: 24, N: 12, D: 7.29. WR: 30:06.2 (Paavo Nurmi)
1. Paavo Nurmi	FIN	30:18.8 OR
2. Vilho ''Ville'' Ritola	FIN	30:19.4

3. Edvin Wide	SWE	31:00.6
4. Jean-Gunnar Lindgren	SWE	31:26.0
5. Anthony Muggridge	GBR	31:31.8
6. Ragnar Magnusson	SWE	31:37.2
7. Toivo Loukola	FIN	—
8. K. Matilainen	FIN	—

Paavo Nurmi earned his ninth and last gold medal in the 10,000 meters flat race, the same event in which he had won his first gold medal. After nine laps only Ritola, Nurmi and Wide were still in contention. During the 18th lap the Swede dropped back. Nurmi dogged Ritola for the remainder of the race, then passed him about 50 yards from the tape and won by two or three meters. Nurmi refused to be congratulated or photographed, and simply picked up his sweatsuit and walked off the track without a smile. The following week he gained two silver medals in the 5000 and the steeplechase.

Nurmi had planned to enter the 10,000 and the marathon in the 1932 Olympics, but was declared a professional by the International Amateur Athletic Federation and banned from competition. For a time Nurmi ran a construction business and then a men's clothing store, eventually gaining considerable financial security as a result of wise real estate investments. His last appearance on a track was a dramatic one. When the 1952 Olympics were held in Helsinki, Finland, the opening ceremonies were staged in the Olympic Stadium, which was graced with a bronze statue of Nurmi in the front. After the athletes had paraded around the track and onto the infield, the audience awaited the arrival of the Olympic torch. When the final runner, whose name had not been announced, appeared from out of the tunnel bearing the torch aloft, the Finnish spectators broke into thunderous applause as they recognized the runner as none other than Paavo Nurmi, whose stride was unmistakable even though he was 55 years old. The athletes of the world broke rank and dashed to the side of the track to catch a glimpse of the legendary "Flying Finn," who bounded up the steps and passed the torch to 62-year-old Hannes Kolehmainen, who lit the Olympic flame.

Paavo Nurmi, who set 29 world records at distances ranging from 1500 meters to 20,000 meters, died on October 2, 1974. Six Finnish gold medal winners served as pallbearers at his funeral. Nurmi left the bulk of his estate to help the cause of heart research.

1932 Los Angeles C: 16, N: 11, D: 7.31. WR: 30:06.2 (Paavo Nurmi)

1. Janusz Kusociński	POL	30:11.4 OR
2. Volmari Iso-Hollo	FIN	30:12.6
3. Lauri Virtanen	FIN	30:35.0
4. John Savidan	NZE	31:09.0
5. Max Syring	GER	31:35.0
6. Jean-Gunnar Lindgren	SWE	31:37.0

Kusociński and Iso-Hollo dueled at close quarters for 24 of 25 laps. Iso-Hollo led by one yard entering the final lap, but then Kusociński sprinted away to a big lead, before slowing to a jog and finishing with ten yards to spare. Among the unplaced entrants were Juan Rodriguez, a Yaqui Indian from Mexico who ran barefooted, and Adalberto Cardoso of Brazil, who got stranded in San Francisco and didn't arrive in Los Angeles until the day of the race.

1936 Berlin C: 30, N: 18, D: 8.2. WR: 30:06.2 (Paavo Nurmi)

1. Ilmari Salminen	FIN	30:15.4
2. Arvo Askola	FIN	30:15.6
3. Volmari Iso-Hollo	FIN	30:20.2
4. Kohei Murakoso	JAP	30:25.0
5. James Burns	GBR	30:58.2
6. Juan Carlos Zabala	ARG	31:22.0
7. Max Gebhardt	GER	31:29.6
8. Donald Lash	USA	31:39.4

Murakoso fought valiantly against the three Finns, who ran a team race that included a good deal of jostling every time one of them passed him. However Murakoso finally had to give in with one lap to go. Salminen, a 33-year-old army sergeant, jumped the others at the start of the last lap, but Askola regained the lead in the backstretch. Salminen caught him again coming out of the final turn and gradually inched ahead for a narrow victory.

1948 London C: 27, N: 15, D: 7.30. WR: 29:35.8 (Viljo Heino)

1. Emil Zátopek	CZE	29:59.6 OR
2. Alain Mimoun O'Kacha	FRA	30:47.4
3. Bertil Albertsson	SWE	30:53.6
4. Martin Stokken	NOR	30:58.6
5. Severt Dennolf	SWE	31:05.0
6. Abdallah ben Said	FRA	31:07.8
7. Stanley Cox	GBR	31:08.0
8. James Peters	GBR	31:16.0

World record holder Viljo Heino was expected to receive a stiff challenge from Czech army lieutenant Emil Zátopek. As it turned out, it was the challenger who controlled the race. Moving in front during the tenth lap, Zátopek ground out the laps at a steady pace until both Heino and his teammate, Heinstrom, were forced to drop out from exhaustion. Eventually Zátopek lapped all but two runners and won by over 300 meters. The incompetent officials in charge of the race became confused by Zátopek's performance and announced the start of the final circuit one lap too soon. Fortunately Zátopek knew better, although others didn't. When the race was over, it was announced that Dennolf of Sweden had finished fourth and Stokken of Norway fifth. The Norwegians protested, but the matter was settled quickly when Dennolf himself supported their case. Sixth place was awarded to Robert Everaert of Belgium, who had actually dropped out of the race over five laps before the finish. Everaert pointed out the mistake, but the judges refused to change their decision until a Belgian official intervened.

1952 Helsinki C: 33, N: 21, D: 7.20. WR: 29:02.6 (Emil Zátopek)

1. Emil Zátopek	CZE	29:17.0 OR
2. Alain Mimoun O'Kacha	FRA	29.32.8
3. Aleksandr Anufriev	SOV	29:28.2
4. Hannu Posti	FIN	29:51.4
5. Frank Sando	GBR	29:51.8
6. Valter Nyström	SWE	29:52.8
7. Gordon Pirie	GBR	30:09.5
8. Fred Norris	GBR	30.09.8

The result was never in doubt as Zátopek wore out his opponents one by one, with Mimoun the last to go, four and a half laps from the finish. Zátopek won by about 100 yards to gain the first part of his unprecedented long-distance triple. Between 1948 and 1954 Emil Zátopek won 38 consecutive races at 10,000 meters.

1956 Melbourne C: 25, N: 15, D: 11.23. WR: 28:30.4 (Vladimir Kuts)

1. Vladimir Kuts	SOV	28:45.6 OR
2. József Kovács	HUN	28:52.4
3. Allan Lawrence	AUS	28:53.6
4. Zdzislaw Kryszkowiak	POL	29:05.0
5. Kenneth Norris	GBR	29:21.6
6. Ivan Chernyavsky	SOV	29:31.6
7. David Power	AUS	29:49.2
8. Gordon Pirie	GBR	29:49.6

Vladimir Kuts was a teenager when the Germans invaded his Ukrainian village in 1943. After the war, he joined the U.S.S.R. navy, and it was only then that he attracted the attention of Soviet coaches, who introduced him to competitive running at the age of 23.

Two months before the Melbourne Olympics, while running in Moscow, Kuts broke the world 10,000 meters record by over 12 seconds. By virtue of this performance, he was considered the favorite. But there were those who remembered that two months before that, Kuts had been beaten in England by Gordon Pirie, and although he had never run the 10,000 faster than 29:17.2, Pirie was also given a good shot at the gold medal.

Kuts took off like a flash and completed the first of 25 laps in only 61.2 seconds. Slowing down only slightly, he had outdistanced everyone but Pirie by the seventh lap. Kuts ran the first half of the race so quickly that he passed the 5000-meter mark at 14:07.0, which almost equaled Emil Zátopek's Olympic record for that distance. And he still had another 5000 meters to run. Between laps 8 and 20, Kuts tried a variety of tactics to rid himself of the stubborn Pirie. Several times he sprinted out at a seemingly insane pace, only to have Pirie catch up each time. Alternatively, Kuts would slow down, move to the outside, and wave Pirie past him. But Pirie refused to bite, preferring to remain at Kuts' shoulder.

Suddenly, at the end of the 20th lap, Kuts stopped so abruptly that Pirie was forced to take the lead. Relieved of the pressure of having Pirie on his heels, Kuts rested for a half lap while he studied his adversary in front of him. Then, just as suddenly as he had slowed, Kuts burst past Pirie to take the lead for good. Pirie struggled to keep pace, but with four laps to go, he gave up, eventually dropping back to eighth place. Kovács and Lawrence finished strongly, but Kuts' victory was never in doubt.

1960 Rome C: 32, N: 20, D: 9.8. WR: 28:30.4 (Vladimir Kuts)

1. Pyotr Bolotnikov	SOV	28:32.2 OR
2. Hans Grodotzki	GDR	28:37.0
3. David Power	AUS	28:38.2
4. Aleksei Desyachikov	SOV	28:39.6
5. Murray Halberg	NZE	28:48.6
6. Max Truex	USA	28:50.2
7. Zdzislaw Krzyszkowiak	POL	28:52.4
8. John Merriman	GBR	28:52.6

Dave Power tried to pull away with seven laps to go, but Bolotnikov, Grodotzki and Desyachikov were able to stay with him. Seven hundred meters from the finish, Bolotnikov, a 30-year-old pupil of Vladimir Kuts, left the others behind, running the last lap in 57.4 seconds and winning by 30 yards. Nine of the first 10 finishers achieved personal records, including Power, who bettered his previous best time by 53.8 seconds.

1964 Tokyo C: 29, N: 17, D: 10.14. WR: 28:15.6 (Ronald Clark)

1. William Mills	USA	28:24.4 OR
2. Mohamed Gammoudi	TUN	28:24.8
3. Ronald Clarke	AUS	28:25.8
4. Mamo Wolde	ETH	28:31.8
5. Leonid Ivanov	SOV	28:53.2
6. Kokichi Tsuburaya	JAP	28:59.4
7. Murray Halberg	NZE	29:10.8
8. Anthony Cook	AUS	29:15.8

The 1964 10,000 meters produced one of the most electrifying upsets in Olympic history. Pregame predictions had the race as a tough battle among defending 5000-meter champion Murray Halberg, defending 10,000 meters champion Pyotr Bolotnikov and the main favorite, world record holder Ron Clarke. By the halfway mark, Clarke, following a strategy of surging every other lap, had managed to eliminate from contention all but four runners: Mohamed Gammoudi and Mamo Wolde, who would both win gold medals four years later in Mexico City, local favorite Kokichi Tsuburaya, and Billy Mills, who had finished second at the U.S. Olympic trials. Tsuburaya was the first to lose contact; then, with two and a half laps to go, Wolde dropped away.

At this point, Ron Clarke appeared assured of victory, since neither Gammoudi or Mills had ever broken 29 minutes. It was surely just a matter of time before Clarke would break away. They reached the final lap with Clarke and Mills running abreast and Gammoudi right behind. The track was cluttered with stragglers, and the three leaders were forced to thread their way through the congestion. It was "like a dash for a train in a peak-hour crowd," Clarke would later recall. In the backstretch Clarke found himself faced with a problem. In front of him was a straggler who wouldn't move aside to be passed. To his right was Mills. Clarke tapped Mills a couple times, but he wouldn't step aside either. So Clarke gave him a shove that sent the American unknown careening to the outside. Clarke turned to apologize, but just then Gammoudi, putting one hand on Clarke and the other on Mills pushed his way to the front and opened a sudden ten-yard lead. Clarke took off after the Tunisian, while Mills appeared to be out of the running. By this time, the audience was already going wild with excitement.

Clarke gradually closed the gap, finally passing Gammoudi at the beginning of the homestretch. But Gammoudi wasn't finished. With a major upset within his grasp, he pulled up to Clarke's shoulder once again. Then came one of those rare moments that sports fans never forget. Billy Mills, fighting his way through still more stragglers, let loose a final sprint that sent Clarke and Gammoudi into shock and carried him across the finish line with a three-yard victory that left the crowd of 75,000 as exhausted as the runners.

During the two weeks that he had spent in the Olympic Village prior to the opening of the games, not one reporter had asked Billy Mills a single question. Now he was besieged by journalists from all over the world, all asking the same question: "Who is Billy Mills?" Humble and calm (after crying on the victory platform), Mills explained that he was $\frac{7}{16}$ Sioux Indian, and had been born in Pine Ridge, South Dakota. Orphaned at 13, he had been sent to Haskell Institute, a school for Native Americans in Lawrence, Kansas. He had taken up running as training to become a boxer, but after losing a couple of fights, he had decided to stick to running. After attending the University of Kansas, he had joined the Marines and was now a motor pool officer at Camp Pendleton in California. His winning time in Tokyo was 46 seconds faster than his previous best (Gammoudi had improved his own personal record by 47 seconds). "I'm flabbergasted," said Mills. "I can't believe it. I suppose I was the only person who thought I had a chance."

1968 Mexico City C: 37, N: 23, D: 10.13. WR: 27:39.4 (Ronald Clarke)

1. Naftali Temu	KEN	29:27.4
2. Mamo Wolde	ETH	29:28.0
3. Mohamed Gammoudi	TUN	29:34.2
4. Juan Martinez	MEX	29:35.0
5. Nikolai Sviridov	SOV	29:43.2
6. Ronald Clarke	AUS	29:44.8
7. Ronald Hill	GBR	29:53.2
8. Wohib Masresha	ETH	29:57.0

When the International Olympic Committee first announced that the 1968 Olympics would be held in Mexico City, there was much criticism that the competitions would be adversely affected by the high altitude. The I.O.C. denied that the altitude would make a difference, but they couldn't have been more wrong.

The 10,000 meters was the first track and field event to be decided. With six laps to go, two runners were carried away on stretchers. The first surprise came after 8900 meters, when Kip Keino dropped out, suffering stomach cramps as a result of a gall bladder infection. Although 11 different men had led over the first 8000 meters, with 800 meters left, the only runners still in contention were Wolde, Clarke, Temu, and Gammoudi. One and a half laps from the finish, Clarke finally lost contact. A 64.4-second 24th lap by Temu got rid of Gammoudi, but just after the bell Wolde shot past Temu and opened up a five-yard gap. However Temu had the most strength left. He caught Wolde 50 meters from the finish line and won by four yards. The first five finishers were all from high-altitude countries or had lived in high-altitude areas of their nations. The first non-high-altitude runner to finish was Ron Clarke, who collapsed and was unconscious for ten minutes.

Temu, a 23-year-old Kisii tribesman, was resentful, as well he should have been, when he learned that his victory was being belittled because of the altitude. In 1966 he had attracted attention by finishing first at the Commonwealth Games in Jamaica. "Now tell me," he said after his win in Mexico City, "I beat that Clarke they were talking about in Jamaica, and tell me . . . were there mountains in Kingston?" Temu was the first Kenyan to earn an Olympic gold medal. The 1968 10,000 meters marked the first time that all three medals in an Olympic event had been won by Africans.

1972 Munich C: 50, N: 34, D: 8.31. WR: 27:39.4 (Ronald Clarke)

1. Lasse Viren	FIN	27:38.4 WR
2. Emiel Puttemans	BEL	27:39.6
3. Miruts Yifter	ETH	27:41.0
4. Mariano Haro Cisneros	SPA	27:48.2
5. Frank Shorter	USA	27:51.4
6. David Bedford	GBR	28:05.4
7. Daniel Korica	YUG	28:15.2
8. Abdelkader Zaddem	TUN	28:18.2

With 50 runners entered, qualifying heats were reinstituted for the first time since 1920. In the first heat, Dave Bedford and Emiel Puttemans pulled away from the field. After reaching 8000 meters in 22:16.2, Bedford turned to Puttemans and asked him if they should go for the world record. Puttemans declined. "But we're so close to the mark," said Bedford. Finally Puttemans convinced him that they should save themselves for the final, not to mention the 5000. The second heat saw the Olympic debut of Lasse Viren, a 23-year-old Finnish policeman from the small village of Myrskyla. Two and a half weeks earlier Viren had defeated Puttemans and Bedford in Stockholm, setting a two-mile world record of 8:14.0.

The third and last heat was highlighted by the appearance of Anilus Joseph of Haiti, who had evidently never taken part in a 10,000 meters race before. Joseph took off as if he was two laps from the finish line. He covered the first lap in 59.6 seconds, opening up a lead of 50 meters. He was still in first place after 800 meters, but then he ran out of steam, and by the 1000-meter mark he was in last place. By the eighth lap he had been lapped by all the other runners and by the twelfth he had been lapped again. When the bell rang to signal the final lap for the leaders, Joseph thought that it meant that he too only had one more lap to go, so he began sprinting again. Informed by an official that even though all the other runners had finished, he still had another mile to run, Joseph finally dropped out. He wasn't seen again in the Olympics, but his performance was only a prelude to the unusual feats that would be accomplished by the Haitian track team four years later in Montreal.

The final, two days later, was a more serious race. Although Bedford set a pace not unlike that of Joseph's, he was able to sustain it for much longer. He was still in the lead after 4600 meters, when a surprising incident occurred behind him.

Running in fifth place, Lasse Viren, without being interfered with, stumbled and fell. Mohamed Gammoudi tripped on Viren and crashed to the ground. Gammoudi, stunned, was forced to give up a couple laps later, but Viren rose quickly and moved up to second place after only 230 meters.

Viren passed Bedford at the 6000-meter mark and Bedford began to fade soon after. Only Yifter, Haro, Puttemans, and Shorter were still in the hunt. The lead changed hands several times during the next few laps. Six hundred meters from the finish, Viren poured it on. Shorter fell back immediately, and Haro lost contact 100 meters later. Yifter fell away in the final backstretch. Puttemans tried desperately to keep up, but Viren had too much strength left and was able to pull away in the final straight to win by about six or seven yards. Viren's times for the last two laps were a remarkable 60.0 and 56.4. Lasse Viren had broken Ron Clarke's seven-year-old world record and won the first of his four gold medals.

1976 Montreal C: 41, N: 26, D: 7.26. WR: 27:30.8 (David Bedford)

1. Lasse Viren	FIN	27:40.38
2. Carlos Sousa Lopes	POR	27:45.17
3. Brendan Foster	GBR	27:54.92
4. Anthony Simmons	GBR	27:56.26
5. Ilie Floroiu	ROM	27:59.93
6. Mariano Haro Cisneros	SPA	28:00.28
7. Mark Smet	BEL	28:02.80
8. Bernard Ford	GBR	28:17.78

The final was a relatively simple race. Lopes took the lead after 3200 meters and eventually drew away from everyone but Viren, who passed him 450 meters from the finish and won easily by 30 meters.

However, the 1976 10,000 meters competition should not be left without making mention of Olmeus Charles of Haiti, whose performance in the opening heat was the ultimate expression of the Olympic ideal that what counts is not the winning, but the taking part. Charles completed the course in 42:00.11, the slowest time ever recorded in the Olympics, almost 14 minutes slower than Carlos Lopes, who won the heat, and over 8½ minutes slower than Chris McCubbins of Canada, who placed next to last. The entire schedule had to be held up while Charles plodded the final six laps alone. In 1972 and 1976 Haitian runners consistently finished in last place. At first reflection, one might feel sympathy for the Haitians. After all, Haiti is the poorest country in the Western Hemisphere, and malnutrition is widespread. However there is no evidence that tryouts were actually held to determine the nation's best runners. Instead, "Baby Doc" Duvalier, the dictator of Haiti, simply chose his friends and other trusted soldiers, and rewarded them with a free trip to Canada. Unfortunately, none of them were athletes. The 1980 Olympics were deprived of the participation of the Haitians when Duvalier chose to support Jimmy Carter's boycott.

1980 Moscow C: 40, N: 26, D: 7.27. WR: 27:22.5 (Henry Rono)

1. Miruts Yifter	ETH	27:42.7
2. Kaarlo Maaninka	FIN	27:44.3
3. Mohammed Kedir	ETH	27:44.7
4. Tolossa Kotu	ETH	27:46.5
5. Lasse Viren	FIN	27:50.5
6. Jörg Peter	GDR	28:05.6
7. Werner Schildhauer	GDR	28:11.0
8. Enn Sellik	SOV	28:13.8

The final resembled a dual meet between Ethiopia and Finland more than an international contest. The Ethiopians dominated the proceedings, changing the pace and the lead every few hundred meters. After lulling the pack into confusion for the first 5000 meters, they set off at a torrid clip until only Viren and Maaninka were left to challenge. In the 22nd lap Maaninka broke ahead, only to be passed by Kedir and Yifter. Then Viren took the lead, but Kedir moved ahead again just before the bell. Finally, the inevitable took place. With 300 meters left in the race, Miruts Yifter sprinted into the lead, covered the last 200 meters in 26.8 seconds, and won by ten meters. Viren faded to fifth, but Maaninka finished strongly to prevent an Ethiopian sweep.

MARATHON

(42,195 Meters — 26 Miles 385 Yards)
1896 Athens C: 17, N: 5, D: 4.10.
(40,000 Meters)

1. Spiridon Louis	GRE	2:58:50
2. Charilaos Vasilakos	GRE	3:06:03
3. Gyula Kellner	HUN	3:06:35

4. Ioannis Vrettos	GRE	—
5. Eleftherios Papasimeon	GRE	—
6. Demetrios Deliyannis	GRE	—
7. Evangelos Gerakakis	GRE	—
8. S. Moussouris	GRE	—

The idea for a marathon race was inspired by the legend of Pheidippides, a professional runner who allegedly carried the news of the Greek victory over the Persians at the Battle of Marathon in 490 B.C. Upon his arrival in Athens, he called out, "Rejoice, we conquer!" and then dropped dead of exhaustion. Actually there is no evidence that this dramatic incident ever took place. The fifth century B.C. historian Herodotus, who thrived on such juicy tidbits, wrote about the Battle of Marathon, but made no mention of Pheidippides's feat. The story didn't appear in print until the second century A.D.—over 600 years after it was alleged to have occurred. The longest race to be included in the ancient Greek Olympics was only 4800 meters.

However, when meetings began to be held in 1894 to organize an international revival of the Olympics, Michel Bréal, a French linguist and historian, proposed that a long-distance race be included. He even offered to present a gold cup to the winner. Invoking the legend of Pheidippides, Bréal and Baron Pierre de Coubertin presented the idea to the Organizing Committee of the Athens Olympics. The Greeks, moved by the presumed historical importance associated with such a race, agreed immediately. Georgious Averoff, designer of the refurbished Pananthenaic Stadium and the primary financial supporter of the Games, added an antique vase to the offer of Bréal's gold cup.

Before long, the marathon race had come to be considered the most important event of the upcoming games, and two preliminary races for Greeks were held along the proposed route from the Marathon Bridge to the stadium in Athens. The first race, on March 10, was won by Charilaos Vasilakos in 3:18:00. He was followed by Spiridon Belokas and Demetrios Deliyannis. The second race was officially designated an Olympic trial and was contested by 38 runners. The winner was Lavrentis (first name unknown), in 3:11:27. In fifth place was a young man of 24 years, from the village of Maroussi, named Spiridon Louis.

On the afternoon of Thursday, April 9, 17 runners were transported from Athens to an inn near the starting point of the race in Marathon. Among them were four foreigners, including the first three finishers in the 1500 meters: Edwin Flack, the London-based Australian accountant, who had won the 800 meters only a couple of hours earlier, Arthur Blake, and Albin Lermusiaux.

The next afternoon, the 17 entrants gathered on the Marathon Bridge and endured a preliminary speech by the starter, Major Papadiamantopoulos, who finally fired a gun to begin the race. There was much excitement among the Greek populace, and all along the route the runners were cheered by curious and enthusiastic peasants. Of the foreigners, only the Hungarian, Gyula Kellner, had ever run a race of such length, having qualified for the trip to Athens by winning a 40-kilometer trial in Budapest. The other three set off relatively quickly and eventually paid for their inexperience. Lermusiaux set the early pace and soon built up a huge lead, which he carried past the halfway mark. At the village of Karavati, the local people had built a triumphal arch. When Lermusiaux approached in first place, the villagers crowned him with a floral victor's wreath. By this time, Blake and several of the Greeks had already dropped out.

Shortly after Karavati, there was an incline, and Lermusiaux began to stagger from exhaustion. A French companion, riding beside him on a bicycle, revived his countryman with an alcohol rubdown, but this delay allowed Flack to pass him and take the lead. Lermusiaux continued for some distance, but finally collapsed. Flack, who had never before run more than ten miles, had overextended himself in his attempt to catch Lermusiaux, and he too began to weave and sway four kilometers short of the stadium. Flack's companion, an Englishman, asked a nearby Greek to keep the Australian from falling over while he rushed off to get a wrap. The delirious Flack, thinking that he was being attacked, smashed the helpful Greek with his fist and knocked him to the ground. Flack was loaded into a carriage and driven to the dressing room at the stadium, where he was tended to by Prince Nicholas himself, and revived with a drink of egg and brandy.

As the race progressed, messengers were sent to the stadium on horseback and bicycle to convey the identity of the leaders. The last news that the 100,000 spectators in and around the stadium heard was that Flack was in front, and their disappointment was great. Then Major Papadiamantopoulos entered the stadium on horseback and rushed to the royal box, where the King and Queen and the rest of the royal family were anxiously awaiting the latest news. The word spread "with the rapidity of lightning," according to the Official Report of the Games. Shouts of "*Elleen! Elleen!*" ("A Greek! A Greek!") announced the joyous news that a Greek was in the lead. Then the Commissioner of Police appeared and formally announced what the growing roar of the crowd in the streets had already implied: the winner had arrived. At last, a small, dusty runner, Spiridon Louis, appeared at the marble entrance to the stadium. Prince George and Crown Prince Constantine rushed down to greet him and, one on each side, ran with him the rest of the way to the finish line, where Louis summoned enough energy to bow to the delighted King George. Louis was kissed and hugged and hauled off to the dressing room upon the shoulders of his admirers, while a collective ecstasy spread from the stadium throughout the city.

Seven minutes later, a second Greek, Charilaos Vasilakos, crossed the finish to be followed shortly by a third Greek, Spiridon Belokas. However, the fourth-place finisher, Gyula Kellner, raised a protest that Belokas had ridden part of the way in a carriage. Belokas admitted his deception, and was stripped of his awards, as well as his shirt, and thoroughly ostracized.

The story of Spiridon Louis is one of which legends are made. In fact, so many legends developed about Louis that it is difficult to sort out the truth. Was he a poor shepherd, a well-to-do farmer, a soldier, a post office messenger? Probably he was a shepherd who served in the army and became a messenger. A modest man, he appeared in the stadium the day after the race to accept his prize, but then returned quickly to his village, allowing journalists to invent whatever details they saw fit. Typical of the rumors that spread was that he had entered the race in hopes of convincing the king to grant clemency to his imprisoned brother—a romantic story that was deflated when it was learned that Louis didn't even have a brother. It is true that merchants throughout Athens tried to shower him with gifts: watches, jewelry, wine, free haircuts, free clothing for life, free meals, monthly stipends. Evidently, Louis graciously turned down all the offers except a horse and cart, which were needed to help transport water to his village.

Amazingly, Spiridon Louis managed to return to a relatively normal life. In 1936, however, he was rediscovered by the German Olympic Organizing Committee, which brought him to Berlin. There he presented a laurel wreath from the sacred grove at Olympia to Adolf Hitler. Louis died on March 27, 1940, and his name entered the Greek language in the expression "egine Louis": "became Louis," or ran quickly. More than any single event, the victory of Spiridon Louis served as an inspiration to keep the Olympics going through the hard times that the movement faced over the next 12 years.

1900 Paris C: 19, N: 5, D: 7.19.
(40,260 Meters)

1. Michel Théato	FRA	2:59:45
2. Emile Champion	FRA	3:04:17
3. Ernst Fast	SWE	3:37:14
4. Eugene Resse	FRA	4:00:43
5. Arthur Newton	USA	4:04:12
6. John Cregan	USA	—
7. Richard Grant	USA	—
8. Ronald McDonald	USA	—

This unfortunate and somewhat controversial event was held in 102 degrees Fahrenheit (39 degrees Centigrade) heat. The course began in the Bois de Boulogne, followed a convoluted and confusing path through the streets of Paris, and ended up back in the Bois. Only 8 of the 19 starters were able to finish. Arthur Newton was convinced that he had taken the lead at the halfway point, and reached the finish line expecting to be declared the victor. Thus it came as a great shock when he learned that he was only fifth, and the winner, Michel Théato, had completed the course over an hour earlier. The Americans accused Théato, a 23-year-old baker's deliveryman, of taking shortcuts, based on his intimate knowledge of the city streets. However, this argument fails to deal with the fact that the third-place finisher was a Swede.

1904 St. Louis C: 32, N: 5, D: 8.30.
(40,000 Meters)

1. Thomas Hicks	USA	3:28:53
2. Albert Corey	FRA	3:34:52
3. Arthur Newton	USA	3:47:33
4. Félix Carvajal	CUB	—
5. Demeter Velouis	GRE	—
6. David Kneeland	USA	—
7. Henry Brawley	USA	—
8. Sidney Hatch	USA	—

The 1904 marathon ranks very high on the list of bizarre events in Olympic history. Among the more unusual entrants in the race was 5-foot-tall Félix Carvajal, a Cuban mail carrier, who raised the money for his trip to St. Louis by staging exhibitions in Havana. He took a boat to the United States and got as far as New Orleans, where he lost the rest of his savings in a crap game. After hitchhiking to St. Louis, he arrived on the starting line wearing heavy street shoes, long trousers, a long-sleeved shirt, and a beret. The start of the race was delayed while Martin Sheridan, the discus thrower, cut off Carvajal's pants at the knees. Also entered were the first two black Africans to participate in the Olympics: Lentauw and Yamasani, Zulu tribesmen who were in St. Louis as part of the Boer War exhibit at the Louisiana Purchase Exposition. Another foreign contestant was Albert Corey, who had taken part in the 1900 Olympic marathon and was intent on vindicating himself in St. Louis after his poor showing four years earlier. Corey was a professional strikebreaker, who had arrived in Chicago in 1903 during a butchers' strike and stayed around, since there was never a shortage of business for him in the Windy City.

Among the American entrants were Sam Mellor, winner of the 1902 Boston Marathon; John Lordon, winner of the 1903 Boston Marathon; Michael Spring, winner of the 1904 Boston Marathon; Thomas Hicks, who had finished second at Boston in 1904; and Arthur Newton, who had finished fifth in Paris in 1900.

Unfortunately, the organizers of the race knew almost nothing about staging such an event. The course included seven hills and was run on dusty roads, made dustier by the many automobiles which the judges, doctors, and journalists used to follow—and lead—the runners. The brutal nature of the contest was made worse by the fact that it was scheduled for the middle of the afternoon in 90 degrees Fahrenheit (32 degrees Centigrade) heat. In addition, the only water available to the runners was from a well located 12 miles from the stadium, where the race began and ended.

With all these obstacles in their path, it is not surprising that only 14 of the 32 starters made it back to the finish line. John Lordon, for example, began vomiting after ten miles and had to withdraw. William Garcia of San Francisco was discovered lying in the road, near death, the membranous wall of his stomach almost destroyed by the clouds of dust kicked up by the automobiles of the officials.

Sam Mellor, the leader at the halfway mark, finally gave up after 16 miles. Meanwhile, Lentauw lost a great deal of valuable time when he was chased off the course and through a cornfield by two large dogs. He still managed to finish ninth. The only runner who didn't seem bothered by all these catastrophes was Félix Carvajal, who stopped a number of times to chat with bystanders, discuss the progress of the race, and practice his English. He also quenched his thirst by snatching a couple of peaches from an official in one of the cars, and by raiding a farmer's orchard of some green apples. The latter detour caused him an attack of stomach cramps.

Back in the stadium, the spectators were unaware of all that had transpired, although the more knowledgeable sports fans may have wondered why three hours had passed without any of the runners showing up. Finally, after 3 hours and 13 minutes, Fred Lorz of New York appeared, and was immediately hailed as the winner. He had already been photographed with Alice Roosevelt, the daughter of the President of the United States, and was about to be awarded the gold medal, when it was discovered that he had actually stopped running after 9 miles, hitched a ride in a car for 11 miles, and then started running again. Lorz readily admitted his practical joke, but A.A.U. officials were not amused, and he was slapped with a lifetime ban. However he was reinstated well before the ban ran out and managed to win the Boston Marathon of 1905.

The real winner of the 1904 Olympic marathon was Thomas Hicks, an English-born brass worker from Cambridge, Massachusetts. If present-day rules had been enforced, however, he would have been disqualified. Second at the halfway point, Hicks found himself in front after Sam Mellor collapsed. Ten miles from the finish Hicks begged to be allowed to lie down, but his handlers wouldn't allow it, even though he had a lead of one and a half miles. Instead they administered to him an oral dose of strychnine sulfate mixed with raw egg white. A few miles later he was given more strychnine, as well as some brandy. He was also bathed with water made warm by being kept next to the boiler of the steam-powered automobile that accompanied him.

Hicks was forced to slow to a walk when faced with a final, steep hill two miles from the stadium, but a couple more doses of strychnine and brandy revived him enough to win the race by six minutes. Needless to say, Hicks was in something of a stupor afterward. He had lost ten pounds during the afternoon, and gladly announced his retirement. When he had finally recovered, he told reporters, "I would rather have won this race than be President of the United States." The athletes who suffered through the 1904 marathon may have received some satisfaction when they learned that two of the officials in charge of patrolling the course were badly injured as well, when their brand-new car swerved to avoid one of the runners and careened down an embankment.

1906 Athens C: 53, N: 15, D: 5.1.
(41,860 Meters)

1. William Sherring	CAN	2:51:23.6
2. John Svanberg	SWE	2:58:20.8
3. William Frank	USA	3:00:46.8
4. Gustaf Törnros	SWE	3:01:00.0
5. John Alepous	GRE	3:09:25.4
6. George Blake	AUS	3:09:35.0
7. Constantinos Karvelas	GRE	3:15:54.0
8. André Roffi	FRA	3:17:49.8

There was great excitement in Athens when it was learned that another Olympic-style marathon would be held. Local merchants offered the winner a statue of Hermes, a loaf of bread every day for a year, three coffees a day for a year, free shaves for life, and a free lunch for six every Sunday for a year—but only if the winner was a Greek.

Billy Sherring of Hamilton, Ontario, had other ideas. Convinced he could win, he gathered his savings from his job as a railway brakeman, but they weren't enough to pay his way to Greece. A local athletic club raised an extra $75, but it still wasn't enough. In desperation, Sherring turned over the $75 to a friendly bartender, who bet the money on a horse named Cicely, who won and paid 6–1 odds. At last Billy Sherring was able to travel to Athens. He arrived two months early and took a job as a railway station porter, training every other day. On March 17, the Greeks staged a trial run that was won in 3:04:29.6. Sherring watched with pleasure, knowing that he had covered the same course, in secret, 20 minutes faster.

When the big day finally came, George Blake of Australia took the early lead. After four miles he was passed by William Frank of New York, who led for three miles before Blake regained the lead. Blake faded, however, and after 15 miles he was passed by Sherring and Frank. The two ran together for three more miles, at which point Sherring turned to Frank and said, "Well, good-bye, Billy." Then he took off and built up such a large lead that he was able to walk part of the way to the finish.

There was great disappointment in the Olympic Stadium when the news spread that the leader was not a Greek. However, when Sherring passed through the marble entrance, he was met by Prince George, who applauded him and ran with him around the track to the finish line, where Sherring bowed to the king, just as Spiridon Louis had done ten years earlier. Billy Sherring had weighed 135 pounds when he left Canada. By the morning of the race he was down to 112, and by the end of the race he had evaporated to 98 pounds. Sherring didn't receive all the goodies that had been offered a Greek winner, but he was presented with a three-foot statue of Athena and a young lamb. Back in Canada he did much better. The city of Hamilton gave him a purse of $5000, while the city of Toronto chipped in $400.

One runner who was overlooked in 1906 was a 20-year-old Italian who developed stomach problems and dropped out after 24 kilometers. His name was Dorando Pietri. Before the decade was out, he would become a living legend.

1908 London C: 56, N: 16, D: 7.24.

—	Dorando Pietri	ITA	2:54:46.4
1.	John Hayes	USA	2:55:18.4 OR
2.	Charles Hefferon	SAF	2:56:06.0
3.	Joseph Forshaw	USA	2:57:10.4
4.	Alton Welton	USA	2:59:44.4
5.	William Wood	CAN	3:01:44.0
6.	Frederick Simpson	CAN	3:04:28.2
7.	Harry Lawson	CAN	3:06:47.2
8.	John Svanberg	SWE	3:07:50.8

July 24, 1908, dawned hot (by English standards) and muggy. The talk of the town was the bitter hostilities that had erupted between the British and the Americans following the controversial running of the 400 meters final the previous day. People had been looking forward to the marathon race with great anticipation, and a large crowd lined the 26-mile route from Windsor Castle to the Olympic Stadium in Shepherd's Bush. The race was scheduled to conclude with 385 yards around the stadium track, so that the finish line would be directly in front of the royal box of Queen Alexandra. As it happened, this random distance of 26 miles and 385 yards would later become the standardized length for marathon races.

The first 26 miles of the 1908 marathon were actually quite exciting, although they were quickly forgotten as a result of the extraordinary incidents which occurred during the final 385 yards. The British runners, under great pressure to perform well, started off at far too fast a clip and later paid the price of their folly. T. Jack of Scotland led for the first five miles, but quickly exhausted himself. Fred Lord and Jack Price took his place in front. Lord began to fade after ten miles. At the halfway mark at Ruislip, Price led by 200 yards. Charles Hefferon had moved into second place, followed by Lord and Dorando Pietri. The American entrants, at this point, were calmly running their own race, unruffled by the fast pace of the leaders.

Shortly after the 14-mile mark, Hefferon passed Price, who dropped out not long after. Lord also began to fade, eventually finishing 15th. The well-known Onondaga Indian Tom Longboat, of Toronto, who had been one of the favorites, came up to challenge, but he too fell back, slowing to a walk and then retiring completely.

By the 18-mile mark, it appeared that only Hefferon and Pietri (or Dorando, as he became better known) had a chance for the gold medal. Hefferon led by 3:18. By 20 miles he had built up a lead of 3 minutes 52 seconds, but then Dorando began to close the gap. Two miles from the stadium, the exhausted Hefferon made a crucial mistake. He accepted a drink of champagne and, within a mile, he had developed stomach cramps and become dizzy. Dorando also committed a major tactical blunder. Urged on by the well-meaning but overzealous crowd, he picked up his pace too early. Meanwhile, Americans John Hayes, Joseph Forshaw, and Alton Welton were drawing closer.

The spectators lining the route, having inadvertently damaged Dorando's chances for victory, now did the same to Hefferon. Hoping to boost his spirits, they slapped him on the back so many times that they sapped him of what little energy he had left. A half-mile from the entrance to the stadium, he was passed by Dorando.

The last report that had been received inside the stadium was that South Africa and Italy were in the lead. All eyes were on the entrance as Dorando Pietri, a small man from the small town of Carpi, near Reggio, made his appearance. However, it immediately became obvious that something was wrong. Dorando appeared dazed and headed off in the wrong direction. Track officials rushed to his aid and pointed him the right way. But after going only a few yards, he collapsed on the track. The audience, which had never before seen or heard of Dorando, immediately became sympathetic. While many people screamed for the officials to help him, others, knowing that such aid would automatically disqualify the plucky Italian, called out to leave him alone. However, in the words of the official report, "It was impossible to leave him there, for it looked as if he might die in the very presence of the Queen . . ." Doctors and officials rushed to help him, and Dorando managed to struggle to his feet and plod on, only to fall again. And again and again. By this time, a second runner had arrived on the track. However, much to the horror of the spectators, he was not Charles Hefferon, a good man of the Empire, but an American, 5-foot 4-inch John Hayes, who had breezed past Hefferon 20 yards before the stadium grounds.

This was too much for the British officials. When Dorando started to collapse for a fifth time, just short of the finish, Jack Andrew, the head organizer of the race, caught him and carried him across the line. The Italian flag was immediately run up the victory pole, even as Hayes, still in good shape, crossed the finish himself. The Americans wasted no time in lodging a protest, and while Dorando, who had been carried away on a stretcher, lay seemingly on the verge of death, the protest was allowed and Hayes was declared the winner.

Remarkably, Dorando was back on his feet the next day, complaining that the British officials should have left him alone and that he could have finished without their assistance. However, photos of the incident make it quite clear that this was highly unlikely, and that the stretcher probably should have been called for the first time he fell. At any rate, Dorando showed up at the stadium the day after the race and was presented with a special gold cup by the Queen. Overnight he became an international celebrity. Even in the United States, songs were written about him, including one by Irving Berlin. Unfortunately, Berlin completely missed the point of what had happened, and portrayed the courageous Italian as a "bigga de flop," entitling his song, "Dorando He'sa Gooda for Not."

Somewhat lost in the excitement was the actual winner, John Hayes, a 22-year-old clerk at Bloomingdale's department store in New York City. Hayes, who had prepared for the big race by resting in bed for two days, had finished fifth in the 1906 Boston Marathon and third in 1907, before winning the 1907 Yonkers Marathon on Thanksgiving Day. Mr. Bloomingdale himself had taken a liking to Hayes, and ordered the construction of a cinder path on the roof of his store so that Hayes could train during his breaks. When Hayes was chosen for the Olympic team, Bloomingdale gave him a full vacation with pay, and when he won the gold medal, Hayes was promoted to manager of the sporting goods department.

But this job was not to last long. Dorando's sensational effort in London had set off a marathon craze that swept around the world. He and Hayes were offered very good money to turn professional. Both of them did, and they each built up a good deal of capital running scores of races over the next couple of years, far more than Hayes could have earned at Bloomingdale's or than Dorando could have earned back in Carpi. The most notable contests were two match races between Hayes and Dorando held in New York City on November 25, 1908, and March 15, 1909, both of which were won by the Italian. Dorando, whose opportunistic brother ran off with his fortune, lived out his life driving a taxi in Italy. He also received a stipend from the Italian government for scouting promising marathon runners.

1912 Stockholm C: 68, N: 19, D: 7.14.
(40,200 Meters) WB:2:42:31.0 (Frederick Barrett)
1. Kenneth McArthur   SAF 2:36:54.8
2. Christian Gitsham   SAF 2:37:52.0
3. Gaston Strobino   USA 2:38:42.4
4. Andrew Sockalexis   USA 2:42:07.9
5. James Duffy   CAN 2:42:18.8
6. Sigfrid "Sigge" Jacobsson SWE 2:43:24.9
7. John Gallahger   USA 2:44:19.4
8. Joseph Erxleben   USA 2:45:47.4

Once again, the Olympic marathon was held on an oppressively hot day that caused half of the runners to retire before the finish. Tatu Kolehmainen, the older brother of Hannes, took the lead before three miles had been covered, and held it until just before the turnaround point, when he was passed by Gitsham. McArthur was third, followed by Fred Lord. After 17 miles, Gitsham and Kolehmainen were running together, with McArthur only a meter or two behind. Two or three miles later, Kolehmainen was forced to retire, and the two South Africans went on alone. Two miles from the stadium they reached a refreshment stand, and Gitsham stopped to take a drink of water. McArthur had said he would wait for his teammate, but instead he kept on going, opening up a lead that Gitsham was unable to close. McArthur was a 30-year-old policeman who had emigrated from Ireland seven years earlier.

The 1912 marathon was marred by a sad note. The 21-year-old Portuguese runner Francisco Lazaro collapsed from sunstroke and heart trouble toward the end of the race and was taken to a hospital, where he died the following day. He was the first of only two athletes to die as a result of their participation in the Olympics.

1920 Antwerp C: 42, N: 17, D: 8.22.
(42,750 Meters) WB: 2:36:06.6 (Alexis Ahlgren)
1. Johannes Kolehmainen   FIN 2:32:35.8 WB
2. Jüri Lossmann   EST 2:32:48.6
3. Valerio Arri   ITA 2:36:32.8
4. Auguste Broos   BEL 2:39:25.8
5. Jaako Tuomikoski   FIN 2:40:10.8
6. Sofus Rose   DEN 2:41:18.0
7. Joseph Organ   USA 2:41:30.8
8. Rudolf Hansen   DEN 2:41:40.9

At last the Olympic marathon was contested on a cool day, and the runners responded with excellent times, particularly considering that the course was longer than ever before. Christian Gitsham took the early lead, but after 15 kilometers he was joined by Hannes Kolehmainen, who had returned from Brooklyn to compete for Finland. They reached the turnaround together, but after 27 kilometers, Kolehmainen moved ahead and began to draw away. Gitsham, suffering from foot trouble after one of his shoes tore open, retired after 35 kilometers. Meanwhile, Jüri Lossman of Estonia closed the gap that separated him from the famous Finn, but Kolehmainen managed to hold on to his lead and win by 70 yards—the closest marathon finish in Olympic history.

In direct contrast to previous marathons, the runners finished in good health. Valerio Arri, the Italian champion, even celebrated his bronze medal by performing three cartwheels as soon as he crossed the finish line.

1924 Paris C: 58, N: 20, D: 7.13. WB: 2:32:35.8 (Johannes Kolehmainen)
1. Albin Stenroos   FIN 2:41:22.6
2. Romeo Bertini   ITA 2:47:19.6
3. Clarence DeMar   USA 2:48:14.0
4. Lauri Halonen   FIN 2:49:47.4
5. Samuel Ferris   GBR 2:52:26.0
6. Miguel Plaza Reyes   CHI 2:52:54.0
7. Boughèra El Ouafi   FRA 2:54:19.6
8. Gustav Kinn   SWE 2:54:33.4

Albin Stenroos, a 35-year-old woodworker, had won a bronze medal in the 1912 10,000 meters race. However he did not run a single marathon between 1909 and May 18, 1924, when he placed second in the Finnish Olympic trial. In Paris, he passed G. Verger of France after 19½ kilometers, and steadily drew away to a huge lead, winning by almost six minutes. Silver medalist Romeo Bertini was 31 years old, while bronze medalist Clarence DeMar was 36. In 1930 DeMar won his seventh Boston Marathon at the age of 42. In the 1924 Olympics, 28 of the 58 starters failed to finish the course.

1928 Amsterdam C: 68, N: 23, D: 8.5. WB: 2: 29:01.8 (Albert Michelsen)

1. Boughèra El Ouafi	FRA	2:32:57.0
2. Miguel Plaza Reyes	CHI	2:33:23.0
3. Martti Marttelin	FIN	2:35:02.0
4. Kanematsu Yamada	JAP	2:35:29.0
5. Joie Ray	USA	2:36:04.0
6. Seiichiro Tsuda	JAP	2:36:20.0
7. Yrjo Korholin-Koski	FIN	2:36:40.0
8. Samuel Ferris	GBR	2:37:41.0

The lead changed several times during the first half of the race, with Joie Ray in first place at the turnaround. Shortly thereafter he was passed by Yamada and Tsuda. These three remained in front past 30 kilometers. By this time two outsiders, Algerian-born Boughèra El Ouafi and Miguel Plaza of Chile, had moved up to challenge. Plaza had evidently decided to run the race on El Ouafi's shoulder, just as he had four years earlier. Three kilometers short of the finish they had taken over second and third place, finally wearing down Yamada during the approach to the stadium. Both El Ouafi and Plaza finished strongly, with El Ouafi winning by about 150 meters. The victor was a former member of the French Colonial Army who had settled in Paris and was employed as an automobile mechanic. Twenty-eight years later, when another French-Arab, Alain Mimoun, won the Olympic marathon, journalists sought out El Ouafi and discovered him unemployed and living in poverty in Paris. French sportsmen got together a fund to help the forgotten hero of Amsterdam. However, three years later, on October 18, 1959, El Ouafi died as a result of a family quarrel. He was 60 years old.

1932 Los Angeles C: 29, N: 15, D: 8.7. WB: 2:29:01:.8 (Albert Michelsen)

1. Juan Carlos Zabala	ARG	2:31:36.0 OR
2. Samuel Ferris	GBR	2:31:55.0
3. Armas Toivonen	FIN	2:32:12.0
4. Duncan McLeod Wright	GBR	2:32:41.0
5. Seiichiro Tsuda	JAP	2:35:42.0
6. Onbai Kin	JAP	2:37:28.0
7. Albert Michelsen	USA	2:39:38.0
8. Oskar Heks	CZE	2:41:35.0

Paavo Nurmi had been considered the favorite to win the 1932 marathon, until he was suspended by the I.A.A.F. one week before the race for accepting payments in excess of his expenses during an exhibition tour. Juan Carlos Zabala, a 20-year-old Argentinian, had set a world record at 30,000 meters in 1931. On June 25, 1932, the *Los Angeles Times* sponsored a marathon race over the Olympic course. Zabala built up an eight-and-a-half-minute lead in that race, but developed foot problems and was ordered to withdraw by his trainer. Albert Michelsen went on to win.

Zabala took the early lead in the Olympics. He was passed briefly by Margarito Baños of Mexico, but regained the lead and held it for over 30 kilometers. At the 31-kilometer mark, Lauri Virtanen, who had already finished third in the 10,000 and 5000, sprinted ahead suddenly and

opened up a 300-meter gap. This shook up the field, and there was much jockeying for position. Duncan Wright, following a well-laid-out British plan, forged to the front after 20 miles (35.5 kilometers), and as Virtanen faded, he moved a full minute ahead of Zabala, with Toivonen another half-minute further back. By 37 kilometers, Virtanen had dropped out and Wright had begun to fade. Zabala moved back into the lead, and Sam Ferris, taking over second place, took off after him. But he had waited too long. Zabala entered the Coliseum with a one-minute lead and was almost three quarters of the way around the track when Ferris appeared, followed closely by Toivonen and Wright. Thus, the crowd was treated to the rare spectacle of the first four finishers of the marathon being on the track at the same time. Zabala struggled across the finish line and then collapsed, whereas Ferris was still full of strength and probably would have won had the race continued for an extra half lap.

1936 Berlin C: 56, N: 27, D: 8.9. WB: 2:26:42.0 (Kee-Chung Sohn)

1. Kee-Chung Sohn (Kitei Son)	JAP/KOR	2:29:19.2 OR
2. Ernest Harper	GBR	2:31:23.2
3. Seung-Yong Nam (Shoryu Nan)	JAP/KOR	2:31:42.0
4. Erkki Tamila	FIN	2:32:45.0
5. Väino Muinonen	FIN	2:33:46.0
6. Johannes Coleman	SAF	2:36:17.0
7. Duncan McNab Robertson	GBR	2:37:06.2
8. Henry Gibson	SAF	2:38:04.0

On November 3, 1935, Kee-Chung Sohn of Korea set a world marathon record of 2:26:42.0. Because Korea was, at the time, occupied by Japanese forces, Sohn's hopes for competing in the Olympics depended on his ability to qualify for the Japanese team. This he accomplished, as did fellow Korean Seung-Yong Nam. Both young men were forced to endure the further insult of adopting Japanese names. Sohn, a fervent nationalist, always signed his Korean name in Berlin, and whenever he was asked where he was from, he made it a point to explain that Korea was a separate nation which was currently a victim of Japanese imperialism.

Defending champion Juan Carlos Zabala had arrived in Berlin months in advance, and during his period of extended training had become a local favorite, particularly in the absence of a serious German threat in the marathon. As usual, Zabala tore into the lead and was 30 seconds in front at the four-kilometer mark. After 15 kilometers he was ahead by 1 minute and 40 seconds. He let the margin slip to 50 seconds at the turnaround, but pumped it back up to 90 seconds after 25 kilometers. For quite some time, Zabala had been followed by Sohn and 34-year-old Ernest Harper, who had been running together since the beginning. However it came as a shock to Zabala when, after 28 kilometers, he was suddenly passed, first by Sohn and, ten meters later, by Harper. Zabala fell, got up, struggled on for four more kilometers, and then retired. Meanwhile, Sohn pulled away and won by over two minutes. Harper finished heroically, holding off the fast-closing Nam despite a bad blister that had filled one of his shoes with blood.

Interviewed by the press afterwards, Sohn used the opportunity to educate the world about the plight of his nation. Few reporters were interested, and most seemed relieved when he turned to the race itself. "The human body can do so much," he said. "Then the heart and spirit must take over."

1948 London C: 41, N: 21, D: 8.7. WB: 2:25:39.0 (Yun-Bok Suh)

1. Delfo Cabrera	ARG	2:34:51.6
2. Thomas Richards	GBR	2:35:07.6
3. Etienne Gailly	BEL	2:35:33.6
4. Johannes Coleman	SAF	2:36:06.0
5. Eusebio Guinez	ARG	2:36:36.0
6. Thomas Sidney Luyt	SAF	2:38:11.0
7. Gustav Ostling	SWE	2:38:40.6
8. John Systad	NOR	2:38:41.0

Twenty-five-year-old Etienne Gailly, running his first race longer than 32.5 kilometers, was in the lead by the ten-kilometer post and had opened up a 41-second gap by 25 kilometers, at which point he was followed by Guinez, Ostling, and Cabrera. The field then began to close in on him, and after 32.5 kilometers he was passed by Yoon-Chil Choi of Korea. At 35 kilometers, Choi led by 28 seconds, with Delfo Cabrera, a 29-year-old fireman also running his first marathon, in second place. Gailly was third and Guinez fourth.

But Choi had used up all his energy and soon retired. Five thousand meters from Wembley Stadium, Cabrera led Gailly by five seconds. Tom Richards, a 38-year-old Welsh nurse, had moved into third place. Gailly gathered his strength and regained the lead. A half mile from the stadium, he led Cabrera by 50 yards and Richards by 100. The exhausted Belgian was the first to enter the stadium, but by now he was barely running. Spectators were immediately reminded of the ordeal endured by Dorando Pietri the last time the Olympics had been held in London. Gailly managed to stay on his feet, but before he had covered 100 yards of the track, he was passed by Cabrera and then by Richards. Gailly staggered on, almost collapsing 60 yards short of his goal. But he did finally cross the finish line and gain a well-earned bronze medal, much to the relief of the sympathetic crowd. In fourth place was 38-year-old Johannes Coleman, who had finished sixth in the last Olympics 12 years earlier.

1952 Helsinki C: 66, N: 32, D: 7.27. WB: 2:20:42.2 (James Peters)

1. Emil Zátopek	CZE	2:23:03.2 OR
2. Reinaldo Gorno	ARG	2:25:35.0
3. Gustav Jansson	SWE	2:26:07.0
4. Yoon-Chil Choi	KOR	2:26:36.0
5. Veikko Karvonen	FIN	2:26:41.8
6. Delfo Cabrera	ARG	2:26:42.4
7. József Dobronyi	HUN	2:28:04.8
8. Erkki Puolakka	FIN	2:29:35.0

Emil Zátopek was born in Koprivnice, Northern Moravia, on September 19, 1922, the exact same day that his wife, Dana, was born. He made his first appearance in the Olympics in 1948, finishing first in the 10,000 meters and second at 5000. Whenever he ran, his face was always contorted by a grimace, and his shoulders and body looked hunched with pain. Observers, on first viewing Zátopek, were sure that he was on the verge of collapse, but it turned out that that was just his style. Years later Zátopek was asked about this idiosyncrasy. He replied, "I was not talented enough to run and smile at the same time."

In 1952 Zátopek became the first runner since Hannes Kolehmainen to win both the 5000- and 10,000-meter races. But that wasn't enough for Zátopek. He decided to attempt an unprecedented triple by also competing in the marathon. The fact that he had never run a marathon before bothered him only slightly. He wasn't concerned about coming up with the necessary endurance, but it did worry him a bit that there might be pacing strategies with which he was not familiar. With this in mind, Zátopek decided to run along with the man whom he considered to be the favorite in the race—Jim Peters of Great Britain, who had run the fastest marathon in history only six weeks earlier. Zátopek took note of Peters' running number in the newspaper, and the next day he located Peters on the starting line and introduced himself.

Peters took off at what seemed to be an outlandish pace, but Zátopek, as well as Gustaf Jansson, kept contact with him. After 15 kilometers Zátopek and Jansson caught up with Peters, and the three ran together for a couple of miles. Then Zátopek turned to Peters and said, in English, "The pace? Is it good enough?" Peters, who had exhausted himself with his early running, pretended that he was still fresh, and replied, "Pace too slow." Zátopek mulled this over for a few moments and then said, "You say, 'too slow.' Are you sure the pace is too slow?" "Yes," came the reply. They continued on in silence for a short while, and then Zátopek zipped by Peters, taking Jansson with him.

They passed the turnaround together, with Peters ten seconds behind. After 20 miles Peters developed a leg cramp and dropped out. By this time Zátopek had shaken off Jansson, and he was able to enter the stadium far ahead of the other runners. The huge crowd greeted him as the hero of the 1952 Games, chanting "Zá-to-pek, Zá-to-pek," as he completed the final lap. The Jamaican relay team hoisted him on their shoulders and carried him around the field. Zátopek was already signing autographs by the time the next runner, the surprising Reinaldo Gorno, arrived. Zátopek greeted him at the finish line with a slice of orange.

Despite his convincing victory, Zátopek later said, "I was unable to walk for a whole week after that, so much did the race take out of me. But it was the most pleasant exhaustion I have ever known."

Emil Zátopek also entered the Olympic marathon in 1956. But six weeks before the Games he had developed a hernia while trying to train with his wife on his shoulders. His doctors told him not to run for two months after his operation, but instead he resumed training the day after he left the hospital. Under the circumstances, his sixth-place finish could hardly be considered a failure.

Zátopek had been a member of the Czech army since 1944. His athletic successes gained him promotion to the rank of lieutenant-colonel, as well as a prominent position in the Communist Party. However, Emil Zátopek was not really a party man. In 1968 he signed the *2000 Words Manifesto,* which supported the establishment of freedom in Czechoslovakia. When Soviet tanks moved in and crushed the growing democratic movement in Czechoslovakia, Zátopek was expelled from the Communist Party and given the job of well-tester. Then he was demoted further to garbage collector. When the Czech people recognized him on his rounds, they insisted on helping him with his work. Realizing that aiding Zátopek had become a symbol of resistance, the Communists fired him. In 1971 he publicly supported the government, and was given a better job with the Czech Geological Research Institute. However, he continued to speak his mind on the subject of freedom, particularly when he was allowed to visit the West. Eventually, an uneasy compromise was reached, and he was employed as a clerk in the Bureau of Sports Information.

No matter what happens to Emil Zátopek in the future, he has left an indelible impression on the world of sports that goes beyond his four gold medals and 18 world records. Unlike his predecessor Paavo Nurmi, Zátopek was greatly loved by his fellow competitors, as well as by all those who have had the good fortune to meet him personally.

1956 Melbourne C: 46, N: 23, D: 12.1 WB: 2:17:39.4 (James Peters)

1.	Alain Mimoun O'Kacha	FRA	2:25:00.0
2.	Franjo Mihalič	YUG	2:26:32.0
3.	Veikko Karvonen	FIN	2:27:47.0
4.	Chang-Hoon Lee	KOR	2:28:45.0
5.	Yoshiaki Kawashima	JAP	2:29:19.0
6.	Emil Zátopek	CZE	2:29:34.0
7.	Ivan Filin	SOV	2:30:27.0
8.	Evert Nyberg	SWE	2:31:12.0

Thirty-five-year-old Algerian-born Alain Mimoun had made a habit of finishing second to Emil Zátopek—three times in the Olympics and twice in the European championships. But he was sure that December 1, 1956, would be his lucky day. Frenchmen had won the Olympic marathon in 1900, and then 28 years later in 1928. Now, 28 more years had passed. In addition, Mimoun was wearing what he considered to be the lucky number 13. As if these weren't enough good omens, he had just learned that he had become a father.

For the first time in Olympic history, there was a false start in the marathon. Mimoun stayed with the leading group for the first half of the race. Then he surged forward during an uphill segment before the turnaround. By the 25-kilometer mark he had opened a 50-second gap, and no one came close to him again. For the third time in a row, the Olympic marathon had been won by a converted track star competing in his first marathon.

At the finish line Mimoun waited for his old friend Emil Zátopek, who trotted home in a trance four and a half minutes later. "Emil," he asked, "why don't you congratulate me? I am an Olympic champion. It was I who won." Zátopek snapped out of his trance, took off his cap, saluted Mimoun, and then embraced him. "For me," Mimoun recalled, "that was better than the medal."

Surprisingly, Mimoun's marathon career had only just begun. He proceeded to win the French championship six times, the last in 1966, when he was 42 years old. At the age of 51, Mimoun completed the 26-mile, 385-yard race in a time of 2:34:36.2.

1960 Rome C: 69, N: 35, D: 9.10. WB: 2:15:17.0 (Sergei Popov)

1.	Abebe Bikila	ETH	2:15:16.2 WB
2.	Rhadi Ben Abdesselem	MOR	2:15:41:6
3.	Barry Magee	NZE	2:17:18.2
4.	Konstantin Vorobiev	SOV	2:19:09.6
5.	Sergei Popov	SOV	2:19:18.8
6.	Thyge Tögersen	DEN	2:21:03.4
7.	Abebe Wakgira	ETH	2:21:10.0
8.	Benaissa Bakir	MOR	2:21:22.0

The 1960 Olympic marathon was the first to be run at night, the first to start and end outside the stadium, and, as it turned out, the first to be won by a black African. After 18 kilometers, two men pulled away from the field: Rhadi Ben Abdesselem, who was one of the favorites, and barefooted Abebe Bikila, who was not. A member of the Ethiopian Imperial Bodyguard, the 28-year-old Abebe was running in his third marathon. The two ran side by side, mile after mile, never looking at each other, along a course lit by torches held by Italian soldiers, and lined by thousands of spectators who had to be restrained from interfering with the runners.

Reconnoitering the route some days earlier, Abebe and his Swedish coach, Onni Niskanen, had noticed that less than a mile from the finish line at the Arch of Constantine was the obelisk of Axum, which had been plundered from Ethiopia by Italian troops and hauled off to Rome. It seemed appropriate that the slight incline that followed the obelisk would be the proper place for Abebe to make his final move. Although none of the experts had even considered that the Ethiopian would still be in contention by that point, Abebe was sure that he would be. Right on schedule, he pulled away from Rhadi, and his lead had increased to almost 200 yards by the time he breasted the tape. His final obstacle was a typical Roman driver, who had lurched his motor scooter onto the course 60 yards from the end.

1964 Tokyo C: 68, N: 35, D: 10.21. WB: 2:13:55.0 (Basil Heatley)

1. Abebe Bikila	ETH	2:12:11.2 WB
2. Basil Heatley	GBR	2:16:19.2
3. Kokichi Tsuburaya	JAP	2:16:22.8
4. Brian Kilby	GBR	2:17:02.4
5. József Sütö	HUN	2:17:55.8
6. Leonard "Buddy" Edelen	USA	2:18:12.4
7. Aurele Vandendriessche	BEL	2:18:42.6
8. Kenji Kimihara	JAP	2:19:49.0

There was no clear-cut favorite in the 1964 marathon, with at least 15 runners in serious contention for the gold medal. Defending champion Abebe Bikila had undergone an appendectomy only 40 days before the race. The Australian Ron Clarke, running his fourth race in a week, rushed to an early lead, followed closely by Jim Hogan of Ireland. Abebe, running this time with shoes and socks, joined them before the seven-kilometer mark, and the three ran together for about half an hour. After 15 kilometers, Bikila, attempting to become the first person in history to win two Olympic marathons, began to apply pressure. By the turning point—Tobitakyu-machi, in Chofu city—Clarke had fallen behind and Abebe was five seconds ahead of Hogan. From 25 kilometers on, Abebe moved ahead steadily until, ten kilometers later, he led Hogan by two and a half minutes. Hogan slowed to a walk and then dropped out, leaving Kokichi Tsuburaya, who was running only the fourth marathon of his career, in second place.

When Abebe Bikila entered the stadium, he was greeted by 75,000 waving and cheering spectators. After crossing the finish line in the fastest marathon time ever recorded, Abebe entertained the crowd by doing stretching and bicycling exercises and generally looking like he was sorry the race had been so short. He told the press that he could have kept up the pace for another ten kilometers. At the medal ceremony later in the day, none of the Japanese officials knew the Ethiopian national anthem, so the band took the opportunity to play the Japanese anthem instead.

Tsuburaya was the second man to enter the stadium, followed ten yards later by Heatley. Despite the encouragement of the hometown crowd, Tsuburaya was exhausted, and when Heatley moved past him before the final curve, he was unable to respond. However, Tsuburaya's third-place finish brought him Japan's first track and field medal in 28 years, and he became a national hero.

Unfortunately, Kokichi Tsuburaya met a tragic end. A member of the Training School of the Japanese Ground Self-Defense Force, after the 1964 race he was ordered to stop seeing his fiancée and to begin training immediately for the 1968 Olympics. But in 1967 he suffered two injuries and was forced to spend three months in the hospital. The doctors declared him completely recovered, but when Tsuburaya started running again, he realized that his body had been irreversibly weakened and that he could not possibly win the next Olympic marathon. On January 9, 1968, two months after his release from the hospital and nine months before the Mexico Olympics, Kokichi Tsuburaya ended his own life by cutting his right carotid artery with a razor blade. Beside him was a piece of paper on which he had written a single phrase: "Cannot run anymore."

Abebe Bikila also came up against tragedy. He entered the 1968 marathon, but had to withdraw after 17 kilometers because of a bone fracture in his leg. The following year he was driving his Volkswagen, a gift from the government following his second gold medal, when he crashed. He suffered a broken neck and a spinal cord injury that left him paralyzed below the waist. Confined to a wheelchair for the rest of his life, he died of a brain hemorrhage on October 25, 1973, at the age of 41.

1968 Mexico City C: 74, N: 41, D: 10.20. WB: 2:09:36.4 (Derek Clayton)

1. Mamo Wolde	ETH	2:20:26.4
2. Kenji Kimihara	JAP	2:23:31.0
3. Michael Ryan	NZE	2:23:45.0
4. Ismail Akcay	TUR	2:25:18.8
5. William Adcocks	GBR	2:25:33.0
6. Merawi Gebru	ETH	2:27:16.8
7. Derek Clayton	AUS	2:27:23.8
8. Timothy Johnston	GBR	2:28:04.4

Mamo Wolde had a long and unusual involvement in the Olympics. His first appearance was in Melbourne in 1956, where he had entered the 800 and 1500, and finished last in his heat in both events. He also ran the third leg for the Ethiopian 4×400 relay team, which finished last in its heat. He did not compete in 1960, but he was back in 1964. He failed to complete the marathon, but placed fourth in the 10,000. In 1968 he finished a close second to Naftali Temu in the 10,000, a week before the marathon. In the later race, Wolde and Temu let others set the pace without allowing the leaders to get too far ahead. Then, about the halfway mark, they picked up the pace considerably and left the others behind. Shortly after 30 kilometers Temu ran out of steam and began to drift back, eventually finishing 19th. This left Wolde with almost a two-minute lead at 35 kilometers. He went on to win as easily as Abebe Bikila had four years earlier. At the age of 36, he had finally come out from the shadow of his famous teammate and won an Olympic gold medal.

1972 Munich C: 69, N: 35, D: 9.10. WB: 2:08:33.6 (Derek Clayton)

1. Frank Shorter	USA	2:12:19.8
2. Karel Lismont	BEL	2:14:31.8
3. Mamo Wolde	ETH	2:15:08.4
4. Kenneth Moore	USA	2:15:39.8
5. Kenji Kimihara	JAP	2:16:27.0
6. Ronald Hill	GBR	2:16:30.6
7. Donald Macgregor	GBR	2:16:34.4
8. Jack Foster	NZE	2:16:56.2

Munich-born Yale graduate Frank Shorter, annoyed by the slow pace, took the lead after ten kilometers and pulled away steadily as the race progressed. He was never challenged. Quite naturally, he entered the stadium expecting to be greeted by cheers and applause. Instead, all he heard was whistling and booing, and he wondered what he had done wrong. Unbeknownst to Shorter, a hoaxster named Norbert Sudhous had appeared on the track a couple of minutes before him and run a full lap before being hustled away by security guards. The sounds of derision had been aimed at Sudhous, not Shorter. The silver medal went to previously undefeated Karel Lismont, and the bronze to Mamo Wolde, who ran his fastest marathon ever at the age of 40. Eighth-place finisher Jack Foster was also 40 years old. After the race, Shorter went back to his room and celebrated his victory by drinking three gins in the bathtub.

1976 Montreal C: 67, N: 35, D: 7.31. WB: 2:08:33.6 (Derek Clayton)

1. Waldemar Cierpinski	GDR	2:09:55.0 OR
2. Frank Shorter	USA	2:10:45.8
3. Karel Lismont	BEL	2:11:12.6
4. Donald Kardong	USA	2:11:15.8
5. Lasse Viren	FIN	2:13:10.8
6. Jerome Drayton	CAN	2:13:30.0
7. Leonid Moseyev	SOV	2:13:33.4
8. Franco Fava	ITA	2:14:24.6

Defending champion Frank Shorter looked like the man to beat in 1976, although Lasse Viren was an unknown quantity. Viren had already run 30,000 meters during the last seven days, including victories in the 10,000 and, 24 hours before the marathon, in the 5,000. This was his first marathon race. Bill Rodgers of the United States, who eventually finished 40th, guided the leading pack through the first ten kilometers, but the real action didn't begin until just before the 25-kilometer mark, when Shorter surged through the rain, leaving the others behind. Viren tried to keep up for 200 meters, but fell back. About four minutes later, Waldemar Cierpinski, a relatively unknown converted steeplechaser from East Germany, who had entered his first marathon on a whim in 1974, decided that Shorter wasn't really running so fast after all, and caught up with him.

"It was a wonderful feeling when I came alongside," Cierpinski later recalled. "I glanced at Shorter as I did so, and looked right into the eyes of the man who was my idol as a marathon runner. I knew all about him. And yet I could tell by the return glance that he didn't know much, if anything, about me. The psychological advantage was mine." Cierpinski's coaches had told him to annoy Shorter by getting as close to his body as possible. This he did, until a couple shoves separated them. Shorter made periodic surges, but each time Cierpinski caught him. Then, after 34 kilometers, they disappeared from the sight of the crowds and the cameras during a short stretch through the campus of McGill University. When they emerged again, Cierpinski had taken the lead and begun to draw away. Shorter tried to close the gap, but couldn't.

Cierpinski entered the stadium just as the band had finished playing the East German national anthem to cele-

brate the victory of the women's relay team. When he reached the finish line, Cierpinski noticed that the lap indicator read "1." Confused, he continued running for another lap and was surprised, when he crossed the finish again, to find Frank Shorter waiting to congratulate him.

Cierpinski's victory came as a shock even to his fellow countrymen. Back in the Olympic Village, the East German soccer team watched the race on television while waiting for their final match against Poland. Goalie Jürgen Croy later recalled, "We just sat there staring at each other, thinking that if this living example of mediocrity can lift himself up and win the marathon, and we don't beat Poland, we are never going to hear the end of it." They won.

1980 Moscow C: 74, N: 40, D: 8.1. WB: 2:08:33.6 (Derek Clayton)

1. Waldemar Cierpinski	GDR	2:11:03.0
2. Gerard Nijboer	HOL	2:11:20.0
3. Setymkul Dzhumanazarov	SOV	2:11:35.0
4. Vladimir Kotov	SOV	2:12:05.0
5. Leonid Moseyev	SOV	2:12:14.0
6. Rodolfo Gomez	MEX	2:12:39.0
7. Dereje Nedi	ETH	2:12:44.0
8. Massimo Magnani	ITA	2:13:12.0

Vladimir Kotov led for the first half of the race. After 24 kilometers, Lasse Viren, who had been running with the leaders, suddenly rushed off into the bushes with diarrhea. He dropped out three kilometers later. Rudolfo Gomez took advantage of Viren's indisposition to jump into the lead, quickly opening a 100-meter gap. At the 30-kilometer mark, he led by 23 seconds. However, five and a half kilometers later he was passed by Gerard Nijboer. Six hundred meters further along, Cierpinski passed them both, and was never headed. He ran the last 200 meters in 33.4 seconds and won by about 80 meters. As he crossed the finish line, there were five runners on the track, an Olympic record. Although he was only two days shy of his 30th birthday, Waldemar Cierpinski was still described by East German sources as a "sports student." After becoming the only person besides Abebe Bikila to win two Olympic marathons, he was elevated to "sports teacher."

110-METER HURDLES

Contestants in this event must clear ten hurdles, each of which is 3 feet 6 inches high.

1896 Athens C: 7, N: 6, D: 4.10. WR(120 yards): 15.4 (Stephen Chase)

1. Thomas Curtis	USA	17.6
2. Grantley Goulding	GBR	17.7e

DNS: William Hoyt (USA) and Alajos Szokolyi (HUN)

1900 Paris C: 10, N: 4, D: 7.14. WR(120 yards): 15.2 (Alvin Kraenzlein)

1. Alvin Kraenzlein	USA	15.4 OR
2. John McLean	USA	15.5

3. Frederick Moloney   USA   —
4. Jean Lécuyer   FRA   —
5. Norman Pritchard   IND   —

Alvin Kraenzlein won the first of his four gold medals at the 1900 Games. Kraenzlein was responsible for introducing the leg-extended style to hurdling.

1904 St. Louis C: 8, N: 2, D: 9.3. WR(120 yards): 15.2 (Alvin Kraenzlein)
1. Frederick Schule   USA   16.0
2. Thaddeus Shideler   USA   16.3
3. Lesley Ashburner   USA   16.4
4. Frank Castleman   USA   —

1906 Athens C: 15, N: 8, D: 5.1. WR(120 yards): 15.2 (Alvin Kraenzlein)
1. Robert Leavitt   USA   16.2
2. A.H. Healey   GBR   16.2
3. Vincent Duncker   SAF   16.3
4. Hugo Friend   USA   16.4
5. Henri Molinié   FRA   —

1908 London C: 25, N: 10, D: 7.25. WR(120 yards):15.2 (Alvin Kraenzlein)
1. Forrest Smithson   USA   15.0 WR
2. John Garrels   USA   15.7
3. Arthur Shaw   USA   —
4. William Rand   USA   —

Smithson, of Portland, Oregon, shot into the lead before the first hurdle and won by five yards.

1912 Stockholm C: 21, N: 9, D: 7.12. WR: 15.0 (Forrest Smithson)
1. Frederick Kelly   USA   15.1
2. James Wendell   USA   15.2
3. Martin Hawkins   USA   15.3
4. John Case   USA   15.3
5. Kenneth Powell   GBR   15.5
DNF: John Nicholson (USA)

1920 Antwerp C: 21, N: 13, D: 8.18. WR(120 yards): 14.4 (Earl Thomson)
1. Earl Thomson   CAN   14.8 WR
2. Harold Barron   USA   15.1
3. Frederick Murray   USA   15.2
4. Harry Wilson   NZE   15.3
5. Walker Smith   USA   —
6. Carl-Axel Christiernsson   SWE   —

Thomson was born in Saskatchewan, but grew up in Southern California from the age of 8. He represented Dartmouth in intercollegiate competition, but because he was still a Canadian citizen, he competed for Canada in the Olympics. Thomson, who survived a near-fatal rifle accident in 1914, took his hurdling very seriously, going so far as to tie his legs to the foot of his bed so that he wouldn't curl up and risk cramping. Thomson spent most of his life as a track coach, including 37 years as head coach of the

Navy team at Annapolis. His Olympic time of 14.8 seconds was accepted as a world record even though his 14.4 for the slightly shorter distance of 120 yards was much more impressive.

1924 Paris: C: 27, N: 15, D: 7.9. WR(120 yards): 14.4 (Earl Thomson)
1. Daniel Kinsey   USA   15.0
2. Sydney Atkinson   SAF   15.0
3. Sten Pettersson   SWE   15.4
4. Carl-Axel Christiernsson   SWE   15.5
5. Karl Anderson   USA   —
DISQ: George Guthrie (USA)

Atkinson was in the lead as he and Kinsey rose to clear the last hurdle. However, the South African clipped the barrier with his rear foot and stumbled. He recovered well, but lost by inches. Guthrie finished third, but was disqualified for knocking over three hurdles.

1928 Amsterdam C: 41, N: 24, D: 8.1. WR(120 yards): 14.4 (Earl Thomson)
1. Sydney Atkinson   SAF   14.8
2. Stephen Anderson   USA   14.8
3. John Collier   USA   14.9
4. Leighton Dye   USA   14.9
5. George Weightman-Smith   SAF   15.0
6. Frederick Gaby   GBR   15.2

In the semifinals, Weightman-Smith set a metric world record of 14.6 seconds. The finalists awaited the draw for lanes with great apprehension, as the inside lane had been severely chewed up by rain and overuse. It was Syd Atkinson, who had come so close to victory four years earlier, who drew the unwanted lane. However, Weightman-Smith walked over to his bitterly disappointed teammate and offered to switch lanes. Atkinson refused, but Weightman-Smith insisted, and the change was made. Taking full advantage of his reprieve, Atkinson finished first, while Weightman-Smith sloshed home in fifth place.

1932 Los Angeles C: 17, N: 10, D: 8.3. WR(120 yards): 14.2 (Percy Beard)
1. George Saling   USA   14.6
2. Percy Beard   USA   14.7
3. Donald Finlay   GBR   14.8
4. Jack Keller   USA   14.8
5. David Burghley   GBR   14.8
DISQ: Willi Welscher (GER)

Jack Keller won the first semifinal in 14.5 and George Saling the second in 14.4. In the final, Keller showed in front first, but hit the fifth hurdle, allowing Beard to move ahead. However, Beard hit the sixth hurdle. Saling then caught up and took the lead. He tripped on the ninth hurdle, but held on to win by a yard. Welscher finished fourth, but was disqualified for knocking over four hurdles, a prohibition that is no longer in the rules. For the first time in Olympic history, the results of a final were changed after a film of the race had been viewed. Originally Keller had been placed third and awarded the bronze medal. When the revised results were announced, Keller sought out Finlay in the Olympic Village and handed over the medal.

1936 Berlin C: 31, N: 20, D: 8.6. WR: 14.1 (Forrest Towns)
1. Forrest Towns   USA   14.2
2. Donald Finlay   GBR   14.4
3. Frederick Pollard USA   14.4
4. Håkan Lidman   SWE   14.4
5. John Thornton   GBR   14.7
6. Lawrence O'Connor CAN   15.0

Forrest "Spec" Towns of Georgia equaled his own world record of 14.1 in the semifinals and then skimmed to a two-yard victory in the final.

1948 London C: 28, N: 18, D: 8.4. WR(120 yards): 13.6 (Harrison Dillard)
1. William Porter   USA   13.9 OR
2. Clyde Scott   USA   14.1
3. Craig Dixon   USA   14.1
4. Alberto Triulzi ARG   14.6
5. Peter Gardner   AUS   —
6. Håkan Lidman   SWE   —

The absence of world record holder Harrison Dillard, eliminated at the U.S. trials, did not prevent the U.S. from sweeping the medals so decisively that the final appeared to be two separate races.

1952 Helsinki C: 30, N: 20, D: 7.24. WR: 13.5 (Richard Attlesey)
1. Harrison Dillard   USA   13.7 OR
2. Jack Davis   USA   13.7
3. Arthur Barnard   USA   14.1
4. Yevgeny Bulanchik   SOV   14.5
5. Kenneth Doubleday   AUS   14.7
6. Raymond Weinberg   AUS   14.8

In 1948 Harrison Dillard was the unquestioned world champion of the high hurdles. However, he lost his stride in the U.S. Olympic trials and failed to finish. He did qualify in the 100-meter dash and went on to win the gold medal. Despite this unexpected triumph, he still wanted to earn an Olympic victory in the hurdles. Four years later, at the age of 29, Dillard got his chance. He was hard-pressed by Jack Davis, who knocked down the ninth hurdle, allowing Dillard to achieve the victory "on which I had set my heart." The usually calm Dillard jumped for joy and exclaimed, "Good things come to those who wait."

1956 Melbourne C: 24, N: 15, D: 11.26. WR: 13.4 (Jack Davis)
1. Lee Calhoun   USA   13.5 OR
2. Jack Davis   USA   13.5
3. Joel Shankle   USA   14.1
4. Martin Lauer   GER   14.5
5. Stanko Lorger   YUG   14.5
6. Boris Stolyarov SOV   14.6

Once again, if each nation had not been limited to three entrants, the final would probably have been an all-American affair. Running into a 1.9 miles per second wind, Calhoun and Davis were even by the eighth hurdle. Using a lunge that he had learned from Davis, Calhoun got his shoulder across the finish line inches ahead. For the second straight time, Jack Davis had recorded the same time as the winner yet had been forced to settle for a silver medal.

1960 Rome C: 36, N: 21 D: 9.5. WR: 13.2 (Martin Lauer, Lee Calhoun)
1. Lee Calhoun   USA   13.8
2. Willie May   USA   13.8
3. Hayes Jones   USA   14.0
4. Martin Lauer   GER   14.0
5. Keith Gardner   JAM   14.4
6. Valentin Chistyakov SOV   14.6

Lee Calhoun had to sit out the 1958 season after being suspended for receiving gifts on the television game show *Bride and Groom*. He was back in uniform in 1960, winning his second gold medal with the same lunge that he had used to win four years earlier, and United States hurdlers achieved their fourth consecutive sweep. Calhoun is the only athlete to win the Olympic high hurdles twice.

1964 Tokyo C: 37, N: 23, D: 10.18. WR: 13.2 (Martin Lauer, Lee Calhoun)
1. Hayes Jones   USA   13.6
2. H. Blaine Lindgren   USA   13.7
3. Anatoly Mikhailov   SOV   13.7
4. Eddy Ottoz   ITA   13.8
5. Gurbachan Randhawa Singh   IND   14.0
6. Marcel Duriez   FRA   14.0
7. Giovanni Cornacchia   ITA   14.1
8. Giorgio Mazza   ITA   14.1

A U.S. sweep was prevented when Willie Davenport, the surprise winner of the U.S. Olympic trials, succumbed to a leg injury and was eliminated in the semifinals. Jones and Lindgren ran evenly for almost the entire race, but Lindgren started his lean too early and was nipped at the tape.

1968 Mexico City C: 33, N: 23, D: 10.17. WR: 13.2 (Martin Lauer, Lee Calhoun, Earl McCullouch)
1. Willie Davenport   USA   13.3 OR
2. Ervin Hall   USA   13.4
3. Eddy Ottoz   ITA   13.4
4. Leon Coleman   USA   13.6
5. Werner Trzmiel   GER   13.6
6. Bo Forssander   SWE   13.7
7. Marcel Duriez   FRA   13.7
8. Pierre Schoebel   FRA   14.0

In 1968, 19 of the world's top 25 high hurdlers were from the United States. Since 1964, Willie Davenport had struggled through four years of injuries to gain another chance at an Olympic gold medal. He was so nervous before the start of the final that he almost fell while taking off his sweat pants, and he never even heard the starter say, "set." Yet "from the first step, the gun," he said, "I knew I had won the race. It was perhaps the only race I ever ran that way, but that first step was so perfect—right on the money. I coasted over the last three hurdles thinking, "It's over, it's over." His time of 13.3 equaled the Olympic record set by Erv Hall in the semifinals.

1972 Munich C: 39, N: 27, D: 9.7. WR: 13.2 (Martin Lauer, Lee Calhoun, Earl McCullouch, Willie Davenport); WR (120 yards): 13.0 (Rodney Milburn)

1. Rodney Milburn	USA	13.24 EWR
2. Guy Drut	FRA	13.34
3. Thomas Hill	USA	13.48
4. Willie Davenport	USA	13.50
5. Frank Siebeck	GBR	13.71
6. Leszek Wodzyński	POL	13.72
7. Lubomir Nadenicek	CZE	13.76
8. Petr Cech	CZE	13.86

Rod Milburn almost pulled a Harrison Dillard in 1972. After going undefeated in 1971 and winning 27 consecutive finals, he hit two hurdles in the U.S. Olympic trials and barely qualified in third place. However, in Munich his superiority was absolute. He was first over the first hurdle and almost two meters in front by the sixth hurdle, winning by one meter over fast-closing Guy Drut.

1976 Montreal C: 23, N: 17, D: 7.28. WR: 13.0 (Guy Drut)

1. Guy Drut	FRA	13.30
2. Alejandro Casañas Ramirez	CUB	13.33
3. Willie Davenport	USA	13.38
4. Charles Foster	USA	13.41
5. Thomas Munkelt	GBR	13.44
6. James Owens	USA	13.73
7. Vyacheslav Kulebyakin	SOV	13.93
8. Victor Myasnikov	SOV	13.94

Early in 1975 Guy Drut predicted that he would win the Olympics in a time of 13.28. By 1976 he was under so much pressure from French sports fans that he was forced to train in secret. The son of a French father and an English mother, he was born in Oignies, on the same street as France's last male track and field medalist, Michel Jazy. Drut got off to a good start, took a slight lead after the third hurdle and held it the rest of the way. He was the first person from a non-English-speaking country to win the high hurdles. Drut was an excellent all-around athlete, whose other feats included pole-vaulting 17 feet 3/4 inches, long-jumping 24 feet 1/2 inches, and high-jumping 6 feet 7 inches.

Thirty-three-year-old bronze medalist Willie Davenport was competing in his fourth Olympics. In 1980 he also took part in the Winter Olympics, in the four-man bobsled event.

1980 Moscow C: 22, N: 16, D: 7.27. WR: 13.00 (Renaldo Nehemiah)

1. Thomas Munkelt	GDR	13.39
2. Alejandro Casañas Ramirez	CUB	13.40
3. Aleksandr Puchkov	SOV	13.44
4. Andrei Prokofev	SOV	13.49
5. Jan Pusty	POL	13.68
6. Arto Bryggare	FIN	13.76
7. Javier Moracho	SPA	13.78
8. Yuri Chervanev	SOV	15.80

Renaldo Nehemiah, Dedy Cooper, and Greg Foster of the United States would have been favorites to finish at least first and second. Without them, the winning time was the slowest since 1964. Thomas Munkelt, a good-humored 27-year-old dental student, commented before the final, "I will drill through my opposition." He ended up winning by the skin of his teeth. Alejandro Casañas, having lost in 1976 by 0.03 seconds, experienced the frustration of coming even closer in 1980—0.01 seconds.

400-METER HURDLES

Contestants in this event must clear ten 3-foot hurdles.

1896 not held

1900 Paris C: 5, N: 4, D: 7.15. WR(440 yards): 57.2 (Godfrey Shaw)

1. John Walter Tewksbury	USA	57.6
2. Henri Tauzin	FRA	58.3
3. George Orton	CAN/USA	—
4. William Lewis	USA	—

The results were a great disappointment to the French, since this event was unfamiliar to the Americans. This didn't prevent Tewksbury from easily defeating the previously unbeaten Tauzin. The "hurdles" were actually 30-foot-long telephone poles. A water jump was added just before the finish.

1904 St. Louis C: 4, N: 1, D: 8.31. WR(440 yards): 57.2 (Godfrey Shaw)

1. Harry Hillman	USA	53.0
2. Frank Waller	USA	53.2
3. George Poage	USA	—
4. George Varnell	USA	—

An oddity in the world of U.S. athletics, Harry Hillman was a 22-year-old bank teller who had never attended college. Writing in the September 1905 issue of *Physical Culture* magazine, Hillman advised aspiring hurdlers to avoid candy, pastries, tobacco and meat, although he did recommend swallowing whole raw eggs, which he claimed were "excellent for the wind and stomach." He concluded by advising young men in the business world to take up athletics because it "gives one the needed virility demanded by modern business life." Hillman's time was not allowed as a world record because he tipped over one hurdle, and because the hurdles were only 2 feet 6 inches high anyway. George Poage was the first black runner to win an Olympic medal. On April 24, 1909, Harry Hillman and Lawson Robertson set a world record of 11.0 seconds in the 100-yard three-legged race.

1906 not held

1908 London C: 15, N: 6, D: 7.22. WR(440 yards): 57.2 (Godfrey Shaw)
1. Charles Bacon   USA   55.0 WR
2. Harry Hillman   USA   55.3
3. Leonard Tremeer   GBR   57.0
DNF: Leslie Burton (GBR)

Bacon won a close and exciting contest despite the fact that he went over a hurdle in the wrong lane midway through the race. When the judges measured the course he had taken, they discovered that he had actually run farther than if he had stayed in his own lane, so he was saved from disqualification.

1912 not held

1920 Antwerp C: 21, N: 10, D: 8.16. WR(440 yards): 54.2 (John Norton)
1. Frank Loomis   USA   54.0 WR
2. John Norton   USA   54.3
3. August Desch   USA   54.5
4. George "Géo" André   FRA   54.6
5. Carl-Axel Christiernsson SWE   54.9
6. Charles Daggs   USA   —

Fourth-place finisher Géo André had won a silver medal in the high jump in 1908.

1924 Paris C: 23, N: 13, D: 7.7. WR: 54.0 (Frank Loomis)
1. F. Morgan Taylor   USA   52.6
2. Erik Vilén   FIN   53.8 OR
3. Ivan Riley   USA   54.2
4. George "Géo" André   FRA   56.2
DISQ: Charles Brookins (USA), F.J. Blackett (GBR)

Taylor's world record time was not allowed because he knocked down one hurdle, thus violating the rules of that time. Brookins finished second, but was disqualified for running out of his lane and clearing a hurdle improperly. Consequently, it was Erik Vilén who was credited with an Olympic record, even though he finished only third.

1928 Amsterdam C: 27, N: 16, D: 7.30. WR: 52.0 (F. Morgan Taylor)
1. David Burghley   GBR   53.4 OR
2. Frank Cuhel   USA   53.6
3. F. Morgan Taylor   USA   53.6
4. Sten Pettersson   SWE   53.8
5. Thomas Livingstone-Learmonth GBR   54.2
6. Luigi Facelli   ITA   55.8

Lord David George Brownlow Cecil Burghley was one of the most popular winners of the 1928 Games. Heir to the Marquess of Exeter, he first appeared in the Olympics in 1924, when he was eliminated in the first round of the 110-meter hurdles. In 1927, during his last year at Cambridge, he caused a sensation by running around the Great Court at Trinity College in the time it took the Trinity Clock to toll 12 o'clock. A completely distorted version of this event was presented in the film *Chariots of Fire*, in which the feat is credited to Harold Abrahams. For this reason, Lord Burghley, who was then 76 years old, reportedly refused to view the film. Actually, Lord Burghley was not the first person to accomplish the Great Court run. It had been done in the 1890s by Sir Walter Borley Fletcher, but in Sir Walter's time the clock took five more seconds to complete its toll.

Burghley was an extremely colorful character, who once set another unusual record by racing around the upper promenade deck of the ocean liner *Queen Mary* in 57 seconds, dressed in street clothes. Once he showed up for a meet in Antwerp, but was denied admission at the main gate, and told to circle the stadium and enter by the competitors' gate. Burghley took a few steps back, tightened his bowler hat on his head, got a firm grip on his attaché case, hurdled the four-foot fence, and dashed off before the astonished guards could react. He was elected to Parliament in 1931, but was granted a leave of absence to compete in the 1932 Olympics in Los Angeles. He later served as governor of Bermuda for three years, as well as president of the International Amateur Athletic Federation for 30 years. He was also chairman of the Organizing Committee of the 1948 Olympics.

1932 Los Angeles C: 18, N: 13, D: 8.1. WR: 52.0 (F. Morgan Taylor)
1. Robert Tisdall   IRL   51.7
2. Glenn Hardin   USA   51.9 WR
3. F. Morgan Taylor   USA   52.0
4. David Burghley   GBR   52.2
5. Luigi Facelli   ITA   53.0
6. Johan Kjell Areskoug SWE   54.6

Bob Tisdall, a well-known athlete while a student at Cambridge, had run the 400-meter hurdles only once when, in March 1932, he decided to try out for the Irish Olympic team. He quit his job in London and, with his wife, moved into a converted railway carriage in an orchard in Sussex, where he spent the next three months training, although he had no hurdles to practice with. He won a match race in early June and then, on June 18, finished first in the All-Ireland Championships in a time of 54.2 seconds. Less than a month later he was on his way to Los Angeles with the rest of the Irish team. Weakened by the two-week journey, he stayed in bed for 15 hours a day until the morning of his first-round heat. Full of energy, he qualified easily. In the semifinals, he surprised even himself by winning in 52.8, equaling the Olympic record that had been set by Glenn Hardin in the first semi. The final was only Tisdall's seventh race at the distance, and he faced not only Hardin, but former champions Morgan Taylor and Lord Burghley as well. Completely relaxed, Tisdall took the lead early and approached the last hurdle five yards ahead of the others. However, he mistimed his leap, knocked over the barrier, and stumbled for five or six yards before regaining his balance. Hardin and Taylor closed fast, but Tisdall beat them to the tape in world record time. According to the rules of the day, which were not changed until 1938, his record was disallowed because he had failed to clear the final barrier. So Glenn Hardin entered the record books as world record holder even though he only finished second.

1936 Berlin C: 32, N: 20, D: 8.4. WR: 50.6 (Glenn Hardin)

1. Glenn Hardin	USA	52.4
2. John Loaring	CAN	52.7
3. Miguel White	PHI	52.8
4. Joseph Patterson	USA	53.0
5. Sylvio de Magalhães Padilha	BRA	54.0
6. Christos Mantikas	GRE	54.2

On July 26, 1934, while running in Stockholm, Glenn Hardin of Louisiana took a full second off the existing world record. His time of 50.6 was not beaten for more than 19 years. Following his second-place finish in the 1932 Olympics, Hardin never lost another race. In Berlin, he caught the fading Joe Patterson in the stretch and won by four yards.

1948 London C: 25, N: 17, D: 7.31. WR: 50.6 (Glenn Hardin)

1. Roy Cochran	USA	51.1 OR
2. Duncan White	SRL	51.8
3. Rune Larsson	SWE	52.2
4. Richard Ault	USA	52.4
5. Yves Cros	FRA	53.3
6. Ottavio Missoni	ITA	54.0

1952 Helsinki C: 40, N: 24, D: 7.21. WR: 50.6 (Glenn Hardin)

1. Charles Moore	USA	50.8 OR
2. Yuri Lituyev	SOV	51.3
3. John Holland	NZE	52.2
4. Anatoly Yulin	SOV	52.8
5. Harry Whittle	GBR	53.1
6. Armando Filiput	ITA	54.4

Remarkably, the six finalists cleared the first five hurdles in unison. Then Moore, whose father had been an alternate on the 1924 U.S. Olympic team, pulled ahead. Lituyev drew even by the eighth hurdle, but Moore moved ahead again and won by four yards. Moore's near-world record time was quite extraordinary considering that the track had been soaked by rain. He also ran 50.8 in the semifinals.

1956 Melbourne C: 28, N: 13, D: 11.24. WR: 49.5 (Glenn Davis)

1. Glenn Davis	USA	50.1 OR
2. Silas "Eddie" Southern	USA	50.8
3. Joshua Culbreath	USA	51.6
4. Yuri Lituyev	SOV	51.7
5. David Lean	AUS	51.8
6. Gerhardus Potgieter	SAF	56.0

On June 29, at the U.S. Olympic trials, Glenn Davis set a world record of 49.5, pressed by Eddie Southern, who ran 49.7. In Melbourne Southern set an Olympic record of 50.1 in the semifinals, then set the pace in the final. Davis caught him midway and surged ahead at the seventh hurdle to win decisively.

1960 Rome C: 34, N: 23, D: 9.2. WR: 49.2 (Glenn Davis)

1. Glenn Davis	USA	49.3 OR
2. Clifton Cushman	USA	49.6
3. Richard Howard	USA	49.7
4. Helmut Janz	GER	49.9
5. Jussi Rintamäki	FIN	50.8
6. Bruno Galliker	SWI	51.0

"Running scared" in what was to be his last race (other than the 4×400 relay a few days later), Glenn Davis ran off stride until the seventh hurdle, when he regained his poise, passed Janz at the ninth hurdle and Howard at the tenth, to win by two meters. Silver medalist Cliff Cushman was lost in action in Vietnam in 1966. Bronze medalist Dick Howard died of a heroin overdose in 1967. They were 28 and 32 years old, respectively.

1964 Tokyo C: 39, N: 25, D: 10.16. WR: 49.1 (Warren "Rex" Cawley)

1. Warren "Rex" Cawley	USA	49.6
2. John Cooper	GBR	50.1
3. Salvatore Morale	ITA	50.1
4. Gary Knoke	AUS	50.4
5. James Luck	USA	50.5
6. Roberto Frinolli	ITA	50.7
7. Vasily Anisimov	SOV	51.1
8. Wilfried Geeroms	BEL	51.4

Rex Cawley ran off stride until the sixth hurdle, and was still three yards behind Frinolli at the eighth hurdle. Then the world record holder turned on his speed and pulled away to a clear victory. Silver medalist John Cooper was one of the 346 people who died in the famous Turkish Air Lines plane crash over France on March 3, 1974. He was 33 years old.

1968 Mexico City C: 30, N: 24, D: 10.15. WR: 48.8 (Geoffrey Vanderstock)

1. David Hemery	GBR	48.12 WR
2. Gerhard Hennige	GER	49.0
3. John Sherwood	GBR	49.0
4. Geoffry Vanderstock	USA	49.0
5. Vyacheslav Skomorokhov	SOV	49.1
6. Ronald Whitney	USA	49.2
7. Rainer Schubert	GER	49.2
8. Roberto Frinolli	ITA	50.1

The 1968 final had all the makings of a spectacular race. The favorites were world record holder Geoff Vanderstock, fellow American Ron Whitney, and David Hemery, who had beaten Vanderstock at the N.C.A.A. championships. Hemery, although born in England, had spent 10 of his 24 years in the United States. Other finalists included John Sherwood, whose wife, Sheila, had won a silver medal in the long jump the day before, Vyacheslav Skomorokhov, who was deaf, and 1964 finalist Roberto Frinolli, who had stripped down to his bikini-style black jock strap before the race, unaware that he was being shown live on U.S. television. Hemery was in Lane 6, just inside Ron Whitney, the man he most feared because of his strong finishing kick.

Frinolli and Vanderstock were off quickest, but Hemery had taken the lead by the third hurdle. He passed the halfway mark in 23.3 and demoralized the rest of the field with an awesome display of speed in which he gained at least a yard between and over each of the next five hurdles. He crossed the finish line with an eight-yard lead, the largest winning margin since 1924. While millions of people around the world marveled at his extraordinary performance, Hemery himself wasn't even sure he had won. He had looked to his right at the end to check for Ron Whitney, but had failed to look to his left. It wasn't until he was approached by a BBC camera crew that his uncertainty was erased. At the victory ceremony, Hemery received his gold medal from David Burghley, who had won the same event 40 years earlier.

Final mention should be made of U.S. hurdler Boyd Gittins, who was eliminated at the U.S. Olympic semitrials when a pigeon dropping hit him in the eye and dislodged his contact lens just before the first hurdle. Fortunately, he won a runoff to qualify for the final Olympic trials, and then made the team. Unfortunately, a leg injury forced him to withdraw from his first-round heat.

1972 Munich C: 37, N: 25, D: 9.2. WR: 48.12 (David Hemery)

1. John Akii-Bua	UGA	47.82 WR
2. Ralph Mann	USA	48.51
3. David Hemery	GBR	48.52
4. James Seymour	USA	48.64
5. Rainer Schubert	GER	49.65
6. Yevgeny Gavrilenko	SOV	49.66
7. Stavros Tziortzis	GRE	49.66
8. Yuri Zorin	SOV	50.25

The second semifinal was filled with misfortune. James Seymour and Australia's Gary Knoke, running in the two outside lanes, mistook the echo of the starter's gun for a second shot and thought a false start had been declared. Seymour, in Lane 7, realized his mistake quickly enough to avoid disaster and win the heat anyway, but Knoke, in Lane 8, was unable to recover, and finished last. As the runners cleared the tenth hurdle, East Germany's Christian Rudolph, in Lane 1, stumbled and fell heavily into Lane 2, right into the path of Dieter-Wolfgang Büther of West Germany, who also fell. Neither man was able to finish. The judges decided not to order a rerun, since Büther was only in fifth place at the time of the mishap.

In the final David Hemery actually set an even faster pace than he had in Mexico City, covering the first 200 meters in 22.8 seconds. Thus it came as quite shock when he discovered that John Akii-Bua, running in Lane 1, was right beside him with 100 meters to go. Akii-Bua surged ahead between the eighth and ninth hurdles and won by six meters. Despite the fact that he had just set a world record, Uganda's first gold medalist kept right on going over the next two flights of hurdles. Akii-Bua, who was also Uganda's decathlon champion, said that he was "scared to death" when he learned that he had drawn Lane 1. "When you are in Lane 1," he said, "you are always the loser. I couldn't sleep that night." Akii-Bua's father had eight wives and 43 children, 29 of whom were still alive in 1972. A police instructor, John Akii-Bua fled Uganda in 1979, following the overthrow of Idi Amin, and spent a month in a Kenyan jail before he was recognized and released.

1976 Montreal C: 22, N: 16, D: 7.25. WR: 47.82 (John Akii-Bua)

1. Edwin Moses	USA	47.64 WR
2. Michael Shine	USA	48.69
3. Yevgeny Gavrilenko	SOV	49.45
4. Quentin Wheeler	USA	49.86
5. José Carvalho	POR	49.94
6. Yanko Bratanov	BUL	50.03
7. Damaso Alfonso	CUB	50.19
8. Alan Pascoe	GBR	51.29

The African boycott prevented a potentially historic showdown. No matter how sympathetic one is to the movement to bring self-determination for blacks in South Africa, it is difficult to not be cynical when you realize that John Akii-Bua was not allowed to compete in Montreal because the leader of his nation's government, Idi Amin, was offended by human rights violations in another country.

With Akii-Bua gone and Alan Pascoe still recovering from a leg injury, the competition turned into a one-man show. Edwin Moses, a 20-year-old physics major at Morehouse College in Atlanta, had entered only one 400-meter hurdles race before March 27, 1976. Thus the Olympics was his first international meet. Moses wore down his last challenger Yevgeny Gavrilenko, by the seventh hurdle and won by eight meters, the largest winning margin in the history of the event. Afterward, Moses said that his major regret was that training for the Olympics had interfered with his studies, allowing his grade-point average to dip to 3.57.

1980 Moscow C: 22, N: 19, D: 7.26. WR: 47.13 (Edwin Moses)

1. Volker Beck	GDR	48.70
2. Vassily Arkhipenko	SOV	48.86
3. Gary Oakes	GBR	49.11
4. Nicolai Vassilev	SOV	49.34
5. Rok Kopitar	YUG	49.67
6. Horia Toboc	ROM	49.84
7. Franz Meier	SWI	50.00
8. Yanko Bratanov	BUL	56.35

The year 1980 saw a severely devalued competition as a result of the Jimmy Carter boycott. The preboycott favorite, Edwin Moses, set a world record of 47.13 on July 3, three weeks before the Olympics. The silver medal had been expected to be a toss-up among Harald Schmid of West Germany and James Walker and David Lee of the United States. In their absence, Volker Beck passed Arkhipenko on the run-in to win the closest 400-meter hurdles final in Olympic history. His winning time was the slowest since 1964. As of September 1983 Edwin Moses has won 87 straight races.

3000-METER STEEPLECHASE

In the steeplechase, runners must negotiate a course of 28 hurdles and 7 water jumps. The hurdles are 3 feet high and are solid, so that they can not be knocked over. The tops of the hurdles are 5 inches wide, allowing the contestants to step on them. The water jump, which is preceded by a hedge, is 12 feet long, with a maximum depth of 2 feet 3½ inches. The steeplechase event appears to have been introduced in Edinburgh in 1828, although the distance was not standardized at 3000 meters until 1920.

1896 not held

1900 Paris C: 6, N: 6, D: 7.2.
(2500 Meters)
1. George Orton	CAN/USA	7:34.4
2. Sidney Robinson	GBR	7:38.0
3. Jacques Chastanié	FRA	—
4. Arthur Newton	USA	—
5. Hermann Wraschtil	AUT	—
6. Franz Duhne	GER	—

1904 St. Louis C: 7, N: 2, D: 8.29.
(2590 Meters)
1. James Lightbody	USA	7:39.6
2. John Daly	IRL	7:40.6
3. Arthur Newton	USA	—
4. W. Frank Verner	USA	—

Lightbody came from behind to win the first of his three gold medals at St. Louis.

1906 not held

1908 London C: 24, N: 6, D: 7.18.
(3200 Meters)
1. Arthur Russell	GBR	10:47.8
2. Archie Robertson	GBR	10:48.4
3. John Eisele	USA	—
4. C. Guy Holdaway	GBR	—
5. H. Sewell	GBR	—
6. William Galbraith	CAN	—

A rather unusual controversy developed during the heats, when some of the American runners showed up wearing white shorts, which were prohibited by A.A.A. rules. They were finally allowed to compete after they had been provided with dark shorts. Russell and Robertson cleared the last hurdle together in the final, but Russell won by two yards in the run-in.

1912 not held

1920 Antwerp C: 16, N: 6, D: 8.20. WR: 9:49.8 (Josef Ternström)
1. Percy Hodge	GBR	10:00.4 OR
2. Patrick Flynn	USA	—
3. Ernesto Ambrosini	ITA	—
4. Gustaf Mattsson	SWE	—
5. Michael Devaney	USA	—
6. Albert Hulsebosch	USA	—
7. Lars Hedvall	SWE	—
8. Raymond Watson	USA	—

The 29-year-old Hodge won easily by 100 yards. Earlier in the year he had entered the A.A.A. steeplechase championship. In the second lap of that race, he was spiked and lost the heel of his shoe. Hodge stopped running, took off his shoe, readjusted and relaced it, and then took off again. He won by 60 yards.

1924 Paris C: 21, N: 9, D: 7.9. WR: 9:33.6 (Paul Bontemps)
1. Vilho "Ville" Ritola	FIN	9:33.6 EWR
2. Elias Katz	FIN	9:44.0
3. Paul Bontemps	FRA	9:45.2
4. E. Marvin Rick	USA	9:56.4
5. Karl Ebb	FIN	9:57.6
6. Evelyn Montague	GBR	—
7. Michael Devaney	USA	—
8. A. Isola	FRA	10:14.9

Paul Bontemps had run a 9:33.4 on June 9, 1924, but was unable to repeat his performance one month later at the Olympics, as Ville Ritola won by 75 meters. Sixth-place finisher Evelyn Aubrey Montague is introduced in the film *Chariots of Fire* as a good friend of Harold Abrahams, whose acquaintance he makes when they both arrive at Cambridge as freshmen. In reality, Abrahams and Montague were rivals, since Montague attended not Cambridge, but Oxford.

1928 Amsterdam C: 22, N: 10, D: 8.4. WR: 9:33.4 (Paul Bontemps)
1. Toivo Loukola	FIN	9:21.8 WR
2. Paavo Nurmi	FIN	9:31.2
3. Ove Andersen	FIN	9:35.6
4. Nils Eklöf	SWE	9:38.0
5. Henri Dartigues	FRA	9:40.0
6. Lucien Duquesne	FRA	9:40.6
7. Melvin Dalton	USA	—
8. W.O. Spencer	USA	—

In the second heat of the qualifying round, Paavo Nurmi fell head over heels into the first water jump and had to be fished out by Lucien Duquesne. Nurmi repaid Duquesne's kindness by pacing him for the rest of the race, the two finishing together. The final marked the last Olympic appearances of Nurmi and Ville Ritola, both of whom were exhausted from their duel in the 5000 meters final the previous day. Ritola dropped out 600 yards short of the finish, but Nurmi held on grimly and placed second, 60 yards behind Toivo Loukola. Five years earlier Loukola had been declared unfit for military service because he had tuberculosis. He had then returned home and taken up running to restore his health.

1932 Los Angeles C: 15, N: 8, D: 8.6. WR: 9:08.4 (George Lermond)
(3460 Meters)
1. Volmari Iso-Hollo	FIN	10:33.4
2. Thomas Evenson	GBR	10:46.0
3. Joseph McCluskey	USA	10:46.2
4. Martti Matilainen	FIN	10:52.4
5. George Bailey	GBR	10:53.2
6. Glen Dawson	USA	—
7. Giuseppe Lippi	ITA	—
8. Walter Pritchard	USA	—

Volmari Iso-Hollo, a 25-year-old typesetter, crossed the finish line with a 40-yard lead, only to discover that there was no tape awaiting him and that the lap counter still read "1." He continued on for an extra lap and won by 75 yards. It was later determined that the lap checker, a substitute for the regular man, who was ill, had forgotten to change the lap count the first time the runners passed by. It didn't make any difference to Iso-Hollo, but the blunder had a profound effect on who won the silver medal. At the end of the regulation distance, McCluskey was in second place and Evenson in third. But during the extra lap Evenson passed McCluskey and beat him to the finish by two yards. This potentially sticky situation was resolved when McCluskey declined to lodge a protest, stating that "a race has only one finish line" and that he was quite satisfied with his bronze medal.

1936 Berlin C: 28, N: 13, D: 8.8. WR: 9:08.2 (Harold Manning)
1. Volmari Iso-Hollo	FIN	9:03.8 WR
2. Kaarlo Tuominen	FIN	9:06.8
3. Alfred Dompert	GER	9:07.2
4. Martti Matilainen	FIN	9:09.0
5. Harold Manning	USA	9:11.2
6. Lars Larsson	SWE	9:16.6
7. W. Wihtols	LAT	9:18.8
8. Glen Dawson	USA	9:21.2

1948 London C: 26, N: 12, D: 8.5. WR: 8:59.6 (Erik Elmsater)
1. Thore Sjöstrand	SWE	9:04.6
2. Erik Elmsäter	SWE	9:08.2
3. Göte Hagström	SWE	9:11.8
4. Alex Guyodo	FRA	9:13.6
5. Pentti Siltaloppi	FIN	9:19.6
6. Petar Šegedin	YUG	9:20.4
7. H. Browning Ross	USA	9:23.2
8. C. Miranda Justo	SPA	9:25.0

The only runner given a chance of defeating the Swedes was the European champion, Raphael Pujazon of France. However Pujazon developed a stomach cramp midway through the final and was forced to retire.

1952 Helsinki C: 35, N: 12, D: 7.25. WR: 8:48.6 (Vladimir Kazantsev)
1. Horace Ashenfelter	USA	8:45.4 WR
2. Vladimir Kazantsev	SOV	8:51.6
3. John Disley	GBR	8:51.8
4. Olavi Rinteenpää	FIN	8:55.2
5. Curt Söderberg	SWE	8:55.6
6. Günther Hesselmann	GER	8:55.8
7. Mikhail Saltykov	SOV	8:56.2
8. Helmut Gude	GER	9:01.4

Twenty-seven-year-old F.B.I. agent Horace Ashenfelter of Glen Ridge, New Jersey, caused something of a stir when he won his preliminary heat in 8:51.0. Not only was it the fastest time of the round, but Ashenfelter's previous best had been an undistinguished 9:06.4. Still, it seemed unlikely that Ashenfelter, who had trained at night, using park benches as hurdles, could seriously challenge world record holder Vladimir Kazantsev. Mikhail Saltykov was the early leader in the final, but before the third lap had ended, Ashenfelter had moved ahead, followed closely by Kazantsev. They continued running together until the final lap. With half a lap to go, Kazantsev forged ahead, and it looked like the race was his. But Kazantsev stumbled slightly at the final water jump, while Ashenfelter breezed through without even breaking stride. Kazantsev had run out of energy, and Ashenfelter pulled away dramatically over the last 150 meters to win by almost 30 yards. Gleeful American sportswriters had a field day—it was the first time that an F.B.I. man had allowed himself to be followed by a Russian.

1956 Melbourne C: 23, N: 13, D: 11.29. WR: 8:35.6 (Semyon Rzhischin)
1. Christopher Brasher	GBR	8:41.2 OR
2. Sándor Rozsnyól	HUN	8:43.6
3. Ernst Larsen	NOR	8:44.0
4. Heinz Laufer	GER	8:44.4
5. Semyon Rzhischin	SOV	8:44.6
6. John Disley	GBR	8:44.6
7. Neil Robbins	AUS	8:50.0
8. Eric Shirley	GBR	8:57.0

Larsen led until two laps from the finish, after which Rzhischin surged ahead. Entering the final curve, Rozsnyói made his move, with Larsen at his shoulder. As they approached the fourth-to-last hurdle, Rozsnyói swung wide to give himself room to clear. Chris Brasher, a 28-year-old oil company executive, saw his chance, elbowed his way between the two leaders, and sprinted away to an unexpected 15-yard victory. Twelve minutes later came an announcement that Brasher had been disqualified for interfering with Larsen. However Larsen made it clear that although he had been bumped, he considered the incident insignificant, and not worthy of disqualification. Rozsnyói, who was considerably more concerned about the fact that he hadn't heard from his wife or children since Soviet troops had invaded Hungary, also supported Brasher. Three hours later, the Jury of Appeal voted unanimously to rescind the disqualification, giving Great Britain its first track and field gold medal since 1936.

1960 Rome C: 32, N: 20, D: 9.3. WR: 8:31.4 (Zdzislaw Krzyszkowiak)

1. Zdzislaw Krzyszkowiak	POL	8:34.2 OR
2. Nikolai Sokolov	SOV	8:36.4
3. Semyon Rzhischin	SOV	8:42.2
4. Gaston Roelants	BEL	8:47.6
5. Gunnar Tjörnebo	SWE	8:58.6
6. Ludwig Müller	GER	9:01.6
7. Charles "Deacon" Jones	USA	9:18.2
8. Aleksei Konov	SOV	9:18.2

The three Soviet runners ran a team race, hoping to wear down Krzyszkowiak. It didn't work. The 31-year-old Polish world record holder glided past Sokolov on the final backstretch and won by 15 yards.

1964 Tokyo C: 29, N: 19, D: 10.17. WR: 8:29.6 (Gaston Roelants)

1. Gaston Roelants	BEL	8:30.8 OR
2. Maurice Herriott	GBR	8:32.4
3. Yvan Belyayev	SOV	8:33.8
4. Manuel de Oliveira	POR	8:36.2
5. George Young	USA	8:38.2
6. Guy Texereau	FRA	8:38.6
7. Adolfas Alekseunas	SOV	8:39.0
8. Lars-Erik Gustafsson	SWE	8:41.8

Ahead by five yards after the first lap, Gaston Roelants broke away from the field and led by 50 yards at the start of the bell lap. Maurice Herriott closed the gap in the final lap, but fell 10 yards short. Between 1961 and 1966 Roelants won 45 straight steeplechase finals. In 1977, at the age of 40, he was clocked in 8:41.5.

1968 Mexico City C: 37, N: 26, D: 10.16. WR: 8:24.2 (Jouko Kuha)

1. Amos Biwott	KEN	8:51.0
2. Benjamin Kogo	KEN	8:51.6
3. George Young	USA	8:51.8
4. Kerry O'Brien	AUS	8:52.0
5. Aleksandr Morozov	SOV	8:55.8
6. Mikhail Chelev	BUL	8:58.4
7. Gaston Roelants	BEL	8:59.4
8. Arne Risa	NOR	9:09.0

No one except the most fanatic track fans had ever heard of Amos Biwott before the 1968 Olympics. But the 20-year-old Kenyan literally leaped to prominence in the third and final elimination heat. Apparently unaware of either racing tactics or steeplechase techniques, Biwott sprinted to a 30-yard lead in the first half lap and led by 70 yards before the first lap had been completed. But what really made the crowd go wild was Biwott's bizarre method of clearing the water jump. Contradicting the teachings of every coach in the world, he would jump onto the hedge and then hop over the water, triple-jump-style, landing on dry ground with the same foot he used to take off. His hurdle style was also unique: he jumped over the barriers with his feet together. In the words of Joe Henderson of *Track and Field News,* "He cleared the hurdles like he feared they had spikes imbedded on the top and leaped the water hazard as if he thought crocodiles were swimming in it." Despite his unorthodox approach, Biwott won his heat by 11.6 seconds.

Naturally, there was a great deal of curiosity as to how well Biwott would stand up in the final two days later against favorites Ben Kogo, Victor Kudinsky, and George Young. Surprisingly, Biwott started slowly, letting Kogo do most of the pace-setting. Unfortunately, Kudinsky withdrew with a hip injury during the second lap. With two laps to go, Gaston Roelants took the lead, while Biwott lingered in ninth place. By the start of the last lap, Kogo was back in the lead. Then, with 300 meters left, Young made his move, passing Kogo on the backstretch. Kogo fought him off, but out of nowhere came Amos Biwott. Kogo was still in front as they cleared the last hurdle, 60 meters from the finish, but Biwott loped right by him and won by three yards.

1972 Munich C: 49, N: 29, D: 9.4. WR: 8:22.0 (Kerry O'Brien)

1. H. Kipchoge Keino	KEN	8:23.6 OR
2. Benjamin Jipcho	KEN	8:24.6
3. Tapio Kantanen	FIN	8:24.8
4. Bronislaw Malinowski	POL	8:28.0
5. Dušan Moravčik	CZE	8:29.2
6. Amos Biwott	KEN	8:33.6
7. Romualdas Bite	SOV	8:34.6
8. Pekka Paivarinta	FIN	8:37.2

The second preliminary heat seemed to be cursed. Sergei Skropka of the Soviet Union lost a shoe with six laps to go, but managed to stay with the leaders until the final water jump, when he slipped and fell headlong into the pond. World record holder Kerry O'Brien had similar bad luck, losing a shoe 200 meters from the finish and smashing into the water jump barrier. In the fourth heat, Amos Biwott set an Olympic record of 8:23.8.

The final was won by Kip Keino, who outkicked his teammate Ben Jipcho. Keino had little steeplechase experience, having entered the race as a challenge. "I had a lot of fun jumping the hurdles," he said, although his lack of experience caused him to jump "like an animal. My style is not good."

1976 Montreal C: 24, N: 16, D: 7.28. WR: 8:09.7 (Anders Gärderud)

1. Anders Gärderud	SWE	8:08.2 WR
2. Bronislaw Malinowski	POL	8:09.2
3. Frank Baumgartl	GDR	8:10.4
4. Tapio Kantanen	FIN	8:12.6
5. Michael Karst	GER	8:20.1
6. Evan Robertson	NZE	8:21.1
7. Dan Glans	SWE	8:21.5
8. Antonio Campos	SPA	8:22.7

The 1976 final was one of the greatest steeplechase races of all time. Antonio Campos led for almost half the race. Then Bronislaw Malinowski, who had issued a warning that he planned to run away from the field in order to make it difficult for "followers" like Anders Gärderud, took over and tried to pull away. But Gärderud and Frank Baumgartl stayed with him. With 300 meters to go, Gärderud, who previously had had trouble living up to expectations in major competitions, flew by Malinowski, with Baumgartl right behind him. Gärderud cleared the final water jump beautifully and opened a five-yard lead. However, the surprising Baumgartl closed the gap as they approached the final hurdle. Gärderud cleared perfectly again, but Baumgartl clipped the barrier with his trail knee and sprawled to the ground. Malinowski jumped over the human hurdle and beat the world record, but he couldn't catch Gärderud. Baumgartl, recalling Lasse Viren's fall in the 1972 10,000 meters, leaped to his feet and salvaged the bronze medal, improving his personal best by 7.2 seconds, despite his mishap.

1980 Moscow C: 31, N: 18, D: 7.31. WR: 8:05.4 (Henry Rono)
1. Bronislaw Malinowski   POL   8:09.7
2. Filbert Bayi   TAN   8:12.5
3. Eshetu Tura   ETH   8:13.6
4. Domingo Ramon   SPA   8:15.8
5. Francisco Sanchez   SPA   8:18.0
6. Guiseppe Gerbi   ITA   8:18.5
7. Boguslaw Mamiński   POL   8:19.5
8. Anatoly Dimov   SOV   8:19.8

No longer contemptuous of those who only follow during the early going, Bronislaw Malinowski was quite content to let Filbert Bayi set the pace in Moscow. Bayi, an air force mechanic from the Mbulu tribe, had little steeplechase experience, whereas Malinowski had been concentrating on the event for 13 years. The offspring of a Polish father and a Scottish mother, Malinowski had finished fourth in 1972 and second in 1976.

Bayi drove into the lead immediately and led by 35 meters with two laps to go, but about a half lap later he suddenly began to tire. Malinowski caught him on the backstretch and won easily, finally achieving his goal of an Olympic gold medal. When asked why he had followed such a suicidal race plan, Bayi replied, "Because it's fun. . . . It is fun to run as fast as one can until you are dead-tired." He was the first Tanzanian ever to win an Olympic medal. Unfortunately, Bronislaw Malinowski was killed in a car crash on September 26, 1981, near his hometown of Grudziak. He was 30 years old.

4 x 100-METER RELAY

This event has been dominated by the United States, which has won it 12 of 15 times. The only U.S. losses have been the result of disqualification (1912 and 1960) and boycott (1980).

1896–1908 not held

1912 Stockholm T: 8, N: 8, D: 7.9
1. GBR   (David Jacobs, Harold Macintosh, Victor   42.4 OR
   d'Arcy, William Applegarth)
2. SWE   (Ivan Möller, Charles Luther, Ture Persson,   42.6
   Knut Lindberg)
DISQ: GER (Otto Röhr, Max Herrmann, Erwin Kern, Richard Rau)

The U.S. team of Courtney, Belote, Wilson, and Cooke won the first semifinal in a time of 42.2, but was disqualified for passing out of the zone. The third semifinal was won by the German team, in 42.3; however they too were disqualified for passing out of the zone in the final, in which they finished second.

1920 Antwerp T: 13, N: 13, D: 8.22. WR: 42.3 (GER—Röhr, Herrmann, Kern, Rau)
1. USA   (Charles Paddock, Jackson Scholz, Loren   42.2 WR
   Murchison, Morris Kirksey)
2. FRA   (René Tirard, René Lorain, René Mourlon,   42.6
   Emile Ali Khan)
3. SWE   (Agne Holmström, William Petersson [Björne-   42.9
   man], Sven Malm, Nils Sandström)
4. GBR   (William Hill, Harold Abrahams, Victor d'Arcy,   —
   Harry Edward)
5. DEN   (Henri Thorsen, Fritjoff Andersen, August Sör-   —
   ensen, Marinus Sörensen)
6. LUX   (Jean Colbach, Paul Hammer, Jean Proess,   —
   Alex Servais)

1924 Amsterdam T: 15, N: 15, D: 7.13. WR: 42.2 (USA—Paddock, Scholz, Murchison, Kirksey)
1. USA   (Francis Hussey, Louis Clarke, Loren Murchi-   41.0 EWR
   son, Alfred Leconey)
2. GBR   (Harold Abrahams, Walter Rangeley, Lance-   41.2
   lot Royle, William Nichol)
3. HOL   (Jacob Boot, Henricus Broos, Jan de Vries,   41.8
   Marinus van den Berge)
4. HUN   (Ferenc Gerö, Lajos Kurunczy, László Mus-   42.0
   kát, Gusztáv Rózsahegyi)
5. FRA   (Maurice Degrelle, Albert Heise, René Mour-   42.2
   lon, André Mourlon)
DISQ: SWI (Karl Borner, Heinz Hemmi, Joseph Imbach, David Moriaud)

A wholesale assault on the world record began in the first heat of the first round, when Great Britain clocked 42.0. The Dutch team equaled this time in the next heat, but in the sixth heat the Americans ran away in 41.2. In the semifinal, the United States recorded a time of 41.0, and repeated this performance in the final. The most surprising aspect of the final was that the U.S. leadoff runner, Francis Hussey of Stuyvesant High School in New York City, beat 100-meter gold medalist Harold Abrahams by two yards.

1928 Amsterdam T: 13, N: 13, D: 8.5. WR: 41.0 (USA—Hussey, Clarke, Murchison, Leconey; Newark Athletic Club, USA—

Bowman, Currie, Pappas, Cumming; Sports Club Eintract, GER—Geerling, Wichmann, Metzner, Salz)

1. USA   (Frank Wykoff, James Quinn, Charles Borah,   41.0 EWR
Henry Russell

2. GER   (Georg Lammers, Richard Corts, Hubert Hou-   41.2
ben, Helmuth Körnig)

3. GBR   (Cyril Gill, Ellis Smouha, Walter Rangeley   41.8
Jack London)

4. FRA   (André Cerbonney, Gilbert Auvergne, Pierre   42.0
Dufau, André Mourlon)

5. SWI   (Emmanuel Goldsmith, Willy Weibel, Willy   42.6
Tschopp, Hans Niggl)

DISQ: CAN (Ralph Adams, John Fitzpatrick, George Hester, Percy Williams)

1932 Los Angeles T: 8, N: 8, D: 8.7. WR: 40.8 (GER—Jonath, Corts, Houben, Körnig; Sports Club Charlotten Burg, GER—Körnig, Grosser, Natan, Schloske; University of Southern California, USA—Delby, Maurer, Guyer, Wykoff)

1. USA   (Robert Kiesel, Emmett Toppino, Hector Dyer,   40.0 WR
Frank Wykoff)

2. GER   (Helmuth Körnig, Friedrich Hendrix, Erich   40.9
Borchmeyer, Arthur Jonath)

3. ITA   (Giuseppe Castelli, Ruggero Maregatti, Ga-   41.2
briele Salviati, Edgardo Toetti)

4. CAN   (Percy Williams, James Brown, Harold Wright,   41.3
Birchall Pearson)

5. JAP   (Takayoshi Yoshioka, Chuhei Nambu, Izuo   41.3
Anno, Itaro Nakajima)

6. GBR   (Donald Finlay, Stanley Fuller, Stanley Engle-   41.4
hart, Ernest Page)

The U.S. team set world records of 40.6 in the preliminaries and 40.0 in the final without having to use their leading sprinters, Eddie Tolan, Ralph Metcalfe, and George Simpson.

1936 Berlin T: 15, N: 15, D: 8.9. WR: 40.0 (USA—Kiesel, Toppino, Dyer, Wykoff)

1. USA   (Jesse Owens, Ralph Metcalfe, Foy Draper,   39.8 WR
Frank Wykoff)

2. ITA   (Orazio Mariani, Gianni Caldana, Elio Ragni,   41.1
Tullio Gonnelli)

3. GER   (Wilhelm Leichum, Erich Borchmeyer, Erwin   41.2
Gillmeister, Gerd Hornberger)

4. ARG   (Juan Lavenas, Antonio Sande, Carlos Hof-   42.2
meister, Tomas Clifford Beswick)

5. CAN   (Samuel Richardson, Arthur Bruce Humber,   42.7
Lee Orr, Howard McPhee)

DISQ: HOL (Tjeerd Boersma, Wijnand van Beveren, Christiaan Berger, Martinus Osendarp)

The 4 × 100-meter relay was the focus of one of the uglier incidents of the 1936 Games, one that caused great embarrassment to the United States. For weeks it had been assumed that the U.S. team would consist of Sam Stoller, Marty Glickman, Frank Wykoff, and Foy Draper, and the foursome spent a good deal of time practicing their baton passing. On August 5, three days before the qualifying heats, Jesse Owens won the 200-meter dash, gaining his third gold medal. When asked if Owens would be added to the relay quartet, coach Lawson Robertson replied, "Owens has had enough glory and collected enough gold medals and oak trees to last him a while. We want to give the other boys a chance to enjoy the '*ceremonie protocolaire*.' Marty Glickman, Sam Stoller, and Frank Wykoff are assured places on the relay team. The fourth choice rests between Foy Draper and Ralph Metcalfe."

Two days later, however, Robertson announced that Owens would probably replace Glickman. Then, on the morning of the heats, the U.S. coaches informed both Glickman and Stoller that they were being dropped from the team and replaced by Owens and Metcalfe. What made the situation ugly was that Stoller and Glickman were the only Jews on the U.S. track squad, and they returned to the United States as the only members of the squad who didn't compete. Robertson's excuse was that he feared the speed of the Dutch and German teams, and wanted to field the fastest foursome possible. Robertson's fears turned out to be unfounded. If he had really been concerned about fielding the best teams possible, he should have paid more attention to the 4 × 400-meter relay team. In that event, Robertson bypassed medal winners Archie Williams, James LuValle, and Glenn Hardin, and stuck with the original foursome, who promptly lost to the British by over 12 yards.

At any rate, the U.S. 4 × 100 team won easily by 15 yards, setting a world record that would last for 20 years. Frank Wykoff, running the anchor leg, won his third straight relay gold medal, setting a world record each time.

1948 London T: 15, N: 15, D: 8.7. WR: 39.8 (USA—Owens, Metcalfe, Draper, Wykoff)

1. USA   (Norwood "Barney" Ewell, Lorenzo Wright, Harri-   40.6
son Dillard, Melvin Patton)

2. GBR   (John Archer, John Gregory, Alistair McCorquo-   41.3
dale, Kenneth Jones)

3. ITA   (Michele Tito, Enrico Perucconi, Antonio Siddi,   41.5
Carlo Monti)

4. HUN   (Ferenc Tima, László Bartha, György Csányi, Béla   41.6
Goldoványi)

5. CAN   (Don McFarlane, James O'Brien, Donald Pettie,   41.9
Edward Haggis)

6. HOL   (Jan Lammers, Johannes Meyer, Gabe Scholten,   41.9
Jan Zwaan)

The U.S. team crossed the finish line six yards ahead of the British, but were disqualified when a judge claimed that the first pass, between Barney Ewell and Lorenzo Wright, had taken place beyond the legal zone. The Americans were dumbfounded and immediately lodged a formal protest. The medal ceremony was held anyway, but three days later a Jury of Appeal viewed films of the race and discovered that the pass had been perfectly legal, and that the track official had been in error. The disqualification was therefore rescinded.

1952 Helsinki T: 22, N: 22, D: 7.27. WR: 39.8 (USA—Owens, Metcalfe, Draper, Wykoff)
1. USA (F. Dean Smith, Harrison Dillard, Lindy Remigino, Andrew Stanfield) 40.1
2. SOV (Boris Tokaryev, Levan Kalyayev, Levan Sanadze, Vladimir Sukharyev) 40.3
3. HUN (László Zarándi, Géza Varasdi, György Csányi Bela Goldoványi) 40.5
4. GBR (Emmanuel McDonald Bailey, William Jack, John Gregory, Brian Shenton) 40.6
5. FRA (Alain Porthault, Etienne Bally, Yves Camus, René Bonino) 40.9
6. CZE (František Brož, Jiři David, Miroslav Horčic, Zdenek Pospišil) 41.2

The United States and the U.S.S.R. were almost even after three legs, but Stanfield drew away from Sukharyev to win by two yards.

1956 Melbourne T: 18, N: 18, D: 12.1. WR: 39.8 (USA—Owens, Metcalfe, Draper, Wykoff)
1. USA (Ira Murchison, Leamon King, W. Thane Baker, Robert Morrow) 39.5 WR
2. SOV (Boris Tokaryev, Vladimir Sukharyev, Leonid Bartenyev, Yuri Konovalov) 39.8
3. GER (Lothar Knörzer, Leonhard Pohl, Heinz Fütterer, Manfred Germar) 40.3
4. ITA (Franco Galbiati, Giovanni Ghiselli, Luigi Gnocchi, Vincenzo Lombardo) 40.3
5. GBR (Kenneth Box, Roy Sandstrom, Brian Shenton, David Segal) 40.6
6. POL (Marian Foik, Janusz Jarzembowski, Edward Schmidt, Zenon Baranowski) 40.6

1960 Rome T: 19, N: 19, D: 9.8. WR: 39.5 (USA—Baker, King, Morrow, Murchison; GER—Steinbach, Lauer, Fütterer, Germar)
1. GER (Bernd Cullmann, Armin Hary, Walter Mahlendorf, Martin Lauer) 39.5 EWR
2. SOV (Gusman Kosanov, Leonid Bartenyev, Yuri Konovalov, Edvin Ozolin) 40.1
3. GBR (Peter Radford, David Jones, David Segal, Neville Whitehead) 40.2
4. ITA (Armando Sardi, Pier Giorgio Cazzola, Salvatore Giannone, Livio Berruti) 40.2
5. VEN (S. Clive Bonas, Lloyd Murad, Emilio Romero, Rafael Romero) 40.7
DISQ: USA (Frank Budd, O. Ray Norton, Stonewall Johnson, David Sime)

The United States had won eight straight 4 × 100-meter relays, but in the opening round the West Germans served notice that they would be serious contenders when they equaled the world record of 39.5. Disaster struck the Americans in the final. Ray Norton, anxious to make up for his disappointing sixth place finishes in the 100 and 200, took off too quickly on his second leg. Leadoff runner Frank Budd yelled at Norton, who came to almost a complete halt. But it was too late. He was already three yards beyond the ten-meter passing zone. Norton didn't realize it at the time, and ran a strong leg anyway, moving the Unit-

ed States from fourth to second. Dave Sime's come-from-behind anchor leg brought the United States through the tape in first place, in world record time, but the disqualification gave the victory to the Germans, who equaled the world record again in the final.

1964 Tokyo T: 21, N: 21, D: 10.21. WR: 39.1 (USA—Jones, Budd, Frazier, Drayton)
1. USA (O. Paul Drayton, Gerald Ashworth, Richard Stebbins, Robert Hayes) 39.0 WR
2. POL (Andrzej Zieliński, Wieslaw Maniak, Marian Foik, Marian Dudziak) 39.3
3. FRA (Paul Genevay, Bernard Laidebeur, Claude Piquemal, Jocelyn Delecour) 39.3
4. JAM (Pablo McNeil, Patrick Robinson, Lynworth Headley, Dennis Johnson) 39.4
5. SOV (Edvin Ozolin, Boris Zubov, Gusman Kosanov, Boris Savchuk) 39.4
6. VEN (Arquimedes Herrera, Lloyd Murad, Rafael Romero, Hortensio Herrera Fucil) 39.5
7. ITA (Livio Berruti, Ennio Preatoni, Sergio Ottolina, Pasquale Giannattasio) 39.5
8. GBR (Peter Radford, Ronald Jones, Walter Campbell, Lynn Davies) 39.6

Poor baton passing put the United States in fifth place, three meters behind France, when Bob Hayes took over for the anchor leg. Hayes then unleashed one of the most awesome and breathtaking displays of sprinting ever seen. He swept into the lead after only 30 yards and crossed the finish line with a three-meter margin of victory. Observers disagreed as to Hayes' time for his 100-meter leg, but the slowest estimate was 8.9 seconds.

1968 Mexico City T: 19, N: 19, D: 10.20. WR: 38.6 (USA—McCulloch, Kuller, Simpson, Miller)
1. USA (Charles Greene, Melvin Pender, Ronnie Ray Smith, James Hines) 38.2 WR
2. CUB (Hermes Ramirez, Juan Morales, Pablo Montes, Enrique Figuerola Camue) 38.3
3. FRA (Gérard Fénouil, Jocelyn Delecour, Claude Piquemal, Roger Bambuck) 38.4
4. JAM (Errol Stewart, Michael Fray, Clifton Forbes, Lennox Miller) 38.4
5. GDR (Heinz Erbstösser, Hartmut Schelter, Peter Haase, Harald Eggers) 38.6
6. GER (Karl-Peter Schmidtke, Gerhard Wucherer, Gert Metz, Joachim Eigenherr) 38.7
7. ITA (Sergio Ottolina, Ennio Preatoni, Angelo Sguazzero, Livio Berruti) 38.7
8. POL (Wieslaw Maniak, Edward Romanowski, Zenon Nowosz, Marian Dudziak) 39.2

With Charlie Greene running with heavily bandaged legs, the United States was beaten to the tape by Cuba in both the opening round and the semifinals. Although Greene ran the final as if uninjured, mediocre baton passing left the United States in only third place when Jim Hines took over for the anchor leg. Five feet behind Enrique Figuerola at the exchange, Hines ripped into the lead after 30 yards and won by a yard. The Cubans mailed their silver medals to activist Stokely Carmichael as a symbol of support for U.S. blacks.

1972 Munich T: 27, N; 27, D: 9.10. WR: 38.2 (USA—Greene, Pender, Smith, Hines)
1. USA (Larry Black, Robert Taylor, Gerald Tinker, 38.19 EWR Edward Hart)
2. SOV (Aleksandr Kornelyuk, Vladimir Lovetski, 38.50 Yuri Silos, Valery Borzov)
3. GER (Jobst Hirscht, Karlheinz Klotz, Gerhard Wu- 38.79 cherer, Klaus Ehl)
4. CZE (Jaroslav Matoušek, Juraj Demeč, Jiři 38.82 Kynos, Ludvik Bohman)
5. GBR (Manfred Kokot, Bernd Borth, Hans-Jürgen 38.90 Bombach, Siegfried Schenke)
6. POL (Stanislaw Wagner, Tadeusz Cuch, Jerzy 39.03 Czerbniak, Zenon Nowosz)
7. FRA (Patrick Bourbeillon, Jean-Pierre Gres, Ge- 39.14 rard Fenouil, Bruno Cherrier)
8. ITA (Vincenzo Guerini, Ennio Preatoni, Luigi 39.41 Benedetti, Pietro Mennea)

For the first time since 1932, the 4 × 100-meter relay was won by a team that did not include the 100-meter gold medalist. Eddie Hart, running the anchor leg for the United States, gained some degree of satisfaction after missing the start of his 100-meter quarterfinal heat.

1976 Montreal T: 20, N: 20, D: 7.31. WR: 38.19 (USA—Black, Taylor, Tinker, Hart)
1. USA (Harvey Glance, John Wesley Jones, Millard 38.33 Hampton, Steven Riddick)
2. GDR (Manfred Kokot, Jörg Pfeifer, Klaus-Dieter Kurrat, 38.66 Alexander Thieme)
3. SOV (Alexander Aksinin, Nikolai Kolesnikov, Yuriy Si- 38.78 lovs, Valery Borzov)
4. POL (Andrzej Świerczyński, Marian Woronin, Bogdan 38.83 Grzejszczak, Zenon Licznerski)
5. CUB (Francisco Gomez, Alejandro Casañas Ramirez, 39.01 Hermes Ramirez, Silvio Leonard Tartabull)
6. ITA (Vincenzo Guerini, Luciano Caravani, Luigi Bene- 39.08 detti, Pietro Mennea)
7. FRA (Claude Amoureux, Joseph Arame, Lucien Rose- 39.16 Sainte, Dominique Chauvelot)
8. CAN (Hugh Sponner, Marvin Nash, Albin Dukowski, 39.47 Hugh Fraser)

1980 Moscow T: 16, N: 16, D: 9.1. WR: 38.03 (USA—Collins, Riddick, Wiley, Williams)
1. SOV (Vladimir Muravyov, Nikolai Sidorov, Aleksandr 38.26 Aksinin, Andrei Prokofiev)
2. POL (Krzysztof Zwoliński, Zenon Licznerski, Leszek 38.33 Duneki, Marian Woronin)
3. FRA (Antoine Richard, Pascal Barré, Patrick Barré, 38.53 Hermann Panzo)

4. GBR (Michael McFarlane, Allan Wells, Cameron 38.62 Sharp, Andrew McMaster)
5. GDR (Sören Schlegel, Eugen Ray, Bernhard Hoff, 38.73 Thomas Munkelt)
6. BUL (Pavel Pavlov, Vladimir Ivanov, Ivailo Karaniotov, 38.99 Peter Petrov)
7. NGR (Hammed Adio, Kayode Elegbede, Samson Oye- 39.12 ledun, Peter Okodogbe)
8. BRA (Milton Costa de Castro, Nelson Rocha Dos San- 39.54 tos, Katsuhico Nakaya, Altevir Araujo Filho)

The French team included 21-year-old twins, Pascal and Patrick Barré.

4 x 400-METER RELAY
1896-1906 not held

1908 London T: 7, N: 7, D: 7.25.
(Medley Relay: 200, 200, 400, 800)
1. USA (William Hamilton, Nathaniel Cartmell, John Tay- 3:29.4 lor, Melvin Sheppard)
2. GER (Arthur Hoffmann, Hans Eicke, Otto Trieloff, — Hanns Braun)
3. HUN (Pàl Simon, Frigyes Mezey-Wiesner, József — Nagy, Ödön Bodor)

The U.S. team clocked 3:27.2 in the first round, but eased up in the final, winning by 25 yards. John Taylor, who ran the third leg, was the first black athlete to win an Olympic gold medal. He was just about to open up practice as a doctor, when he died of typhoid on December 2, 1908, at the age of 24.

1912 Stockholm T: 7, N: 7, D: 7.15. WR: 3:18.2 (USA—Schaaf, Sheppard, Gissing, Rosenberger)
1. USA (Melvin Sheppard, Edward Lindberg, James 3:16.6 WR ''Ted'' Meredith, Charles Reidpath)
2. FRA (Charles Lelong, Robert Schurrer, Pierre Fai- 3:20.7 liot, Charles Poulenard)
3. GBR (George Nicol, Ernest Henley, James Tindal 3:23.2 Soutter, Cyril Seedhouse)

1920 Antwerp T: 6, N: 6, D: 8.23. WR: 3:16.6 (USA—Sheppard, Lindberg, Meredith, Reidpath)
1. GBR (Cecil Griffiths, Robert Lindsay, E. John Ains- 3:22.2 worth-Davis, Guy Butler)
2. SAF (Harry Davel, Clarence Oldfield, Jack Ooster- 3:24.2 laak, Bevil Rudd)
3. FRA (George ''Géo'' André, Gaston Féry, Maurice 3:24.8 Delvart, Jean Devaux)
4. USA (Earl Eby, James ''Ted'' Meredith, Robert Emory, 3:25.2 Frank Shea)
5. SWE (Sven Krokström, Sven Malm, Erik Sundbald, — Nils Engdahl)
6. BEL (Jules Migeot, Auguste Corteyn, Omer Smet, — François Morren)

1924 Paris T: 7, N: 7, D: 7.13. WR: 3:16.4 (American Legion, Pennsylvania, USA—Rodgers, Eby, Brown, Maxam)

1. USA   (Charles "Con" Cochrane, Alan Helffrich,   3:16.0 WR
J. Oliver McDonald, William Stevenson)
2. SWE   (Artur Svensson, Erik Byléhn, Gustaf Wej-   3:17.0
narth, Nils Engdahl)
3. GBR   (Edward Toms, George Renwick, Richard   3:17.4
Ripley, Guy Butler)
4. CAN   (Horace Aylwin, Allan Christie, David John-   3:22.8
ston, William Maynes)
5. FRA   (Raymond Fritz, Gaston Féry, Francis Gal-   3:23.4
tier, Barthélémy Favaudon)
6. ITA   (Guido Cominotto, Alfredo Gargiullo, Ennio   3:28.0
Maffiolini, Luigi Facelli)

The British team was hampered by the absence of Eric Liddell, who was off preaching a sermon, it being a Sunday.

1928 Amsterdam T: 16, N: 16, D: 8.5. WR: 3:16.0 (USA— Cochran, Helffrich, McDonald, Stevenson)

1. USA   (George Baird, Emerson "Bud" Spencer,   3:14.2 WR
Frederick Alderman, Raymond Barbuti)
2. GER   (Otto Neumann, Richard Krebs, Werner   3:14.8
"Harry" Storz, Hermann Engelhard)
3. CAN   (Alexander Wilson, Philip Edwards, Stanley   3:15.4
Glover, James Ball)
4. SWE   (Björn Kugelberg, Bertil von Wachenfeldt,   3:15.8
Erik Byléhn, Sten Pettersson)
5. GBR   (Roger Leigh-Wood, William Craner, John   3:16.4
Rinkel, Douglas Lowe)
6. FRA   (Georges Krotoff, Joseph Jackson, Georges   3:19.4
Dupont, René Féger)

1932 Los Angeles T: 7, N: 7, D: 8.7. WR:3:12.6 (Stanford University, USA—Shore, A. Hables, L. Hables, Eastman)

1. USA   (Ivan Fuqua, Edgar Ablowich, Karl Warner,   3:08.2 WR
William Carr)
2. GBR   (Crew Stoneley, Thomas Hampson, David   3:11.2
Burghley, Godfrey Rampling)
3. CAN   (Raymond Lewis, James Ball, Philip Ed-   3:12.8
wards, Alexander Wilson)
4. GER   (Joachim Büchner, Walter Nehb, Adolf   3:14.4
Metzner, Otto Peltzer)
5. JAP   (Itaro Nakajima, Iwao Masuda, Seikan Oki,   3:14.6
Teiichi Nishi)
6. ITA   (Giacomo Carlini, Giovanni Turba, Mario De   3:17.8
Negri, Luigi Facelli)

The U.S. team set a world record of 3:11.8 in the opening heat. In the final Bill Carr took off with a 12-yard lead. Godfrey Rampling closed the gap to six yards, at which point Carr pulled away and won by over 20 yards.

1936 Berlin T: 12, N: 12, D: 8.9. WR: 3:08.2 (USA—Fuqua, Ablowich, Warner, Carr)

1. GBR   (Frederick Wolff, Godfrey Rampling, William   3:09.0
Roberts, Arthur Godfrey Brown)
2. USA   (Harold Cagle, Robert Young, Edward O'Brien,   3:11.0
Alfred Fitch)

3. GER   (Helmut Hamann, Friedrich von Stülpnagel, Har-   3:11.8
ry Voigt, Rudolf Harbig)
4. CAN   (Marshall Limon, Philip Edwards, William Fritz,   3:11.8
John Loaring)
5. SWE   (Sven Strömberg, Per Edfeldt, Olle Danielsson,   3:13.0
Bertil von Wachenfeldt)
6. HUN   (Tibor Ribényi, Zoltán Zsitavi, József Vadas, Jó-   3:14.8
sef Kovacs)

This race marked the only Olympic appearance of the great German runner Rudolf Harbig. Between August 1938 and September 1940, Harbig won 55 consecutive races at distances ranging from 50 meters to 1000 meters. On July 15, 1939, he ran 800 meters in 1:46.6, setting a world record that would last for 16 years. On August 12, he set a 400-meter world record of 46.0 that wasn't bettered until 1948. Harbig was killed fighting the Russians in World War II, on March 5, 1944.

1948 London T: 15, N: 15, D: 8.7. WR: 3:08.2 (USA—Fuqua, Ablowich, Warner, Carr)

1. USA   (Arthur Harnden, Clifford Bourland, Roy Coch-   3:10.4
ran, Malvin Whitfield)
2. FRA   (Jean Kerebel, François Schewetta, Robert Chef   3:14.8
d'Hotel, Jacques Lunis)
3. SWE   (Kurt Lundkvist, Lars Wolfbrandt, Folke Alnevik,   3:16.0
Rune Larsson)
4. FIN   (Tauno Suvanto, Olli Talja, Runar Holmberg, Ber-   3:24.8
til Storskrubb)

DNF: JAM (V. George Rhoden, Leslie Laing, Arthur Wint, Herbert McKenley), ITA (Giovanni Rocca, Ottavio Missoni, Luigi Paterlini, Antonio Siddi)

1952 Helsinki T: 18, N: 18, D: 7.27. WR: 3:08.2 (USA—Fuqua, Ablowich, Warner, Carr)

1. JAM   (Arthur Wint, Leslie Laing, Herbert McKenley,   3:03.9 WR
V. George Rhoden)
2. USA   (Ollie Matson, Gerald Cole, Charles Moore,   3:04.0
Malvin Whitfield)
3. GER   (Hans Geister, Günther Steines, Heinz Ulz-   3:06.6
heimer, Karl-Friedrich Haas)
4. CAN   (Douglas Clement, John Hutchins, John Car-   3:09.3
roll, James Lavery)
5. GBR   (Leslie Lewis, Alan Dick, Terence Higgins,   3:10.0
Nicholas Stacey)
6. FRA   (Jean-Pierre Goudeau, Robert Bart, Jacques   3:10.1
Degats, Jean-Paul Martin du Gard)

In 1948, the Jamaican relay team had wanted more than anything to defeat the United States and win the gold medal. But Arthur Wint, running the third leg, had pulled a muscle and hobbled off the track in pain and anguish. Four years later the same four Jamaicans were back on the track, ready for another shot at their goal. Before the final began, Wint, Laing, McKenley, and Rhoden locked arms in a circle and said a prayer.

Wint ran the first leg and gave up a slight lead to Ollie Matson. Gerald Cole ran a tremendous second lap for the United States. When Herb McKenley took over for Jamaica, he was 12 yards behind 400-meter hurdles' champion

Charley Moore. McKenley, competing in his fifth Olympic final without ever having won a gold medal, ran like a man inspired. Incredibly, he closed the gap and passed Moore in the last second, running a phenomenal 44.6 to Moore's far from shabby 46.3, and allowing 400-meter gold medalist George Rhoden to take off with a one-yard lead. Victory now seemed assured for the Jamaicans, since Mal Whitfield, the U.S. anchor man, had run a disappointing sixth in the 400-meter final. But Whitfield didn't give in, refusing to yield an inch the entire way. However, Rhoden, wearing the same vest that Wint had worn to run the first leg, also refused to let up, and managed to break the tape exactly one yard ahead of Whitfield. The 20-year-old world record, set at the Los Angeles Games, had been demolished by 4.3 seconds. That night, the Jamaican foursome celebrated in their quarters by drinking whisky with the Duke of Edinburgh, out of the only available vessel—a toothbrush tumbler.

1956 Melbourne T: 15, N: 15, D: 12.1. WR: 3:03.9 (JAM—Wint, Laing, McKenley, Rhoden)
1. USA (Louis Jones, Jesse Mashburn, Charles Jenkins, 3:04.8
         Thomas Courtney)
2. AUS (Leon Gregory, David Lean, Graham Gipson, Ke- 3:06.2
         van Gosper)
3. GBR (John Salisbury, Michael Wheeler, F. Peter Hig- 3:07.2
         gins, Derek Johnson)
4. GER (Jürgen Kühl, Walter Oberste, Manfred Pörschke, 3:08.2
         Karl-Friedrich Haas)
5. CAN (Laird Sloan, Murray Cockburn, Douglas Clem- 3:10.2
         ent, Terry Tobacco)
DISQ: JAM (Keith Gardner, George Kerr, Malcolm Spence, Melville Spence)

1960 Rome T: 19, N: 19, D: 9.8. WR: 3:03.9 (JAM—Wint, Laing, McKenley, Rhoden)
1. USA (Jack Yerman, Earl Young, Glenn Davis, Otis 3:02.2 WR
         Davis)
2. GER (Hans-Joachim Reske, Manfred Kinder, Jo- 3:02.7
         hannes Kaiser, Carl Kaufmann)
3. BWI (Malcolm Spence, James Wedderburn, Keith 3:04.0
         Gardner, George Kerr)
4. SAF (Edward Jefferys, Edgar Davis, Gordon Day, 3:05.0
         Malcolm Spence)
5. GBR (Malcolm Yardley, Barry Jackson, John 3:08.3
         Wrighton, Robbie Brightwell)
6. SWI (René Weber, Ernst Zaugg, Hansrüdi Bruder, 3:09.4
         Christian Wägli)

Otis Davis began the anchor leg six yards ahead of Carl Kaufmann. Kaufmann closed the gap to one yard, but in the middle of the final curve, Davis accelerated and pulled away to win by four yards.

1964 Tokyo T: 17, N: 17, D: 10.21. WR: 3:02.2 (USA—Yerman, Young, G. Davis, O. Davis)
1. USA (Ollan Cassell, Michael Larrabee, Ulis 3:00.7 WR
         Williams, Henry Carr)
2. GBR (Timothy Graham, Adrian Metcalfe, 3:01.6
         John Cooper, Robbie Brightwell)

3. TRI (Edwin Skinner, Kent Bernard, Edwin 3:01.7
         Roberts, Wendell Mottley)
4. JAM (Lawrence Kahn, Malcolm Spence, 3:02.3
         Melville Spence, George Kerr)
5. GER/GDR (Jörg Jüttner, Hans-Ullrich Schulz, Jo- 3:04.3
         hannes Schmitt, Manfred Kinder)
6. POL (Marian Filipiuk, Ireneusz Kluczek, 3:05.3
         Stanislaw Swatowski, Andrzej Ba-
         deński)
7. SOV (Grigory Sverbetov, Victor Bychkov, 3:05.9
         Vasily Anisimov, Vadim Arkhipchuk)
8. FRA (Michel Hiblot, Bernard Martin, Ger- 3:07.4
         main Nelzy, Jean Pierre Boccardo)

1968 Mexico City T: 16, N: 16, D: 10.20. WR: 2:59.6 (USA—Frey, Evans, Smith, Lewis)
1. USA (Vincent Matthews, Ronald Freeman, Larry 2:56.1 WR
         James, Lee Evans)
2. KEN (Daniel Rudisha, Matesi Munyoro Nyamau, 2:59.6
         Naftali Bon, Charles Asati)
3. GER (Helmar Müller, Manfred Kinder, Gerhard 3:00.5
         Hennige, Martin Jellinghaus)
4. POL (Jan Balachowski, Stanislaw Grędziński, Jan 3:00.5
         Werner, Andrzej Badeński)
5. GBR (Martin Winbolt-Lewis, Colin Campbell, David 3:01.2
         Hemery, John Sherwood)
6. TRI (George Simon, Euric Bobb, Benedict Cay- 3:04.5
         enne, Edwin Roberts)
7. ITA (Sergio Ottolina, Giacomo Puosi, Furio Fusi, 3:04.6
         Sergio Bello)
8. FRA (Jean Nallet, Jacques Carette, Gilles Ber- 3:07.5
         tould, Jean Boccardo)

The final was really two separate races: the United States fighting for a world record and the other teams battling it out for second through eighth places. It was Ron Freeman's remarkable second leg that really did the trick for the Americans. His unofficial time of 43.2 is the fastest leg ever recorded in a 4 × 400-meter relay. Anchor man Lee Evans crossed the finish line 30 yards ahead of Charles Asati in second place.

1972 Munich T: 21, N: 21, D: 9.10. WR: 2:56.1 (USA—Matthews, Freeman, James, Evans)
1. KEN (Charles Asati, Hezakiah Nyamau, Robert Ouko, 2:59.8
         Julius Sang)
2. GBR (Martin Reynolds, Alan Pascoe, David Hemery, 3:00.5
         David Jenkins)
3. FRA (Gilles Bertould, Daniel Velasques, Francis Ker- 3:00.7
         biriou, Jacques Carette)
4. GER (Bernd Herrmann, Horst-Rüdiger Schlöske, Herr- 3:00.9
         mann Köhler, Karl Honz)
5. POL (Jan Werner, Jan Balachowski, Zbigniew Jar- 3:01.1
         emski, Andrzej Badeński)
6. FIN (Stig Lönnqvist, Ari Salin, Ossi Karttunen, 3:01.1
         Markku Kukkoaho)
7. SWE (Eric Carlgren, Anders Faager, Kenth Oehman, 3:02.6
         Ulf Roenner)
8. TRI (Arthur Cooper, Pat Marshall, Charles Joseph, 3:03.6
         Edwin Roberts)

Ten days before the heats, each nation submitted a list of six names from which a team of four could be chosen. The names submitted by the United States were Vince Matthews, Wayne Collett, Lee Evans, John Smith, Maurice Peoples, and Tommie Turner. Unfortunately, Matthews and Collett were banned from further competition because of their behavior on the victory platform following the 400-meter final. Meanwhile, Smith had pulled a hamstring muscle and was unable to run. This left the United States without a full team, so they were forced to withdraw.

The final was an exciting race, with the hometown West Germans in first place most of the way. But Julius Sang, running a 43.5 anchor leg, passed the fading Karl Honz 75 meters from the finish and went on to give Kenya a three-meter victory.

1976 Montreal T: 16, N: 16, D: 7.31. WR: 2:56.1 (USA—Matthews, Freeman, James, Evans)

1.	USA	(Herman Frazier, Benjamin Brown, Frederick Newhouse, Maxie Parks)	2:58.65
2.	POL	(Ryszard Podlas, Jan Werner, Zbigniew Jaremski, Jerzy Pietrzyk)	3:01.43
3.	GER	(Franz-Peter Hofmeister, Lothar Krieg, Harald Schmid, Bernd Herrmann)	3:01.98
4.	CAN	(Ian Seale, Don Domansky, Leighton Hope, Brian Saunders)	3:02.64
5.	JAM	(Leighton Priestley, Donald Quarrie, Colin Bradford, Seymour Newman)	3:02.84
6.	TRI	(Michael Solomon, Horace Tuitt, Joseph Coombs, Charles Joseph)	3:03.46
7.	CUB	(Eddy Gutierrez, Damaso Alfonso, Carlos Alvarez, Alberto Juantorena Danger)	3:03.81
8.	FIN	(Hannu Makela, Ossi Karttunen, Stig Lonnqvist, Markku Kukkoaho)	3:06.51

With the defending champions from Kenya boycotted out of the Olympics, the Americans were left unchallenged. The final was run during a hard rain.

1980 Moscow T: 24, N: 24, D: 8.1. WR: 2:56.1 (USA—Mattews, Freeman, James, Evans)

1.	SOV	(Remigius Valiulis, Mikhail Linge, Nikolai Chernetsky, Viktor Markin)	3:01.1
2.	GDR	(Klaus Thiele, Andreas Knebel, Frank Schaffer, Volker Beck)	3:01.3
3.	ITA	(Stefano Malinverni, Mauro Zuliani, Roberto Tozzi, Pietro Mennea)	3:04.3
4.	FRA	(Jacques Fellice, Robert Froissart, Didier Dubois, Francis Demarthon)	3:04.8
5.	BRA	(Paulo Roberto Correia, Antonio Dias Ferreira, Agberto Conceião Guimaraes, Geraldo José Pegado)	3:05.9
6.	TRI	(Joseph Coombs, Charles Joseph, Rafee Mohammed Michael Solomon)	3:06.6
7.	CZE	(Josef Lomicky, Dusan Malovec, Frantisek Brecka, Karel Kolar)	3:07.0

DNF: GBR (Alan Bell, Terry Whitehead, Roderic Milne, Glendon Cohen)

With the top three teams—the United States, West Germany and Kenya—absent because of the anti-Soviet boycott, this was a severely devalued contest. The Soviets, desperate for a victory, rested 400-meter champion Viktor Markin in the opening heat, then claimed that his replacement, Victor Burakov, had been injured, and brought Markin back for the final. They used the same trick to circumvent the anti-replacement rules in the women's 4×400 relay. The rejuvenated Markin fought off a surprisingly strong challenge from 400-meter hurdle gold medalist Volker Beck to gain a victory-at-any-cost for the U.S.S.R. The winning time was the slowest in 20 years. The slowest losing time since 1956 (3:25.0) was recorded by Sierra Leone.

20,000-METER WALK

In walking races, the contestants must keep at least one foot in contact with the ground at all times. If a walker loses contact with the ground, he receives a warning for "lifting." A second infraction results in disqualification. Another rule requires walkers to straighten the leg at each step.

Official world records can only be set in walking races contested on a track. Since Olympic walking events are held on the road, winning times are not eligible for world record consideration.

1896–1952 not held

1956 Melbourne C: 21, N: 10, D: 11.28. WR: 1:27:58.2 (Mikhail Lavrov)

1.	Leonid Spirin	SOV	1:31:27.4
2.	Antanas Mikenas	SOV	1:32:03.0
3.	Bruno Junk	SOV	1:32:12.0
4.	John Ljunggren	SWE	1:32:24.0
5.	Stanley Vickers	GBR	1:32:34.2
6.	Donald Keane	AUS	1:33:52.0
7.	George Coleman	GBR	1:34:01.8
8.	Roland Hardy	GBR	1:34:40.4

So many disputes had developed over the judging of the comparatively fast-paced 10,000-meter walk that it was replaced by the less controversial 20,000-meter event. Mikenas, leading after 15 kilometers, received a warning, and resigned himself to second place, urging on Spirin, who had only been placed tenth at the halfway mark.

1960 Rome C:36, N: 18, D: 9.2. WR: 1:27:05.0 (Vladimir Golubnichiy)

1.	Vladimir Golubnichiy	SOV	1:34:07.2
2.	Noel Freeman	AUS	1:34:16.4
3.	Stanley Vickers	GDR	1:34:56.4
4.	Dieter Lindner	GER	1:35:33.8
5.	Norman Read	NZE	1:36:59.0
6.	Lennart Back	SWE	1:37:17.0
7.	John Ljunggren	SWE	1:37:59.0
8.	Ladislav Moc	CZE	1:38:32.4

Golubnichiy, a 24-year-old Ukrainian who eventually competed in five Olympics, won the first of his five medals. Freeman, who apparently had not gone over the course beforehand, misjudged his closing surge and fell 9.2 seconds short of victory.

1964 Tokyo C: 30, N: 15, D: 10.15. WR: 1:27:05.0 (Vladimir Golubnichiy)
1. Kenneth Matthews	GBR	1:29:34.0 OR
2. Dieter Lindner	GDR	1:31:13.2
3. Vladimir Golubnichiy	SOV	1:31:59.4
4. Noel Freeman	AUS	1:32:06.8
5. Gennady Solodov	SOV	1:32:33.0
6. Ronald Zinn	USA	1:32:43.0
7. Boris Khrolovich	SOV	1:32:45.4
8. John Edgington	GBR	1:32:46.0

Ken Matthews, an electrician at a power station near his hometown of Sutton Coldfield, had collapsed and failed to finish in 1960 after leading for eight kilometers. In 1964 he knew he would win if only his wife, Sheila, could join him in Tokyo. His mates agreed and collected £742 to send her along. Sure enough, Matthews crossed the finish line far ahead of the others. Sheila broke through stadium security, rushed onto the track, and gave her hubby what was probably the longest victory kiss in Olympic history. At the postrace interview, Matthews said, "My legs hurt me at the end of the race. They still do. But I wouldn't mind going dancing now."

Sixth-place finisher Ron Zinn died in the Vietnam War less than nine months later. He was 26 years old.

1968 Mexico City C: 33, N: 20, D: 10.14. WR: 1:27:05.0 (Vladimir Golubnichiy)
1. Vladimir Golubnichiy	SOV	1:33:58.4
2. José Pedraza Zuniga	MEX	1:34:00.0
3. Nikolai Smaga	SOV	1:34:03.4
4. Rudolph Haluza	USA	1:35:00.2
5. Gerhard Sperling	GDR	1:35:27.2
6. Otto Bartsch	SOV	1:36:16.8
7. Hans Reimann	GDR	1:36:31.4
8. Stefan Ingvarsson	SWE	1:36:43.4

After 85 minutes of hard walking, Vladimir Golubnichiy entered the stadium in first place, followed closely by teammate Nikolai Smaga. Then the 60,000-plus spectators went wild as a third walker appeared—José Pedraza, a 31-year-old Mexican soldier. Two hundred meters from the finish, Pedraza passed Smaga and set his sights on Golubnichiy. Pedraza's style seemed far from legal and he received three cautions (one step short of a warning). But it would have taken a suicidal judge to disqualify the determined Pedraza while the stadium echoed with chants of "May-hee-co" and "Pay-drah-zah." An international incident was avoided when Golubnichiy drew away slightly in the homestretch to win by a mere three yards.

1972 Munich C: 24, N: 12, D: 8.31. WR: 1:25:19.4 (Peter Frenkel, Hans Reimann)
1. Peter Frenkel	GDR	1:26:42.4 OR
2. Vladimir Golubnichiy	SOV	1:26:55.2
3. Hans Reimann	GDR	1:27:16.6
4. Gerhard Sperling	GDR	1:27:55.0
5. Nikolai Smaga	SOV	1:28:16.6
6. Paul Nihill	GBR	1:28:44.4
7. Jan Ornoch	POL	1:32:01.6
8. Vittorio Visino	ITA	1:32:30.0

Frenkel, Reimann, and Golubnichiy were even after 15 kilometers, with the deaf walker, Gerhard Sperling, six seconds behind. Approaching the stadium, Golubnichiy moved ahead, but Frenkel had the strongest finishing kick and was able to enter the stadium with a small but growing lead. Frenkel was described in East German press handouts as a "color designer and decorator."

1976 Montreal C: 38, N: 21, D: 7.23. WR: 1:24:45.0 (Bernd Kannenberg)
1. Daniel Bautista Rocha	MEX	1:24:40.6 OR
2. Hans-Georg Reimann	GDR	1:25:13.8
3. Peter Frenkel	GDR	1:25:29.4
4. Karl-Heinz Stadtmüller	GDR	1:26:50.6
5. Raul Gonzalez	MEX	1:28:18.2
6. Armando Zanbaldo	ITA	1:28:25.2
7. Vladimir Golubnichiy	SOV	1:29:24.6
8. Vittorio Visini	ITA	1:29:31.6

The contestants in the 1976 20-kilometer walk covered one of the widest age ranges in the Olympics. Eighteen-year-old Bengt Simonsen of Sweden finished 26th, while 48-year-old Alex Oakley of Canada placed 35th. The winner, Daniel Bautista, brought Mexico its first-ever track and field gold medal. He was so dehydrated at the end that he had to drink 10 cans of soft drinks before he could produce enough urine for the dope test. Bautista's time was not accepted as a world record because it was set on the road rather than on a track.

1980 Moscow C: 34, N: 20, D: 7.24. WR: 1:20:06.8 (Daniel Bautista)
1. Maurizio Damilano	ITA	1:23:35.5 OR
2. Pyotr Pochinchuk	SOV	1:24:45.4
3. Roland Wieser	GDR	1:25:58.2
4. Yevgeny Yevsyukov	SOV	1:26:28.3
5. José Marin	SPA	1:26:45.6
6. Raul Gonzalez	MEX	1:27:48.6
7. Bohdan Bulakowski	POL	1:28:36.3
8. Karl-Heinz Stadtmüller	GDR	1:29:21.7

In 1976 walk officials had been embarrassed by the publication of photographs which clearly showed gold medal winner Daniel Bautista with both feet off the ground during his final lap. In 1980 the officials decided to get tough. With less than 2500 meters to go, Bautista was in first place when he was suddenly disqualified and ordered off the course. This left Anatoly Solomin of the U.S.S.R. in front, but a few hundred meters later he too was disqualified. By the end of the race seven walkers had been ordered off by the judges, including three of the six leaders at the 15-kilometer mark. These crackdowns allowed Maurizio Damilano to win a surprise gold medal. His twin brother, Giorgio, finished 11th. Thipsamay Chanthaphone of Laos, celebrating his 19th birthday, crossed the finish line over a half hour after the other walkers, and 21½ minutes slower than any contestant since the event began in 1952. But, unlike Bautista and Solomin, he *did* finish.

50,000-METER WALK

1896–1928 not held

1932 Los Angeles C: 15, N: 10, D: 8.3. WR: 4:34:03.0 (Paul Sievert)
1. Thomas Green	GBR	4:50:10
2. Jánis Dalinsch	LAT	4:57:20
3. Ugo Frigerio	ITA	4:59:06
4. Karl Hähnel	GER	5:06:06
5. Ettore Rivolta	ITA	5:07:39
6. Paul Sievert	GER	5:16:41
7. Henri Quintric	FRA	5:27:25
8. Ernest Crosbie	USA	5:28:02

Thomas Green, a 38-year-old railway worker, took the lead seven miles from the finish and won easily. Ugo Frigerio added a bronze medal to the three golds he had won in 1920 and 1924.

1936 Berlin C: 33, N: 16, D: 8.5. WR: 4:34:03.0 (Paul Sievert)
1. H. Harold Whitlock	GBR	4:30:41.4 OR
2. Arthur Schwab	SWI	4:32:09.2
3. Adalberts Bubenko	LAT	4:32:42.2
4. Jaroslav Štork	CZE	4:34:00.2
5. Edgar Bruun	NOR	4:34:53.2
6. Fritz Bleiweiss	GER	4:36:48.4
7. Karl Reiniger	SWI	4:40:45.0
8. Etienne Laisne	FRA	4:41:40.0

Harold Whitlock, a 32-year-old auto mechanic, moved into first place after 33 kilometers. However, at the 38-kilometer mark, he began to vomit. His sickness continued for five kilometers, but he kept walking, recovered, and won by a wide margin.

1948 London C: 23, N: 11, D: 7.31. WR: 4:34:03.0 (Paul Sievert)
1. John Ljunggren	SWE	4:41:52
2. Godel Gaston	SWI	4:48:17
3. Tebbs Lloyd-Johnson	GBR	4:48:31
4. Edgar Bruun	NOR	4:53:18
5. Harry Martineau	GBR	4:53:58
6. Rune Bjurström	SWE	4:56:43
7. Pierre Mazille	FRA	5:01:40
8. Claude Hubert	FRA	5:03:12

Ljunggren led from start to finish and won easily. Bronze medalist Tebbs Lloyd-Johnson was 48 years old, the oldest person ever to win an Olympic track and field medal.

1952 Helsinki C: 31, N: 16, D: 7.21. WR: 4:31:21.6 (Antal Roka)
1. Giuseppe Dordoni	ITA	4:28:07.8 OR
2. Josef Doležal	CZE	4:30:17.8
3. Antal Róka	HUN	4:31:27.2
4. George Whitlock	GBR	4:32:21.0
5. Sergey Lobastov	SOV	4:32:34.2
6. Vladimir Ukhov	SOV	4:32:51.6
7. Dumitru Paraschivescu	ROM	4:41:05.2
8. Ionescu Baboie	ROM	4:41:52.8

1956 Melbourne C: 21, N: 10, D: 11.24. WR: 4:21:07.0 (Ladislav Moc)
1. Norman Read	NZE	4:30:42.8
2. Yevgeny Maskinskov	SOV	4:32:57.0
3. John Ljunggren	SWE	4:35:02.0
4. Abdon Pamich	ITA	4:39:00.0
5. Antal Róka	HUN	4:50:09.0
6. Raymond Smith	AUS	4:56:08.0
7. Adolf Weinacker	USA	5:00:16.0
8. Albert Johnson	GBR	5:02:19.0

Norman Read moved from England to New Zealand in 1954. As the Melbourne Olympics approached, he wrote to the British A.A.A. asking for permission to represent Great Britain as a walker. He was rejected. At first he was rejected in New Zealand as well, but a strong showing in races in Australia and New Zealand paved the way for him. He got his naturalization papers and was ready to fulfill his dream. On the day of the 50,000-meter race Read got lost in the corridors of the stadium and didn't find his way to the track until the other runners were already standing on the starting line. Maskinskov led over most of the course, with Read two and a half minutes back after 30 kilometers. At 42 kilometers, however, Read caught the tiring Soviet walker and pulled away to a decisive victory. His unexpected win caused wild cheering in the stadium, and a whole section of the New Zealand contingent had to be restrained from streaming onto the track.

1960 Rome C: 39, N: 20, D: 9.7. WR: 4:16:08.6 (Sergei Lobastov)
1. Donald Thompson	GBR	4:25:30.0 OR
2. John Ljunggren	SWE	4:25:47.0
3. Abdon Pamich	ITA	4:27:55.4
4. Aleksandr Stcherbina	SOV	4:31:44.0
5. Thomas Misson	GBR	4:33:03.0
6. Alexander Oakley	CAN	4:33:08.6
7. Giuseppe Dordoni	ITA	4:33:28.8
8. Zora Singh	IND	4:37:45.0

In 1956, Don Thompson had been in fifth place with only 5000 meters to go, when he collapsed and failed to finish. With this bad memory in mind, he decided to acclimatize himself well in advance. But it is not easy to simulate a hot and humid September day in Rome when you live in Cranford, Middlesex. Fortunately, Don Thompson was quite a resourceful person. Several times each week, the 5-foot 5½-inch fire insurance clerk hauled heaters, hot water, and boiling kettles into his bathroom, sealed the doors and windows, and did his exercises in steaming 100-degree Fahrenheit (38-degree Centigrade) heat.

Sure enough, the race began in 87-degree Fahrenheit (30.5-degree Centigrade) weather, but Don Thompson was ready. At the halfway point, he found himself in first place, following the disqualification of two of the leaders and the early overexertions of several others. Surprisingly, his only challenger was 1948 gold medalist John Ljunggren, who was two days shy of his 41st birthday. With 5000 meters to go, the two men were only one second apart. But then Thompson managed to pull away by 18 seconds over the next two kilometers, a lead that he was able to maintain the rest of the way.

1964 Tokyo C: 34, N: 19, D: 10.18. WR: 4:14:02.4 (Abdon Pamich)

1. Abdon Pamich	ITA	4:11:12.4 OR
2. Paul Nihill	GBR	4:11:31.2
3. Ingvar Pettersson	SWE	4:14:17.4
4. Burkhard Leuschke	GDR	4:15:26.8
5. Robert Gardiner	AUS	4:17:06.8
6. Christoph Höhne	GDR	4:17:41.6
7. Anatoly Vedyakov	SOV	4:19:56.0
8. Kurt Sakowski	GDR	4:20:31.0

The race resolved into a two-man battle between Pamich and Nihill. At the 38-kilometer mark, Pamich was overcome by nausea and forced to take a 15-second vomit break. He regained the lead quickly, however, and fought off Nihill's challenges for the remainder of the race.

1968 Mexico City C: 36, N: 18, D: 10.17. WR: 4:10:41.8 (Christoph Höhne)

1. Christoph Höhne	GDR	4:20:13.6
2. Antal Kiss	HUN	4:30:17.0
3. Larry Young	USA	4:31:55.4
4. Peter Selzer	GDR	4:33:09.8
5. Stig-Erik Lindberg	SWE	4:34:05.0
6. Vittorio Visini	ITA	4:36:33.2
7. Bryan Eley	GBR	4:37:33.0
8. José Pedraza Zuniga	MEX	4:37:52.0

Favorite Christoph Höhne drew away after passing the halfway mark, and won by an incredible ten-minute margin. Paul Nihill, who collapsed after 44 kilometers, suffered his only defeat in 86 races between December 1967 and June 1970. He finished ninth at the 1972 Olympics.

1972 Munich C: 36, N: 18, D: 9.3. WR: 3:52:44.6 (Bernd Kannenberg)

1. Bernd Kannenberg	GER	3:56:11.6 OR
2. Veniamin Soldatenko	SOV	3:58:24.0
3. Larry Young	USA	4:00:46.0
4. Otto Barch	SOV	4:01:35.4
5. Peter Selzer	GDR	4:04:05.4
6. Gerhard Weidner	GER	4:06:26.0
7. Vittorio Visini	ITA	4:08:31.4
8. Gabriel Hernandez	MEX	4:12:09.0

Kannenberg and Soldatenko walked together for 35 kilometers. Kannenberg, who had dropped out in the middle of the 20-kilometer race, noticed that Soldatenko was slow in taking his refreshments at the 35-kilometer food and drink stand, so he decided to pick up the pace. Soldatenko, worried because he had already received a warning, was unable to respond.

1976 not held

1980 Moscow C: 27, N: 14, D: 7.30. WR: 3:41:39.0 (Raul Gonzalez)

1. Hartwig Gauder	GDR	3:49:24.0 OR
2. Jorge Llopart	SPA	3:51:25.0
3. Yevgeny Ivchenko	SOV	3:56:32.0
4. Bengt Simonsen	SWE	3:57:08.0
5. Vyacheslav Fursov	SOV	3:58:32.0
6. José Marin	SPA	4:03:08.0
7. Stanislaw Rola	POL	4:07:07.0
8. Willi Sawall	AUS	4:08:25.0

Gold medalist Hartwig Gauder was born in West Germany, but his family moved to East Germany in 1960. Forty-two-year-old bronze medalist Yevgeny Ivchenko had been credited with a controversial time of 3:37:36.0 on the Olympic course on May 23, 1980.

HIGH JUMP

In high-jump competitions, a contestant may pass at any height. Three successive misses results in elimination, even if the misses are at different heights. Current rules decide ties in the following manner:

1. The competitor with the fewest misses at the last cleared height wins. If there is still a tie, then:
2. The competitor with the fewest total misses wins. If there is still a tie, then:
3. The competitor who has taken the fewest attempts, successful or unsuccessful, wins. If there is still a tie, it is recorded as such, unless the tie is for first place. In which case:
4. Each competitor is given one extra jump. If there is still a tie, then the bar is raised or lowered until the tie is broken.

High-jumpers must take off from one foot. In April 1954, U.S. tumbler Dick Browning reportedly somersaulted over a bar set at 7 feet 6 inches (2.28 meters). In 1962 Gary Chamberlain did a back handspring with a back flip over a bar set at 7 feet 4 inches (2.23 meters). He landed on his feet.

1896 Athens C: 5, N: 3, D: 4.10. WR: 1.97, 6–5 5/8 (Michael Sweeney)

		M	FT.– IN.
1. Ellery Clark	USA	1.81	5-11¼
2. James Connolly	USA	1.65	5-5
2. Robert Garrett	USA	1.65	5-5
4. Henrik Sjöberg	SWE	1.60	5-3
5. Fritz Hofmann	GER	1.55	5-1

Ellery Clark was a 22-year-old Harvard undergraduate who was granted a leave of absence for the Olympics because of his high grade-average.

1900 Paris C: 11, N: 7, D: 7.15. WR: 1.97, 6–5 5/8 (Michael Sweeney)

		M	FT.– IN.
1. Irving Baxter	USA	1.90	6-2¾ OR
2. Patrick Leahy	GBR/IRL	1.78	5-10
3. Lajos Gönczy	HUN	1.75	5-8¾
4. Carl-Albert Andersen	NOR	1.70	5-7
5. Eric Lemming	SWE	1.70	5-7
6. Waldemar Steffens	GER	1.70	5-7
7. Louis Monnier	FRA	1.60	5-3
8. Tore Blom	SWE	1.50	4-11

Two Americans, William Remington and Walter Carroll, refused to take part in the final because it was held on a Sunday. Silver medalist Pat Leahy had reportedly cleared 6 feet 4 inches at least six times back in Ireland, but in Paris he missed three times at 6 feet.

1904 St. Louis C: 6, N: 3, D: 8.29. WR: 1.97, 6–5 5/8 (Michael Sweeney)

		M	FT.– IN.
1. Samuel Jones	USA	1.80	5-11
2. Garrett Serviss	USA	1.77	5-9¾
3. Paul Weinstein	GER	1.77	5-9¾
4. Lajos Gönczy	HUN	1.75	5-9
5. Emil Freymark	USA	—	—
6. Ervin Barker	USA	1.70	5-7

Lajos Gönczy had brought with him to the United States several bottles of potent Hungarian wine, which were confiscated by Hungarian team officials prior to the competition. Unable to clear even 5 feet 9¾ inches, Gönczy finished a disappointing fourth. Several days later, Gönczy took part in an unofficial handicap event and successfully cleared 6 feet 2 inches. When the other Hungarians rushed up to congratulate him, they smelled his breath and discovered that he had found the hidden bottles of wine.

1906 Athens C: 24, N: 10, D: 5.1. WR: 1.97, 6–5 5/8 (Michael Sweeney)

		M	FT.– IN.
1. Cornelius Leahy	GBR/IRL	1.775	5-10
2. Lajos Gönczy	HUN	1.75	5-8¾
3. Themistoklis Diakidis	GRE	1.725	5-8
3. Herbert Kerrigan	USA	1.725	5-8
5. Gunnar Rönström	SWE	1.70	5-7

Herbert Kerrigan had been the favorite, but he was injured when a huge wave hit the ship that carried the U.S. team to Athens.

1908 London C: 20, N: 10, D: 7.21. WR: 1.97, 6–5 5/8 (Michael Sweeney)

		M	FT.– IN.
1. Harry Porter	USA	1.905	6-3 OR
2. George "Géo" André	FRA	1.88	6-2
2. Cornelius Leahy	GBR/IRL	1.88	6-2
2. István Somodi	HUN	1.88	6-2
5. Herbert Gidney	USA	1.853	6-1
5. Thomas Moffitt	USA	1.853	6-1
7. John Neil Patterson	USA	1.83	6-0

DNC: Axel Hedenlund (SWE)

1912 Stockholm C: 26, N: 9, D: 7.8. WR: 2.005, 6–7 (George Horine)

		M	FT.– IN.
1. Alma Richards	USA	1.93	6-4 OR
2. Hans Liesche	GER	1.91	6-3¼
3. George Horine	USA	1.89	6-2¼
4. Egon Erickson	USA	1.87	6-1½
4. James Thorpe	USA	1.87	6-1½
6. Harry Grumpelt	USA	1.85	6-0¾
6. John Johnstone	USA	1.85	6-0¾
8. Karl-Axel Kullerstrand	SWE	1.83	6-0

Alma Richards was a tall, awkward-looking 22-year-old Mormon from Parowan, Utah. On the ship from New York to Stockholm, he became the butt of countless "country boob" jokes made by the other members of the U.S. team. In the final Olympic competition, Richards seemed to have quite a bit of trouble, missing as many jumps as he made. Yet when the bar was raised to 6 feet 3¼ inches, the only jumpers left were Richards, Hans Liesche of Germany, and the favorite, George Horine, inventor of what came to be known as the "western-roll" style of high-jumping. Liesche cleared smoothly on the first try, but Horine missed three times and was eliminated. Richards, however, cleared the bar on his third and final attempt.

The bar was then put up to 6 feet 4 inches. Alma Richards, scheduled to jump first, walked away from the high jump area to be by himself. He closed his eyes and bowed his head, and made a deal with God. "I told the Lord," he later wrote, "that if He would help me to win the high jump in the Olympic Games at Stockholm, I would do my best to be a good boy and set a good example." Without further hesitation, Richards, who had never before come close to jumping 6 feet 4 inches, dashed toward the bar and sailed over with almost two inches to spare. Liesche was completely unnerved. He failed twice. Then, just as he had composed himself for his final attempt, a gun went off to signal the start of a race. Liesche waited for the race to end and then composed himself once more. This time the band began to play. After nine minutes, a Swedish official approached him and asked him to hurry up. This was the final blow. Liesche ran at the bar, but missed completely. Alma Richards, transformed from a country bumpkin into a hero in the eyes of his teammates, went on to be a good boy for the rest of his life.

1920 Antwerp C: 22, N: 8, D: 8.17. WR: 2.01, 6–7¼ (Edward Beeson)

		M	FT.–IN.	
1. Richmond Landon	USA	1.935	6-4	OR
2. Harold Muller	USA	1.90	6-2¾	
3. Bo Ekelund	SWE	1.90	6-2¾	
4. Walter Whalen	USA	1.85	6-0¾	
5. John Murphy	USA	1.85	6-0¾	
6. B. Howard Baker	GBR	1.85	6-0¾	
7. Pierre Lewden	FRA	1.80	5-10¾	
7. Einar Thulin	SWE	1.80	5-10¾	

1924 Paris C: 21, N: 15, D: 7.7. WR: 2.03, 6–8¼ (Harold Osborn)

		M	FT.–IN.	
1. Harold Osborn	USA	1.98	6-6	OR
2. Leroy Brown	USA	1.95	6-4¾	
3. Pierre Lewden	FRA	1.92	6-3½	
4. Thomas Poor	USA	1.88	6-2	
5. Jenö Gáspár	HUN	1.88	6-2	
6. Helge Jansson	SWE	1.85	6-0¾	
7. P. Guilloux	FRA	1.85	6-0¾	
8. S. Helgesen	NOR	1.83	6-0	
8. L. Roberts	SAF	1.83	6-0	

Harold Osborn cleared every height on his first attempt. Five days later he earned a second gold medal in the decathlon.

1928 Amsterdam C: 35, N: 17, D: 7.29. WR: 2.03, 6–8¼ (Harold Osborn)

		M	FT.–IN.
1. Robert King	USA	1.94	6-4½
2. Benjamin Hedges	USA	1.91	6-3¼
3. Claude Ménard	FRA	1.91	6-3¼
4. Simeon Toribio	PHI	1.91	6-3¼
5. Harold Osborn	USA	1.91	6-3¼
6. Kazuo Kimura	JAP	1.88	6-2
7. A. Cherrier (FRA), Pierre Lewden (FRA), Charles McGinnis (USA), Mikio Oda (JAP)		1.88	6-2

Places two through five were decided by a jump-off.

1932 Los Angeles C: 14, N: 10, D: 7.31. WR: 2.03, 6–8¼ (Harold Osborn)

		M	FT.–IN.
1. Duncan McNaughton	CAN	1.97	6-5½
2. Robert Van Osdel	USA	1.97	6-5½
3. Simeon Toribio	PHI	1.97	6-5½
4. Cornelius Johnson	USA	1.97	6-5½
5. Ilmari Reinikka	FIN	1.94	6-4¼
6. Kazuo Kimura	JAP	1.94	6-4¼
7. Misao Ono	JAP	1.90	6-2¾
7. Jerzy Plawczyk	POL	1.90	6-2¾

Bob Van Osdel and Duncan McNaughton were good friends and fellow students at the University of Southern California in Los Angeles. Van Osdel had qualified for the U.S. team, as expected, by clearing 6 feet 6⅝ inches at the U.S. trials. McNaughton, on the other hand, had to wage a one-man campaign to convince the Canadian Olympic Association to let him compete. Undeterred by their constant refusals, McNaughton waited until the Canadian team arrived in Los Angeles, and then badgered them in person until they finally relented.

Van Osdel, McNaughton, Toribio, and 18-year-old Los Angeles High School student Cornelius Johnson all cleared 6 feet 5½ inches, but they all missed at 6 feet 6¾ inches. Following the rules in force at the time, the bar was then raised, lowered, raised and lowered until the contest was decided. After Johnson and Toribio had been eliminated, Van Osdel, who had been informally coaching McNaughton ever since he had first arrived in Los Angeles from Vancouver two years earlier, approached his Canadian friend and advised him on improving his technique. He concluded, "Get your kick working and you will be over." That piece of advice and encouragement did the trick. McNaughton cleared the bar while Van Osdel missed.

If current tie-breaking rules had been used back in 1932, Van Osdel would have won the gold medal, Johnson the silver, and McNaughton the bronze.

1936 Berlin C: 40, N: 24, D: 8.2. WR: 2.07, 6–9¾ (Cornelius Johnson, David Albritton)

		M	FT.–IN.	
1. Cornelius Johnson	USA	2.03	6-8	OR
2. David Albritton	USA	2.00	6-6¾	
3. Delos Thurber	USA	2.00	6-6¾	
4. Kalevi Kotkas	FIN	2.00	6-6¾	
5. Kimio Yada	JAP	1.97	6-5½	
6. Yoshiro Asakuma	JAP	1.94	6-4¼	
6. Lauri Kalima	FIN	1.94	6-4¼	
6. Hiroshi Tanaka	JAP	1.94	6-4¼	
6. Gustav Weinkötz	GER	1.94	6-4¼	

Johnson won the gold medal without a miss and didn't even take off his sweatsuit until the bar had reached 6 feet 6¾ inches. Places 2 through 4 were decided by a jump-off, the last time such a procedure was used in Olympic competition. Adolf Hitler had personally congratulated the winners of the first two events of the day, Germans and Finns, but he left the stadium before the ceremony honoring the three Americans. Both Johnson and Albritton were black.

1948 London C: 26, N: 16, D: 7.30. WR: 2.11, 6–11 (Lester Steers)

			FT.–	
		M	IN.	
1. John Winter	AUS	1.98	6-6	
2. Björn Paulson	NOR	1.95	6-4¾	
3. George Stanich	USA	1.95	6-4¾	
4. Dwight Eddleman	USA	1.95	6-4¾	
5. Georges Damitio	FRA	1.95	6-4¾	
6. Arthur Jackes	CAN	1.90	6-2¾	
7. Alan Paterson	GBR	1.90	6-2¾	
7. Hans Wähli	SWI	1.90	6-2¾	

John Winter, a 23-year-old bank clerk from Perth, injured his back when he cleared 6 feet 4¾ inches. He decided to try one more height anyway, and made 6 feet 6 inches on his first attempt. Then he watched in surprise as the remaining four jumpers, including two Americans who had had to clear 6 feet 7¼ inches just to make the team, failed three times each. For the first time in the Olympics, ties were decided according to fewer misses.

1952 Helsinki C: 36, N: 24, D: 7.20. WR: 2.11, 6–11 (Lester Steers)

			FT.–	
		M	IN.	
1. Walter Davis	USA	2.04	6-8½	OR
2. Kenneth Wiesner	USA	2.01	6-7	
3. José Telles da Conceição	BRA	1.98	6-6	
4. Gösta Svensson	SWE	1.98	6-6	
5. Ronald Pavitt	GBR	1.95	6-4¾	
6. Ion Söter	ROM	1.95	6-4¾	
7. Arnold Betton	USA	1.95	6-4¾	
8. Björn Gundersen	NOR	1.90	6-2¾	

The 6-foot 8-inch , 206-pound Davis was an All-American basketball player from Texas A.& M.. Stricken by polio at the age of 8, he had been unable to walk for three years.

1956 Melbourne C: 28, N: 19, D: 11.23. WR: 2.15, 7–0½ (Charles Dumas)

			FT.–	
		M	IN.	
1. Charles Dumas	USA	2.12	6-11½	OR
2. Charles Porter	AUS	2.10	6-10¾	
3. Igor Kashkarov	SOV	2.08	6-9¾	
4. Stig Pettersson	SWE	2.06	6-9	
5. Kenneth Money	CAN	2.03	6-8	
6. Vladimir Sitkin	SOV	2.00	6-6¾	
7. Phil Reavis	USA	2.00	6-6¾	
7. Colin Ridgeway	AUS	2.00	6-6¾	

When Les Steers jumped 6 feet 11 inches on June 14, 1941, it seemed that the magic 7-foot barrier would be cleared at any time. But it was 12 years before Walt Davis bettered Steer's record with a leap of 6 feet 11½ inches, and even he was unable to go that extra half-inch. It was as if the 7-foot mark was guarded by a protective aura. It is true that 7-foot jumps had been claimed, most notably by Davis in an exhibition, but the first official, in-competition 7-foot jump wasn't achieved until June 29, 1956, when 19-year-old Charley Dumas glided over at the U.S. Olympic trials. There was great interest in Dumas when he arrived in Melbourne, but some of that interest turned to hostility when it turned out that Dumas didn't believe in practicing or even training, other than a few stretching exercises each morning.

However, Dumas knew what he was up to. He won the gold medal with relative ease, despite the spirited challenge of local favorite Chilla Porter, who improved his personal best by two inches.

1960 Rome C: 32, N: 23, D: 9.1. WR: 2.23, 7–3¾ (John Thomas)

			FT.–	
		M	IN.	
1. Robert Shavlakadze	SOV	2.16	7-1	OR
2. Valery Brumel	SOV	2.16	7-1	
3. John Thomas	USA	2.14	7-0¼	
4. Viktor Bolshov	SOV	2.14	7-0¼	
5. Stig Pettersson	SWE	2.09	6-10¼	
6. Charles Dumas	USA	2.03	6-8	
7. Jiři Lansky	CZE	2.03	6-8	
7. Kjell-Ake Nilsson	SWE	2.03	6-8	
7. Theo Püll	GER	2.03	6-8	

American sportswriters boasted that the high jump was one gold medal that was "in the bag" for the Unites States. The U.S. team consisted of 17-year-old Joe Faust, who had cleared 7 feet, defending champion Charley Dumas, and the 6-foot 5-inch world record holder John Thomas, who had jumped 7 feet over 30 times and hadn't been defeated in two years. But Faust, hampered by an ankle injury, was unable to clear 6 feet 6¾ inches. And Dumas, plagued by a knee injury that American officials had tried to convince him was imaginary, bowed out at 6 feet 10¼ inches. This left Thomas to battle it out with three jumpers from the U.S.S.R.: Soviet champion Viktor Bolshov, 18-year-old Siberian-born Valery Brumel, who had suddenly improved three and a half inches in August to 7 feet 1½ inches, and Robert Shavlakadze, a mustachioed 27-year-old from Tbilisi, Georgia.

At 6 feet 11½ inches Thomas passed. Bolshov and Shavlakadze went over the bar on their first attempts, while Brumel missed twice before clearing. This height also saw the departure of Stig Pettersson. The bar was raised to 7 feet ¼ inch. Brumel and Bolshov missed, but Shavlakadze cleared with his first try, the first time he had ever jumped over 7 feet in competition. Thomas missed, but the second time around, he and the other two Soviet jumpers all cleared the bar.

The next height was 7 feet 1 inch. The only one to clear

on the first attempt was Shavlakadze, who had now made seven straight successful jumps since missing his first try of the afternoon at 6 feet 6¾ inches. Brumel cleared on his second try, but Bolshov and Thomas missed all three times. For Robert Shavlakadze, this was the greatest day of his career. For Valery Brumel, it was just the beginning. As for John Thomas, he was disappointed, but proud that he had earned an Olympic medal. Consequently, it came as a shock to the mild-mannered teenager when the very same sportswriters and fans who had been singing his praises only a few days earlier turned on him and accused him of getting carried away with all the publicity that they themselves had spread.

"That was the first time I learned people didn't like me," Thomas later recalled. "They only like winners. They don't give credit to a man for trying. I was called a quitter, a man with no heart. It left me sick." Thomas had nightmares for months until he finally came to accept that American sports fans were fickle. "American spectators are frustrated athletes," he concluded. "In the champion, they see what they'd like to be. In the loser, they see what they actually are, and they treat him with scorn."

1964 Tokyo C: 29, N: 20, D: 10.21. WR: 2.28, 7–5¾ (Valery Brumel)

			FT.–		
		M	IN.	
1. Valery Brumel	SOV	2.18	7-1¾	OR
2. John Thomas	USA	2.18	7-1¾	OR
3. John Rambo	USA	2.16	7-1	
4. Stig Pettersson	SWE	2.14	7-0¼	
5. Robert Shavlakadze	SOV	2.14	7-0¼	
6. Ralf Drecoll	GER	2.09	6-10¼	
6. Kjell-Åke Nilsson	SWE	2.09	6-10¼	
8. Edward Caruthers	USA	2.09	6-10¼	

By 1964 the situation had become easier for John Thomas, since he was no longer the favorite. Instead, the pressure of great expectations had shifted to Valery Brumel, the current world record holder. And Brumel definitely felt that pressure. He lost to Shavlakadze at the 1964 U.S.S.R. championships, and arrived in Tokyo in somewhat of a crisis. Well below form, he worked out in secret so that his image of invincibility wouldn't be tarnished. When he cleared 6 feet 9¾ inches in practice, his coach lied to him and told him the bar had actually been two inches higher.

The Olympic qualifying round was held on October 20. Brumel missed twice at 6 feet 8 inches and was on the verge of not even making it to the final, when he got himself together and cleared the bar successfully, thus preventing a complete disaster.

The next day, for the final, Brumel was more composed. He made it through 6 feet 11½ inches without a miss, a feat matched only by Robert Shavlakadze. Pettersson, Rambo, and Thomas each cleared 6 feet 11½ inches with their second try. At 7 feet ¼ inches, only Rambo went over

the first time, and only Pettersson made it the second time. The three medalists from 1960 were now each one miss from elimination. But all three literally rose to the challenge and sailed over without dislodging the bar. This seemed to be a turning point for Valery Brumel. With renewed confidence, he cleared 7 feet 1 inch on his first attempt. Thomas made it the second time around, and Rambo the third, while Pettersson and Shavlakadze failed at all three attempts. Rambo bowed out at 7 feet 1¾ inches, while Brumel and Thomas both succeeded with their first tries. However, neither man, by now good friends after four years of competition, was able to make it over 7 feet 2½ inches. Brumel and Thomas were both credited with the Olympic record, but Brumel was awarded first place because he had committed fewer misses.

On October 4, 1965, Valery Brumel was riding on the back of a motorcycle being driven by female motorcycle racing champion Tamara Golikova, when they skidded out of control. Although Golikova was unhurt, Brumel was smashed into a concrete pillar and suffered multiple fractures to his right leg. His right foot was hanging limply, barely connected to the rest of his body.

When Brumel had traveled to the United States to compete in a series of competitions against John Thomas, he had been shocked by the behavior of American crowds, which booed Thomas when he missed a jump or, worst of all, when he committed the sin of finishing second. But now that his own sporting career had come to a sudden end, Brumel learned that Soviet fans could be just as harsh. The newspapers lost interest in him, most of his friends drifted away, his wife, perhaps wondering what he had been doing whizzing around on the back of a motorcycle with Tamara Golikova in the first place, divorced him.

After his accident, Brumel had received a telegram that read, "Sometimes a twist of fate seems to have been put there to test a man's strength of character. Don't admit defeat. I sincerely hope you come back to jump again." It was signed "John Thomas." Remarkably, Valery Brumel did jump again. Although he never made it back to international competition, in 1970 he actually cleared 6 feet 11¾ inches. He was also able to channel his energy into other directions, earning a doctorate in sports psychology and publishing a novel about scientists.

1968 Mexico City C: 39, N: 25, D: 10.20. WR: 2.28, 7–5¾ (Valery Brumel)

			FT.–		
		M	IN.	
1. Richard Fosbury	USA	2.24	7-4¼	OR
2. Edward Caruthers	USA	2.22	7-3¼	
3. Valentin Gavrilov	SOV	2.20	7-2½	
4. Valery Skvortsov	SOV	2.16	7-1	
5. Reynaldo Brown	USA	2.14	7-0¼	
6. Giacomo Crosa	ITA	2.14	7-0¼	
7. Gunther Spielvogel	GER	2.14	7-0¼	
8. Lawrie Peckham	AUS	2.12	6-11½	

The 1968 Olympics marked the international debut of Dick Fosbury and his celebrated "Fosbury Flop," which would soon revolutionize high-jumping. Fosbury's technique began by racing up to the bar at great speed and taking off with his left foot. But instead of swinging his right foot up and over the bar, as everyone else did, Fosbury would pivot his right leg back and approach head first with his back to the bar. While the coaches of the world, already exasperated by the steeplechase style of Amos Biwott, shook their heads in disbelief, the Mexico City audience was absolutely captivated by Fosbury. Fosbury cleared every height through 7 feet 3¼ inches without a miss and then achieved a personal record of 7 feet 4¼ inches to win the gold medal. By 1980, 13 of the 16 Olympic finalists were using the Fosbury Flop.

1972 Munich C: 40, N: 29, D: 9.10. WR: 2.29, 7–6 (Ni Chih-chin, Patrick Matzdorf)

		M	FT.–IN.
1. Yuri Tarmak	SOV	2.23	7-3¾
2. Stefan Junge	GDR	2.21	7-3
3. Dwight Stones	USA	2.21	7-3
4. Hermann Magerl	GER	2.18	7-1¾
5. Ádám Szepesi	HUN	2.18	7-1¾
6. John Beers	CAN	2.15	7-0½
6. István Major	HUN	2.15	7-0½
8. Rustam Akhmyetov	SOV	2.15	7-0½

1976 Montreal C: 36, N: 23, D: 7.31. WR: 2.31, 7–7 (Dwight Stones)

		M	FT.–IN.	
1. Jacek Wszola	POL	2.25	7-4½	OR
2. Gregory Joy	CAN	2.23	7-3¾	
3. Dwight Stones	USA	2.21	7-3	
4. Sergei Budalov	SOV	2.21	7-3	
5. Sergei Senyukov	SOV	2.18	7-1¾	
6. Rodolfo Bergamo	ITA	2.18	7-1¾	
7. Rolf Beilschmidt	GDR	2.18	7-1¾	
8. Jesper Torring	DEN	2.18	7-1¾	

In 1972 Dwight Stones had been one of the darlings of the Munich Games. A mere 18 years old, he had delighted the crowd with his exuberance. Four years later in Montreal, it was a completely different story. Now he was the world record holder and heavy favorite. But several days before the competition began, Stones had launched a verbal attack against the French-Canadian organizers of the Games for failing to complete the stadium as planned. Of particular concern to Stones was the nonappearance of a retractable roof, which would have kept out the rain. Fear of rain was an obsession with Stones because his approach to the bar was unusually fast and sharp. Stones called the Olympic organizers "rude" for forcing the athletes to compete in an unfinished stadium. But by the time that his remarks had been translated into the local papers, he was being accused of calling all French-Canadians "rude."

When Stones appeared on the track for the qualifying round, he was loudly booed. Whenever his name was announced, he was booed; whenever he began a jump he was booed; whenever he missed or made a jump he was booed. The situation degenerated rather badly when U.S. fans in the stadium retaliated by booing a French-Canadian high-jumper, Claude Ferragne.

The next day, Stones tried to make peace with the local crowd by wearing a shirt that bore on the back the slogan "I love French Canadians." Track officials made him take it off. Underneath he had on a 1972 Olympic shirt, which he was wearing because it had been made by a company with whom he had a financial relationship. The officials made him take that one off too. By the time the bar had been raised to 7 feet 1¾ inches, a light rain had begun to fall. At 7 feet 3 inches, the rain had become heavy. Huge puddles formed in the high jump area. Stones, exasperated by the ineffectual attempts of the officials to clear the area, grabbed a squeegee and started mopping up the area himself. Other jumpers joined him, including surprise local favorite Greg Joy. For Stones it was a hopeless cause. Even the eventual winner, 19-year-old Jacek Wszola, when asked later at what point he knew he would win, replied, "When it started to rain."

Four days later, in Philadelphia, Dwight Stones broke his own world record with a leap of 7 feet 7¼ inches.

1980 Moscow C: 30, N: 19, D: 8.1. WR: 2.35, 7–8½ (Jacek Wszola, Dietmar Mogenburg)

		M	FT.–IN.	
1. Gerd Wessig	GDR	2.36	7-8¾	WR
2. Jacek Wszola	POL	2.31	7-7	
3. Jörg Freimuth	GDR	2.31	7-7	
4. Henry Lauterbach	GDR	2.29	7-6	
5. Roland Dalhäuser	SWI	2.24	7-4¼	
6. Vaso Komnenić	YUG	2.24	7-4¼	
7. Adrian Proteasa	ROM	2.21	7-3	
8. Aleksandr Grigoriev	SOV	2.21	7-3	

The anticipated showdown between co-world record holders Jacek Wszola and Dietmar Mogenburg was spoiled when West Germany joined the anti-Soviet boycott. As it turned out, however, neither of them held the world record anymore once the competition was over. Gerd Wessig, a 6-foot 5-inch 21-year-old cook from Schwerin, was one of the big surprises of the 1980 Olympics. He had only qualified for the East German team two weeks earlier when he won the national championship with what was then his personal record of 7 feet 6½ inches. In Moscow he improved by over two inches to become the first man to set a world record in the high jump in the Olympics. Oddly enough, Wessig was also the first jumper since 1896 to make a successful jump beyond the height that had won him the gold medal.

POLE VAULT

The tie-breaking rules for the pole vault are the same as those for the high jump.

1896 Athens C: 5, N: 2, D; 4.10. WR: 3.49, 11–5 3/8 (Walter Rodenbaugh)

		FT.–	
		M	IN.
1. Wiliam Welles Hoyt	USA	3.30	10-10
2. Albert Tyler	USA	3.25	10-8
3. Evangelos Damaskos	GRE	2.85	9-4¼
4. Ioannis Theodoropoulos	GRE	2.80	9-2¼
5. Vasilios Xydas	GRE	2.50	8-2½

There is much confusion among Olympic historians as to the actual heights achieved by all the competitors other than Hoyt.

1900 Paris C: 8, N: 5, D: 7.15. WR: 3.62, 11–10½ (Raymond Clapp)

		FT.–	
		M	IN.
1. Irving Baxter	USA	3.30	10-10
2. Michael Colkett	USA	3.25	10-8
3. Carl-Albert Andersen	NOR	3.20	10-6
4. Eric Lemming	SWE	3.10	10-2
4. Jakab Kauser	HUN	3.10	10-2
4. Louis Gontier	FRA	3.10	10-2
7. Karl Gustaf Staaf	SWE	2.80	9-2¼
8. August Nilsson	SWE	2.60	8-6¼

This event was marred by indecision on the part of the officials in charge. Three of the leading American entrants, Bascom Johnson, Charles Dvorak, and D.S. Horton, objected to the scheduling of the pole vault on a Sunday. Johnson and Dvorak showed up anyway, but were told that the event would be rescheduled, so they left. Then the officials changed their minds and went ahead with the contest without Johnson and Dvorak. In their absence, the pole vault was won by Irving Baxter, who also won the high jump that day. The next day he finished second to Ray Ewry in the three standing jump events. A few days later, in order "to appease the indignant visitors from across the seas," a second pole vault contest was staged. This was won by D.S. Horton at 11 feet 3¾ inches with Dvorak second at 11 feet 1¾ inches.

1904 St. Louis C: 7, N: 2, D: 9.3. WR: 3.69, 12–1½ (Norman Dole)

		FT.–	
		M	IN.
1. Charles Dvorak	USA	3.50	11-5¾
2. Leroy Samse	USA	3.43	11-3
3. Louis Wilkins	USA	3.43	11-3
4. Ward McLanahan	USA	3.35	10-11¾
5. Claude Allen	USA	3.35	10-11¾
6. Walter Dray	USA	—	—
7. Paul Weinstein	GER	—	—

1906 Athens C: 11, N: 8, D: 4.25. WR: 3.74, 12–3¼ (Fernand Gonder)

		FT.–	
		M	IN.
1. Fernand Gonder	FRA	3.50	11-5¾
2. Bruno Söderström	SWE	3.40	11-1¾
3. Edward Glover	USA	3.35	10-11¾
4. Theodoris Makris	GRE	3.25	10-8
5. Heikki Åhlmann (Pennola) (FIN), Otto Haug (NOR), I. Kiss (HUN), S. Kountouriotis (GRE), Georgios Banikas (GRE)		3.00	9-10

Gonder won first place by clearing 11 feet 6 inches in a jump-off. When Glover attempted to clear the same height, an official crossed his path. Glover lost his balance and was injured. The Canadian vaulter, Ed Archibald, also had a tough time. His pole disappeared on a train ride through Italy. Olympic officials gave him some local models when he arrived in Athens, but when one of them broke and almost impaled him, he lost confidence and was unable to perform at his usual level.

1908 London C: 14, N: 7. D: 7.24 WR: 3.90, 12–9½ (Walter Dray)

		FT.–		
		M	IN.	
1. Edward Cooke	USA	3.71	12-2	OR
1. Alfred Gilbert	USA	3.71	12-2	OR
3. Ed Archibald	CAN	3.58	11-9	
3. Charles Jacobs	USA	3.58	11-9	
3. Bruno Söderström	SWE	3.58	11-9	
6. Georgios Banikas	GRE	3.50	11-6	
6. Sam Bellah	USA	3.50	11-6	
8. Károly Szathmáry	HUN	3.35	11-0	

Competition in the pole vault was severely disrupted by the sensational incidents surrounding the finish of the marathon. Gold medalist Alfred Gilbert worked his way through Yale as a magician. He is best known today as the inventor of the Erector Set, one of the most popular toys of all time.

1912 Stockholm C: 24, N: 11, D: 7.11. WR: 4.02, 13–2¼ (Marc Wright)

		FT.–		
		M	IN.	
1. Harry Babcock	USA	3.95	12-11½	OR
2. Frank Nelson	USA	3.85	12-7½	
2. Marcus Wright	USA	3.85	12-7½	
4. William Happenny	CAN	3.80	12-5½	
4. Frank Murphy	USA	3.80	12-5½	
4. Bertil Uggla	SWE	3.80	12-5½	
7. Samuel Bellah	USA	3.75	12-3½	
8. Frank Coyle (USA), Gordon Dukes (USA), Bill Fritz (USA)		3.65	11-11¾	

1920 Antwerp C: 14, N: 6, D: 8.20. WR: 4.02, 13–2¼ (Marcus Wright)

| | | FT.– | | |
		M	IN.	
1. Frank Foss	USA	4.09	13-5	WR
2. Henry Petersen	DEN	3.70	12-1½	
3. Edwin Myers	USA	3.60	11-9¾	
4. Edward Knourek	USA	3.60	11-9¾	
5. Ernfrid Rydberg	SWE	3.60	11-9¾	
6. Lauritz Jörgensen	DEN	3.60	11-9¾	
7. Eldon Jenne	USA	3.60	11-9¾	

Foss' world record leap, made in the midst of wind and rain, excited the crowd more than any other event in the 1920 Games. His 15½ inch margin of victory was by far the largest in Olympic history.

1924 Paris C: 20, N: 13, D: 7.10. WR: 4.21, 13–9¾ (Charles Hoff)

| | | FT.– | | |
		M	IN.	
1. Lee Barnes	USA	3.95	12-11½	
2. Glenn Graham	USA	3.95	12-11½	
3. James Brooker	USA	3.90	12-9½	
4. Henry Petersen	DEN	3.90	12-9½	
5. Victor Pickard	CAN	3.80	12-5½	
6. Ralph Spearow	USA	3.70	12-1½	
7. M. Henrijean	BEL	3.66	12-0	

Charles Hoff, the Norwegian world record holder, withdrew because of an injury. In his absence, the event was won by 17-year-old Lee Barnes, a student at Hollywood High School in Los Angeles. In 1927 Barnes appeared in the film *College*, as a stand-in for Buster Keaton in a scene that required him to pole vault into a second-story window.

1928 Amsterdam C: 20, N: 13, D: 8.1. WR: 4.31, 14–1¾ (Lee Barnes)

| | | FT.– | | |
		M	IN.	
1. Sabin Carr	USA	4.20	13-9¼	OR
2. William Droegemuller	USA	4.10	13-5¼	
3. Charles McGinnis	USA	3.95	12-11½	
4. Victor Pickard	CAN	3.95	12-11½	
5. Lee Barnes	USA	3.95	12-11½	
6. Yonataro Nakazawa	JAP	3.90	12-9½	
7. Henry Lindblad	SWE	3.90	12-9½	
8. János Karlovits	HUN	3.80	12-5½	

Sabin Carr of Yale had become the first vaulter to clear 14 feet on May 27, 1927.

1932 Los Angeles C: 8, N: 4, D: 8.3. WR: 4.37, 14–4¼ (William Graber)

| | | FT.– | | |
		M	IN.	
1. William Miller	USA	4.31	14-1¾	OR
2. Shuhei Nishida	JAP	4.30	14-1¼	
3. George Jefferson	USA	4.20	13-9½	
4. William Graber	USA	4.15	13-7½	
5. Shizuo Mochizuki	JAP	4.00	13-1½	
6. Lucio de Castro	BRA	3.90	12-9½	
7. Peter Chlentzos	GRE	3.75	12-3½	

The 1932 competition was expected to provide a clean sweep for the United States, but no one had counted on the unexpected determination of Japan's Shuhei Nishida, who gained the support of the previously partisan crowd with his great performance and sportsmanship. Nevertheless, most of the 80,000 American spectators breathed a sigh of relief when Bill Miller avoided a vault-off by clearing 14 feet 1¾ inches on his third attempt.

1936 Berlin C: 30, N: 21, D: 8.5. WR: 4.43, 14–6½ (George Varoff)

| | | FT.– | | |
		M	IN.	
1. Earle Meadows	USA	4.35	14-3¼	OR
2. Shuhei Nishida	JAP	4.25	13-11¼	
3. Sueo Oe	JAP	4.25	13-11¼	
4. William Sefton	USA	4.25	13-11¼	
5. William Graber	USA	4.15	13-7¼	
6. Kiyoshi Adachi (JAP), Sylvanus Apps (CAN), Péter Bácsalmási (HUN), Josef Haunzwickel (AUT), Danilo Innocenti (ITA), Jan Korejs (CZE), Bo Ljungberg (SWE), Alfred Proksch (AUT), Wilhelm Sznajder (POL), Frederick Webster (GBR), Viktor Zsuffka (HUN)		4.00	13-1½	

On July 4, 1936, George Varoff, a 22-year-old janitor from San Francisco, rose from obscurity to set a world record of 14 feet 6½ inches at the A.A.U. championships in Princeton, New Jersey. Sportswriters rushed in to get his story. They learned that he came from a poor family of Ukrainian immigrants; that he was a music major at Oregon University who played the string fiddle; that he hoped to land a good job in order to help his family. VAROFF TYPIFIES SPIRIT OF AMERICA read a typical headline. But the following week at the U.S. Olympic trials, Varoff bowed out at 14 feet 3 inches and failed to make the U.S. team. The press moved on to other stories.

The 1936 Olympic final was another dramatic duel between the Americans and the Japanese that lasted into the night and finished in the eerie glow of floodlights. After it had been determined that Meadows had finished first and Sefton fourth, Nishida and Oe refused to vault-off for second and third. Instead they decided by lot that Nishida would be placed second and Oe third. Back home in Japan, they brought their medals to a jeweler and had them cut in half lengthwise. Then they were fused back together so that each man had a medal that was half silver and half bronze.

1948 London C: 19, N: 10, D: 8.2. WR: 4.77, 15–7¾ (Cornelius Warmerdam)

		FT.–	
		M	IN.
1. O. Guinn Smith	USA	4.30	14-1¼
2. Erkki Kataja	FIN	4.20	13-9¼
3. Robert Richards	USA	4.20	13-9¼
4. Erling Kaas	NOR	4.10	13-5¼
5. Ragnar Lundberg	SWE	4.10	13-5¼
6. Richmond Morcom	USA	3.95	12-11½
7. Hugo Göllors	SWE	3.95	12-11½
7. Valto Olenius	FIN	3.95	12-11½

The period between the 1936 and 1948 Olympics was dominated by Cornelius "Dutch" Warmerdam, the first person to vault 15 feet. Between 1940 and his retirement in 1944, Warmerdam cleared 15 feet 43 times. No one else accomplished the height until 1951. In fact, when he retired, Warmerdam's best vault was nine inches higher than anyone else's. His world record of 15 feet 7¾ inches, set on May 23, 1942, wasn't broken until April 1957.

The 1948 Olympic final was concluded during a downpour. With ties now decided on the basis of fewer misses, Erkki Kataja was poised for victory if no one could clear 14 feet 1¼ inches. But Guinn Smith made it on his final try, and the U.S. pole vault winning streak was kept alive.

1952 Helsinki C: 25, N: 17, D: 7.22 WR: 4.77, 15–7¾ (Cornelius Warmerdam)

		FT.–		
		M	IN.	
1. Robert Richards	USA	4.55	14-11	OR
2. Donald Laz	USA	4.50	14-9	
3. Ragnar Lundberg	SWE	4.40	14-5¼	
4. Pyotr Denisenko	SOV	4.40	14-5¼	
5. Valto Olenius	FIN	4.30	14-1¼	
6. Bunkichi Sawada	JAP	4.20	13-9¼	
7. Vladimir Bražnik	SOV	4.20	13-9¼	
8. Viktor Knyazev	SOV	4.20	13-9¼	

The competition came down to a duel between Don Laz and "The Vaulting Vicar," Reverend Bob Richards, a theology professor in California. They both missed for the first time at 14 feet 9 inches and then cleared with their second attempts. When they both missed twice at 14 feet 11 inches, discussions began as to how a vault-off would be conducted. But Richards solved the problem quickly by clearing the bar on his third attempt. The year 1952 was the first time that the U.S.S.R. competed in the Olympics, and many politicians, journalists, and athletes looked at the Olympics as a front-line battle in the Cold War. Bob Richards thought otherwise and was a major force in encouraging interaction and friendship between athletes from the United States and the U.S.S.R.

Both Richards and Laz had sons who vaulted higher than their fathers. Bob Richards, Jr., cleared 17 feet 6 inches in 1973, and Doug Laz leaped 17 feet 4¾ inches in 1976.

1956 Melbourne C: 19, N: 12, D: 11.26. WR: 4.77, 15–7¾ (Cornelius Warmerdam)

		FT.–		
		M	IN.	
1. Robert Richards	USA	4.56	14-11½	OR
2. Robert Gutowski	USA	4.53	14-10¼	
3. Georgios Roubanis	GRE	4.50	14-9	
4. George Mattos	USA	4.35	14-3¼	
5. Ragnar Lundberg	SWE	4.25	13-11¼	
6. Zenon Ważny	POL	4.25	13-11¼	
7. Eeles Landström	FIN	4.25	13-11¼	
8. Manfred Preussger	GDR	4.25	13-11¼	

The qualifying round almost saw a major upset when Bob Richards missed twice at the shockingly low height of 13 feet 1½ inches. He cleared on his third attempt and was in control for the rest of the contest. Gusty winds and a patchy runway hampered the quality of performance in the final. As it happened though, the wind actually helped Richards on his winning vault. After missing once at 14 feet 11½ inches, he hit the bar on his second attempt. Richards lay on his back for 30 seconds watching the bar bounce and quiver. "I was scared to change my position in the pit in case the slightest vibration brought it down," he explained. But the wind kept the bar in place and Richards became the only person to win two gold medals and three total medals in the pole vault.

It was silver medalist Bob Gutowski who finally broke Cornelius Warmerdam's world record with a vault of 15 feet 8¼ inches on April 27, 1957. Richards had predicted that Gutowski would someday be the first vaulter to break the 16-foot barrier. However, Bob Gutowski was killed in a car crash at the age of 25 on August 2, 1960.

The 1956 competition was also noteworthy because it saw the first appearance in the pole vault competition of the fiberglass pole, which would revolutionize pole vaulting. It was used by bronze medalist Georgios Roubanis, who improved his personal best by three and a half inches. The first Olympic athlete to use a fiberglass pole was Bob Mathias in the 1952 decathlon.

1960 Rome C: 30, N: 20, D: 9.7. WR: 4.80, 15–9¼ (Donald Bragg)

		FT.–		
		M	IN.	
1. Donald Bragg	USA	4.70	15-5	OR
2. Ronald Morris	USA	4.60	15-1	
3. Eeles Landström	FIN	4.55	14-11	
4. Rolando Cruz	PUR	4.55	14-11	
5. Günter Malcher	GDR	4.50	14-9	
6. Igor Petrenko	SOV	4.50	14-9	
6. Matti Sutinen	FIN	4.50	14-9	
8. Rudolf Tomášek	CZE	4.50	14-9	

Don "Tarzan" Bragg began the final competition cautiously, but gained confidence with each leap and finished strongly. After he had won, Bragg, whose dream it was to play Tarzan in the movies, delighted the crowd by celebrating with a Tarzan yell.

Silver medalist Ron Morris had failed to clear the qualifying height of 14 feet 5¼ inches. However, Olympic rules state that at least 12 men must compete in the final. Since only 10 had made the required height, the three vaulters with the next best records were added to the final. One of them was Morris. Bragg, by the way, never did get to play Tarzan, although he did come close. Shooting had already begun for *Tarzan and the Jewels of Opar* in 1964, and Bragg was in front of the cameras, happily swinging from vines, when a court order halted the production because of copyright infringement. Forced to become a salesman of drug supplies, Bragg later opened a boys' camp in New Jersey.

1964 Tokyo C: 32, N: 20, D: 10.17. WR: 5.28, 17–4 (Frederick Hansen)

			FT.–	
			M	IN.
1. Frederick Hansen	USA	5.10	16-8¾	OR
2. Wolfgang Reinhardt	GER	5.05	16-6¾	
3. Klaus Lehnertz	GER	5.00	16-4¾	
4. Manfred Preussger	GDR	5.00	16-4¾	
5. Gennady Bliznyetsov	SOV	4.95	16-2¾	
6. Rudolf Tomášek	CZE	4.90	16-0¾	
7. Pentti Nikula	FIN	4.90	16-0¾	
8. Billy Pemelton	USA	4.80	15-9	

The pole vault world record was broken 17 times between the Rome Olympics and the Tokyo Olympics, the last two times by Fred Hansen of Cuero, Texas. The 1964 final was a long, drawn-out affair that ended up lasting 8¾ hours. For the first eight hours, Hansen attempted only four vaults, all of them successful. When the bar was raised to 16 feet 6¾ inches, Hansen gambled by passing. Tomášek, Bliznyetsov, Preussger and Lehnertz all bowed out, but Wolfgang Reinhardt, who had beaten Hansen earlier in the year, cleared on his first try. The bar was moved up to 16 feet 8¾ inches and suddenly, after hours of boredom, the pole vault had become a dramatic contest. Hansen and Reinhardt both missed twice. If Hansen missed again, the gold medal would go to Reinhardt and the United States would lose the pole vault for the first time ever (not including the 1906 Intercalated Games). "Please don't think I'm corny," Hansen later said, "but I was thinking what I could do for my country, not for myself." Hansen had the uprights moved back eight inches. Then he prepared himself at great length, raced down the runoff, and cleared the bar by half a foot. Reinhardt had one more attempt, but he missed, and the competition was finally over.

1968 Mexico City C: 23, N: 15, D: 10.16. WR: 5.41, 17–9 (Robert Seagren)

			FT.–	
			M	IN.
1. Robert Seagren	USA	5.40	17-8½	OR
2. Claus Schiprowski	GER	5.40	17-8½	OR
3. Wolfgang Nordwig	GDR	5.40	17-8½	OR
4. Christos Papanicolaou	GRE	5.35	17-6½	
5. John Pennel	USA	5.35	17-6½	
6. Gennady Bliznyetsov	SOV	5.30	17-4½	
7. Herve D'Encausse	FRA	5.25	17-2¾	
8. Heinfried Engel	GER	5.20	17-0¾	

Bob Seagren had set a world record of 17 feet 9 inches at the U.S. Olympic Trials five weeks before the Olympics, but no one expected him to have an easy time of it in Mexico City, as the field was thick with great vaulters. Ignacio Sola of Spain cleared 17 feet 0¾ inches and only placed ninth. Herve D'Encausse cleared 17 feet 2¾ inches. This put him in first place, so he elected to pass the next height of 17 feet 4½ inches. He then watched in horror as the remaining six vaulters all made the height, dropping D'Encausse to seventh, which is where he finished.

At 17 feet 6½ inches, Seagren passed. This was thought to be a dangerous but shrewd gamble, comparable to Fred Hansen's pass four years earlier. Actually it was an error due to Seagren's unfamiliarity with the metric system. "If I'd known the metric system better," he later revealed, "I wouldn't have passed that high—5.35 meters doesn't sound as high as 17 feet 6½ inches." Ironically, Seagren's mistake may have won him the gold medal. At any rate, it was now Seagren's turn to sit on the sidelines and watch as the remaining four competitors all cleared the bar, dropping Seagren from first to fifth.

Next the bar was raised to 17 feet 8½ inches, only one half-inch below Seagren's new world record. Papanicolaou, Nordwig, Seagren, Pennel, and Schiprowski all missed their first attempts. If they continued to miss, the victory would go to Nordwig, since he had only missed once at lower heights. The second time around, Papanicolaou and Nordwig missed again, but Seagren cleared, to move into the lead again. Then John Pennel made a successful clearance, but his pole passed under the bar. The I.A.A.F. had just voted a new rule making such an occurrence legal, but they had also decreed that the rule wouldn't take effect until the following May. Too late for Pennel, who lost out on at least a bronze medal. Schiprowski, whose pre-Olympic best was only 17 feet, then cleared 17 feet 8½ inches, bettering his previous record for the fifth time in one day. Papanicolaou, who would later become the first person to vault 18 feet, and Pennel failed one last time, but Nordwig made it.

The bar then went up to 17 feet 10½ inches, but before Nordwig, Seagren and Schiprowski could start vaulting, the competition was delayed while the victory ceremony for the 200 meters took place. This turned out to be a sensational event, as Tommie Smith and John Carlos staged their now famous black power protest, which was greeted by booing and whistling. This may have disturbed the concentration of the vaulters, but it didn't prevent each of them from making superb efforts at the world record height. None of them succeeded, however, so the medals were decided on the basis of fewer misses. Personal records had been set by five of the top six vaulters and eight of the top 11.

1972 Munich C: 21, N: 12, D: 9.2. WR: 5.63, 18–5¾ (Robert Seagren)

			FT.–	
		M	IN.	
1. Wolfgang Nordwig	GDR	5.50	18-0½	OR
2. Robert Seagren	USA	5.40	17-8½	
3. Jan Johnson	USA	5.35	17-6½	
4. Reinhard Kuretzky	GER	5.30	17-4½	
5. Bruce Simpson	CAN	5.20	17-0¾	
6. Volker Ohl	GER	5.20	17-0¾	
7. Hans Lagerqvist	SWE	5.20	17-0¾	
8. Francois Tracanelli	FRA	5.10	16-8¾	

The U.S. monopoly of the pole vault was finally broken in 1972, but only after a series of disruptive and disturbing events. On July 25, the Technical Committee of the International Amateur Athletic Federation announced that it was banning the new model of Cata-Poles, which was being used by most of the leading vaulters, including Olympic favorites Bob Seagren, Kjell Isaksson of Sweden, and Steve Smith of the United States. The original complaint, lodged by East Germany, was that the poles contained carbon fiber. Manufacturers of the poles pointed out that they didn't contain carbon fiber at all, while the vaulters referred to I.A.A.F. rules, which said that poles could be made of any material, anyway. The I.A.A.F. refused to withdraw the ban on the grounds that the new Cata-Poles "had not been available through normal supply channels" for at least 12 months prior to the Olympics. Once again it was pointed out that the I.A.A.F. rule book made no mention of such a requirement.

On August 27, four days before the competition was to begin, the I.A.A.F. reversed itself and lifted the ban. Relieved vaulters returned to practicing with their usual poles. Then, on August 30, the ban was reimposed. The night before the qualifying round, I.A.A.F. officials went to the athletes' rooms, confiscated all their poles, and brought them off for inspection. Those vaulters who were found to be in possession of the now illegal poles were handed new ones, or rather, new old ones.

The qualifying round turned out to be a pretty sad affair. Only ten men were able to clear the qualifying height of 16 feet 8¾ inches, so four more who had only cleared 16 feet 4¾ inches were added for the final.

The vaulter who had benefited most by the ban of the new model Cata-Pole was Wolfgang Nordwig of East Germany, who had not adapted well to the new Cata-Pole and still used an old model. Nordwig, who kept out the noise of the stadium by stuffing his ears, missed once at 17 feet 4½ inches before clearing, which put him behind Seagren, who reached 17 feet 8½ inches without a miss. Nordwig made

that height with his second attempt, while Seagren needed a third. This reversed their positions. At 17 feet 10½ inches, Nordwig went over the first time, but Seagren missed all three of his attempts. After his final miss, Seagren approached Adriaan Paulen, the I.A.A.F. official who had taken responsibility for the Cata-Pole ban, and thrust his pole into Paulen's lap. Seagren stated that Paulen had given him the unwanted pole and now he was returning it. Nordwig, a 29-year-old precision engineer, had the bar raised once more, and cleared 18 feet for the first time in his life.

1976 Montreal C: 27, N: 13, D: 7.26. WR: 5.70, 18–8¼ (David Roberts)

			FT.–	
		M	IN.	
1. Tadeusz Ślusarski	POL	5.50	18-0½	EOR
2. Antti Kalliomäki	FIN	5.50	18-0½	EOR
3. David Roberts	USA	5.50	18-0½	EOR
4. Patrick Abada	FRA	5.45	17-10½	
5. Wojciech Buciarski	POL	5.45	17-10½	
6. Earl Bell	USA	5.45	17-10½	
7. Jean-Michel Bellot	FRA	5.45	17-10½	
8. Itsuo Takanezawa	JAP	5.40	17-8½	

Pre-Olympic prognostications had the battle for the gold medal among Earl Bell, who had set a world record of 18 feet 7¼ inches on May 29, Dave Roberts, who had broken Bell's record on June 22, and Wladyslaw Kozakiewicz, known for his strong performances in important meets. Surprisingly, Kozakiewicz, hampered by injury, was unable to clear 17 feet 10½ inches. Since he had passed the previous three heights, he ended up in 11th place. Roberts, too was playing a passing game. He didn't even start jumping until 17 feet 6¾ inches. He missed his first attempt, a miss that would later prove crucial, but cleared the second time. Then he passed the next two heights before sailing over 18 feet ½ inch with his first try.

When the bar was raised to 18 feet 2½ inches, there were still six vaulters left in the competition. Roberts, following a strategy he had prepared a month earlier, passed. His reasoning was that the contest would go on for quite some time and that fewer misses and fewer attempts might become crucial. He was absolutely right about that. But then two things happened that were unexpected. All five of the other remaining vaulters missed every one of their attempts at 18 feet 2½ inches, leaving Roberts alone with the bar at 18 feet 4½ inches, and facing the other unexpected element—a strong and unpredictable headwind. He missed all three attempts and ended up in third place.

The silver medal went to surprising Antti Kalliömaki and the gold to Kozakiewicz's Polish teammate Tadeusz Ślusarski. Ślusarski had the same number of misses as Kalliomaki, but had made fewer attempts. As it turned out, if Dave Roberts hadn't missed his initial attempt at 17 feet 6¾ inches, he would have finished in first place.

1980 Moscow C: 19, N: 10, D: 7.30. WR: 5.77, 18–11 (Philippe Houvion)

		FT.–	
		M	IN.
1. Wladyslaw Kozakiewicz	POL	5.78	18-11½ WR
2. Tadeusz Ślusarski	POL	5.65	18-6½
2. Konstantin Volkov	SOV	5.65	18-6½
4. Philippe Houvion	FRA	5.65	18-6½
5. Jean-Michel Bellot	FRA	5.60	18-4½
6. Mariusz Klimczyk	POL	5.55	18-2½
7. Thierry Vigneron	FRA	5.45	17-10½
8. Sergei Kulibaba	SOV	5.45	17-10½

The year 1980 was a banner one for pole vaulting. For the first time ever, three different men set world records in the same season. Wladyslaw Kozakiewicz began the onslaught on May 11 when his jump of 18 feet 9¼ inches broke Dave Roberts' 1976 record. Three weeks later, on June 1, Thierry Vigneron vaulted 18 feet 10¼ inches. On June 29, he repeated this feat. On July 17, less than two weeks before the Olympic competition, Philippe Houvion set a new record of 18 feet 11 inches. The stage was set for a classic showdown, particularly with the addition of defending champion Tadeusz Ślusarski and local favorite, Konstantin Volkov.

Unfortunately, the competition was marred by the incredibly boorish behavior of many of the Soviet fans, who whistled and jeered at the foreign vaulters, particularly the Poles. The 3000 Poles in the audience responded in kind whenever Volkov vaulted. Another unfortunate incident was the forced removal of Sergei Kulibaba, who insisted on giving illegal signals to Volkov as to wind conditions, after he himself had been eliminated. Through it all, Wladyslaw Kozakiewicz seemed unperturbed. Indeed, he seemed to gain strength from the hostility of the Russians. He won the gold medal without a miss and punctuated his winning leap with an obscene gesture to the crowd. Then he had the bar raised, and set a world record on his second attempt, the first pole vault world record to be set in the Olympics since Frank Foss' in 1920. Afterward, Kozakiewicz ran into the stands and shook hands with his compatriots, while the Poles, surrounded by Soviet soldiers, sang "Poland Is Not Beaten. . . ."

LONG JUMP

A valid jump must be made from behind the far edge of the take-off board, which is eight inches wide and level to the ground. Jumps are measured from the nearest impression made in the sand by any part of the jumper's body or limbs. Current competitions begin with a qualifying round, the results of which are not carried over to the final. In the final, each contestant is allowed three jumps. Then the first eight are allowed three more jumps. The long jump has been dominated by U.S. athletes, who have won 17 of 20 times. The only U.S. losses have been by two and a quarter inches, one and a half inches, and one boycott.

1896 Athens C: 9, N: 5, D: 4.7. WR: 7.21, 23-8 (J.J. Mooney)

		FT.–	
		M	IN.
1. Ellery Clark	USA	6.35	20-10
2. Robert Garrett	USA	6.18	20-3½
3. James Connolly	USA	6.11	20-0½
4. Alexandre Tuffère	FRA	5.98	19-7½
5. Alphonse Grisel	FRA	5.83	19-1½
6. Henrik Sjoberg	SWE	5.80	19-0½
7. Alexandros Chalkokondilis	GRE	5.74	18-10
8. Karl Schumann	GER	5.70	18-8½

Each man was allowed three jumps. Clark fouled the first two times. "It was little short of agony," he later wrote. "I shall never forget my feelings as I stood at the end of the path for my third—and last—try. Five thousand miles, I reflected, I had come; and was it to end in this? Three fouls, and then five thousand miles back again, with that for my memory of the games." Fortunately, his last jump was not only valid, but good enough to win.

1900 Paris C: 12, N: 6, D: 7.15. WR: 7.50, 24-7¼ (Meyer Prinstein)

		FT.–	
		M	IN.
1. Alvin Kraenzlein	USA	7.18	23-6¾ OR
2. Meyer Prinstein	USA	7.17	23-6¼
3. Patrick Leahy	GBR/IRL	6.95	22-9¾
4. William Remington	USA	6.82	22-4½
5. Albert Delannoy	FRA	6.75	22-1¾
6. John McLean	USA	6.65	21-10
7. Thaddeus McClain	USA	6.43	21-1¼
8. Waldemar Steffen	GER	6.30	20-8

Prinstein achieved his 23-foot 6¼-inch jump in the qualifying round, which, according to the rules of the time, counted in the final placings. The final was held on the next day, which was a Sunday. The official in charge of the Syracuse team prohibited Prinstein from competing on a Sunday even though Prinstein was Jewish. Kraenzlein did take part in the final and bettered Prinstein's mark by one centimeter. Peter O'Connor of Ireland was entered, but did not compete. The following month he broke Prinstein's world record with a leap of 24 feet 7¾ inches. On August 5, 1901, he jumped 24 feet 11¾ inches to set a record that would last 20 years.

1904 St. Louis C: 10, N: 3, D: 9.1. WR: 7.61, 24-11¾ (Peter O'Connor)

		FT.–	
		M	IN.
1. Meyer Prinstein	USA	7.34	24-1
2. Daniel Frank	USA	6.89	22-7¼
3. Robert Stangland	USA	6.88	22-7
4. Fred Englehardt	USA	6.63	21-9
5. George Van Cleaf	USA	—	—
6. John Hagerman	USA	—	—

Prinstein earned his well-deserved Olympic long-jump championship after a four-year wait.

1906 Athens C: 27, N: 10, D: 4.27. WR: 7.61, 24–11¾ (Peter O'Connor)

			FT.–	
			M	IN.
1.	Meyer Prinstein	USA	7.20	23-7½
2.	Peter O'Connor	GBR/IRL	7.02	23-0½
3.	Hugo Friend	USA	6.96	22-10
4.	Hjalmar Mellander	SWE	6.58	21-7¼
5.	Sidney Abrahams	GBR	6.21	20-4½
6.	Thomas Cronan	USA	6.18	20-3½
7.	Gunnar Rönström	SWE	6.15	20-2¼
8.	István Somodi	HUN	6.05	19-10

Including the Intercalated Games of 1906, Meyer Prinstein won four gold medals and one silver in the long jump and triple jump.

1908 London C: 30, N: 9, D: 7.22. WR: 7.61, 24–11¾ (Peter O'Connor)

			FT.–		
			M	IN.	
1.	Francis ''Frank'' Irons	USA	7.48	24-6½	OR
2.	Daniel Kelly	USA	7.09	23-3¼	
3.	Calvin Bricker	CAN	7.08	23-3	
4.	Edward Cooke	USA	6.97	22-10½	
5.	John Brennan	USA	6.86	22-6¼	
6.	Frank Mount Pleasant	USA	6.82	22-4½	
7.	Albert Weinstein	GER	6.77	22-2¾	
8.	Timothy Ahearne	GBR	6.72	22-0¾	

The victory of 5-foot 5½-inch Frank Irons came as quite a surprise since his pre-Olympic best was only 22 feet 7½ inches. Many British sports enthusiasts were disgusted by the exuberant displays of the Americans whenever a U.S. athlete won an event. One London paper described the American response to Irons' victory: "They were entertained then from the American stand by the singing of 'There'll be a hot time in the old town tonight,' by the fluttering of United States flags, and by the blowing of a new squeaking instrument of torture such as is employed at country fairs [probably a kazoo]. The Americans made themselves a nuisance and behaved in a manner which is happily quite foreign to the athletic grounds of England."

1912 Stockholm C: 32, N: 12, D: 7.13. WR: 7.61, 24–11¾ (Peter O'Connor)

			FT.–		
			M	IN.	
1.	Albert Gutterson	USA	7.60	24-11¼	OR
2.	Calvin Bricker	CAN	7.21	23-8	
3.	Georg Åberg	SWE	7.18	23-6¾	
4.	Harry Worthington	USA	7.03	23-0¾	
5.	Eugene Leroy Mercer	USA	6.97	22-10½	
6.	Fred Allen	USA	6.94	22-9¼	
7.	James Thorpe	USA	6.89	22-7¼	
8.	Robert Pasemann	GER	6.82	22-4½	

Gutterson, of Andover, Vermont, settled the competition with his first jump, which was the best in the world since Peter O'Connor's record of 1901.

1920 Antwerp C: 29, N: 11, D: 8.18. WR: 7.61, 24–11¾ (Peter O'Connor)

			FT.–	
			M	IN.
1.	William Petersson (Björneman)	SWE	7.15	23-5½
2.	Carl Johnson	USA	7.09	23-3¼
3.	Erik Abrahamsson	SWE	7.08	23-2¾
4.	Robert ''Dink'' Templeton	USA	6.95	22-9¾
5.	Erling Aastad	NOR	6.88	22-7
6.	Rolf Franksson	SWE	6.73	22-1
7.	Sol Butler	USA	6.60	21-8
8.	E. Raeder	NOR	6.58	21-7¼

William Petersson, who later changed his last name to Björneman, was preparing to take his first jump when he noticed a silver coin lying on the runway. He picked it up and discovered that it was an American quarter. He put it in his left shoe for good luck and went on to win the gold medal. The favorite, Sol Butler, pulled a tendon on his first jump and had to withdraw. Fourth-place finisher Dink Templeton later became a famous track coach at Stanford.

1924 Paris C: 34, N: 21, D: 7.8. WR: 7.69, 25–3 (Edward Gourdin)

			FT.–	
			M	IN.
1.	William De Hart Hubbard	USA	7.44	24-5
2.	Edward Gourdin	USA	7.27	23-10¼
3.	Sverre Hansen	NOR	7.26	23-10
4.	Vilho Tuulos	FIN	7.07	23-2½
5.	Louis Wilhelme	FRA	6.99	22-11¼
6.	Christopher Macintosh	GBR	6.92	22-8½
7.	Virgilio Tommasi	ITA	6.89	22-7¼
8.	J. Boot	HOL	6.86	22-6¼

De Hart Hubbard was the first black to win an individual Olympic gold medal. His performance, however, was overshadowed by that of Robert LeGendre the day before. LeGendre, who had failed to make the U.S. long jump team, set a world record of 25 feet 5¾ inches while competing in the pentathlon.

1928 Amsterdam C: 41, N: 23, D: 7.31. WR: 7.90, 25–11 (Edward Hamm)

			FT.–		
			M	IN.	
1.	Edward Hamm	USA	7.73	25-4½	OR
2.	Silvio Cator	HAI	7.58	24-10½	
3.	Alfred Bates	USA	7.40	24-3½	
4.	Willi Meier	GER	7.39	24-3	
5.	Erich Köchermann	GER	7.35	24-1½	
6.	Hannes de Boer	HOL	7.32	24-0¼	
7.	Edward Gordon	USA	7.32	24-0¼	
8.	Erik Svensson	SWE	7.29	23-11	

Six weeks after the Olympic competition, silver medalist Silvio Cator became the first man to break the 26-foot barrier with a jump of 26 feet ¼ inch. Cator was also the captain of the Haitian soccer team. As it turned out, five different past and future gold medal winners took part in the 1928 long jump. In addition to Hamm, 1924 winner De Hart Hubbard finished 11th, 1932 winner Ed Gordon placed seventh, 1928 triple jump winner Mikio Oda tied with Hubbard for 11th, and 1932 triple jump winner Chuhei Nambu finished ninth.

1932 Los Angeles C: 12, N: 9, D: 8.2. WR: 7.98, 26–2¼ (Chuhei Nambu)

			FT.–	
		M	IN.	
1. Edward Gordon	USA	7.64	25-0¾	
2. Charles Lambert Redd	USA	7.60	24-11¼	
3. Chuhei Nambu	JAP	7.45	24-5½	
4. Erik Svensson	SWE	7.41	24-3¾	
5. Richard Barber	USA	7.39	24-3	
6. Naoto Tajima	JAP	7.15	23-5½	
7. Hector Berra	ARG	6.66	21-10¼	
8. Clovis de Figueiredo Raposo	BRA	6.43	21-1¼	

1936 Berlin C: 43, N: 27, D: 8.4. WR: 8.13, 26–8¼ (Jesse Owens)

			FT.–	
		M	IN.	
1. Jesse Owens	USA	8.06	26-5½	OR
2. Luz Long	GER	7.87	25-10	
3. Naoto Tajima	JAP	7.74	25-4¾	
4. Wilhelm Leichum	GER	7.73	25-4½	
4. Arturo Maffei	ITA	7.73	25-4½	
6. Robert Clark	USA	7.67	25-2	
7. John Brooks	USA	7.41	24-3¾	
8. Robert Paul	FRA	7.34	24-1	

On May 25, 1935, Jesse Owens had jumped 26 feet 8¼ inches, setting a world record that would last for 25 years and 79 days. He seemed a sure bet to win the Olympic gold medal. But when he walked over to the long jump area, he was surprised to see a tall, blue-eyed, blond German taking practice jumps in the 26-foot range. Owens was fully aware of the Nazis' desire to prove their theory of "Aryan superiority" and he was also fully aware that Hitler and his followers had a particular distaste for Negroes. With this in mind, Jesse, still in his sweatsuit, took a practice run down the runway and into the pit. To his surprise, the officials in charge counted this as his first attempt of the qualifying round. Somewhat rattled, he fouled his second attempt. He was now one foul away from being eliminated from his best event.

At this point, Owens was approached by the tall, blue-eyed, blond German, who introduced himself, in English, as Luz Long.

"Glad to meet you," said Owens tentatively. "How are you?"

"I'm fine," replied Long. "The question is: How are *you*?"

"What do you mean?" asked Owens.

"Something must be *eating* you," said Long, proud to display his knowledge of American slang. "You should be able to qualify with your eyes closed." For the next few minutes the black son of sharecroppers and the white model of Nazi manhood chatted. It turned out that Luz Long didn't believe in the theory of Aryan superiority and the two joked about the fact that he looked the part anyway. Then Long made a suggestion. Since the qualifying distance was only 23 feet 5½ inches, why didn't Owens make a mark several inches before the takeoff board and jump from there to play it safe. Owens did just that, and qualified easily.

The final was held that afternoon. Jesse Owens opened up with an Olympic record of 25 feet 5½ inch and then followed with 25 feet 10 inches. In the fifth of six rounds, Luz Long brought the German crowd to life by matching Owens' jump exactly. Inspired by the challenge, Owens leaped 26 feet ¾ inch. Then, with his final jump, he hit 26 feet 5½ inches, to clinch his second of four gold medals. The first person to congratulate Owens, in full view of Adolf Hitler, was Luz Long. "You can melt down all the medals and cups I have," Jesse Owens later wrote, "and they wouldn't be a plating on the 24-carat friendship I felt for Luz Long at that moment." Long was killed in the Battle of St. Pietro on July 14, 1943, but Owens continued to correspond with his family.

1948 London C: 21, N: 17, D: 7.31. WR: 8.13, 26–8¼ (Jesse Owens)

			FT.–	
		M	IN.	
1. Willie Steele	USA	7.82	25-8	
2. Thomas Bruce	AUS	7.55	24-9¼	
3. Herbert Douglas	USA	7.54	24-9	
4. Lorenzo Wright	USA	7.45	24-5½	
5. Adegboyega Folaranmi Adedoyin	GBR/NGR	7.27	23-10¼	
6. Georges Damitio	FRA	7.07	23-2½	
7. Harry Whittle	GBR	7.03	23-0¾	
8. F. Wurth	AUS	7.00	22-11¾	

Fifth-place finisher Prince Adegboyega Folaranmi Adedoyin was a member of the royal family of the kingdom of Ijabu-Remo in Nigeria. A medical student at Queen's University in Belfast, he represented Great Britain, since Nigeria was not yet considered an independent nation.

1952 Helsinki C: 27, N: 19, D: 7.21. WR: 8.13, 26–8¼ (Jesse Owens)

			FT.–	
		M	IN.	
1. Jerome Biffle	USA	7.57	24-10	
2. Meredith Gourdine	USA	7.53	24-8½	
3. Ödön Földessy	HUN	7.30	23-11½	
4. Ary Facanha de Sá	BRA	7.23	23-8¾	
5. Jorma Valtonen	FIN	7.16	23-6	
6. Leonid Grigoryev	SOV	7.14	23-5¼	
7. Karl-Erik Israelsson	SWE	7.10	23-3½	
8. Paul Faucher	FRA	7.02	23-0½	

George Brown of U.C.L.A. had won 41 straight competitions before placing third at the U.S. Olympic trials. Yet he was still the heavy favorite to win in Helsinki. In the final, however, he fouled three times in a row and was eliminated. Gold medalist Jerome Biffle was an Army private who came out of two years retirement to compete. Neville Price of South Africa jumped 24 feet 1¼ inches in the qualifying round, but was unable to take part in the final because of an injury.

1956 Melbourne C: 32, N: 21, D: 11.24. WR: 8.13, 26–8¼ (Jesse Owens)

			FT.–	
			M	IN.
1. Gregory Bell	USA	7.83	25-8¼	
2. John Bennett	USA	7.68	25-2½	
3. Jorma Valkama	FIN	7.48	24-6½	
4. Dmitri Bondarenko	SOV	7.44	24-5	
5. Karim Olowu	NGR	7.36	24-1¾	
6. Kazimierz Kropidlowski	POL	7.30	23-11½	
7. Neville Price	SAF	7.28	23-10¾	
8. Oleg Fyedoseyev	SOV	7.27	23-10¼	

A short, loose runway and a strong fluctuating wind caused all entrants to perform well below their normal standards.

1960 Rome C: 49, N: 34, D: 9.2. WR: 8.21, 26–11¼ (Ralph Boston)

			FT.–	
			M	IN.
1. Ralph Boston	USA	8.12	26-7¾	OR
2. Irvin "Bo" Roberson	USA	8.11	26-7¼	
3. Igor Ter-Ovanesyan	SOV	8.04	26-4½	
4. Manfred Steinbach	GER	8.00	26-3	
5. Jorma Valkama	FIN	7.69	25-2¾	
6. Christian Collardot	FRA	7.68	25-2½	
7. Henk Visser	HOL	7.66	25-1¾	
8. Dmitri Bondarenko	SOV	7.58	24-10½	

On August 12, 1960, two weeks before the opening of the Rome Olympics, Ralph Boston finally broke Jesse Owens' 25-year-old world record with a leap of 26 feet 11¼ inches. He was expected to receive his stiffest challenge from Armenian Igor Ter-Ovanesyan, who had fouled out of the 1956 final, and who would eventually go on to take part in five Olympics. Ter-Ovanesyan led at 25 feet 11 inches after the first round of the final. Bo Roberson, whose pre-Olympic best had been 26 feet 0 inches, jumped 26 feet 4¼ inches in the second round to take the lead. However the third round saw Boston's big jump of 26 feet 7¾ inches. There were no changes in position during the next two rounds, but the competition was far from over. With his last attempt, Ter-Ovanesyan leaped 26 feet 4½ inches to edge into second place. An exhausted Bo Roberson had considered passing, but now he had to give it one last try. He zoomed seven inches beyond his pre-Olympic record, but landed one centimeter short of a gold medal. This was the first meet in which four different men jumped over 26 feet.

1964 Tokyo C: 32, N: 23, D: 10.18. WR: 8.34, 27–4¼ (Ralph Boston)

			FT.–	
			M	IN.
1. Lynn Davies	GBR	8.07	26-5¾	
2. Ralph Boston	USA	8.03	26-4¼	
3. Igor Ter-Ovanesyan	SOV	7.99	26-2¾	
4. Wariboko West	NGR	7.60	24-11¼	
5. Jean Cochard	FRA	7.44	24-5	
6. Luis Felipe Areta	SPA	7.34	24-1	
7. Mike Ahey	GHA	7.30	23-11½	
8. Andrzej Stalmach	POL	7.26	23-10	

Lynn Davies, a physical education teacher from Nantymoel, Glamorganshire, in Wales, wasn't on anyone's list of potential winners in 1964. In fact, he barely made it into the final, qualifying with his last attempt. But the weather, cold, windy, and raining, was much more familiar to Davies than it was to the favorites, Ralph Boston and Igor Ter-Ovanesyan. The American and Soviet champions tried to convince the officials to reverse the running of the event, so that they would be jumping with the wind behind them instead of against them, but to no avail.

Ter-Ovanesyan took the first round lead at 25 feet 6¼ inches. Boston moved ahead in the second round with a jump of 25 feet 9¼ inches. In the fourth round, he improved to 25 feet 10¼ inches. Entering the fifth round, Lynn Davies was in third place. "I remember thinking, this is it," he recalled. "I glanced up at the flag at the top of the stadium. Boston told me about this in New York, six months previously. 'If the flag drops,' he had said, 'it's a good indication that the wind is about to fade inside the stadium.' And as I looked up at it, it dropped dead." Davies took off down the runway immediately and hit the best jump of his career—26 feet 5¾ inches.

Ter-Ovanesyan followed with 26 feet 2¾ inches to move back into second place. The competition came down to Ralph Boston's final leap. Davies covered his face and peeked through his fingers. Boston's jump was long and Davies prepared himself for disappointment. But the measurement showed Boston had missed by four centimeters, and Lynn Davies had become the first Welshman ever to win an Olympic gold medal.

1968 Mexico City C: 35, N: 22, D: 10.18. WR: 8.35, 27–4¾ (Ralph Boston, Igor Ter-Ovanesyan)

			FT.–	
			M	IN.
1. Robert Beamon	USA	8.90	29-2½	WR
2. Klaus Beer	GDR	8.19	26-10½	
3. Ralph Boston	USA	8.16	26-9¼	
4. Igor Ter-Ovanesyan	SOV	8.12	26-7¾	
5. Tonu Lepik	SOV	8.09	26-6½	
6. Allen Crawley	AUS	8.02	26-3¾	
7. Jacques Pani	FRA	7.97	26-1¾	
8. Andrzej Stalmach	POL	7.94	26-0¾	

All three medalists from 1964, Lynn Davies, Ralph Boston, and Igor Ter-Ovanesyan, were back in 1968, and all three were in good enough shape to win the gold medal. However, none of them was the favorite. That distinction fell to Bob Beamon, a 6-foot 3-inch 22-year-old from South Jamaica in New York. In 1968 Beamon had won 22 of 23 meets, losing only once indoors. But Beamon was by no means a sure bet. Unlike the other leading contenders, he made no checkmarks on the side of the runway to help him with his stride, so he was unusually prone to fouling. In addition, he had been without the benefit of a regular coach since mid-April, when he had been suspended from the track team at the University of Texas at El Paso for refusing to compete against Brigham Young University, as a protest against the racial policies of the Mormon Church.

Beamon almost met disaster in the qualifying round. His first jump took off a full foot after the board and his second jump was also a foul. He was now one foul away from elimination. Remembering the Jesse Owens–Luz Long incident of 1936, Ralph Boston, who had been informally coaching Beamon, walked up to the nervous favorite and had a few words with him. He told Beamon to relax and to take off from a mark a few inches before the takeoff board. Like Jesse Owens 32 years earlier, Bob Beamon made a mark one foot up the runway, then raced down the path and qualified easily.

According to Dick Schaap's biography, *The Perfect Jump,* that night, the night before the most important final of his career, Bob Beamon did something he had never done before: he engaged in sexual intercourse the night before a major competition. At the moment of orgasm, he was suddenly overcome with the horrible feeling that he had blown it, that his chances for a gold medal and for the world record he had boldly predicted he would achieve had been thrown away right there in bed.

The following day was gloomy, with occasional rain, the kind of day that supposedly favored Lynn Davies. There were 17 finalists ready to begin the competition at 3:40 p.m. Beamon's jumping order was fourth, Davies' 12th, Ter-Ovanesyan's 13th, and Ralph Boston's 17th. The first three jumpers fouled. Then it was Bob Beamon's turn. Boston called out to him, "Come on, make it a good one." For 20 seconds Beamon stood at the beginning of the runway, gathering his strength and telling himself, "Don't foul, don't foul." Then he tore down the runway (he was a 9.5 sprinter at 100 yards), hit the takeoff board perfectly, and sailed through the air at what seemed to be an uncommon elevation, estimated by observers to be between five and a half and six feet. He hit the sand so powerfully that he bounced back up and landed outside the pit.

"That's over 28 feet," Ralph Boston said to Lynn Davies. "With his first jump?" replied Davies. "No, it can't be." They trotted over to the pit to get a better look. Officials slid the marker of the sophisticated optical measuring device down its rail to the point where Beamon's feet had hit the sand. But before it got there, the marker fell off the end of the rail. An official turned to Beamon and murmured, "Fantastic. Fantastic." An old-fashioned steel tape was called for. A couple measurements were taken and

then the result was flashed on the electronic scoreboard: 8.90 meters. Beamon knew he had set a record, but being unfamiliar with the metric system, he didn't really understand how far he had jumped. He ran up to Ralph Boston, the man who had helped him so much, and embraced him. Boston then told Beamon, "Bob, you jumped 29 feet."

Beamon was stunned. "What do I do now?" he asked. "Ralph, I know you're gonna kick my ass."

"No, no," said Boston. "It's over for me. I can't jump that far."

"What about the Great Britain dude?" asked Beamon. "And what about the Russian?"

"The Russian," Igor Ter-Ovanesyan, had turned to Lynn Davies and said, "Compared to this jump, we are as children." Davies told Boston, "I can't go on. What is the point? We'll all look silly." Then he turned to Beamon and said, "You have destroyed this event."

By this time, Beamon's jump had been officially converted to 29 feet 2½ inches. Suddenly, Beamon realized what he had done. His legs gave in and he sank to the ground, experiencing what doctors would later describe as a "cataplectic seizure," an "atonic state of the somatic muscles which develops suddenly on the heels of emotional excitement." He was overcome with nausea and tears, and was helped to his feet by Boston and U.S. teammate Charlie Mays, who supported him until he recovered from his dizziness.

The contest continued, but just as Ter-Ovanesyan began his first jump, the skies began pouring rain. Beamon took one more jump of 26 feet 4½ inches, but then passed his last four opportunities. Boston, Ter-Ovanesyan and Davies, (who finished ninth), who had waited four years for another chance at Olympic victory, were dazed and unable to perform up to par. Klaus Beer of East Germany, on the other hand, had had no such grand expectations, and was able to take the silver medal by bettering his personal best by four inches. Lepik and Crawley also had their best jumps ever.

Beamon's 29-foot 2½-inch jump was hailed as the greatest athletic achievement of all time, although detractors criticized the suspicious Mexican wind readings which measured the exact legal maxiumum of 2.0 m.p.s. In the 33 years since Jesse Owens' 1935 jump of 26 feet 8¼ inches, the world record had progressed eight and a half inches. In a matter of seconds, Beamon had added another 21¾ inches. Ironically—since Beamon completely bypassed the 28-foot barrier—the first 28-foot jump didn't take place until the 1980 Olympics.

1972 Munich C: 36, N: 25, D: 9.9. WR: 8.90, 29–2½ (Robert Beamon)

		M	FT.–IN.
1. Randy Williams	USA	8.24	27-0½
2. Hans Baumgartner	GER	8.18	26-10
3. Arnie Robinson	USA	8.03	26-4¼
4. Joshua Owusu	GHA	8.01	26-3½

5. Preston Carrington	USA	7.99	26-2¾
6. Max Klauss	GDR	7.96	26-1½
7. Alan Lerwill	GBR	7.91	25-11½
8. Leonid Barkovsky	SOV	7.75	25-5¼

Nineteen-year-old Randy Williams, the youngest entrant, led the qualifying round with a jump of 27 feet 4¼ inches—over a foot farther than his pre-Olympic, non-wind-aided best. He was followed by Preston Carrington at 26 feet 11¾ inches, 7¾ inches better than *his* pre-Olympic record. Neither American was able to do as well in the final. Williams, who kept a good-luck teddy bear with him at all times, injured his leg warming up before the final, and wisely decided to put all his effort into his first leap, which turned out to be good enough for the gold medal.

1976 Montreal C: 33, N: 25, D: 7.29. WR: 8.90, 29–2½ (Robert Beamon)

			FT.–
		M	IN.
1. Arnie Robinson	USA	8.35	27-4¾
2. Randy Williams	USA	8.11	26-7¼
3. Frank Wartenberg	GDR	8.02	26-3¾
4. Jacques Rousseau	FRA	8.00	26-3
5. Joao Carlos de Oliivera	BRA	8.00	26-3
6. Nenad Stekić	YUG	7.89	25-10¾
7. Valery Podluzhniy	SOV	7.88	25-10¼
8. Hans Baumgartner	GER	7.82	25-8

For the third straight time, the long jump was won with a first round leap, and for the tenth time in 12 Olympics, it was won by a black American.

1980 Moscow C: 32, N: 24, D: 7.28. WR: 8.90, 29–2½ (Robert Beamon)

			FT.–
		M	IN.
1. Lutz Dombrowski	GDR	8.54	28-0¼
2. Frank Paschek	GDR	8.21	26-11¼
3. Valery Podluzhniy	SOV	8.18	26-10
4. László Szalma	HUN	8.13	26-8¼
5. Stanislaw Jaskulka	POL	8.13	26-8¼
6. Viktor Belsky	SOV	8.10	26-7
7. Antonio Corgos	SPA	8.09	26-6½
8. Yordan Yanev	BUL	8.02	26-3¾

Before the Moscow Olympics, the longest jump other than Bob Beamon's had been 27 feet 11½ inches, by Larry Myricks of the United States. Myricks had qualified for the 1976 final, but fractured a bone in his foot and had to withdraw. In 1980, he was kept out again, this time by the Jimmy Carter boycott. Without him, the long jump competition was dominated by Lutz Dombrowski, who put together a tremendous series that averaged 27 feet 3¼ inches. His fifth round jump of 28 feet ¼ inch was the first ever in the 28-foot range. Something of a rebel, Dombrowski kept running away from the schools to which he had been assigned by the East German government, in order to return home to his family, his girl friend, and his soccer team. When he broke his left leg playing soccer in 1979, he finally gave in to the East German coaches, although he continued to insist that he preferred the triple jump to the long jump.

TRIPLE JUMP

This used to be known as the hop, step, and jump, which accurately describes the event. The contestants land on the same foot with which they take off, take one step onto the other foot, and then jump. If their trailing foot touches the ground, the jump is ruled a foul. Other rules are the same as those for the long jump.

1896 Athens C: 10, N: 5, D: 4.6. WR: 15.25, 50–0½ (Daniel Shanahan)

			FT.–
		M	IN.
1. James Connolly	USA	13.71	44-11¾
2. Alexandre Tuffère	FRA	12.70	41-8
3. Ioannis Persakis	GRE	12.52	41-1
4. Alajos Szokolyi	HUN	12.30	40-4¼
5. Christos Zomuis	GRE	—	
6. Alexandros Chalkokondilis	GRE	—	

James Brendan Connolly came from a poor Irish-American family in South Boston, Massachusetts. He was a 27-year-old, self-educated undergraduate at Harvard when he read about the revival of the Olympic Games. As the national triple jump champion, he decided to go to Athens and take part. He asked permission for a leave of absence. When his dean refused, he dropped out and went anyway. Ten American athletes and one trainer spent 16½ days on a ship to Naples, where Connolly's wallet was stolen. Then they took the train to Athens, arriving at nine p.m. on April 5. They thought that they had 12 days to rest up and train, but discovered that the Greeks used a different calendar, and that the Olympics actually started the next day. This didn't stop them from staying up all night enjoying the general festivities which had engulfed the city.

At two p.m. the next day, the first modern Olympic Games were officially opened. Connolly was the last to jump in the triple-jump competition. He surveyed the mark of the leading jumper, Alexandre Tuffère, noted that it was a paltry 41 feet 8 inches, and brazenly threw his cap down a yard beyond the mark. Then he jumped beyond the cap, as the Greeks called out *"Nike, nike"* (victory). James Connolly had become the first Olympic champion since the boxer Barasdates of Armenia in 369 A.D. Actually, Connolly had performed two hops and a jump rather than a hop, step, and jump, but that was considered acceptable at the time.

Connolly later became a noted journalist and war correspondent, and also authored 25 novels and 200 short stories. He was once offered an honorary degree from Harvard, but refused it. Connolly died on January 20, 1957, at the age of 88.

1900 Paris C: 13, N: 6, D: 7.16. WR: 15.25, 50–0½ (Daniel Shanahan)

		FT.–		
		M	IN.	
1. Meyer Prinstein	USA	14.47	47-5¾	OR
2. James Connolly	USA	13.97	45-10	
3. Lewis Sheldon	USA	13.64	44-9	
4. Patrick Leahy	GBR/IRL	—	—	
5. Albert Delannoy	FRA	—	—	
6. Alexandre Tuffère	FRA	—	—	

Prinstein made up for his disappointment at not being allowed to take part in the previous day's long jump final.

1904 St. Louis C: 7, N: 1, D: 9.1. WR: 5.25, 50–0½ (Daniel Shanahan)

		FT.–	
		M	IN.
1. Meyer Prinstein	USA	14.35	47-1
2. Fred Englehardt	USA	13.90	45-7¼
3. Robert Stangland	USA	13.36	43-10
4. John Fuhler	USA	12.91	42-4½
5. George Van Cleaf	USA	—	—
6. John Hagerman	USA	—	—
7. Samuel Jones	USA	—	—

Prinstein won with his sixth and final jump.

1906 Athens C: 21, N: 8, D: 4.30. WR: 15.25, 50–0½ (Daniel Shanahan)

		FT.–	
		M	IN.
1. Peter O'Connor	GBR/IRL	14.075	46-2¼
2. Cornelius Leahy	GBR/IRL	13.98	45-10½
3. Thomas Cronan	USA	13.70	44-11½
4. Oscar Guttormsen	NOR	13.34	43-9¼
5. Dimitrios Müller	GRE	13.125	43-0¾
6. Francis Connolly	USA	12.75	41-10
7. B. Stournares	GRE	12.725	41-9
8. C.F. Pedersen	NOR	12.68	41-7¼

After his victory, O'Connor, who won with his final attempt, climbed the flagpole, pulled down the Union Jack of Great Britain, and replaced it with the green flag of Ireland.

1908 London C: 19, N: 7, D: 7.25. WR: 15.25, 50–0½ (Daniel Shanahan)

		FT.–		
		M	IN.	
1. Timothy Ahearne	GBR/IRL	14.92	48-11¼	OR
2. J. Garfield MacDonald	CAN	14.76	48-5¼	
3. Edvard Larsen	NOR	14.39	47-2¾	
4. Calvin Bricker	CAN	14.10	46-3	
5. Platt Adams	USA	14.07	46-2	
6. Frank Mount Pleasant	USA	13.97	45-10	

1912 Stockholm C: 22, N: 9, D: 7.15. WR: 15.52, 50–11 (Daniel Ahearn)

		FT.–	
		M	IN.
1. Gustaf Lindblom	SWE	14.76	48-5¼
2. Georg Åberg	SWE	14.51	47-7¼
3. Erik Almlöf	SWE	14.17	46-6
4. Erling Vinne	NOR	14.14	46-4¾
5. Platt Adams	USA	14.09	46-2¾
6. Edvard Larsen	NOR	14.06	46-1½
7. Hjalmar Olsson	SWE	14.01	45-11¾
8. N. Fixdal	NOR	13.96	45-9¾

1920 Antwerp C: 19, N: 7, D: 8.21. WR: 15.52, 50–11 (Daniel Ahearn)

		FT.–	
		M	IN.
1. Vilho Tuulos	FIN	14.50	47-7
2. Folke Jansson	SWE	14.48	47-6
3. Erik Almlöf	SWE	14.27	46-9¾
4. Ivar Sahlin	SWE	14.17	46-6
5. Sherman Landers	USA	14.17	46-6
6. Daniel Ahearn	USA	14.08	46-2¼
7. Ossian Nylund	FIN	13.74	45-0½
8. B. Howard Baker	GBR	13.67	44-10

1924 Paris C: 20, N: 12, D: 7.12. WR: 15.52, 50–11 (Daniel Ahearn)

		FT.–		
		M	IN.	
1. Anthony Winter	AUS	15.525	50-11¼	WR
2. Luis Brunetto	ARG	15.42	50-7¼	
3. Vilho Tuulos	FIN	15.37	50-5-7	
4. Väinö Rainio	FIN	15.01	49-3	
5. Folke Jansson	SWE	14.97	49-1½	
6. Mikio Oda	JAP	14.35	47-1	
7. R. Earle Wilson	USA	14.235	46-8	
8. Ivar Sahlin	SWE	14.16	46-5½	

In setting a world record, Nick Winter improved on his pre-Olympic best by 14½ inches.

1928 Amsterdam C: 24, N: 13, D: 8.2. WR: 15.525, 50–11¼ (Anthony Winter)

		FT.–	
		M	IN.
1. Mikio Oda	JAP	15.21	49-11
2. Levi Casey	USA	15.17	49-9¼
3. Vilho Tuulos	FIN	15.11	49-7
4. Chuhei Nambu	JAP	15.01	49-3
5. Toimi Tulikoura	FIN	14.70	48-2¾
6. Erkki Järvinen	FIN	14.65	48-0¾
7. Willem Peters	HOL	14.55	47-9
8. Väinö Rainio	FIN	14.41	47-3½

Mikio Oda of Japan was the first Asian to win an Olympic gold medal.

1932 Los Angeles C: 16, N: 12, D: 8.4. WR: 15.58, 51–1½ (Mikio Oda)

		FT.–		
		M	IN.	
1. Chuhei Nambu	JAP	15.72	51-7	WR
2. Eric Svensson	SWE	15.32	50-3¼	
3. Kenkichi Oshima	JAP	15.12	49-7¼	
4. Eamon Fitzgerald	IRL	15.01	49-3	
5. Willem Peters	HOL	14.93	48-11¾	
6. Sol Furth	USA	14.88	48-10	
7. Sidney Bowman	USA	14.87	48-9½	
8. Rolland Romero	USA	14.85	48-8¾	

Chuhei Nambu was the world record holder in the long jump, but a leg injury prevented him from placing better than third in Los Angeles. Two days later he entered the triple jump and finished first, achieving the rare distinction of holding the world record in both horizontal jump events.

1936 Berlin C: 31, N: 19, D: 8.6. WR: 15.78, 51–9¼ (John Metcalfe)

		FT.–		
		M	IN.	
1. Naoto Tajima	JAP	16.00	52-6	WR
2. Masao Harada	JAP	15.66	51-4½	
3. John Metcalfe	AUS	15.50	50-10¼	
4. Heinz Wöllner	GER	15.27	50-1¼	
5. Rolland Romero	USA	15.08	49-5¾	
6. Kenkichi Oshima	JAP	15.07	49-5½	
7. Erich Joch	GER	14.88	48-10	
8. Dudley Wilkins	USA	14.83	48-8	

Tajima duplicated Nambu's feat of winning the triple jump gold medal two days after he had earned a bronze medal in the long jump. Long jump silver medalist Luz Long placed tenth in the triple jump.

1948 London C: 29, N: 18, D: 8.3. WR: 16.00, 52–6 (Naoto Tajima)

		FT.–	
		M	IN.
1. Arne Åhman	SWE	15.40	50-6¼
2. George Avery	AUS	15.36	50-4¾
3. Ruhi Sarialp	TUR	15.02	49-3½
4. Preben Larsen	DEN	14.83	48-8
5. Geraldo de Oliveira	BRA	14.82	48-7½
6. Valdemar Rautio	FIN	14.70	48-2¾
7. Les McKeand	AUS	14.53	47-8
8. Helio Coutinho da Silva	BRA	14.49	47-6½

1952 Helsinki C: 35, N: 23, D: 7.23. WR: 16.01, 52–6½ (Adhemar Ferreira da Silva)

		FT.–		
		M	IN.	
1. Adhemar Ferreira da Silva	BRA	16.22	53-2¾	WR
2. Leonid Sherbakov	SOV	15.98	52-5¼	

3. Arnoldo Devonish	VEN	15.52	50-11	
4. Walter Ashbaugh	USA	15.39	50-6	
5. Rune Nilsen	NOR	15.13	49-7¾	
6. Yoshio Iimuro	JAP	14.99	49-2¼	
7. Geraldo de Oliveira	BRA	14.95	49-0¾	
8. Roger Norman	SWE	14.89	48-10¼	

Da Silva put on an incredible show, breaking his old world record four times in six attempts in the final. Arnoldo Devonish was the first Venezuelan to win an Olympic medal.

1956 Melbourne C: 32, N: 20, D: 11.27. WR: 16.56, 54 4 (Adhemar Ferreira da Silva)

		FT.–		
		M	IN.	
1. Adhemar Ferreira da Silva	BRA	16.35	53-7¾	OR
2. Vilhjálmur Einarsson	ICE	16.26	53-4¼	
3. Vitold Kreyer	SOV	16.02	52-6¾	
4. William Sharpe	USA	15.88	52-1¼	
5. Martin Rehák	CZE	15.85	52-0	
6. Leonid Sherbakov	SOV	15.80	51-10	
7. Koji Sakurai	JAP	15.73	51-7¼	
8. Teruji Kogake	JAP	15.64	51-3¾	

The second round of the final produced a tremendous shock, when a completely unknown Icelander, 22-year-old Vilhjalmur Einarsson, took the lead with a jump of 53 feet 4¼ inches, improving his personal record by 17 inches. Nevertheless, defending champion da Silva regained the lead in the fourth round and won his second gold medal. Afterward, reporters searched frantically to find an Icelandic interpreter, only to have Einarsson save them the trouble by explaining that he spoke English quite well, since he had just graduated from Dartmouth. Einarrson is Iceland's only Olympic medal winner.

In 1958 Adhemar Ferreira da Silva acted in the internationally acclaimed film *Black Orpheus*.

1960 Rome C: 39, N: 24, D: 9.6. WR: 17.03, 55–10½ (Józef Schmidt)

		FT.–	
		M	IN.
1. Józef Schmidt	POL	16.81	55-2
2. Vladimir Goryayev	SOV	16.63	54-6¾
3. Vitold Kreyer	SOV	16.43	53-11
4. Ira Davis	USA	16.41	53-10¼
5. Vilhjálmur Einarsson	ICE	16.37	53-8½
6. Ryszard Malcherczyk	POL	16.01	52-6½
7. Manfred Hinze	GDR	15.93	52-3¼
8. Kari Rahkamo	FIN	15.84	51-11¾

On August 5, 1960, Józef Schmidt had jumped 55 feet 10½ inches to become the first person to break both the 55-foot barrier and the 17-meter barrier, bettering the world record by 13 inches. In Rome, he won easily.

1964 Tokyo C: 34, N: 21, D: 10.16. WR: 17.03, 55–10½ (Józef Schmidt)

		M	FT.–IN.	
1. Józef Schmidt	POL	16.85	55-3½	OR
2. Oleg Fyedoseyev	SOV	16.58	54-4¾	
3. Viktor Kravchenko	SOV	16.57	54-4½	
4. Frederick Alsop	GBR	16.46	54-0	
5. Şerban Ciochină	ROM	16.23	53-3	
6. Manfred Hinze	GDR	16.15	53-0	
7. Georgi Stoikovski	BUL	16.10	52-10	
8. Hans-Jürgen Rückborn	GDR	16.09	52-9½	

Józef Schmidt had dominated the event for six years. However he underwent an operation to his knee less than two months before the Tokyo Games, and his condition was still in doubt. Competing in pain, needing an injection of novocaine, Schmidt jumped 54 feet 7½ inches in the second round of the final, and then set an Olympic record of 55 feet 3½ inches with his last attempt.

1968 Mexico City C: 34, N: 24, D: 10.17. WR: 17.03, 55–10½ (Józef Schmidt)

		M	FT.–IN.	
1. Viktor Saneyev	SOV	17.39	57-0¾	WR
2. Nelson Prudencio	BRA	17.27	56-8	
3. Giuseppe Gentile	ITA	17.22	56-6	
4. Arthur Walker	USA	17.12	56-2	
5. Nikolai Dudkin	SOV	17.09	56-1	
6. Philip May	AUS	17.02	55-10¼	
7. Józef Schmidt	POL	16.89	55-5	
8. Mamadou Mansour-Dia	SEN	16.73	54-10¾	

Guiseppe Gentile, a bearded 25-year-old law student who later played opposite Maria Callas in the film version of *Medea*, produced a stunning performance in the qualifying round when he leaped 56 feet 1¼ inches to break Józef Schmidt's eight-year-old world record. But this was just a prelude to the extraordinary events of the following day's final.

In the very first round, Gentile hit a whopping 56 feet 6 inches, 19 inches farther than his pre-Olympic best, and it seemed that he had surely put a lock on the gold medal. But in the second round, Nelson Prudencio, who had never jumped beyond 53 feet 5¾ inches before Mexico City, leaped an ominous 55 feet 11¼ inches. In the third round it was the turn of Viktor Saneyev, a graduate of the Georgian Sub-Tropical Plant Cultivation Institute. The pre-Olympic favorite, Saneyev reached 56 feet 6½ inches, to move ahead of Gentile by one centimeter.

In the fifth round, Nikolai Dudkin moved into third place with 56 feet 1 inches. Two jumps later, Prudencio exploded with another world record of 56 feet 8 inches. With his last jump, Prudencio again broke Schmidt's old record with a jump of 56 feet 3¼ inches. Saneyev, Art Walker, and Gentile each had one jump remaining. It was Saneyev who came up with the clutch performance, extending to 57 feet ¾ inches for yet another world record. Walker jumped 56 feet 2 inches, leaving Nikolai Dudkin in fifth place even though he had bettered the pre-Olympic world record. Gentile closed the amazing competition with his fourth foul in five jumps, and had to settle for a bronze medal after twice setting a world record. The best jumps of Saneyev and Prudencio were both accompanied by suspicious wind readings of exactly 2.0 m.p.s., which didn't affect the competition, but did affect their validity as world records, since 2.0 m.p.s. happened to be the maximum allowable wind speed.

1972 Munich C: 36, N: 28, D: 9.4. WR: 17.40, 57–1 (Pedro Perez Dueñas)

		M	FT.–IN.
1. Viktor Saneyev	SOV	17.35	56-11¼
2. Jörg Drehmel	GDR	17.31	56-9½
3. Nelson Prudencio	BRA	17.05	55-11¼
4. Carol Corbu	ROM	16.85	55-3½
5. John Craft	USA	16.83	55-2¾
6. Mamadou Mansour-Dia	SEN	16.83	55-2¾
7. Michal Joachimowski	POL	16.69	54-9¼
8. Kristen Flogstad	NOR	16.44	53-11¼

This was expected to be a dramatic showdown between defending champion Viktor Saneyev and his rival Jörg Drehmel, who had twice beaten Saneyev in important meets. But Saneyev belted out the third best jump of all time in the first round of the final, and Drehmel was unable to even come close until the fifth round. World record holder Pedro Perez withdrew in the middle of the qualifying round because of injury. Nelson Prudencio's final jump was his best since the 1968 Olympic final.

1976 Montreal C: 25, N: 18, D: 7.30 WR: 17.89, 58–8½ (Joao Carlos de Oliveira)

		M	FT.–IN.
1. Viktor Saneyev	SOV	17.29	56-8¾
2. James Butts	USA	17.18	56-4½
3. Joao Carlos de Oliveira	BRA	16.90	55-5½
4. Pedro Perez Dueñas	CUB	16.81	55-2
5. Tommy Haynes	USA	16.78	55-0¾
6. Wolfgang Kolmsee	GER	16.68	54-8¾
7. Eugeniusz Biskupski	POL	16.49	54-1¼
8. Carol Corbu	ROM	16.43	53-11

On October 15, 1975, Joao Carlos de Oliveira, competing at the Pan American Games in Mexico City, triple-jumped 58 feet 8½ inches to better Viktor Saneyev's world record by an incredible 17¾ inches. At the Montreal Olympics, de Oliveira led the qualifying round with a reserved jump of 55 feet 2 inches, followed by Saneyev at 55 feet ¼ inches. In the final, Perez took the first round lead at 55 feet 2 inches, but Saneyev moved ahead in the third round with a jump of 55 feet 11¾ inches. In the fourth round, James

Butts, aiming to become the first U.S. triple jump medalist in 48 years, leaped into the lead at 56 feet 4½ inches. However Saneyev, ever the clutch performer, rebounded in the fifth round with a jump of 56 feet 8¾ inches and that settled the issue. He joined standing jumper Ray Ewry, hammer thrower John Flanagan, and discus champion Al Oerter as the only track and field athletes to win three or more individual gold medals in the same event.

1980 Moscow C: 23, N: 19, D: 7.25 WR: 17.89, 58–8½ (Joao Carlos de Oliveira)

| | | | FT.– |
		M	IN.
1. Jaak Uudmäe	SOV	17.35	56-11¼
2. Viktor Saneyev	SOV	17.24	56-6¾
3. Joao Carlos de Oliveira	BRA	17.22	56-6
4. Keith Connor	GBR	16.87	55-4¼
5. Ian Campbell	AUS	16.72	54-10¼
6. Atanas Chochev	BUL	16.56	54-4
7. Béla Bakosi	HUN	16.47	54-0½
8. Kenneth Lorraway	AUS	16.44	53-11¼

Unfortunately, this event was marred by ugly scenes: Soviet spectators whistling while de Oliveira jumped, and controversial officiating which caused leading non-Soviet contenders de Oliveira and Ian Campbell to be charged with nine fouls in 12 jumps. In the third round Campbell received a no-jump after allegedly dragging his trail leg during the step stage. He argued his case, but the pit was raked before impartial observers could arrive. The very next jump was the gold medal winner for 25-year-old Estonian Jaak Uudmäe. The final round was highlighted by a near world record by de Oliveira that was ruled a foul, and by 34-year-old Viktor Saneyev's noble attempt to match Al Oerter's feat of four consecutive gold medals. He landed four and a half inches short, but did manage to edge past de Oliveira for the silver medal. In January 1982, Joao Carlos de Oliveira was badly injured in an auto accident. After a nine-month battle to salvage his athletic career, his right leg was finally amputated below the knee.

SHOT PUT

A shot is a 16-pound ball made of iron or brass. It must be put rather than thrown and must not drop below the level of the contestant's shoulder.

1896 Athens C: 4, N: 3, D: 4.7. WR: 14.32, 47–0 (George Gray)

| | | | FT.– |
		M	IN.
1. Robert Garrett	USA	11.22	36-9¾
2. Miltiades Gouskos	GRE	11.20	36-9
3. Georgios Papasideris	GRE	10.36	34-0
4. Louis Adler	FRA	—	—

Garrett, who had placed first in the discus the day before, won the shot put with his first attempt.

1900 Paris C: 10, N: 6, D: 7.15. WR: 14.68, 48-2 (Dennis Horgan)

| | | | FT.– |
		M	IN.
1. Richard Sheldon	USA	14.10	46-3¼ OR
2. Josiah McCracken	USA	12.85	42-2
3. Robert Garrett	USA	12.37	40-7
4. Rezsö Crettier	HUN	12.05	39-6½
5. Panagiotis Paraskevopoulos	GRE	11.52	37-9½
6. Gustaf Söderström	SWE	11.18	36-8¼

1904 St. Louis C: 8, N: 2, D: 8.31. WR: 14.68, 48–2 (Dennis Horgan)

| | | | FT.– |
		M	IN.
1. Ralph Rose	USA	14.81	48-7 WR
2. William Coe	USA	14.40	47-3
3. Leon Feuerbach	USA	13.37	43-10½
4. Martin Sheridan	USA	12.39	40-8
5. Charles Chadwick	USA	—	—
6. Albert Johnson	USA	—	—
7. John Guiney	USA	—	—

Ralph Rose was a 6-foot 6-inch, 235-pound giant from California. Before his Olympic career was over, he had won three gold medals, two silver, and one bronze. He died on October 16, 1913, at the age of 29. Nicolaos Georgantas of Greece was also entered in this event, but after his first two attempts were disallowed for throwing, he withdrew in disgust.

1906 Athens C: 18, N: 10, D: 4.27. WR: 15.09, 49–6 (Wesley Coe)

| | | | FT.– |
		M	IN.
1. Martin Sheridan	USA	12.325	40-5¼
2. Mihály Dávid	HUN	11.83	38-9¾
3. Eric Lemming	SWE	11.26	36-11½
4. André Tison	FRA	11.02	36-2

Martin Sheridan was the star of the Intercalated Games, winning two gold medals and three silver medals. In 1908 he added two gold and a silver.

1908 London C: 26, N: 8, D: 7.16. WR: 15.12, 49–7½ (Ralph Rose)

| | | | FT.– |
		M	IN.
1. Ralph Rose	USA	14.21	46-7½
2. Dennis Horgan	GBR/IRL	13.62	44-8¼
3. John Garreis	USA	13.18	43-3
4. William Coe	USA	13.07	42-10½
5. Edmond Barrett	GBR	12.89	42-3½
6. Marquis Horr	USA	12.82	42-1
7. Jalmari Sauli	FIN	12.58	41-3¼
8. Lee Talbott	USA	11.63	38-1¾

Dennis Horgan was 37 years old and past his prime. His second-place performance was particularly noteworthy considering that he had almost been killed the year before.

On duty as a New York City policeman, Horgan tried to break up a brawl and was severely attacked with sticks and shovels. After his surprising recovery, he was given a pension and allowed to return to Ireland.

1912 Stockholm C: 22, N: 14, D: 7.10. WR: 15.545, 51–0 (Ralph Rose)

			FT.–	
		M	IN.	
1. Patrick McDonald	USA	15.34	50-4	OR
2. Ralph Rose	USA	15.25	50-0½	
3. Lawrence Whitney	USA	13.93	45-8½	
4. Elmer Niklander	FIN	13.65	44-9½	
5. George Philbrook	USA	13.13	43-1	
6. Imre Mudin	HUN	12.81	42-0½	
7. Einar Nilsson	SWE	12.62	41-5	
8. P. Quinn	GBR	12.53	41-1½	

McDonald, another New York City policeman, surprised Rose, in the fourth round of six, by achieving the best put of his career.

1920 Antwerp C: 20, N: 10, D: 8.18. WR: 15.545, 51–0 (Ralph Rose)

			FT.–	
		M	IN.	
1. F.W."Ville" Pörhölä	FIN	14.81	48-7¼	
2. Elmer Niklander	FIN	14.155	46-5¼	
3. Harry Liversedge	USA	14.15	46-5¼	
4. Patrick McDonald	USA	14.08	46-2½	
5. Einar Nilsson	SWE	13.87	45-6¼	
6. Harald Tammer	EST	13.605	44-7½	
7. George Bihlman	USA	13.575	44-6½	
8. Howard Cann	USA	13.52	44-4¼	

1924 Paris C: 28, N: 15, D: 7.8. WR: 15.545, 51–0 (Ralph Rose)

			FT.–	
		M	IN.	
1. Clarence"Bud" Houser	USA	14.99	49-2¼	
2. Glenn Hartranft	USA	14.89	48-10¼	
3. Ralph Hills	USA	14.64	48-0½	
4. Hannes Torpo	FIN	14.45	47-5	
5. Norman Anderson	USA	14.29	46-10¾	
6. Elmer Niklander	FIN	14.26	49-9½	
7. F.W."Ville" Pörhölä	FIN	14.10	46-3¼	
8. Bertil Jansson	SWE	13.76	45-1¾	

1928 Amsterdam C: 22, N: 14, D: 7.29. WR: 15.79, 51–9¾ (Emil Hirschfeld)

			FT.–	
		M	IN.	
1. John Kuck	USA	15.87	52-0¾	WR
2. Herman Brix	USA	15.75	51-8¼	
3. Emil Hirschfeld	GER	15.72	51-7	
4. Eric Krenz	USA	14.99	49-2¼	
5. Armas Wahlstedt	FIN	14.69	48-2½	
6. Wilhelm Uebler	GER	14.69	48-2½	
7. Harlow Rothert	USA	14.68	48-2	
8. József Darányi	HUN	14.35	47-1	

On May 6, 1928, Emil Hirschfeld finally broke Ralph Rose's 1909 world record. He was in good form in Amsterdam, but Kuck and Brix were superb. Brix later changed his name to Bruce Bennett and became a well-known movie actor. Among his early roles was Tarzan in *The New Adventures of Tarzan* (1935).

1932 Los Angeles C: 15, N: 10, D: 7.31. WR: 16.05, 52–8 (Zygmont Heljasz)

			FT.–	
		M	IN.	
1. Leo Sexton	USA	16.00	52-6	OR
2. Harlow Rothert	USA	15.67	51-5	
3. František Douda	CZE	15.61	51-2¾	
4. Emil Hirschfeld	GER	15.56	51-0¾	
5. Nelson Gray	USA	15.47	50-9¼	
6. Hans-Heinrich Sievert	GER	15.07	49-5½	
7. József Darányi	HUN	14.67	48-1¾	
8. Jules Noël	FRA	14.53	47-8	

Leo Sexton was a 6-foot 4-inch insurance broker from New York. World record holder Zygmont Heljasz of Poland was able to place only ninth.

1936 Berlin C: 22, N: 14, D: 8.2. WR: 17.40, 57–1 (Jack Torrance)

			FT.–	
		M	IN.	
1. Hans Woellke	GER	16.20	53-1¾	OR
2. Sulo Bärlund	FIN	16.12	52-10¾	
3. Gerhard Stöck	GER	15.66	51-4½	
4. Samuel Francis	USA	15.45	50-8¼	
5. Jack Torrance	USA	15.38	50-5½	
6. Dimitri Zaitz	USA	15.32	50-3¼	
7. František Douda	CZE	15.28	50-1¾	
8. Arnold Viiding	EST	15.23	49-11¾	

Hans Woellke, a 25-year-old policeman, was the first German to win a track and field gold medal. Another policeman, 304-pound world record holder Jack Torrance of Baton Rouge, Louisiana, was out of shape and finished a disappointing fifth.

1948 London C: 24, N: 14, D: 8.3. WR: 17.68, 58–0⅜ (Charles Fonville)

			FT.–	
		M	IN.	
1. Wilbur Thompson	USA	17.12	56-2	OR
2. F. James Delaney	USA	16.68	54-8¾	
3. James Fuchs	USA	16.42	53-10½	
4. Mieczyslaw Lomowski	POL	15.43	50 7½	
5. Gösta Arvidsson	SWE	15.37	50- 5¼	
6. Yrjö Lehtilä	FIN	15.05	49- 4½	
7. J. Jouppila	FIN	14.59	47-10½	
8. C. Kalina	CZE	14.55	47-9	

The American putters were so strong that world record holder Charles Fonville failed to make the U.S. team. At

London the Americans outdistanced the rest of the world by over three feet.

1952 Helsinki C: 20, N: 14, D: 7.21. WR: 17.95, 58–10½ (James Fuchs)

			FT.–	
		M	IN.	
1. W. Parry O'Brien	USA	17.41	57-1½	OR
2. C. Darrow Hooper	USA	17.39	57-0¾	
3. James Fuchs	USA	17.06	55-11¾	
4. Otto Grigalka	SOV	16.78	55-0¾	
5. Roland Nilsson	SWE	16.55	53-3¾	
6. John Savidge	GBR	16.19	53-1½	
7. Georgi Fyodorov	SOV	16.06	52-8¼	
8. Per Stavem	NOR	16.02	52-6¾	

World record holder Jim Fuchs had won 88 consecutive meets when he was beaten at the 1951 A.A.U. championships by Parry O'Brien. At the 1952 U.S. Olympic trials, O'Brien was beaten by Darrow Hooper. It was his last loss for four years, during which time he won 116 straight meets. O'Brien and Hooper were almost the exact same size and weight. Their similarity also extended to their performances in the Olympics. O'Brien, who was two days older than Hooper, outputted him by only two centimeters. Parry O'Brien, a student at the University of Southern California, practiced at the Los Angeles Memorial Coliseum, site of the 1932 and 1984 Olympics, by sneaking over a fence late at night while no one was there. He revolutionized shot putting by introducing a new style in which he began with his back to the front of the throwing circle and then used every bit of momentum he could gather before he let go of the shot.

1956 Melbourne C: 14, N: 10, D: 11.28. WR:19.25, 63–2 (W. Parry O'Brien)

			FT.–	
		M	IN.	
1. W. Parry O'Brien	USA	18.57	60-11¼	OR
2. William Nieder	USA	18.18	59-7¾	
3. Jiři Skobla	CZE	17.65	57-11	
4. Kenneth Bantum	USA	17.48	57-4¼	
5. Boris Balyayev	SOV	16.96	55-7¾	
6. Erik Uddebom	SWE	16.65	54-7½	
7. Karlheinz Wegmann	GER	16.63	54-6¾	
8. Georgios Tsakanikas	GRE	16.56	54-4	

On May 8, 1954, two days after Roger Bannister broke the four-minute mile, Parry O'Brien became the first person to put the shot more than 60 feet, with a toss of 60 feet 5¼ inches. In Melbourne, at the 1956 Olympics, O'Brien overwhelmed the field, recording the five best puts of the competition. Even his worst put was beaten only by Bill Nieder's best. Parry O'Brien became the first reigning world record holder to win the shot put at the Olympics since 1908. Bronze medalist Jiři Skobla was the son of Jaroslav Skobla, who won the heavyweight weightlifting gold medal in 1932.

1960 Rome C: 24, N: 16, D: 8.31. WR: 20.06, 65–10 (William Nieder)

			FT.–	
		M	IN.	
1. William Nieder	USA	19.68	64-6¾	OR
2. W. Parry O'Brien	USA	19.11	62-8½	
3. Dallas Long	USA	19.01	62-4½	
4. Viktor Lipsnis	SOV	17.90	58-8¾	
5. Michael Lindsay	GBR	17.80	58-4¾	
6. Alfred Sosgórnik	POL	17.57	57-7¾	
7. Dieter Urbach	GER	17.47	57-3¾	
8. Martyn Lucking	GBR	17.43	57-2¼	

Bill Nieder had failed to qualify for the U.S. team after finishing fourth in the Olympic trials. But a wrist injury suffered by Dave Davis, and a world record put by Nieder, convinced U.S. officials to make a rare replacement. In Rome, Nieder showed that they had made the right decision. Parry O'Brien led after four rounds, but in the fifth round, Nieder, recalling O'Brien's disparaging remark that he was a "cow pasture performer" who choked in important meets, let loose a monster toss that was almost two feet better than anything the defending champion was able to produce.

1964 Tokyo C: 22, N: 13, D: 10.17. WR: 20.68, 67–10 (Dallas Long)

			FT.–	
		M	IN.	
1. Dallas Long	USA	20.33	66-8½	OR
2. James Randel Matson	USA	20.20	66-3¼	
3. Vilmos Varju	HUN	19.39	63-7½	
4. W. Parry O'Brien	USA	19.20	63-0	
5. Zsigmond Nagy	HUN	18.88	61-11½	
6. Nikolai Karasyov	SOV	18.86	61-10½	
7. Leslie Mills	NZE	18.52	60-9¼	
8. Adolfas Varanauskas	SOV	18.41	60-4¾	

Twenty-four-year-old Dallas Long, a 6-foot 4-inch, 260-pound dentist from Los Angeles, took the lead with a first round toss of 64 feet 4 inches. In the third round, 19-year-old Randy Matson of Pampa, Texas moved ahead at 65 feet 2¾ inches. With his next throw he improved to 66 feet 3¼ inches, a new Olympic record. However, his record was short-lived. Two minutes later, Long countered with a put of 66 feet 8½ inches that held up for first place.

1968 Mexico City C: 19, N: 14, D: 10.14. WR: 21.78, 71–5½ (James Randel Matson)

			FT.–
		M	IN.
1. James Randel Matson	USA	20.54	67-4¾
2. George Woods	USA	20.12	66-0¼
3. Eduard Gushchin	SOV	20.09	65-11
4. Dieter Hoffmann	GDR	20.00	65-7½
5. David Maggard	USA	19.43	63-9
6. Wladyslaw Komar	POL	19.28	63-3¼
7. Uwe Grabe	GDR	19.03	62-5¼
8. Heinfried Birlenbach	GER	18.80	61-8¼

Although he only placed third at the U.S. Olympic trials, 6-foot 6½-inch, 265-pound Randy Matson was still the overwhelming favorite by virtue of the fact that he had completely dominated the event over the previous four years. On May 8, 1965, he had demolished the world record with a put of 70 feet 7¼ inches, bettering the previous record by 2 feet 9¼ inches. By the time of the Mexico City Olympics, Matson had registered 23 of the 25 longest puts in history. He led the qualifying round with an Olympic record of 67 feet 10¼ inches. His first toss of the final was 67 feet 4¾ inches. No one else came close to that for the rest of the competition. U.S. shot putters finished first and second for the fifth straight time. Like many athletes during the Vietnam War period, Randy Matson was declared unfit for military service because of knee problems.

1972 Munich C: 29, N: 19, D: 9.9 WR: 21.78, 71–5½ (James Randel Matson)

			FT.–	
			M	IN.
1. Wladyslaw Komar	POL	21.18	69-6	OR
2. George Woods	USA	21.17	69-5½	
3. Hartmut Briesenick	GDR	21.14	69-4¼	
4. Hans-Peter Gies	GDR	21.14	69-4¼	
5. Allan Feuerbach	USA	21.01	68-11¼	
6. Brian Oldfield	USA	20.91	68-7¼	
7. Heinfried Birlenbach	GER	20.37	66-10	
8. Vilmos Varjú	HUN	20.10	65-11½	

The 6-foot 5¼-inch, 276-pound Wladyslaw Komar had twice been kicked off the Polish team for "misbehavior," including once when he received a "life ban." However, he was back again in Munich for his third Olympics. Ninth in 1964, sixth in 1968, the 32-year-old Komar connected with the greatest put of his career in the first round of the 1972 final, bettering his previous best by seven and a quarter inches. Woods, Briesenick, and Gies all came very, very close, but all fell short by inches. George Woods' last toss caused much controversy since it hit the marker which indicated Komar's best put. Many observers were quite surprised when it was measured at only 69 feet ¾ inches, and Woods himself believed that at the very least he deserved an extra put. But the officials in charge ruled it a valid toss and called an end to the competition. Films of the incident were inconclusive.

1976 Montreal C: 23, N: 18, D: 7.24. WR: 22.00, 72–2¼ (Aleksandr Baryshnikov)

			FT.–	
			M	IN.
1. Udo Beyer	GDR	21.05	69-0¾	
2. Yevgeny Mironov	SOV	21.03	69-0	
3. Aleksandr Baryshnikov	SOV	21.00	68-10¾	
4. Allan Feuerbach	USA	20.55	67-5¼	
5. Hans-Peter Gies	GDR	20.47	67-2	
6. Geoffrey Capes	GBR	20.36	66-9¾	
7. George Woods	USA	20.26	66-5¾	
8. Hans Hoglund	SWE	20.17	66-2¼	

Missing from the Olympics was the number-one shot putter in the world, Brian Oldfield, who owned the four longest unofficial puts in history, including one of 75 feet. Oldfield was a professional and thus ineligible to compete. The amateur record of 72 feet 2¼ inches, was set by Aleksandr Baryshnikov on July 10. Baryshnikov looked good as gold when his one put of the qualifying round sailed 69 feet 11½ inches to break the Olympic record. Baryshnikov also took the lead in the first round of the final with a toss of 67 feet 4¼ inches. In the second round he was passed by Al Feuerbach's 67 feet 5 inches. Baryshnikov boomed back in front with a third-round 68 feet 10¾ inches. Then, in the fifth round, 20-year-old Udo Beyer, the youngest man in the competition, unleashed a put of 69 feet ¾ inch. Beyer had only been added to the East German team one week before the Olympics began. Yevgeny Mironov, who had been mired inconspicuously in sixth place, followed a few minutes later with 69 feet 0 inches and the medals were decided. Most of the leading contenders fell several feet short of their best performances. Although the pressure of the Olympics may have been a contributing factor, most observers felt that the institution of steroid testing played a more important role.

1980 Moscow C: 16, N: 11, D: 7.30. WR: 22.15, 72–8 (Udo Beyer)

			FT.–	
			M	IN.
1. Vladimir Kiselyov	SOV	21.35	70-0½	OR
2. Aleksandr Baryshnikov	SOV	21.08	69-2	
3. Udo Beyer	GDR	21.06	69-1¼	
4. Reijo Ståhlberg	FIN	20.82	68-3¾	
5. Geoffrey Capes	GBR	20.50	67-3¼	
6. Hans-Jürgen Jacobi	GDR	20.32	66-8	
7. Jaromir Vlk	CZE	20.24	66-5	
8. Vladimir Milic	YUG	20.07	65-10¼	

Vladimir Kiselyov was the only shot putter to achieve a personal best, ending Udo Beyer's string of 34 consecutive victories.

DISCUS THROW

The men's discus weighs 2 kilograms (4 pounds 6.55 ounces). The discus throw is the only track and field event in which a world record has never been set in the Olympics.

1896 Athens C: 9, N: 6, D: 4.6.

			FT.–	
			M	IN.
1. Robert Garrett	USA	29.15	95-7½	
2. Panagiotis Paraskevopoulos	GRE	28.955	95-0	
3. Sotirios Versis	GRE	28.78	94-5	
4. Louis Adler	FRA	—	—	
5. Georgios Papasideris	GRE	—	—	
6. George Robertson	GBR	—	—	
7. Henrik Sjöberg	SWE	—	—	

Twenty-year-old Robert Garrett came from a wealthy Baltimore banking family. While a student at Princeton, he was shown a drawing of an ancient Greek discus. He ordered a facsimile made and tried practicing with it, but it proved too heavy and unwieldy and so he lost interest quickly. However, while strolling on the field in Athens, he chanced upon a similar object and was told that this was a real discus, which turned out to be much lighter than his American version. Encouraged, yet risking what he feared would be great embarrassment, he entered the Olympic discus contest. To the disappointment of the Greeks, he won the event with his third and final throw. Before the games were over, Garrett had won two events, placed second in two more, and third in yet another two.

1900 Paris C: 20, N: 8. D: 7.15. WR: 36.20, 118–9 (Charles Henneman)

			FT.–	
		M	IN.	
1. Rudolf (Rezsö) Bauer	HUN	36.04	118-3	OR
2. František Janda-Suk	CZE	35.25	115-7	
3. Richard Sheldon	USA	34.60	113-6	
4. Panagiotis Paraskevopoulos	GRE	34.04	111-8	
5. Rezsö Crettier	HUN	33.65	110-4	
6. Gustaf Soderstrom	SWE	33.30	109-3	
7. Robert Garrett	USA	33.07	108-5	
8. Eric Lemming	SWE	32.50	106-7	
8. Carl Winckler	DEN	32.50	106-7	

1904 St. Louis C: 6, N: 2, D: 9.3. WR: 40.71, 133–6½ (Martin Sheridan)

			FT.–	
		M	IN.	
1. Martin Sheridan	USA	39.28	128-10½	OR
2. Ralph Rose	USA	39.28	128-10½	
3. Nicolaos Georgantas	GRE	37.68	123-7½	
4. John Flanagan	USA	36.14	118-7	
5. John Biller	USA	—	—	
6. James Mitchell	USA	—	—	

Sheridan and Rose finished in a tie, so, for the only time in Olympic history, a throw-off was held to determine first place. Each man was given three throws. Sheridan won by about five feet.

1906 Athens C: 21, N: 9, D: 4.25. WR: 42.14, 138–3 (Martin Sheridan)

			FT.–
		M	IN.
1. Martin Sheridan	USA	41.46	136-0
2. Nicolaos Georgantas	GRE	38.06	124-10
3. Werner Järvinen	FIN	36.82	120-9
4. Eric Lemming	SWE	35.62	116-10
5. André Tison	FRA	34.81	114-2

1908 London C: 41, N: 11, D: 7.16. WR: 42.63, 139–10½ (Martin Sheridan)

			FT.–	
		M	IN.	
1. Martin Sheridan	USA	40.89	134-2	OR
2. Merritt Giffin	USA	40.70	133-6	
3. Marquis Horr	USA	39.44	129-5	
4. Werner Järvinen	FIN	39.42	129-4	
5. Arthur Dearborn	USA	38.52	126-4	
6. György Luntzer	HUN	38.34	125-9	
7. André Tison	FRA	38.30	125-8	
8. W.G. Burroughs	USA	37.42	122-9	

Competing in the 1904, 1906, and 1908 Games, Irish-born policeman Martin Sheridan won five gold medals and four silver.

1912 Stockholm C: 40, N: 15, D: 7.12. WR: 47.58, 156–1 (James Duncan)

			FT.–	
		M	IN.	
1. Armas Taipale	FIN	45.21	148-3	OR
2. Richard Byrd	USA	42.32	138-10	
3. James Duncan	USA	42.28	138-8	
4. Elmer Niklander	FIN	42.09	138-1	
5. Hans Tronner	AUS	41.24	135-4	
6. Arlie Mucks	USA	40.93	134-3	
7. George Philbrook	USA	40.92	134-2½	
8. Emil Magnusson	SWE	39.91	130-11	

1920 Antwerp C: 28, N: 12, D: 8.22. WR: 47.58, 156–1 (James Duncan)

			FT.–
		M	IN.
1. Elmer Niklander	FIN	44.685	146-7
2. Armas Taipale	FIN	44.19	145-0
3. Augustus Pope	USA	42.13	138-2
4. Otto Zallhagen	SWE	41.07	134-9
5. William Bartlett	USA	40.875	134-1
6. Allan Eriksson	SWE	39.41	129-3
7. W. Jenson	DEN	38.23	125-5

1924 Paris C: 32, N: 18, D: 7.13. WR: 47.58, 156–1 (James Duncan)

			FT.–	
		M	IN.	
1. Clarence "Bud" Houser	USA	46.15	151-4	OR
2. Vilho Niittymaa	FIN	44.95	147-5	
3. Thomas Lieb	USA	44.83	147-0	
4. Augustus Pope	USA	44.42	145-9	
5. Ketil Askildt	NOR	43.40	142-5	
6. Glenn Hartranft	USA	42.49	139-4	
7. Elmer Niklander	FIN	42.09	138-1	
8. H. Malmivirta	FIN	41.16	135-0	

Bud Houser also won the shot put five days later. He is the last athlete to achieve such a double in the Olympics.

1928 Amsterdam C: 34: N: 19, D: 8.1. WR: 48.20, 158–2
(Clarence "Bud" Houser)

		FT.–		
		M	IN.	
1. Clarence "Bud" Houser	USA	47.32	155-3	OR
2. L. Antero Kivi	FIN	47.23	154-11	
3. James Corson	USA	47.10	154-6	
4. Harald Stenerud	NOR	45.80	150-3	
5. John Anderson	USA	44.87	147-2	
6. Eino Kenttä	FIN	44.17	144-10	
7. Ernst Paulus	GER	44.15	144-9	
8. J. Trandem	NOR	43.97	144-3	

1932 Los Angeles C: 18, N: 11, D: 8.3. WR: 51.73, 169–9 (Paul
Jessup)

		FT.–		
		M	IN.	
1. John Anderson	USA	49.49	162-4	OR
2. Henri Jean Laborde	USA	48.47	159-0	
3. Paul Winter	FRA	47.85	156-11	
4. Jules Noël	FRA	47.74	156-7	
5. István Donogán	HUN	47.08	154-5	
6. Endre Madarász	HUN	46.52	152-7	
7. Kalevi Kotkas	FIN	45.87	150-5	
8. Paul Jessup	USA	45.25	148-5	

Two of the favorites, József Remecz of Hungary and Paul
Jessup, the 6-foot 7-inch world record holder, failed to
qualify for the final round of six. But the final competition
was still hotly contested, as Anderson and Laborde traded
the lead, with Anderson breaking the previous Olympic record four times in six throws. The Americans may have
won the medals, but it was the fourth-place finisher, Jules
Noël, who made the news. Because the 1932 Olympics
were held in the United States during Prohibition, the
French team had to receive special permission to import
several thousand bottles of wine into the United States.
The French successfully argued that although alcohol
might be illegal in the United States, it was an essential
part of the diet of many of the French athletes.

Evidently, Jules Noël was one of those athletes, as he
caused the American track and field officials great conster-
nation during the competition by making periodic visits to
the dark tunnel which joined the field to the locker rooms.
There he swigged champagne with his compatriots.

On his fourth attempt, Noël lofted a great throw that appeared to land just beyond the flag that marked Anderson's first-place effort. Unfortunately, every one of the
officials in charge of the discus was, at that moment, distracted by the tense proceedings of the pole vault, taking
place nearby, so none of them saw where Noël's discus had
landed. Embarrassed by this blunder, they awarded Noël
an extra throw in addition to the two that he still had coming. However, the Frenchman was unable to come up with
another big throw, and he was forced to return home without a medal.

1936 Berlin C: 31, N: 17, D: 8.5. WR: 53.10, 174–2 (Willy
Schröder)

		FT.–		
		M	IN.	
1. Kenneth Carpenter	USA	50.48	165-7	OR
2. Gordon Dunn	USA	49.36	161-11	
3. Giorgio Oberweger	ITA	49.23	161-6	
4. Reidar Sörlie	NOR	48.77	160-0	
5. Willy Schröder	GER	47.93	157-3	
6. Nicolaos Syllas	GRE	47.75	156-7	
7. Gunnar Bergh	SWE	47.22	154-11	
8. Åke Hedvall	SWE	46.20	151-7	

The two favorites, Harald Andersson of Sweden and Willy
Schröder of Germany, were unable to rise to the occasion.
Andersson, hampered by injury, failed to qualify for the
semifinals, while Schröder only made it to the final group
of six by winning a throw-off against Bergh. Carpenter
overhauled Dunn and Oberweger with his next to last attempt.

1948 London C: 28, N: 18, D: 8.2. WR: 54.93, 180–3 (Robert
Fitch)

		FT.–		
		M	IN.	
1. Adolfo Consolini	ITA	52.78	173-2	OR
2. Giuseppe Tosi	ITA	51.78	169-10	
3. Fortune Gordien	USA	50.77	166-6	
4. Ivar Ramstad	NOR	49.21	161-5	
5. Ferenc Klics	HUN	48.21	158-2	
6. Veikko Nyqvist	FIN	47.33	155-3	
7. Nicolaos Syllas	GRE	47.25	155-0	
8. Stein Johnsen	NOR	46.54	152-8	

Adolfo Consolini held the world record from October 1941
until June 1948. Two months after earning the Olympic
gold medal, he regained the world record.

1952 Helsinki C: 32, N: 20, D: 7.22. WR: 56.97, 186–11 (Fortune
Gordien)

		FT.–		
		M	IN.	
1. Sim Iness	USA	55.03	180-6	OR
2. Adolfo Consolini	ITA	53.78	176-5	
3. James Dillion	USA	53.28	174-10	
4. Fortune Gordien	USA	52.66	172-9	
5. Ferenc Klics	HUN	51.13	167-9	
6. Otto Grigalka	SOV	50.71	166-4	
7. Roland Nilsson	SWE	50.06	164-3	
8. Giuseppe Tosi	ITA	49.03	160-10	

Sim Iness of Tulare, California bettered Consolini's Olympic record with all six of his throws in the final. Nicolaos
Syllas of Greece, who had finished sixth in 1936, was still
able to place ninth 16 years later.

1956 Melbourne C: 20, N: 15, D: 11.27. WR: 59.28, 194–6 (Fortune Gordien)

		M	FT.– IN.	
1. Alfred Oerter	USA	56.36	184-11	OR
2. Fortune Gordien	USA	54.81	179-9	
3. Desmond Koch	USA	54.40	178-6	
4. Mark Pharaoh	GBR	54.27	178-0	
5. Otto Grigalka	SOV	52.37	171-9	
6. Adolfo Consolini	ITA	52.21	171-3	
7. Ferenc Klics	HUN	51.82	170-0	
8. Dako Radosević	YUG	51.69	169-7	

Twenty-year-old Al Oerter of West Babylon, New York, watched the favorites, Adolfo Consolini and Fortune Gordien, make their first round throws. When his turn came, he felt "keyed up" and "inspired" and let loose the best throw of his career—184 feet 11 inches. No one else came within five feet as Oerter ended up with the three longest throws of the competition. On the victory rostrum he suddenly realized that he had actually won. His knees buckled and he almost fell. As it turned out, in the years to come Al Oerter would have plenty of opportunities to get used to standing on the gold medal platform at Olympic medal ceremonies.

1960 Rome C: 35, N: 22, D: 9.7. WR: 59.91, 196–6 (Edmund Piątkowski, Richard "Rink" Babka)

		M	FT.– IN.	
1. Alfred Oerter	USA	59.18	194-2	OR
2. Richard "Rink" Babka	USA	58.02	190-4	
3. Richard Cochran	USA	57.16	187-6	
4. József Szécsényi	HUN	55.79	183-0	
5. Edmund Piątkowski	POL	55.12	180-10	
6. Viktor Kompanyeyets	SOV	55.06	180-8	
7. Carmelo Rado	ITA	54.00	177-2	
8. Kim Bukhantsev	SOV	53.61	175-10	

In 1957 Al Oerter was involved in a near fatal car crash, but he recovered fully and was back in shape before long. Then, at the U.S. Olympic trials, he suffered his first defeat in over two years when he lost to giant Rink Babka. Oerter was still considered a slight favorite at the Olympics, but he was definitely under great pressure. While warming up for the qualifying round, he casually threw the discus beyond the world record marker, and then qualified with an Olympic record of 191 feet 8 inches. But the day of the final he was "so tense I could barely throw." Babka led off with a toss of 190 feet 4 inches. Oerter followed with 189 feet 1 inch, but couldn't get closer over the next three rounds. As Oerter prepared for his fifth throw, Babka told him that he seemed to be "doing something wrong" with his left arm. Oerter then threw his discus 194 feet 2 inches—a personal record. He thanked Babka and wished him luck on his last throw, but Babka fell short and settled for the silver medal.

1964 Tokyo C: 28, N: 21, D: 10.15. WR: 64.54, 211–9 (Ludvik Daněk)

		M	FT.– IN.	
1. Alfred Oerter	USA	61.00	200-1	OR
2. Ludvik Daněk	CZE	60.52	198-7	
3. David Weill	USA	59.49	195-2	
4. L. Jay Silvester	USA	59.09	193-10	
5. József Szécsényi	HUN	57.23	187-9	
6. Zenon Begier	POL	57.06	187-2	
7. Edmund Piątkowski	POL	55.81	183-1	
8. Vladimir Trusenyov	SOV	54.78	179-9	

On May 18, 1962, Al Oerter became the first discus thrower to break officially the 200-foot barrier, with a throw of 200 feet 5 inches. Surprisingly, it was his first world record. It lasted only 17 days, when it was broken by Vladimir Trusenyov. But 27 days later Oerter had the record back again.

In 1964, however, Oerter knew that he would be in for a real struggle if he wanted to win a third gold medal. Not only did he have to face current world record holder Ludvik Daněk, who had won 45 straight competitions, but he had also been suffering for quite some time from a chronic cervical disc injury, which caused him to wear a neck harness. As if that wasn't trouble enough, Oerter tore the cartilage in his lower ribs while practicing in Tokyo less than a week before the competition. Doctors advised him to rest for six weeks, but the day of the preliminary round, he showed up anyway, shot up with novocaine and wrapped with ice packs and tape to prevent internal bleeding. With his first throw Oerter set an Olympic record of 198 feet 8 inches.

Ludvik Daněk opened the final at 195 feet 11 inches. Before the competition, Al Oerter had told a fellow athlete, "If I don't do it on the first throw, I won't be able to do it at all." But his first attempt only went 189 feet 1 inch. After four rounds Oerter was in third place behind Daněk and David Weill. Then, with his fifth throw, Oerter gave it everything he had. While he doubled over in pain, his discus sailed 200 feet 1 inch to set another Olympic record and earn Oerter a third gold medal.

1968 Mexico City C: 27, N: 19, D: 10.15. WR: 68.40, 224–5 (L. Jay Silvester)

		M	FT.– IN.	
1. Alfred Oerter	USA	64.78	212-6	OR
2. Lothar Milde	GDR	63.08	206-11	
3. Ludvik Daněk	CZE	62.92	206-5	
4. Hartmut Losch	GDR	62.12	203-10	
5. L. Jay Silvester	USA	61.78	202-8	
6. Gary Carlsen	USA	59.46	195-1	
7. Edmund Piątkowski	POL	59.40	194-10	
8. Björn Rickard Bruch	SWE	59.28	194-6	

Jay Silvester, the 31-year-old world record holder, was the favorite in Mexico City. And yet, one couldn't help but wonder if Al Oerter might pull off one more miracle. Silvester dampened such speculations in the qualifying round by opening up with an Olympic record of 207 feet 10 inches, 16½ feet less than his own best, but several inches better than anything Oerter had ever done.

The final was delayed an hour because of rain and this seemed to upset Silvester in particular. Lothar Milde took the first round lead with a throw of 204 feet 10 inches, and then improved to 206 feet 11 inches with his second attempt. The third round began with Oerter in fourth place, behind Milde, Losch, and Silvester. But, as if out of a fairy tale, the incomparable Oerter uncorked a throw of 212 feet 6 inches—five feet farther than he had ever thrown before. The rest of the finalists were demoralized, particularly Silvester, who fouled three times in a row. Oerter, meanwhile, added throws of 212 feet 5 inches and 210 feet 1 inch. Al Oerter had become the first athlete to win four gold medals in the same event.

Oerter, after throwing the discus 33,000 times, didn't take part in the 1972 or 1976 Olympics, but then he came out of retirement to try out for the 1980 U.S. team. At the age of 43, he finished fourth at the U.S. Olympic trials, which were held after the anti-Soviet boycott had been declared. But who knows, if the top three had really been assured of going to Moscow instead of settling for symbolic honors, Al Oerter, the ultimate clutch performer, just might have qualified after all.

1972 Munich C: 29, N: 19, D: 9.2. WR: 68.40, 224–5 (L. Jay Silvester, Björn Rickard Bruch)

		M	IN.
		FT.–	
1. Ludvik Daněk	CZE	64.40	211-3
2. L. Jay Silvester	USA	63.50	208-4
3. Björn Rickard Bruch	SWE	63.40	208-0
4. John Powell	USA	62.82	206-1
5. Géza Fejér	HUN	62.62	205-5
6. Detlef Thorith	GDR	62.42	204-9
7. Ferenc Tégla	HUN	60.60	198-10
8. Tim Vollmer	USA	60.24	197-8

With Al Oerter gone, Ludvik Daněk and Jay Silvester, both 35 years old, could finally relax and get down to the business of winning a gold medal. They had previously met 24 times, with Daněk finishing ahead 12 times and Silvester 12 times. In Munich they also had to contend with high-strung, but increasingly consistent Ricky Bruch.

Daněk led the qualifying round with an impressive throw of 211 feet. In the final, Géza Fejér took the first round lead at 205 feet 1 inch. John Powell moved ahead in the second round at 206 feet 1 inch, and then Silvester took over at the halfway mark with 208 feet 4 inches. With one round to go, the order was Silvester, Bruch, Powell, Fejér, and Daněk, who hadn't come within five feet of his qualifying toss. Since no Olympic discus contest had been won in the final round since 1896, it seemed a good bet that Jay

Silvester was on the verge of victory. But Daněk, who had enlisted the aid of a psychologist to help him prepare for just such last-ditch situations, broke tradition and won with a final throw of 211 feet 3 inches.

1976 Montreal C: 30, N: 20, D: 7.25. WR: 70.86, 232–6 (Mac Wilkins)

		M	IN.
		FT.–	
1. Mac Wilkins	USA	67.50	221-5
2. Wolfgang Schmidt	GDR	66.22	217-3
3. John Powell	USA	65.70	215-7
4. Norbert Thiede	GDR	64.30	210-11
5. Siegfried Pachale	GDR	64.24	210-9
6. Pentti Kahma	FIN	63.12	207-1
7. Knut Hjeltnes	NOR	63.06	206-11
8. L. Jay Silvester	USA	61.98	203-4

With his first and only throw of the preliminary round, Mac Wilkins, a 25-year-old schoolteacher from Oregon, set an Olympic record of 224 feet. The next day, his second round throw of 221 feet 5 inch put a quick end to any doubt as to who would win the final. Wilkins was sharply criticized by the U.S. press for congratulating East German silver medallist Wolfgang Schmidt, with whom he had become quite friendly, while ignoring American bronze medalist John Powell, with whom he did not get along. The criticism seemed ironic in view of the concern which was simultaneously being expressed about excessive nationalism in the Olympics.

1980 Moscow C: 18, N: 12, D: 7.28. WR: 71.16, 233–5 (Wolfgang Schmidt)

		M	IN.
		FT.–	
1. Viktor Rashchupkin	SOV	66.64	218-8
2. Imrich Bugár	CZE	66.38	217-9
3. Luis Delis Fournier	CUB	66.32	217-7
4. Wolfgang Schmidt	GDR	65.64	215-4
5. Yuri Dumchev	SOV	65.58	215-2
6. Igor Douguinets	SOV	64.04	210-1
7. Emil Vladimirov	BUL	63.18	207-3
8. Velko Velev	BUL	63.04	206-10

Conspicuously missing because of the anti-Soviet boycott were Knut Hjeltnes of Norway, and Mac Wilkins, John Powell, and Ben Plucknett, each of whom had to throw over 223 feet just to make the U.S. team. With these leading contenders absent, Wolfgang Schmidt seemed a sure bet for the gold medal, but a foot injury upset his performance and he had to settle for fourth place. The first round lead in the final went to Imrich Bugár at 213 feet 8 inches. The lead changed hands four more times before Rashchupkin moved from fourth place to first with his gold-medal-winning fourth round throw. His pre-Olympic best had only been 216 feet 6 inches. The contest ended in controversy, as many observers felt that Luis Delis' final throw had been marked about a foot short, keeping him from a silver medal or maybe even a gold.

HAMMER THROW

The hammer is a 16-pound metal sphere attached to a grip by means of a spring steel wire not longer than 3 feet 11¾ inches (121.5 centimeters). This potentially dangerous sport appears to have had its origins in the practice of sledge-hammer throwing in fifteenth- and sixteenth-century England and Scotland.

1896 not held

1900 Paris C: 5, N: 2, D: 7.16. WR: 51.105, 167–8 (John Flanagan)

			FT.–	
		M	IN.	
1. John Flanagan	USA	49.73	163-1	
2. Thomas Truxtun Hare	USA	49.13	161-2	
3. Josiah McCracken	USA	42.46	139-4	
4. Eric Lemming	SWE	—	—	
5. Karl Gustaf Staaf	SWE	—	—	

Irish-born John Flanagan emigrated to the United States in 1896 and became a policeman in New York City. Truxtun Hare was a four-time All-American football selection from the University of Pennsylvania.

1904 St. Louis C: 6, N: 1, D: 8.29. WR: 52.705, 172–11 (John Flanagan)

			FT.–	
		M	IN.	
1. John Flanagan	USA	51.23	168-1	OR
2. John DeWitt	USA	50.26	164-11	
3. Ralph Rose	USA	45.73	150-0	
4. Charles Chadwick	USA	42.78	140-4	
5. James Mitchell	USA	—	—	
6. Albert Johnson	USA	—	—	

1906 not held

1908 London C: 18, N: 8, D: 7.14. WR: 53.35, 175–0 (Matthew McGrath)

			FT.–	
		M	IN.	
1. John Flanagan	USA	51.92	170-4	OR
2. Matthew McGrath	USA	51.18	167-11	
3. Cornelius Walsh	USA	48.51	159-1	
4. Thomas Nicolson	GBR	48.09	157-9	
5. Lee James Talbott	USA	47.86	157-0	
6. Marquis Horr	USA	46.94	154-0	
7. Simon Gillis	USA	45.58	149-6	
8. Eric Lemming	SWE	43.06	141-3	

With his last attempt, Flanagan won his third straight hammer throw gold medal. On July 24, 1909, Flanagan threw the hammer 184 feet 4 inches to become the oldest world record breaker in the history of track and field. He was 41 years, 196 days old. He returned to Ireland in 1911 and lived there until his death in 1938.

1912 Stockholm C: 14, N: 4, D: 7.14. WR: 57.10, 187–4 (Matthew McGrath)

			FT.–	
		M	IN.	
1. Matthew McGrath	USA	54.74	179-7	OR
2. Duncan Gillis	CAN	48.39	158-9	
3. Clarence Childs	USA	48.17	158-0	
4. Robert Olsson	SWE	46.50	152-7	
5. Carl Johan Lind	SWE	45.61	149-7	
6. Denis Carey	GBR	43.78	143-8	
7. Nils Linde	SWE	43.32	142-1	
8. Carl Jahnzon	SWE	42.58	139-8	

Irish-American policeman Matt McGrath was truly in a class by himself in Stockholm. The *shortest* of his six throws—173 feet 4 inches—was almost 15 feet longer than anyone else's *longest* throw. McGrath's Olympic record held up for 24 years.

1920 Antwerp C: 12, N: 5, D: 8.18. WR: 57.77, 189–6 (Patrick Ryan)

			FT.–	
		M	IN.	
1. Patrick Ryan	USA	52.875	173-5	
2. Carl Johan Lind	SWE	48.43	158-10	
3. Basil Bennet	USA	48.25	158-3	
4. Malcom Svensson	SWE	47.29	155-1	
5. Matthew McGrath	USA	46.67	153-1	
6. Thomas Nicolson	GBR	45.70	149-11	
7. Nils Linde	SWE	44.88	147-3	
8. James McEachern	USA	44.70	146-8	

Pat Ryan emigrated from Ireland to New York in 1910. On August 17, 1913, he set a world record of 189 feet 6 inches that would last for 25 years. It remained as a U.S. record until 1953. In Antwerp Ryan was unchallenged, particularly after Matt McGrath injured his knee and was forced to withdraw after only two throws.

1924 Paris C: 15, N: 10, D: 7.10. WR: 57.77, 189–6 (Patrick Ryan)

			FT.–	
		M	IN.	
1. Frederick Tootell	USA	53.295	174-10	
2. Matthew McGrath	USA	50.84	166-9	
3. Malcolm Nokes	GBR	48.875	160-4	
4. Erik Eriksson	FIN	48.74	159-11	
5. Ossian Skiöld	SWE	45.285	148-7	
6. James McEachern	USA	45.225	148-4	
7. Carl Johan Lind	SWE	44.785	146-11	
8. J. Murdock	CAN	42.48	139-4	

Fred Tootell was the first American-born winner of the hammer throw. Silver medalist Matt McGrath was 45 years old.

1928 Amsterdam C: 16, N: 11, D: 7.30. WR: 57.77, 189–6 (Patrick Ryan)

			FT.–	
---	---	---	M	IN.
1. Patrick O'Callaghan	IRL	51.39	168-7
2. Ossian Skiöld	SWE	51.29	168-3
3. Edmund Black	USA	49.03	160-10
4. Armando Poggioli	ITA	48.37	158-8
5. Donald Gwinn	USA	47.15	154-8
6. Frank Connor	USA	46.75	153-4
7. Federico Kleger	ARG	46.60	152-11
8. R. Bayer	CHI	46.34	152-0

Pat O'Callaghan, of Derrygallon in North Cork, had only been competing for 13 months when he won an Olympic gold medal with his next-to-last throw, improving his personal best by 20 inches.

1932 Los Angeles C: 14, N: 9, D: 8.1. WR: 57.77, 189–6 (Patrick Ryan)

			FT.–	
---	---	---	M	IN.
1. Patrick O'Callaghan	IRL	53.92	176-11
2. F.W. "Ville" Pörhölä	FIN	52.27	171-6
3. Peter Zaremba	USA	50.33	165-1
4. Ossian Skiöld	SWE	49.24	161-6
5. Grant McDougall	USA	49.12	161-2
6. Federico Kleger	ARG	48.33	158-7
7. Gunnar Jansson	SWE	47.79	156-9
8. Armando Poggioli	ITA	46.90	153-10

Ville Pörhölä, who had won the shot put gold medal 12 years earlier in Antwerp, led after five rounds. However, defending champion Dr. Pat O'Callaghan, who had spent every free moment between throws filing down the spikes on his shoes, came through with a dramatic victory on his final attempt.

1936 Berlin C: 27, N: 16, D: 8.3. WR: 57.77, 189–6 (Patrick Ryan)

			FT.–		
---	---	---	M	IN.	
1. Karl Hein	GER	56.49	185-4	OR
2. Erwin Blask	GER	55.04	180-7
3. O. Fred Warngård	SWE	54.83	179-10
4. Gustaf Alfons Koutonen	FIN	51.90	170-3
5. William Rowe	USA	51.66	169-6
6. Donald Favor	USA	51.01	167-4
7. Bernhard Greulich	GER	50.61	166-0
8. K. Annamaa	EST	50.46	165-7

Hein, a 28-year-old Hamburg carpenter, scored an upset victory with his final throw. All three medalists achieved personal records.

1948 London C: 24, N: 16, D: 7.31. WR: 59.02, 193–8 (Imre Németh)

			FT.–	
---	---	---	M	IN.
1. Imre Németh	HUN	56.07	183-11
2. Ivan Gubijan	YUG	54.27	178-0
3. Robert Bennett	USA	53.73	176-3
4. Samuel Felton	USA	53.66	176-0
5. Lauri Tamminen	FIN	53.08	174-2
6. Bo Ericson	SWE	52.98	173-10
7. Teseo Taddia	ITA	51.74	169-9
8. Einar Söderqvist	SWE	51.48	168-11

Imre Németh, who broke Erwin Blask's ten-year-old world record two weeks before the Olympics began, weighed a mere 184 pounds.

1952 Helsinki C: 33, N: 18, D: 7.24. WR: 59.88, 196–5 (Imre Németh)

			FT.–		
---	---	---	M	IN.	
1. József Csérmák	HUN	60.34	197-11	WR
2. Karl Storch	GER	58.86	193-1
3. Imre Németh	HUN	57.74	189-5
4. Jiří Dadák	CZE	56.80	186-4
5. Nikolai Redkin	SOV	56.55	185-6
6. Karl Wolf	GER	56.49	185-4
7. Sverre Strandli	NOR	56.36	184-11
8. Georgi Dybenko	SOV	55.03	180-6

Twenty-year-old József Csérmák, a pupil of defending champion Imre Németh, broke the 60-meter barrier for the first time with his third throw. Silver medalist Karl Storch, who had first cleared 190 feet in 1939, was 38 years old.

1956 Melbourne C: 22, N: 14, D: 11.24. WR: 68.54, 224–10 (Harold Connolly)

			FT.–		
---	---	---	M	IN.	
1. Harold Connolly	USA	63.19	207-3	OR
2. Mikhail Krivonosov	SOV	63.03	206-9
3. Anatoly Samotsvetov	SOV	62.56	205-3
4. Albert Hall	USA	61.96	203-3
5. József Csérmák	HUN	60.70	199-2
6. Krešimir Račić	YUG	60.36	198-0
7. Dmitri Yegorov	SOV	60.22	197-7
8. Sverre Strandli	NOR	59.21	194-3

For several months, Harold Connolly and Mikhail Krivonosov had been carrying on a long-distance duel between Boston and Minsk, breaking each other's most recent records. Krivonosov was a Byelorussian who attracted the attention of athletic coaches during a hand-grenade throwing contest. In 1952 he had hoped to go to the Helsinki Olympics as a discus thrower, but finished only fourth in the U.S.S.R. trials and failed to make the team. Two days later he qualified in the hammer throw instead. In Helsinki he fouled twice, fell once, and failed to register a valid throw. Concentrating on the hammer from then on, Krivonosov set his first world record in 1954. His sixth record, 220 feet 10 inches, was made on October 22, 1956. Eleven days later, Harold Connolly, whose left arm was withered as a result of an accident at birth, broke Krivonosov's record by four feet. Three weeks later the two rivals met at the Melbourne Olympics.

The first-round lead went to Siberia's Anatoly Samotsvetov at 203 feet 9 inches. Krivonosov moved ahead in the second round with a throw of 206 feet 8 inches. His last three attempts were all fouls. Hal Connolly, wearing ballet shoes to improve his footing, finally won the contest with a fifth round heave of 207 feet 3 inches.

What gained Connolly international attention was not his gold medal but his Olympic Village romance with Czechoslovakian discus champion Olga Fikotová. After a great deal of pressure, the Iron Curtain was drawn open long enough for Olga to emigrate to the United States, where the two were married. Harold eventually took part in four Olympics and Olga in five. After the couple divorced in 1975, Harold married three-time Olympian Pat Daniels.

1960 Rome C: 28, N: 18, D: 9.3. WR: 70.33, 230–9 (Harold Connolly)

			FT.-	
		M	IN.	
1. Vasily Rudenkov	SOV	67.10	220-2	OR
2. Gyula Zsivótzky	HUN	65.79	215-10	
3. Tadeusz Rut	POL	65.64	215-4	
4. John Lawlor	IRL	64.95	213-1	
5. Olgierd Cieply	POL	64.57	211-10	
6. Zvonko Bezjak	YUG	64.21	210-7	
7. Anatoly Samotsvetov	SOV	63.60	208-8	
8. Harold Connolly	USA	63.58	208-7	

Harold Connolly broke his own world record only two weeks before the Olympics began, but was troubled by injury and finished a disappointing eighth in Rome. Meanwhile, metal worker Vasily Rudenkov set an Olympic record of 219 feet 10 inches in the qualifying round and then led the final from start to finish.

1964 Tokyo C: 24, N: 13, D: 10.18 WR: 70.66, 231–10 (Harold Connolly)

			FT.-	
		M	IN.	
1. Romuald Klim	SOV	69.74	228-10	OR
2. Gyula Zsivótzky	HUN	69.09	226-8	
3. Uwe Beyer	GER	68.09	223-4	
4. Yuri Nikulin	SOV	67.69	222-1	
5. Yuri Bakarinov	SOV	66.72	218-11	
6. Harold Connolly	USA	66.65	218-8	
7. Edward Burke	USA	65.66	215-5	
8. Olgierd Cieply	POL	64.82	212-8	

Romuald Klim, a 31-year-old from Byelorussia, won with his fourth throw.

1968 Mexico City C: 22, N: 12, D: 10.17. WR: 73.76, 242–0 (Gyula Zsivotsky)

			FT.-	
		M	IN.	
1. Gyula Zsivótzky	HUN	73.36	240-8	OR
2. Romuald Klim	SOV	73.28	240-5	
3. Lázár Lovász	HUN	69.78	228-11	
4. Takeo Sugawara	JAP	69.78	228-11	
5. Sándor Eckschmidt	HUN	69.46	227-11	
6. Gennady Kondrashov	SOV	69.08	226-8	
7. Reinhard Theimer	GDR	68.84	225-10	
8. Helmut Baumann	GDR	68.26	223-11	

On September 4, 1965, Gyula Zsivótzky threw the hammer 241 feet 11 inches to better the world record by a shocking 8 feet 2 inches. Three years later he bumped the record up an extra inch, but at the Olympics he was not the favorite. Romuald Klim, unbeaten in three years, had defeated Zsivótzky nine straight times. Zsivótzky seemed to be held back by a psychological barrier whenever he faced Klim, but he received a big boost when he threw 247 feet 1 inch in practice one week before the competition began.

Klim's first throw of the final was 237 feet, but Zsivótzky, throwing immediately after Klim, gained further confidence by recording 237 feet 9 inches with his second throw. However, the third round saw Klim take the lead at 238 feet 11 inches, while Zsivótzky could only respond with 238 feet, two less than the Olympic record he had set in the qualifying round the previous day. In the fourth round of the final, Klim reached 240 feet 5 inches, while Zsivótzky fouled. However, the Hungarian put it together with his next-to-last throw and won with 240 feet 8 inches.

Takeo Sugawara, the smallest man in the competition at 5 feet 8½ inches and 185 pounds, tied with Lázár Lovász, but Lovász was awarded the bronze medal because his second best throw was one foot longer than Sugawara's.

1972 Munich C: 31, N: 18, D: 9.7. WR: 76.40, 250–8 (Walter Schmidt)

			FT.-	
		M	IN.	
1. Anatoly Bondarchuk	SOV	75.50	247-8	OR
2. Jochen Sachse	GDR	74.96	245-11	
3. Vasily Khmelevski	SOV	74.04	242-11	
4. Uwe Beyer	GER	71.52	234-8	
5. Gyula Zsivótzky	HUN	71.38	234-2	
6. Sándor Eckschmidt	HUN	71.20	233-7	
7. Edwin Klein	GER	71.14	233-5	
8. Shigenobu Murofushi	JAP	70.88	232-6	

The favorite, 32-year-old Anatoly Bondarchuk, settled matters early in the final with an opening throw of 247 feet 8 inches. He claimed to have thrown the hammer 100,000 times in the previous 13 years.

1976 Montreal C: 20, N: 13, D: 7.28. WR: 79.30 260-2 (Walter Schmidt)

		FT.–		
		M	IN.	
1. Yuri Sedykh	SOV	77.52	254-4	OR
2. Aleksei Spiridonov	SOV	76.08	249-7	
3. Anatoly Bondarchuk	SOV	75.48	247-8	
4. Karl-Hans Riehm	GER	75.46	247-7	
5. Walter Schmidt	GER	74.72	245-2	
6. Jochen Sachse	GDR	74.30	243-9	
7. Chris Black	GBR	73.18	240-1	
8. Edwin Klein	GER	71.34	234-1	

On May 19, 1975, Karl-Hans Riehm had a truly remarkable day. Competing at Rehlingen, he bettered the previous world record with all six of his throws, his best of the day being 257 feet 6 inches. Three months later, he lost the record to Walter Schmidt, who was famous for achieving his best performances at minor meets. In Montreal, Riehm led the qualifying round at 244 feet 3 inches, but in the final, he and Schmidt had to take a back seat to the Soviet trio. Yuri Sedykh, a 21-year-old student of Anatoly Bondarchuk, won the competition with his second throw.

1980 Moscow C: 17, N: 12, D: 7.31. WR: 81.66, 267–11 (Sergei Litvinov)

		FT.–		
		M	IN.	
1. Yuri Sedykh	SOV	81.80	268-4	WR
2. Sergei Litvinov	SOV	80.64	264-7	
3. Yuri Tamm	SOV	78.96	259-1	
4. Roland Steuk	GDR	77.54	254-5	
5. Detlef Gerstenberg	GDR	74.60	244-9	
6. Emannouil Dulgherow	BUL	74.04	242-11	
7. Gianpaola Urlando	ITA	73.90	242-5	
8. Ireneusz Golda	POL	73.74	242-11	

Unfortunately missing because of the anti-Soviet boycott was Karl-Hans Riehm, who threw 265 feet 1 inch the day before the Olympic final. Riehm was the only man capable of threatening the Soviets, who dominated hammer throwing so thoroughly that three of their team members set world records during one nine-day period. On May 16, 1980, Sedykh took the record away from Riehm with a throw of 263 feet 8 inches. Then Yuri Tamm entered the circle and threw 263 feet 9 inches. Not to be outdone, Sedykh countered with 264 feet 7 inches. Eight days later, Sergei Litvinov beat them both with a new record of 267 feet 11 inches.

In Moscow Sedykh opened the Olympic final with a world record of 268 feet 4 inches. Litvinov's first throw gained him the silver medal. He followed with five straight fouls.

JAVELIN THROW

A javelin must weigh a minimum of 800 grams (1 pound 12¼ ounces) and measure between 2.60 meters (8 feet 6¼ inches) and 2.70 meters (8 feet 10¼ inches). The shaft may be either wood or metal. For a throw to be considered valid the pointed metal head must break the turf. The javelin is thrown on the run and must be released above the shoulder. Spinning around before throwing is illegal, since this technique could seriously discourage spectators from coming anywhere near the part of the stadium where the javelin competition is taking place.

1896–1904 not held

1906 Athens C: 22, N: 7, D: 7.27. WR: 53.79, 176–5 (Eric Lemming)

		FT.–		
		M	IN.	
1. Eric Lemming	SWE	53.90	176-10	WR
2. Knut Lindberg	SWE	45.17	148-2	
3. Bruno Söderström	SWE	44.92	147-4	
4. Hjalmar Mellander	SWE	44.30	145-4	
5. Werner Järvinen	FIN	44.25	145-2	

Eric Lemming, a 6-foot 3-inch, 26-year-old Stockholm policeman, had dominated javelin throwing since 1899.

1908 London C: 16, N: 6, D: 7.17. WR: 54.40, 178–6 (Eric Lemming)

		FT.–		
		M	IN.	
1. Eric Lemming	SWE	54.825	179-10	WR
2. Arne Halse	NOR	50.57	165-11	
3. Otto Nilsson	SWE	47.105	154-6	
4. Aarne Salovaara	FIN	45.89	150-6	
5. Armas Pesonen	FIN	45.18	148-3	
6. Juho Halme	FIN	—	—	
7. Jalmari Sauli	FIN	—	—	

1912 Stockholm C: 25, N: 7, D: 7.6. WR: 58.27, 191–2 (Eric Lemming)

		FT.–		
		M	IN.	
1. Eric Lemming	SWE	60.64	198-11	WR
2. Julius Juho Saaristo	FIN	58.66	192-5	
3. Mór Kóczán	HUN	55.50	182-1	
4. Juho Halme	FIN	54.65	179-3	
5. Väinö Siikaniemi	FIN	52.43	172-0	
6. Richard Åbrink	SWE	52.20	171-3	
7. Arne Halse	NOR	51.98	170-6	
8. Jonni Myyrä	FIN	51.32	168-4	

Lemming received a standing ovation from the hometown crowd after he made the world's first 60-meter throw. Three days later, while competing in the now discontinued combined left- and right-hand event, Juho Saaristo set a world record of 200 feet 1 inch using his right hand.

1920 Antwerp C: 30, N: 13, D: 8.15. WR: 66.10, 216–10 (Jonni Myyrä)

		FT.– M	IN.	
1. Jonni Myyrä	FIN	65.78	215-10	OR
2. Urho Peltonen	FIN	63.50	208-4	
3. Paavo Jaale-Johansson	FIN	63.095	207-0	
4. Julius Juho Saaristo	FIN	62.395	204-9	
5. Alexander Klumberg	EST	62.39	204-8	
6. Gunnar Lindström	SWE	60.52	198-7	
7. Milton Angier	USA	59.26	194-5	
8. Erik Blomqvist	SWE	58.18	190-10	

1924 Paris C: 30, N: 13, D: 8.15. WR: 66.10, 216–10 (Jonni Myyrä)

		FT.– M	IN.
1. Jonni Myrrä	FIN	62.96	206-7
2. Gunnar Lindström	SWE	60.92	199-10
3. Eugene Oberst	USA	58.35	191-5
4. Yrjö Ekqvist	FIN	57.56	188-10
5. William Neufeld	USA	56.96	186-10
6. Erik Blomqvist	SWE	56.85	186-6
7. Urho Peltonen	FIN	55.66	182-7
8. Paavo Jaale-Johansson	FIN	55.10	180-9

The 32-year-old Myyrä successfully defended his title. However he lost his world record two months later, when Lindström threw 218 feet 7 inches.

1928 Amsterdam C: 28, N: 18, D: 8.2. WR: 69.88, 229–3 (Eino Penttilä)

		FT.– M	IN.	
1. Erik Lundkvist	SWE	66.60	218-6	OR
2. Béla Szepes	HUN	65.26	214-1	
3. Olav Sunde	NOR	63.97	209-10	
4. Paavo Liettu	FIN	63.86	209-6	
5. W. Bruno Schlokat	GER	63.40	208-0	
6. Eino Penttilä	FIN	63.20	207-4	
7. S.A. Lay	NZE	62.89	206-3	
8. J. Meimer	EST	61.46	201-8	

On October 8, 1927, Eino Penttilä recorded a throw of 229 feet 3 inches to improve the world record by an impressive 10 feet 8 inches. In Amsterdam, however, Penttilä suffered from overtraining, the pressure of high expectations, and a sore foot, and was only able to finish sixth. The winner, sign painter Erik Lundkvist, went on to set a world record of 232 feet 11 inches two weeks later.

1932 Los Angeles C: 13, N: 7, D: 8.4. WR: 74.02, 242–10 (Matti Järvinen)

		FT.– M	IN.	
1. Matti Järvinen	FIN	72.71	238-6	OR
2. Matti Sippala	FIN	69.80	229-0	

3. Eino Penttilä	FIN	68.70	225-5
4. Gottfried Weimann	GER	68.18	223-8
5. Lee Bartlett	USA	64.46	211-6
6. Kenneth Churchill	USA	63.24	207-6
7. Malcolm Metcalf	USA	61.89	203-0
8. Kohsaku Sumiyoshi	JAP	61.14	200-7

Three sons of Finland's first gold medal winner, Werner Järvinen, took part in the 1932 Olympics, but only the youngest, Matti, won a gold medal. Matti's first five throws were the best of the competition, and all of them bettered the previous Olympic record. Matti didn't bother to take off the trousers of his track suit until the contest was over and it was time for photographs to be taken. Between 1930 and 1936 Matti Järvinen broke the javelin world record ten times and became known as "Mr. Javelin."

1936 Berlin C: 28, N: 19, D: 8.6. WR: 77.23, 253–4 (Matti Järvinen)

		FT.– M	IN.
1. Gerhard Stöck	GER	71.84	235-8
2. Yrjö Nikkanen	FIN	70.77	232-2
3. Kaarlo Kalervo Toivonen	FIN	70.72	232-0
4. Lennart Attervall	SWE	69.20	227-0
5. Matti Järvinen	FIN	69.18	227-0
6. Alton Terry	USA	67.15	220-4
7. Eugeniusz Lokajski	POL	66.39	217-9
8. József Várszegi	HUN	65.30	214-3

Gerhard Stöck, who had finished third in the shot put four days earlier, was in fifth place after four rounds. It was then that Adolf Hitler arrived in the stadium. Properly inspired, Stöck unleashed a throw of 235 feet 8 inches, which turned out to be sufficient for the gold medal. Matti Järvinen, suffering from a back injury, was only able to place fifth.

1948 London C: 22, N: 15, D: 8.4. WR: 78.70, 258–2 (Yrjö Nikkanen)

		FT.– M	IN.
1. Kai Tapio Rautavaara	FIN	69.77	228-10
2. Steve Seymour	USA	67.56	221-8
3. József Várszegi	HUN	67.03	219-11
4. Pauli Vesterinen	FIN	65.89	216-2
5. Odd Maehlum	NOR	65.32	214-3
6. Martin Biles	USA	65.17	213-9
7. Mirko Vujacic	YUG	64.89	212-10
8. Robert Likens	USA	64.51	211-7

Marty Biles led the qualifying round with a throw of 222 feet, which would have been good enough for a silver medal if he had been able to repeat it in the final. Gold medal winner Tapio Rautavaara later became a successful archer, folk singer, and actor. While posing for a photograph, he fell and hit his head on a concrete floor; he died on September 25, 1979, at the age of 64.

1952 Helsinki C: 26, N: 16, D: 7.23. WR: 78.70, 258–2 (Yrjö Nikkanen)

		FT.–		
		M	IN.	
1. Cyrus Young	USA	73.78	242-1	OR
2. William Miller	USA	72.46	237-9	
3. Toivo Hyytiäinen	FIN	71.89	235-10	
4. Viktor Tsibulenko	SOV	71.72	234-4	
5. Branko Dangubič	YUG	70.55	231-5	
6. Vladimir Kuznetsov	SOV	70.37	230-10	
7. Ragnar Ericzoň	SWE	69.04	226-6	
8. Soini Nikkinen	FIN	68.80	225-9	

The two American medalists presented an unusual contrast. Cy Young, who celebrated his 24th birthday by winning the gold medal, was 6 feet 5 inches, while Bill Miller was only 5 feet 9 inches. When a third American, ninth-place finisher Bud Held, broke Yrjö Nikkanen's 15-year-old world record in 1953, it looked like the United States had found itself another specialty. However, the expected U.S. dominance did not materialize.

1956 Melbourne C: 21, N: 12, D: 26.11. WR: 83.66, 274–6 (Janusz Sidlo)

		FT.–		
		M	IN.	
1. Egil Danielsen	NOR	85.71	281-2	WR
2. Janusz Sidlo	POL	79.98	262-5	
3. Viktor Tsibulenko	SOV	79.50	260-10	
4. Herbert Koschel	GER	74.68	245-0	
5. Jan Kopyto	POL	74.28	243-8	
6. Giovanni Lievore	ITA	72.88	239-1	
7. Michel Macquet	FRA	71.84	235-8	
8. Aleksandr Gorshkov	SOV	70.32	230-8	

Cy Young led the qualifying round with a throw of 245 feet 3 inches. After three rounds of the final, Sidlo was in first place, followed by Tsibulenko and Koschel. For his fourth throw, Tsibulenko abandoned the wooden javelin he had been using and picked up a steel one which had been made in Sweden. He immediately improved his standing by almost 15 feet. Egil Danielsen, who had won 36 consecutive meets but was only in sixth place, asked Tsibulenko if he could borrow his steel javelin. He then let loose an enormous throw that broke the world record and almost landed on the runway of the pole vault. Danielsen danced around, hugging and kissing everyone in the area of the javelin competition, while Tsibulenko was left to laugh, shake his head, and marvel at the result of his good sportsmanship.

1960 Rome C: 28, N: 18, D: 9.8. WR: 86.04, 282–3 (Albert Cantello)

		FT.–	
		M	IN.
1. Viktor Tsibulenko	SOV	84.64	277-8
2. Walter Krüger	GDR	79.36	260-4
3. Gergely Kulcsár	HUN	78.57	257-9
4. Väinö Kuisma	FIN	78.40	257-3
5. Willy Rasmussen	NOR	78.36	257-1
6. Knut Fredriksson	SWE	78.33	256-11
7. Zbigniew Radziwonowicz	POL	77.30	253-7
8. Janusz Sidlo	POL	76.46	250-10

In 1960 the javelin throw turned out to be a strange contest. The preliminary round was led by Janusz Sidlo at 279 feet 4 inches and Al Cantello at 261 feet 6 inches. If Sidlo and Cantello had been able to reproduce their form in the final, they would have finished first and third. Instead, they ended up eighth and tenth. The preliminary round also saw the elimination of defending champion Egil Danielsen and Bill Alley of the United States, who had a pending (and subsequently never ratified) world record of 283 feet 8 inches. The final was settled early with Viktor Tsibulenko's first-round throw of 277 feet 8 inches. Gusty winds and rain disrupted the competition from the second round on, and no one, Tsibulenko included, was able to do better than 257 feet 1 inch after that.

1964 Tokyo C: 25, L: 15, D: 10.14. WR: 91.72, 300–11 (Terje Pedersen)

		FT.–	
		M	IN.
1. Pauli Nevala	FIN	82.66	271-2
2. Gergely Kulcsár	HUN	82.32	270-1
3. Jānis Lūsis	SOV	80.57	264-4
4. Janusz Sidlo	POL	80.17	263-0
5. Urs von Wartburg	SWI	78.72	258-3
6. Jorma Kinnunen	FIN	76.94	252-5
7. Rolf Herings	GER	74.72	245-2
8. Vladimir Kuznetsov	SOV	74.26	243-8

On September 2, 1964, Terje Pedersen shocked the track and field world with a monster throw of 300 feet 11 inches that bettered his own world record by 15 feet 1 inch. Yet six weeks later in Tokyo, he could do no better than 236 feet 6 inches, and failed to qualify for the final. The 1964 Olympic competition, like the one in 1960, was marred by wind and rain. Janusz Sidlo had the best throw of the first round of the final at 263 feet. Jānis Lūsis took the lead in the second round with a throw of 264 feet 4 inches. But the real action took place in the fourth round. Ever-consistent Gergely Kulcsár reached 270 feet 1 inch, only to be topped by unheralded Pauli Nevala at 271 feet 2 inches. Von Wartburg's final throw appeared good enough for a silver medal, but was declared invalid on the grounds that it landed incorrectly, a ruling that raised many eyebrows.

Finnish Olympic officials had been criticized for wasting

their money sending Nevala to Tokyo, particularly after he had failed to win the national championship. "Even if I'm not the Finnish champion," Nevala commented, "at least I've won the Olympics."

1968 Mexico City C: 27, N: 18, D: 10.16. WR: 91.98, 301–9 (Jānis Lūsis)

		FT.–		
		M	IN.	
1. Jānis Lūsis	SOV	90.10	295-7	OR
2. Jorma Kinnunen	FIN	88.58	290-7	
3. Gergely Kulcsár	HUN	87.06	285-7	
4. Wladislaw Nikiciuk	POL	85.70	281-2	
5. Manfred Stolle	GDR	84.42	277-0	
6. Åke Nilsson	SWE	83.48	273-11	
7. Janusz Sidlo	POL	80.58	264-4	
8. Urs von Wartburg	SWI	80.56	264-4	

A surprising thing happened in the 1968 javelin competition. For the first time since 1932, it was won by the favorite. The first-round lead went to 5-foot 9-inch, 165-pound Jorma Kinnunen. Popular Jānis Lūsis of Latvia, who was married to Elvira Ozolina, winner of the 1960 women's javelin, edged ahead by four centimeters in the second round. In the fourth round, Gergely Kulcsar moved in front with a personal and Olympic record of 285 feet 7 inches. And so the situation stood with one round remaining: Kulcsár in first, followed by Lūsis and Kinnunen. Lūsis calmly took his spear in hand and made his last attempt his best—295 feet 7 inches. He had one more moment of concern when Kinnunen also came up with a clutch performance, 290 feet 7 inches, but the Finn had to be content with second place. Janusz Sidlo, competing in his fifth Olympics, finished a creditable seventh.

1972 Munich C:23, N: 15, D: 9.3. WR: 93.80, 307–9 (Jānis Lūsis)

		FT.–		
		M	IN.	
1. Klaus Wolfermann	GER	90.48	296-10	OR
2. Jānis Lūsis	SOV	90.46	296-9	
3. William Schmidt	USA	84.42	277-0	
4. Hannu Siitonen	FIN	84.32	276-8	
5. Björn Grimnes	NOR	83.08	272-7	
6. Jorma Kinnunen	FIN	82.08	269-3	
7. Miklos Németh	HUN	81.98	268-11	
8. Fredrick Luke	USA	80.06	262-8	

Jānis Lūsis dominated javelin throwing between Olympics. In 1972 no one came within 17 feet of his best performance of the year until one week before the Munich Games, when Klaus Wolfermann hit 296 feet 7 inches. In the Olympic final, Lūsis had the first big throw—291 feet 7 inches in the first round. He improved to 293 feet 9 inches with his third attempt. Wolfermann, cheered on by the German crowd, picked up steam in the fourth round with a throw of 290 feet. Then, in the fifth round, he caused the spectators to roar with excitement when he exploded for a per-

sonal best of 296 feet 10 inches. However, Jānis Lūsis still had one attempt left, and many remembered his dramatic last-round victory four years earlier. Sure enough, Lūsis let loose a big one. Wolfermann and his supporters waited anxiously for the measurement. And then it came—296 feet 9 inches. The two-centimeter difference is the smallest unit of measurement used in javelin competitions. One more inch and Lūsis would have won on the basis of a longer second throw.

When Jānis Lūsis was a little boy, he had been forced to watch the execution of his father by German soldiers. Yet as a grown man, he bore no grudge against the German people, and later became good friends with Klaus Wolfermann, even vacationing with him in Bavaria.

1976 Montreal C: 23, N: 15, D: 7.25. WR: 94.08, 308–8 (Klaus Wolfermann)

		FT.–		
		M	IN.	
1. Miklos Németh	HUN	94.58	310-4	WR
2. Hannu Siitonen	FIN	87.92	288-5	
3. Gheorghe Megelea	ROM	87.16	285-11	
4. Pyotr Bielczyk	POL	86.50	283-9	
5. Sam Colson	USA	86.16	282-8	
6. Vasily Yershov	SOV	85.26	279-9	
7. Seppo Hovinen	FIN	84.26	276-5	
8. Jānis Lūsis	SOV	80.26	263-4	

Miklos Németh was less than two years old when his father, Imre, won the gold medal for the hammer throw at the 1948 Olympics in London. His father pressed him to take up the hammer, but Miklos preferred the javelin, and by 1967 he was ranked second in the world. But he never performed well in major championships. In the 1968 Olympics an elbow injury kept Miklos from qualifying for the final. In 1972 he was one of the favorites, but finished a disappointing seventh. His father said he was too gentle. His critics said he was a choker. Miklos himself said, "It is not an easy thing in my country to be the son of an Olympic champion."

Then came Montreal. Now 29 years old and no longer a favorite, Miklos Németh was almost ignored as interest centered on the leading contenders, Hovinen, Siitonen, and Bielczyk. Németh was the tenth man up in the final, and with his first attempt he uncorked a beauty. He tried not to watch it, but kept looking back as the spear sailed on and on until it finally landed 310 feet 4 inches away from the throwing area. It was ten and a half feet farther than Németh had ever thrown before. It was also a new world record.

While Németh jumped for joy, the rest of the javelin throwers were absolutely demoralized. The remaining medals, it turned out, were also decided by first-round throws. Hovinen, who had led the qualifiers at 294 feet 6 inches, could do no better than 276 feet 5 inches. Nineteen-year-old Phil Olson of Canada, who had qualified with a throw of 287 feet 11 inches, finished 11th at 254 feet 11 inches. Németh was so excited that he had to pass the next two rounds. His winning margin was the widest in any field event in Olympic history (excluding the Intercalated Games of 1906). Imre and Miklos Németh are the only father-and-son combination ever to win track and field gold medals at the Olympics.

1980 Moscow C: 18, N: 11, D: 7.27. WR: 96.72, 317–4 (Ferenc Paragi)

		FT.–	
		M	IN.
1. Dainis Kula	SOV	91.20	299-2
2. Aleksandr Makarov	SOV	89.64	294-1
3. Wolfgang Hanisch	GDR	86.72	284-6
4. Kheino Puuste	SOV	86.10	282-6
5. Antero Puranen	FIN	85.12	279-3
6. Pentti Sinersaari	FIN	84.34	276-8
7. Detlef Fuhrmann	GDR	83.50	273-11
8. Miklos Németh	HUN	82.40	270-4

Only once since World War II has the leader of the qualifying round in the javelin gone on to victory, the exception being Klaus Wolfermann in 1972. Unfortunately for world record holder Ferenc Paragi, the jinx continued. After a preliminary throw of 291 feet 2 inches, his best in the final was only 260 feet 11 inches and he placed tenth. After two rounds, the leader was Wolfgang Hanisch, followed by Kheino Puuste. The decisive moment came at the end of the third round. The last man to throw was Dainis Kula, a 21-year-old Latvian. Having fouled on his first two attempts, Kula needed not only a valid throw, but a big one, just to qualify for the extra three attempts accorded the top eight. To most observers, Kula's third try appeared to land tail first and then bounce, which should have led to his immediate elimination. Instead, Soviet officials rushed out to measure it and announced a valid throw of 291 feet 7 inches. Taking advantage of his questionable reprieve, Kula followed with an excellent, and perfectly legal, throw of 299 feet 2 inches that held up for the gold medal.

The U.S. team trials had been won by Rod Ewaliko at 291 feet, but Bruce Kennedy, who finished second, set what must be an Olympic record—and a most unfortunate one. A citizen of Zimbabwe, then known as Rhodesia, Kennedy had gone to Munich in 1972 as part of his nation's Olympic team. However, pressure from black African nations opposed to Rhodesia's white minority government prevented the Rhodesians from competing. In 1976 Kennedy was again selected to compete in the Olym-

pics, but again Rhodesia was excluded. Meanwhile, Kennedy had moved to the United States and married an American. In 1977 he became a U.S. citizen. In 1980 he qualified for the U.S. team, but, for the third time, he was prevented from competing in the Olympics because of politics. Ironically, Zimbabwe, now ruled by blacks, was readmitted into the Olympic movement and allowed to take part in the Moscow Games.

DECATHLON

The decathlon consists of ten events held over a two-day period. On the first day, the athletes take part in the 100-meter dash, long jump, shot put, high jump, and 400-meter run. On the second day they compete in the 110-meter hurdles, discus throw, pole vault, javelin throw and 1500-meter run. Points are scored according to a set of tables approved by the International Amateur Athletic Federation. The tables currently in use were devised in 1962 and revised in 1971 and 1977 to take into account the advent of automatic electronic timing, with accuracy to $\frac{1}{100}$ second. The 1962 equivalent of each athlete's performance is included here for the purpose of historical comparison.

Decathletes tend to show up later as movie actors. Jim Thorpe was an extra in several Westerns, Glenn Morris played Tarzan, Floyd Simmons was in *South Pacific*, Bob Mathias acted with Jayne Mansfield in *It Happened in Athens*. Rafer Johnson and C.K. Yang also appeared in movies. The 1976 gold medalist Bruce Jenner made his screen debut in *Can't Stop the Music*, one of the worst films ever made. Dennis Weaver, who became famous for his roles in the television series *Gunsmoke* and *McCloud*, placed sixth in the 1948 U.S. Olympic trials.

KEY TO ABBREVIATIONS

DISC = Discus throw
H = Hurdles
HAM = Hammer throw
HJ = High jump
JAV = Javelin throw
LJ = Long jump
M = Meters
PV = Pole vault
SP = Shot put

1904 St. Louis C: 7, N: 2, D: 7.4.

			100 YDS.	SP	HJ	800-YD. WALK	HAM	PV	120-YD. H	56-LB. THROW	LJ	MILE	TOTAL POINTS
1.	Thomas Kiely	IRL	11.17	10.82	1.52	3:59.0	36.76	2.74	17.8	8.91	5.94	5:51.0	6036
2.	Adam Gunn	USA	11.13	12.21	1.65	4:13.0	31.40	2.97	17.9	7.22	5.53	5:45.0	5907
3.	Thomas Truxtun Hare	USA	10.8	12.09	1.52	4:20.0	36.28	2.44	18.27	7.59	6.07	5:40.0	5813
4.	John Holloway	IRL	10.9	10.01	1.68	3:59.0	27.51	2.89	18.33	5.98	5.53	5:40.0	5273
5.	Ellery Clark	USA	11.0	10.26	1.62	4:11.0	29.11	DNF					2778
6.	John Grieb	USA	11.13	10.54	1.62	4:49.0	DNF						2199

This competition was known as the "All-Around Championship" and was noteworthy because all ten events were held on the same day. Offered a free trip if he would compete for Great Britain, 35-year-old Tom Kiely refused, paid his own way, and competed for Ireland.

1906-1908 not held

1912 Stockholm C: 29, N: 12, D: 7.13–15.

		100 M	LJ	SP	HJ	400 M	110 H	DISC	PV	JAV	1500 M	TOTAL POINTS		1962 TABLES
1.	James Thorpe	USA	11.2	6.79	12.89	1.87	52.2	15.6	36.98	3.25	45.70	4:40.1	8412	WR	6756
2.	Hugo Wieslander	SWE	11.8	6.42	12.14	1.75	53.6	17.2	36.29	3.10	50.40	4:45.0	7724		6161
3.	Charles Lomberg	SWE	11.8	6.87	11.67	1.80	55.0	17.6	35.35	3.25	41.83	5:12.2	7414		5943
4.	Gösta Holmér	SWE	11.4	5.98	10.98	1.70	53.2	17.0	31.78	3.20	46.28	4:41.9	7348		5956
5.	James Donahue	USA	11.8	6.48	9.67	1.65	51.6	16.2	29.95	3.40	37.09	4:44.0	7083		5836
6.	E. Leroy Mercer	USA	11.0	6.84	9.76	1.65	49.9	16.4	21.95	3.60	32.32	4:46.3	7075		5927
7.	Woldemar Wickholm	FIN	11.5	5.95	11.09	1.60	52.3	17.0	29.78	3.25	42.58	4:33.9	7059		5778
8.	Erik Kugelberg	SWE	12.3	6.20	9.99	1.65	55.7	17.2	31.48	3.00	45.67	4:43.5	6758		5499

James Francis Thorpe was born on May 28, 1888, on a farm near the town of Prague in what was then known as the Oklahoma Territory. His father was part Irish, part Sac and Fox Indian. His mother, who was part Potawatomie and Kickapoo Indian and part French, gave him the Indian name Wa-Tho-Huck, or "Bright Path." Jim's twin brother, Charles, died of pneumonia at the age of 8. His mother died when he was 12 and his father when he was 15. Educated at the government-run Indian schools of Haskell and Carlisle, Jim Thorpe soon became a star athlete.

He first came to national prominence as a football player. In 1911, tiny Carlisle upset Harvard 18–15, with Thorpe scoring all of Carlisle's points on four field goals and a touchdown. The following year against Army, he ran 92 yards for a touchdown, only to have the score nullified because of a penalty. On the next play, he ran 97 yards for a touchdown. Thorpe was chosen as an All-America halfback in both 1911 and 1912. An all-around athlete, he also played baseball and basketball, and so excelled at track and field that he was chosen to represent the United States at the 1912 Olympics.

In Stockholm, Thorpe began by winning the pentathlon. The next day, while the other pentathletes were recuperating, Thorpe was back on the field taking fourth place in the high jump. He also finished seventh in the long jump. Finally, he took part in the decathlon, which was spread over three days because of the large number of entrants. Although he had never before competed in a decathlon, and had never thrown a javelin until two months earlier, he won easily. His performance was so impressive that it would have earned him a silver medal in the *1948* Olympics.

Besides his gold medals, Thorpe was awarded a jewel-encrusted chalice by Czar Nicholas of Russia, in honor of his victory in the decathlon, and a bronze bust of King Gustav V of Sweden for winning the pentathlon. When Gustav handed Jim the bust, he said, "Sir, you are the greatest athlete in the world." To which Thorpe replied shyly, "Thanks, King."

Back in the United States, Jim Thorpe had become a national hero. Honored with a ticker tape parade down Broadway in New York City, Jim marveled at the experience. "I heard people yelling my name—and I couldn't realize how one fellow could have so many friends," he recalled.

But in January 1913, Thorpe received a hard blow. It was revealed that in 1909 and 1910 he had earned $25 a week playing minor league baseball in North Carolina. Thus, by the strictest definition of the word, he had been a professional athlete and therefore ineligible to compete in the Olympics. Thorpe wrote a letter to James E. Sullivan, chairman of the Amateur Athletic Union, admitting what he had done but asking for leniency.

"I hope I will be partly excused by the fact that I was simply an Indian schoolboy and did not know all about such things," he wrote. "In fact, I did not know that I was doing wrong because I was doing what I knew several other college men had done except that they did not use their own names . . .

"I have received offers amounting to thousands of dollars since my victories last summer, but I have turned them all down because I did not care to make money from my athletic skill. . . I hope the Amateur Athletic Union and the people will not be too hard in judging me."

The "people" were not hard in judging Jim Thorpe, and generally rallied to his side. The A.A.U., on the other hand, was very hard in judging him. He was publicly vilified and his name was stricken from all record books. The American Olympic Committee issued a formal apology to the International Olympic Committee, which asked for the return of Thorpe's medals and trophies. The one bright spot in the whole unfortunate affair was that both Hugo Wieslander, who had finished second in the decathlon, and

Ferdinand Bie, who had been runner-up in the pentathlon, refused to accept the trophies which the I.O.C. forwarded to them.

As soon as he had been declared a professional, Thorpe received offers to play major-league baseball. He signed with the New York Giants first, and played as well for the Cincinnati Reds until 1919. He also played professional football between 1915 and 1929. During the Depression, Jim Thorpe drifted from job to job. He was discovered wielding a pick and shovel at a construction site in Los Angeles, and when the 1932 Olympics came to town he was invited to sit with U.S. Vice-President Charles Curtis, who was also part-Indian. Such high spots were few, however. He worked as an extra in Hollywood, mostly playing Indian chiefs, gave lectures, joined the Merchant Marine in 1945, and took a job as a bouncer in 1949.

In February 1950, a poll of sportswriters taken by the Associated Press voted Thorpe the greatest athlete of the first half of the century. The following year *Jim Thorpe—All-American*, a film based on his life and starring Burt Lancaster, was released. Yet two months later, when Jim was hospitalized with cancer of the lip, he was admitted as a charity case because he had no money. He had sold the film rights to his life to MGM in 1931 for $1500. When MGM sold the rights to Warner Bros., Thorpe thought he would be paid again, but he had failed to read the fine print. He died of a heart attack in Lomita, California on March 28, 1953. Thorpe was buried in Mauch Chunk, Pennsylvania, a small town which agreed to change its name to Jim Thorpe in return for the right to have his body.

The movement to reinstate Jim Thorpe's records and trophies began in 1943, but met with no success during his lifetime. "Rules are like steam rollers," he once wrote. "There is nothing they won't do to flatten the man who stands in their way." It is interesting to note that Avery Brundage, who was President of the International Olympic Committee from 1952 to 1972, and who did nothing to help Jim Thorpe's cause, also took part in the 1912 pentathlon and decathlon, placing sixth in the former and failing to finish the latter. Not until October 13, 1982, did the I.O.C. finally lift the ban against Thorpe and allow his name to be returned to the record books. On January 18, 1983, his gold medals were presented to his children.

1920 Antwerp C: 23, N: 12, D: 8.20–21.

		100 M	LJ	SP	HJ	400 M	110 H	DISC	PV	JAV	1500 M	TOTAL POINTS	1962 TABLES
1. Helge Lövland	NOR	12.0	6.28	11.19	1.65	54.8	16.2	37.34	3.20	48.01	4:48.4	6803	5970
2. Brutus Hamilton	USA	11.4	6.325	11.61	1.60	55.0	17.3	36.14	3.30	48.08	4:57.8	6771	5940
3. Bertil Ohlson	SWE	12.0	6.435	11.07	1.65	55.0	17.0	37.78	3.30	39.89	4:50.6	6580	5825
4. Gösta Holmér	SWE	11.8	5.92	11.06	1.70	56.5	16.6	34.82	3.20	47.62	5:01.6	6532	5740
5. Everett Nilsson	SWE	12.2	5.67	11.39	1.75	55.7	20.0	34.77	3.40	49.28	4:45.6	6434	5624
6. Woldemar Wickholm	FIN	11.6	6.12	11.44	1.60	52.8	16.8	32.30	3.00	42.76	4:45.6	6405	5790
7. Gene Vidal	USA	12.0	6.13	11.16	1.65	55.7	17.1	37.30	3.30	35.32	4:46.6	6360	5673
8. Erik Gyllenstolpe	SWE	12.0	6.35	10.69	1.65	55.4	16.8	33.65	2.90	49.31	5:01.4	6332	5653

Lövland passed Hamilton in the last event. If Hamilton had finished the 1500 meters six seconds faster, he would have won the gold medal. In 1952 Brutus Hamilton served as coach of the U.S. Olympic track team.

1924 Paris C: 36, N: 22, D: 7.11–12. WR: 7482/6270 (1962 tables) (Alexander Klumberg);——/6756 (Jim Thorpe)

		100 M	LJ	SP	HJ	400 M	110 H	DISC	PV	JAV	1500 M	TOTAL POINTS		1962 TABLES
1. Harold Osborn	USA	11.2	6.92	11.435	1.97	53.2	16.0	34.51	3.50	46.69	4:50.0	7711	WR	6668
2. Emerson Norton	USA	11.6	6.92	13.04	1.92	53.0	16.6	33.11	3.80	42.09	5:38.0	7351		6340
3. Alexander Klumberg	EST	11.6	6.96	12.27	1.75	54.4	17.6	36.795	3.30	57.70	5:16.0	7329		6260
4. Anton Huusari	FIN	12.0	6.16	12.025	1.70	53.4	16.6	33.15	3.20	53.65	4:37.2	7005		6119
5. Edward Sutherland	SAF	11.6	6.67	10.865	1.80	56.0	16.6	30.83	3.30	51.015	5:19.0	6794		5943
6. Ernst Gerspach	SWI	11.4	6.46	10.355	1.70	53.4	16.8	33.91	3.40	44.82	5:08.2	6744		5959
7. Helge Jansson	SWE	11.6	6.32	12.22	1.83	54.2	17.8	32.08	3.10	47.20	5:22.0	6656		5861
8. Harry Frieda	USA	11.6	5.94	11.01	1.60	54.0	19.0	35.095	3.40	54.90	5:02.6	6618		7574

Norton led after eight events, but fell off badly in the javelin, and barely finished the 1500 meters. Osborn, having already won a gold medal in the high jump on July 7, achieved a unique double.

1928 Amsterdam C: 38, N: 19, D: 8.3-4. WR: 7995/6768 (Paavo Yrjölä)

		100 M	LJ	SP	HJ	400 M	110 H	DISC	PV	JAV	1500 M	TOTAL POINTS		1962 TABLES
1. Paavo Yrjölä	FIN	11.8	6.72	14.11	1.87	53.2	16.6	42.09	3.30	55.70	4:44.0	8053	WR	6774
2. Akilles Järvinen	FIN	11.2	6.87	13.64	1.75	51.4	15.6	36.95	3.30	55.58	4:52.4	7932		6815
3. John Kenneth Doherty	USA	11.6	6.61	11.85	1.80	52.0	15.8	38.72	3.30	56.56	4:54.0	7707		6593
4. James Stewart	USA	11.2	6.61	13.04	1.87	52.8	16.6	40.90	3.30	48.07	5:17.0	7624		6530
5. Thomas Churchill	USA	11.6	6.32	12.28	1.70	52.2	16.8	38.19	3.60	50.93	4:55.0	7417		6364
6. Helge Jansson	SWE	11.4	6.85	13.59	1.87	53.2	16.6	36.83	3.30	41.73	5:27.0	7286		6336
7. L. Vesely	AUT	11.6	6.73	12.58	1.70	52.2	15.8	35.46	3.20	47.44	4:47.0	7274		6393
8. Albert Andersson	SWE	12.0	6.30	12.19	1.75	54.0	15.8	36.64	3.30	45.81	4:44.2	7109		6211

1932 Los Angeles C: 14, N: 9, D: 8.5–6. WR: 8255/7036 (Akilles Järvinen)

		100 M	LJ	SP	HJ	400 M	110 H	DISC	PV	JAV	1500 M	TOTAL POINTS		1962 TABLES
1. James Bausch	USA	11.7	6.95	15.32	1.70	54.2	16.2	44.58	4.00	61.91	5:17.0	8462	WR	6896
2. Akilles Järvinen	FIN	11.1	7.00	13.11	1.75	50.6	15.7	36.80	3.60	61.00	4:47.0	8292		7038
3. Wolrad Eberle	GER	11.4	6.77	13.22	1.65	50.8	16.7	41.34	3.50	57.49	4:34.4	8031		6830
4. Wilson Charles	USA	11.2	7.24	12.56	1.85	51.2	16.2	38.71	3.40	47.72	4:39.8	7985		6901
5. Hans-Heinrich Sievert	GER	11.4	6.97	14.50	1.78	53.6	16.1	44.54	3.20	53.91	5:18.0	7941		6699
6. Paavo Yrjölä	FIN	11.8	6.59	13.68	1.75	52.6	17.0	40.77	3.10	56.12	4:37.4	7688		6566
7. Clyde Clifford Coffman	USA	11.3	6.77	11.86	1.70	51.8	17.8	34.40	4.00	48.88	4:48.0	7534		6480
8. Robert Tisdall	IRL	11.3	6.60	12.58	1.65	49.0	15.5	33.31	3.20	45.26	4:34.4	7327		6557

Akilles Järvinen, older brother of javelin gold medalist Matti Järvinen, was the heavy favorite to win the decathlon. He did in fact break his own world record, but he was only able to place second. The upset winner was ex-University of Kansas football star Jim Bausch. Fifth after the first day's events, Bausch took advantage of splendid performances in the discus and pole vault to build an insurmountable lead. Although Järvinen did win his second silver medal, had the 1962 tables been in use at the time he would have finished first in both 1928 and 1932.

1936 Berlin C: 28, N: 17, D: 8.7–8. WR: 7880/7383 (Glenn Morris)

		100 M	LJ	SP	HJ	400 M	110 H	DISC	PV	JAV	1500 M	TOTAL POINTS		1962 TABLES
1. Glenn Morris	USA	11.1	6.97	14.10	1.85	49.4	14.9	43.02	3.50	54.52	4:33.2	7900	WR	7421
2. Robert Clark	USA	10.9	7.62	12.68	1.80	50.0	15.7	39.39	3.70	51.12	4:44.4	7601		7226
3. Jack Parker	USA	11.4	7.35	13.52	1.80	53.3	15.0	39.11	3.50	56.46	5:07.8	7275		6918
4. Erwin Huber	GER	11.5	6.89	12.70	1.70	52.3	15.8	35.46	3.80	56.45	4:35.2	7087		6811
5. Reindert Brasser	HOL	11.6	6.69	13.49	1.90	51.5	16.2	39.45	3.40	55.75	5:06.0	7046		6758
6. Armin Guhl	SWI	11.3	7.04	12.30	1.80	52.3	15.6	40.97	3.30	51.20	4:49.2	7033		6790
7. Olle Bexell	SWE	11.6	6.68	13.54	1.75	54.9	16.0	38.83	3.70	57.07	4:40.4	7024		6743
8. Helmut Bonnet	GER	11.6	6.66	13.45	1.75	53.7	16.2	39.16	3.60	58.15	4:54.0	6939		6672

A new set of tables were instituted in 1934, which accounts for the lower scores. Just before the running of the 1500 meters, it was announced that Glenn Morris, a 24-year-old automobile salesman from Colorado, needed to run 4:32.0 in order to set a new world record. This was much faster than Morris, who was only competing in his third decathlon, had ever run. When he crossed the finish line in 4:33.2, there was much disappointment. But then it was discovered that an error had been made in computing his score, and that he had in fact broken the record after all.

1948 London C: 35, N: 20, D: 8.5-6. WR: 7900/7421 (Glenn Morris)

		100 M	LJ	SP	HJ	400 M	110 H	DISC	PV	JAV	1500 M	TOTAL POINTS	1962 TABLES
1. Robert Mathias	USA	11.2	6.615	13.04	1.86	51.7	15.7	44.00	3.50	50.32	5:11.0	7139	6826
2. Ignace Heinrich	FRA	11.3	6.895	12.85	1.86	51.6	15.6	40.94	3.20	40.98	4:43.8	6974	6740
3. Floyd Simmons	USA	11.2	6.725	12.80	1.86	51.9	15.2	32.73	3.40	51.99	4:58.0	6950	6711
4. Enrique Kistenmacher	ARG	10.9	7.08	12.67	1.70	50.5	16.3	41.11	3.20	45.06	4:49.6	6929	6726
5. Erik Peter Andersson	SWE	11.6	6.595	12.66	1.75	52.0	15.9	36.07	3.60	51.04	4:34.0	6877	6669
6. Peter Mullins	AUS	11.2	6.645	12.75	1.83	53.2	15.2	33.94	3.40	51.32	5:17.6	6739	6527
7. Per Axel Eriksson	SWE	11.9	6.80	11.96	1.80	52.5	16.2	34.91	3.30	56.70	4:35.8	6731	6552
8. Irving Mondschein	USA	11.3	6.810	12.74	1.83	51.6	16.6	38.74	3.50	36.81	4:49.8	6715	6538

Bob Mathias was only 17 years old when his track coach at Tulare High School in Central California suggested that he take up the decathlon. Mathias learned quickly, and less than three months later he had qualified for the U.S. Olympic team and was on his way to London. His inexperience led to one setback in the shot put. After lofting the 16-pound ball over 45 feet, he was surprised when an official raised the red flag that indicated a foul. The perplexed teenager was informed that he had left the throwing circle from the front, which was against the rules. Nobody had ever told Mathias about this particular rule, but there was nothing he could do about it. His best throw after that was only 42 feet 9¼ inches.

The next event was the high jump, and here Mathias almost met disaster, as he missed twice at the mediocre height of 5 feet 9 inches. Faced with virtual elimination, he ignored formal technique and threw himself over the bar with a jump that was clumsy, but successful. He went on to clear 6 feet 1¼ inches. After the first day's events, Mathias was in third place behind Enrique Kistenmacher and Ignace Heinrich.

The second day's competition began at 10 a.m., but bad weather and general confusion caused it to drag on into the night. The discus was Bob Mathias' specialty, and he connected with a good throw of about 145 feet. Unfortunately, the marker for his throw got knocked over. After a half hour search in the rain and gloom for the hole left by his discus, officials gave him credit for 144 feet 4 inches. Mathias' older brother, Gene, who had gained access to the field by flashing a bogus press pass, raced up to Bob and urged him to press the search. But Bob felt guilty about the delay he was causing, and so accepted his fate. The throw was good enough, however, to put him into first place. By the time he staggered across the finish line at the end of the 1500 meters, it was 10:35 p.m. and Bob Mathias had become the youngest winner of a men's track and field event in the history of the Olympics. In the dressing room afterward, the exhausted teenager was asked how he intended to celebrate his victory. He replied, "I'll start shaving, I guess." In fact, he was so drained that he went right to sleep and had to be awakened to take part in the victory ceremony the next day.

Back home in Tulare, a small farming town of 12,000, the entire population had been on pins and needles waiting for the results from London. When the news came over the radio that Mathias had won, the town went wild. Factory whistles and fire sirens blared for 45 minutes, businesses closed down, and a spontaneous three-hour parade of cars clogged the downtown area and the nearby interstate highway. The local telegraph office had to stay open into the night as friends stood in line to send their congratulations to the hometown boy who had made good. When Mathias finally returned three weeks later, the excitement was so great that the airplane he was on had to delay its landing until the crowd could be cleared from around the runway.

1952 Helsinki C: 28, N: 16, D: 7.25–26. WR: 7825/7453 (Robert Mathias)

		100 M	LJ	SP	HJ	400 M	110 H	DISC	PV	JAV	1500 M	TOTAL POINTS		1962 TABLES
1. Robert Mathias	USA	10.9	6.98	15.30	1.90	50.2	14.7	46.89	4.00	59.21	4:50.8	7887	WR	7731
2. Milton Campbell	USA	10.7	6.74	13.89	1.85	50.9	14.5	40.50	3.30	54.54	5:07.2	6975		7132
3. Floyd Simmons	USA	11.5	7.06	13.18	1.92	51.1	15.0	37.77	3.60	54.69	4:53.4	6788		7069
4. Vladimir Volkov	SOV	11.4	7.09	12.62	1.75	51.2	15.8	38.04	3.80	56.68	4:33.2	6674		7030
5. Josef Hipp	GER	11.4	6.85	13.26	1.75	51.3	16.1	45.84	3.50	54.14	4:57.2	6449		6882
6. Göran Widenfeldt	SWE	11.4	6.76	11.61	1.94	51.3	16.1	39.53	3.50	49.36	4:38.6	6388		6850
7. Kjell Tånnander	SWE	11.4	6.90	12.97	1.85	52.6	15.8	39.30	3.50	52.79	4:57.2	6308		6797
8. Friedel Schirmer	GER	11.7	6.37	12.69	1.80	50.5	16.0	37.01	3.50	54.00	4:47.6	6118		6647

World records for this period get very confusing, since yet another new set of tables was devised in 1950 and revised a few days before the Olympics. It made little difference to Bob Mathias, who won by the largest margin in Olympic history. His only problem developed in the javelin, when his first two throws fell far short of his capabilities. Up in the stands, Jack Weiershauser, Mathias' track coach at Stanford, convinced a bunch of American rooters to chant, "Oh Bob, hey you, don't forget to follow through." Bob got the message, and followed through with a throw of 194 feet 3 inches.

1956 Melbourne C: 15, N: 8, D: 11.29–30. WR: 7985/7758 (Rafer Johnson)

		100 M	LJ	SP	HJ	400 M	110 H	DISC	PV	JAV	1500 M	TOTAL POINTS		1962 TABLES
1. Milton Campbell	USA	10.8	7.33	14.76	1.89	48.8	14.0	44.98	3.40	57.08	4:50.6	7937	OR	7708
2. Rafer Johnson	USA	10.9	7.34	14.48	1.83	49.3	15.1	42.17	3.90	60.27	4:54.2	7587		7568
3. Vassily Kuznyetsov	SOV	11.2	7.04	14.49	1.75	50.2	14.9	44.33	3.95	65.13	4:53.8	7465		7461
4. Uno Palu	SOV	11.5	6.65	13.39	1.89	50.8	15.4	40.38	3.60	61.59	4:35.6	6930		7186
5. Martin Lauer	GER	11.1	6.83	12.86	1.83	48.2	14.7	39.38	3.10	50.66	4:43.8	6853		7072
6. Walter Meier	GDR	11.3	6.80	12.99	1.86	49.3	16.1	37.59	3.70	47.97	4:20.6	6773		7111
7. Torbjörn Lassenius	FIN	11.8	6.62	13.45	1.70	50.8	15.9	41.36	3.80	59.33	4:36.2	6565		6938
8. Yang Chuan-Kwang	TAI	11.2	6.90	11.56	1.95	51.3	15.0	33.92	3.30	57.88	5:00.8	6521		6850

World record holder Rafer Johnson was hampered by injury, but even in full health he probably couldn't have beaten Milt Campbell in Melbourne. Campbell, a 22-year-old sailor from Plainfield, New Jersey, had hoped to qualify for the U.S. Olympic team as a hurdler, but only finished fourth in the final tryouts. "I was stunned," he said. "But then God seemed to reach into my heart and tell me he didn't want me to compete in the hurdles, but in the decathlon."

In the Olympics he led from start to finish. A time of 14.0 in the hurdles earned him 1124 points and assured him the victory. He lost his shot at a world record when he could do no better than 11 feet 1¼ inches in the pole vault, almost 20 inches below his best performance. But, paced and urged on by 11th-place finisher Ian Bruce of Australia, he ran the 1500 meters in 4:50.6 to gain the Olympic record.

1960 Rome C: 30, N: 20, D: 9.5–6. WR: 8683/8063 (Rafer Johnson)

		100 M	LJ	SP	HJ	400 M	110 H	DISC	PV	JAV	1500 M	TOTAL POINTS		1962 TABLES
1. Rafer Johnson	USA	10.9	7.35	15.82	1.85	48.3	15.3	48.49	4.10	69.76	4:49.7	8392	OR	8001
2. Yang Chuan-Kwang	TAI	10.7	7.46	13.33	1.90	48.1	14.6	39.83	4.30	68.22	4:48.5	8334		7930
3. Vassily Kuznyetsov	SOV	11.1	6.96	14.46	1.75	50.2	15.0	50.52	3.90	71.20	4:53.8	7809		7624
4. Yuri Kutyenko	SOV	11.4	6.93	13.97	1.80	51.1	15.6	45.63	4.20	71.44	4:44.2	7567		7513
5. Evert Kamerbeek	HOL	11.3	7.21	13.76	1.80	51.1	14.9	44.31	3.80	57.49	4:43.6	7236		7361
6. Franco Sar	ITA	11.4	6.69	13.89	1.80	51.3	14.7	49.58	3.80	55.74	4:49.2	7195		7291
7. Markus Kahma	FIN	11.5	6.93	14.55	1.75	50.5	15.9	44.93	3.60	60.50	4:22.8	7112		7316
8. Klaus Grogorenz	GDR	10.8	6.93	12.42	1.73	48.0	16.9	40.12	3.70	60.81	4:27.0	7032		7265

Rafer Johnson and Yang Chuan-Kwang grew up in very different circumstances, yet they came together as fellow students at U.C.L.A., and then as friendly rivals at the Rome Olympics. Johnson was born in Hillsboro, Texas. In

1945, when Rafer was 11, his family moved to the small town of Kingsburg, California, less than 25 miles from Bob Mathias' hometown of Tulare. There they lived in a boxcar for a year until things started looking up. Yang was a member of the Takasago ethnic group, which inhabited the island of Formosa long before the Chinese arrived. He visited the United States for a couple of months and decided to stay. At U.C.L.A. Johnson and Yang, now known as C.K. Yang, trained together, but in Rome Johnson represented the United States and Yang, Taiwan.

The first day of competition, interrupted by an 80-minute thunder shower, didn't end until 11 p.m. After five events, Johnson led Yang by only 55 points. They were back on the track again at 9 a.m. for the sixth event, the 110-meter hurdles, which was one of Johnson's specialties. But the poorly rested American hit the first hurdle badly and took 15.3 seconds to reach the finish line, far slower than his best of 13.9. He made up the lost points in the pole vault by achieving a personal record of 13 feet 5½ inches.

With only the 1500 meters left to run, Johnson led Yang by 67 points. This meant that if Yang, whose best time for the distance was 4:36.0, could beat Johnson by ten seconds, he would become Taiwan's first-ever gold medalist. Johnson's 1500 best was the 4:54.2 that he had recorded at the 1956 Olympics. The two very tired rivals took off at 9:15 p.m., with Yang in front and Johnson dogging him the entire way. Yang tried desperately to pull away in the final lap, but Johnson stuck close and earned the gold medal by finishing only six yards behind, in a career best of 4:49.7. Johnson and Yang wobbled on for a few yards and then fell against each other for support. Yang was the first Taiwanese to gain an Olympic medal.

Rafer Johnson later became an actor and television sportscaster before becoming involved in politics. On June 5, 1968, Johnson was walking through the kitchen in the Ambassador Hotel in Los Angeles with Robert Kennedy, when the Presidential candidate was shot and killed.

1964 Tokyo C: 22, N: 14, D: 10.19–20. WR: 8089 (Yang Chuan-Kwang)

			100 M	LJ	SP	HJ	400 M	110 H	DISC	PV	JAV	1500 M	1962 TOTAL POINTS
1.	Willi Holdorf	GER	10.7	7.00	14.95	1.84	48.2	15.0	46.05	4.20	57.37	4:34.3	7887
2.	Rein Aun	SOV	10.9	7.22	13.82	1.93	48.8	15.9	44.19	4.20	59.06	4:22.3	7842
3.	Hans-Joachim Walde	GER	11.0	7.21	14.45	1.96	49.5	15.3	43.15	4.10	62.90	4:37.0	7809
4.	Paul Herman	USA	11.2	6.97	13.89	1.87	49.2	15.2	44.15	4.35	63.35	4:25.4	7787
5.	Yang Chuan-Kwang	TAI	11.0	6.80	13.23	1.81	49.0	14.7	39.59	4.60	68.15	4:48.4	7650
6.	Horst Beyer	GER	11.2	7.02	14.32	1.90	49.8	15.2	45.17	3.80	58.17	4:23.6	7647
7.	Vassily Kuznyetsov	SOV	10.9	6.98	14.06	1.70	49.5	14.9	43.81	4.40	67.87	5:02.5	7569
8.	Mikhail Storozhenko	SOV	11.0	7.22	16.37	1.84	53.6	15.0	43.20	4.00	59.10	5:99.7	7464

On April 28, 1963, Yang Chuan-Kwang had severely disrupted the scoring of the decathlon by pole-vaulting 15 feet 10½ inches, which put him above the maximum height accounted for by the charts then in use. The new charts, known as the 1962 tables, were not released until August, 1964. They tended to equalize the ten events, and were particularly damaging to Yang, whose pole-vault best was suddenly worth 501 points less than it had been. Using the old tables, Yang's best total of 1964 had been 485 points higher than anyone else's. With the new tables, he trailed both Holdorf and Beyer.

At the end of the first day in Tokyo, Holdorf led with 4090 points. He was followed by Walde with 4074 and Aun with 4067. After nine events, Holdorf led Walde by 60 points and Aun by 137. The 1500, however, was one of Aun's strong points. To win, Holdorf had to finish within 17 seconds of Aun, but his best time of the year was more than 30 seconds slower than Aun's. Holdorf's coach, Friedel Schirmer, purposely misled him, telling Holdorf that he had only 12 seconds to spare.

Aun finished in 4:22.3, while Holdorf pushed himself as hard as he could. Forty yards from the finish, he began to weave and appeared on the verge of collapse. But he struggled on until the end, crossing the finish with a time of 4:34.3—exactly 12 seconds slower than Aun. Then he collapsed. Aun tried to congratulate his fallen conqueror, but Holdorf was too dazed to comprehend. Eventually he was revived and shown the scoreboard that displayed his winning score.

1968 Mexico City C: 33, N: 20, D: 10.18–19. WR: 8319 (Kurt Bendlin)

		100 M	LJ	SP	HJ	400 M	110 H	DISC	PV	JAV	1500 M	1962 TOTAL POINTS	
1.	William Toomey	USA	10.4	7.87	13.75	1.95	45.6	14.9	43.68	4.20	62.80	4:57.1	8193	OR
2.	Hans-Joachim Walde	GER	10.9	7.64	15.13	2.01	49.0	14.8	43.54	4.30	71.62	4:58.5	8111	
3.	Kurt Bendlin	GER	10.7	7.56	14.74	1.80	48.3	15.0	46.78	4.60	75.42	5:09.8	8064	
4.	Nikolai Avilov	SOV	10.9	7.64	13.41	2.07	49.9	14.5	46.64	4.10	60.12	5:00.8	7909	
5.	Joachim Kirst	GDR	10.5	7.61	16.43	1.98	50.2	15.6	46.89	4.15	57.02	5:20.1	7861	
6.	Thomas Wadell	USA	11.3	7.47	14.45	2.01	51.2	15.3	43.73	4.50	63.70	5:04.5	7719	
7.	Rick Sloan	USA	11.2	6.72	14.07	2.10	51.0	15.5	45.58	4.85	49.90	4:44.0	7692	
8.	Steen Smidt-Jensen	DEN	10.9	7.17	13.03	1.95	50.2	14.9	41.07	4.85	46.80	4:41.3	7648	

"Behind every good decathlon man, there's a good doctor," Bill Toomey once declared, and he was an expert on the subject. Aside from the usual array of illnesses and pulled muscles, Toomey had suffered through hepatitis, mononucleosis, and a shattered kneecap on his way to an Olympic gold medal. A 29-year-old English teacher from California, Toomey faced his moment of truth in the pole vault. Leading after seven events, he suddenly found himself one miss away from elimination at the opening height of 11 feet 9¾ inches.

"I had done so many things wrong on my first two jumps," he later recalled, "I couldn't figure out how to correct anything. . . . Everything was closing in on me— the people in that huge arena, the people watching on television back home, my whole life, all those years of working and waiting for this moment. If I missed, it would be like dying." Fortunately, Toomey didn't miss. "All the technique I had learned and practiced . . . had been forgotten in the fear and frustration I felt. I was like a beginner, clumsy and uncertain. But I had made that jump on sheer determination. I'm not even sure I needed my pole."

Toomey went on to clear 13 feet 9½ inches, his best ever in competition, and then managed to stave off the competition through the first two events.

1972 Munich C: 33, N: 19, D: 9.7–8. WR: 8417 (William Toomey)

		100 M	LJ	SP	HJ	400 M	110 H	DISC	PV	JAV	1500 M	TOTAL POINTS		1962 TABLES
1. Nikolai Avilov	SOV	11.00	7.68	14.36	2.12	48.45	14.31	46.98	4.55	61.66	4:22.8	8454	WR	8454
2. Leonid Litvinenko	SOV	11.13	6.81	14.18	1.89	48.40	15.03	47.84	4.40	58.94	4:05.9	8035		8045
3. Ryszard Katus	POL	10.89	7.09	14.39	1.92	49.11	14.41	43.00	4.50	59.96	4:31.9	7984		7981
4. Jefferson Bennett	USA	10.73	7.26	12.82	1.86	46.25	15.58	36.58	4.80	57.48	4:12.2	7974		7979
5. Stefan Schreyer	GDR	10.82	7.44	15.02	1.92	49.51	15.00	45.08	4.40	50.42	4:48.2	7950		7954
6. Freddy Herbrand	BEL	11.00	7.30	13.91	2.04	49.78	14.87	47.12	4.40	50.42	4:27.1	7947		7944
7. Steen Smidt-Jensen	DEN	11.07	6.95	13.35	2.01	50.10	14.65	44.80	4.80	55.24	4:24.7	7947		7936
8. Tadeusz Janczenko	POL	10.64	7.28	14.45	2.04	49.10	16.89	45.26	4.50	63.80	5:01.5	7861		7869

The 1972 decathlon looked to be a wide-open affair, with at least four men considered leading contenders: two-time European champion Joachim Kirst of East Germany, Jeff Bannister of the United States, veteran Lennart Hedmark of Sweden, and the fast-improving Ukrainian Nikolai Avilov of the U.S.S.R. Unfortunately, Hedmark, troubled by an injured foot, was forced to withdraw after three events. After five events, Kirst was in first place with 4364 points, followed by Avilov with 4345, and Tadeusz Janczenko and Ryszard Skowronek of Poland with 4266 and 4240, respectively.

The turning point came shortly after 9 a.m. the following morning, in the second heat of the high hurdles. Kirst hit the first hurdle, fell heavily at the next and pulled a muscle. Bannister, in the next lane, was thrown off stride, fell after the fourth hurdle, pushed over the next one, and was disqualified. Janczenko, forced to add the fallen Bannister to the obstacles in his path, was slowed down so much that it may have cost him a medal. Meanwhile, Avilov, unaware of the chaos behind him, finished first with a time of 14.31. In addition to all this, Skowronek had pulled a muscle in his heat and had to retire in the middle of the next event.

Avilov, who suddenly found himself with a huge lead, finished the day brilliantly, eventually recording personal records in seven of the ten decathlon events, and equaling his best in an eighth. A strong finish in the 1500 earned him a world record. Fellow Ukrainian Leonid Litvinenko ran an even better 1500-meter race, enabling him to move from eighth place after nine events to second after ten.

The first to congratulate Avilov was the man whose record he had broken, Bill Toomey, on hand as a television commentator. Both Toomey and Avilov married Olympic medalists. Toomey wed 1964 long-jump champion Mary

Rand, and Avilov married Valentina Kozyr, winner of the bronze medal in the 1968 high jump.

1976 Montreal C: 28, N: 17, D: 7.29–30. WR: 8538 (Bruce Jenner)

			100 M	LJ	SP	HJ	400 M	110 H	DISC	PV	JAV	1500 M	TOTAL POINTS		1962 TABLES
1.	Bruce Jenner	USA	10.94	7.22	15.35	2.03	47.51	14.84	50.04	4.80	68.52	4:12.6	8617	WR	8631
2.	Guido Kratschmer	GER	10.66	7.39	14.74	2.03	48.19	14.58	45.70	4.60	66.32	4:29.1	8411		8397
3.	Nikolai Avilov	SOV	11.23	7.52	14.81	2.14	48.16	14.20	45.60	4.45	62.28	4:26.3	8369		8375
4.	Raimo Pihl	SWE	10.93	6.99	15.55	2.00	47.97	15.81	44.30	4.40	77.34	4:28.8	8218		8224
5.	Ryszard Skowronek	POL	11.02	7.26	13.74	1.91	47.91	14.75	45.34	4.80	62.22	4:29.9	8113		8112
6.	Siegfried Stark	GDR	11.35	6.98	15.08	1.91	49.14	15.65	45.48	4.65	74.18	4:24.9	8048		8032
7.	Leonid Litvinenko	SOV	11.12	6.92	14.20	1.91	48.44	14.71	46.26	4.60	53.66	4:11.4	8025		8031
8.	Lennart Hedmark	SWE	11.36	7.09	15.00	1.91	49.80	14.79	46.42	4.30	78.58	4:44.2	7974		7965

The 1976 decathlon was looked forward to as a classic duel between Nikolai Avilov, the defending champion and holder of the automatically timed world record, and Bruce Jenner, tenth in Munich, but now the holder of the official, albeit hand-timed, world record. From the very first event, however, it was Jenner who was in control. Hoping to be within 200 points of the leaders, Kratschmer and Avilov, at the end of the first day, Jenner found himself only 35 points behind Kratschmer and 17 points behind Avilov. He went to bed completely confident of victory since the second day's events were his best.

By the time eight events had been completed, Jenner's victory was assured, and he began to cry as he realized that his goal was about to be achieved, and that his athletic career was about to come to an end. Encouraged by his wife, Chrystie, who had supported the young couple with her job as an air hostess, Jenner had totally immersed himself in the world of the decathlon. At night, he dreamed about the different events so often that Chrystie could tell which one he was unconsciously practicing. As Jenner rested on the infield in Montreal, his reverie was broken by Leonid Litvinenko, who patted him on the shoulder and said, "Bruce, you going to be Olympic champion."

"Thanks," said Jenner.

Litvinenko stared at Jenner for a few seconds, and then asked, "Bruce, you going to be a millionaire?"

Jenner just laughed.

Unlike most decathletes, who dread the 1500 meters, Jenner actually looked forward to it, and ran his final race full of strength, leaning forward as he crossed the finish line. The North American crowd roared with delight, but eventually Bruce made his way through the adulation, found Chrystie, and told her, "Congratulations. We did it together." When he left the stadium, he didn't even bother to take his vaulting poles with him, because he knew he wouldn't need them where he was going.

Bruce Jenner did become rich and famous, just as Litvinenko had wondered, but his marriage didn't last. Since the media had constantly portrayed Bruce and Chrystie as the All-American couple, their divorce was a difficult one.

Jenner later married Linda Thompson, former girlfriend of Elvis Presley. By 1983 he had four children, two by Chrystie and two by Linda.

1980 Moscow C: 21, N: 12, D: 7.25–26. WR: 8649 (Guido Kratschmer)

		100 M	LJ	SP	HJ	400 M	110 H	DISC	PV	JAV	1500 M	TOTAL POINTS	1962 TABLES
1. Francis "Daley" Thompson	GBR	10.62	8.00	15.18	2.80	48.01	14.47	42.24	4.70	64.16	4:39.9	8495	8496
2. Yuri Kutsenko	SOV	11.19	7.74	14.50	2.08	48.67	15.04	39.86	4.90	68.08	4:22.6	8331	8332
3. Sergei Zhelanov	SOV	11.40	7.60	14.17	2.18	49.27	14.83	42.80	4.60	57.30	4:27.5	8315	8318
4. Georg Werthner	AUT	11.44	7.27	13.45	2.03	49.26	15.08	38.14	4.85	73.66	4:23.4	8050	8055
5. Josef Zeilbauer	AUT	11.29	7.14	15.31	2.03	50.91	14.80	44.00	4.50	64.86	4:30.6	8007	8006
6. Dariusz Ludwig	POL	11.35	7.51	13.32	2.08	50.55	15.38	45.82	4.80	58.38	4:29.7	7978	7963
7. Atanas Andonov	BUL	11.38	6.86	15.59	2.00	50.36	14.83	47.62	4.70	53.54	4:29.2	7927	7924
8. Steffen Grummt	GDR	11.35	6.86	16.15	1.94	49.39	14.82	48.56	4.30	55.24	4:30.2	7892	7883

In Montreal Daley Thompson had been the youngest entrant in the decathlon, finishing 18th at the age of 18. Four years later this gregarious offspring of a Nigerian father and a Scottish mother was expected to face a tough battle for the gold medal against Guido Kratschmer of West Germany. When West Germany joined the Jimmy Carter boycott, Thompson broke training, so that he could compete against Kratschmer. He beat his rival in May, and set a world record of 8622 in the process. Kratschmer responded with another world record of 8649 in June, but he would have been hard-pressed to beat Thompson in Moscow.

At the Olympics, Thompson was not seriously challenged. His nearest rival, Valery Kachanov of the U.S.S.R., pulled a calf muscle during the pole vault and had to withdraw while in second place. Thompson's world record pace was thwarted by rain on the second day, but the Soviet fans, who had been none too friendly to foreign athletes, gave Thompson a standing ovation anyway when he finished the 1500 meters.

Discontinued Events

60 METERS

1900 Paris C: 10, N: 6, D: 7.15.
1. Alvin Kraenzlein — USA — 7.0 — WR
2. John Walter Tewksbury — USA — 7.1
3. Stanley Rowley — AUS — 7.2
4. Edmund Minahan — USA — 7.2

1904 St. Louis C: 15, N: 3, D:8.29. WR: 7.0 (Alvin Kraenzlein)
1. Archie Hahn — USA — 7.0 — EWR
2. William Hogenson — USA — 7.2
3. Fay Moulton — USA — 7.2
4. Clyde Blair — USA — 7.2
5. Meyer Prinstein — USA — —
6. Frank Castleman — USA — —

Hahn won the first of his three gold medals at the St. Louis Games.

5 MILES (8047 METERS)

1906 Athens C: 28, N: 12, D: 4.25. WR: 24:33.4 (Alfred Shrubb)
1. Henry Hawtrey   GBR   26:11.8
2. John Svanberg   SWE   26:19.4
3. Edward Dahl   SWE   26:26.2
4. George Bonhag   USA   —
5. Pericle Pagliani   ITA   —
6. George Blake   AUS   —

John Daly of Ireland finished third, but was disqualified for staggering in front of Dahl and impeding his progress.

1908 London C: 35, N: 14, D: 7.18. WR: 24:33.4 (Alfred Shrubb)
1. Emil Voigt   GBR   25:11.2
2. Edward Owen   GBR   25:24.0
3. John Svanberg   SWE   25:37.2
4. Charles Hefferon   SAF   25:44.0
5. Archie Robertson   GBR   26:13.0
6. Frederick Meadows   CAN   —
7. J.F. Fitzgerald   CAN   —
8. Frederick Bellars   USA   —

Voigt, a 5-foot 5-inch vegetarian from Manchester, sprinted away in the final lap and won by 50 yards.

CROSS-COUNTRY, INDIVIDUAL

1912 Stockholm C: 46, N: 10, D: 7.15.
(ca. 12,000 Meters)
1. Johannes Kolehmainen   FIN   45:11.6
2. Hjalmar Andersson   SWE   45:44.8
3. John Eke   SWE   46:37.6
4. Jalmari Eskola   FIN   46:54.8
5. Josef Ternström   SWE   47:07.1
6. Albin Stenroos   FIN   47:23.4
7. K. Kronen   FIN   47:32.0
8. L. Richardsson   SAF   47:33.5

Hannes Kolehmainen won his third gold medal of the Stockholm Games, having already triumphed in the 5000 meters and 10,000 meters.

1920 Antwerp C: 42, N: 10, D: 8.23.
(ca. 8000 Meters)
1. Paavo Nurmi   FIN   27:15.0
2. Erik Backman   SWE   27:17.6
3. Heikki Liimatainen   FIN   27:37.4
4. James Wilson   GBR   27:45.2
5. Frank Hegarty   GBR   27:57.0
6. Teudor Koskenniemi   FIN   27:57.2
7. Julien van Campenhout BEL   28:00.0
8. Gaston Heuet   FRA   28:10.0

Nurmi and Joseph Guillemot had split the 5000 and 10,000. The cross-country was to be the tie-breaker, but three kilometers from the finish Guillemot stepped in a hole, injured his ankle, and had to withdraw.

1924 Paris C: 38, N: 10, D: 7.12.
(ca. 10,000 Meters)
1. Paavo Nurmi   FIN   32:54.8
2. Vilho "Ville" Ritola   FIN   34:19.4
3. Earl Johnson   USA   35:21.0
4. Ernest Harper   GBR   35:45.4
5. Henri Lauvaux   FRA   36:44.8
6. Arthur Studenroth   USA   36:45.4
7. C. Martinenghi   ITA   37:01.0
8. August Fager   USA   37:40.6

This event proved to be an almost total disaster, which put an end to cross-country races in the Olympics. Thirty-eight runners started off in the afternoon of one of the hottest days in Parisian history. Only fifteen finished. The course was unusually difficult, including stone paths that were covered in knee-high thistles and weeds. The first man to enter the stadium and cross the finish line was Paavo Nurmi. He appeared so fresh and untroubled that the spectators had no reason to suspect that anything was wrong. But as soon as the other runners started to arrive, the horrible situation began to unfold. One after another, strong athletes staggered onto the track. Aguilar of Spain collapsed, hit his head on a marker, and began bleeding. Sewell of Great Britain headed the wrong way. Pointed in the right direction, he collided with another runner. Both of them fell and failed to finish. Out on the roads there had been worse scenes of carnage, as various contestants were overcome by sunstroke and vomiting. Hours later, the Red Cross and Olympic officials were still searching the sides of the road for missing runners.

When the full extent of the tragedy became known, the remarkable performance of Paavo Nurmi was seen as even more impressive. Not only had the race taken place only two days after Nurmi had won the 1500 meters and the 5000 meters on the same day, but the very next day after the catastrophe, while most of the other cross-country runners were recuperating in bed or in the hospital, Nurmi was back again, winning another gold medal in the 3000 meters team race.

3000-METER TEAM RACE

1912 Stockholm T: 5, N: 5, D: 7.13.

		TEAM TOTALS	
1.	USA	9	(1—Tel Berna 8:44.6, 3—Norman Taber 8:45.2, 5—George Bonhag 8:46.6)
2.	SWE	13	(2—Thorild Ohlsson 8:44.6, 4—Ernst Wide 8:46.2, 7—Bror Fock 8:47.1)
3.	GBR	23	(6—William Cottrill 8:46.8, 8—George Hutson 8:47.2, 9—Cyril Porter 8:48.0)

Finland was eliminated in the first-round heat by the well-balanced U.S. team, despite the fact that Hannes Kolehmainen set a world record of 8:36.9.

1920 Antwerp T: 6, N: 6, D: 8.22.

		TEAM TOTALS	
1.	USA	10	(1—Horace Brown 8:45.4, 3—Arlie Schardt, 6—Ivan Dresser)
2.	GBR	20	(5—Charles Blewitt, 7—Albert Hill, 9—William Seagrove)
3.	SWE	24	(2—Erik Backman, 13—Sven Lundgren, 15—Edvin Wide)
4.	FRA	30	(4—Armand Burtin, Gaston Heuet, Edmond Brossard)
5.	ITA	34	(11—Ernesto Ambrosini, Augusto Maccario, Carlo Speroni)

For the team race, only the placings for the first three finishers from each country were counted. This explains why the team totals were less than the combined totals of the individual runners.

1924 Paris T: 9, N: 9, D: 7.13.

		TEAM TOTALS	
1.	FIN	8	(1—Paavo Nurmi 8:32.0, 2—Vilho "Ville" Ritola 8:40.6, 5—Elias Katz 8:45.4)
2.	GBR	14	(3—Bernard McDonald 8:44.0, 4—Harry Johnston, 7—George Webber)
3.	USA	25	(6—Edward Kirby 8:53.0, 8—William Cox, 11—Willard Tibbets)
4.	FRA	31	(9—Paul Bontemps, 10—Armand Burtin, 12—Léonard Mascaux)

Paavo Nurmi, running his seventh race in six days, won his fifth gold medal.

3-MILE TEAM RACE (4828 METERS)

1908 London T: 6, N: 6, D: 7.15.

		TEAM TOTALS	
1.	GBR	6	(1—Joseph Deakin 14:39.6, 2—Archie Robertson, 14:41.0, 3—Wilfred Coales 14:41.6)
2.	USA	19	(4—John Eisele 14:41.8, 6—George Bonhag 15:05.0, 9—Herbert Trube 15:11.0)
3.	FRA	32	(8—Louis de Fleurac 15:08.4, 11—Joseph Dreher 15:40.0, 13—Paul Lizandier 16:03.0)

5000-METER TEAM RACE

1900 Paris T: 2, N: 3, D: 7.22.

		TEAM TOTALS	
1.	GBR/AUS	26	(1—Charles Bennett 15:20.0, 2—John Rimmer, 6—Sidney Robinson, 7—Alfred Tysoe, 10—Stanley Rowley AUS)

2.	FRA	29	(3—Henri Deloge, 4—Gaston Ragueneau, 5—Jacques Chastanié, 8—André Castanet, 9—Michel Champoudry)

CROSS-COUNTRY TEAM RACE

1904 St. Louis T: 2, N: 2, D: 9.3.
(4 Miles, 6437 Meters)

		TEAM TOTALS	
1.	New York A.C.	27	(1—Arthur Newton 21:17.8, 5—George Underwood, 6—Paul Pilgrim, 7—Howard Valentine, 8—David Munson)
2.	Chicago A.A.	28	(2—James Lightbody, 3—William Frank Verner, 4—Lacey Hearn, 9—Albert Corey [FRA], 10—Sidney Hatch)

1906–1908 not held

1912 Stockholm T: 6, N: 6, D: 7.15.
(ca. 12,000 Meters)

		TEAM TOTALS	
1.	SWE	10	(2—Hjalmar Andersson 45:44.8, 3—John Eke 46:37.6, 5—Josef Ternström 47:07.1)
2.	FIN	11	(1—Johannes Kolehmainen 45:11.6, 4—Jalmari Eskola 46:54.8, 6—Albin Stenroos 47:23.4)
3.	GBR	49	(15—Frederick Hibbins 49:18.2, 16—Ernest Glover 49:53.7, 18—Thomas Humphreys 50:28.0)
4.	NOR	61	(19—Olav Hovdenak 50:40.8, 20—Parelius Finnerud 51:16.2, 22—Johannes Andersen 51:47.4)
5.	DEN	63	(14—Lauritz Christiansen 49:06.4, 23—Viggo Pedersen 53:00.8, 26—Carl Alfred Holmberg 54:24.9)

1920 Antwerp T: 7, N: 7, D: 8.23.
(ca. 8000 Meters)

		TEAM TOTALS	
1.	FIN	10	(1—Paavo Nurmi 27:15.0, 3—Heikki Liimatainen 27:37.00 6—Teudor Koskenniemi 27:57.2)
2.	GBR	21	(4—James Wilson 27:45.2, 5—Frank Hegarty 27:57.0, 12—Arthur Nichols)
3.	SWE	23	(2—Erik Backman 27:15.6, 10—Gustaf Mattsson 28:16.0, 11—Hilding Ekman 28:17.0)
4.	USA	36	(9—Patrick Flynn 28:12.0, 15—Frederick Faller, 16—Max Bohland)
5.	FRA	40	(8—Gaston Heuet 28:10.0, 17—Gustave Lauvaux, 21—Joseph Servella)
6.	BEL	48	(7—Julien van Campenhout 28:00.0, 33—Henri Smets, 36—Aimée Proot)
7.	DEN	53	—

1924 Paris T: 7, N: 7, D: 7.12.
(ca. 10,000 Meters)

	TEAM TOTALS	
1. FIN	11	(1—Paavo Nurmi 32:54.8, 2—Vilho "Ville" Ritola 34:19.4, 8—Heikki Liimatainen 38:12.0)
2. USA	14	(3—Earl Johnson 35:21.0, 5—Arthur Studenroth 36:45.44 6—August Fager 37:40.2)
3. FRA	20	(4—Henri Lauvaux 36:44.8, 7—Gaston Heuet 37:52.0, 9—Maurice Norland 41:38.6)

The same horrible race that was the individual cross-country also counted as the team race. In order for Finland to win, at least three men had to cross the finish line. Nurmi and Ritola finished easily, but Liimatainen, staggering along in the oppressive heat, halted 30 meters short of his goal. Delirious, he turned around and began staggering back the way he had come. The crowd shouted at him and he stopped. After standing for a while with his back to the finish line, he finally regained control of his senses, turned around, and walked across the finish. The British, Italian, Spanish, and Swedish teams failed to complete the course.

200-METER HURDLES

1900 Paris C: 8, N: 5, D: 7.16.
1. Alvin Kraenzlein   USA   25.4
2. Norman Pritchard   IND   26.6
3. John Walter Tewksbury   USA   —
4. Eugene Choisel   FRA   —

Kraenzlein won his fourth gold medal of the Paris Games.

1904 St. Louis C: 5, N: 1, D: 9.1.
1. Harry Hillman   USA   24.6   OR
2. Frank Castleman   USA   24.9
3. George Poage   USA   —
4. George Varnell   USA   —
5. Frederick Schule   USA   —

4000-METER STEEPLECHASE

1900 Paris C: 8, N: 5, D:7.16.
1. John Thomas Rimmer   GBR   12:58.4
2. Charles Bennett   GBR   12:58.6
3. Sidney Robinson   GBR   12:58.8
4. Jacques Chastanié   FRA   —
5. George Orton   CAN/USA   —
6. Franz Duhne   GER   —
AC: Alexander Grant (USA), Thaddeus McClain (USA)

1500-METER WALK

1906 Athens C: 9, N: 6, D: 4.30.
1. George Bonhag   USA   7:12.6
2. Donald Linden   CAN   7:19.8
3. Konstantin Spetsiotis   GRE   7:24.0
4. Georgios Saridakis   GRE   —
5. Harilaos Vasilakos   GRE   —
6. Alexandros Kouris   GRE   —
7. György Sztantics   HUN   —
DISQ: Richard Wilkinson (GBR), Eugen Spiegler (AUT)

Wilkinson and Spiegler finished first and second, but were disqualified for illegal technique. This left Bonhag with first place, although he too was disqualified by two of the four judges. The deciding vote in favor of Bonhag was cast by the president of the jury, Prince George. Bonhag had actually never entered a walking race before. Disappointed by his showings in the 5-mile run and the 1500-meter run, in which he had finished fourth and sixth, Bonhag entered the 1500-meter walk hoping to make up for his previous failures.

3000-METER WALK

1906 Athens C: 8, N: 5, D: 5.1.
1. György Sztantics   HUN   15:13.2
2. Hermann Müller   GER   15:20.0
3. Georgios Saridakis   GRE   15:33.0
4. Pandelis Ektoros   GRE   —
5. I. Panagoulopoulos   GRE   —
DISQ: Richard Wilkinson (GBR), Eugen Spiegler (AUT), Konstantin Spetsiotis (GRE)

The day after the controversial 1500-meter walk, a second contest was held at 3000 meters. Once again Wilkinson and Spiegler moved to the front. Fifty meters from the finish, they both began to run and were again disqualified.

1908–1912 not held

1920 Antwerp C: 22, N: 12, D: 8.21. WR: 12:53.8 (Gunnar Rasmussen)
1. Ugo Frigerio   ITA   13:14.2   OR
2. George Parker   AUS   13:20.6
3. Richard Remer   USA   13:23.6
4. Cecil McMaster   SAF   13:25.2
5. Thomas Maroney   USA   13:26.8
6. Charles Dowson   GBR   13:30.0
7. William Hehir   GBR   —
8. William Roelker   USA   —

Ugo Frigerio was such a colorful character that his flamboyance often obscured the fact that he was a superb athlete who combined great speed with perfect style. While other walkers became nervous or annoyed when a judge got down on his hands and knees to scrutinize their style, Frigerio seemed to enjoy the attention, and always made it a point to thank the judge when he was finished. Frigerio also enjoyed the attentions of the crowd, sometimes taking the time to exchange remarks with spectators, and even leading cheers for himself.

Just before the beginning of the 3000-meter walk, Frigerio approached the conductor of the band in the middle of the field and handed him several pages of sheet music, which he requested to be played during the course of the race. Accompanied by the proper background music, Frigerio moved quickly to the front and led the entire race, pausing only once toward the end to admonish the band for not playing at the correct tempo. He won easily by 20 meters.

TRACK AND FIELD

1. Charley Paddock wins the 1920 100 meters with his famous "flying finish." Morris Kirksey (right) placed second and Harry Edward (left) third.

2. (Left to right) Charley Paddock, Jackson Scholz, Loren Murchison, and Morris Kirksey spent anxious hours together before the final of the 100-meter dash in 1920. Six days later they teamed up to win the 4 × 100-meter relay.

CHARIOTS OF FIRE

3. The real Harold Abrahams. Despite the film Chariots of Fire, Abrahams did not run around the courtyard at Trinity College, Cambridge. He did, however, win the 100-meter dash at the 1924 Olympics in Paris.

4. Chariots of Fire portrayed Eric Liddell as learning at the last minute that the final of his specialty, the 100-meter dash, would be held on a Sunday. Actually Liddell was informed of the schedule six months in advance and had plenty of time to adjust his training for the 200 and 400.

JESSE OWENS

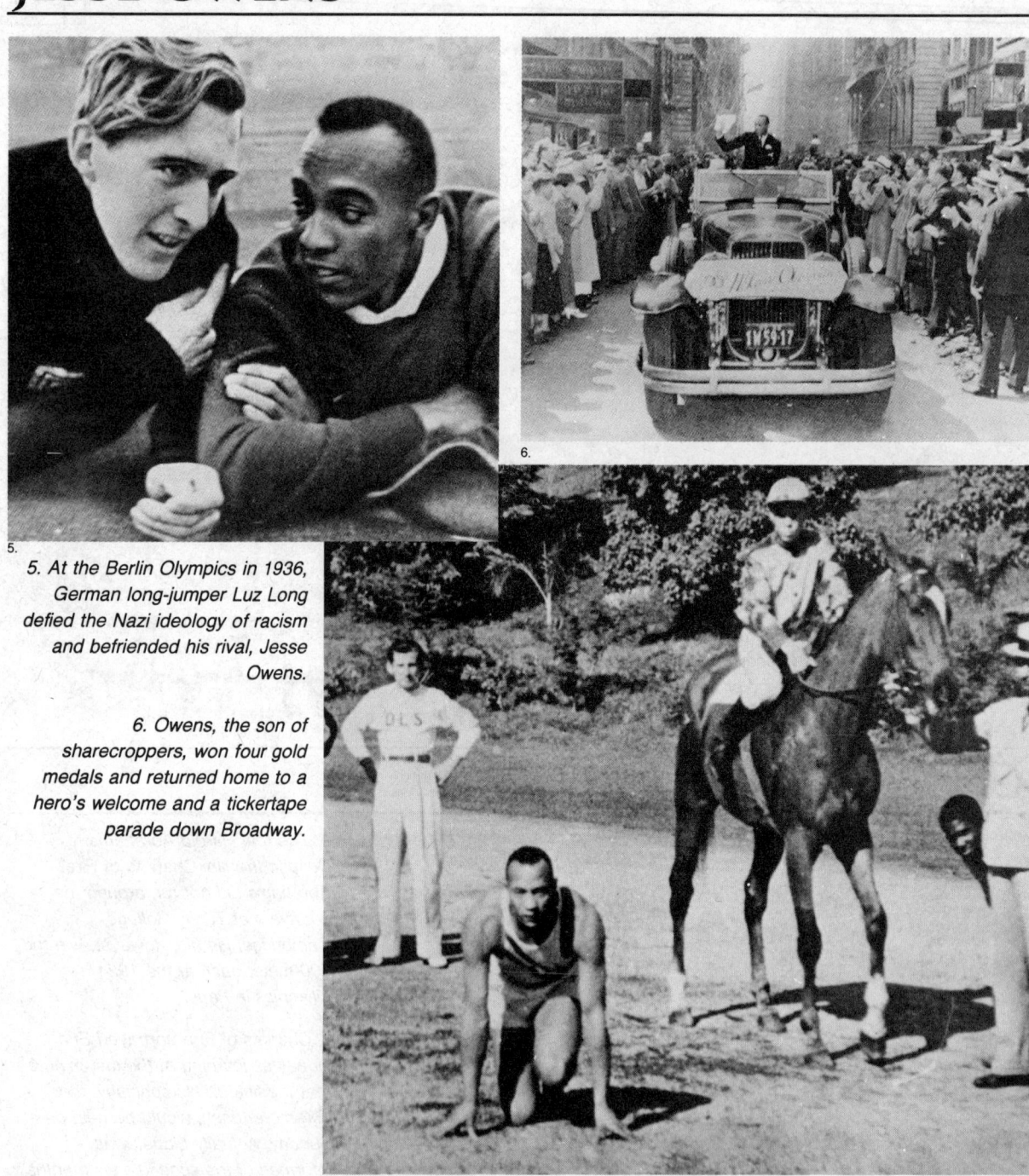

5. At the Berlin Olympics in 1936, German long-jumper Luz Long defied the Nazi ideology of racism and befriended his rival, Jesse Owens.

6. Owens, the son of sharecroppers, won four gold medals and returned home to a hero's welcome and a tickertape parade down Broadway.

7. Jesse Owens' celebrity failed to earn him a living, and he was forced to make ends meet by racing against horses, dogs, and motorcycles. He eventually found his place as a "professional good example."

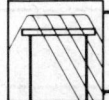

8. The controversial finish of the 1952 100-meter dash. The straight white line down the middle is *not* the finish line, but a flash from a photographer's bulb. To see if Herb McKenley (Lane 2 from top) beat Lindy Remigino (Lane 3), take a piece of transparent lined paper and match one of the lines with the black line below the words "Omega Timer." Slowly move the paper to the left until it reaches one of the runners. Arms and legs don't count; only shoulders and torso.

9. An ecstatic Pietro Mennea pulls ahead of "The Beast" to win the 1980 200 meters.

TOMMIE SMITH

10. Tommie Smith won the 1968 200 meters in world record time. When he raised two clenched fists at the finish line to celebrate his victory he was hailed as a hero . . .

11. . . . but when he raised one clenched fist on the victory platform he was denounced by the I.O.C., suspended by the U.S. Olympic Committee, and ordered to leave Mexico within 48 hours.

12.

14.

13.

15.

12. Unknown Paul Pilgrim scored an upset victory in the 1906 400 meters. The next day he also won the 800 meters. He never again won a major race. Wyndham Halswelle (right), seen here finishing second, was the beneficiary two years later in the famous 400 meters controversy of 1908.

13. James Ball (left) loses the 1928 400 meters to Ray Barbuti by committing the classic mistake of turning his head to check his position.

14. (Left to right) George Rhoden, Leslie Laing, Arthur Wint, and Herb McKenley failed to finish the 4 × 400-meter relay in 1948, when Wint pulled a muscle during the third leg. Four years later the same foursome fought back the challenge of the U.S. team to win the gold medal by one-tenth of a second.

15. Tom Courtney (153) edges Derek Johnson (137) in the 800 meters final of 1956, the most dramatic race of the Melbourne Olympics. Courtney exhausted himself so thoroughly that the award ceremony had to be delayed an extra hour until he recovered.

16. Peter Snell (right) scores a surprise victory over world record holder Roger Moens in the 1960 800 meters.

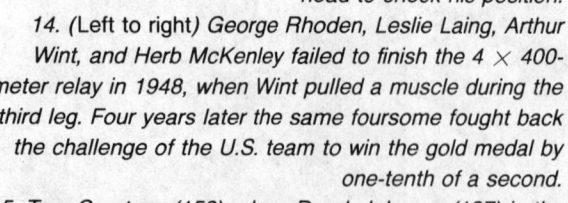
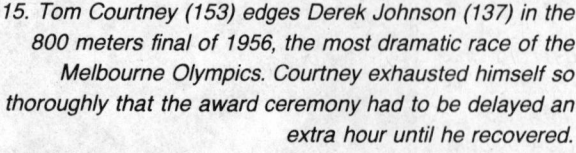

16.

1500 METERS

17.

18.

17. Josy Barthel of Luxembourg wins the 1500 meters in 1952. "Just as I had always dreamed in secret," he later recalled, "I raised my arms, I smiled, and I crossed the finish line."
18. Ron Delany leads the great mass finish of the 1956 1500 meters.

19.

20.

19. After the race, John Landy goes to the aid of Delany, whom he assumes to be doubled over in pain. Instead he discovers that Delany is deep in prayer.
20. Mexico City, 1968: Kip Keino of Kenya scores the most decisive 1500 meters victory in Olympic history.

21.

21. Sebastian Coe winning the 1500 meters in 1980 after his disappointing second-place finish in the 800.

GREAT MOMENTS IN LONG - DISTANCE

22.

23.

24.

22. Hannes Kolehmainen (left) passes Jean Bouin just before the finish of the 1912 5000 meters.

23. Paavo Nurmi checks his watch during the running of the 1924 5000 meters. He is followed by fellow Finn Ville Ritola.

24. Emil Zátopek enters the homestretch of the 1952 5000 meters, followed by Alain Mimoun and Herbert Schade. An exhausted Chris Chataway has fallen after stepping on the curb.

25. Gordon Pirie and Vladimir Kuts, still friendly despite their intense rivalry. In 1956 Kuts defeated Pirie in both the 10,000 meters and the 5000 meters.

25.

26.

26. Murray Halberg, winner of the 5000 meters in 1960, collapses in the infield, still holding the tape that marked his victory.
27. The varied emotions of the finish of the 1964 5000 meters. The joy of the winner, Bob Schul (center), the surprised thrill of silver medalist Harald Norpoth (left) and the agony and disappointment of Michel Jazy (third from left), who was in first place only 50 meters from the tape, but finished only fourth.
28. Mohamed Gammoudi (second from left) pushes his way past Billy Mills (left) and Ron Clarke (right) during the spectacular last lap of the 1964 10,000 meters.

27.

29.

28.

30.

29. Lasse Viren, having fallen halfway through the final of the 1972 10,000 meters, briefly contemplates his fate before regaining his feet. Viren went on to win the first of his four gold medals and set a world record as well.
30. Miruts Yifter celebrates the culmination of his eight-year quest for a gold medal in the 5000 meters. In 1972 he spent too long in the toilet and missed the start of his heat. In 1976 Ethiopia boycotted the Olympics. In 1980 he won at last.

THE 1904 MARATHON

31. Lentauw and Yamasani, the first black Africans to compete in the Olympics. They happened to be in St. Louis as part of the Boer War exhibit at the World's Fair and decided to enter the marathon race.

31.

32. The one and only Félix Carvajal. Financing his own trip from Cuba, he lost all his money in a crap game in New Orleans. He hitchhiked to St. Louis and arrived at the starting line wearing long pants and heavy boots. The start of the race was delayed while a sympathetic U.S. athlete cut off Carvajal's pants at the knees.
33. Thomas Hicks, the winner of the St. Louis marathon, visibly under the influence of the strychnine and brandy that was administered to him during the course of the race.

32.

33.

MARATHON WINNERS

34. Spiridon Louis, 1896.
35. Boughèra El Ouafi, 1928.

36. Delfo Cabrera, 1948.
37. Waldemar Cierpinski, 1976 and 1980.

THE LAST LAP—MARATHON

38. Dorando Pietri collapses within sight of the finish of the 1908 marathon. This photo puts to rest Dorando's contention that he could have completed the course unaided if meddlesome British officials had not interfered with him.

39. A perplexed Frank Shorter wonders why the spectators are booing as he circles the stadium on his way to victory in the 1972 Munich marathon.

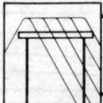

40.  41.  42.

40. *Alvin Kraenzlein won four gold medals in three days at the 1900 Paris Olympics. His wins came in the 60-meter dash, the long jump, and the 110- and 200-meter hurdles.*

41. *Harrison Dillard, the king of the high hurdles, failed to qualify in that event for the 1948 Olympics, but won the 100-meter dash instead. Four years later, in Helsinki, he finally earned his high hurdles gold medal.*

42. *Lord Burghley (center), winner of the 1928 400-meter hurdles, clears a barrier in classic style during a preliminary heat.*

43. *David Hemery (center), the 1968 gold medalist, and John Akii-Bua (right), the 1972 gold medalist, in a heat of the 1972 400-meter hurdles.*

44. *FBI agent Horace Ashenfelter surges past favorite Vladimir Kazantsev at the final water jump of the 1952 steeplechase.*

45. *Amos Biwott, defying accepted technique, soars over the water barrier in the 1968 steeplechase.*

43.

44.

45.

THE 1976 STEEPLECHASE

46. Frank Baumgartl (384) and Anders Gärderud (812) negotiate the final hurdle of the 1976 steeple-chase, followed closely by Bronislaw Malinowski (724).

47. Gärderud makes a successful clearance, but Baumgartl clips the barrier with his knee and falls.

48. Gärderud takes off for the finish line, while Malinowski is forced to add a human hurdle to the obstacles in his path.

49. Gärderud holds off Malinowski for the victory, while Baumgartl gets up to salvage the bronze medal.

WALKS

50.

51.

52.

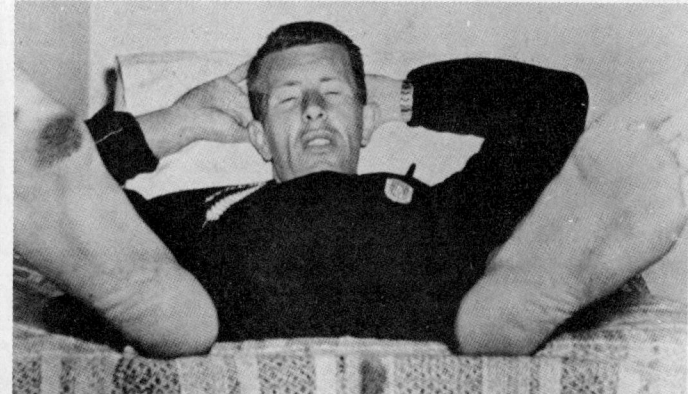

53.

50. Vladimir Golubnichiy holds off a frantic finish of dubious legality by local favorite José Pedraza to win the 20,000-meter walk in Mexico City in 1968.
51. Musically-minded crowd-pleaser Ugo Frigerio won a total of three walking gold medals in 1920 and 1924.
52. Ken Mathews celebrates his victory in the 1964 20,000-meter walk with his wife, Sheila.
53. Norman Read celebrates his victory in the 1956 50,000-meter walk by resting his feet.

HIGH-JUMPERS

54. Duncan McNaughton pestered the Canadian Olympic Association into letting him compete in the 1932 Olympics, since he lived in Los Angeles anyway. He went on to win the gold medal in the high jump.

54.

55.

55. John Thomas (left) congratulates Robert Shavlakadze after the latter's upset victory in the 1960 high jump.

56. The ecstasy of victory: Valery Brumel wins the 1964 high jump.

56.

57.

58.

59.

60.

57.–60. Dick Fosbury introduces the Fosbury Flop at the 1968 Olympics.

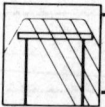

61.

62.

63.

64.

61. With his final attempt, Fred Hansen clears 16 feet 8 ¾ inches to win the 1964 pole vault in Tokyo.
62. Wladyslaw Kozakiewicz of Poland, winner of the 1980 Moscow pole vault, expresses his opinion of the Soviet crowd.
63. William DeHart Hubbard became the first black athlete to win an Olympic gold medal in an individual event when he won the 1924 long jump in Paris.
64. The three medalists in the 1960 long jump: (left to right) Bo Roberson, Ralph Boston, and Igor Ter-Ovanesyan.

BOB BEAMON

65. Bob Beamon stunned the sports world when he bettered the world long jump record by 21 ¾ inches, with a leap of 29 feet 2 ½ inches in 1968.

66. When he realized what he had accomplished, Beamon suffered a cataplectic seizure and fell to the ground in shock.

65.

66.

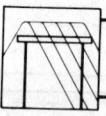

67.

68.

67. James Connolly of Boston became the first Olympic champion in 1527 years when he won the triple jump in 1896. He later became a well-known writer.
68. Viktor Saneyev won three gold medals in the triple jump, in 1968, 1972, and 1976, and came within 4 ½ inches of winning a fourth in 1980.

69. The winners of the 1912 shot put: (left to right) Patrick McDonald (gold), Lawrence Whitney (bronze), and Ralph Rose (silver.) Rose also won gold medals in 1904 and 1908.

69.

70.

71.

72.

70. Al Oerter, the only athlete ever to win the same Olympic track and field event four straight times. He earned four gold medals in the discus throw, in 1956, 1960, 1964, and 1968.

71. Eric Lemming of Sweden dominated the javelin throw from 1899 until 1912.

72. Matti Järvinen pretending to throw the javelin following his victory in 1932. He competed with his sweat pants on and only took them off to pose for photographers.

DECATHLON

73. Jim Thorpe led a tickertape parade in New York City following his victories in the decathlon and pentathlon in 1912. "I heard people yelling my name," he recalled, "and I couldn't realize how one fellow could have so many friends."

74. Glenn Morris was an automobile salesman when he won the Olympic decathlon in Berlin in 1936.

75. Seventeen-year-old Bob Mathias was the youngest winner of a men's track and field gold medal in Olympic history.

77. U.C.L.A. teammates Rafer Johnson (USA) and Yang Chuan-Kwang (Taiwan) collapse against each other after completing the final event of the 1960 decathlon.

76. After his victory in the 1948 decathlon, Mathias returned home to Tulare, California, for the small-town equivalent of a tickertape parade.

78.

78. Nikolai Avilov, winner of the 1972 decathlon, achieved personal bests in eight of the ten events.

79. Bruce Jenner completes his world record performance in the 1976 decathlon.

79.

80. Daley Thompson (center), the 1980 decathlon champion, shows his delight after receiving his gold medal at the award ceremony.

80.

DISCONTINUED TRACK AND FIELD

81.

81. Paavo Nurmi leads the field during the running of the murderous 1924 cross-country race that put an end to cross-country as an Olympic event.

82.

82. Ray Ewry, a victim of childhood polio, won eight gold medals in the standing jump events of 1900, 1904, and 1908, and two more in the Intercalated Games of 1906. He is seen here taking off in the standing high jump.

83. Martin Sheridan earned five gold medals and four silver medals in 1904, 1906, and 1908. In this photo he is standing on the pedestal that was used for the Greek-style discus throw of 1908. Sheridan is also credited with shortening Félix Carvajal's pants at the starting line of the 1904 marathon.

83.

WOMEN'S TRACK AND FIELD

84.

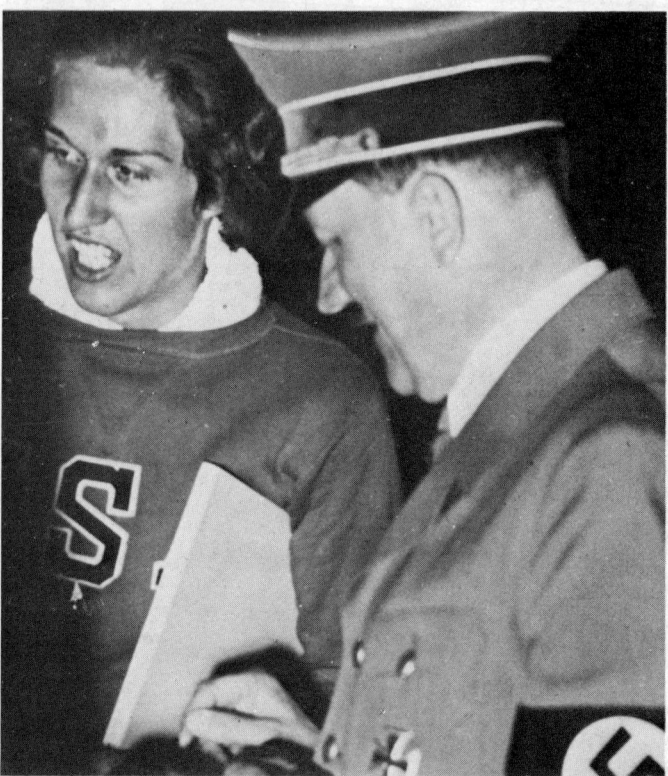

85.

84. What deep, dark secret prevented Stella Walsh from smiling even after she had won the gold medal in the 1932 100-meter dash?

85. Adolf Hitler made advances to Helen Stephens after her victory in the 1936 100 meters, but she turned him down.

86. In 1948 Fanny Blankers-Koen won four of the nine women's track and field events.

86.

87. As a child in rural Tennessee, Wilma Rudolph suffered through polio, double pneumonia, and scarlet fever. Yet she grew up to win three gold medals in 1960, in the 100- and 200-meter dashes and the 4 × 100-meter relay.

88. In 1968 Wyomia Tyus became the only Olympic runner to win the 100-meter dash twice.

87.

88.

89. Between 1964 and 1976 Irena Szewińska earned seven medals in five different events. Here she acknowledges the applause of the crowd after winning the 400 meters in 1976.

90. The 1952 Australian 4 × 100-meter relay team set a world record in their qualifying heat and were on their way to victory in the final, when Winsome Cripps and Marjorie Jackson dropped the baton during the final changeover.

89.

90.

WOMEN'S TRACK AND FIELD

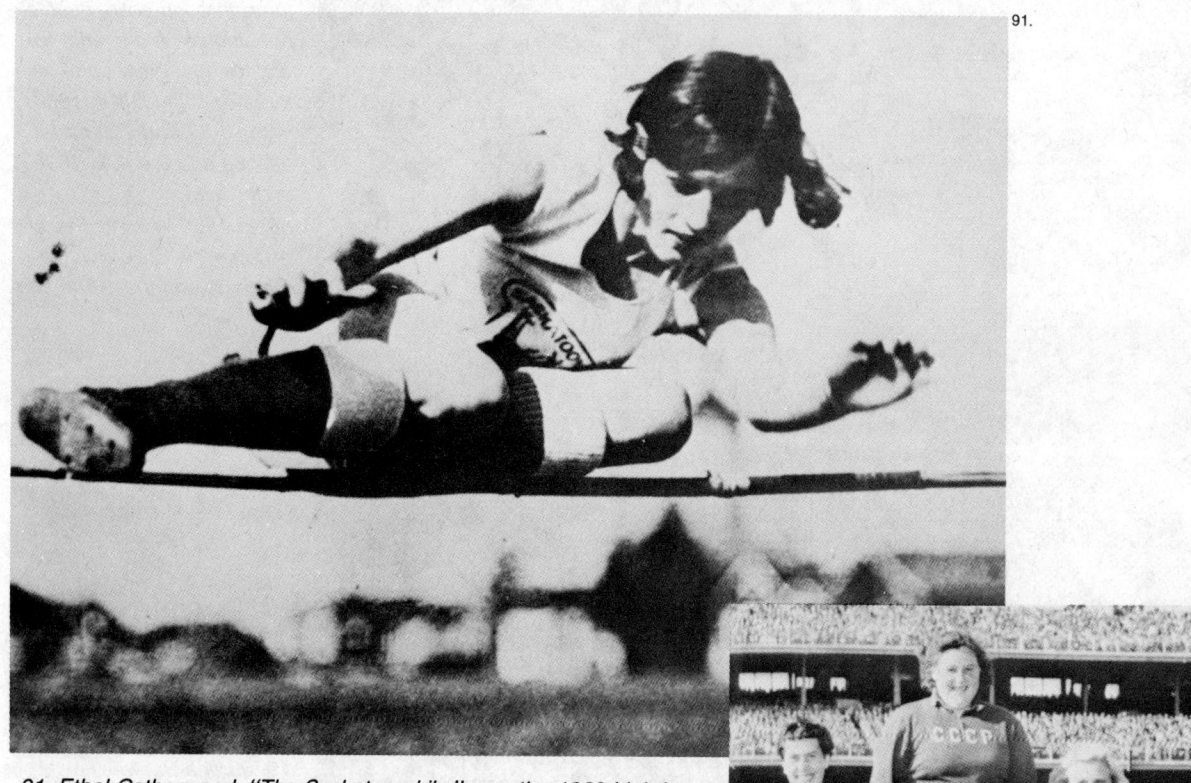

91. Ethel Catherwood, "The Saskatoon Lily," won the 1928 high jump in Amsterdam.

92. The medalists in the 1956 shot put: (left to right) Marianne Werner, Tamara Tyshkevich, and Galina Zybina.

WOMEN OF QUESTIONABLE HORMONAL BALANCE

93. Iolanda Balaş completely dominated the high jump between 1957 and 1967, setting fourteen world records and winning two Olympic gold medals.

94. Tamara Press overwhelmed the opposition in the 1960 and 1964 shot put, but disappeared from international competition when sex tests were introduced.

93.

94.

WOMEN'S TRACK AND FIELD

95.

97.

95. Lia Manoliu, the only track and field athlete to take part in six Olympics, finally won a gold medal on her fifth attempt, in the 1968 discus throw.

96. Babe Didriksen qualified for all five individual women's track and field events in 1932, but was allowed to compete in only three of them. She won the javelin throw and the 80-meter hurdles and set a world record in the high jump, despite being placed second. She was later voted the greatest female athlete of the first half of the twentieth century.

96.

97. Elvira Ozolina, winner of the 1960 javelin throw, was so humiliated at finishing only fifth in 1964 that she shaved off all her hair and refused to wear a scarf to hide her shame.

98. The medalists in the 1972 pentathlon: (left to right) Heidemarie Rosendahl (silver), Mary Peters (gold), and Burglinde Pollak (bronze).

98.

3500-METER WALK

1908 London C: 24, N: 9, D: 7.14.

1. George Larner	GBR	14:55.0
2. Ernest Webb	GBR	15:07.4
3. Harry Kerr	NZE	15:43.4
4. George Goulding	CAN	15:49.8
5. Arthur Rowland	AUS	16:07.0
6. Charles Westergaard	DEN	17:21.8
7. Einar Rothman	SWE	17:50.0

Larner, a 33-year-old Brighton policeman, came out of retirement to take part in the Olympics. He won by 45 yards.

10,000-METER WALK

1912 Stockholm C: 22, N: 11, D: 7.11. WR: 45:15.6 (Ernest Webb)

1. George Goulding	CAN	46:28.4
2. Ernest Webb	GBR	46:50.4
3. Fernando Altimani	ITA	47:37.6
4. Aage Rasmussen	DEN	48:00.0

George Goulding, an English-born Canadian, had competed in the 1908 Olympics as both a walker and a runner, placing fourth in the 3500-meter walk and 22nd in the marathon. In 1912 he kept up such a rapid pace in the 10,000-meter walk that three of the ten finalists dropped out and another three were disqualified for lifting. After his victory, the laconic Canadian sent a telegram to his wife which read simply, "Won—George." Ernest Webb, who earned his third Olympic silver medal, was 40 years old.

1920 Antwerp C: 23, N: 13, D: 8.18. WR: 45:26.4 (Gunnar Rasmussen)

1. Ugo Frigerio	ITA	48:06.2
2. Joseph Pearman	USA	49:40.8 e
3. Charles Gunn	GBR	49:44.4 e
4. Cecil McMaster	SAF	50:02.8 e
5. William Hehir	GBR	50:13.0 e
6. Thomas Maroney	USA	50:20.6 e
7. Joseph Seghers	BEL	—
8. Albert Doyen	BEL	—

Frigerio, as boisterous as ever, won by 250 meters to gain the first of his three gold medals.

1924 Paris C: 23, N: 13, D: 7.13. WR: 45:26.4 (Gunnar Rasmussen)

1. Ugo Frigerio	ITA	47:49.0
2. George Goodwin	GBR	48:37.9
3. Cecil McMaster	SAF	49:08.0
4. Donato Pavesi	ITA	49:17.0
5. Arthur Tell Schwab	SWI	49:50.0
6. Ernest Clarke	GBR	49:59.2 e
7. Armando Valente	ITA	—
8. Luigi Besatra	ITA	—

Frigerio's final gold medal was won by 200 meters.

1928–1936 not held

1948 London C: 19, N: 10, D: 8.7. WR: 42:39.6 (Verner Hardmo)

1. John Mikaelsson	SWE	45:13.2
2. Ingemar Johansson	SWE	45:43.8
3. Fritz Schwab	SWI	46:00.2
4. Charles Morris	GBR	46:04.0
5. Harry Churcher	GBR	46:28.0
6. Emile Maggi	FRA	47:02.8
7. Richard West	GBR	—
8. Giuseppe Dordoni	ITA	—

Mikaelsson set an Olympic record of 45:03.0 in the first round. The final saw the disqualification of the great Verner Hardmo, who set 29 ratified and unratified world records between 1943 and 1945, at distances ranging from 3000 meters to 10 miles.

1952 Helsinki C: 23, N: 12, D: 7.27. WR: 42:39.6 (Verner Hardmo)

1. John Mikaelsson	SWE	45:02.8 OR
2. Fritz Schwab	SWI	45:41.0
3. Bruno Junk	SOV	45:41.0
4. Louis Chevalier	FRA	45:50.4
5. George Coleman	GBR	46:06.8
6. Yvan Yarmysch	SOV	46:07.0
7. Emile Maggi	FRA	46:08.0
8. Bruno Fait	ITA	46:25.6

Mikaelsson was 38 years old when he won his second gold medal. Silver medalist Fritz Schwab was the son of Arthur Schwab, who won the 50-kilometer silver medal in 1936. Both Schwab and Junk began running 30 yards from the finish, making the judges, who had disqualified seven men in the heats and final, look foolish. The controversies which resulted from this race led Olympic officials to drop the 10,000 meters event and replace it with a 20,000 meters contest in 1956.

10-MILE WALK (16,093 METERS)

1908 London C: 25, N: 8, D: 7.17. WR: 1:14:45.0 (J.W. Raby)

1. George Larner	GBR	1:15:57.4
2. Ernest Webb	GBR	1:17:31.0
3. Edward Spencer	GBR	1:21:20.2
4. Frank Carter	GBR	1:21:20.2
5. Ernest Larner	GBR	1:24:26.2

DNF: William Palmer (GBR), Richard Harrison (GBR), Harry Kerr (NZE)

Larner broke the 11-year-old world's amateur record of 1:17:38.4 in winning his second gold medal in four days.

STANDING HIGH JUMP

1900 Paris C: 6, N: 3, D: 7.16. WR: 1.63, 5–4¼ (Raymond Ewry)

		FT.–		
		M	IN.	
1. Raymond Ewry	USA	1.65	5-5	WR
2. Irving Baxter	USA	1.525	5-0	
3. Lewis Sheldon	USA	1.50	4-11	

Ray Ewry won eight Olympic gold medals in 1900, 1904, and 1908, and added two more in the Intercalated Games of 1906. Yet he is almost unknown today because his unprecedented feats were performed in events that are no longer held. Born on October. 18, 1873, in Lafayette, Indiana, Ewry contracted polio as a small boy. Confined to a wheelchair, it was thought that he might be paralyzed for life. However he began exercising on his own, and not only regained the use of his legs, but eventually grew up to be a superb athlete who specialized in the standing jumps. On July 16, 1900, Ewry won three gold medals in Paris, sweeping the standing high jump, the standing long jump, and the standing triple jump. He repeated his sweep in 1904. With the triple jump eliminated from the Games, he had to settle for double victories in 1906 and 1908. The standing jumps were dropped from the Olympics after 1912. Ewry also held the amateur record for the backward standing long jump—9 feet 3 inches. He died on September 27, 1937, at the age of 63.

1904 St. Louis C: 4, N: 1, D: 8.31. WR: 1.65, 5–5 (Raymond Ewry)

		M	FT.–IN.
1. Raymond Ewry	USA	1.60	5-3
2. Joseph Stadler	USA	1.45	4-9
3. Lawson Robertson	USA	1.45	4-9
4. John Biller	USA	1.42	4-8

Joseph Stadler was the first black athlete to win an Olympic medal in a field event. He was awarded second place after a jump-off.

1906 Athens C: 10, N: 6, D: 5.1. WR: 1.65, 5–5 (Raymond Ewry)

		M	FT.–IN.
1. Raymond Ewry	USA	1.56	5-1¼
2. Léon Dupont	BEL	1.40	4-7
2. Lawson Robertson	USA	1.40	4-7
2. Martin Sheridan	USA	1.40	4-7
5. Lajos Gönczy	HUN	1.35	4-5
6. Konstantin Tsiklitiras	GRE	1.30	4-3¼
7. Themistoklis Diakidis	GRE	1.25	4-1¼
7. Paul Weinstein	GER	1.25	4-1¼

1908 London C: 22, N: 11, D: 7.23. WR: 1.65, 5–5 (Raymond Ewry)

		M	FT.–IN.
1. Raymond Ewry	USA	1.575	5-2
2. John Biller	USA	1.55	5-1
2. Constantin Tsiklitiras	GRE	1.55	5-1
4. F. Leroy Holmes	USA	1.525	5-0
5. Platt Adams	USA	1.47	4-10
5. George "Géo" André	FRA	1.47	4-10
5. A. Motté	FRA	1.47	4-10

1912 Stockholm C: 16, N: 8, D: 7.13. WR: 1.65, 5–5 (Raymond Ewry)

		M	FT.–IN.
1. Platt Adams	USA	1.63	5-4¼
2. Benjamin Adams	USA	1.60	5-3
3. Constantin Tsiklitiras	GRE	1.55	5-1
4. Richard Byrd	USA	1.50	4-11
4. Leo Goehring	USA	1.50	4-11
4. Evald Möller	SWE	1.50	4-11

Platt Adams was 27 years old. His brother Ben was 22. In 1980, Rune Alenen of Sweden cleared 6 feet 2¾ inches in the standing high jump.

STANDING LONG JUMP

1900 Paris C: 7, N: 4, D: 7.16.

		M	FT.–IN.
1. Raymond Ewry	USA	3.21	10-6¼
2. Irving Baxter	USA	3.135	10-3¼
3. Emile Torchebouef	FRA	3.03	9-11¼
4. Lewis Sheldon	USA	3.02	9-10¾

1904 St. Louis C: 4, N: 1, D: 9.3.

		M	FT.–IN.	
1. Raymond Ewry	USA	3.476	11-4⅞	WR
2. Charles King	USA	3.28	10-9	
3. John Biller	USA	3.26	10-8¼	
4. Henry Field	USA	3.19	10-5½	

1906 Athens C: 30, N: 10, D: 4.27.

		M	FT.–IN.
1. Raymond Ewry	USA	3.30	10-10
2. Martin Sheridan	USA	3.095	10-1¾
3. Lawson Robertson	USA	3.05	10-0
4. Léon Dupont	BEL	2.975	9-9
5. Axel Ljung	SWE	2.955	9-8¼
6. Istzán Somodi	HUN	2.86	9-4½
7. Constantin Tsiklitiras	GRE	2.84	9-3¾
8. H. Jardin	FRA	2.83	9-3¼
8. Herbert Kerrigan	USA	2.83	9-3¼

1908 London C: 25, N: 11, D: 7.20.

		M	FT.–IN.
1. Raymond Ewry	USA	3.335	10-11¼
2. Constantin Tsiklitiras	GRE	3.235	10-7¼
3. Martin Sheridan	USA	3.23	10-7
4. John Biller	USA	3.215	10-6½
5. Ragnar Ekberg	SWE	3.195	10-5¾
6. Platt Adams	USA	3.11	10-2½
6. F. LeRoy Holmes	USA	3.11	10-2½

1912 Stockholm C: 19, N: 8, D: 7.8.

		M	FT.–IN.
1. Constantin Tsiklitiras	GRE	3.37	11-0¾
2. Platt Adams	USA	3.36	11-0¼
3. Benjamin Adams	USA	3.28	10-9
4. Gustaf Malmsten	SWE	3.20	10-6
5. Leo Goehring	USA	3.14	10-3½
5. Evald Möller	SWE	3.14	10-3½
7. András Baronyi	HUN	3.13	10-3¼
8. Richard Byrd	USA	3.12	10-2¾

In 1962 Johan Evandt of Norway performed a standing long jump of 11 feet 11¾ inches. The claims of professional jumpers are difficult to substantiate. Joe Darby of Great Britain was said to have jumped 12 feet 1½ inches on May 28, 1890, and W. Barker was reputed to have leaped 12 feet 6½ inches in May 1904.

STANDING TRIPLE JUMP

1900 Paris C: 10, N: 4, D: 7.16.

		M	FT.–IN.
1. Raymond Ewry	USA	10.58	34-8½
2. Irving Baxter	USA	9.95	32-7¾
3. Robert Garrett	USA	9.50	31-2
4. Lewis Sheldon	USA	9.45	31-0

1904 St. Louis C: 4, N: 1, D: 9.3.

		M	FT.–IN.
1. Raymond Ewry	USA	10.54	34-7¼
2. Charles King	USA	10.16	33-4
3. Joseph Stadler	USA	9.60	31-6
4. Garrett Serviss	USA	9.53	31-3¼

STONE THROW

(6.40 kg — 14.08 lbs.)

1906 Athens C: 15, N: 8, D: 4.27.

		M	FT.–IN.
1. Nicolaos Georgantas	GRE	19.925	65-4½
2. Martin Sheridan	USA	19.035	62-5½
3. Michel Dorizas	GRE	18.585	60-11¾
4. Eric Lemming	SWE	18.21	59-9

The American favorite, James Mitchell, was unable to compete because he had suffered a dislocated shoulder when the ship carrying the U.S. team to Europe was hit by a large wave.

SHOT PUT (BOTH HANDS)

1912 Stockholm C: 7, N: 4, D: 7.11.

		M	TWO HANDS	FT.–IN.
1. Ralph Rose	USA	27.70	(15.23 + 12.47)	90-10½
2. Patrick McDonald	USA	27.53	(15.08 + 12.45)	90-4
3. Elmer Niklander	FIN	27.14	(14.71 + 12.43)	89-0½
4. Lawrence Whitney	USA	24.09	(13.48 + 10.61)	79-0½
5. Einar Nilsson	SWE	23.37	(12.52 + 10.85)	76-8¼
6. Paavo Aho	FIN	23.30	(12.72 + 10.58)	76-5½
7. M. Megherian	TUR	19.78	(10.85 + 8.93)	64-10¾

The current world record for this event is 121 feet 6¾ inches, set by Al Feuerbach on August 24, 1974. He put 70 feet 1¾ inches with his right hand and 51 feet 5 inches with his left.

56-POUND WEIGHT THROW

(25.4 kg)

1904 St. Louis C: 6, N: 2, D: 9.1.

		M	FT.–IN.
1. Étienne Desmarteau	CAN	10.46	34-4
2. John Flanagan	USA	10.16	33-4
3. James Mitchell	USA	10.13	33-3
4. Charles Henneman	USA	9.18	30-1½
5. Charles Chadwick	USA	—	—
6. Ralph Rose	USA	8.53	28-0 e

Refused a leave of absence from his job as a Montreal policeman to compete in the St. Louis Games, Étienne Desmarteau went anyway and was fired. When it was learned that he had won a gold medal, his dismissal notice was conveniently lost. Unfortunately, Desmarteau, who was Canada's first Olympic champion, died of typhoid the following year at the age of 32. A park was named in his honor.

1906–1912 not held

1920 Antwerp C: 6, N: 4, D: 8.21. WR: 12.36, 40–6¾ (Matthew McGrath)

		M	FT–IN.	
1. Patrick McDonald	USA	11.265	36-11½	OR
2. Patrick Ryan	USA	10.965	35-11½	
3. Carl Johan Lind	SWE	10.25	33-7½	
4. Archie McDiarmid	CAN	10.12	33-2½	
5. Malcolm Svensson	SWE	9.45	31-0	
6. Petter Pettersson	FIN	9.37	30-9	

McDonald is the oldest person ever to win an Olympic track and field gold medal. He was 42 years and 26 days old.

DISCUS (GREEK-STYLE)

1906 Athens C: 21, N: 9, D: 5.1.

		M	FT.–IN.
1. Werner Järvinen	FIN	35.17	115-4½
2. Nicolaos Georgantas	GRE	32.80	107-7
3. István Mudin	HUN	31.91	104-8½
4. Martin Sheridan	USA	—	—

Contestants threw the discus from a pedestal that sloped forward, and they were required to follow a restricted set of movements. The discus had to be released from a standing position, with no spinning allowed. Werner Järvinen had four sons, three of whom competed in the 1932 Olympics.

1908 London C: 24, N: 9, D: 7.18.

		M	FT.–IN.	
1. Martin Sheridan	USA	38.00	124-8	OR
2. Marquis Horr	USA	37.33	122-5½	
3. Werner Järvinen	FIN	36.48	119-8¼	
4. Arthur Dearborn	USA	35.65	116-11½	
5. Michel Dorizas	GRE	33.35	109-4½	
6. Nicolaos Georgantas	GRE	33.20	108-11¼	
7. István Mudin	HUN	33.11	108-7½	
8. W.G. Burroughs	USA	32.73	107-4¾	

DISCUS (BOTH HANDS)

1912 Stockholm C: 20, N: 6, D: 7.13.

		M	TWO HANDS	FT.–IN.
1. Armas Taipale	FIN	82.86	(44.68 + 38.18)	271-10
2. Elmer Niklander	FIN	77.96	(40.28 + 37.68)	255-9
3. Emil Magnusson	SWE	77.37	(40.58 + 36.79)	253-10
4. Einar Nilsson	SWE	71.40	(40.99 + 30.41)	234-3
5. James Duncan	USA	71.13	(39.78 + 31.35)	233-4½
6. Emil Muller	USA	69.56	(39.83 + 29.73)	229-2
7. Folke Fleetwood	SWE	68.22	(34.20 + 33.82)	223-10
8. Carl Johan Lind	SWE	68.02	(34.98 + 32.12)	223-2

JAVELIN (FREESTYLE)

1908 London C: 31, N: 9, D: 7.15. WR: 54.92, 180–2 (Eric Lemming)

		M	FT.–IN.
1. Eric Lemming	SWE	54.45	178-7½
2. Michel Dorizas	GRE	51.36	168-6
3. Arne Halse	NOR	49.73	163-1¾
4. Charalambos Zouras	GRE	48.61	159-5¾
5. Hugo Wieslander	SWE	47.55	156-0
6. Armas Pesonen	FIN	46.04	151-0½
7. Imre Mudin	HUN	45.95	150-9
8. Jalmari Sauli	FIN	43.31	142-1

Since all of the successful throwers held the javelin in the middle, just as they did in the regular javelin event, the freestyle javelin was quickly dropped from the Olympics.

JAVELIN (BOTH HANDS)

1912 Stockholm C: 14, N: 4, D: 7.9.

		M	TWO HANDS	FT.–IN.
1. Juho Julius Saaristo	FIN	109.42	(61.00 WR + 48.42)	359-0
2. Väino Siikaniemi	FIN	101.13	(54.09 WR + 47.04)	331-9½
3. Urho Peltonen	FIN	100.24	(53.58 WR + 46.66)	328-10
4. Eric Lemming	SWE	98.59	(58.33 WR + 40.26)	323-5½
5. Arne Halse	NOR	96.92	(55.05 WR + 41.87)	318-0
6. Richard Åbrink	SWE	93.12	(50.04 WR + 43.08)	305-6
7. D. Johansen	NOR	92.82	(48.78 WR + 44.04)	304-6
8. Otto Nilsson	SWE	88.90	(50.21 WR + 38.69)	291-8

When Finnish officials realized that all three finalists were from Finland, they decided to cancel the final round and let the preliminary results stand.

TRIATHLON

1904 St. Louis C: 118, N: 4, D: 7.1–2.

		PTS.	LJ	SP	100 YARDS
1. Max Emmerich	USA	35.7	21-7	32-2¼	10.6
2. John Grieb	USA	34.0	20-2¼	33-7	11.0
3. William Merz	USA	33.9	19-10¾	31-1	10.8
4. George Mayer	USA	32.4	18-1	36-7	11.4
5. John Bissinger	USA	30.8	18-4¾	32-9½	11.4
6. Phillip Kassel	USA	30.1	19-2¼	28-9½	11.2
7. Christian Busch	GER	30.0	18-10¾	31-3½	11.6
7. Fred Schmind	USA	30.0	19-4¾	30-2¼	11.6

This event was part of a combined gymnastics and track and field competition known as "turning" or "turnverein gymnastics."

PENTATHLON

Unlike the decathlon, the pentathlon was decided according to placement points. After the first three events, all but the top 12 athletes were eliminated. After the fourth event, only the top six could continue. Oddly enough, despite these rules, seven men competed in the final event in 1912, 1920, and 1924. In 1912, it was the result of a tie; in 1920, it was due to a controversy concerning the eligibility of Hugo Lahtinen; and in 1924 it was because of a mistake in computing the point total of Göran Unger. Ties in the final places were decided according to the decathlon tables.

1906 Athens C: 26, N: 10, D: 4.27.
(Standing Long Jump, Greek-Style Discus, 192-Meter Race, Javelin, Greco-Roman Wrestling)

		PTS.
1. Hjalmar Mellander	SWE	24
2. István Mudin	HUN	25
3. Erik Lemming	SWE	29
4. Uno Häggman (Tuomela)	FIN	34
5. Lawson Roberston	USA	36
6. Knut Lindberg	SWE	37
7. E.B. Archibald	CAN	—
8. J. Wagner	GER	—

The events of the 1906 pentathlon were the same as those of the ancient Greek pentathlon.

1908 not held

1912 Stockholm C: 26, N: 11, D: 7.7.

		LJ		JAV		200M		DISC		1500M		TOTAL PTS.
1. James Thorpe	USA	7.07	(1)	46.71	(3)	22.9	(1)	35.75	(1)	4:44.8	(1)	7
2. Ferdinand Bie	NOR	6.85	(2)	46.45	(4)	23.5	(5)	31.79	(4)	5:07.8	(6)	21
3. James Donahue	USA	6.83	(3)	38.28	(10)	23.0	(2)	29.64	(11)	4:51.0	(3)	29
4. Frank Lukeman	CAN	6.45	(6)	36.02	(11)	23.2	(4)	33.76	(3)	5:00.2	(5)	29
5. James Menaul	USA	6.40	(8)	35.85	(12)	23.0	(2)	31.38	(6)	4:49.6	(2)	30
6. Avery Brundage	USA	6.58	(4)	42.85	(7)	24.2	(11)	34.72	(2)	—	(7)	32
7. Hugo Wieslander	SWE	6.27	(10)	49.56	(1)	24.1	(10)	30.74	(7)	4:51.1	(4)	32

1920 Antwerp C: 16, N: 6, D: 8.6.

		LJ		JAV		200M		DISC		1500M		TOTAL PTS.
1. Eero Lehtonen	FIN	6.635	(2)	54.67	(2)	23.0	(1)	34.64	(7)	4:40.2	(2)	14
2. Everett Bradley	USA	6.61	(3)	49.16	(8)	23.0	(1)	36.78	(6)	5:10.0	(6)	24
3. Hugo Lahtinen	FIN	6.59	(4)	54.25	(3)	23.6	(5)	31.12	(13)	4:36.0	(1)	26
4. Robert LeGendre	USA	6.505	(5)	44.60	(11)	23.0	(1)	37.39	(4)	4:46.0	(5)	26
5. Helge Lövland	NOR	6.32	(7)	53.13	(4)	24.0	(10)	39.51	(2)	4:45.8	(4)	27
6. Brutus Hamilton	USA	6.86	(1)	48.36	(10)	23.4	(4)	37.13	(5)	5:12.8	(7)	27
7. Robert Olsson	SWE	6.27	(9)	43.68	(12)	23.6	(5)	39.80	(1)	4:42.8	(3)	30
8. Alexander Klumberg	EST	6.25	(10)	60.76	(1)	25.3	(15)	38.62	(3)	—		—

1924 Paris C: 0, N: 17, D: 7.7.

		LJ		JAV		200M		DISC		1500M		TOTAL PTS.
1. Eero Lehtonen	FIN	6.68	(7)	50.93	(4)	23.0	(1)	40.44	(1)	4:47.1	(1)	14
2. Elemér Somfay	HUN	6.77	(5)	52.07	(2)	23.4	(5)	37.76	(2)	4:48.4	(2)	16
3. Robert LeGendre	USA	7.765	(1)	48.04	(9)	23.0	(1)	36.76	(4)	4:52.6	(3)	18
4. Leo Leino	FIN	6.72	(6)	54.12	(1)	23.2	(4)	33.62	(8)	4:55.4	(4)	23
5. Morton Kaer	USA	6.96	(2)	50.20	(5)	23.0	(1)	32.70	(10)	5:38.6	(6)	24
6. Hugo Lahtinen	FIN	6.895	(3)	48.66	(7)	23.6	(7)	36.08	(5)	4:55.6	(5)	27
7. Brutus Hamilton	USA	6.83	(4)	48.96	(8)	24.25	(18)	37.70	(3)	—		—
8. Göran Unger	SWE	6.56	(8)	48.45	(10)	23.45	(8)	35.11	(6)	—		—

The highlight of this competition was the surprising world record of 25 feet 5¾ inches set in the long jump by Robert LeGendre of Georgetown University. First place was not decided until Lehtonen edged Somfay in the 1500 meters.

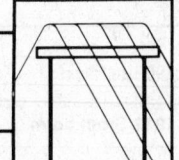

TRACK AND FIELD

WOMEN

100 METERS

1896–1924 not held

1928 Amsterdam C: 31, N: 13, D: 7.31. WR: 12.2 (Elizabeth Robinson)
1. Elizabeth Robinson   USA   12.2   EWR
2. Fanny Rosenfeld   CAN   12.3
3. Ethel Smith   CAN   12.3
4. Erna Steinberg   GER   12.4
DISQ: Myrtle Cook (CAN), Helene "Leni" Schmidt (GER)

This was the first women's track and field event to be contested in the Olympics, so the entrants were unusually nervous, as was the primarily male audience. The men found it particularly unsettling when the three Canadian finalists hugged and kissed each other before the race. First Cook and then Schmidt were disqualified for false-starting twice. The winner, Betty Robinson, was a 16-year-old high school student from Riverdale, Illinois. Three years later she was badly injured in a plane crash, suffering a concussion, a broken leg, a crushed arm, and a severe cut across her forehead and eyelid. She was unconscious for seven weeks and was unable to walk normally for two years. However, she regained the use of her leg, returned to competitive running, and won another gold medal in 1936 as a member of the U.S. 4 × 100-meter relay team.

1932 Los Angeles C: 20, N: 10, D: 8.2. WR: 11.9 (Tollien Schuurman)
1. Stanislawa Walasiewicz   POL   11.9   EWR
2. Hilde Strike   CAN   11.9
3. Wilhelmina Von Bremen   USA   12.0
4. Marie Dollinger   GER   12.2
5. Eileen Hiscock   GBR   12.3
6. Elizabeth Wilde   USA   —

Stanislawa Walasiewicz was born in Rypin, Poland, on April 11, 1911. When she was still an infant her family moved to the United States and settled in Cleveland, Ohio, where she grew up and became known as Stella Walsh. On May 30, 1930, she became the first woman to break the 11-second barrier for 100 yards. By 1932 U.S. track enthusiasts were looking forward to a gold medal from her in the Olympics. But Stella Walsh had a problem: as a result of the worldwide depression, her job with the New York Central Railroad had been eliminated. She was offered a position with the Cleveland Recreation Department, but taking it would have made her ineligible for the Olympics, since Olympic regulations at the time disqualified athletes who made their living from physical education or recreation. With no help forthcoming from her adopted country, Stella Walsh made a major decision in her life. Twenty-four hours before she was scheduled to take out U.S. naturalization papers, she accepted a job offer from the Polish consulate in New York and decided to compete for Poland.

Stella Walsh's performance in Los Angeles was no disappointment. Running with what the Canadian official report called "long man-like strides," Stella Walsh equaled Tollien Schuurman's two-month-old world record in every one of her three races. In the final she was hard-pressed by Hilde Strike, but managed to win by half a yard. While some U.S. observers pointed to the loss of Walsh to Poland as an example of the consequences of the lack of support for women's athletics in the U.S., there were also those who held a grudge against Walsh herself, and she was not granted her naturalization papers until 1947.

1936 Berlin C: 30, N: 15, D: 8.4. WR: 11.6 (Helen Stephens)

1. Helen Stephens	USA	11.5	w
2. Stanislawa Walasiewicz	POL	11.7	
3. Käthe Krauss	GER	11.9	
4. Marie Dollinger	GER	12.0	
5. Annette Rogers	USA	12.2	
6. Emmy Albus	GER	12.3	

Helen Stephens was a 6-foot farm girl from Calloway County, Missouri, who loved to run. When she entered Fulton High School she was routinely timed in the 50-yard dash. Coach Burton Moore was astounded to discover that Stephens had run the race in 5.8 seconds, equaling the existing world record held by Betty Robinson. Moore taught Stephens the various events of track and field and then entered her in the 1935 national A.A.U. meet, which was being held in St. Louis. Wearing a borrowed sweatshirt and shoes, she won the shot put, set a world record in the 200 meters, and set another world record in the standing long jump. But the real sensation came when she beat Stella Walsh in the 50-yard dash, this time officially tying the world record. Walsh was outraged by such impudence and referred to Stephens as a "greenie from the sticks." When Stephens and Walsh met again in the Olympics in Berlin there was never any question as to who would take the gold medal. In the opening round Helen Stephens ran a wind-aided 11.4 to win her heat by ten yards. She ran wind-aided 11.5s in the semifinals and final, finishing the latter two yards ahead of Stella Walsh. After the race, Stephens was taken to meet Adolf Hitler in his private glass-enclosed box. "Hitler comes in and gives me the Nazi salute," she later recalled. "I gave him a good old Missouri handshake. He shook my hand, put his arm around me, pinched me, and invited me to spend a weekend with him." She declined.

After only two and a half years of competition, Helen Stephens retired from amateur athletics with an undefeated record in running events. For a while she made a living playing basketball and softball and then served as a marine during World War II. Later she worked until retirement for the Defense Mapping Agency Aerospace Center in St. Louis.

The rivalry between Helen Stephens and Stella Walsh had an ironic and long-delayed ending. After Stephens' victory in Berlin, a Polish journalist accused her of actually being a man, and German officials were forced to issue a statement that they had given her a sex check and that she

had passed. Forty-four years later, on December 4, 1980, Stella Walsh went to a discount store in Cleveland to buy streamers for a reception for the Polish national basketball team. In the parking lot she got caught in the middle of a robbery attempt and was shot to death. When an autopsy was performed afterward, it turned out that although Helen Stephens may not have had male sexual organs, Stella Walsh did. All the while that Walsh had been setting 11 world records, winning 41 A.A.U. titles and two Olympic medals, she was, in fact, a man.

1948 London C: 38, N: 21, D: 8.2. WR: 11.5 (Helen Stephens)

1. Francina "Fanny" Blankers-Koen	HOL	11.9
2. Dorothy Manley	GBR	12.2
3. Shirley Strickland	AUS	12.2
4. Viola Myers	CAN	—
5. Patricia Jones	CAN	—
6. Cynthia Thompson	JAM	—

Fanny Koen was 18 years old when she was chosen to join the Dutch team for the 1936 Olympics in Berlin. She tied for sixth place in the high jump and was part of the 4×100-meter relay team that finished fifth. The highlight of the games for her was when she got Jesse Owens' autograph. When the Olympics resumed after a 12-year break, Fanny was the holder of six world records—in the 100 yards, the 80-meter hurdles, the high jump, the long jump, and in two relays. In the interim she had also married her coach, Jan Blankers, and given birth to two children. At 30 years of age she was thought by some to be too old to win the Olympic sprints, despite her string of records. She quieted her critics almost immediately by recording the best time of the opening round (12.0), in the 100-meter dash. She went on to win the final in the mud by three yards. Later in the week she also won gold medals in the 80-meter hurdles, the 200 meters, and the 4×100-meter relay. Of the nine women's track and field events included in the 1948 Olympics, Fanny Blankers-Koen won four of them. If she had entered the long jump she probably would have won that too, considering that the winning jump was 20 inches shorter than Fanny's world record. When she returned to Amsterdam she was driven through the crowded streets in an open carriage drawn by four gray horses. Her neighbors gave her a bicycle, "so she won't have to run so much."

1952 Helsinki C: 56, N: 27, D: 7.22. WR: 11.5 (Helen Stephens, Francina "Fanny" Blankers-Koen)

1. Marjorie Jackson	AUS	11.5	EWR
2. Daphne Hasenjager (Robb)	SAF	11.8	
3. Shirley Strickland	AUS	11.9	
4. Winsome Cripps	AUS	11.9	
5. Maria Sander	GER	12.0	
6. Mae Faggs	USA	12.1	

British fans, who had been looking forward to the playing of "God Save the Queen" following the victory of Marjorie Jackson, whom they considered a British subject, were stunned when what they heard instead was "Advance Australia Fair." Back home in Australia, the residents of Jackson's hometown of Lithgow welcomed her with a 250-pound cake to help her break training.

1956 Melbourne C: 34, N: 16, D: 11.26. WR: 11.3 (Shirley Strickland)

1. Betty Cuthbert	AUS	11.5
2. Christa Stubnick	GDR	11.7
3. Marlene Matthews	AUS	11.7
4. Isabelle Daniels	USA	11.8
5. Giuseppina Leone	ITA	11.9
6. Heather Armitage	GBR	12.0

Eighteen-year-old Betty Cuthbert broke the Olympic record in the first round with an 11.4. In the semifinals she was beaten by Stubnick, but in the final she led from start to finish to win by five feet. Betty Cuthbert was as unassuming a heroine as one could hope for. In her autobiography, *Golden Girl,* she wrote, "I broke the tape in 11.5s just like in any other race and there seemed nothing special about it. I couldn't realize then just what I had done and even later, when the telegrams, letters, honours, victory functions and the like started, I was too shy and self-conscious fully to appreciate it.... However, at the time, Mum must have realized what I had done because I looked up in the crowd just after the race was over and saw her crying her eyes out." Four days later Cuthbert won the 200-meter dash and then earned another gold medal as part of the Australian 4×100-meter relay team.

1960 Rome C: 31, N: 18, D: 9.2. WR: 11.3 (Shirley Strickland, Vyera Krepkina)

1. Wilma Rudolph	USA	11.0	w
2. Dorothy Hyman	GBR	11.3	
3. Giuseppina Leone	ITA	11.3	
4. Maria Itkina	SOV	11.4	
5. Catherine Capdeville	FRA	11.5	
6. Jennifer Smart	GBR	12.0	

Wilma Rudolph was born in rural Tennessee on June 23, 1940, the 20th of her father's 22 children. She was born prematurely and weighed only 4½ pounds at birth. She suffered through polio, double pneumonia, and scarlet fever, which caused her to lose the use of her left leg. From the age of 6 she wore a brace. Her mother learned from doctors that rubbing her daughter's leg might help, so each day Wilma received four leg rubs from her brothers, sisters, and mother. Eventually she graduated from a brace to an orthopedic shoe and she joined her brothers playing basketball whenever she could. When Wilma was 11, her mother returned home one day to find her daughter playing basketball barefooted, having thrown away her corrective shoes. By the time she was 16, Wilma had developed into a star runner and had qualified for the U.S. Olympic team. In Melbourne in 1956 she was eliminated in the first round of the 200 meters, but earned a bronze medal running the third leg of the U.S. 4×100-meter relay team. The

same day that she returned from Australia to her home town of Clarksville, Tennessee, she played for her high school's basketball team.

Four years later, the 5-foot 11-inch Rudolph, now a member of the Tennessee State University "Tigerbelles," went to the Rome Olympics as the favorite to succeed Betty Cuthbert as the world's fastest woman. She dominated the competition from the beginning. She actually fell asleep while waiting for her semifinal heat. Well-rested, she swept to a three-yard victory, equaling the world record of 11.3. She won the final by the same wide margin and was clocked in 11.0. However her time was not accepted as a world record because the wind was 2.752 meters per second—above the acceptable limit of 2 meters per second. She went on to match Betty Cuthbert's triple gold by winning the 200 meters and the 4×100-meter relay.

1964 Tokyo C: 44, N: 27, D: 10.16. WR: 11.2 (Wilma Rudolph)

1. Wyomia Tyus	USA	11.4
2. Edith McGuire	USA	11.6
3. Ewa Klobukowska	POL	11.6
4. Marilyn White	USA	11.6
5. Miguelina Cobián	CUB	11.7
6. Marilyn Black	AUS	11.7
7. Halina Górecka	POL	11.8
8. Dorothy Hyman	GBR	11.9

Until the Olympics, 19-year-old Wyomia Tyus of Griffin, Georgia, had been overshadowed by her Tennessee State teammate Edith McGuire. But in Tokyo, Tyus improved her personal best from 11.5 to 11.2 to equal Wilma Rudolph's world record in the second round. She won the final handily by two yards. Bronze medalist Klobukowska was later the subject of much controversy. On September 15, 1967, she was barred from international competition after she failed a sex chromosome test. Although she passed a visual examination she was subsequently stripped of all her records.

1968 Mexico City C: 41, N: 20, D: 10.15. WR: 11.1 (Irena Szewińska [Kirszenstein], Wyomia Tyus, Barbara Ferrell, Lyudmila Samotyosova, Margarett Bailes)

1. Wyomia Tyus	USA	11.0	WR
2. Barbara Ferrell	USA	11.1	
3. Irena Szewińska (Kirszenstein)	POL	11.1	
4. Raelene Boyle	AUS	11.1	
5. Margaret Bailes	USA	11.3	
6. Dianne Burge	AUS	11.4	
7. Chi Cheng	TAI	11.5	
8. Miguelina Cobián	CUB	11.6	

Competition was particularly stiff in 1968. In the first round, all three Americans, Tyus, Bailes, and Ferrell, equaled the Olympic record of 11.2. The second round saw Ferrell and Szewińska tie the world record of 11.1, while Wyomia Tyus ran a wind-aided 11.0. The semifinals, run in the rain, were won by Szewińska and Tyus, as co-world record holder Lyudmila Samotyosova was eliminated. The final matched four of the five world record holders. After false-starting once, Tyus won a clear victory to become the first runner, male or female, to win an Olympic sprint title twice in a row.

1972 C: 47, N: 33, D: 9.2. WR: 11.0 (Wyomia Tyus, Chi Cheng, Renate Stecher, Ellen Stropahl, Eva Gleskova)
1. Renate Stecher	GDR	11.07
2. Raelene Boyle	AUS	11.23
3. Silvia Chibás	CUB	11.24
4. Iris Davis	USA	11.32
5. Annegret Richter	GER	11.38
6. Alice Annum	GHA	11.41
7. Barbara Ferrell	USA	11.45
8. Eva Gleskova	CZE	12.48

Although 17-year-old Silvia Chibás recorded the fastest times of the first two rounds (11.18 and 11.22), there was never any doubt that Stecher would win the gold.

1976 Montreal C: 39, N: 22, D: 7.25. WR: 10.8 (Renate Stecher, Annegret Richter); 11.04 (Inge Helten)
1. Annegret Richter	GER	11.08
2. Renate Stecher	GDR	11.13
3. Inge Helten	GER	11.17
4. Raelene Boyle	AUS	11.23
5. Evelyn Ashford	USA	11.24
6. Chandra Cheeseborough	USA	11.31
7. Andrea Lynch	GBR	11.32
8. Marlies Oelsner	GDR	11.34

Richter defeated Stecher 11.19 to 11.21 in heat number 6 of the first round. In the second round she ran an impressive 11.05. The next day she set a world record of 11.01 in the semifinals, before leading a German sweep in the final. Less than a yard separated the three medalists at the finish.

1980 Moscow C: 40, N: 25, D: 7.26. WR: 10.87 (Marlies Göhr)
1. Lyudmila Kondratyeva	SOV	11.06
2. Marlies Göhr	GDR	11.07
3. Ingrid Auerswald	GDR	11.14
4. Linda Haglund	SWE	11.16
5. Romy Müller	GDR	11.16
6. Kathryn Smallwood	GBR	11.28
7. Chantal Rega	FRA	11.32
8. Heather Hunte	GBR	11.34

Haglund led at the halfway mark, but Kondratyeva and Göhr stormed by her after 60 meters. Göhr edged ahead with a few meters to go, but Kondratyeva came back and, despite pulling a hamstring muscle at the finish, won by the smallest margin imaginable.

200 METERS

1896–1936 not held

1948 London C: 33, N: 17, D: 8.6. WR: 23.6 (Stanislawa Walasiewicz)
1. Francina "Fanny" Blankers-Koen	HOL	24.4
2. Audrey Williamson	GBR	25.1
3. Audrey Patterson	USA	25.2
4. Shirley Strickland	AUS	—
5. Margaret Walker	GBR	—
6. Daphne Robb	SAF	—

Fanny Blankers-Koen had already won two gold medals in the 100-meter dash and the 80-meter hurdles. Far from being exuberant about these accomplishments, she felt tremendous pressure to win a third gold medal and was close to a mental breakdown. Prior to the semifinals of the 200 meters she told her husband, Jan, that she wanted to withdraw. Jan tried to calm her down and gave her words of encouragement, but to no avail. In desperation he evoked memories of her parents and her two children, and she burst into tears. When she finally came out of her cry, she had recovered and was once again eager to run. She went out and won her heat by six yards, establishing an Olympic record of 24.3 seconds. The next day, running on a muddy track, she won the final by seven yards, the largest margin ever recorded in the women's 200 meters.

1952 Helsinki C: 38, N: 21, D: 7.26. WR: 23.6 (Stanislawa Walasiewicz)
1. Marjorie Jackson	AUS	23.7
2. Bertha Brouwer	HOL	24.2
3. Nadezhda Khnykina	SOV	24.2
4. Winsome Cripps	AUS	24.2
5. Helga Klein	GER	24.6
6. Daphne Hasenjager (Robb)	SAF	24.6

The longest-lasting women's track and field world record ever was set by Stanislawa Walasiewicz on August 15, 1935, when she/he ran the 200 meters in 23.6 seconds. Almost 17 years later, Marjorie Jackson tied that record in the first round of the 1952 Helsinki Olympics, and in the first semifinal she ran a 23.4 to finally break it. In the final she reached the tape four yards ahead of her nearest rival.

1956 Melbourne C: 27, N: 12, D: 11.30. WR: 23.2 (Betty Cuthbert)
1. Betty Cuthbert	AUS	23.4	EOR
2. Christa Stubnick	GDR	23.7	
3. Marlene Matthews	AUS	23.8	
4. Norma Croker	AUS	24.0	
5. June Paul (Foulds)	GBR	24.3	
6. Gisela Köhler	GDR	24.3	

For the first and only time in Olympic history, the medalists in the two sprints (100 and 200 meters) finished in the exact same order.

1960 Rome C: 29, N: 17, D: 9.5. WR: 22.9 (Wilma Rudolph)
1. Wilma Rudolph	USA	24.0
2. Jutta Heine	GER	24.4
3. Dorothy Hyman	GBR	24.7
4. Maria Itkina	SOV	24.7
5. Barbara Janiszewska	POL	24.8
6. Giuseppina Leone	ITA	24.9

Wilma Rudolph dominated the event, setting an Olympic record of 23.2 in her opening heat. Silver medalist Jutta

Heine was the daughter of a millionaire, while the father of bronze medalist Dorothy Hyman was a Yorkshire miner.

1964 Tokyo C: 29, N: 21, D: 10.19. WR: 22.9 (Wilma Rudolph, Margaret Burvill)

1.	Edith McGuire	USA	23.0 OR
2.	Irena Kirszenstein	POL	23.1
3.	Marilyn Black	AUS	23.1
4.	Una Morris	JAM	23.5
5.	Lyudmila Samotyosova	SOV	23.5
6.	Barbara Sobotta (Janiszewska)	POL	23.9
7.	Janet Simpson	GBR	23.9
8.	Daphne Arden	GBR	24.0

1968 Mexico City C: 36, N: 21, D: 10.18. WR: 22.7 (Irena Szewińska [Kirszenstein])

1.	Irena Szewińska (Kirszenstein)	POL	22.5 WR
2.	Raelene Boyle	AUS	22.7
3.	Jennifer Lamy	AUS	22.8
4.	Barbara Ferrell	USA	22.9
5.	Nicole Montandon	FRA	23.0
6.	Wyomia Tyus	USA	23.0
7.	Margaret Bailes	USA	23.1
8.	Jutta Stöck	GER	23.2

Irena Kirszenstein was born in Leningrad to Polish parents on May 24, 1946. Beginning in 1964 she competed in five Olympics, winning seven medals in five different events. As an 18-year-old at the 1964 Tokyo Olympics she finished second in the long jump and the 200 meters and ran the second leg on the Polish 4×100-meter relay team, which scored an upset victory. In 1967 she culminated a five-year courtship by marrying Janusz Szewińsk, and when she arrived in Mexico City for the 1968 Olympics she was running under the name Irena Szewińska. She was disappointed in her first two events, failing to qualify for the final of the long jump and finishing third in the 100 meters, but in the final of the 200 meters she overcame a slow start to win in world record time.

Most people attribute the plethora of world records which were set in Mexico City to the altitude, but another factor was the unusual method that the Mexicans used for determining wind conditions. With the acceptable limit for world records set at a wind speed of 2 meters per second, the measurement during the women's 200 meters was exactly 2 m.p.s. The same recording of exactly 2.0 m.p.s. was registered when Bob Beamon made his famous 29-foot 2½-inch leap and when Nelson Prudencio and Viktor Saneyev set world records in the triple jump.

1972 Munich C: 37, N: 27, D: 9.7. WR: 22.4 (Chi Cheng)

1.	Renate Stecher	GDR	22.40 EWR
2.	Raelene Boyle	AUS	22.45
3.	Irena Szewińska (Kirszenstein)	POL	22.74
4.	Ellen Stropahl	GDR	22.75
5.	Christina Heinich	GDR	22.89
6.	Annegret Kroniger	GER	22.89
7.	Alice Annum	GHA	22.99
8.	Rosie Allwood	JAM	23.11

Between August 1970 and June 1974, Renate Stecher won 90 straight outdoor races at 100 meters and 200 meters.

1976 Montreal C: 36, N: 21, D: 7.28. WR: 22.21 (Irena Szewińska [Kirszenstein])

1.	Bärbel Eckert	GDR	22.37 OR
2.	Annegret Richter	GER	22.39
3.	Renate Stecher	GDR	22.47
4.	Carla Bodendorf	GDR	22.64
5.	Inge Helten	GER	22.68
6.	Tatyana Prorochenko	GBR	23.03
7.	Denise Robertson	AUS	23.05
8.	Chantal Rega	FRA	23.09

The first shock came in the semifinals, when five-time sprint finalist Raelene Boyle was disqualified for false-starting twice. Boyle was furious and protested unsuccessfully. The electronic starting device had registered a clean start the first time, but the recall judge claimed that Boyle's shoulders had been moving. Unaware that she had actually been charged with a false start rather than a mere warning, Boyle was stunned when she was disqualified after her next false start. The real surprise was 21-year-old Bäerbel Eckert, East Germany's third-string sprinter. In the quarterfinals she equaled her personal best of 22.85. She won her semifinal heat in 22.71 and then set an Olympic record to win the final.

1980 Moscow C: 35, N: 25, D: 7.30. WR: 21.71 (Marita Koch)

1.	Bärbel Wöckel (Eckert)	GDR	22.03 OR
2.	Natalya Bochina	SOV	22.19
3.	Merlene Ottey	JAM	22.20
4.	Romy Müller	GDR	22.47
5.	Kathryn Smallwood	GBR	22.61
6.	Beverley Goddard	GBR	22.72
7.	Denise Boyd	AUS	22.76
8.	Sonia Lannaman	GBR	22.80

Defending champion Bärbel Eckert of Leipzig, now married, a mother, and renamed Wöckel, made it through to the final without winning a single heat. She finished second each time, once to Lyudmila Maslakova of the U.S.S.R., and twice to Merlene Ottey. Meanwhile, 18-year-old Natalya Bochina ran a 22.26 in the second round to break Wöckel's Olympic record. In the final, however, it was Wöckel who took the lead coming out of the turn and won going away. Missing from the competition were the two women who had clocked the fastest times in the world: Marita Koch, who chose to concentrate on the 400 meters, and Evelyn Ashford, who suffered the double blow of injury and boycott.

400 METERS

1896–1960 not held

1964 Tokyo C: 23, N: 17, D: 10.17. WR: 51.4 (Sin-Kim Dan)

1.	Betty Cuthbert	AUS	52.0 OR
2.	Ann Packer	GBR	52.2

3. Judith Amoore	AUS	53.4
4. Antonia Munkácsi	HUN	54.4
5. Maria Itkina	SOV	54.6
6. Mathilda "Tilly" van der Zwaard	HOL	55.2
7. Gertrud Schmidt	GDR	55.4
8. Evelyne Lebret	FRA	55.5

World record holder Sin-Kim Dan of North Korea was banned from participating because she had taken part in the unauthorized Games of the New Emerging Forces (GANEFO) in Djakarta. In her absence, the inaugural Olympic 400 meters was won by Betty Cuthbert, the remarkable Australian who had earned three gold medals eight years earlier in Melbourne. At the Rome Olympics in 1960 she had suffered a hamstring pull and was forced to withdraw from competition after only one race. In Tokyo she coasted through the opening round and the semifinals, satisfied to qualify for the final. Then, on October 16, she ran what she later called "the only perfect race I have ever run" to finish a long yard ahead of Ann Packer.

1968 Mexico City C: 29, N: 21. D: 10.16. WR: 51.2 (Sin-Kim Dan)

1. Colette Besson	FRA	52.0	EOR
2. Lillian Board	GBR	52.1	
3. Natalya Pechenkina	SOV	52.2	
4. Janet Simpson	GBR	52.5	
5. Aurelia Penton	CUB	52.7	
6. Jarvis Scott	USA	52.7	
7. Helga Henning	GER	52.8	
8. Hermina Van Der Hoeven	HOL	53.0	

The victory of Colette Besson, a 22-year-old physical education teacher from Bordeaux, came as a complete surprise. Her best time previous to the Olympics was 53.8, but she was able to improve by 1.8 seconds when it counted. She passed the favorite, Lillian Board, just before the finish line and won by almost two feet. Although the harsher members of the British sports press were critical of Board for missing the gold medal, she was only 19 years old and seemed a good bet for the 1972 Olympics in Munich. She did make it to Munich, but the circumstances were tragic. In 1970 she developed cancer, complicated by peritonitis. She died in a Munich clinic 13 days after her 22nd birthday.

1972 Munich C: 49, N: 29, D: 9.7. WR: 51.0 (Marilyn Neufville, Monika Zehrt)

1. Monika Zehrt	GDR	51.08	OR
2. Rita Wilden	GER	51.21	
3. Kathy Hammond	USA	51.64	
4. Helga Seidler	GDR	51.86	
5. Mable Fergerson	USA	51.96	
6. Charlene Rendina	AUS	51.99	
7. Dagmar Käsling	GDR	52.19	
8. Györgyi Balogh	HUN	52.39	

Despite the absence of injured co-world record holder Marilyn Neufville of Jamaica, the competition was excel-

lent. The Olympic record was broken by five different women before the final was even run. However 19-year-old Monika Zehrt of Berlin seemed unaffected by the pressure of her opponents or by her role as favorite. She had taken the lead by the halfway mark and held off a late challenge by local favorite Rita Wilden to win by a meter.

1976 Montreal C: 38, N: 19, D: 7.29. WR: 49.75 (Irena Szewińska [Kirszenstein])

1. Irena Szewińska (Kirszenstein)	POL	49.29	WR
2. Christina Brehmer	GDR	50.51	
3. Ellen Streidt	GDR	50.55	
4. Pirjo Häggman	FIN	50.56	
5. Rosalyn Bryant	USA	50.65	
6. Shelia Ingram	USA	59.90	
7. Riita Salin	FIN	50.98	
8. Debra Sapenter	USA	51.66	

The amazing Irena Szewińska had already won Olympic medals in the 100 meters, 200 meters, long jump, and 4×100-meter relay when she switched to the 400 meters in 1973. The following year she became the first woman to break 50 seconds in what was only the second 400 meters race of her career. Early in 1976 her world record was broken by Christina Brehmer. But later in the year Szewińska regained the record, and an Olympic showdown between the 18-year-old Brehmer and the 30-year-old Szewińska was eagerly awaited. Irena coasted through the first two rounds and then set an Olympic record of 50.48 in the semifinals. For the first 300 meters, the final was a close race, but then Szewińska pulled away dramatically to win by almost ten meters. Her total of seven medals (three gold, two silver, and two bronze) ranks her along with Shirley Strickland as one of the most successful female track and field athletes in Olympic history. Between 1974 and 1978 she won 34 straight 400-meter finals, until she was finally beaten by Marita Koch at the European championships. In 1980 Szewińska took part in the Moscow Olympics, but was eliminated in the semifinals when she pulled a muscle.

Pirjo Häggman, who finished fourth in Montreal, later became the first woman to be elected to the I.O.C.

1980 Moscow C: 38, N: 22, D: 7.28. WR: 48.60 (Marita Koch)

1. Marita Koch	GDR	48.88	OR
2. Jarmila Kratochvilová	CZE	49.46	
3. Christina Lathan (Brehmer)	GDR	49.66	
4. Irina Nazarova	GBR	50.07	
5. Nina Zyuskova	GDR	50.17	
6. Gabriele Löwe	GDR	51.33	
7. Pirjo Häggman	FIN	51.35	
8. Linsey MacDonald	GBR	52.40	

Marita Koch had been one of the favoites in 1976, but was forced to withdraw from her semifinal heat because of injury. In 1979 she became the first woman to break 22 seconds for 200 meters as well as the first woman to beat 49 seconds for 400 meters. In Moscow, using the same spikes she had used four years earlier in Montreal, Koch won a clear victory over Kratochvilova and Lathan, both of whom recorded personal bests. The race was the first in history in which three women broke the 50-second barrier.

800 METERS

1896–1924 not held

1928 Amsterdam C: 25, N: 13, D: 8.2. WR: 2:19.6 (Lina Radke)
1. Lina Radke	GER	2:16.8	WR
2. Kinue Hitomi	JAP	2:17.6	
3. Inga Gentzel	SWE	2:17.8	
4. Jenny Thompson	CAN	2:21.6	
5. Fanny Rosenfeld	CAN	2:22.4	
6. Florence McDonald	USA	2:22.6	
7. Marie Dollinger	GER	2:23.0	
8. Gertruda Kilos	POL	2:28.0	

The 1928 women's 800-meter race touched off a major controversy in the athletic world. The competition itself was exciting enough. The three German finalists, Lina Radke, Marie Dollinger, and Elfriede Wever, ran a team race, with Dollinger and Wever wearing down the opposition and keeping a steady pace for Radke, who pulled away in the final 300 meters. Radke's winning time was a world record that lasted for sixteen years. After the race, several of the women collapsed in exhaustion and some had to be given aid. Antifeminists in the press and in the International Amateur Athletic Federation (I.A.A.F.) seized on their condition as evidence that women should be banned from running races of more than 200 meters. The London *Daily Mail* quoted doctors who said that women who took part in races of 800 meters and other such "feats of endurance" would "become old too soon." The president of the International Olympic Committee, Comte de Baillet-Latour, spoke out in favor of eliminating all women's sports from the Olympics and returning to the ancient Greek custom of an all-male affair. But there were those who supported women's athletics, and they pointed out that men frequently fainted after races just as women did. In fact, male rowers were *expected* to be nearly comatose at the finish of important races, such as those between Oxford and Cambridge or Harvard and Yale. In retrospect, of course, the arguments of the antiwomen forces seem foolish and ridiculous, particularly in light of the inclusion of a women's marathon in the 1984 Olympics. What makes the story more of a tragedy than a comedy however, is that the executive committee of the I.A.A.F. actually *did* ban races longer than 200 meters, and no women's race longer than ½ lap was run at the Olympics for another 32 years.

Some of the early women athletes were extremely versatile. Fifth-place finisher Fanny Rosenfeld, who worked in a Toronto chocolate factory, also took second in the 100 meters and first in the 4×100-meter relay. Silver medalist Kinue Hitomi was the world record holder in the 200 meters and the long jump. Since neither event was included in the Olympics program, she took part instead in the 100

meters and 800 meters. At the third Women's World Games, held in Prague in 1930, Hitomi delighted the crowd by winning four medals: a gold in the long jump, a silver in the triathlon, and bronzes in the 60-meter dash and the discus. The following year Kinue Hitomi died at the age of 23.

1932–1956 not held

1960 Rome C: 27, N: 15, D 9.7. WR: 2:04.3 (Lyudmila Shevtsova)
1. Lyudmila Shevtsova	SOV	2:04.3	EWR
2. Brenda Jones	AUS	2:04.4	
3. Ursula Donath	GDR	2:05.6	
4. Vera Kummerfeldt	GER	2:05.9	
5. Antje Gleichfeld	GER	2:06.5	
6. Joyce Jordan	GBR	2:07.8	
7. Gizella Csoka	HUN	2:08.0	
8. Beata Zbikowska	POL	2:11.8	

Dixie Willis of Australia led the field for most of the race, but, with 150 meters to go, she suddenly threw her arms into the air and staggered off the track. Brenda Jones took the lead, but was passed by world record holder Lyudmila Shevtsova just before the finish.

1964 Tokyo C: 23, N: 15, D: 10.20. WR: 1:58.0 (Sin-Kim Dan)
1. Ann Packer	GBR	2:01.1	OR
2. Maryvonne Dupureur	FRA	2:01.9	
3. M. Ann Chamberlain	NZE	2:02.8	
4. Zsuzsa Szabó	HUN	2:03.5	
5. Antje Gleichfeld	GER	2:03.9	
6. Laine Erik	SOV	2:05.1	
7. Gerarda Kraan	HOL	2:05.8	
8. Anne Smith	GBR	2:05.8	

With unofficial world record holder Sin-Kim Dan out because of politics and official world record holder (2:01.2) Dixie Willis out because of illness, the 800 meters looked like an open race. In the semifinals, Maryvonne Dupureur, a housewife and physical education teacher from Lille, set an Olympic record of 2:04.1. In the final Dupureur had a five-yard lead entering the last straightaway, but Britain's Ann Packer, who had already won a silver medal in the 400 meters, turned on a fantastic finishing kick, passed Dupureur with 70 yards to go, and won by five yards. The 800 meters was not really Packer's race. She had finished fifth in her opening heat and third in her semifinal heat. She had considered skipping the final and going shopping instead, but when her fiancé, Robbie Brightwell, finished a disappointing fourth in the men's 400 meters, she decided to go all-out in his honor. "It was so easy, I could not believe I had won," she told reporters afterward. "I was thinking about him and not about myself, and so I wasn't nervous."

1968 Mexico City C: 24, N: 16, D: 10.19. WR: 1:58.0 (Sin-Kim Dan)
1. Madeline Manning	USA	2:00.9	OR
2. Ileana Silai	ROM	2:02.5	

3. Maria Gommers   HOL   2:02.6
4. Sheila Taylor   GBR   2:03.8
5. Doris Brown   USA   2:03.9
6. Patricia Lowe   GBR   2:04.2
7. Abigail Hoffman   CAN   2:06.8
8. Maryvonne Dupureur   FRA   2:08.2

The most shocking incident of the 1968 women's events occurred in the first semifinal heat, when the 20-year-old favorite, and official world record holder (2:00.5) Vera Nikolić of Yugoslavia, overcome by the pressure of being her nation's only hope of a track and field medal, dropped out after 300 meters and left the stadium. Rumors quickly spread that she had gone straight to a nearby bridge and was only prevented from committing suicide by her coach, who had followed her. That race was won by 20-year-old Madeline Manning, a Tennessee State "Tigerbelle" from Cleveland. Two days later, in the final, Manning took the early lead, then, spurred on by the garlicky perspiration of one of the other runners, she pulled away in the backstretch of the final lap and won by over ten meters.

1972 Munich C: 38, N: 26, D: 9.3. WR: 1:58.0 (Sin-Kim Dan)
1. Hildegard Falck   GER   1:58.55   OR
2. Niole Sabaite   SOV   1:58.65
3. Gunhild Hoffmeister   GDR   1:59.19
4. Svetla Zlateva   BUL   1:59.72
5. Vera Nikolić   YUG   1:59.98
6. Ileana Silai   ROM   2:00.04
7. Rosemary Stirling   GBR   2:00.15
8. Abigail Hoffman   CAN   2:00.17

The fireworks started in the second heat of the first round, when Svetla Zlateva slashed three seconds off her personal best to set an Olympic record of 1:58.9. Vera Nikolić finished close behind her in 1:59.6. Previous to this race, the only women to better two minutes had been Sin-Kim Dan, Hildegard Falck, and Vasilena Amzina of Bulgaria, who had run a 1:59.9 a week before the Olympics began. In the fourth heat of the first round Amzina collided with Raisa Ruus of the U.S.S.R. and fell to the ground. She got up and finished the race with blood on her face, but she failed to qualify for the next round. The first semifinal was won by Lithuanian Niole Sabaite and the second by local favorite Hildegard Falck, a 23-year-old schoolteacher. In the second semi, defending champion Madeline Manning was eliminated when she misjudged the finish line and was passed just before the real line by Rosemary Stirling. The final was a thrilling race. Falck, urged on by the partisan crowd, pulled away coming out of the last curve and held off a final burst by Sabaite.

1976 Montreal C: 35, N: 20, D: 7.26. WR: 1:56.0 (Valentina Gerassimova)
1. Tatyana Kazankina   SOV   1:54.94   WR
2. Nikolina Shtereva   BUL   1:55.42
3. Elfi Zinn   GDR   1:55.60
4. Anita Weiss   GDR   1:55.74
5. Svetlana Styrkina   SOV   1:56.44

6. Svetla Zlateva   BUL   1:57.21
7. Doris Gluth   GDR   1:58.99
8. Mariana Suman   ROM   2:02.21

The level of competition was so high that world record holder Valentina Gerassimova, European champion Liliana Tomova of Bulgaria, Commonwealth champion Charlene Rendina of Australia, and 1968 Olympic champion Madeline Jackson (Manning) were all eliminated in the semifinals. Anita Weiss, who lowered the Olympic record by two seconds with a 1:56.53 in her semifinal heat, broke the world record in the final, but didn't even win a medal. Kazankina, a 1500-meter specialist who had been entered in the 800 meters as well on the final day for entries, moved from fifth place to first in the last 50 meters and slashed the world record by over a second.

1980 Moscow C: 28, N: 17, D: 7.27. WR: 1:54.8 (Nadezhda Olizarenko)
1. Nadezhda Olizarenko   SOV   1:53.42   WR
2. Olga Mineyeva   SOV   1:54.9
3. Tatyana Providokhina   SOV   1:55.5
4. Martina Kämpfert   GDR   1:56.3
5. Hildegard Ullrich   GDR   1:57.2
6. Jolanta Januchta   POL   1:58.3
7. Nikolina Shtereva   BUL   1:58.8
8. Gabriella Dorio   ITA   1:59.2

For the first time in Olympic history, all three medals in a women's track event were won by athletes from the same nation. Olizarenko, a 26-year-old military office worker from Odessa, ran a spectacular race, leading from start to finish (a rarity at 800 meters) and clipping almost one and a half seconds from her own world record, set only six weeks earlier.

1500 METERS
1896–1968 not held

1972 Munich C: 36, N: 21, D: 9.9 WR: 4:06.9 (Lyudmila Bragina)
1. Lyudmila Bragina   SOV   4:01.4   WR
2. Gunhild Hoffmeister   GDR   4:02.8
3. Paola Cacchi   ITA   4:02.9
4. Karin Burneleit   GDR   4:04.1
5. Sheila Carey   GBR   4:04.8
6. Ilja Keizer   HOL   4:05.1
7. Tamara Pangelova   SOV   4:06.5
8. Jennifer Orr   AUS   4:12.2

Twenty-nine-year-old Lyudmila Bragina exploded onto the international scene six weeks before the Olympics when she chopped 2.7 seconds off Karin Burneleit's world record by running a 4:06.9 in a *heat* of the Soviet championships. A few weeks later she ran 3000 meters in 8:53.0, to better the world record at that distance by over 16 seconds. In the first heat of the first round of the 1500 meters at Munich, Bragina led from start to finish and broke her own world record in 4:06.47, carrying 17-year-old Glenda Reiser of Canada with her in 4:06.71. Three days later Bragina again broke the world record with a 4:05.07 in her semifinal heat. The semifinals saw 13 women better the pre-Olympic world record. In the final, Bragina moved to the front after two laps and pulled away to a 12-meter lead, which she held for the entire last lap. In a postrace interview, Bragina told reporters, "We shall be running 3 minutes 56 seconds before the next Olympics." She hit it right on the button, as 3:56.0 was exactly the world record at the time of the 1976 Olympics.

1976 Montreal C: 36, N: 19, D: 7.30. WR: 3:56.0 (Tatyana Kazankina)

1. Tatyana Kazankina	SOV	4:05.48
2. Gunhild Hoffmeister	GDR	4:06.02
3. Ulrike Klapezynski	GDR	4:06.09
4. Nikolina Shtereva	BUL	4:06.57
5. Lyudmila Bragina	SOV	4:07.20
6. Gabriella Dorio	ITA	4:07.27
7. Ellen Wellmann	GER	4:07.91
8. Janice Merrill	USA	4:08.54

Bragina's Munich world record went unbeaten until one month before the next Olympics, when Kazankina lowered it by 5.4 seconds. Track fans who had hoped for a new record in the Olympic final were disappointed, as the race turned into a tactical affair. With one lap to go, Bragina took the lead, but 200 meters later, with elbows flying, she was passed by the two East German training mates, Hoffmeister on the inside and Klapezynski on the outside. Meanwhile, Kazankina, who had already won the 800 meters gold medal, steered clear of the elbowing and moved up on the outside to take the lead with 50 meters to go. She won by three meters. Defending champion Lyudmila Bragina had to settle for fifth place, but her career was hardly over. A few days later, at a U.S.A. vs. U.S.S.R. meet, she ran the 3000 meters in 8:27.2, 18.3 seconds faster than the previous world record. This put her only 50 years behind the men's pace, something of a record in women's track events.

1980 Moscow C: 24, N: 14, D: 8.1. WR: 3:55.0 (Tatyana Kazankina)

1. Tatyana Kazankina	SOV	3:56.6	OR
2. Christiane Wartenberg	GDR	3:57.8	
3. Nadezhda Olizarenko	SOV	3:59.6	
4. Gabriella Dorio	ITA	4:00.3	
5. Ulrike Bruns	GDR	4:00.7	
6. Lyubov Smolka	SOV	4:01.3	
7. Maricia Puika	ROM	4:01.3	
8. Ileana Silai	ROM	4:03.0	

Covering the final 800 meters in 1:59.0, Kazankina took the lead with 600 meters to go and had left the other runners 20 meters behind by the time she reached the last curve. Twelve days later she lowered the world record to 3:52.47 and became the first woman to run 1500 meters faster than Paavo Nurmi.

3000 METERS

This event will be held for the first time in 1984.

MARATHON

This event will be held for the first time in 1984.

100-METER HURDLES

1896–1928 not held

1932 Los Angeles C: 9, N: 6, D: 8.4. WR: 11.8 (Marjorie Clark)
(80 Meters)

1. Mildred Didriksen	USA	11.7	WR
2. Evelyne Hall	USA	11.7	
3. Marjorie Clark	SAF	11.8	
4. Simone Schaller	USA	11.9	
5. Violet Webb	GBR	11.9	
6. Alda Wilson	CAN	12.0	

Babe Didriksen had already won a gold medal in the javelin throw when she began competition in the 80-meter hurdles. In her opening heat she tied the world record of 11.8 seconds. In the final she committed one false start and then broke the record, beating Evelyne Hall of Chicago by a mere two inches. Fourth-place finisher Simone Schaller of Pasadena, California, had taken up hurdling only three months earlier.

1936 Berlin C: 22, N: 11, D: 8.6. WR: 11.6 (Ruth Engelhard)
(80 Meters)

1. Trebisonda Valla	ITA	11.7
2. Anni Steuer	GER	11.7
3. Elizabeth Taylor	CAN	11.7
4. Claudia Testoni	ITA	11.7
5. Catharina ter Braake	HOL	11.8
6. Doris Eckert	GER	12.0

The finish was so close that the judges spent 30 minutes studying the photo-finish before they were able to sort out the places and announce the results. In the semifinals, Valla had run a wind-aided 11.6, which was recognized as an Olympic record but not a world record.

1948 London C: 21, N: 12, D: 8.4. WR: 11.0 (Francina "Fanny"Blankers-Koen)
(80 Meters)

1. Francina"Fanny"Blankers-Koen	HOL	11.2	OR
2. Maureen Gardner	GBR	11.2	
3. Shirley Strickland	AUS	11.4	
4. Yvette Monginou	FRA	—	
5. Maria Oberbreyer	AUS	—	
6. Libuše Lomská	CZE	—	

Fanny Blankers-Koen had already won the 100-meter dash, but she was quite nervous about 19-year-old Maureen Gardner in the hurdles. She didn't meet her rival until the day of the opening heats, when Gardner showed up at the warmup track with her own set of hurdles. In the semifinals Gardner hit a hurdle and stumbled, barely qualifying in third place. But in the final it was Blankers-Koen who had a tough race. Left behind at the start, she caught Gardner at the fifth barrier, but hit the hurdle and lurched clumsily to the finish line. It was unclear who had won, and the first three finishers waited impatiently for the results. Suddenly the band struck up "God Save the King" and Fanny thought that meant she had lost. Actually the band was playing not because Maureen Gardner had won, but because the British royal family had just arrived at the stadium. Then the results appeared on the scoreboard, and Fanny Blankers-Koen had gained her second gold medal. The fact that Fanny was a devoted mother and housewife and that Maureen Gardner was a ballet instructor did much to counter the pre-World War II masculine image of women athletes that had been established by Stella Walsh, Babe Didriksen, and Helen Stephens. Bronze medalist Shirley Strickland also finished third in the 100 meters, fourth in the 200, and second in the relay. Her official time of 11.4 is undoubtedly a mistake, since she was less than a meter behind the winner.

1952 Helsinki C: 33, N: 21, D: 7.24. WR: 11.0 (Francina "Fanny" Blankers-Koen)
(80 Meters)

1. Shirley Strickland	AUS	10.9	WR
2. Maria Golubnichaya	SOV	11.1	
3. Maria Sander	GER	11.1	
4. Anneliese Seonbuchner	GER	11.2	
5. Jean Desforges	GBR	11.6	

DNF: Francina "Fanny"Blankers-Koen (HOL)

Shirley Strickland, a 27-year-old teacher from Western Australia, equaled Fanny Blankers-Koen's world record in the first heat. The Dutch defending champion, suffering from a carbuncle on her leg, ran 11.2 and 11.3 to qualify for the final, while Strickland ran a wind-aided 10.8 in the semifinals. In the final, Blankers-Koen hit the first two hurdles and stopped running. Meanwhile, Shirley Strickland streaked to victory in world record time.

1956 Melbourne C: 22, N: 11, D: 11.28. WR: 10.6 (Zenta Gastl)
(80 Meters)

1. Shirley Strickland	AUS	10.7	OR
2. Gisela Köhler	GDR	10.9	
3. Norma Thrower	AUS	11.0	
4. Galina Bystrova	SOV	11.0	
5. Maria Golubnichaya	SOV	11.3	
6. Gloria Cooke	AUS	11.4	

By 1956 Shirley Strickland had become a wife, a mother, and an assistant lecturer in physics and mathematics at Perth Technical College. Her decisive two-yard victory in the 80-meter hurdles and her gold medal in the relay gave her a total of seven Olympic medals: three gold, one silver, and three bronze.

1960 Rome C: 28, N: 17, D: 9.1. WR: 10.5 (Gisela Birkemeyer [Köhler])
(80 Meters)

1. Irina Press	SOV	10.8
2. Carole Quinton	GBR	10.9
3. Gisela Birkemeyer (Köhler)	GDR	11.0
4. Mary Bignal	GBR	11.1
5. Galina Bystrova	SOV	11.2
6. Rimma Koschelyova	SOV	11.2

Irina Press, the younger sister of shot put and discus champion Tamara Press, set an Olympic record of 10.6 in the semifinals before winning a clear start-to-finish victory in the final.

1964 Tokyo C: 27, N: 19, 10.19. WR: 10.5 (Gisela Birkemeyer [Köhler], Betty Moore, Karin Balzer, Irina Press, Draga Stamejčić)
(80 Meters)

1. Karin Balzer	GDR	10.5	w
2. Teresa Ciepla-Wieczorek	POL	10.5	
3. Pamela Kilborn	AUS	10.5	
4. Irina Press	SOV	10.6	
5. Ikuko Yoda	JAP	10.7	
6. Maria Piatkowska	POL	10.7	
7. Draga Stamejčić	YUG	10.8	
8. Rosie Bonds	USA	10.8	

Hometown favorite Ikuko Yoda delighted the crowd with her unusual prerace routine, which included sweeping her lane up to the first hurdle, sucking a lemon, and dabbing cream behind her ears. She led until the third hurdle, but couldn't hold off the favorites. The three medalists finished within 12 inches of one another. Their world record time was disallowed because of a 2.23 meters per second wind. The competition was marred in the opening round when Canadian Marion Snider crashed into a hurdle and was carried away, unconscious, on a stretcher.

1968 Mexico City C: 32, N: 23, D: 10.18. WR: 10.2 (Vyera Korsakova)
(80 Meters)

1. Maureen Caird	AUS	10.3	OR
2. Pamela Kilborn	AUS	10.4	
3. Chi Cheng	TAI	10.4	
4. Patricia Van Wolvelaere	USA	10.5	
5. Karin Balzer	GDR	10.6	
6. Danuta Straszyńska	POL	10.6	
7. Elżbieta Żebrowska	POL	10.6	
8. Tatyana Talysheva	SOV	10.7	

When word spread from the U.S.S.R. that unknown Vyera Korsakova had broken Irina Press's world record, many eyebrows were raised. Cynics doubted her time of 10.2 and said that it was just the Soviets' way of removing from the record books the names of the Press sisters, who had disappeared from competition following the institution of sex tests. Sure enough, Korsakova was eliminated in the semifinals after clocking only 10.6 and 10.8. Pam Kilborn had been undefeated since the Tokyo Olympics, but she suffered a slow start in the final and was unable to catch her 17-year-old teammate Maureen Caird. Chi Cheng, the first Asian woman to win an Olympic track and field medal, was elected to the Taiwan parliament in 1981.

1972 Munich C: 25, N: 15, D: 9.8, WR: 12.5 (Annelie Ehrhardt, Pamela Ryan [Kilborn])

1. Annelie Ehrhardt	GDR	12.59	WR
2. Valeria Bufanu	ROM	12.84	
3. Karin Balzer	GDR	12.90	
4. Pamela Ryan (Kilborn)	AUS	12.98	
5. Teresa Nowak	POL	13.17	
6. Danuta Straszyńska	POL	13.18	
7. Annerose Krumpholz	GDR	13.27	
8. Grażyna Rabsztyn	POL	13.44	

Esther Shakhamorov had the potential of becoming Israel's first Olympic finalist, but she withdrew following the terrorist murder of Israeli athletes, including her coach, Amitzur Shapira. Annelie Ehrhardt was never seriously challenged. The final was noteworthy for the success of the "older women," including 34-year-old Karin Balzer and 33-year-old Pam Ryan.

1976 Montreal C: 27, N: 15, D: 7.29. WR: 12.59 (Annelie Ehrhardt)

1. Johanna Schaller	GDR	12.77
2. Tatiana Anisimova	SOV	12.78
3. Natalya Lebedeva	SOV	12.80
4. Gudrun Behrend	GDR	12.82
5. Grażyna Rabsztyn	POL	12.96
6. Esther Rot (Shakhamorov)	ISR	13.04
7. Valeria Stefanescu	ROM	13.35
8. Ileana Ongar	ITA	13.51

The semifinals saw an unusual incident. In the second heat, Lyubov Kononova of the U.S.S.R. stumbled and smashed into Valeria Stefanescu in the next lane. At first both women were disqualified, but fair play prevailed. Stefanescu was reinstated, and a rerun was ordered for the next day, 75 minutes before the final. This rerun allowed Stefanescu to replace injured defending champion Ehrhardt as the eighth finalist. The final was so close that only one and a half feet separated Schaller from fourth-place finisher Behrend. Esther Shakhamorov, now married and living in Tarzana, California, at last succeeded in becoming Israel's first finalist.

1980 Moscow C: 20, N: 11, D: 7.28. WR: 12.36 (Grażyna Rabsztyn)

1. Vera Komisova	SOV	12.56	OR
2. Johanna Klie (Schaller)	GDR	12.63	
3. Lucyna Langer	POL	12.65	
4. Kerstin Claus	GDR	12.66	
5. Grażyna Rabsztyn	POL	12.74	
6. Irina Litovchenko	SOV	12.84	
7. Bettine Gärtz	GDR	12.93	
8. Zofia Bielczyk	POL	13.08	

Twenty-seven-year-old Vera Komisova was one of the surprise winners of the Moscow Games, as she improved her pre-Olympic best by .28 seconds, even greater than Schaller's 1976 Olympic improvement of .22.

400-METER HURDLES

This event will be held for the first time in 1984.

4×100-METER RELAY

1896–1924 not held

1928 Amsterdam T: 8, N: 8, D: 8.5. WR (440 yards): 49.8 (GBR—Scovler, Haynes, Edwards, Thompson)

1. CAN	(Fanny Rosenfeld, Ethel Smith, Florence Bell, Myrtle Cook)	48.4	WR
2. USA	(Mary Washburn, Jessie Gross, Loretta McNeil, Elizabeth Robinson)	48.8	
3. GER	(Rosa Kellner, Helene "Leni" Schmidt, Anni Holdmann, Helene "Leni" Junker)	49.0	
4. FRA	(Georgette Gagneux, Yvonne Plancke, Marguerite Radideau, Lucienne Velu)	49.6	
5. HOL	(Mechelina Aengenendt, Maria Briejer, Jeannette Hendrika Grooss, Elisabeth ter Horst)	49.8	
6. ITA	(Luisa Bonfanti, Giannina Marchini, Derna Polazzo, Vittorina Vivenza)	53.6	

The relay victory was sweet revenge for the Canadian team, particularly for Fanny Rosenfeld, who had lost first place in the 100 meters on a disputed judges' decision, and for Myrtle Cook, who had cried by the side of the track for a half hour after being disqualified in the 100 meters final. Myrtle Cook later became a sports editor for the Montreal *Star*.

1932 Los Angeles T: 6, N: 6, D: 8.7. WR: 48.4 (CAN—Rosenfeld, Smith, Bell, Cook)

1. USA	(Mary Carew, Evelyn Furtsch, Annette Rogers, Wilhelmina Von Bremen)	46.9	WR
2. CAN	(Mildred Frizzel, Lilian Palmer, Mary Frizzel, Hilda Strike)	47.0	
3. GBR	(Eileen Hiscock, Gwendoline Porter, Violet Webb, Nellie Halstead)	47.6	
4. HOL	(Johanna Dalmolen, Cornelia Aalten, Elisabeth du Mee, Tollina Schurrman)	—	
5. JAP	(Mie Muraoka, Michi Nakanishi, Asa Dogura, Sumiko Watanabe)	—	
6. GER	(Grete Heublein, Ellen Braumüller, Tilly Fleischer, Marie Dollinger)	—	

1936 Berlin T: 8, N: 8, D: 8.9. WR: 46.5 (GER—Albus, Krauss, Dollinger, Dörffeldt)

1. USA	(Harriet Bland, Annette Rogers, Elizabeth Robinson, Helen Stephens)	46.9
2. GBR	(Eileen Hiscock, Violet Olney, Audrey Brown, Barbara Burke)	47.6
3. CAN	(Dorothy Brookshaw, Mildred Dolson, Hilda Cameron, Aileen Meagher)	47.8

4. ITA   (Lydia Bongiovanni, Trebisonda Valla, Fernanda   48.7
          Bullano, Claudia Testoni)
5. HOL   (Catharina ter Braake, Francina "Fanny" Koen,   48.8
          Alida de Vries, Elisabeth Koning)
DISQ: GER (Emmy Albus, Käthe Krauss, Marie Dollinger, Ilse Dörffeldt)

In the opening round the German team set a world record of 46.4 that was to remain unbroken for sixteen years. In the final they led by eight meters as Marie Dollinger prepared to make the final pass to Ilse Dörffeldt. However, as Adolf Hitler, King Boris of Bulgaria, and 100,000 others watched, Ilse Dörffeldt dropped the baton. The U.S. team, anchored by the heroic 1928 100 meters winner Betty Robinson and the 1936 100 meters winner Helen Stephens, took advantage of the German catastrophe and won by eight yards. Hitler was so moved by the sight of Dörffeldt sobbing after the race that he called the four German women to his booth and comforted them.

1948 London T: 10, N: 10, D: 8.7. WR: 46.4 (GER—Albus, Krauss, Dollinger, Dörffeldt)
1. HOL   (Xenia Stad-de Jong, Jeanette Witziers-Timmer,   47.5
          Gerda van der Kade-Koudijs, Francina "Fanny"
          Blankers-Koen)
2. AUS   (Shirley Strickland, June Maston, Elizabeth McKin-   47.6
          non, Joyce King)
3. CAN   (Viola Myers, Nancy Mackay, Diane Foster, Patri-   47.8
          cia Jones)
4. GBR   (Dorothy Manley, Muriel Pletts, Margaret Walker,   48.0
          Maureen Gardner)
5. DEN   (Grete Lövsöe [Nielsen], Bente Bergendorff, Birte   48.2
          Nielsen, Hildegard Nissen)
6. AUS   (Grete Jenny, Elfi Steurer, Grete Pavlousek, Maria   49.2
          Oberbreyer)

Fanny Blankers-Koen took over in fourth place, but was able to race through the field and catch Joyce King just before the finish. She thus became the only woman to win four track and field gold medals in one Olympics.

1952 Helsinki T: 15, N: 15, D: 7.27. WR: 46.4 (GER—Albus, Krauss, Dollinger, Dörffeldt)
1. USA   (Mae Faggs, Barbara Jones, Janet Moreau,   45.9 WR
          Catherine Hardy)
2. GER   (Ursula Knab, Maria Sander, Helga Klein,   45.9 WR
          Marga Petersen)
3. GBR   (Sylvia Cheeseman, June Foulds, Jean Des-   46.2
          forges, Heather Armitage)
4. SOV   (Irina Turova, Yevgenya Setshenova, Na-   46.3
          dezhda Khnykina, Vyera Kalashnikova)
5. AUS   (Shirley Strickland, Verna Johnson, Winsome   46.6
          Cripps, Marjorie Jackson)
6. HOL   (Grietje de Jongh, Bertha Brouwer, Neeltje   47.8
          Büch, Wilhelmina Lust)

The Australians set a new world record of 46.1 in the very first heat. They led by one meter in the final at the last changeover. Winsome Cripps made a clean pass to Marjorie Jackson, winner of both sprints, but as Jackson took off,

her hand hit Cripps's knee and the baton was jarred loose. Jackson caught it on a bounce and raced on, but the delay proved decisive. One of the four black women who made up the U.S. team was 15-year-old Barbara Jones of Chicago, who is the youngest person in Olympic history to win a gold medal in track and field.

1956 Melbourne T: 9, N: 9, D: 12.1 WR: 45.2 (SOV—Krepkina, Itkina, Kocheleva, Botchkaryova)
1. AUS   (Shirley Strickland, Norma Croker,   44.5 WR
          Fleur Mellor, Betty Cuthbert)
2. GBR   (Anne Pashley, Jean Scrivens, June   44.7
          Paul [Foulds], Heather Armitage)
3. USA   (Mae Faggs, Margaret Matthews, Wil-   44.9
          ma Rudolph, Isabelle Daniels)
4. SOV   (Vyera Krepkina, Galina Reschikova,   45.6
          Maria Itkina, Irina Botchkaryova)
5. ITA   (Maria Musso, Letizia Bertoni, Maria   45.7
          Greppi, Giuseppina Leone)
6. GDR/GER (Maria Sander, Christa Stubnick, Gi-   47.2
          sela Köhler, Barbara Mayer)

Pressed by the Germans, the Australian team set a world record of 44.9 in the opening heat. In the final, though, it was the British women who put on the pressure. Heather Armitage finished only half a yard behind Betty Cuthbert (a closer margin than indicated by Great Britain's time of 44.7). Anne Pashley, who ran the opening leg for the British team, later gained renown as a mezzo-soprano.

1960 Rome T 10, N: 10, D: 9.8. WR: 44.5 (AUS—Strickland, Croker, Mellor, Cuthbert)
1. USA   (Martha Hudson, Lucinda Williams, Barbara   44.5
          Jones, Wilma Rudolph)
2. GER   (Martha Langbein, Annie Biechl, Brunhilde Hen-   44.8
          drix, Jutta Heine)
3. POL   (Teresa Wieczorek, Barbara Janiszewska, Celina   45.0
          Jesionowska, Halina Richter)
4. SOV   (Vyera Krepkina, Valentina Maslovskaya, Maria It-   45.2
          kina, Irina Press)
5. ITA   (Letizia Bertoni, Sandra Valenti, Piera Tizzoni, Giu-   45.6
          seppina Leone)
DNF: GBR (Carole Quinton, Dorothy Hyman, Jennifer Smart, Mary Bignal)

Marie Dollinger was one of the two unfortunate German women who dropped their baton in 1936, during the changeover from the third runner to the fourth. Twenty-four years later she sat in the stands in Rome and watched tensely as her daughter, Brunhilde Hendrix, the third runner on the German team, prepared to pass the baton to Jutta Heine. Fortunately all went well, and the 1960 German team finished impressively in second place. The U.S. team from Tennessee State had a two-yard lead that was lost in a sloppy final pass. However Wilma Rudolph was able to regain the lead and cross the tape in first place for the ninth time in the Rome Games. The U.S. women had set a world record of 44.4 in the semifinals.

1964 Tokyo T: 15, N: 15, D: 10.21. WR: 44.3 (USA—White, Pollards, Brown, Rudolph)

1. POL	(Teresa Ciepla [Wieczorek], Irena Kirszenstein, Halina Górecka [Richter], Ewa Klobukowska)	43.6
2. USA	(Willye White, Wyomia Tyus, Marilyn White, Edith McGuire)	43.9
3. GBR	(Janet Simpson, Mary Rand [Bignal], Daphne Arden, Dorothy Hyman)	44.0
4. SOV	(Galina Gaide, Renata Latse, Lyudmila Samotyosova, Galina Popova)	44.4
5. GER	(Karin Frisch, Erika Pollmann, Martha Pensberger [Langbein], Jutta Heine)	44.7
6. AUS	(Dianne Bowering, Marilyn Black, Margaret Burvill, Joyce Bennett)	45.0
7. HUN	(Erzsébet Bartos Heldt, Margit Nemesháì Markó, Antónia Munkácsi, Ida Such)	45.2
8. FRA	(Marlene Canguio, Daniele Gueneau, Michele Lurot, Denise Guenard)	46.1

The Polish team was originally credited with a world record, but their names were later struck from the record books when Ewa Klobukowska became the first athlete to fail a sex test.

1968 Mexico City T: 14, N: 14, D: 10.20. WR: 43.6 (SOV—Zharkova, Bukharina, Popkova, Samotysova)

1. USA	(Barbara Ferrell, Margaret Bailes, Mildrette Netter, Wyomia Tyus)	42.8 WR
2. CUB	(Marlene Elejarde, Fulgencia Romay, Violetta Quesada, Miguelina Cobián)	43.3
3. SOV	(Lyudmila Zharkova, Galina Bukharina, Vyera Popkova, Lyudmila Samotysova)	43.4
4. HOL	(Geertruida Hennipman, Mieke Sterk, Cornelia Bakker, Wilhelmina van den Berg)	43.4
5. AUS	(Jennifer Lamy, Joyce Bennett, Raelene Boyle, Dianne Burge)	43.4
6. GER	(Renate Meyer, Jutta Stöck, Rita Jahn, Ingrid Becker)	43.6
7. GBR	(Anita Neil, Maureen Tranter, Janet Simpson, Lillian Board)	43.7
8. FRA	(Michele Alayrangues, Gabrielle Meyer, Nicole Montandon, Silviane Telliez)	44.2

The American women set a world record of 43.4 in the first heat. This time was equaled, surprisingly, in the second heat by the unheralded Dutch team. In the final the U.S. team overcame mediocre baton-passing with rare speed to win by five yards and establish a new world record.

1972 Munich T: 15, N: 15, D: 9.10. WR:42.8 (USA—Ferrell, Bailes, Netter, Tyus)

1. GER	(Christiane Krause, Ingrid Mickler [Becker], Annegret Richter, Heidemarie Rosendahl)	42.81 EWR
2. GDR	(Evelyn Kaufer, Christina Heinich, Bärbel Struppert, Renate Stecher)	42.95
3. CUB	(Marlene Elejarde, Carmen Valdes, Fulgencia Romay, Silvia Chibás)	43.36

4. USA	(Martha Watson, Mattline Render, Mildrette Netter, Iris Davis)	43.39
5. SOV	(Marina Sidorova, Galina Bukharina, Lyudmila Zharkova, Nadezhda Bezfamilnaya)	43.59
6. AUS	(Maureen Caird, Raelene Boyle, Marion Hoffman, Penelope Gillies)	43.61
7. GBR	(Andrea Lynch, Della Pascoe, Judith Vernon, Anita Neil)	43.71
8. POL	(Helena Flišnik, Barbara Bakulin, Urszula Jóźwik, Danuta Jędrejek)	44.20

The East Germans had edged the West Germans in the European championships. Rematched in a poorly seeded opening heat, the East Germans again finished ahead, 42.88 to 42.97. In the final, however, long jump gold medalist Heide Rosendahl began the anchor leg with a one-meter advantage and raced flat-out to hold off Renate Stecher, who had won both the 100 meters and 200 meters earlier in the games.

1976 Montreal T: 10, N: 10, D: 7.31. WR: 42.51 (GDR—Maletzki, Stecher, Heinich, Eckert)

1. GDR	(Marlies Oelsner, Renate Stecher, Carla Bodendorf, Bärbel Eckert)	42.55	OR
2. GER	(Elvira Possekel, Inge Helten, Annegret Richter, Annegret Kroniger)	42.59	
3. SOV	(Tatyana Prorochenko, Lyudmila Maslakova [Zharkova], Nadezhda Besfamilnaya, Vera Anisimova)	43.09	
4. CAN	(Margaret Howe, Patty Loverock, Joanne McTaggart, Marjorie Bailey)	43.17	
5. AUS	(Barbara Wilson, Deborah Wells, Denise Robertson, Raelene Boyle)	43.18	
6. JAM	(Leleith Hodges, Rose Allwood, Carol Cummings, Jacqueline Pusey)	43.24	
7. USA	(Martha Watson, Evelyn Ashford, Debra Armstrong, Chandra Cheeseborough)	43.35	
8. GBR	(Wendy Clarke, Denise Ramsden, Sharon Colyear, Andrea Lynch)	43.79	

The 200 meters champion, Bärbel Eckert, made up a one-meter deficit on the anchor leg to win by a foot. The East German victory brought Renate Stecher's Olympic medal total to six: three gold, two silver, and one bronze.

1980 Moscow T: 8, N: 8, D: 8.1. WR: 41.85 (GDR—Müller, Wöckel [Eckert], Auerswald, Göhr)

1. GDR	(Romy Müller, Bärbel Wöckel [Eckert], Ingrid Auerswald, Marlies Göhr)	41.60	WR
2. SOV	(Vera Komisova, Lyudmila Maslakova [Zharkova], Vera Anisimova, Natalya Bochina)	42.10	
3. GBR	(Heather Hunte, Kathryn Smallwood, Beverley Goddard, Sonia Lannaman)	42.43	
4. BUL	(Sofka Popova, Liliana Panayotova, Maria Shishkova, Galina Encheva)	42.67	
5. FRA	(Veronique Grandrieux, Chantal Rega, Raymonde Naigre, Emma Sulter)	42.84	

6. JAM   (Leleith Hodges, Jacqueline Pusey, Rosie   43.19
          Allwood, Merlene Ottey)
7. POL   (Lucyna Langer, Elżbieta Stachurska, Zofia   43.59
          Bielczyk, Grażyna Rabsztyn)
DNF: SWE (Linda Haglund, Lena Moller, Ann-Louise Skoglund, Helena Pihl)

Unusually poor baton passing failed to prevent the East Germans from winning by five meters and breaking their own world record.

4×400-METER RELAY
1896–1968 not held

1972 Munich T: 14, N: 14, D: 9.10. WR: 3:28.8 (GDR—Käsling, Seidler, Zehrt, Rohde)
1. GDR   (Dägmar Käsling, Rita Kühne, Helga   3:23.0 WR
          Seidler, Monika Zehrt)
2. USA   (Mable Fergerson, Madeline Manning,   3:25.2
          Cheryl Toussaint, Kathy Hammond)
3. GER   (Anette Rückes, Inge Bödding, Hildegard 3:26.5
          Falck, Rita Wilden)
4. FRA   (Martine Duvivier, Colette Besson, Berna- 3:27.5
          dette Martin, Nicole Duclos)
5. GBR   (Verona Bernard, Janet Simpson, Jannette 3:28.7
          Roscoe, Rosemary Stirling)
6. AUS   (Alison Ross-Edwards, Raelene Boyle,   3:28.8
          Cheryl Peasley, Charlene Rendina)
7. FIN   (Marika Eklund, Pirjo Wilmi, Tuula Rau-   3:29.4
          tanen, Mona-Lisa Strandvall)
8. SOV   (Lyubov Runtso, Olga Syrovatskaya, Nata- 3:31.9
          lya Chistiakova, Nadezhda Kolesnikova)

1976 Montreal T: 11, N: 11, D: 7.31. WR: 3:23.0 (GDR—Käsling, Kühne, Seidler, Zehrt)
1. GDR   (Doris Maletzki, Brigitte Rohde, Ellen   3:19.23 WR
          Streidt, Christina Brehmer)
2. USA   (Debra Sapenter, Sheila Ingram, Pamela   3:22.81
          Jiles, Rosalyn Bryant)
3. SOV   (Inta Klimovocha, Lyudmila Aksenova,   3:24.24
          Natalya Sokolova, Nadezhda Ilyina)
4. AUS   (Judith Canty, Verna Burnand, Charlene   3:25.56
          Rendina, Bethanie Nail)
5. GER   (Claudia Steger, Dagmar Fuhrmann, Elke 3:25.71
          Barth, Rita Wilden)
6. FIN   (Marika Lindholm, Pirjo Häggman, Mona- 3:25.87
          Lisa Pursiainen, Riita Salin)
7. GBR   (Elizabeth Barnes, Gladys Taylor, Verona 3:28.01
          Elder, Donna Murray)
8. CAN   (Margaret Stride, Joyce Yakubowich, Ra- 3:28.91
          chelle Campbell, Yvonne Saunders)

The remarkable East German women won by almost 30 meters.

1980 Moscow T: 11, N: 11, D: 8.1. WR: 3:19.23 (GDR—Maletzki, Rohde, Streidt, Brehmer)
1. SOV   (Tatyana Prorochenko, Tatyana Goistchik, 3:20.2
          Nina Zyuskova, Irina Nazarova)
2. GDR   (Gabriele Löwe, Barbara Krug, Christina   3:20.4
          Lathan [Brehmer], Marita Koch)
3. GBR   (Linsey MacDonald, Michelle Probert, Joslyn 3:27.5
          Hoyte-Smith, Janine Macgregor)
4. ROM   (Iboia Korodi, Niculina Lazarciuc, Maria Sa- 3:27.7
          mungi, Elena Tarita)
5. HUN   (Irén Orosz, Judit Forgacs, Éva Toth, Ilona 3:27.9
          Pal)
6. POL   (Grażyna Oliszewska, Elżbieta Katolik-   3:27.9
          Skowrońska, Jolanta Januchta, Malgorzata
          Dunecka)
7. BEL   (Lea Alaerts, Regine Berg, Anne Michel, Ro- 3:31.6
          sine Wallez)
DNF: BUL (Svobodka Damianova, Rossitza Stamenova, Milena Andonova, Bonka Dimova)

The defeat of the East German 4×400-meter relay team was a major upset, but it took an unusual set of circumstances to produce the result. Current Olympic rules state that the same athletes who run in the heats must run in the final, unless official certificates can be produced proving that they are medically unfit to run. The U.S.S.R. came up with two such certificates to replace Olga Mineyeva and Lyudmila Chernova with two fresh runners—Nina Zyuskova and Irina Nazarova, who had finished fifth and fourth respectively in the individual 400 meters event. At the beginning of the third leg, East Germany's Christine Lathan shot ahead of Zyuskova, but the Soviet runner pushed back in front as Lathan stepped on the curb and lost her rhythm. Nazarova took over with a lead of about 10 meters, but 400 meters champion Marita Koch slowly but surely closed the gap. As they entered the final straight it looked as if Koch would move ahead. However Nazarova, inspired by the wildly cheering hometown crowd of 100,000, managed to hold off Koch's challenge and win by one meter.

HIGH JUMP
1896–1924 not held

1928 Amsterdam C: 20, N: 9, D: 8.5. WR: 1.61, 5–3¼ (Carolina Gisolf)

		M	FT.–IN.
1. Ethel Catherwood	CAN	1.59	5-2½
2. Carolina Gisolf	HOL	1.56	5-1¼
3. Mildred Wiley	USA	1.56	5-1¼
4. Jean Shiley	USA	1.51	4-11½
5. Marjorie Clark	SAF	1.48	4-10¼
6. Helma Notte	GER	1.48	4-10¼
7. Inge Braumüller	GER	1.48	4-10¼
8. Catherine Maguire	USA	1.48	4-10¼

Ethel Catherwood, "The Saskatoon Lily," was a beautiful 18-year-old who became a favorite of the spectators and the photographers. During the three-hour competition she kept herself wrapped up in a big red blanket and didn't even take off her sweatsuit until the five-foot mark had been reached. Before each jump she would face the bar, smile and then go over. Her return to Saskatoon caused the largest celebration since the signing of the 1918 Armistice. She was presented with a $3000 education trust fund to be used to continue her piano studies. When asked about rumors that she had received offers to go to Hollywood, Catherwood replied, "I'd rather gulp poison than try my hand at motion pictures." However she did move to the United States the following year, eventually settling in San Francisco.

1932 Los Angeles C: 10, N: 6, D: 8.7. WR: 1.62, 5–3¾ (Carolina Gisolf)

		M	FT.–IN.	
1. Jean Shiley	USA	1.657	5-5¼	WR
2. Mildred Didriksen	USA	1.657	5-5¼	WR
3. Eva Dawes	CAN	1.60	5-3	
4. Carolina Gisolf	HOL	1.58	5-2¼	
5. Marjorie Clark	SAF	1.58	5-2¼	
6. Annette Rogers	USA	1.58	5-2¼	
7. Helman Notte	GER	1.55	5-1	
8. Yuriko Hirohashi	JAP	1.49	4-10½	

Jean Shiley and Babe Didriksen had tied for first place in the U.S. Olympic trials and they tied again in Los Angeles. Both women cleared 5 feet 5¼ inches but failed at 5 feet 6 inches. A jump-off was ordered, and both cleared a world record height of 5 feet 5¾ inches. At this point the judges intervened and declared that Didriksen's western-roll style caused her head to clear the bar before her body. This was deemed "diving" and ruled illegal. Deprived of her third gold medal, Babe was nonetheless given a share of the world record. Her jumping style was legalized not long afterward.

1936 Berlin C: 17, N: 12, D: 8.7. WR: 1.67, 5–5¾ (Jean Shiley, Mildred Didriksen)

		M	FT.–IN.
1. Ibolya Csák	HUN	1.60	5-3
2. Dorothy Odam	GBR	1.60	5-3
3. Elfriede Kaun	GER	1.60	5-3
4. Dora Ratjen	GER	1.58	5-2¼
5. Marguerite Nicolas	FRA	1.58	5-2¼
6. Doris Carter	AUS	1.55	5-1
6. Francina "Fanny" Koen	HOL	1.55	5-1
6. Annette Rogers	USA	1.55	5-1

Csák was awarded first place after clearing 1.62 meters in a jump-off. If the current tie-breaking rules had been in force, 16-year-old Dorothy Odam would have won the gold medal. Fourth-place finisher Dora Ratjen was barred from competition in 1938, when it was discovered that she was a hermaphrodite, a rare sexual group for which international athletics has made no provisions.

1948 London C: 19, N: 10, D: 8.7. WR: 1.71, 5–7¼ (Francina "Fanny" Blankers-Koen)

		M	FT.–IN.	
1. Alice Coachman	USA	1.68	5-6	OR
2. Dorothy Tyler (Odam)	GBR	1.68	5-6	OR
3. Micheline Ostermeyer	FRA	1.61	5-3¼	
4. Vinton Beckett	CAN	1.58	5-2¼	
4. Doreen Dredge	CAN	1.58	5-2¼	
6. Bertha Crowther	GBR	1.58	5-2¼	
7. I. Steinegger	AUT	1.55	5-1	
8. Dorothy Gardner	GBR	1.55	5-1	

Once again, Dorothy Odam, now Dorothy Tyler, lost a tie despite having fewer misses than the winner. This time Alice Coachman was awarded first place because she cleared the final height on her first try, while Tyler required a second attempt. Coachman was the first black woman to win an Olympic gold medal. Bronze medalist Micheline Ostermeyer had already won the shot put and discus.

1952 Helsinki C: 17, N: 10, D: 7.27. WR: 1.72, 5–7¾ (Sheila Lerwill)

		M	FT.–IN.
1. Esther Brand	SAF	1.67	5-5¾
2. Sheila Lerwill	GBR	1.65	5-5
3. Aleksandra Chudina	SOV	1.63	5-4¼
4. Thelma Hopkins	GBR	1.58	5-2¼
5. Olga Modrachová	CZE	1.58	5-2¼
6. Theodora Schenk-Solms	AUT	1.58	5-2¼
7. Nina Kossova	SOV	1.58	5-2¼
7. Dorothy Tyler (Odam)	GBR	1.58	5-2¼

1956 Melbourne C: 19, N: 12, D: 12.1 WR: 1.75, 5–8¾ (Iolanda Balaş)

		M	FT.–IN.	
1. Mildred McDaniel	USA	1.76	5-9¼	WR
2. Thelma Hopkins	SOV	1.67	5-5¾	
2. Maria Pissaryeva	SOV	1.67	5-5¾	
4. Gunhild Larking	SWE	1.67	5-5¾	
5. Iolanda Balaş	ROM	1.67	5-5¾	
6. Michele Mason	AUS	1.67	5-5¾	
7. Mary Donaghy	NZE	1.67	5-5¾	
8. Hermina Geyser	SAF	1.64	5-4½	
8. Jirina Voborilov	CZE	1.64	5-4½	

1960 Rome C: 23, N: 15, D: 9.8. WR: 1.86, 6–1¼ (Iolanda Balaş)

		M	FT.–IN.	
1. Iolanda Balaş	ROM	1.85	6-0¾	OR
2. Jaroslawa Jóźwiakowska	POL	1.71	5-7¼	
2. Dorothy Shirley	GBR	1.71	5-7¼	
4. Galina Dolya	SOV	1.71	5-7¼	
5. Taisiya Chenchik	SOV	1.68	5-6	
6. Helen Frith	AUS	1.65	5-5	
6. Inga-Britt Lorentzon	SWE	1.65	5-5	
6. Frances Slaap	GBR	1.65	5-5	

Few people have dominated an event as completely as Iolanda Balaş dominated the women's high jump. Following her fifth-place finish at the Melbourne Olympics, she won an incredible 140 consecutive competitions over the next ten and a half years. She set 14 world records and was the first woman to high-jump 6 feet. By the time a second woman, Michele Brown of Australia, had cleared that bar—

rier, Balaş had done it in 46 different meets. On July 16, 1961, the 6-foot Balaş jumped 6 feet 3¼ inches, a height that wasn't beaten until September 4, 1971.

1964 Tokyo C: 27, N: 18, D: 10.15. WR: 1.91, 6–3¼ (Iolanda Balaş)

		M	FT.–IN.	
1. Iolanda Balaş	ROM	1.90	6-2¾	OR
2. Michele Brown (Mason)	AUS	1.80	5-11	
3. Taisiya Chenchik	SOV	1.78	5-10	
4. Aida Dos Santos	BRA	1.74	5-8½	
5. Dianne Gerace	CAN	1.71	5-7¼	
6. Frances Slaap	GBR	1.71	5-7¼	
7. Olga Pluic	YUG	1.71	5-7¼	
8. Eleanor Montgomery	USA	1.71	5-7¼	

1968 Mexico City C: 24, N: 14, D: 10.17. WR: 1.91, 6–3¼ (Iolanda Balaş)

		M	FT.–IN.
1. Miloslava Režková	CZE	1.82	5-11½
2. Antonina Okorokova	SOV	1.80	5-10¾
3. Valentina Kozyr	SOV	1.80	5-10¾
4. Jaroslava Valentová	CZE	1.78	5-10
5. Rita Schmidt	GDR	1.78	5-10
6. Maria Faithová	CZE	1.78	5-10
7. Karin Schulze	GDR	1.76	5-9¼
8. Ilona Gusenbauer	AUT	1.76	5-9¼

Eighteen-year-old Milena Režková was a popular winner. Not only was she a complete outsider who had improved her personal best by 6 inches since the beginning of the year and who jumped 5 inches over her own height, but she was a Czech who won a dramatic showdown against two women from the U.S.S.R. Her victory was gained on her third and final try at 5 feet 11½ inches. Had Režková missed, Okorokova would have won on the basis of fewer misses.

1972 Munich C: 40, N: 22, D: 9.4. WR: 1.92, 6–3½ (Ilona Gusenbauer)

		M	FT.–IN.	
1. Ulrike Meyfarth	GER	1.92	6-3½	EWR
2. Yordanka Blagoeva	BUL	1.88	6-2	
3. Ilona Gusenbauer	AUT	1.88	6-2	
4. Barbara Inkpen	GBR	1.85	6-0¾	
5. Rita Schmidt	GDR	1.85	6-0¾	
6. Sara Simeoni	ITA	1.85	6-0¾	
7. Rosemarie Witschas	GDR	1.85	6-0¾	
8. Deborah Brill	CAN	1.82	5-11½	

If Režková's win in Mexico City was considered an upset, then the victory of 16-year-old Ulrike Meyfarth in Munich was more like a fairy tale. The 6-foot ½-inch Köln-Rodenkirchen schoolgirl, who had only finished third in the West German trials, jumped 2¾ inches higher than her pre-Olympic best. Blagoeva appeared to have cleared the bar on her last attempt at 6 feet 2¾ inches and was already

starting to put her sweatsuit back on, when the bar fell and the judges ruled a miss. The admirably neutral German audience jeered the decision, which was, however, entirely in keeping with the rules of the competition. Gusenbauer looked the other way as Meyfarth equaled the world record that the Austrian had set exactly one year earlier to the day. Three weeks later, Blagoeva raised the world record to 6 feet 4½ inches. Ulrike Meyfarth is the youngest person of either sex to win an individual track and field gold medal in the Olympics.

1976 Montreal C: 35, N: 23, D: 7.28. WR: 1.96, 6–5¼ (Rosemarie Ackermann [Witschas])

		M	FT.–IN.	
1. Rosemarie Ackermann (Witschas)	GDR	1.93	6-4	OR
2. Sara Simeoni	ITA	1.91	6-3¼	
3. Yordanka Blagoeva	BUL	1.91	6-3¼	
4. Mária Mrachnová	CZE	1.89	6-2½	
5. Joni Huntley	USA	1.89	6-2½	
6. Tatyana Shlyahto	SOV	1.87	6-1½	
7. Annette Tannander	SWE	1.87	6-1½	
8. Cornelia Popa	ROM	1.87	6-1½	

The qualifying rounds saw the surprising early elimination of Ulrike Meyfarth, Rita Kirst (Schmidt), Debbie Brill of Canada, and Vera Bradacova of Czechoslovakia, all of whom had cleared 6 feet 3 inches previously. Although the competition was won by the favorite, Rosemarie Ackermann, the field had such depth that 18 women cleared 6 feet and 13 were still in the running after three hours. On August 26, 1977, Ackermann, a shop clerk from Cottbus, became the first woman to jump two meters—9½ inches over her own head.

1980 Moscow C: 20, N: 13, D: 7.26. WR: 2.01, 6–7 (Sara Simeoni)

		M	FT.–IN.	
1. Sara Simeoni	ITA	1.97	6-5½	OR
2. Urszula Kielan	POL	1.94	6-4¼	
3. Jutta Kirst	GDR	1.94	6-4¼	
4. Rosemarie Ackermann (Witschas)	GDR	1.91	6-3¼	
5. Marina Sysoyeva	SOV	1.91	6-3¼	
6. Christine Stanton	AUS	1.91	6-3¼	
6. Andrea Reichstein	GDR	1.91	6-3¼	
8. Cornelia Popa	ROM	1.88	6-2	

The ever-popular Sara Simeoni had switched to high-jumping at the age of 12 after being told that she couldn't be a ballet dancer because she was too tall and her feet were too big. She lost six out of seven meets to Rosemarie Ackermann between 1973 and 1977. Then she beat her in a dramatic showdown at the European championships in Prague in August 1978, and the tide turned. In Moscow Simeoni recorded her first miss at 1.94, but cleared on her second attempt to earn the gold medal. Fifth-place finisher Marina Sysoyeva jumped 6 feet 4 inches earlier in the year to set a women's world record for jumping higher than one's own height—10¼ inches.

LONG JUMP
1896–1936 not held

1948 London C: 26, N: 13, D: 8.4. WR: 6.25, 20–6¼ (Francina "Fanny" Blankers-Koen)

			M	FT.–IN.
1.	Olga Gyarmati	HUN	5.695	18-8¼
2.	Noëmi Simonetto De Portela	ARG	5.60	18-4½
3.	Ann-Britt Leyman	SWE	5.575	18-3¼
4.	Gerda van der Kade-Koudijs	HOL	5.57	18-3¼
5.	Neeltje Karelse	HOL	5.545	18-2¼
6.	Kathleen Russell	JAM	5.495	18-0¼
7.	Judy Canty	AUS	5.38	17-7¾
8.	Yvonne Curtet-Chabot	FRA	5.35	17-6½

The importance of the competition was somewhat muted by the absence of world record holder Fanny Blankers-Koen, who was busy winning gold medals in four other events.

1952 Helsinki C: 34, N: 22, D: 7.23. WR: 6.25, 20–6¼ (Francina "Fanny" Blankers-Koen)

			M	FT.–IN.	
1.	Yvette Williams	NZE	6.24	20-5¾	OR
2.	Aleksandra Chudina	SOV	6.14	20-1¾	
3.	Shirley Cawley	GBR	5.92	19-5¼	
4.	Irmgard Schmelzer	GER	5.90	19-4¼	
5.	Wilhelmina Lust	HOL	5.81	19-0¾	
6.	Nina Tyurkina	SOV	5.81	19-0¾	
7.	Mabel Landry	USA	5.75	18-10½	
8.	Verna Johnson	AUS	5.74	18-10	

Twenty-three-year-old Yvette Williams of Dunedin led the qualifying rounds with a jump of 6.16 meters (20 feet 2½ inches). She faulted twice in the final and was one jump away from elimination. However her third jump of 5.90 meters (19 feet 4¼ inches) was good enough to put her in the top six who qualified for three more jumps. Her fourth attempt was the winning one, and none of the leaders was able to improve after that. Williams also finished sixth in the shot put. However, the real award for versatility in field events went to Chudina, who took second in the long jump, second in the javelin, and third in the high jump.

1956 Melbourne C: 19, N: 11, D: 11.27. WR: 6.35, 20–10 (Elżbieta Krzesińska)

			M	FT.–IN.	
1.	Elżbieta Krzesińska	POL	6.35	20-10	EWR
2.	Willye White	USA	6.09	19-11¾	
3.	Nadezhda Dvalischvili (Khnykina)	SOV	6.07	19-11	
4.	Erika Fisch	GER	5.89	19-4	
5.	Marthe Lambert	FRA	5.88	19-3½	
6.	Valentina Schaprunova	SOV	5.85	19-2¼	
7.	Beverly Weigel	NZE	5.85	19-2¼	
8.	Nancy Borwick	AUS	5.82	19-1¼	

Krzesińska, a 21-year-old medical student, was in a class by herself. Seventeen-year-old Willye White, who was born in Money, Mississippi, was a surprise silver medalist. She read the New Testament between jumps and won second place with her final leap. She also competed in the next four Olympics.

1960 Rome C: 30, N: 18, D: 8.31. WR: 6.40, 21–0 (Hildrun Claus)

			M	FT.–IN.	
1.	Vyera Krepkina	SOV	6.37	20-10¾	OR
2.	Elżbieta Krzesińska	POL	6.27	20-7	
3.	Hildrun Claus	GDR	6.21	20-4½	
4.	Renate Junker	GER	6.19	20-3¾	
5.	Lyudmila Radchenko	SOV	6.16	20-2½	
6.	Helga Hoffmann	GER	6.11	20-0½	
7.	Johanna Bijleveld	HOL	6.11	20-0½	
8.	Valentina Schaprunova	SOV	6.01	19-8¾	

Krepkina's victory came as a complete surprise, since she was better known as a sprinter. In fact, she was co-holder of the world record for the 100 meters.

1964 Tokyo C: 31, N: 20, D: 10.14. WR: 6.70, 21–11¾ (Tatyana Schelkanova)

			M	FT.–IN.	
1.	Mary Rand (Bignal)	GBR	6.76	22-2¼	WR
2.	Irena Kirszenstein	POL	6.60	21-8	
3.	Tatyana Schelkanova	SOV	6.42	21-0¾	
4.	Ingrid Becker	GER	6.40	21-0	
5.	Viorica Viscopoleanu	ROM	6.35	20-10	
6.	Diana Yorgova	BUL	6.24	20-5¾	
7.	Hildrun Laufer (Claus)	GDR	6.24	20-5¾	
8.	Helga Hoffmann	GER	6.23	20-5¼	

In 1960 Mary Rand (then Mary Bignal) had been considered the favorite in the long jump, particularly after she had led the qualifying round with a personal best of 20 feet 9¼ inches. That jump would have won her a silver medal if she had been able to repeat it in the final. Instead she ran through twice and had to settle for ninth place with her third jump. She also finished fourth in the 80-meter hurdles the following day. Four years later in Tokyo, Mary Rand again had the best jump of the qualifying round—21 feet 4¾ inches. This time, though, everything went right in the final. Four of her six jumps were her best ever, and her whole series was so consistent that her worst leap would have earned her a silver medal. Her fifth jump registered 6.76 meters. Unfamiliar with the metric system, she raced back to her bag, pulled out the program, and learned that she had broken the world record. And this despite the fact that she had jumped into a 1.69 meters per second wind. Mary Rand was the first British woman to win an Olympic gold medal in track and field. Later in the week she also won a silver medal in the pentathlon and a bronze in the 4×100-meter relay. In 1967 she went to Mexico City and met her future second husband, the U.S. decathlon champion Bill Toomey.

The woman who finished sixth in 1964, Bulgarian Diana Yorgova, made the news several days later when she and Bulgarian gymnast Nikolai Prodanov held the first-ever Olympic wedding. The ceremony took place in the International Club of the Olympic Village in front of a huge Olympic flag and a photo of the Olympic flame. The couple honeymooned in Kyoto, but returned to Tokyo in time for the closing ceremonies.

1968 Mexico City C: 27, N: 19, D: 10.14. WR: 6.76, 22–2¼ (Mary Rand [Bignal])

		M	FT.–IN.	
1. Viorica Viscopoleanu	ROM	6.82	22-4½	WR
2. Sheila Sherwood	GBR	6.68	21-11	
3. Tatyana Talisheva	SOV	6.66	21-10¼	
4. Burghild Wieczorek	GDR	6.48	21-3¼	
5. Miroslawa Sarna	POL	6.47	21-2¾	
6. Ingrid Becker	GER	6.43	21-1¼	
7. Berit Berthelsen	NOR	6.40	21-0	
8. Heidemarie Rosendahl	GER	6.40	21-0	

Viscopoleanu recorded her winning jump on her first attempt of the final. The 29-year-old Romanian improved on her pre-Olympic personal best by no less than nine inches.

1972 Munich C: 33, N: 19, D: 8.31. WR: 6.84, 22–5¼ (Heidemarie Rosendahl)

		M	FT.–IN.
1. Heidemarie Rosendahl	GER	6.78	22-3
2. Diana Yorgova	BUL	6.77	22-2½
3. Eva Suranová	CZE	6.67	21-10¾
4. Marcia Garbey	CUB	6.52	21-4¾
5. Heidi Schüller	GER	6.51	21-4¼
6. Meta Antenen	SWI	6.49	21-3½
7. Viorica Viscopoleanu	ROM	6.48	21-3¼
8. Margrit Olfert	GDR	6.46	21-2½

Heidemarie Rosendahl brought great joy to the crowd by becoming the first West German gold medal winner of the Munich Games. Her first leap of 6.78 meters appeared to be good enough for first place until the fourth round, when Diana Yorgova, the first Bugarian to win a track and field medal, hit the best jump of her career. But it was one centimeter too short. Yorgova's last jump was also a long one, but was disallowed because her foot went over the board. Later in the Games Rosendahl picked up a silver medal in the pentathlon and another gold in the 4×100-meter relay.

1976 Montreal C: 30, N: 19, D: 7.23. WR: 6.99, 22–11¼ (Siegrun Siegl)

		M	FT.–IN.
1. Angela Voigt	GDR	6.72	22-0¾
2. Kathy McMillan	USA	6.66	21-10¼
3. Lidia Alfeyeva	SOV	6.60	21-8
4. Siegrun Siegl	GDR	6.59	21-7½
5. Ildikó Szabo	HUN	6.59	21-7½
6. Jarmila Nygrynová	CZE	6.54	21-5½
7. Heidimarie Wycisk	GDR	6.39	20-11¾
8. Elena Vintila	ROM	6.38	20-11¼

For the third straight time the women's long jump was won on a first-round jump. Angela Voigt had held the world record for ten days earlier in the year, but she had a reputation for doing poorly in important meets. The last jumper of the competition, 18-year-old Kathy McMillan of Raeford, North Carolina, finished with the longest leap of the day; however, she had stepped an inch or so over the board, and a no-jump was declared.

1980 Moscow C: 19, N: 11, D: 7.31. WR: 7.09, 23–3¼ (Vilma Bardauskiene)

		M	FT.–IN.	
1. Tatiana Kolpakova	SOV	7.06	23-2	OR
2. Brigitte Wujak	GDR	7.04	23-1¼	
3. Tatiana Skachko	SOV	7.01	23-0	
4. Anna Wlodarczyk	POL	6.95	22-9¾	
5. Siegrun Siegl	GDR	6.87	22-6½	
6. Jarmila Nygrýnová	CZE	6.83	22-5	
7. Siegrid Heimann	GDR	6.71	22-0¼	
8. Lidiya Alfeyeva	SOV	6.71	22-0¼	

This was, without question, the most exciting women's Olympic long-jump contest ever. In 1978 Vilma Bardauskiene had become the first woman to break the 7-meter barrier, but two years later, hampered by injuries, she was unable to make the Soviet team. With one round to go Skachko was in first place as a result of her third round leap of 7.01 meters. She was followed by Wujak and Wlodarczyk, with 6.88 each, and Kolpakova with 6.87. Wlodarczyk's final jump of 6.95 put her into second place and had her crying for joy, but she and Skachko watched in horror as the situation changed dramatically in the next two minutes. First Kolpakova, third string on the U.S.S.R. team, jumped into first place with a 7.06—nine inches further than her pre-Olympic best. Then Wujak improved her personal best by 5½ inches to take the silver medal. Skachko, who had been in front for two hours, was forced to settle for a bronze medal, and Wlodarczyk was left without any medal at all. At the postrace press conference, Kolpakova, a shy 20-year-old from Frunze in the Kirghiz Soviet Socialist Republic, summed up the competition by saying, "I think that one should always fight until the end, and my last attempt confirmed it."

SHOT PUT

The women's shot weights 4 kilograms (8 pounds 13 ounces).

1896–1936 not held

1948 London C: 19, N: 12, D: 8.4. WR: 14.89, 48–10¼ (Tatyana Sevryukova)

		M	FT.–IN.
1. Micheline Ostermeyer	FRA	13.75	45-1½
2. Amelia Piccinini	ITA	13.09	42-11½
3. Ine Schäffer	AUT	13.08	42-11
4. Paulette Veste	FRA	12.985	42-7¼
5. Jaroslava Komárková	CZE	12.92	42-4¾
6. Anni Bruk	AUT	12.50	42-0¼
7. Maria Radosaljevic	YUG	12.355	40-6½
8. Bevis Reid	GBR	12.17	39-11¼

Three months before the Olympics, pianist Micheline Ostermeyer had graduated with high honors from the Paris Conservatory of Music. In London she used the hands that so delicately played the piano to win gold medals in both the shot put and discus. Her success in track and field actually hurt her reputation as a concert pianist, and for a long time she was afraid to play Liszt because he was too *"sportif."*

1952 Helsinki C: 20, N: 13, D: 7.26. WR: 15.19, 49–10 (Galina Zybina)

		M	FT.–IN.	
1. Galina Zybina	SOV	15.28	50-1¾	WR
2. Marianne Werner	GER	14.57	47-9¾	
3. Klaudia Tochenova	SOV	14.50	47-7	
4. Tamara Tyshkevich	SOV	14.42	47-3¾	
5. Gertrud Kille	GER	13.84	45-5	
6. Yvette Williams	NZE	13.35	43-9¾	
7. Maria Radosaljevic	YUG	13.30	43-7¾	
8. Meeri Saari	FIN	13.02	42-8¾	

As a ten-year-old child, Galina Zybina had watched her mother and brother die of cold and starvation during World War II. She barely survived herself and entered adolescence thin and sickly. However, ten years after her ordeal, she proved to be the strongest woman in the world. In Helsinki Zybina had the three longest throws of the competition and had already secured first place when she broke the world record on her final attempt. Werner moved from fourth to second on her final throw to prevent a Soviet sweep.

1956 Melbourne C: 18, N: 9, D: 11.30 WR: 16.76, 55–0 (Galina Zybina)

		M	FT.–IN.	
1. Tamara Tyshkevich	SOV	16.59	54-5¼	OR
2. Galina Zybina	SOV	16.53	54-2¾	
3. Marianne Werner	GER	15.61	51-2¾	
4. Zinaida Doynikova	SOV	15.54	51-0	
5. Valerie Sloper	NZE	15.34	50-4	
6. Earlene Brown	USA	15.12	49-7¼	
7. Regina Branner	AUS	14.60	47-10¾	
8. Nadya Kotlusek	YUG	14.56	47-9¼	

Zybina took the lead in the first round and appeared to be headed for a second gold medal. However, in the final round her 231-pound teammate, Tamara Tyshkevich, scored a dramatic victory by heaving the shot 2¼ inches further than Zybina's best. Los Angeles housewife Earlene Brown made a great impression on the Australians and became a local favorite. Arriving in Melbourne early, she took part in a regional meet and won. When a fan informed her that she had just broken the Victoria state record, Brown replied, "I'm sorry, honey, If I'd known I was going to do that I wouldn't have thrown it so far."

1960 Rome C: 18, N: 12, D: 9.2. WR: 17.78, 58–4 (Tamara Press)

		M	FT.–IN.	
1. Tamara Press	SOV	17.32	56-10	OR
2. Johanna Lüttge	GDR	16.61	54-6	
3. Earlene Brown	USA	16.42	53-10½	
4. Valerie Sloper	NZE	16.39	53-9¼	
5. Zinaida Doynikova	SOV	16.13	52-11	
6. Renate Garisch	GDR	15.94	52-3¾	
7. Galina Zybina	SOV	15.56	51-0¾	
8. Wilfriede Hoffmann	GDR	15.14	49-8¼	

Tamara Press and her younger sister Irina were two nice Jewish girls from Leningrad (hometown of Galina Zybina). Between them they set 26 world records and won five Olympic gold medals and one silver. The only trouble was that they may not have been women at all. When sex tests were instituted at international competitions, the careers of both Press "sisters" came to a sudden halt. Probably they did not actually have male sex organs, but rather had been injected with an excessive amount of male sex hormones.

1964 Tokyo C: 16, N: 11, D: 10.20. WR: 18.55, 60–10½ (Tamara Press)

		M	FT.–IN.	
1. Tamara Press	SOV	18.14	59-6¼	OR
2. Renate Garisch-Culmberger	GDR	17.61	57-9½	
3. Galina Zybina	SOV	17.45	57-3	
4. Valerie Young-Sloper	NZE	17.26	56-7½	
5. Margitta Helmboldt	GDR	16.91	55-5¾	
6. Irina Press	SOV	16.71	54-10	
7. Nancy McCredie	CAN	15.89	52-1¾	
8. Ana Salagean	ROM	15.83	51-11¼	

Tamara Press won the discus gold the day before the shot put. Zybina's bronze gave her a complete set of Olympic medals.

1968 Mexico City C: 14, N: 10, D: 10.20. WR: 18.87, 61–11 (Margitta Gummel [Helmboldt])

		M	FT.–IN.	
1. Margitta Gummel (Helmboldt)	GDR	19.61	64-4	WR
2. Marita Lange	GDR	18.78	61-7½	
3. Nadezhda Chizhova	SOV	18.19	59-8¼	
4. Judit Bognar	HUN	17.78	58-4	
5. Renate Boy (Garisch-Culmberger)	GDR	17.72	58-1¾	
6. Ivanka Hristova	BUL	17.25	56-7¼	
7. Marlene Fuchs	GER	17.11	56-1¾	
8. Els Van Noorduyn	HOL	16.23	53-3	

In the very first round Marita Lange heaved the shot 61 feet 7½ inches to improve her personal best by over a yard. Gummel broke the world record in the third round and then unleashed an amazing fifth-round toss of 64 feet 4 inches to better her own pre-Olympic world record by 29 inches.

1972 Munich C: 18, N: 11, D: 9.7. WR: 20.63, 67–8¼ (Nadezhda Chizhova)

		M	FT.–IN.	
1. Nadezhda Chizhova	SOV	21.03	69-0	WR
2. Margitta Gummel (Helmboldt)	GDR	20.22	66-4¼	
3. Ivanka Hristova	BUL	19.35	63-6	
4. Svet Krachevska	SOV	19.24	63-1½	
5. Marianne Adam	GDR	18.94	62-1¾	
6. Marita Lange	GDR	18.85	61-10¼	
7. Helena Fibingerová	CZE	18.81	61-8½	
8. Yelena Stoyanova	BUL	18.34	60-2	

Siberian-born Nadezhda Chizhova put the championship out of reach on her first attempt with a world record of 69 feet.

1976 Montreal C: 13, N: 8, D: 7.31. WR: 21.89, 71–10 (Ivanka Hristova)

		M	FT.–IN.	
1. Ivanka Hristova	BUL	21.16	69-5¼	OR
2. Nadezhda Chizhova	SOV	20.96	68-9¼	
3. Helena Fibingerová	CZE	20.67	67-9¾	
4. Marianne Adam	GDR	20.55	67-5¼	
5. Ilona Schoknecht	GDR	20.54	67-4¾	
6. Margitta Droese	GDR	19.79	64-11¼	
7. Eva Wilms	GER	19.29	63-3½	
8. Yelena Stoyanova	BUL	18.89	61-11¾	

The 1976 shot put competition matched the world record holder against three former world record holders. Defending champion Chizhova led after the first round with a throw of 68 feet 4½ inches. In the second round Hristova hit 68 feet 6 inches, but Chizhova responded with 68 feet 9¼ inches. However Chizhova slipped and injured her leg and was unable to come up with another serious throw. Her lead held up until the fifth round, when Hristova secured the victory with a new Olympic record of 69 feet 5¼ inches. Hristova's win culminated a steady rise in her career. In the 1964 Olympics she finished tenth. In 1968 she was sixth, and in 1972 she was third. Finally, at the age of 34, she won a gold medal, the first ever by a Bulgarian track and field athlete. Chizhova matched Galina Zybina's feat of earning a complete set of medals.

1980 Moscow C: 14, N: 8, D: 7.24. WR: 22.45, 73–8 (Ilona Slupianek [Schoknecht])

		M	FT.–IN.
1. Ilona Slupianek (Schoknecht)	GDR	22.41	73-6¼
2. Svetlana Krachevskaya	SOV	21.42	70-3½
3. Margitta Pufe (Droese)	GDR	21.20	69-6¾
4. Nunu Abashicze	SOV	21.15	69-4¾
5. Verginia Vesselinova	BUL	20.72	67-11¾
6. Elena Stoyanova	BUL	20.22	66-4¼
7. Nataliya Akhrimenko	SOV	19.74	64-9¼
8. Ines Reichenbach	GDR	19.66	64-6

Slupianek was forced to sit out the 1978 season when she was caught taking steroids. In Moscow she put on an ex-traordinary performance, outclassing the opposition. The last to throw, she broke the Olympic record on her first attempt and then went over 70 feet on each of her five remaining throws. Her *worst* put, 70 feet 3½ inches, was equal to the *best* put of silver medalist Svetlana Krachevskaya.

DISCUS THROW

The women's discus weighs 1 kilogram (2 pounds 3.27 ounces).

1896–1924 not held

1928 Amsterdam C: 21, N: 12, D: 7.31. WR: 39.18, 128–6 (Halina Konopacka)

		M	FT.–IN.	
1. Halina Konopacka	POL	39.62	129-11¾	WR
2. Lillian Copeland	USA	37.08	121-8	
3. Ruth Svedberg	SWE	35.92	117-10	
4. Emilie "Milly" Reuter	GER	35.86	117-8	
5. Grete Heublein	GER	35.56	116-8	
6. Liesl Perkaus	AUT	33.54	110-0½	
7. Maybelle Reichardt	USA	33.52	110-0	
8. Genowefa Kobielska	POL	32.72	107-4	

1932 Los Angeles C: 9, N: 4, D: 8.2. WR: 42.43, 139–2½ (Jadwiga Wajs)

		M	FT.–IN.	
1. Lillian Copeland	USA	40.58	133-2	OR
2. Ruth Osburn	USA	40.12	131-7	
3. Jadwiga Wajs	POL	38.74	127-1	
4. Tilly Fleischer	GER	36.12	118-6	
5. Grete Heublein	GER	34.66	113-8	
6. Stanislawa Walasiewicz	POL	33.60	110-3	
7. Mitsue Ishizu	JAP	33.52	110-0	
8. Ellen Braümuller	GER	33.15	108-9	

Twenty-seven-year-old Lillian Copeland, a student at the nearby University of Southern California, won the contest on her final throw. She told reporters, "The only thing I could think of as I stood there waiting for my last throw of the day was Dr. O'Callaghan, who won the hammer throw [the previous day] on *his* last throw of the day."

1936 Berlin C: 19, N: 11, D: 8.4. WR: 48.31, 158–6 (Gisela Mauermayer)

		M	FT.–IN.	
1. Gisela Mauermayer	GER	47.63	156-3	OR
2. Jadwiga Wajs	POL	46.22	151-8	
3. Paula Mollenhauer	GER	39.80	130-7	
4. Ko Nakamura	JAP	38.24	125-5	
5. Hide Mineshima	JAP	37.35	122-6	
6. Birgit Lundström	SWE	35.92	117-10	
7. Anna Niesink	HOL	35.21	115-6	
8. Gertrude Wilhemsen	USA	34.43	112-11½	

Three weeks before the games began, Gisela Mauermayer heaved the discus 158 feet 6 inches to set a world record that would last for twelve years. Mauermayer was a modest 22-year-old, a 6-foot blonde, who was hailed in Germany as the perfect example of Aryan womanhood. She gave the Nazi salute on the victory stand and joined the Nazi party. During World War II she was a teacher in Munich. After the war she lost her job because of her Nazi party membership. Starting over at the Zoological Institute of Munich University she gained a doctor's degree by studying the social behavior of ants. Like Helen Stephens, another star of the 1936 games, Mauermayer eventually settled down as a librarian.

1948 London C: 21, N: 1, D: 7.30 WR: 48.31, 158–6 (Gisela Mauermayer)

		M	FT.–IN.
1. Micheline Ostermeyer	FRA	41.92	137-6
2. Edera Cordiale Gentile	ITA	41.17	135-0
3. Jacqueline Mazeas	FRA	40.47	132-9
4. Jadwiga Wajś-Marcinkiewicz	POL	39.30	128-11
5. Charlotte "Lotte" Haidegger	AUT	38.81	127-3
6. Anna Panhorst Niesink	HOL	38.74	127-1
7. Majken Aberg	SWE	38.48	126-3
8. Ingeborg Mello	ARG	38.44	126-1

1952 Helsinki C: 20, N: 16, D: 7.20. WR: 53.37, 175–1 (Nina Dumbadze)

		M	FT.–IN.
1. Nina Romaschkova	SOV	51.42	168-8 OR
2. Yelisaveta Bagryantseva	SOV	47.08	154-5
3. Nina Dumbadze	SOV	46.29	151-10
4. Toyoko Yoshino	JAP	43.81	143-8
5. Charlotte "Lotte" Haidegger	AUT	43.49	142-8
6. Lia Manoliu	ROM	42.65	139-11
7. Ingeborg Pfuller (Mello)	ARG	41.73	136-11
8. Ilona Jozsa	HUN	41.61	136-6

Romaschkova was well known to British fans as a result of an incident in London in which she had been arrested for shoplifting a hat. Her margin of victory in Helsinki was extraordinary, particularly considering the presence of world record holder Nina Dumbadze. The following month Romaschkova broke Dumbadze's record, but on October 18, Dumbadze threw the discus 187 feet 1½ inches to set a world record that would last for almost eight years. Olympic silver medalist Yelisaveta Bagryantseva was the mother of Irina Bagryantseva, who won a gold medal in the 4×400-meter relay in 1980.

1956 Melbourne C: 22, N: 12, D: 11.23. WR: 57.04, 187-1½ (Nina Dumbadze)

		M	FT.–IN.
1. Olga Fikotová	CZE	53.69	176-1 OR
2. Irina Beglyakova	SOV	52.54	174-4
3. Nina Ponomaryeva (Romaschkova)	SOV	52.02	170-8
4. Earlene Brown	USA	51.35	168-5
5. Albina Yelkina	SOV	48.20	158-2
6. Isabel Ercilia Avellán	ARG	46.73	153-3
7. Jiřina Voborilova	CZE	45.84	150-5
8. Stepanka Martova	CZE	45.78	150-2

A former member of the Czechoslovakian national basketball team, Fikotová gained great fame as a result of her Cold War-thawing romance with and marriage to U.S. hammer thrower Harold Connolly. The couple eventually settled in California, although they were later divorced. Olga took part in four more Olympics, finishing seventh in 1960, 12th in 1964, sixth in 1968, and 16th in 1972.

1960 Rome C: 24, N: 15, D: 9.5. WR: 57.04, 187–1½ (Nina Dumbadze)

		M	FT.–IN.
1. Nina Ponomaryeva (Romaschkova)	SOV	55.10	180-9 OR
2. Tamara Press	SOV	52.59	172-4
3. Lia Manoliu	ROM	52.36	171-9
4. Krimhild Hausmann	GER	51.47	168-10
5. Yevgenya Kuznyetsova	SOV	51.43	168-8
6. Earlene Brown	USA	51.29	168-3
7. Olga Connolly (Fikatová)	USA	50.95	167-2
8. Jiřina Nemcova (Voborilova)	CZE	50.12	164-5

The 1960 discus competition matched two former gold medal winners and two future gold medal winners. Ponomaryeva took the lead in the second round and won with the contest's three longest throws. A week later, Tamara Press set a world record of 57.15 meters (187 feet 6 inches).

1964 Tokyo C: 21, N: 15, D: 10.19. WR: 59.28, 194–5¾ (Tamara Press)

		M	FT.–IN.
1. Tamara Press	SOV	57.27	187-10 OR
2. Ingrid Lotz	GDR	57.21	187-8
3. Lia Manoliu	ROM	56.97	186-10
4. Virzhinia Mikhailova	BUL	56.70	186-0
5. Yevgenya Kuznyetsova	SOV	55.17	181-0
6. Jolán Kleiber	HUN	54.87	180-0
7. Krimhild Limberg (Hausmann)	GER	53.81	176-6
8. Olimpia Catarama	ROM	53.08	173-11

After four rounds, world record holder Tamara Press was only in fourth place. Her fifth attempt, however, stretched two inches beyond Ingrid Lotz's first-round mark and gave Press the closest victory in Olympic discus history.

1968 Mexico City C: 15, N: 8, D: 10.18. WR: 62.54, 205–2¼ (Liesel Westermann)

		M	FT.–IN.
1. Lia Manoliu	ROM	58.28	191-2 OR
2. Liesel Westermann	GER	57.76	189-6
3. Jolán Kleiber	HUN	54.90	180-1
4. Anita Otto	GDR	54.40	178-6
5. Antonina Popova	SOV	53.42	175-3
6. Olga Connolly (Fikatová)	USA	52.96	173-9
7. Christine Speilberg	GDR	52.86	173-5
8. Brigitte Berendonk	GER	52.80	173-3

On November 5, 1967, while competing in Brazil, Liesel Westermann became the first woman to throw the discus over 200 feet, with a heave of 201 feet (61.26 meters). In Mexico City she was one of the three favorites, along with the East German Christine Speilberg and the Romanian Lia Manoliu, who was taking part in her fifth Olympics. In 1952 Manoliu had finished sixth, in 1956 ninth, in 1960 third, and in 1964 third again. Manoliu entered the competition in 1968 with a sore elbow, so she decided to put everything she had into her first throw. It went 191 feet 2 inches, good enough to take the lead after the first round. After that she fouled three times, passed once, and got off one poor throw. However a rainstorm arrived during the second round, and the rest of the competition was severely impaired as the throwing circle became wetter and wetter. It turned out that Lia Manoliu's first toss held up to take first place, and the 36-year-old Manoliu became the oldest woman in Olympic history to win a track and field gold medal. She took part in one more Olympics in 1972, finishing ninth. No other track and field athlete of either sex has taken part in six different Olympic Games.

1972 Munich C: 17, N: 10, D: 9.10. WR: 66.76, 219–0¼ (Faina Melnik)

		M	FT.–IN.	
1. Faina Melnik	SOV	66.62	218-7	OR
2. Argentina Menis	ROM	65.06	213-5	
3. Vassilka Stoeva	BUL	64.34	211-1	
4. Tamara Danilova	SOV	62.86	206-3	
5. Liesel Westermann	GER	62.18	204-0	
6. Gabriele Hinzmann	GDR	61.72	202-6	
7. Carmen Ionescu	ROM	60.42	198-3	
8. Lyudmila Muraviova	SOV	59.00	193-7	

Argentina Menis, who wore makeup and false eyelashes while competing, led after three rounds, with world champion Faina Melnik struggling in fifth place. However Melnik, who yelled at the top of her lungs with each throw, came within 3½ inches of her best ever on her fourth attempt. Menis gave one last mighty effort on her final try, nearly decapitating a marker judge with a throw of 212 feet 11 inches. Less than two weeks later Menis set a world record of 220 feet 10 inches.

1976 Montreal C: 15, N: 9, D: 7.29. WR: 70.50, 231–3½ (Faina Melnik)

		M	FT.–IN.	
1. Evelin Schlaak	GDR	69.00	226-4	OR
2. Maria Vergova	BUL	67.30	220-9	
3. Gabriele Hinzmann	GDR	66.84	219-3	
4. Faina Melnik	SOV	66.40	217-10	
5. Sabine Engel	GDR	65.88	216-2	
6. Argentina Menis	ROM	65.38	214-6	
7. Maria Betancourt	CUB	63.86	209-6	
8. Natalya Gorbachova	SOV	63.46	208-2	

Twenty-year-old Schlaak shocked the opposition with a 69-meter first throw that held up for the victory. It was originally announced that Faina Melnik had taken second place by virtue of her fifth-round toss of 225 feet 1 inches. However the throw was later ruled illegal because Melnik had stepped in front of the circle twice before taking her shot. Danuta Rosani of Poland qualified for the final, but

was disqualified after failing the test for anabolic steroids. She was the first Olympic track and field athlete to be disqualified for taking drugs.

1980 Moscow C: 17, N: 10, D: 8.1. WR: 71.80, 235–7 (Maria Petkova [Vergova])

		M	FT.–IN.	
1. Evelin Jahl (Schlaak)	GDR	69.96	229-6	OR
2. Maria Petkova (Vergova)	BUL	67.90	222-9	
3. Tatyana Lesovaya	SOV	67.40	221-1	
4. Gisela Beyer	GDR	67.08	220-1	
5. Margitta Pufe (Droese)	GDR	66.12	216-11	
6. Florenţa Ţacu	ROM	64.38	211-2	
7. Galina Murashova	SOV	63.84	209-5	
8. Svetla Gunleva	BUL	63.14	207-1	

Now married and a first lieutenant in the army, Jahl had lost her world record to Petkova a few weeks before the games. However, in Moscow she posted the four longest throws of the competition after Petkova had taken the opening-round lead.

JAVELIN THROW

The women's javelin must weigh a minimum of 600 grams (26.16 ounces) and measure between 2.20 meters (7 feet 2⅔ inches) and 2.30 meters (7 feet 6½ inches).

1896–1928 not held

1932 Los Angeles C: 8, N: 4, D: 7.31. WR: 46.75, 153–4½ (Nan Gindele)

		M	FT.–IN.	
1. Mildred Didriksen	USA	43.68	143-4	OR
2. Ellen Braumüller	GER	43.49	142-8	
3. Tilly Fleischer	GER	43.00	141-1	
4. Masako Shimpo	JAP	39.07	128-2	
5. Nan Gindele	USA	37.95	124-6	
6. Gloria Russell	USA	36.73	120-6	
7. Maria Uribe Jasso	MEX	33.66	110-5	
8. Mitsue Ishizu	JAP	30.81	101-1	

Born in Port Arthur, Texas and raised in nearby Beaumont, Mildred "Babe" Didriksen* was already an all-American basketball player when she gained sudden and dramatic national attention as a track and field star. On July 4, 1932, the women's A.A.U. championships, which also served as the Olympic trials, were held in Evanston, Illinois, on the campus of Northwestern University. Babe caused a sensation at the opening parade when she appeared as the entire team representing the Employers Casualty Insurance Company of Dallas, for whom she worked as an 85 w.p.m. typist. In the next three hours she took part in eight of the ten events and won six of them. She set world records in the 80-meter hurdles, the javelin, and the high jump, in which she tied with Jean Shiley. She also won the shot put, long jump, and baseball throw, and

*Preferred family spelling.

finished fourth in the discus. When the point totals were tallied, it was announced that Babe Didriksen had won the team title with 30 points. In second place with 22 points was the University of Illinois, which had sent a 22-woman contingent.

Olympic rules limited Babe to only three events, even though she had qualified for five, so she chose the three at which she had set world records. On the train across the country to the Los Angeles Olympics, the 18-year-old Babe irritated her fellow teammates by playing the harmonica, exercising in the aisles, and bragging about her numerous feats, which included earning a blue ribbon for sewing at the Texas State Fair. The same qualities that annoyed the athletes delighted the reporters. Upon arrival in California, she told them, "I am out to beat everybody in sight, and that's just what I'm going to do." Her first event was the javelin, in which her first throw of 143 feet 4 inches was good enough for the gold medal even though the javelin slipped out of her hand. Before the Olympics were over she had recorded new world marks in the 80-meter hurdles and the high jump.

Overnight Babe Didriksen became a celebrity. But before the year was out she had been barred from amateur competition because she had allowed a photo of herself and an interview to be used in an automobile ad campaign. She tried her hand on the vaudeville circuit, telling jokes, shot-putting, playing harmonica, and performing various athletic feats. For a time she toured as the only female and only nonbearded member of the House of David baseball team. She even pitched an inning against the Philadelphia Athletics during an exhibition game with the St. Louis Cardinals. After loading the bases with no outs, she got out of the inning on a double play and a fly ball to the outfield. Eventually she turned to golf, and it was there that she gained her greatest success. Encouraged by her 285-pound husband, wrestler George Zaharias, she became the greatest woman golfer in the world. During one 12-month period from 1946 to 1947, she won 14 straight tournaments and became the first American woman to win the British Amateur Open.

In 1953 Babe learned that she had cancer and was forced to undergo an emergency colostomy. Three and a half months after the surgery she was back on the circuit, finishing third in a minor tournament. The following year she won the U.S. Open by 12 strokes. But the cancer returned, and on September 17, 1956, Babe Didriksen, who had been voted the greatest female athlete of the half-century by an Associated Press poll, died at the age of 42.

1936 Berlin C: 14, N: 10, D: 8.2. WR: 46.75, 153–4½ (Nan Gindele)

		M	FT.–IN.	
1. Tilly Fleischer	GER	45.18	148-3	OR
2. Luise Krüger	GER	43.29	142-8	
3. Maria Kwaśniewska	POL	41.80	137-2	
4. Hermine "Herma" Bauma	AUT	41.66	136-8	
5. Sadako Yamamoto	JAP	41.45	135-11	
6. Lydia Eberhardt	GER	41.37	135-8	
7. Gertrude Wilhelmsen	USA	37.35	122-6	
8. Gerda de Kock	HOL	36.93	121-2	

1948 London C: 15, N: 10, D: 7.31. WR: 50.32, 165–1 (Klavdia Mayuchaya)

		M	FT.–IN.	
1. Hermine "Herma" Bauma	AUT	45.57	149-6	OR
2. Kaisa Parviainen	FIN	43.79	143-8	
3. Lily Carlstedt	DEN	42.08	138-1	
4. Dorothy Dodson	USA	41.96	137-8	
5. Johanna Tenunissen Waalboer	HOL	40.92	134-3	
6. Johanna Koning	HOL	40.33	132-3	
7. Dana Ingrova	CZE	39.64	130-0	
8. Elly Dammers	HOL	38.23	125-5	

1952 Helsinki C: 19, N: 13, D: 7.24. WR: 53.41, 175–2¾ (Nina Smirnitskaya)

		M	FT.–IN.	
1. Dana Zátopková (Ingrova)	CZE	50.47	165-7	OR
2. Aleksandra Chundina	SOV	50.01	164-0	
3. Yelena Gorchakova	SOV	49.76	163-3	
4. Galina Zybina	SOV	48.35	158-7	
5. Lily Kelsby-Carlstedt	DEN	46.23	151-8	
6. Marlies Müller	GER	44.37	145-6	
7. Maria Ciach	POL	44.31	145-4½	
8. Jutta Kruger	GER	44.30	145-4	

Shortly before the competition began, Dana Zátopková's husband, Emil Zatopek, was awarded a gold medal for winning the 5000 meters. After the ceremony, she rushed up to him and said, "You've won! Splendid! Show me that medal." After examining it, she added, "I'll take it with me for luck." She put it in her bag and left. On her first throw she set an Olympic record and earned a gold medal of her own. That evening Emil claimed that he deserved partial credit for his wife's gold medal because he had inspired her. Naturally, Dana was quite offended and replied, "What? All right, go and inspire some other girl and see if she throws a javelin fifty meters."

1956 Melbourne C: 19, N: 12, D: 11.28. WR: 55.48, 182–0 (Nadezhda Konyayeva)

		M	FT.–IN.	
1. Inese Jaunzeme	SOV	53.86	176-8	OR
2. Marlene Ahrens	CHI	50.38	165-3	
3. Nadezhda Konyayeva	SOV	50.28	164-11½	
4. Dana Zátopková (Ingrova)	CZE	49.83	163-5½	
5. Ingrid Almqvist	SWE	49.74	163-2	
6. Urszula Figwer	POL	48.16	158-0	
7. Erszébeth Vig	HUN	48.07	157-8½	
8. Karen Anderson	USA	48.00	157-5½	

1960 Rome C: 20, N: 14, D: 9.1. WR: 59.54, 195–4 (Elvira Ozolina)

		M	FT.–IN.	
1. Elvira Ozolina	SOV	55.98	183-8	OR
2. Dana Zátopková (Ingrova)	CZE	53.78	176-5	
3. Birute Kalediene	SOV	53.45	175-4	
4. Vlasta Pesková	CZE	52.56	172-5	
5. Urszula Figwer	POL	52.33	171-8	
6. Anna Pazera	AUS	51.15	167-9	
7. Susan Platt	GBR	51.01	167-4	
8. Alevtina Shastitko	SOV	50.92	167-1	

Ozolina unleashed her winning throw at her first attempt. Zátopková was 18 days shy of her 38th birthday when she won her second Olympic medal. Not only was she the oldest woman in Olympic history to win a track and field medal, but two years earlier she had thrown the javelin 182 feet 10 inches to become the oldest female world record breaker.

In the third round, Susan Platt of Great Britain threw past the 177-foot mark. However she was so excited that she stepped over the line on her way to see where the spear had fallen. The judge immediately ruled a foul and Platt had to settle for seventh place.

1964 Tokyo C: 16, N: 10, D: 10.16. WR: 61.38, 201–4½ (Elvira Ozolina)

		M	FT.–IN.
1. Mihaela Peneş	ROM	60.54	198-7
2. Márta Rudas	HUN	58.27	191-2
3. Yelena Gorchakova	SOV	57.06	187-2
4. Birute Kalediene	SOV	56.31	184-8
5. Elvira Ozolina	SOV	54.81	179-9
6. Maria Diaconescu	ROM	53.71	176-2
7. Hiroko Sato	JAP	52.48	172-2
8. Anneliese Gerhards	GER	52.37	171-10

The 1964 javelin competition was full of surprises. On the very first throw of the qualification round, 31-year-old Yelena Gorchakova set a world record of 62.40 meters (204 feet 9 inches). This boosted her up to co-favorite along with defending champion Elvira Ozolina. However, when the final began a few hours later, it was 17-year-old high school student Mihaela Peneş of Bucharest who stunned the crowd with a throw of 198 feet 7 inches—17 feet further than she had ever thrown before. No one came close to her for the rest of the competition. Ozolina fouled on her last four attempts and had to settle for fifth place. She was so distressed by her performace that she went straight to the hairdresser at the Olympic Village and asked to have her head shaved. When the Japanese hairdresser refused, Ozolina took the clippers herself and removed a chunk of her long tresses. The hairdresser finished the job and Ozolina left the parlor bald, refusing a scarf to hide her shame. Ozolina was not the first Olympic athlete to react to defeat by having her head shaved, although she was the first woman. Four years earlier, in Rome, the entire Japanese

wrestling team had had their heads shaved after an all-around poor showing.

1968 Mexico City C: 16, N: 11, D: 10.14. WR: 62.40, 204–8¾ (Yelena Gorchakova)

		M	FT.–IN.
1. Angéla Németh	HUN	60.36	198-0
2. Mihaela Peneş	ROM	59.92	196-7
3. Eva Janko	AUT	58.04	190-5
4. Márta Rudas	HUN	56.38	185-0
5. Daniela Jaworska	POL	56.06	183-11
6. Nataša Urbančič	YUG	55.42	181-10
7. Ameli Koloska	GER	55.20	181-1
8. Kaisa Launela	FIN	53.96	177-0

1972 Munich C: 19, N: 10, D: 9.1. WR: 65.06, 213–5½ (Ruth Fuchs)

		M	FT.–IN.	
1. Ruth Fuchs	GDR	63.88	209-7	OR
2. Jacqueline Todten	GDR	62.54	205-2	
3. Kathryn Schmidt	USA	59.94	196-8	
4. Liutvian Mollova	BUL	59.36	194-9	
5. Nataša Urbančič	YUG	59.06	193-9	
6. Eva Janko	AUT	58.56	192-1	
7. Ewa Gryziecka	POL	57.00	187-0	
8. Svetlana Korolyova	SOV	56.36	184-11	

Yelena Gorchakova's 1964 qualifying toss of 204 foot 8¾ inches had been in the books as a world record for over seven and a half years when it was suddenly beaten twice in one day. On June 11, 1972, Ewa Gryziecka, competing in Bucharest, threw the javelin 205 feet 8 inches (62.70 meters). One half hour later, in Potsdam, East Germany, Ruth Fuchs began her domination of women's javelin with a throw of 213 feet 5½ inches (65.06 meters). Two and a half months later, at the Munich Olympics, Fuchs took the lead from Kate Schmidt in the second round, improved in the fourth round, and broke the Olympic record in the fifth round. The competition ended on an exciting note when Urbančič's final throw almost skewered a wandering photographer.

1976 Montreal C: 15, N: 10, D: 7.24. WR: 69.12, 226–9¼ (Ruth Fuchs)

		M	FT.–IN.	
1. Ruth Fuchs	GDR	65.94	216-4	OR
2. Marion Becker	GER	64.70	212-3	
3. Kathryn Schmidt	USA	63.96	209-10	
4. Jacqueline Hein (Todten)	GDR	63.84	209-5	
5. Sabine Sebrowski	GDR	63.08	206-11	
6. Svetlana Babich (Korolyova)	SOV	59.42	194-11	
7. Nadezhda Yakubovich	SOV	59.16	194-1	
8. Karin Smith	USA	57.50	188-8	

Marion Becker reached the victory platform in Montreal after an unusual odyssey. Born in Hamburg in West Germany in 1950, she was nonetheless raised in East Germany. After marrying, she moved to Romania and represented Romania at the 1972 Olympics in Munich, finishing seventeenth. After the games, she stayed behind in West Germany and four years later competed for the nation of her birth in the 1976 Olympics. In the qualifying round she broke the Olympic record with a throw of 213 feet 8 inches (65.14 meters). However, in the competition proper, Ruth Fuchs knocked out her opposition with an opening throw of 216 feet 4 inches (65.94 meters).

1980 Moscow C: 21, N: 14, D: 7.25. WR: 70.08, 229–10 (Tatyana Biryulina)

		M	FT.–IN.	
1. Maria Colon Rueñes	CUB	68.40	224-5	OR
2. Saida Gunba	SOV	67.76	222-2	
3. Ute Hommola	GDR	66.56	218-4	
4. Ute Richter	GDR	66.54	218-4	
5. Ivanka Vancheva	BUL	66.38	217-9	
6. Tatyana Biryulina	SOV	65.08	213-6	
7. Eva Raduly-Zorgo	ROM	64.08	210-3	
8. Ruth Fuchs	GDR	63.94	209-9	

Ruth Fuchs continued to be the queen of javelin throwing all the way into 1980. On April 29 she set a world record of 69.96 meters (229 feet 6 inches) and she looked poised to become the first woman to break the 70-meter barrier.

However, on July 12 a complete unknown, Tatyana Biryulina, improved her personal best by 27½ feet with a throw of 70.08. Less than two weeks later, at the Olympics, Biryulina could do no better than 65.08 and sixth place. In fact, the women with the four best pre-Olympic records all had disappointing performances. Fuchs finished eighth, Raduly was seventh, and Tessa Sanderson, who had thrown 69.70, failed to qualify for the final. It was left to Maria Colon to win the competition on her first throw. She was the first Cuban woman to win an Olympic gold medal. Fuchs needn't have felt ashamed by her loss. From 1970 through 1980 she took part in 129 meets and won 113 of them, including 30 straight from 1972 to 1974.

PENTATHLON/HEPTATHLON

In 1984 the pentathlon will be replaced by the heptathlon, which will include the javelin and the 200 meters as well as the 100-meter hurdles, the shot put, high jump, long jump and 800 meters.

Points are scored according to a set of tables approved by the International Amateur Athletic Federation.

1896–1960 not held

1964 Tokyo C: 20, N: 15, D: 10.17. WR: 5194 (Irina Press)

		80M H	SP	HJ	LJ	200M	TOTAL	
1. Irina Press	SOV	10.7	17.16	1.63	6.24	24.7	5246	WR
2. Mary Rand	GBR	10.9	11.05	1.72	6.55	24.2	5035	
3. Galina Bystrova	SOV	10.7	14.47	1.60	6.11	25.2	4956	
4. Mary Peters	GBR	11.0	14.48	1.60	5.60	25.4	4797	
5. Draga Stamejčič	YUG	10.9	12.73	1.54	6.19	25.2	4790	
6. Helga Hoffman	GER	11.2	10.67	1.60	6.44	25.0	4737	
7. Patricia Winslow	USA	12.0	13.04	1.63	5.90	24.6	4724	
8. Ingrid Becker	GER	11.6	11.62	1.60	6.17	24.6	4717	

Press's margin of victory was provided in the shot put, where she outpointed Rand 1173 to 789 with a throw of 56 feet 2½ inches, which was 16½ inches farther than she was able to throw in the shot put competition three days later.

1968 Mexico City C: 33, N: 24, D: 10.16. WR: 5246 (Irina Press)

		80M H	SP	HJ	LJ	200M	TOTAL
1. Ingrid Becker	GER	10.9	11.48	1.71	6.43	23.5	5098
2. Elisabeth "Liese" Prokop	AUT	11.2	14.61	1.68	5.97	25.1	4966
3. Annamária Tóth	HUN	10.9	12.68	1.59	6.12	23.8	4959
4. Valentina Tichomirova	SOV	11.2	14.12	1.65	5.99	24.9	4927
5. Manon Bornholdt	GER	11.0	12.37	1.59	6.42	24.8	4890
6. Patricia Winslow	USA	11.4	13.33	1.65	5.97	24.5	4877
7. Ingeborg Bauer	GDR	11.4	13.00	1.59	6.22	24.5	4849
8. Meta Antenen	SWI	10.7	11.06	1.62	6.30	24.9	4848

Heidemarie Rosendahl of West Germany was considered the pre-Games favorite, but she pulled a muscle while warming up and was unable to compete. Liese Prokop was the surprise leader after four events, but Ingrid Becker, competing in her third Olympics, ran the fastest 200 meters of the competition to take the gold medal.

1972 Munich C: 28, N: 18, D: 9.3. WR: 4775 (Burglinde Pollack)   I

		100M H	SP	HJ	LJ	200M	TOTAL	
1. Mary Peters	GBR	13.29	16.29	1.82	5.98	24.08	4801	WR
2. Heidemarie Rosendahl	GER	13.34	13.86	1.65	6.83	22.96	4791	
3. Burglinde Pollak	GDR	13.53	16.04	1.76	6.21	23.93	4768	
4. Christine Bodner	GDR	13.25	12.51	1.76	6.40	23.66	4671	
5. Valentina Tikhomirova	SOV	13.77	14.64	1.74	6.15	24.25	4597	
6. Nedialka Angelova	BUL	13.84	13.96	1.68	6.32	24.58	4496	
7. Karen Mack	GER	14.45	14.10	1.76	6.11	24.72	4449	
8. Ilona Bruzsenyák	HUN	13.65	12.48	1.65	6.29	24.35	4419	

In 1971, the 80-meter hurdles was replaced by the 100-meter hurdles, necessitating a change in the scoring tables and a reevaluation of the world record. Mary Peters, a 33-year-old English-born secretary from Belfast, Northern Ireland, finished fourth at Tokyo in 1964 and ninth in Mexico City in 1968. During the first day of competition in Munich she recorded personal bests in two of the three events—the 100-meter hurdles and the high jump. The high jump was a particularly magical moment for her, as the German crowd rooted her on and chanted her name despite the fact that she was competing against local favorite Heide Rosendahl, who had won the long jump two days earlier. At the end of the first day, Peters was 97 points head of Pollak and 301 points ahead of Rosendahl, who was in fifth place. But the two events of the second day, the long jump and the 200 meters, were Rosendahl's best and Peters' worst. Sure enough, Rosendahl jumped 22 feet 5 inches, 1 centimeter short of her world record. The 200 meters saw both women achieve personal bests. If Mary Peters had run one-tenth second slower she would have lost the gold medal. Afterward she told the press that she had become so exhausted in the last 50 meters of the 200 that her legs felt like jelly. In her autobiography, *Mary P.,* she revised her description and wrote that her legs felt like lead.

1976 Montreal C: 20, N: 13, D: 7.26. WR: 4932 (Burglinde Pollack)

		100M H	SP	HJ	LJ	200M	TOTAL
1. Siegrun Siegl	GDR	13.31	12.92	1.74	6.49	23.09	4745
2. Christine Laser (Bodner)	GDR	13.55	14.29	1.78	6.27	23.48	4745
3. Burglinde Pollak	GDR	13.30	16.25	1.64	6.30	23.64	4740
4. Liudmila Popovskaya	SOV	13.33	15.02	1.74	6.19	24.10	4700
5. Nadezhda Tkachenko	SOV	13.41	14.90	1.80	6.08	24.61	4669
6. Diane Jones	CAN	13.79	14.58	1.80	6.29	25.33	4582
7. Jane Frederick	USA	13.54	14.55	1.76	5.99	24.70	4566
8. Margit Papp	HUN	14.14	14.80	1.78	6.35	25.43	4535

Anyone who enjoys close finishes need look no further than the 1976 pentathlon. With four events finished and only the 200 meters to be run, the standings were as follows:

1. Tkachenko	3788		5. Laser	3757
2. Popovskaya	3772		6. Papp	3726
3. Pollak	3768		7. Siegl	3718
4. Jones	3764		8. Frederick	3693

All the leaders were matched against one another in the final heat. When the dust cleared 26 seconds later, officials and fans hurriedly consulted their scoring tables. It was discovered that Siegl, the world record holder in the long jump, and Laser, who had achieved personal records in the high jump and 200, had finished with the exact same point total, while Pollak was only five points behind. Siegl was finally awarded first place on the basis of having beaten Laser in three of the five events. Had Pollak run six one-hundredths of a second faster she would have won the gold medal. Instead she had to settle for her second straight bronze. While Siegl jumped from seventh to first in one event, Tkachenko had the misfortune of dropping from first to fifth in less than 25 seconds.

1980 Moscow C: 19, N: 12, D: 7.24. WR (with 800m): 4856 (Olga Kuragina)

			100M H	SP	HJ	LJ	800M	TOTAL	
1.	Nadezhda Tkachenko	SOV	13.29	16.84	1.84	6.73	2:05.2	5083	WR
2.	Olga Rukavishnikova	SOV	13.66	14.09	1.88	6.79	2:04.8	4937	
3.	Olga Kuragina	SOV	13.26	12.49	1.84	6.77	2:03.6	4875	
4.	Ramona Neubert	GDR	13.93	13.68	1.77	6.63	2:07.7	4698	
5.	Margit Papp	HUN	13.96	14.94	1.74	6.35	2:15.8	4562	
6.	Burglinde Pollak	GDR	13.74	16.67	1.68	5.93	2:14.4	4553	
7.	Valentina Dimitrova	BUL	14.39	15.65	1.74	5.91	2:15.5	4458	
8.	Emilia Kounova	BUL	13.73	11.98	1.74	6.10	2:11.1	4431	

The 1980 pentathlon saw tremendous performances by all three Soviet athletes, each of whom broke the existing world record. Thirty-one-year-old Nadezhda Tkachenko followed a long road to her gold medal. Ninth in Munich, fifth in Montreal, she won the European title in 1978 only to lose it after failing a test for anabolic steroids. Handed an 18-month suspension by the I.A.A.F., she was back in time for the 1980 Olympics. In Moscow she achieved personal bests in four of the five events and fell only three-quarters of an inch short of her lifetime record in the shot put. Rukavishnikova has the unusual distinction of setting the shortest-lived world record in history—two-fifths of a second. When she crossed the finish line of the 800 meters she became world record holder in the pentathlon. But when Tkachenko finished right behind her, a new record was set.

ARCHERY

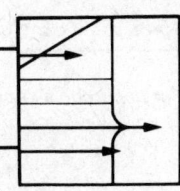

MEN
Discontinued Events | **WOMEN**
Discontinued Events

MEN

Competitors in men's Olympic archery shoot two F.I.T.A. rounds. One F.I.T.A. round consists of 36 arrows at each of four distances: 90, 70, 50, and 30 meters. The target is divided into ten rings. The inner ring is worth ten points and the outer ring one point. Thus, a perfect score for a F.I.T.A. round would be 1440 points. Modern bows are incredibly complicated and are augmented by bowsights, bowmarks, foresights, and stabilizers.

1896–1968 not held

1972 Munich C: 55, N: 24, D: 9.10 WR: 2445 (John Williams)

			1st ROUND		2nd ROUND	TOTAL POINTS	
1.	John Williams	USA	1268	WR	1260	2528	WR
2.	Gunnar Jarvil	SWE	1229		1252	2481	
3.	Kyösti Laasonen	FIN	1213		1254	2467	
4.	Robert Cogniaux	BEL	1205		1240	2445	
5.	Edwin Eliason	USA	1193		1245	2438	
6.	Donald Jackson	CAN	1225		1212	2437	
7.	Victor Sidorouk	SOV	1205		1222	2427	
8.	Arne Jacobsen	DEN	1188		1235	2423	

The reigning world champion, John Williams, was an 18-year-old army private from Cranesville, Pennsylvania, who spent 42 hours a week in training. In the first F.I.T.A. round he broke Arne Jacobsen's single round world record despite missing the target completely with one arrow.

1976 Montreal C: 37, N: 23, D: 7.30. WR: 2570 (Darrell Pace)

			1st ROUND	2nd ROUND	TOTAL POINTS	
1.	Darrell Pace	USA	1264	1307	2571	WR
2.	Hiroshi Michinaga	JAP	1226	1276	2502	
3.	Giancarlo Ferrari	ITA	1220	1275	2495	
4.	Richard McKinney	USA	1230	1241	2471	
5.	Vladimir Chendarov	SOV	1217	1250	2467	
6.	Willi Gabriel	GER	1203	1232	2435	
7.	Dave Mann	CAN	1190	1241	2431	
8.	Takanobu Nishi	JAP	1191	1231	2422	

1980 Moscow C: 38, N: 25, D: 8.2. WR (single round): 1341 (Darrell Pace)

			1st ROUND	2nd ROUND	TOTAL POINTS
1.	Tomi Poikolainen	FIN	1220	1235	2455
2.	Boris Isachenko	SOV	1217	1235	2452
3.	Giancarlo Ferrari	ITA	1215	1234	2449
4.	Mark Blenkarne	GBR	1224	1222	2446
5.	Béla Nagy	HUN	1225	1221	2446
6.	Vladimir Yesheyev	SOV	1222	1210	2432
7.	Kyösti Laasonen	FIN	1212	1207	2419
8.	Tiny Reniers	HOL	1205	1213	2418

Discontinued Events

1900 Paris C: 68, N: 2, D: 5.28.
Au cordon doré—50 Meters

			PTS.
1.	Henri Herouin	FRA	31
2.	Hubert van Innis	BEL	29
3.	Emile Fisseux	FRA	28

Au chapelet—50 Meters

1.	Eugène Mougin	FRA	—
2.	Henri Helle	FRA	—
3.	Emile Mercier	FRA	—

Au cordon doré—33 Meters

1.	Hubert van Innis	BEL
2.	Victor Thibaud	FRA
3.	Charles Frédéric Petit	FRA

Au chapelet—33 Meters

1.	Hubert van Innis	BEL
2.	Victor Thibaud	FRA
3.	Charles Frédéric Petit	FRA

Sur la perche a la herse

1.	Emmanuel Foulon	FRA	—
2.	Serrurier	FRA	—
3.	Druart, Jr.	BEL	—

Sur la perche a la pyramide
1. Emile Grumiaux   FRA   —
2. Louis Glineux   BEL   —

1904 St. Louis C: 16, N: 1, D: 9.20.
Double York Round (100 Yards—80 Yards—60 Yards)

		PTS.
1. George Phillip Bryant	USA	820
2. Robert Williams	USA	819
3. William Thompson	USA	816
4. Wallace Bryant	USA	618
5. Benjamin Keys	USA	532
6. Ernest Frentz	USA	528
7. Homer Taylor	USA	506
8. C.S. Woodruff	USA	487

1904 St. Louis C: 22, N: 1, D: 9.19.
Double American Round (60 Yards—50 Yards—4 Yards)

		PTS.
1. George Philipp Bryant	USA	1048
2. Robert Williams	USA	991
3. William Thompson	USA	949
4. C.S. Woodruff	USA	907
5. William Clark	USA	880
6. Benjamin Keys	USA	840
7. Wallace Bryant	USA	818
8. Cyrus Dallin	USA	816

1904 St. Louis T: 4, N: 1, D: 9.21.
Team Round (60 Yards)

	PTS.
1. (Potomac Archers, Washington D.C.—William Thompson, Robert Williams, Louis Maxson, Galen Spencer)	1344
2. (Cincinnati Archers—C.S. Woodruff, William Clark, Charles Hubbard, S.H. Duvall)	1341
3. (Boston Archers—George Phillip Bryant, Wallace Bryant, Cyrus Dallin, Henry Richardson)	1268
4. (Chicago Archers—Benjamin Keys, Homer Taylor, Edward Weston, Edward Bruce)	942

1908 London C: 34, N: 3, D: 7.17–18, 20.
York Round (100 Yards—80 Yards—60 Yards)

		PTS.
1. W. Dod	GBR	815
2. R.B. Brooks-King	GBR	768
3. Henry Richardson	USA	760
4. J. Penrose	GBR	709
5. J.H. Bridges	GBR	687
6. H.V. James	GBR	652

Dod had the distinction of being part of the first father-daughter Olympic medalists. His daughter, Lottie, a former golf and tennis champion, won the silver medal in the women's national round.

Continental Style (50 Meters)

		PTS.
1. E.G. Grisot	FRA	263
2. Louis Vernet	FRA	256
3. Gustave Cabaret	FRA	255
4. C. Aubras	FRA	231
5. C. Querviel	FRA	223
6. A. Dauchez	FRA	222

An unofficial entrant, R.O. Backhouse of Great Britain, finished second with a score of 260 and was awarded a certificate for special merit.

1920 Antwerp C: 30, N: 3, D: 8.3–8. 8.22-29.
Fixed Bird Target

		PTS.
1. Edmond van Moer	BEL	11
2. Louis van de Perck	BEL	8
3. Joseph Hermans	BEL	6

Large Birds

		PTS.
1. Edouard Cloetens	BEL	13
2. Louis van de Perck	BEL	11
3. Firmin Flamand	BEL	7

Moving Bird Target
28 Meters:

		PTS.
1. Hubert van Innis	BEL	144
2. Léonce Quentin	FRA	115

33 Meters:

		PTS.
1. Hubert van Innis	BEL	139
2. Julien Brulé	FRA	94

50 Meters:

		PTS.
1. Julien Brulé	FRA	134
2. Hubert van Innis	BEL	106

Teams
28 Meters:

	PTS.
1. HOL	3087
(Adrianus Theeuwes, Hendrikus van Bussel, Jan Packbiers, Adrianus van Merrienboer, Jan Babtiest Josef van Gestel. Theodorus Willems, Petrus de Brouwer, Johannes van Gastel)	
2. BEL	2924
(Hubert van Innis, Alphonse Allaert, Edmond de Knibber, Louis Delcon, Jérome de Mayer, Louis van Beeck, Pierre van Thielt, Louis Fierens)	
3. FRA	2328
(Léonce Quentin, Julien Brulé, Pascal Fauvel, E.G. Grisot, Eugène Richez, Leroy, Mabellon, Epin)	

33 Meters:

		PTS.
1. BEL		2958

(Hubert van Innis, Alphonse Allaert, Edmond de Knibber, Louis Delcon, Jérome de Mayer, Louis van Beeck, Pierre van Thielt, Louis Fierens)

2. FRA		2586

(Léonce Quentin, Julien Brulé, Pascal Fauvel, E.G. Grisot, Eugene Richez, Leroy, Mabellon, Epin)

50 Meters:

		PTS.
1. BEL		2701

(Hubert van Innis, Alphonse Allaert, Edmond de Knibber, Louis Delcon Jérome de Mayer, Louis van Beeck, Pierre van Thielt, Louis Fierens)

2. FRA		2493

(Léonce Quentin, Julien Brulé, Pascal Fauvel, E.G. Grisot, Eugene Richez, Leroy, Mabellon, Epin)

WOMEN

Women's Olympic archery consists of two F.I.T.A. rounds. A single round is 36 arrows shot at each of four distances: 70, 60, 50, and 30 meters.

1896–1968 not held

1972 Munich C: 40, N: 21, D: 9.10. WR: 2380 (Emma Gaptchenko)

		1st ROUND	2nd ROUND	TOTAL POINTS	
1. Doreen Wilber	USA	1198	1226	2424	WR
2. Irena Szydlowska	POL	1224	1183	2407	
3. Emma Gaptchenko	SOV	1201	1202	2403	
4. Keto Lossaberidze	SOV	1195	1207	2402	
5. Linda Myers	USA	1200	1185	2385	
6. Maria Maczyńska	POL	1173	1198	2371	
7. Ho-Gu Kim	PRK	1195	1174	2369	
8. Alla Peounova	SOV	1180	1184	2364	

Wilber was a 42-year-old housewife from Jefferson, Iowa.

1976 Montreal C: 27, N: 16, D: 7.30. WR: 2465 (Zebiniso Rustamova)

		1st ROUND	2nd ROUND	TOTAL POINTS	
1. Luann Ryon	USA	1217	1282	2499	WR
2. Valentina Kovpan	SOV	1182	1278	2460	
3. Zebiniso Rustamova	SOV	1202	1205	2407	
4. Sun-Yong Jang	PRK	1200	1205	2405	
5. Lucille Lemay	CAN	1181	1220	2401	
6. Jadwiga Wilejto	POL	1200	1195	2395	
7. Linda Myers	USA	1180	1213	2393	
8. Maria Urban	GER	1216	1160	2376	

Ryon, a 23-year-old student from Riverside, California, had never before competed in an international tournament.

1980 Moscow C: 29, N: 19, D: 8.2. WR (Single Round): 1321 (Natalya Butuzova)

		1st ROUND	2nd ROUND	TOTAL POINTS
1. Keto Losaberidze	SOV	1257	1234	2491
2. Natalya Butuzova	SOV	1251	1226	2477
3. Päivi Meriluoto	FIN	1217	1232	2449
4. Ždenka Padevetova	CZE	1206	1199	2405
5. Gwang-Sun O	PRK	1195	1206	2401
6. Catherina Floris	HOL	1186	1196	2382
7. Maria Szeliga	POL	1190	1175	2365
8. Lotti Tschanz	SWI	1184	1162	2346

Discontinued Events

1904 St. Louis C: 6, N: 1, D: 9.19.
Double Columbia Round (50 Yards—40 Yards—30 Yards)

		PTS.
1. Lida Howell	USA	867
2. Emma Cooke	USA	630
3. Jessie Pollock	USA	630
4. Laura Woodruff	USA	547
5. Mabel Taylor	USA	243
6. Louise Taylor	USA	229

1904 St. Louis C: 6, N: 1, D: 9.20.
Double National Round (60 Yards—50 Yards)

		PTS.
1. Lida Howell	USA	620
2. Emma Cooke	USA	419
3. Jessie Pollock	USA	419
4. Laura Woodruff	USA	234
5. Mabel Taylor	USA	160
6. Louise Taylor	USA	159

1904 St. Louis T: 2, N: 1, D: 9.21.
Team Round

	PTS.
1. (Cincinnati Archers—Lida Howell, Jessie Pollock, Laura Woodruff, Louise Taylor)	—
2. Potomac Archers, Washington, D.C.	—

1908 London C: 25, N: 1, D: 7.20.
National Round (60 Yards—50 Yards)

		PTS.
1. Q.F. Newall	GBR	688
2. Lottie Dod	GBR	642
3. Hill-Lowe	GBR	618
4. A.H. Wadworth	GBR	605
5. G.W. Honnywill	GBR	587
6. S.H. Armitage	GBR	582

BASKETBALL

MEN

1896–1932 not held

1936 Berlin T: 21, N: 21, D: 8.14.

		W	L	PF	PA
1. USA	(Ralph Bishop, Joe Fortenberry, Carl Knowles, Jack Ragland, Carl Shy, William Wheatley, Francis Johnson, Samuel Balter, John Gibbons, Frank Lubin, Arthur Mollner, Duane Swanson, Willard Schmidt)	4	0	152	69
2. CAN	(Gordon Aitchison, Jan Allison, Arthur Chapman, Charles Chapman, Douglas Peden, James Stewart, Malcolm Wiseman, Edward John Dawson, Irving Meretsky)	5	1	176	104
3. MEX	(Carlos Borja Morca, Victor Hugo Borja Morca, Raúl Fernández Robert, Francisco Martinez Cordero, Jesus Olmos Moreni, Greer Skousen Spilsbury, Luis Ignacio de la Vega Leija, Rodolfo Choperno Irizarri, José Pamplona Lecuanda, Andrés Gómez Dominguez, Silvio Hernandez del Valle)	4	2	160	115
4. POL	(Zdzislaw Filipkiewicz, Florian Grzechowiak, Jakub Kopowski, Edwaryst Lój, Andrzej Pluciński, Zenon Różycki, Edward Szostak, Zdzislaw Kasprzak, Janusz Patrzykont, Pavel Stok)	1	4	119	180
5. PHI	(Charles Bork, Jacinto Cruz Ciria, Franco Marquicias, Primitivo Martinez, Jesús Marzan, Amador Obordo, Ambrosio Padilla, Bibiano Ouano, Fortunato Yamboa)	4	1	159	145
6. URU	(Gregorio Agos, Rodolfo Braseili, Leandro Gomez Harley, Alejo Gonzalez Roig, Victor Latou Jaime, Prudencio de Pena, Tabaré Quintans, Humberto Bernasconi, Carlos Gabin)	2	3	125	136
7. ITA	(Castelli, Dondi, Franeschini, Giasetti, Marinelli, Paganella, Premiani, Basso)	3	2	160	129

Final: USA 19—8 CAN
3rd Place: MEX 26—12 POL
5th Place: PHI 33—23 URU

The first official Olympic basketball tournament was held outdoors in a tennis stadium on courts of clay and sand. Half the U.S. squad was was made up of members of the winner of the U.S. trials—the team from Universal Studios. During the tournament, the International Basketball Federation passed a rule that banned all players who were taller than 6 feet 3 inches. The United States, which would have lost three of its players, objected, and the rule was withdrawn. The day of the final saw heavy rain, which turned the courts into mud. The players found it quite difficult to dribble on wet sand, which undoubtedly contributed to the low score. The United States led 15–4 at the half. Six-foot 8-inch center Joe Fortenberry of McPherson, Kansas, scored eight points to match the score of the entire Canadian team.

1948 London T: 23, N: 23, D: 8.13.

		W	L	PF	PA
1. USA	(Clifford Barker, Donald Barksdale, Ralph Beard, Lewis Beck, Vincent Boryla, Gordon Carpenter, Alexander Groza, Wallace Jones, Robert Kurland, Raymond Lumpp, Robert Pitts, Jesse Renick, Robert Robinson, Kenneth Rollins)	8	0	524	256
2. FRA	(André Barrais, Michel Bonnevie, André Buffière, René Chocat, René Dérency, Maurice Desaymonnet, André Even, Maurice Girardot, Fernand Guillou, Raymond Offner, Jacques Perrier, Yvan Quénin, Lucien Rebuffic, Pierre Thiolon)	5	2	331	281
3. BRA	(Zenny de Azevedo, João Francisco Bráz, Marcus Vinicius Dias, Alfonso Azevedo Evora, Ruy de Freitas, Alexandre Gemignani, Alberto Marson, Alfredo Rodrigues da Motta, Nilton Pacheco de Oliveira, Massinet Sorcinelli)	7	1	374	263
4. MEX	(Angel Acuna Lizaña, Isaac Alfaro Loza, Alberto Bienvenu Barajas, José de la Cruz Cabrera Gándara, Jorge Cardiel Gaitán, Rodolfo Diaz	5	2	314	264

Mercado, Francisco Galinda Chávez, Jorge Gudiño Goya, Héctor Guerrero Delgado, Emilio López Enriquez, Ignacio Romo Porches, José Rojas Herrera, Fernando Rojas Herrera, José Santos de León)

		W	L	PF	PA
5.	URU (Martin Acosta y Lara, Néstor Anton, Victorio Cieslinskas, Nelson Demarco, Miguel Diab, Abraham Eidlin, Eduardo Folle, Héctor Garcia Otero, Eduardo Gordon, Adesio Lombardo, Roberto Lovera, Gustavo Margariños, Carlos Rosselló, Héctor Ruiz)	5	3	369	301
6.	CHI (Eduardo Cordero Fernandez, Exequil Figueroa Reyes, Juan Gallo Chinchilla, R. Hammer Casadio, E. Kapstein Suckel, M. Ledesma Barraies, Victor Mahana Badrie, G.L. Marmentini, A. Mitrovic Guic, A. Moreno Rodillo, E. Parra Rojas, H. Raffo Abarca, Marcos Sanchez Carmona, G. Yanez Verdugo)	4	4	391	301
7.	CZE (J. Belohradsky, C. Benacek, Z. Chlup, J. Drvota, J. Ezr, J. Kalina, J. Kozak, V. Krasa, Z. Krenicky, J. Krepela, I. Mrazek, J. Siegel, J. Toms, L. Trpkos)	5	3	315	294
8.	KOR (B. Ahn, W. Bang, Chin-Ri Chang, Joon-Deuk Chyo, Hyun-Bong Kang, Shin-Chung Kim, Yung-Choon Lee, Hoon-Sang Lee, Chul-Soo Oh)	3	5	364	279

Final: USA 65—21 FRA
3rd Place: BRA 52—47 MEX

The 1948 tournament had some unusual highlights: A British referee was knocked unconscious during a preliminary game between Chile and Iraq. A Chinese player dribbled between the legs of America's 7-foot center, Bob Kurland, and followed through by scoring a basket. In the fiercely contested match for third place, da Motta of Brazil lost his pants and had to retire to the dressing room. Iraq lost by 100 points twice—to Korea and China (which finished eighteenth), and gave up an average of 104 points per game while scoring only 23.5. Ireland's offense was even less effective, averaging only 17 points a game. Meanwhile, the U.S. team survived an early 59–57 scare against Argentina and then breezed through the rest of its games. The halftime score in the final was 28–9. J. Llanusa Gobel of the Cuban team went on to become Minister of Education under Fidel Castro.

1952 Helsinki T: 23, N: 23, D:8.2.

		W	L	PF	PA
1.	USA (Charles Hoag, William Hougland, Melvin Dean Kelley, Robert Kenney, Clyde Lovellette, Marcus Freiberger, Victor Wayne Glasgow, Frank McCabe, Daniel Pippin, Howard Williams, Ronald Bontemps, Robert Kurland, William Lienhard, John Keller)	8	0	562	406
2.	SOV (Viktor Vlassov, Styapas Butautas, Yvan Lysov, Kazis Petkyavichus, Nodar Dshordshikiya, Anatoly Konyev, Otar Korkiya, Ilmar Kullam, Yuri Ozerov, Aleksandr Moiseyev, Heino Kruus, Yustinas Lagunavichus, Maigonis Valdmanis, Stassis Stonkus)	6	2	468	431
3.	URU (Martin Acosta y Lara, Enrique Baliño, Victorio Cies-linskas, Héctor Costa, Nelson Demarco, Héctor Garcia Otero, Roberto Lovera, Adesio Lombardo, Tabaré Larre Borges, Sergio Matto, Wilfredo Pelaez, Carlos Rosselló)	5	3	486	471
4.	ARG (Ruben Francisco Menini, Hugo Oscar del Vecchio, Leo-poldo, Contarbio, Raúl Perez Varela, Juan Gazso, Roberto Viau, Juan Gazso, Roberto Viau, Ricardo Primitiva Gonzalez, Juan Carlos Uder, Omar Monza, Ruben Pagliari, Rafael Liedo, Oscar Alberto Furlong, Alberto Lopez, Ignacio Poletti)	5	3	600	523
5.	CHI (Juan Gallo Chinchilla, Victor Mahana Badrie, Exequiel Figueroa, Reyes, Eduardo Cordero Fernandez, Rufino Bernedo Zorzano, Alvaro Salvadores Salvi, Eric Maehn Godoy, Herman Ramos Muñoz, Hugo Fernandez Diaz, Orlando Silva Infante, Hernan Raffo Abarca, Pedro Araya Zabala, Juan Ostoic Ostoic)	4	4	447	508
6.	BRA (Zenny de Azevedo, Sebastião Gimenez, Ruy de Freitas, Mayr Facci, Raymundo Carvalho dos Santos, Angelo Bonfietti, João Francisco Bráz, Alfredo Rodrigues da Motta, Almir Nelson de Almeida, Mario Jorge da Fonseca Hermes, Thales Monteiro, José Luiz Santos Azevedo, Helio Marquez Pereira)	4	4	469	436
7.	BUL (Kiril Semov, Hristo Donchev, Vasil Manchenko, Peter Shishkov, Georgi Panov, Konstantin Totev, Anton Kuzov, Gencho Rashkov, Ivan Nikolov, Veselin Penkov, Konstantin Georgiev, Vladimir Slavov)	4	4	451	506
8.	FRA (Bernard Planque, Robert Monclar, René Chocat, Jean Perniceni, Louis Devoti, Robert Guillin, Robert Crost, Jacques Dessemme, André Buffière, André Vacheresse, André Chavet, Jean-Paul Beugnot, Roger Haudegand, Jean-Pierre Salignon)	4	4	468	460

Final: USA 36—25 SOV
3rd Place: URU 68—59 ARG
5th Place: CHI 58—49 BRA
7th Place: BUL 58—44 FRA

Having been crushed by the United States 86–58, in the semifinal round, the Soviet team decided to freeze the ball in the final match. After ten minutes, the United States led 4–2. At halftime the score was still only 17–15. With five minutes to play, Clyde Lovellette scored a basket to give the United States a lead of 31–25. The next time the Americans got the ball, it was their turn to stall. One Soviet player became so exasperated that he sat down on the floor until his coach ordered him to stand up.

The tournament was enlivened by the participation of Uruguay. In the semifinal round, France had a 66–64 lead over the team from South America, which had been reduced to three players due to excessive fouling. With one minute to play, Uruguay tied the score, whereupon the American referee, Vincent Farrell, whistled a foul against Uruguay. The Uruguayan team rushed off the bench and abused Farrell for five minutes until he was finally able to communicate that the foul had occurred *after* the basket and that the 2 points had not been disallowed. France took the ball out of bounds and worked the ball to Jacques Dessemme, who scored an easy layup to win the game. At this point Uruguayan players and spectators attacked Farrell again. This time he was kicked in the groin and had to be carried from the court. Two Uruguayan players were banned from further competition. Three days later it was the U.S.S.R.'s turn to face the volatile Uruguayans. In the second half, three Soviet players had to receive first aid. The following day, the now exhausted Uruguayans faced their bitter rival, Argentina, in the match for third place. They mustered up enough energy for one more brawl with 25 people involved. So many fouls were called that Uruguay finished the game with only four players and Argentina with only three.

1956 Melbourne T: 15, N: 15, D: 12.1.

			W	L	PF	PA
1.	USA	(Carl Cain, William Hougland, K.C. Jones, William Russell, James Walsh, William Evans, Burdette Haldorson, Ronald Tomsic, Richard Boushka, Gilbert Ford, Robert Jeangerard, Charles Darling)	8	0	793	365
2.	SOV	(Valdis Muischnieks, Maigonis Valdmanis, Vladimir Torban, Stassis Stonkus, Kazis Petkyavichus, Arkady Bochkaryov, Yanis Kruminsch, Mikhail Semyonov, Algirdas Lauritenas, Yuri Ozerov, Viktor Zubkov, Mikhail Studenetsky)	5	3	574	524
3.	URU	(Carlos Blixen, Ramiro Cortes, Héctor Costa, Nelson Chelle, Nelson Demarco, Héctor Garcia Otero, Carlos González, Sergio Matto, Oscar Moglia, Raúl Mera, Ariel Olascoaga, Milton Scarón)	6	2	568	559
4.	FRA	(Roger Haudegand, Christian Baltzer, Robert Monclar, Roger Veyron, Gérard Sturla, Henri Rey,	5	3	542	497

Roger Antoine, Henri Grange, Yves Gominon, Maurice Buffière, Andrè Schlupp, Jean-Paul Beugnot)

5.	BUL	(Atanas Atanasov, Vladimir Slavov, Ilia Mirchev, Victor Radev, Georgi Kunev, Vasil Manchenko, Georgi Panov, Konstantin Totev, Tsviatko Slavov, Lyubomir Panov, Nikola Ilov)	5	3	568	545
6.	BRA	(Zenny de Azevedo, Noel Marques Lisboa, Wlamir Marques, Angelo Bonfietti, Jamil Gedeão, Wilson Bombarda, Jorge Dortas Olivieri, Mayr Facci, Edson Bispo dos Santos, José Luiz Santos Azevedo, Fausto Sucena Rasga Filho, Amary Antônio Pasos)	3	4	500	535
7.	PHI	(Ramon Manulat, Ramon Campos, Carlos Badion, Loreto Carbonel, Martin Urra, Rafael Barretto, Leonardo Marquicias, Antonio Villamor, Mariano Tolentino, Carlos Loyzaga, Antonio Genato, Eduardo Lim)	4	4	534	599
8.	CHI	(Luis Salvadores, Juan Ostoic, Maximiliano Garafulic, Pedro Araya, Rufino Bernedo, Victor Mahana, Orlando Silva, Raul Urra, Hernán Raffo, Orlando Etcheverregaray, J. Arrendondo, Rolando Etchepare)	2	5	490	518

Final: USA 89—55 SOV
3rd Place: URU 71—62 FRA
5th Place: BUL 64—52 BRA
7th Place: PHI 75—68 CHI

Led by Bill Russell and K.C. Jones, who later became great professional stars with the Boston Celtics, the United States won all eight of their games by at least 30 points and scored over 100 points four times. Their average score was 99–46.

1960 Rome T: 16, N: 16, D: 9.10.

			W	L	PF	PA
1.	USA	(Jay Arnette, Walter Bellamy, Robert Boozer, Terry Dischinger, Jerry Lucas, Oscar Robertson, Adrian Smith, Burdette Haldorson, Darrall Imhoff, Allen Kelley, Lester Lane, Jerry Lucas, Jerry West)	8	0	815	476
2.	SOV	(Yuri Korneyev, Yanis Kruminsch, Guram Minaschvill, Valdis Muischnieks, Cesar Ozers, Aleksandr Petrov, Mikhail Semyonov, Vladimir Ugrekhelidze, Maigonis Valdmanis, Albert Valtin, Gennady Volnov, Viktor Zubkov)	6	2	596	497
3.	BRA	(Edson Bispo dos Santos, Moyses Blas, Waldemar Blatkauskas, Zenny de Azevedo, Carmo de Souza, Carlos Domingos Massoni, Waldyr Geraldo Boccardo, Wlamir Marques, Amaury Antonio Pasos, Fernando	6	2	568	573

Pereira de Freitas, Antônio Salvador
Sucar, Jatyr Eduardo Schall)

4. ITA	(Augusto Giomo, Gabriele Vianello, Alessandro Riminucci, Gianfranco Lombardi, Gianfranco Pieri, Alessandro Gamba, Mario Alesini, Achille Canna, Antonio Calebotta, Paolo Vittori, Giovanni Gavagnin, Gianfranco Sardagna)	4	4	603	653
5. CZE	(Jaroslav Tetiva, Josef Kinský, Zdeněk Bobrovský, Boris Lukašik, František Konvička, Zdeněk Konečný, Dušan Lukašik, Bohuslav Rylich, Jiři Baumruk, Vladimir Pištělák, Jiři Štastný, Bohumil Tomášek)	5	3	632	594
6. YUG	(Slobodan Gordič, Ivo Daneu, Sreten Dragojlovič, Josip Djerdja, Nemanja Djurič, Marjan Kandus, Radivoje Korač, Boris Kristančič, Miha Lokar, Miodrag Nikolič, Zvonimir Petricevič, Radovan Radovič)	4	4	582	603
7. POL	(Jerzy Piskun, Janusz Wichowski, Andrzej Pstrokoński, Andrzej Nartowski, Jerzy Mlynarczyk, Ryszard Olszewski, Krzysztof Sitkowski, Mieczyslaw Lopatka, Zbigniew Dregier, Bogdan Przywarski, Tadeusz Pacula, Dariusz Świerczewski)	4	4	582	653
8. URU	(Sergio Matto, Raul Mera, Nelson Chelle, Waldemar Rial, Washington Poyet, Carlos Blixen, Milton Scaron, Aldofo Lubnicki, Hector Costa, Danilo Coito, Edison Ciavattone, Manuel Gadea)	2	6	548	678

Final Round: USA 81—57 SOV
BRA 78—75 ITA
USA 112—81 ITA
SOV 64—62 BRA
SOV 78—70 ITA
USA 90—63 BRA

The 1960 U.S. squad was without question the greatest Olympic team ever assembled. Ten members of the team went on to play professionally in the National Basketball Association. The team was so strong that future Boston Celtic star John Havlicek qualified only as an alternate. Led by Jerry Lucas and Oscar Robertson, both of whom averaged 17 points a game, the Americans won every game by at least 24 points despite a much improved international field. The U.S. team averaged 102 points per game while giving up only 59.5. In the final match against Brazil, the United States built up a 41–14 lead after only 14 minutes and coasted for the rest of the game.

1964 Tokyo T: 16, N: 16, D: 10.23.

		W	L	PF	PA
1. USA	(James Barnes, William Bradley, Lawrence Brown, Joseph Caldwell, Mel Counts, Richard Davies, Walter Hazzard, Lucius Jackson, John McCaffrey, Jeffrey Mullins, Jerry Shipp, George Wilson)	9	0	704	434
2. SOV	(Valdis Muischnieks, Nikolai Bagley, Armenak Alachachyan, Aleksandr Travin, Vyacheslav Khrynin, Yanis Kruminsch, Levan Mosechvili, Yuri Korneyev, Aleksandr Petrov, Gennady Voinov, Yaak Lipso, Yuris Kaininsch)	8	1	674	544
3. BRA	(Amaury Antônio Pasos, Wlamir Marques, Ubiratan Pereira Maciel, Carlos Domingos Massoni, Friedrich Wilhelm Braun, Carmo de Souza, Jatyr Eduardo Schall, Edson Bispo dos Santos, Antonio Salvador Sucar, Victor Mirshawka, Sergio de Toledo Machado, Jose Edvar Simões)	6	3	596	565
4. PUR	(William McCadney, Evelio Droz Ramos, Ruben Adorno Melendez, Teofilo Cruz Downs, Juan Vicens Sastre, Alberto Zamot Bula, Martin Anza Ortiz, Jaime Frontera Colley, Juan Ramon Baez Marino, Angel Garcia Lucas, Angel Cancel Acevedo, Thomas Gutierrez Ferrer)	5	4	595	592
5. ITA	(Augusto Giomo, Giusto Pellanera, Gianfranco Lombardi, Gianfranco Pieri, Gianfranco Bertini, Paolo Vittori, Gianfranco Sardagna, Ottorino Flaborea, Massimo Masini, Sauro Bufalini, Gabriele Vianello, Giovanni Gavagnin)	6	3	649	602
6. POL	(Janusz Wichowski, Andrzej Pstrokonski, Tadeusz Blauth, Andrzej Perka, Stanislaw Olejniczak, Krystian Czernichowski, Zbigniew Dregier, Kazimierz Frelkiewicz, Bogdan Liszko, Mieczyslaw Lopatka, Jerzy Piskun, Krzysztof Sitkowski)	5	4	608	596
7. YUG	(Slobodan Gordic, Radivoje Korač, Trajko Rajkovič, Dragan Kovacic, Josip Djerdja, Dragoslav Ražnatuvič, Ivo Daneu, Zvonko Petricevic, Vital Eiselt, Vladimir Cvetkovič, Menamja Djuric, Miodrag Nikolic)	6	3	670	583
8. URU	(Washington Poyet, Walter Marquez, Julio Cesar Gomez, Luis Eduardo Koster, Edison Ciavattone, Alvaro Eduardo Roca, Sergio Pisano, Luis Agustin Garcia, Manuel Roberto Gadea, Ramiro Eduardo de Leon, Waldemar Jose Rial, Jorge Maya)	4	5	596	642

Final: USA 73—59 SOV
3rd Place: BRA 76—60 PUR
5th Place: ITA 79—59 POL
7th Place: YUG 78—55 URU

Once again the Americans went through the tournament undefeated and were pressed only by the Yugoslavs, whom they beat 69–61. In the final, the U.S.S.R. led 16–13 after the first ten minutes, but the United States went on an 18–4 spurt and were never headed again. The Peruvian team sported four brothers, Ricardo, Enrique, Raul, and Luis Duarte, each of whom was over 6 feet 2½ inches.

1968 Mexico City T: 16, N: 16, D: 10.25.

		W	L	PF	PA
1. USA	(John Clawson, Kenneth Spain, Joseph "Jo-Jo" White, Michael Barrett, Spencer Haywood, Charles Scott, William Hosket, Calvin Fowler, Michael Silliman, Glynn Saulters, James King, Donald Dee)	9	0	739	505
2. YUG	(Aljoša Žorga, Radivoje Korač, Zoran Maroevič, Trajko Rajkovič, Vladimir Cvetkovič, Dragoslav Ražnatovič, Ivo Daneu, Krešimir Čosić, Damir Šolman, Nikola Plečas, Dragutin Čermak, Petar Skansi,)	7	2	705	638
3. SOV	(Anatoly Krikun, Modestas Paulauskas, Zurab Sakandelidze, Vadim Kapranov, Yuri Selikhov, Anatoly Polivoda, Sergei Belov, Priit Tomson, Sergei Kovalenko, Gennady Volnov, Yaak Lipso, Vladimir Andreyev)	8	1	774	524
4. BRA	(Sergio de Toledo Machado, Wlamir Marques, Ubiratan Pereira Maciel, Celso Luiz Scarpini, Helio Rubens Garcia, Carmo de Souza, José Aparecido dos Santos, Luiz Claudio Menon, Antonio Salvador Suctar, José Edvar Simões, José Geraldo de Castro, Carlos Domingos Massoni)	6	3	677	563
5. MEX	(Rafael Heredia Estrella, Arturo Guerrero, Fernando Tiscareño, Miguel Arellano, Antonio Ayala, Oscar Asiain, Luis Grajeda, Alejandro Guzman, Carlos Quintanar, Ricardo Pontvianne, John Hatch, Mañuel Raga)	7	2	641	580
6. POL	(Grzegorz Korcz, Wlodzimierz Trams, Czeslaw Malec, Henryk Cegielski, Andrzej Kasprzak, Edward Jurkiewicz, Adam Niemiec, Bogdan Likszo, Mieczyslaw Lopatka, Kazimierz Frelkiewicz, Boleslaw Kwiatkowski, Andrzej Pasiorowski)	5	4	604	631
7. SPA	(Juan Martinez, Vicente Ramos, Luis Santiago, Jesus Codina, Enrique Margall, Antonio Nava, Emiliano Rodriguez, Clifford Luyk, José Vela Sagi, Francisco Buscato, Lorenzo Alocen, Alfonso Martinez)	5	4	717	693
8. ITA	(Carlo Recalcati, Giusto Pellanera, Gianfranco Lombardi, Enrico Bovone, Massimo Masini, Paolo Vittori,	5	4	686	693

Gabriele Vianello, Guido Gatti, Ottorino Flaborea, Sauro Fufalini, Massimo Cosmelli, Gianluigi Jessi)

Final: USA 65—50 YUG
3rd Place: SOV 70—53 BRA
5th Place: MEX 76—65 POL
7th Place: SPA 88—72 ITA

The best of the U.S. college players stayed away from the Olympic trials for various reasons. Notable absentees included Elvin Hayes, who had signed a professional contract, and Lew Alcindor (Kareem Abdul-Jabbar), who gave two reasons: not wanting to take time off from his studies and support for the threatened black boycott of the Olympics. But the U.S. team, although held to a 5-point victory by Puerto Rico, made it to the final by beating Brazil 75–63. In the other semifinal, Yugoslavia's captain, Ivo Daneu, sank two free throws with four seconds to play to upset the U.S.S.R. 63–62. At the end of the first half of the final, the Yugoslavs trailed the United States by only three points, 32–29. But at the beginning of the second half Spencer Haywood and Jo-Jo White went on a rampage, as the U.S. outscored Yugoslavia 22–3 to put the game out of reach. The vocal Mexican crowd, which had been rooting for the underdog Yugoslavs, was so impressed by the display of Haywood and White that they switched allegiance. The only incident of the tournament occurred when some photographers attempted to shoot pictures of the weeping Cuban team, which had just lost to Mexico by one point. The Cubans took out their frustrations by chasing the photographers across the court. There were no injuries.

1972 Munich T: 16, N: 16, D: 9.10.

		W	L	PF	PA
1. SOV	(Anatoly Polivoda, Modestas Paulauskas, Zurab Sakandelidze, Alshan Sharmukhamedov, Aleksandr Boloshev, Ivan Edeshko, Sergei Belov, Mishako Korkia, Ivan Dvorni, Gennady Volnov, Aleksandr Belov, Sergei Kovalenko)	9	0	757	590
2. USA	(Kenneth Davis, Douglas Collins, Thomas Henderson, Michael Bantom, Robert Jones, Dwight Jones, James Forbes, James Brewer, Tommy Burleson, Thomas McMillen, Kevin Joyce, Ed Ratleff)	8	1	660	401
3. CUB	(Juan Domecq, Ruperto Herrera, Juan Roca, Pedro Chappé, José Miguel Alvarez Pozo, Rafael Canizares, Conrado Perez, Miguel Calderon, Tomas Herrera, Oscar Varona, Alejandro Urgelles, Franklin Standard)	7	2	687	577
4. ITA	Ottorino Flaborea, Giuseppe Brumatti, Giorgio Giomo, Mauro Cerioni, Massimo Masini, Renzo Bariviera, Marino Zanatta, Dino Meneghin, Pierluigi Marzorati, Luigi Serafini, Ivan Bisson, Giulio Jellini)	5	4	650	605

5. YUG (Ratko Tvrdič, Ljubodrag Simonovič, 7 2 734 617
Vinko Jelovač, Zarko Knezevič, Mir-
oljub Damnjanovič, Dragan Kapicič,
Blagoje Georgievski, Krešimir Čosič,
Damir Solman, Nikola Plecas, Dra-
gutin Cermak, Milun Marovič)

6. PUR (Joe Hatton, Neftali Rivera, James 6 3 743 683
Thordsen, Ruben Rodriguez, Eric
William Baum, Hector Blondet, Earl
Brown, Mariano Ortiz, Teofilo Cruz
Downs, Raymond Dalmau, Ricardo
Calzada)

7. BRA (Joseph Washington, Radvilas Gor- 3 5 625 642
auskas, Maciel Pereira Ubiratan,
Sergio Francisco Garcia, Rubens
Helio Garcia, Abdalla Marcos Leite,
Jose Aparecido dos Santos, Luiz
Claudio Menon, Adilson de Nasci-
mento, Jose Edivar Simoes, Jose
Geraldo de Castro, Carlos Domingos
Massoni)

8. CZE (Petr Noviky, Zdenek Dousa, Jiři 4 5 625 642
Konopasek, Jiři Pospisil, Zdenek
Kos, Jiři Balastik, Jiři Zidek, Jiři Zed-
nicek, Jan Bobrovsky, Kamil Bra-
benec, Jan Blazek, Jiři Ruzicka)

Final: SOV 51—50 USA
3rd Place: CUB 66—65 ITA
5th Place: YUG 86—70 PUR
7th Place: BRA 87—69 CZE

One of the greatest controversies in the history of international sports took place in Munich in the early morning
hours of Sunday, September 10. The United States entered
the final match with a record of 62 wins and no losses in
Olympic basketball competition. The game began at 11:45
p.m., in order to accommodate U.S. television. The
U.S.S.R. scored first, led 26–21 at the half, and were ahead
by eight points with 6:07 to play. The United States closed
the gap, but still trailed by one point with six seconds left.
Then the Soviet star Sasha Belov inadvertently threw the
ball toward Doug Collins of Illinois State. With three seconds left, Collins was fouled intentionally by Sako Sakan-
delidze. Collins calmly sank two free throws to give the
United States its first lead of the game, 50–49. The Soviet
team in-bounded the ball, but two seconds later head referee Renato Righetto of Brazil noted a disturbance at the
scorer's table and called an administrative time out. The
U.S.S.R. coach, Vladimir Kondrashkin, claimed that he
had called a time out after Collins' first shot. Indeed, the
time out horn had gone off just as Collins released his second free throw attempt. Both Righetto and André Cho-
pard, who was the timekeeper, thought that one second
remained. But at this point Great Britain's R. William
Jones, the Secretary-General of the International Amateur
Basketball Federation (F.I.B.A.), intervened and ordered
the clock set back to three seconds. Technically, Jones had
no right to make any decisions, but he ruled F.I.B.A. with
an iron hand, and hardly anyone dared to question his au-

thority. Kondrashkin brought in Ivan Yedeshko, who
threw a long pass to Sasha Belov. Belov caught the pass
perfectly, pushed past two defenders, and scored the winning basket. The United States filed a protest, which was
heard by a five-man Jury of Appeal. Jones appointed Terence Hepp of Hungary to be chairman of the committee,
and Hepp provided the deciding vote in favor of the
U.S.S.R. He was joined by representatives of Poland and
Cuba, while representatives of Italy and Puerto Rico voted
to disallow Belov's basket. The U.S. team voted unanimously to refuse their silver medals. Coach Hank Iba felt
doubly robbed. At two a.m., while he was signing the official protest, his pocket was picked and he lost $370.

UNITED STATES' BASKETBALL WINNING STREAK

1936			1960		
USA	52—28	EST	USA	88—54	ITA
USA	56—23	PHI	USA	125—66	JAP
USA	25—10	MEX	USA	107—63	HUN
USA	19—8	CAN	USA	104—42	YUG
1948			USA	108—50	URU
USA	86—21	SWI	USA	81—57	SOV
USA	53—28	CZE	USA	112—81	ITA
USA	59—57	ARG	USA	90—63	BRA
USA	66—28	EGY	**1964**		
USA	61—33	PER	USA	78—45	AUS
USA	63—28	URU	USA	77—51	FIN
USA	71—40	MEX	USA	60—45	PER
USA	65—21	FRA	USA	83—28	URU
1952			USA	69—61	YUG
USA	66—48	HUN	USA	86—53	BRA
USA	72—47	CZE	USA	116—50	KOR
USA	57—44	URU	USA	62—42	PUR
USA	86—58	SOV	USA	73—59	SOV
USA	103—55	CHI	**1968**		
USA	57—53	BRA	USA	81—46	SPA
USA	85—76	ARG	USA	93—36	SEN
USA	36—25	SOV	USA	96—75	PHI
1956			USA	73—58	YUG
USA	98—40	JAP	USA	95—50	PAN
USA	101—29	THA	USA	100—61	ITA
USA	121—53	PHI	USA	61—56	PUR
USA	84—44	BUL	USA	75—63	BRA
USA	113—51	BRA	USA	65—50	YUG
USA	85—55	SOV	**1972**		
USA	101—38	URU	USA	66—35	CZE
USA	89—55	SOV	USA	81—55	AUS
			USA	67—48	CUB
			USA	61—54	BRA
			USA	96—31	EGY
			USA	72—56	SPA
			USA	99—33	JAP
			USA	68—38	ITA

1976 Montreal T: 12, N: 12, D: 7.27.

		W	L	PF	PA
1. USA	(Phil Ford, Steve Sheppard, Adrian Dantley, Walter Davis, William "Quinn" Buckner, Ernie Grunfeld, Kenneth Carr, Scott May, Michel Armstrong, Thomas La Garde, Philip Hubbard, Mitchell Kupchak)	7	0	584	500
2. YUG	(Blagoje Georgijevski, Dragan Kicanović, Vinko Jelovac, Rajko Žižić, Željko Jerkov, Andro Knego, Zoran Slavnić, Krešimir Čošić, Damir Solman, Žarko Varajić, Dražen Dalipagić, Mirza Delibašić)	5	2	527	522
3. SOV	(Vladimir Arzamaskov, Aleksandr Salnikov, Valery Miloserdov, Alshan Sharmukhamedov, Andrei Makeev, Ivan Edeshko, Sergei Belov, Vladimir Tkachenko, Anatoly Myshkin, Mikhail Korkiya, Aleksandr Belov, Vladimir Zhigily)	6	1	732	535
4. CAN	(Alexander Devlin, Martin Riley, Bill Robinson, John Cassidy, Derek Sankey, Robert Sharpe, Cameron Hall, James Russell, Robert Town, Romel Raffin, Lars Hansen, Phillip Tollestrup)	4	3	595	611
5. ITA	(Giulio Jellini, Carlo Recalcati, Luciano Vendemini, Fabrizio Della Fiori, Renzo Bariviera, Marino Zanatta, Dino Meneghin, Pier Luigi Marzorati, Liugi Serafini, Ivan Bisson, Gianni Bertolotti)	5	2	526	491
6. CZE	(Vladimir Ptaček, Petr Vojtech, Jiří Konopašek, Justin Sedlak, Stanislav Kropilak, Jaroslav Kanturek, Zedenek Kos, Jiří Pospišil, Vladimir Padrta, Kamil Brabeneč, Zdenek Douša, Gustav Hraška)	3	4	584	580
7. CUB	(Juan Domecq, Ruperto Herrera, Juan Roca, Pedro Alejandro Ortiz, Rafael Canizares, Daniel Scott, Angel Padron, Tomas Herrera, Oscar Varona, Alejandro Urgelles, Felix Morales)	4	3	616	574
8. AUS	(Andrew Campbell, Ian Watson, Robert Cadee, Anthony Barnett, Edward Palubinskas, Andris Blicavs, Michael Tucker, Perry Crosswhite, Russell Simon, Peter Walsh, John Maddock, Ray Tomlinson)	2	5	625	652

Final: USA 95—74 YUG
3rd Place: SOV 100—72 CAN
5th Place: ITA 98—75 CZE
7th Place: CUB 92—81 AUS

For four years the United States waited to gain revenge for their loss to the U.S.S.R., but their train was almost derailed by a young man from New York who also had something to prove. Butch Lee of Marquette University had been prevented from trying out for the U.S. team when his college coach, Al McGuire, sent another player to the tryouts instead. Lee returned to his birthplace of Puerto Rico and made the team there. Puerto Rico faced the United States in the second game of the Olympic tournament: Lee shot 15 of 18 from the field and scored 35 points, while his teammate Neftali Rivera added 26. But the gutsy Puerto Ricans fell one point short and lost 95–94. However, the U.S.–U.S.S.R. showdown was not to be. In the semifinals, an inspired Yugoslav team upset the Soviets 89–84. The final was no contest, as the Americans took an 8–0 lead and never looked back. High scorer in the tournament for the United States was Adrian Dantley of Notre Dame, who averaged 19.3 points a game.

1980 Moscow T: 12, N: 12, D: 7.30.

		W	L	PF	PA
1. YUG	(Andro Knego, Dragan Kicanović, Rajko Žižić, Mihovil Nakić, Zeljko Jerkov, Branko Skroce, Zoran Slavnić, Krešimir Čošić, Rtko Radovanović, Duje Krstulović, Dražen Dalipagić, Mirze Delibašić)	9	0	920	768
2. ITA	(Romeo Sacchetti, Roberto Brunamonti, Michael Sylvester, Enrico Gilardi, Fabrizio Della Fiori, Marco Solfrini, Marco Bonamico, Dino Meneghin, Renato Villalta, Renzo Vecchiato, Pier Luigi Marzorati, Pietro Generali)	5	4	744	757
3. SOV	(Stanislav Eremin, Valery Miloserdov, Sergei Tarakanov, Aleksandr Salnikov, Andrey Lopatov, Nikolai Deruguin, Sergei Belov, Vladimir Tkachenko, Anatoly Myshkin, Sergei Yovaysha, Aleksandr Belostenny, Vladimir Zhigily)	7	2	943	797
4. SPA	(Wayne Brabender, José Luis Llorente, Candido-Antonio Sibilio, José Maria Margall, Manuel Flores, Fernando Roman, Luis-Miguel Santillana, Juan-Antonio Corbalan, Ignacio Solozabal, Juan-Domingo Delacruz, Juan Lopeziturriaga, Juan Antonio Sanepifanio)	4	5	871	843
5. BRA	(André Ernesto Stoffel, Luiz Gustavo De Lage, José Carlos Saiani, Milton Setrini, Jr., Machado Da Silva Wagner, Marcos Abdalla Leite, Jesus De Gilson Trindade, Marcel Ramon De Souza, Adilson De Nascimento, Marcelo Vido, Oscar Daniel Schmidt, Ricardo Cardoso Guimaraes)	4	4	745	712
6. CUB	(Jorge More Rojas, Ruperto Herrera Tabio, Alejandro Ortiz Herrara, Noangel Luaces Rodriguez, Generoso Marquez Saes, Raul Dubois Cumbath, Pedro Abreu Pascual, Miguel Calderon Gomez, Tomas Herre-	2	6	660	704

ra Martinez, Daniel Scott Brice, Alejandro Urgelles Guibot, Felix Morales Alphonso)

			W	L	PF	PA
7.	POL	(Dariusz Zelig, Leszek Doliński, Wojciech Rosinski, Eugeńiusz, Kijewski, Jerzy Bińkowski, Andrzej Michalski, Ireneusz Mulak, Justyn Weglorz, Mieczyslaw Mylarnski, Zdzislaw Myrda, Ryszard Prostak, Kryzstof Fikiel)	5	3	709	656
8.	AUS	(Melvyn Dalgeish, Gordon McLeod, Philip Smyth, Larry Sengstock, Peter Ali, Michael Tucker, Stephan Berheny, Les Riddle, Ian Davies, Peter Walsh, Danny Morseu, Perry Crosswhite)	6	2	641	596

Final: YUG 86—77 ITA
3rd Place: SOV 117—94 SPA

The Yugoslavs were led by Dalipagić and Kicanović, who averaged 24.4 and 23.6 points per game respectively. The team from India brought back memories of the 1948 Iraqi squad, losing their eight matches by an average score of 65.5 to 116.

WOMEN

1896–1972 not held

1976 Montreal T: 6, N: 6, D: 7.27.

			W	L	PF	PA
1.	SOV	(Angele Rupshene, Tatyana Zakharova, Raisa Kurvyakova, Olga Barisheva, Tatyana Ovechkina, Nadezhda Shubaeva, Iuliyana Semenova, Nadezhda Zakharova, Nelly Feriabnikova, Olga Sukharnova, Tamara Daunene, Natalya Klimova)	5	0	504	346
2.	USA	(Cindy Brogdon, Susan Rojcewicz, Ann Meyers, Lusia Harris, Nancy Dunkle, Charlotte Lewis, Nancy Lieberman, Gail Marquis, Patricia Roberts, Mary Anne O'Connor, Patricia Head, Julienne Simpson)	3	2	415	417
3.	BUL	(Nadka Golcheva, Penka Metodieva, Petkana Makaveeva, Snezhana Mihailova, Krassima Gyurova, Krassimira Bogdanova, Todorka Yordanova, Diana Dilova, Margarita Shturkelova, Maria Stoyanova, Girgina Skerlatova, Penka Stoyanova)	3	2	365	377
4.	CZE	(Ludmila Kraliková, Dana Ptačkova, Pavla Davidová, Ludmila Chmeliková, Martina Balaštiková, Ivana Korinkova, Marta Pechová, Hana Doušová, Božena Miklošovičová)	2	3	351	359

			W	L	PF	PA
5.	JAP	(Kazuko Kadoya, Kimi Wakitashiro, Mieko Fukui, Miyako Otsuka, Miho Matsuoka, Kazuyo Hayashida, Teruko Miyamoto, Keiko Namai, Reiko Aonuma, Sachiyo Yamamoto, Misako Satake)	2	3	405	400
6.	CAN	(Joyce Douthwright, Joanne Sargent, Anne Hurley, Christine Critelli, Beverly Bland, Coleen Dufresne, Sheila Strike, Sylvia Sweeney, Carol Turney, Donna Hobin, Angela Johnson, Beverly Barnes)	0	5	336	477

The Soviet women's basketball team had not lost a game for five years and was undefeated in international tournament competition since 1958. Not surprisingly, they won the Olympic gold medal with ease. High scorer for the Soviets was 6-foot 10½-inch, 284-pound Iuliyana Semenova of Riga, who averaged 19.4 points and 12.4 rebounds a game, despite the fact that she spent more than half the time on the bench. The United States was awarded second place by virtue of its 95–79 victory over Bulgaria.

1980 Moscow T: 6, N: 6, D: 7.30.

			W	L	PF	PA
1.	SOV	(Angele Rupshene, Lyubov Sharmay, Vida Besselene, Olga Korosteleva, Tatiana Ovechkina, Nadezhda Olkhova, Iuliyana Semenova, Lyudmila Rogozina, Nelly Feriabnikova, Olga Sukharnova, Tatiana Nadyrova, Tatiana Ivinskaya)	6	0	657	389
2.	BUL	(Nadka Golcheva, Penka Metodieva, Petkana Makaveeva, Snezhana Mihailova, Vania Dermandzhieva, Krassimira Bogdanova, Angelina Mihailova, Diana Brainova, Evladia Zakatanova, Kostadinka Radkova, Silvia Germanova, Penka Stoyanova)	4	2	513	509
3.	YUG	(Vera Djurasković, Mersada Becirspahić, Jelica Komnenović, Mira Bjedov, Vukica Mitić, Sanja Ozegović, Sofija Pekić, Marija Tonković, Zorica Djurković, Vesna Despotović, Biljana Majstorović, Jasmina Perazić)	4	2	424	429
4.	HUN	(Éva Gulyás, Ágnes Németh, Ilona Kovács, Györgyi Vertetics, Zsuzsa Boksay, Ilona Lőrincz, Katalin Szuchy, Magda Gulyás, Ildikó Gulyás, Judit Medgyesi, Lenke Kiss, Erzsébet Szentesi)	2	4	409	475
5.	CUB	(Leonor Borrell Hernandez, Nancy Aties Sanchez, Barbara Becquer Rivero, Maria Moret Hernandez, Inocenta Corbea Aguirre, Caridad Despaigne Savig, Matilde Charro Mendoza, Maria de Los Santos Igle-	1	4	346	403

	W	L	PF	PA
sias, Sonia de La Paz Galan, Virginia Perez Viart, Margarita Skeet Quiñones, Vicenta Salom Smith)				
6. ITA (Chiara Guzzonato, Nunziata Serradimigni, Roberta Faccin, Lidia Gorlin, Emanuela Silimbani, Wanda Sandon, Bianca Rossi, Antonietta Baistrocchi, Marinella Draghetti, Rosanna Vergnano, Mariangela Piancastelli, Orietta Grossi)	0	5	308	452

Final: SOV 104—73 BUL
3rd Place: YUG 68—65 HUN

The U.S.S.R. had an even easier time than they had had in 1976, winning all their games by 31 points or more. Their average score was 109.5 to 65. Semenova, now 27 years old, was high scorer in the tournament, with 21.8 points a game. She also averaged 12.5 rebounds. In fact, Semenova and her 6-foot 3-inch teammate Olga Sukharnova pulled down more rebounds than the entire 12-woman Italian team.

BOXING

Light Flyweight
Flyweight
Bantamweight
Featherweight
Lightweight
Light Welterweight

Welterweight
Light Middleweight
Middleweight
Light Hevyweight
Heavyweight
Super Heavyweight

Amateur boxing matches consist of three 3-minute rounds. Defeated quarterfinalists are listed as tied for fifth place. Beginning in 1952, third-place matches were no longer held, and defeated semifinalists were both awarded bronze medals.

LIGHT FLYWEIGHT

(48 kg-106 lbs)

1896–1964 not held

1968 Mexico City C: 24, N: 24, D: 10.26.

			FINAL MATCH
1.	Francisco Rodriguez	VEN	Dec 3–2
2.	Yong-ju Jee	KOR	
3.	Harlan Marbley	USA	
3.	Hubert Skrzypczak	POL	
5.	Joseph Donovan (AUS), Hatha Karunaratne (SRL), Alberto Morales (MEX), Gabriel Ogun (NGR)		

After Rodriguez's victory was announced, few in the crowd could fail to be moved by the sight of the 23-year-old Venezuelan joyfully weeping into the national flag that his seconds had draped over his shoulders.

1972 Munich C: 31, N: 31, D: 9.10.

			FINAL MATCH
1.	György Gedó	HUN	Dec 5–0
2.	U-Gil Kim	PRK	
3.	Ralph Evans	GBR	

| 4. | Enrique Rodriguez | SPA | |
| 5. | Rafael Carbonell (CUB), Chanyalew Haile (ETH), Vladimir Ivanov (SOV), James Odwori (UGA) | | |

1976 Montreal C: 27, N: 27, D: 7.31.

			FINAL MATCH
1.	Jorge Hernandez	CUB	Dec 4–1
2.	Byong-Uk Li	PRK	
3.	Orlando Maldonado	PUR	
3.	Payao Pooltarat	THA	
5.	György Gedó (HUN), Armando Guevara (VEN), Chan-Lee Park (KOR), Hector Patri (ARG)		

Hernandez was the reigning world amateur and Pan-American champion. Eighteen-year-old bronze medalist Payao Pooltarat from Prachub Khirikhan was the first Thai athlete to win an Olympic medal. He accomplished this by outpointing defending champion Gedó in the quarterfinals.

1980 Moscow C: 22, N: 22, D: 8.2.

			FINAL MATCH
1.	Shamil Sabyrov	SOV	Dec 3–2
2.	Hipolito Ramos	CUB	
3.	Byong-Uk Li	PRK	
3.	Ismail Hjuseinov	BUL	
5.	György Gedó (HUN), Dietmar Geilich (GDR), Dumitru Schiopu (ROM), Ahmed Siad (ALG)		

FLYWEIGHT

(51 kg–112½ lbs)

1896–1900 not held

1904 St. Louis C: 2, N: 1, D: 9.22.
(47.63 kg–105 lbs)

		FINAL MATCH
1. George Finnegan	USA	RSC 1
2. Miles Burke	USA	

For some unknown reason Burke was allowed to compete even though he was almost three pounds over the weight limit.

1906–1912 not held

1920 Antwerp C: 12, N: 7, D: 8.26.
(50.80 kg–112 lbs)

		FINAL MATCH
1. Frank Di Gennara	USA	Dec
2. Anders Petersen	DEN	
3. William Cuthbertson	GBR	
4. J. Albert	FRA	
5. Rampignon (FRA), Zegwaard (HOL), Peter Zivic (USA)		

Seven and a half years later, Di Gennara, fighting under the name Frankie Genaro, won the World Flyweight title by defeating Frenchy Belanger in Toronto.

1924 Paris C: 19, N: 13, D: 7.20.
(50.80 kg–112 lbs)

		FINAL MATCH
1. Fidel LaBarba	USA	Dec
2. James McKenzie	GBR	
3. Raymond Fee	USA	
4. Rinaldo Castellenghi	ITA	
5. Oscar Bergström (SWE), R. Biete-Berdes (SPA), J. MacGregor (CAN), S. Rennie (CAN)		

LaBarba, an 18-year-old Los Angeles high school student, went on to a successful professional career. In 1925 he defeated Frankie Genaro for the American Flyweight title, and in 1927 he won the vacant World Flyweight title. He later worked as a screenwriter in Hollywood.

1928 Amsterdam C: 19, N: 19, D: 8.11.
(50.80 kg–112 lbs)

		FINAL MATCH
1. Antal Kocsis	HUN	Dec
2. Armand Appell	FRA	
3. Carlo Cavagnoli	ITA	
4. H. Lebenon	SAF	
5. Hubert Ausböck (GER), B. Bril (HOL), Alfred Gaona (MEX), Cuthbert Taylor (GBR)		

In the first contest of the tournament, 16-year-old Hyman Miller of California appeared to have easily defeated Marcel Santos of Belgium. When the decision was announced in Santos's favor, Miller's confident smile turned to convulsive sobbing. The U.S. boxing team was so outraged that they requested permission to withdraw all their boxers from the Olympics. However the president of the U.S. Olympic Committee, Major-General Douglas MacArthur, refused permission, stating, "Americans never quit." The eventual winner, Antal Kocsis, was Hungary's first Olympic gold medalist in boxing. The following year he turned professional and emigrated to the United States.

1932 Los Angeles C: 12, N: 12, D: 8.13.
(50.80 kg–112 lbs)

		FINAL MATCH
1. István Énekes	HUN	Dec
2. Francisco Cabañas	MEX	
3. Louis Salica	USA	
4. Thomas Pardoe	GBR	
5. Isaac Duke (SAF), Kiyonobu Murakami (JAP), Edelweis Rodriguez (ITA), Werner Spannagel (GER)		

1936 Berlin C: 25, N: 25, D: 8.15.
(50.80 kg–112 lbs)

		FINAL MATCH
1. Willi Kaiser	GER	Dec
2. Gavino Matta	ITA	
3. Louis Daniel Laurie	USA	
4. Alfredo Carlomagno	ARG	
5. R. Degryse (BEL), W.I. Passmore (SAF), Edmund Sobkowiak (POL), F. Tricanico (URU)		

1948 London C: 26, N: 26, D: 8.13.

		FINAL MATCH
1. Pascual Perez	ARG	Dec
2. Spartaco Bandinelli	ITA	
3. Soo-Ann Han	KOR	
4. František Majdloch	CZE	
5. Alex Bollaert (BEL), H.A.H. Corman (HOL), Luis Martinez Zapata (SPA), Frank Sodano (USA)		

Pascual Perez, a 22-year-old clerk in the Chamber of Deputies in Buenos Aires, faced his most difficult challenge *before* the fighting began. Perez was unexpectedly disqualified for being overweight. However, it was later discovered that officials had confused him with his bantamweight teammate Arnoldo *Pares*.

1952 Helsinki C: 28, N: 28, D: 8.2.

		FINAL MATCH
1. Nathan Brooks	USA	Dec 3–0
2. Edgar Basel	GER	
3. Anatoly Bulakov	SOV	
3. William Toweel	SAF	

5. Thorbjorn Clausen (NOR), David Dower (GBR), Mircea Dobrescu (ROM), Soo-Ann Han (KOR)

1956 Melbourne C: 19, N: 19, D: 12.1.

		FINAL MATCH
1. Terence Spinks	GBR	Dec
2. Mircea Dobrescu	ROM	
3. John Caldwell	IRL	
3. René Libeer	FRA	

5. Warner Batchelor (AUS), Ray Perez (USA), Vladimir Stolnikov (SOV), Kenji Yonekura (JAP)

1960 Rome C: 33, N: 33, D: 9.5.

		FINAL MATCH
1. Gyula Török	HUN	Dec 3–2
2. Sergey Sivko	SOV	
3. Abdelmoneim Elguindi	UAR	
3. Kiyoshi Tanabe	JAP	

5. Humberto Barrera (USA), Miguel Botta (ARG), Mircea Dobrescu (ROM), Manfred Homberg (GER)

1964 Tokyo C: 28, N: 28, D: 10.23.

		FINAL MATCH
1. Fernando Atzori	ITA	Dec 4–1
2. Artur Olech	POL	
3. Robert Carmody	USA	
3. Stanislav Sorokin	SOV	

5. Otto Babiasch (GER), Dong-Kih Choh (KOR), Constantin Ciuca (ROM), John McCafferty (IRL)

After one minute and six seconds of the first round of his quarterfinal bout against Stanislaw Sorokin, Korean boxer Dong-Kih Choh was disqualified for holding his head too low. Unable to accept this verdict, Dong sat down in the middle of the ring and refused to leave. His sitdown strike continued for 51 minutes, until officials persuaded him to leave. Ironically, Sorokin was forced to withdraw before his next fight because of a cut that wasn't healing. The winner, Sardinian house-painter Fernando Atzori, fought the final with a black eye.

1968 Mexico City C: 26, N: 26, D: 10.26.

		FINAL MATCH
1. Ricardo Delgado	MEX	Dec 5–0
2. Artur Olech	POL	

3. Servilio Oliveira BRA
3. Leo Rwabwogo UGA

5. Tibor Badari (HUN), Joseph Destimo (GHA), Tetsuaki Nakamura (JAP), Nicolai Novikov (SOV)

Heriberto Cintron of Puerto Rico was standing in the ring waiting for his first-round bout with Polish policeman Artur Olech when he was suddenly disqualified for being younger than the minimum age of 17 years. He was, in fact, 16 years and one month old.

1972 Munich C: 37, N: 37, D: 9.10.

		FINAL MATCH
1. Georgi Kostadinov	BUL	Dec 5–0
2. Leo Rwabwogo	UGA	
3. Leszek Blazyński	POL	
3. Douglas Rodriguez	CUB	

5. Neil McLaughlin (IRL), Calixto Perez (COL), Chong-Man You (KOR), Boris Zoriktuev (SOV)

Most Olympic boxers who went on to become world champions were also Olympic champions, or at least medalists. But there is one boxing star who made little impression in his Olympic debut. As an underage 15-year-old representative of Puerto Rico, Wilfredo Gomez lost a 4–1 decision in the first round to Mohamed Selin of Egypt, who was in turn knocked out in his next fight. Less than five years later, on May 21, 1977, Gomez won the World Super Bantamweight championship and on March 9, 1979, he won the Junior Featherweight title.

1976 Montreal C: 26, N: 26, D: 7.31.

		FINAL MATCH
1. Leo Randolph	USA	Dec 3–2
2. Ramon Duvalon	CUB	
3. Leslek Blazyński	POL	
3. David Torosyan	SOV	

5. Ian Clyde (CAN), Jo-Ung Jong (PRK), David Larmour (IRL), Alfrede Perez (VEN)

Leo Randolph, an 18-year-old high school student from Tacoma, Washington, called his surprise victory "the best thing that happened to me since I became a Christian in 1969."

1980 Moscow C: 20, N: 20, D: 8.2.

		FINAL MATCH
1. Peter Lessov	BUL	RSC 2 2:08
2. Viktor Miroshnichenko	SOV	
3. Hugh Russell	IRL	
3. János Váradi	HUN	

5. Roman Gilberto (MEX), Daniel Radu (ROM), Henryk Średnicki (POL), Ryon-Sik Yo (PRK)

BANTAMWEIGHT

(54 kg–119½ lbs)

1896–1900 not held

1904 St. Louis C: 2, N: 1, D: 9.22.
(52.16 kg–115 lbs)

			FINAL MATCH
1.	Oliver Kirk	USA	RSC 3
2.	George Finnegan	USA	

1906 not held

1908 London C: 6, N: 2, D: 10.27.
(52.62 kg–116 lbs)

			FINAL MATCH
1.	A. Henry Thomas	GBR	Dec
2.	John Condon	GBR	
3.	W. Webb	GBR	
4.	P. Mazior (FRA), F. McGurk (GBR), H. Perry (GBR)		

1912 not held

1920 Antwerp C: 8, N: 8, D: 8.26.
(53.52 kg–118 lbs)

			FINAL MATCH
1.	Clarence Walker	SAF	Dec
2.	Chris Graham	CAN	
3.	James McKenzie	GBR	
4.	Henri Hebrants	BEL	
5.	Edward Earl Hartman (USA), Maurice Herschman (USA), Ricard (FRA), Voss (NOR)		

1924 Paris C: 21, N: 15, D: 7.20.
(53.52 kg–118 lbs)

			FINAL MATCH
1.	William Smith	SAF	Dec
2.	Salvatore Tripoli	USA	
3.	Jean Ces	FRA	
4.	Oscar Andrén	SWE	
5.	A. Barber (GBR), A. Sanchez Dietz (SPA), J. Lemouton (FRA), Benjamin Pertuzzo (ARG)		

Joe Lazarus of Cornell University had the unusual misfortune of knocking out his opponent, Oscar Andrén of Sweden, and yet being declared the loser. As Andrén was being revived, the referee announced that Lazarus was disqualified for hitting during a clinch a few seconds before the knockout punch. Swedish officials were so embarrassed by the ruling that they offered to have the bout refought, but Olympic officials wouldn't allow it.

1928 Amsterdam C: 18, N: 18, D: 8.11.
(53.52 kg–118 lbs)

			FINAL MATCH
1.	Vittorio Tamagnini	ITA	Dec
2.	John Daley	USA	
3.	Harry Isaacs	SAF	
4.	Edward Traynor	IRL	
5.	John Garland (GBR), Vincent Glionna (CAN), Carmelo Robledo (ARG), János Széles (HUN)		

1936 Berlin C: 24, N: 24, D: 8.15.
(53.52 kg–118 lbs)

			FINAL MATCH
1.	Ulderico Sergo	ITA	Dec
2.	Jack Wilson	USA	
3.	Fidel Ortiz	MEX	
4.	Stig Cederberg	SWE	
5.	J. Cornelis (BEL), O. de Larrazal (PHI), A.L. Hannan (SAF), S. Hashioka (JAP)		

1948 London C: 30, N: 30, D: 8.13.

			FINAL MATCH
1.	Tibor Csik	HUN	Dec
2.	Giovanni Battista Zuddas	ITA	
3.	Juan Venegas	PUR	
4.	Alvaro Vicente Domenech	SPA	
5.	James Carruthers (AUS), Celestine Gonzalez Henriquez (CHI), Willie Lenihan (IRL) Albert Perera (SRL)		

Argentina's Arnoldo Pares, although innocent of any wrongdoing, was the center of much confusion and controversy. At the weigh-in he was found to be overweight. In a panic, his supporters cut off his hair, rubbed him down with a towel, scrubbed the soles of his feet, and blew the dust off the scales. He even wept for a few minutes which further reduced his weight. It was no use: he still couldn't make the limit. The Argentinians filed a protest, and weights and measures experts were sent for. Sure enough, it turned out that the scales were inaccurate, and Pares was allowed to compete. In his first match the nearly bald Pares won a disputed decision from Vic Toweel of South Africa. Toweel didn't let this setback hurt his career. He turned professional and, less than two years later, won the World Bantamweight title, which he held for two and a half years before losing to Jimmy Carruthers of Australia, who happened to have been Arnoldo Pares' second opponent at the 1948 Olympics. Carruthers won that fight but sustained an eye injury that forced him to withdraw from his quarterfinal bout with Tibor Csik. The unusually lucky Csik was thus able to move on to the semifinals even though he had fought only one regular fight. (His first-round opponent had been disqualified.)

1952 Helsinki C: 23, N: 23, D: 8.2.

			FINAL MATCH
1.	Pentti Hämäläinen	FIN	Dec 2–1
2.	John McNally	IRL	
3.	Gennady Garbuzov	SOV	
3.	Joon-Ho Kang	KOR	
5.	Vincenzo Dall'osso (ITA), František Majdloch (CZE), David Moore (USA), Helmuth Von Gravenitz (SAF)		

The victory of Hämäläinen, a 23-year-old typewriter mechanic from Kotka, was greeted with great enthusiam by the local Finnish crowd, although the Irish felt they had gotten a raw deal. Nevertheless, Belfast's John McNally was the first Irishman to win an Olympic boxing medal.

1956 Melbourne C: 18, N: 18, D: 12.1.

			FINAL MATCH
1.	Wolfgang Behrendt	GDR	Dec
2.	Soon-Chun Song	KOR	
3.	Claudio Barrientos	CHI	
3.	Frederick Gilroy	IRL	
5.	Eder Jofre (BRA), Owen Reilly (GBR), Mario Sitri (ITA), Carmelo Adolfo Tomaselli (ARG)		

Twenty-year-old Berlin machine-fitter Wolfgang Behrendt was the first Olympic champion from the German Democratic Republic (East Germany).

1960 Rome C: 33, N: 33, D: 9.5.

			FINAL MATCH
1.	Oleg Grigoryev	SOV	Dec
2.	Primo Zamparini	ITA	
3.	Brunon Bendig	POL	
3.	Oliver Taylor	AUS	
5.	Jerry Armstrong (USA), Fernandez Alfred Carbajo (SPA), Horst Rascher (GER), Myint Thein (BUR)		

In the third round of competition, Oleg Grigoryev won a much-disputed split decision over 17-year-old Frankie Taylor of Great Britain. Although a British protest was rejected, all three judges who voted for Grigoryev were fired, as were no less than half of the 30 referees and judges involved in the Olympic tournament.

1964 Tokyo C: 32, N: 32, D: 10.23.

			FINAL MATCH	
1.	Takao Sakurai	JAP	RSC 2	1:18
2.	Shin-Cho Chung	KOR		
3.	Juan Fabila Mendoza	MEX		
3.	Washington Rodriguez	URU		
5.	Fermin Espinosa (CUB), Oleg Grigoryev (SOV), Nicolae Puiu (ROM), Karimu Young (NGR)			

The final contest was stopped after Sakurai had knocked down Chung four times in less than four and a half minutes. After a brief career as a professional, Sakurai opened a coffee shop in Tokyo called "The Medalist."

1968 Mexico City C: 39, N: 39, D: 10.26.

			FINAL MATCH	
1.	Valery Sokolov	SOV	RSC 2	2:15
2.	Eridari Mukwanga	UGA		
3.	Kyou-Chull Chang	KOR		
3.	Eiji Morioka	JAP		
5.	Roberto Cervantes (MEX), Michael Dowling (IRL), Samuel Mbugua (KEN), Horst Rascher (GER)			

1972 Munich C: 38, N: 38, D: 9.10.

			FINAL MATCH
1.	Orlando Martinez	CUB	Dec 5–0
2.	Alfonso Zamora	MEX	
3.	Ricardo Carreras	USA	
3.	George Turpin	GBR	
5.	Ferry Egberty Moniaga (INS), John Mwaura Nderu (KEN), Juan Francisco Rodriguez (SPA), Vassily Solomin (SOV)		

Martinez was the first Cuban to win an Olympic gold medal since Ramon Forst, the fencer, in 1904.

1976 Montreal C: 24, N: 24, D: 7.31.

			FINAL MATCH
1.	Yong-Jo Gu	PRK	Dec 5–0
2.	Charles Mooney	USA	
3.	Patrick Cowdell	GBR	
3.	Victor Rybakov	SOV	
5.	Stefan Förster (GDR), Reynaldo Fortaleza (PHI), Chul-Soon Hwang (KOR), Veerachat Saturngrum (THA)		

1980 Moscow C: 33, N: 33, D: 8.2.

			FINAL MATCH
1.	Juan Hernandez	CUB	Dec 5–0
1.	Bernardo José Pinango	VEN	
3.	Michael Anthony	GUY	
3.	Dumitru Cipere	ROM	
5.	Geral Issaick (TAN), Samson Khachatrian (SOV), John Sirakibbe (UGA), Daniel Zaragoza (MEX)		

Seventeen-year-old Hernandez was the second youngest boxer at the Moscow Olympics. He stopped two African boxers before the fights had gone the distance, and he defeated his other three opponents with clear-cut decisions.

FEATHERWEIGHT

(57 kg–126 lbs)

1896–1900 not held

1904 St. Louis C: 3, N: 1, D: 9.22.
(56.70 kg–125 lbs)

		FINAL MATCH
1. Oliver Kirk	USA	Dec
2. Frank Haller	USA	
3. Fred Gilmore	USA	

Kirk is the only person to win two boxing titles at a single Olympics. The importance of his achievement is certainly muted by the fact that he fought only one bout in each division (Bantamweight and Featherweight).

1906 not held

1908 London C: 8, N: 2, D: 10.27.
(57.15 kg–126 lbs)

		FINAL MATCH
1. Richard Gunn	GBR	Dec
2. C.W. Morris	GBR	
3. Hugh Roddin	GBR	
4. T. Ringer	GBR	

At 37, Gunn was the oldest fighter ever to win an Olympic championship. He had been Bristish amateur champion from 1894 to 1896. Unfortunately, his superiority over other British featherweights was so pronounced that his entry in a tournament caused others to drop out. Consequently, Gunn, the true sportsman, retired from competition. He came out of retirement for the London Olympics and defeated one Frenchman and two Englishmen to win the gold medal. Then he retired again, having lost only one fight in 15 years.

1912 not held

1920 Antwerp C: 15, N: 9, D: 8.26.
(57.15 kg–126 lbs)

		FINAL MATCH
1. Paul Fritsch	FRA	Dec
2. Jean Gachet	FRA	
3. Edoardo Garzena	ITA	
4. Jack Zivic	USA	
5. Bovy (BEL), Cater (GBR), Clausen (DEN), Erdal (NOR)		

1924 Paris C: 24, N: 17, D: 7.20.
(57.15 kg–126 lbs)

		FINAL MATCH
1. John Fields	USA	Dec
2. Joseph Salas	USA	
3. Pedro Quartucci	ARG	
4. Jean Devergnies	BEL	
5. C. Abarca-Gonzalez (CHI), M. Depont (FRA), H. Dingley (GBR), B. Petrarca (ITA)		

Jackie Fields and Joe Salas were best friends back home in Los Angeles. At 16, Fields, whose real name was Jacob Finkelstein, was the youngest boxer at the Paris Olympics. After his victory over Salas in the final, Fields was so upset at having defeated his buddy that he went back to the dressing room and cried. In 1929 Fields won the World Welterweight title.

1928 Amsterdam C: 18, N: 18, D: 8.11.
(57.15 kg–126 lbs)

		FINAL MATCH
1. Lambertus van Klaveren	HOL	Dec
2. Victor Peralta	ARG	
3. Harold Devine	USA	
4. Lucien Biquet	BEL	
5. George Boireau (FRA), Jan Górny (POL), Frederick Perry (GBR), Olavi Vakeva (FIN)		

There seemed little question in anyone's mind that Peralta had outclassed van Klaveren. Anyone, that is, except the judges who awarded the decision to the Dutch fighter. "It was as plain as a pike-staff which was the master," wrote the reporter for the London *Daily Telegraph*. A battle ensued between Argentinian spectators and Dutch police, and the commotion was still bubbling when the decision of the next match, the Lightweight championship, set off outrage among the Americans in the crowd.

1932 Los Angeles C: 10, N: 10, D: 8.13.
(57.15 kg–126 lbs)

		FINAL MATCH
1. Carmelo Robledo	ARG	Dec
2. Josef Schleinkofer	GER	
3. Carl Carlsson	SWE	
4. Gaspare Alessandri	ITA	
5. John Hines (USA), John Keller (CAN), Ernest Smith (IRL)		

1936 Berlin C: 25, N: 25, D: 8.15.
(57.15 kg–126 lbs)

		FINAL MATCH
1. Oscar Casanovas	ARG	Dec
2. Charles Catterall	SAF	
3. Josef Miner	GER	
4. Dezső Frigyes	HUN	

5. Theodore Ernst Kara (USA), W. Marquart (CAN), Aleksander Polus (POL), J.W. Treadaway (GBR)

1948 London C: 30, N: 30, D: 8.13.
(58 kg–128 lbs)

		FINAL MATCH
1. Ernesto Formenti	ITA	Dec
2. Dennis Shephard	SAF	
3. Aleksy Antkiewicz	POL	
4. Francisco Nunez	ARG	

5. Edward Johnson (USA), Edward Kerschbaumer (AUT), Armand Savoie (CAN), Bung-Nan Su (KOR)

A new style in Olympic boxing protests was created following the announcement that American Eddie Johnson had been declared the winner over 33-year-old Basilio Alves of Uruguay in their second-round match. While the crowd booed for more than fifteen minutes, Alves' supporters hoisted him on their shoulders and stormed the table of the Jury of Appeal. In the semifinals, it was the turn of the Argentinians to protest. Upset over the loss of Nunez to Shephard, they grabbed Nunez, who had refused to leave the ring, lifted him to their shoulders, and attempted a Uruguayan charge toward the Jurors' table. Repulsed by a phalanx of twelve attendants, the Argentinians listened to speeches by two of their officials and were finally convinced to end their protest by an Argentinian member of the Jury of Appeal, Señor Oriani. The final saw Shephard enter the ring with six stitches over his right eye, the result of a cut that had been opened in four of his five preliminary bouts. He fought gamely but was finally worn down by Formenti in the final minute and a half.

1952 Helsinki C: 30, N: 30, D: 8.2.

		FINAL MATCH
1. Jan Zachara	CZE	Dec 2–1
2. Sergio Caprari	ITA	
3. Leonard Leisching	SAF	
3. Joseph Ventaja	FRA	

5. Edson Brown (USA), Leszek Drogosz (POL), János Erdei (HUN), Leonard Walters (CAN)

1956 Melbourne C: 18, N: 18, D: 12.1.

		FINAL MATCH
1. Vladimir Safronov	SOV	Dec
2. Thomas Nicholls	GBR	
3. Pentti Hämäläinen	FIN	
3. Henryk Niedźwiedzki	POL	

5. Andre De Sousa (FRA), Tristan Octavio Falfan (ARG), Shinetsu Suzuki (JAP), Jan Zachara (CZE)

Sarfonov, an artist from Siberia, gained the U.S.S.R's first Olympic boxing title. He was added to the team at the last minute when Soviet champion Aleksandr Zasukhin injured his hand in training.

1960 Rome C: 31, N: 31, D: 9.5.

		FINAL MATCH
1. Francesco Musso	ITA	Dec 4–1
2. Jerzy Adamski	POL	
3. Jorma Limmonen	FIN	
3. William Meyers	SAF	

5. Abel Bekker (ZIM), Ernest Chervet (SWI), Constantin Gheorghiu (ROM), Boris Nikanorov (SOV)

In the first round of the tournament, Boris Nikanorov outpointed Nick Spanakos to become the first Soviet boxer ever to defeat an American.

1964 Tokyo C: 32, N: 32, D: 10.23.

		FINAL MATCH
1. Stanislav Stepashkin	SOV	Dec 3–2
2. Anthony Villanueva	PHI	
3. Charles Brown	USA	
3. Heinz Schulz	GDR	

5. Constantin Crudu (ROM), Jose Duran Aguirre (MEX), Piotr Gutman (POL), Tun Tin (BUR)

After all the hoopla and uproar that had gone on as a result of unpopular decisions in Olympic boxing, it was left to Spanish featherweight Valentin Loren to register the ultimate protest. Disqualified for repeated holding and open-glove hitting in the second round of his first fight, Loren turned on the Hungarian referee, György Sermer, and punched him in the face. This unfortunate indiscretion caused the Saragoza southpaw to receive a lifetime ban from international amateur boxing. Silver medalist Anthony Villanueva was the son of Cely Villanueva, who had won the Bantamweight bronze medal at the 1932 Olympics in Los Angeles. Anthony tried a brief career as a movie actor and then turned professional boxer. Stepashkin won his first four fights by knockout and technical knockout before gaining a split decision over Villanueva.

1968 Mexico City C: 28, N: 28, D: 10.26.

		FINAL MATCH
1. Antonio Roldan	MEX	DISQ 2
2. Albert Robinson	USA	
3. Ivan Mihailov	BUL	
3. Philipp Waruinge	KEN	

5. Miguel Garcia (ARG), Abdel Khallaf (UAR), Valery Plotnikov (SOV), Seyfi Tatar (TUR)

The final match came to a sudden end when Robinson was disqualified for butting. Although the Mexican crowd was delighted with the victory, Roldan himself seemed apologetic. As the first disqualified finalist since Ingemar Johanson in 1952, Robinson was prevented from receiving his silver medal. After a protest by American officials, Robinson was finally awarded the medal ofter his return to the United States.

1972 Munich C: 45, N: 45, D: 9.10.

		FINAL MATCH
1. Boris Kousnetsov	SOV	Dec 3–2
2. Philip Waruinge	KEN	
3. András Botos	HUN	
3. Clemente Rojas	COL	

5. Kazuo Kobayashi (JAP), Jouko Lindberg (FIN), Gabriel Pometcu (ROM), Antonio Rubio (SPA)

1976 Montreal C: 26, N: 26, D: 7.31.

		FINAL MATCH
1. Angel Herrera	CUB	KO 2 2:18
2. Richard Nowakowski	GDR	
3. Leszek Kosedowski	POL	
3. Juan Paredes	MEX	

5. Davey Armstrong (USA), Choon-Gil Choi (KOR), Gheorghe Ciochina (ROM), Angel Pacheco (VEN), Bratislav Ristic (YUG)

1980 Moscow C: 35, N: 35, D: 8.2.

		FINAL MATCH
1. Rudi Fink	GDR	Dec 4–1
2. Adolfo Horta	CUB	
3. Krzysztof Kosedowski	POL	
3. Viktor Rybakov	SOV	

5. Tzacho Andreikovski (BUL), Sidnei Dalrovere (BRA), Winfred Kabunda (ZAM), Luis Pizarro (PUR)

LIGHTWEIGHT

(60 kg–132 lbs)

1896–1900 not held

1904 St. Louis C: 8, N: 1, D: 9.22.
(61.24 kg–135½ lbs)

		FINAL MATCH
1. Harry Spanger	USA	Dec
2. James Eagan	USA	
3. Russell Van Horn	USA	
4. Peter Sturholdt	USA	

A well-known local boxer, Carroll Burton, entered the tournament and won his first match. However it was then discovered that the victor was not Burton at all, but a man named Bollinger posing as Burton. Bollinger was disqualified and his opponent, Sturholdt, was advanced to the next round.

1906 not held

1908 London C: 12, N: 3, D: 10.27.
(63.50 kg–140 lbs)

		FINAL MATCH
1. Frederick Grace	GBR	Dec
2. Frederick Spiller	GBR	
3. H.H. Johnson	GBR	
4. H. Holmes (GBR), G. Jessup (GBR), M. Wells (GBR)		

Early in the second round, the two finalists swung hard at each other. Both missed and fell on their faces.

1912 not held

1920 Antwerp C: 12, N: 12, D: 8.26.
(61.24 kg–135½ lbs)

		FINAL MATCH
1. Samuel Mosberg	USA	Dec
2. Gotfred Johansen	DEN	
3. Clarence Newton	CAN	
4. Beland	SAF	

5. Frederick Grace (GBR), Muyzen (BEL), Saterhang (NOR)

1924 Paris C: 30, N: 22, D: 7.20.
(61.24 kg–135½ lbs)

		FINAL MATCH
1. Hans Nielsen	DEN	Dec
2. Alfredo Copello	ARG	
3. Frederick Boylstein	USA	
4. J. Tholey	FRA	

5. Beland (SAF), D. Genon (BEL), H. Hansen (NOR), Ben Rothwell (USA)

1928 Amsterdam C: 24, N: 24, D: 8.11.
(61.24 kg–135½ lbs)

		FINAL MATCH
1. Carlo Orlandi	ITA	Dec
2. Stephen Michael Halaiko	USA	
3. Gunnar Berggren	SWE	
4. Hans Nielsen	DEN	

5. Dirk Baan (HOL), Cecil Bissett (ZIM), Pascual Bonfiglio (ARG), Jorge Diaz Hernandez (CHI)

1932 Los Angeles C: 13, N: 13, D: 8.13.
(61.24 kg–135½ lbs)

		FINAL MATCH
1. Lawrence Stevens	SAF	Dec
2. Thure Ahlqvist	SWE	
3. Nathan Bor	USA	
4. Mario Bianchini	ITA	

5. Frank Genovese (CAN), Franz Kartz (GER), Gaston Mayor (FRA)

1936 Berlin C: 26, N: 26, D: 8.15.
(61.24 kg–135½ lbs)

			FINAL MATCH
1.	Imre Harangi	HUN	Dec
2.	Nikolai Stepulov	EST	
3.	Erik Ågren	SWE	
4.	Poul Kops	DEN	

5. C. Lillo (CHI), L.J. Oliver (ARG), Jose Padilla (PHI), Andrew Scrivani (USA)

Prior to the Olympics, Harangi was urged by doctors to retire from boxing and undergo an operation on his nose, which had been badly injured in previous fights. Harangi refused and went on to win the gold medal in Berlin. One unfortunate competitor was Hamilton-Brown of South Africa. In the opening-round match, he lost a split decision to Lillo of Chile. However it was later discovered that one of the judges had mistakenly reversed his scores for the two boxers and that Hamilton-Brown was in fact the winner and thus eligible to move on to the next round. Unfortunately, Hamilton-Brown, who had had trouble making the weight limit, had softened the disappointment of his loss by going on an eating binge. By the time the South African manager found him it was after midnight and the boxer had put on nearly five pounds. Desperately his trainer tried to boil him down, but it was no use. The next day Hamilton-Brown, still over the weight limit, was disqualified.

1948 London C: 28, N: 28, D: 8.13.
(62 kg–135½ lbs)

			FINAL MATCH
1.	Gerald Dreyer	SAF	Dec
2.	Joseph Vissers	BEL	
3.	Svend Wad	DEN	
4.	Wallace Smith	USA	

5. O. Breiby (NOR), Edward Haddad (CAN), Maxie McCullagh (IRL), R. Benedito Zumbano (BRA)

1952 Helsinki C: 27, N: 27, D: 8.2.

			FINAL MATCH
1.	Aureliano Bolognesi	ITA	Dec 2–1
2.	Aleksy Antkiewicz	POL	
3.	Gheorghe Fiat	ROM	
4.	Erkki Pakkanen	FIN	

5. Americo Bonetti (ARG), István Juhász (HUN), Vincente Matute (VEN), Frederick Reardon (GBR)

1956 Melbourne C: 18, N: 18, D: 12.1.

			FINAL MATCH
1.	Richard McTaggart	GBR	Dec
2.	Harry Kurschat	GER	
3.	Anthony Byrne	IRL	

3. Anatoly Lagetko   SOV
5. Edward Beattie (CAN), Zygmunt Milewski (POL), Louis Molina (USA), André Vairolatto (FRA)

1960 Rome C: 34, N: 34, D: 9.5.

			FINAL MATCH
1.	Kazimierz Paździor	POL	Dec 4–1
2.	Sandro Lopopolo	ITA	
3.	Abel Laudonio	ARG	
3.	Richard McTaggart	GBR	

5. Vellikton Barannikov (SOV), Harry Campbell (USA), Ferenc Kellner (HUN), Salah Shokweir (UAR)

Paździor, a 25-year-old blacksmith from Padom, used his experience of 175 fights to outpoint five straight opponents, although he had a tough time with McTaggart in the semifinals.

1964 Tokyo C: 34, N: 34, D: 10.23.

			FINAL MATCH
1.	Józef Grudzień	POL	Dec
2.	Velikton Barannikov	SOV	
3.	Ronald Harris	USA	
3.	James McCourt	IRL	

5. Rodolfo Arpon (PHI), Domingo Barrera (SPA), János Kajdi (HUN), Stoyan Pilichev (BUL)

1968 Mexico City C: 37, N: 37, D: 10.26.

			FINAL MATCH
1.	Ronald Harris	USA	Dec 5–0
2.	Józef Grudzień	POL	
3.	Calistrat Cutov	ROM	
3.	Zvonimir Vujin	YUG	

5. Luis Minami (PER), Mohamed Muruli (UGA), Enzo Petriglia (ITA), Stoyan Pilichev (BUL)

Grudzień had defeated Harris in the semifinals four years earlier, but in Mexico City Harris won a clear, unanimous decision.

1972 Munich C: 37, N: 37, D: 9.10.

			FINAL MATCH
1.	Jan Szczepański	POL	Dec 5–0
2.	László Orbán	HUN	
3.	Samuel Mbugua	KEN	
3.	Alfonso Pérez	COL	

5. Eraslan Doruk (TUR), Tai-ho Kim (KOR), Charles Nash (IRL), Sven Erik Paulsen (NOR)

The 32-year-old European champion, Szczepański, was almost upset in the third round when he won the closest of split decisions over Chaidau Altankhuiag of Mongolia. He won his next two fights on a disqualification and a walkover, due to the last-minute withdrawal of the Africans.

Then he took a close but unanimous decision from Orbán, the 1969 European champion.

1976 Montreal C: 23, N: 23, D: 7.31.

		FINAL MATCH
1. Howard Davis	USA	Dec 5–0
2. Simion Cutov	ROM	
3. Ace Rusevski	YUG	
3. Vasily Solomin	SOV	

5. András Botos (HUN), Yves Jeudy (HAI), Ove Lundby (SWE), Tsvetan Tsvetkov (BUL)

The year 1976 was a full one for Howard "John John" Davis. The father of a 2-year-old boy, Davis played guitar in a rock and soul group, having previously played drums for James Brown. In January he graduated from Glen Cove High School on Long Island. In February he turned 20. In July he went to Montreal with the intention of beating the favorite, European champion Simion Cutov. Two days before the start of the Olympics, Davis' mother, Catherine, died of a heart attack. Davis, deciding to honor his mother by winning the gold medal, was voted the Val Barker Award for most outstanding boxer of the Olympics. Two of his five fights were stopped in the first round and the other three were won by unanimous decision.

1980 Moscow C: 29, N: 29, D: 8.2.

		FINAL MATCH	
1. Angel Herrera	CUB	RSC 3	0:13
2. Viktor Demianenko	SOV		
3. Kazimierz Adach	POL		
3. Richard Nowakowski	GDR		

5. Galsandorj Batbileg (MON), George Gilbody (GBR), Yordan Lessov (BUL), Florian Livadaru (ROM)

Herrera, who had won the 1976 Olympic Featherweight title, moved up successfully to Lightweight four years later, winning four unanimous decisions on his way to the final.

LIGHT WELTERWEIGHT
(63.5 kg–140 lbs)

1896–1948 not held

1952 Helsinki C: 28, N: 28, D: 8.2.

		FINAL MATCH
1. Charles Adkins	USA	Dec 2–1
2. Viktor Mednov	SOV	
3. Erkki Mallenius	FIN	
3. Bruno Visintin	ITA	

5. Terence Milligan (IRL), Jean Paternotte (BEL), Alexander Webster (SAF), René Weismann (FRA)

The final saw the first-ever boxing match between fighters from the United States and the U.S.S.R. Adkins, a 20-year-

old police administration student from Gary, Indiana, had had no trouble with his preliminary fights. Mednov, on the other hand, entered the ring with stitches over both eyes, the result of a brutal second-round fight with Ambrus of Romania, which was finally stopped by a doctor due to injuries to both men. Fortunately for Mednov, his semifinal opponent, Erkki Mallenius, injured his hand and had to withdraw, allowing the Soviet boxer an extra day to heal. In the final bout Mednov fought gallantly, but was no match for Adkins' powerful two-handed hooking.

1956 Melbourne C: 22, N: 22, D: 12.1.

		FINAL MATCH
1. Vladimir Yengibaryan	SOV	Dec
2. Franco Nenci	ITA	
3. Constantin Dumitrescu	ROM	
3. Henry Loubscher	SAF	

5. Ei-Kyung Hwang (KOR), Antonio Salvador Marcilla (ARG), Claude Saluden (FRA), Joseph Shaw (USA)

1960 Rome C: 34, N: 34, D: 9.5.

		FINAL MATCH
1. Bohumil Nemeček	CZE	Dec 5–0
2. Clement "Ike" Quartey	GHA	
3. Quincey Daniels	USA	
3. Marian Kasprzyk	POL	

5. Piero Brandi (ITA), Sayed Elnahas (UAR), Duck-Bong Kim (KOR), Vladimir Yengibaryan (SOV)

The final matched two underdogs and was won by Bohumil Nemeček, a 22-year-old railway worker from Decin. Ike Quartey, however, gained distinction by becoming the first black African to win an Olympic medal.

1964 Tokyo C: 35, N; 35, D: 10.23

		FINAL MATCH
1. Jerzy Kulej	POL	Dec 5–0
2. Yevgeny Frolov	SOV	
3. Eddie Blay	GHA	
3. Habib Galhia	TUN	

5. Felix Betancourt (CUB), Joao Henrique da Silva (BRA), Vladimir Kucera (CZE), Iosif Mihalic (ROM)

1968 Mexico City C: 35, N: 35, D: 10.26.

		FINAL MATCH
1. Jerzy Kulej	POL	Dec 3–2
2. Enrique Regueiferos	CUB	
3. Arto Nilsson	FIN	
3. James Wallington	USA	

5. Yevgeny Frolov (SOV), Sa-Yong Kim (KOR), Peter Stoichev (BUL), Peter Tiepold (GDR)

Policeman Jerzy Kulej beat Enrique Requeiferos, a strong puncher eight years his junior, to win a rare repeat Olympic boxing title.

1972 Munich C: 32, N: 32, D: 9.10

		FINAL MATCH
1. Ray Seales	USA	Dec 3-2
2. Angel Angelov	BUL	
3. Issaka Daborg	NIG	
3. Zvonimir Vujin	YUG	
5. Srisook Bantow (THA), Andres Molina (CUB), Graham Moughton (GBR), Kyoji Shinohara (JAP)		

The final between Angel Angelov and "Sugar Ray" Seales of Tacoma, Washington, was a surprisingly dull affair. Many observers felt that Sugar Ray's mother, who rooted him on enthusiastically from ringside, had shadow boxed a better fight than her son's. Seales turned professional and was reasonably successful until his career was ended by encroaching blindness.

1976 Montreal C: 32, N: 32, D: 7.31.

		FINAL MATCH
1. Ray Leonard	USA	Dec 5-0
2. Andrés Aldama	CUB	
3. Vladimir Kolev	BUL	
3. Kazimierz Szczerba	POL	
5. Ulrich Beyer (GDR), Calistrat Cutov (ROM), Clinton McKenzie (GBR), József Nagy (HUN), Luis Portillo (ARG)		

Ray Leonard, of Palmer Park, Maryland, made it two in a row for light welterweights nicknamed "Sugar Ray." He faced a tough customer in Andrés Aldama, who had stopped his first three opponents in the second round and knocked out Kolev in the semifinals. But Sugar Ray, wearing a photo of his girlfriend and their 2-year-old son on his shoes, won a clear victory. He turned professional a few months later and won the World Welterweight championship on November 30, 1979. He lost the title to Roberto Duran on June 20, 1980, but regained it later in the year. In 1982 he retired as a result of an eye injury.

1980 Moscow C: 30, N: 30, D: 8.2

		FINAL MATCH
1. Patrizio Oliva	ITA	Dec 4-1
2. Serik Konakbaev	SOV	
3. José Aguilar	CUB	
3. Anthony Willis	GBR	
5. Faruok Chanchoun Jawad (IRQ), William Lyimo (TAN), Jose Angel Molina (PUR), Ace Rusevski (YUG)		

Bronze medalist Tony Willis followed in the great British tradition of middleweight Chris Finnegan and hurdler David Hemery when he required three hours, an orangeade, and a glass of water to produce enough urine to be used for a drug test. He passed.

WELTERWEIGHT
(67 kg–148 lbs)

1896–1900 not held

1904 St. Louis C: 4, N: 1, D: 9.22.
(65.77 kg–145 lbs)

		FINAL MATCH
1. Albert Young	USA	Dec
2. Harry Spanger	USA	
3. Jack Eagan	USA	
3. Joseph Lydon	USA	

1906–1912 not held

1920 Antwerp C: 15, N: 10, D: 8.26.
(66.68 kg–147 lbs)

		FINAL MATCH
1. Albert Schneider	CAN	Dec
2. Alexander Ireland	GBR	
3. Frederick Colberg	USA	
4. William Clark	USA	
5. Gillet (FRA), Steen (NOR), Stocksgad (NOR), Suhr (DEN)		

Bert Schneider of Canada was actually a U.S. citizen. Born in Cleveland, his family moved to Montreal when he was 9 years old. Unaware that boxing was an Olympic sport, Schneider learned that he had been chosen for the Canadian team when he read it in a newspaper. His final bout with Ireland ended in a draw, so the referee ordered the two exhausted fighters to square off for an extra round. Schneider had the most energy left and earned the gold medal.

1924 Paris C: 29, N: 18, D: 7.26.
(66.68 kg–147 lbs)

		FINAL MATCH
1. Jean Delarge	BEL	Dec
2. Héctor Méndez	ARG	
3. Douglas Lewis	CAN	
4. Patrick Dwyer	IRL	
5. Hugh Haggerty (USA), Ingram (SAF), Al Mello (USA), T. Stauffer (SWI)		

The first two rounds of the final match were all Delarge's, as Méndez tried unsuccessfully to land his notorious knockout right. He finally caught the Belgian in the third round and pummeled him around the ring. But it was too late. Delarge wouldn't go down, and he had already built up a big enough lead to secure the victory. When the verdict was announced, pandemonium broke loose as thousands of Argentinians began chanting, "Méndez! Méndez! Méndez!" A furious Belgian rushed in among them and unfurled a Belgian flag, which led to further chaos. The demonstration went on for over fifteen minutes before order was restored. This incident was actually a mere anticlimax to what had occurred following a preliminary match three days earlier. On that day an English referee, T.H. Walker, disqualified an Italian boxer named Oldani for persistent holding of his opponent. Oldani fell to the floor, sobbing, while his supporters pelted Walker with sticks, coins, and walking stick knobs. This went on for almost an hour, until Walker was finally escorted from the arena by a contingent of British, American, and South African boxers, headed by the 265-pound wrestler Con O'Kelly.

1928 Amsterdam C: 22, N: 22, D: 8.11.
(66.68 kg–147 lbs)

			FINAL MATCH
1.	Edward Morgan	NZE	Dec
2.	Raúl Landini	ARG	
3.	Raymond Smillie	CAN	
4.	R. Galataud	FRA	
5.	C.F.J. Blommers (HOL), R. Caneva (ITA), K.J. Hellstron (FIN), Kintaro Usuda (JAP)			

1932 Los Angeles C: 16, N: 16, D: 8.13.
(66.68 kg–147 lbs)

			FINAL MATCH
1.	Edward Flynn	USA	Dec
2.	Erich Campe	GER	
3.	Bruno Ahlberg	FIN	
4.	David McCleave	GBR	
5.	Robert Barton (SAF), Luciano Fabbroni (ITA), Lucien Laplace (FRA), Carl Jensen (DEN)			

After the Olympics Flynn turned professional and fought just long enough to finance his way through dental school, eventually setting up practice in New Orleans.

1936 Berlin C: 25, N: 25, D: 8.15.
(66.68 kg–147 lbs)

			FINAL MATCH
1.	Sten Suvio	FIN	Dec
2.	Michael Murach	GER	
3.	Gerhard Petersen	DEN	
4.	Roger Tritz	FRA	
5.	S. De Castro (PHI), H.G. Dekkers (HOL), Imre Mándi (HUN), R.H. Rodriguez (ARG)			

1948 London C: 26, N: 26, D: 8.13.

			FINAL MATCH
1.	Julius Torma	CZE	Dec
2.	Horace Herring	USA	
3.	Alessandro D'Ottavio	ITA	
4.	Douglas Du Preez	SAF	
5.	William Boyce (AUS), Zygmunt Chychla (POL), Aurelio Cadabeda Diaz (SPA), Eladio Herrera (ARG)			

Before his second-round bout with C.G. Blackburn of Canada, Julius Torma of Czechoslovakia attempted to shake hands with his opponent in the dressing room. When Blackburn refused, Torma became angry and decided to give the Canadian a lesson in the ring. This he did, with the referee stopping the fight in the second round. However er Torma's final left hook fractured a bone in his hand and it looked as if he might have to withdraw. Instead the 26-year-old Hungarian-born store clerk was able to hide his injury from his next three opponents, winning with careful defense and judicious use of his right hand.

1952 Helsinki C: 29, N: 29, D: 8.2.

			FINAL MATCH
1.	Zygmunt Chychla	POL	Dec 3–0
2.	Sergei Scherbakov	SOV	
3.	Günther Heidemann	GER	
3.	Victor Jörgensen	DEN	
5.	Nicholaas Linneman (HOL), Ron Norris (IND), Julius Torma (CZE), Franco Vescovi (ITA)			

1956 Melbourne C: 16, N: 16, D: 12.1.

			FINAL MATCH
1.	Nicolae Linca	ROM	Dec 3–2
2.	Frederick Tiedt	IRL	
3.	Nicholas Gargano	GBR	
3.	Kevin John Hogarth	AUS	
5.	Nicholas André (SAF), András Döri (HUN), Francisco Gelabert (ARG), Pearce Allen Lane (USA)			

Tiedt actually received more total points than Linca, but the Romanian was given the nod by three of the five judges.

1960 Rome C: 33, N: 33, D: 9.5.

			FINAL MATCH
1.	Giovanni Benvenuti	ITA	Dec 4–1
2.	Yuri Radonyak	SOV	
3.	Leszek Drogosz	POL	
3.	James Lloyd	GBR	
5.	A. Phil Baldwin (USA), Henry Loubscher (SAF), Shishman Mitsev (BUL), Andres Moreno Navarro (SPA)			

The European amateur Light Middleweight champion, Benvenuti dropped down in weight class for the Olympics. He floored Radonyak toward the end of the first round, but the Soviet boxer came back strongly and was the aggressor in the final round. Benvenuti turned professional in 1961 and won the World Junior Middleweight title in 1965. On April 17, 1967, he defeated Emile Griffith for the World Middleweight championship, a title which he held for three of the next three and a half years.

1964 Tokyo C: 30, N: 30, D: 10.23.

			FINAL MATCH
1.	Marian Kasprzyk	POL	Dec 4–1
2.	Richardas Tamulis	SOV	
3.	Silvano Bertini	ITA	
3.	Pertti Purhonen	FIN	
5.	Issaka Dabore (NIG), Kichijiro Hamada (JAP), Ernest Powell Mabwa (UGA), Michael Varley (GBR)		

1968 Mexico City C: 33, N: 33, D: 10.26.

			FINAL MATCH
1.	Manfred Wolke	GDR	Dec 4–1
2.	Joseph Bessala	CAM	
3.	Mario Guilloti	ARG	
3.	Vladimir Mussalimov	SOV	
5.	Armando Muniz (USA), Alfonso Ramirez Gutierrez (MEX), Celal Sandal (TUR), Victor Zilberman (ROM)		

1972 Munich C: 37, N: 37, D: 9.10.

			FINAL MATCH
1.	Emilio Correa	CUB	Dec 5–0
2.	János Kajdi	HUN	
3.	Dick Tiger Murunga	KEN	
3.	Jesse Valdez	USA	
5.	Maurice Hope (GBR), Anatoliy Khohlov (SOV), Sergio Lozano (MEX), Güenter Meier (GER)		

The final matched the 19-year-old Pan American champion, Emilio Correa, and the 32-year-old European titleholder, János Kajdi. The Cuban won a close but unanimous decision.

1976 Montreal C: 31, N: 31, D: 7.31.

			FINAL MATCH
1.	Jochen Bachfeld	GDR	Dec 3–2
2.	Pedro Gamarro	VEN	
3.	Reinhard Skricek	GER	
3.	Victor Zilberman	ROM	
5.	Clinton Jackson (USA), Michael McCallum (JAM), Carmen Rinke (CAN), Carlos Santos (PUR)		

Silver medalist Pedro Gamarro was the surprise of the tournament. In his third bout he stopped defending Olympic and world amateur champion Correa, and in the quarterfinals he defeated favorite Clinton Jackson on a split decision. The 21-year-old Venezuelan almost went all the way, but he lost a close split decision in the title match to 24-year-old Jochen Bachfeld.

1980 Moscow C: 29, N: 29, D: 8.2.

			FINAL MATCH
1.	Andrés Aldama	CUB	Dec 4–1
2.	John Mugabi	UGA	

3.	Karl-Heinz Krüger	GDR
3.	Kazimierz Szczerba	POL
5.	Memet Bogujevci (YUG), Ionel Budusan (ROM), Joseph Frost (GBR), Plamen Yankov (BUL)	

John Mugabi needed a total of only nine minutes to knock out his first three opponents. He got by Kazimierz Szczerba on a split decision but was defeated by Andrés Aldama, who had won the Light Welterweight silver medal four years earlier.

LIGHT MIDDLEWEIGHT
(71 kg–156 lbs)

1896–1948 not held

1952 Helsinki C: 23, N: 23, D: 8.2.

			FINAL MATCH
1.	László Papp	HUN	Dec 3–0
2.	Theunis van Schalkwyk	SAF	
3.	Eladio Herrera	ARG	
3.	Boris Tischin	SOV	
5.	Paulo De Jesus Cavalheiro (BRA), Guido Mazzinghi (ITA), Erich Schöppner (GER), Peter Stankov (BUL)		

Papp had a tough time with van Schalkwyk until the final round of their bout, when a right hook dropped the South African to his knees for an eight-count.

1956 Melbourne C: 14, N: 14, D: 12.1.

			FINAL MATCH
1.	László Papp	HUN	Dec
2.	José Torres	USA	
3.	John McCormack	GBR	
3.	Zbigniew Pietrzykowski	POL	
5.	Ulrich Kienast (GER), Boris Georgiev (BUL), Alberto Manuel Saenz (ARG), Franco Scisciani (ITA)		

In defeating Torres, the 30-year-old Papp became the first boxer to win three Olympic gold medals (he had won the Middleweight title in 1948). In 1965 Torres won the World Light Heavyweight professional title by knocking out Willie Pastrano.

1960 Rome C: 23, N: 23, D: 9.5.

			FINAL MATCH
1.	Wilbert McClure	USA	Dec 4–1
2.	Carmelo Bossi	ITA	
3.	William Fisher	GBR	
3.	Boris Lagutin	SOV	
5.	John Bukowski (AUS), Henryk Dempc (POL), Souleymane Diallo (FRA), Celedonio Lima (ARG)		

"Skeeter" McClure of Toledo, Ohio, survived two very close split decisions over Lima and Lagutin to qualify for the final. Against Bossi, he used his strong in-fighting abilities to wear down the aggressive Italian. McClure later became a professor at Northeastern University in Boston.

1964 Tokyo C: 25, N: 25, D: 10.23.

			FINAL MATCH
1.	Boris Lagutin	SOV	Dec 4–1
2.	Joseph Gonzales	FRA	
3.	Józef Grzesiak	POL	
3.	Nojim Maiyegun	NGR	
5.	Anthony Barber (AUS), Tom Bogs (DEN), Eddie Davies (GHA), Vasile Mirza (ROM)		

Boris Lagutin's path to the finals included a victory by disqualification over Jose Chirino of Argentina, who was penalized for punching the referee, and a walkover in the quarterfinals. After two rounds with Gonzales, Lagutin had matters well in hand. But in the third round he decided to mix it up and received for his efforts a cut eye and a warning for pulling Gonzales. Maiyegun was the first Nigerian to win an Olympic medal.

1968 Mexico City C: 27, N: 27, D: 10.26.

			FINAL MATCH
1.	Boris Lagutin	SOV	Dec 5–0
2.	Rolando Garbey	CUB	
3.	John Baldwin	USA	
3.	Günther Meier	GER	
5.	Mario Benitez (URU), Eric Blake (GBR), David Jackson (UGA), Ianos Kovacs (ROM)		

The 30-year-old Lagutin outclassed all of his opponents to win his third straight medal. His final match with Garbey was an ugly, brawling affair, which led the crowd to boo and throw coins and burning newspapers at the Korean referee for failing to take action.

1972 Munich C: 33, N: 33, D: 9.10.

			FINAL MATCH
1.	Dieter Kottysch	GER	Dec 3–2
2.	Wieslaw Rudkowski	POL	
3.	Alan Minter	GBR	
3.	Peter Tiepold	GDR	
5.	Rolando Garbey (CUB), Loucif Hamani (ALG), Mohamed Majeri (TUN), Emeterio Villanueva (MEX)		

Kottysch eked out controversial split decisions over Minter and Rudkowski to take the gold medal. However, the most disputed verdict came in the opening round of the tournament when a battered and bleeding Valery Tregubov of the U.S.S.R. was declared the winner against Reggie Jones of the United States. The announcement was met by a quarter-hour of international catcalls, which continued throughout the next bout.

1976 Montreal C: 23, N: 23, D: 7.31.

			FINAL MATCH
1.	Jerzy Rybicki	POL	Dec 5–0
2.	Tadija Kacar	YUG	
3.	Rolando Garbey	CUB	
3.	Victor Savchenko	SOV	
5.	Vasile Didea (ROM), Wilfredo Guzman (PUR), Kalevi Kosunen (FIN), Alfredo Lemus (VEN)		

1980 Moscow C: 23, N: 23, D: 8.2.

			FINAL MATCH
1.	Armando Martinez	CUB	Dec 4–1
2.	Aleksandr Koshkin	SOV	
3.	Ján Franek	CZE	
3.	Detlef Kästner	GDR	
5.	Francisco Carlos Jesus (BRA), Wilson Kaoma (ZAM), Leonidas Njunwa (TAN), Nicholas Colin Wilshire (GBR)		

MIDDLEWEIGHT
(75 kg–165½ lbs)
1896–1900 not held

1904 St. Louis C: 2, N: 1, D: 9.22.
(71.67 kg–158 lbs)

			FINAL MATCH
1.	Charles Mayer	USA	RSC 3 1:40
2.	Benjamin Spradley	USA	

1906 not held

1908 London C: 10, N: 3, D: 10.27.
(71.67 kg–158 lbs)

			FINAL MATCH
1.	John Douglas	GBR	Dec
2.	Reginald Baker	AUS	
3.	W. Philo	GBR	
4.	R.C. Warnes	GBR	
5.	W. Childs	GBR	

Douglas was a well-known cricketer, known as "Johnny Won't Hit Today" Douglas because of his defensive batting. Silver medalist Reginald Baker also took part in the springboard diving competition at the 1908 Olympics.

1912 not held

1920 Antwerp C: 15, N: 8, D: 8.26.
(72.57 kg–160 lbs)

		FINAL MATCH
1. Harry Mallin	GBR	Dec
2. Georges Prudhomme	CAN	
3. Montgomery "Moe" Herscovitch	CAN	
4. Hjalmar Strömme	NOR	
5. Bradley (SAF), Samuel Lagonia (USA), Olsen (DEN), Pegoliet (FRA)		

1924 Paris C: 23, N: 14, D: 7.20.
(72.57 kg–160 lbs)

		FINAL MATCH
1. Harry Mallin	GBR	Dec
2. John Elliott	GBR	
3. Joseph Beecken	BEL	
4. Leslie Black	CAN	
5. Roger Brousse, (FRA), Daney (FRA), Henning (CAN), Murphy (IRL)		

Olympic boxing has a long and glorious history of protests, demonstrations, and general outrages. But of all the incidents and controversies, the real gold medal winner was the Brousse-Mallin Affair, which occurred in Paris in 1924. Mallin, the defending champion, was a 32-year-old London policeman. In the quarterfinals he faced 23-year-old Roger Brousse of France. As soon as the fight ended, Mallin approached the Belgian referee and displayed several well-defined teeth marks on his chest. The referee ignored him and proceeded to read out the verdict. Although most ringside observers gave the fight to Mallin, it was Brousse who won the decision, 2–1. The Italian judge and the Belgian referee voted for Brousse, while the South African judge sided with Mallin. Mallin, who had never lost a fight, left the ring without further comment. However a protest was lodged by Mr. Soderland, a Swedish member of the International Boxing Association, and an inquiry was held. Examination of Mallin's chest revealed that he had most definitely been bitten, and quite robustly at that. In fact, in his previous bout Brousse had also been accused of biting his opponent, Gallardo of Argentina. Brousse's supporters claimed that he had an odd habit of snapping his jaw whenever he threw a punch. What had happened, they said, was that Mallin had ducked one of Brousse's punches and, coming back up, bumped his chest against Brousse's snapping mouth. The Jury of Appeal ruled that Brousse's bite had been unintentional, but disqualified him anyway. When this decision was announced at the Velodrome d'Hiver the following evening, Brousse leapt to his feet and burst into tears. Immediately the hall became a scene of turmoil. Brousse was hoisted upon the shoulders of his loyal fans and paraded about the arena. Hundreds of demonstrators hooted and hollered and attempted to enter the ring. They were repulsed by the police. After about a half hour the commotion died down, but Brousse's supporters continued to launch attacks against the judges and referees for the rest of the evening.

The boxing finals were held the following night. The evening began with the announcement that two Italian boxers, flyweight Rinaldo Castellenghi and light heavyweight Carlo Saraudi, had withdrawn from the tournament to protest the poor officiating. After the Mendez-Delarge welterweight final the arena was in an uproar, with hundreds of Argentinians expressing their outrage and anger vociferously. The confusion was added to when Mallin and Elliot entered the ring, for the mere sight of Mallin set off the French spectators in their own chorus of catcalls. Not surprisingly, the two English middleweights had a hard time concentrating on their contest, which Mallin won in an uncharacteristically uninspired manner. The official report of the British Olympic Association included this account of the bout: "Mallin eventually won a close fight, but we are unable to give a more detailed description, owing to the fact that we were seated in the centre of a group of excited and gesticulating Frenchmen, who, not content with making themselves ridiculous ... also refused to allow anyone in their proximity to get a view of the fight." The British press had a field day with the affair. "It was found necessary," said the *Daily Sketch,* "to substitute for a mere boxer a man-eating expert named Brousse, whose passion for raw meat led him to attempt to bite off portions of his opponents' anatomies." Another reporter wrote, "Having got his teeth into a piece of Argentine meat during one of the earlier contests, M. Brousse decided to vary the menu by sampling some of the unroasted human beef of Old England." Less light-hearted observers called for an end to boxing, an end to the Olympics, and, at the very least, an end to the French. However life did go on and so did boxing and so did the Olympics and so did the French.

1928 Amsterdam C: 17, N: 17, D: 8.11.
(72.57 kg–160 lbs)

		FINAL MATCH
1. Piero Toscani	ITA	Dec
2. Jan Heřmánek	CZE	
3. Leonard Steyaert	BEL	
4. Fred Mallin	GBR	
5. John Chase (IRL), Humberto Curi (ARG), Harry Henderson (USA), Oscar Kjällander (SWE)		

Wild scenes and alleged injustice hit the Middleweight division again in Amsterdam. In the final Heřmánek appeared to be the winner, but Toscani was awarded the gold medal. Heřmánek was hoisted on the shoulders of his countrymen and dumped at the feet of the judges, where he argued his case while the demonstration spread, erupting into violence in the back of the hall. While the light heavyweight finalists, Avendano and Pistulla, prepared for their bout, Hĕrmánek's seconds tried to push him back into the ring. Finally the police intervened, and action *inside* the ring resumed.

1932 Los Angeles C: 10, N: 10, D: 8.13.
(72.57 kg–160 lbs)

		FINAL MATCH
1. Carmen Barth	USA	Dec
2. Amado Azar	ARG	
3. Ernest Pierce	SAF	
4. Roger Michelot	FRA	
5. Hans Bernlöhr (GER)		

1936 Berlin C: 19, N: 19, D: 8.15.
(72.57 kg–160 lbs)

		FINAL MATCH
1. Jean Despeaux	FRA	Dec
2. Henry Tiller	NOR	
3. Raúl Villareal	ARG	
4. Henryk Chmielewski	POL	
5. Adolf Baumgarten (GER), James Clark (USA), G.C. Dekkers (HOL), J. Hrubes (CZE)		

1948 London C: 25, N: 25, D: 8.13.
(73 kg–161 lbs)

		FINAL MATCH
1. László Papp	HUN	Dec
2. John Wright	GBR	
3. Ivano Fontana	ITA	
4. Michael McKeon	IRL	
5. A. Cavignac (BEL), Aime-Joseph Escudie (FRA), Dogomar Martinez (URU), Jan Schubart (HOL)		

This was the first milestone in László Papp's illustrious career. In 1952 he would go on to win the Light Middleweight gold medal and in 1956 he would successfully defend his title. The following year, at the age of 31, Papp gained permission from the Hungarian government to become the first boxer from a Communist country to fight professionally. He won the European Middleweight championship, but the Hungarian government refused to let him challenge for the world championship. He retired undefeated in 1965 and became a coach for the Hungarian Olympic team.

1952 Helsinki C: 23, N: 23, D: 8.2.

		FINAL MATCH	
1. Floyd Patterson	USA	KO 1	1:14
2. Vasile Tită	ROM		
3. Boris Georgiev	BUL		
3. Stig Sjölin	SWE		
5. Leonardus Jansen (HOL), Anthony Madigan (AUS), Walter Sentimenti (ITA), Dieter Wemhöner (GER)			

Seventeen-year-old Floyd Patterson of Brooklyn breezed through his four bouts in the easiest manner imaginable. When the bell sounded at the start of the final, Patterson spun around in a circle, which earned him a warning from the Polish referee. A tremendous uppercut to Tită's chin ended the contest after 74 seconds. Four years later Patterson knocked out Archie Moore to win the vacant World Heavyweight title.

1956 Melbourne C: 14, N: 14, D: 12.1.

		FINAL MATCH
1. Gennady Schatkov	SOV	KO 1
2. Rámon Tapia	CHI	
3. Gilbert Chapron	FRA	
3. Victor Zalazar	ARG	
5. Giulio Rinaldi (ITA), Roger Rouse (USA), Julius Torma (CZE), Dieter Wemhöner (GER)		

1960 Rome C: 25, N: 25, 9.5.

		FINAL MATCH
1. Edward Crook	USA	Dec 3–2
2. Tadeusz Walasek	POL	
3. Evgeny Feofanov	SOV	
3. Ion Monea	ROM	
5. Hans Buechi (SWI), Lo Pu Chang (TAI), Luigi Napoleoni (ITA), Frederik Van Rooyen (SAF)		

The announcement of Crook's victory over Walasek was greeted by prolonged booing and whistling, which caused a delay in the awards ceremony.

1964 Tokyo C: 20, N: 20, D: 10.23.

		FINAL MATCH	
1. Valery Popenchenko	SOV	RSC 1	2:05
2. Emil Schulz	GER		
3. Franco Valle	ITA		
3. Tadeusz Walasek	POL		
5. Joe Darkey (GHA), Ahmed Hassan (UAR), Ion Monea (ROM), Guillermo Slinas (CHI)			

1968 Mexico City C: 22, N: 22, D: 10.26.

		FINAL MATCH
1. Christopher Finnegan	GBR	Dec 3–2
2. Aleksei Kisselyov	SOV	
3. Alfred Jones	USA	
3. Agustin Zaragoza	MEX	
5. Simeon Georgiev (BUL), Jan Hejdik (CZE), Parlov Mate (YUG), Wieslaw Rudkowski (POL)		

Chris Finnegan, a 24-year-old bricklayer from Iver, Buckinghamshire, won his semifinal bout by gaining an unpopular 4–1 decision over Al Jones of Detroit. In the final he faced Aleksei Kisselyov who had won the Light Heavyweight silver medal four years earlier. Kisselyov started strong, but was already tiring by the second round. The fight was close, but Finnegan thought he had won. "Then we were called to the centre of the ring for the announcement," he recalled in his autobiography *Finnegan: Self-Portrait of a Fighting Man*. "At first I couldn't cotton on to the jabber, but all of a sudden I heard the magic word which sounds the same in any language—FINNEGAN!" Three judges had voted 59–58 for Finnegan and two had voted 59–58 for Kisselyov. "I shall never be able to properly describe my feelings as I climbed up on that rostrum for the medal presentation," he went on. "The nearest I've felt to it was when walking down the aisle with my old woman after our wedding . . . . Only there was no gold medal at the end of that—only the golden rivet."

But Finnegan's most difficult challenge was still ahead: the urine test for drugs. As Finnegan put it: "Now if there's one thing I've never been able to do, it's have a piss while someone's watching me. I can never stand at those long urinals you get in gents' bogs, with all the other blokes having a quick squint." Sure enough, he was unable to produce. People turned on water faucets, whistled, whispered encouragement. He drank several glasses of water. Still nothing. Then he downed three or four pints of beer, but still without the desired result. After giving a television interview, Finnegan was hauled off to a local restaurant for a victory meal. Two Olympic officials tagged along with the necessary collection equipment. Finally, at 1:40 a.m., Finnegan jumped up and shouted, "Who wants some piss?" The officials followed him to the men's room, secured their sample, and returned to the lab. The test, of course, proved negative.

1972 Munich C: 22, N: 22, D: 9.10.

			FINAL MATCH	
1.	Vyacheslav Lemechev	SOV	KO 1	2:17
2.	Reima Virtanen	FIN		
3.	Prince Amartey	GHA		
3.	Marvin Johnson	USA		
5.	Poul Knudsen (DEN), Nazif Kuran (TUR), Alejandro Montoya (CUB), Witold Stachurski (POL)			

Lemechev's performance was so impressive that only one of his five opponents lasted the full three rounds. In the semifinals he stopped Marvin Johnson in the second round to avenge an earlier loss in the Soviet Union. In the final, Lemechev, a great counterpuncher, scored a sharp right cross over Virtanen's left lead that put the Finnish boxer out cold for a minute.

1976 Montreal C: 19, N: 19, D: 7.31.

			FINAL MATCH	
1.	Michael Spinks	USA	RSC 3	1:54
2.	Rufat Riskiev	SOV		
3.	Luis Martinez	CUB		
3.	Alec Nastac	ROM		
5.	Siraj Din (PAK), Fernando Martins (BRA), Ryszard Pasiewicz (POL), Dragomir Vujkovic (YUG)			

Twenty-year-old Michael Spinks of St. Louis won the gold medal even though he fought only two fights—his path to the title included one bye and two forfeits. Six months earlier Spinks had been beaten by Riskiev in Tashkent, but in the third round of the final in Montreal, Spinks landed a tremendous blow to the Russian's stomach, causing Riskiev to double up in pain and the referee to stop the contest.

1980 Moscow C: 19, N: 19, D: 8.2.

			FINAL MATCH
1.	José Gomez	CUB	Dec 4–1
2.	Viktor Savchenko	SOV	
3.	Jerzy Rybicki	POL	
3.	Valentin Silaghi	ROM	
5.	Bong-Mun Jang (PRK), Mark Kaylor (GBR), Peter Odhiambo (UGA), Manfred Trauten (GDR)		

Savchenko won his first four fights by technical knockouts, but Gomez, the favorite, was too much for him in the final.

LIGHT HEAVYWEIGHT
(81 kg–179 lbs)
1896–1912 not held

1920 Antwerp C: 8, N: 6, D: 8.26.
(79.38 kg–175 lbs)

			FINAL MATCH
1.	Edward Eagan	USA	Dec
2.	Sverre Sörsdal	NOR	
3.	H. Franks	GBR	
4.	H. Brown	GBR	
5.	Andersen (DEN), Hohstock (SAF), Prachelle (FRA), Edwin Schell (USA)		

A Yale graduate who later attended Oxford as a Rhodes scholar, Eagan was a member of the four-man bobsled team that won a gold medal at the Lake Placid Olympics in 1932.

1924 Paris C: 21, N: 15, D: 7.20.
(79.38 kg–175 lbs)

			FINAL MATCH
1.	Harry Mitchell	GBR	Dec
2.	Thyge Petersen	DEN	
3.	Sverre Sörsdal	NOR	
4.	Carlo Saraudi	ITA	
5.	Courtis (GBR), Thomas Kirby (USA), George Mulholland (USA), Rossignon (FRA),		

1928 Amsterdam C: 16, N: 16, D: 8.11.
(79.38 kg–175 lbs)

			FINAL MATCH
1.	Victor Avendaño	ARG	Dec
2.	Ernst Pistulla	GER	
3.	Karl Leendert Miljon	HOL	
4.	Donald McCorkindale	SAF	
5.	Donald Carrick (CAN), Alfred Jackson (GBR), Juozas Vinca (LIT), William Murphy (IRL)		

1932 Los Angeles C: 8, N: 8, D: 8.13.
(79.38 kg–175 lbs)

			FINAL MATCH
1.	David Carstens	SAF	Dec
2.	Gino Rossi	ITA	
3.	Peter Jörgensen	DEN	
4.	James Murphy	IRL	
5.	Hans Berger (GER), Rafael Lang (ARG), Nikolaos Mastoridis (GRE), John Miler (USA)		

1936 Berlin C: 22, N: 22, D: 8.15.
(79.38 kg–175 lbs)

			FINAL MATCH
1.	Roger Michelot	FRA	Dec
2.	Richard Vogt	GER	
3.	Francisco Risiglione	ARG	
4.	Sydney Leibbrandt	SAF	
5.	T.J. Griffin (GBR), F. Havelka (CZE), B. Holm (DEN), J.E. Koivunen (FIN)		

1948 London C: 24, N: 24, D: 8.13.
(80 kg–177 lbs)

			FINAL MATCH
1.	George Hunter	SAF	Dec
2.	Donald Scott	GBR	
3.	Maurio Cia	ARG	
4.	Adrian Holmes	AUS	
5.	Giacomo Di Segni (ITA), Hugh O'Hagan (IRL), Harry Siljander (FIN), Franciszek Szymura (POL)		

Before the match for third place, Maurio Cia had his broken right hand shot up with cocaine, then used it to knock down Adrian Holmes, who broke his ankle when he fell. Gold medalist George Hunter, a 21-year-old boilermaker, was awarded the Val Barker trophy for the best boxer of the Olympics.

1952 Helsinki C: 18, N: 18, D: 8.2.

			FINAL MATCH
1.	Norvel Lee	USA	Dec 3–0
2.	Antonio Pacenza	ARG	
3.	Anatoly Perov	SOV	
3.	Harri Siljander	FIN	
5.	Giovanni Battista Alfonsetti (ITA), Lucio Grotone (BRA), Tadeusz Grzelak (POL), Karl Kistner (GER)		

Norvel Lee went to Helsinki as a reserve heavyweight. Informed that he could compete as a light heavyweight if he made the weight limit, he lost twelve pounds and won the gold medal. An exception among boxers, Lee already had a master's degree, from Howard University.

1956 Melbourne C: 11, N: 11, D: 12.1.

			FINAL MATCH
1.	James Boyd	USA	Dec
2.	Gheorghe Negrea	ROM	
3.	Carlos Lucas	CHI	
3.	Romualdas Murauskas	SOV	
5.	Rodolfo Luciano Diaz (ARG), Anthony Madigan (AUS), Ottavio Panunzi (ITA), Andrzej Wojciechowski (POL)		

1960 Rome C: 19, N: 19, D: 9.5.

			FINAL MATCH
1.	Cassius Clay	USA	Dec 5–0
2.	Zbigniew Pietrzykowski	POL	
3.	Anthony Madigan	AUS	
3.	Giulio Saraudi	ITA	
5.	Gennady Schatkov (SOV), Rafael Gargiulo (ARG), Gheorghe Negrea (ROM), Peter Stankov (BUL)		

Long before Muhammad Ali became one of the most famous people in the world, he was Cassius Marcellus Clay, a brash and friendly 18-year-old who traveled to Rome from his hometown of Louisville, Kentucky, with hopes of winning a gold medal. Clay thrived in the atmosphere of the Olympic Village, garrulously introducing himself to people of all countries, joking with them, having his picture taken with them.

In the ring he was equally in his element. After stopping Yan Becaus of Belgium in the second round, he defeated the 1956 Olympic Middleweight champion, Gennady Schatkov, and the Australian Tony Madigan, by unanimous decisions. In the final he met the three-time European champion, Zbigniew Pietrzykowski who was a veteran of 231 fights. Clay spent the first two rounds nimbly avoiding everything Pietrzykowski threw at him. Then in the last round he overwhelmed the Pole to earn a clear, unanimous decision.

At a press conference after the fight, a Soviet journalist asked Clay how he, as a Negro, felt about the fact that he wasn't allowed to eat at certain restaurants back home. Sensing an attempt to exploit him, Clay shot back, "Russian, we got qualified men working on that problem. We got the biggest and the prettiest cars. We get all the food we can eat. America is the greatest country in the world, and as far as places I can't eat goes, I got lots of places I can eat—more places I can than I can't."

And so Cassius Marcellus Clay achieved his goal of winning a gold medal. But the story of what happened to that medal tells volumes about the state of race relations in America at the beginning of the 1960s. Clay loved his medal. He slept with it, he ate with it, he wore it all the time. He wore it so much in fact that the gold began to wear off, revealing a common lead base. He returned to a hero's welcome in Louisville. The porch of his house was decorated with American flags, and his father had painted the steps red, white and blue. Cassius posed for photographers with his father—and his medal—while his father sang "The Star-Spangled Banner."

It wasn't long before Cassius turned professional and signed a contract with ten white Louisville millionaires, who agreed to sponsor his career. The millionaires gave him a slip of paper with all their phone numbers on it in case he ever needed help.

One day the mayor of Louisville asked Clay to come to his office so he could show off the gold medal to some visiting dignitaries. The mayor boasted to his visitors about the response Cassius had given to the Soviet reporter about the status of Negroes in the United States. The mayor told them, "Why, Cassius stood up tall, 'Look here, Commie . . . I'd rather live here in Louisville than in Africa cause at least I ain't fightin' off no snakes and alligators and livin' in mud huts.' He sho' told' em! He's our own boy, Cassius, our next world champion."

By now Clay was sorry he had responded to the Soviet journalist the way he had. On the way home, he and a friend, Ronnie King, stopped at a whites-only restaurant and attempted to order two hamburgers and two vanilla milk shakes. They were refused service. "Miss," Clay told the waitress, "I'm Cassius Clay, the Olympic champion," and he showed off his gold medal with its red, white, and blue ribbons. The waitress turned to the owner of the restaurant who boomed out, "I don't give a damn who he is! I done told you, we don't serve no niggers!" Several members of a white motorcycle gang happened to be in the restaurant and they rose and joined the owner by the counter. Ronnie King pulled out the paper with the names and numbers of Clay's millionaire sponsors and urged his friend to call them up for help. But Cassius just couldn't ask. In his book, *The Greatest*, Ali wrote, "I had earned my Gold Medal without their permission. It should mean something without their permission. I wanted that medallion to mean that I owned myself. And to call seemed to me to be exchanging one Owner for the Other."

Clay and Ronnie King left the restaurant. "Whatever illusions I'd built up in Rome as the All-American Boy were gone. My Olympic honeymoon was over." In the parking lot Clay was approached by one of the gang members, who ordered him to hand over his gold medal. Instead, he and Ronnie King raced off on their motor bikes, well aware that this gang had already seriously beaten several blacks who had been caught in white neighborhoods. Two of the gang leaders caught up with Clay and King at the Jefferson County Bridge on the Indiana border. A violent confrontation followed, which left the gang members bleeding and badly injured. When they left, Clay and King walked down to the river to wash the blood off their bodies and clothes. Ronnie King took the gold medal, cleaned it carefully, and hung it over his neck. It was the first time the medal had been away from Clay's chest. "For the first time" he wrote, "I saw it as it was. Ordinary, just an object." King put the gold medal back around Clay's neck, and the two friends walked back to the bridge. When they got to the middle of the bridge, Cassius Clay walked over to the side, pulled the gold medal off his chest, and threw it into the Ohio River. Later Ali wrote, "The medal was gone, but . . . I felt calmly relaxed, confident. My holiday as a White Hope was over. I felt a new, secret strength."

1964 Tokyo C: 19, N: 19, D: 10.23.

		FINAL MATCH
1. Cosimo Pinto	ITA	Dec 3–2
2. Aleksei Kisselyov	SOV	
3. Alexander Nikolov	BUL	
3. Zbigniew Pietrzykowski	POL	
5. Rafael Luis Gargiulo (ARG), Sayed Mersal (UAR), Frantisek Polacek (CZE), Jürgen Schlegel (GDR)		

1968 Mexico City C: 18, N: 18, D: 10.26.

		FINAL MATCH
1. Dan Poznyak	SOV	Default
2. Ion Monea	ROM	
3. Stanislaw Dragan	POL	
3. Georgi Stankov	BUL	
5. Fatai Ayinia (NGR), Walter Facchinetti (ITA), Bernard Malherbe (FRA), Jürgen Schlegel (GDR)		

Monea suffered a broken nose in his semifinal victory over Dragan and was unable to compete in the final.

1972 Munich C: 28, N: 28, D: 9.10.

		FINAL MATCH
1. Mate Parlov	YUG	RSC 2 2:39
2. Gilberto Carrillo	CUB	
3. Janusz Gortat	POL	
3. Isaac Ikhouria	NGR	
5. Nikolai Anfimov (SOV), Miguel Angel Cuello (ARG), Rudi Hornig (GER), Harald Skog (NOR)		

Parlov blasted his way through the tournament, winning one walkover and stopping three of his other four opponents in the second round. Parlov turned professional in 1975 and three years later won the World Light Heavyweight title.

1976 Montreal C: 18, N: 18, D: 7.31.

			FINAL MATCH	
1.	Leon Spinks	USA	RSC 3	1:09
2.	Sixto Soria	CUB		
3.	Costica Dafinoiu	ROM		
3.	Janusz Gortat	POL		
5.	Robert Burgess (BER), Wolfgang Gruber (GER), Ottomar Sachse (GDR), Juan Suarez (ARG)			

Marine Corps Lance Corporal Leon Spinks stepped into the ring for his Olympic final immediately after his younger brother, Michael, had won the Middleweight championship. He faced knockout artist Sixto Soria, who had required only 9 minutes and 5 seconds to dispose of his first three opponents. However the Cuban met his match in Spinks, who knocked him down in the first round and continued to batter him until the referee stopped the fight. A year and a half later Spinks defeated Muhammad Ali to win the World Heavyweight championship.

1980 Moscow C: 15, N: 15, D: 8.2.

			FINAL MATCH
1.	Slobodan Kacar	YUG	Dec 4–1
2.	Pawel Skrzeck	POL	
3.	Herbert Bauch	GDR	
3.	Ricardo Rojas	CUB	
5.	Georgica Donici (ROM), David Kvachadze (SOV), Michael Madsen (DEN), Geoffrey Pike (AUS)		

HEAVYWEIGHT

(91 kg–200¹/₂ lbs)
This weight division will be included for the first time in 1984.

SUPER HEAVYWEIGHT

(Over 91 kg–200 ¹/₂ lbs)
This division, which is the unlimited weight class, was known as Heavyweight from 1904–1980.

1896–1900 not held

1904 St. Louis C: 3, N: 1, D: 9.22.
(Over 71.67 kg–158 lbs)

			FINAL MATCH
1.	Samuel Berger	USA	Dec
2.	Charles Mayer	USA	
3.	William Michaels	USA	

1906 not held

1908 London C: 6, N: 1, D: 10.27.
(Over 71.67 kg–158 lbs)

			FINAL MATCH	
1.	A.L. Oldham	GBR	KO 1	2:00
2.	S.C.H. Evans	GBR		
3.	Frederick Parks	GBR		
4.	H. Brewer (GBR), A. Ireton (GBR), I. Myrams (GBR),			

1912 not held

1920 Antwerp C: 8, N: 6, D: 8.26.
(Over 79.38 kg–175 lbs)

			FINAL MATCH
1.	Ronald Rawson	GBR	Dec
2.	Sören Petersen	DEN	
3.	Xavier Eluere	FRA	
4.	William Spengler	USA	
5.	Creusen (BEL), Dore (GBR), Holl (NOR), Samuel Stewart (USA)		

1924 Paris C: 15, N: 10, D: 7.20.
(Over 79.38 kg–175 lbs)

			FINAL MATCH
1.	Otto von Porat	NOR	Dec
2.	Sören Petersen	DEN	
3.	Alfredo Porzio	ARG	
4.	Henk de Best	HOL	
5.	Bertazzolo (ITA), Clifton (GBR), H.G. Greathouse (USA), Larsen (DEN)		

The final was a popular battle that saw Petersen almost knocked out in the first round and von Porat almost put away in the second. The Norwegian rebounded in the final round to earn the victory.

1928 Amsterdam C: 10, N: 10, D: 8.11.
(Over 79.38 kg–175 lbs)

			FINAL MATCH
1.	Arturo Rodriguez Jurado	ARG	RSC 1
2.	Nils Ramm	SWE	
3.	M. Jacob Michaelsen	DEN	
4.	Sverre Sörsdal	NOR	
5.	Georges Gardebois (FRA), Alexander Kaletchetz (USA), Sam Oliji (NZE), Hans Schonrath (GER)		

1932 Los Angeles C: 6, N: 6, D: 8.13.
(Over 79.38 kg–175 lbs)

			FINAL MATCH
1.	Santiago Lovell	ARG	Dec
2.	Luigi Rovati	ITA	
3.	Frederick Feary	USA	
4.	George Maughan	CAN	
5.	Gunnar Barlund (FIN), Heinz Kohlhaas (GER)		

1936 Berlin C: 17, N: 17, D: 8.15.
(Over 79.38 kg–175 lbs)

		FINAL MATCH
1. Herbert Runge	GER	Dec
2. Guillermo Lovell	ARG	
3. Erling Nilsen	NOR	
4. Ferenc Nagy	HUN	
5. J. Feans (URU), V.A. Stuart (GBR), Olle Tandberg (SWE), E. Toussaint (LUX)		

1948 London C: 17, N: 17, D: 8.13.
(Over 80 kg–176½ lbs)

		FINAL MATCH
1. Rafael Iglesias	ARG	KO 2
2. Gunnar Nilsson	SWE	
3. John Arthur	SAF	
4. Hans Müller	SWI	
5. Uber Baccilieri (ITA), Adam Faul (CAN), Jack Gardner (GBR), E. Jay Lambert (USA),		

1952 Helsinki C: 22, N: 22, D: 8.2.
(Over 81 kg–179 lbs)

		FINAL MATCH
1. H. Edward Sanders	USA	DISQ 2
2. Ingemar Johansson	SWE	
3. Ilkka Koski	FIN	
3. Andries Nieman	SAF	
5. Giacomo Di Segni (ITA), Edgar Hearn (GBR), Tomislav Krizmanic (YUG), Algirdas Schocikas (SOV)		

Evidently the punishment that Sanders inflicted on his first three opponents made a great impression on Ingemar Johansson, because the Swede spent all his time in the ring back-pedaling, without throwing a single punch. After receiving several warnings from the referee, he was finally disqualified for not "giving of his best." Because of the disqualification, he was not awarded his silver medal. Ironically, it was not Sanders but Johansson who went on to a successful professional career, knocking out Floyd Patterson in 1959 to win the World Heavyweight championship. He was finally awarded his silver medal in 1982. Sanders died of a brain hemorrhage on December 12, 1954, after being knocked out in his ninth professional bout.

1956 Melbourne C: 11, N: 11, D: 12.1.
(Over 81 kg–179 lbs)

		FINAL MATCH	
1. T. Peter Rademacher	USA	RSC 1	2:27
2. Lev Mukhin	SOV		
3. Daniel Bekker	SAF		
3. Giacomo Bozzano	ITA		
5. Thorner Åhsman (SWE)			

The final looked as if it would be a classic. Mukhin had beaten all three of his opponents by knockout or technical knockout, coming off the floor himself in two of the fights. Rademacher, a soldier from Yakima, Washington, never gave Mukhin a chance to make a third comeback. He knocked down the Soviet boxer in the first 50 seconds. Mukhin got up, but Rademacher flattened him twice more in the next 80 seconds, and the referee finally stopped the fight. Eight and a half months later, Rademacher became the first boxer to fight for the Heavyweight title in his first professional contest. Rademacher, who had never gone more than three rounds, sent champion Floyd Patterson to the canvas in the second round, but Patterson came back to win in round 6.

1960 Rome C: 17, N: 17, D: 9.5.
(Over 81 kg–179 lbs)

		FINAL MATCH	
1. Franco De Piccoli	ITA	KO 1	1:30
2. Daniel Bekker	SAF		
3. Josef Nemec	CZE		
3. Günter Siegmund	GDR		
5. Andrey Abramov (SOV), Vasile Mariutan (ROM), Percy Price (USA), Obrad Sretenovic (YUG)			

1964 Tokyo C: 14, N: 14, D: 10.23.
(Over 81 kg–179 lbs)

		FINAL MATCH
1. Joseph Frazier	USA	Dec 3–2
2. Hans Huber	GER	
3. Giuseppe Ros	ITA	
3. Vadim Yemelyanov	SOV	
5. Santiago Alberto Lovell (ARG), Vasile Mariutan (ROM), Athol McQueen (AUS)		

Philadelphia butcher's apprentice Joe Frazier was a last-minute substitute for 293-pound Buster Mathis, who had broken his knuckle. Despite the fact that he himself was fighting with a broken right hand, Frazier demolished his first three opponents and then won a much tamer split decision over Regensburg bus driver Hans Huber in the final. In 1970 Frazier won the World Heavyweight championship, and in 1980 he was elected to the Boxing Hall of Fame.

1968 Mexico City C: 14, N: 14, D: 10.23.
(Over 81 kg–179 lbs)

		FINAL MATCH
1. George Foreman	USA	RSC 2
2. Ionas Chepulis	SOV	
3. Giorgio Bambini	ITA	
3. Joaquin Rocha	MEX	
5. Ion Alexe (ROM), Bernd Anders (GDR), Rudolfus Lubbers (HOL), Kiril Pandov (BUL)		

The relatively inexperienced Foreman, who had fought only 18 times before the Olympics, had little trouble winning the gold medal. After his final victory he paraded around the ring holding aloft a small U.S. flag. On January 22, 1973, Foreman knocked out Joe Frazier to win the World Heavyweight title.

1972 Munich C: 14, N: 14, D: 9.10.
(Over 81 kg–179 lbs)

		FINAL MATCH
1. Teófilo Stevenson	CUB	Default
2. Ion Alexe	ROM	
3. Peter Hussing	GER	
3. Hasse Thomsén	SWE	
5. Duane Bobick (USA), Jürgen Fanghänel (GDR), Carroll Morgan (CAN)		

Teófilo Stevenson, a handsome 6-foot 3½-inch Cuban from Las Tunas, Oriente, was the most impressive Olympic boxer since Cassius Clay. After disposing of Poland's Ludwik Denderys in one round, he faced Duane Bobick of the U.S. Navy. In 1971 Bobick had beaten Stevenson in the semifinals of the Pan-American Games. Now, at the Munich Olympics, Bobick wasn't too worried about Stevenson. "I know he's tall and strong," he told reporters, "but the last time all he had was a good jab—no right hand." Unbeknownst to Bobick, the Cuban had spent twelve months working on just that problem. Using a stinging left jab and a now powerful right hand, Stevenson plastered Bobick until the fight was stopped in the third round.

Stevenson's semifinal opponent was Peter Hussing of Germany. He lasted 4 minutes and 3 seconds. "I have never been hit so hard in all my 212 bouts," said the good-natured Hussing. "You just don't see his right hand. All of a sudden it is there—on your chin." The other semifinal matched Alexe of Romania and Thomsén of Sweden, both of whom had previously been knocked out by Stevenson. Some observers suggested that the *loser* should be forced to face Stevenson in the final.

In fact, neither of them did. Alexe won a unanimous decision over Thomsén, but showed up for the final with his hand in plaster, the result of a broken thumb. Although capitalist fight promoters drooled at the prospect, Stevenson refused to turn professional, stating that he was more interested in his studies and in revolution than he was in making a million dollars. In fact, he turned down an offer of $2,000,000. "Professional boxing treats a fighter like a commodity to be bought and sold and discarded when he is no longer of use," he said. "I wouldn't exchange my piece of Cuba for all the money they could give me."

1976 Montreal C: 15, N: 15, D: 7.31.
(Over 81 kg–179 lbs)

		FINAL MATCH	
1. Teófilo Stevenson	CUB	KO 3	2:35
2. Mircea Simon	ROM		
3. Clarence Hill	BER		
3. Johnny Tate	USA		
5. Peter Hussing (GER), Atanas Souvandzhiev (BUL)			

In the four years since the Munich Olympics, Stevenson had lost two fights—both to Igor Vysotsky of the U.S.S.R., who had knocked out the Cuban in Minsk three months before the 1976 Olympics. However, Vysotsky was unable to compete in Montreal because of eye injuries, and the road seemed clear for Stevenson to defend his title. He demolished his first three opponents in a record 7 minutes and 22 seconds. His last victim was Mircea Simon, who avoided Stevenson completely for the first two rounds. Although this same tactic had earned Ingemar Johansson a disqualification 24 years earlier, it seemed quite understandable in Simon's case. When Stevenson finally hit Simon in the third round, the Romanian's seconds immediately threw in the towel. Simon later defected to the United States.

1980 Moscow C: 14, N: 14, D: 8.2.
(Over 81 kg–179 lbs)

		FINAL MATCH
1. Teófilo Stevenson	CUB	Dec 4–1
2. Pyotr Zaev	SOV	
3. Jürgen Fanghänel	GDR	
3. István Levai	HUN	
5. Francesco Damiani (ITA), Grzegorz Skrzecz (POL), Peter Stoimenov (BUL)		

In the semifinals, Levai ran around the ring for three rounds, becoming the first Olympic boxer to go the distance against Stevenson. Stevenson, in turn, became the first boxer to win three Olympic gold medals in the same division.

CANOEING

MEN
Kayak Singles 500 Meters
Kayak Singles 1000 Meters
Kayak Pairs 500 Meters
Kayak Pairs 1000 Meters
Kayak Fours 1000 Meters
Canadian Singles 500 Meters
Canadian Singles 1000 Meters
Canadian Pairs 500 Meters
Canadian Pairs 1000 Meters
Discontinued Events

WOMEN
Kayak Singles 500 Meters
Kayak Pairs 500 Meters
Kayak Fours 500 Meters
Discontinued Events

MEN

Olympic canoeing events are divided into two types, depending on the kind of paddle that is used. In *kayak* events, a paddle with a blade on each end is used. The canoeist alternately paddles one blade on the left side and the other blade on the right side. The paddle in *Canadian* canoeing has only one blade. The canoeist sits in a half-kneeling position, switching the blade from side to side.

Canoeing contests begin with qualifying heats. The eight fastest qualifiers advance directly to the semifinals, while the rest take part in a repêchage, or second-chance round (repêchage being the French word for "fishing again").The four fastest participants in the repêchage races join the semifinals. The top six semifinalists take part in the final, while the other six take part in a *petit final* to determine seventh through twelfth places.

KAYAK SINGLES 500 METERS

1896–1972 not held

1976 Montreal C: 18, N: 18, D: 7.30
1. Vasile Diba   ROM   1:46.41
2. Zoltán Sztanity   HUN   1:46.95
3. Rüdiger Helm   GDR   1:48.30
4. Herminio Menendez   SPA   1:48.40
5. Grzegorz Śledziewski POL   1:48.49

6. Sergei Lizunov   SOV   1:49.21
7. Oreste Perri   ITA   1:50.27
8. Douglas Parnham   GBR   1:50.33

1980 Moscow C: 17, N: 17, D: 8.1.
1. Vladimir Parfenovich SOV   1:43.43
2. John Sumegi   AUS   1:44.12
3. Vasile Diba   ROM   1:44.90
4. Milan Janic   YUG   1:45.63
5. Frank-Peter Bischof GDR   1:45.97
6. Anders Andersson   SWE   1:46.32
7. Ian Ferguson   NZE   1:47.36
8. Felix Masar   CZE   1:48.18

Parfenovich, a 21-year-old physical education instructor from Minsk, won three gold medals at the Moscow Olympics.

KAYAK SINGLES 1000 METERS

1896–1932 not held

1936 Berlin C: 15, N: 15, D: 8.8.
1. Gregor Hradetzky   AUT   4:22.9
2. Helmut Cämmerer   GER   4:25.6
3. Jacobus Kraaier   HOL   4:35.1
4. Ernest Riedel   USA   4:38.1
5. Joel Rahmqvist   SWE   4:39.5
6. Henri Eberhardt   FRA   4:41.2
7. B. Johansson   FIN   4:42.2
8. Iversen   NOR   4:44.2

1948 London C: 15, N: 15, D: 8.12.

1.	Gert Fredriksson	SWE	4:33.2
2.	Johan Frederik Kobberup	DEN	4:39.9
3.	Henri Eberhardt	FRA	4:41.4
4.	Hans Martin Gulbrandsen	NOR	4:41.7
5.	Willem Frederik van der Kroft	HOL	4:43.5
6.	Harry Åkerfelt	FIN	4:44.2
7.	Lubomir Vambera	CZE	4:44.3
8.	W. Piemann	AUT	4:50.3

In the first heat Fredriksson showed his superiority by casually lying in fourth place for the first 950 meters and then sprinting at the end to take first. The final was no contest, as Fredriksson attained the longest winning margin in any Olympic kayak final other than 10,000 meters.

1952 Helsinki C: 20, N: 20, D: 7.28.

1.	Gert Fredriksson	SWE	4:07.9
2.	Thorvald Strömberg	FIN	4:09.7
3.	Louis Gantois	FRA	4:20.1
4.	Willem Frederik van der Kroft	HOL	4:20.8
5.	Meinrad Miltenberger	GER	4:21.6
6.	Lubomir Vambera	CZE	4:24.0
7.	Hendrik Verbrugghe	BEL	4:25.0
8.	Lev Nikitin	SOV	4:26.2

Fredriksson started a long, sustained sprint from the halfway mark, which wore down his opponents and allowed him to turn the tables on Strömberg, who had beaten him the previous evening in the 10,000 meters.

1956 Melbourne C: 13, N: 13, D: 12.1.

1.	Gert Fredriksson	SWE	4:12.8
2.	Igor Pissaryev	SOV	4:15.3
3.	Lajos Kiss	HUN	4:16.2
4.	Stefan Kaplaniak	POL	4:19.8
5.	Louis Gantois	FRA	4:22.1
6.	Ladislav Čepčianský	CZE	4:23.2
7.	Villy Christiansen	DEN	4:25.2
8.	Ernst Steinhauer	GER	4:25.5

Fredriksson earned his fifth individual Olympic gold medal.

1960 Rome C: 22, N: 22, D: 8.29.

1.	Erik Hansen	DEN	3:53.00
2.	Imre Szöllösi	HUN	3:54.02
3.	Gert Fredriksson	SWE	3:55.89
4.	Ibragim Khasanov	SOV	3:56.38
5.	Ronald Rhodes	GBR	4:01.15
6.	Rolf Olsen	NOR	4:02.31
7.	Wolfgang Lange	GDR	4:03.05
8.	Simo Kuismanen	FIN	4:03.66

1964 Tokyo C: 15, N: 15, D: 10.22.

1.	Rolf Peterson	SWE	3:57.13
2.	Mihály Hesz	HUN	3:57.28
3.	Aurel Vernescu	ROM	4:00.77
4.	Erich Suhrbier	GER	4:01.62
5.	Günther Pfaff	AUT	4:03.56
6.	Antonius Geurts	HOL	4:04.48

7.	Erik Hansen	DEN	4:04.72
8.	Alistair Wilson	GBR	4:05.80

Mihály Hesz and Aurel Vernescu, the reigning world champion, were the favorites, but were upset by Rolf Peterson, a 22-year-old student from Halmstead.

1968 Mexico City C: 20, N: 20, D: 10.25.

1.	Mihály Hesz	HUN	4:02.63
2.	Aleksandr Shaparenko	SOV	4:03.58
3.	Erik Hansen	DEN	4:04.39
4.	Wladyslaw Szuszkiewicz	POL	4:06.36
5.	Rolf Peterson	SWE	4:07.86
6.	Václav Mára	CZE	4:09.35
7.	Andrei Contolenco	ROM	4:09.96
8.	Wolfgang Lange	GDR	4:10.03

Lying fifth at the halfway mark, Hesz waited to make his move until there were only 200 meters to go. In the last 100 meters he passed Hansen, the 1960 Olympic champion, and Shaparenko, the reigning world champion.

1972 Munich C: 24, N: 24, D: 9.9.

1.	Aleksandr Shaparenko	SOV	3:48.06
2.	Rolf Peterson	SWE	3:49.38
3.	Géza Csapó	HUN	3:49.38
4.	Jean-Pierre Burny	BEL	3:50.29
5.	Ladislav Souček	CZE	3:51.05
6.	Joachim Mattern	GDR	3:51.94
7.	Erik Hansen	DEN	3:52.15
8.	Grzegorz Śledziewski	POL	3:53.22

1976 Montreal C: 19, N: 19, D: 7.31.

1.	Rüdiger Helm	GDR	3:48.20
2.	Géza Csapó	HUN	3:48.84
3.	Vasile Diba	ROM	3:49.65
4.	Oreste Perri	ITA	3:51.13
5.	Aleksandr Shaparenko	SOV	3:51.45
6.	Berndt Andersson	SWE	3:52.46
7.	Douglas Parnham	GBR	3:52.64
8.	Grzegorz Śledziewski	POL	3:54.29

In the opening heats Oreste Perri, the world champion, and Vasile Diba were disqualified for using underweight boats. However, the decision was reversed when the judges announced that the super sensitive electronic scales had responded to a change in atmospheric pressure. Helm made his move in the last quarter of the race, passed Csapó, and shouted with joy as he stormed across the finish line. At 19, he was the youngest competitor in the event.

1980 Moscow C: 20, N: 20, D: 8.2.

1.	Rüdiger Helm	GDR	3:48.77
2.	Alain Lebas	FRA	3:50.20
3.	Ion Birladeanu	ROM	3:50.49
4.	John Sumegi	AUS	3:50.63
5.	Oreste Perri	ITA	3:51.95
6.	Felix Masár	CZE	3:52.19
7.	Milan Janic	YUG	3:53.50
8.	Ian Ferguson	NZE	3:53.78

Two hours after this race, Helm joined his teammates in winning the Kayak Fours, to bring his Olympic medal total to five: three gold and two bronze.

KAYAK PAIRS 500 METERS

1896–1972 not held

1976 Montreal T: 21, N: 21, D: 7.28.
1. Joachim Mattern, Bernd Olbricht   GDR   1:35.87
2. Sergei Nagorny, Vladimir Romanovsky   SOV   1:36.81
3. Larion Serghei, Policarp Malihin   ROM   1:37.43
4. José Seguin, Guiller Del Riego   SPA   1:38.50
5. József Deme, János Rátkai   HUN   1:38.81
6. Hannu Kojo, Kari Markkanen   FIN   1:39.59
7. Anders Andersson, Lars Andersson   SWE   1:39.63
8. John Southwood, John Sumegi   AUS   1:39.77

1980 Moscow T: 18, N: 18, D: 8.1.
1. Vladimir Parfenovich, Sergei Chukhrai SOV   1:32.38
2. Herminio Menendez, Guillermo Del Riego SPA   1:33.65
3. Rüdiger Helm, Bernd Olbricht   GDR   1:34.00
4. Francis Hervieu, Alain Lebas   FRA   1:36.22
5. Barry Kelly, Robert Lee   AUS   1:36.45
6. Alexandru Giura, Ion Birladeanu   ROM   1:36.96
7. Waldemar Merk, Zdzislaw Szubski   POL   1:37.20
8. László Szabó, Zoltán Romhányi   HUN   1:37.66

KAYAK PAIRS 1000 METERS

1896–1932 not held

1936 Berlin T: 12, N: 12, D: 8.8.
1. Adolf Kainz, Alfons Dorfner   AUT   4:03.8
2. Ewald Tilker, Fritz Bondroit   GER   4:08.9
3. Nicolaas Tates, Willem Frederik van der Kroft   HOL   4:12.2
4. František Brzák-Felix, Josef Dusil   CZE   4:15.2
5. Rudolf Vilim, Werner Klingelfuss   SWI   4:22.8
6. Edward Deir, Francis Willis   CAN   4:24.5
7. Lovgreen, Svenden   DEN   4:26.6
DISQ: Sixten Jansson, Gunnar Lundqvist (SWE)

1948 London T: 16, T: 16, D: 8.12.
1. Hans Berglund, Lennart Klingström SWE   4:07.3
2. Ejvind Hansen, Bernhard Jensen   DEN   4:07.5
3. Thor Axelsson, Nils Björklof   FIN   4:08.7
4. Ivar Mathisen, Knut Östbye   NOR   4:09.1
5. Otto Kroutil, Miloš Pech   CZE   4:09.8
6. Cornelis Gravesteyn, Willem Pool   HOL   4:15.8
7. G. Covey, H. Harper   CAN   4:56.8
DISQ: János Toldi, Gyula Andrási (HUN)

Toldi and Adrasi were disqualified for "hanging" in the wake of another canoe. It was thought by many that the ruling was a harsh one.

1952 Helsinki T: 19, N: 19, D: 7.28.
1. Kurt Wires, Yrjö Hietanen   FIN   3:51.1
2. Lars Glassér, Ingemar Hedberg   SWE   3:51.1
3. Max Raub, Herbert Wiedermann   AUT   3:51.4
4. Gustav Schmidt, Helmut Noller   GER   3:51.8
5. Ivar Mathisen, Knut Östbye   NOR   3:54.7
6. Maurice Graffen, Marcel Renaud   FRA   3:55.1
7. István Granek, János Kulcsár   HUN   3:55.1
8. Cornelis Koch, Abraham Klingers   HOL   3:55.8

Wires and Hietanen, who had already won the 10,000 meter pairs, were awarded a second set of gold medals only after a photo-finish had been studied.

1956 Melbourne T: 15, N: 15, D: 7.28.
1. Michael Scheuer, Meinrad Miltenberger   GER   3:49.6
2. Mikhail Kaaleste, Anatoly Demitkov   SOV   3:51.4
3. Maximilian Raub, Herbert Wiedermann   AUT   3:55.8
4. Mircea Anastasescu, Stavru Teodorov   ROM   3:56.1
5. Maurice Graffen, Michel Meyer   FRA   3:58.3
6. Henri Verbrugghe, Germain van de Moere   BEL   3:58.7
7. Walter Brown, Dennis Green   AUS   3:59.1
8. Miroslav Jemelka, Rudolph Klabouch   CZE   4:01.4

1960 Rome T: 23, N: 23, D: 8.29.
1. Gert Fredriksson, Sven-Olov Sjödelius   SWE   3:34.73
2. György Mészáros, András Szente   HUN   3:34.91
3. Stefan Kaplaniak, Wladislaw Zielinski   POL   3:37.34
4. Nikolas Rudzinskas, Ivan Golovachev   SOV   3:37.48
5. Kaj Schmidt, Vagn Schmidt   DEN   3:39.06
6. František Riha, František Vršovsky   CZE   3:40.78
7. Rudolf Knuppe, Antonius Geurts   HOL   3:41.01
8. Wolfgang Lange, Dieter Krause   GDR   3:41.46

Fredriksson completed his Olympic career with six gold medals, one silver medal, and one bronze medal. Four years later in Tokyo he was the coach of the Swedish team.

1964 Tokyo T: 14, N: 14, D: 10.22.
1. Sven-Olov Sjödelius, Nils Gunnar Utterberg SWE   3:38.54
2. Antonius Geurts, Paul Hoekstra   HOL   3:39.30
3. Heinz Büker, Holger Zander   GER   3:40.69
4. Haralambie Ivanov, Vasile Nicoară   ROM   3:41.12
5. György Mészáros, Imre Szöllösi   HUN   3:41.39
6. Cesare Beltrami, Cesare Zilioli   ITA   3:43.55
7. Erik Kalugin, Ibragim Khasanov   SOV   3:44.19
8. Gordan Jeffery, Adrian Powell   AUS   3:44.52

1968 Mexico City T: 20, N: 20, D: 10.25.
1. Aleksandr Shaparenko, Vladimir Morozov   SOV   3:37.54
2. Csaba Giczi, István Timár   HUN   3:38.44
3. Gerhard Seibold, Günther Pfaff   AUT   3:40.71
4. Paul Hoekstra, Antonius Geurts   HOL   3:41.36
5. Lars Andersson, Nils Gunnar Utterberg   SWE   3:41.99
6. Atanase Sciotnic, Aurel Vernescu   ROM   3:45.18
7. Jean-Pierre Burny, Herman Naegels   BEL   3:45.21
8. Cesare Beltrami, Cesare Zilioli   ITA   3:46.08

1972 Munich T: 25, N: 25, D: 9.9.
1. Nikolai Gorbachev, Viktor Kratassyuk   SOV   3:31.23
2. József Deme, János Rátkai   HUN   3:32.00
3. Wladyslaw Szuszkiewicz, Rafal Piszcz   POL   3:33.83
4. Reiner Kurth, Alexander Slatnow   GDR   3:34.16
5. Costel Coşnită, Vasile Simiocenco   ROM   3:35.66
6. Jean-Pierre Cordebois, Didier Niquet   FRA   3:36.51
7. Günther Pfaff, Helmut Hediger   AUT   3:36.61
8. Hans-Juer Riemenschneider, Horst Mattern GER   3:38.67

1976 Montreal T: 24, N: 24, D: 7.31.
1. Sergei Nagorny, Vladimir Romanovsky   SOV   3:29.01
2. Joachim Mattern, Bernd Olbricht   GDR   3:29.33
3. Zoltán Bakó, István Szabó   HUN   3:30.36
4. Jean-Paul Hanquier, Alain Lebas   FRA   3:33.05
5. Guillermo Del Riego, José Seguin   SPA   3:33.16
6. Jean-Pierre Burny, Paul Hoekstra   BEL   3:33.86
7. Policarp Malihin, Larion Serghei   ROM   3:34.27
8. Steve King, Denis Barre   CAN   3:34.46

1980 Moscow T: 16, N: 16, D: 8.2.
1. Vladimir Parfenovich, Sergei Chukhrai   SOV   3:26.72
2. István Szabó, István Joós   HUN   3:28.49
3. Luis Ramos-Misione, Herminio Menendez   SPA   3:28.66
4. Alexandru Giura, Nicolae Ticu   ROM   3:28.94
5. Peter Hempel, Harry Nolte   GDR   3:31.02
6. Jose Marrero Rodriguez, Reynaldo Cunill Infante   CUB   3:31.12
7. Ron Stevens, Gert Lebbink   HOL   3:33.18
8. Alan Thompson, Geoffrey Walker   NZE   3:33.83

KAYAK FOURS 1000 METERS
1896–1960 not held

1964 Tokyo T: 14, N: 14, D: 10.22.
1. SOV   (Nikolai Chuzhikov, Anatoly Grischin, Vyaches-   3:14.67
          lav Ionov, Vladimir Morozov)
2. GER   (Günther Perleberg, Bernhard Schulze, Fried-   3:15.39
          helm Wentzke, Holger Zander)
3. ROM   (Simion Cuciuc, Atanase Sciotnic, Mihai Tur-   3:15.51
          caş, Aurel Vernescu)
4. HUN   (Imre Kemecsey, György Mészáros, András   3:16.24
          Szente, Imre Szöllösi)
5. SWE   (Rolf Peterson, Sven-Olov Sjödellus, Nils Gun-   3:17.47
          nar Utterberg, Carl von Gerber)
6. ITA   (Claudio Agnisetta, Cesare Beltrami, Angelo   3:19.32
          Pedroni, Cesare Zilioli)
7. HOL   (Paul Hoekstra, Theodorus van Halteren, Guil-   3:19.36
          laume Weijzen, Jan Wittenberg)
8. YUG   (Dragan Desancic, Vladimir Ignjatijevic, Alek-   3:19.79
          sandar Kercov, Stanisa Radmanovic)

1968 Mexico City T: 19, N: 19, D: 10.25.
1. NOR   (Steinar Admundsen, Egil Söby, Tore Berger,   3:14.38
          Jan Johansen)
2. ROM   (Anton Calenic, Dimitrie Ivanov, Haralambie   3:14.81
          Ivanov, Mihai Turcaş)

3. HUN   (Csaba Giczi, Istvan Timár, Imre Szöllösi, István   3:15.10
          Csizmadia)
4. SWE   (Per Larsson, Hans Nilsson, Tord Sahlén, Åke   3:16.68
          Sandin)
5. FIN   (Karl-Gustav von Alfthan, Heikki Mäkelä, Jorma   3:17.28
          Lehtosalo, Ilkka Nummisto)
6. GDR   (Joachim Wenzke, Klaus-Uwe Will, Erhard Rie-   3:18.03
          drich, Klaus-Peter Ebeling)
7. AUS   (Helmut Hediger, Kurt Lindlgruber, Günther   3:18.95
          Pfaff, Gerhard Seibold)
8. POL   (Ewald Janusz, Ryszard Marchlik, Rafal Piszcz,   3:22.10
          Wladyslaw Zieliński)

Much credit for the Norwegians' upset victory went to their trainer, Sten Jonsson, who had successfully coached track and field, skiing, and speed skating before trying his hand at canoeing.

1972 Munich T: 20, N: 20, D: 9.9.
1. SOV   (Yuri Filatov, Yuri Stezenko, Vladimir Morozov,   3:14.02
          Valery Didenko)
2. ROM   (Aurel Vernescu, Mihai Zafiu, Roman Vartolo-   3:15.07
          meu, Atanase Sciotnic)
3. NOR   (Egil Söby, Steinar Amundsen, Tore Berger,   3:15.27
          Jan Johansen)
4. ITA   (Alberto Ughi, Pier Angelo Congiu, Mario Pe-   3:15.60
          dretti, Oreste Perri)
5. GER   (Rudolf Blass, Eberhard Fischer, Rainer   3:16.63
          Hennes, Hans-Erich Pasch)
6. HUN   (István Szabó, Peter Várhelyi, Zoltán Bakó,   3:16.88
          Csongor Vargha)
7. FIN   (Kari Markkanen, Heikki Mäkelä, Ilkka Num-   3:16.92
          misto, Jorma Lehtosalo)
8. SWE   (Lars Andersson, Nils Gunnar Utterberg, Per   3:17.39
          Larsson, Hans Nilsson)

1976 Montreal T: 20, N: 20, D: 7.31.
1. SOV   (Sergei Chuhray, Aleksandr Degtiarev, Yuri Fi-   3:08.69
          latov, Vladimir Morozov)
2. SPA   (José Celorrio, José Diaz-Flor, Herminio Me-   3:08.95
          nendez, Luis Ramos Misione)
3. GDR   (Peter Bischof, Bernd Duvigneau, Rüdiger   3:10.76
          Helm, Jürgen Lehnert)
4. ROM   (Nicusor Eseanu, Vasile Simioncenco, Neculai   3:11.35
          Simioncenco, Mihai Zafiu)
5. POL   (Henryk Budzicz, Kazimierz Górecki, Grzegorz   3:12.17
          Koltan, Ryszard Oborski)
6. NOR   (Morten Moerland, Einar Rasmussen, Olaf   3:12.28
          Soeyland, Jostein Stiege)
7. BUL   (Ivan Manev, Bojidar Milenkov, Nikolai Nachev,   3:12.94
          Vasil Chilingirov)
8. HUN   (József Deme, Csaba Giczi, János Rátkai, Zol-   3:14.67
          tán Romhányi)

The Soviet team came from third place in the last 250 meters to nose out Spain, which had been the surprise winner of the 1975 world championship.

1980 Moscow T: 12, N: 12, D: 8.2.
1. GDR (Rüdiger Helm, Bernd Olbricht, Harald Marg, Bernd Duvigneau) 3:13.76
2. ROM (Mihai Zafiu, Vasile Diba, Ion Geanta, Nicusor Esanu) 3:15.35
3. BUL (Borislav Borissov, Bozhidar Milenkov, Lazar Hristov, Ivan Manev) 3:15.46
4. POL (Ryszard Oborski, Grzegorz Koltan, Daniel Welna, Grzegorz Śledziewski) 3:16.33
5. HUN (József Deme, János Rátkai, József Kosztyán, Zoltán Sztaniti) 3:17.27
6. FRA (Francois Barouh, Patrick Berard, Philippe Boccara, Patrick Lefoulon) 3:17.60
7. SOV (Gennady Makhnev, Sergei Nagornyi, Aleksandr Avdyev, Vladimir Tainikov) 3:19.83
8. AUS (Barry Kelly, Robert Lee, Ken Vidler, Crosbie Baulch) 3:19.87

CANADIAN SINGLES 500 METERS
1896–1972 not held

1976 Montreal C: 15, N: 15, D: 7.30.
1. Aleksandr Rogov SOV 1:59.23
2. John Wood CAN 1:59.58
3. Matija Ljubek YUG 1:59.60
4. Borislav Ananiev BUL 1:59.92
5. Wilfried Stephan GDR 2:00.54
6. Károly Szegedi HUN 2:01.12
7. Ivan Patzaichin ROM 2:01.40
8. Ulrich Eicke GER 2:02.30

John Wood thrilled the Canadian crowd of 5000 by leading from the start until the last few strokes, when he was overtaken by the favorite, Aleksandr Rogov.

1980 Moscow C: 11, N: 11, D: 8.1.
1. Sergei Postrekhin SOV 1:53.37
2. Lyubomir Lyubenov BUL 1:53.49
3. Olaf Heukrodt GDR 1:54.38
4. Tamás Wichmann HUN 1:54.58
5. Marek Lbik POL 1:55.90
6. Timo Grönlund FIN 1:55.94
7. Lipat Varabiev ROM 1:56.80
8. Radomir Blazik CZE 1:56.83

CANADIAN SINGLES 1000 METERS
1896–1932 not held

1936 Berlin C: 6, N: 6, D: 8.8.
1. Francis Amyot CAN 5:32.1
2. Bohuslav Karlik CZE 5:36.9
3. Erich Koschik GER 5:39.0
4. Otto Neumüller AUT 5:47.0
5. Joseph Hasenfus USA 6:02.6
6. Joe Treinen LUX 7:39.5

Amyot, who once saved three Ottawa Rough Riders football players from drowning, took an early lead but was passed by Karlik at the 750-meter mark. A 31-year-old veteran, Amyot refused to be rattled and continued stroking smoothly, until he had burst past Karlik with 50 meters to go. Amyot was Canada's only gold medal winner at the Berlin Olympics, thus embarrassing the Canadian Olympic Committee, which had refused to pay his way.

1948 London C: 6, N: 6, D: 8.12.
1. Josef Holeček CZE 5:42.0
2. Douglas Bennett CAN 5:53.3
3. Robert Boutigny FRA 5:55.9
4. Ingemar Andersson SWE 6:08.0
5. Frank Havens USA 6:14.3
6. H. Maidment GBR 6:37.0

1952 Helsinki C: 10, N: 10, D: 7.28.
1. Josef Holeček CZE 4:56.3
2. János Parti HUN 5:03.6
3. Olavi Ojanperä FIN 5:08.5
4. Frank Havens USA 5:13.7
5. Ingemar Andersson SWE 5:15.0
6. Ralf Berckhan GER 5:22.8
7. Jean Molle FRA 5:24.1
8. Vladimir Kotyrev SOV 5:24.5

1956 Melbourne C: 9, N: 9, D: 12.1.
1. Leon Rotman ROM 5:05.3
2. István Hernek HUN 5:06.2
3. Gennady Bukharin SOV 5:12.7
4. Karel Hradil CZE 5:15.9
5. Franz Johannsen GER 5:18.6
6. Verner Wettersten SWE 5:28.0
7. Bryan Harper AUS 5:37.6
8. George Bossy CAN 5:39.4

1960 Rome C: 13, N: 13, D: 8.29.
1. János Parti HUN 4:33.93
2. Aleksandr Silayev SOV 4:34.41
3. Leon Rotman ROM 4:35.87
4. Ove Emanuelsson SWE 4:36.46
5. Tibor Polakovič CZE 4:39.28
6. Detlef Lewe GER 4:39.72
7. Don Stringer CAN 4:40.65
8. Bogdan Ivanov BUL 4:42.52

1964 Tokyo C: 11, N: 11, D: 10.22.
1. Jürgen Eschert GDR 4:35.14
2. Andrei Igorov ROM 4:37.89
3. Yevgeny Penyayev SOV 4:38.31
4. András Törö HUN 4:39.95
5. Ove Emanuelsson SWE 4:42.70
6. Bogdan Ivanov BUL 4:44.76
7. Paul Stahl CAN 5:04.79
8. Dennis Van Valkenburgh USA 5:12.55

1968 Mexico City C: 12, N: 12, D: 10.25.

1. Tibor Tatai	HUN	4:36.14
2. Detlef Lewe	GER	4:38.31
3. Vitaly Galkov	SOV	4:40.42
4. Jiři Čtvrtečka	CZE	4:40.74
5. Boris Lyubenov	BUL	4:43.43
6. Ove Emanuelsson	SWE	4:45.80
7. Ivan Patzaichin	ROM	4:49.32
8. Andreas Weigand	USA	4:50.42

Tibor Tatai made the Hungarian team only as a reserve, but he drove the other finalists to exhaustion and won decisively.

1972 Munich C: 13, N: 13, D: 9.9.

1. Ivan Patzaichin	ROM	4:08.94
2. Tamás Wichmann	HUN	4:12.42
3. Detlef Lewe	GER	4:13.63
4. Dirk Weise	GDR	4:14.38
5. Vassili Yurchenko	SOV	4:14.43
6. Boris Lyubenov	BUL	4:14.65
7. Jiři Čtvrtečka	CZE	4:14.98
8. Roberto Altamirano	MEX	4:20.39

1976 Montreal C: 15, N: 15, D: 7.31.

1. Matija Ljubek	YUG	4:09.51
2. Vassily Urchenko	SOV	4:12.57
3. Tamás Wichmann	HUN	4:14.11
4. Borislav Ananiev	BUL	4:14.41
5. Ivan Patzaichin	ROM	4:15.08
6. Roland Iche	FRA	4:18.23
7. Wilfried Stephan	GDR	4:22.43
8. Ulrich Eicke	GER	4:22.77

Ljubek, a carpenter from Belisce, was the only finalist to paddle the second half of the race faster than the first. He was fourth at the halfway mark but won going away.

1980 Moscow C: 12, N: 12, D: 8.2.

1. Lyubomir Lyubenov	BUL	4:12.38
2. Sergei Postrekhin	SOV	4:13.53
3. Eckhard Leue	GDR	4:15.02
4. Libor Dvořák	CZE	4:15.25
5. Lipat Varabiev	ROM	4:16.68
6. Timo Grönlund	FIN	4:17.37
7. Thomas Falk	SWE	4:20.66
8. Matija Ljubek	YUG	4:22.40

CANADIAN PAIRS 500 METERS
1896–1972 not held

1976 Montreal T: 15, N: 15, D: 7.30.

1. Sergei Petrenko, Aleksandr Vinorgadov	SOV	1:45.81
2. Andrzej Gronowicz, Jerzy Opara	POL	1:47.77
3. Tamás Buday, Oszkár Frey	HUN	1:48.35
4. Gheorghe Danilov, Gheorghe Simionov	ROM	1:48.84
5. Gerald Delacroix, Jean-François Millot	FRA	1:49.74
6. Ivan Burchin, Krasimir Hristov	BUL	1:50.43
7. Gregory Smith, John Wood	CAN	1:50.74
8. Jiři Čtvrtečka, Tomáš Sach	CZE	1:50.85

1980 Moscow T: 10, N: 10, D: 8.1.

1. László Foltán, István Vaskuti	HUN	1:43.39
2. Petre Capusta, Ivan Patzaichin	ROM	1:44.12
3. Borislav Ananiev, Nikolai Ilkov	BUL	1:44.83
4. Jerzy Dunajski, Marek Wisla	POL	1:45.10
5. Petr Kubiček, Jiři Vrdlovec	CZE	1:46.48
6. Sergei Petrenko, Aleksandr Vinogradov	SOV	1:46.95
7. Santos Magaz, Narciso Suarez	SPA	1:48.18
8. Bernt Lindelof, Erik Zeidlitz	SWE	1:48.69

CANADIAN PAIRS 1000 METERS
1896–1932 not held

1936 Berlin T: 5, N: 5, D: 8.8.

1. Vladimir Syrovátka, Jan Brzák-Felix	CZE	4:50.1
2. Rupert Weinstabl, Karl Proisl	AUT	4:53.8
3. Frank Saker, Harvey Charters	CAN	4:56.7
4. Hans Wedemann, Heinrich Sack	GER	5:00.2
5. Clarence McNutt, Robert Graf	USA	5:14.0

1948 London T: 8, N: 8, D: 8.12.

1. Jan Brzák-Felix, Bohumil Kudrna	CZE	5:07.1
2. Stephen Lysak, Stephan Macknowski	USA	5:08.2
3. Georges Dransart, Georges Gandil	FRA	5:15.2
4. Douglas Bennett, Harry Poulton	CAN	5:20.7
5. Karl Molnar, Viktor Salmhofer	AUT	5:37.3
6. Gunnar Johansson, Verner Wettersten	SWE	5:44.9
7. J. Symons, H. Van Zwanenberg	GBR	5:50.8

DNF: H. Coomans, J. Dubois (BEL), man overboard

Jan Brzák was one of the few gold medal winners at the Berlin Olympics who was able to retain his championship 12 years later in London. In 1955, when he was 43 years old, Brzak teamed with 46-year-old Bohuslav Karlik to paddle the 118 miles from Ceske Budejovice to Prague in 20 hours.

1952 Helsinki T: 11, N: 11, D: 7.28.

1. Bent Peder Rasch, Finn Haunstoft	DEN	4:38.3
2. Jan Brzák-Felix, Bohumil Kudrna	CZE	4:42.9
3. Egon Drews, Wilfried Soltau	GER	4:48.3
4. Georges Dransart, Armand Loreau	FRA	4:48.6
5. István Bodor, József Tuza	HUN	4:51.9
6. Kurt Liebhart, Englebert Lulla	AUT	4:55.8
7. John Haas, Frank Krick	USA	4:59.0
8. Arthur Johnson, Thomas Hodgson	CAN	5:01.4

1956 Melbourne T: 10, N: 10, D: 12.1.

1. Alexe Dumitru, Simion Ismailciuc	ROM	4:47.4
2. Pavel Kharine, Gratsian Botev	SOV	4:48.6
3. Károly Wieland, Ferenc Mohácsi	HUN	4:54.3
4. Georges Dransart, Marcel Renaud	FRA	4:57.7
5. William Jones, Thomas Ohman	AUS	5:03.0
6. Otto Schindler, Walter Waldner	AUT	5:04.4
7. William Collins, Bert Oldershaw	CAN	5:11.0

DISQ: Kai Sylvan, Gerner Christiansen (DEN)

1960 Rome T: 11, N: 11, D: 8.29.
1. Leonid Geischtor, Sergei Makarenko — SOV — 4:17.94
2. Aldo Dezi, Francesco La Macchia — ITA — 4:20.77
3. Imre Farkas, András Törö — HUN — 4:20.89
4. Igor Lipalit, Alexe Dumitru — ROM — 4:22.36
5. Jiří Kodeš, Václav Vokal — CZE — 4:27.66
6. Marin Gopov, Toma Sokolov — BUL — 4:31.52
7. Willi Mehlberg, Werner Ulrich — GDR — 4:31.68
8. Georges Turlier, Michel Picard — FRA — 4:35.48

1964 Tokyo T: 12, N: 12, D: 10.22.
1. Andrey Khimich, Stepan Oschepkov — SOV — 4:04.64
2. Jean Boudehen, Michel Chapuis — FRA — 4:06.52
3. Peer Norrbohm Nielsen, John Sörensen — DEN — 4:07.48
4. Antal Hajba, Árpád Soltesz — HUN — 4:08.97
5. Igor Lipalit, Achim Sidorov — ROM — 4:09.88
6. Klaus Böhle, Detlef Lewe — GER — 4:13.18
7. Andor Elbert, Fred Heese — CAN — 4:21.99
8. Miloslav Houzim, Rudolf Penkava — CZE — 4:22.89

1968 Mexico City T: 12, N: 12, D: 10.25.
1. Ivan Patzaichin, Serghei Covaliov — ROM — 4:07.18
2. Tamás Wichmann, Gyula Petrikovics — HUN — 4:08.77
3. Naum Prokupets, Mikhail Zamotin — SOV — 4:11.30
4. Juan Martinez, Felix Altamirano — MEX — 4:15.24
5. Bernt Lindelöf, Erik Zeidlitz — SWE — 4:16.60
6. Jürgen Harpke, Helmut Wagner — GDR — 4:22.53
7. Roland Kapf, Klaus Lewandwsky — GER — 4:26.36
8. Ivan Vulov, Alexander Damianov — BUL — 4:26.74

Ivan Patzaichin and Serghei Covaliov were fishermen from the village of Crisan-Mila, in the Danube delta. Silver medalist Tamás Wichmann was a chef.

1972 Munich T: 16, N: 16, D: 9.9.
1. Vladas Chessyunas, Yuri Lobanov — SOV — 3:52.60
2. Ivan Patzaichin, Serghei Covaliov — ROM — 3:52.63
3. Fedia Damianov, Ivan Burchin — BUL — 3:58.10
4. Hans-Peter Hoffmann, Hermann Glaser — GER — 3:59.24
5. Miklós Darvas, Péter Povázsay — HUN — 4:00.42
6. Roland Muhlen, Andreas Weigand — USA — 4:01.28
7. Dirk Weise, Dieter Lichtenberg — GDR — 4:01.50
8. Berndt Lindeloef, Eric Zeidlitz — SWE — 4:01.60

Chessyunas and Lobanov took an early lead, but at the 700-meter mark Patzaichin and Covaliov mounted a furious challenge that brought them to the finish line only three one-hundredths of a second too late.

1976 Montreal T: 15, N: 15, D: 7.31.
1. Sergei Petrenko, Aleksandr Vinogradov — SOV — 3:52.76
2. Gheorghe Danielov, Gheorghe Simionov — ROM — 3:54.28
3. Tamás Buday, Oszkár Frey — HUN — 3:55.66
4. Jerzy Opara, Andrzej Gronowicz — POL — 3:59.56
5. Detlef Bothe, Hans-Jürgen Tode — GDR — 4:00.37

6. Jiří Čtvrtečka, Tomáš Sach — CZE — 4:01.48
7. Ivan Burchin, Krasimir Hristov — BUL — 4:02.44
8. Hermann Glaser, Heinz Lucke — GER — 4:03.86

1980 Moscow T: 11, N: 11, D: 8.2.
1. Ivan Patzaichin, Toma Simionov — ROM — 3:47.65
2. Olaf Heukrodt, Uwe Madeja — GDR — 3:49.93
3. Vassily Yurchenko, Yuri Lobanov — SOV — 3:51.28
4. Matija Ljubek, Mirko Nisović — YUG — 3:51.30
5. Jiří Vrdlovec, Petr Kubiček — CZE — 3:52.50
6. Marek Dopiérala, Jan Pinczura — POL — 3:53.01
7. Raiko Kurmadzhiev, Kamen Koutzev — BUL — 3:53.89
8. Tamás Buday, Oszkár Frey — HUN — 3:54.31

Discontinued Events

KAYAK SINGLES 10,000 METERS
1896–1928 not held

1936 Berlin C: 15, N: 15, D: 8.7.
1. Ernst Krebs — GER — 46:01.6
2. Fritz Landertinger — AUT — 46:14.7
3. Ernest Riedl — USA — 47.23.9
4. Jacobus van Tongeren — HOL — 47:31.0
5. Evert Johansson — FIN — 47:35.5
6. František Brzák-Felix — CZE — 47:36.8
7. Lips — SWI — 48:01.2
8. Sasso Sant — ITA — 49:20.0

1948 London C: 13, N: 13, D: 8.11.
1. Gert Fredriksson — SWE — 50:47.7
2. Kurt Wires — FIN — 51:18.2
3. Eivind Skabo — NOR — 51:35.4
4. Knud Ditlevsen — DEN — 51:54.2
5. Henri Eberhardt — FRA — 52:09.0
6. Jochem Bobeldijk — HOL — 52:13.2
7. Czeslaw Sobieraj — POL — 52:51.0
8. A. Cobiaux — BEL — 53:23.5

1952 Helsinki C: 17, N: 17, D: 7.27.
1. Thorvald Strömberg — FIN — 47:22.8
2. Gert Fredriksson — SWE — 47:34.1
3. Michael Scheuer — GER — 47:54.5
4. Ejvind Hansen — DEN — 47:58.8
5. Hans Martin Gulbrandsen — NOR — 48:12.9
6. Miloš Pech — CZE — 48:25.8
7. Ivan Sotnikov — SOV — 48:36.8
8. Jochem Bobeldijk — HOL — 49:36.2

Fredriksson spent most of the race hanging in the wake of Stromberg's bow, but when he finally made his move, the 21-year-old Finnish fisherman had saved enough for a spurt of his own and pulled away to victory.

1956 Melbourne C: 11, N: 11, D: 11.30.

1. Gert Fredriksson	SWE	47:43.4
2. Ferenc Hatlaczky	HUN	47:53.3
3. Michael Scheuer	GER	48:00.3
4. Thorvald Strömberg	FIN	48:15.8
5. Igor Pissaryev	SOV	49:58.2
6. Ladislav Čepciansky	CZE	50:08.2
7. Svend Fromming	DEN	50:10.0
8. Knut Östbye	NOR	51:28.2

FOLDING KAYAK SINGLES 10,000 METERS

1936 Berlin C: 13, N: 13, D: 8.7.

1. Gregor Hradetzky	AUT	50:01.2
2. Henri Eberhardt	FRA	50:04.2
3. Xaver Hörmann	GER	50:06.5
4. Lennart Dozzi	SWE	51:23.8
5. František Svoboda	CZE	51:52.5
6. Hans Mooser	SWE	52:43.8
7. Nordberg	FIN	52:45.8
8. Lawton	GBR	52:50.0

KAYAK PAIRS 10,000 METERS

1936 Berlin T: 12, N: 12, D: 8.7.

1. Paul Wevers, Ludwig Landen	GER	41:45.0
2. Viktor Kalisch, Karl Steinhuber	AUT	42:05.4
3. Tage Fahlborg, Helge Larsson	SWE	43:06.1
4. Verner Lövgreen, Axel Svendsen	DEN	44:39.8
5. Hendrik Starreveld, Gerardus Siderius	HOL	45:12.5
6. Werner Zimmermann, Othmar Bach	SWI	45:14.6
7. William Gaehler, William Lofgren	USA	45:15.4
8. Cernicky, Humpal	CZE	46:05.4

1948 London T: 15, N: 15, D: 8.11.

1. Gunnar Åkerlund, Hans Wetterström	SWE	46:09.4
2. Ivar Mathisen, Knut Östbye	NOR	46:44.8
3. Thor Axelsson, Nils Björklof	FIN	46:48.2
4. Alfred Christensen, Finn Rasmussen	DEN	47:17.5
5. Gyula Andrási, János Urányi	HUN	47:33.1
6. Cornelius Koch, Hendrik Stroo	HOL	47:35.6
7. Ludvik Klima, K. Lomecky	CZE	48:14.9
8. D. Deprez, J. Massy	BEL	48:23.1

1952 Helsinki T: 18, N: 18, D: 7.27.

1. Kurt Wires, Yrjö Hietanen	FIN	44:21.3
2. Gunnar Åkerlund, Hans Wetterström	SWE	44:21.7
3. Ferenc Varga, József Gurovits	HUN	44:26.6
4. Max Raub, Herbert Wiedermann	AUT	44:29.1
5. Ivar Mathiesen, Knut Östbye	NOR	45:04.7
6. Karl-Heinz Schäfer, Meinrad Miltenberger	GER	45:15.2
7. Rudolf Klabouch, Bedřich Dvořák	CZE	45:39.6
8. Ingvard Norregaard, Svend Fromming	DEN	45:59.6

Although Wires and Hietanen led from start to finish, they won by only half a meter.

1956 Melbourne T: 12, N: 12, D: 11.30.

1. János Urányi, László Fábián	HUN	43:37.0
2. Fritz Briel, Theo Kleine	GER	43:40.6
3. Dennis Green, Walter Brown	AUS	43:43.2
4. Hans Wetterström, Carl-Axel Sundin	SWE	44:06.7
5. Yevgeny Yatsynyenki, Sergei Klimov	SOV	45:49.3
6. Miloslav Jemelka, Rudolf Klabouch	CZE	46:13.1
7. Yrjö Hietanen, Simo Kuismanen	FIN	46:40.4
8. Brian Bullivant, Raymond Blick	GBR	47:03.7

FOLDING KAYAK PAIRS 10,000 METERS

1936 Berlin T: 13, N: 13, D: 8.7.

1. Sven Johansson, Eric Bladström	SWE	45:48.9
2. Willi Horn, Erich Hanisch	GER	45:49.2
3. Pieter Wijdekop, Cornelis Wijdekop	HOL	46:12.4
4. Adolf Kainz, Alfons Dorfner	AUT	46:26.1
5. Otokar Kouba, Ludvik Klima	CZE	47:46.2
6. Eugen Knoblauch, Emil Bottlang	SWI	47:54.4
7. John Lysak, James O'Rourke	USA	49:46.0
8. Pagnoulle, Pasquier	BEL	49:57.1

KAYAK SINGLES RELAY 4×500 METERS

1960 Rome T: 18, N: 18, D: 8.29.

1. GDR/GER	(Paul Lange, Günter Perleberg, Friedhelm Wentzke, Dieter Krause)		7:39.43
2. HUN	(Imre Szöllösi, Imre Kemecsey, András Szente, György Mészáros)		7:44.02
3. DEN	(Helmuth Sörensen, Arne Höyer, Erling Jessen, Erik Hansen)		7:46.09
4. POL	(Stefan Kaplaniak, Wladislaw Zieliński, Ryszard Skwarski, Ryszard Marchlik)		7:49.93
5. SOV	(Igor Pissaryev, Anatoly Kononyenko, Fyodor Lyakhovsky, Vladimir Natalukha)		7:50.72
6. ROM	(Mircea Anastasescu, Aurel Vernescu, Ion Sideri, Stavru Teodorov)		7:53.00

KAYAK SLALOM SINGLES

1972 Munich C: 37, T: 15, D: 8.28.

		PTS
1. Siegbert Horn	GDR	268.56
2. Norbert Sattler	AUT	270.76
3. Harald Gimpel	GDR	277.95
4. Ulrich Peters	GER	282.82
5. Alfred Baum	GER	288.01
6. Marian Havliček	CZE	289.56
7. Eric Evans	USA	296.34
8. Jürgen Bremer	GDR	303.15

This unusual event, also known as white water canoeing, requires the canoeist to paddle down an obstacle course in much the same manner as the slalom races in skiing. Each competitor runs the course twice, with only the better run, as defined by both time and penalty points, counting. The West Germans spent 17 million marks ($4 million) constructing an artificial river at Augsburg for the competition, and they hoped to gain several medals at the Olympics. However a year before the Munich games, the East Germans came over, studied the facilities at Augsburg, and built an exact replica back home. In 1972 East Germany won all four canoe slalom events. Their first winner was Siegbert Horn, a 22-year-old army sergeant from Leipzig. Horn keeled over in the first run and finished 17th. But the second time he paddled a smooth race and, although his time was only the eighth best, he picked up so few penalty points that he won anyway.

CANADIAN SINGLES 10,000 METERS

1948 London C: 5, N: 5, D: 8.11.

1. František Čapek   CZE   1:02:05.2
2. Frank Havens   USA   1:02:40.4
3. Norman Lane   CAN   1:04:35.3
4. Raymond Argentin   FRA   1:06:44.2
5. Ingemar Andersson   SWE   1:07:27.1

Čapek, a 33-year-old bank clerk from Prague, used a "crooked" canoe which curved at the keel, allowing him to paddle on one side and not waste energy maintaining a straight course.

1952 Helsinki C: 10, N: 10, D: 7.27.

1. Frank Havens   USA   57:41.1
2. Gábor Novák   HUN   57:49.2
3. Alfréd Jindra   CZE   57:53.1
4. Bengt Backlund   SWE   59:02.8
5. Norman Lane   CAN   59:26.4
6. Jarl Fagerström   FIN   59:45.9
7. Franz Johannsen   GER   1:00.26.5
8. Robert Boutigny   FRA   1:01.15.2

Jindra led most of the way, but Havens, a 28-year-old auto insurance adjuster from Arlington, Virginia, overtook him on the home stretch of the last lap and won by about 18 yards.

1956 Melbourne C: 9, N: 9, D: 11.30.

1. Leon Rotman   ROM   56:41.0
2. János Parti   HUN   57:11.0
3. Gennady Bukharin   SOV   57:14.5
4. Jiří Vokněr   CZE   57:44.5
5. Franz Johannsen   GER   58:50.1
6. Verner Wettersten   SWE   59:24.7
7. Donald Stringer   CAN   59:57.5
8. Frank Havens   USA   1:01:23.6

CANADIAN PAIRS 10,000 METERS

1936 Berlin T: 5, N: 5, D: 8.7.

1. Václav Mottl, Ždenek Škrdlant   CZE   50:35.5
2. Frank Saker, Harvey Charters   CAN   51:15.8
3. Rupert Weinstabl, Karl Proisl   AUT   51:28.0

4. Walter Schuur, Christian Holzenberg   GER   52:35.6
5. Joseph Hasenfus, Walter Hasenfus   USA   57:06.2

1948 London T: 6, N: 6, D: 8.11.

1. Stephen Lysack, Stephan Macknowski   USA   55:55.4
2. Václav Havel, Jiří Pecka   CZE   57:38.5
3. Georges Dransart, Georges Gandil   FRA   58:00.8
4. Karl Molnar, Viktor Salmhofer   AUT   58:59.3
5. Bert Oldershaw, William Stevenson   CAN   59:48.4
6. Gunnar Johansson, Verner Wettersten   SWE   1:03:34.4

Stephen Lysack, age 26, and Stephen Macknowski, age 33, of Yonkers, New York, using a homemade mahogany canoe, took the lead after only five strokes and went on to win by an enormous margin.

1952 Helsinki T: 9, N: 9. D: 7.27.

1. Georges Turlier, Jean Laudet   FRA   54:08.3
2. Kenneth Lane, Donald Hawgood   CAN   54:09.9
3. Egon Drews, Wilfried Soltau   GER   54:28.1
4. Valentin Orischenko, Nikolai
   Perevozchikov   SOV   54:36.6
5. John Haas, Frank Krick   USA   54:42.5
6. Bohuslav Karlík, Oldřich Lomecky   CZE   55:10.9
7. Ernö Söptei, Róbert Söptei   HUN   55:35.3
8. Rune Blomqvist, Harry Lindbeck   SWE   55:41.3

1956 Melbourne T: 10, N: 10, D: 11.30.

1. Pavel Kharin, Gratsian Botev   SOV   54:02.4
2. Georges Dransart, Marcel Renaud   FRA   54:48.3
3. Imre Farkas, József Hunics   HUN   55:15.6
4. Egon Drews, Wilfried Soltau   GER   55:21.1
5. Alexe Dumitru, Simion Ismailciuc   ROM   55:51.1
6. Aksel Duun, Finn Haunstoft   DEN   55:54.3
7. William Jones, Thomas Ohman   AUS   56:18.6
8. Otto Schindler, Wálter Waldner   AUT   56:48.7

SLALOM CANADIAN SINGLES

1972 Munich C: 22, N: 9, D: 7.28.

		PTS
1. Reinhard Eiben	GDR	315.84
2. Reinhold Kauder	GER	327.89
3. Jamie McEwan	USA	335.95
4. Jochen Förster	GDR	354.42
5. Wolfgang Peters	GER	356.25
6. Jürgen Köhler	GDR	372.88
7. Karel Tresnak	CZE	385.07
8. Petr Sodomka	CZE	391.11

The victory of Reinhard Eiben, a 20-year-old industrial blacksmith from Zwickau, came as a complete surprise. He had placed 13th at the 1971 world championships and only sixth in the East German championships. However, at the Olympics he recorded the best time in both rounds to finish well ahead of the favorite, Reinhold Kauder.

SLALOM CANADIAN PAIRS

1972 Munich T: 20, N: 9, D: 8.30.

		PTS
1. Walter Hofmann, Rolf-Dieter Amend	GDR	310.68
2. Hans Otto Schumacher, Wilhelm Baues	GER	311.90
3. Jean-Louis Olry, Jean-Claude Olry	FRA	315.10
4. Jürgen Kretschmer, Klaus Trummer	GDR	329.57
5. Jan Frączek, Ryszard Seruga	POL	366.21
6. Janez Andrijasić, Peter Guzelj	YUG	368.01
7. Michael Reimann, Olaf Fricke	GER	371.86
8. Heimo Müllneritsch, Helmar Steindl	AUT	375.14

WOMEN

KAYAK SINGLES 500 METERS

1896–1936 not held

1948 London C: 10, N: 10, D: 8.12.
1. Karen Hoff	DEN	2:31.9
2. Alida van der Anker-Doedens	HOL	2:32.8
3. Fritzi Schwingl	AUT	2:32.9
4. Klára Bánfalvi	HUN	2:33.8
5. Ružena Koštalová	CZE	2:38.2
6. Sylvi Saimo	FIN	2:38.4
7. A. Van Marcke	BEL	2:43.4
8. C. Vautrin	FRA	2:44.4

1952 Helsinki C: 13, N: 13, D: 7.28.
1. Sylvi Saimo	FIN	2:18.4
2. Gertrude Liebhart	AUT	2:18.8
3. Nina Savina	SOV	2:21.6
4. Alida van der Anker-Doedens	HOL	2:22.3
5. Bodil Svendsen	DEN	2:22.7
6. Cecília Hartmann	HUN	2:23.0
7. Marta Kroutilová	CZE	2:23.8
8. Josefa Köster	GER	2:25.9

1956 Melbourne C: 10, N: 10, D: 12.1.
1. Yelisaveta Dementyeva	SOV	2:18.9
2. Therese Zenz	GER	2:19.6
3. Tove Soby	DEN	2:22.3
4. Cecília Berkes (Hartmann)	HUN	2:23.5
5. Edith Cochrane	AUS	2:23.8
6. Daniela Walkowiak	POL	2:24.1
7. Patricia Moody	GBR	2:25.3
8. Eva Marion	FRA	2:27.9

Dementyeva false-started once, then spurted into the lead and held on to win by six feet. Zenz had competed at the 1952 Helsinki Olympics as a representative of the then independent nation of Saar.

1960 Rome C: 13, N: 13, D: 8.29.
1. Antonina Seredina	SOV	2:08.08
2. Therese Zenz	GER	2:08.22
3. Daniela Walkowiak	POL	2:10.46
4. Annemarie Werner-Hansen	DEN	2:13.88
5. Klára Fried-Bánfalvi	HUN	2:14.02
6. Else Marie Lindmark	SWE	2:14.17
7. Alberta Zanardi	ITA	2:14.31
8. Eva Kutova	CZE	2:15.30

1964 Tokyo C: 13, N: 13, D: 10.22.
1. Lyudmila Khvedosyuk	SOV	2:12.87
2. Hilde Lauer	ROM	2:15.35
3. Marcia Jones	USA	2:15.68
4. Elke Felten	GER	2:15.94
5. Else Marie Ljungdahl (Lindmark)	SWE	2:16.00
6. Hanneliese Spitz	AUT	2:16.11
7. Daniela Pilecka	POL	2:17.52
8. Mária Roka	HUN	2:17.85

1968 Mexico City C: 13, N: 13, D: 10.25.
1. Lyudmila Pinayeva (Khvedosyuk)	SOV	2:11.09
2. Renate Breuer	GER	2:12.71
3. Victoria Dumitru	ROM	2:13.22
4. Marcia Smoke (Jones)	USA	2:14.68
5. Ivona Vávrová	CZE	2:14.78
6. Anita Nüssner	GDR	2:16.02
7. Ingmärie Svensson	SWE	2:16.04
8. Mieke Jaapies	HOL	2:18.38

In the middle of the race the ninth finalist, Anna Pfeffer of Hungary, spun over in the water and was rescued by a special emergency craft following the kayakists. One and a half hours later she was back in action, winning a silver medal in the kayak pairs.

1972 Munich C: 15, N: 15, D: 9.5.
1. Yulia Ryabchinskaya	SOV	2:03.17
2. Mieke Jaapies	HOL	2:04.03
3. Anna Pfeffer	HUN	2:05.50
4. Irene Pepinghege	GER	2:06.55
5. Bettina Müller	GDR	2:06.85
6. Maria Nichiforov	ROM	2:07.13
7. Kate Olsen	DEN	2:07.16
8. Ingmärie Svensson	SWE	2:07.61

1976 Montreal C: 15, N: 15, D: 7.30.
1. Carola Zirzow	GDR	2:01.05
2. Tatiana Korshunova	SOV	2:03.07
3. Klára Rajnai	HUN	2:05.01
4. Ewa Kamińska	POL	2:05.16
5. Maria Mihoreanu	ROM	2:05.40
6. Anastazie Hajná	CZE	2:06.72
7. Julie Leach	USA	2:06.92
8. Irene Peppinghege	GER	2:07.80

East German boat designers spent a month in Montreal studying the layout of the Olympic course. Then they went home and constructed special fiberglass canoes and kayaks that curved inward when placed in the water, becoming longer and faster. Using one of these kayaks, Carola Zirzow, a 5-foot 10-inch, 21-year-old student of physiotherapy, overcame a poor start to take first place.

1980 Moscow C: 11, N: 11, D: 8.1.
1. Birgit Fischer   GDR   1:57.96
2. Vania Gesheva   BUL   1:59.48
3. Antonina Melnikova   SOV   1:59.66
4. Maria Stefan   ROM   2:00.90
5. Ewa Eichler   POL   2:01.23
6. Agneta Andersson   SWE   2:01.33
7. Katalin Povázsán   HUN   2:01.52
8. Beatrice Knopf   FRA   2:02.91

KAYAK PAIRS 500 METERS
1896–1956 not held

1960 Rome T: 11, N: 11, D: 8.29.
1. Maria Chubina, Antonina Seredina   SOV   1:54.76
2. Therese Zenz, Ingrid Hartmann   GER   1:56.66
3. Klára Fried-Bánfalvi, Vilma Egresi   HUN   1:58.22
4. Daniela Walkowiak, Janina Mendalska   POL   1:59.03
5. Annemarie Werner-Hansen, Birgit Jensen   DEN   2:01.36
6. Maria Szekeli, Elena Lipalit   ROM   2:01.68
7. Gabriella Cotta Ramusino, Luciana Guindani   ITA   2:02.47
8. Eva Kutova, Eva Kolinska   CZE   2:02.76

1964 Tokyo T: 10, N: 10, D: 10.22.
1. Roswitha Esser, Annemarie Zimmermann   GER   1:56.95
2. Francine Fox, Gloriane Perrier   USA   1:59.16
3. Hilde Lauer, Cornelia Sideri   ROM   2:00.25
4. Nina Gruzintseva, Antonina Seredina   SOV   2:00.69
5. Birthe Hansen, Annemarie Werner-Hansen   DEN   2:00.88
6. Else-Marie Ljungdahl (Lindmark), Eva-Britt Sisth   SWE   2:02.24
7. Katalin Benkö, Mária Roka   HUN   2:03.67
8. Izabella Antonowicz, Daniela Pilecka   POL   2:04.31

Silver medalist Francine Fox was only 15 years old.

1968 Mexico City T: 11, N: 11, D: 10.25.
1. Roswitha Esser, Annemarie Zimmermann   GER   1:56.44
2. Anna Pfeffer, Katalin Rozsnyói   HUN   1:58.60
3. Lyudmila Pinayeva (Khvedosyuk), Antonina Seredina   SOV   1:58.61
4. Valentina Serghei, Viorica Dumitru   ROM   1:59.17
5. Anita Kobuss, Karin Haftenberger   GDR   2:00.18
6. Mieke Jaapies, Tjeertje Bergers-Duif   HOL   2:02.02
7. Sperry Rademaker, Marcia Smoke (Jones)   USA   2:02.97
8. Lesley Oliver, Barbara Mean   GBR   2:03.70

1972 Munich T: 12, N: 12, D: 9.9.
1. Lyudmila Pinayeva (Khvedosyuk), Ekaterina Kuryshko   SOV   1:53.50
2. Ilse Kaschube, Petra Grabowski   GDR   1:54.30
3. Maria Nichiforov, Victoria Dumitru   ROM   1:55.01
4. Anna Pfeffer, Katalin Hollósy   HUN   1:55.12
5. Roswitha Esser, Renate Breuer   GER   1:55.64
6. Izabella Antonowicz-Szuszkiewicz, Ewa Grajkowska   POL   1:57.45
7. Mieke Jaapies, Maria van der Holst   HOL   1:58.11
8. Natasha Petrova, Petrana Koleva   BUL   1:59.40

1976 Montreal T: 14, N: 14, D: 7.30.

1. Nina Gopova, Galina Kreft	SOV	1:51.15
2. Anna Pfeffer, Klára Rajnai	HUN	1:51.69
3. Bärbel Köster, Carola Zirzow	GDR	1:51.81
4. Nastasia Nichitov, Agafia Orlov	ROM	1:53.77
5. Barbara Lewe-Pohlmann, Heiderose Wallbaum	GER	1:53.86
6. Maria Kazanecka, Katarzyna Kulczak	POL	1:55.05
7. Maria Mincheva, Natasha Yanakieva	BUL	1:55.95
8. Anne Dodge, Susan Holloway	CAN	1:56.75

1980 Moscow T: 12, N: 12, D: 8.1.

1. Carsta Genäuss, Martina Bischof	GDR	1:43.88
2. Galina Alexeyeva, Nina Trofimova	SOV	1:46.91
3. Éva Rakusz, Mária Zakariás	HUN	1:47.95
4. Elisabeta Babeanu, Agafia Buhaev	ROM	1:48.04
5. Agneta Andersson, Karin Olsson	SWE	1:49.27
6. Anne-Marie Loriot, Valerie Leclerc	FRA	1:49.48
7. Ewa Eichler, Ewa Wojtaszek	POL	1:51.31
8. Frances Wetherall, Lesley Smither	GBR	1:52.76

Genäuss and Bischof achieved the most decisive victory ever in women's Olympic canoeing.

KAYAK FOURS 500 METERS

This event will be held for the first time in 1984.

Discontinued Events

KAYAK SLALOM SINGLES

1972 Munich C: 22, N: 10, D: 8.30.

		PTS
1. Angelika Bahmann	GDR	364.50
2. Gisela Grothaus	GER	398.15
3. Magdalena Wunderlich	GER	400.50
4. Maria Ćwiertniewicz	POL	432.30
5. Kunegunda Godawska	POL	441.05
6. Victoria Brown	GBR	443.71
7. Ulrike Deppe	GER	456.44
8. Bohumila Kapplova	CZE	460.16

CYCLING

MEN
1000-Meter Sprint (Scratch)
1000-Meter Time Trial
4000-Meter Individual Pursuit
4000-Meter Team Pursuit
Individual Road Roace
Team Road Race
Individual Points Race
Discontinued Events

WOMEN
Individual Road Race
Individual Points Race

MEN

1000-METER SPRINT (SCRATCH)

The individual sprint, or scratch, is a tactical, and some-times violent, race in which two or three cyclists make three laps of the track. For the first 800 meters they care-fully maneuver for position, usually trying to avoid taking the lead so that they can take advantage of the slipstream created by the leading cyclist. Then they sprint for the fin-ish line. Times are usually taken only for the final 200 me-ters.

Since 1928 separate races have been held to determine first place and third place. Since 1976 all four defeated quarterfinalists have raced off for places 5 through 8.

1896 Athens C: 4, N: 3, D: 4.11
(2000 Meters)

1. Paul Masson	FRA	4:58.2
2. Stamatios Nikolopoulos	GRE	5:00.2
3. Léon Flameng	FRA	—
4. Joseph Rosemeyer	GER	—

1900 Paris C: 26, N: 5, D: 9.13
(2000 Meters)

1. Georges Taillandier	FRA	2:52.0 (last 200 meters 13.0)
2. Fernand Sanz	FRA	—
3. John Henry Lake	USA	—

1904 not held

1906 Athens C: 26, N: 9, D: 4.23.

1. Francesco Verri	ITA	1:42.2
2. H.C. Bouffler	GBR	—
3. Eugène Debongnie	BEL	—

1908 London C: 40, N: 9, D: 7.16.
The final was declared void because the time limit was ex-ceeded. The finalists were: 1. Maurice Schilles (FRA), 2. Ben Jones (GBR). DNF: Victor Johnson (GBR) and Charles Kingsbury (GBR).

Johnson suffered a punctured wheel shortly after the start. The other three crawled around the track, carefully jockeying for position. At the beginning of the last bank, Kingsbury also punctured. Then the remaining two raced to the finish line, with Schilles winning by inches. Howev-er, the time limit of 1 minute 45 seconds had been exceed-ed, so the race was declared void. Much to the surprise of most of those present, the judges of the National Cyclists' Union refused to allow the race to be rerun.

1912 not held

1920 Antwerp C: 18, N: 7, D: 8.12.

1. Maurice Peeters	HOL	1:38.3
2. Thomas Johnson	GBR	—
3. Harry Ryan	GBR	—

1924 Paris C: 31, N: 17, D: 7.27.

1. Lucien Michard	FRA	12.8 (last 200 meters)
2. Jacob Meijer	HOL	—
3. Jean Cugnot	FRA	—

1928 Amsterdam C: 18, N: 18, D: 8.7.

1. Roger Beaufrand	FRA	13.2 (last 200 meters)
2. Antoine Mazairac	HOL	—
3. Willy Falck-Hansen	DEN	—
4. Hans Bernhardt	GER	—
5. Jerzy Koszutski (POL), A. Malvassi (ARG), J.E. Standen (AUS), Y. van Massenhove (BEL)		

1932 Los Angeles C: 9, N: 9, D: 8.3.

		1ST RACE	2ND RACE	3RD RACE
1. Jacobus van Egmond	HOL	—	12.6	12.6
2. Louis Chaillot	FRA	12.5	—	—
3. Bruno Pellizzari	ITA			
4. Edgar Gray	AUS			
5. Ernest Henry Chambers (GBR), Willy Gervin (DEN), Leo Marchiori (CAN), Robert Thomas (USA)				

Beginning in 1932, it was necessary to win two out of three races. Louis Chaillot won the first race of the final by inches. But Jacobus van Egmond set the pace in the second, leading all the way to the finish. He then won the tie-breaker by a foot.

1936 Berlin C: 20, N: 20, D: 8.7.

		1ST RACE	2ND RACE
1. Toni Merkens	GER	11.8	11.8
2. Arie van Vliet	HOL	—	—
3. Louis Chaillot	FRA		
4. Benedetto Pola	ITA		
5. Henri Collard (BEL), Edgar Gray (AUS), Carl Magnussen (DEN), Werner Wagelin (SWI)			

As Arie van Vliet began to overtake Toni Merkens in the first race of the final, the German swerved to his right and blatantly interfered with his rival. No foul was called, and a disconcerted Van Vliet lost the second race as well. The Dutch team protested. In a bizarre twist, cycling officials decided not to disqualify Merkens, but to fine him 100 marks instead. The next day, Van Vliet returned to win the 1000-meter time trial. Merkens died toward the end of World War II, while fighting the Russians.

1948 London C: 23, N: 23, D: 8.9.

		1ST RACE	2ND RACE
1. Mario Ghella	ITA	12.2	12.0
2. Reginald Harris	GBR	—	—
3. Axel Schandorff	DEN		
4. Charles Bazzano	AUS		
5. John Heid (USA), M. Masanes Gimeno (CHI), L. Rocca (URU), E. Van de Velde (BEL)			

Reg Harris, the reigning world sprint champion, was struck from the British team a few days before the Olympics because he insisted on staying in his hometown of Manchester instead of training with the rest of the team in London. After a public outcry, Harris was reinstated, but not until he had won a ride-off against his tandem partner, Alan Bannister. In the final he faced 20-year-old Mario Ghella, a student from Turin. In the first race, Ghella caught Harris in a moment of inattention with 350 meters to go, slipped inside of him, and won easily. In the second race, Ghella fought off three challenges from Harris to earn a dramatic and emotional victory.

1952 Helsinki C: 27, N: 27, D: 7.31.

1. Enzo Sacchi	ITA	12.0
2. Lionel Cox	AUS	—
3. Werner Potzernheim	GER	
4. Cyril Peacock (GBR), Raymond Robinson (SAF), Béla Szekeres (HUN)		

1956 Melbourne C: 19, N: 19, D: 12.6. WR: 11.0 (Arie van Vliet)

		1ST RACE	2ND RACE
1. Michel Rousseau	FRA	11.4	11.4
2. Guglielmo Pesenti	ITA	—	—
3. Richard Ploog	AUS		
4. Warren Johnston	NZE		
5. Jack Disney (USA), Ladislav Fouček (CZE), Boris Romanov (SOV), Thomas Shardelow (SAF)			

1960 Rome C: 30, N: 18, D: 8.29. WR: 10.8 (Antonio Maspes)

		1ST RACE	2ND RACE
1. Sante Gaiardoni	ITA	11.1	11.5
2. Leo Sterckx	BEL	—	—
3. Valentino Gasparella	ITA		
4. Ronald Baensch	AUS		
5. Anesio Argenton (BRA), Lloyd Binch (GBR), Antoine Pellegrina (FRA) August Rieke (GER)			

For the third straight time, the Olympic sprint championship was won by the reigning world champion. The 5-foot 6-inch 174-pound Gaiardoni had already won the 1000-meter time trial when he swept through the sprint competition without being seriously challenged.

1964 Tokyo C: 39, N: 22, D: 10.19. WR: 10.8 (Antonio Maspes)

		1ST RACE	2ND RACE
1. Giovanni Pettenella	ITA	13.85	13.69
2. Sergio Bianchetto	ITA	—	—
3. Daniel Morelon	FRA		
4. Pierre Trentin	FRA		
5. Willi Fuggerer (GER), Patrick Sercu (BEL), Mario Vanegas Jimenez (COL), Zbyslaw Zając (POL)			

In the semifinals Pettenella and Trentin set an Olympic record by standing still for 21 minutes 57 seconds.

1968 Mexico City C: 46, N: 27, D: 19.10. WR: 10.61 (Omari Phakadze)

		1ST RACE	2ND RACE
1. Daniel Morelon	FRA	11.27	10.68
2. Giordano Turrini	ITA	—	—
3. Pierre Trentin	FRA		
4. Omari Phakadze	SOV		
5. Jürgen Barth (GER), Johannes Jansen (HOL), Leijn Loevesijn (HOL), Dino Verzini (ITA)			

The tactical highlight of the competition came in the first race of the quarterfinal contest between Dino Verzini and Omari Pkhakadze. The first time out they stood and watched each other until a restart was ordered. The second attempt saw them both stop again, with Phakadge slipping off the banking and causing both of them to slide into the infield. The next restart, the two cyclists stopped for 4 minutes 47 seconds before continuing. This time they made it all the way to the finish with Verzini in the lead. However, Phakadge won the next two races and advanced to the semifinals, where he lost two out of three to Daniel Morelon, the eventual gold medalist. Morelon was a police officer from Bourg-en-Bresse, northeast of Lyon.

1972 Munich C: 51, N: 29, D: 9.2. WR: 10.61 (Omari Phakadze)

		1ST RACE	2ND RACE
1. Daniel Morelon	FRA	11.69	11.25
2. John Nicholson	AUS	—	—
3. Omari Phakadze	SOV		
4. Klaas Balk	HOL		

5. Niels Fredborg (DEN), Hans-Jürgen Geschke (GDR), Massimo Marino (ITA), Peter van Doorn (HOL)

1976 Montreal C: 25, N: 25, D: 7.24. WR: 10.61 (Omari Phakadze)

		1ST RACE	2ND RACE	3RD RACE
1. Anton Tkáč	CZE	10.78	—	11.17
2. Daniel Morelon	FRA	—	11.58	—
3. Hans-Jürgen Geschke	GDR			
4. Dieter Berkmann	GER			
5. Sergei Kravtsov	SOV			
6. Yoshika Cho	JAP			
7. Niels Fredborg	DEN			
8. Giorgio Rossi	ITA			

This was the first time that Olympic cycling events were held indoors. The Czech team got off to a bad start at the Montreal Olympics when all of their wheels and spare tires were inadvertently picked up by garbage collectors and fed into a trash compactor. The final was held the day before the 32nd birthday of Daniel Morelon, the sentimental as well as the betting favorite. But Anton Tkáč, a pipe fitter from Bratislava, jumped early in the tie-breaker, took a five-length lead, and was too strong to be caught. In the first race Tkac had crossed the finish line at almost 42 miles per hour. Morelon's second-place finish earned him his fifth Olympic medal: two golds, one silver, and one bronze in the sprint, and one more gold in the tandem.

1980 Moscow C: 15, N: 15, D: 7.26. WR: 10.61 (Omari Phakadze)

		1ST RACE	2ND RACE	3RD RACE
1. Lutz Hesslich	GDR	11.40	—	12.01
2. Yave Cahard	FRA	—	10.86	—

3. Sergei Kopylov	SOV	—	—	—
4. Anton Tkáč	CZE	—	—	—
5. Henrik Salee	DEN	—	—	—
6. Heinz Isler	SWI	—	—	—
7. Kenrick Tucker	AUS	—	—	—
8. Octavio Dazzan	ITA	—	—	—

1000-METER TIME TRIAL

In the time trial, the competitors take turns racing against the clock.

1896 Athens C: 8, N: 4, D: 4.11.
(333.33 Meters)
1. Paul Masson   FRA   24.0
2. Stamatios Nikolopoulos   GRE   25.4
3. Adolf Schmal   AUT   26.6

1900–1904 not held

1906 Athens C: 24, N: 9, D: 4.23.
(333.33 Meters)
1. Francesco Verri   ITA   22.8
2. H. Crowther   GBR   22.8
3. Menjou   FRA   23.2
4. Emile Demangel   FRA   23.2
5. Debougnie   BEL   23.6
6. F. Della Ferrera   ITA   23.8
7. A. Verdesopoulos   GRE   23.8
8. H.C. Bouffler (GBR), Bruno Götze (GER), Max Götze (GER), 24.2 John Matthews (GBR)

Crowther was awarded second place after winning a race-off. His time was 22.8, while Menjou clocked 23.2 and De-mangel 23.6.

1908–1924 not held

1928 Amsterdam C: 14, N: 14, D: 8.7.
1. Willy Falck Hansen   DEN   1:14.4
2. Gerard Bosch van Drakestein   HOL   1:15.2
3. Edgar Gray   AUS   1:15.6
4. Octave Dayen   FRA   1:16.0
5. Kurt Einsiedel   GER   1:17.2
6. E.J. Kerridge   GBR   1:18.0
6. Józef Lange   POL   1:18.0
8. J. Aerts   BEL   1:18.6

1932 Los Angeles C: 9, N: 9, D: 8.1.
1. Edgar Gray   AUS   1:13.0 OR
2. Jacobus van Egmond   HOL   1:13.3
3. Charles Rampelberg   FRA   1:13.4
4. Luigi Consonni   ITA   1:14.7
4. William Harvell   GBR   1:14.7
6. Lewis Rush   CAN   1:15.6
7. Harald Christensen   DEN   1:16.0
8. Bernard Mammes   USA   1:18.0

1936 Berlin C: 19, N: 19, D: 8.8.
1. Arie van Vliet   HOL   1:12.0   OR
2. Pierre Georget   FRA   1:12.8
3. Rudolf Karsch   GER   1:13.2
4. Benedetto Pola   ITA   1:13.6
5. Arne Pedersen   DEN   1:14.0
5. László Orczán   HUN   1:14.0
7. Raymond Hicks   GBR   1:14.8
8. George Giles   NZE   1:15.0

1948 London C: 21, N: 21, D: 8.11. WR: 1:10.0 (F. Battesini)
1. Jacques Dupont   FRA   1:13.5
2. Pierre Nihant   BEL   1:14.5
3. Thomas Godwin   GBR   1:15.0
4. Hans Fluckiger   SWI   1:15.3
5. Axel Schandorff   DEN   1:15.5
6. Sidney Patterson   AUS   1:15.7
7. John Heid   USA   1:16.2
8. W. Freitag   AUT   1:16.8

1952 Helsinki C: 27, N: 27, D: 7.31. WR: 1:09.8 (Reginald Harris)
1. Russell Mockridge   AUS   1:11.1   OR
2. Marino Morettini   ITA   1:12.7
3. Raymond Robinson   SAF   1:13.0
4. Clodomiro Cortoni   ARG   1:13.2
5. Donald McKellow   GBR   1:13.3
6. Ib Vagn Hansen   DEN   1:14.4
7. Ion Ioniță   ROM   1:14.4
8. Johannes Hijzelendoorn HOL   1:14.5

Russell Mockridge believed that cycling was somewhat boring, but he felt compelled to keep returning to it because it was clearly something that he was very good at. Mockridge worked as a journalist but quit his job. He studied art but dropped out. After competing in the 1948 London Olympics and winning two gold medals at the 1950 British Empire Games, Mockridge told the press, "I feel there is a lot more to this life than riding a bicycle," and announced that he was giving up cycling to become a minister in the Church of England. A few months later he changed his mind again and returned to competitive cycling.

Mockridge seemed assured a place on the 1952 Australian Olympic team until he refused to sign a statement that he would refrain from turning professional for two years. While the controversy over his participation was reaching the floor of Parliament, Mockridge was racing in Europe. A month before the Olympics he became the first amateur to win the Paris Open Grand Prix. Back in Australia, Mockridge's hometown of Geelong worked out a face-saving compromise with the Australian Olympic Federation by which the agreement was limited to one year.

Mockridge arrived in Helsinki four days before he was scheduled to compete. On July 31 he won the gold medal for the time trial and then teamed with Lionel Cox to win a second goal medal in the tandem. Six years later Mockridge was in Melbourne, competing in the 140-mile Tour of Gippsland. Three miles after the start, Mockridge and five other cyclists, followed in a car by Mockridge's wife and 3-year-old daughter, were crossing an intersection when a bus came up on the right and struck Mockridge, killing him instantly. He was 30 years old.

1956 Melbourne C: 22, N: 22, D: 12.6. WR: 1:08.6 (Reginald Harris)
1. Leandro Faggin   ITA   1:09.8   OR
2. Ladislav Fouček   CZE   1:11.4
3. Alfred Swift   SAF   1:11.6
4. Warren Scarfe   AUS   1:12.1
5. Alan Danson   GBR   1:12.3
5. Louis Serra   URU   1:12.3
5. Boris Savostin   SOV   1:12.3
8. Warwick Dalton   NZE   1:12.6

1960 Rome C: 25, N: 25, D: 8.26. WR: 1:07.5 (Sante Gaiardoni)
1. Sante Gaiardoni   ITA   1:07.27   WR
2. Dieter Gieseler   GER   1:08.75
3. Rostislav Vargashkin   SOV   1:08.86
4. Pieter van der Touw   HOL   1:09.20
5. Ian Chapman   AUS   1:09.55
6. Anesio Argenton   BRA   1:09.96
7. Jean Govaerts   BEL   1:10.23
8. Josef Helbling   SWI   1:10.42

1964 Tokyo C: 27, N: 27, D: 10.16. WR: 1:07.27 (Sante Gaiardoni)
1. Patrick Sercu   BEL   1:09.59
2. Giovanni Pettenella   ITA   1:10.09
3. Pierre Trentin   FRA   1:10.42
4. Pieter van der Touw   HOL   1:10.68
5. Jiři Pecka   CZE   1:10.70
6. Lothar Claesges   GER   1:10.86
7. Waclaw Latocha   POL   1:11.12
8. Roger Gibbon   TRI   1:11.19

1968 Mexico City C: 32, N: 32, D: 10.17. WR: 1:04.61 (Gianni Sartori)
1. Pierre Trentin   FRA   1:03.91   WR
2. Niels Fredborg   DEN   1:04.61
3. Janusz Kierzkowski   POL   1:04.63
4. Gianni Sartori   ITA   1:04.65
5. Roger Gibbon   TRI   1:04.66
6. Leijn Loevesijn   HOL   1:04.84
7. Jocelyn Lovell   CAN   1:05.18
8. Sergei Kravtsov   SOV   1:05.21

Trentin won three medals in Mexico City: a gold in the time trial, a gold in the tandem, and a bronze in the sprint.

1972 Munich C: 32, N: 32, D: 8.31. WR: 1:03.91 (Pierre Trentin)
1. Niels Fredborg   DEN   1:06.44
2. Daniel Clark   AUS   1:06.87
3. Jürgen Schütze   GDR   1:07.02
4. Karl Köther   GER   1:07.21
5. Janusz Kierzkowski   POL   1:07.22
6. Dimo Angelov   BUL   1:07.55
7. Christian Brunner   SWI   1:07.71
8. Eduard Rapp   SOV   1:07.73

One of the favorites, Eduard Rapp of the U.S.S.R. was eliminated due to an unfortunate incident. He started before the gun and, assuming he would be ordered to restart, he stopped racing. But the officials ruled his start to be legal, and he was disqualified for stopping.

1976 Montreal C: 30, N: 30, D: 7.20. WR: 1:03.91 (Pierre Trentin)

1. Klaus-Jürgen Grünke	GDR	1:05.927	
2. Michel Vaarten	BEL	1:07.516	
3. Niels Fredborg	DEN	1:07.617	
4. Janusz Kierzkowski	POL	1:07.660	
5. Eric Vermeulen	FRA	1:07.846	
6. Hans Michalsky	GER	1:07.878	
7. Harald Bundli	NOR	1:08.093	
8. Walter Baeni	SWE	1:08.112	

1980 Moscow C: 18, N: 18, D: 7.22. WR: 1:04.225 (José Ruchansky)

1. Lothar Thoms	GDR	1:02.955	WR
2. Aleksandr Panfilov	SOV	1:04.845	
3. David Weller	JAM	1:05.241	
4. Guido Bontempi	ITA	1:05.478	
5. Yave Cahard	FRA	1:05.584	
6. Heinz Isler	SWI	1:06.273	
7. Petr Kocek	CZE	1:06.368	
8. Bjarne Carl Sorensen	DEN	1:07.422	

4000-METER INDIVIDUAL PURSUIT

In pursuit races, two cyclists or teams of cyclists start off on opposite sides of the track. If one cyclist, or team, catches the other, the race is over. Otherwise, the winner is the first one to cross the finish line. Two cyclists or teams take part in the race for first place and two in the race for third. For this reason, the times for third and fourth place are often faster than those for first and second.

1896–1960 not held

1964 Tokyo C: 24, N: 24, D: 10.17. WR: 4:51.20 (Van Looy)

1. Jiři Daler	CZE	5:04.75
2. Giorgio Ursi	ITA	5:05.96
3. Preben Isaksson	DEN	5:01.90
4. Tiemen Groen	HOL	5:04.21
5. Lucjan Józefowicz (POL), Stanislav Moskvin (SOV), Hugh Porter (GBR), Lothar Spiegelberg (GER)		

1968 Mexico City C: 28, N: 28, D: 10.18. WR: 4:45.94 (Jiri Daler)

1. Daniel Rebillard	FRA	4:41.71
2. Mogens Frey Jensen	DEN	4:42.43
3. Xaver Kurmann	SWI	4:39.42
4. John Bylsma	AUS	4:41.60
5. Cipriano Chamello (ITA), Paul Crapez (BEL), Rupert Kratzer (GER), Radamés Treviño (MEX)		

Jensen set a world record of 4:37.54 in the quarterfinals to defeat the favorite, Chamello.

1972 Munich C: 28, N: 28, D: 9.1. WR: 4:37.54 (Mogens Frey Jensen)

1. Knut Knudsen	NOR	4:45.74
2. Xaver Kurmann	SWI	4:51.96
3. Hans Lutz	GER	4:50.80
4. John Christopher Bylsma	AUS	4:54.93
5. Carlos Miguel Alvarez (ARG), Luciano Borgognoi (ITA), Luis Diaz (COL), Roy Schuiten (HOL)		

Knut Knudsen was such an outsider that he didn't even get nervous until the final. Using wheels lent to him by the Danish team, the 21-year-old welder from Levanger took the lead from Kurmann after the fourth of 14 laps and pulled away to win comfortably.

1976 Montreal C: 28, N: 28, D: 7.22. WR: 4:37.54 (Mogens Frey Jensen)

1. Gregor Braun	GER	4:47.61
2. Herman Ponsteen	HOL	4:49.72
3. Thomas Huschke	GDR	4:52.71
4. Vladimir Osokin	SOV	4:57.34
5. Jan Iversen (NOR), Michal Klasa (CZE), Orfeo Pizzoferrato (ITA), Garry Sutton (AUS)		

The crucial match-up occurred in the semifinals, when the 20-year-old Braun upset Osokin by 0.17 seconds, as both men recorded personal bests.

1980 Moscow C: 14, N: 14, D: 7.24. WR: 4:34.66 (Uwe Unterwalder)

1. Robert Dill-Bundi	SWI	4:35.66
2. Alain Bondue	FRA	4:42.96
3. Hans-Henrik Örsted	DEN	4:36.54
4. Harald Wolf	GDR	4:37.58
5. Pierangelo Bincoletto (ITA), Vladimir Osokin (SOV), Martin Penc (CZE), Sean Yates (GBR)		

In the semifinals Robert Dill-Bundi set a world record of 4:32.29. After his victory in the final he got off his bike and kissed the track.

4000-METER TEAM PURSUIT

1896–1906 not held

1908 London T: 5, N: 5, D: 7.17.
(1810.5 Meters)

1. GBR	(Leonard Meredith, Benjamin Jones, Ernest Payne, Charles Kingsbury)	2:18.6
2. GER	(Hermann Martens, Bruno Götze, Karl Neumer, Richard Katzer)	2:28.6
3. CAN	(William Morton, Walter Andrews, Frederick McCarthy, William Anderson)	2:29.6
4. HOL	(Johasses van Spengen, Antonie Gerrits, Dorotheus Nijland, Gerard Bosch van Drakestein)	2:44.0

1912 not held

1920 Antwerp T: 5, N: 5, D: 8.12.
1. ITA   (Franco Giorgetti, Ruggero Ferrario, Arnaldo   5:20.0
         Carli, Primo Magnani)
2. GBR   (Albert White, H. Thomas Johnson, William Stew-
         art, Cyril Albert Alden)
3. SAF   (James Walker, William Smith, Henry Justaves
         Kaltenbrun, Harry Goosen)
4. BEL   (Albert de Buinne, Charles van Doorselaer, Gus-
         tave Deschryver, Jean Janssens)

The British team actually finished first, but a protest of interference was allowed and Italy was awarded first place.

1924 Paris T: 10, N: 10, D: 7.27.
1. ITA   (Angelo De Martino, Alfredo Dinale, Aleardo   5:15.0
         Menegazzi, Francesco Zucchetti)
2. POL   (Józef Lange, Jan Lazarski, Tomasz Stan-   —
         kiewicz, Franciszek Szymczyk)
3. BEL   (Léonard Daghelinckx, Henri Hoevenaers, Fer-   —
         nand Saive, Jean van den Bosch)
4. FRA   (Lucien Choury, Joseph Vuillemin, R. Hournon,   —
         Marcel Renaud)

The French team set an Olympic record of 5:11.4 in the
heats.

1928 Amsterdam T: 12, N: 12, D: 8.7.
1. ITA   (Luigi Tasselli, Giacomo Gaioni, Cesare   5:01.8
         Facciani, Mario Lusiani)
2. HOL   (Adriaan Braspenninx, Jacobus Maas, Johannes   5:06.2
         Pijnenburg, Piet van der Horst)
3. GBR   (Frank Wyld, Leonard Wyld, Percy Wyld, M.   —
         George Southall)
4. FRA   (André Aumerle, Octave Dayen, René Brossy,   —
         André Trantoul)
5. BEL (G. Meuleman, Y. van Massenhove, A. Muylle, J. van
   Buggenhout), CAN (L.R. Elder, J. Davies, A. Houting, W.S.
   Peden), GER (Josef Steger, Anton Joksch, Kurt Einsiedel, Hans
   Dornebach), POL (Jozef Lange, Artur Reul, Jan Zybert, Józef
   Oksiutycz)

The British team set on Olympic record of 5:11.2 in the
quarter finals. Three of the four British riders were the
Wyld brothers from Derby: Frank, Leonard, and Percy.

1932 Los Angeles T: 5, N: 5, D: 8.3.
1. ITA   (Marco Cimatti, Paolo Pedretti, Alberto Ghilardi,   4:53.0
         Nino Borsari)
2. FRA   (Amédée Fournier, René Legrèves, Henri Mouil-   4:55.7
         lefarine, Paul Chocque)
3. GBR   (Ernest Johnson, William Harvell, Frank Southall,   4:56.0
         Charles Holland)
4. CAN   (Lewis Rush, Glen Robbins, Russell Hunt, Fran-   6:04.0
         cis Elliott)

The Italian team set an Olympic record of 4:52.9 in the
heats.

1936 Berlin T: 13, N: 13, D: 8.8.
1. FRA   (Robert Charpentier, Jean Goujan, Guy Lapébie,   4:45.0
         Roger Le Nizerhy)

2. ITA   (Bianco Bianchi, Mario Gentili, Armando Latini,   4:51.0
         Severino Rigoni)
3. GBR   (Harry Hill, Ernest Johnson, Charles King, Ernest   4:53.6
         Mills)
4. GER   (Erich Arndt, Heinz Hasselberg, Heiner Hoffman,   4:55.0
         Karl Klockner)

The French team set an Olympic record of 4:41.8 in the
heats.

1948 London T: 15, N: 15, D: 8.9.
1. FRA   (Charles Coste, Serge Blusson, Ferdinand De-   4:57.8
         canali, Pierre Adam)
2. ITA   (Arnaldo Benfenati, Guido Bernardi, Anselmo   5:36.7
         Citterio, Rino Pucci)
3. GBR   (Alan Geldard, Thomas Godwin, David Ricketts,   4:55.8
         Wilfred Waters)
4. URU   (Atilio François, Juan De Armas, Luis De Los   5:04.4
         Santos, W. Bernatsky)
5. AUS (S. Patterson, E. Nestor, J. Hoobin, Russell Mockridge),
   BEL (J. DeBeukelaere, M. Blomme, G. van Brabant, R. Glorieux),
   DEN (M. Jorgensen, B. Gissel, B. Mortensen, B. Schnoor), SWI
   (W. Bucher, G. Gerosa, E. Kamber, Hans Pfenninger)

1952 Helsinki T: 22, N: 22, D: 7.29.
1. ITA   (Marino Morettini, Guido Messina, Mino De Ros-   4:46.1
         si, Loris Campana)
2. SAF   (Thomas Shardelow, Alfred Swift, Robert Fowler,   4:53.6
         George Estman)
3. GBR   (Ronald Stretton, Alan Newton, George New-   4:51.5
         berry, Donald Burgess)
4. FRA   (Henri Andrieux, Pierre Michel, Jean-Marie Jou-   4:51.9
         bert, Claude Brugerolles)
5. BEL (Gabriel Glorieux, José Pauwels, Robert Raymond, Paul de
   Paepe), DEN (Knud Andersen, Edvard Preben Lundgren-Kristen-
   sen, J. Hansen, Bent Jorgensen), HOL (Johannes Plantaz,
   Adrianus Voorting, Daniël de Groot, Jules Maenen), SWI (Hans
   Pfenninger, Heini Müller, Max Wirth, Oscar von Büren)

1956 Melbourne T: 16, N: 16, D: 12.4.   4:37.4 OR
1. ITA   (Leandro Faggin, Valentino Gasparella, An-
         tonio Domenicali, Franco Gandini)
2. FRA   (Michel Vermeulin, Jean-Claude Lecante,   4:39.4
         René Bianchi, Jean Graczyk)
3. GBR   (Donald Burgess, Michael Gambrill, John   4:42.4
         Geddes, Thomas Simpson)
4. SAF   (Alfred Swift, Robert Fowler, Charles Jonker,   4:43.8
         Anne-Jan Hettema)
5. BEL (André Bar, Gustave de Smet, François de. Wagheneire,
   Guillaume Van Tongerloo), CZE (Jaroslav Cihlar, Jiři. Opavsky,
   Jiři Nouza, František Jursa), NZE (Warwick Dalton, Donald Eagle, Leonard Kent, Neil Ritchie), SOV (Victor Iliine, Vladimir Mi-
   tine, Rodislav Tchijikov, Edouard Goussev)

Great Britain won its sixth straight bronze medal in the
team pursuit.

1960 Rome T: 19, N: 19, D: 8.29.
1. ITA   (Luigi Arienti, Franco Testa, Mario Vallotto, Mari-   4:30.90
         no Vigna)

2. GDR (Siegfried Köhler, Peter Gröning, Manfred 4:35.78
Klieme, Bernd Barleben)
3. SOV (Stanislav Moskvin, Viktor Romanov, Leonid Ko- 4:34.05
lumbet, Arnold Belgardt)
4. FRA (Marcel Delattre, Jacques Suire, Guy Claud, Mi- 4:35.72
chel Nedelec)
5. ARG (Alberto Trillo, Ernesto Contreros, Hector Agosta, Juan
Brotto), CZE (Slavoy Cerny, Ferdinand Duchon, Jan Chlistovsky,
Josef Volf), DEN (John Lundgren, Leif Larsen, Jens Sorensen,
Kurt Stein), HOL (Jacob Oudkerk, Theodorus Nikkessen, Hendrix Nijdam, Petrus van der Lans)

The Italian team set an Olympic record of 4:28.88 in the
semifinals.

1964 Tokyo T: 18, N: 18, D: 10.21. WR: 4:26.60 (West Germany)
1. GER (Lothar Claesges, Karlheinz Henrichs, Karl Link, 4:35.67
Ernst Streng)
2. ITA (Luigi Roncaglia, Vincenzo Mantovani, Carlo 4:35.74
Rancati, Franco Testa)
3. HOL (Gerard Koel, Hendrik Cornelissen, Jacob Oud- 4:38.99
kerk, Cornelis Schuuring)
4. AUS (Kevin Brislin, Robert Baird, Victor Browne, Hen- 4:39.42
drikus Vogels)
5. ARG (Carlos Alvarez, Ernesto Contreras, Juan Alberto Merlos,
Alberto Trillo), CZE (Jiři Daller, Antonin Kritz, Jiři Pecka, František
Rezac), DEN (Bent Kurt Hansen, Preben Isaksson, Alf Johansen,
Kurt Vid Stein), SOV (Zintars Latsis, Leonid Kolumbet, Stanislav
Moskvin, Sergei Terechenkov)

The world champion German team broke the Italian pursuit monopoly in dramatic fashion. The two teams raced
evenly for the last quarter of the contest. The finish was so
close that it took ten minutes to determine the winner, despite the use of electronic timing devices.

1968 Mexico City T: 20, N: 20, D: 10.21. WR: 4:20.64 (Italy)
1. DEN (Gunnar Asmussen, Per Pedersen Lyngemark, 4:22.44
Reno Olsen, Mogens Frey Jensen)
2. GER (Udo Hempel, Karl Link, Karlheinz Henrichs, Jür- 4:18.94
gen Kissner)
3. ITA (Lorenzo Bosisio, Cipriano Chemello, Luigi Ron- 4:18.35
caglia, Giorgio Morbiato)
4. SOV (Dzintars Latsis, Stanislav Moskvin, Vladimir 4:33.39
Kuznyetsov, Mikhail Kolyuschev)
5. BEL (Ernest Bens, Ronny Vanmarcke, Willy Debosscher, Paul
Crapez), CZE (Jiři Daler, Pavel Kondr, Milan Puzrla, František
Rezac), FRA (Bernard Darmet, Daniel Rebillard, Jack Mourioux,
Alain Van Lancker), POL (Wojciech Matusiak, Janusz Kierzkowski, Waclaw Latocha, Rajmund Zieliński)

In the qualifying round the West Germans set a world record of 4:19.90, which was broken quickly by the Italians
at 4:16.10. In the first semifinal the Germans took back the
record by beating the Italians 4:15.76 to 4:16.21. The final
saw the exhausted West Germans hold on to finish first.
But with one lap to go, Jürgen Kissner touched his teammate Karlheinz Henrichs on the back. The Danes protested that the "touch" had been an illegal shove. Their
protest was upheld, and West Germany was disqualified.

At first it was announced that Italy would receive the silver medal and the U.S.S.R. the bronze, but a post-Olympic
decision allowed the Germans to retain second place.

1972 Munich T: 22, N: 22, D: 9.4.
1. GER (Jürgen Colombo, Günter Haritz, Udo Hempel, 4:22.14
Günther Schumacher)
2. GDR (Thomas Huschke, Heinz Richter, Herbert Rich- 4:25.25
ter, Uwe Unterwalder)
3. GBR (Michael Bennett, Ian Hallam, Ronald Keeble, 4:23.78
William Moore)
4. POL (Bernard Kręczyński, Pawel Kaczorowski, Jan- 4:26.06
usz Kierzkowski, Mieczyslaw Nowicki)
5. BUL (Nikifor Petrov, Plamen Timchev, Dimo Angelov, Ivan Stan-
oev), HOL (Ad Dekkers, Gerard Kamper, Herman Ponsteen, Roy
Schuiten), SOV (Viktor Bykov, Vladimir Kuznyetsov Anatoly Ste-
panenko, Aleksandr Yudin), SWI (Martin Steger, Xaver Kurmann,
René Savary, Christian Brunner)

The dramatic confrontation between the two German
teams turned out to be a one-sided affair, as the West Germans took an early lead and were up by 3.82 seconds with
1000 meters to go.

1976 Montreal T: 16, N: 16, D: 7.24.
1. GER (Gregor Braun, Hans Lutz, Günther Schu- 4:21.06
macher, Peter Vonhof)
2. SOV (Vladimir Osokin, Aleksandr Perov, Vitaly Petra- 4:27.15
kov, Victor Sokolov)
3. GBR (Ian Banbury, Michael Bennett, Robin Croker, Ian 4:22.41
Hallam)
4. GDR (Norbert Dürpisch, Thomas Huschke, Uwe Un- 4:22.75
terwalder, Matthias Wiegand)
5. CZE (Ždenek Dohnal, Michal Klasa, Petr Koček, Jiři Pokorny),
HOL (Gerrit Mohlmann, Peter Nieuwenhuis, Herman Ponsteen,
Gerrit Slot), ITA (Sandro Callari, Cesare Cipollini, Rino de Can-
dido, Giuseppe Saronni), POL (Jan Jankiewicz, Czeslaw Lang,
Krzysztof Sujka, Zbigniew Szczepkowski)

The world champion West German team filled their tires
with helium instead of air because it was lighter. They also
arrived in Montreal with one-piece silk racing suits, which
they were not allowed to use because of the unfair aerody-
namic advantage it would have given them.

1980 Moscow C: 13, N: 13, D: 7.26.
1. SOV (Vikton Manakov, Valery Movchan, Vladimir 4:15.70
Osokin, Vitaly Petrakov)
2. GDR (Gerald Mortag, Uwe Unterwalder, Matthias 4:19.67
Wiegand, Volker Winkler)
3. CZE (Teodor Černý, Martin Penc, Jiři Pokorný, Igor Over-
Sláma) took
4. ITA (Pierangelo Bincoletto, Guido Bontempi, Ivano
Maffei, Silvestro Milani)
5. AUS (Colin Fitzgerald, Kevin Nichols, Kelvin Poole, Garry Sutton)
FRA (Alain Bondue, Philippe Chevalier, Pascal Poisson, Jean-
Marc Rebiere), GBR (Anthony Doyle, Malcolm Elliott, Glen Mitch-
ell, Sean Yates), SWI (Robert Dill-Bundi, Urs Fleuler, Hans
Kaenel, Hans Ledermann)

The Soviet team set a world record of 4:14.64 in the quarterfinals, achieving a speed of 56.55 kilometers per hour.

INDIVIDUAL ROAD RACE

1896 Athens C: 6, N: 3, D: 4.12.
87 KM

1. Aristidis Konstantinidis	GRE	3:22:31.0
2. August Goedrich	GER	3:42:18.0
3. F. Battel	GBR	—
4. Minas Konstantinou	GRE	—
4. G. Aspiotis	GRE	—
4. M. Iatrou	GRE	—

The cyclists raced from Athens to Marathon, where they signed their names, and then rode back again on the same road. Konstantinidis had to use three different bicycles, as his first two broke down.

1900–1904 not held

1906 Athens C: 24, N: 9, D: 5.1.
84 KM

1. Fernand Vast	FRA	2:41:28.0
2. Maurice Bardonneau	FRA	2:41:28.4
3. Edmond Luguet	FRA	2:41:28.6
4. Prospère Verschelden-Romeo	BEL	—
5. Ad. Böhm	GER	—
6. I. Petritsas	GRE	—
7. C. Andreasen	DEN	—
8. Hans Holly	AUT	—

1908 not held

1912 Stockholm C: 123, N: 16, D: 7.7.
320 KM

1. Rudolph "Okey" Lewis	SAF	10:42:39.0
2. Frederick Grubb	GBR	10:51:24.2
3. Carl Schutte	USA	10:52:38.8
4. Leonard Meredith	GBR	11:00:02.6
5. Frank Brown	CAN	11:01:00.0
6. Antti Raita	FIN	11:02:20.3
7. Eric Friborg	SWE	11:04:17.0
8. Ragnar Malm	SWE	11:08:14.5

This grueling 199-mile race around Lake Malan was begun at 2:00 a.m. The competitors were sent out on the course at two-minute intervals over the next four hours. "Okey" Lewis of South Africa began at an unusually fast pace and held an 11½-minute lead at the 120 km control station. He increased this lead to 17 minutes at 200km and held on for the last 4¼ hours to win by 8¾ minutes. While racing in Germany, Lewis got caught up in World War I. He was wounded several times and incarcerated in prison camps. He returned to Johannesburg after the war in very poor health, but survived until 1933.

There was one terrible accident at the beginning of the race. A few hundred meters after the start, Karl Landsberg

of Sweden was hit by a motor-wagon and dragged along for some distance before the wagon stopped.

1920 Antwerp C: 46, N: 13, D: 8.9.-12.
175 KM

1. Harry Stenqvist	SWE	4:40:01.8
2. Henry Kaltenbrun	SAF	4:41:26.6
3. Fernand Canteloube	FRA	4:42:54.4
4. Jean Janssens	BEL	4:44:20.6
5. Albert de Buinne	BEL	4:45:23.4
6. Georges Detreille	FRA	4:46:13.4
7. Ragnar Malm	SWE	—
8. Piet Ikelaar	HOL	—

The course was intersected by six railway crossings which might be closed at any time. Timekeepers were posted at each crossing to record any delays. At first it appeared that Kaltenbrun had won, and his victory was acknowledged by triumphant music in the stadium. However, it was later learned that Stenqvist had been held up for four minutes at a railway crossing, and the subtraction from his time put him into first place.

1924 Paris C: 72, N: 22, D: 7.23.
188 KM

1. Armand Blanchonnet	FRA	6:20:48.0
2. Henri Hoevenaers	BEL	6:30:27.0
3. René Hamel	FRA	6:30:51.6
4. Gunnar Sköld	SWE	6:33:36.2
5. Albert Blattmann	SWE	6:34:09.0
6. Alphonse Pardondry	BEL	6:35:57.0
7. Eric Bohlin	SWE	6:36:12.4
8. Georges Wambst	FRA	6:38:34.4

1928 Amsterdam C: 63, N: 21, D: 8.7.
168 KM

1. Henry Hansen	DEN	4:47:18.0
2. Frank Southall	GBR	4:55:06.0
3. Gösta Carlsson	SWE	5:00:17.0
4. Allegro Grandi	ITA	5:02:05.0
5. Jack Lauterwasser	GBR	5:02:57.0
6. Gottlieb Amstein	SWI	5:04:48.0
7. Leo Nielsen	DEN	5:05:37.0
8. A. Aumerle	FRA	5:07:12.0

1932 Los Angeles C: 33, N: 11, D: 8.4.
100 KM

1. Attilio Pavesi	ITA	2:28:05.6
2. Guglielmo Segato	ITA	2:29:21.4
3. Bernhard Britz	SWE	2:29:45.2
4. Giuseppe Olmo	ITA	2:29:48.2
5. Frode Sörensen	DEN	2:30:11.2
6. Frank Southall	GBR	2:30:16.2
7. Giovanni Cazzulani	ITA	2:31:07.2
8. Sven Hoglund	SWE	2:31:29.4

The contestants were not allowed outside assistance during the race. According to *Time* magazine, Pavesi carried with him a bowl of soup, a bucket of water, bananas, cinnamon rolls, jam, cheese sandwiches, spaghetti, and two spare tires.

1936 Berlin C: 100, N: 29, D: 8.10.
100 KM

1.	Robert Charpentier	FRA	2:33:05.0
2.	Guy Lapébie	FRA	2:33:05.2
3.	Ernst Nievergelt	SWI	2:33:05.8
4.	Fritz Scheller	GER	2:33:06.0
4.	Charles Holland	GBR	2:33:06.0
4.	Robert Dorgebray	FRA	2:33:06.0
7.	Pierino Favalli	ITA	2:33:06.2
8.	Auguste Garrebeek	BEL	2:33:06.6
8.	Armand Putzeys	BEL	2:33:06.6
8.	Tuncalp	TUR	2:33:06.6

For the first time, all the competitors started together rather than at intervals. This, coupled with the narrow road, caused numerous accidents and injuries during the last five kilometers. Charpentier had already won a gold medal in the team pursuit two days earlier.

1948 London C: 101, N: 29, D: 8.13.
194.63 KM

1.	José Beyaert	FRA	5:18:12.6
2.	Gerardus Petrus Voorting	HOL	5:18:16.2
3.	Lode Wouters	BEL	5:18:16.2
4.	Léon Delathouwer	BEL	5:18:16.2
5.	Nils Johansson	SWE	5:18:16.2
6.	Robert Maitland	GBR	5:18:16.2
7.	J. Hoobin	AUS	5:18:18.2
8.	Gordon Thomas	GBR	5:18:18.2

Beyaert, a 22 year-old shoemaker from Lens, sprinted ahead with half a mile to go and won by 8 lengths.

1952 Helsinki C: 112, N: 30, D: 8.2.
190.4 KM

1.	André Noyelle	BEL	5:06:03.4
2.	Robert Grondelaers	BEL	5:06:51.2
3.	Edi Ziegler	GER	5:07:47.5
4.	Lucien Victor	BEL	5:07:52.0
5.	Dino Bruni	ITA	5:10:54.0
6.	Vincenzo Zucconelli	ITA	5:11:16.5
7.	Gianni Ghidini	ITA	5:11:16.8
8.	Oscar Zeissner	GER	5:11:18.5

1956 Melbourne C: 88, N: 28, D: 12.7.
187.73 KM

1.	Ercole Baldini	ITA	5:21:17.0
2.	Arnaud Geyre	FRA	5:23:16.0
3.	Alan Jackson	GBR	5:23:16.0
4.	Hörst Tuller	GDR	5:23:16.0
5.	Gustav-Adolf Schur	GDR	5:23:16.0
6.	A. Stanley Brittain	GBR	5:23:40.0
7.	Arnaldo Pambianco	ITA	5:23:40.0
8.	Maurice Moucheraud	FRA	5:23:40.0

The year 1956 was known as "Baldini's Year," because the 23-year-old Italian won the world championship in the 4000-meter pursuit, set a world record for the one-hour race, and won the Olympic road race by a full mile. His victory was protested by the French and British, who charged that in the later stages of the race he had been protected from the hot sun by the Olympic film unit van that rode alongside him. The protest was rejected. The start of the race was delayed fifteen minutes when it was discovered that two "unauthorized" Irish bicyclists, butcher Tom Gerrard and carpenter Paul Fitzgerald, were in the middle of the 88 starters. After they were removed, they joined 200 supporters in passing out Irish nationalist literature.

1960 Rome C: 148, N: 42, D: 8.30.
175.38 KM

1.	Viktor Kapitonov	SOV	4:20:37.0
2.	Livio Trapé	ITA	4:20:37.0
3.	Willy van den Berghen	BEL	4:20:57.0
4.	Yuri Melikhov	SOV	4:20:57.0
5.	Ion Cosma	ROM	4:20:57.0
6.	Stanislaw Gazda	POL	4:20:57.0
7.	Benoni Beheyt	BEL	4:20:57.0
8.	Janez Zirovnik	YUG	4:20:57.0

Kapitonov sprinted to the finish line to defeat Trape by inches, only to discover that he still had one more 14½-km lap to go. Twenty-four minutes later, the scene was repeated but this time Kapitonov's victory was official. Kapitonov later joined the editorial board of *Theory and Practice of Physical Culture* magazine and became the manager of the U.S.S.R. cycling team.

The race, which was run in 93-degree heat, was marred by the death of Danish cyclist Knut Jensen, who collapsed from sunstroke and suffered a fractured skull. It was later determined that before the race Jensen had taken Ronicol, a blood circulation stimulant. Jensen was the first person to die in Olympic competition since the 1912 marathon.

1964 Tokyo C: 132, N: 35, D: 10.22.
194.83 KM

1.	Mario Zanin	ITA	4:39:51.63
2.	Kjell Åkerström Rodian	DEN	4:39:51.65
3.	Walter Godefroot	BEL	4:39:51.74
4.	Raymond Bilney	AUS	4:39:51.74
5.	José Lopez Rodriguez	SPA	4:39:51.74
6.	Wilfried Peffgen	GER	4:39:51.74
7.	Gösta Pettersson	SWE	4:39:51.74
8.	Delmo Delmastro	ARG	4:39:51.74

A spectacular finish saw Zanin, a mechanic from Treviso, emerge from the pack with 20 meters to go and win by a wheel. Sture Pettersson of Sweden finished only sixteen-hundredths of a second behind Zanin, yet he ended up in 51st place.

1968 Mexico City C: 144, N: 44, D: 10.23.
196.2 KM

1. Pierfranco Vianelli	ITA	4:41:25.24
2. Leif Mortensen	DEN	4:42:49.71
3. Gösta Pettersson	SWE	4:43:15.24
4. Stephan Abrahamian	FRA	4:43:36.54
5. Marinus Pijnen	HOL	4:43:36.81
6. Jean-Pierre Monsère	BEL	4:43:51.77
7. Tomas Pettersson	SWE	4:43:58.11
8. Giovanni Bramucci	ITA	4:43:58.19

1972 Munich C: 163, N: 48, D: 9.7.
182.4KM

1. Hennie Kuiper	HOL	4:14:37.0
2. Kevin Clyde Sefton	AUS	4:15:04.0
— Jaime Huelamo	SPA	4:15:04.0
3. Bruce Bidole	NZE	4:15:04.0
4. Philip Bayton	GBR	4:15:07.0
5. Philip Edwards	GBR	4:15:13.0
6. Wilfried Trott	GER	4:15:13.0
7. Francesco Moser	ITA	4:15:13.0
8. Miguel Samaca	COL	4:15:21.0

The four Dutch contestants rode a team race with Cees Priem and Fedor Den Hertog protecting Kuiper and fighting off challengers. Freddy Maertens was so frustrated by Priem's dogged persistance in sticking to his wheel that he tried to hit Priem in the face. Said Priem, "We worked for Hennie because he is one of the nicest blokes around." Four Irish Republican Army cyclists joined the race to protest the fact that the Irish Cycling Federation competed against cyclists from Northern Ireland. One of them tried to run Irish Olympian Noel Taggart into a ditch. The 4 IRA cyclists were arrested but later released without charge.

Third-place finisher Jaime Huelamo was disqualified after he failed a test for drugs.

1976 Montreal C: 134, N: 40, D: 7.26.
175 KM

1. Bernt Johansson	SWE	4:46:52.0
2. Giuseppe Martinelli	ITA	4:47:23.0
3. Mieczyslaw Nowicki	POL	4:47:23.0
4. Alfons de Wolf	BEL	4:47:23.0
5. Nikolai Gorelov	SOV	4:47:23.0
6. George Mount	USA	4:47:23.0
7. Jean René Bernaudeau	FRA	4:47:23.0
8. Vittorio Algeri	ITA	4:47:23.0

Peter Thaler of Germany crossed the finish line in second place, but was demoted to ninth because he had interfered with Martinelli in the final sprint.

1980 Moscow C: 112, N: 32, D: 7.28.
189 KM

1. Sergei Sukhoruchenkov	SOV	4:48:28.9
2. Czeslaw Lang	POL	4:51:26.9
3. Yuri Barinov	SOV	4:51:29.9
4. Thomas Barth	GDR	4:56:12.9
5. Tadeusz Wojtas	POL	4:56:12.9
6. Anatoly Yarkin	SOV	4:56:54.9
7. Adri van der Poel	HOL	4:56:54.9
8. Christian Faure	FRA	4:56:54.9

Sukhoruchenkov pulled away with 20 miles to go to win by the largest Olympics margin since 1928.

TEAM ROAD RACE

Until 1960 the results of the individual road race were used to determine the team winner. However, starting with the 1960 Rome Olympics a separate team event was held.

1896–1908 not held

1912 Stockholm T: 15, N: 15, D: 7.7.
320 KM

		COMBINED TIME
1. SWE	(Eric Friborg, Ragnar Malm, Axel Persson, Algot Lönn)	44:35:33.6
2. GBR	(Frederick Grubb, Leonard Meredith, Charles Moss, Victor Hammond)	44:44:39.2
3. USA	(Carl Schutte, Alvin Loftes, Albert Krushel, Walter Martin)	44:47:55.5
4. GBR	(John Wilson, Robert Thompson, John Miller, D.M. Stevensen)	46:29:55.1
5. FIN	(Antti Raita, V.O. Tilkanen, J.W. Kankonnen, Hjalmar Väre)	46:34:03.5
6. GER	(Franz Lemnitz, Rudolf Baier, Oswald Rathmann, Georg Warsow)	46:35:16.1
7. AUT	(Robert Rammer, Adolf Kofler, Rudolf Kramer, Josef Hellensteiner)	46:57:26.4
8. DEN	(O. Meyland-Smith, Charles Hansen, C.J. Reinwald, Hans Olsen)	47:16:07.0

1920 Antwerp T: 11, N: 11, D: 8.9.
175 KM

		COMBINED TIME
1. FRA	(Fernand Canteloube, Georges Detreille, Achille Souchard, Marcel Gobillot)	19:16:43.2
2. SWE	(Harry Stenqvist, Ragnar Malm, Axel Persson, Sigfrid Lundberg)	19:23:10.0
3. BEL	(Jean Janssens, Albert de Buinne, André Vercruysse, Albert Wyckmans)	19:28:44.4
4. DEN	(Christian Johansen, Arnold Lundgren, Christian Frisch, Ahrensberg Clausen)	19:52:35.0
5. ITA	(Federico Gay, Pietro Bestetti, Camillo Arduino, Dante Guindani)	20:24:44.0
6. HOL	(Petrus Ikelaar, Nico de Jong, Arie Gerrit van der Stel, Pieter Kloppenburg)	20:28:39.2

1924 Paris T: 16, N: 16, D: 7.23.
188 KM

		COMBINED TIME
1. FRA	(Armand Blanchonnet, René Hamel, Georges Wambst)	19:30:14.0

2. BEL (Henri Hoevenaers, Alphonse Parfondry, 19:46:55.4
Jean van den Bosch)
3. SWE (Gunnar Sköld, Erik Bohlin, Ragnar Malm) 19:59:41.6
4. SWI (Albert Blattmann, Otto Lehner, Georg An- 20:11:15.0
tenen)
5. ITA (Ardito Bresciani, Antonio Negrini, Nello 20:19:59.2
Ciaccheri)
6. HOL (C. Heeren, Jan Maas, Phillippus Hendrik 20:37:27.8
Innemee)

1928 Amsterdam T: 15, N: 15, D: 8.7.
168 KM

		COMBINED TIME
1. DEN	(Henry Hansen, Leo Nielsen, Orla Jörgensen)	15:09:14.0
2. GBR	(Frank Southall, Jack Lauterwasser, John Middleton)	15:14:49.0
3. SWE	(Gösta Carlsson, Erik Jansson, E. Georg Johnsson)	15:27:49.0
4. ITA	(Allegro Grandi, Michele Orecchia, Ambrogio Beretta)	15:33:12.0
5. BEL	(Jean Aerts, Pierre Houdé, Joseph Lowagie)	15:33:50.0
6. SWI	(Gottlieb Amstein, Jakob Caironi, Tütel Wanzenried)	15:35:21.0
7. FRA	(A. Aumerle, L. Bessiere, O. Dayen)	15:38:20.0
8. ARG	(C. Saavedra, F. Bonvehi, J. Lopez)	15:42:55.0

1932 Los Angeles T: 8, N: 8, D: 8.4.
100 KM

		COMBINED TIME
1. ITA	(Attilio Pavesi, Guglieimo Segato, Giuseppe Olmo)	7:27:15.2
2. DEN	(Frode Sörensen, Leo Nielsen, Henry Hansen)	7:38:50.2
3. SWE	(Bernhard Britz, Sven Höglund, A. Arne Berg)	7:39:12.6
4. GBR	(Frank Southall, Charles Holland, Stanley Butler)	7:44:53.0
5. FRA	(Paul Chocque, Amédée Fournier, Henri Mouillefarine)	7:46:31.8
6. USA	(Henry O'Brien, Frank Connell, Otto Luedeke)	7:51:55.6
7. CAN	(Frances Elliott, James Jackson, Francis Robbins)	8:01:38.0
8. GER	(Hubert Ebner, W. Lange-Wittich, Julius Maus)	8:21:21.2

1936 Berlin T: 22, N: 22, D: 8.10.
100 KM

		COMBINED TIME
1. FRA	(Robert Charpentier, Guy Lapébie, Robert Dorgebray)	7:39:16.2
2. SWI	(Ernst Nievergelt, Edgar Buchwalder, Kurt Ott)	7:39:20.4
3. BEL	(Auguste Garrebeek, Armand Putzeys, Francois Vandermette)	7:39:21.0

4. ITA (Pierino Favalli, Glauco Servadei, Corrado 7:39:22.0
Ardizzoni)
5. AUT (Virgilius Altmann, Hans Höfner, Hans 7:39:24.0
Schnalek)

1948 London T: 25, N: 25, D: 8.13.
194.63 KM

		COMBINED TIME
1. BEL	(Lode Wouters, Léon Delathouwer, Eugène van Roosbroeck)	15:58:17.4
2. GBR	(Robert Maitland, Gordon Thomas, C.S. Ian Scott)	16:03:31.6
3. FRA	(José Beyaert, Alain Moineau, Jacques Dupont)	16:08:19.4
4. ITA	(Alfo Ferrari, Silvio Pedroni, Franco Fanti)	16:13:05.2
5. SWE	(Nils Johansson, Harry Snell, Åke Olivestedt)	16:20:26.6
6. SWI	(Jakob Schenk, Jean Brun, Walter Reiser)	16:23:04.2
7. ARG	(C. Perone, D. Benvenuti, M. Sevillano)	16:39:46.2

1952 Helsinki T: 27, N: 27, D: 8.2.
190.4 KM

		COMBINED TIME
1. BEL	(André Noyelle, Robert Grondelaers, Lucien Victor)	15:20:46.6
2. ITA	(Dino Bruni, Vincenzo Zucconelli, Gianni Ghidini)	15:33:27.3
3. FRA	(Jacques Anquetil, Alfred Tonello, Claud Rover)	15:38:58.1
4. SWE	(Yngve Lundh, Stig Mårtensson, Allan Carlsson)	15:41:34.3
5. GER	(Edi Ziegler, Oskar Zeissner, Paul Maue)	15:43:50.5
6. DEN	(Hans Andersen, Jörgen Rasmussen, Poul Östergaard)	15:48:02.0
7. LUX	(André Moes, Roger Ludwig, Nicolas Morn)	15:49:04.0
8. HOL	(Arend Van't Hof, Johannes Planatz, Adrianus. Voorting)	15:52:22.7

1956 Melbourne T: 20, N: 20, D: 12.7.
187.73 KM

		PTS.
1. FRA	(2—Arnaud Geyre, 8—Maurice Moucheraud, 12—Michel Vermeulin)	22
2. GBR	(3—Alan Jackson, 6—Arthur Stanley Brittain, 14—William Holmes)	23
3. GDR/ GER	(4—Horst Tüller, 5—Gustav-Adolf Schur, 18— Reinhold Pommer)	27
4. ITA	(1—Ercole Baldini, 7—Arnaldo Pambianco, 28—Dino Bruni	36
5. SWE	(10—Lars Nordwall, 17—Karl-Ivan Andersson, 20—Roland Ströhm)	47
6. SOV	(15—Anatoly Cherepovich, 16—Nikolai Kolumbet, 32—Viktor Kapitonov)	63
7. BEL	(23—Norbert Verougstraete, 24—Gustave De Smet, 42—François van den Bosch)	89
8. COL	(13—Ramon Hoyos Vallejo, 39—Pablo Hurtada Castañeda 40—Jaime Villegas)	92

In 1956 the placings in the team road race were determined not by combined times, but by adding together the individual placings of the team members. Great Britain lost its chance for a gold medal when Billy Holmes crashed into a photographer who had stepped onto the course. Holmes was injured, but worse still, was delayed two and a half minutes while he changed a wheel. Holmes caught up with the leaders eleven miles later, but had he finished one second earlier, Britain would have taken first place.

1960 Rome T: 32, N: 32, D: 8.26.
100 KM

			COMBINED TIME
1.	ITA	(Antonio Bailetti, Ottavio Cogilati, Giacomo Fornoni, Livio Trapé)	2:14:33.53
2.	GDR	(Gustav-Adolf Schur, Egon Adler, Erich Hagen, Günter Lörke)	2:16:56.31
3.	SOV	(Viktor Kapitonov, Yevgeny Klevzov, Yuri Melikhov, Aleksei Petrov)	2:18:41:67
4.	HOL	(Johannes Hugens, Cornelis Lotz, Albert Sluis, Pieter van Kreuningen)	2:19:15.71
5.	SWE	(Owe Adamson, Gunnar Göransson, Oswald Johansson, Gösta Pettersson)	2:19:36.37
6.	ROM	(Ion Cosma, Gabriel Moiceanu, Aurel Selaru, Ludovic Zanoni)	2:20:18.91
7.	FRA	(Henri Duez, François Hamon, Roland Lacombe, Jacques Simon)	2:20:36.38
8.	SPA	(Ignacio Astigarraga Uriarte, Juan Sanchez Camero, José Momene Campo, Ramon Saez Marzo)	2:21:34:59

1964 Tokyo T: 33, N: 33, D: 10.14.
109.89 KM

			COMBINED TIME
1.	HOL	(Evert Dolman, Gerben Karstens, Johannes Pieterse, Hubertus Zoet)	2:26:31.19
2.	ITA	(Severino Andreoli, Luciano Dalla Bona, Pietro Guerra, Ferrucio Manza)	2:26:55.39
3.	SWE	(Sven Hamrin, Erik Pettersson, Gösta Pettersson, Sture Pettersson)	2:27:11.52
4.	ARG	(Hector Acosta, Roberto Breppe, Delmo Delmastro, Ruben Placanica)	2:27:58.55
5.	SOV	(Yuri Melikhov, Anatoly Olizarenko, Aleksei Petrov, Gaynan Saidkhuschin)	2:28:26.48
6.	FRA	(Marcel-Ernest Bidault, Georges Chappe, André Desvages, Jean-Claude Wuillemin)	2:28:52.74
7.	DEN	(Flemming Hansen, Henning Petersen, Ole Pedersen, Ole Ritter)	2:29:10.33
8.	SPA	(José Goyeneche, José Lopez, Mariano Diaz, Luis Santamarina)	2:30:55.26

1968 Mexico City T: 30, N: 30, D: 10.15.
104 KM

			COMBINED TIME
1.	HOL	(Fedor den Hertog, Jan Krekels, Marinus Pijnen, Gerardes Zoetemelk)	2:07:49.06
2.	SWE	(Erik Pettersson, Gösta Pettersson, Sture Pettersson, Tomas Pettersson)	2:09:26.60
3.	ITA	(Giovanni Bramucci, Vittorio Marcelli, Mauro Simonetti, Pierfranco Vianelli)	2:10:18.74
4.	DEN	(Verner Blaudzun, Jörgen Emil Hansen, Ole Hojlund Pedersen, Leif Mortensen)	2:12:41.41
5.	NOR	(Thorleif Andresen, Ornulf Andresen, Tore Milsett, Leif Yli)	2:14:32.85
6.	POL	(Jan Magiera, Zenon Czechowski, Marian Kegel, Andrzej Blawdzin)	2:14:40.98
7.	ARG	(Juan Merlos, Carlos Alvarez, Roberto Breppe, Ernesto Contreras)	2:15:34.24
8.	GER	(Burkhard Ebert, Jürgen Tschan, Ortwin Czarnowski, Dieter Koslar)	2:15:37.25

The four Swedish silver medalists were all brothers. All four of them subsequently changed their last names, from Pettersson to that of their home village, Fåglum.

1972 Munich T: 35, N: 35, D: 9.6.
100 KM

			COMBINED TIME
1.	SOV	(Boris Chouhov, Valery Iardy, Gennady Komnatov, Valery Likhachev)	2:11:17.8
2.	POL	(Lucjan Lis, Edward Barcik, Stanislaw Szozda, Ryszard Szurkowski)	2:11:47.5
—.	HOL	(Fedor den Hertog, Hennie Kuiper, Cees Priem, Aad van den Hoek)	2:12:27.1
3.	BEL	(Ludo Delcroix, Gustaaf Hermans, Gustaaf Van Cauter, Louis Verreydt)	2:12:36.7
4.	NOR	(Thorleif Andresen, Arve Haugen, Knut Knudsen, Magne Orre)	2:13:20.7
5.	SWE	(Lennart Fagerlund, Tord Filipsson, Leif Hansson, Sven-Åke Nilsson)	2:13:36.9
6.	HUN	(Tibor Debreceni, Imre Géra, József Peterman, András Takács)	2:14:18.8
7.	SWI	(Gilbert Bischoff, Bruno Hubschmid, Roland Schaer, Ulrich Sutter)	2:14:33.6
8.	ITA	(Osvaldo Castellan, Pasqualino Moretti, Francesco Moser, Giovanni Tonoli)	2:14:36.2

The Dutch team was disqualified after it was determined that one of their members, Aad van den Hoek, had taken Coramine, a drug which was permitted by the International Cyclists' Union but forbidden by the International Olympic Committee. It was decided that the Belgian team would not be awarded the bronze medal, since its members had not been tested for drugs.

1976 Montreal T: 28, N: 28, D: 7.18.
100 KM

			COMBINED TIME
1.	SOV	(Anatoly Chukanov, Valery Chaplygin, Vladimir Kaminsky, Aavo Pikkuus)	2:08:53.0
2.	POL	(Tadeusz Mytnik, Mieczyslaw Nowicki, Stanislaw Szozda, Ryszard Szurkowski)	2:09:13.0
3.	DEN	(Verner Blaudzun, Gert Frank, Jörgen Hansen, Törgen Lund)	2:12:20.0

4. GER   (Hans-Peter Jakst, Olaf Paltian, Friedrich   2:12:35.0
          von Löffelholz, Peter Weibel)
5. CZE   (Petr Buchaček, Petr Matoušek, Milan   2:12:56.0
          Puzrla, Vladimir Vondraček)
6. GBR   (Paul Carbutt, Philip Griffiths, Dudley Hay- 2:13:10.0
          ton, William Nickson)
7. SWE   (Tord Filipsson, Bernt Johansson, Sven-   2:13.13.0
          Åke Nilsson, Tommy Prim)
8. NOR   (Stein Brathen, Geir Digerud, Arne Kla-   2:13:17.0
          venes, Magne Orre)

1980 Moscow T: 23, N: 23, D: 7.20.
101 KM   COMBINED
                                                      TIME

1. SOV   (Yuri Kashirin, Oleg Logvin, Sergei Shelpa- 2:01:21.7
          kov, Anatoly Yarkin)
2. GDR   (Falk Boden, Bernd Drogan, Olaf Ludwig,   2:02:53.2
          Hans-Joachim Hartnick)
3. CZE   (Michal Klasa, Vlastibor Konečný, Alipi   2:02:53.9
          Kostadinov, Jiři Škoda)
4. POL   (Stefan Ciekanski, Jan Jankiewicz, Czes-   2:04:13.8
          law Lang, Witold Plutecki)
5. ITA   (Mauro De Pellegrin, Gianni Giacomini, Iva- 2:04:36.2
          no Maffei, Alberto Minetti)
6. BUL   (Borislav Assenov, Venelin Houbenov, Yor-   2:05:55.2
          dan Penchev, Nencho Staikov)
7. FIN   (Harry Hannus, Kari Puisto, Patrick Wack-   2:05:58.2
          strom, Sixten Wackstrom)
8. YUG   (Bruno Bilic, Vinko Poloncic, Bojan Ropret, 2:07:12.0
          Bojan Udovic)

Discontinued Events
ONE-LAP RACE
(603.49 Meters)
1908 London C: 46, N: 9, D: 7.15.
1. Victor Johnson   GBR   51.2
2. Emile Demangel   FRA   —
3. Karl Neumer   GER   —
4. Daniel Flynn   GBR   —

5000-METER TRACK RACE
1906 Athens C: 26, N: 9, D: 4.23.
1. Francesco Verri   ITA   7:28.6
2. H. Crowther   GBR   —
3. Fernand Vast   FRA   —
AC: Emile Demangel (FRA), Max Götze (GER)

1908 London C: 42, N: 8, D: 7.18.
1. Benjamin Jones   GBR   8:36.2
2. Maurice Schilles   FRA   —
3. André Auffray   FRA   —
4. E. Maréchal   FRA   —
5. Charles Kingsbury   GBR   —
6. Johannes van Spengen   HOL   —
7. Gerard Bosch van Drakestein HOL   —

In the final of the 1000-meter sprint, Schilles beat Jones by inches. However the race was declared void because the time limit was exceeded. Two days later in the 5000 meters, it was Jones who held off Schilles' finishing sprint to win by 6 inches.

10 KM TRACK RACE
1896 Athens C: 6, N: 4, D: 4.11.
1. Paul Masson   FRA   17:54.2
2. Léon Flameng   FRA   17:54.2
3. Adolf Schmal   AUT   —
4. Joseph Rosemeyer GER   —
DNF: G. Kolettis (GRE), Aristidis Konstantinidis (GRE)

20 KM TRACK RACE
1906 Athens C: 24, N: 9, D: 4.23.
1. William Pett   GBR   29:00.0
2. Maurice Bardonneau FRA   29:30.0
3. Fernand Vast   FRA   29:32.0
4. Hans Holly   AUT   —
5. Eduard Dannenberg GER   —
AC: Ad. Böhm (GER), Edmond Luguet (FRA)

1908 London C: 44, N: 11, D: 7.14.
1. Charles Kingsbury GBR   34:13.6
2. Benjamin Jones   GBR   —
3. Joseph Werbrouck   BEL   —
4. L.J. Weintz   USA   —

Kingsbury, of Portsmouth, won by 3 inches.

50 KM TRACK RACE
1920 Antwerp C: 29, N: 11, D: 8.12.
1. Henry George   BEL   1:16:43.2
2. Cyril Alden   GBR   —
3. Piet Ikelaar   HOL   —
4. Ruggero Ferrario ITA   —
5. Herbert McDonald CAN   —
6. Franco Giorgetti ITA   —

Eyewitnesses said that Ikelaar actually finished second. The Jury of Appeal eventually agreed, but refused to reverse the judges' verdict, since it had already been announced.

1924 Paris C: 36, N: 16, D: 7.27.
1. Jacobus Willems   HOL   1:18:24.0
2. Cyril Alden   GBR   —
3. Frank Wyld   GBR   —
4. Angelo De Martino ITA   —
5. Józef Lange   POL   —
6. Alfredo Dinale   ITA   —

100 KM TRACK RACE
1896 Athens C: 9, N: 5, D: 4.8.
1. Léon Flameng   FRA   3:08:19.2
2. G. Kolettis   GRE   —

The race required 300 circuits of the track. Once, when Kolettis' bike needed repair, Flameng stopped and waited for him. Flameng fell towards the end of the race, but still won by six or seven laps.

1908 London C: 43, N: 11, D: 7.16.
1. Charles Bartlett   GBR   2:41:48.6
2. Charles Denny   GBR   —
3. Octave Lapize   FRA   —
4. William Pett   GBR   —
5. P. Texier   FRA   —
6. Walter Andrews   CAN   —
7. D.C. Robertson   GBR   —
8. S.F. Bailey   GBR   —

This was considered the most important cycling contest of the 1908 Olympics, and there were so many entrants that qualifying heats had to be run to cut down the field. In the second of these heats, a bad accident occurred when Harry Venn, a walking official, walked right onto the track and collided with Coeckelberg of Belgium. Coeckelberg fell to the ground and was cut on the thigh and head, but he managed to finish the race, qualifying for the final as a consequence of his having led much of the way. In the final, with more than two and a half hours gone and only one lap of the track remaining, the race had come down to Octave Lapize of France and three representatives of Great Britain, Charles Denny, Charles Bartlett, and William Pett. The four were moving around at a crawl when Bartlett suddenly darted to the inside, took the lead, and sprinted home to win by almost a length.

12-HOUR RACE

1896 Athens C: 7, N: 4, D: 4.13.

		KM
1. Adolf Schmal	AUT	300.000
2. F. Keeping	GBR	299.667

DNF: Georgios Paraskevopoulos (GRE), Minas Konstantinou (GRE), Leoverdas (GRE), Tryfiatis (GRE), Josef Welzenbacher (GER)

2000-METER TANDEM

1896–1904 not held

1906 Athens T: 6, N: 4, D: 4.23.
1. GBR   (John Matthews, Arthur Rushen)   2:15.0
2. GER   (Max Götze, Bruno Götze)   —
3. GER   (Eduard Dannenberg, Otto Küpferling)   —

1908 London T: 17, N: 7, D: 7.15.
1. FRA   (Maurice Schilles, André Auffray)   3:07.6
2. GBR   (Frederick Hamlin, H. Thomas Johnson)   —
3. GBR   (Colin Brooks, Walter Isaacs)   —

Schilles and Auffray had never ridden together before the first round of this contest.

1912 not held

1920 Antwerp T: 5, N: 5, D: 8.12.
1. GBR   (Harry Ryan, Thomas Lance)   2:49.4
2. SAF   (James Walker, William Smith)   —
3. HOL   (Frans de Vreng, Piet Ikelaar)   —

1924 Paris T: 5, N: 5, D: 7.27.

1. FRA	(Lucien Choury, Jean Cugnot)	12.6 (last 200 meters)
2. DEN	(Willy Falck Hansen, Edmund Hansen)	—
3. HOL	(Gerard Bosch van Drakestein, Maurice Peeters)	—

1928 Amsterdam T: 7, N: 7, D: 8.7.

1. HOL	(Bernhard Leene, Daniel van Dijk)	11.8 (last 200 meters)
2. GBR	(John Sibbit, Ernest Henry Chambers)	—
3. GER	(Karl Köther, Hans Bernhardt)	—
4. ITA	(Francesco Malatesta, Adolf Corsi)	—

1932 Los Angeles T: 5, N: 5, D: 8.3.

1. FRA	(Maurice Perrin, Louis Chaillot)	12.0 (last 200 meters)
2. GBR	(Ernest Henry Chambers, Stanley Chambers)	—
3. DEN	(Willy Gervin, Harald Christensen)	—
4. HOL	(Bernhard Leene, Jacobus van Egmond)	—

1936 Berlin T: 11, N: 11, D: 8.8.

		1ST RACE	2ND RACE
1. GER	(Ernst Ihbe, Carl Lorenz)	11.0	11.0
2. HOL	(Bernhard Leene, Hendrik Ooms)	—	—
3. FRA	(Pierre Georget, Georges Maton)	—	—
4. ITA	(Carlo Legutti, Bruno Loatti)	—	—

5. BEL (Cools, Pirotte), DEN (Dissing, Stieler), GBR (Chambers, Sibbit), USA (William Logan, Albert Sellinger)

1948 London T: 10, N: 10, D: 8.11.

		1ST RACE	2ND RACE	3RD RACE
1.	ITA (Ferdinando Teruzzi, Renato Perona)	—	11.3	11.6
2.	GBR (Reginald Harris, Alan Bannister)	11.1	—	—
3.	FRA (René Faye, Georges Dron)	—	—	—
4.	SWI (Jean Roth, Max Aeberli)	—	—	—

5. BEL (L. van Schill, R. de Pauw), DEN (H. Andersen, E. Klamer), HOL (N. Buchly, M. van Gelder), USA (Marvin Thomson, Alfred Stiller)

In a thrilling finish, held in the dark, Teruzzi and Perona won the tie-breaker by a mere six inches.

1952 Helsinki T: 14, N: 14, D: 7.31.
1. AUS (Lionel Cox, Russell Mockridge) 11.0
2. SAF (Raymond Robinson, Thomas Shardelow) —
3. ITA (Antonio Maspes, Cesare Pinarello)
4. FRA (Franck Le Normand, Robert Vidal)
5. DEN (Jens Eriksen, Olaf Holmstrup), GBR (Leslie Wilson, Alan Bannister), HUN (István Schillerwein, Imre Furmen), NZE (Colin Dickinson, Clarence Simpson)

1956 Melbourne T: 10, N: 10, D: 6.12.
1. AUS (Ian Browne, Anthony Marchant) 10.8
2. CZE (Ladislav Fouček, Václav Machek) —
3. ITA (Giuseppe Ogna, Cesare Pinarello)
4. GBR (Peter Brotherton, Eric Thompson)
5. FRA (Robert Vidal, André Gruchet), NZE (Richard Johnston, Warren Johnston), SAF (Thomas Shardelow, Raymond Robinson), USA (James Rossi, Donald Ferguson)

1960 Rome T: 12, N: 12, D: 8.27.

		1ST RACE	2ND RACE
1.	ITA (Giuseppe Beghetto, Sergio Bianchetto)	10.7	10.8
2.	GDR (Jürgen Simon, Lothar Stäber)	—	—

3. SOV (Boris Vassilyev, Vladimir Leonov)
4. HOL (Marinus Paul, Melis Gerritsen)
5. CZE (Juraj Miklusica, Dusan Skvarenina), FRA (Roland Surrugue, Michael Scob), GBR (David Handley, Eric Thompson), USA (Jack Hartman, David Sharp)

1964 Tokyo T: 13, N: 13, D: 10.20.

		1ST RACE	2ND RACE	3RD RACE
1.	ITA (Angelo Damiano, Sergio Bianchetto)	—	10.85	10.75
2.	SOV (Imant Bodnieks, Viktor Logunov)	10.80	—	—
3.	GER (Willi Fuggerer, Klaus Kobusch)			
4.	HOL (Arie de Graaf, Peiter van der Touw)			

5. AUS (Ian Browne, Daryl Perkins), CZE (Karel Paar, Karel Stark), DEN (Niels Fredborg, Per Jorgensen), HUN (Richárd Bicskey, Ferenc Habony)

1968 Mexico City T: 14, N: 14, D: 10.21.

		1ST RACE	2ND RACE
1.	FRA (Daniel Morelon, Pierre Trentin)	10.03	9.83
2.	HOL (Johannes Jansen, Leijn Loevesijn)	—	—
3.	BEL (Daniel Goens, Robert van Lancker)		
4.	ITA (Walter Gorini, Luigi Borghetti)		

5. CZE (Ivan Kucirek, Milos Jelinek), GDR (Werner Otto, Jürgen Geschke), GER (Klaus Kobusch, Martin Stenzel), SOV (Igor Tselovalnikov, Imant Bodnieks)

1972 Munich T: 14, N: 14, D: 9.3.

		1ST RACE	2ND RACE	3RD RACE
1.	SOV (Vladimir Semenets, Igor Tselovalnikov)	—	10.52	10.60
2.	GDR (Jürgen Geschke, Werner Otto)	10.68	—	—
3.	POL (Andrzej Bek, Benedykt Kocot)			
4.	FRA (Daniel Morelon, Pierre Trentin)			

5. BEL (Manu Snellinx, Noel Soetaert), CZE (Ivan Kucirek, Vladimir Popelka), GER (Jürgen Barth, Rainer Müller), HOL (Klaas Balk, Peter van Doorn)

WOMEN
INDIVIDUAL ROAD RACE
This event will be held for the first time in 1984.

INDIVIDUAL POINTS RACE
This event will be held for the first time in 1984.

EQUESTRIAN

Three-Day Event, Individual
Three-Day Event, Team
Jumping (Prix des Nations), Individual
Jumping (Prix des Nations), Team
Dressage, Individual
Dressage, Team
Discontinued Events

THREE-DAY EVENT, INDIVIDUAL

The three-day event consists of three parts: dressage, endurance, and show jumping. The dressage and jumping portions follow the same basic rules and scoring as the regular dressage and jumping events. The endurance phase is a long-distance obstacle run broken into four sections: two "road and tracks," one "steeplechase," and one "cross-country." Penalty points are assessed for falls and overtime, while bonus points can be accumulated by completing any of the four sections of the endurance run under the set time limit.

1896–1908 not held

1912 Stockholm C: 27, N: 7, D: 7.17.

		MOUNT	PTS.
1. Axel Nordlander	SWE	Lady Artist	46.59
2. Friedrich von Rochow	GER	Idealist	46.42
3. Jean Cariou	FRA	Cocotte	46.32
4. Nils Adlercreutz	SWE	Atout	46.31
5. Ernst Casparsson	SWE	Irmelin	46.16
5. Rudolf Graf von Schaesberg-Tannheim	GER	Grundsee	46.16
7. Eduard von Lütcken	GER	Blue Boy	45.90
8. John Montgomery	USA	Deceive	45.88

1920 Antwerp C: 25, N: 8, D: 9.10.

		MOUNT	PTS.
1. Helmer Mörner	SWE	Germania	1775.00
2. Åge Lundström	SWE	Ysra	1738.75
3. Ettore Caffaratti	ITA	Traditore	1733.75
4. Roger Moeremans d'Emaus	BEL	Sweet Girl	1652.50
5. Garibaldi Spighi	ITA	Virginia	1647.50
6. Harry Chamberlin	USA	Harebell	1568.75

The competition consisted of jumping, a 20-kilometer course, and a 50-kilometer course, but no dressage.

1924 Paris C: 44, N: 13, D: 7.26.

		MOUNT	DRESSAGE	ENDURANCE	JUMPING	TOTAL PTS.
1. Adolph van der Voort van Zijp	HOL	Silver Piece	174.0	1402.0	400.0	1976.0
2. Frode Kirkebjerg	DEN	Meteor	164.0	1409.5	280.0	1853.5
3. Sloan Doak	USA	Pathfinder	156.0	1369.5	320.0	1845.5
4. Charles Pahud de Mortanges	HOL	Johnny Walker	174.0	1334.0	320.0	1828.0
5. Claës König	SWE	Bojar	166.0	1284.0	280.0	1730.0
6. Beaudouin de Brabandère	BEL	Modestie	138.0	1190.5	400.0	1728.5
6. Edward de Fonblanque	GBR	Copper	133.0	1275.5	320.0	1728.5
8. Frank Carr	USA	Proctor	154.0	1333.0	240.0	1727.0

1928 Amsterdam C: 46, N: 17, D: 8.11.

		MOUNT	DRESSAGE	ENDURANCE	JUMPING	TOTAL PTS.
1. Charles Pahud de Mortanges	HOL	Marcroix	237.82	1432.0	300.0	1969.82
2. Gerard de Kruyff	HOL	Va-t-en	251.26	1416.0	300.0	1967.26
3. Bruno Neumann	GER	Ilja	208.42	1436.0	300.0	1944.42
4. Adolph van der Voort van Zijp	HOL	Silver Piece	224.60	1404.0	300.0	1928.60
5. Hans Olof von Essen	FIN	El Kaid	180.64	1444.0	300.0	1924.64
6. Bjart Ording	NOR	And Over	200.98	1412.0	300.0	1912.98
7. Nils Kettner	SWE	Caesar	197.66	1404.0	300.0	1901.66
8. Arthur Quist	NOR	Hidalgo	221.14	1404.0	270.0	1895.14

1932 Los Angeles C: 14, N: 5, D: 8.13.

		MOUNT	DRESSAGE	ENDURANCE	JUMPING	TOTAL PTS.
1. Charles Pahud de Mortanges	HOL	Marcroix	311.833	− 58.0	−40.00	1813.83
2. Earl Thomson	USA	Jenny Camp	300.000	− 29.0	−60.00	1811.00
3. Clarence von Rosen	SWE	Sunnyside Maid	310.666	− 58.5	−42.75	1809.42
4. Harry Chamberlin	USA	Pleasant Smiles	340.333	− 192.5	−60.00	1687.83
5. Ernst Hallberg	SWE	Marokan	290.333	− 171.0	−40.00	1679.33
6. Karel Johan Schummelketel	HOL	Duiveltje	267.500	− 195.0	−58.00	1614.00
7. Morishige Yamamoto	JAP	Kingo	257.333	− 207.5	−40.25	1609.58
8. Edwin Argo	USA	Honolulu Tomboy	333.000	− 392.5	− 0.75	1539.25

Lieutenant Pahud de Mortanges completed his Olympic career with four gold medals and one silver.

1936 Berlin C: 50, N: 19, D: 8.16.

		MOUNT	DRESSAGE	ENDURANCE	JUMPING	TOTAL PTS.
1. Ludwig Stubbendorff	GER	Nurmi	− 96.7	+69	−10	− 37.7
2. Earl Thomson	USA	Jenny Camp	− 127.9	+38	−10	− 99.9
3. Hans Mathiesen-Lunding	DEN	Jason	− 134.2	+42	−10	− 102.2
4. Vincens Grandjean	DEN	Grey Friar	− 115.9	+11	0	− 104.9
5. Agoston Endrödy	HUN	Pandur	− 134.7	+39	−10	− 105.7
6. Rudolf Lippert	GER	Fasan	− 118.6	+27	−20	− 111.6
7. Alec Scott	GBR	Bob Clive	− 152.3	+45	−10	− 117.3
8. Mario Mylius	SWI	Saphir	− 122.0	+57	−20	− 145.0

The course was so difficult that three horses met their deaths and only 27 of the 50 entrants finished the competition.

1948 London C: 45, N: 16, D: 8.10.

		MOUNT	DRESSAGE	ENDURANCE	JUMPING	TOTAL PTS.
1. Bernard Chevallier	FRA	Aiglonne	−104	+108	0	+ 4
2. Frank Henry	USA	Swing Low	−117	+ 96	0	−21
3. Robert Selfelt	SWE	Claque	−109	+ 84	0	−25
4. Charles Anderson	USA	Reno Palisade	−111	+ 96	−11.5	−25.5
5. Joaquin Nogueras Marquez	SPA	Epsom	−128	+ 87	0	−41
6. Erik Carlsen	DEN	Ezja	−113	+ 69	0	−44
7. Aecio Morrot Coelho	BRA	Guapo	−114	+ 72	−10	−52
8. Fernando Marques Caveleiro	POR	Satari	−135	+ 90	−10	−55
8. Fabio Mangilli	ITA	Guerriero da Capestrano	− 85	+ 72	−42	−55

1952 Helsinki C: 59, N: 21, D: 8.2.

		MOUNT	DRESSAGE	ENDURANCE	JUMPING	TOTAL PTS.
1. Hans von Blixen-Finecke, Jr.	SWE	Jubal	−123.33	+105	−10	−28.33
2. Guy Lefrant	FRA	Verdun	−119.50	+ 75	−10	−54.50
3. Wilhelm Büsing	GER	Hubertus	−103.50	+ 48	0	−55.50
4. Pedro Mercado	ARG	Mandinga	−130.80	+ 78	−10	−62.80
5. Klaus Wagner	GER	Dachs	−109.66	+ 54	−10	−65.66
6. Piero D'Inzeo	ITA	Pagoro	−118.80	+ 52	0	−66.80
7. Albert Hill	GBR	Stella	−126.33	+ 69	−10	−67.33
8. Olof Stahre	SWE	Komet	−108.66	+ 81	−41.75	−69.41

Blixen-Finecke's father won a gold medal in the 1912 team dressage.

1956 Stockholm C: 57, N: 19, D: 6.14.

		MOUNT	DRESSAGE	ENDURANCE	JUMPING	TOTAL PTS.
1. Petrus Kastenman	SWE	Iluster	−116.40	+69.87	−20	− 66.53
2. August Lütke-Westhues	GER	Trux von Kamax	−129.60	+64.73	−20	− 84.87
3. Francis Weldon	GBR	Kilbarry	−103.20	+37.72	−20	− 85.48
4. Lev Baklychkine	SOV	Guimnast	−119.20	+42.55	−20	− 96.65
5. Genko Rashkov	BUL	Euphoria	−146.00	+44.77	−10	−111.23
6. A. Laurence Rook	GBR	Wild Venture	−101.60	− 4.29	−13.75	−119.64
7. Giancarlo Gutierrez	ITA	Wiston	−138.80	+12.37	−10	−136.43
8. Juan Martín Merbilháa	ARG	Gitana I	−150.00	+23.54	−10	−136.46

1960 Rome C: 73, N: 19, D: 9.10.

		MOUNT	DRESSAGE	ENDURANCE	JUMPING	TOTAL PTS.
1. Lawrence Morgan	AUS	Salad Days	−106.00	+128.4	−15.25	+ 7.15
2. Neale Lavis	AUS	Mirrabooka	−124.50	+108.0	0	−16.50
3. Anton Bühler	SWI	Gay Spark	− 89.01	+ 50.8	−13	−51.21
4. Michael Bullen	GBR	Cottage Romance	−129.00	+ 66.4	0	−62.60
5. Saibattal Mursalimov	SOV	Satrap	− 79.00	+ 46.0	−30.75	−63.75
6. Jack Le Goff	FRA	Image	−108.51	+ 55.6	−20	−72.91
7. Lev Baklychkine	SOV	Bazis	−103.50	+ 58.4	−20.25	−85.35
8. Marian Babirecki	POL	Volt	−127.00	+ 61.6	−20	−85.40

The endurance course was unnecessarily dangerous, and two horses were killed. The Italian organizers seemed unprepared for such disasters. The Danish horse Rolf II had to wait two and a half hours for the arrival of a veterinarian, and the Romanian horse Mures II, driven across the finish line despite a fatal injury, lay dead for hours before he was finally removed. Only 35 of the 73 entrants completed the competition.

1964 Tokyo C: 48, N: 12, D: 10.19.

		MOUNT	DRESSAGE	ENDURANCE	JUMPING	TOTAL PTS.
1. Mauro Checcoli	ITA	Surbean	−54.00	+118.4	0	+64.40
2. Carlos Moratorio	ARG	Chalan	−42.00	+ 98.4	0	+56.40
3. Fritz Ligges	GER	Donkosak	−32.00	+ 91.2	−10	+49.20
4. Michael Page	USA	Grasshopper	−43.00	+ 90.4	0	+47.40
5. Anthony Cameron	IRL	Black Salmon	−70.67	+117.2	0	+46.53
6. Horst Karsten	GER	Condora	−49.00	+ 95.6	−10	+36.60
7. James Roycroft	AUS	Eldorado	−65.00	+ 97.2	0	+32.20
8. Richard Meade	GBR	Barberry	−52.67	+118.4	−36	+29.73

Mauro Checcoli, a 21-year-old student from Bologna, won the gold medal, but it was the 33rd-place finisher who made equestrian history. Helena Dupont of the United States became the first woman to compete in the Olympic three-day event.

1968 Mexico City C: 49, N: 13, D: 10.21.

		MOUNT	DRESSAGE	ENDURANCE	JUMPING	TOTAL PTS.
1. Jean-Jacques Guyon	FRA	Pitou	− 73.01	+44.4	−10.25	−38.86
2. Derek Allhusen	GBR	Lochinvar	− 85.01	+44.4	0	−41.61
3. Michael Page	USA	Foster	−107.51	+59.2	− 4	−52.31
4. Richard Meade	GBR	Cornishman V	− 97.01	+54.8	−22.25	−64.46
5. Reuben Jones	GBR	The Boacher	− 68.51	+ 4.4	− 5.75	−69.86
6. James Wofford	USA	Kilkenny	−101.51	+71.2	−43.75	−74.06
7. Juliet Jobling-Purser	IRL	Jenny	− 72.51	+ 5.6	− 1	−79.11
8. Wayne Roycroft	AUS	Zhivago	−103.50	+21.2	−12.75	−95.05

Two more horses were killed during the endurance competition. This time they died of exhaustion.

1972 Munich C: 73, N; 19, D: 9.1.

		MOUNT	DRESSAGE	ENDURANCE	JUMPING	TOTAL PTS.
1. Richard Meade	GBR	Laurieston	−50.6	+108.4	0	−57.73
2. Alessandro Argenton	ITA	Woodland	−48.6	+ 92.0	0	−43.33
3. Jan Jönsson	SWE	Sarajevo	−50.3	+ 90.0	0	−39.67
4. Mary Gordon-Watson	GBR	Cornishman V	−51.3	+ 81.6	0	−30.27
5. Kevin Freeman	USA	Good Mixture	−51.3	+ 91.2	−10	−29.87
6. William Roycroft	AUS	Warrathoola	−36.0	+ 65.6	0	−29.60
7. Richard Sands	AUS	Depeche	−64.3	+ 99.2	−10	−24.87
8. Bruce Davidson	USA	Plain Sailing	−40.3	+ 74.8	−10	−24.47

1976 Montreal C: 49, N: 13, D: 7.25.

		MOUNT	DRESSAGE	ENDURANCE	JUMPING	TOTAL PTS.
1. Edmund Coffin	USA	Bally-Cor	− 64.59	− 50.4	0	−114.99
2. John Plumb	USA	Better & Better	− 66.25	− 49.6	−10	−125.85
3. Karl Schultz	GER	Madrigal	− 46.25	− 63.2	−20	−129.45
4. Richard Meade	GBR	Jacob Jones	− 73.75	− 57.6	−10	−141.35
5. Wayne Roycroft	AUS	Laurenson	− 80.84	− 97.2	0	−178.04
6. Gerard Sinnott	IRL	Croghan	−101.25	− 77.6	0	−178.85
7. Jean Valat	FRA	Vampire	− 92.50	− 95.2	0	−187.70
8. Yuri Salnikov	SOV	Rumpel	− 86.66	−102.8	0	−189.46

1980 Moscow C:28, N: 7, D: 7.27.

			MOUNT	DRESSAGE	ENDURANCE	JUMPING	TOTAL PTS.
1.	Euro Federico Roman	ITA	Rossinan	−54.4	− 49.2	− 5	−108.6
2.	Aleksandr Blinov	SOV	Galzun	−64.4	− 56.4	0	−120.8
3.	Yuri Salnikov	SOV	Pintset	−53.0	− 93.6	− 5	−151.6
4.	Valery Volkov	SOV	Tskheti	−54.0	−125.6	− 5	−184.6
5.	Tzvetan Donchev	BUL	Medisson	−66.4	−114.4	− 5	−185.8
6.	Miroslaw Sziapka	POL	Erywan	−52.4	−184.4	− 5	−241.8
7.	Anna Casagrande	ITA	Daleye	−61.2	−190.0	−15	−266.2
8.	Mauro Roman	ITA	Dourakine 4	−63.4	−218.0	0	−281.4

The equestrian events were badly hit by the boycott, and an alternative competition was held in August at Fontaine-bleau, France, with 42 riders representing 14 nations. The winner was Nils Haagensen of Denmark, with Americans James Wofford and Torrance Watkins finishing second and third.

THREE-DAY EVENT, TEAM

According to current rules, each team has four members, but the scores of only the top three finishers are counted.

1896–1908 not held

1912 Stockholm T: 7, N: 7, D: 7.17.

	MOUNT		TOTAL PTS.
1. SWE			139.06
Axel Nordlander	Lady Artist	46.59	
Nils Adlercreutz	Atout	46.31	
Ernst Casparsson	Irmelin	46.16	
2. GER			138.48
Friedrich von Rochow	Idealist	46.42	
Rudolf Graf von			
Schaesberg-Tannheim	Grundsee	46.16	
Eduard von Lütcken	Blue Boy	45.90	
3. USA			137.33
Benjamin Lear	Poppy	45.91	
John Montgomery	Deceive	45.88	
Guy Henry	Chiswell	45.54	
4. FRA			136.77
Jean Cariou	Cocotte	46.32	
Bernard Meyer	Allons-y	45.30	
Seigner	Dignité	45.15	

1920 Antwerp T: 6, N: 6, D: 9.10.

	MOUNT		TOTAL PTS.
1. SWE			5057.50
Helmer Mörner	Germania	1775.00	
Åge Lundström	Yrsa	1738.75	
Georg von Braun	Diana	1543.75	
2. ITA			4735.00
Ettore Caffaratti	Traditore	1733.75	
Garibaldi Spighi	Virginia	1647.50	
Giulio Cacciandra	Fortunello	1353.75	

3. BEL   4560.00

	MOUNT	
Roger Moeremans d'Emaus	Sweet Girl	1652.50
Oswald Lints	Martha	1515.00
Jules Bonvalet	Weppelghem	1392.50

4. USA   4477.50

	MOUNT	
Harry Chamberlin	Harebell	1568.75
William West	Prince	1558.75
John Barry	Singian	1350.00

1924 Paris T: 10, N: 10, D: 7.26.

	MOUNT		TOTAL PTS.
1. HOL			5297.5
Adolph van der Voort van Zijp	Silver Piece	1976.0	
Charles Pahud de Mortanges	Johnny Walker	1828.0	
Gerard de Kruyff	Addio	1493.5	
2. SWE			4743.5
Claës König	Bojar	1730.0	
Carl Torsten Sylvan	Amita	1678.0	
Gustaf Hagelin	Varius	1335.5	
3. ITA			4512.5
Alberto Lombardi	Pimplo	1572.0	
Alessandro Alvisi	Capiligio	1536.0	
Emanuele di Pralormo	Mount Felix	1404.5	
4. SWI			4338.5
Hans Bühler	Mikosch	1477.5	
Charles Stoffel	Kreuzritter	1466.0	
Werner Fehr	Prahihans	1395.0	
5. BEL			4233.5
Beaudouin de Brabandère	Modestie	1728.5	
Jules Bonvalet	Weppelghem	1428.0	
Joseph Fallon	Lè Divorce	1077.0	
6. GBR			4064.5
Edward de Fonblanque	Copper	1728.5	
K.W. Hervey	Wild Gal	1354.0	
F. Tod	White Surrey	982.0	
7. POL			3571.5
Karol Rómmel	Krechowiak	1648.5	
Kazimierz Szosland	Helusia	961.5	
Kazimierz Rostowo-Suski	Lady	958.5	

1928 Amsterdam T: 14, N: 14, D: 8.11.

	MOUNT		TOTAL PTS.
1. HOL			5865.68
Charles Pahud de Mortanges	Marcroix	1969.82	
Gerard de Kruyff	Va-t-en	1967.26	
Adolph van der Voort van Zijp	Silver Piece	1928.60	
2. NOR			5395.68
Bjart Ording	And Over	1912.98	
Arthur Quist	Hidalgo	1895.14	
Eugen Johansen	Baby	1587.56	
3. POL			5067.92
Michal Antoniewicz	Moja Mita	1822.50	
Józef Trenkwald	Lwi Pazur	1645.20	
Karol Rómmel	Doneuse	1600.22	

1932 Los Angeles T: 4, N: 4, D: 8.13.

	MOUNT		TOTAL PTS.
1. USA			5038.083
Earl Thomson	Jenny Champ	1811.000	
Harry Chamberlin	Plesant Smiles	1687.833	
Edwin Argo	Honolulu Tomboy	1539.250	
2. HOL			4689.083
Charles Pahud de Mortanges	Marcroix	1813.833	
Karel Johan Schummelketel	Duiveltje	1614.500	
Aernout van Lennep	Henk	1260.750	

1936 Berlin T: 14, N: 14, D: 8.16.

	MOUNT		TOTAL PTS.
1. GER			— 676.65
Ludwig Stubbendorff	Nurmi	— 37.70	
Rudolf Lippert	Fasan	— 111.60	
Konrad Freiherr von Wangenheim	Kurfurst	— 527.35	
2. POL			— 991.70
Henryk Rojcewicz	Arlekin III	— 253.00	
Zdzislaw Kawecki	Bambino	— 300.70	
Seweryn Kulesza	Tosca	— 438.00	
3. GBR			— 9195.50
Alec Scott	Bob Clive	— 117.30	
Edward Howard-Vyse	Blue Steel	— 324.00	
Richard Fanshawe	Bowie Knife	— 8754.20	
4. CZE			—18952.70
Václav Procházka	Harlekyn	— 324.30	
Josef Dobes	Leskov	— 497.70	
Otomar Bureš	Mirko	—18130.70	

Lieutenant Konrad Freiherr von Wangenheim was one of the German heroes of the Berlin Games. During the steeplechase portion of the endurance run, his horse, Kurfurst, stumbled at the fourth obstacle, a hurdle and pond, throwing the 26-year-old von Wangenheim to the ground and breaking his collarbone. Knowing that the German team would be disqualified if he failed to finish, von Wangenheim remounted and negotiated the remaining 32 obstacles without a fault. But the jumping competition still remained. The next day von Wangenheim appeared in the stadium with his arm in a sling. Just before he mounted Kurfurst, the sling was removed and his arm was tightly bound. However, at one of the early obstacles, a double jump, Kurfurst rushed ahead and von Wangenheim was forced to pull the reins with both hands. The horse reared up, fell backward, and landed on von Wangenheim, who managed to crawl out from underneath. Kurfurst lay still and was thought to be dead, but suddenly jumped back up. Von Wangenheim remounted and again completed the course without another fault. The stadium crowd of 100,000 gave von Wangenheim a prolonged standing ovation, as Germany won the gold medal.

The unusually enormous number of penalty points accumulated by Lieutenant Bureš of Czechoslovakia were a result of his taking 2 hours 46 minutes and 36 seconds to complete the eight-kilometer cross-country course, for which the time limit was 17 minutes 46 seconds.

1948 London T: 14, N: 14, D: 8.12.

	MOUNT	TOTAL PTS.
1. USA		−161.50
Frank Henry	Swing Low	− 21.00
Charles Anderson	Reno Palisade	− 26.50
Earl Thomson	Reno Rhythm	−114.00
2. SWE		−165.00
Robert Selfelt	Claque	− 25.00
Olof Stahre	Komet	− 70.00
Sigurd Svensson	Dust	− 70.00
3. MEX		−305.25
Humberto Mariles Cortés	Parral	− 61.75
Raúl Campero	Tarahumara	−120.50
Joaquin Solano Chagoya	Malinche	−123.00
4. SWI		−404.50
Alfred Blaser	Mahmud	− 59.25
Anton Bühler	Amour Amour	− 95.00
Pierre Musy	Franzosin	−250.25
5. SPA		−422.50
Joaquin Nogueras Marquez	Epsom	− 41.00
Fernando Gazapo de Sarraga	Vivian	−179.25
Santiago Martinez Larraz	Fogoso	−202.25

1952 Helsinki T: 19, N: 19, D: 8.2.

	MOUNT	TOTAL PTS.
1. SWE		−221.94
Hans von Blixen-Finecke, Jr.	Jubal	− 28.33
Olof Stahre	Komet	− 69.41
Karl Folke Frölén	Fair	−124.20
2. GER		−235.49
Wilhelm Büsing	Hubertus	− 55.50
Klaus Wagner	Dachs	− 65.66
Otto Rothe	Trux von Kamax	−114.33
3. USA		−587.16
Charles Hough	Cassivellannus	− 70.66
Walter Staley	Craigwood Park	−168.50
John Wofford	Benny Grimes	−348.00
4. POR		−618.00
Fernando Marques Cavaleiro	Caudel	−183.00
Antonio Pereira de Almeida	Florentina	−216.20
Joaquim Miguel Duarte Silva	Faial	−218.80
5. DEN		−828.86
Hans Andersen	Tom	−222.20
Otto Acthon	Sirdar	−267.66
Aage Rybaek-Nielsen	Sahara	−339.00
6. IRL		−953.52
Henry Freeman-Jackson	Cuchulain	−268.66
Ian Dudgeon	Hope	−269.20
Mark Darley	Emily Little	−415.66

1956 Stockholm T: 19, N: 19, D: 6.14.

	MOUNT		TOTAL PTS.
1. GBR			− 355.48
Frank Weldon	Kilbarry	− 85.48	
A. Laurence Rook	Wild Venture	−119.64	
Albert Hill	Countryman III	−150.36	
2. GER			− 475.91
August Lütke-Westhues	Trux von Kamax	− 84.87	
Otto Rothe	Sissi	−158.04	
Klaus Wagner	PrinzeB	−233.00	
3. CAN			− 572.72
John Rumble	Cilroy	−162.53	
James Elder	Colleen	−193.69	
Brian Herbinson	Tara	−216.50	
4. AUS			− 619.98
Brian Crago	Radar	−147.42	
Wyatt Thompson	Brown Sugar	−155.06	
Ernest Barker	Dandy	−317.50	
5. ITA			− 691.14
Giancarlo Gutierrez	Wiston	−136.43	
Adriano Capuzzo	Tuft of Heather	−139.41	
Giuseppe Molinari	Uccello	−415.30	
6. ARG			− 724.18
Juan Martín Merbilháa	Gitana I	−136.46	
Eduardo Cano	Why	−242.01	
Carlos de la Serna	Fanion	−345.71	
7. SOV			−1112.33
Lev Baklychkine	Guimnast	− 96.65	
Nikolai Chelenkov	Satrap	−297.68	
Valerian Kouibychev	Perekop	−718.00	
8. SWI			−1360.90
Emil-Otto Gmür	Romeo	−378.51	
Roland Perret	Erlfried	−405.18	
Samuel Koechlin	Goya	−577.21	

1960 Rome T: 18, N: 18, D: 9.10.

	MOUNT		TOTAL PTS.
1. AUS			−128.18
Lawrence Morgan	Salad Days	+ 7.15	
Neale Lavis	Mirrabooka	− 16.50	
William Roycroft	Our Solo	−118.83	
2. SWI			−386.02
Anton Bühler	Gay Spark	− 51.21	
Hans Schwarzenbach	Burn Trout	−131.45	
Rudolf Günthardt	Atbara	−203.36	
3. FRA			−515.71
Jack Le Goff	Image	− 72.91	
Guy Lefrant	Nicias	−208.50	
Jean Raymond Le Roy	Gardem	−234.30	
4. GBR			−516.21
Michael Bullen	Cottage Romance	− 62.60	
Albert Hill	Wild Venture	−215.60	
Frank Weldon	Samuel Johnson	−238.01	
5. ITA			−528.21
Lucio Tasca	Rahin	−125.80	
Ludovico Nava	Arcidosso	−161.91	
Giovanni Grignolo	Court Hill	−240.50	

6. IRL			−674.00
Edward Harty	Harlequin	−112.30	
Anthony Cameron	Sonnet	−251.55	
Ian Dudgeon	Corrigneagh	−310.15	

Suffering from a concussion and a broken collarbone as a result of a fall during the endurance course, 45-year-old Bill Roycroft insisted on leaving his hospital bed to compete in the jumping test, thus ensuring that the gold medal would go to Australia.

1964 Tokyo T: 12, N: 12, D: 10.19.

	MOUNT		TOTAL PTS.
1. ITA			+ 85.80
Mauro Checcoli	Surbean	+ 64.40	
Paolo Angioni	King	+ 17.87	
Giuseppe Ravano	Royal Love	+ 3.53	
2. USA			+ 65.86
Michael Page	Grasshopper	+ 47.40	
Kevin Freeman	Gallopade	+ 17.13	
J. Michael Plumb	Bold Minstrel	+ 1.33	
3. GER/GDR			+ 56.73
Fritz Ligges	Donkosak	+ 49.20	
Horst Karsten	Condora	+ 36.60	
Gerhard Schulz	Balza X	− 29.07	
4. IRL			+ 42.86
Anthony Cameron	Black Salmon	+ 46.53	
Thomas Brennan	Kilkenny	+ 1.13	
John Harty	San Michele	− 4.80	
5. SOV			− 19.63
German Gazyumov	Gran	+ 23.47	
Boris Konkov	Rumb	− 10.97	
Pavel Deyev	Satrap	− 32.13	
6. ARG			− 34.80
Carlos Moratorio	Chalan	+ 56.40	
Elvio Flores	Legitima	− 2.73	
Juan Gesualdi	Morrina	− 88.47	
7. AUS			− 67.27
James Roycroft	Eldorado	+ 32.20	
Brien Cobcroft	Stony Crossing	+ 8.40	
John Kelly	Brigalow	−107.87	
8. FRA			−133.87
Jack Le Goff	Leopard	− 37.87	
J. De Croutte de St. Martin	Mon Clos	− 38.47	
Hugues Landon	Laurier	− 57.53	

1968 Mexico City T: 12, N: 12, D: 10.21.

	MOUNT		TOTAL PTS.
1. GBR			−175.93
Derek Allhusen	Lochinvar	− 41.61	
Richard Meade	Cornishman V	− 64.46	
Reuben Jones	The Poacher	− 69.86	
2. USA			−245.87
Michael Page	Foster	− 52.31	
James Wofford	Kilkenny	− 74.06	
J. Michael Plumb	Plain Sailing	−119.50	

3. AUS			−331.26
Wayne Roycroft	Zhivago	− 94.95	
Brien Cobcroft	Depeche	−108.76	
William Roycroft	Joburg	−359.71	
4. FRA			−505.83
Jean-Jacques Guyon	Pitou	− 38.86	
André Le Goupil	Olivette B	−107.26	
Jean Sarrazin	Joburg	−359.71	
5. GER			−518.22
Horst Karsten	Adagio	−102.96	
Jochen Mehrdorf	Lapis Lazuli	−199.41	
Klaus Wagner	Abdulla	−215.85	
6. MEX			−631.56
Ernesto Del Castillo	Coficioso	−170.60	
Ramon Mejia	Centinela	−182.90	
Evaristo Avalos	Ludmilla II	−278.06	
7. GDR			−690.72
Karl-Heinz Fuhrmann	Saturn	−218.25	
Uwe Plank	Kranich	−231.01	
Helmut Hartmann	Ingwer	−241.46	
8. CAN			−787.68
Robin Hahn	Taffy	− 95.41	
Norman Elder	Questionnaire	−332.46	
Barry Sonshine	Durlas Eile	−359.81	

Australia's bronze medalist team included a father-son combination: Bill and Wayne Roycroft. The Roycrofts repeated their performance in 1976, when father Bill was 61 years old.

1972 Munich T: 18, N: 18, D: 9.1.

	MOUNT		TOTAL PTS.
1. GBR			− 95.53
Richard Meade	Laurieston	+ 57.73	
Mary Gordon-Watson	Cornishman V	+ 30.27	
Bridget Parker	Cornish Gold	+ 7.53	
2. USA			− 10.81
Kevin Freeman	Good Mixture	+ 29.87	
Bruce Davidson	Plain Sailing	+ 24.47	
J. Michael Plumb	Free and Easy	− 43.53	
3. GER			− 18.00
Harry Klugmann	Christopher Rob	+ 8.00	
Ludwig Goessing	Chikago	− 0.40	
Karl Schultz	Pisco	− 25.60	
4. AUS			− 27.86
William Roycroft	Warrathoola	+ 29.60	
Richard Sands	Depeche	+ 24.87	
Brian Schrapel	Wakool	− 82.33	
5. GDR			−127.93
Rudolf Beerbohm	Ingolf	+ 3.80	
Jens Niehls	Big-Ben	− 60.00	
Joachim Brohmann	Uranio	− 71.73	
6. SWI			−156.43
Paul Hürlimann	Grand Times	− 11.03	
Anton Bühler	Wukari	− 19.87	
Alfred Schwarzenbach	Big Boy	−125.53	

7. SOV			−190.06
Sergei Mukhin	Reisfeder	− 0.13	
Valentin Gorelkin	Rok	− 34.93	
Vladimir Lanugin	Zimar	−155.00	
8. ITA			−203.58
Alessandro Argenton	Woodland	− 43.33	
Dino Costantini	Lord Jim	− 98.18	
Mario Turner	Forgotten Fred	−148.73	

1976 Montreal T: 12, N: 12, D: 7.25.

	MOUNT		TOTAL PTS.
1. USA			−441.00
Edmund Coffin	Bally-Cor	−114.99	
J. Michael Plumb	Better & Better	−125.85	
Bruce Davidson	Irish-Cap	−200.16	
2. GER			−584.60
Karl Schultz	Madrigal	−129.45	
Herbert Blöcker	Albrant	−213.15	
Helmut Rethemeier	Pauline	−242.00	
3. AUS			−599.54
Wayne Roycroft	Laurenson	−178.04	
Mervyn Bennett	Regal Reign	−206.04	
William Roycroft	Version	−215.46	
4. ITA			−682.24
Euro Federico Roman	Shamrock	−194.14	
Mario Turner	Tempest Blisland	−213.19	
Alessandro Argenton	Woodland	−274.91	
5. SOV			−721.55
Yuri Salnikov	Rumpel	−189.46	
Valery Dvorianinov	Zeila	−218.25	
Viktor Kalinin	Araks	−313.84	
6. CAN			−808.81
Juliet Graham	Sumatra	−202.69	
Cathy Wedge	City Fella	−286.76	
Robin Hahn	L'Esprit	−319.36	

1980 Moscow T: 7, N: 7, D: 7.27.

	MOUNT		TOTAL PTS.
1. SOV			457.00
Aleksandr Blinov	Galzun	120.80	
Yuri Salnikov	Pintset	151.60	
Valery Volkov	Tskheti	184.60	
2. ITA			656.20
Euro Federico Roman	Rossinan	108.60	
Anna Casagrande	Daleye	266.20	
Mauro Roman	Dourakine 4	281.40	
3. MEX			1172.8
Manuel Mendivil Yocupicio	Remember	319.75	
David Barcena Rios	Bombon	362.50	
José Luis Perez Soto	Quelite	490.60	
4. HUN			1603.40
László Cseresnyes	Fapipa	436.20	
István Grozner	Biboros	498.60	
Zoltán Horvath	Lamour	668.60	

The substitute three-day event, held in August at Fountainbleau, was won by France, with West Germany second and Australia third.

JUMPING (PRIX DES NATIONS), INDIVIDUAL

Each horse and rider jumps two rounds. Fault points are assessed if an obstacle is knocked down, if the horse balks at an obstacle, and if the time limit is exceeded. In case of a tie, a jump-off is held. If the jump-off results in a tie, the fastest finisher is declared the winner.

1896 not held

1900 Paris C: 45, N: 5, D: 5.29.

		MOUNT	
1. Aimé Haegeman	BEL	Benton II	2:16.0
2. Georges van de Poele	BEL	Windsor Squire	2:17.6
3. M. de Champsavin	FRA	Terpsichore	2:26.0

1904–1908 not held

1912 Stockholm C: 31, N: 8, D: 7.16.

		MOUNT	FAULTS	JUMP-OFF
1. Jean Cariou	FRA	Mignon	4	5
2. Rabod Wilhelm von Kröcher	GER	Dohna	4	7
3. Emanuel de Blommaert de Soye	BEL	Clonmore	5	
4. H. S. L. Scott	GBR	Shamrock	6	
5. Sigismund Freyer	GER	Ultimus	7	
6. Wilhelm Graf von Hohenau	GER	Pretty girl	9	
6. Nils Adlercreutz	SWE	Ilex	9	
6. Ernst Casparsson	SWE	Kiriki	9	

1920 Antwerp C: 25, N: 6, D: 7.16.

		MOUNT	FAULTS
1. Tommaso Lequio	ITA	Trebecco	2
2. Alessandro Valerio	ITA	Cento	3
3. Carl-Gustaf Lewenhaupt	SWE	Mon Coeur	4
4. Paul Michelet	NOR	Raon	5
5. Ferdinand de la Serna	BEL	Arsinoe	6
5. Lars von Stockenström	SWE	Reward	6

1924 Paris C: 43, N: 11, D: 7.27.

		MOUNT	FAULTS	
1. Alphonse Gemuseus	SWI	Lucette	6	
2. Tommaso Lequio	ITA	Trebecco	8.75	
3. Adam Królikiewicz	POL	Picador	10	
4. P.E. Bowden-Smith	GBR	Billy Boy	10.5	
5. Antonio Borges d'Almeida	POR	Reginald	12	2:28.8
6. Åke Thelning	SWE	Loke	12	2:30.4
7. Axel Ståhle	SWE	—	12.25	
8. Nicolas Leroy	BEL	—	14.75	

1928 Amsterdam C: 46, N: 16, D: 8.12.

		MOUNT	FAULTS	1ST JUMP-OFF	2ND JUMP-OFF	
1. František Ventura	CZE	Eliot	0	0	0	
2. Pierre Bertran de Balanda	FRA	Papillon	0	0	2	
3. Charley Kuhn	SWI	Pepita	0	0	4	
4. Kazimierz Gzowski	POL	Mylord	0	2		1:33.0
5. José Navarro Morenés	SPA	Zapatazo	0	2		1:36.0
6. Karl Hansen	SWE	Gerold	0	2		1:39.0
7. K. Fourquet	ITA	Joe Aleshire	0	DISQ.		
8. Alphonse Gemuseus	SWI	Lucette	2			

1932 Los Angeles C: 11, N: 4, D: 8.14.

		MOUNT	FAULTS
1. Takeichi Nishi	JAP	Uranus	8
2. Harry Chamberlin	USA	Show Girl	12
3. Clarence von Rosen, Jr.	SWE	Empire	16
4. William Bradford	USA	Joe Aleshire	24
5. Ernst Hallberg	SWE	Kornett	50.5

Takeichi Nishi was a lieutenant in the Japanese army when he won his gold medal. Promoted to colonel toward the end of World War II, he was made commander of a tank battalion on Iwo Jima. During the fierce fighting on that island, some of the U. S. officers learned that Nishi was on the island and hoped to meet him. They never got a chance. Nishi, who had many American friends, including Will Rogers, Mary Pickford, and Douglas Fairbanks, refused to surrender and instead joined a mass Japanese suicide.

1936 Berlin C: 54, N: 18, D: 8.16.

		MOUNT	FAULTS	JUMP-OFF	
1. Kurt Hasse	SWE	Tora	4	4	59.2
2. Henri Rang	ROM	Delfis	4	4	1:12.8
3. József Platthy	HUN	Sello	8	0	1:02.6
4. Georges van der Meersch	BEL	Ibrahim	8	0	1:09.0
5. Carl Raguse	USA	Dakota	8	4	
6. José Beltrão	POR	Biscuit	12		
6. Xavier Bizard	FRA	Bagatelle	12		
6. Johan Jacob Greter	HOL	Ernica	12		
6. Maurice Gudin de Vallerin	FRA	Ecuyere	12		
6. Cevat Koula	TUR	Sapkin	12		

1948 London C: 44, N: 15, D: 8.14.

		MOUNT	FAULTS	JUMP-OFF	
1. Humberto Mariles Cortés	MEX	Arete	6.25		
2. Rubén Uriza	MEX	Harvey	8	0	
3. Jean François d'Orgeix	FRA	Sucre de Pomme	8	4	38.9
4. Franklin Wing	USA	Democrat	8	4	40.1
5. Jaime Garcia Cruz	SPA	Bizarro	12		
5. Eric Sörensen	SWE	Blatunga	12		
7. M. Fresson	FRA	Decametre	16		
7. Harry Llewellyn	GBR	Foxhunter	16		
7. Henry Nicoll	GBR	Kilgeddin	16		

General Mariles won the title in dramatic fashion. The last rider to enter the arena, he needed to incur fewer than eight faults to win the gold medal. This he did, clearing every obstacle but the water jump and losing 2¼ points for being eight seconds overtime. On the night of August 14, 1964, the 51-year-old Mariles was driving home from a party in his honor in Mexico City when another motorist attempted to force him off the road. At the next traffic light Mariles pulled out a gun and shot the man. He was sent to prison, but later released by presidential pardon. In 1972 he was arrested in Paris for drug-smuggling, but died in prison before coming to trial.

1952 Helsinki C: 51, N: 20, D: 8.3.

			MOUNT	FAULTS	JUMP-OFF	
1.	Pierre Jonquères d'Oriola	FRA	Ali Baba	8	0	
2.	Oscar Cristi	CHI	Bambi	8	4	
3.	Fritz Thiedemann	GER	Meteor	8	8	38.5
4.	Eloi Massey Oliveira de Menezes	BRA	Bigua	8	8	45.0
5.	Wilfred White	GBR	Nizefella	8	12	
6.	Humberto Mariles Cortés	MEX	Petrolero	8.75		
7.	Cesar Mendoza	CHI	Pillan	12		3:08.8
8.	Argentino Molinuevo	ARG	Discutido	12		3:13.0

1956 Stockholm C: 66, N: 24, D: 6.16.

			MOUNT	FAULTS
1.	Hans-Günter Winkler	GER	Haila	4
2.	Raimondo D'Inzeo	ITA	Merano	8
3.	Piero D'Inzeo	ITA	Uruguay	11
4.	Fritz Thiedemann	GER	Meteor	12
4.	Wilfred White	GBR	Nizefella	12
6.	Pierre Jonquères d'Oriola	FRA	Voulette	15
7.	Henrique Callado	POR	Martingil	16
8.	Carlos Delía	ARG	Discutido	19

1960 Rome C: 60, N: 23, D: 9.7.

			MOUNT	FAULTS
1.	Raimondo D'Inzeo	ITA	Posillipo	12
2.	Piero D'Inzeo	ITA	The Rock	16
3.	David Broome	GBR	Sunslave	23
4.	George Morris	USA	Simjon	24
5.	Hans-Günter Winkler	GER	Halla	25
6.	Fritz Thiedemann	GER	Meteor	25.5
7.	Naldo Dasso	ARG	Final	28
7.	Bert de Fombelle	FRA	Buffalo	28
7.	Hugh Wiley	USA	Master William	28

1964 Tokyo C: 46, N: 17, D: 10.24.

			MOUNT	FAULTS	JUMP-OFF
1.	Pierre Jonquères d'Oriola	FRA	Lutteur	9	
2.	Hermann Schridde	GER	Dozent	13.75	
3.	Peter Robeson	GBR	Firecrest	16	0

		MOUNT	FAULTS	JUMP-OFF
4. Thomas Fahey	AUS	Bonvale	16	8
5. Joaquim Miguel Duarte Silva	POR	Juene France	20	
5. Nelson Pessoa Filho	BRA	Huipil	20	
7. Frank Chapot	USA	San Lucas	20.5	
8. Kurt Jarasinski	GER	Torro	22.25	

1968 Mexico City C: 41, N: 15, D: 10.23

		MOUNT	FAULTS	JUMP-OFF	
1. William Steinkraus	USA	Snowbound	4		
2. Marion Coakes	GBR	Stroller	8		
3. David Broome	GBR	Mister Softee	12	0	35.3
4. Frank Chapot	USA	San Lucas	12	0	36.8
5. Hans-Günter Winkler	GER	Enigk	12	0	37.5
6. James Elder	CAN	The Immigrant	12	0	39.2
7. Monika Bachmann	SWI	Erbach	16		
7. Piero D'Inzeo	ITA	Fidux	16		
7. Argentino Molinuevo	ARG	Don Gustavo	16		
7. Alwin Schockemöhle	GER	Donal Rex	16		

1972 Munich C: 56, N: 22, D: 9.3.

		MOUNT	FAULTS	JUMP-OFF
1. Graziano Mancinelli	ITA	Ambassador	8	0
2. Ann Moore	GBR	Psalm	8	3
3. Neal Shapiro	USA	Sloopy	8	8
4. James Day	CAN	Steelmaster	8.75	
4. Hugo Simon	AUT	Lavendel	8.75	
4. Hartwig Steenken	GER	Simona	8.75	
7. Jean-Marcel Rozier	FRA	Sans Souci	12	
8. Alfonso Segovia	SPA	Tic Tac	16	
8. Fritz Ligges	GER	Robin	16	

For a long time Mancinelli was a rider for the Milan horse-dealing company of Fratelli Rivolta. Consequently he was considered a professional, and many observers were surprised when he was included as a member of the Italian team in Tokyo in 1964. Banned from the team the day before the competition was to begin, he was reinstated at the last minute. The ruling turned in his favor when it was revealed that he was the adopted son of one of the Rivolta brothers—part of the family and therefore not a professional. Eight years later in Munich, Mancinelli rode a perfect round in the jump-off to earn the individual gold medal.

1976 Montreal C: 48, N: 20, D: 7.27.

		MOUNT	FAULTS	JUMP-OFF
1. Alwin Schockemöhle	GER	Warwick Rex	0	
2. Michel Vaillancourt	CAN	Branch County	12	4
3. François Mathy	BEL	Gai Luron	12	8
4. Debbie Johnsey	GBR	Moxy	12	15.25
5. Frank Chapot	USA	Viscount	16	
5. Guy Creighton	AUS	Mr. Dennis	16	
5. Marcel Rozier	FRA	Bayard de Maupas	16	
5. Hugo Simon	AUT	Lavendel	16	

A 39-year-old factory owner, Alwin Schockemöhle was the first rider to complete the Olympic competition without a fault since František Ventura in 1928.

1980 Moscow C: 14, N: 7, D: 8.3.

		MOUNT	FAULTS	JUMP-OFF	
1. Jan Kowalczyk	POL	Artemor	8		
2. Nikolai Korolkov	SOV	Espardron	9.5		
3. Joaquin Perez Heras	MEX	Alymony	12	4	43.23
4. Oswaldo Mendez Herbruger	GUA	Pampa	12	4	43.59
5. Viktor Poganovsky	SOV	Topky	15.5		
6. Wieslaw Hartman	POL	Norton	16		
7. Barnabas Hevesi	HUN	Bohem	24		
8. Marian Kozicki	POL	Bremen	24.5		

The Rotterdam Show Jumping Festival for Olympic boycotters was won by Hugo Simon of Austria, with John Whitager of Great Britain second and Melanie Smith of the United States third.

JUMPING (PRIX DES NATIONS), TEAM
1896–1908 not held

1912 Stockholm T: 6, N: 6, D: 7.17.

	MOUNT	FAULTS	TOTAL PTS.
1. SWE			25
Carl-Gustaf Lewenhaupt	Medusa	2	
Gustaf Kilman	Gatan	10	
Hans von Rosen	Lord Iron	13	
2. FRA			32
Michel d'Astafort	Amazone	5	
Jean Cariou	Mignon	8	
Bernard Meyer	Allons-y	19	
3. GER			40
Sigismund Freyer	Ultimus	9	
Wilhelm Graf von Hohenau	Pretty Girl	13	
Ernst-Hubertus Deloch	Hubertus	18	
4. USA			43
John Montgomery	Deceive	10	
Guy Henry	Chiswell	16	
Benjamin Lear	Poppy	17	
5. RUS			50
Aleksandr Rodzianko	Eros	14	
Michel Plechkov	Yvette	18	
Alexis Selikhov	Tugela	18	
6. BEL			60
Emanuel de Blommaert de Soye	Clonmore	2	
Gaston de Trannoy	Capricieux	28	
Paul Convert	La Sioute	30	

1920 Antwerp T: 5, N: 5, D: 9.12.

	MOUNT	TOTAL PTS.
1. SWE		14.00
Hans von Rosen	Poor Boy	
Claes König	Tresor	
Daniel Norling	Eros II	
2. BEL		16.25
Herman d'Oultremont	Lord Kitchener	
André Coumans	Lisette	
Herman de Gaiffier d'Hestroy	MiB	
3. ITA		18.75
Ettore Caffaratti	Traditore	
Giulio Cacciandra	Fortunello	
Alessandro Alvisi	Raggio di Sole	
4. FRA		34.75
Henri Horment	Dignite	
Auguste de Laissardière	Othello	
Edouard Saint Poulof	Flirt	
5. USA		42.00
Harry Dwight Chamberlin	Nigra	
K.C. Greenwald	Moses	
Sloan Doak	Rabit Red	

1924 Paris T: 11, N: 11, D: 7.27.

	MOUNT	FAULTS	TOTAL PTS.
1. SWE			42.25
Åke Thelning	Loke	12.00	
Axel Ståhle	Cecil	12.25	
Åge Lundström	Anvers	18.00	
2. SWI			50.00
Alphonse Gemuseus	Lucette	6.00	
Werner Stüber	Glrandole	20.00	
Hans Bühler	Sailor Boy	24.00	
3. POR			53.00
Antonio Borges d'Almeida	Reginald	12.00	
Helder de Souza Martins	Avro	19.00	
José Mousinho d'Albuquerque	Hetrugo	22.00	
4. BEL			57.00
Nicolas Leroy	Vif Argent	14.75	
Jacques Misonne	Torino	19.50	
Gaston Mesmaekers	As de Pique	22.75	
5. ITA			57.50
Tommaso Lequio di Assaba	Trebecco	8.75	
Leone Valle	Struffo	20.00	
Alessandro Alvisi	Grey Fox	28.75	
6. POL			58.50
Adam Królikiewicz	Picador	10.00	
Karol Rómmel	Faworyt	18.00	
Zdzislaw Dziadulski	Zefer	30.50	
7. GBR			65.75
P. Bowden-Smith		10.50	
C. Brunker		25.50	
G. Brocke		29.75	
8. SPA			73.75
José Alvarez de Bohorques		18.00	
N. Martinez Hombre		22.00	
José Navarro Morenes		33.75	

1928 Amsterdam T:15, N: 15, D: 8.12.

	MOUNT	FAULTS	TOTAL PTS.
1. SPA			4
José Navarro Morenes	Zapatazo	0	
José Alvarez de las Asturias y Bohorques			
(de los Trujillos)	Zalamero	2	
Julio Garcia Fernandez	Revistada	2	
2. POL			8
Kazimierz Gzowski	Mylord	0	
Kazimierz Szosland	Ali	2	
Michal Antoniewicz	Readgleadt	6	
3. SWE			10
Karl Hansen	Gerold	0	
Carl Björnstierna	Kornett	2	
Ernst Hallberg	Loke	8	
4. FRA			12
Pierre Bertran de Balanda	Papillon	0	
G. J. Couderc de Fonlongue	Vangerville	4	
Pierre Clavé	Le Trouvere	8	
4. ITA			12
Francesco Forquet	Capineca	0	
Alessandro Bettoni-Cazzago	Aladino	6	
Tommaso Lequio di Assaba	Trebecco	6	
4. POR			12
Luiz Ivens Ferraz	Marco Visconti	4	
Henrique de Sousa Martins	Avro	4	
José Mousinho d'Albuquerque	Hebraico	4	
7. GER			14
Eduard Krüger	Donauwelle	2	
Richard Sahla	Correggio	4	
Carl Friedrich Freiherr von Langen-Parow	Falkner	8	
8. SWI			18
Charles Kuhn	Pepita	0	
Alphonse Gemuseus	Lucette	2	
P. de Muralt	Notas	16	

1932 Los Angeles T: 3, N: 3, D: 8.14.
No nation completed the course with three riders.

1936 Berlin T: 18, N: 18, D: 8.16.

	MOUNT		TOTAL PTS.
1. GER			44.00
Kurt Hasse	Tora	4.00	
Marten von Barnekow	Nordland	20.00	
Heinz Brandt	Alchimist	20.00	
2. HOL			51.50
Johan Jacob Greter	Ernica	12.00	
Jan Adrianus de Bruine	Trixie	15.00	
Henri Louis van Schaik	Santa Bell	24.50	
3. POR			56.00
José Beltrão	Biscuit	12.00	
Luis Marquéz do Funchal	Merle Blanc	20.00	
Luis Mena e Silva	Faussette	24.00	
4. USA			72.50
Carl Raguse	Dakota	8.00	
William Bradford	Don	27.00	
Cornelius Jadwin	Ugly	37.50	

5. SWI			74.50
Arnold Mettler	Durmitor	15.00	
Jürg Fehr	Corona	29.00	
Max Iklé	Exile	30.50	
6. JAP			75.00
Manabu Iwahashi	Falaise	15.25	
Takeichi Nishi	Uranus	20.75	
Hirotsugu Inanami	Asafuji	39.00	
7. FRA			75.25
— Bizard	Bagatelle	12.00	
— Gudin de Vallerin	Ecuyère	12.00	
— de Tilière	Adriano	51.25	

1948 London T: 14, N: 14, D: 8.14.

	MOUNT		TOTAL PTS.
1. MEX			34.25
Humberto Mariles Cortés	Arete	6.25	
Rubén Uriza	Harvey	8.00	
Alberto Valdes	Chihuchoc	20.00	
2. SPA			56.50
Jaime Garcia Cruz	Bizarro	12.00	
José Navarro Morenes	Quorum	20.00	
Marcelino Gavilán y			
Ponce de Leon	Forajido	24.50	
3. GBR			67.00
Harry Llewellyn	Foxhunter	16.00	
Henry Nicoll	Kilgeddin	16.00	
Arthur Carr	Monty	35.00	

The course was so difficult that only three of the 14 teams managed to finish intact.

1952 Helsinki T: 15, N: 15, D: 8.3.

	MOUNT		TOTAL PTS.
1. GBR			40.75
Wilfred White	Nizefella	8.00	
Douglas Stewart	Aherlow	16.00	
Harry Llewellyn	Foxhunter	16.75	
2. CHI			45.75
Oscar Cristi	Bambi	8.00	
Cesar Mendoza	Pillan	12.00	
Ricardo Echeverria	Lindo Peal	25.75	
3. USA			52.25
William Steinkraus	Hollandia	13.25	
Arthur John McCashin	Miss Budweiser	16.00	
John Russell	Democrat	23.00	
4. BRA			56.50
Eloi Massey Oliveira de Menezes	Bigua	8.00	
Renyldo Guimaraes Ferreira	Bibelot	20.50	
Alvaro Dias de Toledo	Eldorado	28.00	
5. FRA			59.00
Pierre Jonquères d'Oriola	Ali Baba	8.00	
Bertran Pernot du Breuil	Tourbillon	20.00	
Jean-François d'Orgeix	Arlequin D.	31.00	
6. GER			60.00
Fritz Theidemann	Meteor	8.00	
Georg Höltig	Fink	20.00	
Hans-Hermann Evers	Baden	32.00	

	MOUNT		TOTAL PTS.
7. ARG			60.75
Sergio Dellacha	Santa Fe	12.00	
Argentino Molinuevo	Discutido	12.00	
Julio Sagasta	Don Juan	36.75	
8. POR			64.00
João Craveiro Lopes	Raso	20.00	
Henrique Alves Calado	Caramulo	20.00	
José Alves Carvalhosa	Mondina	24.00	

1956 Stockholm T: 20, N: 20, 6.15, 6.16.

	MOUNT		TOTAL PTS.
1. GER			40.00
Hans-Günter Winkler	Halla	4.00	
Fritz Thiedemann	Meteor	12.00	
Alfons Lütke-Westhues	Ala	24.00	
2. ITA			66.00
Raimondo D'Inzeo	Merano	8.00	
Piero D'Inzeo	Uruguay	11.00	
Salvatore Oppes	Pagoro	47.00	
3. GBR			69.00
Wilfred White	Nizefella	12.00	
Patricia Smythe	Flanagan	21.00	
Peter Robeson	Scorchin	36.00	
4. ARG			99.50
Carlos Delía	Discutido	19.00	
Pedro Mayorga	Coriolano	32.00	
Naldo Dasso	Ramito	48.50	
5. USA			104.50
Hugh Wiley	Trail Guide	24.00	
William Steinkraus	Night Owl	28.00	
Frank Chapot	Belair	52.25	
6. SPA			117.25
Carlos López Quesada	Tapatio	27.75	
Francisco Goyoaga	Fahnenkonig	28.00	
Carlos Figueroa Castillejo	Gracieux	61.50	
7. IRL			131.25
Kevin Barry	Ballyneety	35.00	
William Ringrose	Liffey Vale	44.00	
Patrick Kiernan	Ballynonty	52.25	
8. FRA			154.50
Pierre Jonquères d'Oriola	Voulette	15.00	
Bernard Jevardat de Fombelle	Doria	52.75	
Georges Calmon	Virtuoso	86.75	

1960 Rome T: 18, N: 18, 9.11.

	MOUNT		TOTAL PTS.
1. GER			46.50
Hans-Günter Winkler	Halla	13.25	
Fritz Thiedemann	Meteor	16.00	
Alwin Schockemöhle	Ferdl	17.25	

2. USA			66.00
Frank Chapot	Trail Guide	20.00	
William Steinkraus	Ksar d'Esprit	21.50	
George Morris	Sinjon	24.50	
3. ITA			80.50
Raimondo D'Inzeo	Posillipo	8.00	
Piero D'Inzeo	The Rock	32.00	
Antonio Oppes	The Scholar	40.50	
4. UAR			135.50
Gamal Harres	Nefertiti	24.00	
Mohamed Zaki	Artos	48.00	
Alwi Gazi	Mabrouk	63.50	
5. FRA			168.75
Bernard Jevardat de Fombelle	Buffalo	32.50	
Max Fresson	Grand Veneur	50.25	
Pierre Jonquères d'Oriola	Eclaire au Chocolat	86.00	
6. ROM			175.00
Vasile Pinciu	Barsan	41.50	
Virgil Barbuceanu	Robot	57.75	
Gheorghe Langa	Rubin	75.75	

1964 Tokyo T: 14, N: 14, D: 10.24.

	MOUNT		TOTAL PTS.
1. GER			68.50
Hermann Schridde	Dozent	13.75	
Kurt Jarasinski	Torro	22.25	
Hans-Günter Winkler	Fidelitas	32.50	
2. FRA			77.75
Pierre Jonquères d'Oriola	Lutteur	9.00	
Janou Lefebvre	Kenavo D	32.00	
Guy Lefrant	Monsieur de Littry	36.75	
3. ITA			88.50
Piero D'Inzeo	Sunbeam	24.50	
Raimondo D'Inzeo	Posillipo	28.00	
Graziano Mancinelli	Rockette	36.00	
4. GBR			97.25
Peter Robeson	Firecrest	16.00	
David Broome	Jacopo	37.00	
William Barker	North Flight	44.25	
5. ARG			101.00
Jorge Canaves	Confinado	29.50	
Hugo Arrambide	Chimbote	34.25	
Carlos Delia	Popin	37.25	
6. USA			107.00
Frank Chapot	San Lucas	20.50	
Kathryn Kusner	Untouchable	29.75	
Mary Mairs	Tomboy	56.75	
7. AUS			109.00
Thomas John Fahey	Bonvale	16.00	
Bridget Anne MacIntyre	Coronation	39.50	
Kevin Ashley Bacon	Ocean Foam	53.50	
8. SPA			118.75
Fernando Goyoaga	Kif-Kif B.	35.00	
Enrique Martinez de Vallejo	Eolo IV	40.00	
A. Queipo de Llano	Infernal	43.75	

1968 Mexico City T: 15, N: 15, D: 10.27.

	MOUNT		TOTAL PTS.
1. CAN			102.75
James Elder	The Immigrant	27.25	
James Day	Canadian Club	36.00	
Thomas Gayford	Big Dee	39.50	
2. FRA			110.50
Janou Lefebvre	Rocket	29.75	
Marcel Rozier	Quo vadis	33.50	
Pierre Jonquères d'Oriola	Nagir	47.25	
3. GER			117.25
Alwin Schockemöhle	Donald Rex	18.75	
Hans-Günter Winkler	Enigk	28.25	
Hermann Schridde	Dozent	70.25	
4. USA			117.50
Frank Chapot	San Lucas	25.00	
Kathryn Kusner	Untouchable	44.50	
Mary Chapot	White Lightning	48.00	
5. ITA			129.25
Raimondo D'Inzeo	Bellevue	24.25	
Piero D'Inzeo	Fidux	47.50	
Graziano Mancinelli	Donerailo	57.50	
6. SWI			136.75
Paul Weier	Satan	36.75	
Monica Bachmann	Erbach	49.50	
Arthur Blickenstorfer	Marianka	50.50	
7. BRA			138.00
Nelson Pessoa	Pass-Op	38.75	
Lucia Faria	Rush du Camp	44.75	
Jose Reynoso	Cantal	54.50	
8. GBR			159.50
David Broome	Mr. Softee	20.00	
R. Harvey Smith	Madison Time	45.00	
Marion Coakes	Stroller	94.50	

1972 Munich T: 17. N: 17. D: 9.11.

	MOUNT		TOTAL PTS.
1. GER			32.00
Fritz Ligges	Robin	8.00	
Gerhard Wiltfang	Askan	12.00	
Hartwig Steenken	Simona	12.00	
Hans-Günter Winkler	Torphy	16.00	
2. USA			32.25
William Steinkraus	Main Spring	4.00	
Neal Shapiro	Sloopy	8.25	
Kathryn Kusner	Fleet Apple	32.00	
Frank Chapot	White Lightning	36.00	
3. ITA			48.00
Vittorio Orlandi	Fulmer Feather	8.00	
Raimondo D'Inzeo	Fiorello II	12.00	
Graziano Mancinelli	Ambassador	28.00	
Piero D'Inzeo	Easter Light	135.25	
4. GBR			51.00
Michael Saywell	Hideaway	16.00	
R. Harvey Smith	Summertime	20.00	
David Broome	Manhaton VI	20.00	
Ann Moore	Psalm	32.00	

5. SWI			61.25
Monica Weier	Erbach	17.75	
Paul Weier	Wulf	20.00	
Max Hauri	Haiti	23.50	
Hermann von Siebenthal	Royal Havana	135.25	
6. CAN			64.00
James Elder	Houdini	8.00	
James Day	Happy Fellow	24.00	
Terrance Miller	Le Dauphin	35.00	
Ian Miller	Shoeman	44.00	
7. SPA			66.00
Alfonso Segovia	Tic Tac	19.00	
Enrique Martinez Vallejo	Val de Loire	19.00	
Luis Alvarez Cervera	Acorn	28.00	
Duque de Aveyro	Sunday Beau	115.25	
8. ARG			121.00
Hugo Arrambide	Camalote	27.00	
Roberto Tagle	Simple	46.00	
Jorge Llambi	Okey Amigo	48.00	
Argentino Molinuevo	Abracadabra	135.25	

Beginning in 1972, team totals were determined by adding the three best scores for each round rather than the three best scores for both rounds combined.

1976 Montreal T: 14. N: 14. D: 8.1.

	MOUNT		TOTAL PTS.
1. FRA			40.00
Hubert Parot	Rivage	12.00	
Marcel Rozier	Bayard de Maupas	12.00	
Marc Roguet	Belle de Mars	24.00	
Michel Roche	Un Espoir	32.00	
2. GER			44.00
Alwin Schockemöhle	Warwik Rex	12.00	
Hans-Günter Winkler	Torphy	16.00	
Sönke Sönksen	Kwepe	20.00	
Paul Schockemöhle	Agent	24.00	
3. BEL			63.00
Eric Wauters	Gute Sitte	15.00	
François Mathy	Gai Luron	20.00	
Edgar Gupper	Le Champion	28.00	
Stanny van Paeschen	Porsche	36.00	
4. USA			64.00
Frank Chapot	Viscount	16.00	
Robert Ridland	South Side	20.00	
William Brown	Sandsablaze	28.00	
Michael Matz	Grande	40.00	
5. CAN			64.50
James Day	Sympatico	20.00	
Michel Vaillancourt	Branch County	20.50	
Ian Millar	Countdown	27.50	
James Elder	Raffles II	36.00	
6. SPA			71.00
Luis Alvarez-Cervera	Acorne	16.00	
Alfonso Segovia	Val de Loire	23.00	
José Rosillo	Agamenon	36.00	
Eduardo Amoros	Limited Edition	39.00	

7. GBR 76.00

	MOUNT	
Debbie Johnsey	Moxy	24.00
Roland Fernyhough	Bouncer	31.00
Peter Robeson	Law Court	32.00
Graham Fletcher	Hideaway	36.00

8. MEX 76.25

	MOUNT	
Fernando Hernandez	Fascination	24.00
Fernando Senderos	Jet Run	24.00
Luis Razo	Pueblo	28.50
Carlos Aguirre	Consejero	38.25

1980 Moscow T:6. N:6. D: 7.29.

	MOUNT		TOTAL PTS.
1. SOV			20.25
Vyacheslav Chukanov	Gepatit	4.00	
Viktor Poganovsky	Topky	8.25	
Viktor Asmaev	Reis	11.25	
Nikolai Korolkov	Espadron	12.00	
2. POL			56.00
Jan Kowalczyk	Artemor	12.00	
Wieslaw Hartman	Norton	24.00	
Marian Kozicki	Bremen	37.50	
Janusz Bobik	Szampan	40.00	
3. MEX			59.75
Joaquin Perez Heras	Alymony	12.00	
Alberto Valdes Lacarra	Lady Mirka	20.75	
Gerardo Tazzer Valencia	Caribe	31.75	
Jesus Gomez Portugal	Massacre	35.25	
4. HUN			124.00
Barnabás Hevesy	Bohem	28.00	
Ferenc Krucsó	Vadrozsa	32.00	
József Varró	Gambrinusz	97.75	
András Balogi	Artemis	101.75	
5. ROM			150.50
Alexandru Bozan	Prejmer	43.75	
Dania Popescu	Sonor	53.00	
Dumitru Velea	Fudul	73.75	
Ion Popa	Licurici	95.50	
6. BUL			159.50
Nikola Dimitrov	Vals	46.75	
Dimitar Ghenov	Makbet	56.00	
Boris Pavlov	Monblan	60.75	
Hristo Katchov	Povdo	73.00	

The surprise winners of the Rotterdam Show Jumping Festival were the Canadians. Great Britain was second and Austria was third.

DRESSAGE, INDIVIDUAL

The dressage competition requires the rider to put the horse through a series of movements which display the degree of communication and cooperation between human and animal. Points are awarded for the proper execution of each movement.

1896–1908 not held

1912 Stockholm C: 21, N: 8, D: 7.15.

		MOUNT	PTS.
1. Carl Bonde	SWE	Emperor	15
2. Gustaf-Adolf Boltenstern, Sr.	SWE	Neptun	21
3. Hans von Blixen-Finecke, Sr.	SWE	Maggie	32
4. Friedrich von Oesterley	GER	Condor	36
5. Carl Rosenblad	SWE	Miss Hastings	43
6. Oskar af Ström	SWE	Irish Lass	47
7. Felix Burkner	GER	King	51
8. Carl Kruckenberg	SWE	Kartusch	51

1920 Antwerp C: 13, N: 5, D: 9.9.

		MOUNT	PTS.
1. Janne Lundblad	SWE	Uno	27,937
2. Bertil Sandström	SWE	Sabel	26,312
— Gustaf-Adolf Boltenstern, Sr.	SWE	Iron	26,187
3. Hans von Rosen	SWE	Running Sister	25,125
4. Wilhelm von Essen	SWE	Nomeg	24,875
5. Hédoin de Maillé	FRA	Cheribiribi	23,937
6. Michel Artola	FRA	Plumard	23,437

Colonel Boltenstern, on Iron, finished in third place, but was disqualified for practicing in the ring before the competition began.

1924 Paris C: 24, N: 9, D: 7.25.

		MOUNT	PTS.
1. Ernst Linder	SWE	Piccolomini	276.4
2. Bertil Sandström	SWE	Sabel	275.8
3. Xavier Lesage	FRA	Plumard	265.8
4. Wilhelm von Essen	SWE	Zobel	260.0
5. Victor Ankarcrona	SWE	Corona	256.5
6. Emanuel Thiel	CZE	Ex	256.2
7. R. Wallon	FRA	Magister	243.2
7. H. von der Weid	SWI	Uhlard	243.2

1928 Amsterdam C: 29, N: 12, D: 8.11.

		MOUNT	PTS.
1. Carl Friedrich Freiherr von Langen-Parow	GER	Draufganger	237.42
2. Charles Marion	FRA	Linon	231.00
3. Ragnar Ohlson	SWE	Gunstling	229.78
4. Janne Lundblad	SWE	Blackmar	226.70
5. Emanuel Thiel	CZE	Loki	225.96
6. Hermann Linkenbach	GER	Gimpel	224.26
7. L.E.R. Wallon	FRA	Clough-banck	224.08
8. Jan van Reede	HOL	Hans	220.70

1932 Los Angeles C: 10, N: 4, D: 8.10.

		MOUNT	POINTS	ORDINALS
1. Xavier Lesage	FRA	Taine	343.75	6
2. Charles Marion	FRA	Linon	305.42	14
3. Hiram Tuttle	USA	Olympic	300.50	14
4. Thomas Byström	SWE	Guliver	293.50	16
5. André Jousseaume	FRA	Sorelta	290.42	17
6. Isaac Kitts	USA	American Lady	282.08	17
7. Alvin Moore	USA	Water Pat	276.33	20
8. Gustaf-Adolf Boltenstern, Jr.	SWE	Ingo	277.83	21

Bertil Sandström of Sweden came in second but was relegated to last place for encouraging his horse, Kreta, by making clicking noises. He claimed that the noises were actually made by a creaking saddle, but the Jury of Appeal was not convinced. Moore was awarded seventh place, ahead of Boltenstern, because places were determined not by total points but by the rankings of the judges, using a system of ordinals such as is used in figure skating.

1936 Berlin C: 29, N: 11, D: 8.13.

		MOUNT	PTS.
1. Heinz Pollay	GER	Kronos	1760.0
2. Friedrich Gerhard	GER	Absinth	1745.5
3. Alois Podhajsky	AUT	Nero	1721.5
4. Gregor Adlercreutz	SWE	Teresina	1675.0
5. André Jousseaume	FRA	Favorite	1642.5
6. Gérard de Ballore	FRA	Debaucheur	1634.0
7. Peder Jensen	DEN	His Ex	1596.0
8. Pierre Versteegh	HOL	Ad Astra	1579.0

1948 London C: 19, N: 9, D: 8.9.

		MOUNT	PTS.
1. Hans Moser	SWI	Hummer	492.5
2. André Jousseaume	FRA	Harpagon	480.0
3. Gustaf-Adolf Boltenstern, Jr.	SWE	Trumf	477.5
4. Robert Borg	USA	Klingson	473.5
5. Henri Saint Cyr	SWE	Djimm	444.5
— Gehnäll Persson	SWE	—	444.0
6. Jean Saint Fort Paillard	FRA	Sous les Ceps	439.5
7. Alois Podhajsky	AUT	Teja	437.5
8. Earl Thomson	USA	Pancraft	421.0

The absurdity of the rules governing Olympic dressage reached its pinnacle in 1948, when sixth-place finisher Gehnäll Persson was disqualified when it was discovered that he was only a noncommissioned officer and thus ineligible to compete.

1952 Helsinki C: 27, N: 10, D: 7.29.

		MOUNT	PTS.
1. Henri Saint Cyr	SWE	Master Rufus	561.0
2. Lis Hartel	DEN	Jubilee	541.5
3. André Jousseaume	FRA	Harpagon	541.0
4. Gustaf-Adolf Boltenstern, Jr.	SWE	Krest	531.0
4. Gottfried Trachsel	SWI	Kursus	531.0
6. Henri Chammartin	SWI	Wohler	529.5

7. Gustav Fischer	SWI	Soliman	518.5
7. Heinz Pollay	GER	Adular	518.5

Between 1948 and 1952 dressage competition underwent a radical change. Not only were noncommissioned officers allowed to enter in 1952, so were other enlisted men. And not only were enlisted men allowed to enter, so were men who were civilians. And not only were men who were civilians allowed to enter, but for the first time in Olympic equestrian history, four women were allowed to compete against men. One of those women was Lis Hartel of Denmark. In 1944 Lis Hartel, a 23-year-old pregnant mother, was one of Denmark's leading riders. Then, one morning in September, she awoke with a headache and a strange stiffness in her neck. A few days later paralysis began spreading throughout her body—she had become a victim of polio. But Lis Hartel was determined to regain her health. First she learned to lift her arm, then she regained the use of her thigh muscles. Then she gave birth to a healthy daughter. Soon she was crawling, and eight months after the attack, she was able to walk a bit by using crutches. Her friends hailed her recovery, but she was not finished. She insisted on mounting a horse. Reactivating the muscles necessary to keep from falling was so exhausting that she had to rest for two weeks before she tried a second time. Slowly but surely, Lis Hartel improved until, three years after her polio attack, she was able to compete in the Scandinavian riding championship, finishing second in the women's dressage. She remained paralyzed below the knees, but learned to do without those muscles. In 1952 she was chosen to represent Denmark in the Olympics, and she responded by earning the silver medal, even though she had to be helped on and off her horse. When gold medalist Henri Saint Cyr helped her up onto the victory platform for the medal presentation, it was one of the most emotional moments in Olympic history. Four years later, in Stockholm, she won another silver medal.

1956 Stockholm C: 36, N: 17, D: 6.16.

		MOUNT	PTS.
1. Henri Saint Cyr	SWE	Juli	860.0
2. Lis Hartel	DEN	Jubilee	850.0
3. Liselott Linsenhoff	GER	Adular	832.0
4. Gehnäll Persson	SWE	Knaust	821.0
5. André Jousseaume	FRA	Harpagon	814.0
6. Gottfried Trachsel	SWI	Kursus	807.0
7. Gustaf-Adolf Bolterstern, Jr.	SWE	Krest	794.0
8. Henri Chammartin	SWI	Woehler	789.0

The judging caused something of a scandal. The German judge, General Berger, ranked the three German riders first, second, and third and the Swedish judge, General Colliander, ranked the three Swedish riders first, second, and third. First-place finisher Henri Saint Cyr completed his harvest of four gold medals. The fifth-place finisher, 61-year-old André Jousseaume, was competing in his fifth

Olympics. Between 1932 and 1952 he won two gold medals, two silver, and one bronze.

1960 Rome C: 17, N: 10, D: 9.6.

		MOUNT	PTS.
1. Sergei Filatov	SOV	Absent	2144.0
2. Gustav Fischer	SWI	Wald	2087.0
3. Josef Neckermann	GER	Asbach	2082.0
4. Henri Saint Cyr	SWE	L'Etoile	2064.0
5. Ivan Kalita	SOV	Korbey	2007.0
6. Patricia Galvin	USA	Rathpatrick	995.0
7. Rosemarie Springer	GER	Doublette	985.0
8. Henri Chammartin	SWI	Wolfdietrich	978.0

Finishing in 16th place was Kroum Lekarshi of Bulgaria, whose first Olympic appearance has been in the three-day event in 1924.

1964 Tokyo C: 22, N: 9, D: 10.23.

		MOUNT	PTS.
1. Henri Chammartin	SWI	Woermann	1504.0
2. Harry Boldt	GER	Remus	1503.0
3. Sergei Filatov	SOV	Absent	1486.0
4. Gustav Fischer	SWI	Wald	1485.0
5. Josef Neckermann	GER	Antoinette	1429.0
6. Reiner Klimke	GER	Dux	1404.0
7. Marianne Gossweiler	SWI	Stephan	802.0
8. Patricia de la Tour	USA	Rath Patrick	783.0

1968 Mexico City C: 26, N: 9, D: 10.25.

		MOUNT	PTS.
1. Ivan Kizimov	SOV	Ikhor	1572.0
2. Josef Neckermann	GER	Mariano	1546.0
3. Reiner Klimke	GER	Dux	1537.0
4. Ivan Kalita	SOV	Absent	1519.0
5. Horst Köhler	GDR	Neuschnee	1475.0
6. Yelena Petushkova	SOV	Pepel	1471.0
7. Gustav Fischer	SWI	Wald	1465.0
8. Liselott Linsenhoff	GER	Piaff	855.0

1972 Munich C: 33, N: 13, D: 9.7.

		MOUNT	PTS.
1. Liselott Linsenhoff	GER	Piaff	1229.0
2. Yelena Petushkova	SOV	Pepel	1185.0
3. Josef Neckermann	GER	Venetia	1177.0
4. Ivan Kizimov	SOV	Ikhor	1159.0
6. Ivan Kalita	SOV	Tarif	1130.0
5. Ulla Håkansson	SWE	Ajax	1126.0
7. Karin Schlueter	GER	Liostroa	1113.0
8. Maud von Rosen	SWE	Lucky Boy	1088.0

Twenty-one of the 33 riders were women, including Liselott Linsenhoff, the first female individual gold medalist. Second-place finisher Petushkova was a professor of biology at the University of Moscow and was, for some time, married to high-jumper Valery Brumel.

1976 Montreal C: 12, N: 7, D: 7.30.

			MOUNT	PTS.
1.	Christine Stückelberger	SWI	Granat	1486.0
2.	Harry Boldt	GER	Woycek	1435.0
3.	Reiner Klimke	GER	Mehmed	1395.0
4.	Gabriela Grillo	GER	Ultimo	1257.0
5.	Dorothy Morkis	USA	Monaco	1249.0
6.	Viktor Ugriumov	SOV	Said	1247.0
7.	Chris Boylen	CAN	Gaspano	1217.0
8.	Ulla Petersen	DEN	Chigwell	1192.0

1980 Moscow C: 12, N: 6, D: 8.1.

			MOUNT	PTS.
1.	Elisabeth Theurer	AUT	Mon Cherie	1370.0
2.	Yuri Kovshov	SOV	Igrok	1300.0
3.	Viktor Ugryumov	SOV	Shkval	1234.0
4.	Vera Misevich	SOV	Plot	1231.0
5.	Kyra Kyrklund	FIN	Piccolo	1121.0
6.	Anghelache Donescu	ROM	Dor	960.0
7.	Georgi Gadzhev	BUL	Vnimatelen	881.0
8.	Svetoslav Ivanov	BUL	Aleko	850.0

Theurer was the only leading dressage rider to enter the Olympics. All the rest took part in the Dressage Festival the following week, which was won by Christine Stückelberger.

DRESSAGE, TEAM

1896–1924 not held

1928 Amsterdam T: 8, N: 8, D: 8.11.

	MOUNT		TOTAL PTS.
1. GER			669.72
Carl Friedrich Freiherr von Langen-Parow	Draufganger	237.42	
Hermann Linkenbach	Gimpel	224.26	
Eugen Freiherr von Lotzbeck	Caracalla	208.04	
2. SWE			650.86
Ragnar Ohlson	Gunstling	229.78	
Janne Lundblad	Blackmar	226.70	
Carl Bonde	Ingo	194.38	
3. HOL			642.96
Jan van Reede	Hans	220.70	
Pierre Versteegh	His Excellence	216.44	
Gérard Le Heux	Valerine	205.82	
4. FRA			642.18
Charles Marion	Linon	231.00	
Robert Wallon	Cloughbank	224.08	
Pierre Danloux	Rempart	187.10	
5. CZE			637.94
Emanuel Thiel	Loki	225.96	
Otto Schöniger	Ex	210.28	
Jaroslav Hauf	Elegant	201.70	
6. AUT			600.40
Arthur von Pongracz	Turridu	204.28	
Wilhelm Jaich	Graf	204.16	
Gustav Grachegg	Daniel	191.96	

7. BEL		499.70
R.G.G. Delrue	Dreypuss	146.14
H.J. Laame	Belga	167.70
O.G.H. Lints	Rira-t-elle	185.86
8. SWI		569.08
W. Stuber	Ulhard	175.12
O. Frank	Solon	190.62
A. Mercier	Queen-Mary	203.34

1932 Los Angeles T: 3, N: 3, D: 8.10.

	MOUNT	TOTAL PTS.
1. FRA		2818.75
Xavier Lesage	Taine	1031.25
Charles Marion	Linon	916.25
André Jousseaume	Sorelta	871.25
2. SWE		2678.00
Thomas Byström	Gulliver	880.50
Gustaf-Adolf Boltenstern, Jr.	Ingo	833.50
Bertil Sandström	Kreta	964.00
3. USA		2576.75
Hiram Tuttle	Olympic	901.50
Isaac Kitts	American Lady	846.25
Alvin Moore	Water Pat	829.00

1936 Berlin T: 9, N: 9, D: 8.13.

	MOUNT	TOTAL PTS.
1. GER		5074.0
Heinz Pollay	Kronos	1760.0
Friedrich Gerhard	Absinth	1745.5
Hermann von Oppeln-Bronikowski	Gimpel	1568.5
2. FRA		4846.0
André Jousseaume	Favorite	1642.5
Gerard de Ballore	Debaucheur	1634.0
Daniel Gillois	Nicolas	1569.5
3. SWE		4660.5
Gregor Adlercreutz	Teresina	1675.0
Sven Colliander	Kal	1530.5
Folke Sandström	Pergoia	1455.0
4. AUT		4627.5
Alois Podhajsky	Nero	1721.5
Albert Dolleschall	Infant	1476.0
Arthur von Pongracz	Georgine	1430.0
5. HOL		4382.0
Pierre Versteegh	Ad Astra	1579.0
Gérard Le Heux	Zonnetje	1422.0
Daniel Camerling-Helmolt	Wodan	1381.0
6. HUN		4090.0
Gusztáv von Pados	Ficsur	1424.0
Lászlo von Magasházy	Tucsok	1415.5
Pál Kerméry	Csintaian	1250.5
7. NOR		4050.5
Quist	Jaspis	1438.0
Johansen	Sorte Mand	1388.0
Bjornseth	Invictus	1224.5
8. CZE		4026.0
Jandl	Nestor	1453.0
Pechmann	Ideal	1319.0
Schöniger	Helios	1254.0

The oldest competitor at the Berlin Olympics was 72-year-old General Arthur von Pongracz, of Austria's fourth-place team. Von Pongracz made his Olympic debut in Paris in 1924, when he was a mere youngster of 60.

1948 London T: 5, N: 5, D: 8.9.

	MOUNT		TOTAL PTS.
— SWE			1366.0
Gustav-Adolf Boltenstern, Jr.	Trumf	477.5	
Henri Saint Cyr	Djimm	444.5	
Gehnäll Persson	—	444.0	
1. FRA			1269.0
André Jousseaume	Harpagon	480.0	
Jean Saint Fort Paillard	Sous les Ceps	439.5	
Maurice Buret	Saint Ouen	349.5	
2. USA			1256.0
Robert Borg	Klingson	473.5	
Earl Thomson	Pancraft	421.0	
Frank Henry	Reno Overdo	361.5	
3. POR			1182.0
Fernando Pais da Silva	Matamas	411.0	
Francisco Valadas	Feitico	405.0	
Luiz Mena e Silva	Fascinante	366.0	
4. ARG			1005.5
Justo Iturralde	Pajarito	397.0	
Humberto Terzano	Bienvenido	327.0	
Oscar Goulu	Grillo	281.5	

The first-place Swedish team was disqualified when it was learned that Persson, who had been entered as an officer, was actually only a noncommissioned officer.

1952 Helsinki T: 8, N: 8, D: 7.29.

	MOUNT		TOTAL PTS.
1. SWE			1597.5
Henri Saint Cyr	Master Rufus	561.0	
Gustaf-Adolf Boltenstern, Jr.	Krest	531.0	
Gehnäll Persson	Knaust	505.5	
2. SWI			1579.0
Gottfried Trachsel	Krusus	531.0	
Henri Chammartin	Wohler	529.5	
Gustav Fischer	Solimon	518.5	
3. GER			1501.0
Heinz Pollay	Adular	518.5	
Ida von Nagel	Afrika	503.0	
Fritz Thiedemann	Chronist	479.5	
4. FRA			1423.5
André Jousseaume	Harpagon	541.0	
Jean Peiterin de Saint André	Vol au vent	479.0	
Jean Saint Fort Paillard	Tapir	403.5	
5. CHI			1340.5
José Larrain	Rey de Oros	473.5	
Hector Clavel	Frontalera	452.0	
Ernesto Silva	Viareggio	415.0	
6. USA			1253.5
Robert Borg	Bill Biddle	492.0	
Marjorie Haines	The Flying Dutchman	446.0	
Hartmann Pauly	Reno Overde	315.5	

7. SOV   1205.5

7. SOV		**1205.5**
Vladimir Raspopov	Imeninnik	433.5
Vassily Tihonov	Pevec	395.0
Nikolai Sitko	Cesar	377.0
8. POR		**1196.5**
Antonio Reymão Nogueira	Napeiro	428.4
Francisco Valadas Júnior	Feitico	422.0
Fernando Silva Paes	Matamas	346.0

1956 Stockholm T: 8, N: 8, D: 6.16.

	MOUNT		TOTAL PTS.
1. SWE			2475.0
Henri Saint Cyr	Juli	860.0	
Gehnäll Persson	Knaust	821.0	
Gustaf-Adolf Boltenstern, Jr.	Krest	794.0	
2. GER			2346.0
Liselott Linsenhoff	Adular	832.0	
Hannelore Weygand	Perkunos	785.0	
Anneliese Küppers	Afrika	729.0	
3. SWI			2346.0
Gottfried Trachsel	Kursus	807.0	
Henri Chammartin	Wohler	789.0	
Gustav Fischer	Vasello	750.0	
4. SOV			2170.0
Sergei Filatov	Ingas	744.0	
Aleksandr Vtorov	Repertoir	726.0	
Nikolai Sitko	Skatschek	700.0	
5. DEN			2167.0
Lis Hartel	Jubilee	850.0	
Hermann Zobel	Monty	673.0	
Inger Lemvigh-Müller	Bel Ami	644.0	
6. FRA			2016.0
André Jousseaume	Harpagon	814.0	
Jean-Albert Brau	Vol d'Amour	648.0	
Jean Salmon	Kipling	554.0	
7. NOR			1912.5
Else Christophersen	Diva	739.0	
Anne Lise Kielland	Clary	601.5	
Bodil Russ	Corona	572.0	
8. ROM			1862.0
Gheorghe Teodorescu	Palatin	721.0	
Nicolae Mihalcea	Mihnea	625.0	
Niculae Marcoci	Corvin	516.0	

1960 not held

1964 Tokyo T: 6, N: 6, D: 10.23.

	MOUNT		TOTAL PTS.
1. GER			2558.0
Harry Boldt	Remus	889.0	
Reiner Klimke	Dux	837.0	
Josef Neckermann	Antoinette	832.0	
2. SWI			2526.0
Henri Chammartin	Wormann	870.0	
Gustav Fischer	Wald	854.0	
Marianne Gossweiler	Stepan	802.0	

	MOUNT		TOTAL PTS.
3. SOV			2311.0
Sergei Filatov	Absent	847.0	
Ivan Kizimov	Ikhor	758.0	
Ivan Kalita	Moar	706.0	
4. USA			2130.0
Patricia de la Tour	Rath Patrick	783.0	
Anne Newberry	Forstrat	707.0	
Karen McIntosh	Malteser	640.0	
5. SWE			2068.0
William Hamilton	Delicado	777.0	
Hans Wikne	Gaspari	753.0	
Bengt Ljungquist	Karat	538.0	
6. JAP			1779.5
Kikuko Inoue	Katsunobori	648.0	
Nagahira Okabe	Seiha	589.5	
Yoritsune Matsudaira	Hamachidori	542.0	

1968 Mexico City T: 8, N: 8, D: 10.24.

	MOUNT		TOTAL PTS.
1. GER			2699.0
Josef Neckermann	Mariano	948.0	
Reiner Klimke	Dux	896.0	
Liselott Linsenhoff	Piaff	855.0	
2. SOV			2657.0
Ivan Kizimov	Ikhor	908.0	
Ivan Kalita	Absent	879.0	
Yelena Petushkova	Pepel	870.0	
3. SWI			2547.0
Gustav Fischer	Wald	866.0	
Henri Chammartin	Wolfdietrich	845.0	
Marianne Gossweiler	Stephan	836.0	
4. GDR			2357.0
Horst Köhler	Neuschnee	875.0	
Gerhard Brockmüller	Tristan	789.0	
Wolfgang Müller	Marios	693.0	
5. GBR			2332.0
Domini Lawrence	San Fernando	793.0	
H. Lorna Johnstone	El Guapo	777.0	
Johanna Hall	Conversano Caprice	762.0	
6. CHI			2015.0
Guillermo Squella	Colchaguino	693.0	
Antonio Piraino	Ciclon	672.0	
Patricio Escudero	Prete	650.0	
7. CAN			2012.0
Inez Fischer-Credo	Marius	732.0	
Christilot Hanson	Bonheur	677.0	
Zoltan Sztehlo	Virtuose	603.0	
8. USA			1919.0
Kyra Downton	Cadet	657.0	
Edith Master	Helios	646.0	
Donnan Plumb	Attache	616.0	

1972 Munich T: 10, N: 10, D: 9.7.

	MOUNT		TOTAL PTS.
1. SOV			5095.0
Yelena Petushkova	Pepel	1747.0	
Ivan Kizimov	Ikhor	1701.0	
Ivan Kalita	Tarif	1647.0	

2. GER			5083.0
Liselott Linsenhoff	Piaff	1763.0	
Josef Neckermann	Venetia	1706.0	
Karin Schlüter	Lisotro	1614.0	
3. SWE			4849.0
Ulla Håkansson	Ajax	1649.0	
Ninna Swaab	Casanova	1622.0	
Maud Von Rosen	Lucky Boy	1578.0	
4. DEN			4606.0
Aksel Mikkelsen	Talisman	1597.0	
Ulla Petersen	Chigwell	1534.0	
Charlotte Ingemann	Souliman	1475.0	
5. GDR			4552.0
Gerhard Brockmüller	Marios	1545.0	
Wolfgang Müller	Semafor	1521.0	
Horst Köhler	Imanuel	1486.0	
6. CAN			4418.0
Christilot Hanson	Armagnac III	1615.0	
Cynthia Neal	Bonne Annee	1424.0	
Lorraine Stubbs	Venezuela	1379.0	
7. SWI			4383.0
Christine Stückelberger	Granat	1528.0	
Hermann Duer	Sod	1466.0	
Marita Aeschbacher	Charlamp	1389.0	
8. HOL			4309.0
Annie van Doorne	Pericles	1480.0	
Friederie Benedictus	Turista	1420.0	
John Swaab	Maharadscha	1409.0	

1976 Montreal T: 8, N: 8, D: 7.29.

	MOUNT		TOTAL PTS.
1. GER			5155.0
Harry Boldt	Woycey	1863.0	
Reiner Klimke	Mehmed	1751.0	
Gabriela Grillo	Ultimo	1541.0	
2. SWI			4684.0
Christine Stückelberger	Granat	1869.0	
Ulrich Lehmann	Widin	1425.0	
Doris Ramseier	Roch	1390.0	
3. USA			4647.0
Hilda Gurney	Keen	1607.0	
Dorothy Morkis	Monaco	1559.0	
Edith Master	Dahlwitz	1481.0	
4. SOV			4542.0
Viktor Ugriumov	Said	1597.0	
Ivan Kalita	Tarif	1520.0	
Ivan Kizimov	Rebus	1425.0	
5. CAN			4538.0
Christilot Boylen	Gaspano	1590.0	
Lorraine Stubbs	True North	1549.0	
Barbara Stracey	Jungherr II	1399.0	
6. DEN			4448.0
Ulla Petersen	Chigwell	1552.0	
Tonny Jensen	Fox	1521.0	
Niels Haagensen	Lowenstern	1375.0	
7. HOL			4380.0
Jo Rutten	Banjo	1533.0	
Louky Van Olphen	Aleric	1449.0	
Marjolyn Greeve	Lucky Boy	1398.0	

8. GBR			4076.0
Sarah Whitmore	Junker	1375.0	
Jennie Loriston Clarke	Kadett	1375.0	
Diana Mason	Special Ed	1326.0	

1980 Moscow T: 4, N: 4, D: 7.31.

	MOUNT		TOTAL PTS.
1. SOV			4383.0
Yuri Kovshov	Igrok	1588.0	
Viktor Ugryumov	Shkval	1541.0	
Vera Misevich	Plot	1254.0	
2. BUL			3580.0
Peter Mandazhiev	Stchibor	1244.0	
Svetoslav Ivanov	Aleko	1190.0	
Georgi Gadjev	Vnimatelen	1146.0	
3. ROM			3346.0
Anghelache Donescu	Dor	1255.0	
Dumitru Veliku	Decebal	1076.0	
Petre Rosca	Derbist	1015.0	
4. POL			2945.0
Józef Zagor	Helios	1061.0	
Elżbieta Morciniec	Sum	954.0	
Wanda Waśowska	Damask	930.0	

The Goodwood Dressage Festival, held as an alternative to the Olympics, was won by West Germany, with Switzerland second and Denmark third.

Discontinued Events

HIGH JUMP

1900 Paris C: 18, N: 5, D: 6.2.

		MOUNT	M
1. Dominique Maximien Gardéres	FRA	Canela	1.85
1. Gian Giorgio Trissino	ITA	Oreste	1.85
3. Georges van de Poele	BEL	Ludlow	1.70
4. Gian Giorgio Trissino	ITA	Melopo	1.70

LONG JUMP

1900 Paris C: 17, N: 5, D: 5.31.

		MOUNT	M
1. Constant van Langhendonck	BEL	Extra Dry	6.10
2. Gian Giorgio Trissino	ITA	Oreste	5.70
3. de Bellegarde	FRA	Tolla	5.30
4. Prince Napoléon Murat	FRA	Bayard	—

FIGURE RIDING

1920 Antwerp C: 17, N: 3, D: 9.11.

		PTS.
1. Bouckaert	BEL	30.5
2. Fiel	FRA	29.5
3. Finet	BEL	29.0
4. van Ranst	BEL	—
5. van Schauwbroeck	BEL	—
6. van Cauwenberg	BEL	—

Teams
1. BEL (Bouckaert, Finet, van Ranst)
2. FRA (Fiel, Salins, Cauchy)
3. SWE (Carl Green, Oskar Nilsson, Anders Märtensson)

This event was open only to soldiers below the rank of noncommisioned officers.

FENCING

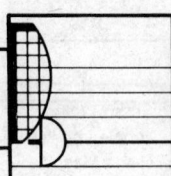

MEN	WOMEN
Foil, Individual	Foil, Individual
Foil, Team	Foil, Team
Epée, Individual	
Epée, Team	
Sabre, Individual	
Sabre, Team	
Discontinued Events	

MEN

The three swords used in fencing competitions are the foil, the épée, and the sabre.

The *foil* has a flexible rectangular blade and a blunt point. Touches must be made with the point on the trunk of the body, between the collar and the hipbones.

The *épée* has a rigid triangular blade with a point that is covered by a cone with barbed points. Touches may be made on any part of the body.

The *sabre* is a flexible triangular blade with a blunt point. Both the point and the cutting edges can be used to score touches, which must be made on the body, above the waist.

Fencing tournaments are run on a round-robin basis. For the first round, the fencers are divided into pools. The leaders of each pool advance to the next round. When sixteen fencers remain, a double elimination tournament is held. The six survivors then move on to the final pool. The last two fencers to be eliminated from the double eliminations are awarded joint seventh place.

Currently, ties for medal-winning positions are decided by *barrage*, or fence-offs. Ties for other places are decided by comparing the differential between touches (or hits) given and received. If a tie still exists, it is won by the fencer who has received the fewest touches.

Fencing bouts are won by the first fencer to score five touches.

FOIL, INDIVIDUAL

1896 Athens C: 8, N: 2, D: 4.7.

		W	L	TG	TR
1. Eugene-Henri Gravelotte	FRA	4	0	12	6
2. Henri Callot	FRA	3	1	11	7
3. Perikles Pierrakos-Mavromichalis	GRE	2	1	7	4
3. A. Vouros	GRE	2	1	5	4
5. de Laborde	FRA	1	2	5	7
5. Konstantinos Komnios-Milliotis	GRE	1	2	5	4
7. Balakakis	GRE	0	3	2	9
7. Ioannis Poulos	GRE	0	3	3	9

1900 Paris C: 54, N: 3, D: 5.21.

		W	L
1. Emile Coste	FRA	6	1
2. Henri Masson	FRA	5	2
3. Marcel Jacques Boulenger	FRA	4	3
4. Debax	FRA	4	3
5. Pierre d'Hugues	FRA	3	4
6. Senat	FRA	3	4
7. Georges Dillon-Cavanagh	FRA	2	5
8. Rudolf Brosch	AUT	1	6

1904 St. Louis C: 9, N: 3, D: 9.7.

		W	L
1. Ramón Fonst	CUB	3	0
2. Albertson Van Zo Post	USA	2	1
3. Charles Tatham	USA	1	2
4. Gustav Casmir	GER	0	3

1906 Athens C: 37, N: 12, D: 4.28.
1. Georges Dillon-Cavanagh   FRA
2. Gustav Casmir   GER
3. Pierre d'Hugues   FRA
4. Martin Harden   AUT
5. S. Okker   HOL
6. Federico Cesarano   ITA

1908 not held

1912 Stockholm C: 104, N: 16, D: 7.8.

		W	L	TG	TR
1. Nedo Nadi	ITA	7	0	35	8
2. Pietro Speciale	ITA	5	2	29	24
3. Richard Verderber	AUT	4	3	27	25
4. László Berti	HUN	4	3	23	25
5. Edoardo Alajmo	ITA	4	3	27	26
6. Edgar Seligman	GBR	3	4	23	29
7. Béla Bekessy	HUN	1	6	20	34
8. Robert Montgomerie	GBR	0	7	22	35

Nadi was a mere 18 years old when he won his first Olympic gold medal. The French team boycotted the competition after their proposal to include the upper arm as an attackable surface was rejected.

1920 Antwerp C: 64, N: 8, D: 8.23.

		W	L	TR
1. Nedo Nadi	ITA	10	1	—
2. Philippe Cattiau	FRA	9	2	14
3. Roger Ducret	FRA	9	2	19
4. André Labatut	FRA	7	4	—
5. Aldo Nadi	ITA	6	5	19
6. Fernand de Montigny	BEL	6	5	27

Nadi's performance at Antwerp was nothing short of spectacular, as he won an unprecedented and unequaled five gold medals. Not only did he win both the individual foil and sabre, but he was also the leader of the winning Italian teams in the foil, épée, and sabre.

1924 Paris C: 49, N: 17, D: 7.4.

		W	L	TG	TR
1. Roger Ducret	FRA	6	0	30	14
2. Philippe Cattiau	FRA	5	1	29	11
3. Maurice van Damme	BEL	4	2	23	16
4. Jacques Coutrot	FRA	3	3	18	25
5. Roberto Larraz	ARG	2	4	21	25
6. Ivan Osiier	DEN	1	5	14	27
7. Balthazar de Beuckelaer	BEL	0	6	13	30

DNS: Edgar Seligman (GBR)

In the absence of the Italians, who had withdrawn following an incident during the team foil, the individual competition was dominated by the French. Particularly formidable was Philippe Cattiau, who whipped through the tournament with an outstanding record of 23 wins and one loss and 119 touches given, as opposed to only 54 received. Unfortunately, his only loss was in the final pool to 36-year-old Roger Ducret, who beat Cattiau five touches

to four to win the gold medal. Ducret had suffered six defeats (against 13 wins) on his way to the final.

1928 Amsterdam C: 54, N: 23, D: 8.1.

						BARRAGE			
		W	L	TG	TR	W	L	TG	TR
1. Lucien Gaudin	FRA	9	2	49	24	2	0	10	5
2. Erwin Casmir	GER	9	2	49	33	1	1	6	8
3. Giulio Gaudini	ITA	9	2	53	34	0	2	7	10
4. Oreste Puliti	ITA	8	3	51	27				
5. Philippe Cattiau	FRA	7	4	43	32				
6. Raymond Bru	BEL	7	4	42	41				
7. Ugo Pignotti	ITA	4	7	40	48				
8. Fritz August Gazzera	GER	4	7	37	49				

Lucien Gaudin and Oreste Puliti entered the finals undefeated, but Puliti lost to Gaudin, Erwin Casmir, and Raymond Bru. In the final Casmir beat Gaudin 5–4, but in the barrage Gaudin was the victor, 5–1. Gaudin was 41 years old.

1932 Los Angeles C: 26, N: 12, D: 8.5.

		W	L	TG	TR
1. Gustavo Marzi	ITA	9	0	45	17
2. Joseph Levis	USA	6	3	38	35
3. Giulio Gaudini	ITA	5	4	34	27
4. Gioacchino Guaragna	ITA	5	4	37	33
5. Erwin Casmir	GER	5	4	36	34
6. John Emrys Lloyd	GBR	5	4	36	34
7. Roberto Larraz	ARG	3	6	33	31
8. René Bougnol	FRA	3	6	28	41

Twenty-three-year-old Gustavo Marzi completed the tournament with a record of 21–2.

1936 Berlin C: 62, N: 22, D: 8.6.

		W	L	TG	TR
1. Giulio Gaudini	ITA	7	0	35	20
2. Edward Gardère	FRA	6	1	33	25
3. Giorgio Bocchino	ITA	4	3	28	22
4. Erwin Casmir	GER	4	3	31	29
5. Gioacchino Guaragna	ITA	3	4	30	28
6. Raymond Bru	BEL	3	4	25	31
7. André Gardère	FRA	1	6	23	32
8. Georges de Bourguignon	BEL	0	7	17	35

Between 1928 and 1936 the 6-foot 6-inch Gaudini won three gold medals, four silver, and two bronze. The 1936 foil was his only individual gold.

1948 London C: 63, N: 25, D: 8.4.

		W	L	TG	TR
1. Jehan Buhan	FRA	7	0	35	14
2. Christian d'Oriola	FRA	5	2	29	18
3. Lajos Maszlay	HUN	4	3	25	22
4. John Emrys Lloyd	GBR	4	3	23	29
5. René Bougnol	FRA	3	4	28	26
6. Manlio Di Rosa	ITA	3	4	22	27
7. Paul Valcke	BEL	1	6	23	31
8. Ivan Ruben	DEN	1	6	15	33

The 36-year-old Buhan had gone to London to compete in the épée and was only entered in the foil at the last minute. Runner-up d'Oriola had surprised the fencing world in 1947 by winning the world championship in Lisbon at the tender age of 18. Buhan finished the tournament with a record of 24–1.

1952 Helsinki C: 61, N: 25, D: 7.24.

		W	L	TG	TR
1. Christian d'Oriola	FRA	8	0	40	12
2. Edoardo Mangiarotti	ITA	6	2		21
3. Manlio Di Rosa	ITA	5	3		22
4. Jacques Lataste	FRA	4	4		31
5. Jehan Buhan	FRA	4	4	29	33
6. Mahmoud Younes	EGY	4	4	27	33
7. Salah Dessouki	EGY	2	6		35
8. Giancarlo Bergamini	ITA	2	6		36

All three medalists were left-handed.

1956 Melbourne C: 32, N: 14, D: 11.26.

						BARRAGE			
		W	L	TG	TR	W	L	TG	TR
1. Christian d'Oriola	FRA	6	1	33	17				
2. Giancarlo Bergamini	ITA	5	2	33	26	1	0	5	4
3. Antonio Spallino	ITA	5	2	30	21	0	1	4	5
4. Allan Jay	GBR	4	3	29	26				
5. József Gyuricza	HUN	3	4	21	25				
6. Claude Netter	FRA	3	4	19	30				
7. Mark Midler	SOV	2	5	19	30				
8. Raymond Paul	GBR	0	7	15	35				

D'Oriola was a 27-year-old law student when he became the first man since Nedo Nadi to win two individual foil gold medals. D'Oriola, a native of Perpignan, had some trouble adapting to the new electric foil, but he solved it quite well in time for the Melbourne Olympics.

1960 Rome C: 78, N: 31, D: 8.30.

						BARRAGE			
		W	L	TG	TR	W	L	TG	TR
1. Viktor Zhdanovich	SOV	7	0	35	20				
2. Yuri Sissikin	SOV	4	2	27	21				
3. Albert Axelrod	USA	3	3	23	24	2	0	10	7
4. Witold Woyda	POL	3	3	24	23	1	1	9	7
5. Mark Midler	SOV	3	4	28	25	0	2	5	10
6. Roger Closset	FRA	2	2	14	16				
7. Henry Hoskyns	GBR	2	5	21	33				
8. Christian d'Oriola	FRA	1	6	22	32				

A 22-year-old student-teacher from Leningrad, Zhdanovich was the first Soviet fencer to win a gold medal. As such, he became a hero and was known in the newspapers as "Viktor the Victor."

1964 Tokyo C: 55, N: 21, D: 10.14.

		W	L	TG	TR
1. Egon Franke	POL	3	0	15	9
2. Jean-Claude Magnan	FRA	2	2	14	10
3. Daniel Revenu	FRA	1	3	12	11
4. Roland Losert	AUT	0	3	4	15
5. Jenő Kamuti	HUN				
6. Tim Gerresheim	GER				
7. Henry Hoskyns	GBR				
7. Sandor Syabo	HUN				

Egon Franke, a 29-year-old technical administrator from the small town of Gliwice, was an unexpected and popular winner.

1968 Mexico City C: 64, N: 25, D: 10.16.

						BARRAGE			
		W	L	TG	TR	W	L	TG	TR
1. Ionel Drimbă	ROM	4	1	22	15				
2. Jenő Kamuti	HUN	3	2	19	14	1	0	5	4
3. Daniel Revenu	FRA	3	2	22	17	0	1	4	5
4. Christian Noël	FRA	2	3	14	18				
5. Jean-Claude Magnan	FRA	2	3	18	22				
6. Mihai Tiu	ROM	1	4	14	23				
7. Tanase Muresan	ROM								
7. German Sveshnikov	SOV								

Ion Drimbă, a 26-year-old physical training instructor, went through the tournament with a record of 19–2. Two years later he defected to the West and retired from competition.

1972 Munich C: 58, N: 26, D: 8.30.

		W	L	TG	TR
1. Witold Woyda	POL	5	0	25	7
2. Jenő Kamuti	HUN	4	1	23	19
3. Christian Noël	FRA	2	3	17	18
4. Mihai Tiu	ROM	2	3	17	20
5. Vladimir Denissov	SOV	2	3	17	21
6. Marek Dabrowski	POL	0	5	10	25

Thirty-three-year-old Witold Woyda qualified for the final with a modest record of 14–6, but then he completely dominated his last five opponents to take the gold medal.

1976 Montreal C: 56, N: 23, D: 7.21.

						BARRAGE			
		W	L	TG	TR	W	L	TG	TR
1. Fabio Dal Zotto	ITA	4	1	24	15	1	0	5	1
2. Aleksandr Romankov	SOV	4	1	21	13	0	1	1	5
3. Bernard Talvard	FRA	3	2	19	21				
4. Vassily Stankovich	SOV	2	3	19	18				
5. Frédéric Pietruszka	FRA	2	3	13	19				
6. Gregory Benkö	AUS	0	5	15	25				
7. Vladimir Denissov	SOV								
7. Christian Noël	FRA								

Dal Zotto, a student from Venice, celebrated his 19th birthday three days before the competition began.

1980 Moscow C: 37, N: 16, D: 7.23.

					BARRAGE			
		W	L	TG	TR	W	L	TG	TR
1. Vladimir Smirnov	SOV	4	1	24	16	1	1	9	5
2. Paskal Jolyot	FRA	4	1	24	17	1	1	5	5
3. Aleksandr Romankov	SOV	4	1	22	15	1	1	5	9
4. Sabiryhan Ruziev	SOV	2	3	20	19				
5. Lech Koziejowski	POL	1	4	15	21				
6. Petru Kuki	ROM	0	5	8	25				
7. Frédéric Pietruszka	FRA								
7. István Szelei	HUN								

Two years after winning the Olympic gold medal, Smirnov was defending his world championship in Rome when the foil of his opponent, Mattias Behr of West Germany, snapped and pierced Smirnov's mask. The 28-year-old Soviet fencer died nine days later.

FOIL, TEAM

Current rules allow each team to have six members, four of whom take part in each contest. Each contest consists of 16 matches, with each member of a team fencing against each other member of the opposing team. Ties are decided by total touches. Very often a contest will end as soon as one team has clinched the victory.

1896–1900 not held

1904 St. Louis T: 2, N: 2, D: 9.8.

		WON
1. CUB/USA	(Ramón Fonst—CUB, Manuel Diaz—CUB, Albertson Van Zo Post—USA)	7
2. USA	(Charles Tatham, Fitzhugh Townsend, Arthur Fox)	2

1906–1912 not held

1920 Antwerp T: 8, N: 8, D: 8.23.

		WON	LOST	MATCHES W	L
1. ITA	(Baldo Baldi, Tommaso Constantino, Aldo Nadi, Nedo Nadi, Abelardo Olivier, Oreste Puliti, Pietro Speciale, Rodolfo Terlizzi)	4	0	50	14
2. FRA	(Lionel Bony de Castellane, Gaston Amson, Phillippe Cattiau, Roger Ducret, André Labatut, Georges Trombert, Marcel Perrot, Lucien Gaudin)	3	1	44	18

3. USA	(Henry Breckinridge, Francis Honeycutt, Arthur Lyon, Harold Rayner, Robert Sears)	2	2	22	42
4. DEN	(Ivan Osiier, Georg Hegner, Ejnar Levison, Poul Rasmussen, Kay Schröder)	1	3	25	37
5. GBR	(Edgar Seligman, R.M.P. Willoughby, P.G. Doyne, Robert Montgomerie, H. Evan James, C.A. Kershaw)	0	4	17	47
6. BEL	7. HOL	8. CZE			

1924 Paris T: 12, N: 12, D: 6.30.

		WON	LOST	MATCHES W	L
1. FRA	(Lucien Gaudin, Philippe Cattiau, Jacques Coutrot, Roger Ducret, Henri Jobier, André Labatut, Guy de Luget, Joseph Peroteaux)	3	0	31	6
2. BEL	(Désiré Beaurain, Charles Crahay, Fernand de Montigny, Maurice van Damme, Marcel Bérré, Albert de Roocker)	2	1	12	20
3. HUN	(László Berti, Sándor Posta, Zoltán Schenker, Ödön Tersztyánszky, István Lichteneckert)	1	2	9	23
4. ITA	(Oreste Puliti, Giorgio Pessina, Valentino Argento, Giorgio Chiavacci, Giulio Gaudini, Aldo Boni, Luigi Cuomo, Dante Carniel)	0	3	1	4
5. ARG	(F.C. Bollini, Carmelo Camet, H.A. Casco, C. Guerrico, Roberto Larraz, Luis Lucchetti, A. Santamarina, J.N. Sosa)				

When the French and Italian teams met in the final pool at the Velodrome d'Hiver, it was assumed that the winner would go on to take the gold medal. France took a 3–1 lead. In the fifth assault, Lucien Gaudin and Aldo Boni were tied at four touches each when the jury awarded a decisive fifth touth to Gaudin. Boni was incensed and launched a verbal attack against Kovács, the Hungarian judge. Kovács approached the Jury of Appeal and demanded an apology, whereupon Boni denied everything. Kovács then produced a witness, the Italian-born Hungarian fencing master Italo Santelli, who reluctantly supported Kovács' allegations of abusive language. The Italian team withdrew in protest, and their remaining matches were declared forfeited. Lost in the excitement was a brilliant performance by Gaudin, who scored 22 victories without a defeat and recorded 110 touches while receiving only 21.

However, the affair was not over. Back in Italy, the Italian foil team issued a statement which accused Santelli of testifying against them because he feared the Italians would defeat the Hungarian team, which he had coached. When he heard about this insult, Santelli, who was over 60 years old, challenged Adolfo Contronei, the Italian captain, to a real duel. Government permission was obtained to fight the duel, but before the two men could meet, Santelli's 27-year-old son, Giorgio, invoked the *code duello* and demanded that he fight in his father's place. In the small town of Abazzia near the Hungarian border, Giorgio and Contronei met and fought with heavy sabres. After two minutes the younger Santelli slashed Contronei deeply on the side of the head, drawing blood. Doctors rushed in and halted the duel. Giorgio Santelli later moved to the United States, where he became the coach of the U.S. team. He taught fencing to 8,000 people and spent over 100,000 hours with a sword in his hand, but he never again engaged in a real duel.

1928 Amsterdam T: 16, N: 16, D: 7.30.

				MATCHES	
		WON	LOST	W	L
1. ITA	(Ugo Pignotti, Oreste Puliti, Giulio Gaudini, Giorgio Pessina, Giorgio Chiavacci, Gioacchino Guaragna)	3	0	34	14
2. FRA	(Lucien Gaudin, Philippe Cattiau, Roger Ducret, André Labatut, Raymond Flacher, André Gaboriaud)	2	1	23	25
3. ARG	(Roberto Larraz, Raúl Anganuzzi, Luis Lucchetti, Hector Lucchetti, Carmelo Camet)	1	2	23	25
4. BEL	(Max Janlet, Pierre Pecher, Raymond Bru, Albert de Roocker, Jean Verbrugghe, Charles Crahay)	0	3	16	32
5. HUN	(Ödön Tersztyánszky, György Rozgonyi, György Piller, József Rády, Gusztáv Kálniczky, Péter Toth)				
5. USA	(George Calnan, René Peroy, Joseph Levis, Harold Rayner, Henry Breckinridge, Dernell Every)				

In Amsterdam the Italians gained their revenge against the French with a 10–6 victory. The Italian team was led by Chiavacci, who finished the tournament with 22 wins and two losses, and Gaudini, who was 30–2, including four straight victories against the French.

1932 Los Angeles T: 6, N: 6, D: 8.1.

				MATCHES		BARRAGE		MATCHES	
		WON	LOST	W	L	WON	LOST	W	L
1. FRA	(Philippe Cattiau, Edward Gardère, René Lemoine, René Bondoux, Jean Piot, René Bougnol)	2	1	26	22	2	0	19	13
2. ITA	(Giulio Gaudini, Gustavo Marzi, Ugo Pignotti, Giorgio Pessina, Gioacchino Guaranga, Rodolfo Terlizzi)	2	1	31	17	1	1	17	9
3. USA	(George Calnan, Joseph Levis, Hugh Allesandroni, Dernell Every, Richard Steere, Frank Righeimer)	2	1	22	26	0	2	6	20
4. DEN	(Axel Bloch, Erik Kofoed-Hansen, Aage Leidersdorff, Ivan Osiier)	0	3	17	31				

Italy and France tied in the barrage, 8–8, but France was awarded the victory on fewer touches received, 58–62.

1936 Berlin T: 18, N: 18, D: 8.4.

				MATCHES	
		WON	LOST	W	L
1. ITA	(Giulio Gaudini, Gioacchino Guaranga, Gustavo Marzi, Giorgio Bocchino, Manlio Di Rosa, Ciro Verratti)	3	0	38	7
2. FRA	(Jacques Coutrot, André Gardère, René Lemoine, René	2	1	27	18

Bougnol, Edward Gardère,
René Bondoux)

		WON	LOST	W	L
3. GER	(Siegfried Lerdon, August Heim, Julius Eisenecker, Erwin Casmir, Stefan Rosenbauer, Otto Adam)	1	2	13	33
4. AUT	(Hans Lion, Roman Fischer, Hans Schönbaumsfeld, Ernst Baylon, Josef Losert, Karl Sudrich)	0	3	13	33
5. BEL	(Georges de Bourguignon, André van de Werve de Vorsselaer, Henri Paternoster, Raymond Bru, Heremans, Paul Valcke)				
5. USA	(Joseph Levis, Hugh Alessandroni, John Potter, John Hurd, Warren Dow, William Pecora)				
7. ARG	(Roberto Larraz, Hector Lucchetti, Gorordo Palacios, Luis Luccheti, Valenzuela, M. Torrente)				
7. HUN	(Jószef Hatszeghy Hatz, Lajos Maszlay, Aladár Gerevich, Béla Bay, Ottó Hatszeghy Hatz, Antal Zirczy)				

France was the slight favorite, but the Italians breezed through the tournament with 104 wins and 19 losses. Verratti was 23–1 and Marzi 18–1. The deciding match with France was halted when Italy achieved an unbeatable 9–4 advantage.

1948 London T: 16, N: 16, D: 7.31.

		WON	LOST	W	L
1. FRA	(André Bonin, René Bougnol, Jehan Buhan, Jacques Lataste, Christian d'Oriola, Adrian Rommel)	3	0	28	18
2. ITA	(Renzo Nostini, Manlio Di Rosa, Edoardo Mangiarotti, Giuliano Nostini, Giorgio Pellini, Saverio Ragno)	2	1	28	15
3. BEL	(Georges de Bourguignon, Henry Paternoster, Edouard Yves, Raymond Bru, André van de Werwe de Vorsselaer, Paul Valcke)	1	2	19	27
4. USA	(Daniel Bukantz, Dean Cetrulo, Dernell Every, Silvio Giolito, Nathaniel Lubell, Austin Prokop)	0	3	14	29
5. ARG	(José Rodriguez, Fulvio Galami, M. Torrente, Felix Galimi)				
5. EGY	(Osman Abdel Hafeez, Salah Dessouki, Mahmoud Younes, Mohamet Zulficar, H. Tewfik, M. Abdine)				

		WON	LOST	W	L
5. GBR	(R. Paul, A. Smith, Harry Cooke, John Emrys Lloyd, P. Turquet, Ulrich Wendon)				
5. HUN	(Béla Bay, Aladár Gerevich, Jószef Hatszeghy Hatz, Lajos Maszlay, Pál Dunay, Endre Palócz)				

An incident marred the semifinal round. Dissatisfied with a call by the president of the judges, the Argentine team gave three cheers for their opponents, the Belgians, and withdrew in protest. A more pleasant kind of event took place in the semifinal match between Great Britain and the United States. Harry Cooke of Britain was trailing Dean Cetrulo 3–4, when the two men collided. Cooke's mask smashed into his face, cutting his nose. The American team immediately administered first aid to their opponent. After a rest Cooke returned to action and rallied to win 5–4. In the deciding match, France took a 6–3 lead over Italy, but the Italians came from behind to win five of the last seven fights. However, France won anyway on fewer touches received, 60–62.

1952 Helsinki T: 15, N: 15, D: 7.22.

				MATCHES	
		WON	LOST	W	L
1. FRA	(Jehan Buhan, Christian d'Oriola, Adrian Rommel, Claude Netter, Jacques Noël, Jacques Lataste)	3	0	35	11
2. ITA	(Giancarlo Bergamini, Antonio Spallino, Manlio Di Rosa, Giorgio Pellini, Renzo Nostini, Edoardo Mangiarotti)	2	1	34	12
3. HUN	(Endre Tilli, Aladár Gúrevich, Endre Palócz, Lajos Maszlay, Tibor Berczelly, József Sákovics)	1	2	16	31
4. EGY	(Salah Dessouki, Mohamed Ali Riad, Osman Abdel-Hafiz, Mahmoud Younes, Mohamed Zulficar, Hassan Hosni Tawfik)	0	3	8	39
5. ARG	(Fulvio Galimi, José Rodriguez, Eduardo Sastre, Felix Galimi, Santaigo Massini)				
5. BEL	(Pierre van Houdt, André Verhalle, Alex Bourgeois, Paul Valcke, Edouard Yves, Gustave Balister)				

As usual, France and Italy dominated all other countries, entering their final showdown with match records of 54–9 and 55–6, respectively. Christian d'Oriola was the star of the tournament, winning ten matches without a loss. In the deciding confrontation he swept all four Italians by the scores of 5–0, 5–0, 5–1, and 5–2, leading the French team to an 8–6 victory.

1956 Melbourne T: 9, N: 9, D: 11.23.

		MATCHES			
		WON	LOST	W	L
1. ITA	(Edoardo Mangiarotti, Giancarlo Bergamini, Antonio Spallino, Luigi Carpaneda, Manlio Di Rosa, Vittorio Lucarelli)	3	0	26	22
2. FRA	(Christian d'Oriola, Bernard Baudoux, Claude Netter, Jacques Lataste, Roger Closset, René Coicaud)	2	1	28	20
3. HUN	(József Gyuricza, József Sákovics, Mihály Fülöp, Endre Tilli, Lajos Somodi, Sr., József Marosi)	1	2	22	24
4. USA	(Albert Axelrod, Daniel Bukantz, Harold Goldsmith, Byron Kreiger, Nathaniel Lubell, Sewall Shurtz)	0	3	18	28
5. GBR	(René Paul, Henry Hoskyns, Raymond Paul, Allan Jay, Arnold Ralph Cooperman)				
5. SOV	(Yuri Roudov, Yuri Ossipov, Mark Midler, Aleksandr Ovsiankine, Viktor Zhdanovich, Yuri Ivanov)				

Once again the championship was between France and Italy, and once again d'Oriola swept the Italians, receiving only seven hits in four assaults. This time, though, Italy's team was better balanced. Going into the last bout, Italy led 8–7, but because the touches were even at 57, whoever won the last bout, which matched Spallino and Netter, would win the gold medal. Netter took an early lead, but Spallino came from behind to tie 4–4 and then win the championship for Italy on the final touch.

1960 Rome T: 16, N: 16, D: 9.2.
1. SOV   (Viktor Zhdanovich, Mark Midler, Yuri Sissikin, German Sveshnikov, Yuri Rudov)
2. ITA   (Alberto Pellegrino, Luigi Carpaneda, Mario Curletto, Aldo Aureggio, Edoardo Mangiarotti)
3. GER   (Jürgen Brecht, Tim Gerresheim, Eberhard Mehl, Jürgen Theuerkauff)
4. HUN   (Ferenc Czvikovsky, Jenő Kamuti, Mihály Fülöp, László Kamuti, József Gyuricza, József Sákovics)
5. FRA   (Jacky Courtillat, Jean-Claude Magnan, Guy Barrabino, Claude Netter, Christian D'Oriola)
5. GBR   (Henry Hoskyns, Allan Jay, Arnold Ralph Cooperman, Angus McKenzie, Raymond Paul)
5. POL   (Egon Franke, Ryszard Parulski, Janusz Różycki, Ryszard Kunze, Witold Woyda)
5. USA   (Gene Glazer, Harold Goldsmith, Joseph Paletta, Albert Axelrod, Daniel Bukantz)
Final: SOV 9–4 ITA
3rd Place: GER 9–5 HUN

The Soviet Union became the first team since 1904 to break the Franco-Italian monopoly of the team foil event.

In the final, Zhdanovich and Midler provided seven of nine Soviet wins.

1964 Tokyo T: 16, N: 16, D: 10.16.
1. SOV   (German Sveshnikov, Yuri Sissikin, Mark Midler, Viktor Zhdanovich, Yuri Scharov)
2. POL   (Zbigniew Skrudlik, Witold Woyda, Egon Franke, Ryszard Parulski, Janusz Różycki)
3. FRA   (Daniel Revenu, Jacky Courtillat, Pierre Rodocanachi, Christian Nöel, Jean-Claude Magnan)
4. JAP   (Kazuhiko Tabuchi, Fujio Shimizu, Kazuo Mano, Heizaburo Okawa, Sosuke Toda)
5. GER   (Jürgen Brecht, Dieter Wellmann, Eberhard Mehl, Tim Gerresheim, Jürgen Theuerkauff)
6. ROM   (Tănase Mureşan, Ionel Drimbă, Iuliu Falb, Sefan Haukler, Atila Csipler)
7. HUN   (Jenő Kamuti, László Kamuti, József Gyuricza, Sándor Szabó, Béla Gyarmati)
7. ITA   (Gianguido Milanesi, Pasquale La Ragione, Arcangelo Pinelli, Nicola Granieri)
Final: SOV 9–7 POL
3rd Place: FRA 9–4 JAP
5th Place: GER 8(60)–8(57)ROM

1968 Mexico City T: 17, N: 17, D: 10.19.
1. FRA   (Daniel Revenu, Gilles Berolatti, Christian Nöel, Jean-Claude Magnan, Jacques Dimont)
2. SOV   (German Sveshnikov, Yuri Scharov, Vassily Stankovich, Viktor Putiatin, Yuri Sissikin)
3. POL   (Witold Woyda, Ryszard Parulski, Egon Franke, Zbigniew Skrudlik, Adam Lisewski)
4. ROM   (Ionel Drimbă, Mihai Tiu, Ştefan Haukler, Tănase Mureşan, Iuliu Falb)
5. HUN   (Sándor Szabó, Jenő Kamuti, László Kamuti, Gábor Füredi, Attila May)
6. GER   (Jürgen Theuerkauff, Friedrich Wessel, Tim Gerresheim, Jürgen Brecht, Dieter Wellmann)
7. ITA   (Pasquale La Ragione, Alfredo Del Francia, Nicola Granieri, Archangelo Pinelli, Michelle Maffei)
7. JAP   (Masaya Fukuda, Heizaburo Ohkawa, Fujio Shimizu, Kazuhiko Wakasugi, Kazuo Mano)
Final: FRA 9–6 SOV
3rd Place: POL 9–3 ROM
5th Place: HUN 9–4 GER

1972 Munich T: 13, N: 13, D: 9.2.
1. POL   (Lech Koziejowski, Witold Woyda, Marek Dabrowski, Jerzy Kaczmarek, Arkadiusz Godel)
2. SOV   (Vassily Stankovich, Viktor Poutiatin, Leonid Romanov, Anatoly Kotescev, Vladimir Denissov)
3. FRA   (Daniel Revenu, Bernard Talvard, Gilles Berolatti, Jean-Claude Magnan, Christian Nöel)
4. HUN   (Sándor Szabó, Csaba Fenyeesi, László Kamuti, István Marton, Jenő Kamuti)
5. GER   (Klaus Reichert, Friedrich Wessel, Harald Hein, Dieter Wellmann, Erk Sens-Gorius)
6. JAP   (Shiro Maruyama, Masaya Fukuda, Hiroshi Nakajima, Kiyoshi Uehara, Ichiro Serizawa)

7. CUB (Evelio Gonzalez, Eduardo Jhons, Jesus Gil, Enrique Salvat, Jorge Garbey)
7. ROM (Iuliu Falb, Ştefan Haukler, Mihai Tiu, Tănase Mureşan, Aurel Stefan)
   Final: POL 9–5 SOV
   3rd Place: FRA 9–7 HUN
   5th Place: GER 9–7 JAP

Poland secured the gold medal despite an early loss to Germany. In the same round, the U.S.S.R. was defeated by Japan. The match for first place was highlighted by Woyda's sweep of the four Soviet fencers. The French had been the favorites, but they lost in the semifinals, 9–6, to the Soviet Union.

1976 Montreal T: 14, N: 14, D: 7.24.
1. GER (Harald Hein, Thomas Bach, Erk Sens-Gorius, Klaus Reichert, Matthias Behr)
2. ITA (Fabio Dal Zotto, Attilio Calatroni, Carlo Montano, Stefano Simoncelli, Giovan Battista Coletti)
3. FRA (Daniel Revenu, Christian Nöel, Didier Flament, Bernard Talvard, Frédéric Pietruszka)
4. SOV (Sabirzhan Ruziev, Aleksandr Romankov, Vladimir Denissov, Vassily Stankovich)
5. POL (Leszek Martewicz, Lech Koziejowski, Ziemowit Wojciechowski, Arkadiusz Godel, Marek Dabrowski)
6. GBR (Geoffrey Grimmett, Barry Paul, Robert Bruniges, Graham Paul, Nicholas Bell)
7. HUN (József Komatits, Csaba Fenyvesi, Lajos Somodi, Jr., Jenő Kamuti, Sándor Erdös)
7. USA (Martin Lang, Edward Ballinger, Edward Wright, Edward Donofrio, Brooke Mackler)
   Final: GER 9–6 ITA
   3rd Place: FRA 9–4 SOV
   5th Place: POL 9–1 GBR

1980 Moscow T: 9, N: 9, D: 7.26.
1. FRA (Didier Flament, Paskal Jolyot, Frédéric Pietruszka, Philippe Bonnin, Paskal Jolyot, Bruno Boscherie)
2. SOV (Aleksandr Romankov, Vladimir Smirnov, Ashot Karagyan, Vladimir Lapitsky, Sabirzhan Ruziev)
3. POL (Boguslaw Zych, Adam Robak, Marian Sypniewski, Lech Koziejowski)
4. GDR (Siegmar Gutzeit, Hartmuth Behrens, Adrian Germanus, Klaus Kotzmann, Klaus Haertter)
5. ROM (Petru Kuki, Mihai Tiu, Sorin Roca, Tudor Petrus)
6. HUN (István Szelei, Ernő Kolczonay, András Papp, László Demény, Jenő Pap)
7. CUB (Efigenio Favier, Guillermo Betancourt, Heriberto Gonzalez, Pedro Hernandez)
8. GBR (John Llewellyn, Steven Paul, Robert Bruniges, Pierre Harper, Neal Mallett)
   Final: FRA 8(68)–8(60)SOV
   3rd Place: POL 9–5 GDR
   5th Place: ROM 9–7 HUN

In the semifinals, Soviet world champion Vladimir Lapitsky was accidentally run through the chest when his Polish opponent's foil broke his leather protective clothing. The sword severed a blood vessel but missed his heart.

France's victory marked their 13th team foil medal in 14 Olympics.

ÉPÉE, INDIVIDUAL
1896 not held

1900 Paris C: 101, N: 4, D: 6.14.
1. Ramón Fonst   CUB
2. Louis Perrée   FRA
3. Léon Sée   FRA
4. Georges de la Falaise FRA
5. Camet   FRA
6. Edmond Wallace   FRA
7. Gaston Alibert   FRA
8. Leon Thiebaut   FRA

Ramón Fonst was only 16 years old when he won the Olympic championship. His teacher, Albert Ayot, won the competition for masters.

1904 St. Louis C: 5, N: 3, D: 9.7.
1. Ramón Fonst   CUB
2. Charles Tatham   USA
3. Albertson Van Zo Post USA
4. Gustav Casmir   GER
5. Fitzhugh Townsend   USA

Not only did Fonst achieve a rare double victory in winning both the foil and épée, but he is also the only repeat winner in the individual épée.

1906 Athens C: 29, N: 10, D: 4.28.
1. Georges de la Falaise   FRA
2. Georges Dillon-Cavanagh   FRA
3. Alexander van Blijenburgh   HOL
4. Raphael Vigeveno   HOL
5. Emil Schön   GER
6. Maurits Jacob van Löben Sels HOL

1908 London C: 84, N: 13, D: 7.24.

		W	L	T	BARRAGE W	L
1. Gaston Alibert	FRA	5	0	2		
2. Alexandre Lippmann	FRA	4	2	1	2	0
3. Eugène Olivier	FRA	4	3	0	1	1
4. Robert Montgomerie	GBR	4	1	2	0	2
5. Paul Anspach	BEL	2	5	0		
5. Cecil Haig	GBR	2	5	0		
5. Alfred Joan Labouchère	HOL	2	3	2		
8. Martin Holt	GBR	1	5	1		

Gaston Alibert completed the tournament with 21 wins, no losses, and two double hits, or ties. Two other contestants worth noting were Alfred Labouchère, who attracted quite a bit of attention because he was 6 feet 9 inches tall and Ivan Osiier, a 19-year-old from Denmark. Osiier ultimately competed in seven Olympics, making his first and final appearances in London—40 years apart. Along the way he qualified for nine finals, achieving his greatest success in

1912, when he won the individual épée silver medal. His wife, Ellen, was the first woman Olympic fencing champion.

1912 Stockholm C: 112, N: 16, D: 7.13.

		W	L	T
1. Paul Anspach	BEL	6	1	0
2. Ivan Osiier	DEN	5	2	0
3. Philippe Le Hardy de Beaulieu	BEL	4	2	1
4. Victor Boin	BEL	4	2	1
5. Einar Sörensen	SWE	3	4	0
6. Edgar Seligman	GBR	2	4	1
7. Léon Tom	BEL	1	6	0
8. Martin Holt	GBR	0	4	3

The Italian Fencing Federation proposed that the length of the épée blade be extended to 94 cm. When this was rejected, the Italians refused to participate. Between 1908 and 1920 Paul Anspach won a total of four medals: two gold, one silver, and one bronze.

1920 Antwerp C: 46, N: 12, D: 8.23.

		WON
1. Armand Massard	FRA	9
2. Alexandre Lippmann	FRA	7
3. Gustave Buchard	FRA	6
4. Ernest Gevers	BEL	6
5. E. Moreau	FRA	5
6. Antonio Mascarenhas de Menezes	POR	5
7. —	—	—
8. S. Casanova	FRA	—

1924 Paris C: 67, N: 18, D: 7.11.

		WON	LOST	1st BARRAGE W	1st BARRAGE L	2nd BARRAGE W	2nd BARRAGE L
1. Charles Delporte	BEL	8	3				
2. Roger Ducret	FRA	7	4	2	1	1	0
3. Nils Hellsten	SWE	7	4	2	1	0	1
4. Emile Cornereau	FRA	7	4	1	2	1	0
5. Armand Massard	FRA	7	4	1	2	0	1
6. Virgilio Mantegazza	ITA	6	5				
7. Gustave Buchard	FRA	5	6				
7. Léon Tom	BEL	5	6				

1928 Amsterdam C: 59, N: 22, D: 8.7.

		W	L	T	TG	TR	EXTRA FINAL W	EXTRA FINAL L	EXTRA FINAL TG	EXTRA FINAL TR
1. Lucien Gaudin	FRA	8	0	1	18	5	2	0	20	12
2. Georges Buchard	FRA	7	2	0	15	8	1	1	19	21
3. George Calnan	USA	6	3	0	14	9	1	1	21	19
4. Léon Tom	BEL	6	2	1	15	9	0	2	12	20
5. Nils Hellsten	SWE	5	4	0	12	13				
6. Charles Delporte	BEL	4	5	0	11	13				
7. Charles Debeur	BEL	3	6	0	10	15				
8. S. Cicurel	EGY	3	6	0	10	15				

Gaudin's record for the tournament was an impressive 34 wins and five losses, as he became the only fencer besides Ramón Fonst to win both the foil and épée.

1932 Los Angeles C: 28, N: 12, D: 8.9.

		W	L	T	TG	TR
1. Giancarlo Cornaggia-Medici	ITA	8	1	2	31	18
2. Georges Buchard	FRA	8	3	0	27	17
3. Carlo Agostoni	ITA	7	3	1	30	17
4. Saverio Ragno	ITA	7	4	0	27	20
5. Bernard Schmetz	FRA	7	4	0	26	22
6. Philippe Cattiau	FRA	6	5	0	23	22
7. George Calnan	USA	6	5	0	22	22
8. Balthazar de Beuckelaer	BEL	4	7	0	19	25

1936 Berlin C: 68, N: 26, D: 8.11.

		W	L	T	TG	TR
1. Franco Riccardi	ITA	5	1	3	25	18
2. Saverio Ragno	ITA	6	3	0	24	15
3. Giancarlo Cornaggia-Medici	ITA	6	3	0	22	16
4. Hans Drakenberg	SWE	4	3	2	20	20
5. Charles Debeur	BEL	4	4	1	21	21
6. Henrique da Silveira	POR	4	5	0	18	19
7. R. Stasse	BEL	3	4	2	21	21
8. I.D. Campbell-Gray	GBR	3	4	2	18	24

Riccardi's total record was 24 wins, three losses, and four ties. In the quarterfinal pool, defending champion Cornaggia-Medici demonstrated his acute awareness of distance. Perplexed by the call of two straight double hits, he insisted that his opponent's blade was the wrong length. Measurement showed that it was in fact a half-inch too long.

1948 London C: 66, N: 25, D: 8.9.

		W	L	TG	TR	BARRAGE TG	BARRAGE TR
1. Luigi Cantone	ITA	7	2	24	15		
2. Oswald Zappelli	SWI	5	4	20	17	3	0
3. Edoardo Mangiarotti	ITA	5	4	20	17	0	3
4. Henri Guérin	FRA	5	4	20	19		
5. Jean Radoux	BEL	5	4	19	20		
6. Henri Lepage	FRA	4	5	19	20		
7. Carlo Agostoni	ITA	4	5	22	21		
8. Emile Gretsch	LUX	3	6	16	22		

Thirty-one-year-old Luigi Cantone was allowed to compete at the last minute after Dario Mangiarotti injured his foot and had to withdraw. In the final pool, which took five and a half hours, Cantone lost his first two bouts to Carlo Agostoni and Edoardo Mangiarotti. Then he won seven straight to take first place without a barrage.

1952 Helsinki C: 76, N: 29, D: 7.28.

		W	L	TR
1. Edoardo Mangiarotti	ITA	7	2	12
2. Dario Mangiarotti	ITA	6	3	16
3. Oswald Zappelli	SWI	6	3	18

					1st BARRAGE				2nd BARRAGE			
4. Léon Buck	LUX	6	3	19								
5. József Sákovics	HUN	5	4	17								
6. Carlo Pavesi	ITA	4	5	21								
7. Per Carleson	SWE	3	6	20								
8. Carl Forsell	SWE	3	6	23								

Milanese fencing master Giuseppe Mangiarotti began giving his sons lessons when they turned eight years old. Although both were right-handed, Giuseppe converted the younger boy, Edoardo, into a left-hander because he considered it an advantage in competition. When he was 11, Edoardo won the Italian junior foil title. But Giuseppe had been Italian professional épée champion 17 times, so when Edoardo turned 15 his father started training him with that weapon. At age 17, Edoardo was a member of the Italian épée team that won the gold medal at Berlin. By 1960 Edoardo had won 13 Olympic medals: four gold and one silver in team épée, one gold and two bronze in individual épée, one gold and three silver in team foil, and one silver in individual foil. His older brother, Dario, gained one gold and two silver.

1956 Melbourne C: 40, N: 17, D: 11.30.

		W	L	TG	TR	1st BARRAGE				2nd BARRAGE			
						W	L	TG	TR	W	L	TG	TR
1. Carlo Pavesi	ITA	5	2	29	20	1	1	9	7	2	0	10	5
2. Giuseppe Delfino	ITA	5	2	30	27	1	1	7	7	1	1	10	8
3. Edoardo Mangiarotti	ITA	5	2	30	17	1	1	7	9	0	2	3	10
4. Richard Pew	USA	4	3	25	28								
5. Lajos Balthazár	HUN	4	3	30	29								
6. René Queyroux	FRA	3	4	29	25								
7. Per Carleson	SWE	2	5	22	29								
8. Rolf Wiik	FIN	0	7	15	35								

Giuseppe Delfino came within one touch of winning the gold, but lost 5–4 to Richard Pew and was forced into the barrage.

1960 Rome C: 79, N: 32, D: 9.6.

		W	L	TG	TR	BARRAGE	
						TG	TR
1. Giuseppe Delfino	ITA	5	2	39	32	5	2
2. Allan Jay	GBR	5	2	39	23	2	5
3. Bruno Khabarov	SOV	4	3	32	23	8	7
4. József Sákovics	HUN	4	3	30	31	7	8
5. Roger Achten	BEL	3	4	31	30		
6. Yves Dreyfus	FRA	3	4	30	30		
7. Armand Mouyal	FRA	3	4	25	30		
8. Giovanni Breda	ITA	1	6	19	34		

The 38-year-old Delfino utilized a rather unusual style to achieve his long-awaited gold medal. Rather than waste his energy going for a five-touch victory, he would content himself with a tie until time ran out. Then he would concentrate on, and usually win, the single sudden-death overtime hit. This tactic defeated Allan Jay in the final pool to force the barrage.

1964 Tokyo C: 65, N: 25, D: 10.19.

		W	L	TG	TR	BARRAGE W	L	TG	TR
1. Grigory Kriss	SOV	2	1	12	11	1	0	5	2
2. Henry Hoskyns	GBR	2	1	15	12	0	1	2	5
3. Guram Kostava	SOV	1	2	12	12	1	0	5	0
4. Gianluigi Saccaro	ITA	1	2	10	14	0	1	0	5
5. Bogdan Gonsior	POL								
6. Claude Bourquard	FRA								
7. Orvar Lindwall	SWE								
8. Franz Rompza	GER								

In the final pool Kriss, a 23-year-old soldier from Kiev, defeated Hoskyns in a bout that saw four straight double (or simultaneous) hits. Hoskyns was a 33-year-old Somerset fruit farmer.

1968 Mexico City C: 73, N: 28, D: 10.22.

		W	L	TG	TR	BARRAGE W	L	T	TG	TR
1. Gyözö Kulcsár	HUN	4	1	24	14	2	0	0	10	5
2. Grigory Kriss	SOV	4	1	25	19	0	1	1	8	10
3. Gianluigi Saccaro	ITA	4	1	21	19	0	1	1	7	10
4. Viktor Modzalevsky	SOV	2	3	20	23					
5. Herbert Polzhuber	AUT	1	4	17	24					
6. Jean-Pierre Allemand	FRA	0	5	17	25					
7. Peter Loetscher	SWI									
7. Henryk Nielaba	POL									

The hero of Hungary's team épée victory four years earlier in Tokyo, Kulcsár completed the 1968 individual tournament with 17 wins and only one loss.

1972 Munich C: 72, N: 28, D: 9.6.

		W	L	TG	TR
1. Csaba Fenyvesi	HUN	4	1	25	10
2. Jacques la Degaillerie	FRA	3	2	23	19
3. Gyözö Kulcsár	HUN	3	2	20	19
4. Anton Alex Pongratz	ROM	3	2	19	20
5. Rolf Edling	SWE	1	4	15	22
6. Jacques Brodin	FRA	0	5	13	25

Two of the three medals went to fencers from Budapest. Csaba Fenyvesi was a 29-year-old physician, Gyözö Kulcsár a 31-year-old engineer.

1976 Montreal C: 64, N: 25, D: 7.23.

		W	L	TG	TR	BARRAGE W	L	TG	TR
1. Alexander Pusch	GER	3	2	22	18	2	0	10	7
2. Jürgen Hehn	GER	3	2	18	20	1	1	9	7
3. Gyözö Kulcsár	HUN	3	2	22	19	0	2	5	10
4. Istvan Osztrics	HUN	2	3	18	19				
5. Jerzy Janikowski	POL	2	3	20	21				
6. Rolf Edling	SWE	2	3	18	21				
7. Csaba Fenyvesi	HUN								
7. Göran Floodström	SWE								

In the barrage Pusch defeated Hehn, 5–4, in a seesaw battle, and then scored the last two touches to beat Kulcsár 5–3. Pusch was only 21 years old.

1980 Moscow C: 42, N: 16, D: 7.28.

		W	L	TG	TR
1. Johan Harmenberg	SWE	4	1	22	21
2. Ernö Kolczonay	HUN	3	2	23	19
3. Philippe Riboud	FRA	3	2	20	17
4. Rolf Edling	SWE	3	2	18	16
5. Alexandr Mozhaev	SOV	1	4	18	22
6. Ioan Popa	ROM	1	4	18	24
7. Jaroslav Jurka	CZE				
7. Boris Lukomsky	SOV				

ÉPÉE, TEAM

1896–1904 not held

1906 Athens T: 6, N: 6, D 4.28.
1. FRA   (Pierre d'Hugues, Georges Dillon-Cavanaugh, Mohr, Georges de la Falaise)
2. GBR   (William Desborough, Cosmo Duff-Gordon, Charles Robinson, Edgar Seligman)
3. BEL   (Constant Cloquet, Fernand de Montigny, Edmond Crahay, Philippe Le Hardy de Beaulieu)

In the first round Germany was due to meet Great Britain. However a misunderstanding of the schedule found the Germans asleep at their hotel at the time the match was to start. Quickly roused, the Germans rushed to the fencing grounds and were easily beaten, 9–2. The final resulted in a tie. The rematch was held immediately; France won, 9–6.

1908 London T: 9, N: 9, D: 7.23.
1. FRA   (Gaston Alibert, Bernard Gravier, Alexandre Lippmann, Eugène Olivier, Henri-Georges Berger, Charles Collignon, Jean Stern)
2. GBR   (Edward Amphlett, C. Leaf Daniell, Cecil Haig, Robert Montgomerie, Martin Holt, Edgar Seligman)
3. BEL   (Paul Anspach, Fernand Bosmans, Fernand de Montigny, François Rom, Victor Willems, Désiré Beaurain, Ferdinand Feyerick)
4. ITA   (Marcello Bertinetti, Giuseppe Mangiarotti, Riccardo Nowak, Abelardo Olivier)
Final: FRA 9–7 BEL
Pool for 2nd: GBR 9–8 DEN; GBR 9–5 BEL

1912 Stockholm T: 11, N: 11, D: 7.10.

		W	L	TR
1. BEL	(Paul Anspach, Henri Anspach, Robert Hennet, Fernand de Montigny, Jacques Ochs,	3	0	

François Rom, Gaston Salmon, Victor Willems)
2. GBR   (Edgar Seligman, Edward Amphlett, Robert Montgomerie, John Blake, Percival Davson, Arthur Everitt, Sydney Martineau, Martin Holt) — 1 2 28
3. HOL   (Adrianus E. W. de Jong, Willem P. Hubert van Blijenburgh, Jetze Doorman, Leonardus Salomonson, George van Rossem) — 1 2 30
4. SWE   (Einar Sörensen, Gustaf Lindblom, Pontus von Rosen, Louis Sparre, Georg Branting) — 1 2 32

1920 Antwerp T: 11, N: 11, D: 8.23.

		WON	LOST	MATCHES W	MATCHES L
1. ITA	(Nedo Nadi, Aldo Nadi, Abelardo Olivier, Tullio Bozza, Giovanni Canova, Andrea Marrazi, Dino Urbani, Antonio Allocchio, Tommaso Constantino, Paolo Thaon di Revel)	5	0	40	23
2. BEL	(Ernest Gevers, Paul Anspach, Felix Goblet d'Alviella, Victor Boin, Joseph de Craecker, Léon Tom, Maurice de Wée, Philippe Le Hardy de Beaulieu)	4	1	39	34
3. FRA	(Armand Massard, Alexandre Lippmann, Gustave Buchard, Georges Trombert, S. Casanova, Gaston Amson, E. Moreau)	3	2	40	30
4. POR	(Antonio Mascarenhas de Menezes, Jorge Paiva, Rui Mayer, João Sassetti, Henrique da Silveira, Frederico Paredes, Manuel Queiroz)	2	3	30	35
5. SWI	(Henri Jacquet, Léopold Montagnier, Franz Wilhelm, Frédéric Fitting, Eugène Empeyta, Louis de Tribolet, John Laurent Albaret, Edouard Fitting)	1	4	33	41
6. USA	(William Russell, Ray Dutcher, Henry Breckinridge, Arthur Lyon, Robert Sears, Harold Rayner)	0	5	19	38

Two competitors worth noting were Nedo Nadi of Italy and Victor Boin of Belgium. Nadi, who won five gold medals in foil and sabre, was not as well known as an épéeist. His father, Beppe, considered the épée to be an "undisciplined" weapon and forbade the use of it in his *salle*. So Nedo would sneak out to enjoy the taboo sword. His insubordination paid off with a team épée gold medal in 1920. Boin's silver medal as part of the Belgian team was his third Olympic medal. His first two, however were earned not in fencing but in water polo: a silver in 1908 and a bronze in 1912. Boin also enjoyed swimming, skating, flying, ice hockey, and motorcycle racing. He was founder of the International Association of Sports Journalists and President of the Belgian Olympic Committee.

1924 Paris T: 16, N: 16, D: 7.9.

		WON	LOST	MATCHES W	L
1. FRA	(Lucien Gaudin, Georges Buchard, Roger Ducret, André Labatut, Lionel Liottel, Alexandre Lippmann, Georges Tainturier)	3	0	29	16
2. BEL	(Paul Anspach, Joseph de Craecker, Charles Delporte, Fernand de Montigny, Ernest Gevers, Léon Tom)	2	1	24	22
3. ITA	(Giulio Basletta, Marcello Bertinetti, Giovanni Canova, Vincenzo Cuccia, Virgilio Mantegazza, Oreste Moricca)	1	2	21	26
4. POR	(Antonio Mascarenhas de Menezes, Jorge Paiva, Paulo d'Eca Leal, Rui Mayer, Henrique da Silveira, Mário de Noronha, Frederico Paredes, Antonio Pinto Leite)	0	3	18	28
5. SPA	(J. Delgado, F. De Pomes-Soler, Diez de Rivera, F. Garcia-Bilbao, D. Garcia-Montoro, J. Lopez-Lara-Mallor, C. Miguel de los Reyes, M. Zabalza de la Fuente)				
5. USA	(Henry Breckinridge, George Breed, George Calnan, Arthur Lyon, Allen Millner, William Russell, Leon Shore, Donald Waldhaus)				

1928 Amsterdam T: 18, N: 18, D: 8.5.

		WON	LOST	MATCHES W	L
1. ITA	(Carlo Agostoni, Marcello Bertinetti, Giancarlo Cornaggia-Medici, Renzo Minoli, Giulio Basletta, Franco Riccardi)	3	0	28	19
2. FRA	(Armand Massard, Georges Buchard, Gaston Amson, Emile Cornic, Bernard Schmetz, René Barbier)	2	1	24	22
3. POR	(Paulo d'Eca Leal, Mário de Noronha, Jorge Paiva, João Sassetti, Frederico Paredes, Henrique de Silveira)	1	2	21	26

4. BEL	(Emile Barbier, Balthazar de Beuckalaer, Charles Delporte, Charles Debeur, Léon Tom, Georges Dambois)	0	3	20	26
5. CZE	(M. G. Harden, J. Jungmann, F. Kriz, J. Tille, M. Beznoska, J. Cernohorsky)				
5. HOL	(L. Kuypers, Adrianus E. W. de Jong, H. J. M. Wijnoldy Daniels, W. Driebergen, Alfred Joan Labouchère, Jr. K. J. van den Brandeler)				
5. SPA	(J. M. de Tejada, D. Garcia Montoro, D. Diez de Rivera, F. de Pomes Soler, F. Gonzalez Badia)				
5. USA	(Arthur Lyon, George Calnan, Allen Milner, Harold Rayner, Henry Breckinridge, Edward Barnett)				

1932 Los Angeles T: 7, N: 7, D: 8.7.

		WON	LOST	MATCHES W	L
1. FRA	(Philippe Cattiau, Georges Buchard, Bernard Schmetz, Jean Piot, Fernand Jourdant, Georges Tainturier)	3	0	30.5	17.5
2. ITA	(Carlo Agostoni, Giancarlo Cornaggia-Medici, Renzo Minoli, Franco Riccardi, Saverio Ragno)	2	1	27.5	20.5
3. USA	(George Calnan, Gustave Heiss, Frank Righeimer, Tracy Jaeckel, Curtis Shears, Miguel de Capriles)	1	2	20.5	22.5
4. BEL	(Raoul Hankart, André Poplimont, Max Janlet, Balthazar de Beuckelaer, Albert Mund)	0	3	12.5	30.5

1936 Berlin T: 21, N: 21, D: 8.8.

		WON	LOST	MATCHES W	L
1. ITA	(Saverio Ragno, Alfredo Pezzana, Giancarlo Cornaggia-Medici, Edoardo Mangiarotti, Franco Riccardi, Giancarlo Brusati)	3	0	26	11
2. SWE	(Hans Granfelt, Sven Thofelt, Gösta Almgren, Gustaf Dyrssen, Hans Drakenberg, Birger Cederin)	2	1	21	22

3. FRA	(Michel Pécheux, Bernard Schmetz, Georges Buchard, Henri Dulieux, Paul Wormser, Philippe Cattiau)	1	2	21	23
4. GER	(Siegfried Lerdon, Joseph Uhlmann, Hans Esser, Eugen Geiwitz, Ernst Röthig, Otto Schröder)	0	3	11	23
5. BEL	(R. Stasse, T'Sas, Charles Debeur, de Monceau, Plumier, Heim)				
5. POL	(Jerzy Staszewicz, Teodor Zaczyk, Rajmund Karwicki, Roman Kantor, Kazimierz Szempliński, Antoni Franz)				
5. POR	(Henrique de Silveira, Paulo d'Eca Leal, Antonio Mascarenhas de Menezes, Sasseti, Carinhas)				
5. USA	(Frank Righeimer, Thomas Sands, Tracy Jaeckel, Gustave Heiss, Miguel de Capriles, Andrew Boyd)				

1948 London T: 21, N: 21, D: 8.6

		WON	LOST	MATCHES W	L
1. FRA	(Henri Guérin, Henri Lepage, Marcel Desprets, Michel Pécheux, Edouard Artigas, Maurice Huet)	3	0	31	10
2. ITA	(Luigi Cantone, Antonio Mandruzzato, Dario Mangiarotti, Edoardo Mangiarotti, Fiorenzo Marini, Carlo Agostoni)	2	1	25	21
3. SWE	(Per Carleson, Frank Cervell, Carl Forssell, Bengt Ljungquist, Sven Thofelt, H. Arne Tollbom)	1	2	18	26
4. DEN	(Mogens Lüchow, Erik Andersen, Ib Benjamin Nielsen, René Dybkaer, Jacob Lyng, Kenneth Flindt)	0	3	12	29
5. BEL	(R. Stasse, L. Hauben, R. Bru, J. Radoux, R. Henkart, Charles Debeur)				
5. HUN	(Imre Hennyey, Pál Dunay, Béla Rerrich, Béla Mikla, Lajos Balthazár, Béla Bay)				
5. LUX	(Fernand Leischen, Paul Anen, Emile Gretsch, G. Lamesch, E. Putz)				
5. SWI	(F. Thiebaud, R. Lips, J. Hauert, Oswald Zappelli, Otto Rufenach, M. Chamay)				

France qualified for the final pool despite being upset 10–5 in the semifinal pool by Belgium. The French team was led by Michel Pécheux, a last-minute addition, who was 11–0 in the final pool and 23–3 total.

1952 Helsinki T: 19, N: 19, D: 7.26.

		WON	LOST	MATCHES W	L
1. ITA	(Dario Mangiarotti, Edoardo Mangiarotti, Franco Bertinetti, Carlo Pavesi, Giuseppe Delfino, Roberto Battaglia)	3	0	32	11
2. SWE	(Bengt Ljundquist, Berndt-Otto Rehbinder, Sven Fahlman, Per Carleson, Carl Forssell, Lennart Magnusson)	2	1	26	17
3. SWI	(Otto Rüfenacht, Paul Meister, Oswald Zappelli, Paul Barth, Willy Fitting, Mario Valota)	1	2	18	24
4. LUX	(Emile Gretsch, Fernand Leischen, Paul Anen, Léon Buck)	0	3	9	33
5. DEN	(Raimondo Carnera, Erik Swane-Lund, René Dybkaer, Mogens Lüchow, Ib Benjamin Nielsen, Jacob Lyng)				
5. HUN	(Lajos Balthazár, Barnabás Berzsenyi, Béla Rerrich, József Sákovics, Imre Hennyey)				

The 1952 Olympics saw the downfall of defending champion France, eliminated in the second round after losses to Luxemburg and Hungary. Italy defeated Sweden 8–5 in the deciding match, despite the efforts of Bengt Ljundquist who beat all four Italians.

1956 Melbourne T: 11, N: 11, D: 11.28.

		WON	LOST	MATCHES W	L
1. ITA	(Giuseppe Delfino, Alberto Pelligrino, Edoardo Mangiarotti, Carlo Pavesi, Giorgio Anglesio, Franco Bertinetti)	3	0	34	10
2. HUN	(József Sákovics, Béla Rerrich, Lajos Balthazár, Ambrus Nagy, József Marosi, Barnabás Berzsenyi)	2	1	22	22
3. FRA	(Armand Mouyal, Claude Nigon, Daniel Dagallier, Yves Dreyfus, René Queyroux)	1	2	17	27
4. GBR	(René Paul, Michael Howard, Henry William Hoskyns, Allen Jay)	0	3	15	29
5. BEL	(François Dehez, Roger Achten, Ghislain Delaunois, Marcel Vanderauwera, Jacques Debeur)				
5. SOV	(Arnold Chernushevich, Valentin Chernikov, Lev Saitchouk, Revas Tsirekidze, Iosas Oudras)				

1960 Rome T: 21, N: 21, D: 9.9.
1. ITA (Giuseppe Delfino, Alberto Pellegrino, Carlo Pavesi, Edoardo Mangiarotti, Fiorenzo Marini, Gianluigi Saccaro)
2. GBR (Allan Jay, Michael Howard, John Pelling, Henry William Hoskyns, Raymond Harrison, Michael Alexander)
3. SOV (Guram Kostava, Bruno Khabarov, Arnold Chernushevich, Valentin Chernikov, Aleksandr Pavlovsky)
4. HUN (József Marosi, Tamás Gábor, István Kausz, József Sákovics, Árpád Bárány)
5. GER (Paul Gnaier, Fritz Zimmermann, Dieter Fänger, Georg Neuber, Helmut Anschütz, Walter Kostner)
5. LUX (Roger Theisen, Edouard Schmit, Robert Schiel, Rodolphe Kugeler, Edmond Gutenkauff)
5. SWE (Hans Lagerwall, Göran Abrahamsson, Ling Vannerus, Berndt Rehbinder, Carl-Wilhem Engdahl, Orvar Lindwall)
5. SWI (Hans Baessler, Amez Droz, Paul Meister, Charles Ribordy, Claudio Polledri, Michel Steininger)
Final: ITA 9–5 GBR
3rd Place: SOV 9–5 HUN

The Italian squad included the last three individual épée champions: Mangiarotti (1952), Pavesi (1956), and Delfino (1960), as well as 21-year-old Gianluigi Saccaro, who fenced with a patch over his injured right eye. In Italy's semifinal match against the U.S.S.R., the usually subdued Delfino found himself trailing Chernikov 4–1 with 13 seconds left. He then scored three hits in 12 seconds to force an overtime bout, which he also won.

1964 Tokyo T: 18, N: 18, D: 10.21.
1. HUN (Győzö Kulcsár, Zoltán Nemere, Támás Gábor, István Kausz, Árpád Bárány)
2. ITA (Gianluigi Saccaro, Giovanni Battista Breda, Gianfranco Paolucci, Giuseppe Delfino, Alberto Pellegrino)
3. FRA (Claude Brodin, Yves Dreyfus, Claude Bourquard, Jack Guittet, Jacques Brodin)
4. SWE (Ivar Genesjö, Orvar Lindwall, Hans Lagerwall, Göran Abrahamson, Carl-Wilhem Engdahl)
5. POL (Henryk Nielaba, Mikolaj Pomarnacki, Bogdan Gonsior, Bogdan Andrzejewski, Jerzy Pawlowski)
6. GER (Franz Rompza, Max Geuter, Volkmar Würtz, Paul Gnaier, Haakon Stein)
7. SOV (Bruno Khabarov, Guram Kostava, Yuri Smoliakov, Grigory Kriss, Alexsei Nikanchikov)
7. SWI (Claudio Polledri, Paul Meister, Walter Bar, Jean Gontier, Michel Steininger)
Final: HUN 8–3 ITA
3rd Place: FRA 8(64)–8(59) SWE
5th Place: POL 8(66)–8(62) GER

Hungary broke the 44-year Italian–French domination of team épée, as Győzö Kulcsár won all 20 of his bouts.

1968 Mexico City T: 20, N: 20, D: 10.25.
1. HUN (Csaba Fenyvesi, Zoltán Nemere, Pál Schmitt, Győzö Kulcsár, Pál Nagy)

2. SOV (Grigory Kriss, Yosif Vitebsky, Aleksei Nikanchikov, Yuri Smoliakov, Viktor Modzelevsky)
3. POL (Bohdan Andrzejewski, Michal Butkiewicz, Bohdan Gonsior, Henryk Nielaba, Kazimierz Barburski)
4. GER (Dieter Jung, Franz Rompza, Fritz Zimmerman, Max Geuter, Paul Gnaier)
5. GDR (Bernd Uhlig, Klaus Dumke, Harry Fiedler, Hans-Peter Schulze)
6. ITA (Gianfranco Paolucci, Claudio Francesconi, Giovanni Battista Breda, Gianluigi Saccaro, Antonio Albanese)
7. FRA (François Jeanne, Claude Bourquard, Yves Boissier, Jacques Ladegaillerie, Jean-Pierre Allemand)
7. GBR (Nicholas Halsted, Owen Bourne, Henry Hoskyns, Ralph Johnson, Peter Jacobs)
Final: HUN 7–4 SOV
3rd Place: POL 9–6 GER
5th Place: GDR 9–6 ITA

For the first time in 60 years, Italy failed to finish among the top three.

1972 Munich T: 20, N: 20, D: 9.9.
1. HUN (Istvan Osztrics, Sándor Erdös, Csaba Fenyvesi, Pál Schmitt, Győzö Kulcsár)
2. SWI (Peter Löetscher, Christian Kauter, Guy Evéquoz, Daniel Giger, François Suchanecki)
3. SOV (Georgy Zajitsky, Grigory Kriss, Viktor Modzelevsky, Igor Valetov, Sergei Paramonov)
4. FRA (François Jeanne, Jacques Brodin, Pierre Marchand, Jean-Pierre Allemand, Jacques La Degaillerie)
5. ROM (Constantin Dutu, Costică Bărăgan, Anton Alex Pongratz, Alexandru Istrate, Nicolae Iorgu)
6. POL (Bohdan Andrzejewski, Jerzy Janikowski, Henryk Nielaba, Kazimierz Barburski, Bohdan Gonsior)
7. NOR (Jan Von Koss, Jeppe Normann, Ole Morch, Claus Morch)
7. SWE (Hans Wieselgren, Carl Von Essen, Orvar Joensson, Rolf Edling, Per Sundberg)
Final: HUN 8–4 SWI
3rd Place: SOV 9–4 FRA
5th Place: ROM 9–3 POL

1976 Montreal T: 19, N: 19, D: 7.29.
1. SWE (Hans Jacobson, Orvar Jonsson, Carl Von Essen, Leif Högström, Göran Flodström, Rolf Edling)
2. GER (Alexander Pusch, Jürgen Hehn, Hanns Jana, Reinhold Behr, Volker Fischer)
3. SWI (Jean-Blaise Evéquoz, Michel Poffet, Daniel Giger, Christian Kauter, François Suchanecki)
4. HUN (Csaba Fenyvesi, Sándor Erdös, István Osztrics, Pál Schmitt, Győzö Kulcsár)
5. SOV (Aleksandr Aboushahmetov, Viktor Modzelevsky, Vassilly Stankovich, Aleksandr Bykov, Boris Loukomski)
6. ROM (Ioan Popa, Anton Pongratz, Nicolae Iorgu, Paul Szabo)
7. ITA (John Pezza, Nicola Granieri, Fabio Dal Zotto, Marcello Bertinetti, Giovan Battista Coletti)

7. NOR   (Nils Koppang, Jeppe Normann, Kjell Moe, Baard Vonen, Ole Moerch)
   Final: SWE 8–5 GER
   3rd Place: SWI 9–3 HUN
   5th Place: SOV 9–2 ROM

The world champion Swedish team received a setback in the first bout of the final match, when Göran Flodström was knocked out. Carl Von Essen was brought in as a replacement and won two crucial bouts, including one against Alexander Pusch, which took place while Flodström was being carried out on a stretcher.

1980 Moscow T: 11, N: 11, D: 7.31.
1. FRA   (Philippe Riboud, Patrick Picot, Hubert Gardas, Michel Salesse, Philippe Boisse)
2. POL   (Piotr Jablkowski, Andrzej Lis, Mariusz Strzalka, Ludomir Chronowski, Leszek Swornowski)
3. SOV   (Boris Lukomsky, Aleksandr Abushakhmetov, Vladimir Smirnov, Ashot Karagan, Aleksandr Mozhaev)
4. ROM   (Ioan Popa, Octavian Zidaru, Anton Pongratz, Costica Baragan, Petru Kuki)
5. SWE   (Johan Harmenberg, Rolf Edling, Leif Högström, Göran Malkar, Hans Jacobsen)
6. CZE   (Jaroslav Jurka, Jaromír Holub, Jiři Douba, Jiři Adam, Oldřich Kubišta)
7. GBR   (Steven Paul, John Patrick Llewellyn, Neal Pelham Mallett, Robert John Bruniges)
8. HUN   (Ernö Kolczonay, István Osztrics, Laszlo Petö, Jenö Pap, Péter Takács)
   Final: FRA 8–4 POL
   3rd Place: SOV 9–5 ROM
   5th Place: SWE 9–2 CZE
   7th Place: GBR 16–0 HUN (forfeit)

Led by Philippe Riboud's 16–2 effort, France pulled off a major upset and won the team épée gold medal for the first time in 32 years.

SABRE, INDIVIDUAL
1896 Athens C: 5, N: 3, D: 4.9.

		W	L	TG	TR
1. Jean Georgiadis	GRE	4	0	12	6
2. Telemachos Karakalos	GRE	3	1	11	5
3. Holger Nielsen	DEN	2	2	10	9
4. Adolf Schmal	AUT	1	3	7	11
5. Georgios Iatridis	GRE	0	4	3	12

1900 Paris C: 32, N: 10, D: 6.25.
1. Georges de la Falaise   FRA
2. Léon Thiébaut   FRA
3. Siegfried Flesch   AUT
4. Ámon von Gregurich   HUN
5. Gyula von Iványi   HUN
6. de Boissière   FRA
7. Heinrich Terner   AUT
8. Camillo Müller   AUT

1904 St. Louis C: 5, N: 2, D: 9.8.

		W	L	TG	BARRAGE W	L
1. Manuel Diaz	CUB	3	0	21		
2. William Grebe	USA	2	1	20	1	0
3. Albertson Van Zo Post	USA	2	1	18	0	1
4. Theodore Carstens	USA	1	2			
5. Arthur Fox	USA	0	4			

1906 Athens C: 29, N: 8, D: 4.28.
1. Jean Georgiadis   GRE
2. Gustav Casmir   GER
3. Federico Cesarano   ITA
4. Georges de la Falaise   FRA
5. Ervin Mészáros   HUN
6. Jěno Apáthy   HUN

1908 London C: 76, N: 11, D: 7.24.

		W	L	T	BARRAGE W	L
1. Jenö Fuchs	HUN	6	0	1	1	0
2. Béla Zulavszky	HUN	6	1	0	0	1
3. Vilém Goppold von Lobsdorf	BOH	4	2	1		
4. Jenö Szántay	HUN	3	3	1		
5. Péter Tóth	HUN	3	4	0		
6. Lajos Werkner	HUN	2	5	0		
7. Jetze Doorman	HOL	1	5	1		
7. Georges de la Falaise	FRA	1	6	0		

Dr. Jenö Fuchs, the winner of four sabre gold medals in 1908 and 1912, recorded 22 wins, two losses, and one draw in the individual competition. Fuchs was also active in rowing and bobsledding.

1912 Stockholm C: 40, N: 9, D: 8.23.

		W	L	TG	TR
1. Jenö Fuchs	HUN	6	1	18	10
2. Béla Békéssy	HUN	5	2	17	11
3. Ervin Mészáros	HUN	5	2	17	12
4. Zoltán Schenker	HUN	4	3	17	13
5. Nedo Nadi	ITA	4	3	16	17
6. Péter Tóth	HUN	2	5	12	17
7. Lajos Werkner	HUN	1	6	13	19
8. Deysö Földes	HUN	1	6	9	20

1920 Antwerp C: 40, N: 9, D: 8.23.

		W	L	TR
1. Nedo Nadi	ITA	11	0	—
2. Aldo Nadi	ITA	9	2	—
3. Adrianus de Jong	HOL	7	4	—
4. Oreste Puliti	ITA	6	5	19
5. Jan van der Wiel	HOL	6	5	22
6. Robert Hennet	BEL	5	6	24
6. Léon Tom	BEL	5	6	24
6. Henri Wijnoldij-Daniels	HOL	5	6	24

The only break in Hungary's incredible 60-year domination of individual sabre occurred in 1920. Having been on the losing side of World War I, Hungary was not invited to the Antwerp Olympics.

1924 Paris C: 47, N: 15, D: 7.18.

						BARRAGE		
		W	L	TG	TR	W	L	TG	TR
1. Sándor Posta	HUN	5	2	26	20	2	0	8	1
2. Roger Ducret	FRA	5	2	22	18	1	1	4	7
3. János Garay	HUN	5	2	23	20	0	2	4	8
4. Zóltan Schenker	HUN	4	3	24	21	1	0	4	3
5. Adrianus de Jong	HOL	4	3	24	21	0	1	3	4
6. Ivan Osiier	DEN	2	5	15	24	1	0	4	2
7. G.J. Conraux	FRA	2	5	23	22	0	1	2	4
8. H.A. Casco	ARG	1	6	16	27				

The Italians, led by Oreste Puliti, had already defeated the Hungarians to win the team sabre title, and another show-down seemed certain in the individual championship as four Italians and three Hungarians were among the twelve who qualified for the final round. The final matches began with the Official Jury of Appeal ordering the four Italians—Puliti, Bertinetti, Bini, and Sarrocchi—to fight off against each other. As expected, Puliti beat the other three with ease. But the judges were not satisfied. Led by Kovács, the Hungarian judge, they maintained that the other three had thrown their matches against Puliti in order to increase his chances for a gold medal.

Outraged by these accusations, Puliti threatened to cane Judge Kovács. Puliti was disqualified, and Bertinetti, Bini, and Sarrocchi walked out in protest. Two days later Puliti and Kovács ran into each other at a music hall and renewed their argument. When Kovács haughtily told Puliti that he couldn't understand the furious fencer because he didn't speak Italian, Puliti hit the Hungarian in the face and said that Kovács surely couldn't fail to understand that. The two men were pulled apart, but further words were exchanged and a formal duel was proposed.

Four months later Puliti and Kovács met again, at Nagykanizsa on the Yugoslav-Hungarian border. This time they were accompanied by seconds, swords, and spectators. After slashing away at each other for an hour, the two were finally separated by spectators, who had become concerned about the wounds which both men had received. Their honor restored, Puliti and Kovács shook hands and made up.

As for the Olympic competition, it was won by Sándor Posta in a three-way fence-off against fellow Hungarian János Garay and the French champion Roger Ducret, who left the 1924 Olympics with three gold medals and two silver.

1928 Amsterdam C: 44, N: 17, D: 8.11.

						BARRAGE	
		W	L	TG	TR	TG	TR
1. Ödön Tersztyánszky	HUN	9	2	51	33	5	2
2. Attila Petschauer	HUN	9	2	52	28	2	5
3. Bino Bini	ITA	8	3	49	32		
4. Gustavo Marzi	ITA	8	3	49	34		
5. Sándor Gombos	HUN	8	3	49	38		
6. Erwin Casmir	GER	6	5	44	32		
7. Arturo De Vecchi	ITA	5	6	44	36		
8. Roger Ducret	FRA	5	6	42	47		

Lieutenant Colonel Tersztyánszky died in an auto accident outside Budapest ten months after winning his gold medal. He was 40 years old.

1932 Los Angeles C: 25, N: 12, D: 8.13.

		W	L	TG	TR
1. György Piller (Jekelfalussy)	HUN	8	1	42	19
2. Giulio Gaudini	ITA	7	2	39	28
3. Endre Kabos	HUN	5	4	36	29
4. Erwin Casmir	GER	5	4	32	30
5. Attila Petschauer	HUN	5	4	37	32
6. John Huffman	USA	5	4	38	35
7. Ivan Osiier	DEN	4	5	32	35
8. Arturo De Vecchi	ITA	3	6	27	36

Colonel Piller completed the tournament with a record of 19–2.

1936 Berlin C: 71, N: 26, D: 8.15.

		W	L	TG	TR
1. Endre Kabos	HUN	7	1	37	20
2. Gustavo Marzi	ITA	6	2	35	22
3. Aladár Gerevich	HUN	6	2	37	26
4. László Rajcsányi	HUN	5	3	34	25
5. Vincenzo Pinton	ITA	5	3	32	28
6. Giulio Gaudini	ITA	3	5	27	28
7. Antoni Sobik	POL	2	6	22	34
8. Josef Losert	AUT	2	6	20	36

As a student, Kabos received a fencing outfit as a birthday gift from his godfather. He hid it in his wardrobe, but his friends came across it and teased him. The next day he enrolled in a fencing club to spite them. At the Berlin Olympics Kabos compiled a record of 24–1 to win the gold medal. Kabos was killed during World War II when the Budapest Margaret Bridge blew up, the day before his 38th birthday.

1948 London C: 60, N: 24, D: 8.13.

		W	L	TG	TR
1. Aladár Gerevich	HUN	7	0	35	18
2. Vincenzo Pinton	ITA	5	2	32	23
3. Pál Kovács	HUN	5	2	33	24
4. Jacques Lefèvre	FRA	4	3	27	26
5. George Worth	USA	2	5	26	27
6. Gastone Darè	ITA	2	5	25	30
7. Tibor Nyilas	USA	2	5	20	31
8. Antonio Oliva Haro	MEX	1	6	15	34

Aladár Gerevich competed in six Olympics between 1932 and 1960 (when he was 50 years old). He won seven gold medals, one silver, and two bronze. In winning his only individual gold medal Gerevich scored 19 victories against only one defeat.

1952 Helsinki C: 66, N: 26, D: 8.1.

		W	L	TR
1. Pál Kovács	HUN	8	0	19
2. Aladár Gerevich	HUN	7	1	16
3. Tibor Berczelly	HUN	5	3	22
4. Gastone Darè	ITA	5	3	27
5. Werner Plattner	AUT	4	4	34
6. Jacques Lefèvre	FRA	3	5	25
7. Vincenzo Pinton	ITA	2	6	32
8. Heinz Lechner	AUT	2	6	35

Kovács was the third straight Hungarian to win the sabre gold after winning the bronze in the previous Olympics. Kovács was 40 years old and had first won the world sabre championship fifteen years earlier. In the final pool he needed one last victory to clinch the gold medal. Trailing Pinton 4–2, he scored three hits in the final minute to secure the championship with an undefeated record of 19–0. A mechanic, Kovács ultimately earned six Olympic gold medals.

1956 Melbourne C: 35, N: 17, D: 12.5

						BARRAGE	
		W	L	TG	TR	TG	TR
1. Rudolf Kárpáti	HUN	6	1	32	19		
2. Jerzy Pawlowski	POL	5	2	30	22		
3. Lev Kuznyetsov	SOV	4	3	29	24	5	2
4. Jacques Lefèvre	FRA	4	3	27	25	2	5
5. Aladár Gerevich	HUN	3	4	30	31		
6. Wojciech Zablocki	POL	2	5	17	29		
7. Pál Kovács	HUN	2	5	25	30		
8. Luigi Narduzzi	ITA	2	5	21	31		

The 36-year-old Kárpáti, eventual winner of six Olympic gold medals, earned his first individual championship by putting together 18 victories against only one loss (to Pawlowski). Kárpáti believed that his love of music contributed to his skills as a fencer, since both are based rhythm and timing.

1960 Rome C: 70, N: 29, D: 9.8.

						BARRAGE			
		W	L	TG	TR	W	L	TG	TR
1. Rudolf Kárpáti	HUN	5	2	31	25				
2. Zoltán Horváth	HUN	4	3	29	26	2	1	14	8
3. Wladimiro Calarese	ITA	4	3	31	29	2	1	13	12
4. Claude Arabo	FRA	4	3	31	29	2	1	11	12
5. Wojciech Zablocki	POL	4	3	27	26	0	3	9	15
6. Jerzy Pawlowski	POL	3	4	28	28				
7. David Tyshler	SOV	2	5	24	29				
8. Yakov Rylsky	SOV	2	5	21	32				

Following the quarterfinal round, the French team lodged a protest against Kárpáti, claiming the defending champion had purposely lost to Rohonyi of Romania in order to ensure that he, instead of Lefèvre of France, would advance to the next round. The protest was overruled. In the semifinals Kárpáti's loss to Arabo allowed the Frenchman

to qualify for the final without a barrage. This time no protest was made.

1964 Tokyo C: 52, N: 21, D: 10.20.

						BARRAGE	
		W	L	TG	TR	TG	TR
1. Tibor Pézsa	HUN	2	1	13	13	5	2
2. Claude Arabo	FRA	2	1	14	9	2	5
3. Umar Mavlikhanov	SOV	1	2	9	13	5	3
4. Yakov Rylsky	SOV	1	2	11	12	3	5
5. Emil Ochyra	POL						
6. Marcel Parent	FRA						
7. Walter Köstner	GER						
8. Dieter Wellmann	GER						

Pézsa won despite a relatively unimpressive overall record of 12 wins and seven losses.

1968 Mexico City C: 40, N: 16, D: 10.17.

						BARRAGE	
		W	L	TG	TR	TG	TR
1. Jerzy Pawlowski	POL	4	1	22	18	5	4
2. Mark Rakita	SOV	4	1	24	16	4	5
3. Tibor Pézsa	HUN	3	2	20	16		
4. Vladimir Nazlymov	SOV	3	2	21	17		
5. Rolando Rigoli	ITA	1	4	11	21		
6. Józef Nowara	POL	0	5	15	25		
7. Umar Mavlikhanov	SOV						
8. Serge Panizza	FRA						

In June, Pawlowski, a 35-year-old major in the Polish Army, received his master's degree in law, having written his dissertation on "A Critique of Hayek's Neo-Liberal Conception of Liberty and Law." In the final pool Pawlowski defeated world champion Mark Rakita 5–4. Then he beat him again by the same score in the barrage, to achieve a final win-loss total of 16–2. Pawlowski became interested in fencing at age 16 when he saw films of the 1948 London Olympics. He was world sabre champion three times (in 1957, 1965, 1966) and runner-up four times. In his military pursuits, Pawlowski was considered a protégé of General Wojciech Jaruzelski, who later became Premier of Poland. In 1981 Pawlowski was asked by the Polish government to become a spy. When he refused, he was charged with *being* a spy and sentenced to twenty-five years in prison. His name has also been removed from all Polish books about the Olympics.

1972 Munich C: 54, N: 23, D: 8.31.

		W	L	TG	TR
1. Viktor Sidiak	SOV	4	1	23	15
2. Péter Maróth	HUN	3	2	21	20
3. Vladimir Nazlymov	SOV	3	2	21	21
4. Michele Maffei	ITA	3	2	20	21
5. Regis Bonissent	FRA	1	4	19	22
6. Tamás Kovács	HUN	1	4	17	22

Maffei, Kovács, and Sidiak each entered the final pool with records of 17–3, but Sidiak, emitting a growl each time he scored a hit, prevailed.

1976 Montreal C: 46, N: 18, D: 7.22

		W	L	TG	TR
1. Viktor Krovopuskov	SOV	5	0	25	14
2. Vladimir Nazlymov	SOV	4	1	23	18
3. Viktor Sidiak	SOV	3	2	22	20
4. Ioan Pop	ROM	2	3	22	20
5. Mario Montano	ITA	1	4	16	21
6. Michele Maffei	ITA	0	5	13	25
7. Francisco de Latorre	CUB				
7. Imre Gedövári	HUN				

1980 Moscow C: 30, N: 12, D: 7.25.

		W	L	TG	TR	BARRAGE TG	TR
1. Viktor Krovopuskov	SOV	4	1	24	17	5	3
2. Mikhail Burtsev	SOV	4	1	23	18	3	5
3. Imre Gedovari	HUN	3	2	23	21		
4. Vassil Etropolski	BUL	2	3	17	23		
5. Hristo Etropolski	BUL	1	4	19	21		
6. Michele Maffei	ITA	1	4	15	21		
7. Ferdinando Meglio	ITA						
7. Vladimir Nazlymov	SOV						

Burtsev beat Krovopuskov in the final pool, 5–4, but Krovopuskov turned the tables in the barrage to become the third repeat winner in individual sabre.

SABRE, TEAM

1896–1904 not held

1906 Athens T: 4, N: 4, D: 4.28.
1. GER (Gustav Casmir, Jacob Erckrath de Bary, August Petri, Emil Schön)
2. GRE (Jean Georgiadis, Menelaos Sakorraphos, Ch. Zorbas, Triantaphylos Kordogiannis)
3. HOL (James Melvill van Carnbee, Johannes Franciscus Osten, George vann Rossem, Maurits Jacob van Löben Sels)
4. HUN (Péter Tóth, Jĕno Apáthy, Ervin Mészáros, B. Nagy)

1908 London T: 8, N: 8, D: 7.23.
1. HUN (Jĕno Fuchs, Oszkár Gerde, Péter Tóth, Lajos Werkner, Dezsö Földes)
2. ITA (Riccardo Nowak, Alessandro Pirzio-Biroli, Abelardo Olivier, Marcello Bertinetti, Sante Ceccherini)
3. BOH (Vilém Goppold von Lobsdorf, Jaroslav Tuček, Vlastimil Lada-Sázavsky, Otakar Lada, Bedřich Schejbal)
4. FRA (Georges de la Falaise, B. de Lesseps, Marc Perrodon, Jean Joseph Renaud)
   Semi-Final: HUN 11–5 ITA; BOH 9–7 FRA
   Final: HUN 9–7 BOH; ITA 10–4 GER

Péter Tóth of the Hungarian team became involved in a fight with a fellow student at age 15 and was challenged to a duel. After consultation with their classmates, the boys decided to postpone the duel until after final examinations. In the meantime Tóth enrolled in a fencing school and became so proficient that when final exams were over his opponent decided to drop the matter. Eleven years later Tóth won the first of his team sabre gold medals. Dr. Dezsö Földes, another member of the Hungarian team, emigrated to the United States in 1912 and set up a clinic for the poor in Cleveland.

1912 Stockholm T: 11, N: 11, D: 7.15.
1. HUN (Jenö Fuchs, László Berti, Ervin Mészáros, Dezsö Földes, Oszkár Gerde, Zoltán Schenker, Péter Tóth, Lajos Werkner)
2. AUT (Richard Verderber, Otto Herschmann, Rudolf Cvetko, Friedrich Golling, Andreas Suttner, Albert Bogen, Reinhold Trampler)
3. HOL (Willem Hubert van Blijenburgh, George van Rossem, Adrianus de Jong, Jetze Doorman, Dirk Scalongne, Hendrik de Iongh)
4. BOH (Vilém Goppold von Lobsdorf, Otakar Svorcik, Josef Javurek, František Křiž, Zdeněk Bárta, Josef Pfeiffer, Bedřich Schejbal, Josef Čipera)
5. BEL, GBR, GER, RUS

1920 Antwerp T: 8, N: 8, D: 8.23.

			WON	LOST	MATCHES W	L
1. ITA	(Nedo Nadi, Aldo Nadi, Oreste Puliti, Baldo Baldi, Francesco Gargano, Giorgio Santelli, Dino Urbani)		6	0	76	20
2. FRA	(Georges Trombert, J. Margraff, Marc Perrodon, Henri de Saint Germain, Jean Lacroix, Mondielli)		5	1	54	42
3. HOL	(Jan van der Wiel, Adrianus de Jong, Jetze Doorman, William Hubert van Blijenburgh, Louis Albert Delaunoy, Salomon Zeidenrust, Henri Wijnoldij-Daniels)		4	2	51	45
4. BEL	(Robert Hennet, Pierre Calle, Alexis Simonson, Léon Tom, Robert Feyerick, Charles Delporte, Harry Dombeeck)		3	3	47	47
5. USA	(E. G. Fullinwidder, Arthur Lyon, J. Brooks Parker, John Dimond, F. J. Cunningham, C. J. Walker, C. Bradford Fraley, Roscoe Bowman)		2	4	37	59
6. DEN	(Ivan Osiier, Poul Rasmussen, Ejnar Levison, Aage Berntsen, William Bonde)		1	5	39	55
7. CZE	—		0	2	9	23
7. GBR	—		0	4	21	43

1924 Paris T: 14, N: 14, D: 7.15.

		WON	LOST	MATCHES W	L
1. ITA	(Renato Anselmi, Guido Bal-zarini, Marcello Bertinetti, Bino Bini, Vincenzo Cuccia, Oreste Moricca, Oreste Puliti, Giulio Sarrocchi)	3	0	28	20
2. HUN	(László Berti, János Garay, Sándor Pósta, Jozsef Rády, Zoltán Schenker, Laszlo Széchy, Ödön Tersztyánszky, Jenő Uhlyárik)	2	1	33	15
3. HOL	(Adrianus de Jong, Jetze Doorman, Hendrik Scherpen-huizen, Jan van der Wiel, Maarten van Dulm, Henri Wij-noldij-Daniels)	1	2	18	30
4. CZE	(František Dvořak, Alexander Bárta, Josef Jungmann, Luděk Oppl, Otakar Švorčik)	0	3	17	31
5. ARG	(C. F. Camet, H. A. Casco, C. Guerrico, C. Merlo, P. Nazar-Anchorena, A. Ponce-Costa, R. Sola, S. Torres Blanco)				
5. FRA	(G. J. Conraux, De Saint-Ger-main, J. F. Jannekeyn, L. Lifs-chitz, J. A. Margraff, M. M. J. Perrodon, M. M. Taillandier, G. O. E. Trombert)				

The crucial match between Italy and Hungary ended in an 8–8 tie, but Italy won by four touches, 46 to 50. Puliti was the star of the tournament, winning 26 of 28 bouts and scoring 110 touches while receiving only 39.

1928 Amsterdam T: 12, N: 12, D: 8.9.

		WON	LOST	MATCHES W	L
1. HUN	(Ödön Tersztyánszky, Sándor Gombos, Attila Petschauer, János Garay, József Rády, Gyula Glykais)	2	0	23	9
2. ITA	(Bino Bini, Renato Anselmi, Gustavo Marzi, Oreste Puliti, Emilio Salafia, Giulio Sarroc-chi)	1	1	21	11
3. POL	(Adam Papée, Tadeusz Frie-drich, Kazimierz Laskowski, Wladyslaw Segda, Alek-sander Malecki, Jerzy Za-bielski)	1	1	11	21
4. GER	(Erwin Casmir, Heinrich Moos, Hans Halberstadt, Hans Thomson)	0	2	9	23
5. FRA	(R. G. Fristeau, Roger Ducret, Jean Lacroix, M. M. Taillan-				

dier, J. Piot, P. A. V. Oziol de Pignol)

5. HOL	(C. W. Ekkart, H. G. Hagens, Maarten van Dulm, Jan van der Wiel, Adrianus de Jong, Henri Wijnoldij-Daniels)				
7. BEL	(J. Stordeur, M. Cuypers, J. Kesteloot, E. Yves, G. Kaanen)				
7. TUR	(T. Mouhiddin, E. Fouad, D. Nami, E. Enver)				

Hungary defeated Italy 9–7 in the decisive match. The Hungarian team was led by the high-strung 23-year-old Attila Petschauer of Budapest, who won all 20 of his bouts. Petschauer died in 1943 while fighting on the Russian front. In the words of Olympic historian Ferenc Mezo, "He fell victim to the blind political hatred of one of his superiors."

1932 Los Angeles T: 6, N: 6, D: 8.11.

		WON	LOST	MATCHES W	L
1. HUN	(György Piller, Endre Kabos, Attila Petschauer, Ernő Nagy, Gyula Glykais, Aladár Gere-vich)	3	0	31	6
2. ITA	(Renato Anselmi, Arturo De Vecchi, Emilio Salafia, Ugo Pignotti, Gustavo Marzi, Giulio Gaudini)	2	1	20	14
3. POL	(Adam Papée, Tadeusz Frie-drich, Wladyslaw Segda, Les-zek Lubicz-Nyzz, Wladyslaw Dobrowolski, Marian Suski)	1	2	10	26
4. USA	(Peter Bruder, John Huffman, Norman Armitage, Nickolas Muray, Harold van Buskirk, Ralph Faulkner)	0	3	15	30

Hungary won 56 bouts and lost only nine.

1936 Berlin T: 21, N: 21, D: 8.13.

		WON	LOST	MATCHES W	L
1. HUN	(Tibor Berczelly, László Rajc-sányi, Pál Kovács, Aladár Ger-evich, Imre Rajczy, Endre Kabos)	3	0	32	10
2. ITA	(Vincenzo Pinton, Giulio Gau-dini, Aldo Masciotta, Gustavo Marzi, Aldo Montano, Athos Tanzini)	2	1	25	17
3. GER	(Richard Wahl, Julius Eisen-ecker, Erwin Casmir, August Heim, Hans Esser, Hans Jörger)	1	2	14	25

			WON	LOST	MATCHES W	L
4.	POL	(Antoni Sobik, Wladyslaw Sagda, Wladyslaw Dobrowolski, Adam Papée, Marian Suski, Teodor Zaczyk)	0	3	10	29
5.	AUT	(Losert, Weczerek, Sudrich, Loisel, Hanisch, Kaschka)				
5.	FRA	(Faure, Gramain, E. Gardere, J.Piot, Barisien, A. Gardere)				
5.	HOL	(Faber, Montfoort, Mosman, van Wieringen, Schriever)				
5.	USA	(Peter Bruder, Miguel de Capriles, Bela de Nagy, John Huffman, Samuel Stewart, Norman Armitage)				

The Hungarians won their first seven matches by scores of 13–3 or better, and then defeated Italy 9–6 to win the gold medal. Their final bout total was 106 wins and 16 losses. Leading Hungarian scorers were Berczelly (24–3), Kovacs (21–2), Rajcsányi (20–4) and Gerevich (17–2).

1948 London T: 17, N: 17, D: 8.11.

			WON	LOST	MATCHES W	L
1.	HUN	(Tibor Berczelly, Rudolf Kárpáti, Aladár Gerevich, Pál Kovács, László Rajcsányi, Bertalan Papp)	3	0	29	13
2.	ITA	(Gastone Darè, Carlo Turcato, Vincenzo Pinton, Mauro Racca, Aldo Montano, Renzo Nostini)	2	1	24	24
3.	USA	(Norman Armitage, George Worth, Tibor Nyilas, Dean Cetrulo, Miguel de Capriles, James Flynn)	1	2	24	23
4.	BEL	(Robert Bayot, Georges de Bourguignon, Ferdinand Jassogne, Eugène Laermans, Marcel Nys, Edouard Yves)	0	3	12	29
5.	ARG	(M. Aguero, Jose Luis D'Andrea Mohr, Edgardo Pomini, J. Cermesoni, F. Huergo, Daniel Sande)				
5.	FRA	(Jean-François Tournon, J. Parent, M. Gramain, Jacques Lefèvre, Jean Levavasseur, G. Leveque)				
5.	HOL	(H. Ter Weer, A. Hoevers, W. Van den Berg, F. Mosman, L. Kuijpers)				
5.	POL	(Antoni Sobik, Boleslaw Banaś, Teodor Zaczyk, Jerzy Wójcik, Jan Nawrocki)				

Berczelly had a 15–2 record, including four straight victories in the final 10–6 defeat of Italy. Hungary's total for the tournament was 65 wins and 20 losses.

1952 Helsinki T: 19, N: 19, D: 7.30.

			WON	LOST	MATCHES W	L
1.	HUN	(Bertalan Papp, László Rajcsányi, Rudolf Kárpáti, Aladár Gerevich, Pál Kovács, Tibor Berczelly)	3	0	34	13
2.	ITA	(Vincenzo Pintoh, Mauro Racca, Roberto Ferrari, Gastone Darè, Renzo Nostini, Giorgio Pellini)	2	1	32	15
3.	FRA	(Jacques Lefèvre, Jean Laroyenne, Maurice Piot, Jean Levavasseur, Bernard Morel, Jean-François Tournon)	1	2	14	32
4.	USA	(Norman Armitage, Miguel de Capriles, Tibor Nyilas, Alex Treves, George Worth, Allan Kwartler)	0	3	13	33
5.	AUT	(Werner Plattner, Heinz Putzl, Hubert Loisel, Heinz Lechner, Paul Kerb)				
5.	BEL	(Marcel van der Auwera, Gustave Balister, François Heyvaert, Robert Bayot, Georges de Bourguignon, Edouard Yves)				
5.	GBR	(Roger Tredgold, Olgierd Porebski, Robert Andersson, William Beatley, Ulrich Luke Wendon)				
5.	POL	(Jerzy Twardokens, Leszek Suski, Jerzy Pawlowski, Wojciech Zablocki, Zygmunt Pawlas)				

Great tension built in the final contest as Hungary's string of 35 victories and four Olympic gold medals appeared in jeopardy when Italy took a 7–5 lead. Then Berczelly beat Nostini 5–0 and Kárpáti beat Ferrari 5–0 to even the match at 7–7. Gerevich, who had lost his other three bouts against the Italians, recovered to defeat Enzo Pinton 5–3 and give Hungary an insurmountable lead of 8–7, with a 14-touch advantage. Hungary's tournament totals were 111 wins and 25 losses.

1956 Melbourne T: 8, N: 8, D: 12.3.

			WON	LOST	MATCHES W	L
1.	HUN	(Attila Keresztes, Pál Kovács, Rudolf Kárpáti, Aladár Gerevich, Jenö Hámori, Dániel Magay)	3	0	30	15
2.	POL	(Jerzy Pawlowski, Wojciech Zablocki, Marek Kuszewski, Zygmunt Pawlas, Ryszard Zub, Andrzej Piatkowski)	2	1	23	22
3.	SOV	(Lev Kuznyetsov, Yakov Rylsky, Yevgeny Chere-	1	2	22	25

povsky, David Tyschler, Leonid Bogdanov)

4. FRA	(Claude Gamot, Jacques Lefèvre, Bernard Morel, Jacques Roulot)	0	3	17	30

By 1956 the sabre contests were the only ones which were not using electronic scoring. Tensions were high during the match between Hungary and the U.S.S.R., since the Soviets had just invaded Hungary. The Hungarians were victorious, 9–7. After the Olympics Keresztes, Hámori, and Magay defected to the West. Keresztes and Hámori fenced for the United States in the 1964 Olympics.

1960 Rome T: 16, N: 16, D: 9.10.
1. HUN   (Zoltán Horváth, Rudolf Kárpáti, Tamás Mendelényi, Pál Kovács, Gábor Delneky, Aladár Gerevich)
2. POL   (Andrzej Piatkowski, Emil Ochyra, Wojciech Zablocki, Jerzy Pawlowski, Ryszard Zub, Marek Kuszewski)
3. ITA   (Wladimiro Calarese, Gianpaolo Calanchini, Pierluigi Chicca, Mario Ravagnan, Roberto Ferrari)
4. USA   (Allan Kwartler, George Worth, Michael D'Asaro, Alfonso Morales, Tiborz Nyilas, R. Richard Dyer)
5. FRA   (Marcel Parent, Claude Gamot, Jacques Lefèvre, Jacques Roulot, Claude Arabo)
5. GER   (Dieter Lohr, Jürgen Theuerkauff, Wilfried Wohler, Peter von Peter von Krockov, Walter Köstner)
5. ROM   (Dimitri Mustata, Cornel Pelmus, Ion Szanto, Ladislau Rohonyi, Emeric Arus)
5. SOV   (Yevgeny Cherepovsky, Umar Mavlikhanov, Nugzar Asatiani, David Tyschler, Yakov Rylsky)
Final: HUN 9–7 POL
3rd Place: ITA 9–6 USA

In the match for first place, Poland took a 3–0 lead. Then Hungary won five in a row, but Poland came back to tie it, 6–6. Finally Kárpáti beat Pawlowski 5–3 to secure the gold medal. Gerevich, 50 years old, won his sixth straight team sabre gold medal.

1964 Tokyo T: 13, N: 13, D: 10.23.
1. SOV   (Yakov Rylsky, Nugzar Asatiani, Mark Rakita, Umar Mavlikhanov, Boris Melnikov)
2. ITA   (Wladimiro Calarese, Cesare Salvadori, Gianpaolo Calanchini, Pierluigi Chicca, Mario Ravagnan)
3. POL   (Emil Ochyra, Jerzy Pawlowski, Ryszard Zub, Andrzej Piatkowski, Wojciech Zablocki)
4. FRA   (Jean Ramez, Jacques Lefèvre, Claude Arabo, Marcel Parent, Robert Fraisse)
5. HUN   (Péter Bakonyi, Miklós Meszéna, Attila Kovács, Zoltan Horvath, Tibor Pézsa)
6. GER   (Dieter Wellmann, Klaus Allissat, Walter Köstner, Jürgen Theuerkauff, Percy Borucki)
7. ROM   (Attila Csipler, Octavian Vintila, Tanase Muresan, Ionel Drimba)
7. USA   (Alfonso Morales, Robert Blum, Eugene [Jenö] Hamori, Attila Keresztes, Thomas Orley)
Final: SOV 9–6 ITA
3rd Place: POL 8(60)–8(59) FRA
5th Place: HUN 9–3 GER

In the semifinals Hungary's winning streak was finally stopped at 46 when they were upset by Italy, 9–7. It was Italy that had handed the Hungarians their last defeat 40 years earlier in Paris.

HUNGARY'S TEAM SABRE WINNING STREAK

1924			1936			1956		
14	HOL	2	16	DEN	0	9	USA	1
11	CZE	5	14	URU	2	12	FRA	4
			15	GER	1	9	SOV	4
1928			15	HOL	1	9	POL	4
14	USA	2	14	USA	2			
13	GBR	3	13	GER	3	**1960**		
12	GER	4	10	POL	1	9	BEL	3
12	FRA	4	9	ITA	6	9	ROM	3
14	POL	2				9	ITA	6
9	ITA	7	**1948**			9	POL	7
11	DEN	1	9	EGY	3			
			15	ARG	1	**1964**		
1932			12	POL	3	9	ARG	2
14	MEX	2	10	USA	6	9	ROM	0
13	USA	3	9	BEL	1			
9	ITA	2	10	ITA	6			
9	POL	1						
			1952					
			15	POR	1			
			15	SAA	1			
			9	DEN	0			
			13	FRA	3			
			13	BEL	3			
			12	AUT	4			
			13	FRA	3			
			13	USA	3			
			8	ITA	7			

1968 Mexico City T: 12, N: 12, D: 10.21.
1. SOV   (Vladimir Nazlymov, Eduard Vinokurov, Viktor Sidyak, Mark Rakita, Umar Mavlikhanov)
2. ITA   (Wladimiro Calarese, Cesare Salvadori, Michele Maffei, Pierluigi Chicca, Rolando Rigoli)
3. HUN   (Tamás Kóvács, Miklós Meszéna, Janos Kalmar, Péter Bakonyi, Tibor Pézsa)
4. FRA   (Marcel Parent, Claude Arabo, Bernard Vallée, Serge Panizza, Jean Ramez)
5. POL   (Jerzy Pawlowski, Józef Nowara, Franciszek Sobczak, Zygmunt Kawecki, Emil Ochyra)
6. USA   (Alex Orban, Alfonso Morales, Anthony Keane, Robert Blum, Thomas Balla)
7. GBR   (Alexander Leckie, Rodney Craig, David Acfield, Richard Oldcorn)
7. GER   (Percy Borucki, Walter Köstner, Paul Wischeidt, Klaus Allisat, Volker Duschner)
Final: SOV 9–7 ITA
3rd Place: HUN 9–5 FRA
5th Place: POL 9–5 USA

1972: Munich T: 13, N: 13, D: 9.4.
1. ITA   (Michele Maffei, Mario Aldo Montano, Cesare Salvadori, Mario Tullio Montano, Rolando Rigoli)
2. SOV   (Mark Rakita, Eduard Vinokurov, Viktor Bajenov, Victor Sidiak, Vladimir Nazlymov)
3. HUN   (Pál Gerevich, Támás Kovács, Péter Marót, Tibor Pézsa, Péter Bakonyi)
4. ROM   (Dan Irimiciuc, Iosif Budahazi, Gheorghe Culcea, Constantin Nicolae, Octavian Vintila)
5. POL   (Józef Nowara, Krzysztof Grzegorek, Zygmunt Kawecki, Jerzy Pawlowski, Janusz Majewski)
6. CUB   (Hilario Hipolito, Guzman Salazar, Francisco de la Torre, Manuel Ortiz, Manuel Suarez)
7. FRA   (Regis Bonissent, Bernard Dumont, Bernard Vallee, Philippe Bena, Serge Panizza)
7. GER   (Walter Convents, Volker Duschner, Knut Höhne, Dieter Wellmann, Paul Wischeidt)
Final: ITA 9–5 SOV
3rd Place: HUN 8–7 ROM
5th Place: POL 9–5 CUB

Maffei defeated all four Soviet fencers in the final, but it was Aldo Montano who won the decisive bout with Vinokurov, 5–1. Montano had previously been warned by the officials not to remove his mask before a decision had been announced. When he scored the winning hit the 205-pound Montano leaped up and down while his team manager and his cousin (and teammate), Tullio Montano, desperately held on to his helmet until the official call was made.

1976 Montreal T: 13, N: 13
1. SOV   (Edouard Vinokurov, Viktor Krovopuskov, Mikhail Burtsev, Viktor Sidiak, Vladimir Nazlymov)
2. ITA   (Mario Aldo Montano, Michele Maffei, Angelo Arcidiacono, Tommaso Montano, Mario Tullio Montano)
3. ROM   (Dan Irimiciuc, Ioan Pop, Marin Mustata, Corneliu Marin, Alexandru Nilca))
4. HUN   (Péter Marót, Tamás Kovács, Imre Gedövari, Ferenc Hammang, Csaba Körmöczi)
5. CUB   (Manuel Ortiz, Francisco de Latorre, Guzman Salazar, Ramon Hernandez, Lazaro Mora)
6. POL   (Leszek Jablonowski, Sylwester Królikowski, Jacek Bierkowski, Józef Nowara)
7. USA   (Paul Apostol, Peter Westbrook, Stephen Kaplan, Thomas Losonczy, Alex Orban)
7. FRA   (Philippe Bena, Regis Bonnissent, Bernard Dumont, Didier Flament, Patrick Quivrin)
Final: SOV 9–4 ITA
3rd Place: ROM 9–4 HUN
5th Place: CUB 9–6 POL

1980 Moscow T: 8, N: 8, D: 7.29.
1. SOV   (Mikhail Burtsev, Viktor Krovopuskov, Viktor Sidiak, Vladimir Nazlymov, Nikolai Alyokhin)
2. ITA   (Michele Maffei, Mario Aldo Montano, Marco Romano, Ferdinando Meglio)
3. HUN   (Imre Gedövari, Rudolf Nebald, Pál Gerevich, Ferenc Hammang, György Nebald)

4. POL   (Tadeusz Pigula, Leszek Jablonowski, Jacek Bierkowski, Andrzej Kostrzewa)
5. ROM   (Ioan Pop, Marin Mustata, Corneliu Marin, Ion Pantelimonescu, Alexandruu Nilca)
6. GDR   (Rüdiger Müller, Hendrik Jung, Peter Ulbrich, Frank-Eberhard Höltje, Gerd May)
7. CUB   (Manuel Ortiz, Jesus Ortiz, Jose Laverdecia, Guzman Salazar)
8. BUL   (Hristo Etropolski, Nikolai Marincheshki, Vassil Etropolski, Georgi Chomakov, Marin Ivanov)
Final: SOV 9–2 ITA
3rd Place: HUN 9–6 POL
5th Place: ROM 9–6 GDR

Discontinued Events
MASTERS FOIL FENCING
1896 Athens C: 2, N: 2, D: 4.7.

		TG	TR
1. Leon Pyrgos	GRE	3	1
2. M. Perronnet	FRA	1	3

Pyrgos, although a professional, was the first Greek winner of the modern Olympic Games.

1900 Paris C: 64, N: 7, D: 5.22.

		W	L	W	L
				BARRAGE	
1. Lucien Mérignac	FRA	6	1	1	0
2. Alphonse Kirchhoffer	FRA	6	1	0	1
3. Jean-Baptiste Mimiague	FRA	4	3	1	0
4. Antonio Conte	ITA	4	3	0	1
5. Jules Rossignol	FRA	3	4		
6. Leopold Ramus	FRA	2	5		
7. Italo Santelli	ITA	0	7		
8. Adolphe Rouleau	FRA	3	4		

Rouleau was placed last because he withdrew from his bout with Mimiague "under the pretext of a sore thumb."

MASTERS ÉPÉE FENCING
1900 Paris C: 54, N: 3?, D: 6.14.
1. Albert Ayat   FRA
2. Emile Bougnol   FRA
3. Henri Laurent   FRA
4. Hippolyte-Jacques Hyvernaud   FRA
5. Damotte   FRA
6. Brassart   FRA
7. Lezard   FRA
8. Jourdan   FRA

1904 not held

1906 Athens C: 3, N: 3, D: 4.28.
1. Cyrille Verbrugge   BEL
2. Mario Gubiani   ITA
3. Ioannis Raissis   GRE

ÉPÉE FOR AMATEURS AND MASTERS

1900 Paris C: 8, N: 2, D: 6.15.
1. Albert Ayat   FRA
2. Ramón Fonst   CUB
3. Léon Sée   FRA
4. Georges de la Falaise   FRA
5. Louis Perrée   FRA
5. Henri Laurent   FRA
5. Emile Bougnol   FRA
5. Hippolyte-Jacques Hyvernaud   FRA

This event brought together the first four finishers in the amateur and masters tournaments. Ayot won without receiving a hit and was awarded a prize of 3000 francs.

MASTERS SABRE FENCING

1900 Paris C: 44, N: 10, D: 6.27.

		W	L
1. Antonio Conte	ITA	7	0
2. Italo Santelli	ITA	6	1
3. Milan Neralić	AUT	4	3
4. François Delibes	BEL	3	4
5. Michaux	RUS/FRA	3	4
6. Xavier Anchetti	FRA	2	5
7. Zachavrot	RUS	2	5
8. Hebrant	BEL	1	6

1904 not held

1906 Athens C: 2, N: 2, D: 4.28.
1. Cyrille Verbrugge   BEL
2. Ioannis Raissis   GRE

THREE-CORNERED SABRE

1906 Athens C: 22, N: 6, D: 4.28.
1. Gustav Casmir   GER
2. George van Rossem   HOL
3. Péter Tóth   HUN
4. Emil Schön   GER
5. Jěno Apáthy   HUN
6. Ernst Königsgarten   AUT

SINGLE STICKS

1904 St. Louis C: 3, N: 1, D: 9.10.

		TG
1. Albertson Van Zo Post	USA	11
2. William Scott O'Connor	USA	8
3. William Grebe	USA	2

WOMEN
FOIL, INDIVIDUAL

1896–1920 not held

1924 Paris C: 25, N: 9, D: 7.4.

		W	L	TG	TR
1. Ellen Osiier	DEN	5	0	25	14
2. Gladys Davis	GBR	4	1	23	16
3. Grete Heckscher	DEN	3	2	22	16
4. Muriel Freeman	GBR	2	3	17	20
5. Yutha Barding	DEN	1	4	20	22
6. Gizella Tary	HUN	0	5	6	25

The first female Olympic fencing champion was 33-year-old Ellen Ottilia Osiier, who won all 16 of her bouts. She scored 80 touches and received only 34. One of the U.S. entrants was Adeline Gehrig, sister of the great New York Yankee baseball player Lou Gehrig.

1928 Amsterdam C: 27, N: 11, D: 8.1.

		W	L	TG	TR
1. Helene Mayer	GER	7	0	35	9
2. Muriel Freeman	GBR	6	1	32	19
3. Olga Oelkers	GER	4	3	25	27
4. Erna Sondheim	GER	3	4	22	29
5. Gladys Daniell	GBR	2	5	23	27
6. Jenny Addams	BEL	2	5	23	30
6. Margit Dany	HUN	2	5	23	30
8. Johanna de Boer	HOL	2	5	23	33

A German Jew, 17-year-old Helene Mayer swept through the tournament with surprising ease, winning 18 bouts and losing two.

1932 Los Angeles C: 17, N: 11, D: 8.3.

		W	L	TG	TR	BARRAGE TG	BARRAGE TR
1. Ellen Preis	AUT	8	1	44	27	5	3
2. J. Heather Guinness	GBR	8	1	43	19	3	5
3. Erna Bogáthy Bogen	HUN	7	2	38	30		
4. Jenny Addams	BEL	6	3	37	29		
5. Helene Mayer	GER	5	4	38	27		
6. Johanna de Boer	HOL	5	4	30	35		
7. Gerda Munck	DEN	2	7	29	39		
8. Marion Lloyd	USA	2	7	26	42		
8. Grete Olsen	DEN	2	7	31	42		

Preis won by defeating Guinness 5–3 in both the final pool and the barrage. She eventually competed in five Olympics. Bronze medalist Erna Bogen was the daughter of Albert Bogen, who won a silver medal in team sabre in 1912. She later married seven-time sabre gold medalist Aladár Gerevich. Their son, Pál, earned two bronze medals in team sabre in 1972 and 1980.

1936 Berlin C: 41, N: 17, D: 8.5.

		W	L	TG	TR
1. Ilona Schacherer-Elek	HUN	6	1	33	17
2. Helene Mayer	GER	5	2	33	19
3. Ellen Preis	AUT	5	2	32	20
4. Hedwig Hass	GER	5	2	30	23
5. Karen Lachmann	DEN	3	4	23	24
6. Jenny Addams	BEL	2	5	18	28
7. Ilona Vargha	HUN	2	5	17	31
8. Grasser	AUT	0	7	11	35

In 1932 Helene Mayer left her family behind in Konigstein, Germany, and moved to the United States, where she taught German at Mills College in Oakland, California. Under pressure from the U.S., the Nazis invited her back to compete in the Olympics. The Nazis rationalized their leniency toward her by stating that although she was Jewish, she had two "Aryan" grandparents. Also competing at Berlin were the defending Olympic champion, Ellen Preis and the European champion, Ilona Schacherer, later Elek. In the final pool, Schacherer-Elek defeated Mayer 5–4 and Preis 5–3, losing only to Hedwig Hass. On the victory platform Helene Mayer pleased the large German crowd by giving a "Heil Hitler" salute.

1948 London C: 39, N: 15, D: 8.2.

		W	L	TG	TR
1. Ilona Elek	HUN	6	1	31	15
2. Karen Lachmann	DEN	5	2	24	11
3. Ellen Müller-Preis	AUT	5	2	24	16
4. Maria Cerra	USA	5	2	23	16
5. Fritzi Filz	AUT	4	3	20	21
6. Margit Elek	HUN	1	6	10	26
7. Velleda Cessari	ITA	1	6	15	27
8. Mary Glen Haig	GBR	1	6	10	27

Ilona Elek's retention of her Olympic title after a 12-year interlude was a tremendous achievement in itself. But the manner in which she won added to the drama. In her next-to-last bout she trailed Maria Cerra 2–0 before scoring four straight hits. Then, with the winner earning the gold medal, she defeated Karen Lachmann 4–2 as well.

1952 Helsinki C: 37, N: 15, D: 7.27.

					BARRAGE			
		W	L	TR	W	L	TG	TR
1. Irene Camber	ITA	5	2	22	1	0	4	3
2. Ilona Elek	HUN	5	2	21	0	1	3	4
3. Karen Lachmann	DEN	4	3	22	3	0	12	4
4. Janice Lee York	USA	4	3	25	2	1	8	7
5. Maxine Mitchell	USA	4	3	23	1	2	9	8
6. Renée Garilhe	FRA	4	3	24	0	3	2	12
7. Lylian Lecomte-Guyonneau	FRA	1	6	30				
8. Magdolna Kovács-Nyári	HUN	1	6	32				

The 45-year-old Elek appeared well on her way to her third gold medal when she won her first 20 bouts, includ-

ing five in the final pool. But then she lost to Mitchell and then to Camber, 4–3. Forced into a barrage, she was again defeated by Camber, 4–3.

1956 Melbourne C: 23, N: 11, D: 11.29.

						BARRAGE	
		W	L	TG	TR	TG	TR
1. Gillian Sheen	GBR	6	1	26	20	4	2
2. Olga Orban	ROM	6	1	27	17	2	4
3. Renée Garilhe	FRA	5	2	26	14		
4. Janice Lee Romary (York)	USA	4	3	23	21		
5. Kate Delbarre	FRA	3	4	20	25		
6. Karen Lachmann	DEN	2	5	17	20		
7. Ellen Müller-Preis	AUT	1	6	20	25		
8. Bruna Colombetti	ITA	1	6	14	27		

Sheen, a 28-year-old London dental surgeon, barely qualified for the final by winning a barrage to finish fourth in her semifinal pool. She lost 4–2 to Orban, but won the rest of her bouts to force a barrage. This time she defeated the Romanian, 4–2.

1960 Rome C: 56, N: 24, D: 9.1.

						BARRAGE			
		W	L	TG	TR	W	L	TG	TR
1. Heidi Schmid	GER	6	1	26	13				
2. Valentina Rastvorova	SOV	5	2	24	12				
3. Maria Vicol	ROM	4	3	23	18	2	0	8	5
4. Galina Gorokhova	SOV	4	3	22	19	1	1	7	6
5. Olga Szabo (Orban)	ROM	4	3	20	20	0	2	4	8
6. Elzbieta Pawlas	POL	2	5	14	24				
7. Maria del Pilar Roldan	MEX	2	5	13	25				
8. Waltraut Ebert	AUT	1	6	14	27				

Heidi Schmid was a left-handed 21-year-old music teacher from Augsburg. She scored 18 wins against only two losses, one of which occurred after she had clinched the championship.

1964 Tokyo C: 39, N:17, D: 10.15.

						BARRAGE			
		W	L	TG	TR	W	L	TG	TR
1. Ildikó Ujlaki-Rejtö	HUN	2	1	10	5	2	0	8	1
2. Helga Mees	GER	2	1	8	9	1	1	4	6
3. Antonella Ragno	ITA	2	1	9	7	0	2	3	8
4. Galina Gorokhova	SOV	0	3	6	12				
5. Katalin Juhász	HUN								
6. Giovanna Masciotta	ITA								
7. Bruna Colombetti	ITA								
7. Catherine Rousselet	FRA								

Ildikó Ujilaki-Rejtö was born deaf on May 11, 1937. When she began fencing at age 14 her coaches communicated their instructions on pieces of paper. A factory worker, she faced Helga Mees, a 27-year-old secretary from Saarbrücken, for the championship. Mees had already beaten Uj-laki-Rejtö twice, in the first round and in the final round, but in the barrage the Hungarian won, 4–0.

1968 Mexico City C: 38, N: 16, D: 10.20.

		W	L	TG	TR
1. Yelena Novikova	SOV	4	1	19	11
2. Maria del Pilar Roldan	MEX	3	2	17	14
3. Ildikó Ujlaki-Rejtö	HUN	3	2	14	16
4. Brigitte Gapais	FRA	2	3	15	15
5. Kerstin Palm	SWE	2	3	17	17
6. Galina Gorokhova	SOV	1	4	10	19
7. Giovanna Masciotta	ITA				
7. Heidi Schmid	GER				

Novikova, a tall 21-year-old student-teacher, compiled a record of 15 wins and two losses. Silver medalist Roldan, a mother of two, came out of retirement to compete in the Olympics before a hometown crowd.

1972 Munich C: 44, N: 20, D: 9.3.

		W	L	TG	TR
1. Antonella Ragno-Lonzi	ITA	4	1	19	13
2. Ildikó Bóbis	HUN	3	2	17	14
3. Galina Gorokhova	SOV	3	2	16	14
4. Marie-Chantal Demaille	FRA	3	2	14	16
5. Yelena Belova (Novikova)	SOV	2	3	15	13
6. Kerstin Palm	SWE	0	5	9	20

1976 Montreal C: 48, N: 20, D: 7.24.

						BARRAGE	
		W	L	TG	TR	TG	TR
1. Ildikó Schwarczenberger	HUN	4	1	21	15	5	4
2. Maria Consolata Collino	ITA	4	1	24	12		5
3. Yelena Belova (Novikova)	SOV	3	2	21	19		
4. Brigitte Dumont-Gapais	FRA	2	3	17	17		
5. Cornelia Hanisch	GER	1	4	13	22		
6. Ildikó Bóbis	HUN	1	4	13	24		
7. Valentina Sidorova	SOV						
7. Ecaterina Stahl (Jencic)	ROM						

The reigning world champion, Ecaterina Stahl, ran up a 15–2 record before being eliminated in the prefinal round by Ildikó Schwartzenberger. The final pool turned into an exciting three-way affair. Collino defeated Schwarczen-berger 5–1, which appeared to end the Hungarian's chance for a gold medal. Then Yelena Belova beat Collino on the last hit to put Schwarzenberger back into a tie for first place. In her final match, Belova faced Ildikó Bóbis, who had lost all of her other final pool matches. A win would put her into a triple barrage. However, Bóbis summoned all her skill and defeated Belova 5–4. Inspired by her team-mate's effort, Schwarczenberger won the final hit against Collino to take the championship.

1980 Moscow C: 33, N: 14, D: 7.24.

		W	L	TG	TR
1. Pascale Trinquet	FRA	4	1	21	16
2. Magda Maros	HUN	3	2	23	17
3. Barbara Wysoczańska	POL	3	2	19	18
4. Ecaterina Stahl (Jencic)	ROM	2	3	19	21
5. Brigitte Gaudin (Latrille)	FRA	2	3	20	22
6. Dorina Vaccaroni	ITA	1	4	14	22
7. Katarina Loksova	CZE				
7. Delfina Skapska	POL				

FOIL, TEAM

1896–1956 not held

1960 Rome T: 12, N: 12, D: 9.3.
1. SOV (Tatyana Petrenko, Valentina Rastvorova, Lyudmila Schi-shova, Valentinaa Prudskova, Aleksandra Zabelina, Ga-lina Gorokhova)
2. HUN (Györgyi Szekely, Ildikó Ujlaki-Rejtö, Magdolna Kovács-Nyári, Katalin Juhász, Lidia Dömölky)
3. ITA (Irene Camber, Velleda Cesari, Antonella Ragno, Bruna Colombetti, Claudia Pasini)
4. GER (Heidi Schmid, Helga Mees, Helga Stroh, Helmi Höhle, Gudrun Theuerkauff, Rosemarie Weiss)
5. FRA (Monique Leroux, Regine Veronnet, Françiose Mailliard, Renée Garilhe, Kate Delbarre)
5. HOL (Nina Kleyweg, Daniel Van Rossem, Helena Kokkes, Elisa Botbjil)
5. POL (Elżbieta Pawlas, Silwia Julito, Barbara Orzechowska, Genowefa Migas, Wanda Kaczmarczyk)
5. ROM (Ecaterina Lazar, Eugenia Mateianu, Olga Szabó-Orban, Maria Vicol)
Final: SOV 9–3 HUN
3rd Place: ITA 9–2 GER

The Soviets received their only scare in the quarterfinals, when they had to rally from a 3–8 deficit to defeat France by two touches. Their final win-loss total was 48–21.

1964 Tokyo T: 10, N: 10, D: 10.17.
1. HUN (Ildikó Ujlaki-Rejtö, Katalin Juhász-Nagy, Lidia Sákovics-Dömölky, Judit Mendelényi-Ágoston, Paula Földessy-Marosi)
2. SOV (Galina Gorokhova, Valentina Prudskova, Tatyana Samu-senko, Lyudmila Schishova, Valentina Rastvorova)
3. GER (Heidi Schmid, Helga Mees, Rosemarie Scherberger, Gudrun Theuerkauff)
4. ITA (Antonella Ragno, Giovanna Masciotta, Irene Camber, Natalina Sanguineti, Bruna Colombetti)
5. ROM (Olga Szabó-Orban, Ileana Gyulai, Ana Dersidan, Maria Vicol, Ecaterina Jencic)
6. FRA (Catherine Rousselet, Marie-Chantal Depetris, Brigitte Ga-pais, Annick Level, Colette Revenu)
Final: HUN 9–7 SOV
3rd Place: GER 9–5 ITA
5th Place: ROM 9–6 FRA

1968 Mexico City T: 10, N: 10, D: 10.24.
1. SOV (Aleksandra Zabelina, Yelena Novikova, Galina Gorok-hova, Tatyana Samusenko, Svetlana Chirkova)
2. HUN (Ildikó Bóbis, Lidia Sákovics, Ildikó Ujlaki-Rejtö, Mária Gulácsy, Paula Földessey-Marosi)
3. ROM (Ecatrina Stahl [Jencic], Ileana Drimbă, Olga Szabó [Or-ban], Maria Vicol, Ana Ene-Dersidan)
4. FRA (Cathérine Ceretti, Brigitte Gapais, Marie-Chantal Depe-tris, Claudette Herbster, Annick Level)
5. GER (Heidi Schmid, Helga Koch, Gudrun Theuerkauff, Monika Pulch, Helga Volz-Mees)
6. ITA (Antonella Ragno, Giulia Lorenzoni, Giovanna Masciotta, Bruna Colombetti, Silvana Sconciafurno)
Final: SOV 9–3 HUN
3rd Place: ROM 8(47)–8(45)FRA
5th Place: GER 8–7 ITA

1972 Munich T: 11, N: 11, D: 9.8.
1. SOV (Yelena Belova [Novikova], Alexandra Zabelina, Tatyana Semusenko, Galina Gorokhova, Svetlana Chirkova)
2. HUN (Ildikó Ságiné-Rejtö [Ujlaki-Rejtö], Ildikó Schwarczen-berger [Tordasi], Ildikó Matuscakné-Ronay, Maria Szol-noki, Ildikó Bóbis)
3. ROM (Ileana Gyulai, Ana Pascu, Ecaterina Stahl [Jencic], Olga Szabó-Orban)
4. ITA (Antonnella Ragno-Lonzi, Giulia Lorenzoni, Reka Der Ci-priani, Maria Consolata Collino, Giuseppina Bersani)
5. GER (Gudrun Theuerkauff, Irmela Broniecki, Karin Giessel-mann, Monika Pulch, Erika Bethmann)
6. FRA (Marie-Chantal Demaille, Catherine Ceretti, Claudie Jos-land, Brigitte Dumont-Gapais)
7. POL (Halina Balon, Krystyna Urbánska-Machnicka, Jolanta Bebel-Rzymowska, Kamila Skladanowska, Elżbieta Franke)
7. USA (Ruth White, Natalia Clovis, Tanya Adamovich, Harriet King, Ann O'Donnell)
Final: SOV 9–5 HUN
3rd Place: ROM 9–7 ITA
5th Place: GER 8–7 FRA

The Soviet team compiled a record of 52 wins and 20 losses. They were led by Belova (17–3) and Zabelina (14–4).

1976 Montreal T: 13, N: 13, D: 7.28.
1. SOV (Yelena Belova [Novikova], Olga Kniazeva, Valentina Si-dorova, Nailia Guiliazova, Valentina Nikonova)

2. FRA (Brigitte Latrille, Brigitte Dumont-Gapais, Christine Muzio, Veronique Trinquet, Claudie Josland)
3. HUN (Ildikó Schwarczenberger [Tordasi], Edit Kovács, Magda Maros, Ildikó Ságiné-Rejtö [Ujlaki-Rejtö], Ildikó Bóbis)
4. GER (Karin Rutz, Cornelia Hanisch, Ute Kircheis, Brigitte Oer-tel, Jutta Höhne)
5. ITA (Maria Consolata Collino, Giulia Lorenzoni, Doriana Pig-liapoco, Susanna Batazzi, Carola Mangiarotti)
6. POL (Jolanta Bebel-Rzymowska, Barbara Wysoczańska, Ka-milla Mazurowska-Skladanowska, Krystyna Urbańska-Machnicka, Grażyna Staszak-Makowska)
7. GBR (Wendy Ager, Susan Wrigglesworth, Hilary Cawthorne, Clare Halsted, Susan Green)
7. ROM (Ileana Jenei, Marcela Moldovan, Ecaterina Stahl [Jen-cic], Ana Pascu, Magdalena Bartos)
Final: SOV 9–2 FRA
3rd Place: HUN 9–4 GER
5th Place: ITA 9–7 POL

The U.S.S.R. won almost without competition, with 50 wins and only 13 losses. Belova was 13–0 and Kniazeva 11–2. The final victory came on Belova's 29th birthday.

1980 Moscow T: 9, N: 9, D: 7.27.
1. FRA (Brigitte Gaudin [Latrille], Pascale Trinquet, Isabelle Boeri-Begard, Veronique Brouquier, Christine Muzio)
2. SOV (Valentina Sidorova, Nailia Guiliazova, Yelena Belova [Novikova], Irina Ushakova, Larisa Tsagaraeva)
3. HUN (Ildikó Schwarczenberger [Tordasi], Magda Maros, Ger-trud Stefanek, Zsuzsa Szöcz, Edit Kovács)
4. POL (Delfina Skapska, Agnieszka Dubrawska, Jolanta Króli-kowska, Barbara Wysoczańska, Kamila Mazurowska-Skladanowska)
5. ITA (Dorina Vaccaroni, Anna Rita Sparaciari, Susanna Ba-tazzi, Carola Mangiarotti, Clara Mochi)
6. CUB (Margarita Rodriguez Vargas, Marlene Font Kindelan, Maria Garcia Pascau, Clara Alfonso Freire, Mercedes del Risco Randich)
7. GBR (Susan Wriggleworth, Ann Brannon, Wendy Grant, Linda Martin, Hilary Cawthorne)
8. GDR (Mandy Niklaus, Gabriele Janke, Sabine Hertrampf, Beate Schubert, Marion Schulze)
Final: FRA 9–6 SOV
3rd Place: HUN 9–7 POL
5th Place: ITA 9–6 CUB

FIELD HOCKEY

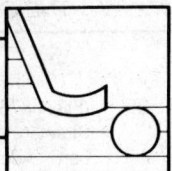

MEN

A field hockey match is divided into two 35-minute halves. In the event of a draw, two 7½-minute extra periods are played. A continued draw is decided by "sudden death."

1896–1906 not held

1908 London T: 6, N: 3, D: 10.31.

			W	L	T	PF	PA
1.	GBR	England (H. I. Wood, Harold Scott-Freeman, L. C. Baillon, John Robinson, Edgar Page, Alan Noble, Percy Rees, Gerald Logan, Stanley Shoveller, Reginald Pridmore, Eric Green)	3	0	0	24	3
2.	IRL	Ireland (E. P. C. Holmes, Henry Brown, Walter Peterson, William Graham, Walter Campbell, Henry Murphy, C. F. Power, G. S. Gregg, Eric Allman-Smith, Frank Robinson, Robert Kennedy, W. G. McCormick)	1	1	0	4	9
3.	GBR	Scotland (John Burt, Hugh Neilson, Colin Foulkes, Hew Fraser, Alexander Burt, Andrew Dennistoun, Norman Stevenson, Ivan Laing, John Harper-Orr, Hugh Walker, William Orchardson)	1	1	0	5	6
3.	GBR	Wales (Bruce Turnbull, E. W. G. Richards, Llewellyn Evans, C. W. Shephard, R. Lyne, F. Connah, F. Gordon Phillips, A. A. Law, P. B. Turnbull, J. Ralph Williams, W. J. Pallott)	0	1	0	1	3

Final: ENG 8–1 IRL

1912 not held

1920 Antwerp T: 4, N: 4, 9.5.

			W	L	T	PF	PA
1.	GBR	(Harry Haslam, John Bennett, Charles Atkin, Harold Cooke, Eric Crockford, Cyril Wilkinson, William Smith, George McGrath, John McBryan, Stanley Shoveller, Rex Crummack, Arthur Leighton, H. K. Cassels, Colin Campbell, Charles Marcom)	3	0	0	17	2

			W	L	T	PF	PA
2.	DEN	(Andreas Rasmussen, Hans Christian Herlak, Frans Faber, Erik Husted, Henning Holst, Hans Jörgen Hansen, Hans Adolf Bjerrum, Thorvald Eigenbrod, Svend Blach, Steen Due, Ejvind Blach)	2	1	0	15	8
3.	BEL	(Charles Delelienne, Maurice van den Bemden, Raoul Daufresne de la Chevalerie, René Strauwen, Fernand de Montigny, Adolphe Goemaere, Pierre Chibert, Andre Becquet, Raymond Keppens, Pierre Valcke, Jean van Nerom, Robert Gevers, Louis Diercxens)	1	2	0	6	19
4.	FRA	(Paul Haranger, Robert Lelong, Pierre Estrabant, Georges Breuille, Jacques Morise, Edmond Loriol, Désiré Guard, Roland Bedel, André Bounal, Gaston Rogot, Pierre Rollin)	0	3	0	3	12

1924 not held

1928 Amsterdam T: 9, N: 9, D: 5.26.

			W	L	T	PF	PA
1.	IND	(Richard Allen, Leslie Hammond, Michael Rocque, Sayed Yusuf, Broome Eric Pinniger, Rex Norris, Ernest Goodsir-Cullen, Frederic Seaman, Dhyan Chand, George Marthins, Maurice Gateley, Jaipal Singh, Shaukat Ali, Feroze Khan)	5	0	0	29	0
2.	HOL	(Adrian Katte, Reindert de Waal, Albert Tresling, Jan Ankerman, Emile Duson, Johannes Brand, August Kop, Gerrit Jannink, Paulus van de Rovaert, Robert van der Veen, Hendrik Visser t'Hooft)	3	1	0	8	5
3.	GER	(Georg Brunner, Heinz Wöltje, Werner Proft, Erich Zander, Theodor Haag, Werner Freyberg, Herbert Kemmer, Herbert Hobein, Bruno Boche, Herbert Müller, Friedrich Horn, Erwin Franzkowiak, Hans Haussmann, Karl-Heinz Irmer, Aribert Heymann, Kurt Haverbeck, Rolf Wollner, Gerd Strantzen, Heinz Förstendorf)	3	1	0	11	3

		W	L	T	PF	PA
4. BEL	(Etienne Soubre, Johnny van der Straeten, Corneille Wellens Lambert Adelot, Claude Baudoux, Adolphe Goemaere, André Seeldrayers, Charles Delheid, Louis Diercxens, Yvon Baudoux, Charles Koning, Freddy Cattoir, Louis de Deken, Emile Vercken, Auguste Goditiabois, Georges Grosjean, René Mallieux)	3	2	0	8	12

Final: IND 3–0 HOL
3rd Place: GER 3–0 BEL

The first Indian hockey clubs were formed in Calcutta in 1885. In 1926 India played its initial international matches against New Zealand. But it was the 1928 Olympics in Amsterdam that established India as the world's number-one power in field hockey. Led by 22-year-old Dhyan Chand, an army captain from Uttar Pradesh, the Indians whipped through the tournament without giving up a single goal. Chand eventually won three Olympic gold medals and later became coach of the Indian national team.

1932 Los Angeles T: 3, N: 3, D: 8.11.

		W	L	T	PF	PA
1. IND	(Richard Allen, Arthur Hind, Carlyle Tapsell, Leslie Hammond, Masud Minhas, Broome Eric Pinniger, Lal Shah Bokhari, Richard Carr, Gurmit Singh Kullar, Dhyan Chand, Roop Singh, Sayed Mohammed Jaffar)	2	0	0	35	2
2. JAP	(Shumkichi Hamada, Akio Sohda, Sadayoshi Kobayashi, Katsumi Shibata, Yoshio Sakai, Eiichi Nakamura, Haruhiko Kon, Hiroshi Nagata, Kenichi Konishi, Toshio Usami, Junzo Inohara)	1	1	0	10	13
3. USA	(Harold Brewster, Samuel Ewing, Leonard O'Brien, Henry Greer, James Gentle, Horace Disston, Lawrence Knapp, Charles Shaeffer, Amos Deacon, William Boddington, David McMullin, Frederick Wolters)	0	2	0	3	33

Interest in hockey spread rapidly throughout India following the Olympic triumph of 1928. When it came time to raise money to send a team to the Los Angeles Olympics, a journalist representing the Indian Hockey Federation approached Mahatma Gandhi and asked him to issue an appeal to the masses. Gandhi's only reply was, "What's hockey?" Nevertheless, an Indian team did make it to Los Angeles, paying its way by playing exhibition matches in Europe on the way home. The Indians had no problems with the competition, defeating Japan, 11–1, and the United States, 24–1. In the latter game, which had the highest score ever achieved in an international match, Roop Singh scored ten goals and Dhyan Chand eight.

1936 Berlin T: 11, N: 11, D: 8.15.

		W	L	T	PF	PA
1. IND	(Richard Allen, Carlyle Tapsell, Mohammed Hussain, Baboo Narsoo Nimal, Ernest Goodsir-Cullen, Joseph Galibardy, Shabban Shahab ud Din, Dara Singh, Dhyan Chand, Roop Singh, Sayed Mohammed Jaffar, Cyril Michie, Paul Peter Fernandes, Paul Peter, Joseph Phillip, Garewal Gurcharan Singh, Ahsan Mohomed Khan, Ahmed Sher Khan, Lionel Emmett, Mirza Nasir-ud-Din Masood)	5	0	0	38	1
2. GER	(Karl Dröse, Herbert Kemmer, Erich Zander, Alfred Gerdes, Erwin Keller, Heinrich Schmalix, Harald Huffmann, Werner Hamel, Kurt Weiss, Hans Scherbart, Fritz Messner, Tito Warnholtz, Detlef Okrent, Hermann Auf der Heide, Heinrich Peter, Carl Menke, Heinz Raack, Paul Mehlitz, Ludwig Beisiegel, Karl Ruck, Erich Cuntz, Werner Kubitzki)	3	1	0	14	9
3. HOL	(Jan de Looper, Reindert de Waal, Max Westerkamp, Hendrik de Looper, Rudolf Jacob van der Haar, Antoine Robert van Lierop, Pieter Adriaan Gunning, Henri Schnitger, Ernst Willem van den Berg, Agathon de Roos, René Sparenberg, Carl Erich Haybroek)	3	1	1	13	10
4. FRA	(Raymond Tixier, Guy Chevalier, Paul Imbault, Claude Graveraux, Félix Grimonprez, Francois Verger, Paul Sartorius, Anatole Vologe, Joseph Goubert, Claude Soulé, Claude Roques, Etienne Guibal, Michel Verkindere, Marcel Lachmann, Guy Hénon, Emmanuel Gonat, Jean Rouget, Charles Imbault, Robert Rousse)	2	3	0	7	19

Final: IND 8–1 GER
3rd Place: HOL 4–3 FRA

As a British colony, India was forced to march behind the flag of Great Britain. But in the dressing room before their final match against Germany, the Indian team saluted the tricolor flag of the Indian National Congress. The Germans fought hard and trailed only 1–0 at halftime. But the Indians wore them down after the break, winning 8–1, with Dhyan Chand scoring six goals while playing barefoot.

1948 London T: 13, N: 13, D: 8.13.

		W	L	T	PF	PA
1. IND	(Leo Pinto, Trilochan Singh, Randhir Singh Gentle, Keshava Datt, Amir Kumar, Maxie Vaz, Kishan	5	0	0	25	2

Lal, Kunwar Digvijay Singh, Grahanandan Singh, Patrick Jansen, Lawrie Fernandes, Ranganandhan Francis, Akhtar Hussain, Leslie Claudius, Jaswant Rajput, Reginald Rodrigues, Latifur Rehman, Balbir Singh, Walter D'Souza, Gerry Glacken)

			W	L	T	PF	PA
2. GBR	(David Brodie, George Sime, William Lindsay Michael Walford, Frank Reynolds, Robin Lindsay, John Peake, Neil White, Robert Adlard, Norman Borrett, William Griffiths, Ronald Davies)		3	1	1	21	4
3. HOL	(Antonius Richter, Henri Jean Derckx, Johan Frederik Drijver, Jenne Langhout, Hermanus Pieter Loggere, Edouard Tiel, Willem van Heel, Andries Boerstra, Pieter Marie Bromberg, Jan Hendrik Kruize, Rius Esser, Henricus Bouwman)		4	2	1	17	11
4. PAK	(M. Anwar Beg Moghal, Mohamad Niaz Khan, Mohamad Abdul Razzao, Hamid Ullah Khan Burki, Abdul Ghafoor Khan, Shah-Rukh Shahzada, Ahmed Masud, M. Shaikh, Iqtidar Ali Shah Dara, Abdul Aziz, Rhamat Ullah Shaikh, Sayed Mohamed Saleem, S. Khurrum, Mohamed Khawaja Taki, Mukhtar Bhatti, Abdul Hamid, M. D'Mello, Abdul Qayyum Khan, Azziz-ur-Rahman Khan, Mohmood Ul Hassan)		4	2	1	25	7

Final: IND 4–0 GBR
3rd Place: HOL 1–1 PAK
3rd Place Replay: HOL 4–1 PAK

Ever since India first appeared on the international field hockey scene, Great Britain had studiously avoided playing the Indian team, apparently afraid of the embarrassment of losing to one of its colonies. However in 1948 India gained not only its independence from Britain, but also a chance to face its former mentor in what had now become the Indian national sport. The match for first place turned out to be no contest, as Great Britain, which had advanced to the final without giving up a goal, was itself shut out, 4–0.

1952 Helsinki T: 12, N: 12, D: 7.24.

			W	L	T	PF	PA
1. IND	(Ranganandhan Francis, Dharam Singh, Randhir Singh Gentle, Leslie Claudius, Keshava Datt, Govind Perumal, Raghbir Lal, Kunwar Digvijay Singh, Balbir Singh, Udham Singh, Muniswamy Rajgopal, Chinadorai Deshmutu, Meldric St. Clair Daluz, Grahanandan Singh)		3	0	0	13	2

			W	L	T	PF	PA
2. HOL	(Laurentz Mulder, Henri Jean Derckx, Johan Frederik Drijver, Julius Ancion, Hermanus Pieter Loggere, Edouard Tiel, Willem van Heel, Rius Esser, Jan Hendrik Kruize, Andries Boerstra, Leonard Wery, Andries Cornelis Dirk)		2	1	0	3	6
3. GBR	(Graham Dadds, Roger Midgley, Denys Carnill, John Cockett, Dennis Eagan, Anthony Robinson, Anthony Nunn, Robin Fletcher, Richard Norris, John Conroy, John Taylor, Derek Day, Neil Nugent)		2	1	0	4	4
4. PAK	(Abdul Waheed Qazl, Mohamad Niaz Khan, Asghar Ali Khan, Jack Britto, Manzoor Hussain Atif, Habib Ali Kiddi, Mahmudal Hassan, Abdul Hamid, Abdul Aziz Mallick, Habibur Rehman, Latifur Rehman, Abdul Latif Mir, Safdor Bahul, Mohamad Rafique Khan, Fazar Ur Rehman, Abdul Qayyum Khan, Azmat)		1	2	0	7	3

Final: IND 6–1 HOL
3rd Place: GBR 2–1 PAK

Nine of India's 13 goals were scored by Balbir Singh, a police inspector from Punjab.

1956 Melbourne T: 12, N: 12, D: 12.6

			W	L	T	PF	PA
1. IND	(Shankar Laxman, Bakshish Singh, Randhir Singh Gentle, Leslie Claudius, Amir Kumar, Govind Perumal, Raghbir Lal, Gurdev Singh, Balbir Singh, Udham Singh, Raghbir Singh Bhola, Charles Stephen, Ranganandhan Francis, Balkrishnan Singh, Amit Singh Bakshi, Hari Pal Kaushik, Hardyal Singh)		5	0	0	38	0
2. PAK	(Zakir Hussain, Munir Ahmad Dar, Manzoor Hussain Atif, Ghulam Rasul, Anwar Ahmad Khan, Hussain Mussarat, Noor Alam, Abdul Hamid, Habibur Rehman, Nasir Ahmad, Mutih Ullah, Latifur Rehman, Hussein Akhtar, Habib Ali Kiddi)		3	1	1	10	4
3. GER	(Alfred Lücker, Helmut Nonn, Günther Brennecke, Werner Delmes, Eberhard Ferstl, Hugo Dollheiser, Heinz Radzikowski, Wolfgang Nonn, Hugo Budinger, Werner Rosenbaum, Günther Ullerich)		2	1	2	8	6
4. GBR	(David Archer, John Strover, Denys Carnill, John Cockett, Francis Davis, Anthony Robinson, Frederick Hugh Scott, Neil Forster, David Thomas, John Conroy, Michael Doughty, Stephan Johnson, Colin Dale, Geoffrey Cutter)		2	2	2	9	10

		W	L	T	PF	PA
5. AUS	(Louis Hailey, Alan Barblett, Desmond Spackman, Kevin Carton, Keith Leeson, Dennis Kemp, Raymond Whiteside, Ian Dick, Melville Pearce, Eric Pearce, Gordon Pearce, Maurice Foley)	2	2	0	6	5
6. NZE	(David Goldsmith, Brian Johnston, Reginald Johansson, John Tynan, Murray Loudon, John Abrams, Archie Currie, Noel Hobson, Guy McGregor, Bruce Turner, Ivan Armstrong, Phillip Bygrave, William Schaefer)	1	2	0	8	10

Final: IND 1–0 PAK
3rd Place: GER 3–1 GBR

India began confidently with victories of 14–0 over Afghanistan and 16–0 over the United States. However they barely got by a roughhouse German team, 1–0, in the semifinal, and they won the final by the same score on a short corner hit by Gentle midway through the second half.

1960 Rome T: 16, N: 16, D: 9.9.

		W	L	T	PF	PA
1. PAK	(Abdul Rashid, Bashir Ahmad, Manzoor Hussain Atif, Ghulam Rasul, Anwar Ahmad Khan, Habib Ali Kiddi, Noor Alam, Abdul Hamid, Abdul Waheed, Nasir Ahmad, Mutih Ullah, Mushtaq Ahmad, Munir Ahmad Dar, Khurshid Aslam)	6	0	0	25	1
2. IND	(Shankar Laxman, Prithipal Singh, Jaman Lal Sharma, Leslie Claudius, Joseph Antic, Mohinder Lal, Joginder Singh, John Peter, Jaswant Singh, Udham Singh, Raghbir Singh Bhola, Charanjit Singh, Govind Sawant)	5	1	0	19	2
3. SPA	(Pedro Amat Fontanals, Francisco Caballer Soteras, Juan Angel Calzado de Castro, José Colomer Rivas, Carlos Del Coso Iglesias, José Antonio Dinares Massagué, Eduardo Dualde Santos de Lamadrid, Joaquin Dualde Santos de Lamadrid, Rafael Egusquiza Basterra, Ignacio Macaya Santos de Lamadrid, Pedro Murúa Leguizamon, Pedro Roig Junyent, Luis Maria Usoz Quintana, Narciso Ventalló Surralles)	4	1	1	11	4
4. GBR	(Harold Cahill, John Neill, Denys Carnill, Charles Jones, Howard Davis, Neil Livingstone, Ian Taylor, John Hindle, Stuart Mayes, Frederick Scott, Derek Miller, Peter Croft, John Bell, Griffiths Saunders, Patrick Austen)	3	2	1	7	5
5. NZE	(William Schaefer, John Abrams, Ian Kerr, Bruce Turner, John Cullen, John Ross Gillespie, Anthony Hayde, Guy McGregor, Noel Hobson, Mervyn McKinnon, Phillip Bygrave, James Barclay, Kelvin Percy, Murray Mathieson)	4	3	1	10	9
6. AUS	(Louis Hailey, William Spackman, Mervyn Crossman, John McBryde, Kevin Carton, Julian Pearce, Gordon Pearce, Michael Craig, Raymond Evans, Eric Pearce, Donald Currie, Phillip Pritchard, Graham Wood, Errol Bill, Barry Malcolm)	4	3	2	16	10
7. GER	(Wolfgang End, Helmut Nonn, Günther Ullerich, Dieter Krause, Werner Delmes, Eberhard Ferstl, Klaus Woller, Keller, Hugo Budinger, Norbert Schuler, Herbert Winters, Christian Buchting, Willi Brendel, Klaus Greinert)	2	3	0	11	4
7. KEN	(George Saudi, Anthony Vaz, Sohal Avtar Singh, Jagnandan Singh, Deol Surjeet Singh, Fernandes Silvester, Fernades Edgar, Fernandes Hilary, Panaser Surjeet Singh, Sandhu Pritan Singh, John Levon, Simonian, Kirpal Singh, Gurarian, Fernandes Egbert, Aloysius Mendonca, Aggarwal Krishan, Sehmi Cursarah Singh)	2	2	2	11	5

Final: PAK 1–0 IND
3rd Place: SPA 2–1 GBR

The early rounds saw some surprising incidents. In the quarterfinal contest between Germany and Pakistan, the score was tied 1–1 with only a few minutes to play. A penalty was called against Ullerich of Germany for illegally blocking a shot with his hand. The referee, Asselmann of Belgium, ordered a bully, or face-off. When a bully is called, two players, one from each team, touch sticks three times and then go after the ball. Ullerich bullied off for the Germans, but only touched sticks twice. The referee caught him and ordered the bully repeated. Again Ullerich struck before the third touch. This time the referee awarded a goal to Pakistan, a goal which gave Pakistan a 2–1 victory. The next day a consolation match was held between France and Belgium. With the score 0–0 and the French attacking, an Italian traffic policeman, on duty just outside the field, blew his whistle. The Belgians thought it was an umpire's whistle and stopped playing, whereupon the French team knocked the ball into the net for what proved to be the only goal of the game. Meanwhile India was forced into double overtime in the quarterfinals before they were able to defeat Australia, 1–0. But that was nothing compared to the Great Britain–Kenya match that followed. That contest went into six overtimes before Saunders of Great Britain scored to give the British a 2–1 victory after 127 minutes of play.

The semifinals were tense affairs, with both Pakistan and India scoring early and holding on for 1–0 wins over Spain and Great Britain, respectively. Entering the final, India had a cumulative Olympic record of 30 wins and no losses, their teams having scored 197 goals while allowing only eight. Unintimidated, the Pakistanis attacked aggressively from the beginning. After 12 minutes Nasir Ahmad of Pakistan pushed a goal into the corner of the net. Despite vigorous play on both sides, that was the only score of the match. The Pakistanis were ecstatic, and most observers were thrilled to have seen such a hard-fought match. But back in India the loss to Pakistan was considered a national tragedy, and plans were immediately made to regain the Olympic title in Tokyo in 1964.

INDIA'S FIELD HOCKEY WINNING STREAK

1928	**1948**	**1960**
IND 6–0 AUS	IND 8–0 AUS	IND 10–0 DEN
IND 9–0 BEL	IND 9–1 ARG	IND 4–1 HOL
IND 5–0 DEN	IND 2–0 SPA	IND 3–0 NZE
IND 5–0 SWI	IND 2–1 HOL	IND 1–0 AUS
IND 3–0 HOL	IND 4–0 GBR	IND 1–0 GER
1932	**1952**	
IND 11–1 JAP	IND 4–0 AUS	
IND 24–1 USA	IND 3–1 GBR	
	IND 6–1 HOL	
1936		
IND 4–0 HUN	**1956**	
IND 7–0 USA	IND 14–0 AFG	
IND 9–0 JAP	IND 16–0 USA	
IND 10–0 FRA	IND 6–0 SIN	
IND 8–1 GER	IND 1–0 GER	
	IND 1–0 PAK	

1964 Tokyo T: 15, N: 15, D 10.23.

		W	L	T	PF	PA
1. IND	(Shankar Laxman, Prithipal Singh, Dharam Singh, Mohinder Lal, Charanjit Singh, Gurbux Singh, Joginder Singh, John Peter, Harbinder Singh, Hari Pal Kaushik, Darshan Singh, Jagjit Singh, Bandu Patil, Udham Singh, Ali Sayeed)	7	0	2	22	5
2. PAK	(Abdul Hamid, Munir Ahmad Dar, Manzoor Hussain Atif, Saeed Anwar, Anwar Ahmad Khan, Muhammad Rashid, Khalid Mahmood, Zaka-ud-Din, Muhammad Afzal Manna, Mohammad Asad Malik, Mutih Ullah, Tariq Niazi, Zafar Hayat, Khurshid Azam, Khizar Nawaz, Tariq Aziz)	7	1	0	20	44
3. AUS	(Paul Dearing, Donald McWatters,	5	3	0	20	10

Brian Glencross, John McBryde, Julian Pearce, Graham Wood, Robin Hodder, Raymond Evans, Eric Pearce, Patrick Nilan, Donald Smart, Antony Waters, Mervyn Crossman, Desmond Piper)

4. SPA	(Carlos Del Coso Iglesias, José Colomer Rivas, Julio Solaun Garteizgogeascoa, Juan Angel Calzado de Castro, José Antonio Dinares Massagué, Narciso Ventalló Surralles, Ignacio Macaya Santos de Lamadrid, Jaime Amat Fontanais, Eduardo Dualde Santos de Lamadrid, Jorge Vidal Mitjans, Jaime Echevarria Arteche, Luis Maria Usoz Quintana, Pedro Amat Fontanais, Francisco Amat Fontanais)	4	2	3	18	9
5. GDR	(Rainer Stephan, Axel Thieme, Klaus Vetter, Horst Brennecke, Klaus Bahner, Horst Dahmlos, Reiner Hanschke, Rolf Westphal, Lothar Lippert, Dieter Ehrlich, Adolf Krause, Karl-Heinz Freiberger)	4	0	5	17	5
6. KEN	(John Simonian, Anthony Querobino Vaz, Avtar Singh Sohal, Surjeet Singh Panesar, Silvester Fernandes, Leo Fernandes, Edgar Simon Fernandes, Egbert Carmo Fernandes, Amar Singh Mangat, Aloysius Mendonca, Saude André George, Krishan Kumar Aggarwal, Tejparkash Singh Brar, Reynold Anthony D'Souza Santokh Singh Matharu)	4	3	1	10	13
7. HOL	(Joost Boks, Jacob Pieter Leemhuis, Jan Van Gooswilligen, Johan Pieter Fokker, Franciscus Fiolet, Theodorus Terlingen, Th. J. M. V. Van Vroonhoven, Arie Leendert de Keyzer, Guillaum Zweerts, Jacob Voigt, Nicolaas Bernard Spits, Jan Veentjer, John Robert Elffers, Leendert Gerhardus Krol, Jan Francis Van Hooft, Johan Mijnarends, Eric van Rossem, C. V. Coster Van Voorhout)	4	3	1	21	7
7. JAP	(Hiroshi Miwa, Tsuneya Yuzaki, Akio Takashima, Katsuhiro Yuzaki, Tetsuya Wakabayashi, Toshihiko Yamaoka, Kenji Takizawa, Shigeo Kadku, Hiroshi Tanaka, Michio Okabe, Seiji Kihara, Junichi Yamaguchi, Kunio Iwahashi)	3	4	0	7	11

Final: IND 1–0 PAK
3rd Place: AUS 3–2 SPA
5th Place: GER 3–0 KEN

India struggled through to the final, surviving 1–1 ties with Germany and Spain. Pakistan, on the other hand, won seven straight matches. However, in the deciding contest, with five minutes gone in the second half, Munir Ahmad Dar of Pakistan was penalized for stopping a shot with his foot. Mohinder Lal converted the penalty shot for the only goal of the game.

1968 Mexico City T: 16, N: 16, D: 10.26.

			W	L	T	PF	PA
1.	PAK	(Zakir Hussain, Tanvir Ahmad Dar, Tariq Aziz, Saeed Anwar, Riaz Ahmed, Guirez Akhtar, Khalid Mahmood Hussain, Mohammad Ashfaq, Abdul Rashid, Mohammad Asad Malik, Jahangir Ahmad Butt, Riaz Ud Din, Tariq Niazi)	9	0	0	26	5
2.	AUS	(Paul Dearing, James Mason, Brian Glencross, Gordon Pearce, Julian Pearce, Robert Haigh, Donald Martin, Raymond Evans, Ronald Riley, Patrick Nilan, Donald Smart, Desmond Piper, Eric Pearce, Frederick Quinn)	5	3	1	15	8
3.	IND	(Rajendra Absolem Christy, Gurbux Singh, Prithipal Singh, Balbir Singh II, Ajitpal Singh, Krishna Murtay Perumal, Balbir Singh III, Balbir Singh I, Harbinder Singh, Inamur Rehman, Inder Singh, Munir Sait, Harmik Singh, Jagjit Singh, John Peter, Tarsem Singh Gurbaksh Singh)	7	2	0	23	7
4.	GER	(Wolfgang Rott, Günter Krauss, Utz Aichinger, Dirk Michel, Klaus Greinert, Ulrich Vos, Michael Krause, Norbert Schuler, Fritz Schmidt, Carsten Keller, Ulrich Sloma, Wolfgang Müller, Eckart Suhl, Friedrich-Wilhelm Josten, Jürgen Wein, Detlef Kittstein, Wolfgang Baumgart, Hermann End)	5	3	1	16	8
5.	HOL	(Joost Boks, Theodorus Terlingen, Heiko Tiberius Locker van Staveren, Charles de Lanoy Meijer, Johan Pieter Fokker, John Robert Elffers, Frans Gerhard Spits, Otto Boudewijn ter Haar, Charles Thole, Petrus Johannes Weemers, Arie Leendert de Keyzer, Aernout S. Brederode, Ewaldus Kist, Sebo Onno Ebbens, Theo van Vroonhoven, Gerardus Hijikema, Edo Buma)	6	3	0	15	12
6.	SPA	(Carlos Del Coso Iglesias, Antonio Nogues, Julio Solaun Garteizgogeascoa, Francisco Fábregas, José Antonio Dinares Massagué, Juan Amat, Juan Quintana, José Salles, Francisco Amat Fontanais, Pedro Amat Fontanais, Agustin Masana,	3	3	3	9	7

José Colomer Rivas, Jorge Fábregas, Narciso Ventalló Surralles, Rafael Camina, Jorge Vidal Mitjans, Juan José Alvear Calleja)

			W	L	T	PF	PA
7.	NZE	(Ross McPherson, Roger Capey, Alan Patterson, Keith Thomson, Selwyn Maister, John Anslow, Bruce Judge, John Chistensen, Alan McIntyre, Barry Maister, Jan Borren, Edwin Salmon, John Hicks)	3	1	4	9	7
8.	KEN	(John Simonion, Kirpal Bhardwaj, Avtar Singh Sohal, Harvinder Marwa, Surjeet Singh Panesar, Silvester Fernandes, Leo Fernandes, Santokh Singh Matharu, Davinder Deegan, Hillary Fernandes, Aloysius Mendonca, Mohamed Malik, Egbert Fernandes, Reynold Pereira)	4	3	1	12	8

Final: PAK 2–1 AUS
3rd Place: IND 2–1 GER
5th Place: HOL 1–0 SPA
7th Place: NZE 2–0 KEN

With the score tied 0–0 after 55 minutes in a preliminary match between India and Japan, a penalty stroke was awarded to India. The Japanese were so upset that they laid down their sticks and walked off the field, forfeiting the game. Earlier, India had lost to New Zealand, 2–1 — the first time that India had given up more than one goal in an Olympic match. They lost their semifinal match to Australia by the same score. In the final, the winning goal was scored by Mohammad Asad Malik after 56 minutes of play.

1972 Munich T: 16, N: 16, D: 9.10.

			W	L	T	PF	PA
1.	GER	(Wolfgang Rott, Michael Peter, Dieter Freise, Michael Krause, Eduard Thelen, Horst Dröese, Carsten Keller, Ulrich Klaes, Wolfgang Baumgart, Uli Vos, Peter Trump, Peter Kraus, Werner Kaessmann, Wolfgang Ströedter, Detlef Kittstein, Rainer Seifert, Eckart Suhl, Fritz Schmidt)	8	1	0	21	5
2.	PAK	(Saleem Sherwani, Akhtarul Islam, Munawaruz Zaman, Saeed Anwar, Rasool Akhtar, Fazalur Rehman, Mudassar Asghar, Islahud Din, Abdul Rashid, Mohammad Asad Malik, Mohammad Shahnaz, Riaz Ahmed, Iftikhar Ahmed, Muhammad Zahid, Jahangir Ahmad Butt)	6	2	1	19	7
3.	IND	(Manuel Frederick, Mukhbain Singh, Michael Kindo, Krishna Murtay Perumal, Ajitpal Singh, Harmik Singh, Ganesh Mollerapoovayya, Harbinder Singh, Kulwant Singh, Ashok Kumar, Harcharan Singh,	6	1	2	27	11

4. HOL (Andre Bolhuis, Thijs Kaanders, Coen Kranenberg, Thies Kruize, Maarten Sikking, Frans Spits, Nico Spits, Bart Taminiau, Charles Thole, Piet Weemers, Jeroen Zweerts, Wouter Leefers, Flip van Lidth de Jeude, Paul Litjens, Marinus Dijkerman, Irving van Nes) — Govin Billimogaputtaswamy, Singh Virinder, Cornelius Charles) — 5 3 1 21 14

5. AUS (Brian Glencross, Robert Haigh, Richard Charlesworth, Paul Dearing, Thomas Colder, James Mason, Terry McAskell, Patrick Nilan, Desmond Piper, Ronald Riley, Donald Smart, Gregor Browning, Robert Andrew, Graham Reid, Ronald Wilson, Wayne Hammond) — 5 2 2 22 10

6. GBR (Austin Savage, Paul Svehlik, Tony Ekins, Keith Sinclair, Bernard Cotton, Rui Saldanha, Richard Oliver, Michael Crowe, Michael Corby, Peter Marsh, John French, Dennis Hay, Terry Gregg, Peter Mills, Sheik M. Ahmad, Graham Evans, Christopher Langhorne) — 5 3 1 18 12

7. SPA (Alberto Carera, Jorge Fábregas, Francisco Seguar, Juan Amat, Francisco Fábregas, José Salles, José Alustiza, José Borrell, Francisco Amat, Ramon Quintana, Juan Arbos, Jaime Arbos, Jaime Amat, Juan Quintana, Luis Towse, Jorge Camina, Antonio Nogues, Agustin Churruca) — 3 2 4 11 11

8. MAL (Khairuddin Bin Zainal, A. Francis Belavantheran, Sri Shanmuganathan, Poh Meng Phang, Wong Choon Hin, S. Balasingam, Sion Ming Yang, Franco Louis D'Cruz, K. Mahendran, Singh Harnahal, R. Pathmarajah, Mohinder Razali Yeop Omar, Sayed Samat, Sulaiman Saibot, Brian Sta Maria) — 4 4 1 11 11

Final: GER 1–0 PAK
3rd Place: IND 2–1 HOL
5th Place: AUS 2–1 GBR
7th Place: SPA 2–1 MAL

The final was a bitter and violent contest, with Michael Krause of Germany scoring the only goal of the game with ten minutes to play. The Pakistani team and their supporters in the stands were so angry at the officiating that they stormed the judges' table and poured water on Rene Frank, President of the International Hockey Federation. At the medal ceremony, several of the Pakistani players refused to face the German flag during the playing of the German national anthem. All 11 Pakistani finalists were banned for life by the International Olympic Committee.

1976 Montreal T: 11, N: 11, D: 7.30.

			W	L	T	PF	PA
1.	NZE	(Paul Ackerley, Jeff Archibald, Thur Borren, Alan Chesney, John Christensen, Greg Dayman, Tony Ineson, Alan McIntyre, Neil McLeod, Barry Maister, Selwyn Maister, Trevor Manning, Arthur Parkin, Mohan Patel, Ramesh Patel, Les Wilson)	3	1	2	9	9
2.	AUS	(Robert Haigh, Richard Charlesworth, David Bell, Gregory Browning, Ian Cooke, Barry Dancer, Douglas Golder, Wayne Hammond, James Irvine, Malcolm Poole, Robert Proctor, Graham Reid, Ronald Riley, Trevor Smith, Terry Walsh)	4	3	0	16	8
3.	PAK	(Saleem Sherwani, Manzoor Hassan, Munawaruz Zaman, Saleem Nazim, Rasool Akhtar, Iftikhar Syed, Islah Islahuddin, Manzoor Hussain, Abdul Rashid, Shanaz Sheikh, Samiulah Khan, Qamar Zia, Arshad Mahmood, Arshad Ali Chaudry, Mudassar Asghar, Haneef Khan)	4	1	1	20	11
4.	HOL	(Maarten Sikking, Andre Bolhuis, Tim Steens, Geert van Eijk, Theodoor Doyer, Coen Kranenburg, Rob Toft, Wouter Leefers, Hans Jorritsma, Hans Kruize, Jan Albers, Paul Litjens, Imbert Jebbink, Ron Steens, Bart Taminiau, Wouter Kan)	5	2	0	14	8
5.	GER	(Wolfgang Rott, Klaus Ludwiczak, Michael Peter, Dieter Freise, Fritz Schmidt, Michael Krause, Horst Dröese, Werner Kaessmann, Uli Vos, Peter Caninenberg, Peter Trump, Hans Montag, Wolfgang Ströedter, Heiner Dopp, Rainer Seifert, Ralf Lauruschkat)	3	2	1	22	13
6.	SPA	(Luis Alberto Carrera, Juan Amat, Jaime Arbos, Juan Arbos, Ricardo Cabot, Juan Colomer, Francisco Codina, Agustin Churruca, Francisco Frabregas, Jorge Fabregas, Agustin Masana, Juan Pellon, Ramon Quintana, José Salles, Francisco Segura, Luis Alberto Twose)	2	2	2	12	17
7.	IND	(Ajitpal Singh, Vaduvelu Phillips, Baldev Singh, Ashok Diwan, Bilimogga Govinda, Ashok Singh, Varinder Singh, Harcharan Singh, Mohinder Singh, Aslam Khan, Syed Ali, Birbhadur Chattri, Chand Singh, Ajit Singh, Surjit Singh, Vasudevan Baskaran)	4	3	0	16	12
8.	MAL	(Khailuddin Zainal, Azraai Md. Zain, Srishanmuganath Naganathy, Francis Anthonysamy, Kok Ming Lam,	2	5	0	4	11

Mohindar Singh Amar, Choon Hin Wong, Balasingam Singaram, Palanisamy Nallasamy, Rama Krishnan Rengasamy, Medhendran Murugesan, Singh Avtar Gill, Antony Cruz, Fook Loke Poon, Pathmarajah Ramalingam, Soon Kooi Ow)

Final: NZE 1–0 AUS
3rd Place: PAK 3–2 HOL
5th Place: GER 9–1 SPA
7th Place: IND 2–0 MAL

New Zealand didn't exactly overwhelm their opposition; in fact, they didn't even outscore them. But they scored when it counted, including a penalty shot by Tony Ineson early in the second half that gave them a 1–0 victory over Australia in the final.

1980 Moscow T: 6, N: 6, D: 7.26.

		W	L	T	PF	PA
1. IND	(Allan Schofield, Chettri Bir Bhadur, Dung Dung Sylvanus, Rajinder Singh, Davinder Singh, Gurmail Singh, Ravinder Pal Singh, Vasudevan Baskaran, Somaya Maneypanda, Marahaj Krishon Kaushik, Charanjit Kumar, Mervyn Fernandis, Amarjit Rana Singh, Shahid Mohamed, Zafar Iqbal, Surinder Singh)	4	0	2	43	9
2. SPA	(José Garcia, Juan Amat, Santiago Malgosa, Rafael Garralda, Francisco Fabregas, Juan Luis Coghen, Ricardo Cabot, Jaimes Arbos, Carlos Roca, Juan Pellon, Miguel de Paz, Miguel Chavez, Juan Arbos, Javier Cabot, Paulino Monsalve, Jaime Zumalacarregui)	4	1	1	36	7
3. SOV	(Vladimir Pleshakov, Vyacheslav Lampeev, Leonid Pavlovsky, Sos Airapetyan, Farit Zigangirov, Valery Belyakov, Sergei Klevtsov, Oleg Zagoroonev, Aleksandr Gusev, Sergei Pleshakov, Mikhail Nichepurenko, Minneula Azizov, Aleksandr Sytchev, Aleksandr Myasnikov, Viktor Deputatov, Aleksandr Goncharov)	4	2	0	32	12
4. POL	(Zygfryd Józefiak, Andrzej Mikina, Krystian Bąk, Wlodzimierz Stanislawski, Leszek Hensler, Jan Sitek, Jerzy Wybieralski, Leszek Tórz, Zbigniew Rachwalski, Henryk Horwat, Andrzej Myśliwiec, Leszek Andrzejczak, Jan Mielniczak, Mariusz Kubiak, Adan Dolatowski, Krzysztof Glodowski)	2	3	1	20	17
5. CUB	(Angel Mora Parra, Severo Frometa Conte, Bernabe Izquierdo Martinez, Edgardo Vazquez Marquez, Hector Pedroso Garcia, Manuel Varela Perez, Raul Garcia Cabrera, Jorge Mico Gutierrez, Rudolfo Delgado Orabñez, Lazaro Hernandez Rangel, Juan Blanco Peñalver, Juan Caballero Perez, Roberto Ramirez Hernandez, Angel Fontane Escobar, Ricardo Campos Hernandez, Juan Rios Alvarez)	2	4	0	11	43
6. TAN	(Leopold Gracias, Benedict Mendes, Soter Da Silva, Abraham Sykes, Yusuf Manwar, Jaypal Singh, Mohamed Manji, Rajabu Rajab, Jasbir Virdee, Islam Islam, Stephen D'Silva, Frederick Furtado, Taherali Hassanali, Anoop Mukundan, Patrick Toto, Julius Peter)	0	6	0	4	58

Final: IND 4–3 SPA
3rd Place: SOV 2–1 POL
5th Place: CUB 4–1 TAN

The 1980 field hockey tournament was decimated by the boycott. Of the 11 teams that competed in Montreal in 1976, only Spain and India were represented in Moscow. Cuba and Tanzania were added to fill the field even though they had little experience with the sport. It was like old times for India, trouncing Tanzania 18–0 and Cuba 13–0. However, they had a tougher match with Poland, salvaging a 2–2 tie when Mervyn Fernandis scored a goal with five seconds to play. India also scraped through with a 2–2 tie against Spain. The two teams met again in the final. India took a 3–0 lead and held on to win, 4–3, despite the fact that Juan Amat of Spain scored three goals in twelve minutes.

WOMEN

1896–1976 not held

1980 Moscow T: 6, N: 6, D: 7.31.

		W	L	T	PF	PA
1. ZIM	(Sarah English, Ann Mary Grant, Brenda Phillips, Patricia McKillop, Sonia Robertson, Patricia Davies, Maureen George, Linda Watson, Susan Huggett, Gillian Cowley, Elizabeth Chase, Sandra Chick, Helen Volk, Chistine Prinsloo, Arlene Boxhall, Anthea Stewart)	3	0	2	13	4
2. CZE	(Jarmila Kralicková, Berta Hruba, Iveta Sranková, Lenka Vymazalová, Jirina Krizova, Jirina Kadlecová, Jir-	3	1	1	10	5

ina Čermaková, Marta Urbanová, Kveta Petricková, Marie Sykorová, Ida Hubacková, Milada Blazková, Jana Lahodová, Alena Kyselicová, Jirina Hajková, Viera Podhanyiová)

3. SOV	(Galina Inzhuvatova, Nelli Gorbatkova, Valentina Zazdravnykh, Nadezhda Ovechkina, Natella Krasnikova, Natalya Bykova, Lidiya Glubokova, Galina Vyuzhanina, Natalya Buzunova, Lyailya Akhmerova, Nadezhda Filippova, Yelena Gureva, Tatyana Yembakhtova, Tatyana Shvyganova, Alina Kham, Lyudmila Frolova)	3	2	0	11	5
4. IND	(Margaret Toscano, Sudha Chaudhry, Gangotri Bhandari, Rekha Mundphan, Rupa Kumari Saini, Varsha Soni, Eliza Nelson, Prem Maya Sonir, Naazleen Madraswalla, Selma D'Silva, Lorraine Fernandes, Harpreet Gill, Balwinder Kaur Bhatia, Geeta Sareen, Nisha Sharma, Hutoxi Bagli)	2	2	1	9	6
5. AUT	(Patricia Lorenz, Sabine Blemenschuetz, Elisabeth Pistauer, Andrea Kozma, Briggitta Pecanka, Brigette Kindler, Friederike Stern, Regina Lorenz, Eleonore Pecanka, Ilse Stipanovsky, Andrea Porsch, Erika	2	3	0	6	11
	Csar, Dorit Ganster, Ulrike Kleinhansl, Eva Cambal, Jana Cejpek)					
6. POL	(Malgorzata Gajewska, Bogumila Pajor, Jolanta Sekulak, Jolanta Blędowska, Lucyna Matuszna, Danuta Stanislawska, Wieslawa Rylko, Lidia Zgajewska, Maria Kornek, Malgorzata Lipska, Halina Koldras, Lucyna Siejka, Dorota Bielska, Dorota Zalęczna, Michalina Plekaniec, Jadwiga Koldras)	0	5	0	0	18

When five of the six nations scheduled to compete in the inaugural women's field hockey tournament withdrew as part of the Jimmy Carter boycott, it set the stage for a true Cinderella story. As white-ruled Rhodesia, Zimbabwe had been banned from the Olympics, but when the black majority took power, the ban was lifted. Desperate to fill the field, the Soviet Union and the International Olympic Committee contacted Zimbabwe five weeks before the start of the Games and offered to subsidize the sending of a team, the members of which were not selected until the weekend before the Olympics opened. Ironically, the team that represented Zimbabwe was all white. They were held to ties by Czechoslovakia and India, but they were the only team to avoid defeat. A 4–1 victory over Austria assured them of gold medals. Each member of the Zimbabwe team was also awarded an ox by the Zimbabwean minister of sport.

FOOTBALL (SOCCER)

Olympic soccer matches consist of two 45-minute halves.

1896 not held

1900 Paris T: 3, N: 3, D: 9.23.

			W	L	PF	PA
1. GBR	(Upton Park Football Club—J. H. Jones, Claude Buckenham, Grosling, A. Chalk, T. E. Burridge, W. Quash, R. R. Turner Spackman, J. Nicholas, J. Zealley, Haslam)		1	0	4	0
2. FRA	(Union des sociétés françaises de sports athletiques—Huteau, Bach, Pierre Allemane, Gaillard, Bloch, Macaire, Fraysse, Garnier, Lambert, Grandjean, Fernand Canelle, Duparc, Peltier)		1	1	7	8
3. BEL	(Marcel Leboutte, R. Kelcom, Ernest Moreau, Alphonse Renier, Georges Pelgrims, C. van Hoorden, E. Neefs, Erich Thornton, Albert Delbecque, H. Spaunoghe, van Heuckelum, Londot)		0	1	4	7

1904 St. Louis T: 3, N: 2, D: 11.25

		W	L	T	PF	PA
1. CAN	(Galt Football Club—Ernest Linton, George Ducker, John Gourley, John Fraser, Albert Johnson, Robert Lane, Tom Taylor, Frederick Steep, Alexander Hall, Gordon McDonald, William Twaits)	2	0	0	11	0
2. USA	(Christian Brothers College—Louis Menges, Joseph Lydon, Thomas January, John January, Charles January, Peter Ratican, Warren Brittingham, Alexander Cudmore, Charles Bartliff, Oscar Brockmeyer, Raymond Lawler)	1	1	1	2	7
3. USA	(St. Rose School—Frank Frost, George Cooke, Henry Jameson, Joseph Brady, Martin Dooling, Dierkes, Cormic Cosgrove, O'Connell, Claude Jameson, Harry Tate, Thomas Cooke, Johnson)	0	2	1	0	6

The St. Rose team managed to put one ball into the net. Unfortunately, it was into the goal they were defending.

1906 Athens T: 4, N: 2, D: 4.24.

			W	L	PF	PA
1. DEN	(Viggo Andersen, Peter Petersen, Charles Buchwald, Parmo Ferslew, Stefan Rasmussen, Aage Andersen, Oscar Nielsen-Nörland, Carl Frederick Petersen, Holger Fredriksen, August Lindgreen, Henry Rambusch, Hjalmar Heerup, A. Hansen)		2	0	14	1
2. INT	Smyrna (Edwin Charnaud, Zareck Couyoumdzian, Edouard Giraud, Jacques Giravd, Henri Joly, Percy de la Fontaine, Donald Whittal, Albert Whittal, Godfrey Whittal, Herbert Whittal, Edward Whittal)		1	1	13	5
3. GRE	Thessaloniki (Georgios Vaporis, Nicolaos Pindos, A. Tegon, Nicolaos Pentzikis, Ioannis Kyrou, Georgis Sotiriadis, V. Zarkadis, Dimitrios Michitsopoulos, A. Karangonidis, Ioannis Saridakis, Ioannis Abbot)		0	2	0	17

The Athens team was supposed to play off for scond place, but refused on the grounds that they had already beaten Thessaloniki. The team from Smyrna was an international one.

1908 London T: 6, N: 5, D: 10.24.

			W	L	PF	PA
1. GBR	(Harold Bailey, William Corbett, Herbert Smith, Kenneth Hunt, Frederick Chapman, Robert Hawkes, Arthur Berry, Vivian Woodward, Hubert Stapley, Claude Purnell, Harold Hardman)		3	0	18	1
2. DEN	(Ludvig Drescher, Charles Buchwald, Harald Hansen, Harald Bohr, Kristian Middelboe, Nils Middelboe, Oscar Nielsen-Nörland, August Lindgreen, Sophus Nielsen, Vilhelm Wolffhagen, Björn Rasmussen, Marius Andersen, Johannes Gandil)		2	1	26	3

		W	L	PF	PA

3. HOL (Reinier Beeuwkes, Karel Heijting, Lou Otten, Johan Sol, Johannes de Korver, Emil Mundt, Jan Welcker, Edu Snethlage, Gerard Reeman, Jan Thomée, Georges de Bruyn Kops, Johan Kok) — 1 1 2 4

4. SWE (Oskar Bengtsson, Ake Fjästad, Teodor Malm, Sven Olsson, Hans Lindman, Olof Olsson, Sune Almkvist, Gustaf Bergström, Sven Ohlsson, Karl Ansén, Nils Andersson, Valter Lidén, Arvid Fagrell, Karl Gustafsson) — 0 2 1 14

Final: GBR 2–0 DEN
3rd Place: HOL 2–0 SWE

France entered two teams, both of which were thrashed by Denmark. In the 17–1 defeat of the French "B" team, Sophus Nielsen of Denmark scored 10 goals.

1912 Stockholm T: 11, N: 11, D: 7.5.

		W	L	PF	PA
1. GBR	(Ronald Brebner, Thomas Burn, Arthur Knight, Douglas McWhirter, Horace Littlewort, James Dines, Arthur Berry, Vivian Woodward, Harold Walden, Gordon Hoare, Ivan Sharpe, Edward Hanney, Gordon Wright, Harold Stamper)	3	0	13	5
2. DEN	(Sophus Hansen, Nils Middelboe, Harald Hansen, Charles Buchwald, Emil Jörgensen, Poul Berth, Oscar Nielsen-Nörland, Axel Thufason, Anton Olsen, Sophus Nielsen, Vilhelm Wolffhagen, Hjalmar Christoffersen, Aksel Petersen, Ivar Seidelin-Nielsen, Poul Nielsen)	2	1	13	5
3. HOL	(Marius Jan Göbel, David Wijnveldt, Piet Bouman, Gerardus Fortgens, Constant Feith, Nicolaas de Wolf, Dirk Lotsy, Johannes Boutmy, Jan van Breda Kolff, Huug de Groot, Caesar ten Cate, Jan van der Sluis, Jan Vos, Nicolaas Bouvy, Johannes de Korver)	3	1	17	7
4. FIN	(August Syrjäläinen, Jalmari Holopainen, Gösta Löfgren, Knut Lund, Eino Soinio, Viljo Lietola, Lauri Tanner, Bror Wiberg, Jarl Öhman, Artturi Nyyssönen, Algot Niska, Ragnar Wickström, Kaarlo Soinio)	2	2	5	16
5. HUN	(Gáspár Borbás, Imre Schlosser, Mihály Pataky, Sándor Bodnár, Béla Sebestyén, Antal Vágó, Jenö Károly, Gyula Biró, Imre Payer, Gyula Rumbold, László Domonkos)	2	1	6	8
6. AUT	(Müller, Neubauer, Studnicka, Merz, Hussack, Cimera, Braunsteiner, Brandstetter, Graubard Kurpiel, Noll)	3	2	11	8
7. GER	(Julius Hirsch, E. Kipp, Willi Worpitzky, Adölf Jager, Karl Wegele, Hermann Bosch, Max Breunig, Georg Krogmann, Ernst Hollstein, Helmut Röpnack, Albert Weber, Gottfried Fuchs)	1	2	18	8

		W	L	PF	PA
7. ITA	(D. Mariani, C. Sardi, F. Berardo, F. Bontadini, E. Zuffi, B. Leone, G. Milano, C. Demarchi, B. Devecchi, A. Binaschi, P. Campelli)	1	2	4	8

Final: GBR 4–2 DEN
3rd Place: HOL 9–0 FIN

Great Britain was leading 2–1 when Buchwald of Denmark was injured and had to be helped from the field. Denmark was forced to continue with only ten players, and Britain quickly capitalized by scoring two goals in three minutes. The Danes then adjusted to playing shorthanded, but it was too late and they lost, 4–2. In a consolation match against Russia, Gottfried Fuchs of Germany scored ten goals to match Nielsen's feat of four years earlier.

1920 Antwerp T: 14, N: 14, D: 9.5.

		W	L	PF	PA
1. BEL	(Jan de Bie, Armand Swartenbroeks, Oscar Verbeeck, Joseph Musch, Emile Hanse, André Fierens, Louis van Hege, Henri Larnoe, Mathieu Bragard, Robert Coppée, Désiré Bastin, Félix Balyu, Fernand Nisot, Georges Hebdin)	3	0	8	1
2. SPA	(Ricardo Zamora, Pedro Vallana, Mariano Arrate, José Samitier, José Maria Belaustequigoita, Agustin Sancho, Ramón Equiazábal, Félix Sesúmaga, Patricio Arabolaza, Rafael Moreno, Domingo Acedo, Juan Artola, Francisco Pagazaurtundúa, Louis Otero, Joaquin Vázquez, Ramón Moncho Gil, Sabino Bilbao, Silverio Izaguirre)	4	1	9	5
3. HOL	(Robert McNeill, Henri Dénis, Bernard Verweij, Leonard Bosschart, Frederik Kuipers, Hermanus Steeman, Oscar van Rappard, Jan van Dort, Bernardus Groosjohan, Herman van Heijden, Jacob Bulder, Johannes de Natris, Evert Bulder, Adrianus Bieshaar)	2	2	9	10
4. ITA	(Piero Campelli, Giacovanni Giacone, Antonio Bruna, Renzo de Vecchi, Virginio Rosetta, Calo di Nardo, Ettore Reinaudi, Mario Meneghetti, Giuseppe Parodi, Luigi Burlando, Rinaldo Roggero, Giustiniano Barucco, Pio Ferraris, Giuseppe Forlivesi, Cesare Lovati, Celeste Sardi, Adolfo Baloncieri, Emilio Badini, Guglielmo Brezzi, Emilio Santamaria Aristodemo, Alevildo de Marchi.)	2	2	6	7
5. SWE	(Rune Bergström, Albin Dahl, Karl Gustafsson, Fritjof Hillén, Herbert Karlsson, Waldus Lund, Bertil Nordenskjöld, Albert Olsson, Mauritz Sandberg, Ragnar Wicksell, Robert Zander, Albert Öjermark)	1	2	14	7
5. NOR	—	1	2	4	7

2nd Place: SPA 3–1 HOL

The final matched the home team, Belgium, against the Czechoslovakians, who had outscored their opponents 15–1, on their way to the final. A partisan crowd of 40,000 watched with pleasure as Belgium took a 2–0 lead. But after several controversial calls, the Czech team had had enough and walked off the field en masse in protest. This threw the tournament into chaos. With Czechoslovakia disqualified, a playoff for second place was ordered. But France, which had lost to Czechoslovakia in the semifinals, refused to participate since many of the leading French players had already gone home. Eventually Spain defeated Sweden and Italy to qualify for the second-place match against Holland.

1924 Paris T: 22, N: 22, D: 6.9.

			W	L	T	PF	PA
1.	URU	(Andrés Mazali, José Nasazzi, Pedro Arispe, José Leandro Andrade, Jose Vidal, Alfredo Ghierra, Santos Urdinarán, Hector Scarone, Pedro Petrone, Pedro Céa, Angel Romano, Umberto Tomasina, José Naya, Alfredo Zibechi, Antonio Urdinaran)	5	0	0	20	2
2.	SWI	(Hans Pulver, Adolphe Reymond, Rudolf Ramseyer, August Oberhauser, Paul Schmiedlin, Aron Pollitz, Karl Ehren-bolger, Robert Pache, Walter Dietrich, Max Abegglen, Paul Fässler, Felix Bédouret, Adolphe Mengotti, Paul Sturzenegger, Edmond Kramer)	4	1	1	15	6
3.	SWE	(Sigfrid Lindberg, Axel Alfredsson, Fritjof Hillén, Gunnar Holmberg, Sven Friberg, Harry Sundberg, Evert Lundqvist, Sven Rydell, Per Kaufeldt, Tore Keller, Rudolf Kock, Gustaf Carlson, Charles Brommesson, Thorsten Svensson, Albin Dahl, Konrad Hirsch, Sven Lindqvist, Sten Mellgren)	3	1	1	18	5
4.	HOL	(Gejus van der Meulen, Henri Dénis, Hendrik Vermetten, Albert Oosthoek, Gerardus Krom, Gerardus Horstén, Johannes de Natris, Gerrit Visser, André Lefèvre, Ocker Formenoy, Marinus Sigmond, Bernard Verweij, Johannes Tetzner, Evert van Linge, Klaas Jan Breeuwer, Bernardus Groosjohan, Cornelis Pijl, Albert Snouck-Hurgronje, Johannes ter Beek)	2	2	1	11	7
5.	EGY	(Abaza Sayed Fahmi, Abdel Hamid Moharren, Abdel Kader Mohammed, El Hassany Aly-Fahmy, Mohammed El Mahdwy, Fouad Mahmoud, Iaghen Ibrahim, Hamdy Abdel-Salam Hegozi Hussein, Henein Rizkalla, Housny Khalil, Ismail El Sayed, Ismail Mahmoud, Mansour	1	1	0	3	5

Ahmed, Marey Mahmoud, Moktar Mahmoud, Osman Gamil, Riad Aly Mohammed Rouston, Salim Ahmed, Shawky Riad, Taha Kamel)

			W	L	T	PF	PA
5.	FRA	(Bard, Batmale, Baumann, Bonnardel, Bover, Canthelou, Chayrigues, Chessneau, Cottenet, Crut, Devaquez, Domergue, Dufour, Dubly, Gravier, Gross, Huot, Isbecque, Jourda, Parachini, Renier)	1	1	0	8	5
5.	IRL	(Aungier, Cawzer, Crawford, Dowdali, Duncan, Dykes, Farrell, Ghent, Hannon, Healy, Heaney, Hendrick, Kerr, Lea, MacCarthy, MacRay, Muldoon, Murphy, Murray, O'Reilly, Robinson, Thomas)	1	1	0	2	2
5.	ITA	(Aliberti, Ardizone, Baldi, Baloncieri, Barbieri, Antonio Bruna, Luigi Burlando, Calvi, Giampiero Combi, Conti, Della-Valle, De Pra, Renzo de Vecchi, Fayenz, Antonio Janni, Virgilio Levratto, Mario Magnozzi, Martin, Monti, Virginio Rosetta, Rosso)	2	1	0	4	2

Final: URU 3–0 SWI
3rd Place: SWE 1–1 HOL
           SWE 3–1 HOL

The tournament opened with an upset as Italy defeated one of the favorites, Spain, 1–0, on a goal that was actually kicked through the net by the Spanish captain, Vallana. The Uruguayan team caught the fancy of the crowd with its 2–1 come-from-behind win over Holland in the semifinals. Holland lodged a protest, but it was denied. Then, when a Dutch referee was assigned to the final, it was Uruguay's turn to protest. Their protest was accepted, and the Dutch official was replaced by a Frenchman. The stadium was packed with 60,000 people for the final match and another 5000 were left outside, causing a crush that led to several injuries. The Swiss struggled vigorously but were unable to stop the Uruguayans, who led 1–0 at the break before winning 3–1.

1928 Amsterdam T: 17, N: 17, D: 6.13.

			W	L	T	PF	PA
1.	URU	(Andres Mazáli, José Nasazzi, Pedro Arispe, José Leandro Andrade, Lorenzo Fernández, Juan Piriz, Alvaro Gestido, Santos Urdináran, Hector Castro, Pedro Petrone, Pedro Cea, Antonio Campolo, Adhemar Canavesi, Juan Arremón, René Borjas, Hector Scarone, Roberto Figueroa)	4	0	1	12	5
2.	ARG	(Angelo Bosio, Fernando Paternoster, Ludovico Bidoglio, Juan Evaristo, Luis Monti, Segundo Medici, Raimundo Orsi, Enrique Gainzarain, Manuel Ferreyra, Domingo Taras-	3	1	1	25	8

coni, Adolfo Carricaberry, Feliciano Angel Perducca, Octavio Diaz, Roberto Cherro, Rudolfo Orlandini, Saúl Calandra)

3. ITA	(Giampiero Combi, Delfo Bellini, Umberto Caligaris, Alfredo Pitto, Fulvio Bernardini, Piertro Genovesi, Adolfo Baloncieri, Elvio Banchero, Angelo Schiavio, Mario Magnozzi, Virgilio Levratto, Giovanni Deprà, Virginio Rosetta, Silvio Piertroboni, Antonio Janni, Enrico Rivolta, Gino Rossetti)	3	1	1	25	11
4. EGY	(Abdelhamid Hamdi, Sayed Fahmy Abaza, Mohammed Ahmad Shemais, Gaber Yacout El-Soury Fahmy El-Hassani, Abdelhalim Younis Hassan, Elsaid Ismail Mohamed Hooda, Aly Mohamed Riad, Mohmoud Ismail Mohamed Hooda, Moosa Hassan Moussa El-Ezam, Mohamed Gamil El-Zobeir, Mohamed Aly Rostam, Ahmed Mohamed Salem, Mohamed Ezz Eldin Gamal, Mahmoud Mokhtar Refaee, Ahmed Mahmoud Soliman)	2	2	0	12	19
5. BEL	(J. de Bie, S.J.M. Verhulst, H.V.B. Bierna, G. Despae, L. Versyp, H.C. Ditzler, H.M.J. de Deken, A.P. Ruyssevelt, J. Diddens, J. Moeschal, R.E.M. Braine, G.J. de Vos, P.E.E. Braine, B. Voorhoof, F. van Halme, G. Boesman, J. Lavigne, N.H. Hoydonckx, J.E. Caudron)	1	1	0	5	4
5. POR	(A. Fernandes Roquette, C. Alves Jr., J. Gomes Vieira R. Soares Figueiredo, A. Silva, C. Matos Rodrigues, W. Motta Fonesca, J.M. Soares Louro, V. Marcolino da Silva, A. Martins, J.M. Martins, C. Santos Nunes, O. Maia Vasques de Carvalho, A.J. João, A. Ramos, J. Conçalves Tavares, R. Ornellas, J. Santos, L. dos Santos)	1	1	0	3	3
5. SPA	(J. M. Yermo Solaegui, M. Marculeta Barberia, L. Regueiro Pagola, J. Quinococes Lopez, J. M. Jauregui Lagunas, L. Iruretagoyena Ayestaran, A. Mariscal Ibeuba, T. Arizcorreta Sein, F. Gamborena Hernandorena, A. Labarta Rey, P. Vallana Jeanaguenat, C. Errasti Suinaga, D. de Zaldua Anabitarte, J. Legarreta Abaitua, A. Conzales de Audicana Inchaurraga, M. Sagarzazu Martinez, I. Alcorta y Hermoso, J. Errazquin Aumas, J. Izaguirre Goena, A. Villaverde Llanos, F. Bienzobas Ocariz, R. Bilbar, Echevarria)	1	1	1	9	9

Final: URU 1–1 ARG
URU 2–1 ARG
3rd Place: ITA 11–3 EGY

The first final ended in a draw and had to be replayed.

1932 Los Angeles not held

1936 Berlin T: 16, N: 16, D: 8.15.

		W	L	PF	PA
1. ITA	(Bruno Venturini, Alfredo Foni, Pietro Rava, Giuseppe Baldo, Achille Piccini, Ugo Locatelli, Annibale Frossi, Libero Marchini, Sergio Bertoni, Carlo Biagi, Francesco Gabriotti, Luigi Scarabello, Giulio Cappelli, Alfonso Negro)	4	0	13	2
2. AUT	(Eduard Kainberger, Ernst Künz, Martin Kargl, Anton Krenn, Karl Wahlmüller, Max Hofmeister, Walter Werginz, Adolf Laudon, Klement Steinmetz, Karl Kainberger, Franz Fuchsberger, Franz Mandl, Josef Kitzmüller)	2	1	7	4
3. NOR	(Henry Johansen, Nils Eriksen, Öivind Holmsen, Fritjof Ulleberg, Jörgen Juve, Rolf Holmberg, Magdalon Monsen, Reidar Kvammen, Alf Martinsen, Odd Frantzen, Arne Brustad, Fredrik Horn, Sverre Hansen, Magnar Isaksen)	3	1	10	4
4. POL	(Spirydion Albanski, Wladyslaw Szczepaniak, Antoni Galecki, Wilhelm Góra, Franciszek Cebulak, Ewald Dytko, Walerian Kisielinski, Michal Matyas, Teodor Peterek, Hubert God, Gerhard Wdarz, Henryk Martyna, Józef Kotlarczyk, Jan Wasiewicz, Ryszard Piec, Walenty Musielak, Fryc Scherfke)	2	2	11	10
5. GBR	(H.H.C. Hill, Holmes, Fulton, Gardiner, Joy, Pettit, Crawford, Kyle, Dodds, Edelston, Finch)	1	1	6	5
5. GER	(Hans Jakob, Reinhold Münzenberg, Heinz Ditgens, Rudolf Gramlich, Ludwig Goldbrunner, Robert Bernard, Ernst Lehner, Otto Siffling, August Lenz, Adolf Urban, Wilhelm Simetsreiter)	1	1	9	2
5. JAP	(Sano, Suzuki, Takeuchi, Tatsuhara, Oita, Kin, Matsunaga Ukon, Kawamoto, T. Kamo, Sh. Kamo)	1	1	3	10
5. PER	(Valdivieso, Fernandez, A. Lavalle, Tovar, Castillo, Jordan, Magallanes, Alcalde, Fernandez, Villanueva, Morales)	1	0	7	3

Final: ITA 2–1 AUT
3rd Place: NOR 3–2 POL

The status of Olympic soccer, already weakened by the introduction of the World Cup in 1930 and the exclusion of the sport from the 1932 Olympic Games, received another blow when the 1936 tournament was marred by unruly incidents. First came the match between Italy and the United States, in which two Americans were injured. When the

German referee, Weingartner, ordered Achille Piccini of Italy to leave the game, he refused to go. Several Italian players surrounded Weingartner, pinned his arms to his sides, and covered his mouth with their hands. The game continued with Piccini still in the lineup, and Italy won 1–0.

This unfortunate affair was nothing compared to what took place five days later, during the quarterfinal contest between Peru and Austria. Austria led 2–0 at the interval, but Peru tied the game with two goals in the last 15 minutes. A 15-minute overtime period was then played without further scoring, so a second overtime was ordered. By this time the small but vocal group of Peruvian spectators had become frantic with emotion. What followed depends on which continent is telling the story. Evidently, the Peruvian fans rushed onto the field while the game was still in progress and actually attacked one of the Austrian players. The Peruvian team took advantage of the chaos to score two quick goals and win the game, 4–2. Austria protested immediately, and a Jury of Appeal, composed of five European men, ordered the match replayed two days later. The jury also decreed that the game be played behind locked doors with no spectators allowed. The Peruvians refused to show up, and the entire Peruvian Olympic contingent withdrew from the games, as did the Colombians, who supported their South American neighbors. Back in Lima, Peruvian demonstrators threw stones at the German consulate, while Peru's president, Oscar Benavides denounced "the crafty Berlin decision." When German diplomats appealed to Benavides and pointed out that the decision had been made not by Germans but by officials of F.I.F.A., the international football federation, the president changed his position and blamed the demonstrations on Communists.

Meanwhile, back in Berlin, a bitterly contested final was fought out between Italy and Austria. The first 45-minute half ended without a score. Midway in the second half, Annibale Frossi, Italy's inside right wing, scored the first goal of the game. Eleven minutes later Karl Kainberger, Austria's inside left, tied the score and the match went into overtime. A quick goal by Frossi proved decisive, and Italy won the gold medal, 2–1.

1948 London T: 18, N:18, D: 8.13.

		W	L	PF	PA
1. SWE	(Torsten Lindberg, Knut Nordahl, Erik Nilsson, Birger Rosengren, Bertil Nordahl, Sune Andersson, Kjell Rosén, Gunnar Gren, Gunnar Nordahl, Henry Carlsson, Nils Liedholm Börje Leander)	4	0	22	3
2. YUG	(Ljubomir Lovrič, Miroslav Brozovič, Branislav Stanovič, Zlatko Čajkovski, Miodrag Jovanovič, Zvonko Cimermančič, Rajko Mitić, Stjepan Bobek, Željko Čajkovski, Bernard Vukas, Franjo Soštarič, Prvoslav Mihajlovič, Fränjo Wolfl, Kosta Tomaševič)	3	1	13	6
3. DEN	(Ejgil Nielsen, Viggo Jensen, Knud Börge Overgaard, Axel Pilmark, Dion Örnvoid, Ivan Jensen, Johannes Plöger, Knud Lundberg, Carl Aage Praest, John Hansen, Jörgen Sörensen, Holger Seebach, Karl Aage Hansen)	3	1	15	11
4. GBR	(Ronald Simpson, C. R. "Jack" Neale, Andrew Carmichel, J. Robert Hardisty, Eric Lee, Eric Fright, J. Alan Boyd, A. Aitken, Harry McIlvenny, J. Rawlings, William Amor, Kevin McAlinden, G. T. Manning, James McColl, Douglas McBain, Frank Donovan, Thomas Hopper, Denis Kelleher, Frederick Peter Kippax)	2	2	9	11
5. FRA	(G. Rouxel, R. Krug, B. Bienvenu, R. Persillon, M. Colau, G. Robert, J. Heckel, J. Strappe, R. Hebinger, J. Paluch, R. Courbin)	1	1	2	2
5. ITA	(G. Casari, G. Giovannini, A. Stellin, T. Maestrelli, M. Neri, G. Mari, E. Cavigioli,, A. Turconi, F. Pernigo, V. Cassani, E. Caprile)	1	1	12	5
5. KOR	(Duk-Yung Hong, Kyoo-Chung Pak, Dai-Chong Pak, Soon-Gon Choi, Kyoo-Whan Kim, B.D. Min, Zung-Whan Woo, C. Bai, Nam-Sik Chung, Yong-Sik Kim, Kook-Chin Chung)	1	1	5	13
5. TUR	(C. Arman, M. Alyuz, V. Tosuncuk, N. Ozkaya, B. Eken, H. Saygin, F. Kircan, E. Keskin, G. Kilic, K. Andonyadis, S. Gulesin)	1	1	5	3

Final:SWE 3–1 YUG
3rd Place: DEN 5–3 GBR

By 1948 the best players of Western Europe and South America were turning professional, and Olympic soccer began to be dominated by the state-sponsored "amateur" teams of Eastern Europe. Sweden was the last non-Communist team to win an Olympic football tournament. Their team included three brothers, Gunnar, Bertil, and Knut Nordahl, as well as three firemen, including Gunnar Nordahl.

1952 Helsinki T: 25, N: 25, D:8.2.

		W	L	T	PF	PA
1. HUN	(Gyula Grosics, Jenö Buzánszky, Mihály Lantos, József Bozsik, Gyula Lóránt, József Zakariás, Nándor Hidegkuti, Sándor Kocsis, Péter Palotás, Ferenc Puskás, Zoltán Czibor, Jenö Dalnoki, Imre Kovács, László Budai II, Lajos Csordás)	5	0	0	20	2
2. YUG	(Vladimir Beara, Branislav Stankovič, Tomislav Crnkovič, Zlatko Čajkovski, Ivan Horvat, Vujadin Boškov, Tihomir Ognjanov, Rajko	4	1	1	1	13

Mitič, Bernard Vukas, Stjepan Bobek, Branko Zebec)

			W	L	T	PF	PA
3.	SWE	(Karl Svensson, Lennart Samuelsson, Erik Nilsson, Olof Ahlund, Bengt Gustavsson, Gösta Lindh, Sylve Bengtsson, Gösta Löfgren, Ingvar Rydell, Yngve Brodd, Gösta Sandberg, Holger Hansson)	3	1	0	9	8
4.	GER	(Rudolf Schönbeck, Hans Eberle, Herbert Jäger, Kurt Sommerlatt, Herbert Schäfer, Alfred Post, Ludwig Hinterstocker, Georg Stollenwerk, Hans Zeitler, Willi Schröder, Kurt Ehrmann, Erich Gleixner, Matthias Mauritz, Karl Klug)	2	2	0	8	8
5.	AUT	(Fritz Nikolai, Walter Kollmann, Anton Krammar, Anton Wolf, Josef Walter, Robert Fendler, Hermann Hochleitner, Franz Feldinger, Erich Stumpf, Herbert Grohs, Otto Gollnhuber)	1	1	0	5	6
5.	BRA	(Carlos Martins Cavalheiro, Mauro Torres Homen Rodrigues, Waldir Villas Boas, Zozimo Alves Calanzan, Adesio Alves Machado, Edison Campos Martins, Larry Pinto de Faria, Milton Pessanha, Edvaldo Neto, Humberto Barbosa Tozzi, Jansen Moreira)	2	1	0	9	6
5.	DEN	(Jorgen Johansen, Poul Erik Petersen, Svend Nielsen, Erik Terkelsen, Poul Andersen, Steen Blicher, Jorgen Hansen, Poul Eyvind Petersen, Jens Hansen, Knud Lundberg, Holger Seebach)	2	1	0	7	6
5.	TUR	(Erdoğan Akin, Necdet Sentürk, Ridvan Bolatli, Mustafa Ertan, Basri Dirimilili, Ercüment Güder, Vasif Cetinel, Tekin Bilge, Yalçin Çaka, Muzaffer Tokac, Macit Gürdal)	1	1	0	3	8

Final: HUN 2–0 YUG
3rd Place: SWE 2–0 GER

1956 Melbourne T: 11, N: 11, D: 12.8.

			W	L	T	PF	PA
1.	SOV	(Lev Yashin, Anatoly Bashashkin, Mikhail Ogognikov, Boris Kuznyetsov, Igor Netto, Anatoly Maslyonkin, Boris Tatushin, Anatoly Issayev, Nikita Simonyan, Sergei Salnikov, Anatoly Ilyun, Nikolai Tichenko, Aleksei Paramonov, Eduard Streltsov, Valentin Ivanov, Vladimir Ryjkin, Yosif Betsa, Boris Rasinsky)	4	0	1	9	2
2.	YUG	(Petar Radenkovič, Mladen Koščak, Nikola Radovič, Ivan Šantek, Ljubisa Spajič, Dobroslav Krstič, Dragoslav Šekularac, Zlatko Pa-	2	1	0	13	3

pec, Sava Antič, Todor Veselinovič, Muhamed Mujič, Blagoje Vidinic, Ibrahim Biogradič, Luka Lipošinovič)

			W	L	T	PF	PA
3.	BUL	(Yosif Yosilov, Kiril Rakarov, Nikola Kovatschev, Stefan Stefanov, Manol Manolov, Gavril Stojanov, Dimiter Milanov, Georgy Dimitrov, Panayot Panayotov, Ivan Kolev, Todor Diyev, Georgy Naydenov, Miltscho Goranov, Krum Yanev)	2	1	0	10	3
4.	IND	(Narayan Subramaniam, Syed Khaja Aziz, Shaikh Abdul Lateef, Mohamed Kempiah, Noor Muhamed, Ahmed Husain, Mohamed Kannayan, Neville Stephen D'Souza, Krishna Chandra Pal, Nikhil Kumar Nunday, Krishna Swamy Kittu, T. Abdul Rahaman, Muhamed Abdus Salam, Pradip Kuma Banerjee, Tulsidas Balaram, Peter Ramaswamy Thangaraj, Samar Banerjee)	1	2	0	10	3
5.	AUS	(Ronald Lord, Robert Bignell, John Pettigrew, George Arthur, William Sander, Bruce Morrow, Francis Loughran, Jack Lennard, Graham McMillan, Edward Smith, Alwyn Warren)	1	1	0	4	4
5.	GBR	(Harry Sharratt, Donald Stoker, Leslie Thomas Farrer, Lawrence Topp, Stanley Prince, Herbert Dodkins, James Lewis, John Hardisty, John Laybourne, George Bromilow, Charles Twissell)	1	1	0	10	6

Final: SOV 1–0 YUG
3rd Place: BUL 3–0 IND

The winning goal was headed in early in the second half by Anatoly Ilyun. The Soviet victory was preserved when a goal by Yugoslavia's Zlatko Papec was disallowed because of an offside penalty.

1960 Rome T: 16, N: 16, D: 9.10.

			W	L	T	PF	PA
1.	YUG	(Blagoje Vidinič, Novak Roganovič, Fahrudin Jusufi, Zeljko Perušič, Vladimir Durkovič, Ante Žanetič, Andrija Ankovič, Zeljko Matuš, Milan Galič, Tomislav Knez, Borivoje Kostič, Milutin Soskič, Velimir Sombolac, Aleksandar Kozlina, Silvester Takač, Dusan Maravič)	3	0	2	17	7
2.	DEN	(Henry From, Poul Andersen, Poul Jensen, Bent Hansen, Hans Nielsen, Flemming Nielsen, Poul Pedersen, Tommy Troelsen, Harald Nielsen, Henning Enoksen, Jörn Sörensen, John Danielsen)	4	1	0	11	7

	W	L	T	PF	PA
3. HUN (Gábor Török, Zoltán Dudás, Jenő Dalnoki, Ernő Solymosi, Pál Várhidi, Ferenc Kovács, Imre Sátori, János Göröcs, Flórián Albert, Pál Orosz, János Dunai, Lajos Faragó, Dezső Novák, Oszkár Vilezsál, Gyula Rákosi, László Pál, Tibor Pál)	4	1	0	17	6
4. ITA (Luciano Alfieri, Tarcisio Burgnich, Mario Trebbi, Paride Tumburus, Sandro Salvadore, Giovanni Trappatoni, Giancarlo Cella, Giovanni Rivera, Ugo Tomeazzi, Giacomo Bulgarelli, Giorgio Rossano, Orazio Rancati, Giorgio Ferrini, Giovanni Fanello, Gilberto Noletti, Luciano Magistrelli)					

Final: YUG 3–1 DEN
3rd Place: HUN 2–1 ITA

Three-time-runner-up Yugoslavia shocked Denmark when their captain, Milan Galič, scored a goal from 30 meters out in the first minute of play. Ten minutes later, Zeljko Matuš made it 2–0 and it looked like a rout might be in the making. However, late in the first half, Galič was ejected for insulting a referee, and Yugoslavia played the rest of the game with only ten players. Nevertheless, they held on to their lead and prevailed 3–1. It is worth noting that Yugoslavia tied with Bulgaria in their preliminary pool and qualified for the semifinals only because they won a coin toss.

1964 Tokyo T: 14, N: 14, D: 10.23.

	W	L	T	PF	PA
1. HUN (Antal Szentmihályi, Dezső Novák, Kálman Ihász, Gusztáv Szepesi, Árpád Orban, Ferenc Nógrádi, János Farkas, Tibor Csernai, Ferenc Bene, Imre Komora, Sándor Katona, József Gelei, Károly Palotai, Zoltán Varga)	5	0	0	22	6
2. CZE (František Schmucker, Anton Urban, Karel Zdenek Pičman, Josef Vojta, Vladimir Weiss, Jan Geleta, Jan Brumovsky, Ivan Mráz, Karel Lichtnégl, Vojtech Masny, František Valošek, Anton Svajlen, Karel Knesl, Stefan Matlak, Karel Nepomucky, František Knebort, Ludevit Cvetler)	5	1	0	19	5
3. GDR (Hans Jürgen Heinsch, Peter Rock, Manfred Geisler, Herbert Pankau, Manfred Walter, Gerhard Körner, Hermann Stöcker, Otto Frässdorf, Henning Frenzel, Jürgen Nöldner, Eberhard Vogel, Horst Weigang, Klaus Urbanczyk, Bernd Bauchspiess, Klaus-Dieter Seehaus, Werner Unger, Wolfgang Barthels, Klaus Lisiewicz, Dieter Engelhardt)	4	1	1	12	4
4. UAR (Reda Ahmed, Yaken Zaki, Amin Elisnawi, Mohamed Kotb, Raafat Attia, Mohamed Abdelat Elsherbini, Seddik Mohamed, Ibrahim Riad, Mohamed Badawi, Nabil Nosseir, K. Aly Etman, F. Aly Korshed, Darwish Amin, Rifaat Elfanagili, Ahmed Moust Gad, Kalil Shahin, Mahmoud Hassan, Taha Ismail, Farouk Mahmoud)	2	3	1	18	16
5. GHA (Dodoo-Ankrah, Samuel Okai, Emmanuel Oblitey, Sam Acquah, Addo-Odametey, Emmanuel Nkansah, Gyau Agyemang, Wilberforce Mfum, Edward Aggrey Fynn, Edward Acquah, Kofi Pare)	1	1	1	5	8
5. JAP (Kenzo Yokoyama, Hiroshi Katayama, Yoshitada Yamaguchi, Ryozo Suzuki, Aritatsu Ogi, Mitsuo Kamata, Saburo Kawabuchi, Shigeo Yaegashi, Kunishige Kamamoto, Teruki Miyamoto, Masashi Watanabe)	1	2	0	5	9
5. ROM (Ilie Datcu, Ilie Greavu, Bujdr Halmageanu, Emil Petru, Ion Nunweiller, Niculae Georgescu, Ion Pircalah, Ghedrghe Constantin, Ion Ionescu, Dan Coe, Carol Creinicheanu)	2	1	0	5	4
5. YUG (Ivan Curkovic, Hirsad Fazlagic, Svetozar Vujovic, Rudolf Belin, Milan Cop, Jovan Miladinovic, Spasoje Samardzic, Slaven Zambata, Ivan Osin, Lazar Radovic, Dragan Dzajic)	1	2	0	8	8

Final: HUN 2–1 CZE
3rd Place: GDR 3–1 UAR

Most of the fireworks took place before the tournament even started. Beginning in 1952, so many nations began applying to compete in the Olympics that pre-Olympic soccer tournaments had to be held to decide the 16 Olympic teams. On May 24, 1964, one such qualifying match took place in Lima between Peru and Argentina. Argentina led 1–0, but with two minutes to play Peru scored to tie the game. However the Uruguayan referee, Angel Eduardo Payos, nullified the goal because of rough play by the Peruvians. While the crowd of 45,000 booed its disapproval, two spectators leaped onto the field and attacked the referee. They were quickly arrested, which angered the crowd even more. Then Payos ordered the game suspended, claiming, with obvious justification, that police protection on the field was inadequate. The incensed crowd surged onto the field while the police hustled Payos and the players to safety. Some spectators began breaking windows and before long mounted police appeared and began herding the rioters toward the exits, many of which were, unfortunately, locked. Tear-gas grenades were fired by the police, while the Peruvian soccer fans responded by throwing stones and bottles and setting part of the stadium on fire. The fighting spilled into the streets of Lima, and before the night was out, 328 people had been killed and over 500 injured. Most of those killed had been trampled to death, but at least four persons were shot by police bullets. The Peruvian government declared a national "state of siege" and suspended the constitution. Meanwhile, demonstrators marched to the National Palace demanding an end to police brutality and the declaration of a tie in the match with Argentina. Neither demand was met. Argentina, by the way, went to Tokyo but lost both of their games.

When the Olympic tournament finally commenced, two of the 16 qualifying teams were missing. North Korea dropped out after some of its track and swimming athletes were suspended for competing in the unsanctioned Games of the New Emerging Forces (GANEFO) in Jakarta. Italy, the only Western European team to qualify for the Tokyo tournament, withdrew following accusations that several of its players were actually professionals. This charge was fairly hard to deny considering that three members of the Italian Olympic team were also members of the Inter-Milan team, which was the reigning European Cup champion. In fact, Sandro Mazzola scored two of the goals that defeated Real Madrid in the Cup final.

The Olympic tournament itself was not very impressive, particularly after all that had preceded it. However, the final between Hungary and Czechoslovakia was an exciting match. Hungary's first goal, scored at the beginning of the second half, was actually put through the net by Josef Vojta of Czechoslovakia, who inadvertently deflected a Hungarian pass past his own goalie. Thirteen minutes later, Hungarian center forward Ferenc Bene outran the Czech defense and blasted in a second goal, which proved to be decisive.

1968 Mexico City T:16, N: 16, D: 10.26.

		W	L	T	PF	PA
1.	HUN (Károly Fatér, Dezsö Novák, Lajos Dunai, Miklós Páncsics, Iván Menczel, Lajos Szűca, László Fazekas, Antal Dunai, László Nagy, Ernö Noskó, István Juhász, Lajos Kocsis, Istvan Básti, László Keglovich, István Sárközi)	5	0	1	18	3
2.	BUL (Stoyan Yordanov, Atanas Gerov, Georgi Hristakiev, Milko Gaidarski, Kiril Ivkov, Ivailo Georgiev, Tsvetan Veselinov, Yevgeny Yanchovski, Peter Zhekov, Atanas Hristov, Asparuh Nikodimov, Kiril Stankov, Todor Krustev, Mihail Gionin, Yancho Dimitrov, Georgi Tsetkov, Ivan Zafirov, Georgi Vasilev)	3	1	2	16	10
3.	JAP (Kenzo Yokoyama, Hiroshi Katayama, Yoshitada Yamaguchi, Mit-	3	3	0	10	9

suo Kamata, Takaji Mori, Aritatsu Ogi, Teruki Miyamoto, Masashi Watanabe, Kunishige Kamamoto, Ikuo Matsumoto, Ryuichi Sugiyama, Masakatsu Miyamoto, Yasuyuki Kuwahara, Shigeo Yaegashi)

		W	L	T	PF	PA
4.	MEX (Javier Vargas, Juan Mañuel Alejándrez, Héctor Sanabria, Mario Pérez, Luis Regueiro, Luis Estrada, Vicente Pereda, Cesáreo Victorino, Javier Sánchez Galindo, Ignacio Basaguren, Albino Morales, Humberto Medina, Héctor Pulido, Elias Muñoz, Fernando Bustos)	3	3	0	10	9
5.	FRA (Jean Lempereur, Freddy Zix, Michel Verhoeve, Gilbert Plante, Jean-Michel Larque, Jean Louis Hodoul, Daniel Perrigaud, Daniel Hortaville, Marc Case, Gerard Hallet, Henri Ribul)	2	2	0	9	8
5.	GUA (Alberto Lopez, Llijon Leon, Roberto Camposeco, Hugo Montoya, Armando Melgar, Jorge Roldan, Hugo Torres, Carlos Valdez, Hugo Pena, David Stokes, Julio Garcia)	2	2	0	6	4
5.	ISR (Haim Levin, Menacham Bello, Zvi Rosen, Shaia Shwager, Shmuel Rosenthal, Rachamim Talbi, Giora Shpigal, Jehoshua Faygenbaum, Mordechai Shpiegler, Itzhak Druker, George Borba)	2	1	1	9	7
5.	SPA (Pedro Mora, Gregorio Benito, Francisco Espildora, Miguel Ochoa, Isidro Sala, Juan Asensi, Rafael Jean, Juan Fernandez, José Garzon, José Grande, Fernando Ortuno)	2	1	1	4	2

Final: HUN 4–1 BUL
3rd Place: JAP 2–0 MEX

Morocco qualified for the final tournament, but refused to participate against Israel. They were replaced by Ghana. The Ghana-Israel game, won by Israel 5–3, disintegrated into brawling, which continued back at the Olympic Village. A match between Czechoslovakia and Guatemala was also disrupted by fighting. The final pitted defending champion Hungary against Bulgaria, which qualified only after their tied quarterfinal game with Israel was decided by the toss of a coin. Bulgaria scored first on a header by Dimitrov, but four minutes before the end of the first half, Menczel of Hungary evened the score. A minute later Dunai of Hungary put in another goal. At this point the situation deteriorated drastically. Referee Diego De Leo, an Italian-born naturalized Mexican, ejected Dimitrov for rough play. Seconds later another Bulgarian, Kiril Ivkov, was thrown out. An angry teammate, Atanas Hristov, kicked the ball toward the referee, and he too was ejected. The Mexican crowd was none too pleased with the actions of Mr. De Leo. Having already disrupted the third-place game by throwing cushions onto the field, they used the same tactic to show their disapproval and cause delay in the final. The ejections effectively ended the contest, as Bulgaria was forced to play the second half with only eight players. Juhász of Hungary was eventually banished as well, but the Hungarians still outnumbered the Bulgarians 10–8 and won easily, 4–1.

1972 Munich T: 16, N: 16, D: 9.10.

			W	L	T	PF	PA
1.	POL	(Hubert Kostka, Zbigniew Gut, Jerzy Gorgon, Zygmunt Anczok, Leslaw Cmikiewicz, Zygmunt Maszczyk, Jerzy Kraska, Kazimierz Deyna, Zygfryd Szoltysik, Wlodzimierz Lubanski, Robert Gadocha, Ryszard Szymczak, Antoni Szymanowski, Marian Ostafinski, Grzegorz Lato, Joachim Marx, Kazimierz Kmiecik)	6	0	1	21	5
2.	HUN	(István Géczi, Péter Vépi, Miklós Páncsics, Péter Juhász, Lajos Szücs, Mihály Kozma, Antal Dunai, Lajos Kü, Béla Váradi, Ede Dunai, László Bálint, Lajos Kocsis, Kálmán Tóth, Jozsef Kovács, László Branikovits, Csaba Vidáts, Ádám Rothermel)	5	1	1	18	5
3.	GDR	(Jürgen Croy, Manfred Zapf, Konrad Weise, Bernd Bransch, Jürgen Pommerenke, Jürgen Sparwasser, Hans-Jürgen Kreische, Joachim Streich, Wolfgang Seguin, Peter Ducke, Frank Ganzera, Lothar Kurbjuweit, Eberhard Vogel, Ralf Schulenberg, Reinhard Häfner, Harald Irmscher, Siegmar Wätzlich)	4	2	1	23	9
3.	SOV	(Oleg Blochin, Murtaz Hurcilava, Yuri Istomin, Vladimir Kaplichnyi, VikViktor Kolotov, Yevgeny Lovchev, Sergei Olshanskiy, Yevgeny Rudakov, Vyacheslav Semenov, Gennady Yevrushikhin, Oganes Zanazanian, Andrei Yakubik, Arkadiy Andriasian)	5	1	1	17	6
5.	DEN	(Mogens Therkilosen, Flemming Ahlberg, Svend Andresen, Per Rontved, Jorgen Rasmussen, Jack Hansen, Kresten Nygaard, Allan Simonsen, Max Rasmussen, Arvo Heino Hansen, Keld Bak, Leif Prinzlau, Hans Ewald Hansen)	3	2	1	11	10
5.	GER	(Hans Jürgen Bradler, Heiner Baltes, Reiner Hollmann, Egon Schmitt, Friedhelm, Jürgen Kalb, Hermann Bitz, Ulrich Hoeness, Ottmar Hitzfeld, Bernd Nickel, Klaus	3	2	1	17	8

			W	L	T	PF	PA
		Wunder, Ronald Worm, Rudi Seliger)					
5.	MEX	(Jesus Rico, José Luis Trejo, Juan Alvarez, Enrique Martin Del Campo, Alejandro Hernandez, Fernando Blanco, Manuel Manzo, Daniel Razo, Leonardo Cuellar, Horacio Sanchez, Alejandro Peña, Alfredo Hernandez)	2	3	1	4	14
5.	MOR	(Mohamed Hazzaz, Mohamed Elfilali, Boujamaa Benkhrif, Abdallah Tazi, Ahmed Faras, Mohamed Merzaq, Ahmed Belkorchi, Larbi Ihardane, Khalifa Elbakhti, Abdelali, Mustapha Yaghcha, Ghazouani Mouhoub)	1	4	1	7	14

Final: POL 2–1 HUN
3rd Place: GDR 2–2 SOV

Hungary entered the final having lost only one of their last 21 Olympic matches going back to 1960. The game was played in torrential rain and near gale-force wind. Hungary led 1–0 at the interval, but when the teams switched sides for the second half Poland took advantage of having the wind at their backs and scored two goals to gain the victory.

1976 Montreal T: 13, N: 13, D: 7.31.

			W	L	T	PF	PA
1.	GDR	(Jürgen Croy, Gerd Weber, Hans-Jürgen Dörner, Konrad Weise, Lothar Kurbjuweit, Reinhard Lauck, Gert Heidler, Reinhard Häfner, Hans-Jürgen Riediger, Bernd Bransch, Martin Hoffman, Gerd Kische, Wolfram Löwe, Hartmut Schade, Dieter Riedel, Hans-Ullrich Grapenthin, Wilfried Gröbner)	4	0	1	10	2
2.	POL	(Jan Tomaszewski, Antoni Szymanowski, Jerzy Gorgoń, Wojciech Rudy, Wladyslaw Żmuda, Zygmunt Maszczyk, Grzegorz Lato, Henryk Kasperczak, Kazimierz Deyna, Andrzej Szarmach, Kazimierz Kmiecik, Piotr Mowlik, Henryk Wawrowski, Henryk Wieczorek, Leslaw Ćmikiewicz, Jan Beniger, Roman Ogaza)	3	1	1	11	5
3.	SOV	(Vladimir Astapovskiy, Anatoly Konkov, Viktor Matvienko, Mikhail Fomenko, Stefan Reshko, Vladimir Troshkin, David Kipiani, Vladimir Onishenko, Victor Kolotov, Vladimir Veremeev, Oleg Blochin, Leonid Buriak, Vladimir Feodorov, Aleksandr Minaev, Viktor Zviagintsev, Leonid Nazarenko, Aleksandr Prokhorov)	4	1	0	10	4

		W	L	T	PF	PA
4. BRA	(Carlos, Rosemiro, Tecâo, Edinho, Junior, Alberto, Marinho, Batista, Eudes, Erivelto, Santos, Mauro, Julinho, Chico Fraga, Jarbas, Edval, Ze Carlos)	2	2	1	6	6
5. FRA	(Jean-Claude Larrieu, Henri Orlandini, Patrick Battiston, Claude Chazottes, Francis Meynieu, Michel Pottier, Alexandre Strassievitch, Henri Zambelli, Michel Couge, Jean Fernandez, Michel Platini, Francisco Rubio, Loic Amisse, Bruno Baronchelli, Eric Pecout, Olivier Rouyer, Jean Marc Schaer)	2	2	1	9	7
5. IRN	(Mansour Rashidi, Hassan Nazavi, Andranik Eskandarian, Bijan Zolfoqalnassab, Parviz Qelichkhani, Ali Parvin, Nasrollah Abdollahi, Nasser Nouraii, Hassan Rowshan, Ali-reza Khorshidi, Hassan Nayebagha, Gholam Mazloomi, Saham Mirfakhrai, Ghafoor Jahani, Ali-Reza Azizi, Nasser Hejazi)	1	2	0	4	5
5. ISR	(Itzhak Vissoker, Abrahm Lev, Yaron Oz, Haim Bar, Moshe Shani, Itzak Peretz, Itzhak Shum, Elimeleh Leventhal, Rifaat Tourk, Gideon Damti, Josef Sorynow, Meir Nimni, Oded Nachness, Avraham Cohen, Joshoua Gal, Ehud Ben-Tovim, Alon Ben-Dor)	0	1	3	4	7
5. PRK	(In-Chol Jin, Gwangsok Kim, Il-Nam Kim, Myong-Song Kim, Jong-U Ma, Jong-Hun Pak, Se-Uk An, Song-Nam Hong, Jong-Sok Cha, Sung-Gyu Kim, Song-Guk Yang, Gil-Wan An, Hi-Yon Li, Dong-Chan Myong, Kyong-Won Pak)	1	2	0	3	9

Final: GDR 3–1 POL
3rd Place: SOV 2–0 BRA

Again the Olympic soccer final was played in heavy rain, and again it was dominated by the professional amateurs of Eastern Europe, including ten members of Poland's 1974 World Cup team. In the final match, East Germany scored two goals in the first 15 minutes and scored again with six minutes to play to secure the gold medal.

1980 Moscow T: 16, N: 16, D: 8.2.

		W	L	T	PF	PA
1. CZE	(Stanislav Seman, Luděk Macela, Josef Mazura, Libor Radimec, Zdeněk Rygel, Petr Němec, Ladislav Vizek, Jan Berger, Jindřich Svoboda, Lubos Pokluda, Werner Lička, Rostislav Václaviček, Jaroslav Netolicka, Oldřich Rott, František Štambacher, František Kunzo)	4	0	2	10	1
2. GDR	(Bodo Rudwaleit, Artur Ullrich, Lothar Hause, Frank Uhlig, Frank Baum, Rüdiger Schnuphase, Frank Terletzki, Wolfgang Steinbach, Jürgen Bähringer, Werner Peter, Dieter Kühn, Norbert Trieloff, Matthias Liebers, Bernd Jakubowski, Wolf-Rüdiger Netz, Matthias Müller)	4	1	1	12	2
3. SOV	(Rinat Dasaev, Tengiz Sulakvelidze, Aleksandr Chivadze, Vagiz Khidiyatullin, Oleg Romantsev, Sergei Shavlo Sergei Andreev, Vladimir Bessonov, Yuri Gavrilov, Fyodor Cherenkov, Valery Gazzaev, Vladimir Pilguj, Sergei Baltacha, Sergei Nikulin, Khoren Oganesyan, Aleksandr Prokopenko)	5	1	0	10	3
4. YUG	(Dragan Pantelić, Nikica Cukrov, Ivan Gudelj, Milos Hrstic, Milan Jovin, Nikica Klincarski, Miso Krsticević, Dzevad Secerbegović, Vladimir Matijević, Dušan Pestić, Tomislav Ivković, Boro Primorać, Srebrenko Repcić, Milos Sestić Zlatko Vujović, Zoran Vujović)	3	2	1	9	7
5. ALG	(Mourad Ahara, Mahmoud Guendouz, Bouzid Mahiduz, Chaabane Merzekane, Mohamed Kheddis, Rabah Madjer, Ali Fergani, Tadj Bensaoula, Lakhdar Belloumi, Salah Assad, Mohamed Rahmani, Salah Larbes, Djamel Menad, Abderrahmane Derquaz, Hocine Yahi, Mohamed Quamar Ghrib)	1	2	1	4	4
5. CUB	(Jose Reinoso, Miguel Lopez, Raimundo Frometa, Luis Sanchez, Luis Dreke, Roberto Espinosa, Andres Roldan Amado Povea, Dagoberto Lara, Ramon Nũnez, Calixto Martinez, Roberto Pereira, Jorge Masso, Fermin Madera Carlos Loredo, Luis Hernandez)	2	2	0	3	12
5. IRQ	(Abdul Fatah Jassim, Adnan Derchal Hutar, Jamal Ali Hamza, Saad Jassih Mohammed, Hassan Farhan Hassoun, Alaa Ahmed Khdhayir, Adil Khohayrr Hafidh, Falah Hassan Jasim, Hadi Ahmed Basheer, Hussain Saeed Muhammed, Thamir Assoufi Elias, Ibrahim Ali Kadhum, Wathiq Aswad Muhyi, Nazar Asmraf Salman, Ali Kadhum Nasir, Kadom Shibib Abdulsada)	1	1	2	4	5
5. KUW	(Ahmad Altarabulsi, Najeem Hubarak, Mahboub Hubarak, Jamal Alqabendi, Waleed Almubarak, Saed Alhouti, Fathi Marzouq, Jasem Sultan, Mujayed Alhaddad, Hamad Bohamad, Yousef	1	1	2	4	5

Alsuwayed, Ahmad Hasan, Humoud Alshemmari, Sami Alhashash, Faisal Aldaakhil, Abdulnabi Alkhaldi)

Final: CZE 1–0 GDR
3rd Place: SOV 2–0 YUG

Seven of the 16 qualifying teams withdrew as part of the anti-Soviet boycott and were replaced by lesser teams. The only goal of the final was scored by a substitute, Jindřich Svoboda, who entered the game with 19 minutes to play and put in a header six minutes later. For the third straight time, the Olympic final was played in a rainstorm.

ARCHERY

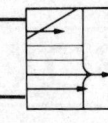

99.

99. Q.F. Newall, winner of the 1908 women's archery competition.

BASKETBALL

100.

100. The greatest basketball team in Olympic history: the 1960 U.S. team. Ten of its members went on to successful careers in professional basketball.

101. Iuliyana Semenova guards 6-foot 3-inch Lucy Harris (with ball) in 1976.

101.

BOXING PROTESTS

102. In 1964 South Korean flyweight Dong-Kih Choh staged a 51-minute sitdown strike after being disqualified for holding his head too low.

103.

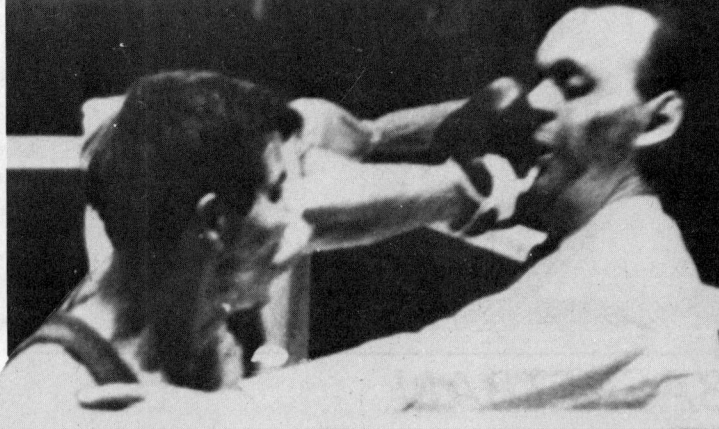

102.

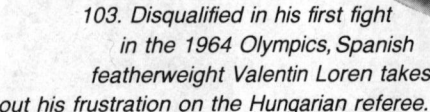

103. Disqualified in his first fight in the 1964 Olympics, Spanish featherweight Valentin Loren takes out his frustration on the Hungarian referee.

104. Supporters of Uruguayan featherweight Basilio Alves storm the table of the Jury of Appeal following Alves' 1948 loss to American Eddie Johnson.

104.

BOXING

105.

106.

107.

108.

105. At 37, 1908 Feather-
weight champion Richard
Gunn was the oldest boxing
gold medalist in Olympic
history.

106. László Papp, the first boxer to win three Olympic gold
medals. He was Middleweight
champion in 1948 and Light
Middleweight champion in
1952 and 1956.

107. "Unroasted human beef
of Old England": Harry Mallin,
the 1920 and 1924 Middle-
weight gold medalist.

108. Outspoken Chris Finnegan, on his way to victory in
the 1968 Middleweight division.
His biggest challenge was providing a urine sample for the
post-fight drug test.

BOXING

, U. S.

109.

110.

109. Eddie Eagan won the Light Heavyweight gold medal in 1920. Twelve years later, as a member of the winning four-man bobsled team, he became the first person to earn gold medals in both the Summer and Winter Games.
110. Cassius Clay, later Muhammad Ali (center), flanked by fellow 1960 gold medalists Edward Crook and Wilbert McClure.

CYCLING

111.

111. In 1968 the four Pettersson brothers of Sweden joined forces to win silver medals in the cycling team road race.

EQUESTRIAN

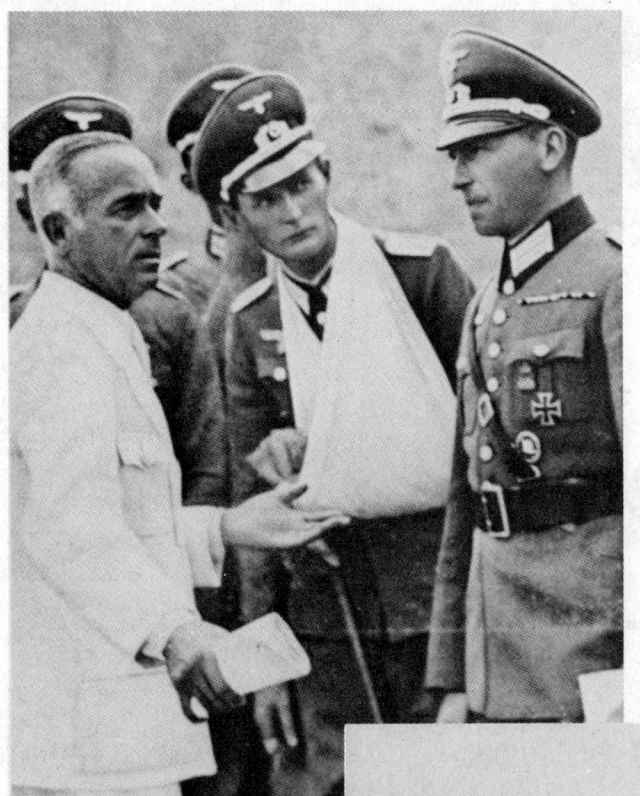

112.

112. *A leading German hero of the 1936 Berlin Olympics, Konrad von Wangenheim broke his collarbone during the steeplechase portion of the equestrian three-day event. The next day he was thrown from his horse a second time, but completed the competition, enabling the German team to win the gold medal.*

113. *In 1952 Lis Hartel of Denmark won a silver medal in the individual dressage event only eight years after being stricken with polio. Paralyzed below the knees, she had to be helped on and off her horse.*

113.

FENCING

114.

115.

114. Nedo Nadi won gold medals in five of the six fencing events of 1920.

115. Aladar Gerevich (left) won seven gold medals, one silver, and two bronze between 1932 and 1960 (when he was 50 years old). Pál Kovács (right) earned six gold medals and one bronze between 1936 and 1960.

116.

116. The award ceremony for the 1936 women's foil: (left to right) Ellen Preis (bronze), Ilona Elek (gold), and German Jew Helene Mayer (silver).

GYMNASTICS

118.

117. Lyudmila Tourisheva won the 1972 All-Around champion- ship, but received little attention from the Western press, which was more interested in her less accomplished but more charismatic teammate . . .

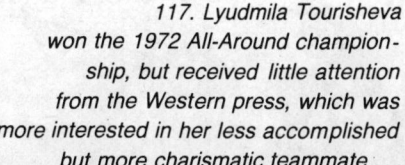

119.

118. . . . Olga Korbut, the Munchkin of Munich.
119. Nadia Comaneci, a vet- eran of 18 at the Moscow Olympics in 1980.

117.

ROWING

120. Jack Kelly, father of Princess Grace of Monaco, won three rowing gold medals in 1920 and 1924.

120.

SHOOTING

121. Károly Takács was a champion shooter when his right hand, his pistol hand, was shattered by a grenade. Ten years later, in 1948, Takacs won his first Olympic gold medal—using his left hand.

122. Gerald Ouellette shot 60 straight bull's-eyes to win the 1956 smallbore rifle (prone) event.

121.

122.

GYMNASTICS

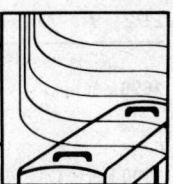

MEN
All-Around
Horizontal Bar
Parallel Bars
Long Horse Vault
Side Horse (Pommeled Horse)

Rings
Floor Exercises
Team Combined Exercises
Discontinued Events

MEN

Gymnastics competitions are divided into three parts. On the first two days, all gymnasts perform compulsory and optional exercises on all apparatuses. Their scores are then used to determine the winners of the team event. The 36 gymnasts who achieve the highest combined individual scores then move on to the individual All-Around finals, in which they once again compete on each apparatus. According to the rules to be used in 1984, only three gymnasts from each nation may compete in the individual All-Around finals. The top eight scorers on each apparatus, based on combined scores from the team and All-Around finals, then move on to the apparatus finals.

Prior to 1984, only six gymnasts participated in the finals of each apparatus. The 1984 rules limit the number of gymnasts from each nation to two for each apparatus. In 1984, for the first time, an age limit will be imposed in the gymnastics competitions. Men must be at least 16 years old and women at least 15. Had this rule been in effect in 1976, Nadia Comaneci would not have been allowed to compete.

ALL-AROUND

HB = Horizontal bar	100 = 100-yard run
PB = Parallel bars	SP = Shot put
LHV = Long horse vault	LJ = Long jump
SH = Side horse (pommeled horse)	RC = Rope climb
R = Rings	CLHJ = Combined long and high jump
FE = Floor exercises	PV = Pole vault
SHV = Side horse vault	H = Heaving a 50 kg stone
CLSV = Combined long and side horse vaults	

1896 not held

1900 Paris C: 134, N: 6? D: 7.30.
Events: HB, PB, LHV, SH, R, FE, LJ, RC, CLHJ, PV, H

		PTS.
1. Gustave Sandras	FRA	302
2. Nöel Bas	FRA	295
3. Lucien Démanet	FRA	293
4. Pierre Payssé	FRA	290
4. Jules Rolland	FRA	290
6. Gustave Fabry	FRA	283
7. J. Martinez	FRA/ALG	277
8. Marcel Lalu	FRA	275
8. Mauvezain	FRA	275

1904 St. Louis C: 119, N: 4, D: 7.2.

		PB	HB	CLSV	FT.–IN. LJ	SP	TIME 100	TOTAL PTS.
1. Julius Lenhart	AUT	14.40	14.60	14.00	18-0	28-6	12.0	69.80
2. Wilhelm Weber	GER	14.17	13.93	13.50	18-1	30-1	12.0	69.10
3. Adolf Spinnler	SWI	14.53	14.53	14.43	16-2¼	29-7	12.4	67.99
4. Ernest Mohr	GER	12.90	13.00	13.00	18-8¼	30-0	11.4	67.90
5. Otto Wiegand	GER	14.20	13.12	13.50	17-6	30-4¾	12.0	67.82
6. Otto Steffen	USA	12.80	14.10	12.63	18-1	30-9½	12.0	67.03
7. John Bissinger	USA	13.10	12.37	12.10	18-4¾	32-9½	11.4	66.57
8. Hugo Peitsch	GER	14.03	14.30	13.23	16-10¾	27-4¾	12.0	66.56

1906 Athens C: 37, N: 8, D: 5.1.
Events: HB, PB, LHV, R, CLHJ

		PTS.
1. Pierre Payssé	FRA	97
2. Alberto Braglia	ITA	95
3. Georges Charmoille	FRA	94
4. Carl Ohms	GER	93
5. Vitaliano Masotti	ITA	92
6. Pissié	FRA	91

7. Nicolaos Aliprantis (GRE), Béla Erody (HUN), Mario Gubiani (ITA), B. Hunzatko (BOH), Joseph Krämer (GER), D. Lavielle (FRA), Carl Schwarz (GER), Wilhelm Weber (GER)—90

1906 Athens C: 17, N: 6, D: 5.1.
Events: HB, PB, LHV, SH, R, CLHJ

		PTS.
1. Pierre Payssé	FRA	116
2. Alberto Braglia	ITA	115
3. Georges Charmoille	FRA	113
4. Carl Ohms	GER	112
5. Vitaliano Masotti	ITA	111
6. Béla Erody	HUN	110
6. Mario Gubiani	ITA	110
6. Pissié	FRA	110
6. Wilhelm Weber	GER	110

This event combined the results of the five apparatuses in the previous event with the results of one more apparatus: the side or pommeled horse.

1908 London C: 97, N: 12, D: 7.15.
Events: HB, PB, SH, R, RC

		PTS.
1. Alberto Braglia	ITA	317.0
2. S.W. Tysal	GBR	312.0
3. Louis Ségura	FRA	297.0
4. Curt Steuernagel	GER	273.5
5. Friedrich Wolf	GER	267.0
6. Samuel Hodgetts	GBR	266.0
7. Marcel Lalu	FRA	258.75
8. R. Diaz	FRA	258.5

1912 Stockholm C: 44, N: 9, D: 7.12.

		HB	PB	R	SH	TOTAL PTS.
1. Alberto Braglia	ITA	32.75	34.75	31.75	35.75	135.0
2. Louis Ségura	FRA	30.0	35.75	32.25	34.5	132.5
3. Adolfo Tunesi	ITA	30.25	35.0	30.5	35.75	131.5
4. Guido Boni	ITA	29.75	35.25	28.25	34.75	128.0
4. Giorgio Zampori	ITA	29.0	35.0	30.75	33.25	128.0
6. Pietro Bianchi	ITA	29.5	33.75	30.75	33.75	127.75
7. Marcel Lalu	FRA	29.25	35.5	30.5	31.75	127.0
7. Marcos Torres	FRA	30.25	35.0	31.0	30.75	127.0

1920 Antwerp C: 44, N: 9, D: 8.29.
Events: HB, PB, SH, R

		PTS.
1. Giorgio Zampori	ITA	88.35
2. Marco Torrès	FRA	87.62
3. Jean Gounot	FRA	87.45
4. Félicien Kempeneers	BEL	86.25
5. Georges Thurnherr	FRA	86.00
6. Laurent Grech	FRA	85.65
7. Luigi Maiocco	ITA	85.38
8. Luigi Costigliolo	ITA	84.90

1924 Paris C: 72, N: 9, D: 7.20.

		HB	PB	LHV	SH	R	SHV	RC	TOTAL PTS.
1. Leon Štukelj	YUG	19.73 (1)	20.40 (20)	9.91 (4)	19.37 (10)	21.33 (4)	9.60 (17)	10.0 (10)	110.340
2. Robert Pražak	CZE	18.73 (9)	21.26 (2)	9.73 (9)	18.97 (13)	21.483 (2)	9.80 (8)	10.0 (13)	110.323
3. Bedřich Supčik	CZE	17.86 (16)	21.26 (8)	9.33 (15)	17.53 (24)	21.12 (5)	9.83 (6)	10.0 (1)	106.930
4. Ferdinando Mandrini	ITA	18.12 (14)	20.21 (24)	9.75 (7)	16.06 (30)	20.943 (8)	8.73 (21)	10.0 (18)	105.583
5. Miroslav Klinger	CZE	16.47 (26)	21.13 (10)	9.75 (7)	19.67 (7)	20.73 (11)	9.75 (12)	8.0 (21)	105.500
6. Ladislav Vácha	CZE	14.70 (39)	21.31 (6)	9.70 (10)	18.33 (17)	21.43 (3)	9.83 (6)	10.0 (4)	105.300
7. August Güttinger	SWI	18.886 (8)	21.63 (1)	9.08 (17)	19.60 (8)	17.57 (37)	8.41 (29)	10.0 (3)	105.176
8. Jean Gounot	FRA	19.043 (6)	20.15 (25)	9.00 (18)	17.30 (27)	19.73 (19)	9.93 (2)	10.0 (6)	105.153

Štukelj, a lawyer from Novo Mesto, eventually won three gold medals, one silver, and two bronze in his Olympic career, including a silver in the rings in 1936, when he was 37 years old.

1928 Amsterdam C: 88, N: 11, D: 8.10.

		HB		PB		LHV		SH		R		TOTAL PTS.
1. Georges Miez	SWI	57.5	(1)	49.75	(30)	28.25	(4)	57.75	(2)	54.25	(8)	247.500
2. Hermann Hänggi	SWI	56.5	(4)	54.25	(3)	27.125	(18)	59.25	(1)	49.5	(36)	246.625
3. Leon Štukelj	YUG	53.75	(21)	53.5	(7)	26.625	(28)	53.25	(12)	57.75	(1)	244.875
4. Romeo Neri	ITA	57.0	(2)	53.0	(12)	27.25	(16)	51.5	(19)	56.0	(4)	244.750
5. Josip Primožič	YUG	56.0	(6)	55.5	(2)	28.25	(4)	51.75	(18)	52.5	(18)	244.000
6. Mauri Nybert-Noroma	FIN	54.0	(16)	53.5	(7)	26.75	(26)	54.5	(7)	55.0	(5)	243.750
6. Heikki Savolainen	FIN	54.5	(13)	51.75	(17)	27.25	(16)	56.5	(3)	53.75	(12)	243.750
8. Eugen Mack	SWI	56.73	(3)	51.0	(21)	28.75	(1)	54.25	(9)	52.50	(18)	243.250

At the Amsterdam Games, 23-year-old Georges Miez won three gold medals and one silver. Between 1924 and 1936 his Olympic total was four gold, three silver, and one bronze.

1932 Los Angeles C: 24, N: 5, D: 8.12.

		HB		PB		LHV		SH		R		TOTAL PTS.
1. Romeo Neri	ITA	28.9	(2)	28.1	(3)	27.525	(3)	28.0	(4)	28.0	(3)	140.625
2. István Pelle	HUN	29.15	(1)	27.9	(6)	24.675	(9)	24.85	(11)	28.34	(1)	134.925
3. Heikki Savolainen	FIN	27.25	(7)	28.4	(1)	22.925	(15)	28.35	(3)	27.65	(5)	134.575
4. Mario Lertora	ITA	28.2	(3)	27.25	(8)	27.25	(4)	23.35	(14)	28.35	(1)	134.400
5. Savino Guglielmetti	ITA	28.2	(3)	28.4	(1)	28.325	(1)	22.6	(16)	26.85	(6)	134.375
6. Frank Haubold	USA	26.9	(10)	28.0	(4)	25.725	(7)	28.45	(1)	23.45	(16)	132.525
7. Oreste Capuzzo	ITA	27.5	(6)	27.3	(7)	23.7	(10)	26.15	(9)	27.8	(4)	132.450
8. Frederick Meyer	USA	27.1	(9)	26.43	(14)	27.55	(2)	28.4	(2)	22.15	(19)	131.650

1936 Berlin C: 111, N: 14, D: 8.11.

		HB		PB		LHV		SH		R		FE		TOTAL PTS.
1. Alfred Schwarzmann	GER	19.23	(3)	18.967	(3)	19.2	(1)	19.0	(7)	18.534	(4)	18.166	(10)	113.100
2. Eugen Mack	SWI	18.9	(9)	18.834	(5)	18.967	(2)	19.167	(2)	18.0	(13)	18.466	(3)	112.334
3. Konrad Frey	GER	19.267	(2)	19.067	(1)	17.666	(20)	19.333	(1)	17.733	(18)	18.466	(3)	111.532
4. Alois Hudec	CZE	18.834	(10)	18.966	(4)	17.867	(18)	17.966	(26)	19.433	(1)	18.133	(11)	111.199
5. Martti Uosikkinen	FIN	19.0	(7)	18.433	(11)	18.3	(6)	19.066	(4)	17.634	(22)	18.267	(8)	110.700
5. Michael Reusch	SWI	18.566	(18)	19.034	(2)	18.266	(7)	19.0	(7)	18.434	(6)	17.400	(22)	110.700
7. Matthias Volz	GER	18.8	(11)	17.033	(38)	18.467	(3)	18.766	(10)	18.667	(3)	18.366	(5)	110.099
8. Willi Stadel	GER	18.7	(14)	18.133	(18)	18.033	(14)	18.887	(9)	16.966	(36)	18.3	(6)	108.999

1948 London C: 123, N: 16, D: 8.13.

		HB		PB		LHV		SH		R		FE		TOTAL PTS.
1. Veikko Huhtanen	FIN	39.2	(3)	39.3	(2)	38.4	(6)	38.7	(1)	37.8	(11)	36.3	(34)	229.7
2. Walter Lehmann	SWI	39.4	(12)	39.0	(5)	38.1	(8)	37.6	(11)	38.4	(4)	36.5	(29)	229.0
3. Paavo Aaltonen	FIN	38.4	(12)	38.8	(7)	39.1	(1)	38.7	(1)	37.3	(17)	36.5	(29)	228.8
4. Josef Stalder	SWI	39.7	(1)	39.1	(3)	36.9	(33)	37.7	(8)	38.3	(5)	37.0	(16)	228.7
5. Christian Kipfer	SWE	38.6	(9)	39.1	(3)	37.9	(14)	37.2	(14)	37.8	(11)	36.5	(29)	227.1
6. Emil Studer	SWI	38.8	(4)	37.8	(21)	38.0	(10)	37.7	(8)	38.3	(5)	36.0	(41)	226.6
7. Zdenek Ružička	CZE	37.9	(17)	38.8	(7)	36.6	(46)	36.3	(30)	38.5	(3)	38.1	(3)	226.2
8. Kalevi Laitinen	FIN	38.1	(14)	38.1	(16)	38.0	(10)	36.9	(19)	37.4	(16)	37.15	(13)	225.65

1952 Helsinki C: 185, N: 29, D: 7.21.

		HB		PB		LHV		SH		R		FE		TOTAL PTS.
1. Viktor Chukarin	SOV	19.4	(5)	19.6	(2)	19.2	(1)	19.5	(1)	19.55	(2)	18.45	(29)	115.7
2. Grant Shaginyan	SOV	19.05	(14)	19.35	(4)	18.5	(35)	19.4	(2)	19.75	(1)	18.90	(8)	114.95
3. Josef Stalder	SWI	19.5	(2)	19.5	(3)	18.8	(13)	19.2	(5)	19.1	(11)	18.65	(19)	114.75
4. Valentin Muratov	SOV	19.2	(9)	19.25	(9)	18.7	(19)	18.3	(32)	19.35	(5)	18.85	(11)	113.65
5. Hans Eugster	SWI	19.15	(11)	19.65	(1)	18.95	(5)	18.55	(25)	19.4	(3)	17.7	(66)	113.40
6. Vladimir Belyakov	SOV	18.8	(23)	19.25	(8)	18.5	(35)	19.1	(7)	18.95	(14)	18.75	(14)	113.35
6. Yevgeny Korolkov	SOV	18.8	(23)	19.3	(5)	18.4	(44)	19.4	(2)	19.15	(7)	18.3	(35)	113.35
8. Jean Tschabold	SWI	19.35	(6)	19.3	(5)	18.7	(19)	19.05	(8)	18.75	(23)	18.15	(41)	113.30

Chukarin, a Ukrainian who had spent four years in a concentration camp during World War II, earned six medals at Helsinki—four gold and two silver.

1956 Melbourne C: 63, N: 18, D: 12.6.

		HB		PB		LHV		SH		R		FE		TOTAL PTS.
1. Viktor Chukarin	SOV	19.25	(4)	19.2	(1)	18.6	(7)	19.1	(3)	19.0	(7)	19.1	(2)	114.25
2. Takashi Ono	JAP	19.6	(1)	19.1	(1)	18.5	(16)	19.2	(2)	19.05	(5)	18.75	(8)	114.20
3. Yuri Titov	SOV	19.4	(2)	18.85	(8)	18.75	(3)	19.0	(5)	18.85	(10)	18.95	(5)	113.80
4. Masao Takemoto	JAP	19.3	(3)	19.1	(3)	18.65	(6)	18.9	(7)	19.1	(3)	18.5	(16)	113.55
5. Valentin Muratov	SOV	18.6	(25)	18.7	(16)	18.85	(1)	18.8	(9)	19.15	(2)	19.2	(1)	113.30
6. Helmut Bantz	GER	19.15	(6)	18.8	(6)	18.85	(1)	18.75	(12)	18.6	(18)	18.75	(8)	112.90
7. Albert Azaryan	SOV	18.95	(8)	19.0	(5)	18.55	(11)	18.75	(12)	19.35	(1)	17.95	(40)	112.55
8. Boris Shakhlin	SOV	18.75	(13)	18.85	(8)	18.7	(4)	19.25	(1)	18.7	(15)	18.25	(28)	112.50

Chukarin, now a 35-year-old teacher, added to his medal collection three gold, one silver, and one bronze at Melbourne, for a remarkable total of 11 Olympic medals.

1960 Rome C: 130, N: 23, D: 9.7.

		HB		PB		LHV		SH		R		FE		TOTAL PTS.
1. Boris Shakhlin	SOV	19.55	(2)	19.4	(1)	19.2	(3)	19.35	(1)	19.5	(2)	18.95	(7)	115.95
2. Takashi Ono	JAP	19.6	(1)	19.4	(1)	19.3	(1)	19.15	(4)	19.45	(3)	19.0	(4)	115.9
3. Yuri Titov	SOV	19.5	(4)	19.2	(6)	19.0	(5)	19.2	(3)	19.45	(3)	19.25	(2)	115.6
4. Shuji Tsurumi	JAP	19.25	(8)	19.15	(8)	19.0	(5)	19.1	(6)	19.2	(9)	18.85	(13)	114.55
5. Yukio Endo	JAP	19.45	(6)	19.2	(6)	19.05	(4)	18.85	(10)	19.0	(12)	18.9	(10)	114.45
5. Masao Takemoto	JAP	19.55	(2)	19.25	(4)	19.0	(5)	18.6	(26)	19.25	(8)	18.8	(14)	114.45
7. Nobuyuki Aihara	JAP	19.0	(13)	19.25	(4)	18.85	(9)	18.6	(26)	19.4	(5)	19.3	(1)	114.4
8. Miroslav Cerar	YUG	19.5	(4)	19.15	(8)	18.75	(13)	19.05	(7)	19.05	(11)	18.75	(17)	114.25

Boris Shakhlin, a Ukrainian from the small town of Ishin, won four gold medals, two silver, and one bronze at the Rome Games to add to the two gold medals he had won at Melbourne four years earlier.

1964 Tokyo C: 130, N: 30, D: 10.20.

		HB		PB		LHV		SH		R		FE		TOTAL PTS.
1. Yukio Endo	JAP	19.4	(3)	19.55	(1)	19.4	(3)	18.7	(16)	19.5	(1)	19.4	(1)	15.95
2. Viktor Lisitsky	SOV	19.25	(6)	19.5	(2)	19.5	(1)	18.75	(13)	19.1	(9)	19.3	(2)	115.4
2. Boris Shakhlin	SOV	19.55	(1)	19.25	(9)	19.35	(4)	18.9	(7)	19.4	(4)	18.95	(14)	115.4
2. Shuji Tsurumi	JAP	18.9	(21)	19.5	(2)	19.3	(6)	19.25	(3)	19.35	(5)	19.1	(9)	115.4
5. Franco Menichelli	ITA	19.25	(6)	19.3	(6)	19.05	(24)	18.8	(10)	19.45	(2)	19.3	(2)	115.15
6. Haruhiro Yamashita	JAP	19.25	(6)	19.3	(6)	19.5	(1)	19.15	(4)	18.75	(21)	19.15	(7)	115.1
7. Miroslav Cerar	YUG	19.3	(5)	19.5	(2)	19.1	(19)	19.45	(1)	19.05	(12)	18.65	(30)	115.05
8. Takuji Hayata	JAP	19.1	(12)	19.15	(10)	19.15	(16)	18.9	(7)	19.45	(2)	19.15	(7)	114.9

1968 Mexico City C: 117, N: 28, D: 10.24.

		HB		PB		LHV		SH		R		FE		TOTAL PTS.
1. Sawao Kato	JAP	19.45	(3)	19.35	(3)	18.9	(5)	19.0	(8)	19.55	(1)	19.65	(1)	115.9
2. Mikhail Voronin	SOV	19.5	(1)	19.45	(2)	19.0	(2)	19.2	(2)	19.45	(3)	19.25	(4)	115.85
3. Akinori Nakayama	JAP	19.5	(1)	19.55	(1)	18.85	(7)	18.85	(12)	19.5	(2)	19.4	(2)	115.65
4. Eizo Kenmotsu	JAP	19.35	(5)	19.25	(5)	18.95	(4)	19.1	(4)	19.0	(7)	19.25	(4)	114.9
5. Takeshi Kato	JAP	19.1	(11)	19.3	(4)	19.05	(1)	18.65	(21)	19.4	(4)	19.35	(3)	114.85
6. Sergei Diomidov	SOV	19.3	(6)	18.9	(23)	18.9	(5)	19.0	(4)	19.05	(6)	18.95	(9)	114.1
7. Vladimir Klimenko	SOV	19.1	(11)	19.25	(5)	18.85	(7)	19.1	(4)	18.9	(9)	18.75	(13)	113.95
8. Yukio Endo	JAP	19.25	(7)	19.15	(9)	19.0	(2)	18.4	(26)	18.95	(8)	18.80	(11)	113.55

1972 Munich C: 113, N: 26, D: 8.30.

		HB		PB		LHV		SH		R		FE		TOTAL PTS.
1. Sawao Kato	JAP	19.525	(2)	19.275	(1)	19.0	(2)	18.9	(3)	19.15	(4)	18.8	(6)	114.650
2. Eizo Kenmotsu	JAP	19.3	(3)	19.1	(4)	19.0	(2)	19.15	(1)	19.05	(5)	18.975	(3)	114.575
3. Akinori Nakayama	JAP	19.275	(4)	19.275	(1)	18.75	(7)	18.75	(7)	19.25	(1)	19.025	(1)	114.325
4. Nikolai Andrianov	SOV	19.25	(5)	18.925	(6)	19.35	(1)	18.7	(8)	19.0	(6)	18.975	(3)	114.200
5. Shigeru Kasamatsu	JAP	19.25	(5)	18.825	(10)	18.625	(10)	19.075	(2)	18.9	(7)	19.025	(1)	113.700
6. Viktor Klimenko	SOV	18.755	(18)	19.275	(1)	18.8	(6)	18.875	(4)	18.7	(13)	18.675	(9)	113.075
6. Klaus Köste	GDR	18.975	(11)	19.1	(4)	18.875	(4)	18.4	(17)	18.85	(9)	18.875	(5)	113.075
8. Mitsuo Tsukahara	JAP	19.675	(1)	18.625	(15)	18.35	(22)	18.15	(20)	19.225	(2)	18.75	(8)	112.775

The 5-foot 3-inch, 125-pound Kato became the third repeat winner of the men's All-Around championship, joining Alberto Braglia of Italy (1908 and 1912) and Viktor Chukarin of the Soviet Union (1952 and 1956).

1976 Montreal C: 90, N: 20, D: 7.21.

		HB		PB		LHV		SH		R		FE		TOTAL PTS.
1. Nikolai Andrianov	SOV	19.3	(4)	19.4	(2)	19.475	(1)	19.425	(3)	19.6	(1)	19.45	(1)	116.65
2. Sawao Kato	JAP	19.5	(2)	19.475	(1)	19.1	(8)	19.3	(5)	19.075	(6)	19.2	(3)	115.65
3. Mitsuo Tsukahara	JAP	19.525	(1)	19.375	(3)	19.45	(2)	19.2	(7)	19.0	(9)	19.025	(7)	115.575
4. Aleksandr Dityatin	SOV	19.0	(11)	19.05	(5)	19.275	(6)	19.35	(4)	19.5	(2)	19.35	(2)	115.525
5. Hiroshi Kajiyama	JAP	19.225	(7)	19.325	(4)	19.325	(5)	19.275	(6)	19.2	(3)	19.075	(6)	115.425
6. Andrzej Szajna	POL	19.1	(9)	19.05	(5)	19.35	(4)	18.95	(10)	19.075	(6)	19.1	(5)	114.625
7. Michael Nikolay	GDR	19.2	(8)	18.725	(12)	18.725	(21)	19.575	(2)	18.8	(16)	18.575	(16)	113.6
8. Imre Molnár	HUN	18.875	(16)	18.875	(9)	19.375	(3)	19.2	(7)	18.7	(19)	18.55	(17)	113.575

The 5-foot 5½-inch Andrianov, who had collected a complete set of medals in 1972, added seven more in Montreal—four gold, two silver, and one bronze.

1980 Moscow C: 65, N: 14, D: 7.24.

		HB		PB		LHV		SH		R		FE		TOTAL PTS.
1. Aleksandr Dityatin	SOV	19.8	(2)	19.7	(2)	19.875	(1)	19.8	(3)	19.875	(1)	19.6	(3)	118.65
2. Nikolai Andrianov	SOV	19.725	(3)	19.6	(4)	19.8	(2)	19.7	(4)	19.725	(3)	19.675	(1)	118.225
3. Stoyan Deltchev	BUL	19.825	(1)	19.675	(3)	19.725	(5)	19.65	(6)	19.775	(2)	19.35	(6)	118.0
4. Aleksandr Tkachyov	SOV	19.525	(4)	19.775	(1)	19.75	(4)	19.675	(5)	19.675	(6)	19.3	(8)	117.7
5. Roland Brückner	GDR	19.075	(17)	19.45	(5)	19.775	(3)	19.625	(7)	19.725	(3)	19.65	(2)	117.3
6. Michael Nikolay	GDR	19.475	(6)	19.35	(7)	19.575	(11)	19.875	(2)	19.525	(8)	18.95	(13)	116.75
7. Lutz Hoffmann	GDR	19.4	(9)	19.05	(11)	19.7	(6)	19.125	(14)	19.425	(10)	19.325	(7)	116.025
8. Jiři Tabák	CZE	19.225	(11)	18.975	(15)	19.675	(7)	18.675	(22)	19.6	(7)	19.525	(4)	115.675

Handsome Aleksandr Dityatin became the first person to win eight medals in one Olympic celebration. He gained three gold, four silver, and one bronze. Dityatin also became the first male gymnast to receive a ten in any Olympic competition, with his longhorse vault. Four more tens were awarded in rapid succession to Stoyan Deltchev on the rings, Aleksandr Tkachyov on the horizontal bar, and Zoltán Magyar and Michael Nicolay on the side horse. Meanwhile, Nikolai Andrianov added two gold, one silver, and one bronze to his collection for a grand career total of 14 Olympics medals—seven gold, four silver, and three bronze.

HORIZONTAL BAR

1896 Athens C: 16, N: 5, D: 4.9.
1. Hermann Weingärtner   GER
2. Alfred Flatow   GER
3. Petmezas   GRE
4. —   —
5. Charles Champov   BUL

1900 not held

1904 St. Louis C: 9, N: 1, D: 10.28.

		PTS.
1. Anton Heida	USA	40
1. Edward Hennig	USA	40
3. George Eyser	USA	39

1908–1920 not held

1924 Paris C: 72, N: 9, D: 7.20.

		PTS.
1. Leon Štukelj	YUG	19.730
2. Jean Gutweniger	SWI	19.236
3. André Higelin	FRA	19.163
4. Antoine Rebetez	SWI	19.053
4. Georges Miez	SWI	19.053
6. Jean Gounot	FRA	19.043
7. François Gangloff	FRA	18.933
8. August Güttinger	SWI	18.886

1928 Amsterdam C: 86, N: 11, D: 8.10.

		PTS.
1. Georges Miez	SWI	19.17
2. Romeo Neri	ITA	19.00
3. Eugen Mack	SWI	18.92
4. Hermann Hänggi	SWI	18.83
4. Vittorio Lucchetti	ITA	18.83
6. Josip Primožič	YUG	18.67
7. Hans Grieder	SWI	18.58
7. August Güttinger	FRA	18.58

1932 Los Angeles C: 12, N: 6, D: 8.11.

		PTS.
1. Dallas Bixler	USA	18.33
2. Heikki Savolainen	FIN	18.07
3. Einari Teräsvirta	FIN	18.07
4. Veikko Pakarinen	FIN	17.27
4. István Pelle	HUN	17.27
6. Michael Schuler	USA	15.57
7. Miklós Péter	HUN	15.13
8. Mahito Haga	JAP	12.47

Savolainen and Teräsvirta tied for second. While the judges discussed a method for deciding which one should get the silver medal, the two Finns talked it out and agreed that Savolainen should receive the silver and Teräsvirta the bronze. The judges abided by their decision.

1936 Berlin C: 111, N: 14, D: 8.11.

		PTS.
1. Aleksanteri Saarvala	FIN	19.367
2. Konrad Frey	GER	19.267
3. Alfred Schwarzmann	GER	19.233
4. Innozenz Stangl	GER	19.167
5. Heikki Savolainen	FIN	19.133
6. Veikko Pakarinen	FIN	19.067
7. Martti Uosikkinen	FIN	19.00
8. Walter Steffens	GER	18.966

1948 London C: 123, N: 16, D: 8.13.

		PTS.
1. Josef Stalder	SWI	19.85
2. Walter Lehmann	SWI	19.70
3. Veikko Huhtanen	FIN	19.60
4. Raymond Dot	FRA	19.40
4. Aleksanteri Saarvala	FIN	19.40
4. Lajos Sántha	HUN	19.40
4. Emil Studer	SWI	19.40
8. Einari Teräsvirta	FIN	19.35

1952 Helsinki C: 185, N: 29, D: 7.21.

		PTS.
1. Jack Günthard	SWI	19.55
2. Alfred Schwarzmann	GER	19.50
2. Josef Stalder	SWI	19.50
5. Heikki Savolainen	FIN	19.45
5. Viktor Chukarin	SOV	19.40
6. Jean Tschabold	SWI	19.35
7. Helmut Bantz	GER	19.25
7. Melchior Thalmann	SWI	19.25

1956 Melbourne C: 63, N: 18, D: 12.6.

		PTS.
1. Takashi Ono	JAP	19.60
2. Yuri Titov	SOV	19.40
3. Masao Takemoto	JAP	19.30
4. Pavel Stolbov	SOV	19.25
4. Viktor Chukarin	SOV	19.25
6. Helmut Bantz	GER	19.15
7. John Beckner	USA	19.00
8. Albert Azaryan	SOV	18.95

1960 Rome C: 130, N: 28, D: 9.10.

		PTS.
1. Takashi Ono	JAP	19.60
2. Masao Takemoto	JAP	19.525
3. Boris Shakhlin	SOV	19.475
4. Yukio Endo	JAP	19.425
5. Miroslav Cerar	YUG	19.40
5. Yuri Titov	SOV	19.40

1964 Tokyo C: 130, N: 24, D: 10.23.

			PTS.
1.	Boris Shakhlin	SOV	19.625
2.	Yuri Titov	SOV	19.550
3.	Miroslav Cerar	YUG	19.50
4.	Viktor Lisitsky	SOV	19.325
5.	Yukio Endo	JAP	19.050
6.	Takashi Ono	JAP	19.00

1968 Mexico City C: 115, N: 27, D: 10.26.

			PTS.
1.	Akinori Nakayama	JAP	19.55
1.	Mikhail Voronin	SOV	19.55
3.	Eizo Kenmotsu	JAP	19.375
4.	Klaus Köste	GDR	19.225
5.	Sergei Diomidov	SOV	19.15
6.	Yukio Endo	JAP	19.025

1972 Munich C: 113, N: 26, D: 9.1.

			PTS.
1.	Mitsuo Tsukahara	JAP	19.725
2.	Sawao Kato	JAP	19.525
3.	Shigeru Kasamatsu	JAP	19.45
4.	Eizo Kenmotsu	JAP	19.35
5.	Akinori Nakayama	JAP	19.225
6.	Nikolai Andrianov	SOV	19.10

1976 Montreal C: 90, N: 20, D: 7.23.

			PTS.
1.	Mitsuo Tsukahara	JAP	19.675
2.	Eizo Kenmotsu	JAP	19.50
3.	Henry Boërio	FRA	19.475
3.	Eberhard Gienger	GER	19.475
5.	Gennadi Kryssin	SOV	19.25
6.	Ferenc Donáth	HUN	19.20

1980 Moscow C: 65, N: 14, D: 7.25.

			PTS.
1.	Stoyan Deltchev	BUL	19.825
2.	Alexandr Dityatin	SOV	19.75
3.	Nikolai Andrianov	SOV	19.675
4.	Ralf-Peter Hemmann	GDR	19.525
4.	Michael Nikolay	GDR	19.525
6.	Sergio Suarez Aime	CUB	19.45

PARALLEL BARS

1896 Athens C: 18, N; 4, D: 4.10.
1. Alfred Flatow   GER
2. Jules Zutter   SWI
3. Hermann Weingärtner GER

1900 not held

1904 St. Louis C: ?, N: 1, D: 10.28.

			PTS.
1.	George Eyser	USA	44
2.	Anton Heida	USA	43
3.	John Duha	USA	40

Eyser's gymnastic feats were all the more impressive considering that one of his legs was made of wood. He also won a gold in the long horse vault, two silver in the pommeled horse and combined competition, and a bronze in the horizontal bar.

1908–1920 not held

1924 Paris C: 72, N: 9, D: 7.20.

			PTS.
1.	August Güttinger	SWI	21.63
2.	Robert Pražak	CZE	21.61
3.	Giorgio Zampori	ITA	21.45
4.	Josef Wilhelm	SWI	21.40
5.	Mario Lertora	ITA	21.33
6.	Ladislav Vácha	CZE	21.31
7.	J. Kos	CZE	21.28
8.	Jean Gutweniger	SWI	21.26

1928 Amsterdam C: 85, N: 11, D: 8.10.

			PTS.
1.	Ladislav Vácha	CZE	18.83
2.	Josip Primožič	YUG	18.50
3.	Hermann Hänggi	SWI	18.08
4.	Jan Gajdoš	CZE	17.92
4.	André Lemoine	FRA	17.92
4.	Bedrich Supčik	CZE	17.92
7.	Mario Lertora (ITA), Mauri Nyberg-Noroma (FIN), Leon Štukelj (YUG), Melchior Wetzel (SWI)		17.83

1932 Los Angeles C: 15, N: 6, D: 8.12.

			PTS.
1.	Romeo Neri	ITA	18.97
2.	István Pelle	HUN	18.60
3.	Heikki Savolainen	FIN	18.27
4.	Mauri Nyberg-Noroma	FIN	17.80
5.	Mario Lertora	ITA	17.53
6.	Alfred Jochim	USA	17.47
7.	József Hegedüs	HUN	17.30
7.	Miklós Péter	HUN	17.30

1936 Berlin C: 111, N: 14, D: 8.11.

			PTS.
1.	Konrad Frey	GER	19.067
2.	Michael Reusch	SWI	19.034
3.	Alfred Schwarzmann	GER	18.967
4.	Alois Hudec	CZE	18.966
5.	Eugen Mack	SWI	18.834
6.	Walter Bach	SWI	18.733
7.	Heikki Savolainen	FIN	18.633
8.	Eduard "Edi" Steinemann	SWI	18.500

1948 London C: 123, N: 16, D: 8.13.

		PTS.
1. Michael Reusch	SWI	19.75
2. Veikko Huhtanen	FIN	19.65
3. Christian Kipfer	SWI	19.55
3. Josef Stalder	SWI	19.55
5. Walter Lehmann	SWI	19.50
6. Heikki Savolainen	FIN	19.45
7. Paavo Aaltonen	FIN	19.40
7. Zdenek Ružička	CZE	19.40

1952 Helsinki C: 185, N: 29, D: 7.21.

		PTS.
1. Hans Eugster	SWI	19.65
2. Viktor Chukarin	SOV	19.60
3. Josef Stalder	SWI	19.50
4. Grant Schaginyan	SOV	19.35
5. Ferdinand Daniš	CZE	19.30
5. Yevgeny Korolkov	SOV	19.30
5. Jean Tschabold	SWI	19.30
8. Vladimir Belyakov	SOV	19.25
8. Valentin Muratov	SOV	19.25

1956 Melbourne C: 63, N: 18, D: 12.6.

		PTS.
1. Viktor Chukarin	SOV	19.20
2. Masami Kubota	JAP	19.15
3. Takashi Ono	JAP	19.10
3. Masao Takemoto	JAP	19.10
5. Albert Azaryan	SOV	19.00
6. Nobuyuki Aihara	JAP	18.90
7. Bengt Lindfors	FIN	18.90
8. Onni Lappalainen (FIN), Olavi Leimuvirta (FIN), Shinsaku Tsukawai (JAP)		18.85

1960 Rome C: 130, N: 28, D: 9.10.

		PTS.
1. Boris Shakhlin	SOV	19.40
2. Giovanni Carminucci	ITA	19.375
3. Takashi Ono	JAP	19.35
4. Nobuyuki Aihara	JAP	19.275
5. Yuri Titov	SOV	19.20
6. Masao Takemoto	JAP	19.125

1964 Tokyo C: 130, N: 29, D: 10.23.

		PTS.
1. Yukio Endo	JAP	19.675
2. Shuji Tsurumi	JAP	19.45
3. Franco Menichelli	ITA	19.35
4. Sergey Diomidov	SOV	19.225
5. Viktor Lisitsky	SOV	19.20
6. Miroslav Cerar	YUG	18.45

1968 Mexico City C: 117, N: 28, D: 10.26.

		PTS.
1. Akinori Nakayama	JAP	19.475
2. Mikhail Voronin	SOV	19.425
3. Vladimir Klimenko	SOV	19.225
4. Takeshi Kato	JAP	19.20
5. Eizo Kenmotsu	JAP	19.175
6. Václav Kubička	CZE	18.95

1972 Munich C: 113, N: 26, D: 9.1.

		PTS.
1. Sawao Kato	JAP	19.475
2. Shigeru Kasamatsu	JAP	19.375
3. Eizo Kenmotsu	JAP	19.25
4. Viktor Klimenko	SOV	19.125
5. Akinori Nakayama	JAP	18.875
6. Nikolai Andrianov	SOV	17.975

1976 Montreal C: 90, N: 20, D: 7.23.

		PTS.
1. Sawao Kato	JAP	19.675
2. Nikolai Andrianov	SOV	19.50
3. Mitsuo Tsukahara	JAP	19.475
4. Bernd Jäger	GDR	19.20
5. Miloslav Netušil	CZE	19.125
6. Andrzej Szajna	POL	18.95

1980 Moscow C: 65, N: 14, D: 7.25.

		PTS.
1. Aleksandr Tkachyov	SOV	19.775
2. Aleksandr Dityatin	SOV	19.75
3. Roland Brückner	GDR	19.65
4. Michael Nikolay	GDR	19.60
5. Stoyan Deltchev	BUL	19.575
6. Roberto Leon Richards-Aguiar	CUB	19.50

LONG HORSE VAULT

1896 Athens C: 17, N: 6, D: 4.9.

1. Karl Schumann	GER
2. Jules Zutter	SWI
3. Hermann Weingärtner	GER

1900 not held

1904 St. Louis C: ?, N: 1, D: 10.28.

		PTS.
1. George Eyser	USA	36
1. Anton Heida	USA	36
3. William Merz	USA	31

1908–1920 not held

1924 Paris C: 70, N: 9, D: 7.20.

			PTS.
1.	Frank Kriz	USA	9.98
2.	Jan Koutny	CZE	9.97
3.	Bohumil Mořkovsky	CZE	9.93
4.	Leon Štukelj	YUG	9.91
5.	Max Wandrer	USA	9.85
6.	Ivan Porenta	YUG	9.76
7.	Miroslav Klinger	CZE	9.75
7.	Ferdinando Mandrini	ITA	9.75

1928 Amsterdam C: 85, N: 11, D: 8.10.

			PTS.
1.	Eugen Mack	SWI	9.58
2.	Emanuel Löffler	CZE	9.50
3.	Stane Derganc	YUG	9.46
4.	Georges Miez	SWI	9.42
4.	Josip Primožič	YUG	9.42
6.	Georges Leroux	FRA	9.33
7.	August Güttinger	SWI	9.28
7.	Ivan Porenta	YUG	9.28
7.	Herman Witzig	USA	9.28

1932 Los Angeles C: 10, N: 4, D: 8.10.

			PTS.
1.	Savino Guglielmetti	ITA	18.03
2.	Alfred Jochim	USA	17.77
3.	Edward Carmichael	USA	17.53
4.	Einari Teräsvirta	FIN	17.53
5.	Marcel Gleyre	USA	17.46
6.	István Pelle	HUN	17.13
7.	Miklós Péter	HUN	16.97
8.	Mario Lertora	ITA	16.40

1936 Berlin C: 110, N: 14, D: 8.11.

			PTS.
1.	Alfred Schwarzmann	GER	19.20
2.	Eugen Mack	SWI	18.967
3.	Matthias Volz	GER	18.467
4.	Walter Bach	SWI	18.40
5.	Walter Beck	SWI	18.367
6.	Martti Uosikkinen	FIN	18.30
7.	Michael Reusch	SWI	18.266
8.	Georges Miez	SWI	18.234
8.	Josef Walter	SWI	18.234

1948 London C: 123, N: 16, D: 8.13.

			PTS.
1.	Paavo Aaltonen	FIN	19.55
2.	Olavi Rove	FIN	19.50
3.	János Mogyorósi-Klencs	HUN	19.25
3.	Ferenc Pataki	HUN	19.25
3.	Leo Sotornik	CZE	19.25
6.	Veikko Huhtanen	FIN	19.20
7.	Einari Teräsvirta	FIN	19.15
8.	Walter Lehmann	SWI	19.05
8.	Sulo Salmi	FIN	19.05

1952 Helsinki C: 185, N: 29, D: 7.21.

			PTS.
1.	Viktor Chukarin	SOV	19.20
2.	Masao Takemoto	JAP	19.15
3.	Takashi Ono	JAP	19.10
3.	Tadao Uesako	JAP	19.10
5.	Hans Eugster	SWI	18.95
5.	Theo Wied	GER	18.95
7.	Yosef Berdiyev	SOV	18.90
7.	Ernst Fivian	SWI	18.90

1956 Melbourne C: 63, N: 18, D: 12.6.

			PTS.
1.	Helmut Bantz	GER	18.85
1.	Valentin Muratov	SOV	18.85
3.	Yuri Titov	SOV	18.75
4.	Boris Shakhlin	SOV	18.70
4.	Theo Wied	GER	18.70
6.	Masao Takemoto	JAP	18.65
7.	John Beckner (USA), Jakob Kiefer (GER), Robert Klein (GER), Viktor Chukarin (SOV)		18.60

1960 Rome C: 130, N: 28, D: 9.10.

			PTS.
1.	Takashi Ono	JAP	19.35
1.	Boris Shakhlin	SOV	19.35
3.	Vladimir Portnoi	SOV	19.225
4.	Yuri Titov	SOV	19.20
5.	Yukio Endo	JAP	19.175
6.	Shuji Tsurumi	JAP	19.15

1964 Tokyo C: 130, N: 29, D: 10.23.

			PTS.
1.	Haruhiro Yamashita	JAP	19.60
2.	Viktor Lisitsky	SOV	19.325
3.	Hannu Rantakari	FIN	19.30
4.	Shuji Tsurumi	JAP	19.225
5.	Boris Shakhlin	SOV	19.20
6.	Yukio Endo	JAP	19.075

Yamashita executed a handspring in a piked position, a vault that became known as a "yamashita." One of the judges, Dr. Widmer of Switzerland, was so impressed that he gave Yamashita a ten—the highest mark possible.

1968 Mexico City C: 116, N: 28, D: 10.26.

			PTS.
1.	Mikhail Voronin	SOV	19.00
2.	Yukio Endo	JAP	18.95
3.	Sergei Diomidov	SOV	18.925
4.	Takeshi Kato	JAP	18.775
5.	Akinori Nakayama	JAP	18.725
6.	Eizo Kenmotsu	JAP	18.65

1972 Munich C: 113, N: 26, D: 9.1.

			PTS.
1.	Klaus Köste	GDR	18.85
2.	Viktor Klimenko	SOV	18.825

3. Nikolai Andrianov   SOV   18.80
4. Sawao Kato   JAP   18.55
4. Eizo Kenmotsu   JAP   18.55
6. Peter Rohner   SWI   18.525

Performing a yamashita and a forward somersault, the 5-foot 4½-inch Köste won East Germany's first gold medal in men's gymnastics.

1976 Montreal C: 90, N: 20, D: 7.23.

		PTS.
1. Nikolai Andrianov	SOV	19.45
2. Mitsuo Tsukahara	JAP	19.375
3. Hiroshi Kajiyama	JAP	19.275
4. Dănut Grecu	ROM	19.20
5. Zoltán Magyar	HUN	19.15
5. Imre Molnár	HUN	19.15

1980 Moscow C: 65, N: 14, D: 7.25.

		PTS.
1. Nikolai Andrianov	SOV	19.825
2. Aleksandr Dityatin	SOV	19.80
3. Roland Brückner	GDR	19.775
4. Ralf-Peter Hemmann	GDR	19.75
5. Stoyan Deltchev	BUL	19.70
6. Jiří Tabák	CZE	19.525

SIDE HORSE (POMMELED HORSE)

1896 Athens C: 17, N: 5, D: 4.9.
1. Jules Zutter   SWI
2. Hermann Weingärtner GER
3. Gyula Kakas   HUN

1900 not held

1904 St. Louis C: 9, N: 1, D: 10.28.

		PTS.
1. Anton Heida	USA	42
2. George Eyser	USA	33
3. William Merz	USA	29

1908–1920 not held

1924 Paris C: 70, N: 9, D: 7.20.

		PTS.
1. Josef Wilhelm	SWI	21.23
2. Jean Gutweniger	SWI	21.13
3. Antoine Rebetez	SWI	20.73
4. Carl Widmer	SWI	20.50
5. Giuseppe Paris	ITA	20.10
6. Stane Derganc	YUG	19.93
7. Miroslav Klinger	CZE	19.67
8. August Güttinger	SWI	19.60

1928 Amsterdam C: 87, N: 11, D: 8.10.

		PTS.
1. Hermann Hänggi	SWI	19.75
2. Georges Miez	SWI	19.25

3. Heikki Savolainen   FIN   18.83
4. Eduard "Edi" Steinemann   SWI   18.67
5. August Güttinger   SWI   18.58
6. Georges Leroux   FRA   18.25
7. Mauri Nyberg-Noroma   FIN   18.17
7. Melchior Wetzel   SWI   18.17

1932 Los Angeles C: 10, N: 5, D: 8.11.

		PTS.
1. István Pelle	HUN	19.07
2. Omero Bonoli	ITA	18.87
3. Frank Haubold	USA	18.57
4. Frank Cumiskey	USA	18.23
5. Péter Boros	HUN	17.57
6. Alfred Jochim	USA	17.07
7. Heikki Savolainen	FIN	17.00
8. Veikko Pakarinen	FIN	16.63

1936 Berlin C: 110, N: 14, D: 8.11.

		PTS.
1. Konrad Frey	GER	19.333
2. Eugen Mack	SWI	19.167
3. Albert Bachmann	SWI	19.067
4. Martti Uosikkinen	FIN	19.066
5. Walter Steffens	GER	19.033
5. Walter Bach	SWI	19.033
7. Michael Reusch	SWI	19.00
7. Alfred Schwarzmann	GER	19.00

1948 London C: 123, N: 16, D: 8.13.

		PTS.
1. Paavo Aaltonen	FIN	19.35
1. Veikko Huhtanen	FIN	19.35
1. Heikki Savolainen	FIN	19.35
4. Luigi Zanetti	ITA	19.15
5. Guido Figone	ITA	19.10
6. Frank Cumiskey	USA	18.95
7. Michael Reusch	SWI	18.90
8. Aleksanteri Saarvala	FIN	18.85
8. Josef Stalder	SWI	18.85
8. Emil Studer	SWI	18.85

Between 1928 and 1952 Heikki Savolainen of Joensuu won two gold medals, one silver, and six bronze. When he received his last medal, as a member of the third-place Finnish team in Helsinki, Savolainen was 44 years old.

1952 Helsinki C: 185, N: 29, D: 7.21.

		PTS.
1. Viktor Chukarin	SOV	19.50
2. Evgeny Korolkov	SOV	19.40
2. Grant Shaginyan	SOV	19.40
4. Mikhail Perelman	SOV	19.30
5. Josef Stalder	SWI	19.20
6. Hans Sauter	AUT	19.15
7. Vladimir Belyakov	SOV	19.10
8. Jean Tschabold	SWI	19.05

1956 Melbourne C: 63, N: 18, D: 12.6.

			PTS.
1.	Boris Shakhlin	SOV	19.25
2.	Takashi Ono	JAP	19.20
3.	Viktor Chukarin	SOV	19.10
4.	Josef Škvor	CZE	19.05
5.	Yuri Titov	SOV	19.00
6.	Jaroslav Bim	CZE	18.95
7.	Pavel Stolbov	SOV	18.90
7.	Masao Takemoto	JAP	18.90

1960 Rome C: 130, N: 28, D: 9.10.

			PTS.
1.	Eugen Ekman	FIN	19.375
1.	Boris Shakhlin	SOV	19.375
3.	Shuji Tsurumi	JAP	19.15
4.	Takashi Mitsukuri	JAP	19.125
5.	Yuri Titov	SOV	18.95
6.	Takashi Ono	JAP	18.525

1964 Tokyo C: 130, N: 29, D: 10.22.

			PTS.
1.	Miroslav Cerar	YUG	19.525
2.	Shuji Tsurumi	JAP	19.325
3.	Yuri Tsapenko	SOV	19.20
4.	Haruhiro Yamashita	JAP	19.075
5.	Harald Wigaard	NOR	18.925
6.	Takashi Mitsukuri	JAP	18.65

1968 Mexico City C: 114, N: 27, D: 10.26.

			PTS.
1.	Miroslav Cerar	YUG	19.325
2.	Olli Eino Laiho	FIN	19.225
3.	Mikhail Voronin	SOV	19.20
4.	Wilhelm Kubica	POL	19.15
5.	Eizo Kenmotsu	JAP	19.05
6.	Viktor Klimenko	SOV	18.95

1972 Munich C: 113, N: 26, D: 9.1.

			PTS.
1.	Viktor Klimenko	SOV	19.125
2.	Sawao Kato	JAP	19.00
3.	Eizo Kenmotsu	JAP	18.95
4.	Shigeru Kasamatsu	JAP	18.925
5.	Mikhail Voronin	SOV	18.875
6.	Wilhelm Kubica	POL	18.75

1976 Montreal C: 90, N: 20, D: 7.23.

			PTS.
1.	Zoltán Magyar	HUN	19.70
2.	Eizo Kenmotsu	JAP	19.575
3.	Nikolai Andrianov	SOV	19.525
3.	Michael Nikolay	GDR	19.525
5.	Sawao Kato	JAP	19.40
6.	Aleksandr Dityatin	SOV	19.35

1980 Moscow C: 65, N: 14, D: 7.25.

			PTS.
1.	Zoltán Magyar	HUN	19.925
2.	Aleksandr Dityatin	SOV	19.80
3.	Michael Nikolay	GDR	19.775
4.	Roland Brückner	GDR	19.725
5.	Aleksandr Tkachyov	SOV	19.475
6.	Ferenc Donáth	HUN	19.40

RINGS

1896 Athens C: 12, N: 3, D: 4.9.

1.	Ioannis Mitropoulos	GRE
2.	Hermann Weingärtner	GER
3.	Petros Persakis	GRE

Mitropoulos was the first announced Greek victor in the modern Olympics.

1900 not held

1904 St. Louis C: 10, N: 1, D: 10.28.

			PTS.
1.	Hermann Glass	USA	45
2.	William Merz	USA	35
3.	Emil Voight	USA	32

1908–1920 not held

1924 Paris C: 70, N: 9, D: 7.20.

			PTS.
1.	Francesco Martino	ITA	21.553
2.	Robert Pražak	CZE	21.483
3.	Ladislav Vácha	CZE	21.430
4.	Leon Štukelj	YUG	21.330
5.	Bedřich Supčik	CZE	21.120
6.	Bohumil Mořkovsky	CZE	21.083
7.	Jan Koutny	CZE	21.053
8.	Ferdinando Mandrini	ITA	20.943

1928 Amsterdam C: 87, N: 11, D: 8.10.

			PTS.
1.	Leon Štukelj	YUG	19.25
2.	Ladislav Vácha	CZE	19.17
3.	Emanuel Löffler	CZE	18.83
4.	Romeo Neri	ITA	18.67
5.	Mauri Nyberg-Noroma	FIN	18.33
6.	Bedřich Supčik	CZE	18.25
7.	Paul Krempel	USA	18.17
8.	Jan Gajdoš	CZE	18.08
8.	Georges Miez	SWI	18.08
8.	Armand Solbach	FRA	18.08

1932 Los Angeles C: 14, N: 6, D: 8.12.

			PTS.
1.	George Gulack	USA	18.97
2.	William Denton	USA	18.60
3.	Giovanni Lattuada	ITA	18.50
4.	Richard Bishop	USA	18.47
5.	Oreste Capuzzo	ITA	18.27
6.	Franco Tognini	ITA	18.03
7.	Heikki Savolainen	FIN	17.70
8.	Toshihiko Sasano	JAP	17.47

1936 Berlin C: 111, N: 14, D: 8.11.

			PTS.
1.	Alois Hudec	CZE	19.433
2.	Leon Štukelj	YUG	18.867
3.	Matthias Volz	GER	18.667
4.	Alfred Schwarzmann	GER	18.534
5.	Franz Beckert	GER	18.533
6.	Michael Reusch	SWI	18.434
7.	Jaroslav Kollinger	CZE	18.433
8.	Heikki Savolainen	FIN	18.40

1948 London C: 123, N: 16, D: 8.13.

			PTS.
1.	Karl Frei	SWI	19.80
2.	Michael Reusch	SWI	19.55
3.	Zdenek Ružička	CZE	19.25
4.	Walter Lehmann	SWI	19.20
5.	Josef Stalder	SWI	19.15
5.	Emil Studer	SWI	19.15
7.	Vladimir Karas	CZE	19.10
8.	Heikki Savolainen	FIN	19.05

1952 Helsinki C: 185, N: 29, D: 7.21.

			PTS.
1.	Grant Shaginyan	SOV	19.75
2.	Viktor Chukarin	SOV	19.55
3.	Hans Eugster	SWI	19.40
3.	Dimitri Leonkin	SOV	19.40
5.	Valentin Muratov	SOV	19.35
6.	Masao Takemoto	JAP	19.20
7.	Attia Ali Alizaky (EGY),		
	Ferenc Kemény (HUN),		
	Yevgeny Korolkov (SOV),		
	Berndt Lindfors (FIN)		19.15

1956 Melbourne C: 63, N: 18, D: 12.6.

			PTS.
1.	Albert Azaryan	SOV	19.35
2.	Valentin Muratov	SOV	19.15
3.	Masami Kubota	JAP	19.10
3.	Masao Takemoto	JAP	19.10
5.	Nobuyuki Aihara	JAP	19.05
5.	Takashi Ono	JAP	19.05
7.	Viktor Chukarin	SOV	19.00
7.	Shinsaku Tsukawaki	JAP	19.00

1960 Rome C: 130, N: 28, D: 9.10.

			PTS.
1.	Albert Azaryan	SOV	19.725
2.	Boris Shakhlin	SOV	19.50
3.	Velik Kapsazov	BUL	19.425
3.	Takashi Ono	JAP	19.425
5.	Nobuyuki Aihara	JAP	19.40
6.	Yuri Titov	SOV	19.275

1964 Tokyo C: 130, N: 29, D: 10.22.

			PTS.
1.	Takuji Haytta	JAP	19.475
2.	Franco Menichelli	ITA	19.425
3.	Boris Shakhlin	SOV	19.40
4.	Viktor Leontyev	SOV	19.35
5.	Shuji Tsurumi	JAP	19.275
6.	Yukio Endo	JAP	19.25

1968 Mexico City C: 117, N: 28, D: 10.26.

			PTS.
1.	Akinori Nakayama	JAP	19.45
2.	Mikhail Voronin	SOV	19.325
3.	Sawao Kato	JAP	19.225
4.	Mitsuo Tsukahara	JAP	19.125
5.	Takeshi Kato	JAP	19.05
6.	Sergei Diomidov	SOV	18.975

1972 Munich C: 113, N: 26, D: 9.1.

			PTS.
1.	Akinori Nakayama	JAP	19.35
2.	Mikhail Voronin	SOV	19.275
3.	Mitsuo Tsukahara	JAP	19.225
4.	Sawao Kato	JAP	19.15
5.	Eizo Kenmotsu	JAP	18.95
5.	Klaus Köste	GDR	18.95

1976 Montreal C: 90, N: 20, D: 7.23.

			PTS.
1.	Nikolai Andrianov	SOV	19.65
2.	Aleksandr Dityatin	SOV	19.55
3.	Dǎnut Grecu	ROM	19.50
4.	Ferenc Dónath	HUN	19.20
5.	Eizo Kenmotsu	JAP	19.175
6.	Sawao Kato	JAP	19.125

1980 Moscow C: 65, N: 14, D: 7.25.

			PTS.
1.	Aleksandr Dityatin	SOV	19.875
2.	Aleksandr Tkachyov	SOV	19.725
3.	Jiří Tabak	CZE	19.60
4.	Roland Brückner	GDR	19.575
5.	Stoyan Deltchev	BUL	19.475
6.	Dǎnut Grecu	ROM	10.85

FLOOR EXERCISES

1896–1928 not held

1932 Los Angeles C: 25, N: 6, D: 8.8.

		PTS.
1. István Pelle	HUN	9.60
2. Georges Miez	SWI	9.47
3. Mario Lertora	ITA	9.23
4. Frank Haubold	USA	9.00
4. Romeo Neri	ITA	9.00
6. Heikki Savolainen	FIN	8.97
7. Alfred Jochim	USA	8.80
7. Martti Uosikkinen	FIN	8.80

1936 Berlin C: 110, N: 14, D: 8.11.

		PTS.
1. Georges Miez	SWI	18.666
2. Josef Walter	SWI	18.50
3. Konrad Frey	GER	18.466
3. Eugen Mack	SWI	18.466
5. Matthias Volz	GER	18.366
6. Willi Stadel	GER	18.30
6. Walter Steffens	GER	18.30
8. Martti Uosikkinen	FIN	18.267

1948 London C: 123, N: 16, D: 8.13.

		PTS.
1. Ferenc Pataki	HUN	19.35
2. János Mogyorósi-Klencs	HUN	19.20
3. Zdenek Ružička	CZE	19.05
4. Raymond Dot	FRA	18.90
5. Elkana Grönne	DEN	18.825
6. Pavel Benetka	CZE	18.80
6. Leo Sotornik	CZE	18.80
8. Vladimir Karas	CZE	18.10

As a teenager in Budapest, Ferenc Pataki wanted to become an actor. His first role was a walk-on part in which he performed some acrobatic moves. His skill was immediately noticed and he was rerouted into gymnastics.

1952 Helsinki C: 185, N: 29, D: 7.21.

		PTS.
1. K. William Thoresson	SWE	19.25
2. Jerzy Jokiel	POL	19.15
2. Tadao Uesako	JAP	19.15
4. Takashi Ono	JAP	19.05
5. Onni Lappalainen	FIN	19.00
6. Kalevi Laitinen	FIN	18.95
6. Anders Lindh	SWE	18.95
8. Ferdinand Daniš	CZE	18.90
8. Robert Stout	USA	18.90

1956 Melbourne C: 63, N: 18, D: 12.6.

		PTS.
1. Valentin Muratov	SOV	19.20
2. Nobuyuki Aihara	JAP	19.10
2. K. William Thoresson	SWE	19.10
2. Viktor Chukarin	SOV	19.10

5. Yuri Titov	SOV	18.95
6. Ferdinand Daniš	CZE	18.80
6. Mintscho Todorov	BUL	18.80
8. Helmut Bantz	GER	18.75
8. Takashi Ono	JAP	18.75

1960 Rome C: 130, N: 28, D: 9.10.

		PTS.
1. Nobuyuki Aihara	JAP	19.45
2. Yuri Titov	SOV	19.325
3. Franco Menichelli	ITA	19.275
4. Takashi Mitsukuri	JAP	19.20
4. Takashi Ono	JAP	19.20
6. Jaroslav Štastny	CZE	19.05

1964 Tokyo C: 130, N: 29, D: 10.22.

		PTS.
1. Franco Menichelli	ITA	19.45
2. Yukio Endo	JAP	19.35
2. Viktor Lisitsky	SOV	19.35
4. Viktor Leontyev	SOV	19.20
5. Takashi Mitsukuri	JAP	19.10
6. Yuri Tsapenko	SOV	18.85

1968 Mexico City C: 117, N: 28, D: 10.26.

		PTS.
1. Sawao Kato	JAP	19.475
2. Akinori Nakayama	JAP	19.40
3. Takeshi Kato	JAP	19.275
4. Mitsuo Tsukuhara	JAP	19.05
5. Valery Karassev	SOV	18.95
6. Eizo Kenmotsu	JAP	18.925

1972 Munich C: 113, N: 26, D: 9.1.

		PTS.
1. Nikolai Andrianov	SOV	19.175
2. Akinori Nakayama	JAP	19.125
3. Shigeru Kasamatsu	JAP	19.025
4. Eizo Kenmotsu	JAP	18.925
5. Klaus Köste	GDR	18.825
6. Sawao Kato	JAP	18.75

1976 Montreal C: 90, N: 20, D: 7.23.

		PTS.
1. Nikolai Andrianov	SOV	19.45
2. Vladimir Marchenko	SOV	19.425
3. Peter Kormann	USA	19.30
4. Roland Brückner	GDR	19.275
5. Sawao Kato	JAP	19.25
6. Eizo Kenmotsu	JAP	19.10

1980 Moscow C: 65, N: 14, D: 7.25.

		PTS.
1. Roland Brückner	GDR	19.75
2. Nikolai Andrianov	SOV	19.725
3. Aleksandr Dityatin	SOV	19.70
4. Jiří Tabák	CZE	19.675
5. Péter Kovács	HUN	19.425
6. Lutz Hoffmann	GDR	18.725

TEAM COMBINED EXERCISES

1896–1900 not held

1904 St. Louis T: 13, N: 1, D: 7.2.

		TOTAL PTS.
1.	Turngemeinde Philadelphia Julius Lenhart 69.80 (1), Philipp Kassel 64.56 (11), Anton Heida 62.72 (17), Max Hess 59.29 (31), Ernst Reckeweg 56.15 (46), John Grieb 55.21 (50)	374.43
2.	New Yorker Turnverein Otto Steffen 67.03 (6), John Bissinger 66.57 (7), Emil Beyer 59.70 (30), Max Wolf 57.85 (33), Julian Schmitz 54.58 (56), Arthur Rosenkampf 48.34 (87)	356.37
3.	Central Turnverein Chicago George Meyer 61.66 (21), John Duha 61.02 (24), Edward Siegler 59.03 (32), Philipp Schuster 55.44 (49), Robert Mayack 54.53 (57), Charles Krause 53.01 (66)	349.69
4.	Concordia Turnverein St. Louis William Merz 65.26 (10), Georges Stapf 61.97 (20), John Dellert 57.41 (35), Emil Voigt 54.33 (59), George Eyser 52.10 (70), Hy. Meyland 48.52 (86)	344.01
5.	South St. Louis Turverein Charles Umbs 63.39 (16), Andy Neu 61.21 (23), William Tritschler 54.73 (54), Christian Deubler 54.63 (55), Edward Tritschler 53.16 (65), John Leichinger 50.00 (81)	338.65
6.	Norwegischer Turnverein Brooklyn Ragnar Berg 60.24 (28), Charles Sörum 57.40 (36), Oliver Olsen 57.27 (38), Harry Hansen 55.00 (51), Oluf Landnes 53.64 (72), Bergin Nilsen 50.45 (80)	334.00

1906 Athens T: 6, N: 5, D: 4.22.

		TOTAL PTS.
1. NOR	(Carl Albert Andersen, Oskar Bye, Conrad Carlsrud, Harald Anders Eriksen, Osvald Falch, Christian Fjeringen, Yngvar Fredriksen, Karl Johan Haagensen, Harald Halvorsen, Petter Hol, Andreas Hagelund, H. Hemsen, Eugen Ingebretsen, Matthias Jespersen, Fin Münster, Fridtjof Olsen, Carl Alfred Pedersen, Rasmus Pettersen, Thorleif Pettersen, Thorleif Rehn, Johan Stumpf)	19.00
2. DEN	(Carl Andersen, Halvor Birch, H. Bukdahl, Kaj Gnudtzmann, Knud Holm, Erik Klem, Harald Klem, R. Kraft, Edvard Larsen, J. Lorentzen, Robert Madsen, Carl Manicus-Hansen, Oluf Olsen, Christian Petersen, Hans Pedersen, Niels Petersen, Viktor Rasmussen, Marius Skram-Jensen, Marius Thuesen)	18.00
3. ITA	Pistoia (Manlio Pastorini, Spartaco Nerozzi, Federico Bertinotti, Vitaliano Masotti, Raffaello Gianoni, Quintilio Mazzoncini, Azeglio Innocenti, Filiberto Innocenti, Ciro Civinini, Maurizio Masetti)	16.71
4. ITA	Roma (Cesare Tifi, Dante Aloisi, Enrico Brignoli, Pierino Caccialupi, Guido Colavini, Romeo Giannotti, Mario Gubiani, Venceslao Rossi, Romolo Tuzzi, Amadeo Zinzi)	16.60
5. GER	(O. Franke, Cassius Hermes, Fritz Hofmann, Julius Keyl, Bruno Mahler, Carl Ohms, Wilhelm Weber, Otto Wiegand)	16.25
6. HUN	(Béla Dáner, Arpád Erdös, Béla Erödi, Frigyes Gráf, Gyula Kakas, Nándor Kovács, Kálmán Szabó, Vilmos Szücs)	14.45

1908 London T: 8, N: 8, D: 7.18.

		TOTAL PTS.
1. SWE	(Gösta Åsbrink, Per Bertilsson, Andreas Cervin, Hjalmar Cedercrona, Rudolf Degermark, Carl Folcker, Sven Forssman, Erik Granfelt, Carl Hårleman, Nils Hellsten, Gunnar Höjer, Arvid Holmberg, Carl Holmberg, Osvald Holmberg, Hugo Jahnke, John Jarlén, Harald Johnsson, Rolf Johnsson, Nils Kantzow, Sven Landberg, Olle Lanner, Axel Jung, Osvald Moberg, Carl Martin Norberg, Erik Norberg, Thor Norberg, Axel Norling, Daniel Norling, Gösta Olsson, Leonard Peterson, Sven Rosen, Gustav Rosenqvist, Axel Sjöblom, Birger Sörvik, Haakon Sorvik, Karl Johan Svensson [Sarland], Gustaf Vinqvist, Nils Widforss)	438
2. NOR	(Arthur Amundsen, Carl Albert Andersen, Otto Authen, Hermann Bohne, Trygve Böysen, Oscar Bye, Conrad Carlsrud, Sverre Gröner, Harald Halvorsen, Harald Hansen, Petter Hol, Eugen Ingebretsen, Ole Iversen, Mathias Jespersen, Sigge Johannesen, Nicolai Kiör, Karl Klaeth, Thor Larsen, Rolf Lefdahl, Hans Lem, Anders Moen, Frithjof Olsen, Carl Alfred Pedersen, Paul Pedersen, John Skrataas, Harald Smedvik, Sigvard Sivertsen, Andreas Strand, Olaf Syvertsen, Thomas Thorstensen)	425
3. FIN	(Eino Forsström, Otto Granström, Johan Kemp, Jivari Kyykoski, Heikki Lehmusto, John Lindroth, Yrjö Linko, Edvard Linna, Matti Markanen, Kaarlo Mikkolainen, Veli Nieminen, Kaarlo Kustaa Paasia, Arvi Pohjanpää, Aarne Pohjonen, Eino Railio, Heikki Riipinen, Arno Saarinen, Einari Verner Sahlstein, Arne Salovaara, Kaarlo Sandelin, Elias Sipilä, Viktor Smeds, Kaarlo Soinio, Kurt Enoch Stenberg, Väinö Tiiri, Magnus Wegelius)	405
4. DEN	(Carl Andersen, Hans Bredmose, Jens Chiewitz, Arvor Hansen, Christian Hansen, Ingvardt Hansen, Einar Hermann, Knud Holm, Paul Holm, O. Husted-Nielsen, Charles Jensen, Gorm Jensen, Hendrik Johansen, Harald Klem, Robert Madsen, Viggo Meulengracht-Madsen, Lucas Nielsen, Oluf Olsen, Niels Petersen, Nicolaj Philipsen, R.H. Rasmussen, Victor Rasmussen, Marius Thuesen, Niels Turin-Nielsen)	378
5. FRA	(L. Bogart, A. Borizée, H. de Breyne, N. Constant, C. A. Courtois, L. Delattre, A. Delecluse, L. Delecluse, G. Demarle, J. Derov, C. Desmarcheliers, Charles Desmarcheliers, E. Dharaney, G. Donnet, E. Duhamel, A. Duponcheel, P. Durin, A.	319

TOTAL PTS.

Eggremont, G. Guiot, L. Hennebioq, H. Hubert, D. Hudels, E. Labitte, L. Lestienne, R. Lis, V. Magnier, G. Nys, J. Parent, L. Pappe, V. Polidori, G. Pottier, A. Pinoy, L. Sandray, E. Schmoll, E. Steffe, E. Vercruysse, H. Vergin, E. Vicogne, J. Walmée, G. Warlouzer)

6. ITA   (Alfredo Accorsi, Nemo Agodi, Umberto Agliorini, Adriano Andreani, Vincenzo Blo, Flaminio Bottoni, Bruto Buozzi, Giovanni Bonati, Pietro Borsetti, Adamo Borzani, Gastone Calabresi, Carlo Celada, Tito Collevati, Antonio Cotechini, Guido Cristofori, Stanislao Dichiara, Giovanni Gasperini, A. Marchi, Carlo Marchiandi, Ettore Massari, Roberto Nardini, Geatano Preti, Decio Pavani, Gino Ravenna, Massimo Ridolfi, Gustavo Taddia, Giannetto Termanini, Ugo Savonuzzi, Gioacchino Vaccari)   316

7. HOL   (C.L.J. Becker, M. Biel, J. de Boer, R.J.C. Blom, J. Bolt, E. Brouwer, C. van Daalen, J.H. Flemer, G.C. Goekel, J. Gondeket, D. Janssen, J.J. Kiefl, S. Kongin, H. N. van Leeuwen, A. Mok, A. d'Oliviera, J.J. Posthumus, J.H.A.G. Schmitt, J. Slier, J. Stikkelman, H.J.F. Thyssen, G.J. Wesling)   297

8. GBR   (P.A. Baker, W.F. Barrett, R. Bonney, J.H. Catley, M. Clay, E. Clough, J. Cotterell, W. Cowy, G.C. Cullen, F. Denby, Herbert Drury, W. Fitt, H. Gill, A.S. Harley, A.E. Hawkins, W.O. Hoare, J.A. Horridge, H.J. Huskinson, J.W. Jones, E. Justice, N.J. Keighley, R. Laycock, R. McGaw, J. McPhail, W. Manning, W.G. Merrifield, C.J. Oldaker, G. Parrott, E. Parsons, E.F. Richardson, J. Robertson, George Ross, D. Scott, J. F. Simpson, W.R. Skeeles, J. Speight, H. Stell, C.V. Suderman, W. Tilt, Charles Vigurs, H. Waterman, E. Walton, E.A. Watkins, John Whitaker, F. Whitehead)   196

1912 Stockholm T: 5, N: 5, D: 7.11.

TOTAL PTS.

1. ITA   (Guido Boni, Giuseppe Domenichelli, Luciano Savorini, Guido Romano, Angelo Zorzi, Giorgio Zampori, Giovanni Mangiante, Lorenzo Mangiante, Adolfo Tunesi, Pietro Bianchi, Paolo Salvi, Alberto Braglia, Alfredo Gollini, Serafino Mazzarocchi, Francesco Loi, Carlo Fregosi)   265.75

2. HUN   (Lajos Aradi-Kmetykó, József Berkes-Bittenbinder, Imre Erdödy, Samu Fóti, Imre Gellért, Gyözö Halmos-Haberfeld, Ottó Helmich, István Herczeg, József Keresztessy, János Korponai-Krizmanich, Elemér Pászty, Árpád Pétery, Jenö Réti-Rittich, Ferenc Szücs, Ödön Téry, Géza Tuli)   227.25

3. GBR   (Albert Betts, Harry Dickason, Samuel Hodgetts, Alfred Messenger, Edward Pepper, Charles Vigurs, Samuel Walker, John Whitaker, Sidney   184.50

Cross, Bernard Franklin, Edward Potts, Reginald Potts, George Ross, Henry Oberholzer, Charles Simmons, Arthur Southern, Ronald McLean, Charles Luck, Herbert Drury, William McKune, William Titt, William Cowhig, Leonard Hanson)

4. LUX   (Nicolas Adam, Charles Behm, André Bordang, Jean-Pierre Frantzen, François Hentges, Pierre Hentges, Michal Hemmerling, Jean-Baptiste Horn, Nicolas Kanivé, Emile Knepper, Nicolas Kummer, Marcel Langsam, Emile Lanners, Jean-Pierre Thommes, François Wagner, Antoine Wehrer, Ferdinand Wirtz, Joseph Zuang, Maurice Palgen)   179.75

5. GER   (Walter Engelmann, Adolf Seebass, Alfred Staats, Hans Roth, Arno Glockauer, Alexander Sperling, Kurt Reichenbach, Rudolf Körner, Erwin Buder, Wilhelm Brülle, Heinrich Pahner, Johannes Reuschle, Walter Jesinghaus, Eberhard Sorge, Karl Richter, Erich Worm, Karl Jordan, Hans Werner)   162.00

1920 Antwerp T: 5, N: 5, D: 8.29.

TOTAL PTS.

1. ITA   (Arnaldo Andreoli, Pietro Bianchi, Ettore Bellotto, Luigi Cambiaso, Luigi Contessi, Carlo Costigliolo, Luigi Costigliolo, Fernando Bonatti, Giuseppe Domenichelli, Roberto Ferrari, Carlo Fregosi, Romualdo Ghiglione, Ambrogio Levati, Francesco Loi, Vittorio Lucchetti, Luigi Maiocco, Ferdinando Mandrini, Giovanni Mangiante, Lorenzo Mangiante, Antonio Marovelli, Michele Mastromarino, Giuseppe Paris, Manlio Pastorini, Ezio Roselli, Paolo Salvi, Giovanni Battista Tubino, Giorgio Zampori, Angelo Zorzi)   359.855

2. BEL   (Eugenius Auwerkerken, Théophile Bauer, François Claessens, Auguste Cootmans, Frans Gibens, Jean van Guysse, Albert Haepers, Dominique Jacobs, Félicien Kempeneers, Jules Labéeu, Hubert Lafortune, Auguste Landrieu, Charles Lannie, Constant Loriot, Alphonse van Mele, Ferdinand Minnaert, Nicolas Maerloos, Louis Stoop, François Verboven, Jean Verboven, Julien Verdonck, Joseph Verstraeten, Georges Vivex, Jules Julianus Wagemans)   346.785

3. FRA   (Emile Bouchès, Paul Joseph Durin, Paulin Alexandre Lemaire, Georges Berger, Léon Delsarte, Georges Duvant, Louis Kempe, Lucien Démanet, Auguste Hoël, René Boulanger, Fernand Fauconnier, Albert Hersoy, Georges Lagouge, Ernest Lepinasse, Jules Pirard, Julien Wartelle, Paul Wartelle, Emile Martel, Georges Thurnherr, Alfred Buyenne, Eugène Pollet, Eugène Cordonnier, Arthur Hermann, André Higelin)   340.100

4. CZE (Josef Bochniček, Ladislav Bubeniček, Josef 305.255
Czada, Stanislav Indruch, Miroslav Klinger, Jo-
sef Maly, Zdenek Opočensky, Josef Pagáč,
František Pecháček, Robert Pražak, Josef Sto-
lař, Svatopluk Svoboda, Ladislav Vắcha,
František Vaneček, Jaroslav Velda, Václav
Virt)

5. GBR (S. Andrew, Albert Betts, A.G. Cocksedge, Wil- 290.215
liam Cotterill, William Cowhig, Sidney Cross,
H.S. Dawswell, J.E. Dingley, S. Domville, H.W.
Doncaster, R.E. Edgecombe, W. Edwards, H.J.
Finchett, Bernard Wallis Franklin, J. Harris,
Samuel Hodgetts, J. Cotterill, Stanley Leigh, G.
Masters, Ronald McLean, O. Morris, E.P. Ness,
A.E. Page, A.O. Pinner, E. Pugh, H.W. Taylor,
J.A. Walker, R.H. Zandell)

1924 Paris T: 9, N: 9, D: 7.20.

		TOTAL PTS.

1. ITA (Fernando Mandrini 105.583 [4], Mario Letora 839.058
103.619 [10], Vittorio Lucchetti 102.803 [12],
Francesco Martino 101.529 [16], Luigi Cambiaso 101.320 [17], Giuseppe Paris 101.169
[18], Giorgio Zampori 96.549 [26], Luigi
Maiocco 92.486 [33])

2. FRA (Jean Gounot 105.153 [8], Léon Delsarte 820.528
104.739 [9], Albert Séquin 102.326 [15], Eugène Cordonnier 99.906 [21], François Gangloff 98.796 [23], Arthur Hermann 95.716 [27],
André Higelin 92.133 [34], Joseph Huber,
88.119 [39])

3. SWI (August Güttinger 105.176 [7], Jean Gutwen- 816.661
iger 102.342 [14], Hans Grieder 99.646 [22],
Georges Miez 98.796 [24], Josef Wilhelm
97.096 [25], Otto Pfister 95.746 [28], Carl
Widmer 94.936 [32], Antoine Rebetez 89.583
[38])

4. YUG (Leon Štukelj 110.340 [1], Ivan Porenta 762.101
100.172 [20], Stane Zilič 95.523 [29], Stane
Derganc 95.293 [30], Miha Osvald 91.066
[36], Slavko Hlastan 81.248 [44], Rastko Polj-
šak 77.665 [45], Josip Primožič 77.393 [47])

5. USA (Frank Kriz 100.293 [19], Alfred Jochim 715.117
95.090 [31], John Pearson 89.852 [37], Frank
Safanda 86.953 [41], Curtis Rottman 82.946
[42], Rudolph Novak 77.593 [46], Max
Wandrer 76.320 [48], John Mais 72.770 [53])

6. GBR (Stanley Leigh 91.266 [35], H. Brown 87.059 637.790
[40], H.J. Finchett 81.710 [43], F. Hawkins
73.796 [49], T. Hopkins 72.350 [54], E. Leigh
69.200 [55], S. Humphreys 64.656 [64], A.
Spencer 64.253 [65])

7. FIN (Jaakko Kunnas 73.473 [51], O. Suhonen 521.998
72.843 [52], Ak. Roine 66.503 [56], Aa. Roine
65.46 [59], M. Hamalainen 65.23
Karonen 65.18 [63], E. Kerttula 62.863 [66], E.
Kostamo 50.443 [70])

8. LUX (C. Quaino 73.569 [50], T. Jeitz 65.98 [57], E. 514.529
Munhofen 65.556 [58], M. Erang 65.356 [60],
A. Neumann 65.196 [62], J. Palzer 61.563
[67], P. Tolar 58.713 [68], M. Weishaupt
58.596 [69])

1928 Amsterdam T: 11, N: 11, D: 8.10.

		TOTAL PTS.

1. SWI (Georges Miez 247.500 [1], Hermann Hänggi 1718.625
246.625 [2], Eugen Mack 243.625 [8], Mel-
chior Wetzel 240.875 [12], Eduard "Edi"
Steinemann 237.875 [15], August Güttinger
237.750 [16], Hans Grieder 234.125 [18],
Otto Pfister 230.875 [24])

2. CZE (Ladislav Vácha 242.875 [9], Emanuel Löffler 1712.25
242.500 [10], Jan Gajdoš 240.625 [13], Jo-
sef Effenberger 238.875 [14], Josef Effenberger 238.875 [14], Bedřich Šupčik 233.250
[10], Václav Vesely 227.625 [28], Jan Koutny
225.250 [31], Ladislav Tikal 217.750 [37])

3. YUG (Leon Štukelj 244.875 [3], Josip Primožič 1648.75
244.000 [5], Anton Malej 228.875 [25],
Eduard Antonijevič 228.000 [26], Boris Gre-
gorka 221.000 [33], Ivan Porenta 220.250
[34], Stane Derganc 211.875 [43], Dragutin
Ciotti 210.000 [45])

4. FRA (Armand Solbach 241.625 [11], Georges Ler- 1620.75
oux 235.750 [17], André Lemoine 232.000
[22], Jean Larrouy 226.500 [29], E. Schmitt
219.125 [35], Jean Gounot 216.750 [39], A.
Chatelain 202.375 [54], Alfred Kraus 100.25
[DNF])

5. FIN (Heikki Savolainen 243.750 [6], Mauri Ny- 1609.25
berg 243.750 [6], Martti Uosikkinen 231.875
[23], Jaakko Kunnas 217.500 [38], U.K. Korhonen 209.875 [46], Rafael Ylönen 188.750
[61], Kaiku Kinos 185.375 [62], Birger Sten-
man 179.750 [66])

6. ITA (Romeo Neri 244.750 [4], Mario Lertora 1599.125
233.375 [19], Vittorio Lucchetti 228.000 [26],
Fernando Mandrini 226.250 [30], Giuseppe
Lupi 224.000 [32], Mario Tambini 212.500
[41], Giuseppe Paris 203.250 [53], Ezio Roselli 192.625 [58])

7. USA (Alfred Jochim 218.250 [36], Glenn Berry 1519.125
212.750 [40], Frank Kriz 211.625 [44], Frank
Haubold 209.375 [47], Harold Newhart
209.375 [47], John Pearson 208.75 [50],
Herman Witzig 206.250 [51], Paul Krempel
203.625 [52])

8. HOL (E.H. Melkman 199.500 [56], P.J. van Dam 1364.875
199.375 [59], M. Jacobs 199.000 [60], I.
Wijnschenk 182.625 [64], W.B. Pouw
182.125 [65], K. Boot 169.000 [71], J.F. van
d. Vinden 169.000 [71], H.G. Licher 143.500
[85])

1932 Los Angeles T: 5, N: 5, D: 8.10.

		TOTAL PTS.
1. ITA	(Romeo Neri 140.625 [1], Mario Lertora 134.400 [4], Savino Guglielmetti 134.375 [5], Oreste Capuzzo 132.450 [7])	541.850
2. USA	(Frank Haubold 132.525 [6], Frederick Meyer 131.650 [9] Alfred Jochim 129.075 [11], Frank Cumiskey 129.025 [12])	522.275
3. FIN	(Heikki Savolainen 134.575 [3], Mauri Nyberg-Noroma 129.800 [10], Veikko Pakarinen 122.700 [14], Einari Teräsvirta 122.700 [14])	509.995
4. HUN	(István Pelle 134.925 [2], Miklós Péter 119.200 [17], Péter Boros 105.775 [20], József Hegedüs 105.750 [21])	465.650
5. JAP	(Toshihiko Sasano 108.475 [19], Shigeo Honma 103.100 [22], Takashi Kondo 101.925 [23], Yoshitaki Takeda 88.500 [24])	402.000

1936 Berlin T: 14, N: 14, D: 8.11.

		TOTAL PTS.
1. GER	(Alfred Schwarzmann 113.100 [1], Konrad Frey 111.532 [3], Matthias Volz 110.099 [7], Willi Stadel 108.999 [8], Franz Beckert 107.200 [15], Walter Steffens 106.500 [17])	657.430
2. SWI	(Eugen Mack 112.334 [2], Michael Reusch 110.700 [5], Eduard ''Edi'' Steinemann 108.633 [10], Walter Bach 108.299 [11], Albert Bachmann 107.502 [13], Georges Miez 107.334 [14])	654.802
3. FIN	(Martti Uosikkinen 110.700 [5], Heikki Savolainen 108.766 [9], Mauri Nyberg-Noroma 106.801 [16], Aleksanteri Saarvala 105.235 [19], Esa Seeste 103.934 [24], Veikko Pakarinen 103.032 [28])	638.468
4. CZE	(Alois Hudec 111.199 [4], Jaroslav Kollinger 104.733 [23], Jan Sládek 103.399 [26], Jan Gajdoš 103.065 [27], Vratislav Petraček 101.966 [34], Jindřich Tintera 101.401 [38])	625.763
5. ITA	(Savino Guglielmetti 107.699 [12], Oreste Capuzzo 102.500 [30], Egidio Armelloni 101.601 [36], Danilo Fioravanti 101.467 [37], Franco Tognini 101.266 [39], Nicolo Tronci 100.600 [41])	615.133
6. YUG	(Konrad Gralc 103.632 [25], Josip Primožič 102.367 [31], Leon Štukelj 102.300 [32], Miroslav Forte 99.200 [46], Jože Vadnov 95.934 [56], Janoz Pristov 94.933 [61])	598.366
7. HUN	(István Pelle 105.566 [18], Lajos Tóth 101.867 [35], Miklós Péter 99.034 [47], Gábor Kecskeméti 97.766 [51], István Sárkány 94.565 [64], Jósef Sarlós 93.132 [71])	591.930
8. FRA	(Walter 98.933 [49], Armand Solbach 97.633 [52], Lucien Masset 97.233 [53], Herold 96.168 [55], Antoine Schildwein 95.633 [59], Rousseau 94.666 [62])	580.266

1948 London T: 16, N: 16, D: 8.13.

		TOTAL PTS.
1. FIN	(Veikko Huhtanen 229.70 [1], Paavo Aaltonen 228.80 [3], Kalevi Laitinen 225.65 [8], Olavi Rove 225.20 [10], Einari Teräsvirta 225.00 [12], Heikki Savolainen 223.95 [14])	1358.30
2. SWI	(Walter Lehmann 229.00 [2], Josef Stalder 228.70 [4], Christian Kipfer 227.10 [5], Emil Studer 226.60 [6], Robert Lucy 223.30 [15], Michael Reusch 222.00 [18])	1356.70
3. HUN	(Lajos Tóth 225.20 [10], Lajos Sántha 224.30 [13], László Baranyai 222.40 [16], Ferenc Pataki 221.30 [19], János Mogyorósi-Klencs 218.95 [27], Ferenc Varkői 218.70 [29])	1330.85
4. FRA	(Raymond Dot 220.80 [20], Michel Mathiot 220.40 [22], Lucien Masset 219.95 [24], André Weingand 219.80 [25], Antoine Schlindwein 216.50 [34], Alphonse Anger 216.40 [35])	1313.85
5. ITA	(Guido Figone 225.30 [9], Luigi Zanetti 219.00 [26], Savino Guglielmetti 217.20 [32], Domenico Grosso 214.10 [40], Quinto Vadi 214.00 [42], Danilo Fioravanti 210.70 [51])	1300.30
6. CZE	(Zdenek Ružička 226.20 [7], Pavel Benetka 220.30 [23], Miroslav Málek 212.90 [47], Vladimir Karas 212.20 [48], Leo Sotornik 210.80 [50], František Wirth 209.70 [52])	1292.10
7. USA	(Edward Scrobe 213.9 [44], Vincent D'Autorio 211.3 [49], William Roetzheim 209.1 [53], Joseph Kotys 208.5 [55], Frank Cumiskey 205.15 [62], Raymond Sorensen 204.55 [63])	1252.50
8. DEN	(Paul Jessen 214.3 [38], T. Gronne 213.5 [45], F. Jensen 208.35 [56], A. Thomsen 206.25 [58], V. Moller 201.75 [68], P. Jensen 201.25 [70])	1245.40

1952 Helsinki T: 29, N: 29, D: 7.21.

		TOTAL PTS.
1. SOV	(Viktor Chukarin 115.70 [1], Grant Shaginyan 114.95 [2], Valentin Muratov 113.65 [4], Yevgeny Korolkov 113.35 [6], Vladimir Belyakov 113.35 [6], Yosif Berdiyev 113.10 [10], Mikhail Perelman 112.50 [11], Dimitri Leonkin 103.75 [78])	574.40
2. SWI	(Josef Stalder 114.75 [3], Hans Eugster 113.40 [5], Jean Tschabold 113.30 [8], Jack Günthard 111.60 [17], Melchior Thalmann 110.75 [25], Ernst Gebendinger 109.75 [39], Hans Schwarzentruber 108.40 [52], Ernst Fivian 107.95 [55])	567.50
3. FIN	(Onni Lappalainen 111.85 [14], Berndt Lindfors 111.45 [19], Paavo Aaltonen 111.40 [20], Kaino Lempinen 110.60 [28], Heikki Savolainen 110.45 [29], Kalevi Laitinen 110.10 [35], Kalevi Viskari 109.80 [38], Olavi Rove 109.45 [42])	564.20

4. GER (Helmut Bantz 113.25 [9], Adalbert Dickhut 561.20
110.85 [24], Theo Wied 110.70 [26], Alfred
Schwarzmann 110.65 [27], Hans Pfann 110.20
[33], Erich Wied 109.70 [40], Friedel Overwien
108.65 [48], Jakob Kiefer 91.70 [150])

5. JAP (Takashi Ono 112.20 [12], Tadao Uesako 556.90
111.65 [15], Masao Takemoto 111.65 [15], Aki-
tomo Kaneko 111.30 [21], Tetsumi Nabeya
110.10 [35])

6. HUN (Lajos Santha 111.50 [18], Ferenc Pataki 555.80
110.90 [23] József Fekete 108.90 [46], Karoly
Kocsis 108.65 [48], Ferenc Kemény 108.40
[52], Sándor Rétl 107.75 [57], Lajos Tóth
107.45 [58], János Mogyorósi-Klencs 106.80
[61])

7. CZE (Ferdinand Daniš 112.00 [13], Zdenek Ružička 555.55
110.40 [30], J. Svoboda 110.05 [37], Lee Sotor-
nik 109.50 [41], Josef Škvor 109.10 [44], J. Mi-
kulec 108.95 [45], Vladimir Kejř 108.15 [54], M.
Kolejka 106.70 [63])

8. USA (Edward Scrobe 110.40 [30], Robert Stout 543.15
110.15 [34], William Roetzheim 107.05 [59],
Donald Holder 103.50 [80], John Beckner
103.40 [81], Charles Simms 102.40 [89], W.
Blattmann 102.35 [90], Vincent D'Antorio
101.20 [100])

1956 Melbourne T: 7, N: 7, D: 12.6.

		TOTAL PTS.
1. SOV	(Viktor Chukarin 114.25 [1], Yuri Titov 113.80 [3], Valentin Muratov 113.30 [5], Albert Azaryan 112.55 [7], Boris Shakhlin 112.50 [8], Pavel Stolbov 111.75 [14])	568.25
2. JAP	(Takashi Ono 114.20 [2], Masao Takemoto 113.55 [4], Masami Kubota 112.50 [8], No-buyuki Aihara 112.45 [10], Shinsaku Tsukawaki 112.20 [12], Akira Kono 111.55 [16])	566.40
3. FIN	(Kalevi Suoniemi 112.35 [11], Berndt Lindfors 111.60 [15], Martti Mansikka 110.60 [20], Onni Lappalainen 110.45 [22], Olavi Leimuvirta 109.35 [27], Raimo Heinonen 108.10 [37])	555.95
4. CZE	(Ferdinand Daniš 111.90 [13], Josef Škvor 110.85 [18], Vladimir Kejř 110.30 [23], Zdenek Ružička 109.65 [26], Jaroslav Mikoška 109.35 [27], Jaroslav Bim 108.25 [26])	554.10
5. GER	(Helmut Bantz 112.90 [6], Robert Klein 110.60 [20], Theo Wied 109.90 [25], Hans Pfann 109.15 [29], Erich Wied 107.50 [29], Jakob Kiefer 107.45 [42])	552.45
6. USA	(John Beckner 111.00 [17], Jose Armando Vega 108.45 [31], Charles Simms 108.40 [32], Rich-ard Beckner 108.30 [35], Abraham Grossfeld 107.75 [39], William Tom 107.35 [43])	547.50
7. AUS	(Brian Blackburn 91.40 [58], Graham Bond 96.40 [54], David Gourlay 95.90 [55], John Lees 93.05 [56], Alexander Punton 85.75 [59], Bruce Sharp 92.95 [57])	477.15

1960 Rome T: 20, N: 20, D: 9.7.

		TOTAL PTS.
1. JAP	(Takashi Ono 115.90 [2], Shuji Tsurumi 114.55 [4], Yukio Endo 114.55 [5], Masao Takemoto 114.45 [5], Nobuyuki Aihara 114.40 [7], Taka-shi Mitsukuri 114.10 [9])	575.20
2. SOV	(Boris Shakhlin 115.95 [1], Yuri Titov 115.60 [3], Albert Azaryan 113.35 [11], Vladimir Port-noi 113.30 [12], Nikolai Miligulo 113.05 [13], Valery Kerdemelidi 111.95 [17])	572.70
3. ITA	(Franco Menichelli 113.80 [10], Giovanni Car-minucci 112.30 [14], Angelo Vicardi 110.90 [24], Pasquale Carminucci 110.40 [31], Orlan-do Polmonari 109.95 [38], Gianfranco Marzolla 109.05 [50])	559.05
4. CZE	(Ferdinand Daniš 112.10 [15], Jaroslav Štastny 111.50 [18], Jaroslav Bim 111.00 [23], Pavel Gajdoš 110.60 [28], Josef Trmal 110.25 [33], Ladislav Pazdera 108.85 [54])	557.15
5. USA	(Larry Banner 111.05 [21], John Beckner 110.85 [25], Donald Tonry 110.75 [27], Abra-ham Grossfeld 110.05 [36], Fred Orlofsky 109.45 [44], Garland O'Quinn 109.00 [53])	555.20
6. FIN	(Otto Kestola 112.00 [16], Eugen Ekman 110.45 [30], Olavi Leimuvirta 110.25 [33], Kauko Heikkinen 109.85 [40], Raimo Heinonen 109.60 [42], Sakkari Olkkonnen 109.40 [45])	554.45
7. GDR/GER	(Günter Lyhs 110.80 [26], Siegfried Fülle 110.60 [28], Erwin Koppe 109.05 [50], Günter Nachtigall 108.75 [59], Karlheinz Friedrich 108.00 [67], Philipp Fürst 106.65 [76])	553.35
8. SWI	(Ernst Fivian 111.05 [21], Max Benker 110.00 [37], Fritz Feuz 109.85 [40], André Brullmann 109.15 [47], Hans Schwarzentruber 109.15 [47], Edy Thomi 108.35 [63])	551.45

Masao Takemoto, a member of the Japanese team, had won a total of two silver medals and three bronze in 1952 and 1956, but he didn't win a gold medal until 1960, when he was 40 years old. He is the oldest gymnast to win a gold medal in Olympic history. In 1960 he also gained another silver medal on the horizontal bar.

1964 Tokyo T: 18, N: 18, D: 10.20.

		TOTAL PTS.
1. JAP	(Yukio Endo 115.95 [1], Shuji Tsurumi 115.40 [2], Haruhiro Yamashita 115.10 [6], Takuji Hayata 114.90 [8], Takashi Mitsukuri 114.80 [9], Takashi Ono 114.40 [11])	577.95
2. SOV	(Boris Shakhlin 115.40 [2], Viktor Lisitsky 115.40 [2], Viktor Leontyev 114.50 [10], Yuri Tsapenko 114.40 [11], Yuri Titov 114.35 [13], Sergei Diomidov 114.20 [14])	575.45
3. GER/GDR	(Siegfried Fülle 114.10 [15], Klaus Köste 112.75 [18], Erwin Koppe 112.45 [19], Peter	565.10

TOTAL PTS.

Weber 112.35 [21], Philipp Fürst 112.25 [24], Günter Lyhs 111.70 [29])

4. ITA (Franco Menichelli 115.15 [5], Luigi Cimnaghi 560.90 112.35 [21], Giovanni Carminucci 111.80 [27], Pasquale Carminucci 110.70 [42], Angelo Vicardi 109.40 [63], Bruno Franceschetti 108.70 [75])

5. POL (Mikolaj Kubica 113.20 [16], Aleksander Rokosa 111.95 [25], Wilhelm Kubica 111.10 [35], Alfred Kucharczyk 111.05 [37], Jan Jankowicz 110.60 [45], Andrzej Konopka 108.70 [75]) 559.50

6. CZE (Bohumil Mudřik 111.50 [30], Ladislav Pazdera 110.70 [42], Václav Kubička 110.65 [44], Přemysl Krbec 110.60 [45], Karel Klečka 110.35 [52], Pavel Gajdoš 101.75 [106]) 558.15

7. USA (Makoto Sakamoto 112.40 [20], Russell Mitchell 111.20 [32], Ronald Barak 110.95 [39], Larry Banner 110.05 [55], Gregor Weiss 109.90 [59], Arthur Shurlock 109.10 [68]) 556.95

8. FIN (Eino Laiho 111.85, Hannu Rantakara 110.50, Eugen Ekman 111.15, Raimo Heinonen 110.95, Otto Kestola 109.95, Kauko Heikkinen 109.35) 556.20

1968 Mexico City T: 16, N: 16, D: 10.24.

TOTAL PTS.

1. JAP (Sawao Kato 115.90 [1], Akinori Nakayama 575.90 115.65 [3], Eizo Kenmotsu 114.90 [4], Takeshi Kato 114.85 [5], Yukio Endo 113.55 [8], Mitsuo Tsukahara 111.50 [18])

2. SOV (Mikhail Voronin 115.85 [2], Sergei Diomidov 571.10 114.10 [6], Viktor Klimenko 113.95 [7], Valery Karassev 113.25 [10], Viktor Lisitsky 112.60 [14], Valery Ilyinykh 111.90 [15])

3. GDR (Matthias Brehme 112.85 [12], Klaus Köste 557.15 111.85 [16], Siegfried Fülle 111.10 [21], Peter Weber 110.15 [26], Gerhard Dietrich 109.70 [34], Günter Beier 108.20 [51])

4. CZE (Václav Kubička 111.30 [19], Jiři Fejtek 111.20 557.10 [20], František Bocko 111.00 [22], Bohumil Mudřik 109.95 [28], Miloslav Netusil 109.40 [37], Václav Skoumal 109.30 [38])

5. POL (Wilhelm Kubica 113.15 [11], Mikolaj Kubica 555.40 112.80 [13], Sylwester Kubica 109.80 [31], Andrzej Gonera 109.25 [39], Aleksander Rokosa 108.85 [44], Jerzy Kruza 108.15 [53])

6. YUG (Miroslav Cerar 113.30 [9], Janez Brodnik 550.75 110.75 [23], Milenko Kersnič 109.85 [30], Milko Vratič 108.90 [42], Damir Anić 105.80 [75], Martin Šrot 104.80 [84])

7. USA (David Thor 110.6 [24], Fred Roethlisberger 548.90 109.7 [34], Stephen Hug 109.6 [36], Stephen Cohen 108.75 [46], Sidney Freudenstein 108.0 [57], Kanati Allen 105.45 [80])

8. GER (Heinz Häussler 108.8 [45], Helmut Tepasse 548.35 108.35 [50], Heiko Reinemer 108.2 [51], Hermann Hopfner 108.1 [55], Erich Hess 107.75 [60])

1972 Munich T: 16, N; 16, D: 8.29.

TOTAL PTS.

1. JAP (Sawao Kato 115.10 [1], Eizo Kenmotsu 114.75 571.25 [2], Shigeru Kasamatsu 114.40 [3], Akinori Nakayama 114.25 [4], Mitsuo Tsukahara 112.25 [11], Teruichi Okamura 111.20 [14])

2. SOV (Nikolai Andrianov 113.80 [5], Mikhail Voronin 564.05 112.95 [7], Viktor Klimenko 112.65 [8], Edvard Mikhaelian 112.50 [9], Aleksandr Maleev 110.70 [18], Vladimir Shukin 110.20 [20])

3. GDR (Klaus Köste 113.25 [6], Matthias Brehme 559.70 112.45 [10], Wolfgang Thüne 112.15 [12], Wolfgang Klotz 111.05 [16], Reinhard Rychly 109.95 [21], Jürgen Paeke 109.35 [28])

4. POL (Mikolaj Kubica 111.25 [13], Andrzej Szajna 551.70 111.15 [15], Sylwester Kubica 110.75 [16], Wilhelm Kubica 109.90 [22], Mieczyslaw Strzalka 106.45 [47], Jerzy Kruza 106.35 [49])

5. GER (Eberhard Gienger 109.75 [23], Walter Mössinger 109.70 [24], Günter Spies 108.70 [30], Bernd Effing 107.75 [37], Reinhard Ritter 106.80 [43], Heinz Häussler 106.25 [51]) 546.40

6. PRK (Song-Sob Li 110.75 [16], Song-Yu Kim 109.45 545.05 [25], Song-Il Kim 108.25 [32], Heung-Do Shin 107.75 [37], Yun-Hang Ho 106.45 [47], Jong-Ryol Jo 106.15 [53])

7. ROM (Petre Mihaiuc 109.30 [29], Dănut Grecu 108.10 538.90 [33], Gheorghe Paunescu 107.25 [41], Mircea Gheorghiu 105.00 [62], Nicolae Oprescu 104.60 [66], Constantin Petrescu 103.70 [73])

8. HUN (Imre Molnár 110.55 [19], Zoltán Magyar 538.60 108.70 [30], István Kiss 106.65 [45], Béla Herczeg 105.60 [56], Antal Kisteleki 105.30 [61], István Bérczi 104.95 [63])

1976 Montreal T: 12, N: 12, D: 7.20

TOTAL PTS.

1. JAP (Sawao Kato 115.90 [2], Mitsuo Tsukahara 576.85 115.75 [3], Hiroshi Kajiyama 115.25 [5], Eizo Kenmotsu 115.15 [6], Hisato Igarashi 113.55 [15], Shun Fujimoto 84.55 [89])

2. SOV (Nikolai Andrianov 116.50 [1], Aleksandr Dityatin 115.15 [6], Gennady Kryssin 114.25 [8], Vladimir Marchenko 113.85 [11], Vladimir Tikhonov 112.15 [23]) 576.45

3. GDR (Lutz Mack 113.00 [17], Bernd Jäger 112.95 564.65 [18], Michael Nikolay 112.90 [19], Roland Brückner 112.00 [24], Wolfgang Klotz 111.95 [25], Rainer Hanschke 111.50 [28])

4. HUN   (Zoltán Magyar 114.25 [8], Imre Molnár 113.65   564.45
         [13], Ferenc Donáth 113.60 [14], Béla Laufer
         111.60 [26], Árpád Farkas 109.65 [40], Imre
         Bánrévi 109.15 [48])

5. GER   (Eberhard Gienger 113.30 [16], Volker Rohr-   557.40
         wick 112.20 [22], Edgar Jorek 111.25 [29],
         Werner Steinmetz 110.30 [34], Reinhard Dietze
         108.80 [53], Reinhard Ritter 107.75 [61])

6. ROM   (Dănut Grecu 114.10 [10], Nicolae Oprescu   557.30
         110.30 [34], Sorin Cepoi 109.95 [36], Ionel
         Checiches 109.85 [37], Mihai Bors 109.75 [38],
         Stefan Gall 109.15 [48])

7. USA   (Wayne Young 111.55 [27], Kurt Thomas   556.10
         111.05 [30], Peter Kormann 110.75 [31], Thom-
         as Beach 110.55 [32], Marshall Avener 109.45
         [43], Bart Conner 109.35 [46])

8. SWI   (Robert Bretscher 112.35 [21], Ueli Bachmann   550.60'
         109.60 [41], Philippe Gaille 109.40 [44], Bern-
         hard Locher 108.30 [55], Peter Rohner 108.25
         [56], Armin Vock 81.45 [90])

The entire team competition came down to the horizontal
bar routine of the Japanese star, Mitsuo Tsukahara. A
score above 9.5 would give Japan first place, while a score
below 9.5 would turn over the gold medal to the U.S.S.R.
Tsukahara came through in superb fashion and earned a
9.9 to ensure the fifth straight Japanese team victory.

1980 Moscow T: 9, N: 9, D: 7.22

		TOTAL PTS.
1. SOV	(Aleksandr Dityatin 118.40 [1], Nikolai Andrianov 118.15 [2], Eduard Azaryan 117.40 [4], Aleksandr Tkachyov 117.40 [4], Bogdan Makuts 116.95 [6], Vladimir Markelov 116.40 [9]	598.60
2. GDR	(Roland Brückner 116.90 [7], Michael Nikolay 116.50 [8], Lutz Hoffmann 115.75 [13], Ralf-Peter Hemmann 115.70 [14], Andreas Bronst 114.85 [15], Lutz Mack 114.00 [20])	581.15
3. HUN	(Ferenc Donáth 115.90 [11], Zoltán Magyar 115.85 [12], Péter Kovács 114.70 [18], György Guczoghy!113.85 [21], István Vamos 113.10 [27], Zoltán Kelemen 112.70 [33])	575.00
4. ROM	(Dănut Grecu 114.85 [15], Kurt Szilier 114.80 [17], Aurelian Georgescu 113.75 [22], Sorin Cepoi 113.55 [25], Nicolae Oprescu 112.95 [28], Romulus Bucuroiu 112.75 [32])	572.30
5. BUL	(Stoyan Delchev 117.50 [3], Dancho Yordanov 113.75 [22], Plamen Petkov 113.50 [26], Roumen Petkov 112.50 [34], Ognyan Bangiev 112.05 [39], Yanko Radanchev 111.60 [42])	571.55
6. CZE	(Jiří Tabák 115.95 [10], Rudolf Babiak 114.10 [19], Dan Zoulík 113.70 [24], Miroslav Kučeřik 112.10 [38], Jan Migdau 111.95 [40], Jozef Konečný 111.35 [43])	569.80
7. CUB	(Sergio Suarez Aime 112.50 [34], Roberto Leon Richards-Aguiar 112.45 [36], Miguel Arroyo 112.15 [37], Enrique Bravo 111.75 [41], Mario Castro 111.15 [46], Jorge Roche 83.40 [65])	563.20

8. FRA   (Michel Boutard 112.95 [28], Willi Moy 112.85   559.20
         [30], Henry Boerio 111.35 [43], Joel Suty
         111.25 [45], Yves Boquel 108.65 [59], Marc
         Touchais 108.10 [62])

Discontinued Events

COMBINED COMPETITION (4 EVENTS)

1904 St. Louis C: 10, N: 1, D: 10.29.

Events: PB, HB, PH, LHV

		PTS.
1. Anton Heida	USA	161
2. George Eyser	USA	152
3. William Merz	USA	135
4. John Duha	USA	—
5. Edward Hennig	USA	—

COMBINED COMPETITION (9 EVENTS)

1904 St. Louis C: 119, N: 3, D: 7.2.

		PTS.
1. Adolf Spinnler	SWI	43.49
2. Julius Lenhart	AUT	43.00
3. Wilhelm Weber	GER	41.60
4. Hugo Peitsch	GER	41.56
5. Otto Wiegand	GER	40.82
6. Otto Steffen	GER	39.53

ROPE CLIMBING

1896 Athens C: 5, N: 4, D: 4.10.

| 1. Nicolaos Andriakopoulos | GRE | 23.4 |
| 2. Thomas Xenakis | GRE | — |

1904 St. Louis C: ?, N: 1, D: 10.28.

1. George Eyser	USA	7.0
2. Charles Krause	USA	7.8
3. Emil Voigt	USA	9.8

1906 Athens C: 17, N: 4, D: 4.25.

1. Georgios Aliprantis	GRE	11.4
2. Béla Erody	HUN	13.8
3. Konstantinos Kozanitas	GRE	13.8
4. G. Georgantopoulos	ITA	14.0
5. Nicolaos Aliprantis	GRE	14.2
6. K. Pantzopoulos	GRE	14.8
7. G. Koemzopoulos	GRE	15.2
8. P. Pavlides	GRE	15.6

1908–1920 not held

1924 Paris C: 70, N: 9, D: 7.20.
1. Bedřich Supčik   CZE   7.2
2. Albert Séguin   FRA   7.4
3. August Güttinger   SWI   7.8
3. Ladislav Vácha   CZE   7.8
5. Stane Žilič   YUG   8.0
6. Jean Gounot   FRA   8.4
6. Arthur Hermann   FRA   8.4
6. Frank Kriz   USA   8.4
6. Ivan Porenta   YUG   8.4

Supčik was Czechoslovakia's first Olympic champion.

1928 not held

1932 Los Angeles C: 5, N: 2, D: 8.10.
1. Raymond Bass   USA   6.7
2. William Galbraith   USA   6.8
3. Thomas Connelly   USA   7.0
4. Miklós Péter   HUN   11.5
5. Péter Boros   HUN   11.6

CLUB SWINGING
1904 St. Louis C: 9, N: 1, D: 10.28.

                  PTS.
1. Edward Hennig   USA   13.0
2. Emil Voigt   USA   9.0
3. Ralph Wilson   USA   5.0

Hennig remained active in club swinging and won the American championship as late as 1951, when he was 71 years old.

1906–1928 not held

1932 Los Angeles C: 4, N: 2, D: 8.9.

                  PTS.
1. George Roth   USA   8.97
2. Philip Erenberg   USA   8.90
3. William Kuhlmeier   USA   8.63
4. Francisco Alvarez   MEX   8.47

SIDEHORSE VAULT
1924 Paris C: 70, N: 9, D: 7.20.

                  PTS.
1. Albert Séguin   FRA   10.00
2. François Gangloff   FRA   9.93
2. Jean Gounot   FRA   9.93
4. Slavko Hlastan   YUG   9.86
5. Stane Derganc   YUG   9.85
6. Bedřich Supčik   CZE   9.83
6. Ladislav Vácha   CZE   9.83
8. Eugene Cordonnier (FRA),
    M. Erang (LUX), Frank Kriz
    (USA), Robert Pražak
    (CZE)   9.80

TUMBLING
1932 Los Angeles C: 4, N: 2, D: 8.10.

                  PTS.
1. Rowland Wolfe   USA   18.90
2. Edward Gross   USA   18.67
3. William Hermann   USA   18.37
4. István Pelle   HUN   15.43

PARALLEL BARS—TEAM
1896 Athens T: 3, N: 2, D: 4.9.
1. GER   (Conrad Böcker, Alfred Flatow, Gustav Felix Flatow, Georg Hilmar, Fritz Manteuffel, Karl Neukirch, Richard Röstel, Gustav Schuft, Karl Schumann, Hermann Weingärtner)
2. GRE   (Panhellenic Club of Athens—Sotirios Athanasopoulos, Nicolaos Andriakopoulos, Petros Persakis, Thomas Yenakis)
3. GRE   (National Gymnastic Club of Athens—Ioannis Chrysaphis, Ioannis Mitropoulos, Dimitrios Loundras, Phillippos Karvelas)

HORIZONTAL BAR—TEAM
1896 Athens T: 1, N: 1, D: 4.9.
1. GER   (Conrad Böcker, Alfred Flatow, Gustav Felix Flatow, Georg Hilmar, Fritz Manteuffel, Karl Neukirch, Richard Röstel, Gustav Schuft, Karl Schumann, Hermann Weingärtner)

FREE EXERCISES AND APPARATUS—TEAM
1912 Stockholm T: 5, N: 5, D: 7.10.

                  TOTAL PTS.
1. NOR   (Isak Abrahamsen, Hans Beyer, Hartmann Björnson, Alfred Engelsen, Sigurd Jörgensen, Bjarne Johnsen, Knud Knudsen, Alf Lie, Rolf Lie, Tor Lund, Petter Martinsen, Per Mathiesen, Jacob Opdahl, Nils Opdahl, Bjarne Pettersen, Frithjof Saelen, Öistein Schirmer, Georg Selenius, Sigvard Sivertsen, Robert Sjursen, Einar Ström, Gabriel Thorstensen, Thomas Torstensen, Nils Voss)   114.25
2. FIN   (Kaarlo Ekholm, Eino Forsström, Ero Hyvarinen, Mikko Hyvärinen, Ilmari Keinänen, Hjalmari Kivenheimo, Karl Fredrick Lund, Arvid Rydman, Eino Saastamoinen, Aarne Salovaara, Heikki Sammallahti, Hannes Sirola, Klaus Uno Suomela, Lauri Tanner, Väino Tiiri, Kaarlo Vähämäki, Kaarlo Vasama, Tauno Ilmoniemi, Aarne Pelkonen, Ilmari Pernaja)   109.25
3. DEN   (Aksel Andersen, Hjalmar Andersen, Halvor Birch, Herman Grimmelmann, Aage Hansen, Arvor Hansen, Christian Hansen, Charles Jensen, Poul Jörgensen, Hjalmar Johansen, Poul Krebs, Viggo Madsen, Lucas Nielsen, Richard Nord-   106.25

ström, Oluf Olsen, Steen Olsen, Carl Pedersen, Christian Petersen, Niels Petersen, Christian Svendsen)

4. GER (Walter Engelmann, Adolf Seebass, Alfred Staats, Hans Roth, Arno Glockauer, Alexander Sperling, Kurt Reichenbach, Rudolf Korner, Erwin Buder, Wilhelm Brülle, Heinrich Pahner, Johannes Reuschle, Walter Jesinghaus, Eberhard Sorge, Karl Richter, Erich Worm, Karl Jordan, Hans Werner) — 84.25

5. LUX (Nicolas Adam, Charles Behm, André Bordang, Jean-Pierre Frantzen, François Hentges, Pierre Hentges, Michel Hemmerling, Jean-Baptiste Horn, Nicolas Kanivé, Emile Knepper, Nicolas Kummer, Marcel Langsam, Emile Lanners, Jean-Pierre Thommes, François Wagner, Antoine Wehrer, Ferdinand Wirtz, Joseph Zuang, Maurice Palgen) — 81.50

SWEDISH SYSTEM—TEAM

1912 Stockholm T: 3, N: 3, D: 7.8.

		TOTAL PTS.
1. SWE	(Per Daniel Bertilsson, Carl-Ehrenfried Carlberg, Nils Daniel Granfelt, Curt Hartzell, Oswald Holmberg, Anders Hylander, Axel Janse, Anders Boo	937.46

Kullberg, Sven Landberg, Per Nilsson, Benkt Rudolf Norelius, Axel Norling, Sven Rosén, Nils Silfverskiöld, Carl Silfverstrand, John Sörensson, Yngve Stiernspetz, Carl Erik Svensson, Karl Johan Svensson [Sarland], Knut Torell, Edvard Wennerholm, Claës Wersäll, David Wiman, Daniel Norling)

2. DEN (Sören Christensen, Ingvald Eriksen, Georg Falche, Thorkild Garp, Hans Trier Hansen, Johannes Hansen, Rasmus Hansen, Jens Kristian Jensen, Sören Alfred Jensen, Valdemar Jensen, Karl Kirk, Jens Kirkegaard, Olav Kjems, Carl Otto Larsen, Jens Peter Laursen, Marius Lefevre, Poul Sörensen Mark, Ejnar Olsen, Hans Pedersen, Hans Ejlert Pedersen, Aksel Sörensen, Martin Hansen Thau, Sören Thorborg, Kristen Möller Vadgaard, Peder Villemoes, Johannes Larsen Vinther, Olaf Pedersen, Peder Larsen Pedersen) — 898.84

3. NOR (Arthur Amundsen, Jorgen Andersen, Trygve Boyesen, Georg Brustad, Conrad Christensen, Oscar Engelstad, Marius Eriksen, Axel Henry Hansen, Petter Hol, Eugen Ingebretsen, Olof Ingebretsen, Olof Jacobsen, Erling Jensen, Thor Jensen, Fritjof Olsen, Oscar Olstad, Edvin Paulsen, Carl Alfred Pedersen, Rolf Roback, Sigurd Smebye, Thorleif Thorkildsen, Paul Pedersen) — 857.21

GYMNASTICS

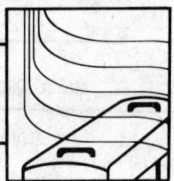

WOMEN
All-Around
Side Horse Vault
Asymmetrical (Uneven) Bars
Balance Beam

Floor Exercises
Team Combined Exercises
Rhythmic All-Around
Discontinued Events

WOMEN

ALL-AROUND

HV = Horse vault
AB = Asymmetrical (uneven) bars
BB = Balance beam
FE = Floor exercises

1896–1948 not held

1952 Helsinki C: 134, N: 18, D: 7.23.

			HV		AB		BB		FE		TOTAL PTS.
1.	Maria Gorokhovskaya	SOV	19.19	(2)	19.26	(2)	19.13	(2)	19.20	(2)	76.78
2.	Nina Bocharova	SOV	19.03	(6)	18.99	(4)	19.22	(1)	18.70	(10)	75.94
3.	Margit Korondi	HUN	18.40	(22)	19.40	(1)	19.02	(3)	19.00	(3)	75.82
4.	Galina Minaicheva	SOV	19.16	(3)	18.89	(8)	18.66	(10)	18.96	(6)	75.67
5.	Galina Urbanovich	SOV	19.10	(5)	18.62	(12)	18.93	(5)	18.99	(4)	75.64
6.	Ágnes Keleti	HUN	18.10	(41)	19.16	(3)	18.96	(4)	19.36	(1)	75.58
7.	Pelageya Danilova	SOV	18.62	(12)	18.99	(7)	18.76	(9)	18.60	(11)	75.03
8.	Galina Shamrai	SOV	18.93	(7)	18.39	(23)	18.79	(8)	18.86	(8)	74.97

1956 Melbourne C: 65, N: 15, D: 12.5.

			HV		AB		BB		FE		TOTAL PTS.
1.	Larissa Latynina	SOV	18.833	(1)	18.333	(2)	18.533	(4)	18.733	(1)	74.933
2.	Ágnes Keleti	HUN	18.133	(23)	18.966	(1)	18.80	(1)	18.733	(1)	74.633
3.	Sofia Muratova	SOV	18.666	(5)	18.80	(3)	18.433	(10)	18.566	(4)	74.466
4.	Elena Leuştean	ROM	18.633	(6)	18.533	(10)	18.50	(6)	18.70	(3)	74.366
4.	Olga Tass	HUN	18.733	(3)	18.633	(6)	18.466	(7)	18.533	(7)	74.366
6.	Tamara Manina	SOV	18.80	(2)	18.333	(16)	18.633	(2)	18.466	(9)	74.233
7.	Eva Bosáková	CZE	18.166	(22)	18.733	(4)	18.633	(2)	18.566	(4)	74.10
8.	Helena Rakoczy	POL	18.50	(7)	18.70	(5)	18.133	(16)	18.366	(14)	73.70

The 1956 competition was dominated by 35-year-old Ágnes Keleti and 21-year-old Larissa Latynina. Keleti captured gold medals on three of the four apparatuses, but a lapse on the vault lost her the All-Around title to Latynina, a Ukrainian from Kherson. Starting with the team event of 1948 and continuing through 1956 Keleti won ten Olympic medals: five gold, four silver, and one bronze. After the games she decided not to return to Hungary. Instead she stayed in Australia and eventually settled in Israel.

1960 Rome C: 124, N: 27, D: 9.8.

		HV		AB		BB		FE		TOTAL PTS.
1. Larissa Latynina	SOV	18.966	(3)	19.433	(2)	19.066	(3)	19.566	(1)	77.031
2. Sofia Muratova	SOV	19.032	(2)	19.299	(3)	19.132	(2)	19.233	(4)	76.696
3. Polina Astakhova	SOV	18.766	(4)	19.633	(1)	18.233	(28)	19.532	(2)	76.164
4. Margarita Nikolayeva	SOV	19.10	(1)	18.799	(20)	18.966	(4)	18.966	(15)	75.831
5. Sonia Iovan	ROM	18.732	(6)	19.266	(4)	18.60	(11)	19.199	(5)	75.797
6. Keiko Ikeda (Tanaka)	JAP	18.432	(18)	19.266	(4)	18.932	(5)	19.066	(12)	75.696
7. Lidiya Ivanova	SOV	18.566	(8)	19.053	(7)	18.699	(8)	19.133	(7)	75.431
8. Vera Čáslavská	CZE	18.699	(7)	18.733	(21)	18.766	(6)	19.10	(9)	75.298

1964 Tokyo C: 86, N: 24, D: 10.21.

		HV		AB		BB		FE		TOTAL PTS.
1. Vera Čáslavská	CZE	19.50	(1)	19.432	(1)	19.366	(1)	19.266	(3)	77.564
2. Larissa Latynina	SOV	19.166	(5)	19.133	(4)	19.233	(3)	19.466	(1)	76.998
3. Polina Astakhova	SOV	19.032	(7)	19.333	(2)	19.20	(5)	19.40	(2)	76.965
4. Birgit Radochla	GDR	19.366	(2)	18.933	(13)	18.933	(9)	19.199	(5)	76.431
5. Hana Ružičková	CZE	18.866	(18)	19.033	(7)	19.232	(4)	18.966	(10)	76.097
6. Keiko Ikeda (Tanaka)	JAP	18.999	(9)	18.766	(16)	19.166	(6)	19.10	(7)	76.031
7. Toshiko Aihara (Shirasu)	JAP	19.233	(3)	19.099	(5)	18.599	(29)	19.066	(8)	75.997
8. Yelena Volchetskaya	SOV	19.233	(3)	18.633	(24)	18.966	(7)	18.933	(13)	75.765

Latynina collected six more Olympic medals to bring her career total to an unprecedented 18: nine gold, five silver, and four bronze. But in Tokyo she lost the All-Around title to a new star, Vera Čáslavská, a 22-year-old secretary from Prague.

1968 Mexico City C: 101, N: 24, D: 10.25.

		HV		AB		BB		FE		TOTAL PTS.
1. Vera Čáslavská	CZE	19.75	(1)	19.50	(1)	19.45	(2)	19.55	(2)	78.25
2. Zinaida Voronina	SOV	19.40	(5)	19.25	(4)	18.80	(15)	19.40	(4)	76.85
3. Natalya Kuchinskaya	SOV	19.45	(3)	18.10	(37)	19.60	(15)	19.60	(1)	76.75
4. Larissa Petrik	SOV	19.20	(8)	18.95	(11)	19.00	(5)	19.55	(2)	76.70
4. Erika Zuchold	GDR	19.65	(2)	19.05	(6)	19.00	(5)	19.00	(8)	76.70
6. Karin Janz	GDR	19.20	(8)	19.30	(2)	19.05	(4)	19.00	(8)	76.55
7. Olga Karasseva	SOV	19.15	(10)	19.00	(7)	18.70	(18)	19.15	(5)	76.00
7. Bohumila Řimnácová	CZE	18.70	(24)	19.30	(2)	18.85	(10)	19.15	(5)	76.00

The undisputed heroine of the Mexico City Olympics was defending All-Around champion Vera Čáslavská. She arrived in Mexico with the rest of the Czech team two months after her country had been occupied by troops from the U.S.S.R. After one of her performances on the balance beam received a 9.6, the audience spent ten minutes booing, howling, and chanting "Ver-a, Ver-a," until finally her mark was upped to 9.8. The last performer in the final event, Čáslavská thrilled her admirers by performing her floor exercise to the tune of "The Mexican Hat

Dance." She eventually earned four gold medals and two silver to add to the three gold and two silver she had won four years earlier in Tokyo. In the floor exercises she shared first place with Larissa Petrik of the Soviet Union, which meant that the two women stood together on the top platform at the medal ceremony and listened first to Czechoslovakia's national anthem and then to the U.S.S.R.'s. Political observers noted that Čáslavská bowed her head and turned away during the playing of the Soviet anthem. Twenty-four hours later Čáslavská topped off her week by marrying Czechoslovak 1500-meter champion Josef Odlozil. After a civil ceremony at the Czechoslovakian ambassador's house, the happy couple pushed their way through a mob of 10,000 people to get to the altar of the Roman Catholic church in Xocalo Square.

1972 Munich C: 118, N: 23, D: 10.30

		HV		AB		BB		FE		TOTAL PTS.
1. Lyudmila Tourischeva	SOV	19.30	(1)	19.275	(3)	18.80	(5)	19.65	(1)	77.025
2. Karin Janz	GDR	19.275	(2)	19.475	(1)	18.825	(4)	19.30	(3)	76.875
3. Tamara Lazakovitch	SOV	19.00	(6)	19.225	(4)	19.325	(1)	19.30	(3)	76.85
4. Erika Zuchold	GDR	19.275	(2)	19.30	(2)	18.80	(5)	19.075	(6)	76.45
5. Liubov Burda	SOV	19.075	(5)	18.875	(8)	18.675	(8)	19.15	(5)	75.775
6. Angelika Hellmann	GDR	18.925	(7)	19.15	(5)	18.425	(14)	19.05	(7)	75.55
7. Olga Korbut	SOV	19.175	(4)	17.15	(35)	19.30	(2)	19.475	(2)	75.10
8. Elvira Saadi	SOV	18.80	(9)	18.70	(15)	18.625	(10)	18.95	(9)	75.075

Vera Čáslavská had played a major role in popularizing women's gymnastics, but the real turning point came at the 1972 Munich Olympics. The All-Around championship was won by 19-year-old world champion Lyudmila Tourischeva, and the silver medal went to Karin Janz of Berlin, who also took first place on the horse vault and the uneven parallel bars. But it was neither of these capable young women who focused the attention of the world on gymnastics. Instead it was the seventh-place finisher, a 4-foot 11-inch, 85-pound 17-year-old from Grodno in Byelorussia—Olga Korbut.

Korbut was trained by the eccentric Renald Knysh, who kept a card file on all the young married couples in Grodno, particularly those whom he thought might produce future gymnasts. Olga qualified for the Olympics as an alternate and was allowed to compete only after a teammate was injured. During the team competition she caught the public's eye with a spectacular routine on the uneven parallel bars. By the end of the day it looked as if Olga had a good chance of pulling an upset and depriving Tourischeva of the All-Around championship. But the next day disaster struck. The crowd watched in silence as she started her performance on the uneven bars. She scuffed her feet on the mat as she mounted, then slipped off the bars during a later move; finally, she missed a simple kip to remount. The judges gave her a 7.5, and she was effectively eliminated from the race for All-Around champion. She returned to her seat to weep with disappointment.

Twenty hours later Olga Korbut was back in the arena to compete for the championships on the four individual apparatuses. With millions of people all over the world watching, Olga regained her form, finished second to Karin Janz on the uneven parallel bars, and won the gold medal for both the balance beam and the floor exercises. In the United States, despite antipathy to the U.S.S.R, little Olga Korbut's dramatic cycle of success, failure, and success captured the national imagination. Korbut never did beat Tourischeva, though, and it must have been confusing, at the very least, to the Soviet champion to realize that no matter how successful she was, she could never achieve the popularity of Olga Korbut.

1976 Montreal C: 86, N: 18, D: 7.19.

		HV		AB		BB		FE		TOTAL PTS.
1. Nadia Comaneci	ROM	19.625	(4)	20.00	(1)	19.95	(1)	19.70	(3)	79.275
2. Nelli Kim	SOV	19.85	(1)	19.725	(2)	19.30	(5)	19.80	(2)	78.675
3. Lyudmila Tourischeva	SOV	19.75	(2)	19.575	(9)	19.475	(3)	19.825	(1)	78.625
4. Teodora Ungureanu	ROM	19.425	(7)	19.80	(2)	19.70	(2)	19.45	(5)	78.375
5. Olga Korbut	SOV	19.525	(6)	19.80	(2)	19.325	(4)	19.375	(6)	78.025
6. Gitta Escher	GDR	19.65	(3)	19.625	(8)	19.125	(7)	19.35	(8)	77.75
7. Márta Egervári	HUN	19.60	(5)	19.775	(4)	18.725	(10)	19.225	(9)	77.325
8. Marion Kische	GDR	19.325	(10)	19.70	(6)	18.55	(14)	19.375	(6)	76.95

Soviet women's gymnastics went through a period of turmoil and crisis between 1972 and 1976. When a Soviet team made an exhibition tour of the United States, the leader of the group was Lyudmila Tourischeva and the highlighted performer was their up-and-coming star Nelli Kim. But Americans showed little interest in Tourischeva and Kim; instead they turned out by the thousands to see Olga Korbut, the Munchkin of Munich. It didn't take long for Olga to realize that huge profits were being made on her popularity, and she became more demanding of rewards for herself. When she insisted on going shopping for gifts for her family, Soviet officials were forced to allow it.

Back home, however, where heroes were measured by the number of medals they won and by their willingness to follow orders and be team players, Olga Korbut had become a thorn in the side of the Soviet bureaucracy. The situation was also hard on Tourischeva, who had always toed the party line and yet was forced to play second fiddle to an inferior gymnast. In his book *The Big Red Machine*, Yuri Brodkin tells of the shock and betrayal experienced by Tourischeva when, two days before the opening of the Montreal Olympics, the Soviet Training Council decided to remove her from her role of team captain and give the designation to Olga Korbut instead.

However the real threat to the competitive success of the Soviet team came not from internal dissension, but from a 4-foot 11-inch Romanian named Nadia Comaneci. Born in Onesti, Moldavia, Nadia had been trained as a gymnast since the age of 6. In 1975 she dethroned five-time European champion Tourischeva. At Montreal she was considered a slight favorite to take the All-Around championship even though she was only 14 years old. During the team competition she made Olympic history by receiving the first perfect scores of ten for her performances on the uneven bars and the balance beam. Before the Olympics were over, Nadia had been awarded seven 10s, while Nelli Kim had earned two perfect scores for her vault and floor exercise. Despite their superb performances, Korbut and Tourischeva were left with tears of disappointment. Tourischeva, in fact, won four medals, to bring her Olympic totals to four gold, two silver, and three bronze.

Nadia Comaneci didn't have the charisma of Olga Korbut, but she was an incredible athlete who was absolutely unafraid of dangerous moves and seemingly oblivious to the millions of people watching her. The most difficult part of the Olympics for Nadia were the obligatory press conferences. Many journalists seemed to forget her age. When one asked what her greatest wish was, she replied, "I want to go home." When another asked if she had plans for retirement, Nadia reminded him, "I'm only 14."

In an attempt to lessen the dominance of the nations strongest in gymnastics, a ruling had been passed prior to the Olympics that only three gymnasts from each country could compete in the final round of 36. The absurdity of this decision was shown when Elvira Saadi, who had achieved the seventh highest score during the individual competitions, was eliminated because she was the fourth-best Soviet performer, while Monique Bolleboom of Holland was allowed to continue even though she ranked 62nd out of 86. Not surprisingly, Bolleboom finished last in the final round.

1980 Moscow C: 62, N: 16, D: 7.24.

		HV		AB		BB		FE		TOTAL PTS.
1. Yelena Davydova	SOV	19.80	(4)	19.70	(6)	19.70	(4)	19.80	(5)	79.15
2. Nadia Comaneci	ROM	19.85	(1)	19.45	(12)	19.90	(1)	19.85	(1)	79.075
2. Maxi Gnauck	GDR	19.85	(1)	19.95	(1)	19.70	(4)	19.85	(1)	79.075
4. Natalya Shaposhnikova	SOV	19.80	(4)	19.75	(3)	19.75	(3)	19.85	(1)	79.025
5. Nelli Kim	SOV	19.65	(7)	19.75	(3)	19.70	(4)	19.85	(1)	78.425
6. Emilia Eberle	ROM	19.60	(8)	19.90	(2)	19.80	(2)	19.80	(5)	78.40
7. Rodica Dunka	ROM	19.70	(6)	19.50	(11)	19.70	(4)	19.60	(8)	78.35
8. Steffi Kräker	GDR	19.85	(1)	19.75	(3)	19.55	(9)	19.35	(13)	78.20

The contest for All-Around champion came down to the final apparatus. If Nadia Comaneci could score 9.95 on the balance beam, she would win outright. If she scored 9.9 she would share the gold medal with a surprising 18-year-old: 4-foot 10-inch Yelena Davydova. Since Nadia had previously been awarded a 9.9 and a 10 on the balance beam, it was quite possible that she could earn the higher mark. With the arena in complete silence, she went through her routine magnificently with only the slightest flaw following a forward flip with a half-twist. It seemed as if she had made it. But her score was not forthcoming. For 28 minutes the judges argued. Finally Nadia's score was flashed on the computer: 9.85, thanks to 9.8s awarded by the judges from Poland and the U.S.S.R. The next day Nadia took first place in the beam and the floor exercise events, giving her an Olympic total of five gold medals, three silver, and one bronze.

SIDE HORSE VAULT
1896–1948 not held

1952 Helsinki C: 134, N: 18, D: 7.23.

		PTS.
1. Yekaterina Kalinchuk	SOV	19.20
2. Maria Gorokhovskaya	SOV	19.19
3. Galina Minaicheva	SOV	19.16
4. Medeya Dschugeli	SOV	19.13
5. Galina Urbanovich	SOV	19.10
6. Nina Bocharova	SOV	19.03
7. Karin Lindberg	SWE	18.79
7. Helena Rakoczy	POL	18.79

1956 Melbourne C: 65, N: 15, D: 12.5.

		PTS.
1. Larissa Latynina	SOV	18.833
2. Tamara Manina	SOV	18.80
3. Ann-Sofi Colling-Pettersson	SWE	18.733
3. Olga Tass	HUN	18.733
5. Sofia Muratova	SOV	18.666
6. Elena Leuştean	ROM	18.633
7. Natalia Kot	POL	18.50
7. Helena Rakoczy	POL	18.50

1960 Rome C: 124, N: 27, D: 9.9.

		PTS.
1. Margarita Nikolayeva	SOV	19.316
2. Sofia Muratova	SOV	19.049
3. Larissa Latynina	SOV	19.016
4. Adolfina Tačová	CZE	18.783
5. Sonia Iovan	ROM	18.766
6. Polina Astakhova	SOV	18.716

1964 Tokyo C: 82, N: 23, D: 10.22.

		PTS.
1. Vera Čáslavská	CZE	19.483
2. Larissa Latynina	SOV	19.283
2. Birgit Radochla	GDR	19.283
4. Toshiko Aihara (Shirasu)	JAP	19.282
5. Yelena Volchetskaya	SOV	19.149
6. Ute Starke	GDR	19.116

1968 Mexico City C: 101, N: 24, D: 10.25.

		PTS.
1. Vera Čáslavská	CZE	19.775
2. Erika Zuchold	GDR	19.625
3. Zinaida Voronina	SOV	19.50
4. Maria Krajčirová	CZE	19.475
5. Natalya Kutschinskaya	SOV	19.375
6. Miroslava Skleničková	CZE	19.325

1972 Munich C: 118, N: 23, D: 8.31.

		PTS.
1. Karin Janz	GDR	19.525
2. Erika Zuchold	GDR	19.275
3. Lyudmila Tourischeva	SOV	19.25
4. Lyubov Burda	SOV	19.225
5. Olga Korbut	SOV	19.175
6. Tamara Lazakovitch	SOV	19.05

1976 Montreal C: 86, N: 18, D: 7.22.

		PTS.
1. Nelli Kim	SOV	19.80
2. Carola Dombeck	GDR	19.65
2. Lyudmila Tourischeva	SOV	19.65
4. Nadia Comaneci	ROM	19.625
5. Gitta Escher	GDR	19.55
6. Márta Egervári	HUN	19.45

1980 Moscow C: 62, N: 16, D: 7.25.

		PTS.
1. Natalya Shaposhnikova	SOV	19.725
2. Steffi Kräker	GDR	19.675
3. Melita Rühn	ROM	19.65
4. Yelena Davydova	SOV	19.575
5. Nadia Comaneci	ROM	19.35
6. Maxi Gnauck	GDR	19.30

ASYMMETRICAL (UNEVEN) BARS
1896–1948 not held

1952 Helsinki C: 134, N: 19, D: 7.23.

		PTS.
1. Margit Korondi	HUN	19.40
2. Maria Gorokhovskaya	SOV	19.26
3. Ágnes Keleti	HUN	19.16
4. Nina Bocharova	SOV	18.99
4. Pelageya Danilova	SOV	18.99
6. Edit Perényi-Weckinger	HUN	18.96
7. Galina Shamrai	SOV	18.93
8. Galina Minaicheva	SOV	18.89

1956 Melbourne C: 65, N: 15, D: 12.5.

		PTS.
1. Ágnes Keleti	HUN	18.966
2. Larissa Latynina	SOV	18.833
3. Sofia Muratova	SOV	18.80
4. Eva Bosáková	CZE	18.733
5. Helena Rakoczy	POL	18.70
6. Alíz Kertész	HUN	18.633
6. Olga Tass	HUN	18.633
8. Natalia Kot	POL	18.60

1960 Rome C: 124, N: 27, D: 9.9.

		PTS.
1. Polina Astakhova	SOV	19.616
2. Larissa Latynina	SOV	19.416
3. Tamara Lyukhina	SOV	19.399
4. Sofia Muratova	SOV	19.382
5. Keiko Ikeda (Tanaka)	JAP	19.333
6. Sonia Iovan	ROM	19.099

The audience was so upset by the low scoring of Ikeda's final routine that they booed for ten minutes until Astakhova stepped up for her turn.

1964 Tokyo C: 82, N: 23, D: 10.22.

		PTS.
1. Polina Astakhova	SOV	19.332
2. Katalin Makray	HUN	19.216
3. Larissa Latynina	SOV	19.199
4. Toshiko Aihara (Shirasu)	JAP	18.782
5. Vera Čáslavská	CZE	18.416
6. Tamara Zamotailova (Lyukhina)	SOV	17.833

1968 Mexico City C: 101, N: 24, D: 10.25.

		PTS.
1. Vera Čáslavská	CZE	19.65
2. Karin Janz	GDR	19.50
3. Zinaida Voronina	SOV	19.425
4. Bohumila Řimnácová	CZE	19.35
5. Erika Zuchold	GDR	19.325
6. Miroslava Skleničková	CZE	18.20

1972 Munich C: 118, N: 23, D: 8.31.

		PTS.
1. Karin Janz	GDR	19.675
2. Olga Korbut	SOV	19.45
2. Erika Zuchold	GDR	19.45
4. Lyudmila Tourischeva	SOV	19.425
5. Ilona Békési	HUN	19.275
6. Angelika Hellmann	GDR	19.20

1976 Montreal C: 86, N: 18, D: 7.22.

		PTS.
1. Nadia Comaneci	ROM	20.00
2. Teodora Ungureanu	ROM	19.80
3. Márta Egervári	HUN	19.775
4. Marion Kische	GDR	19.75
5. Olga Korbut	SOV	19.30
6. Nelli Kim	SOV	19.225

1980 Moscow C: 62, N: 16, D: 7.25.

		PTS.
1. Maxi Gnauck	GDR	19.875
2. Emilia Eberle	ROM	19.85
3. Maria Filatova	SOV	19.775
3. Steffi Kräker	GDR	19.775
3. Melita Rühn	ROM	19.775
6. Nelli Kim	SOV	19.725

BALANCE BEAM

1896–1948 not held

1952 Helsinki C: 134, N: 18, D: 7.23.

		PTS.
1. Nina Bocharova	SOV	19.22
2. Maria Gorokhovskaya	SOV	19.13
3. Margit Korondi	HUN	19.02
4. Ágnes Keleti	HUN	18.96
5. Galina Urbanovich	SOV	18.93
6. Tsvetana Stancheva	BUL	18.86
6. Olga Tass	HUN	18.86
8. Galina Shamrai	SOV	18.79

1956 Melbourne C: 65, N: 15, D: 12.5.

		PTS.
1. Ágnes Keleti	HUN	18.80
2. Eva Bosáková	CZE	18.633
2. Tamara Manina	SOV	18.633
4. Larissa Latynina	SOV	18.533
4. Anna Marejkova	CZE	18.533
6. Elena Leuştean	ROM	18.50
7. Margit Korondi	HUN	18.466
7. Olga Tass	HUN	18.466
7. Lyudmila Yegorova	SOV	18.466

1960 Rome C: 124, N: 27, D: 9.9.

		PTS.
1. Eva Bosáková	CZE	19.283
2. Larissa Latynina	SOV	19.233
3. Sofia Muratova	SOV	19.232
4. Margarita Nikolayeva	SOV	19.183
5. Keiko Ikeda (Tanaka)	JAP	19.132
6. Vera Čáslavská	CZE	19.083

1964 Tokyo C: 83, N: 24, D: 10.23.

		PTS.
1. Vera Čáslavská	CZE	19.449
2. Tamara Manina	SOV	19.399
3. Larissa Latynina	SOV	19.382
4. Polina Astakhova	SOV	19.366
5. Hana Růžčková	CZE	19.349
6. Keiko Ikeda (Tanaka)	JAP	19.216

1968 Mexico City C: 101, N: 24, D: 10.25.

		PTS.
1. Natalya Kuchinskaya	SOV	19.65
2. Vera Čáslavská	CZE	19.575
3. Larissa Petrik	SOV	19.25
4. Karin Janz	GDR	19.225
4. Linda Metheny	USA	19.225
6. Erika Zuchold	GDR	19.150

1972 Munich C: 118, N: 23, D: 8.31.

			PTS.
1.	Olga Korbut	SOV	19.40
2.	Tamara Lazakovitch	SOV	19.375
3.	Karin Janz	GDR	18.975
4.	Mónika Császár	HUN	18.925
5.	Lyudmila Tourischeva	SOV	18.80
6.	Erika Zuchold	GDR	18.70

1976 Montreal C: 86, N: 18, D: 7.22.

			PTS.
1.	Nadia Comaneci	ROM	19.95
2.	Olga Korbut	SOV	19.725
3.	Teodora Ungureanu	ROM	19.70
4.	Lyudmila Tourischeva	SOV	19.475
5.	Angelika Hellmann	GDR	19.45
6.	Gitta Escher	GDR	19.275

1980 Moscow C: 62, N: 16, D: 7.25.

			PTS.
1.	Nadia Comaneci	ROM	19.80
2.	Yelena Davydova	SOV	19.75
3.	Natalya Shaposhnikova	SOV	19.725
4.	Maxi Gnauck	GDR	19.70
5.	Radka Zemanová	CZE	19.65
6.	Emilia Eberle	ROM	19.40

FLOOR EXERCISES

1896–1948 not held

1952 Helsinki C: 134, N: 18, D: 7.23.

			PTS.
1.	Ágnes Keleti	HUN	19.36
2.	Maria Gorokhovskaya	SOV	19.20
3.	Margit Korondi	HUN	19.00
4.	Erzsébet Gulyás	HUN	18.99
4.	Galina Urbanovich	SOV	18.99
6.	Galina Minaicheva	SOV	18.96
7.	Olga Tass	HUN	18.89
8.	Galina Shamrai	SOV	18.86

1956 Melbourne C: 65, N: 15, D: 12.5.

			PTS.
1.	Ágnes Keleti	HUN	18.733
1.	Larissa Latynina	SOV	18.733
3.	Elena Leuştean	ROM	18.70
4.	Eva Bosáková	CZE	18.566
4.	Sofia Muratova	SOV	18.566
4.	Keiko Tanaka	JAP	18.566
7.	Olga Tass	HUN	18.533
8.	Doris Hedberg	SWE	18.50

1960 Rome C: 124, N: 27, D: 9.9.

			PTS.
1.	Larissa Latynina	SOV	19.583
2.	Polina Astakhova	SOV	19.532
3.	Tamara Lyukhina	SOV	19.449
4.	Eva Bosáková	CZE	19.383
5.	Sofia Muratova	SOV	19.349
6.	Sonia Iovan	ROM	19.232

1964 Tokyo C: 83, N: 24, D: 23.10.

			PTS.
1.	Larissa Latynina	SOV	19.599
2.	Polina Astakhova	SOV	19.50
3.	Anikó Jánosi-Ducza	HUN	19.30
4.	Birgit Radochla	GDR	19.299
5.	Ingrid Föst	GDR	19.266
6.	Vera Čáslavská	CZE	19.099

1968 Mexico City C: 101, N: 24, D: 10.20.

			PTS.
1.	Vera Čáslavská	CZE	19.675
1.	Larissa Petrik	SOV	19.675
3.	Natalya Kuchinskaya	SOV	19.650
4.	Zinaida Voronina	SOV	19.550
5.	Olga Karasseva	SOV	19.325
5.	Bohumila Řimnácová	CZE	19.325

1972 Munich C: 118, N: 23, D: 10.25.

			PTS.
1.	Olga Korbut	SOV	19.575
2.	Lyudmila Tourischeva	SOV	19.55
3.	Tamara Lazakovitch	SOV	19.45
4.	Karin Janz	GDR	19.40
5.	Lyubov Burda	SOV	19.10
5.	Angelika Hellmann	GDR	19.10

1976 Montreal C: 86, N: 18, D: 7.22.

			PTS.
1.	Nelli Kim	SOV	19.85
2.	Lyudmila Tourischeva	SOV	19.825
3.	Nadia Comaneci	ROM	19.75
4.	Anna Pohludková	CZE	19.575
5.	Marion Kische	GDR	19.475
6.	Gitta Escher	GDR	19.45

1980 C: 62, N: 16, D: 7.25.

			PTS.
1.	Nadia Comaneci	ROM	19.875
1.	Nelli Kim	SOV	19.875
3.	Maxi Gnauck	GDR	19.825
3.	Natalya Shaposhnikova	SOV	19.825
5.	Emilia Eberle	ROM	19.75
6.	Jana Labáková	CZE	19.725

TEAM COMBINED EXERCISES
1896–1924 not held

1928 Amsterdam T: 5, N: 5, D: 8.10.

			TOTAL PTS.
1.	HOL	(Petronella van Randwijk, Jacomina van den Berg, Annie Polak, Helena Nordheim, Alida Johanna van den Bos, Hendrika Alida van Rumt, Anna Maria van der Vegt, Elka de Levie, Jacoba Cornelia Stelma, Estella Agsteribbe, Petronella Burgerhof, Jud Simons)	316.75
2.	ITA	(Bianca Ambrosetti, Lavinia Gianoni, Luigina Perversi, Diana Pizzavini, Luigina Giavotti, Anna Tanzini, Carolina Tronconi, Ines Vercesi, Rita Vittadini, Virginia Giorgi, Germana Malabarba, Clara Marangoni)	289.00
3.	GBR	(Margaret Hartley, E. Carrie Pickles, Annie Broadbent, Amy Jagger, Ada Smith, Lucy Desmond, Doris Woods, Jessie Kite, Queenie Judd, Midge Moreman, Ethel Seymour, Hilda Smith)	258.25
4.	HUN	(Mária Hámos, Aranka Hennyei, Anna Kael, Margit Pályi, Erzsébet Rudas, Nandorné Szeiler, Ilona Szöllösi, Judit Tóth, Rudolfné Herpich, Irén Hennyey, Margit Kövessy, Irén Rudas)	256.50
5.	FRA	(Honorine Delescluse, Louise Delescluse, R. Oger, Georgette Meulebrouck, Mathilde Bataille, Galuelle Dhont, Valentine Héméryck, Jeanne Vanoverloop, Paulette Houteer, Berthe Verstraete, Genevieve Vankiersbilck, Antonie Straeteman)	247.50

1932 not held

1936 Berlin T: 8, N: 8, D: 8.12.

			TOTAL PTS.
1.	GER	(Trudi Meyer 67.55 [1], Erna Bürger 67.45 [2], Käthe Sohnemann 67.05 [3], Isolde Frölian 65.75 [8], Anita Bärwirth 65.45 [9], Paula Pöhlsen 65.00 [12], Friedel Iby 63.75 [17], Julie Schmitt 62.10 [27])	506.50
2.	CZE	(Vlasta Foltová 66.45 [5], Vlasta Dekanová 65.95 [6], Zdenka Veřmiřovska 65.90 [7], Matylda Pálfyová 64.10 [16], Anna Hřebřinová 62.70 [21], Božena Dobešová 62.65 [22], Marie Vetrovská 60.25 [38], Marie Bajerová 59.35 [45])	503.60
3.	HUN	(Margit Csillik 65.30 [11], Judit Tóth 64.70 [13], Margit Sándor-Nagy 64.55 [15], Gabriella Mészáros 63.05 [19], Eszter Voit 62.90 [20], Olga Törös 61.90 [30], Ilona Madary 61.25 [33], Margit Kalocsai 59.85 [41])	499.00

4.	YUG	(Dušica Radivojevič 62.30 [25], Lidica Rupnik 62.25 [26], Marta Pustišek 62.00 [28], Olga Rajkovič 62.00 [28], Drogana Djordjevič 61.20 [34], Angelina Kopurenko 60.75 [35], Katarina Hribar 60.60 [36], Maja Veršec 58.65 [46])	485.60
5.	USA	(Consetta Caruccio 66.85 [4], Jennie Caputo 65.45 [9], Irma Haubold 62.45 [23], Margaret Duff 60.50 [37], Ada Lunardoni 60.25 [38], Adelaide Meyer 56.55 [50], Mary Wright 55.10 [54], Marie Kibler 5.75 [injured])	471.60
6.	POL	(Klara Sierońska 64.65 [14], Marta Majowska 63.15 [18], Matylda Osadnik 62.45 [23], Wislawa Noskiewicz 61.40 [32], Janina Skirlińska 60.20 [40], Alina Cichecka 59.70 [44], Julia Wojciechowska 57.87 [47], Stefania Krupowa 56.95 [49])	470.30
7.	ITA	(Canella 61.75 [31], Bimbocci 59.75 [42], Cividino 59.75 [42], Toso 57.60 [48], Cipriotto 55.35 [52], A. Avanzini 55.20 [53], V. Avanzini 54.75 [55], Guaita 51.40 [59])	442.05
8.	GBR	(Heaton 56.15 [51], Kelly 53.70 [56], Ridgewell 53.00 [57], Blake 52.45 [58], Crowe 49.00 [60], Hanson 49.00 [60], Wharton 46.95 [62], Gross 43.84 [63])	408.30

1948 London T: 11, N: 11, D: 8.14.

			TOTAL PTS.
1.	CZE	(Zdenka Honsová 54.85 [1], Miloslava Misáková 53.40 [4], Vera Ružičkova 53.00 [7], Božena Srncová 52.95 [8], Milena Mullerová 52.50 [10], Zdenka Veřmiřovská 50.00 [23], Olga Silhanová 49.95 [24], Marie Kovářová 49.60 [26])	445.45
2.	HUN	(Edit Perényi-Weckinger 54.25 [2], Mária Kova 53.40 [4], Irén Kárpàti-Karcsics 53.26 [6], Erzébet Gulyás-Köteles 52.25 [12], Erzsébet Balázs 52.10 [13], Olga Tass 51.45 [15], Anna Fehér 49.15 [28], Margit Sandor-Nagy 39.10 [74])	440.55
3.	USA	(Helen Schifano 51.70 [14], Clara Schroth 51.05 [17], Meta Elste 50.90 [18], Marian Barone 50.30 [19], Ladislava Bakanic 50.10 [20], Consetta Lenz [Caruccia] 49.10 [29], Anita Simonis 47.80 [39], Dorothy Dalton 47.65 [41])	422.63
4.	SWE	(Karin Lindberg 52.70 [9], Kerstin Bohman 51.40 [16], Ingrid Sandahl 51.00 [18], Göta Pettersson 50.10 [21], Gunnel Johansson 49.10 [29], Märta Andersson 49.05 [30], E. Ingrid Andersson 47.10 [47], Stina Haage 39.10 [74])	417.95
5.	HOL	(Jacoba Tonneman 52.50 [10], Helena Gerrietsen 49.50 [27], Jacoba Wijnands 47.25 [44], Johanna Ros 45.75 [54], Anna Maria van Geene 45.45 [57], Klassje Post 44.80 [62], Geertruida Heil-Bonnet 42.55 [67], Barendina Meijer-Haantjes 38.30 [78])	408.35
6.	AUT	(Gertrude Fesl 51.05 [17], Gretchen Hehenberger 50.00 [23], Gertrude Kolar 48.65 [36], Edeltraud Schramm 45.10 [60], Erika Enzenhofer 38.95 [76])	405.45

7. YUG (V. Gerbec 49.00 [34], D. Djordjevic 47.60 [42],   397.90
R. Vojsk 47.20, [45] D. Djipalovic 47.15 [46],
Tanja Zutic 45.25 [58], D. Basletic 42.70 [66],
Z. Mijatovic 40.35 [72], N. Cerne 24.70 [88])

8. ITA (L. Micheli 53.65 [3], E. Santoni 47.55 [43], Li-   394.20
cia Macchini 46.3 [52], V. Nuti 45.75 [54], L.
Torriani 45.10 [60], Renata Bianchi 43.25 [65],
N. Jcardi 40.70 [70], L. Pezzoni 28.2 [85])

In gymnastics, as in other sports in which scoring is dependent on subjective judging, controversies and partisan decisions are commonplace. But a special level of incompetence was displayed by one of the judges in the 1948 women's gymnastics competition when, scoring on a scale of one through ten, she awarded one gymnast a 13.1. The major benefactors of the strange scoring standards of 1948 were the Czechoslovakians, who won the gold medal under dramatic circumstances. Shortly after the Czech team arrived in London, one of its members, 22-year-old Eliska Misáková, was taken ill and confined to an iron lung. The day of her team's appearance at the Olympics, she died of infantile paralysis. The Czech team, which included her older sister, Miloslava, went ahead with its performance and was awarded first place. When the Czech flag was raised for the medal ceremony, it was bordered with a black ribbon. After the Olympics, Marie Provaznikova, the leader of the Czech women's team and the president of the Women's Technical Commission, refused to return to Czechoslovakia because "there is no freedom of speech, of the press or of assembly." She was the first Olympic participant to defect, although hardly the last.

1952 Helsinki T: 18, N: 18, D: 7.24.

		TOTAL PTS.
1. SOV	(Maria Gorokhovskaya 76.78 [1], Nina Bocharova 75.94 [2], Galina Minaicheva 75.67 [4], Galina Urbanovich 75.64 [5], Pelageya Danilova 75.03 [7], Galina Schamrai 74.97 [8], Yekaterina Kalinchuk 73.91 [13])	527.03
2. HUN	(Margit Korondi 75.82 [3], Agnes Keleti 75.58 [6], Edit Perényi-Weckinger 74.77 [10], Olga Tass 74.71 [11], Erzsébet Gulyás 74.61 [12], Mária Zalai-Kövi 73.87 [15], Andrea Bodó 71.67 [28], Irén Daruházi-Karcscics 70.87 [40])	520.96
3. CZE	(Eva Vechtová 73.87 [14], Alena Chadimová 72.25 [20], Jana Rabasová 72.13 [21], Božena Srncová 72.08 [22], Hana Bobková 71.52 [31], Matylda Šinová 71.47 [33], Vera Vančurová 71.38 [34], Alena Reichová 70.40 [47])	503.32
4. SWE	(Karin Lindberg 73.13 [17], Gun Röring 72.07 [23], Evy Berggren 71.07 [36], Göta Pettersson 70.97 [37], Ann-Sofi Colling-Pettersson 70.71 [44], Ingrid Sandahl 69.68 [57], Hjördis Nordin 69.28 [65], Vanja Blomberg 67.84 [83])	501.83
5. GER	(Irma Walther 71.95 [24], Hanna Grages 71.77 [26], Elisabeth Ostermeier 70.91 [38], Wolfgard	495.20

Voss 70.00 [53], Inge Sedlmaeier 69.83 [54], Lydia Zeitlhofer 69.57 [60], Brigitte Kiesier 67.98 [80], Hilde Koop 63.40 [118])

6. ITA (Lidia Pitteri 71.60 [30], Miranda Cicognani   494.74
71.50 [32], Licia Macchini 71.24 [35], Liliana
Scaricabarozzi 70.81 [41], Grazia Bozzo 70.77
[42], Luciana Reali 70.62 [45], Elisabetta Durelli
70.39 [48], Renata Bianchi 69.76 [55])

7. BUL (Tsvetana Stancheva 73.67 [16], Ivanka Doldz-   493.77
heva 72.81 [18], Saltirka Turpova 72.30 [19],
Vasilka Stancheva 71.64 [29], Raina Grigorova
70.18 [49], Yordanka Yovkova 66.37 [98],
Stoyanka Angelova 64.85 [110], Penka Prisa-
dashka 62.91 [122])

8. POL (Stefania Świerzy 71.68 [27], Stefania   483.72
Reindlowa 70.91 [38], Helena Rakoczy 70.74
[43], Zofia Kowalczyk 69.20 [67], Honorata
Marcińczak 68.85 [69], Barbara Wilk-Slizowska
68.14 [76], Dorota Horzonek, 67.57 [86], Ursula
Lukomska 62.90 [123])

1956 Melbourne T: 9, D: 9, D: 12.7.

		TOTAL PTS.
1. SOV	(Larissa Latynina 74.933 [1], Sofia Muratova 74.466 [3], Tamara Manina 74.233 [6], Lyudmila Yegorova 73.533 [10], Polina Astakhova 72.700 [17], Lidiya Kalinina 72.033 [21])	444.80
2. HUN	(Ágnes Keleti 74.633 [2], Olga Tass 74.366 [4], Margit Korondi 73.333 [12], Andrea Bodó 72.900 [14], Erzsébet Gulyás-Köteles 72.200 [18], Alíz Kertész 63.400 [61])	443.50
3. ROM	(Elena Leuştean 74.366 [4], Sonia Iovan 72.900 [14], Georgeta Hurmuzachi 72.733 [16], Emilia Vătăşoiu 72.100 [20], Elena Margarit 72.033 [21], Elena Săcalici 71.433[30])	438.20
4. POL	(Helena Rakoczy 73.700 [8], Natalia Kot 73.633 [9], Danuta Nowak-Stachow 71.800 [25], Dorota Jokiel 71.666 [27], Barbara Ślizowska 70.533 [45], Lidia Szczerbińska 70.300 [47])	436.50
5. CZE	(Eva Bosáková [Vechtova] 74.100 [7], Hana Marejková 73.500 [11], Matylda Šinová 71.800 [25], Vera Drazdiková 71.33 [32], Alena Reichová 70.866 [39], Miroslava Brdičková 70.833 [40])	435.356
6. JAP	(Keiko Tanaka 73.100 [13], Mitsuka Ikeda 71.900 [23], Kazuko Sogabe 71.833 [24], Shizuko Sakashita 71.500 [29], Kyoko Kubota 71.133 [34], Suzuko Seki 71.000 [35])	433.653
7. ITA	(Miranda Cicognani 71.60 [28], Luciana Reali 70.933 [37], Rosella Cicognani 70.766 [42], Elisa Calsi 70.733 [43], Elena Lagorara 70.70 [44], Luciana Lagorara 69.70 [50])	428.654
8. SWE	(Ann-Sofi Colling-Pettersson 71.40 [31], Eva Rönström 70.933 [37], Doris Hedberg 70.466 [46], Karin Lindberg 70.033 [48], Evy Berggren 69.966 [49], Maude Karlén 68.80 [53])	428.60

1960 Rome T: 17, T: 17, D: 9.8.

		TOTAL PTS.

1. SOV (Larissa Latynina 77.031 [1], Sofia Muratova 76.696 [2], Polina Astakhova 76.164 [3], Margarita Nikolayeva 75.831 [4], Lidiya Ivanova [Kalinina] 75.431 [7], Tamara Lyukhina 66.664 [89]) — 382.320

2. CZE (Vera Čáslavská 75.298 [8], Eva Bosáková [Vechtova] 75.197 [10], Ludmila Svédová 74.565 [13], Adolfina Tačová 74.564 [14], Matylda Matoušková [Sinova] 73.265 [26], Hana Ruzickova 72.732 [33]) — 373.323

3. ROM (Sonia Iovan 75.797 [5], Elena Leuştean 74.865 [11], Emilia Liţă 74.264 [16], Atanasia Ionescu 73.564 [21], Uta Poreceanu 73.197 [27], Elena Niculescu 70.563 [67]) — 372.053

4. JAP (Keiko Ikeda [Tanaka] 75.696 [6], Kiyoko Ono 75.398 [15], Kimiko Tsukada 73.398 [22], Toshiko Shirasu 73.298 [24], Ginko Abukawa 72.311 [43], Kazuko Sogabe 17.598 [56]) — 371.422

5. POL (Natalia Kot 74.864 [12], Danuta Stachow 73.930 [17], Barbara Eustachiewicz 732298 [24], Eryka Madra 72.764 [32], Gizela Niedurna 72.647 [37], Brygida Dziuba 71.898 [52]) — 368.620

6. GDR (Ingrid Föst 75.265 [9], Roselore Sonntag 72.964 [29], Ute Starke 72.798 [31], Gretel Schiener 72.697 [34], Renate Schneider 72.029 [48], Karin Boldemann 71.298 [59]) — 367.754

7. HUN (Judit Füle 73.831 [19], Anikó Jánosi-Ducza 73.398 [22], Klára Förstner 72.697 [34], Katalin Müller 72.530 [38], Olga Tass 72.397 [40], Mária Bencsik 72.030 [46]) — 367.054

8. BUL (Raina Grigorova 73.898, Ivanka Doldzheva 72.332 [42], Saltirka Turpova 72.064 [45], Tsvetana Rangelova 71.996 [49], Elisaveta Mileva 71.964 [50], Stanka Pavlova 71.697 [54]) — 364.920

1964 Tokyo T: 10, N: 10, D: 10.21.

		TOTAL PTS.

1. SOV (Larissa Latynina 76.998 [2], Polina Astakhova 76.965 [3], Yelena Volchetskaya 75.765 [8], Tamara Zamotailova [Lyukhina] 75.398 [13], Tamara Manina 75.397 [14], Lyudmila Gromova 74.398 [30]) — 380.890

2. CZE (Vera Čáslavská 77.564 [1], Hana Ružičková 76.097 [5], Jaroslava Sedlačková 75.598 [11], Adolfina Tkačiková [Tačová] 75.331 [19], Mária Krajčirová 74.898 [21], Jana Posnerová 74.765 [23]) — 379.989

3. JAP (Keiko Ikeda [Tanaka] 76.031 [6], Toshiko Aihara [Shirasu] 75.997 [7], Kiyoko Ono 75.665 [9], Taniko Nakamura 75.198 [19], Ginko Chiba [Abukawa] 74.665 [24], Hiroko Tsuji 74.597 [25]) — 377.889

4. GER (Birgit Radochla 76.431 [4], Ute Starke 75.632 [10], Ingrid Föst 75.465 [12], Karin Mannewitz 74.363 [31], Christel Felgner 74.014 [35], Barbara Stolz 73.430 [44]) — 376.038

5. HUN (Anikó Janosi-Ducza 75.33 [16], Katalin Makray 75.330 [18], Mária Tressel 74.932 [21], Gyöngyi Kovacs-Mák 74.597 [26], Katalin Müller 74.565 [27], Márta Erdösi-Talnai 74.231 [32]) — 375.455

6. ROM (Sonia Iovan 75.397 [14], Elena Popescu-Leuştean 75.130 [20], Elena Ceampelea 73.831 [37], Atanasia Ionescu 73.698 [41], Emilia Liţă 72.995 [48], Cristina Doboşan 72.497 [54]) — 371.984

7. POL (Gerda Brylka 74.563, Malgorzata Wilczek 74.563, Elżbieta Apostolska 73.831, Dorota Miller 73.465, Gizela Niedurny 72.365, Barbara Eustachiewicz 72.197) — 371.287

8. SWE (Anna Marie Lundquist 73.798, Laila Egman 73.764, Ewa Rydell 73.599, Ulla Lindstrom 72.898, Anne-Marie Lambert 72.796, Gercla Lindahl) 72.763 — 367.888

1968 Mexico City T: 14, N: 14, D: 10.23.

		TOTAL PTS.

1. SOV (Zinaida Voronina 76.85 [2], Natalya Kuchinskaya 76.75 [3], Larissa Petrik 76.70 [4], Olga Karasseva 76.00 [4], Lyudmila Tourischeva 74.50 [24], Lyubov Burda 74.20 [25]) — 382.85

2. CZE (Vera Čáslavská 78.25 [1], Bohumila Řimnácová 76.00 [7], Miroslava Skleničková 75.85 [9], Máriana Krajčirová 75.85 [9], Hana Lišková 75.65 [11], Jana Kubičkova [Posnerová] 75.05 [15]) — 382.20

3. GDR (Erika Zuchold 76.70 [4], Karin Janz 76.55 [6], Maritta Bauerschmidt 75.45 [12], Ute Starke 74.65 [22], Marianne Noack 74.10 [27], Magdalena Schmidt 73.95 [29]) — 379.10

4. JAP (Kazue Hanyu 75.30 [13], Miyuki Matsuhisa 74.90 [17], Taniko Mitsukuri 74.85 [18], Chieko Oda 74.80 [19], Mitsuko Kandori 74.65 [22], Kayoko Hashiguchi 73.15 [33]) — 375.45

5. HUN (Ágnes Bánfai 75.10 [14], Anikó Jánosi-Ducza 74.80 [19], Katalin Schmitt-Makray 74.15 [26], Márta Erdösi-Tolnai 72.45 [35], Katalin Száll-Müller 72.45 [38], Ilona Békési 71.85 [38]) — 369.80

6. USA (Cathy Rigby 74.95 [16], Linda Metheny 74.00 [28], Joyce Tanac 73.65 [30], Kathy Gleason 73.60 [31], Colleen Mulvihill 73.05 [34], Wendy Cluff 71.80 [39]) — 369.75

7. FRA (Evelyne Letourneur 74.80 [19], Jacqueline Brisepierre 72.45 [35], Mireille Cayre 71.75 [40], Françoise Nourry 70.75 [46], Dominique Lauvard 70.15 [57], Nicole Bourdiau 69.05 [69]) — 361.75

8. BUL (Maria Karashka 73.30 [32], Vania Marinova 71.30 [44], Veselina Pasheva 70.45 [51], — 355.10

Neli Stoyanova 70.45 [51], Raina Atanasova 69.60 [65])

1972 Munich T: 19, N: 19, D: 9.28.

		TOTAL PTS.
1. SOV	(Lyudmila Tourischeva 76.85 [1], Olga Korbut 76.70 [3], Tamara Lazakovitch 76.40 [4], Lyubov Burda 75.35 [6], Elvira Saadi 74.65 [8], Antonina Koshel 73.00 [20])	380.50
2. GDR	(Karin Janz 76.85 [1], Erika Zuchold 76.00 [5], Angelika Hellmann 75.30 [7], Irene Abel 73.75 [13], Christine Schmitt 73.70 [14], Richarda Schmeisser 73.20 [17])	376.55
3. HUN	(Ilona Békési 74.40 [9], Mónika Császár 73.85 [12], Krisztina Medveczky 73.60 [15], Anikó Kéry 73.40 [16], Márta Kelemen 73.00 [20], Zsuzsanna Nagy 71.45 [41])	368.25
4. USA	(Cathy Rigby 74.25 [10], Kimberly Chace 73.05 [18], Roxanne Pierce 72.55 [25], Joan Moore 72.50 [26], Linda Metheny 72.50 [26], Nancy Thies 71.95 [35])	365.90
5. CZE	(Mariana Némethová [Krajčirová] 74.00 [11], Zdena Dornáková 72.90 [23], Sona Brázdová 72.80 [24], Zdena Bujnáčková 72.50 [26], Hana Lišková 72.05 [33], Marcela Váchová 71.95 [35])	365.00
6. ROM	(Elena Ceampelea 73.05 [18], Alina Goreac 72.25 [30], Anca Grigoraş 72.10 [31], Elisabeta Turcu 71.20 [44], Paula Ion 71.10 [46], Marcela Păunescu 70.50 [55])	360.70
7. JAP	(Miyuki Matsuhisa 72.50 [26], Takako Hasegawa 72.00 [34], Eiko Hirashima 71.95 [35], Kayoko Saka 71.80 [40], Kazue Hanyu 71.30 [43], Toshiko Miyamoto 70.00 [60])	359.75
8. GER	(Uta Schorn 72.10 [31], Jutta Oltersdorf 71.95 [35], Andrea Niederheide 71.10 [46], Angelika Kern 70.95 [48], Ulrike Weyh 70.85 [50], Ingrid Santer 68.85 [76])	357.95

1976 Montreal T: 12, N: 12, D: 7.19.

		TOTAL PTS.
1. SOV	(Nelli Kim 78.25 [2], Lyudmila Tourischeva 78.25 [2], Olga Korbut 77.95 [5], Elvira Saadi 77.45 [7], Maria Filatova 77.05 [9], Svetlana Grozdova 77.05 [9]	466.00
2. ROM	(Nadia Comaneci 79.05 [1], Teodora Ungureanu 78.05 [4], Mariana Constantin 76.75 [14], Anca Grigoras 76.70 [15], Gabriela Trusca 76.10 [18], Georgeta Gabor 75.70 [21])	462.35
3. GDR	(Gitta Escher 77.60 [6], Marion Kische 77.20 [8], Kerstin Gerschau 77.00 [12], Angelika Hellmann 76.90 [13], Steffi Kräker 75.70 [21], Carola Dombeck 74.90 [33])	459.30
4. HUN	(Márta Egervári 77.05 [9], Kriszta Medveczky 76.15 [17], Margit Tóth 76.05 [19], Éva Ovári	454.45

75.40 [25], Mária Lövei 75.15 [20], Márta Kelemen 74.65 [34])

5. CZE	(Anna Pohludková 76.40 [16], Ingrid Holkovičova 75.60 [23], Jana Knopová 75.10 [28], Eva Porádková 75.05 [29], Drahomira Smoliková 75.05 [29], Alena Černáková 74.55 [40])	451.75
6. USA	(Kimberly Chace 75.45 [24], Debra Willcox 75.05 [29], Leslie Wolfsberger 74.65 [34], Colleen Casey 74.50 [41], Carrie Englert 74.40 [42], Doris Howard 74.15 [46])	448.20
7. GER	(Andrea Bieger 75.95 [20], Petra Kurbjuweit 74.60 [36], Jutta Oltersdorf 74.60 [36], Traudi Schubert 73.60 [55], Uta Schorn 73.55 [56], Beate Renschler 73.25 [59])	445.55
8. JAP	(Satoko Okazaki 75.30 [26], Miyuki Hironaki 75.00 [32], Nobue Yamazaki 73.85 [50], Chieko Kikkawa 73.65 [53], Sakiko Nozawa 73.45 [57], Kyoko Mano 72.80 [65])	444.05

1980 Moscow T: 8, N: 8, D: 7.23.

		TOTAL PTS.
1. SOV	(Natalya Shaposhnikova 79.15 [2], Yelena Davydova 79.00 [5], Nelli Kim 78.95 [6], Maria Filatova 78.80 [7], Stella Zakharova 78.75 [8], Yelena Naimuschina 78.40 [12])	394.90
2. ROM	(Emilia Eberle 79.10 [3], Nadia Comaneci 79.05 [4], Rodica Dunka 78.50 [10], Melita Rühn 78.30 [13], Cristina Elena Grigoras 78.00 [15], Dumitrita Turner 77.25 [22])	393.50
3. GDR	(Maxi Gnauck 79.35 [1], Katharina Rensch 78.55 [9], Steffi Kräker 78.50 [10], Birgit Süss 77.90 [17], Silvia Hindorff 77.35 [21], Karola Sube 77.20 [23])	392.55
4. CZE	(Eva Marečková 78.05 [14], Jana Labáková 77.85 [18], Katarina Šarišská 77.55 [19], Dana Brydlová 77.05 [26], Anita Sauerová 76.05 [33])	388.80
5. HUN	(Erika Csányi 77.50 [29], Erika Flander 77.20 [23], Márta Egervári 76.50 [27], Lenke Almási 76.25 [29], Éva Óvári 76.25 [29], Erzsébet Hanti 75.35 [36])	384.30
6. BUL	(Silvia Topalova 77.20 [23], Galina Marinova 76.50 [27], Krassimira Toneva 76.25 [29], Kamelia Eftimova 75.60 [34], Dimitrinka Filipova 75.50 [35], Antoaneta Rahneva 74.35 [40])	382.10
7. POL	(Lucja Matraszek-Chydzińska 76.15 [32], Malgorzata Majza 75.20 [37], Anita Jokiel 74.95 [38], Wieslawa Zelaskowska 74.30 [41], Agata Jaroszek 73.65 [42], Katarzyna Snopko 73.45 [44])	376.25
8. PRK	(Jong-Sil Choe 74.85 [39], Myong-Ok Sin 72.50 [46], Myong-Suk Kang 72.35 [47], Chun-Son Kim 71.40 [51], Myong-Hui Choe 71.20 [53], Ok-Sil Lo 70.50 [58])	364.05

RHYTHMIC ALL-AROUND

This event will be held for the first time in 1984.

Discontinued Events

TEAM EXERCISE WITH PORTABLE APPARATUS

1952 Helsinki T: 16, N: 16, D: 7.24.

			TOTAL PTS.
1.	SWE	(Karin Lindberg, Gun Röring, Evy Berggren, Göta Pettersson, Ann-Sofi Colling-Pettersson, Ingrid Sandahl, Hjördis Nordin, Vanja Blomberg)	74.20
2.	SOV	(Maria Gorokhovskaya, Nina Bocharova, Galina Minaicheva, Galina Urbanovich, Pelageya Danilova, Galina Schamrai, Medeya Dschugeli, Yekaterina Kalinchuk)	73.00
3.	HUN	(Margit Korondi, Ágnes Keleti, Edit Perényi-Weckinger, Olga Tass, Erzsébet Gulyás, Mária Zalai-Kövi, Andrea Bodó, Irén Daruházi-Karcscics)	71.60
4.	GER	(Irma Walther, Hanna Grages, Elisabeth Ostermeier, Wolfgard Voss, Inge Sedelmeier, Lydia Zeitlhofer, Brigitte Kiesler, Hilde Koop)	71.20
5.	FIN	(Raili Tuominen, Vappu Salonen, Arja Lehtinen, Raili Hoviniemi, Pirkko Vilppunen, Maila Nisula, Pirkko Pyykönen, Raija Simola)	70.60
6.	CZE	(Eva Vechtová, Alena Chadimová, Jana Rabasová, Božena Srncová, Hana Bobková, Matylda Šinová, Vera Vančurová, Alena Reichová)	70.00
6.	HOL	(Helena Gerrietsen, Huiberdina Krul van der Nolk van Gogh, Johanna Cox-Ladru, Catharina Selbach, Jacoba Kampen, Johanna Ros, Bertha Selbach, Anna Simon)	70.00
8.	YUG	(Sonja Rožman, Tanja Žutić, Anka Drinic, Nada Spasic, Milica Rožman, Ada Smolnikar, Marija Ivandekič, Tereza Kočiš)	69.20

1956 Melbourne T: 9, N: 9, D: 12.7.

			TOTAL PTS.
1.	HUN	(Ágnes Keleti, Margit Korondi, Olga Tass, Andrea Bodó, Aliz Kertész, Erzsébet Gulyás-Köteles)	75.20
2.	SWE	(Ann-Sofi Colling-Pettersson, Karin Lindberg, Eva Rönström, Evy Berggren, Doris Hedberg, Maude Karlén)	74.20
3.	POL	(Helena Rakoczy, Natalia Kot, Dorota Jokiel, Danuta Nowak-Stachow, Barbara Ślizowska, Lidia Szczerbińska)	74.00
3.	SOV	(Tamara Manina, Larissa Latynina, Sofia Muratova, Lidiya Kalinina, Polina Astakhova, Lyudmila Yegorova)	74.00
5.	ROM	(Georgeta Hurmuzachi, Sonia Iovan, Elena Leuştean, Elena Margarit, Elena Săcălici, Emilia Vătăşoiu)	73.40
6.	JAP	(Mitsuka Ikeda, Keiko Tanaka, Kazuko Sogabe, Kyoko Kubota, Suzuko Seki, Shizuko Sakashita)	73.20
7.	CZE	(Eva Bosáková, [Vechtová], Hana Marejková, Matylda Šinová, Vera Drazdikova, Alena Reichová. Miraslava Brdičková)	73.00
8.	ITA	(Miranda Cicognani, Luciana Reali, Rosella Cicognani, Elisa Calsi, Elena Lagorora, Luciana Lagorara)	72.80

TEAM HANDBALL

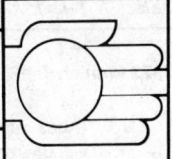

MEN

Team handball is an exciting sport that deserves greater popularity. It is basically a combination of soccer and basketball. The ball is moved down the field as in basketball, but instead of being shot through a hoop it is thrown past a goalkeeper and into a net. There are two 30-minute halves.

1896–1932 not held

1936 Berlin T: 6, N: 6, D: 8.14.

			W	L	PF	PA
1.	GER	(Heinz Körvers, Arthur Knautz, Willy Bandholz, Hans Keiter, Wilhelm Brinkmann, Georg Dascher, Erich Hermann, Hans Theilig, Helmut Berthold, Alfred Klingler, Fritz Fromm, Carl Kreutzberg, Heinrich Keimig, Wilhelm Müller, Kurt Dossin, Rudolf Stahl, Hermann Hansen, Fritz Spengler, Edgar Reinhardt, Günther Ortmann, Wilhelm Baumann, Helmuth Braselmann)	5	0	96	19
2.	AUT	(Alois Schnabel, Franz Bartl, Johann Tauscher, Otto Licha, Emil Juracka, Leopold Wohlrab, Jaroslav Volak, Alfred Schmalzer, Ludwig Schubert, Ferdinand Kiefler, Anton Perwein, Fritz Maurer, Franz Brunner, Fritz Wurmböck, Siegfried Purner, Hans Zehetner, Hans Houschka, Franz Bistricky, Franz Berghammer, Walter Reisp, Josef Krejci, Siegfried Powolny)	4	1	60	29
3.	SWI	(Willy Gysi, Robert Studer, Erich Schmitt, Rolf Faes, Erland Herkenrath, Burkhard Gantenbein, Werner Meyer, Max Streib, Georg Mischon, Ernst Hufschmid, Eugen Seiterle, Edy Schmid, Max Blösch, Werner Scheurmann, Willy Schäfer, Willy Hufschmid, Rudolf Wirz)	2	3	33	52
4.	HUN	(Antal Ujváry, János Koppány, István Serényi, Lajos Kutasi, Frigyes Rakosi, Lőrinc Galgóczy, Ferenc Cziráki, Gyula Takács, Miklós Fodor, Endre Salgó, Sándor Cséffai, Tibor Máté, Antal Benda, Imre Páli, Ferenc Velkei, Sándor Szomori)	1	4	25	64
5.	ROM	(Stefan Zoller, Carol Haffer, Ludovic Haffer, Bruno Holtzträger, Stefan Höchsmann, Robert Speck, Georg Herzog, Frederic Halmen, Wilhelm Kirschner, Wilhelm Heidel, Günther Schörsten, Peter Fesci, Dr. Ion Zikeli, Wilhelm Zaharias, Hertog Hermannstädter)	1	2	19	27
6.	USA	(Henry Oehler, Charles Dauner, Alfred Roseco, Herbert Carl Oehmichen, Edmund Schallenberg, William Ahlemeyer, Gerard Yantz, Joe Kaylor, Willy Renz, Walter Bowden, Fred Leinweber, Edward John Hagen, Otto Oehler, Philip Schupp)	0	3	6	46

Final: GER 10–6 AUT
3rd Place: SWI 10–5 HUN
5th Place: ROM 10–3 USA

Field handball was invented in Germany, so when the Germans were given the opportunity to add one sport to the 1936 Olympics, they chose handball. In 1936 the game was played outdoors with 11 men on a side. Not surprisingly, Germany dominated the tournament, defeating the United States 29–1, Hungary 22–0 and 19–6, and Switzerland 16–6. Austria put up the best fight, trailing only 8–6 with five minutes to play.

1948–1968 not held

1972 Munich T: 16, N: 16, D: 9.11.

		W	L	T	PF	PA
1. YUG	(Abaz Arslanagić, Zoran Živko-vić, Miroslav Pribanić, Hrvoje Horvat, Djoko Lavrnić, Zdravko Miljak, Slobodan Mišković, Bran-islav Pokrajać, Nebojša Popović, Milan Lazarević, Milorad Karalić, Albin Vidović, Zdenko Zorbo, Pe-tar Fajdrić)	7	0	0	140	105
2. CZE	(Ivan Satrapa, Vladimir Jarý, Jiři Kavan, Vladimir Haber, Jindřich Krepindl, Ladislav Beneš, Vin-cent Lafko František Bruna, Petr Pospišil, Jaroslav Konecny, Pa-vel Mikes, Jaroslav Škarvan, František Králik, Andrej Lubósik, Zdenek Skara, Arnošt Limčik)	3	3	1	114	99
3. ROM	(Cornel Penu, Gavril Kicsid, Va-lentin Samungi, Ştefan Birtalan, Cristian Gatu, Roland Gunesch, Simion Schöbel, Gheorghe Gruia, Constantin Tudosie, Alex-andru Dincă, Werner Stöckl, Dan Marin, Ghită Licu, Radu Voina, Adrias Cosma)	6	1	0	111	92
4. GDR	(Reiner Frieske, Peter Randt, Klaus Langhoff, Reiner Gans-chow, Wolfgang Lakenmacher, Rainer Würdig, Jürgen Hilde-brandt, Udo Röhrig, Wolfgang Böhme, Harry Zörnack, Josef Rose, Siegfried Voigt, Klaus Weiss, Rainer Zimmerman, Horst Jankhöfer, Peter Larisch)	5	2	0	103	85
5. SOV	(Nikolai Semenov, Mikhail Is-chenko, Aleksandr Panov, Vladi-mir Maksimov, Valentin Kulev, Vassily Ilyin, Anatoly Shev-chenko, Yuri Klimov, Mikhail Lut-senko, Aleksandr Rezanov, Valery Gassi, Albert Oganezov, Yuri Lagutin, Ivan Ussatiy, Yan Vilson)	3	1	3	91	84
6. GER	(Klaus Kater, Uwe Rathjen, Her-wig Ahrendsen, Wolfgang Braun, Peter Bucher, Diethard Finkel-mann, Klaus Lange, Herbert Lübking, Heiner Möller, Hans-Pe-ter Neuhaus, Herbert Rogge, Herbert Wehnert, Hans-Jürgen Bode, Jochen Feldhoff, Josef Karrer, Klaus Westebbe)	2	4	1	98	106
7. SWE	(Sten Olsson, Frank Ström, Björn Andersson, Dan Eriksson, Len-nart Eriksson, Johan Fischer-ström, Benny Johansson, Jan Jonsson, Michael Koch, Thomas Persson, Goeran Hard Af Seger-stad, Bertil Söderberg)	2	2	3	93	92
8. HUN	(József Horváth, Sándor Kaló, Károly Vass, István Varga, István Szabó, István Marosi, Sándor Vass, Lajos Simó, János Ador-ján, Sándor Takács, János Stil-ler, László Szabó)	2	5	0	126	119

Final: YUG 21–16 CZE
3rd Place: ROM 19–16 GDR
5th Place: SOV 17–16 GER
7th Place: SWE 19–18 HUN

With the Olympics back in Germany, team handball was returned to the schedule, but this time there were seven men on a side. The decisive match was the second-round contest between Yugoslavia and world champion Roma-nia. With 15 minutes to play, Milan Lazarević scored to give Yugoslavia a 10–9 lead. Four minutes later Djoko Lavrnić scored again, and Yugoslavia had the first two-goal lead of the game. They built their lead to 14–11 and survived two late goals to win, 14–13. The final against Czechoslovakia was anticlimactic; Yugoslavia led 12–5 at halftime and 18–8 with 13 minutes to play.

1976 Montreal T: 11, N: 11, D: 7.28.

		W	L	T	PF	PA
1. SOV	(Mikhail Ishchenko, Anatoly Fe-dyukin, Vladimir Maximov, Ser-gei Kushniryuk, Vassily Ilyin, Vladimir Kravzov, Yuri Klimov, Yuri Lagutin, Aleksandr Anpilo-gov, Yevgeny Chernyshov, Vale-ry Gassiy, Anatoly Tomin, Yuri Kidyaev, Aleksandr Rezanov)	5	1	0	130	92
2. ROM	(Cornel Penu, Gavril Kicsid, Cris-tian Gatu, Cezar Draganita, Radu Voina, Roland Gunesch, Alexan-dru Folker, Ştefan Birtalan, Adri-an Cosma, Constantin Tudosie, Nicolae Munteanu, Werner Stöckl, Mircea Grabovschi, Ghită Licu)	3	1	1	106	90
3. POL	(Andrzej Szymczak, Piotr Cjeśla, Zdzislaw Antczak, Zygfryd Kuchta, Jerzy Klempel, Janusz Brzozowski, Ryszard Przbysz, Jerzy Melcer, Andrzej Soko-lowski, Jan Gmyrek, Henryk Roz-miarek, Alfred Kaluźiński, Wlodzimierz Zieliński, Mieczys-law Wojczak)	4	1	0	101	89
4. GER	(Manfred Hofmann, Jürgen Hahn, Günter Bottcher, Kurt Klühspies, Peter Kleibrink, Walter Oepen, Horst Spengler, Gerd Becker, Bernhard Busch, Jo-achim Deckarm, Rudolf Rauer, Arno Ehret, Heiner Brand, Peter Jaschke)	4	2	0	115	97

		W	L	T	PF	PA
5. YUG	(Abaz Arslanagić, Vlado Bojović, Ždravko Radjennović, Milorad Karalić, Radisav Pavicević, Žvonimir Serdarusić, Hrvoje Horvat, Branislav Pokrajać, Radivoj Krivokapić, Predrag Timko, Ždravko Miljak, Ždenko Žorko, Nebojsa Popović, Željko Nims)	5	1	0	131	112
6. HUN	(Béla Bartalos, Ferenc Buday, Péter Kovács, István Varga, Mihály Süvöltös, István Szilágyi, József Kenyeres, László Janovszki, Károly Vass, Ernö Gubányi Zsolt Kontra, Gábor Veröci)	2	3	0	111	103
7. CZE	(Jan Packa, František Sulc, Ivan Satrapa, Vladimir Jary, Jiři Kavan, Stefan Katusak, Vladimir Haber, Jindrich Krepindl, Jiři Hanzl, Jaroslav Papiernik, Jozef Dobrotka, Bohumil Cepak, Jiři Liska, Pavel Mikes)	2	2	1	110	103
8. DEN	(Kay Jorgensen, Palle Jensen, Anders Dahl-Nielsen, Lars Bock, Jorgen Frandsen, Claus From, Thomas Pazyj, Bent Larsen, Soren Andersn, Morten Christenen, Henrik Jacobsgaard, Johnny Pechnik, Thor Munkager, Jesper Petersen)	2	4	0	113	127

Final: SOV 19–15 ROM
3rd Place: POL 21–18 GER
5th Place: YUG 21–19 HUN
7th Place: CZE 25–21 DEN

Again Romania entered the Olympics as defending world champions and again they were unable to win the tournament. They survived the preliminary pool undefeated to qualify for the final. The other pool was won by the Soviet Union despite a 20–18 loss to Yugoslavia, which was unlucky to finish fifth considering they lost only one match— to West Germany, 18–17. The U.S.S.R. took control of the final early, led 10–6 at halftime, and was never behind.

1980 Moscow T: 12, N: 12, D: 7.30.

		W	L	T	PF	PA
1. GDR	(Siegfried Voigt, Günter Dreibrodt, Peter Rost, Klaus Gruner, Hans-Georg Beyer, Dietmar Schmidt, Hartmut Krüger, Lothar Döering, Ernst Gerlach, Frank-Michael Wahl, Ingolf Wiegert, Wieland Schmidt, Rainer Höft, Hans-Georg Jaunich)	5	0	1	131	114
2. SOV	(Mikhail Ishchenko, Viktor Makhorin, Sergei Kushniryuk, Aleksandr Karshakevich, Vladimir Kravzov, Vladimir Belov, Anatoly Fedyukin, Aleksandr Anpilogov, Yevgeny Chernyshov, Aleksei Zhuk, Nikolai Tomin, Yuri Kidyaev, Vladimir Repiev, Valdemar Novitsky)	4	2	0	156	98
3. ROM	(Nicolae Munteanu, Marian Dumitru, Iosif Boros, Maricel Voinea, Vasile Stinga, Radu Voina, Cezar Draganita, Cornel Durau, Ştefan Birtalan, Alexandru Folker, Neculai Vasilca, Lucian Vasilache, Adrian Cosma, Claudiu Eugen Ionescu)	5	1	0	139	106
4. HUN	(Béla Bartalos, László Szabó, Péter Kovács, Sándor Vass, János Fodor, István Szilágyi, József Kenyeres, László Jánovszki, Ambrus Lele, Ernö Gubányi, Zsolt Kontra, Alpár Jegenyés, Árpád Pál, Miklós Kovácsics)	3	1	2	114	108
5. SPA	(José Maria Pagoaga, Juan José Cabanas, Juan José Maria Albisu, Vicente Calabuig, Juan Al de la Puente, Leon Rafael Lopez, José Ignacio Novoa, Juan José Uria, Agustin Milian, Francisco Lopez, Eugenio Serrano, Gregorio Lopez, Juan Pedro de Miguel, Juan Francisco Munoz)	3	2	1	126	129
6. YUG	(Zlatan Arnautović, Momir Rnić, Enver Koso, Drago Jovović, Stjepan Obran, Jasmin Mrkonja, Peter Mahne, Pavle Jurina, Goran Nerić, Jovica Cvetković, Velibor Nenadić, Adnan Dizdar, Mile Isaković, Jovica Elezović)	4	2	0	155	116
7. POL	(Andrzej Kącki, Zbigniew Gawlik, Piotr Czaczka, Marek Panas, Jerzy Klempel, Janusz Brzozowski, Zbigniew Tluczyński, Grzegorz Kosma, Daniel Waszkiewicz, Ryszard Jedliński, Henryk Rozmiarek, Alfred Kaluziński, Jerzy Garpiel, Mieczyslaw Wojczak)	3	2	1	146	119
8. SWI	(Edi Wickli, Ernst Zuellig, Robert Jehle, Roland Brand, Max Schaer, Peter Haag, Walter Müeller, Rudolf Weber, Hans Huber, Konrad Affolter, Hanspter Lutz, Ugo Jametti, Peter Jehle, Martin Ott)	2	4	0	132	121

Final: GDR 23–22 SOV
3rd Place: ROM 20–18 HUN
5th Place: SPA 24–23 YUG
7th Place: POL 23–22 SWI

The final was a particularly exciting match, as neither team ever led by more than two goals. As time ran out, East Germany led 20–19, but Aleksandr Anpilogov of the

U.S.S.R. made a penalty shot with 22 seconds to play and the game went into overtime. Anpilogov also scored the first goal of the ten-minute extra period, but the Soviet Union was held scoreless for the next eight and a half minutes while the Germans took a 23–21 lead. Anpilogov scored the final goal of the game with 51 seconds left to play. East Germany's last point was put in by 23-year-old Hans-Georg Beyer, whose older brother, Udo, was winning the bronze medal in the shot put at the exact same time. Two days later, their sister, Gisela, finished fourth in the discus. Last-place finisher Kuwait had a tough tournament, including losses of 44–10 to Yugoslavia and 38–11 to the U.S.S.R.

WOMEN

Women's handball consists of two 25-minute halves; as in men's handball, there are seven players on a team.

1896–1972 not held

1976 Montreal T: 6, N: 6, D: 7.28.

		W	L	T	PF	PA
1.	SOV	5	0	0	92	40

(Natalya Sherstyuk, Rafiga Shabanova, Lyubov Berezhnaya, Zinaida Turchina, Tatyana Makarez, Maria Litoshenko, Lyudmila Bobrus, Tatyana Gluschenko, Lyudmila Shubina, Galina Zakharova, Aldona Čhesaitité, Nina Lobova, Lyudmila Pantchuk, Larissa Karlova)

		W	L	T	PF	PA
2.	GDR	3	1	1	89	47

(Hannelore Zober, Gabriele Badorek, Evelyn Matz, Roswitha Krause, Christina Rost, Petra Uhlig, Christina Voss, Liane Michaelis, Silvia Siefert, Marion Tietz, Kristina Richter, Eva Paskuy, Waltraud Kretzschmar, Hannelore Burosch)

		W	L	T	PF	PA
3.	HUN	3	1	1	85	55

(Ágota Bujdosó, Márta Magyeri, Borbála Tóth-Harsányi, Katalin Laki, Amália Sterbinszky, Ilona Nagy, Klára Csík, Rozália Lelkes, Mária Vadász, Erzsébet Németh, Éva Angyal, Mária Berzsenyi, Marianna Nagy, Zsuzsanna Kezi)

		W	L	T	PF	PA
4.	ROM	2	3	0	73	83

(Elisabeta Ionescu, Rozalia Sos, Simona Arghir, Georgeta Lacusta, Doina Furcoiu, Niculina Sasu, Cristina Petrovici, Constantina Pitigoi, Doina Cojocaru, Magdalena Miklos, Maria Bosi, Viorica Doina Ionica, Maria Lackovics, Juliana Hobincu)

		W	L	T	PF	PA
5.	JAP	1	4	0	72	115

(Shoko Wada, Hiroko Kosahara, Natsue Shimada, Terumi Kurata, Mikiko Kato, Hitomi Matsushita, Emiko Yamashita, Kuriko Komori, Eiko Kawada, Mihoko Hozumi, Nanami Kino, Tokuko Kubo)

		W	L	T	PF	PA
6.	CAN	0	5	0	35	106

(Danielle Chenard, Louise Hurtubise, Denise Lemaire, Francine Boulay-Parizeau, Joanes Rail, Nicole Genier, Lucie Balthazar, Hélène Tetreault, Manon Charette, Monique Prud'Homme, Louise Beaumont, Mariette Houle, Nicole Robert, Johanne Valois)

1980 Moscow T: 6, N: 6, D: 7.29.

		W	L	T	PF	PA
1.	SOV	5	0	0	99	52

(Natalya Timoshkina, Larissa Karlova, Irina Palchikova, Zinaida Turchina, Tatyana Kochergina [Makerez], Lyudmila Poradnik [Bobrus], Larissa Savkina, Aldona Nenenene [Čhesaitité], Yulia Safina, Olga Zubareva, Valentina Lutaeva, Lyubov Odinokova [Berechnaya], Sigita Strechen)

		W	L	T	PF	PA
2.	YUG	3	1	1	107	67

(Ana Titlić, Slavica Jeremić, Zorica Vojinovic, Radmila Drljaca, Katica Iles, Mirjana Ognjenović, Svetlana Anastasovski, Rada Savić, Svetlana Kitić, Mirjana Djurica, Biserka Visnjić, Vesna Radović, Jasna Merdan, Vesna Milosević)

		W	L	T	PF	PA
3.	GDR	3	1	1	91	58

(Hannelore Zober, Katrin Krüger, Evelyn Matz, Roswitha Krause, Christina Rost, Petra Uhlig, Claudia Wunderlich, Sabine Röther, Kornelia Kunisch, Marion Tietz, Kristina Richter, Waltraud Kretzschmar, Birgit Heinecke, Renate Rudolph)

		W	L	T	PF	PA
4.	HUN	1	3	1	65	74

(Mária Berzsenyi, Erzsébet Csajbok [Németh], Rozália Lelkes, Éva Csulik, Amália Sterbinszky, Klára Csik, Marianna Nagy, Ilona Mihályka, Mária Vadász, Erzsébet Balogh, Eva Angyal, Györgyi Ori, Piroska Budai, Klára Bonyhádi)

		W	L	T	PF	PA
5.	CZE	1	3	1	65	78

(Mária Končeková, Elena Boledovičová, Daniela Nováková, Katerina Lamrichová, Alena Horalová, Jolana Nemethová, Viola Pavlasová, Piroska Polačekova, Jana Kutková, Věra Datinská, Mi-

lena Foltýnová, Elena Brezan-
yová, Petra Kominková)

6. CON	(Madeleine Mitsotso, Pascaline Bobeka, Angelik Abebame, Nicole Oba, Henriette Koula, Solange Koulinka, Isabelle Azanga, Micheline Okemba, Viviane Okoula, Germaine Djimbi, Yolande Kada-Gango, Lopez-Pemba, Julienne Malaki, Yvonne Makouala)	0	5	0	46	159

The U.S.S.R. faced its only threat against Hungary when they led 12–11 with just five minutes to play. The Soviets then scored four straight goals and won, 16–12. Roswitha Krause of the bronze-medal-winning East German team had won a silver medal in the freestyle swimming relay 12 years earlier in Mexico City.

JUDO

Bantamweight | Middleweight
Featherweight | Light Heavyweight
Lightweight | Heavyweight
Light Middleweight | Open

JUDO TERMS

Scoring

Ippon	Full point
Waza-ari	Almost Ippon
Yuko	Almost Waza-ari
Koka	Almost Yuko

Penalties

Hansoku make (= ippon)	Disqualification
Keikoku (= Waza-ari)	Warning
Chui (= Yuko)	Caution
Shido (= Koka)	Note

Throws and Holds

Harai-goshi	Sweeping loin throw
Kami-shiho-gatame	Upper four quarters hold
Kesa-gatame	Sash hold
Kuzure-kami-shiho-gatame	Modified upper four quarters hold
O-soto-gari	Major outside reaping throw (outside clip or kick-back throw)
O-uchi-gari	Major inner reaping throw (inside clip or innercut throw)
Seoi-nage	Over-the-shoulder throw
Tai-otoshi	Body drop
Uchi-mata	Inner thigh throw
Yoko-shiho-gatame	Side four quarters hold

Other Terms

Awasewaza	Combination of two techniques
Katsu	A system of resuscitation
Kinsa	Slight superiority or close decision
Shime-waza	Strangulation techniques
Yushi-gachi	Win by superiority (referee's decision)

A judo match is won by the first person to hold his opponent immobile on his back for 30 seconds. If neither contestant is able to do this within the time limit, which is six minutes in preliminary matches, eight minutes in semifinals, and ten minutes in finals, then a decision is rendered by the referee and two judges.

BANTAMWEIGHT
(60 kg—132 lbs)

1896–1976 not held

1980 Moscow C: 29, N: 29, D: 8.1.

			FINAL MATCH
1. Thierry Rey	FRA		Koka 7:00
2. Rafael Rodriguez Carbenell	CUB		
3. Aramby Emizh	SOV		
3. Tibor Kincses	HUN		
5. John Holliday	GBR		
5. Pavel Petrikov	CZE		
7. Samir Elnajjar	SYR		
7. Reino Fagerlund	FIN		

FEATHERWEIGHT
(65 kg—143 lbs)

1896-1976 not held

1980 Moscow C: 29, N: 29, D: 7.31.

			FINAL MATCH
1. Nikolai Solodukhin	SOV		Koka/shido 7:00
2. Tsendying Damdin	MON		
3. Iliyan Nedkov	BUL		
3. Janusz Pawlowski	POL		
5. Yves Delvingt	FRA		
5. Torsten Reissmann	GDR		
7. Wolfgang Biedron	SWE		
7. Jaroslav Kriz	CZE		

LIGHTWEIGHT
(71 kg—156.5 lbs)

1896–1960 not held

1964 Tokyo C: 25, N: 18, D: 10.20
(68 kg—150 lbs)

		FINAL MATCH
1. Takehide Nakatani	JAP	Awasewaza 1:15
2. Eric Hänni	SWI	
3. Aron Bogolyubov	SOV	
3. Oleg Stepanov	SOV	
5. Won-Ku Chang (TAI), Paul Maruyama (USA), Chung-Sam Park (KOR), Gerhard Zotter (AUT)		

1968 not held

1972 Munich C: 29, N: 29, D: 9.4.
(63 kg—139 lbs)

		FINAL MATCH
1. Takao Kawaguchi	JAP	Kami-shiho-gatame 0:39
— Bakhaavaa Buidaa	MON	
3. Yong-Ik Kim	PRK	
3. Jean-Jacques Mounier	FRA	
5. Wolfram Koppen	GER	
5. Hector Rodriguez Torres	CUB	
7. Chi-Hsiang Cheng	TAI	
7. Ferenc Szabó	HUN	

Buidaa lost his silver medal when he became the first person in judo history to fail a drug test.

1976 Montreal C: 32, N: 32, D: 7.26.
(63 kg—139 lbs)

		FINAL MATCH
1. Hector Rodriguez Torres	CUB	Uchi-mata 10:00
2. Eun-Kyung Chang	KOR	
3. Felice Mariani	ITA	
3. József Tuncsik	HUN	
5. Erich Pointner	AUT	
5. Marian Standowicz	POL	
7. Brad Farrow	CAN	
7. Jose Pinto Gomes	POR	

Surprisingly, two-time world champion Yoshiharu Minami was eliminated in his first match by Yves Delvingt of France. The final was a rugged contest, which was interrupted at one point to allow Rodriguez's ribs to be wrapped up by a doctor. Rodriguez told reporters that he began practicing judo to protect himself from his six older brothers.

1980 Moscow C: 30, N: 30, D: 7.30.

		FINAL MATCH
1. Ezio Gamba	ITA	Yushi-gachi 7:00
2. Neil Adams	GBR	
3. Ravdan Davaadalai	MON	
3. Karl-Heinz Lehmann	GDR	
5. Edward Alksnin	POL	
5. Christian Dyot	FRA	
7. Byong-Gun Kim	PRK	
7. Michael Picken	AUS	

European champion Neil Adams needed less than four minutes to defeat his first three opponents, but in the final he lost a unanimous decision to his 21-year-old nemesis, Ezio Gamba.

LIGHT MIDDLEWEIGHT
(78 kg—172 lbs)

1896–1968 not held

1972 Munich C: 29, N: 29, D: 9.3.
(70 kg—154 lbs)

		FINAL MATCH
1. Toyokazu Nomura	JAP	Seoi-nage 0:27
2. Antoni Zajkowski	POL	
3. Dietmar Hötger	GDR	
3. Anatoli Novikov	SOV	
5. Engelbert Doerbandt	GER	
5. Antal Hetényi	HUN	
7. Jong-She Wang	TAI	
7. Reto Zinsli	SWI	

Nomura disposed of his five opponents in a total of ten minutes and 49 seconds.

1976 Montreal C: 29, N: 29, D: 7.29.
(70 kg—154 lbs)

		FINAL MATCH
1. Vladimir Nevzorov	SOV	Tai-otoshi 10:00
2. Koji Kuramoto	JAP	
3. Marian Talaj	POL	
3. Patrick Vial	FRA	
5. Chang-Sun Lee	KOR	
5. Vaccinuf Morrison	GBR	
7. Juan Carlos Rodriguez	SPA	
7. John Van Hoek	AUS	

1980 Moscow C: 29, N: 29, D: 7.29.

		FINAL MATCH
1. Shota Khabareli	SOV	Yuko 7:00
2. Juan Ferrer La Hera	CUB	
3. Harald Heinke	GDR	
3. Bernard Tchoullouyan	FRA	
5. Mircea Fratica	ROM	
5. Ignacio Sanz	SPA	
7. Georgi Petrov	BUL	
7. Slavko Sikiric	YUG	

MIDDLEWEIGHT
(86 kg—189.5 lbs)

1896–1960 not held

1964 Tokyo C: 25, N: 20, D: 10.21.
(80 kg—176 lbs)

		FINAL MATCH	
1. Isao Okano	JAP	Yoko-shiho-gatame	1:36
2. Wolfgang Hofmann	GER		
3. James Bregman	USA		
3. Eui-Tae Kim	KOR		
5. Lionel Grossain (FRA), Rodolf Perez (ARG), Lhoffei Shiozawa (BRA), Petrus Snijders (HOL)			

In the quarterfinal match between Okano and Grossain, both the referee and Okano failed to notice that Grossain had been rendered unconscious by a Shime-waza. When the Japanese coach called their attention to the Frenchman's condition, Okano revived his opponent through the use of Katsu.

1968 not held

1972 Munich C: 35, N: 35, D: 9.2.
(80 kg—176 lbs)

		FINAL MATCH	
1. Shinobu Sekine	JAP	Yushi-gachi	10:00
2. Seung-Lip Oh	KOR		
3. Jean-Pâul Coché	FRA		
3. Brian Jacks	GBR		
5. Guram Gogalauri	SOV		
5. Lutz Lischka	AUT		
7. Gerd Egger	GER		
7. Petr Jaekl	CZE		

Sekine, the All-Japan open category champion, actually lost to Oh in the preliminary pool. But he was able to fight his way into the final through repêchage, or second-chance matches, and won by a split decision, to the great relief of all the Japanese who were present.

1976 Montreal C: 32, N:32, D: 7.28.
(80 kg—176 lbs)

		FINAL MATCH	
1. Isamu Sonoda	JAP	O-uchi-gari	10:00
2. Valery Dvoinikov	SOV		
3. Slavko Obadov	YUG		
3. Young-Chul Park	KOR		
5. José Luis Frutos	SPA		
5. Fred Marhenke	GER		
7. Paul Buganey	AUS		
7. Suheyl Yesilnur	TUR		

Policeman Isamu Sonoda upset three-time world champion Shozo Fujii in the All-Japan championships, which served as Japan's Olympic qualifying tournament.

1980 Moscow C: 27, N: 27, D: 7.28.

		FINAL MATCH	
1. Jürg Röthlisberger	SWI	Yuko	7:00
2. Isaac Azcuy Oliva	CUB		
3. Aleksandr Iatskevich	SOV		
3. Detlef Ultsch	GDR		
5. Walter Carmona	BRA		
5. Bertil Ström	SWE		
7. Peter Donnelly	GBR		
7. Henri-Richard Lobe	CAM		

LIGHT HEAVYWEIGHT
(95 kg—209 lbs)

1896–1968 not held

1972 Munich C: 30, N: 30, D: 9.1.
(93 kg—205 lbs)

		FINAL MATCH	
1. Shota Chochoshvili	SOV	Yushi-gachi	10:00
2. David Starbrook	GBR		
3. Paul Barth	GER		
3. Chiaki Ishii	BRA		
5. Helmut Howiller	GDR		
5. James Wooley	USA		
7. Pierre Albertini	FRA		
7. Terry Farnsworth	CAN		

Two-time world champion Fumio Sasahara of Hokkaido, Japan, was unexpectedly thrown and defeated by 22-year-old Shota Chochoshvili of Tbilissi, Georgia. Chochoshvili then lost a split decision to Dave Starbrook, the operator of a newspaper, tobacco, and sweet shop in Hackney. The two met again in the finals, and this time Chochoshvili prevailed with a unanimous decision.

1976 Montreal C: 35, N: 35, D: 7.27.
(93 kg—205 lbs)

		FINAL MATCH	
1. Kazuhiro Ninomiya	JAP	Keikoku	10:00
2. Ramaz Harshiladze	SOV		
3. Jürg Röthlisberger	SWI		
3. David Starbrook	GBR		
5. Jeaki Cho	KOR		
5. Dietmar Lorenz	GDR		
7. Ung-Nam An	PRK		
7. Abdoulaye Djiba	SEN		

Ninomiya, who won three of his four preliminary fights in one minute or less, had to lose over 25 pounds to make the weight limit.

1980 Moscow C: 23, N: 23, D: 7.27.

		FINAL MATCH	
1. Robert Van de Walle	BEL	Koka	7:00
2. Tengiz Khubuluri	SOV		
3. Dietmar Lorenz	GDR		
3. Henk Numan	HOL		
5. István Szepesi	HUN		

5. R. José Tornes Bastardo	CUB	
7. Daniel Radu	ROM	
7. Jean-Luc Rouge	FRA	

HEAVYWEIGHT
(Over 95 kg—209 lbs)

1896–1960 not held

1964 Tokyo C: 15, N: 13, D: 10.22.
(80 kg—176 lbs)

		FINAL MATCH
1. Isao Inokuma	JAP	Kinsa 15:00
2. Alfred Rogers	CAN	
3. Anzor Kiknadze	SOV	
3. Parnaoz Chikviladze	SOV	
5. Jong-Dal Kim	KOR	

Inokuma and Rogers were used to practicing together in Japan, so the final was a relatively quiet affair. The lightest entrant in the heavyweight division, Inokuma weighed only 192 pounds, compared to Rogers' 260 pounds.

1968 not held

1972 Munich C: 21, N: 21, D: 8.31.
(93 kg—205 lbs)

		FINAL MATCH
1. Willem Ruska	HOL	Harai-goshi 1:43
2. Klaus Glahn	GER	
3. Motoki Nishimura	JAP	
3. Givi Onashvili	SOV	
5. Jean-Claude Brondani	FRA	
5. Douglas Nelson	USA	
7. Tijive Bankassou	HOL	
7. M'Bagnik Mebodj	SEN	

1976 Montreal C: 20, N: 20, D: 7.26.
(93 kg—205 lbs)

		FINAL MATCH
1. Sergei Novikov	SOV	O-soto-gari 1:19
2. Günther Neureuther	GER	
3. Allen Coage	USA	
3. Sumio Endo	JAP	
5. Gunsem Jalaa	MON	
5. Keith Remfry	GBR	
7. Abdoulaye Kote	SEN	
7. Radomir Kovacevic	YUG	

A most unusual sight was the repêchage match between 5-foot 6½-inch, 259-pound Sumio Endo and 7-foot 0-inch, 350-pound Jong-Gil Pak of North Korea. Endo, the defending world champion, was the victor.

1980 Moscow C: 18, N: 18, D: 7.27.

		FINAL MATCH
1. Angelo Parisi	FRA	Ippon 6:14
2. Dimitur Zapryanov	BUL	

3. Radomir Kovacevic	YUG	
3. Vladímir Kocman	CZE	
5. Myong-Gyu Kim	PRK	
5. Paul Radburn	GBR	
7. Wojciech Reszko	POL	

Parisi was a former member of the British team who married a Frenchwoman and changed citizenship.

OPEN

1896–1960 not held

1964 Tokyo C: 9, N: 9, D: 10.23.

		FINAL MATCH
1. Antonius Geesink	HOL	Kesa-gatame 9:22
2. Akio Kaminaga	JAP	
3. Theodore Boronovskis	AUS	
3. Klaus Glahn	GER	

Geesink's victory was a shocking blow to the Japanese, even though he was two-time world champion and the clear favorite. In 1961 the 6-foot 6-inch, 267-pound judo instructor from Utrecht had become the first non-Japanese to win a world championship. Geesink had won his semifinal fight with Boronovskis in only 12 seconds. Although he failed to gain the gold medal, Kaminaga set an Olympic speed record in the repêchage round when he threw Thomas Ong of the Philippines in four seconds.

1968 not held

1972 Munich C: 29, N: 29, D: 9.9.

		FINAL MATCH
1. Willem Ruska	HOL	Yoko-shiho-gatame 3:58
2. Vitali Kusnezov	SOV	
3. Jean-Claude Brondani	FRA	
3. Angelo Parisi	GBR	
5. Klaus Glahn	GER	
5. Douglas Rogers	CAN	
7. Tijini Benkassow	MOR	
7. Chiaki Ishii	BRA	

Having previously swept to victory in the heavyweight class, Ruska became the only person ever to win two Olympic gold medals in judo. In the open division, Ruska lost an early unanimous decision to Kusnezov, but was able to pin him when they met again in the final.

1976 Montreal C: 30, N: 30, D: 7.31.

		FINAL MATCH
1. Haruki Uemura	JAP	Kuzure-kami-shiho-gatame 7:28
2. Keith Remfry	GBR	
3. Jeaki Cho	KOR	
3. Shota Chochoshvili	SOV	
5. Jorge Portelli	ARG	
5. Jean-Luc Rouge	FRA	
7. Gunther Neureuther	GER	
7. Jong-Gil Pak	PRK	

1980 Moscow C: 21, N: 21, D: 8.2.

		FINAL MATCH	
1. Dietmar Lorenz	GDR	Yushi-gachi	7:00
2. Angelo Parisi	FRA		
3. Arthur Mapp	GBR		
3. András Ozsvár	HUN		
5. Sergei Novikov	SOV		
5. Dambajan Tsend-Auish	MON		
7. Pavelj Dragoi	ROM		

Lorenz, a car mechanic and army officer, had the rare distinction of being a sixth Dan red-and-white belt judoka. At 5 feet 11 inches, he was also the shortest entrant in the open category.

MODERN PENTATHLON

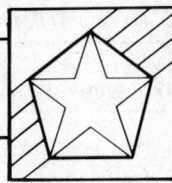

Individual
Team

The basic premise behind the modern pentathlon is that a soldier is ordered to deliver a message. He starts out on the back of an unfamiliar horse, but is forced to dismount and fight a duel with swords. He escapes, but is trapped and has to shoot his way out with a pistol. Then he swims across a river, and finally he finishes his assignment by running 4000 meters through the woods.

Between 1912 and 1952 the scoring was based on an athlete's placing in each of the five events. Since 1956, the modern pentathlon has been scored like the decathlon, with a set of charts assigning a point total to each performance.

INDIVIDUAL

1896–1908 not held

1912 Stockholm C: 32, N: 10, D: 7.12.

			SHOOTING	SWIMMING	FENCING	RIDING	RUNNING	TOTAL
1.	Gösta Lilliehöök	SWE	3	10	5	4	5	27
2.	Gösta Åsbrink	SWE	1	4	15	7	1	28
3.	Georg de Laval	SWE	2	3	10	3	12	30
4.	Åke Grönhagen	SWE	18	5	1	1	10	35
5.	George Patton	USA	21	7	4	6	3	41
6.	Sidney Stranne	SWE	11	9	3	8	11	42
7.	Karl Mannström	SWE	14	14	16	2	9	55
8.	E. Bernhardt	AUT	26	2	6	12	14	60

The fifth-place finisher was a 26-year-old army lieutenant, George S. Patton, Jr. who later went on to considerable fame as a general during World War II. Ironically, Patton might have won the event had he not been such a poor marksman, placing a mediocre 21st in a field of 32 in the shooting competition.

If Lilliehöök had taken five more seconds to finish the 4000-meter cross-country run, he would have lost the gold medal.

1920 Antwerp C: 22, N: 8, D: 8.27.

		SHOOTING	SWIMMING	FENCING	RIDING	RUNNING	TOTAL
1. Gustaf Dyrssen	SWE	6	2	2	6	2	18
2. Erik de Laval	SWE	1	13	5	1	3	23
3. Gösta Runö	SWE	4	1	16	5	1	27
4. Bengt Uggla	SWE	13	5	10	13	5	46
5. Marius Erik Christensen	DEN	12	7	3	7	18	47
6. Harold Rayner	USA	5	12	13	14	4	48
7. Hagelberg	FIN	10	3	21	9	8	51
8. Robert Sears	USA	3	8	9	11	20	51

1924 Paris C: 38, N: 11, D: 7.17.

		SHOOTING	SWIMMING	FENCING	RIDING	RUNNING	TOTAL
1. Bo Lindman	SWE	9	1	3	4	1	18
2. Gustaf Dyrssen	SWE	20	4	1	3	11.5	39.5
3. Bertil Uggla	SWE	7	21	5	5	7	45
4. Ivan Duranthon	FRA	4	18	17.5	11	4	54.5
5. Harry Avellan	FIN	17	6	17.5	1	14	55.5
6. Helge Jensen	DEN	2	19	11.5	9.5	19	61
7. G. Vokins	GBR	24	11	10	8	11.5	64.5
8. C. Tonnet	HOL	22	12	13.5	16	2	65.5

1928 Amsterdam C: 37, N: 14, D: 8.4.

		SHOOTING	SWIMMING	FENCING	RUNNING	RIDING	TOTAL
1. Sven Thofelt	SWE	6	2	4	21	14	47
2. Bo Lindman	SWE	15	5	22	3	5	50
3. Helmuth Kahl	GER	10	9	2	19	12	52
4. Ingvar Berg	SWE	3	11	36	7	1	58
5. Heinz Hax	GER	1	15	21	20	2	59
6. D. Torquand-Young	GBR	24	7	15	9	10	65
7. Hermann Hölter	GER	16	8	11	21	13	69
7. C. Tonnet	HOL	8	24	27	6	4	69

1932 Los Angeles C: 25, N: 10, D: 8.6.

		RIDING	FENCING	SHOOTING	SWIMMING	RUNNING	TOTAL
1. Johan Oxenstierna	SWE	4	14	2	5	7	32
2. Bo Lindman	SWE	1	2.5	19	9	4	35.5
3. Richard Mayo	USA	2	4.5	1	14	17	38.5
4. Sven Thofelt	SWE	15	1	9	1	13	39
5. Willy Remer	GER	12	10	4	13	8	47
6. Conrad Miersch	GER	10	10	5	17	6	48
7. Elemér Somfay	HUN	20	4.5	6	12	10	52.5
8. Digby Legard	GBR	6	18	10	18	1	53

1936 Berlin C: 42, N: 16, D: 8.6.

		RIDING	FENCING	SHOOTING	SWIMMING	RUNNING	TOTAL
1. Gotthardt Handrick	GER	2.5	2	4	9	14	31.5
2. Charles Leonard	USA	15	10	1	6	7.5	39.5
3. Silvano Abba	ITA	1	15.5	10	14	5	45.5
4. Sven Thofelt	SWE	8.5	5.5	6	3	24	47
5. Nándor Orbán	HUN	4	12.5	21	2	16	55.5
6. Hermann Lemp	GER	31	3.5	11	1	21	67.5
7. Alfred Starbird	USA	8.5	8.5	23	20	7.5	67.5
8. Rezsö Bartha	HUN	27	12.5	3	12	22	76.5

In the pistol-shooting portion of the competition, Lieutenant Charles Leonard of St. Petersburg, Florida, became the first person in the history of the event to achieve a perfect score of 200.

1948 London C: 45, N: 16, D: 8.4.

		RIDING	FENCING	SHOOTING	SWIMMING	RUNNING	TOTAL
1. William "Wille" Grut	SWE	1	1	5	1	8	16
2. George Moore	USA	2	3	21	17	4	47
3. Gösta Gärdin	SWE	6	17	10	11	5	49
4. Lauri Vilkko	FIN	17	38	4	3	2	64
5. Olavi Larkas	FIN	26	3	7	19	16	71
6. Bruno Riem	SWI	19	9	1	36	9	74
7. F. Hegner	SWI	24	13	3	7	29	79
8. Richard Gruenther	USA	13	12	14	24	19	81

Captain William Grut, a 33-year-old artillery officer, accomplished the most decisive victory in the history of the modern pentathlon, finishing first in three of the five events.

1952 Helsinki C: 51, N: 19, D: 7.25.

		RIDING	FENCING	SHOOTING	SWIMMING	RUNNING	TOTAL
1. Lars Hall	SWE	1	7	15	1	8	32
2. Gábor Benedek	HUN	8	2	9	18	2	39
3. István Szondy	HUN	3	4	12	5	17	41
4. Igor Novikov	SOV	24	13	4	4	10	55
5. Frederick Denman	USA	9	11	6	17	19	62
5. Olavi Mannonen	FIN	2	37	10	9	4	62
7. Lauri Vilkko	FIN	1	8	38	11	5	63
8. W.Thad McArthur	USA	29	3	23	12	1	68

Twenty-five-year-old Lars Hall was the first nonmilitary winner of the modern pentathlon. A carpenter from Gothenburg, Hall had two lucky breaks. The horse that he drew for the equestrian competition was discovered to be lame. The horse that he was assigned as a substitute turned out to be the best horse in Finland, and Hall's only challenge was to keep from falling off as the horse raced through the course. Two days later, Hall arrived 20 minutes late for the pistol-shooting, but was saved from disqualification due to a Soviet protest that was still being sorted out.

1956 Melbourne C: 40, N: 16, D: 11.28.

		RIDING	FENCING	SHOOTING	SWIMMING	RUNNING	TOTAL
1. Lars Hall	SWE	1035 (4)	889 (4)	720(24)	1030 (2)	1159(12)	4833
2. Olavi Mannonen	FIN	997.5 (5)	815 (8)	880 (5)	920(15)	1162 (7)	4774
3. Väinö Korhonen	FIN	885 (9)	963 (2)	880 (5)	905(16)	1117(12)	4750
4. Igor Novikov	SOV	802.5(14)	815 (8)	920 (2)	935 (6)	1192 (4)	4714
5. George Lambert	USA	1070 (1)	667(17)	900 (4)	975 (7)	1081(15)	4693
6. Gábor Benedek	HUN	860 (11)	889 (4)	920 (2)	855(18)	1126(10)	4650
7. William André	USA	887.5 (5)	889 (4)	860 (8)	870(17)	1123(11)	4629
8. Aleksandr Tarassov	SOV	810 (13)	778(10)	880 (5)	825(21)	1186 (5)	4479

1960 Rome C: 60, N: 23, D: 8.31.

		RIDING	FENCING	SHOOTING	SWIMMING	RUNNING	TOTAL
1. Férenc Németh	HUN	1009(31)	977 (2)	880(10)	990 (6)	1168 (7)	5024
2. Imre Nagy	HUN	1048(19)	1000 (1)	840(23)	935(18)	1165 (8)	4988
3. Robert Beck	USA	1039(24)	977 (2)	940 (3)	1010 (4)	1015(24)	4981
4. András Balczó	HUN	1037(20)	885 (6)	760(36)	1075 (1)	1216 (2)	4973
5. Igor Novikov	SOV	982(33)	839 (9)	860(15)	1035 (2)	1246 (1)	4962
6. Nikolai Tatarinov	SOV	1138 (5)	747(19)	820(27)	885(28)	1168 (6)	4758
7. Stanislaw Przybylski	POL	1111(13)	747(20)	860(16)	815(39)	1198 (3)	4731
8. Jack Daniels	USA	1024(27)	793(12)	900 (6)	1015 (3)	985(26)	4717

1964 Tokyo C: 37, N: 15, D: 10.15.

		RIDING	FENCING	SHOOTING	SWIMMING	RUNNING	TOTAL
1. Ferenc Török	HUN	1070(15)	1000 (1)	960(10)	960(23)	1126 (5)	5116
2. Igor Novikov	SOV	1040(26)	856 (5)	1020 (3)	1055 (5)	1096 (6)	5067
3. Albert Mokeyev	SOV	970(33)	748(15)	1060 (1)	1045 (7)	1216 (1)	5039
4. Peter Macken	AUS	1070(19)	640(21)	1020 (4)	1035 (8)	1132 (3)	4897
5. Viktor Mineyev	SOV	1040(24)	820 (9)	960(13)	1050 (6)	1024(15)	4894
6. James Moore	USA	1070(16)	676(20)	960(12)	990(15)	1195 (2)	4891
7. Imre Nagy	HUN	1040(3))	892 (2)	960 (9)	940(28)	1042(11)	4874
8. Bo-Herman Jansson	SWE	1100 (3)	748(16)	780(28)	1075 (1)	1057(10)	4760

1968 Mexico City C: 48, N: 18, D: 10.17.

		RIDING	FENCING	SHOOTING	SWIMMING	RUNNING	TOTAL
1. Björn Ferm	SWE	1100 (5)	885 (9)	934(12)	1075 (2)	970 (5)	4964
2. András Balczó	HUN	1010(22)	931 (6)	934(13)	1054 (5)	1024 (2)	4953
3. Pavel Lednev	SOV	1070 (8)	839(16)	934(10)	1060 (4)	892(16)	4795
4. Karl-Heinz Kutschke	GDR	1070(10)	632(42)	846(27)	1126 (1)	1090 (1)	4764
5. Boris Onischenko	SOV	995(29)	885 (9)	912(16)	1054 (5)	910(13)	4756
6. Raoul Gueguen	FRA	1040(14)	954 (5)	912(14)	1000(10)	850(20)	4756
7. István Moná	HUN	1010(20)	1040 (2)	868(23)	943(24)	847(22)	4714
— Hans-Gunnar Liljenvall	SWE	1010(24)	908 (7)	956 (7)	955(20)	835(23)	4664
8. Jeremy Fox	GBR	1010(21)	862(13)	890(19)	1006 (9)	895(15)	4663

Ferm, a 24-year-old economics student, kept busy during the 12-hour fencing competition by reading detective stories. When it came down to the final cross-country run, he needed to beat 14 minutes 30 seconds to win the gold medal. Ferm struggled through the unfamiliar rarefied air and crossed the finish line with only four seconds to spare. An ugly incident had marred the riding event. Hans-Jürgen Todt of West Germany drew a beautiful but stubborn horse named Ranchero, which balked three times at one of the obstacles. After completing the course, Todt, disconsolate at seeing his years of training gone to waste because of bad luck, attacked the horse and had to be pulled away by his teammates.

1972 Munich C: 59, N: 21, D: 8.31.

		RIDING	FENCING	SHOOTING	SWIMMING	RUNNING	TOTAL
1. András Balczó	HUN	1060(17)	1057 (2)	956(12)	1060(25)	1279 (3)	5412
2. Boris Onischenko	SOV	945(42)	1076 (1)	1066 (2)	1128(11)	1120(21)	5335
3. Pavel Lednev	SOV	1060(14)	1019 (3)	1022 (4)	1092(18)	1135(14)	5328
4. Jeremy Fox	GBR	1100 (2)	1019 (3)	868(22)	1024(32)	1300 (1)	5311
5. Vladimir Shmelev	SOV	920(47)	962 (7)	1022 (5)	1176 (6)	1222 (6)	5302
6. Björn Ferm	SWE	1100 (4)	943(10)	978 (7)	1112(13)	1150(10)	5283
7. Heiner Thade	GER	1065(12)	962 (7)	956(13)	1012(37)	1150 (9)	5145
8. Risto Hurme	FIN	950(40)	981 (5)	1044 (3)	1068(24)	1051(33)	5094

Five-time world champion András Balczó finally won an Olympic individual gold medal at the age of 34. Tied for third place after four events, Balczó, a typewriter mechanic, set off on the cross-country course at a terrific pace and staggered home a winner. Quite an uproar developed when it was discovered through drug tests that 14 pentathletes had taken the tranquilizers Valium and Librium before going out on the shooting range. These drugs were banned by the International Modern Pentathlon Union, but were considered acceptable by the International Olympic Committee. For this reason no disqualifications were made.

1976 Montreal C: 47, N: 15, D: 7.22

		RIDING	FENCING	SHOOTING	SWIMMING	RUNNING	TOTAL
1. Janusz Pyciak-Peciak	POL	1066(23)	928 (5)	1044 (3)	1164(17)	1318 (3)	5520
2. Pavel Lednev	SOV	1032(32)	1096 (1)	1022 (6)	1092(30)	1243(10)	5485
3. Jan Bártu	CZE	1100 (1)	976 (3)	1044 (5)	1184(13)	1162(22)	5466
4. Daniele Masala	ITA	1090(14)	832(13)	1066 (2)	1244 (6)	1201(17)	5433
5. Adrian Parker	GBR	1100 (1)	712(30)	868(29)	1240 (7)	1378 (1)	5298
6. John Fitzgerald	USA	1036(25)	952 (4)	1000 (9)	1232 (8)	1066(42)	5286
7. Jorn Steffensen	DEN	1100 (1)	856 (9)	1044 (4)	1068(38)	1213(14)	5281
8. Boris Mosolov	SOV	1036(25)	856 (9)	934(20)	1212 (9)	1162(22)	5200

Pyciak-Peciak was only in fifth place after four events, but he ran a strong 4000 meters and finished with 12 seconds to spare in 12:29.70.

1980 Moscow C: 43, N: 19, D: 7.24.

		RIDING	FENCING	SHOOTING	SWIMMING	RUNNING	TOTAL
1. Anatoly Starostin	SOV	1068(13)	1000 (4)	1110 (2)	1216(10)	1174 (8)	5568
2. Tamás Szombathelyi	HUN	1100 (2)	1026 (2)	1088 (3)	1144(24)	1144(11)	5502
3. Pavel Lednev	SOV	1026(21)	1026 (2)	1022(15)	1104(31)	1204 (4)	5382
4. Svante Rasmuson	SWE	936(40)	922 (7)	1000(17)	1332 (2)	1183 (6)	5373
5. Tibor Maracskó	HUN	980(32)	964 (6)	956(27)	1208(12)	1171 (9)	5279
6. Janusz Pyciak-Peciak	POL	1070(12)	844(13)	978(25)	1172(14)	1204 (5)	5268
7. Lennart Pettersson	SWE	1050(18)	922 (7)	1088 (6)	1156(19)	1027(32)	5243
8. Milan Kadlec	CZE	1084 (8)	792(20)	1088 (4)	1088(34)	1177 (7)	5229

TEAM
1896–1948 not held

1952 Helsinki T: 15, N: 15, D: 7.25.

		RIDING	FENCING	SHOOTING	SWIMMING	RUNNING	TOTAL
1. HUN	Gábor Benedek István Szondy Aladár Kovácsi	21 (2)	16 (1)	45 (4)	46 (5)	38 (3)	166
2. SWE	Lars Hall Torsten Lindqvist Claes Egnell	18 (1)	16 (1)	68 (8)	29 (2)	51 (6)	182
3. FIN	Olavi Mannonen Lauri Vilkko Olavi Rokka	38 (4)	90(10)	30 (1)	27 (1)	28 (1)	213
4. USA	Frederick Denman W. Thad McArthur Guy Troy	27 (3)	50 (5)	41 (2)	49 (6)	48 (4)	215
5. SOV	Igor Novikov Pavel Rakityansky Aleksandr Dehayev	76 (6)	69 (6)	81(11)	37 (4)	30 (2)	293
6. BRA	Eduardo Leal Medeiros Aloysio Alves Borges Eric Tinoco Marques	94(11)	42 (3)	70 (9)	34 (3)	73 (9)	313
7. CHI	Nilo Floody Buxton Hernán Fuentes Besoain Luis Carmona Barrales	77 (7)	42 (3)	42 (3)	90(11)	81(11)	336
8. ARG	Luis Riera Carlos Velazquez Jorge Caceres Monie	53(15)	98(12)	52 (5)	75 (9)	77(10)	355

1956 Melbourne T: 12, N: 12, D: 11.28.

		RIDING	FENCING	SHOOTING	SWIMMING	RUNNING	TOTAL
1. SOV	Igor Novikov Aleksandr Tarassov Ivan Deryugin	2457.5(3)	2194(2)	2850(1)	2880(1)	3579(1)	13690.5
2. USA	George Lambert William André Jack Daniels	3020 (1)	2008(4)	2560(2)	2780(2)	3114(5)	13482
3. FIN	Olavi Mannonen Väinö Korhonen Berndt Katter	2512.5(2)	2008(4)	2520(4)	2755(3)	3390(3)	13185.5
4. HUN	Gábor Benedek János Bódy Antal Moldrich	1727.5(4)	2566(1)	2460(5)	2660(4)	3141(4)	12554.5
5. MEX	José Pérez Mier Antonio Almada Félix David Romero Vargas	1700 (5)	2008(4)	2560(2)	2640(5)	2073(8)	10981
6. ROM	Cornel Vena Dumitru Tintea Victor Teodorescu	1160 (8)	2194(2)	2160(6)	2195(8)	2904(6)	10613
7. GBR	Donald Cobley Thomas Hudson George Norman	335 (11)	1574(7)	1340(8)	2560(6)	3417(2)	9226
8. AUS	Neville Sayers Sven Coomer George Nicoll	1060 (9)	1264(8)	2040(7)	2220(7)	2241(7)	8825

1960 Rome T: 17, N: 17, D: 8.31.

			RIDING	FENCING	SHOOTING	SWIMMING	RUNNING	TOTAL
1.	HUN	Ferenc Németh Imre Nagy András Balczó	3094 (5)	2740 (1)	2480(6)	3000 (1)	3549 (2)	14863
2.	SOV	Igor Novikov Nikolai Tatarinov Hanno Selg	3087 (6)	2326 (5)	2460(7)	2845 (4)	3591 (1)	14309
3.	USA	Robert Beck Jack Daniels George Lambert	3228 (4)	2402 (3)	2580(2)	3000 (2)	2982 (7)	14192
4.	FIN	Kurt Lindeman Berndt Katter Eero Lohi	2929(13)	2480 (2)	2580(3)	2705 (7)	3171 (5)	13865
5.	POL	Stanislaw Przybylski Kazimierz Paszkiewicz Kazimierz Mazur	3315 (3)	1804(11)	2660(1)	2535(12)	3432 (3)	13746
6.	SWE	Per-Erik Ritzén Sture Ericson Björn Thofelt	3078 (8)	2352 (4)	2360(9)	2585(11)	2841(10)	13216
7.	GBR	Patrick Harvey Donald Cobley Peter Little	3060 (9)	1700(15)	2400(8)	2670 (8)	3273 (4)	13103
8.	MEX	Antonio Almada Félix Sergio Escobedo José Pérez Mier	3393 (1)	2184 (6)	2540(4)	2625 (9)	2103(16)	12845

1964 Tokyo T: 11, N: 11, D: 10.15.

			RIDING	FENCING	SHOOTING	SWIMMING	RUNNING	TOTAL
1.	SOV	Igor Novikov Albert Mokeyev Viktor Mineyev	3050(11)	2385 (3)	3040(1)	3150 (2)	3336(1)	14961
2.	USA	James Moore David Kirkwood Paul Pesthy	3240 (3)	2262 (4)	2640(5)	2915 (6)	3132(3)	14189
3.	HUN	Ferenc Török Imre Nagy Otto Török	3150 (8)	2590 (1)	2380(9)	2885 (7)	3168(2)	14173
4.	SWE	Bo-Herman Jansson Rolf Junefelt Hans-Gunnar Liljenwall	3240 (4)	2057 (6)	2460(8)	3200 (1)	3099(4)	14056
5.	AUS	Peter Macken Donald McMiken Duncan Page	3210 (5)	1770 (7)	2880(2)	2990 (4)	2853(6)	13703
6.	GER	Wolfgang Gödicke Uwe Adler Elmar Frings	3130 (9)	1729 (8)	2800(4)	2955 (5)	2985(5)	13599
7.	FIN	Jorma Hotanen Keijo Vanhala Kari Kaaja	3120(10)	2221 (5)	2560(6)	2885 (8)	2754(9)	13540
8.	JAP	Yoshihide Fukutome Shigeaki Uchino Shigeki Mino	3210 (6)	1524(10)	2860(3)	2865 (9)	2943(6)	13402

1968 Mexico City T: 15, N: 15, D: 10.17.

		RIDING	FENCING	SHOOTING	SWIMMING	RUNNING	TOTAL
1. HUN	András Balczó István Móna Ferenc Török	2940 (6)	3130 (1)	2714 (2)	2877 (7)	2664 (4)	14325
2. SOV	Pavel Lednev Boris Onischenko Stasis Schaparnis	3135 (1)	2558 (3)	2648 (6)	3141 (1)	2766 (2)	14248
– SWE	Björn Ferm Hans-Gunnar Liljenvall Hans Jacobson	3135 (2)	2818 (2)	2736 (1)	2976 (3)	2523 (6)	14188
3. FRA	Raoul Gueguen Lucien Guiguet Jean-Pierre Giudicelli	2855 (9)	2168(12)	2626 (7)	2931 (4)	2709 (3)	13289
4. USA	James Moore Robert Beck M. Thomas Lough	3030 (3)	2324 (8)	2670 (5)	2844 (8)	2412 (9)	13280
5. FIN	Seppo Aho Martti Ketelä Jorma Hotanen	2890 (7)	2558 (3)	2384(14)	2799 (9)	2607 (5)	13238
6. GDR	Karl-Heinz Kutschke Jörg Tscherner Wolfgang Lüderitz	2485(13)	2194(11)	2626 (7)	3093 (2)	2769 (1)	13167
7. JAP	Toshio Fukui Yuso Makihira Katsuaki Tashiro	2980 (5)	2428 (6)	2428(10)	2796(10)	2451 (7)	13083
8. GBR	Jeremy Fox Barry Lillywhite Robert Phelps	2790(10)	2324(10)	2670 (3)	2952 (3)	2157(12)	12893

The Swedish team finished third with 14,188 points, but was disqualified when one of its members, Hans-Gunnar Liljenvall, failed the drug test for alcohol. It was a common practice for pentathletes to steady their nerves with a bit of alcohol before the shooting contest, but Liljenvall, who finished eighth individually, was found to have a blood alcohol concentration well above the acceptable limit, despite the fact that he claimed he had only drunk two beers.

1972 Munich T: 19, N: 19, D: 8.31.

		RIDING	FENCING	SHOOTING	SWIMMING	RUNNING	TOTAL
1. SOV	Boris Onischenko Pavel Lednev Vladimir Shmelev	2925(13)	3060 (1)	3110 (1)	3396(2)	3477 (2)	15968
2. HUN	András Balczó Zsigmond Villányi Pál Bakó	2975(10)	2820 (2)	2736 (2)	3280(5)	3537 (1)	15348
3. FIN	Risto Hurme Veikko Salminen Martti Ketelä	3010 (6)	2580 (4)	2670 (3)	3300(3)	3252 (9)	14812
4. USA	Charles Richards John Fitzgerald Scott Taylor	3115 (3)	2280(10)	2450(10)	3564(1)	3393 (5)	14802
5. SWE	Björn Ferm Bo-Herman Jansson Hans-Gunnar Liljenvall	3125 (2)	2640 (3)	2428(11)	3236(7)	3279 (8)	14708

		RIDING	FENCING	SHOOTING	SWIMMING	RUNNING	TOTAL
6. GER	Heiner Thade Walter Esser Hole Rössler	3010 (7)	2520 (7)	2626 (4)	3232(8)	3294 (7)	14682
7. FRA	Michel Gueguen Jean-Pierre Giudicelli Raoul Gueguen	2990 (8)	2320 (9)	2538 (8)	3252(6)	3459 (3)	14559
8. POL	Ryszard Wach Janusz Pyciak-Peciak Stanislaw Skwira	2955(11)	2420 (8)	2362(13)	3296(4)	3252(10)	14285

1976 Montreal T: 14, N: 14, D: 7.22.

		RIDING	FENCING	SHOOTING	SWIMMING	RUNNING	TOTAL
1. GBR	Adrian Parker Robert Nightingale Jeremy Fox	3212 (3)	2256 (8)	2648 (8)	3492 (5)	3951 (1)	15559
2. CZE	Jan Bártu Bohumil Starnovsky Jiři Adam	2962(10)	2783 (1)	3000 (1)	3400 (8)	3306(12)	15451
3. HUN	Tamás Kancsal Tibor Maracskó Szvetiszláv Sasics	2772(12)	2773 (2)	2758 (5)	3528 (4)	3564 (5)	15395
4. POL	Janusz Pyciak-Peciak Krzysztof Trybusiewicz Zbigniew Pacelt	3170 (6)	2132(11)	2912 (3)	3544 (3)	3585 (2)	15343
5. USA	John Fitzgerald Michael Burley Robert Nieman	3140 (7)	2535 (4)	2296(12)	3768 (1)	3546 (7)	15285
6. ITA	Daniele Masala Pier Paolo Cristofori Mario Medda	3194 (4)	2256 (8)	2670 (6)	3428 (7)	3483 (8)	15031
7. FIN	Risto Hurme Jussi Pelli Heikki Hulkkonen	2794(11)	2597 (3)	2802 (4)	3228(10)	3579 (3)	15000
8. SWE	Hans Lager Bengt Lager Gunnar Jacobson	3268 (1)	2318 (7)	2340(11)	3468 (6)	3552 (6)	14946

In 1976 the noble sport of modern pentathlon was wracked by controversy. First of all, Captain Orben Greenwald, a member of the U.S. team, was prevented from competing when his team manager, Lieutenant-Colonel Donald Johnson of the U.S. Modern Pentathlon Training Center, court-martialed him for insubordination. Although the charge was thrown out as soon as an investigation was begun, Greenwald was refused accreditation when he arrived in Montreal.

The real shock came on the second day of competition, during the fencing tournament. The favored Soviet team was fencing against the team from Great Britain, when the British pentathletes noticed something odd about the defending silver medalist, Army Major Boris Onischenko. In his fight against Adrian Parker, the automatic light registered a hit for the Ukrainian even though he didn't appear to have touched his opponent. Veteran Jeremy Fox was next to be drawn against Onischenko. When he too lost a hit without being touched, it became obvious that something was wrong with Onischenko's épée. The weapon was

taken away to be examined by the Jury of Appeal. Onischenko continued with a different sword, but an hour or so
later the news came that he had been disqualified.

Evidently Onischenko, desperate for victory in his final
international competition, had wired his sword with a well-
hidden push-button circuit breaker which enabled him to
register a hit whenever he wanted. It is unknown how long
Onischenko had been using this trick, but his fencing
scores, which were already high, had showed a marked up-
ward surge beginning in 1970. He was spirited away from
the Olympic Village almost immediately and was never
seen outside the U.S.S.R. again.

Onischenko's disqualification eliminated the Soviets
from the team competition, leaving an open field. After
four events the British team was in fifth place, 547 points
behind Czechoslovakia. But running was their specialty,
and Parker, the first runner of the day, inspired the others
to victory by completing the 4000-meter course in 12 minutes 9 seconds, the fastest time ever recorded in Olympic
competition. Strong performances by Nightingale and Fox
assured Britain of the unexpected victory.

1980 Moscow T: 12, N: 12, D: 7.24.

		RIDING	FENCING	SHOOTING	SWIMMING	RUNNING	TOTAL
1. SOV	Anatoly Starostin Pavel Lednev Yevgeny Lipeev	3194 (2)	2896 (2)	2956(7)	3552 (4)	3528 (1)	16126
2. HUN	Tamás Szombathelyi Tibor Maracskó László Horváth	3088 (5)	3042 (1)	3000(6)	3428 (9)	3354 (4)	15912
3. SWE	Svante Rasmuson Lennart Pettersson George Horvath	3022 (8)	2714 (3)	3220(1)	3640 (1)	3249 (7)	15845
4. POL	Janusz Pyciak-Peciak Jan Olesiński Marek Bajan	3208 (1)	2506 (5)	2846(8)	3576 (3)	3498 (2)	15634
5. FRA	Paul Four Joel Bouzou Alani Cortes	3070 (6)	2600 (4)	3088(3)	3464 (8)	3123(10)	15345
6. CZE	Milan Kadlec Jan Bártu Bohumil Starnovsky	3154 (3)	2298 (8)	3044(5)	3504 (5)	3339 (6)	15339
7. FIN	Heikki Hulkkonen Jussi Pelli Pekka Santanen	2851(11)	2480 (6)	3132(2)	3384(10)	3240 (8)	15087
8. GBR	Robert Nightingale Peter Whiteside Nigel Clark	2946(10)	2246(10)	2824(9)	3584 (2)	3462 (3)	15062

ROWING

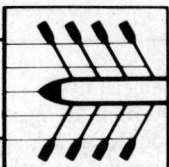

MEN	WOMEN
Single Sculls	Single Sculls
Double Sculls	Double Sculls
Quadruple Sculls	Quadruple Sculls With Coxswain
Pair-Oared Shell Without Coxswain	Pair-Oared Shell Without Coxswain
Pair-Oared Shell With Coxswain	Four-Oared Shell With Coxswain
Four-Oared Shell Without Coxswain	Eight-Oared Shell With Coxswain
Four-Oared Shell With Coxswain	
Eight-Oared Shell With Coxswain	
Discontinued Events	

MEN

Since 1964 rowing contests have begun with qualifying tests. The eight fastest qualifiers advance directly to the semifinals, while the rest take part in a *repêchage,* or second-chance round (*repêchage* being the French word for "fishing again"). The four fastest participants in the repêchage races join the semifinals. The top six semifinalists take part in the final, while the other six take part in a *"petit-final,"* to determine seventh through 12th places.

Men's races are rowed on a 2000-meter course, women's on a 1000-meter course, no matter what the event.

SINGLE SCULLS
1896 not held

1900 Paris C: 10, N: 2, D: 8.26.
1. Henri Barrelet   FRA   7:35.6
2. André Gaudin   FRA   7:41.6
3. George Saint Ashe   GBR   8:15.6
4. Robert d'Heilly   FRA   8:16.0
DNF: Louis Prével (FRA)

1904 St. Louis C: 4, N: 1, D: 7.30.
1. Frank Greer   USA   10:08.5
2. James Juvenal   USA   —
3. Constance Titus   USA   —
4. Dave Duffield   USA   —

1906 not held

1908 London C: 9, N: 6, D: 7.31.
1. Harry Blackstaffe   GBR   9:26.0
2. Alexander McCulloch   GBR   —
3. Bernhard von Gaza   GER   —
3. Károly Levitzky   HUN   —

The 40-year-old Blackstaffe was twice the age of McCulloch, his opponent in the final. Yet he was able to finish more strongly and win by one and a quarter lengths.

1912 Stockholm C: 13, N: 11, D: 7.19.
1. William Kinnear   GBR   7:47.6
2. Polydore Veirman   BEL   7:56.0
3. Everard Butler   CAN   —
3. Mikhail Kusik   RUS   —

1920 Antwerp C: 10, N: 10, D: 8.29.
1. John Kelly, Sr.   USA   7:35.0
2. Jack Beresford   GBR   7:36.0
3. D. Clarence Hadfield d'Arcy   NZE   7:48.0
4. Frits Evert Eyken   HOL   —

Philadelphia bricklayer Jack Kelly, who once won 126 straight races, was barred from competing in London's famous Diamond Sculls race at Henley because the Vesper Boat Club, of which he was a member, had been accused of professionalism three years earlier. Kelly got his revenge a few weeks later in the Olympics, when he defeated the Diamond Sculls winner, Jack Beresford, in the final. The two men were so exhausted after the race that they were unable to shake hands. Nevertheless, Kelly managed to recover sufficiently to win a second gold medal in the double sculls 30 minutes later. Kelly had two illustrious offspring. His son John, Jr., who competed in four Olympics himself, brought his father great joy when he won the Diamond Sculls at Henley in 1947 and 1949. His daughter was Grace Kelly, the famous film actress who later became Princess of Monaco.

1924 Paris C: 8, N: 8, D: 7.17.
1. Jack Beresford   GBR   7:49.2
2. William Garrett Gilmore   USA   7:54.0
3. Josef Schneider   SWI   8:01.1
DNF: A. Bull (AUS)

In 1924 the system of repêchage was introduced, in which the second-place finishers in the preliminary heats are allowed a row-off for a place in the final. This was a break for Beresford, who lost to Gilmore in the opening round. Qualifying through the repêchage, Beresford turned the tables on Gilmore in the final and won by two and a half lengths. Despite his defeat, Gilmore had fond memories of the race. "During the last 200 meters," he later wrote, "when the sun seemed to get hotter with every stroke and I was making a supreme effort to grasp victory, a kindly breeze swept across the Seine, carrying a strong but pleasant scent from a perfumery which was not within sight. It was truly so strong that it first gagged me, but in a moment I was rowing on as if in a flowing river of the perfume itself."

1928 Amsterdam C: 15, N: 15, D: 8.10.
1. Henry Pearce   AUS   7:11.0
2. Kenneth Myers   USA   7:20.8
3. Theodore Collet   GBR   7:29.8
4. Lambertus Gunther   HOL   7:31.6
5. Joseph Wright   CAN
6. Josef Straka   CZE
7. E. Candeveau   SWI
8. V. Savrin   FRA

Henry Pearce, a third-generation sculling champion from Sydney, faced an unexpected challenge in the middle of the final when a family of ducks passed single-file in front of his boat. Pearce let them pass and then sculled to a popular five-length victory. He had hoped that his Olympic win would allow him to row in the Diamond Sculls at Henley, but he was refused admission because he was a carpenter. Back in Sydney he was unable to find work due to the Depression. When Lord Dewar, the Canadian whisky manufacturer, learned of Pearce's plight, he offered him a job as a salesman. Ironically, this new position made Pearce eligible for Henley, since he was no longer a laborer. In 1931 he went to London and won the Diamond Sculls by six lengths. Although he moved to Hamilton, Ontario, in Canada, Pearce represented Australia again in 1932 and won a second gold medal.

1932 Los Angeles C: 5, N: 5, D: 8.13.
1. Henry Pearce   AUS   7:44.4
2. William Miller   USA   7:45.2
3. Guillermo Douglas   URU   8:13.6
4. Leslie Southwood   GBR   8:33.6

1936 Berlin C: 20, N: 20, D: 8.14.
1. Gustav Schäfer   GER   8:21.5
2. Josef Hasenöhrl   AUT   8:25.8
3. Daniel Barrow   USA   8:28.0
4. Charles Campbell   CAN   8:35.0
5. Ernst Rufli   SWI   8:38.9
6. Pascual José Giorgio   ARG   8:57.5
7. Roger Verey   POL
7. H.L. Warren   GBR

1948 London C: 14, N: 14, D: 8.9.
1. Mervyn Wood   AUS   7:24.4
2. Eduardo Risso   URU   7:38.2
3. Romolo Catasta   ITA   7:51.4
4. Tranquilo Cappozzi   ARG
4. John Kelly, Jr.   USA
4. J. Sepheriades   FRA
7. A. Rowe   GBR

1952 Helsinki C: 18, N: 18, D: 7.23.
1. Yuri Tyukalov   SOV   8:12.8
2. Mervyn Wood   AUS   8:14.5
3. Teodor Kocerka   POL   8:19.4
4. J. Anthony Fox   GBR   8:22.5
5. Ian Stephen   SAF   8:31.4

1956 Melbourne C: 12, N: 12, D: 11.27.
1. Vyacheslav Ivanov   SOV   8:02.5
2. Stuart Mackenzie   AUS   8:07.7
3. John Kelly, Jr.   USA   8:11.8
4. Teodor Kocerka   POL   8:12.9

Mackenzie, who made his living as a chicken-sexer, seemed to have the race well in hand, but Ivanov made a sensational spurt with 200 meters to go and won going away. Eighteen-year-old Ivanov was so thrilled when he was presented with his gold medal that he jumped up and down with joy—and dropped the medal into Lake Wendouree. He immediately dived to the bottom of the water, but came back up empty-handed. After the games were over he was given a replacement medal by the I.O.C. He earned two more gold medals in 1960 and 1964.

1960 Rome C: 13, N: 13, D: 9.3.
1. Vyacheslav Ivanov   SOV   7:13.96
2. Achim Hill   GDR   7:20.21
3. Teodor Kocerka   POL   7:21.26
4. James Hill   NZE   7:23.98
5. Harry Parker   USA   7:29.26
6. Savino Rebek   ITA   7:31.09

1964 Tokyo C: 13, N: 13, D: 10.15.
1. Vyacheslav Ivanov   SOV   8:22.51
2. Achim Hill   GDR   8:26.24
3. Gottfried Kottmann   SWI   8:29.68
4. Alberto Demiddi   ARG   8:31.51
5. Murray Watkinson   NZE   8:35.57
6. Donald Spero   USA   8:37.53
7. Robert Groen   HOL
8. Leif Gotfredsen   CAN

Ivanov staged another one of his famous finishing bursts, gaining 11 seconds on Hill in the last 500 meters. Actually he made such a tremendous effort that he blacked out before the finish line. In his book, *Winds of Olympic Lakes*, Ivanov wrote, "I don't remember how long it was before consciousness gradually returned. . . . I mustered the last ounce of my strength, raised my head and couldn't believe it: there was clear water ahead of me and nobody in front of me in those last 50 meters to the finish. I wondered whether it was a case of delirium and that I was having hallucinations. . . . I managed to find an extra bit of strength, picked up the oars and crossed the line first."

1968 Mexico City C: 17, N: 17, D: 10.19.
1. Henri Jan Wienese   HOL   7:47.80
2. Jochen Meissner   GER   7:52.00
3. Alberto Demiddi   ARG   7:57.19
4. John Van Blom   USA   8:00.51
5. Achim Hill   GDR   8:06.09
6. Kenneth Dwan   GBR   8:13.76
7. Zdzsislaw Bromek   POL
8. Niels Secher   DEN

1972 Munich C: 18, N: 18, D: 9.2.
1. Yuri Malishev   SOV   7:10.12
2. Alberto Demiddi   ARG   7:11.53
3. Wolfgang Güldenpfennig GDR 7:14.45
4. Udo Hild   GER   7:20.81
5. James Dietz   USA   7:24.81
6. Melchior Bürgin   SWI   7:31.99
7. John Drea   IRL
8. Yordan Vulchev   BUL

1976 Montreal C: 15, N: 15, D: 7.25.
1. Pertti Karppinen   FIN   7:29.03
2. Peter-Michael Kolbe   GER   7:31.67
3. Joachim Dreifke   GDR   7:38.03
4. Sean Drea   IRL   7:42.53
5. Nikolai Dovgan   SOV   7:57.39
6. Ricardo Ibarra   ARG   8:03.05
7. James Dietz   USA
8. Edward Hale   AUS

Karppinen, a 6-foot 7-inch fireman from Parsio, won Finland's first rowing gold medal by coming from behind to upset world champion Kolbe and co-favorite Dreifke.

1980 Moscow C: 14, N: 14, D: 7.27.
1. Pertti Karppinen   FIN   7:09.61
2. Vassily Yakusha   SOV   7:11.66
3. Peter Kersten   GDR   7:14.88
4. Vladek Lacina   CZE   7:17.57
5. Hans Svensson   SWE   7:19.38
6. Hugh Matheson   GBR   7:20.28
7. Bernard Destraz   SWI
8. Konstantinos Kontomanolis GRE

DOUBLE SCULLS

1896–1900 not held

1904 St. Louis T: 3, N: 1, D: 7.30.
1. USA   (Atalanta Boat Club, New York—John Mulcahy,   10:03.2
         William Varley)
2. USA   (Ravenswood Boat Club, Long Island—John   —
         Hoben, James McLoughlin)
3. USA   (Independent Rowing Club, New Orleans—John   —
         Wells, Joseph Ravanack)

1906–1912 not held

1920 Antwerp T: 5, N: 5, D: 8.29.
1. USA   (John Kelly, Sr., Paul Costello, Sr.)   7:09.0
2. ITA   (Erminio Dones, Pietro Annoni)   7:19.0
3. FRA   (Alfred Plé, Gaston Giran)   7:21.0

1924 Paris T: 5, N: 5, D: 7.17.
1. USA   (Paul Costello, Sr., John Kelly, Sr.)   6:34.0
2. FRA   (Marc Detton, Jean-Pierre Stock)   6:38.0
3. SWI   (Rudolf Bosshard, Heinrich Thoma)   —
4. BRA   (Edumundo Castello-Branco, Carlos Castello-Branco)   —

1928 Amsterdam T: 10, N: 10, D: 7.17.
1. USA   (Paul Costello, Sr., Charles McIlvaine)   6:41.4
2. CAN   (Joseph Wright, Jack Guest)   6:51.0
3. AUT   (Leo Losert, Viktor Flessl)   6:48.8
4. GER   (Horst Hoeck, Gerhard Voigt)   6:48.2
5. HOL   (Henri Cox, Constant Pieterse)   6:52.8
6. SWI   (Rudolf Bosshard, Maurice Rieder)   6:53.4

Costello won his third straight double sculls gold medal with relative ease. He and McIlvaine were never seriously challenged and won the final against Wright and Guest by five lengths.

1932 Los Angeles T: 5, N: 5, D: 8.13.
1. USA   (Kenneth Myers, William Garrett Gilmore) 7:17.4
2. GER   (Herbert Buhtz, Gerhard Boetzelen)   7:22.8
3. CAN   (Charles Pratt, Noël de Mille)   7:27.6
4. ITA   (Orfeo Paroli, Mario Moretti)   7:49.2

Veteran Olympians Myers and Gilmore were 36 and 37 years old, respectively.

1936 Berlin T: 12, N: 12, D: 8.14.

1. GBR (Jack Beresford, Leslie Southwood) 7:20.8
2. GER (Willy Kaidel, Joachim Pirsch) 7:26.2
3. POL (Roger Verey, Jerzy Ustupski) 7:36.2
4. FRA (André Giriat, Robert Jacquet) 7:42.3
5. USA (John Houser, William Dugan) 7:44.8
6. AUS (William Dixon, Herbert Turner) 7:45.1

Beresford and Southwood were beaten by Kaidel and Pirsch in the first round, but qualified for the final through repêchage. The Germans led from the start, but the British pair caught them at 1800 meters, rowed neck and neck for 100 meters, and then pulled away to win by two and a half lengths. The 37-year-old Beresford was competing in his fifth Olympic Games. Each time he won a medal: in 1920 a silver in the single sculls; in 1924 a gold in the same event; in 1928 a silver in the eights; in 1932 a gold in the coxwainless fours; and finally, in 1936, this third gold, in the double sculls. Considering that he and Southwood won the Double Sculls Challenge Cup at Henley in 1939, it is quite possible that Beresford would have won a sixth medal had not World War II intervened.

1948 London T: 15, N: 15, D: 8.9.

1. GBR (Richard Burnell, Bertram Bushnell) 6:51.3
2. DEN (Ebbe Parsner, Aage Larsen) 6:55.3
3. URU (William Jones, Juan Rodriguez) 7:12.4

1952 Helsinki T: 16, N: 16, D: 7.23.

1. ARG (Tranquilo Cappozzo, Eduardo Guerrero) 7:32.2
2. SOV (Georgi Zhilin, Igor Yemchuk) 7:38.3
3. URU (Miguel Seijas, Juan Rodriguez) 7:43.7
4. FRA (Jacques Maillet, Achille Giovannoni) 7:46.8
5. CZE (Antonín Malinković, Jiří Vykoukal) 7:53.8
6. AUS (John Rogers, Murray Riley), BEL (Robert George, Joseph Van Stichel), ITA (Silvio Bergamini, Lodovico Sommaruga)

1956 Melbourne T: 8, N: 8, D: 11.27.

1. SOV (Aleksandr Berkutov, Yuri Tyukalov) 7:24.0
2. USA (Bernard Paul Costello, Jr., James Gardiner) 7:32.2
3. AUS (Murray Riley, Mervyn Wood) 7:37.4
4. GER (Thomas Schneider, Kurt Hipper) 7:41.7

1960 Rome T: 16, N: 16, D: 9.3.

1. CZE (Václav Kozák, Pavel Schmidt) 6:47.50
2. SOV (Aleksandr Berkutov, Yuri Tyukalov) 6:50.49
3. SWI (Ernst Hürlimann, Rolf Larcher) 6:50.59
4. FRA (René Duhamel, Bernard Monnereau) 6:52.22
5. HOL (Peter Bakker, Jacobus Rentmeester) 6:53.86
6. BEL (Gérard Higny, Jean Lemaire) 6:56.40

Václav Kozák was a 23-year-old noncommissioned officer. His partner was 30-year-old Pavel Schmidt, a psychiatrist from Bratislava.

1964 Tokyo T: 13, N: 13, D: 10.15.

1. SOV (Cleg Tyurin, Boris Dubrovsky) 7:10.66
2. USA (Seymour Cromwell, James Storm) 7:13.16

3. CZE (Vladimir Andrs, Pavel Hofmann) 7:14.23
4. SWI (Melchior Bürgin, Martin Studach) 7:24.97
5. GER (Helmut Lebert, Josef Steffes-Mies) 7:30.03
6. FRA (René Duhamel, Bernard Monnereau) 7:41.80
7. GBR (Michael Clay, Peter Webb)
8. HOL (Max Alwin, Peter Bots)

1968 Mexico City T: 13, N: 13, D: 10.19.

1. SOV (Anatoly Sass, Aleksandr Timoshinin) 6:51.82
2. HOL (Leendert Frans van Dis, Henricus Droog) 6:52.80
3. USA (William Maher, John Nunn) 6:54.21
4. BUL (Atanas Schelev, Yordan Valtschev) 6:58.48
5. GDR (Hans-Ulrich Schmied, Manfred Haake) 7:04.92
6. GER (Wolfgang Glock, Udo Hild) 7:12.20
7. BRA (Harri Klein, Edgard Gijsen)
8. ROM (Alexandru Aposteanu, Octavian Pavelescu)

1972 Munich T: 18, N: 18, D: 9.2.

1. SOV (Aleksandr Timoshinin, Gennady Korshikov) 7:01.77
2. NOR (Frank Hansen, Svein Thögersen) 7:02.58
3. GDR (Joachim Böhmer, Hans-Ulrich Schmied) 7:05.55
4. DEN (Niels Secher, Jörgen Engelbrecht) 7:14.19
5. GBR (Timothy Crooks, Patrick Delafield) 7:16.29
6. CZE (Josef Straka, Vladek Lacina) 7:17.60
7. HOL (Jan Bruyn, Paul Veenemans)
8. SWI (Hans Ruckstuhl, Ulrich Isler)

Timoshinin and Korshikov took the lead shortly before the halfway mark and held on to win in the closest double sculls finish in Olympic history.

1976 Montreal T: 13, N: 13, D: 7.25.

1. NOR (Frank Hansen, Alf Hansen) 7:13.20
2. GBR (Chris Baillieu, Michael Hart) 7:15.26
3. GDR (Hans-Ulrich Schmied, Jürgen Bertow) 7:17.45
4. SOV (Yevgeny Barbakov, Gennady Korshikov) 7:18.87
5. GER (Peter Becker, Gerhard Kroschewski) 7:22.15
6. FRA (Jean-Noël Ribot, Jean-Michel Izart) 7:50.18
7. ITA (Umberto Ragazzi, Silvio Ferrini)
8. USA (William Belden, Lawrence Klecatsky)

Two years after Frank Hansen won the silver medal in the double sculls at the Munich Olympics, he asked his younger brother, Alf, to become his new partner. Together they took first place at the 1975 world championships and then went on to win the Olympics the following year. Frank, 30, was an electrician; Alf, 28, worked for the telephone company.

1980 Moscow T: 9, N: 9, D: 7.27.

1. GDR (Joachim Dreifke, Klaus Kröppelien) 6:24.33
2. YUG (Zoran Pancic, Milorad Stanulov) 6:26.34
3. CZE (Zdeněk Pecka, Václav Vochoska) 6:29.07
4. GBR (Tim Clark, Chris Baillieu) 6:31.13
5. SOV (Aleksandr Fomchenko, Yevgeny Duleyev) 6:35.34
6. POL (Wieslaw Kujda, Piotr Tobolski) 6:39.66
7. SPA (Jose Ramon Oyarzabal, Jose Luis Corta)
8. FRA (Marc Boudoux, Didier Gallet)

QUADRUPLE SCULLS

1896-1972 not held

1976 Montreal T: 11, N: 11, D: 7.25.
1. GDR (Wolfgang Güldenpfennig, Rüdiger Reiche, 6:18.65
Karl-Heinz Bussert, Michael Wolfgramm)
2. SOV (Yevgeny Duleev, Yuri Yakomov, Aivar Lazden- 6:19.89
ieks, Vitautas Butkus)
3. CZE (Jaroslav Helebrand, Vaclav Vochoska, Ždenek 6:21.77
Pecka, Vladek Lacina)
4. GER (Norbert Kothe, Helmut Krause, Michael 6:24.81
Gentsch, Helmut Wolber)
5. BUL (Yordan Vulchev, Mincho Nikolov, Hristo Zhe- 6:32.04
lev, Eftim Gerzilov)
6. USA (Peter Cortes, Kenneth Foote, Neil Halleen, 6:34.33
John van Blom)
7. FRA (Roland Weill, Roland Thibaut, Patrick Morin-
eau, Charles Imbert)
8. SWI (Hans Ruckstuhl, Denis Oswald, Jürg Weitnauer, Reto Wyss)

Martin Winter of the East German team had to undergo
an emergency appendectomy and was replaced at the last
minute by Bussert. The sudden change caused the team
some problems in the opening round, and they lost to the
U.S.S.R. But by the final they were all straightened out
and won a hard-fought race. Winter finally won his gold
medal in 1980.

1980 Moscow T: 12, N: 12, D: 7.27.
1. GDR (Frank Dundr, Karsten Bunk, Uwe Heppner, 5:49.81
Martin Winter)
2. SOV (Yuri Shapochka, Yevgeny Barbakov, Valery 5:51.47
Kleshnev, Nikolai Dovgan)
3. BUL (Mincho Nikolov, Lubomir Petrov, Ivo Roussev, 5:52.38
Bogdan Dobrev)
4. FRA (Christian Marquis, Jean Raymond Peltier, 5:53.45
Charles Imbert, Roland Weill)
5. SPA (Juan Solano, Jesus Gonzalez, Manuel Vera, 6:01.19
Julio Oliver)
6. YUG (Milan Arezina, Darko Zibar, Dragan Obradovic, 6:10.76
Nikola Stefanovic)
7. POL (Andrzej Skowroński, Zbigniew Andrusz-
kiewicz, Ryszard Burak Stanislaw Wierzbicki)
8. HOL (Victor Schheffers, Jeroen Vervoorrt, Rob Rob-
bers, Ronald Vervoort)

PAIRED-OARED SHELL WITHOUT COXSWAIN

1896-1900 not held

1904 St. Louis T: 3, N: 1, D: 7.30.
1. USA (Seawanhaka Boat Club, Brooklyn, New York— 10:57.0
Robert Farnam, Joseph Ryan)
2. USA (Atalanta Boat Club, New York—John Mulcahy, —
William Varley)
3. USA (Western Rowing Club, St. Louis, Missouri— —
John Joachim, Joseph Buerger)

1906 not held

1908 London T: 4, N: 3, D: 7.31.
1. GBR (Leander Club I—J.R.K. Fenning, Gordon Thom- 9:41.0
son)
2. GBR (Leander Club II—George Fairbairn, Philip Ver- —
don)

1912-1920 not held

1924 Paris T: 3, N: 3, D: 7.17.
1. HOL (Antonie Beijnen, Wilhelm Rösingh) 8:19.4
2. FRA (Maurice Bouton, Georges Piot) 8:21.6
DNS: GBR (Gordon Killick, C.T. Southgate)

1928 Amsterdam T: 8, N: 8, D: 8.10.
1. GER (Bruno Müller, Kurt Moschter) 7:06.4
2. GBR (Terence O'Brien, R. Archibald Nisbet) 7:08.6
3. USA (Paul McDowell, John Schmitt) 7:20.4
4. ITA (Romeo Sisti, Nino Bolzoni) 7:24.4
5. SWI (Alois Reinhard, Wilhelm Müller) 7:29.1
6. HOL (C.A. van Wankum, Hendrik van Suylekom) 7:30.2

1932 Los Angeles T: 6, N: 6, D: 8.13.
1. GBR (Hugh Arthur Edwards, Lewis Clive) 8:00.0
2. NZE (Cyril Stiles, Frederick Thompson) 8:02.4
3. POL (Henryk Budziński, Janusz Mikolajczak) 8:08.2
4. HOL (Godfried Röel, Pieter Roelofsen) 8:08.4
5. FRA (Fernand Vandernotte, Marcel Vandernotte)

1936 Berlin T: 13, N: 13, D: 8.14.
1. GER (Willi Eichhorn, Hugo Strauss) 8:16.1
2. DEN (Richard Olsen, Harry Larsen) 8:19.2
3. ARG (Horacio Podestá, Julio Curatella) 8:23.0
4. HUN (Károly Györy, Tibor Mamusich) 8:25.7
5. SWI (Wilhelm Klopfer, Karl Müller) 8:33.0
6. POL (Ryszard Borzuchowski, Edward Kobyliński) 8:41.9

1948 London T: 12, N: 12, D: 8.6.
1. GBR (John Wilson, William Laurie) 7:21.1
2. SWI (Hans Kalt, Josef Kalt) 7:23.9
3. ITA (Felice Fanetti, Bruno Boni) 7:31.5

Wilson and Laurie were best friends who joined the Colonial Service and were sent to the Sudan. Returning to London on leave in 1938, they entered the Henley Regatta and
took first place. Then they went back to the Sudan and
didn't touch an oar for ten years. In 1948 they found themselves in Britain on another leave and decided to take up
rowing again. After six weeks' training they entered the
Henley Regatta and won again. This gained them an invitation to represent Great Britain at the Olympics, and they
were granted six months' leave to prepare. Rowing on their
favorite course at Henley, "the Desert Rats," as they were
known, took the lead after 1150 meters and fought off a
late challenge from the Kalt brothers to secure the gold
medal.

1952 Helsinki T: 16, N: 16, D: 7.23.

1. USA	(Charles Logg, Thomas Price)	8:20.7
2. BEL	(Michel Knuysen, Robert Baetens)	8:23.5
3. SWI	(Kurt Schmid, Hans Kalt)	8:32.7
4. GBR	(David Callender, Christopher Davidge)	8:37.4
5. FRA	(Jean-Pierre Souche, René Guissart)	8:48.8

Logg and Price, of Rutgers University, were the Cinderella pair of 1952. Neither man had sat in a pair-oared shell until two months before the Olympics, and the 19-year-old Price had only started rowing in January.

1956 Melbourne T: 9, N: 9, D: 11.27.

1. USA	(James Fifer, Duvall Hecht)	7:55.4
2. SOV	(Igor Buldakov, Viktor Ivanov)	8:03.9
3. AUT	(Alfred Sageder, Josef Kloimstein)	8:11.8
4. AUS	(Peter Adrian Raper, Maurice Grace)	8:22.2

1960 Rome T: 18, N: 18, D: 9.3.

1. SOV	(Valetin Boreyko, Oleg Golovanov)	7:02.01
2. AUT	(Alfred Sageder, Josef Kloimstein)	7:03.69
3. FIN	(Veli Lehtelä, Toimi Pitkänen)	7:03.80
4. GDR	(Jochen Neuling, Heinz Weigel)	7:08.81
5. USA	(Ted Frost, Robert Rogers)	7:17.08
6. YUG	(Nikola Čupin, Antun Ivankovic)	7:20.91

1964 Tokyo T: 14, N: 14, D: 10.15.

1. CAN	(George Hungerford, Roger Jackson)	7:32.94
2. HOL	(Steven Blaisse, Ernst Venemans)	7:33.40
3. GER	(Michael Schwan, Wolfgang Hottenrott)	7:38.63
4. GBR	(James Lee Nicholson, Stewart Farquharson)	7:42.00
5. DEN	(Peter Fich Christiansen, Hans Jórgen Boye)	7:48.13
6. FIN	(Toimi Pitkänen, Veli Lehtelä)	8:05.74
7. SWI	(Peter Bolliger, Nicolas Gobet)	
8. POL	(Czeslaw Nawrot, Alfons Ślusarski)	

Sent to Tokyo as reserves for the Canadian eights team, Hungerford and Jackson were allowed to enter the coxless pairs as compensation. Given only six weeks to get used to each other, they had their first race together ever in the opening round of the Olympics. To compound their problems, Hungerford had not yet recovered from an attack of mononucleosis. In the final they stroked to a one-and-a-half-length lead at the 1500-meter mark and hung on desperately to win Canada's only victory of the 1964 Olympics. Hungerford and Jackson were considered such long shots that no Canadian journalists were present for their race. The two young men celebrated their victory by drinking seven Cokes each. The shell that they used had been loaned to them by the University of Washington; it was the same shell that had been used by Fifer and Hecht when they won the gold medal in 1956.

1968 Mexico City T: 18, N: 18, D: 10.19.

1. GDR	(Jörg Lucke, Hans-Jürgen Bothe)	7:26.56
2. USA	(Lawrence Hough, Philip "Tony" Johnson)	7:26.71
3. DEN	(Peter Christiansen, Ib Ivan Larsen)	7:31.84

4. AUT	(Dieter Ebner, Dieter Losert)	7:41.80
5. SWI	(Fred Rüssli, Werner Zwimpfer)	7:46.79
6. HOL	(Roelof Luynenburg, Rudolf Stokvis)	—
7. AUS	(David Ramage, Paul Guest)	
8. POL	(Alfons Ślusarski, Jerzy Broniec)	

An exciting nip-and-tuck battle saw the favored team of Hough and Johnson take the lead with 500 meters to go, only to have Lucke and Bothe pass them in the last ten meters and win by a mere four feet.

1972 Munich T: 20, N: 20, D: 9.2

1. GDR	(Siegfried Brietzke, Wolfgang Mager)	6:53.16
2. SWI	(Heinrich Fischer, Alfred Bachmann)	6:57.06
3. HOL	(Roelof Luynenburg, Rudolf Stokvis)	6:58.70
4. CZE	(Lubomir Zapletal, Petr Lakomý)	6:58.77
5. POL	(Alfons Ślusarski, Jerzy Broniec)	7:02.74
6. ROM	(Ilie Oantă, Dumitru Grumezescu)	7:42.90
7. GER	(Erwin Haas, Lutz Ulbricht)	
8. SOV	(Vladimir Poliakov, Nikolai Vasiliev)	

In 1968 a comedian named Heinz Quermann appealed over radio and TV for tall young people in East Germany to register with the rowing section of the Leipzig Sports Club. Among the respondents were two 16-year-olds, Siegfried Brietzke and Wolfgang Mager. When they began to achieve competitive success they became known as the "Quermann pair."

1976 Montreal T: 15, N: 15, D: 7.25.

1. GDR	(Jörg Landvoigt, Bernd Landvoigt)	7:23.31
2. USA	(Calvin Coffey, Michael Staines)	7:26.73
3. GER	(Peter Vanroye, Thomas Strauss)	7:30.03
4. YUG	(Žlatko Celent, Duško Mrduljas)	7:34.17
5. BUL	(Valentin Stoev, Georgi Georgiev)	7:37.42
6. CZE	(Miroslav Knapek, Vojtech Časka)	7:51.06
7. SOV	(Gennady Kinko, Tiit Khelmyia)	
8. FIN	(Leo Ahonen, Kari Hanska)	

The Landvoigt twins were 25-year-old steelworkers from Potsdam. The U.S. team, besides being the only American rowers to win medals at Montreal, were also noteworthy for their unusual combination of names—Coffey and Staines.

1980 Moscow T: 15, N: 15, D: 7.27.

1. GDR	(Bernd Landvoigt, Jörg Landvoigt)	6:48.01
2. SOV	(Yuri Pimenov, Nikolai Pimenov)	6:50.50
3. GBR	(Charles Wiggin, Malcolm Carmichael)	6:51.47
4. ROM	(Constantin Postoiu, Valer Toma)	6:53.49
5. CZE	(Miroslav Vrastil, Miroslav Knapek)	7:01.54
6. SWE	(Anders Larson, Anders Wilgotson)	7:02.52
7. IRL	(Pat Gannon, William Ryan)	
8. FRA	(Jean-Claude Roussel, Dominique Lecointe)	

The medal ceremony presented a bizarre sight, as the gold-medal-winning Landvoigt twins stood beside the silver-medal-winning Pimenov twins.

PAIRED-OARED SHELL WITH COXSWAIN

1896 not held

1900 Paris T: 6, N: 3, D: 8.26.
1. HOL (Minerva, Amsterdam—François Antoine Brandt, Roelof Klein, Hermanus Brockmann) 7:34.2
2. FRA (Société Nautique de la Marne—Louis Martinet, Waleff, coxswain unknown) 7:34.4
3. FRA (Rowing Club Castillon—Carlos Deltour, Antoine Védrenne, Paoli) 7:57.2
4. FRA (Cercle Nautique de Reims—Mathieu, Ferlin, coxswain unknown) 8:01.0

Brockmann was coxswain for the Dutch crew in the opening heat, which they lost to the Société Nautique de la Marne. It was decided that Brockmann was too heavy, so he was replaced in the final by a small French boy whose name is unknown. This boy, who was under 10 years old and may have been as young as 7, is presumed to be the youngest competitor in Olympic history.

1904 not held

1906 Athens T: 8, N: 5, D: 4.26.
(1000 Meters)
1. ITA (Bucintoro, Venice—Enrico Bruna, Emilio Fontanella, Giorgio Cesana) 4:23.0
2. ITA (Barion—Luigi Diana, Francesco Civera, Emilio Cesarana) 4:30.0
3. FRA (Société Nautique de la Basse Seine—Gaston Delaplane, Charles Delaporte, Marcel Frebourg) —
4. FRA (Société Nautique de Bayonne—Adolphe Bernard, Joseph Halcet, Jean-Baptiste Mathieu) —
5. BEL (Club Nautique—Max Orban, Remy Orban, Th. Psiliakos) —

1906 Athens T: 7, N: 5, D: 4.26.
(1609 Meters)
1. ITA (Bucintoro, Venice—Enrico Bruna, Emilio Fontanella, Giorgio Cesana) 7:32.4
2. BEL (Société Nautique de Gand—Max Orban, Remy Orban, Th. Psiliakos) 8:00.0
3. FRA (Société Nautique de Bayonne—Adolphe Bernard, Joseph Halcet, Jean-Baptiste Mathieu) 8:08.6
4. DEN (H. Oestergaard, H. Rasmussen, H. Steinthal) —

Psiliakos was a young Greek who offered to cox for the Belgian pair.

1908–1912 not held

1920 Antwerp T: 4, N: 4, D: 8.29.
1. ITA (Ercole Olgeni, Giovanni Scatturin, Guido De Filip) 7:56.0
2. FRA (Gabriel Poix, Maurice Bouton, Ernest Barberolle) 7:57.0
3. SWI (Edouard Candeveau, Alfred Felber, Paul Piaget) —

1924 Paris T: 5, N: 5, D: 7.17.
1. SWI (Edouard Candeveau, Alfred Felber, Emile Lachapelle) 8:39.0
2. ITA (Ercole Olgeni, Giovanni Scatturin, Gino Sopracordevole) 8:39.1
3. USA (Leon Butler, Harold Wilson, Edward Jennings) —
4. FRA (Eugène Constant, Raymond Talleux, Marcel Lepan) —

The final was, by all accounts, a thrilling race, and was won by the Swiss by only two feet.

1928 Amsterdam T: 6, N: 6, D: 8.10.
1. SWI (Hans Schöchlin, Karl Schöchlin, Hans Bourquin) 7:42.6
2. FRA (Armand Marcelle, Edouard Marcelle, Henri Préaux) 7:48.4
3. BEL (Léon Flament, François de Coninck, Georges Anthony) —
4. ITA (R. Vestrini, P.L. Vestrini, C. Milani) —

1932 Los Angeles T: 4, N: 4, D: 8.13.
1. USA (Joseph Schauers, Charles Kieffer, Edward Jennings) 8:25.8
2. POL (Jerzy Braun, Janusz Ślązak, Jerzy Skolimowski) 8:31.2
3. FRA (Anselme Brusa, André Giriat, Pierre Brunet) 8:41.2
4. BRA (José Ramalho, Estevam Strata, Francisco Bricio) 8:53.2

1936 Berlin T: 12, N: 12, D: 8.14.
1. GER (Gerhard Gustmann, Herbert Adamski, Dieter Arend) 8:36.9
2. ITA (Almiro Bergamo, Guido Santin, Luciano Negrini) 8:49.7
3. FRA (Georges Tapie, Marceau Fourcade, Nöel Vandernotte) 8:54.0
4. DEN (Raymond Larsen, Carl Berner, Aage Jensen) 8:55.8
5. SWI (Georges Gschwind, Hans Appenzeller, Rolf Spring) 9:10.9
6. YUG (Ivo Fabris, Elko Mrduljaš, Line Ljubičič) 9:19.4

1948 London T: 9, N: 9, D: 8.9.
1. DEN (Finn Pedersen, Tage Henriksen, Carl-Ebbe Andersen) 8:00.5
2. ITA (Giovanni Steffe, Aldo Tarlao, Alberto Radi) 8:12.2
3. HUN (Antal Szendey, Béla Zsitnik, Róbert Zimonyi) 8:25.2
4. FRA (Ampelio Sartor, Aristide Sartor, R. Crezen),
   YUG (V. Ristic, M. Horvatin, D. Djordjevic)

1952 Helsinki T: 15, N: 15, D: 7.23.
1. FRA (Raymond Salles, Gaston Mercier, Bernard Malivoire) 8:28.6
2. GER (Heinz-Joachim Manchen, Helmut Heinhold, Helmut Noll) 8:32.1
3. DEN (Svend Pedersen, Poul Svendsen, Jörgen Frandsen) 8:34.9
4. ITA (Giuseppe Ramani, Aldo Tarlao, Luciano Marion) 8:38.4
5. FIN (Veijo Mikkolainen, Toimi Pitkänen, Erkki Lyijynen) 8:40.8

1956 Melbourne T: 8, N: 8, D: 11.27.
1. USA (Arthur Ayrault, Conn Findlay, A. Kurt Seiffert) 8:26.1
2. GER (Karl-Heinrich von Groddeck, Horst Arndt, Rainer Borkowsky) 8:29.2
3. SOV (Igor Yemtschuk, Georgy Schilin, Vladimir Petrov) 8:31.0
4. POL (Henryk Jagodziński, Zbigniew Szwarcer, Berthold Mainka) 8:31.5

1960 Rome T: 18, N: 18, D: 9.3.
1. GER (Bernhard Knubel, Heinz Renneberg, Klaus Zerta) 7:29.14
2. SOV (Antanas Bogdanavichus, Zigmas Yukna, Igor Rudakov) 7:30.17
3. USA (Richard Draeger, Conn Findlay, H. Kent Mitchell) 7:34.58
4. DEN (Jens Behrendt Jensen, Knud Nielsen, Sven Lysholt Hansen) 7:39.20
5. ITA (Giancarlo Piretta, Renzo Ostino, Vincenzo Bruno) 7:40.92
6. ROM (Stefan Kureska, Gheorghe Riffelt, Mircea Roger) 7:49.57

1964 Tokyo T: 16, N: 16, D: 10.15.
1. USA (Edward Ferry, Conn Findlay, H. Kent Mitchell) 8:21.23
2. FRA (Jacques Morel, Georges Morel, Jean-Claude Darouy) 8:23.15
3. HOL (Jan Bos, Herman Rouwé, Frederik Hartsuiker) 8:23.42
4. SOV (Nikolai Safronov, Leonid Rakovschik, Igor Rudakov) 8:24.85
5. CZE (Václav Chalupa, Jiři Palko, Zdenek Mejstřik) 8:36.21
6. POL (Kazimierz Maskręcki, Marian Siejkowski, Stanislaw Kozera) 8:40.00
7. GDR (Günter Bergau, Peter Gorny, Karl-Heinz Danielowski)
8. AUT (Alfred Sageder, Josef Kloimstein, Peter Salzbacher)

1968 Mexico City T: 18, N: 18, D: 10.19.
1. ITA (Primo Baran, Renzo Sambo, Bruno Cipolla) 8:04.81
2. HOL (Herman Suselbeek, Hadriaan van Nes, Roderick Rijnders) 8:06.80
3. DEN (Jörn Krab, Harry Jörgensen, Preben Krab) 8:08.07
4. GDR (Helmut Wollmann, Wolfgang Gunkel, Klaus-Dieter Neubert) 8:08.22
5. USA (William Hobbs, Richard Edmunds, Stewart MacDonald) 8:12.60
6. GER (Bernhard Hiesinger, Rolf Hartung, Lutz Benter) 8:41.51
7. SWI (Urs Frankhauser, Urs Bitterli, Beat Wirz)
8. BUL (Georgi Atanasov, Georgi Nikolov, Veselin Staevski)

1972 Munich T: 21, N: 21, D: 9.2.
1. GDR (Wolfgang Gunkel, Jörg Lucke, Klaus-Dieter Neubert) 7:17.25
2. CZE (Oldřich Svojanovský, Pavel Svojanovský, Vladimir Petřiček) 7:19.57

3. ROM (Ştefan Tudor, Petre Ceapura, Ladislau Lowrenschi) 7:21.36
4. GER (Heinz Mussmann, Bernd Krause, Stefan Kuhnke) 7:21.52
5. SOV (Vladimir Eshinov, Nikolai Ivanov, Yuri Lorenson) 7:24.44
6. POL (Wojciech Repsz, Wieslaw Dlugosz, Jacek Rylski) 7:28.92
7. NOR (Rolf Andreassen, Arne Bergodd, Thor Egil Olsen)
8. GBR (David Maxwell, Michael Hart, Alan Inns)

1976 Montreal T: 17, N: 17, D: 7.25.
1. GDR (Harald Jährling, Friedrich-Wilhelm Ulrich, Georg Spohr) 7:58.99
2. SOV (Dmitri Bekhterev, Yuri Shurkalov, Yuri Lorenson) 8:01.82
3. CZE (Oldřich Svojanovský, Pavel Svojanovský, Ludvik Vebr) 8:03.82
4. BUL (Rumen Hristov, Tsvetan Petkov, Tosho Kishev) 8:11.27
5. ITA (Primo Baran, Annibale Venier, Franco Venturnin) 8:15.97
6. POL (Ryszard Stadniuk, Grzegorz Stellak, Ryszard Kubiak) 8:23.02
7. GBR (Neil Christie, James Macleod, David Webb)
8. GER (Winfried Ringwald, Klaus Jaeger, Holger Hocke)

1980 Moscow T: 11, N: 11, D: 7.20.
1. GDR (Harald Jährling, Friedrich-Wilhelm Ulrich, Georg Spohr) 7:02.54
2. SOV (Viktor Pereverzev, Gennady Kryuchkin, Aleksandr Lukyanov) 7:03.35
3. YUG (Dusko Mrduljas, Zlatko Celent, Josip Reic) 7:04.92
4. ROM (Petre Ceapura, Gabriel Bularda, Ladislau Lovrenski) 7:07.17
5. BUL (Tsvetan Petkov, Rumen Hristov, Tosho Kishev) 7:09.21
6. CZE (Josef Plaminek, Milan Škopek, Oldřich Hejdušek) 7:09.41
7. ITA (Antonio Dell'Aquila, Giuseppe Abbagnale, Giuseppe Di Capua)
8. FRA (Serge Fornara, Herve Bourqvel, Jean-Pierre Huguet-Balenx)

FOUR-OARED SHELL WITHOUT COXSWAIN

1896–1900 not held

1904 St. Louis T: 3, N: 1, D: 7.30.
1. USA (Century Boat Club, St. Louis—George Dietz, August Erker, Albert Nasse, Arthur Stockhoff) 9:05.8
2. USA (Mound City Rowing Club, St. Louis—Charles Aman, Michael Begley, Martin Fromanack, Frederick Suerig) —
3. USA (Western Rowing Club, St. Louis—Gustav Voerg, John Freitag, Louis Helm, Frank Dummerth) —

1906 not held

1908 London T: 4, N: 3, D: 7.31.
1. GBR (Magdalen College B.C., Oxford—C. Robert Cud- 8:34.0
   more, James Gillan, Duncan McKinnon, John
   Somers-Smith)
2. GBR (Leander Club—Philip Filleul, Harold Barker, —
   J.R.K. Fenning, Gordon Thomson)

1912–1920 not held

1924 Paris T: 4, N: 4, D: 7.17.
1. GBR (Charles Eley, James MacNabb, Robert Morri- 7:08.6
   son, Terrence Sanders)
2. CAN (Colin Finlayson, Archibald Black, George 7:18.0
   Mackay, William, Wood)
3. SWI (Emile Albrecht, Alfred Probst, Eugen Sigg-
   Bächthold, Hans Walter)
4. FRA (Théo Cremnitz, Jean Camuset, Henri Bonzano,
   Albert Bonzano)

1928 Amsterdam T: 6, N: 6, D: 8.10.
1. GBR (John Lander, Michael Warriner, Richard Beesly, 6:36.0
   Edward Vaughan Bevan)
2. USA (Charles Karle, William Miller, George Heales, Er- 6:37.0
   nest Bayer)
3. ITA (Cesare Rossi, Pietro Freschi, Umberto Bonadè, 6:37.6
   Paolo Gennari)
4. GER (Henry Zänker, Wolfgang Goedecke, Günther DNS
   Roll, Werner Zschieke)

The semifinal race between Great Britain and Germany
saw a dramatic finish. The Germans led by half a length
with 50 meters to go, when Zschieke, their stroke, suddenly collapsed and fell forward on his oars. His teammates
stopped rowing and watched the British crew shoot past to
victory. In the final, the British team, which was from
Trinity College, Cambridge, trailed the U.S. crew for almost the entire race, caught them with 20 yards to go and
spurted ahead to a half-length win.

1932 Los Angeles T: 5, N: 5, D: 8.13.
1. GBR (John Badcock, Hugh Edwards, Jack Beresford, 6:58.2
   Rowland George)
2. GER (Karl Aletter, Ernst Gaber, Walter Flinsch, Hans 7:03.0
   Maier)
3. ITA (Antonio Ghiardello, Francesco Cossu, Giliante 7:04.0
   D'Este, Antonio Provenzani)
4. USA (John McCosker, George Mattson, Thomas 7:14.2
   Pierie, Edgar Johnson)

1936 Berlin T: 9, N: 9, D: 8.14.
1. GER (Rudolf Eckstein, Anton Rom, Martin Karl, Wil- 7:01.8
   helm Menne)

2. GBR (Thomas Bristow, Alan Barrett, Peter Jackson, 7:06.5
   John Duncan Sturrock)
3. SWI (Hermann Betschart, Hans Homberger, Alex 7:10.6
   Homberger, Karl Schmid)
4. ITA (Antonio Ghiardello, Luigi Luscardo, Aldo Pelliz- 7:12.4
   zoni, Francesco Pittaluga)
5. AUT (Rudolf Höpfler, Camillo Winkler, Wilhelm Pichler, 7:20.5
   Johann Binder)
6. DEN (Knud Olsen, Keld Karise, Björn Dröyer, Boye 7:26.3
   Emil Jensen)

1948 London T: 10, N: 10, D: 8.9.
1. ITA (Giuseppe Moioli, Elio Morille, Giovanni Inver- 6:39.0
   nizzi, Franco Faggi)
2. DEN (Helge Halkjaer, Aksel Bonde Hansen, Helge 6:43.5
   Schröder, Ib Storm Larsen)
3. USA (Frederick John Kingsbury, Stuart Griffing, Greg- 6:47.7
   ory Gates, Robert Perew)
4. GBR (P. Kirkpatrick, H. Rushmere, T. Christie, A. —
   Butcher)
5. HOL (H. Van Suylekom, S. Haarsma, J. Dekker, J. —
   Van den Berg)
6. SAF (E. Ramsay, A. Ikin, D. Mayberry, C. Kietzman) —

1952 Helsinki T: 17, N: 17, D: 7.23.
1. YUG (Duje Bonačič, Velimir Valenta, Mate Trojanovič, 7:16.0
   Petar Šegvič)
2. FRA (Pierre Blondiaux, Jacques Guissart, Marc 7:18.9
   Bouissou, Roger Gautier)
3. FIN (Veikko Lommi, Kauko Wahlsten, Oiva Lommi, 7:23.3
   Lauri Nevalainen)
4. GBR (Harry Almond, John Jones, James Crowden, 7:25.2
   George Cadbury)
5. POL (Edward Schwarzer, Zbigniew Schwarzer, Hen- 7:28.2
   ryk Jagodziński, Zbigniew Żarnowiecki)

1956 Melbourne T: 12, N: 12, D: 11.27.
1. CAN (Archibald McKinnon, Lorne Loomer, Walter 7:08.8
   D'Hondt, Donald Arnold)
2. USA (John Welchli, John McKinlay, Arthur McKinlay, 7:18.4
   James McIntosh)
3. FRA (René Guissart, Yves Delacour, Gaston Mercier, 7:20.9
   Guy Guillabert)
4. ITA (Giuseppe Moioli, Attilio Cantoni, Giovanni Zuc- 7:22.5
   chi, Abbondio Marcelli)

The Canadian crew consisted of four small-town boys from
the University of British Columbia, three of whom had
only been rowing for a year. In the final they were so nervous that they almost missed the water with their first
stroke and were left behind. However, they were able to
catch up by the halfway mark and pull away to a five-
length victory. The four Canadians returned to the Olympics four years later in Rome and won silver medals as part
of the eights crew.

1960 Rome T: 16, N: 16, D: 9.3.
1. USA   (Arthur Ayrault, Ted Nash, John Sayre, Richard   6:26.26
         Wailes)
2. ITA   (Tullio Baraglia, Renato Bosatta, Giancarlo   6:28.78
         Crosta, Giuseppe Galante)
3. SOV   (Igor Akhremchik, Yuri Bachurov, Valentin Mor-   6:29.62
         kovkin, Anatoly Tarabrin)
4. CZE   (Jindřich Blažek, Miroslav Jiska, René Libal,   6:34.30
         Jaroslav Starosta)
5. GBR   (J. Michael Beresford, Christopher Davidge,   6:36.18
         Colin Porter, John Vigurs)
6. SWI   (Paul Kölliker, Gottfried Kottmann, Kurt Schmid,   6:38.81
         Rolf Streuli)

1964 Tokyo T: 14, N: 14, D: 10.15.
1. DEN   (John Hansen, Björn Haslöv, Erik Petersen, Kurt   6:59.30
         Helmudt)
2. GBR   (John Michael Russell, Hugh Arthur Wardell-   7:00.47
         Yerburgh, William Barry, John James)
3. USA   (Geoffrey Picard, Richard Lyon, Theodore Mit-   7:01.37
         tet, Theodore Nash)
4. HOL   (Sjoerd Wartena, Jaap Enters, Herman Boelen,   7:09.98
         Spike Castelein)
5. ITA   (Romano Sgheiz, Fulvio Balatti, Giovanni Zuc-   7:10.05
         chi, Luciano Sgheiz)
6. GER   (Günter Schrörs, Horst Effertz, Albrecht Müller,   7:10.33
         Manfred Misselhorn)
7. SOV   (Tselestinas Yutsis, Eugenius Levitskas, Ionas
         Mateyunas, Pavilas Liutkaitis)
8. AUT   (Dieter Ebner, Horst Kuttelwascher, Dieter Lo-
         sert, Manfred Kraushar)

1968 Mexico City T: 11, N: 11, D: 10.19.
1. GDR   (Frank Forberger, Dieter Grahn, Frank Rühle,   6:39.18
         Dieter Schubert)
2. HUN   (Zoltán Melis, György Sarlós, József Csermely,   6:41.64
         Antal Melis)
3. ITA   (Renato Bosatta, Tullio Baraglia, Pier Angelo   6:44.01
         Conti Manzini, Abramo Albini)
4. SWI   (Roland Altenburger, Nicolas Noël Gobet,   6:45.78
         Franz Rentsch, Alfred Meister)
5. USA   (Peter Raymond, Raymond Wright, Charles   6:47.70
         Hamlin, Lawrence Terry)
6. GER   (Thomas Hitzbleck, Manfred Weinreich, Volk-   7:08.22
         hart Buchter, Jochen Heck)
7. ROM   (Pavel Cichi, Dumitru Ivanov, Emanoil Stratan,
         Anton Chirlacopschi)
8. MEX   (Roberto Retolaza, Arcadio Padilla, Jesus Tos-
         cano, David Trejo)

1972 Munich T: 20, N: 20, D: 9.2.
1. GDR   (Frank Forberger, Frank Rühle, Dieter Grahn,   6:24.27
         Dieter Schubert)
2. NZE   (Dick Tonks, Dudley Storey, Ross Collinge,   6:25.64
         Noel Mills)
3. GER   (Joachim Ehrig, Peter Funneköetter, Franz   6:28.41
         Held, Wolfgang Plottke)

4. SOV   (Anatoly Tkachuk, Igor Kashurov, Aleksandr   6:31.92
         Motin, Vitaly Sapronov)
5. ROM   (Emeric Tusa, Adalbert Agh, Mihai Naumencu,   6:35.60
         Francisc Papp)
6. DEN   (Willy Poulsen, Peter Fich Christiansen, Egon   6:37.28
         Peterson, Rolf Andersen)
7. GBR   (Frederick Smallbone, Leonard Robertson,
         James Clark, Mason William)
8. BUL   (Biser Boyadzhiev, Borislav Vasilev, Nikolai Ko-
         lev, Metodi Halvadzhiiski)

Forberger, Rühle, Grahn, and Schubert had been rowing
together for 11 years. In winning their second Olympic title, the Dresden four completed six years of unbeaten rowing in which they also won two world championships and
two European championships. The lead changed hands six
times in their exciting final race with the crew from New
Zealand.

1976 Montreal T: 15, N: 15, D: 7.25.
1. GDR   (Siegfried Brietzke, Andreas Decker, Stefan   6:37.42
         Semmler, Wolfgang Mager)
2. NOR   (Ole Nafstad, Arne Bergodd, Finn Tveter, Rolf   6:41.22
         Andreassen)
3. SOV   (Raul Arnemann, Nikolai Kuznetsov, Valery Do-   6:42.52
         linin, Anushavan Gasan-Dzhalalov)
4. NZE   (Bob Murphy, Grant McAuley, Des Lock, David   6:43.23
         Lindstrom)
5. CAN   (Brian Dick, Philip Monckton, Andrew van Ruy-   6:46.11
         ven, Ian Gordon)
6. GER   (Bernhard Foelkel, Klaus Roloff, Wolfgang   6:47.44
         Horak, Johann Gabriel Konertz)
7. BUL   (Dimiter Vulov, Dimiter Yanakiev, Todor Mrun-
         kov, (Rumen Hristov)
8. USA   (Tony Brooks, James Moroney, Gary Piante-
         dosi, Hugh Stevenson)

1980 Moscow T: 11, N: 11, D: 7.27.
1. GDR   (Jürgen Thiele, Andreas Decker, Stefan   6:08.17
         Semmler, Siegfried Brietzke)
2. SOV   (Aleksey Kamkin, Valery Dolinin, Aleksandr Ku-   6:11.81
         lagin, Vitaly Yeliseyev)
3. GBR   (John Beattie, Ian McNuff, David Townsend,   6:16.58
         Martin Cross)
4. CZE   (Vojtěch Caska, Jiři Prudil, Josef Neštický, Lu-   6:18.63
         bomir Zapletal)
5. ROM   (Daniel Voiculescu, Carolică Ilies, Petru Iosub,   6:19.45
         Nicolae Simion)
6. SWI   (Jürg Weitnauer, Bruno Saile, Hans-Konrad   6:26.46
         Trümpler, Stefan Netzle)
7. FRA   (Jean-Pierre Bremer, Nicolas Lourdaux, Ber-
         nard Bruand, Dominique Basset)
8. POL   (Miroslaw Jarzembowski, Mariusz Trzciński,
         Henryk Trzciński, Marek Niedzialkowski)

Siegfried Brietzke became only the fourth rower to win
gold medals in three different Olympics, joining company
with Paul Costello, Jack Beresford, and Vyacheslav

Ivanov. In 1980 the East Germans dominated rowing so thoroughly that they won 11 of 14 finals. Every one of their 54 oarsmen and women went home with a medal.

FOUR-OARED SHELL WITH COXSWAIN

1896 not held

1900 T: 8, N: 4, D: 8.26, 8.29.
First Final
1. FRA (Cercle de l'Aviron de Roubaix—Emile Delchambre, Jean Cau, Henri Bouckaert, Henri Hazebrouck, Charlot) 7:11.0
2. FRA (Union Nautique de Lyon—Charles Perrin, Daniel Soubeyran, Emile Wegelin, Georges Lumpp, coxswain unknown) 7:18.0
3. GER (R.C. Favorite Hammonia, Hamburg—Hugo Rüster, Wilhelm Carstens, Julius Körner, Adolf Möller, Gustav Moths, Max Ammermann) 7:18.2

Second Final
1. GER (Germania Rowing Club, Hamburg—Oscar Gossler, Walther Katzenstein, Waldemar Tietgens, Gustav Gossler, Carl Gossler) 5:59.0
2. HOL (Minerva Amsterdam—Gerhard Lotsy, Coenraad Hiebendaal, Paulus Jan Lotsy, Johannes Terwogt, Hermanus Brockmann) 6:33.0
3. GER (Ludwigshafener R.V.—Carl Lehle, Ernst Feller, Hermann Wilker, Otto Fickeisen, Franz Kröwerath) 6:35.0

Incompetence on the part of regatta officials resulted in the unusual development of two separate finals in the 1900 Olympics in this event. At first it was declared that the winners of three heats would qualify for the final as would the second-place finisher in heat 3, which included four of the eight entrants. When it was discovered that the losers in heats 2 and 3 had recorded faster times than the winner of heat 1, the officials announced that an extra qualifying heat would have to be run. However, they were unable to notify all of the crews, so the extra heat was cancelled. It was then decided that the three heat winners would be joined in the final by the three fastest losers. But since the course was laid out for only four boats, the heat winners protested and refused to participate in the final. So the first final was run off with only Roubaix of the original qualifiers in the water. The result was obviously ridiculous, so a second final was announced for the three heat winners. Participants in both finals were awarded prizes.

1904 not held

1906 Athens T: 8, N: 4, D: 4.24.
1. ITA (Bucintoro Venice—Enrico Bruna, Emilio Fontanella, Riccardo Jandinoni, Giorgio Cesana, Giuseppe Poli) 8:13.0
2. FRA (Société Nautique de la Basse Seine, Paris—Gaston Delaplane, Charles Delaporte, Leon Delignières, Paul Echard, Marcel Frebourg) —
3. FRA (Société Nautique de Bayonne—Adolphe Bernard, Joseph Halcet, Jean-Baptiste Laporte, Jean-Baptiste Mathieu, Pierre Sourbe) —
4. DEN (K.Bay, E. Saugmann, F. Bielefeldt, H. Rasmussen, H. Oestergaard) —
5. GRE (N. Viaguinis, J. Kountouris, P. Nomikos, G. Tsakonas, Ch. Brisimitzakis) —
6. GRE (N. Zamanos, G. Georgitseas, N. Bertos, P. Saousopoulos, D. Rediadis) —
7. TUR (D. Whittal, N. Petroppulos, P. Pavlidis, J. Gounaris, N. Mardelis) —
DNF: GRE (Ch. Liambeis, Ch. Rangos, M. Sakorrafos, G. Bouboulis, K. Athanasiadis)

1908 not held

1912 Stockholm T: 11, N: 9, D: 7.19.
1. GER (Ludwigshafener R.V.—Albert Arnheiter, Otto Fickeisen, Rudolf Fickeisen, Hermann Wilker, Otto Maier) 6:59.4
2. GBR (Thames R.C.—Julius Beresford, Charles Vernon, Charles Rought, Bruce Logan, Geoffrey Carr) —
3. DEN (Polytehnic Roklub—Erik Bisgaard, Rasmus Peter Frandsen, Magnus Simonsen, Poul Thymann, Eigil Clemmensen) —
3. NOR (Christiana Roklub—Henry Larsen, Matias Torstensen, Theodor Klem, Håkon Tönsager, Ejnar Tönsager) —

1920 Antwerp T: 9, N: 9, D: 8.29.
1. SWI (Willy Brüderlin, Max Rudolf, Paul Rudolf, Hans Walter, Paul Staub) 6:54.0
2. USA (Kenneth Myers, Carl Otto Klose, Franz Federschmidt, Erich Federschmidt, Sherman Clark) 6:58.0
3. NOR (Birger Var, Theodor Klem, Henry Larsen, Per Gulbrandsen, Thoralf Hagen) 7:02.0

1924 Paris T: 10, N: 10, D: 7.17.
1. SWI (Emile Albrecht, Alfred Probst, Eugen Sigg-Bächthold, Hans Walter, Emile Lachapelle) 7:18.4
2. FRA (Eugène Constant, Louis Gressier, Georges Lecointe, Raymond Talleux, Marcel Lepan) 7:21.6
3. USA (Robert Gerhardt, Sidney Jelinek, Edward Mitchell, Henry Welsford, John Kennedy) 7:23.0
4. ITA (Renato Berninzone, Marcello Casanova, Gastone Cerato, Jean Cipollina, Massimo Ballestrero) —
DNF: HOL (Johannes Brandsma, Jacob Brandsma, Dirk Fortuin, Jean van Silfhout, Louis Dekker)

1928 Amsterdam T: 11, N: 11, D: 8.10.
1. ITA (Valerio Peretin, Giliante D'Este, Nicolo Vittori, 6:47.8 Giovanni Delise, Renato Petronio)
2. SWI (Ernst Haas, Joseph Meyer, Otto Bucher, Karl 7:03.4 Schwegler, Fritz Bösch)
3. POL (Franciszek Bronikowski, Edmund Jankowski, 7:12.8 Leon Birkholc, Bernard Ormanowski, Bdeslaw Drewek)
4. GER (Karl Golzo, Hans Nickel, Karl Hoffmann, Werner 7:26.4 Kleine, Alfred Krohn)
5. BEL (Maurice Delplanck, Théo Wambeke, Alphonse 7:30.2 Dewette, Charles van Son, Jean Bauwens)

1932 Los Angeles T: 7, N: 7, D: 8.13.
1. GER (Hans Eller, Horst Hoeck, Walter Meyer, Joachim 7:19.0 Spremberg, Karl-Heinz Neumann)
2. ITA (Bruno Vattovaz, Giovanni Plazzer, Riccardo Di- 7:19.2 vora, Bruno Parovel, Giovanni Scherl)
3. POL (Jerzy Braun, Janusz Ślązak, Stanislaw Urban, 7:26.8 Edward Kobyliński, Jerzy Skolimowski)
4. NZE (Noel Pope, Somers Cox, Charles Saunders, 7:32.6 John Solomon, Delmont Gullery)

A spectacular finish saw the Germans win by a mere one foot.

1936 Berlin T: 16, N: 16, D: 8.14.
1. GER (Hans Maier, Walter Volle, Ernst Gaber, Paul 7:16.2 Söllner, Fritz Bauer)
2. SWI (Hermann Betschart, Hans Homberger, Alex 7:24.3 Homberger, Karl Schmid, Rolf Spring)
3. FRA (Fernand Vandernotte, Marcel Vandernotte, Mar- 7:33.3 cel Cosmat, Marcel Chauvigné, Noël Vander- notte)
4. HOL (Martinus Schoorl, Hotse Sjoerd Bartlema, John 7:34.7 Regout, Simon de Wit, Gerard Hallie)
5. HUN (Miklós Mihók, Vilmos Éden, Ákos Inotay, Alajos 7:35.6 Szilassy-Szymiczek, László Molnár)
6. DEN (Hans Mikkelsen, Ibsen Sörensen, Flemming 7:40.4 Jensen, Svend Aage Sörensen, Aage Jensen)

Coxswain for the French bronze medalists was 12-year-old Noël Vandernotte, whose father, Fernand, and uncle, Marcel, were also members of the crew.

1948 London T: 16, N: 16, D: 8.9.
1. USA (Warren Westlund, Robert Martin, Robert Will, 6:50.3 Gordon Giovanelli, Allen Morgan)
2. SWI (Rudolf Reichling, Erich Schriever, Emile 6:53.3 Knecht, Pierre Stebler, André Moccand)
3. DEN (Erik Larsen, Börge Nielsen, Henry Larsen, Har- 6:58.6 ry Knudsen, Jörgen Ib Olsen)
4. FRA (J. Pieddeloup, R. Lotti, G. Maquat, Jean-Pierre Souche, M. Boigegrain); HUN (Miklós Zágon, Lajos Nagy, B. Nyilasi, Tibor Nádas, Róbert Zimonyi); ITA (R. Polloni, F. Gotti, R. Macario, R. Cerutti, Dominico Cambieri)

1952 Helsinki T: 17, N: 17, D: 7.23.
1. CZE (Karel Mejta, Jiři Havlis, Jan Jindra, Stanislav 7:33.4 Lusk, Miroslav Koranda)
2. SWI (Enrico Bianchi, Karl Weidmann, Heinrich 7:36.5 Scheller, Emile Ess, Walter Leiser)
3. USA (Carl Lovested, Alvin Ulbrickson, Richard Wahl- 7:37.0 ström, Matthew Leanderson, Albert Rossi)
4. GBR (Roderick MacMillan, Graham Fisk, Laurence 7:41.2 Guest, Peter de Giles, Paul Massey)
5. FIN (Kurt Grönholm, Paul Stråhlman, Birger Karlsson, 7:43.8 Karl-Erik Johansson, Antero Tukiainen)

1956 Melbourne T: 10, N: 10, D: 11.27.
1. ITA (Alberto Winkler, Romano Sgheiz, Angelo Van- 7:19.4 zin, Franco Trincavelli, Ivo Stefanoni)
2. SWE (Olof Larsson, Gösta Eriksson, Ivar Aronsson, 7:22.4 Sven Ever Gunnarsson, Bertil Göransson)
3. FIN (Kauko Hänninen, Reino Poutanen, Veli Lehtelä, 7:30.9 Toimi Pitkänen, Matti Niemi)
4. AUS (Gordon Cowey, Kevin McMahon, Reginald Lib- 7:31.1 bis, Ian Allen, John Jenkinson)

1960 Rome T: 21, N: 21, D: 9.3.
1. GER (Gerd Cintl, Horst Effertz, Klaus Rieckemann, 6:39.12 Jürgen Litz, Michael Obst)
2. FRA (Robert Dumontois, Claude Martin, Jaques Mo- 6:41.62 rel, Guy Nosbaum, Jean-Claude Klein)
3. ITA (Fulvio Balatti, Romano Sgheiz, Franco Trinca- 6:43.72 velli, Giovanni Zucchi, Ivo Stefanoni)
4. SOV (Oleg Aleksandrov, Igor Khokhlov, Boris Fyo- 6:45.67 dorov, Valentin Zanin, Igor Rudakov)
5. AUS (Graeme Allen, Maxwell Annett, John Hudson, 6:45.80 Roland Waddington, Lionel Robberds)
6. HUN (Tibor Bedekovics, Csaba Kovács, László Mun- 6:51.65 teán, Pál Wágner, Gyula Lengyel)

1964 Tokyo T: 16, N: 16, D: 10.15.
1. GER (Peter Neusel, Bernhard Britting, Joachim Wer- 7:00.44 ner, Egbert Hirschfelder, Jürgen Oelke)
2. ITA (Renato Bosatta, Emilio Trivini, Giuseppe Ga- 7:02.84 lante, Franco De Pedrina, Giovanni Spinola)
3. HOL (Alex Mullink, Jan van de Graaf, Frederick van 7:06.46 de Graaf, Robert van de Graaf, Marius Klumper- beek)
4. FRA (Yves Fraisse, Claude Pache, Gérard Jacques- 7:13.92 son, Michel Dumas, Jean Claude Darouy)
5. SOV (Anatoly Tkatchuk, Vitaly Kurdchenko, Boris 7:16.05 Kuzmin, Anatoly Luzgin, Vladimir Yevseyev)
6. POL (Szczepan Grajczyk, Marian Leszczyński, Rys- 7:28.15 zard Lubicki, Andrzej Nowaczyk, Jerzy Paw- lowski)
7. USA (Paul Gunderson, Harry Pollock, Thomas Pol- lock, James Tew, Edward Washburn)
8. NZE (Darien Boswell, Alistair Dryden, Peter Masfen, Robert Page, Dudley Storey)

1968 Mexico City T: 13, N: 13, D: 10.19.
1. NZE (Richard Joyce, Dudley Storey, Ross Hounsell Collinge, Warren Cole, Simon Dickie) 6:45.62
2. GDR (Peter Kremtz, Roland Göhler, Manfred Gelpke, Klaus Jakob, Dieter Semetzky) 6:48.20
3. SWI (Denis Oswald, Hugo Waser, Peter Bolliger, Jakob Grob, Gottlieb Fröhlich) 6:49.04
4. ITA (Romano Sgheiz, Emilio Trivini, Giuseppe Galante, Luciano Sgheiz, Mariano Gottifredi) 6:49.54
5. USA (Luther Jones, William Purdy, Anthony Martin, Gardner Cadwalader, John Hartigan) 6:51.41
6. SOV (Anatoly Mentyrev, Nikolai Surov, Aleksei Mischin, Arkady Kudinov, Viktor Mikheyev) 7:00.00
7. ROM (Reinhold Batschi, Petre Ceapura, Stefan Tudor, Francisco Papp, Ladislau Lovrensky)
8. ARG (Hugo Aberastegui, Jose Robledo, Juan Gomez, Guillermo Segurado, Rolando Locatelli)

1972 Munich T: 14, N: 14, D: 9.2.
1. GER (Peter Berger, Hans-Johann Färber, Gerhard Auer, Alois Bierl, Uwe Benter) 6:31.85
2. GDR (Dietrich Zander, Reinhard Gust, Eckhard Martens, Rolf Jobst, Klaus-Dieter Ludwig) 6:33.30
3. CZE (Otakar Mareček, Karel Neffe, Vladimir Jánoš, František Provaznik, Vladimir Petříček) 6:35.64
4. SOV (Vladimir Sterlik, Vladimir Soloviev, Aleksandr Lyubaturov, Yuri Shamaev, Igor Rudakov) 6:37.71
5. USA (David Sawyier, Charles Ruthford, Chad Rudolph, Michael Vespoli, Stewart MacDonald) 6:41.86
6. NZE (Warren Cole, Chris Nilsson, John Clark, David Lindstrom, Peter Lindsay) 6:42.55
7. HOL (Wim Grothuis, Evert Kroes, Jan Woudenberg, Johan ter Haar, Cornelis de Korver)
8. SWI (Hanspeter Leuthi, Urs Frankhauser, Franz Rentsch, Denis Oswald, Rolf Stadelmann)

1976 Montreal T: 14, N: 14, D: 7.25.
1. SOV (Vladimir Eshinov, Nikolai Ivanov, Mikhail Kuznetsov, Aleksandr Klepikov, Aleksandr Lukianov) 6:40.22
2. GDR (Andreas Schulz, Rüdiger Kunze, Walter Diessner, Ullrich Diessner, Johannes Thomas) 6:42.70
3. GER (Hans-Johann Färber, Ralph Kubail, Siegfried Fricke, Peter Niehusen, Hartmut Wenzel) 6:46.96
4. CZE (Otakar Mareček, Karel Neffe, Milan Suchopar, Vladimir Jánoš, Vladimir Petříček) 6:50.15
5. BUL (Luchezar Boichev, Nasko Minchev, Ivan Botev, Kiril Kirchev, Nenko Dobrev) 6:52.88
6. NZE (Viv Haar, Danny Keane, Tim Logan, Ian Boserio, David Simmons) 7:00.17
7. IRL (Michael Ryan, James Muldoon, Willyam Ryan, Christy O'Brien, Liam Redmond)
8. POL (Jerzy Broniec, Adam Tomasiak, Jerzy Ulczyński, Ryszard Burak, Wlodzimierz Chmielewski)

1980 Moscow T: 12, N: 12, D: 7.27.
1. GDR (Dieter Wendisch, Ullrich Diessner, Walter Diessner, Gottfried Döhn, Andreas Gregor) 6:14.51
2. SOV (Artur Garonskis, Dimant Krišhianis, Dzintars Krišhianis, Zhorzh Tikmers, Yüris Berzynsh) 6:19.05
3. POL (Grzegorz Stellak, Adam Tomasiak, Grzegorz Nowak, Ryszard Stadniuk, Ryszard Kubiak) 6:22.52
4. SPA (Manuel Bermudez, Isidro Martin, Salvador Verges, Luis Maria Lasurtegui, Javier Sabria) 6:26.23
5. BUL (Hristo Aleksandrov, Vilhem Germanov, Georgi Petkov, Stoyan Stoyanov, Nenko Dobrev) 6:28.13
6. SWI (Daniel Homberger, Peter Rahn, Roland Stocker, Peter Stocker, Karl Graf) 6:30.26
7. GBR (Leonard Robertson, Gordon Rankine, Colin Seymour, John Roberts, Alan Inns)
8. BRA (Laildo Machado, Wandir Kuntze, Walter Soares, Henrique Johann, Manoel Novo)

EIGHT-OARED SHELL WITH COXSWAIN

1896 not held

1900 Paris T: 4, N: 4, D: 8.26.
1. USA (Vesper Boat Club, Philadelphia—Louis Abell, Harry Debaecke, William Carr, John Exley, John Geiger, Edward Hedley, James Juvenal, Roscoe Lockwood, Edward Marsh) 6:09.8
2. BEL (Royal Club Nautique de Gand—Marcel van Crombrugghe, Maurice Hemelsoet, Oscar de Cock, Maurice Verdonck, Prospère Bruggeman, Oscar de Somville, Frank Odberg, Jules de Bisschop, Alfred Vanlandeghem) 6:13.8
3. HOL (Minerva, Amsterdam—Walter Thijssen, Ruurd Leegstra, Johannes van Dijk, Henricus Tromp, Hendrik Offerhaus, Roelof Klein, François Brandt, Walter Middelberg, Hermanus Brockmann) 6:23.0
4. GER (Germania, Hamburg—Oscar Gossler, Walther Katzenstein, Ernst Ascan Jencquel, Theodor Alphons Lauezzari, Waldemar Tietgens, Arthur Warncke, Edgar Katzenstein, Gustav Gossler, Alexander Gleichmann von Oven) 6:33.0

1904 St. Louis T: 2, N: 2, D: 7.30.
1. USA (Vesper Boat Club, Philadelphia—Louis Abell, Joseph Dempsey, Michael Gleason, Frank Schell, James Flanigan, Charles Armstrong, Harry Lott, Frederick Cresser, John Exley) 7:50.0
2. CAN (Argonaut Rowing Club, Toronto—Joseph Wright, Donald MacKenzie, William Wadsworth, George Strange, Phil Boyd, George Reiffenstein, W. Rice, A.B. Bailey, Thomas Loudon) —

1906 not held

1908 London T: 6, N: 5, D: 7.31.
1. GBR (Leander Club—Albert Gladstone, Frederick Kel- 7:52.0
ly, Banner Johnstone, Guy Nickalls, Charles Burnell, Ronald Sanderson, Raymond Ethering-
ton-Smith, Henry Bucknall, Gilchrist MacLagan)
2. BEL (Royal Club Nautique de Gand—Oscar Taelman, —
Marcel Morimont, Rémy Orban, Georges Mijs,
François Vergucht, Polydore Veirman, Oscar de
Somville, Rodolphe Poma, Alfred Vanlandeghem)
3. CAN (Argonaut Rowing Club, Toronto—Irvine Robert- —
son, George Wright, Julius Thomson, Walter
Lewis, Gordon Bruce Balfour, Becher Gale,
Charles Riddy, Geoffrey Taylor, Douglas Kert-
land)
3. GBR (Cambridge University Boating Club—Frederick —
Jerwood, Eric Powell, Guy Carver, Edward Williams, Henry Goldsmith, Harold Kitching, John
Burn, Douglas Stuart, Richard Boyle)

1912 Stockholm T: 11, N: 7, D: 7.19.
1. GBR (Leander Club—Edgar Burgess, Sidney Swahn, 6:15.0
Leslie Wormald, Ewart Horsfall, Angus James
Gillan, Arthur Garton, Alister Kirby, Philip Fleming, Henry Wells)
2. GBR (New College, Oxford—William Fison, William 6.19.0
Parker, Thomas Gillespie, Beaufort Burdekin,
Frederick Pitman, Arthur Wiggins, Charles Little-
john, Robert Bourne, John Walker)
3. GER (Berliner Ruder-Gesellschaft—Otto Liebing, Max
Bröske, Max Vetter, Willi Bartholomä, Fritz Bartholomä, Werner Dehn, Rudolf Reichelt, Hans
Mathiä, Kurt Runge)

1920 Antwerp T: 8, N: 8, D: 8.30.
1. USA (Virgil Jacomini, Edwin Graves, William Jordan, 6:02.6
Edward Moore Allen Sanborn, Donald Johnston,
Vincent Gallagher, Clyde King, Sherman Clark)
2. GBR (Ewart Horsfall, Guy Nickalls, Richard Lucas, 6:05.0
Walter James, John Campbell, Sebastian Earl,
Ralph Shove, Sidney Swann, Robin Johnstone)
3. NOR (Theodor Nag, Conrad Olsen, Adolf Nilsen, Hå- 6:36.0
kon Ellingsen, Thore Michelsen, Arne Mortensen,
Karl Nag, Tollef Tollefsen, Thoralf Hagen)
4. FRA (Albert Diebold, Charles Hahn, Frédéric Gross- 6:42.6
mann, Robert Fleig, Henri Barbenès, Frédéric
Fleig, Charles Schlewer, Emile Ruhlmann, Emile
Barberolle)

The winning crew represented the U.S. Naval Academy.
Regatta officials first awarded the bronze medals to the
Swiss team because they had recorded the third fastest
time in the preliminary heats when they lost to Great Britain. But after a protest, it was decided that the semifinal
losers, Norway and France, should row off for third place;
however, this race was never held. Most Olympic historians credit Norway with third place, since their semifinal
time was faster than that of France.

1924 Paris T: 10, N: 10, D: 7.17.
1. USA (Leonard Carpenter, Howard Kingsbury, Daniel 6:33.4
Lindley, John Miller, James Rockefeller, Frederick Sheffield, Benjamin Spock, Alfred Wilson,
Laurence Stoddard)
2. CAN (Arthur Bell, Robert Hunter, William Langford, 6:49.0
Harold Little, John Smith, Warren Snyder, Norman Taylor, William Wallace, Ivor Campbell)
3. ITA (Antonio Cattalinich, Francesco Cattalinich, Sim- —
eon Callalinich, Giuseppe Crivelli, Latino Ga-
lasso, Pietro Ivanov, Bruno Sorich, Carlo Toniatti,
Vittorio Gliubich)
4. GBR (R. Bare, C.G.Chandler, H.B. Debenham, H.W. —
Dulley, S. Ian Fairbairn, A.F. Long, H.L. Morphy,
C.H. Rew, J.S. Godwin)

Bill Havens was a member of the Yale University team
that won the right to represent the United States. However, he chose not to make the trip to Paris because his wife
was expecting their first child. That child, a boy named
Frank, was born five days after the closing of the 1924
Olympics. Twenty-eight years later, the Havens family finally got their Olympic gold medal when Frank won the
10,000 meters Canadian canoeing singles event in Helsinki.

One Yale crew member who did compete in 1924 and
win was a gangly 6-foot 4-inch junior named Ben Spock.
After graduating from medical school, Spock became a pe-
diatrician. In 1945 he finished writing a book called *The
Common Sense Book of Baby and Child Care,* which eventually sold over 25 million copies and gained its author international fame as "Dr. Spock, the baby expert." In 1972
he was the presidential candidate of the People's Party.

1928 Amsterdam T: 11, N: 11, D: 8.10.
1. USA (Marvin Stalder, John Brinck, Francis Frederick, 6:03.2
William Thompson, William Dally, James Work-
man, Hubert Caldwell, Peter Donlon, Donald
Blessing)
2. GBR (James Hamilton, Guy Nickalls, John Badcock, 6:05.6
Donald Gollan, Harold Lane, Gordon Killick, Jack
Beresford, Harold West, Arthur Sulley)
3. CAN (Frederick Hedges, Frank Fiddes, John Hand, 6:03.8
Herbert Richardson, Jack Murdock, Athol
Meech, Edgar Norris, William Ross, John Don-
nelly)
4. POL (Otto Gordzialkowski, Stanislaw Urban, Andrzej 6:42.2
Soltan, Marian Wodziański, Janusz Ślązak, Waclaw Michalski, Józef Laszewski, Henryk Nieza-
bitowski, Jerzy Skolimowski)
5. GER (Karl Aletter, Ernst Gaber, Willi Reichert, Erwin 6:42.8
Hoffstätter, Hermann Herbold, Gustav Maier,
Robert Huber, Hans Maier, Fritz Bauer)
6. ITA (Medardo Lamberti, Arturo Moroni, Vittore Stoc- 6:44.4
chi, Guglielmo Carubbi, Amilcare Canevari, Medardo Galli, Giulio Lamberti, Benedetto Borella,
Angelo Polledri)

The United States was represented by the crew from the
University of California at Berkeley. *New York Times* cor-

respondent Wythe Williams described the work of coxswain Don Blessing as "one of the greatest performances of demoniacal howling ever heard on a terrestrial planet. . . . He gave the impression of a terrier suddenly gone mad. But such language and what a vocabulary! . . . One closed his eyes and waited for the crack of a cruel whip across the backs of the galley slaves." After they had won the Olympic championship, the galley slaves, following custom, grabbed their tormentor and threw him into the middle of Sloten Canal.

1932 Los Angeles T: 8, N: 8, D: 8.13.

1. USA (Edwin Salisbury, Jemes Blair, Duncan Gregg, David Dunlap, Burton Jastram, Charles Chandler, Harold Tower, Winslow Hall, Norris Graham) 6:37.6
2. ITA (Vittorio Cioni, Mario Balleri, Renato Bracci, Dino Barsotti, Roberto Vestrini, Guglielmo Del Bimbo, Enrico Garzelli, Renato Barbieri, Cesare Milani) 6:37.8
3. CAN (Earl Eastwood, Joseph Harris, Stanley Stanyar, Harry Fry, Cedric Liddell, William Thoburn, Donald Boal, Albert Taylor, George MacDonald) 6:40.4
4. GBR (Lewis Luxton, Donald McCowen, Harold Rickett, Charles Sergel, William Sambell, Thomas Askwith, Kenneth Payne, David Haig-Thomas, John Ranking) 6:40.8

The U.S. team from the University of California and the Italian team from the University of Pisa staged a dramatic battle, which the Californians won by a foot with their very last stroke.

1936 Berlin T: 14, N: 14, D: 8.14.

1. USA (Herbert Morris, Charles Day, Gordon Adam, John White, James McMillin, George Hunt, Joseph Rantz, Donald Hume, Robert Moch) 6:25.4
2. ITA (Guglielmo Del Bimbo, Dino Barsotti, Oreste Grossi, Enzo Bartolini, Mario Checcacci, Dante Secchi, Ottorino Quaglierini, Enrico Garzelli, Cesare Milani) 6:26.0
3. GER (Alfred Rieck, Helmut Radach, Hans Kuschke, Heinz Kaufmann, Gerd Völs, Werner Löckle, Hans-Joachim Hannemann, Herbert Schmidt, Wilhelm Mahlow) 6:26.4
4. GBR (Annesley Kingsford, Thomas Askwith, McAlister Pender Lonnon, Desmond Kingsford, John Cherry, John Couchman, Hugh Mason, William Laurie, John Duckworth) 6:30.1
5. HUN (Pál Domonkos, Sándor Korompay, Hugo Ballya, Imre Kapossy, Antal Szendey, Gábor Alapy, Frigyes Hollósi-Jung, László Szabó, Ervin Kereszthy) 6:30.3
6. SWI (Werner Schweizer, Fritz Feldmann, Rudolf Homberger, Oskar Neuenschwander, Hermann Betschart, Hans Homberger, Alex Homberger, Karl Schmid, Rolf Spring) 6:35.8

An exciting blanket finish was won by the crew of the University of Washington, which moved up from fifth place at the halfway mark.

1948 London T: 12, N: 12, D: 8.9.
(Ca. 1900 Meters)

1. USA (Ian Turner, David Turner, James Hardy, George Ahlgren, Lloyd Butler, David Brown, Justus Smith, John Stack, Ralph Purchase) 5:56.7
2. GBR (Christopher Barton, Maurice Lapage, Guy Richardson, E. Paul Bircher, Paul Massey, C. Brian Lloyd, David Meyrick, Andrew Mellows, Jack Dearlove) 6:06.9
3. NOR (Kristoffer Lepsöe, Torstein Kråkenes, Hans Egil Hansen, Halfdan Gran Olsen, Harald Kråkenes, Leif Naess, Thor Pedersen, Carl Henrik Monssen, Sigurd Monssen) 6:10.3

The victorious University of California at Berkeley crew had barely qualified for the Olympics, winning the U.S. tryouts by a mere one-tenth second over the University of Washington. But when they got to London they discovered that their most difficult challenge was behind them, as they won all three of their races by at least ten seconds.

1952 Helsinki T: 14, N: 14, D: 7.23.

1. USA (Franklin Shakespeare, William Fields, James Dunbar, Richard Murphy, Robert Detweiler, Henry Proctor, Wayne Frye, Edward Stevens, Charles Manring) 6:25.9
2. SOV (Yevgeny Brago, Vladimir Rodimushkin, Aleksei Komarov, Igor Borisov, Slava Amiragov, Leonid Gissen, Yevgeny Samsonov, Vladimir Krukov, Igor Polyakov) 6:31.2
3. AUS (Robert Tinning, Ernest Chapman, Nimrood Greenwood, Mervyn Finlay, Edward Pain, Phillip Cayzer, Thomas Chessel, David Anderson, Geoffrey Williamson) 6:33.1
4. GBR (David Macklin, Alastair MacLeod, Nicholas Clack, Roger Sharpley, Edward Worlidge, Charles Lloyd, William Windham David Jennens, John Hinde) 6:34.8
5. GER (Anton Reinartz, Michael Reinartz, Roland Freiloff, Heinz Zünkler, Peter Betz, Stefan Reinartz, Hans Betz, Toni Siebenhaar, Hermann Zander) 6:42.8

The winning crew was from the U.S. Naval Academy.

1956 Melbourne T: 10, N: 10, D: 11.27.

1. USA (Thomas Charlton, David Wight, John Cooke, Donald Beer, Caldwell Esselstyn, Charles Grimes, Richard Wailes, Robert Morey, William Becklean) 6:35.2
2. CAN (Philip Kueber, Richard McClure, Robert Wilson, David Helliwell, Donald Pretty, William McKerlich, Douglas McDonald, Lawrence West, Carlton Ogawa) 6:37.1
3. AUS (Michael Aikman, David Boykett, Angus Benfield, James Howden, Garth Manton, Walter Howell, Adrian Monger, Bryan Doyle, Harold Hewitt) 6:39.2
4. SWE (Olof Larsson, Lennart Andersson, Kjell Hansson, Rune Ivar Andersson, Sture Lennart Hanson, Gösta Eriksson, Ivar Aronsson, Sven Gunnarsson, Bertil Göransson) 6:48.1

The United States, represented by the Yale crew, finished third to Australia and Canada in the opening round, but qualified for the semifinal through repêchage. No Olympic eights had ever been won by a team that lost its opening race, but the Yale crew broke this tradition to give the United States its eighth straight win in the eights.

1960 Rome T: 14, N: 14, D: 9.3.

1.	GER	(Klaus Bittner, Karl-Heinz Hopp, Hans Lenk, Manfred Rulffs, Frank Schepke, Kraft Schepke, Walter Schröder, Karl-Heinrich von Groddeck, Willi Padge)	5:57.18
2.	CAN	(Donald Arnold, Walter D'Hondt, Nelson Kuhn, John Lecky, Lorne Loomer, Archibald McKinnon, William McKerlich, Glen Mervyn, Sohen Biln)	6:01.52
3.	CZE	(Bohumil Janoušek, Jan Jindra, Jiří Lundak, Stanislav Lusk, Václav Pavkovič, Ludek Pojezny, Jan Švéda, Josef Ventus, Miroslav Koniček)	6:04.84
4.	FRA	(Christian Puibaraud, Jean Bellet, Emile Clerc, Jean Ledoux, Gaston Mercier, Bernard Meynadier, Joseph Moroni, Michel Viaud, Alain Bouffard)	6:06.57
5.	USA	(Joseph Baldwin, Peter Bos, Mark Moore, Lyman Perry, Warren Sweetser, Gayle Thompson, Robert Wilson, Howard Winfree, William Long)	6:08.06
6.	ITA	(Paolo Amorini, Vasco Cantarello, Giancarlo Casalini, Luigi Prato, Vincenzo Prina, Mazzareno Simonato, Luigi Spozio, Armido Torri, Giuseppe Pira)	6:12.73

The U.S. winning streak was finally broken by a combined crew from Ratzeburg and Ditmarsia Kiel rowing clubs. The Germans led from the start and were never headed.

1964 Tokyo T: 14, N: 14, D: 10.15.

1.	USA	(Joseph Amlong, Thomas Amlong, Harold Budd, Emory Clark, Stanley Cwiklinski, Hugh Foley, William Knecht, William Stowe, Robert Zimonyi)	6:18.23
2.	GER	(Klaus Aeffke, Klaus Bittner, Karl-Heinrich von Groddeck, Hans-Jürgen Wallbrecht, Klaus Behrens, Jürgen Schröder, Jürgen Plagemann, Horst Meyer, Thomas Ahrens)	6:23.29
3.	CZE	(Petr Čermák, Jiří Lundak, Jan Mrvik, Julius Toček, Josef Ventus, Ludek Pojezny, Bohumil Janoušek, Richard Novy, Miroslav Koniček)	6:25.11
4.	YUG	(Boris Klavora, Jadran Barut, Joža Berc, Vjekoslav Skalak, Marko Mandič, Alojz Colja, Pavajo Martič, Lucijan Kelva, Zdenko Balaš)	6:27.15
5.	SOV	(Yozanas Yagelavichus, Yuri Suslin, Piatras Karla, Vitautas Briedis, Vladimir Sterlik, Zigmas Yukna, Antanas Bogdanavichus, Rischard Voitkevich, Yuri Lorentson)	6:30.69
6.	ITA	(Dario Giani, Sergio Tagliapetra, Gianpietro Gilardi, Francesco Glorioso, Pietro Polti, Giuseppe Schiavon, Orlando Savarin, Sereno Brunello, Ivo Stefanoni)	6:42.78

7.	FRA	(André Fevret, Pierre Maddaloni, André Sloth, Joseph Moroni, Robert Dumontois, Jean Pierre Grimaud, Bernard Meynadier, Michel Viaud, Alain Bouffard)	
8.	AUS	(David Ramage, David Boykett, Terence Davies, Robert Lachal, Paul Guest, Martin Tomanovits, Brian Vear, Graeme McCall, Kevin Wickham)	

The Vesper Club of Philadelphia, the first noncollegiate eight to represent the United States in 60 years, scored a one-and-a-quarter-length upset victory over the crew from Ratzeburg, Germany. The Vesper coxswain was Bob Zimonyi, a 46-year-old accountant who had defected after being a member of the 1956 Hungarian squad. Zimonyi's first Olympic appearance had been in the coxed fours of 1948.

1968 Mexico City T: 12, N: 12, D: 10.19.

1.	GER	(Horst Meyer, Dirk Schreyer, Rüdiger Henning, Wolfgang Hottenrott, Lutz Ulbricht, Egbert Hirschfelder, Jörg Siebert, Nikolaus "Nico" Ott, Günther Tiersch)	6:07.00
2.	AUS	(Alfred Duval, Michael Morgan, Joseph Fazio, Peter Dickson, David Douglas, John Ranch, Gary Pearce, Robert Shirlaw, Alan Grover)	6:07.98
3.	SOV	(Zigmas Yukna, Antanas Bogdanavichus, Vladimir Sterlik, Yozanas Yagelavichus, Aleksandr Martyschkin, Vitautas Briedis, Valentin Kravtchuk, Viktor Suslin, Yuri Lorentson)	6:09.11
4.	NZE	(Alan Webster, Gerard Veldman, Alistair Dryden, John Hunter, Mark Brownlee, John Gibbons, Thomas Just, Gilbert Cawood, Robert Page)	6:10.43
5.	CZE	(Vladimir Jánoš, Zdeněk Kuba, Oldřich Svojanovský, Karel Kolesa, Pavel Svojanovský, Jan Walisch, Otakar Mareček, Petr Čermák, Jiří Pták)	6:12.17
6.	USA	(Stephen Brooks, Curtis Canning, Andrew Larkin, Scott Steketee, Franklin Hobbs, Jacques Fiechter, Cleve Livingston, David Higgins, Paul Hoffman)	6:14.34
7.	GDR	(Günter Bergau, Klaus-Dieter Bähr, Claus Wilke, Peter Gorny, Reinhard Zerfowski, Peter Hein, Manfred Schneider, Peter Prompe, Karl-Heinz Danielowski)	
8.	HOL	(Maarten Kloosterman, Pieter Bon, Eric Nieche, Jaap Reesink, Gerard Van Enst, Jan Steinhauser, Izak Wesdrop, Jan Van Laarhoven, Arthur Koning)	

The victorious Ratzeburg crew used a shell that was 75 pounds lighter than the shells of the other teams.

1972 Munich T: 15, N: 15, D: 9.2.

1.	NZE	(Tony Hurt, Wybo Veldman, Dick Joyce, John Hunter, Lindsay Wilson, Athol Earl, Trevor Coker, Gary Robertson, Simon Dickie)	6:08.94
2.	USA	(Lawrence Terry, Fritz Hobbs, Peter Raymond, Timothy Mickelson, Eugene Clapp, William	6:11.61

Hobbs, Cleve Livingston, Michael Livingston, Paul Hoffman)

3. GDR (Hans-Joachim Borzym, Jörg Landvoigt, Harold Dimke, Manfred Schneider, Hartmut Schreiber, Manfred Schmorde, Bernd Landvoigt, Heinrich Mederow, Dietmar Schwarz) — 6:11.67

4. SOV (Aleksandr Riazankin, Viktor Dementiev, Sergei Koliaskin, Aleksandr Shitov, Valery Bissarnov, Boris Vorobiev, Vladimir Savelov, Aleksandr Martishkin, Viktor Mikheev) — 6:14.48

5. GER (Reinhard Wendemuth, Frithjof Henckel, Norbert Kindlmann, Wolfgang Hottenrott, Hans-Ulrich Buchholz, Günter Petermann, Bernd Truschinski, Winfried Ringwald, Manfred Klein) — 6:14.91

6. POL (Jerzy Ulczyński, Marian Siejkowski, Krzysztof Marek, Jan Mlodzikowski, Grzegorz Stellak, Marian Drążdżewski, Ryszard Gilo, Slawomir Maciejowski, Ryszard Kubiak) — 6:29.35

7. HUN (Zoltán Melis, András Pályi, Antal Gelley, Béla Zsitnik, László Romvári, Péter Kokas, Imre Dávid, Ágoston Bányai, Robert Oelschleger)

8. AUS (John Clark, Michael Morgan, Bryan Curtin, Richard Curtin, Robert Paver, Kerry Jelbart, Gary Pearce, Malcolm Shaw, Alan Grover)

The New Zealand team raised the $45,000 needed to support their training and trip to Munich by holding a series of bingo games, as well as a raffle for a "dream kitchen."

1976 Montreal T: 13, N: 13, D: 7.25.

1. GDR (Bernd Baumgart, Gottfried Döhn, Werner Klatt, Hans-Joachim Lück, Dieter Wendisch, Roland Kostulski, Ulrich Karnatz, Karl-Heinz Prudöhl, Karl Heinz Danielowski) — 5:58.29

2. GBR (Richard Lester, John Yallop, Timothy Crooks, Hugh Matheson, David Maxwell, James Clark, Fred Smallbone, Leonard Robertson, Patrick Sweeney) — 6:00.82

3. NZE (Ivan Sutherland, Trevor Coker, Peter Dignan, Lindsay Wilson, Athol Earl, Dave Rodger, Alex Mclean, Tony Hurt, Simon Dickie) — 6:03.51

4. GER (Reinhard Wendemuth, Bernd Truschinski, Frank Schütze, Frithjof Henckel, Wolfram Thiem, Volker Sauer, Otmar Kaufhold, Wolf-Dieter Oschlies, Helmut Latz) — 6:06.15

5. AUS (Islay Lee, Ian Clubb, Timothy Conrad, Robert Paver, Gary Eubergang, Athol MacDonald, Peter Shakespear, Brian Richardson, Stuart Carter) — 6:09.75

6. CZE (Pavel Konvička, Vaclav Mls, Josef Plaminek, Josef Pokorny, Karel Mejta, Josef Nesticky, Lubomir Zapletal, Miroslav Vrastil, Jiři Pták) — 6:14.29

7. SOV (Aleksandr Shitov, Antanas Chikotas, Vassily Potapov, Aleksandr Plyushkin, Anatoly Nemtyrev, Igor Konnov, Anatoly Ivanov, Vladimir Vasilyev, Vladimir Zharov)

8. CAN (Edgar Smith, Dirk Gidney, George Tintor, James Henniger, Patrick Croskerry, Melvin La Forme, Ronald Burak, Alexander Manson, Robert Choquette)

The East German team included a butcher, a plumber, a gardener, a mechanic, and a student.

1980 Moscow T: 9, N: 9, D: 7.27.

1. GDR (Bernd Krauss, Hans-Peter Koppe, Ulrich Kons, Jörg Friedrich, Jens Doberschütz, Ulrich Karnatz, Uwe Dühring, Bernd Höing, Klaus-Dieter Ludwig) — 5:49.05

2. GBR (Duncan McDougall, Allan Whitwell, Henry Clay, Chris Mahoney, Andrew Justice, John Pritchard, Malcolm McGowan, Richard Stanhope, Colin Moynihan) — 5:51.92

3. SOV (Viktor Kokoshin, Andrey Tishchenko, Ionas Pintskus, Ionas Normantas, Andrei Lugin, Aleksandr Mantsevich, Igor Maistrenko, Grigory Dmitrienko, Aleksandr Tkachenko) — 5:52.66

4. CZE (Pavel Pevný, Lubomir Janko, Ctirad Jungmann, Karel Neffe, Karel Mejta, Dušan Vičik, Milan Doleček, Milan Kyselý, Jiři Pták — 5:53.75

5. AUS (Islay Lee, Stephen Handley, William Dankbaar, Andrew Withers, Timothy Willoughby, James Lowe, Timothy Young, Brian Richardson, David England) — 5:56.74

6. BUL (Dimitur Yanakiev, Todor Mrunkov, Bozhidar Rogelov, Ivan Botev, Yani Ignatov, Mikhail Petrov, Petur Patzev, Vesselin Shterev, Ventzislav Kunchev) — 6:04.05

7. HUN (Ferenc Kiss, Péter Tóvári, Róbert Sass, Attila Strochmayer, András Kormos, Zoltán Sztárcsevics, Kálmán Toronyi, László Kiss, Miklós Bálint)

8. CUB (Wenceslao Borroto, Ismael Same, Juan Alfonso, Juan Bueno, Francisco Mora, Hermenegildo Palacio, Jorge Alvarez, Antonio Riano, Enrique Carrillo)

Discontinued Events

SIX-MAN NAVAL ROWING BOATS

1906 Athens T: 4, N: 2, D: 4.24.
(2000 Meters)

1. ITA (Varese) 10:45.0
2. GRE (Spetzia) —
3. GRE (Hydra) —
4. GRE (Psara) —

SIXTEEN-MAN NAVAL ROWING BOATS

1906 Athens T: 5, N: 2, D: 4.24.
(3000 Meters)

1. GRE (Poros) 16:35.0
2. GRE (Hydra) 17:09.6
3. ITA (Varese) —
4. GRE (Psara) —
5. GRE (Spetzia) —

COXED FOURS INRIGGERS

1912 Stockholm T: 6, N: 4, D: 7.18.
1. DEN   (Ejlert Allert, Jörgen Hansen, Carl Möller, Carl   7:47.0
         Petersen, Poul Hartmann)
2. SWE   (Ture Rosvall, William Bruhn-Möller, Conrad   7:56.2
         Brunkman, Herman Dahlbäck, Wilhelm Wilkens)
3. NOR   (Claus Hoyer, Reidar Holter, Magnus Herseth,   —
         Frithjof Olstad, Olaf Bjornstad)

WOMEN

SINGLE SCULLS

All women's races are rowed on a 1000-meter course.

1896–1972 not held

1976 Montreal C: 11, N: 11, D: 7.24.
1. Christine Scheiblich	GDR	4:05.56
2. Joan Lind	USA	4:06.21
3. Elena Antonova	SOV	4:10.24
4. Rositsa Spasova	BUL	4:10.86
5. Ingrid Munneke	HOL	4:18.71
6. Mariann Ambrus	HUN	4:22.59
7. Annick Anthoine	FRA	
8. Christel Agrikola	GER	

1980 Moscow C: 11, N: 11, D: 7.26.
1. Sanda Toma	ROM	3:40.69
2. Antonina Makhina	SOV	3:41.65
3. Martina Schröter	GDR	3:43.54
4. Rositsa Spasova	BUL	3:47.22
5. Beryl Mitchell	GBR	3:49.71
6. Beata Dziadura	POL	3:51.45
7. Frances Cryan	IRL	
8. Mariann Ambrus	HUN	

DOUBLE SCULLS

1896–1972 not held

1976 Montreal T: 10, N: 10, D: 7.24.
1. BUL   (Svetla Otsetova, Zdravka Yordanova)   3:44.36
2. GDR   (Sabine Jahn, Petra Boesler)   3:47.86
3. SOV   (Leonora Kaminskaite, Genovate Ramoshkene)   3:49.93
4. NOR   (Solfrid Johansen, Ingunn Brechan)   3:52.18
5. USA   (Jan Palchikoff, Diane Braceland)   3:58.25
6. CAN   (Cheryl Howard, Beverley Cameron)   4:06.23
7. HOL   (Andrea Vissers, Hellie Klaasee)
8. CZE   (Miluse Neffova, Zuzana Prokesova)

1980 Moscow T: 7, N: 7, D: 7.26.
1. SOV   (Yelena Khloptseva, Larissa Popova)   3:16.27
2. GDR   (Cornelia Linse, Heidi Westphal)   3:17.63
3. ROM   (Olga Homeghi, Valeria Răcilă-Roşca)   3:18.91
4. BUL   (Svetla Otsetova, Zdravka Yordanova)   3:23.14
5. POL   (Hanna Jarkiewicz, Janina Klucznik)   3:27.25
6. HUN   (Ilona Bata, Klara Pétervári-Langhoffer)   3:35.70

QUADRUPLE SCULLS WITH COXSWAIN

1896–1972 not held

1976 Montreal T: 9, N: 9, D: 7.19.
1. GDR   (Anke Borchmann, Jutta Lau, Viola Poley, Ros-   3:29.99
         wietha Zobelt, Liane Weigelt)
2. SOV   (Anna Kondrachina, Mira Bryunina, Larissa   3:32.49
         Aleksandrova, Galina Ermolaeva, Nadezhda
         Chernysheva)
3. ROM   (Ioana Tudoran, Maria Micsa, Felicia Afrasi-   3:32.76
         loaia, Elisabeta Lazar, Elena Giurca)
4. BUL   (Iskra Velinova, Verka Aleksieva, Troyanka Va-   3:34.13
         sileva, Svetla Gincheva, Stanka Georgieva)
5. CZE   (Anna Marešová, Marie Bartaková, Jarmila Pat-   3:42.53
         ková, Hana Kavková, Alena Svobodová)
6. DEN   (Kirsten Thomsen, Else Maersk-Kristensen, Ju-   3:46.99
         dith Andersen, Karen Nielsen, Kirsten Plum-
         Jensen)
7. USA   (Karen McCloskey, Lisá Hansen, Elizabet Hills,
         Claudia Schneider, Irene Moreno)
8. HUN   (Ilona Bata, Kamilla Kosztolányi, Valéria Gyi-
         mesi, Ágnes Szijj, Erzsébet Nagy)

1980 Moscow T: 7, N: 7, D: 7.26.
1. GDR   (Sybille Reinhardt, Jutta Ploch, Jutta Lau, Ros-   3:15.32
         wietha Zobelt, Liane Buhr [Weigelt])
2. SOV   (Antonina Pustovit, Yelena Matievskaya, Olga   3:15.73
         Vasilchenko, Nadezhda Lyubimova, Nina Cher-
         emisina)
3. BUL   (Mariana Serbezova, Roumeliana Boneva, Do-   3:16.10
         lores Nakova, Ani Bakova, Stanka Georgieva)
4. ROM   (Marta Macoviciuc, Aneta Mihaly, Sofia Bano-   3:16.82
         vici, Mariana Zaharia, Elena Giurca)
5. POL   (Boguslawa Tomasiak, Mariola Abrahamczyk,   3:20.95
         Maria Kobylińska, Aleksandra Kaczyńska, Ma-
         ria Dzieźa)
6. HOL   (Ineke Donkervoort, Lily Meeuwisse, Greet Hel-   3:22.64
         lemans, Jos Compaan, Monique Pronk)

PAIR-OARED SHELL WITHOUT COXSWAIN

1896–1972 not held

1976 Montreal T: 11, N: 11, D: 7.24.
1. BUL   (Siika Kelbecheva, Stoyanka Grouicheva)   4:01.22
2. GDR   (Angelika Noack, Sabine Dähne)   4:01.64

3. GER   (Edith Eckbauer, Thea Einöder)   4:02.35
4. SOV   (Natalya Gorodilova, Anna Karnaushenko) 4:03.27
5. CAN   (Tricia Smith, Elisabeth Craig)   4:08.09
6. ROM   (Marlena Predescu, Marinela Maxim)   4:15.44
7. USA   (Susan Morgan, Laura Staines)
8. POL   (Anna Karbowiak, Malgorzata Kowalska)

1980 Moscow T: 6, N: 6, D: 7.26.
1. GDR   (Ute Steindorf, Cornelia Klier)   3:30.49
2. POL   (Malgorzata Dlużewska, Czeslawa Kościańska) 3:30.95
3. BUL   (Siika Barboulova [Kelbecheva], Stoyanka 3:32.39
         Kourbatova [Grouicheva])
4. ROM   (Florica Dospinescu, Elena Oprea)   3:35.14
5. SOV   (Larissa Zavarzina, Galina Stepanova)   4:12.53

Despite the fact that there were only six entrants, regatta officials insisted that two elimination heats and a repêchage be run in order to trim the field in the final to five.

FOUR-OARED SHELL WITH COXSWAIN

1896–1972 not held

1976 Montreal T: 8, N: 8, D: 7.24.
1. GDR   (Karin Metze, Bianka Schwede, Gabriele Lohs, 3:45.08
         Andrea Kurth, Sabine Hess)
2. BUL   (Ginka Gyurova, Liliana Vaseva, Reni Yordan- 3:48.24
         ova, Mariika Modeva, Kapka Georgieva)
3. SOV   (Nadezhda Sevostyanova, Lyudmila Krokhina,   3:49.38
         Galina Mishenina, Anna Pasokha, Lidiya Kry-
         lova)
4. ROM   (Elena Oprea, Florica Petcu, Filigonia Tol, Aure- 3:51.17
         lia Marinescu, Aneta Matei)
5. HOL   (Liesbeth Vosmaer-De Bruin, Hette Borrias,   3:54.36
         Myrian van Rooyen, Ans Gravesteyn, Monique
         Pronk)
6. USA   (Pamela Behrens, Catherine Menges, Nancy   3:56.50
         Storrs, Julia Geer, Mary Kellogg)
7. CAN   (Linda Schaumleffel, Dolores Young, Monica
         Draeger, Joy Fera, Barbara Mutch)
8. GBR   (Gillian Webb, Pauline Bird, Clare Grove, Diana
         Bishop, Pauline Wright)

1980 Moscow T: 6, N: 6, D: 7.26.
1. GDR   (Ramona Kapheim, Silvia Fröhlich, Angelika 3:19.27
         Noack, Romy Saalfeld, Kirsten Wenzel)
2. BUL   (Ginka Gyurova, Mariika Modeva, Rita Todor- 3:20.75
         ova, Iskra Velinova, Nadezhda Filipova)
3. SOV   (Mariya Fadeyeva, Galina Sovetnikova, Marina 3:20.92
         Studneva, Svetlana Semyonova, Nina Chere-
         misina)
4. ROM   (Georgeta Masca Militaru, Florica Szilaghy, 3:22.08
         Maria Tănasa, Valeria Cătescu, Aneta Matei)
5. AUS   (Anne Chirnside, Verna Westwood, Pamela   3:26.37
         Westendorf, Sally Harding, Susanne Palfrey-
         man)

EIGHT-OARED SHELL WITH COXSWAIN

1896–1972 not held

1976 Montreal T: 8, N: 8, D: 7.24.
1. GDR   (Viola Goretzki, Christiane Knetsch, Ilona Rich- 3:33.32
         ter, Brigitte Ahrenholz, Monika Kallies, Henriet-
         ta Ebert, Helma Lehmann, Irina Müller, Marina
         Wilke)
2. SOV   (Lyubov Talalayeva, Nadezhda Roshchina,   3:36.17
         Klavdiya Kozenkova, Elena Zubko, Olga Kol-
         kova, Nelli Tarakanova, Nadezhda Rozgon,
         Olga Guzenko, Olga Pugovskaya)
3. USA   (Jacqueli Zoch, Anita DeFrantz, Carie Graves, 3:38.68
         Marion Greig, Anne Warner, Peggy McCarthy,
         Carol Brown, Gail Ricketson, Lynn Silliman)
4. CAN   (Carol Eastmore, Rhonda Ross, Nancy Higgins, 3:39.52
         Mazina DeLure, Susan Antoft, Wendy Pullan,
         Christine Neuland, Gail Cort, Illoana Smith)
5. GER   (Waltraud Roick, Erika Endriss, Monika Zip- 3:41.06
         plies, Birgit Kiesow, Hiltrud Gürtler, Isolde Ei-
         sele, Marianne Weber, Eva Dick, Ingrid
         Huhn-Wagner)
6. ROM   (Elena Oprea, Florica Petcu, Filigonia Tol, Aure- 3:44.79
         lia Marinescu, Georgeta Militaru, Iuliana Mun-
         teanu, Elena Avram, Marioara Constantin,
         Aneta Matei)
7. POL   (Anna Brandysiewicz, Boguslawa Kozlowska,
         Barbara Wenta-Wojciechowska, Danuta Kon-
         kalec, Róża Data, Mieczyslawa Franczyk, Ma-
         ria Stadnicka, Aleksandra Kaczyńska, Dorota
         Zdanowska)
8. HOL   (Karin Abma, Joke Dierdorf, Barbara Dejong,
         Annette Schortingshuis, Marleen Van Ry, Maria
         Kusters, Liesbeth Pascal, Loes Schutte, Evelien
         Koogje)

1980 Moscow T: 6, N: 6, D: 7.26.
1. GDR   (Martina Boesler, Kersten Neisser, Christiane 3:03.32
         Köpke [Knetsch], Birgit Schütz, Gabriele Kühn
         [Lohs], Ilona Richter, Marita Sandig, Karin
         Metze, Marina Wilke)
2. SOV   (Olga Pivovarova, Nina Umanets, Nadezhda   3:04.29
         Prishchepa, Valentina Zhulina, Tatyana Stet-
         senko, Yelena Tereshina, Nina Preobrazhens-
         kaya, Mariya Pazyun, Nina Frolova)
3. ROM   (Angelica Aposteanu, Marlena Zagoni, Rodica 3:05.63
         Frintu, Florica Bucur, Rodica Puscatu, Ana
         Iliuta, Maria Constantinescu, Elena Bondar,
         Elena Dobritoiu)
4. BUL   (Daniela Stavreva, Stefka Koleva, Todorka   3:10.03
         Vassileva, Snezhka Hristeva, Roumiana Kos-
         tova, Veneta Karamandtzoukova, Mariana Min-
         cheva, Valentina Aleksandrova, Stanka
         Georgieva)
5. GBR   (Gillian Hodges, Joanna Toch, Penelope   3:13.85
         Sweet, Lin Clark, Elizabeth Paton, Rosemary
         Clugston, Nicola Boyes, Beverley Jones, Pau-
         line Wright)

SHOOTING

MEN	WOMEN
Rapid-Fire Pistol	Pistol Match
Free Pistol	Standard Rifle
Small-Bore Rifle, Prone	Air Rifle
Small-Bore Rifle, Three Positions	
Trap Shooting	
Skeet Shooting	
Moving Target	
Air Rifle	
Discontinued Events	

MEN

International shooting competitions have employed a wide variety of tie-breaking rules, including shoot-offs (designated by slash lines in the following charts) and by the positions of the bullets on the target. Current practice in case of ties is to award the victory to whichever shooter recorded the most 10s, or bull's-eyes, in a row, counting backward from the last shot.

Every few years someone conquers a target and achieves a perfect score. At this point the officials of the International Shooting Union alter the target by decreasing the size of the bull's-eye and the rings. It is for this reason that the world records for various events sometimes go down instead of up.

RAPID-FIRE PISTOL

Since 1948 the rapid-fire pistol event has consisted of two 30-shot courses at five silhouettes 25 meters away. The shooter, using a .22 caliber pistol, has eight seconds to fire at each of the five targets. Then the targets reappear and he has six seconds to fire. Finally he must attempt shots at each of the targets within four seconds. This set of 15 shots is repeated four times.

1896 Athens C: 4, N: 3, D: 4.10.

		PTS.
1. Ioannis Phrangoudis	GRE	344
2. Georgios Orphanidis	GRE	249
3. Holger Nielsen	DEN	—
DNF: Merlin (GBR)		

1900 Paris C: ?, N: ?, D: 8.4.

		PTS.
1. Maurice Larrouy	FRA	58
2. Léon Moreaux	FRA	57
3. Eugène Balme	FRA	57
4. Paul Moreau	FRA	57
5. Paul Probst	SWI	57
6. Joseph Labbé	FRA	57

1904 not held

1906 Athens C: 28, N: 8, D: 4.26.

		PTS.
1. Maurice Lecoq	FRA	258
2. Léon Moreaux	FRA	249
3. Aristides Rangavis	GRE	244
4. Louis Richardet	SWI	241
5. Johan Hübner von Holst	SWE	239
6. Cesare Liverziani	ITA	238
7. Hermann Martin	FRA	236
8. Thephtsakis	GRE	235

1908 London C: 43, N: 7, D: 7.11.

		PTS.
1. Paul van Asbroeck	BEL	490
2. Réginald Storms	BEL	487
3. James Gorman	USA	485
4. Charles Axtell	USA	480
5. J.A. Wallingford	GBR	467
6. A. Barbillat	FRA	466
7. W. Ellicott	GBR	458
8. Ira Calkins	USA	457

1912 Stockholm C: 42, N: 10, D: 6.29.

			PTS.
1.	Alfred Lane	USA	287
2.	Paul Palén	SWE	286
3.	Johan Hübner von Holst	SWE	283
4.	John Dietz	USA	283
5.	Curt Törnmark	SWE	280
6.	Eric Carlberg	SWE	278
7.	Georg de Laval	SWE	277
8.	Walter Winans	USA	276

1920 Antwerp C: 38, N: 14, D: 8.3.

			PTS.
1.	Guilherme Paraense	BRA	274
2.	Raymond Bracken	USA	272
3.	Fritz Zulauf	SWI	269
4.	Carl Frederick	USA	262

1924 Paris C: 55, N: 17, D: 6.28.

			PTS.
1.	Henry Bailey	USA	18
2.	Wilhelm Carlberg	SWE	18
3.	Lennart Hannelius	FIN	18
4.	Lorenzo Amaya	ARG	18
5.	M. Osinaldi	ARG	18
6.	A. de Castelbajac	FRA	18
7.	U.B. Sarlin	FIN	18
8.	Einar Liberg	NOR	18

The 1924 match consisted of three series of six shots at six silhouettes in ten seconds. Eight of the 55 competitors achieved perfect scores and, according to the rules of the day, shot off another round of six shots, but this time within eight seconds. All eight shooters had perfect scores, so a second shoot-off string was ordered. This time three of the shooters missed. The third round saw Osinaldi fall by the wayside, the fourth round Amaya, and the fifth round Hannelius. Bailey and Carlberg had now each hit 48 straight targets. A sixth shoot-off was called, and again the two men had perfect scores. Bailey, a 31-year-old gunnery sergeant in the U.S. Marine Corps, fired first in the seventh shoot-off. After calling for the silhouettes, he attempted to fire his first shot. But his .22 autoloader malfunctioned and the cartridge stuck in the breech. Rather than give up, Bailey coolly pulled the spent case out with his fingers, closed the breech, and got off five shots in what remained of his eight seconds. All five shots hit their targets. Carlberg, who had already won three gold medals, three silver, and one bronze since the 1906 Games, was either unnerved or gracious, for he missed two of his next six shots and Bailey won the match.

1928 not held

1932 Los Angeles C: 18, N: 7, D: 8.12.

			PTS.
1.	Renzo Morigi	ITA	36
2.	Heinz Hax	GER	36
3.	Domenico Matteucci	ITA	36
4.	Walter Boninsegni	ITA	35
4.	José Gonzalez Delgado	SPA	35
4.	Arturo Villanueva	MEX	35

The first three series of six shots were shot at eight seconds each. Those with perfect scores took another six shots in six seconds. The eleven survivors shot again at four seconds. Six men were still perfect and shot another round in three seconds. Boninsegni, Delgado, and Villanueva each missed once, leaving Hax, Morigi, and Matteucci still in the contest. The next round required shooting six shots at six turning silhouettes in two seconds. Major Morigi amazed the crowd, which consisted mostly of Los Angeles policemen, by hitting all six targets, the last one after it had already started to turn away.

1936 Berlin C: 53, N: 22, D: 8.7.

			PTS.
1.	Cornelius van Oynn	GER	30/6
2.	Heinz Hax	GER	30/5
3.	Torsten Ullman	SWE	30/4/4
4.	Angelos Papadimas	GRE	30/4/1
5.	Helge Meuller	SWE	30/3
6.	Walter Boninsegni	ITA	29/6/3
7.	Kazimierz Suchorzewski	POL	29/6/1
8.	Haralds Marwe	LAT	29/3

1948 London C: 59, N: 22, D: 8.4. WR: 570 (Carlos Enrique Diaz Sáenz Valiente)

			PTS.	
1.	Károly Takács	HUN	580	WR
2.	Carlos Enrique Diaz Sáenz Valiente	ARG	571	
3.	Sven Lundqvist	SWE	569	
4.	Torsten Ullman	SWE	564	
5.	Leonard Ravilo	FIN	563/36	
6.	Väinö Heusala	FIN	563/34	
7.	Lajos Borzsonyi	HUN	562	
8.	B. Anderson	NOR	559	

Károly Takács was a member of the Hungarian world champion pistol shooting team in 1938 when, while serving as a sergeant in the army, a grenade exploded in his right hand— his pistol hand—and shattered it completely. Undaunted, Takács taught himself to shoot with his left hand, and ten years later, at the age of 38, he won an Olympic gold medal.

1952 Helsinki C: 53, N: 28, D: 7.28. WR: 582 (Huelet Benner)

			PTS.
1.	Károly Takács	HUN	579
2.	Szilárd Kun	HUN	578
3.	Gheorghe Lichiardopol	ROM	578
4.	Carlos Enrique Diaz Sáenz Valiente	ARG	577
5.	Pentti Linnosvuo	FIN	577
6.	Panait Calcai	ROM	575
7.	William McMillan	USA	575
8.	Vassily Frolov	SOV	573

1956 Melbourne C: 35, N: 22, D: 12.5. WR: 589 (Carlos Enrique Diaz Sáenz Valiente)

			PTS.	
1.	Stefan Petrescu	ROM	587	OR
2.	Yevgeny Cherkassov	SOV	585	
3.	Gheorghe Lichiardopol	ROM	581	
4.	Pentti Linnosvuo	FIN	581	
5.	Oscar Cervo	ARG	580	
6.	Szilárd Kun	HUN	578	
7.	Kalle Sievänen	FIN	576	
8.	Károly Takács	HUN	575	

1960 Rome C: 57, N: 35, D: 9.9. WR: 592 (Aleksandr Kropotin, Aleksandr Zabelin)

			PTS.	
1.	William McMillan	USA	587/147	EOR
2.	Pentti Linnosvuo	FIN	587/139	
3.	Aleksandr Zabelin	SOV	587/135	
4.	Hansrüdi Schneider	SWI	586	
5.	Stefan Petrescu	ROM	585	
6.	Gavril Maghiar	ROM	583	
7.	Czeslaw Zając	POL	582	
8.	Jiři Hrnecek	CZE	582	

1964 Tokyo C: 53, N: 34, D: 10.19. WR: 595 (Aleksandr Kropotin)

			PTS.	
1.	Pentti Linnosvuo	FIN	592	OR
2.	Ion Tripşa	ROM	591	
3.	Lubomir Nacovsky	CZE	590	
4.	Hans Albrecht	SWI	590	
5.	Szilárd Kun	HUN	589	
6.	Marcel Roşca	ROM	588	
7.	Igor Bakalov	SOV	588	
8.	Kanji Kubo	JAP	587	

Pentti Linnosvuo became only the second shooter to win gold medals in both the rapid-fire and free pistol events. Alfred Lane won both in the same year (1912), while Linnosvuo's victories were eight years apart.

1968 Mexico City C: 56, N: 34, D: 10.23. WR: 596 (Virgil Atanasiu)

			PTS.	
1.	Józef Zapędzki	POL	593	OR
2.	Marcel Roşca	ROM	591/147	
3.	Renart Suleimanov	SOV	591/146/148	
4.	Christian Düring	GDR	591/146/147	
5.	Erich Masurat	GER	590	
6.	Gerhard Dommrich	GDR	589	
7.	Lubomir Nacovsky	CZE	588	
8.	Giovanni Liverzani	ITA	588	

1972 Munich C: 62, N: 38, D: 9.1. WR: 598 (Giovanni Liverzani)

			PTS.	
1.	Józef Zapędzki	POL	595	OR
2.	Ladislav Falta	CZE	594	
3.	Victor Torshin	SOV	593	
4.	Paul Buser	SWI	592	

5.	Jaime Gonzalez	SPA	592
6.	Giovanni Liverzani	ITA	591
7.	Dencho Denev	BUL	590
8.	Gerhard Petritsch	AUT	590

The 43-year-old Zapędzki was a major in the Polish army when he won his second gold medal. After the competition he visited nearby Dachau and laid a wreath at the grave of his father, who had been killed by the Nazis thirty years earlier.

1976 Montreal C: 48, N: 30, D: 7.23. WR: 598 (Giovanni Liverzani)

			PTS.	
1.	Norbert Klaar	GDR	597	OR
2.	Jürgen Wiefel	GDR	596	
3.	Roberto Ferraris	ITA	595	
4.	Afanasy Kuzmin	SOV	595	
5.	Corneliu Ion	ROM	595	
6.	Erwin Glock	GER	594	
7.	Gerhard Petritsch	AUT	594	
8.	Marin Stan	ROM	594	

Bill McMillan of the United States, competing in his sixth Olympics, scored only one point below his gold-medal-winning performance of 1960. However the quality of marksmanship had improved so much in 16 years that he was able to finish in only a tie for 16th place in 1976. The winner, Norbert Klaar, was a 26-year-old car mechanic from the small industrial town of Wittenberge on the river Elbe. He shot a perfect 300 in the second course.

1980 Moscow C: 40, N: 26, D: 7.25. WR: 598 (Giovanni Liverzani, Corneliu Ion)

			PTS.
1.	Corneliu Ion	ROM	596/148/147/148
2.	Jürgen Wiefel	GDR	596/148/147/147
3.	Gerhard Petritsch	AUT	596/146
4.	Vladas Turla	SOV	595
5.	Roberto Ferraris	ITA	595
6.	Afanasy Kuzmin	SOV	595
7.	Marin Stan	ROM	595
8.	Rafael Rodriguez	CUB	594

FREE PISTOL

The free pistol event is a leisurely affair in which the shooter has two and a half hours in which to fire 60 shots at a target 50 meters (55 yards) away. The 10-ring, or bull's-eye, of the target is only two inches in diameter.

1896 Athens C: 5, N: 3, D: 4.11.

			PTS.
1.	Sumner Paine	USA	442
2.	Holger Nielsen	DEN	285

Sumner Paine was working in Paris when his brother John showed up as part of the Boston Athletic Association team that was on its way to the Olympic Games. John convinced his brother to join him, so the two, not knowing the events or conditions, loaded up with eight guns and 3500 rounds of ammunition (they used only 96) and took the next train to Athens.

1900 Paris C: 20, N: 4, D: 8.1.

		PTS.
1. Conrad Karl Röderer	SWI	503
2. Achille Paroche	FRA	466
3. Konrad Stäheli	SWI	453
4. Louis Richardet	SWI	448
5. Louis Duffoy	FRA	442
6. G. van Haan	HOL	437
7. Friedrich Luthi	SWI	435
7. Léon Moreau	FRA	435

1904 not held

1906 Athens C: 21, N: 8, D: 4.23.

		PTS.
1. Georgios Orphanidis	GRE	221
2. Jean Fouconnier	FRA	219
3. Aristides Rangavis	GRE	218
4. Konrad Stäheli	SWI	206
5. Konstantinos Skarlotos	GRE	206
6. Maurice Lecoq	FRA	205
7. L. Ternajgo	AUT	199
8. Cesare Liverziani	ITA	199

1908 not held

1912 Stockholm C: 54, N: 12, D: 7.2.

		PTS.
1. Alfred Lane	USA	499
2. Peter Dolfen	USA	474
3. Charles Stewart	GBR	470
4. Georg de Laval	SWE	470
5. Erik Boström	SWE	468
6. Horatio Poulter	GBR	461
7. Henry Sears	USA	459
8. Nikolai Panin (Kolomenkin)	RUS	457

Alfred Lane of New York City was only 20 years old when he went to Stockholm and won three gold medals. Eight years later in Antwerp he added two more gold medals and one bronze. Eighth-place finisher Kolomenkin, a ten-time Russian pistol champion, was also a well-known figure skater who had won a gold medal in the special figures event of 1908.

1920 Antwerp C: 36, N: 13, D: 8.2.

		PTS.
1. Karl Frederick	USA	496
2. Afranio da Costa	BRA	489
3. Alfred Lane	USA	481
4. Lauritz Larsen	DEN	475
5. Niels Larsen	DEN	470
6. Wilhelm Andersson	SWE	467

Da Costa used a new Colt .22 that had been loaned to the Brazilian team by the U.S. team, and ammunition given to him by Alfred Lane.

1924-1932 not held

1936 Berlin C: 43, N: 19, D: 8.7. WR: 547 (Torsten Ullman)

		PTS.	
1. Torsten Ullman	SWE	559	WR
2. Erich Krempel	GER	544	
3. Charles des Jammonières	FRA	540	
4. Marcel Bonin	FRA	538	
5. Tapio Vartiovaara	FIN	537	
6. Elliott Jones	USA	536	
7. Georges Stathis	GRE	532	
8. Aatto Nuora	FIN	532	

Earlier in the day Ullman had won a bronze medal in the rapid-fire pistol event.

1948 London C: 50, N: 22, D: 8.2. WR: 559 (Torsten Ullman)

		PTS.
1. Edwin Vasquez Cam	PER	545
2. Rudolf Schnyder	SWI	539/60/21
3. Torsten Ullman	SWE	539/60/16
4. Huelet Benner	USA	539/58
5. Beat Rhyner	SWI	536
6. Angel León de Gozalo	SPA	534
7. Ambrus Balogh	HUN	532
8. M. LaFortune	BEL	530

Vasquez is the only Peruvian ever to win an Olympic medal.

1952 Helsinki C: 48, N: 28, D: 7.25. WR: 559 (Torsten Ullman)

		PTS.	
1. Huelet Benner	USA	553	OR
2. Angel León de Gozalo	SPA	550	
3. Ambrus Balogh	HUN	549	
4. Konstantin Martazov	SOV	546	
5. Lev Vainshtein	SOV	546	
6. Torsten Ullman	SWE	543	
7. Klaus Lahti	FIN	541	
8. Beat Rhyner	SWI	539	

1956 Melbourne C: 33, N: 22, D: 11.30. WR: 566 (Anton Yasinsky)

		PTS.	
1. Pentti Linnosvuo	FIN	556/26	OR
2. Makhmud Umarov	SOV	556/24	OR
3. Offutt Pinion	USA	551	
4. Choji Hosaka	JAP	550/24	
5. Anton Yasinsky	SOV	550/20	
6. Torsten Ullman	SWE	549	
7. Åke Lindbolm	SWE	542	
8. Leonard Tolhurst	AUS	541	

1960 Rome C: 67, N: 40, D: 9.6. WR: 566 (Anton Yasinsky)

		PTS.	
1. Aleksei Gustchin	SOV	560	OR
2. Makhmud Umarov	SOV	552/26	
3. Yoshihisa Yoshikawa	JAP	552/20	
4. Torsten Ullman	SWE	550	
5. Stanislaw Romik	POL	548	
6. Alfred Späni	SWI	546	
7. Vladimir Kudrna	CZE	545	
8. Horst Kadner	GDR	544	

Fourth-place finisher Ullman was now 52 years old.

1964 Tokyo C: 52, N: 42, D: 10.18. WR: 566 (Anton Yasinsky)

		PTS.	
1. Väinö Markkanen	FIN	560	EOR
2. Franklin Green	USA	557	
3. Yoshihisa Yoshikawa	JAP	554/26	
4. Johann Garreis	GDR	554/24	
5. Anthony Chivers	GBR	552	
6. Antonio Vita Segura	PER	550	
7. Leif Larsson	SWE	549	
8. Thomas Smith	USA	548	

1968 Mexico City C: 69, N: 42, D: 10.18. WR: 566 (Anton Yasinsky)

		PTS.	
1. Grigory Kossykh	SOV	562/30	OR
2. Heinz Mertel	GER	562/26	OR
3. Harald Vollmar	GDR	560	
4. Arnold Vitarbo	USA	559	
5. Pawel Malek	POL	556	
6. Helmut Artelt	GDR	555	
7. Nelson Onate	CUB	555	
8. Neagu Bratu	ROM	554	

1972 Munich C: 59, N: 37, D: 8.28. WR: 572 (Grigory Kosskyh)

		PTS.	
1. Ragnar Skanåker	SWE	567	OR
2. Dan Iuga	ROM	562	
3. Rudolf Dollinger	AUT	560	
4. Rajmund Stachurski	POL	559	
5. Harald Vollmar	GDR	558	
6. Hynek Hromada	CZE	556	
7. Kornel Marosvari	HUN	555	
8. Grigory Kosskyh	SOV	555	

1976 Montreal C: 47, N: 32, D: 7.18. WR: 572 (Grigory Kosskyh, Harald Vollmar)

		PTS.	
1. Uwe Potteck	GDR	573	WR
2. Harald Vollmar	GDR	567	
3. Rudolf Dollinger	AUT	562	
4. Heinz Mertel	GER	560	
5. Ragnar Skanåker	SWE	559	
6. Vincenzo Tondo	ITA	559	
7. Grigory Kosskyh	SOV	559	
8. Dencho Denev	BUL	557	

1980 Moscow C: 33, N: 19, D: 7.20. WR: 577 (Moritz Minder, Paavo Palokangas)

		PTS.	
1. Aleksandr Melentev	SOV	581	WR
2. Harald Vollmar	GDR	568	
3. Ljubcho Diakov	BUL	565	
4. Gil-San Soh	PRK	565	
5. Seppo Saarenpää	FIN	565	
6. Sergei Pyzhianov	SOV	564	
7. Ragnar Skanåker	SWE	563	
8. Paavo Palokangas	FIN	561	

SMALL-BORE RIFLE, PRONE

The small-bore rifle, prone match is shot at a distance of 50 meters with a .22 rimfire rifle. Originally the 10-ring bull's-eye was .89 inches in diameter. When high scores became too common, it was scaled down in 1958 to .487 inches. The shooter must keep his wrist at least six inches above the ground. He is given two hours in which to take 60 shots and is also allowed 15 sighting shots, which can only be taken between the strings of ten record shots.

1896-1906 not held

1908 London C: 19, N: 5, D: 7.11.

		PTS.
1. A.A. Carnell	GBR	387
2. Harry Humby	GBR	386
3. George Barnes	GBR	385
4. M.K. Matthews	GBR	384
5. Edward Amoore	GBR	383
6. William Pimm	GBR	379
7. A.E. Taylor	GBR	376
8. H.I. Hawkins	GBR	374

1912 Stockholm C: 41, N: 9, D: 7.4.

		PTS.
1. Frederick Hird	USA	194
2. William Milne	GBR	193
3. Harry Burt	GBR	192
4. Edward Lessimore	GBR	192
5. Francis Kemp	GBR	190
5. Robert Murray	GBR	190
7. William Leushner	USA	189
8. Erik Bostrom	SWE	189

1920 Antwerp C: 50, N: 10, D: 8.2.

		PTS.
1. Lawrence Nuesslein	USA	391
2. Arthur Rothrock	USA	386
3. Dennis Fenton	USA	385

1924 Paris C: 66, N: 19, D: 6.23.

		PTS.
1. Pierre Coquelin de Lisle	FRA	398
2. Marcus Dinwiddie	USA	396
3. Josias Hartmann	SWI	394
4. Erik Saetter-Lassen	DEN	393
4. Anders Peter Nielsen	DEN	393
4. Johannes Theslöf	FIN	393
7. Viktor Knutsson	SWE	392
7. Jakob Reich	SWI	392

Silver medalist Marcus Dinwiddie was a 17-year-old schoolboy from Washington, D.C. His record score of 396 out of 400 held up for most of the match, until the 23-year-old Coquelin de Lisle hit a sensational set of 100, 100, 99, and 99.

1928 not held

1932 Los Angeles C: 26, N: 9, D: 8.13.

		PTS.
1. Bertil Rönnmark	SWE	294/296
2. Gustavo Huet	MEX	294/290
3. Zoltán Hradetzky-Soós	HUN	293
4. Mario Zorzi	ITA	293
5. Gustaf Andersson	SWE	292
5. William Harding	USA	292
5. Karl Larsson	SWE	292
5. Francisco Real	POR	292

Antonius Lemberkovits of Hungary fired one bull's-eye which he had unfortunately aimed at the wrong target. He called out his mistake to the officials, who ruled the shot a complete miss. Had he not made this error and had he not been so honest, Lemberkovits would have won the gold medal.

1936 Berlin C: 66, N: 25, D: 8.8.

		PTS.	
1. Willy Rögeberg	NOR	300	WR
2. Ralph Berzsenyi	HUN	296	
3. Wladyslaw Karaś	POL	296	
4. Martin Gison	PHI	296	
5. José Trindade Mello	BRA	296	
6. Jacques Mazoyer	FRA	296	
7. Gustavo Huet	MEX	296	
8. Bertil Rönnmark	SWE	295	

The 30-year-old Rögeberg fired the first perfect score ever recorded in international competition. Fourth-place finisher Gison was captured by the Japanese during World War II and forced to take part in the infamous Bataan death

march. He survived and was able to compete in the 1948 Olympics in London.

1948 London C: 71, N: 26, D: 8.3.

		PTS.	
1. Arthur Cook	USA	599/43	WR
2. Walter Tomsen	USA	599/42	WR
3. Jonas Jonsson	SWE	597/44	
4. Halvor Kongsjorden	NOR	597/39	
5. Thore Skredegaard	NOR	597/39	
6. Enrique Baldwin Ponte	PER	596/39	
7. J. Ravila	FIN	596/39	
8. Willy Rögeberg	NOR	596/37	

Cook and Tomsen each missed the 10-ring only once in 60 shots, but Cook was awarded first place because he had fired one shot more than Tomsen within the ⅜-inch inner bull's-eye.

1952 Helsinki C: 58, N: 32, D: 7.29. WR: 400 (T. Manttari)

		PTS.	
1. Iosif Sârbu	ROM	400/33	EWR
2. Boris Andreyev	SOV	400/28	EWR
3. Arthur Jackson	USA	399/28	
4. Gilmour Boa	CAN	399/28	
5. Erich Spörer	GER	399/25	
6. Otto Horber	SWI	398/29	
7. Veikko Leskinen	FIN	398/28	
8. Severino Moreira	BRA	398/22	

1956 Melbourne C: 44, N: 25, D: 12.5. WR: 598 (Gilmour Boa)

		PTS.
1. Gerald Ouellette	CAN	600
2. Vassily Borissov	SOV	599
3. Gilmour Boa	CAN	598
4. Otakar Hořinek	CZE	598
5. Iosif Sârbu	ROM	598
6. Sándor Krebs	HUN	598
7. Erling Kongshaug	NOR	598
8. Severino Moreira	BRA	597

After he had done poorly in the three-position small-bore event, Ouellette and his teammate Gilmour Boa decided that they should both use Boa's rifle for the prone competition, even though this meant that they both had to shoot within the same two-and-a-half-hour time limit. Boa went first and, coached by Ouellette, matched his world record of 598. Then, with half the time remaining, it was Ouellette's turn. Coached by Boa, who encouraged the Windsor, Ontario, tool designer to take two breaks to ease the pressure, Ouellette shot 60 straight bull's-eyes for a perfect score. Unfortunately, his score was not accepted as a world record because the Australian officials had set the targets one and a half meters too close. Ouellette's second appearance in the Olympics didn't come until 12 years later, when he finished sixth in the three-position event in Mexico City.

1960 Rome C: 85, N: 46, D: 9.10. WR: 595 (János Holup)

		PTS.
1. Peter Kohnke	GER	590
2. James Hill	USA	589
3. Enrico Forcella Pelliccioni	VEN	587
4. Vassily Borissov	SOV	586
5. Arthur Skinner	GBR	586
6. Yukio Inokuma	JAP	586
7. Daniel Puckel	USA	585
8. Marcel Koen	BUL	585

Eighteen-year-old Peter Kohnke of Bremervorde was the youngest of the 85 entrants in the prone event.

1964 Tokyo C: 73, N: 43, D: 10.16. WR: 595 (János Holup, Rudolf Bortz)

		PTS.	
1. László Hammerl	HUN	597	WR
2. Lones Wigger	USA	597	WR
3. Tommy Pool	USA	596	
4. Gilmour Boa	CAN	595	
5. Nicolae Rotaru	ROM	595	
6. Akihiro Rinzaki	JAP	594	
7. Karl Wenk	GER	594	
8. Traian Cogut	ROM	593	

László Hammerl was a 22-year-old medical student from Budapest. He was awarded the victory on the basis of a tie-breaking rule which stated that whoever had the highest score in the final string of ten shots was the winner.

1968 Mexico City C: 86, N: 45, D: 10.19. WR: 598 (David Boyd, Alfons Meyer)

		PTS.	
1. Jan Kurka	CZE	598	EWR
2. László Hammerl	HUN	598	EWR
3. Ian Ballinger	NZE	597	
4. Nicolae Rotaru	ROM	597	
5. John Palin	GBR	596	
6. Jean Loret	FRA	596	
7. Bjorn Bakken	NOR	595	
8. Gary Anderson	USA	595	

This time Hammerl lost the gold medal because of the same tie-breaking rule from which he had benefited four years earlier. Eulalia Rolińska of Poland and Gladys de Seminario of Peru had the distinction of being the first women to compete in Olympic shooting. They finished 22nd and 31st, respectively.

1972 Munich C: 101, N: 59, D: 8.28. WR: 598 (David Boyd, Alfons Meyer, Jan Kurka, László Hammerl, Peter Gorewski, Wolfram Waibel, Manfred Fiess, Esa Kervinen)

		PTS.	
1. Ho-Jun Li	PRK	599	WR
2. Victor Auer	USA	598	
3. Nicolae Rotaru	ROM	598	
4. Giuseppe de Chirico	ITA	597	
5. Jiří Vogler	CZE	597	
6. Jaime Santiago	PUR	597	
7. Lones Wigger	USA	597	
8. László Hammerl	HUN	597	

After his victory, Li was asked by reporters to what he attributed his brilliant performance. He replied, "I thought I was shooting at my enemies. Our Prime Minister, Kim-Il Sung, told us prior to our departure to shoot as if we were fighting our enemies. And that's exactly what I did." This attitude was considered to be unsportsmanlike, and so a second press conference was called at which Li claimed he had been misquoted. Second-place finisher Vic Auer was a North Hollywood TV scriptwriter who had written for *Death Valley Days*, *Gunsmoke*, and *Bonanza*.

1976 Montreal C: 76, N: 49, D: 7.19. WR: 599 (Ho Jun Li, Karel Bulan, Mircea Ilca)

		PTS.	
1. Karlheinz Smieszek	GER	599	EWR
2. Ulrich Lind	GER	597	
3. Gennady Lushchikov	SOV	595	
4. Anton Müller	SWI	595	
5. Walter Frescura	ITA	594	
6. Arne Sörensen	CAN	593	
7. Henning Clausen	DEN	593	
8. Desanka Pesut	YUG	592	

Smieszek, a 27-year-old insurance agent, was a surprise winner who had never before won a major shooting title.

1980 Moscow C: 56, N: 33, D: 7.21. WR: 599 (Ho-Jun Li, Karel Bulan, Mircea Ilca, Karlheinz Smieszek, Alistair Allan, Lones Wigger)

		PTS.	
1. Károly Varga	HUN	599	EWR
2. Hellfried Heilfort	GDR	599	EWR
3. Petur Zapianov	BUL	598	
4. Krzysztof Stefaniak	POL	598	
5. Timo Hagmaan	FIN	597	
6. Aleksandr Mastianin	SOV	597	
7. Nonka Matova	BUL	597	
8. Walter Frescura	ITA	597	

Varga broke his shooting hand playing soccer two days before the competition and had to wear a bandage while he shot. After winning the gold medal he explained that the injury had actually helped him, because it forced him to squeeze the trigger more delicately.

SMALL-BORE RIFLE, THREE POSITIONS

In the small-bore rifle, three-position event, each entrant shoots 40 shots prone, 40 kneeling, and 40 standing, with a .22 rifle at a target 50 meters away. The target is the same as that used in the prone event.

1896-1948 not held

1952 Helsinki C: 44, N: 25, D: 7.29. WR: 1167 (K. Steigelmann)

			PRONE		KNEELING		STANDING	TOTAL PTS.
1.	Erling Kongshaug	NOR	397		387		380	1164/53
2.	Vilho Ylönen	FIN	397		394	WR	373	1164/53
3.	Boris Andreyev	SOV	400	WR	387		376	1163
4.	Ernst Huber	SWI	397		390		375	1162
5.	Pyotr Avilov	SOV	395		385		382	1162
6.	Iosif Sârbu	ROM	400	WR	383		378	1161
7.	Uno Berg	SWE	396		388		374	1158
8.	Veikko Leskinen	FIN	398		390		369	1157

1956 Melbourne C: 44, N: 28, D: 12.4. WR: 1176 (Ole Jensen)

			PRONE		KNEELING	STANDING	TOTAL PTS.	
1.	Anatoly Bogdanov	SOV	396		392	384	1172	OR
2.	Otakar Hořinek	CZE	393		395	384	1172	OR
3.	Nils Johan Sundberg	SWE	397		396	374	1167	
4.	Vassily Borrisov	SOV	395		391	377	1163	
5.	Vilho Ylönen	FIN	394		386	381	1161	
6.	Gilmour Boa	CAN	400	WR	391	368	1159	
7.	Iosif Sârbu	ROM	397		392	368	1157	
8.	Anders Kvissberg	SWE	394		389	373	1156	

1960 Rome C: 75, N: 40, D: 9.8. WR: 1149 (Klaus Zähringer)

			PRONE	KNEELING	STANDING	TOTAL PTS.	
1.	Viktor Shamburkin	SOV	394	386	369	1149	EWR
2.	Marat Niyasov	SOV	384	388	373	1145	
3.	Klaus Zähringer	GER	394	381	364	1139	
4.	Dušan Houdek	CZE	387	386	366	1139	
5.	Jerzy Nowicki	POL	394	378	365	1137	
6.	Esa Kervinen	FIN	392	381	364	1137	
7.	Daniel Puckel	USA	390	385	361	1137	
8.	János Holup	HUN	394	384	356	1134	

1964 Tokyo C: 75, N: 40, D: 9.8. WR: 1157 (Gary Anderson)

			PRONE	KNEELING	STANDING	TOTAL PTS.	
1.	Lones Wigger	USA	398	394	372	1164	WR
2.	Velichko Velichkov	BUL	396	384	372	1152	
3.	László Hammerl	HUN	397	387	367	1151	
4.	Harry Köcher	GDR	394	389	365	1148	
5.	Jerzy Nowicki	POL	396	389	362	1147	
6.	Tommy Pool	USA	393	392	362	1147	
7.	Ion Olarescu	ROM	393	391	360	1144	
8.	Kurt Müller	SWI	390	386	367	1143	

U.S. Army Captain Lones Wigger of Carter, Montana, had never shot before a large crowd before. Teammate Gary Anderson advised him not to be afraid of the crowd but to feel a part of it. Wigger set a world record in the prone event, but lost on a tie-breaker. Four days later he set another world record in the three-position event, but this time he finished 12 points ahead of the nearest competitor. Eight years later, at the Munich Olympics, Wigger won another gold medal in the 300-meter free rifle event.

1968 Mexico City C: 62, N: 35, D: 10.21. WR: 1165 (Gary Anderson)

			PRONE	STANDING	KNEELING		TOTAL PTS.
1.	Bernd Klingner	GER	394	367	396	WR	1157
2.	John Writer	USA	395	370	391		1156
3.	Viktor Parkhimovich	SOV	395	366	393		1154
4.	John Foster	USA	394	369	390		1153
5.	José Gonzales	MEX	397	376	379		1152
6.	Gerald Ouellette	CAN	396	364	391		1151
7.	Peter Kohnke	GER	395	368	388		1151
8.	Kurt Müller	SWI	390	373	388		1151

1972 Munich C: 69, N: 41, D: 8.30. WR: 1165 (Gary Anderson, Oleg Lapkin)

			PRONE	STANDING		KNEELING	TOTAL PTS.	
1.	John Writer	USA	395	381	WR	390	1166	WR
2.	Lanny Bassham	USA	390	375		392	1157	
3.	Werner Lippoldt	GDR	393	372		388	1153	
4.	Petr Kovařik	CZE	397	368		388	1153	
5.	Vladimir Agishev	SOV	392	369		391	1152	
6.	Andrzej Sieledcow	POL	395	369		387	1151	
7.	Gottfried Kustermann	GER	397	364		388	1149	
8.	Nicolae Rotaru	ROM	397	361		390	1148	

1976 Montreal C: 57, N: 35, D: 7.21. WR: 1167 (Lones Wigger)

			PRONE	STANDING	KNEELING	TOTAL PTS.
1.	Lanny Bassham	USA	397	373	392	1162
2.	Margaret Murdock	USA	398	376	388	1162
3.	Werner Seibold	GER	397	377	386	1160
4.	Srecko Pejovic	YUG	391	379	386	1156
5.	Sven Johansson	SWE	394	367	391	1152
6.	Ho-Jun Li	PRK	390	373	389	1152
7.	Zdravko Milutinovic	YUG	394	394	389	1152
8.	Aleksandr Mitrofanov	SOV	394	369	388	1151

After finishing second in 1972, Lanny Bassham, a rancher from Fort Worth, Texas, became convinced that his technical skill had to be supplemented by mental training. He went to the Montreal Olympics as the favorite. His U.S. teammate was Margaret Murdock, a 33-year-old nurse from Topeka, Kansas. In 1970 Murdock had won the standing event at the world championships while she was four months' pregnant. At the 1976 Olympics, Bassham and Murdock finished in a tie at 1162. Bassham was awarded the gold medal because he had scored three 100s to Murdock's two. Bassham felt that the tie-breaker was a silly rule, and at the medal ceremony he pulled Murdock up to the first place platform and they stood together for the playing of the U.S. national anthem. Murdock was probably less upset about the tie-breaking rule, since it was the same rule that had allowed her to gain a place on the U.S. team when she and John Writer finished with the same scores at the U.S. tryouts. Bassham later started a mental management business to help people become better shooters and make more money. Murdock was the first woman to win an Olympic shooting medal.

1980 Moscow C: 39, N: 21, D: 7.23. WR: 1172 (Nonka Matova)

		PRONE	STANDING	KNEELING	TOTAL PTS.	
1. Viktor Vlasov	SOV	398	378	397	1173	WR
2. Bernd Hartstein	GDR	399	374	393	1166	
3. Sven Johansson	SWE	398	379	388	1165	
4. Mauri Röppänen	FIN	397	379	388	1164	
5. Aleksandr Mitrofanov	SOV	397	378	389	1164	
6. Nonka Matova	BUL	396	377	390	1163	
7. Hellfried Heilfort	GDR	394	378	390	1162	
8. Eugeniusz Pędzisz	POL	397	368	391	1156	

TRAP SHOOTING

In the trap or clay pigeon event, clay saucers about four and a half inches in diameter are flung into the air at various angles. The shooter is allowed two shots with a shotgun at each saucer (or bird).

1896 not held

1900 Paris C: 51, N: 4, D: 7.15.

		PTS.
1. Roger de Barbarin	FRA	17
2. René Guyot	FRA	17
3. Justinien de Clary	FRA	17
4. Cesar Bettex	FRA	16
5. Hilaret	FRA	15
6. Edouard Geynet	FRA	13
7. Merlin	GBR	12
8. De Schonen	?	12

1904 St. Louis not held

1906 Athens C: 12, N: 4, D: 4.26.
Single Shot

		PTS.
1. Gerald Merlin	GBR	24
2. Ioannis Peridis	GRE	24
3. Sidney Merlin	GBR	23
4. Maurice Faure	FRA	22
5. K. Oxyopoulos	GRE	16
6. I. Delpopoulos	GRE	14
7. Sándor Török	HUN	12
8. D. P. Petropoulos	GRE	7

1906 Athens C: 10, N: 4, D: 4.26.
Double Shot

		PTS.
1. Sidney Merlin	GBR	15
2. Anastasios Metaxas	GRE	13
3. Gerald Merlin	GBR	12
4. I. Theofilakis	GRE	11
5. Maurice Faure	FRA	9
6. Jean Fouconnier	FRA	8
6. K. Tanopoulos	GRE	8
6. Sándor Török	HUN	8

1908 London C: 61, N: 8, D: 8.11.

		PTS.
1. Walter Ewing	CAN	72
2. George Beattie	CAN	60
3. Alexander Maunder	GBR	57
3. Anastasios Metaxas	GRE	57
5. Charles Palmer	GBR	55
5. A.W. Westover	CAN	55
7. Mylie Fletcher	CAN	53
7. R. Hutton	GBR/IRL	53
7. J.W. Wilson	HOL	53

1912 Stockholm C: 61, N: 11, D: 7.2.

		PTS.
1. James Graham	USA	96
2. Alfred Göldel	GER	94
3. Harry Blau	RUS	91
4. Harry Humby	GBR	88
4. Anastasios Metaxas	GRE	88
4. Albert Preuss	GER	88
4. Gustaf Adolf Schnitt	FIN	88
4. Freiherr von Zeidlitz und Leipe	GER	88

1920 Antwerp C: 48, N: 8, D: 7.23.

		PTS.
1. Mark Arie	USA	95
2. Frank Troeh	USA	93
3. Frank Wright	USA	87
4. Horace Bonser	USA	87
4. Frederick Plum	USA	87
6. Nordal Lunde	NOR	85

1924 Paris C: 44, N: 14, D: 7.8.

		PTS.	
1. Gyula Halasy	HUN	98/8	OR
2. Konrad Huber	FIN	98/7	OR
3. Frank Hughes	USA	97	
4. James Montgomery	CAN	97	
5. Louis d'Heur	BEL	96/8	
6. George Beattie	CAN	96/7	
6. Samuel Sharman	USA	96/7	
6. Samuel Vance	CAN	96/7	

1928–1948 not held

1952 Helsinki C: 40, N: 22, D: 7.26.

		PTS.
1. George Généreux	CAN	192
2. Knut Holmqvist	SWE	191
3. Hans Liljedahl	SWE	190
4. František Čapek	CZE	188
5. Konrad Huber	FIN	188
6. Ioannis Koutsis	GRE	187
7. Galliano Rossini	ITA	187
8. Italo Bellini	ITA	186

George Généreux, of Saskatoon, Saskatchewan, was only 17 years old when he won the Olympic championship. Holmqvist needed to score a perfect 25 on his last round to tie Généreux, but he missed his next to last shot.

1956 Melbourne C: 32, N: 18, D: 12.1.

		PTS.	
1. Galliano Rossini	ITA	195	OR
2. Adam Smelczyński	POL	190	
3. Alessandro Ciceri	ITA	188/24	
4. Nikolai Mogilevsky	SOV	188/23	
5. Yuri Nikandrov	SOV	188/22	
6. František Čapek	CZE	187	
7. Knut Holmqvist	SWE	188	
8. Hans Liljedahl	SWE	177	

1960 Rome C: 51, N: 28, D: 10.1.

		PTS.
1. Ion Dumitrescu	ROM	192
2. Galliano Rossini	ITA	191
3. Sergei Kalinin	SOV	190
4. James Clark	USA	188
5. Hans Aasnes	NOR	185
5. Joseph Wheater	GBR	185
7. Adam Smelczyński	POL	184
8. Claude Foussier	FRA	183
8. Karni Singh	IND	183

1964 Tokyo C: 51, N: 28, D: 10.17.

		PTS.	
1. Ennio Mattarelli	ITA	198	OR
2. Pavel Senichev	SOV	194/25	
3. William Morris	USA	194/24	
4. Galliano Rossini	ITA	194/23	
5. Ion Dumitrescu	ROM	193	
6. Mario Lira	CHI	193	
7. John Braithwaite	GBR	192	
8. Joachim Marscheider	GDR	191	

1968 Mexico City C: 59, N: 34, D: 10.19. WR: 198 (Ennio Mattarelli)

		PTS.	
1. John Braithwaite	GBR	198	EWR
2. Thomas Garrigus	USA	196/25/25	
3. Kurt Czekalla	GDR	196/25/23	

4. Pavel Senichev	SOV	196/22
5. Pierre Candelo	FRA	195
6. Adam Smelczyński	POL	195
7. Aleksandr Alipov	SOV	195
8. John Primrose	CAN	194

The 43-year-old Braithwaite missed two of his first 13 shots, but then hit the last 187 in a row. A veterinary surgeon from Preston, near Liverpool, Braithwaite took up clay pigeon shooting because he could no longer stand to shoot real birds and animals and see them suffer.

1972 Munich C: 57, N: 33, D: 8.29. WR: 198 (Ennio Mattarelli, John Braithwaite, Silvano Basagni)

		PTS.	
1. Angelo Scalzone	ITA	199	WR
2. Michel Carrega	FRA	198	
3. Silvano Basagni	ITA	195	
4. Burckhardt Hoppe	GDR	193	
5. Johnny Påhlsson	SWE	193	
6. James Poindexter	USA	192	
7. John Primrose	CAN	192	
8. Marcos Olsen	BRA	191	

1976 Montreal C: 44, N: 29, D: 7.20. WR: 199 (Angelo Scalzone, Michel Carrega)

		PTS.
1. Donald Haldeman	USA	190
2. Armando Silva Marques	POR	189
3. Ubaldesco Baldi	ITA	189
4. Burckhardt Hoppe	GDR	186
5. Aleksandr Androshkin	SOV	185
6. Adam Smelczyński	POL	183
7. John Primrose	CAN	183
8. Bernard Blondeau	FRA	182

The low scores were due to poor weather conditions. In a sport where contestants are known to calm their nerves with alcohol or tranquilizers, it came as a shock when 65-year-old Paul Cerutti of Monaco was disqualified after it was found that he had been taking amphetamines. The stimulants did him little good anyway. He finished 43rd out of a field of 44.

1980 Moscow C: 34, N: 22, D: 7.22. WR: 199 (Angelo Scalzone, Michel Carrega)

		PTS.
1. Luciano Giovannetti	ITA	198
2. Rustam Yambulatov	SOV	196/24/25
3. Jörg Damme	GDR	196/24/24
4. Josef Hojny	CZE	196/23
5. Eladio Vallduvi	SPA	195
6. Aleksandr Asanov	SOV	195
7. Silvano Basagni	ITA	194
8. Burckhardt Hoppe	GDR	192

The 34-year-old Giovannetti celebrated his victory by tossing his cap into the air and shooting a hole through it.

SKEET SHOOTING

Skeet shooting is similar to trap shooting in that the shooter, using a shotgun, fires at a flung four-and-a-half-inch clay saucer. However in the skeet match, the shooter moves around to eight different stations and is sometimes thrown two "birds" at a time. The birds may be thrown up to three seconds after they are called. Whereas trap birds are sent out from ground level, in skeet they are released from two towers, one high, one low.

1896–1964 not held

1968 Mexico City C: 52, N: 30, D: 10.22. WR: 198 (J. Faber, Konrad Wirnhier)

		PTS.	
1. Yevgeny Petrov	SOV	198/25	EWR
2. Romano Garagnani	ITA	198/24/25	EWR
3. Konrad Wirnhier	GER	198/24/23	EWR
4. Yuri Tsuranov	SOV	196	
5. Pedro Gianella	PER	194	
6. Nicolas Atalah	CHI	194	
7. Jorge Jottar	CHI	194	
8. Panagiotis Xanthakos	GRE	194	

1972 Munich C: 63, N: 37, D: 9.2. WR: 200 (Yevgeny Petrov, Yuri Tsuranov)

		PTS.
1. Konrad Wirnhier	GER	195/25
2. Yevgeny Petrov	SOV	195/24
3. Michael Buchheim	GDR	195/23
4. Joe Neville	GBR	194
5. Roberto Castrillo Garcia	CUB	194
6. Klaus Reschke	GDR	193
7. Elie Penot	FRA	193
8. Paschalis Georgiou	GRE	192

World champion Yuri Tsuranov of the U.S.S.R. was so upset by a judge's call against him that he walked off the field. The jury decided to penalize him three birds for leaving, but permitted him to continue the round. He ended up three points shy of a tie for first place and finished ninth instead.

1976 Montreal C: 68, N: 41, D: 7.24. WR: 200 (Yevgeny Petrov, Yuri Tsuranov, Jariel Zhgentii Hans Kjeld Rasmussen, Wieslaw Gawlikowski)

		PTS.	
1. Josef Panaček	CZE	198	EOR
2. Eric Swinkels	HOL	198	EOR
3. Wieslaw Gawlikowski	POL	196	
4. Klaus Reschke	GDR	196	
5. Franz Schitzhofer	AUT	195	
6. Edgardo Zachrisson	GUA	194	
7. Juan Avalos	SPA	194	
8. Jean Petitpied	FRA	194	

1980 Moscow C: 46, N: 25, D: 7.26. WR: 199 (Joseph Clemmons)

			PTS.
1.	Hans Kjeld Rasmussen	DEN	196/25/25
2.	Lars-Göran Carlsson	SWE	196/25/24
3.	Roberto Castrillo García	CUB	196/25/23
4.	Pavel Pulda	CZE	196/24
5.	Celso Giardini	ITA	196/24
6.	Guillermo Torres	CUB	195
7.	Francisco Perez	SPA	195
8.	Ari Westergard	FIN	195

Because too many perfect scores had been achieved, the rules were changed to make the match speedier and more difficult.

MOVING TARGET

The moving target or running boar event consists of 60 shots at 50 meters. The target, a life-size reproduction of a wild boar with a two-inch 10-ring, crosses a ten-meter gap. The boar does 30 fast runs at two and a half seconds and 30 slow runs at five seconds.

1896 not held

1900 Paris, C: ?, N: 3, D: 7.17.

			PTS.
1.	Louis Debray	FRA	20
2.	P. Nivet	FRA	20
3.	Comte de Lambert	FRA	19
4.	Gabriel Veyre	FRA	19
5.	de Schlumberger	FRA	19
6.	Paul Desart	FRA	19

1904–1968 not held

1972 Munich C: 28, N: 16, D: 9.1. WR: 566 (Göete Gåård)

			PTS.	
1.	Lakov Zhelezniak	SOV	569	WR
2.	Helmut Bellingrodt	COL	565	
3.	John Kynoch	GBR	562	
4.	Valery Postoianov	SOV	560	
5.	Christoph-Michael Zeisner	GER	554	
6.	Göete Gåård	SWE	553	
7.	Guenther Danne	GER	551	
8.	Karl-Axel Karlsson	SWE	551	

1976 Montreal C: 27, N: 16, D: 7.23. WR: 577 (Helmut Bellingrodt, Valery Postoianov)

			PTS.	
1.	Aleksandr Gazov	SOV	579	WR
2.	Aleksandr Kedyarov	SOV	576	
3.	Jerzy Greszkiewicz	POL	571	
4.	Thomas Pfeffer	GDR	571	
5.	Wolfgang Hamberger	GER	567	
6.	Helmut Bellingrodt	COL	567	
7.	Karl Karlsson	SWE	565	
8.	Louis Theimer	USA	564	

1980 Moscow C: 19, N: 11, D: 7.24. WR: 581 (Thomas Pfeffer)

			PTS.	
1.	Igor Sokolov	SOV	589	WR
2.	Thomas Pfeffer	GDR	589	
3.	Aleksandr Gazov	SOV	587	
4.	András Doleschall	HUN	584	
5.	Tibor Bodnár	HUN	584	
6.	Jorma Lievonen	FIN	584	
7.	Giovanni Mezzani	ITA	582	
8.	Hans-Jürgen Helbig	GDR	579	

AIR RIFLE

This event will be held for the first time in 1984.

Discontinued Events

MILITARY REVOLVER

1896 Athens C: 16, N: 3, D: 4.10.
(25 Meters)

			PTS.
1.	John Paine	USA	442
2.	Sumner Paine	USA	380
3.	Nikolaos Morakis	GRE	205

The Paine brothers set a precedent for family involvement in the Olympics by taking first and second.

1906 Athens C: 31, N: 9, D: 4.24.
(20 Meters)

			PTS.
1.	Louis Richardet	SWI	253
2.	Alexandros Theophilakis	GRE	250
3.	Georgios Skotadis	GRE	240
4.	Konrad Stäheli	SWI	240
5.	Léon Moreaux	FRA	239
6.	L. Ternajgo	AUT	235
7.	M. Triantaphilades	GRE	235
8.	Anastasios Metaxas	GRE	233

1906 Athens C: 31, N: 9, D: 4.23.
(20 Meters—Model 1873–74)

			PTS.
1.	Jean Fouconnier	FRA	219
2.	Raoul de Boigne	FRA	216
3.	Hermann Martin	FRA	215
4.	Maurice Lecoq	FRA	211
5.	L. Ternajgo	AUT	208
6.	Aristides Rangavis	GRE	201
7.	Louis Richardet	SWI	199
8.	A. Hronis	GRE	198

This contest required the use of a Gras-type revolver first made in France in 1873.

MILITARY REVOLVER TEAMS

1900 Paris T: 4, N: 4, D: 8.1.
(50 Meters)

			TOTAL PTS.
1.	SWI	(Conrad Karl Röderer, Konrad Stäheli, Louis Richardet, Friedrich Lüthi, Paul Probst)	2271
2.	FRA	(Achille Paroche, Louis Duffoy, Léon Moreaux, Trinité, Maurice Lecoq)	2203
3.	HOL	(G. van Haan, Henrik Sillem, Antonius Bouwens, Solko van den Bergh, Anthony Sweus)	1876
4.	BEL	(Rooman, Thèves, Victor Robert, Eichorn, Lebègue)	1823

1904–1906 not held

1908 London T: 7, N: 7, D: 7.11.
(50 Yards)

			TOTAL PTS.
1.	USA	(James Gorman, Ira Calkins, John Dietz, Charles Axtell)	1914
2.	BEL	(Paul van Asbroeck, Réginald Storms, Charles Paumier du Verger, René Englebert)	1863
3.	GBR	(I.A. Wallingford, Geoffrey Coles, Henry Lynch-Staunton, W. Ellicott)	1817
4.	FRA	(A. Barbillat, André Regaud, Léon Moreaux, Jean Depassis)	1750
5.	SWE	(Wilhelm Carlberg, Eric Carlberg, Johan Hübner von Holst, Frans Albert Schartau)	1732
6.	HOL	(J. van der Kop, G.A. van den Bergh, Jan Johannes de Blécourt, Petrus ten Bruggencate)	1632
7.	GRE	(Frangiskos Mavromatis, Alexandros Theophilakis, Ioannis Theophilakis, Georgios Orphanidis)	1576

1912 Stockholm T: 7, N: 7, D: 6.29.
(30 Meters)

			TOTAL PTS.
1.	SWE	(Wilhelm Carlberg, Eric Carlberg, Johan Hübner von Holst, Paul Palén)	1145
2.	RUS	(Amos de Kasch, Nikolai de Melnitsky, Pavel de Voyloshnikov, Georgi de Panteleymonov)	1091/118
3.	GBR	(Hugh Durant, Albert Kempster, Charles Stewart, Horatio Poulter)	1107/117
4.	USA	(Alfred Lane, Reginald Sayre, Walter Winans, John Dietz)	1097/117
5.	GRE	(Konstantinos Skarlatos, Ioannis Theophilakis, Frangiskos Mavromatis, Georgios Petropoulos)	1057
6.	FRA	(Edmond Sandoz, Charles de Jaubert, Marquis de Crequi-Montfort, Maurice Faure)	1041
7.	GER	(Bernhard Wandollek, Gerhard Bock, Georg Meyer, Heinrich Hoffmann)	890

1912 Stockholm T: 5, N: 5, D: 7.2.
(50 Meters)

			TOTAL PTS.
1.	USA	(Alfred Lane, Henry Sears, Peter Dolfen, John Dietz)	1916
2.	SWE	(Georg de Laval, Eric Carlberg, Wilhelm Carlberg, Erik Boström)	1849
3.	GBR	(Horatio Poulter, Hugh Durant, Albert Kempster, Charles Stewart)	1804
4.	RUS	(Nikolai Panin [Kolomenkin], Grigory de Schesterikov, Pavel de Voyloshnikov, Nikolai de Melnitsky)	1801
5.	GRE	(Frangiskos Mavromatls, Ioannis Theophilakis, Konstantinos Skarlatos, Alexandros Theophilakis)	1731

1920 Antwerp T: 8, N: 8, D: 8.3.
(30 Meters)

			TOTAL PTS.
1.	USA	(Louis Harant, Alfred Lane, Carl Frederick, James Snook, Michael Kelly)	1310
2.	GRE	(Alexandros Theophilakis, Ioannis Theophilakis, Georgios Moraitinis, Georgios Vaphiadis, Iason Zappas)	1285
3.	SWI	(Fritz Zulauf, Fritz Kuchen, Willy Schnyder, Caspar Widmer, August Wiederkehr)	1270
4.	BRA	(Afranio Da Costa, Sebastião Wolf, Dario Barbosa, Fernando Soledade, Guilherme Paraense)	1261
5.	FRA	(Pecchia, Maujean, Léon Johnson, Boitout, André Regaud)	1239
6.	SPA	(José Bento, Luis Calvet, Antonio Bonilla, Anotonio Vasquez, José Miro)	1224
7.	BEL		1221
8.	POR		1184

1920 Antwerp T: 12, N: 12, D: 8.2.
(50 Meters)

			TOTAL PTS.
1.	USA	(Carl Frederick, Alfred Lane, James Snook, Michael Kelly, Raymond Bracken)	2372
2.	SWE	(Anders Andersson, Casimir Reuterskiöld, Gunnar Gabrielsson, Sigge Hultcrantz, Anders Johnsson)	2289
3.	BRA	(Afranio da Costa, Guilherme Paraense, Sebastião Wolf, Dario Barbosa, Fernando Soledade)	2264
4.	GRE	(Alexandros Theophilakis, Ioannis Theophilakis, Georgios Moraitinis, Georgios Valphiadis, Iason Zappas)	2240
5.	BEL	(Paul van Asbroeck, Conrad Adriansens, Arthur Balbaert, Joseph Haesaerts, François Heyens)	2229
6.	FRA	(Pecchia, Maujean, Léon Johnson, Boitout, Gandon, André Regaud)	2228
7.	ITA		2224
8.	DEN		2159

DUELING PISTOL

1906 Athens C: 24, N: 7, D: 4.24.
(20 Meters)

			PTS.
1.	Léon Moreaux	FRA	242
2.	Cesare Liverziani	ITA	233
3.	Maurice Lecoq	FRA	231
4.	Konstantinos Skarlatos	GRE	221
5.	L. Ternajgo	AUT	218
6.	Frangiskos Mavromatis	GRE	214

1906 Athens C: 22, N: 7, D: 4.25.
(25 Meters)

			BULL'S-EYE/PTS.
1.	Konstantinos Skarlatos	GRE	29/133
2.	Johann Hubner von Holst	SWE	27/115
3.	Wilhelm Carlberg	SWE	26/115
4.	Gerald Merlin	GBR	26/103
5.	Sándor Török	HUN	25/104
6.	Léon Moreaux	FRA	23/104
7.	Sidney Merlin	GBR	23/103
8.	L. Ternajgo	AUT	23/103

FREE RIFLE

1896 Athens C: 106, N: 6, D: 4.9.
(200 Meters)

			PTS.
1.	Pantelis Karasevdas	GRE	2320
2.	Paulos Pavlidis	GRE	1978
3.	Nicolaos Tricoupes	GRE	1718
4.	Anastasios Metaxas	GRE	1701
5.	Georgios Orphanidis	GRE	1698
6.	Viggo Jensen	DEN	1640

1906 Athens C: 25, N: 5, D: 4.28.
(300 Meters, Any Position)

			PTS.
1.	Marcel Meyer de Stadelhofen	SWI	243
2.	Konrad Stäheli	SWI	238
3.	Léon Moreaux	FRA	234
4.	Gudbrand Skatteboe	NOR	230
5.	Albert Helgerud	NOR	230
6.	Julius Braathe	NOR	224
7.	Raoul de Boigne	FRA	224
8.	Jean Fouconnier	FRA	223

1908 London C: 49, N: 8, D: 7.11.
(1000 Yards)

			PTS.
1.	Joshua "Jerry" Millner	GBR	98
2.	Kellogg Kennon Casey	USA	93
3.	Maurice Blood	GBR	92
4.	R.W. Barnett	GBR	92
5.	Ted Ranken	GBR	92
6.	T. Caldwell	GBR	91
7.	J.C. Sellars	GBR	91
8.	S.H. Kerr	CAN	91

The target for this long-range event was six feet by ten feet, with a 36-inch bull's-eye. Colonel Millner was well over 60 years old.

FREE RIFLE TEAMS

1906 Athens T: 4, N: 5, D: 4.28.
(300 Meters)

			TOTAL PTS.
1.	SWI	(Konrad Stäheli, Jean Reich, Louis Richardet, Marcel Meyer de Stadelhofen, Alfred Grutter)	4596
2.	NOR	(Gudbrand Skatteboe, Albert Helgerud, Julius Braathe, Johann Möller, O. Holm)	4534
3.	FRA	(Jean Fouconnier, Léon Moreaux, Maurice Faure, Raoul de Boigne, Maurice Lecoq)	4511

1908 London T: 9, N: 9, D: 7.11.
(300 Meters)

			TOTAL PTS.
1.	NOR	(Albert Helgerud, Ole Saether, Gudbrand Skatteboe, Olaf Saether, Einar Liberg, Julius Braathe)	5055
2.	SWE	(G. Adolf Jonsson, P. Olof Avidsson, Axel Jansson, Gustav Adolf Sjöberg, Claes Rundberg, Janne Gustafsson)	4711
3.	FRA	(Léon Johnson, Eugène Balme, André Parmentier, Albert Courquin, Maurice Lecoq, Raoul de Boigne)	4652
4.	DEN	(Niels Andersen, Lars Jörgen Madsen, Ole Olsen, Kristian Christensen, Christian Petersen, Hans Kristian Schultz)	4543
5.	BEL	(Charles Paumier du Verger, Paul van Asbroeck, Ernest Ista, Henri Sauveur, Joseph Geens, Edouard Poty)	4509
6.	GBR	(J.A. Wallingford, H.I. Hawkins, C.W. Churcher, T.W. Raddall, J. Bostock, R.H. Brown)	4355
7.	HOL	(G.A. Van den Bergh, C. Brosch, C. Van Altenburg, A.W.J. de Gee, U. Vuurman, P.J. Bruyaard)	4130
8.	FIN	(F. Nassling, G.R. Nyman, H. Huttunen, W.W. Kolko, E. Nassling, H. Tuiskunen)	3962

1912 Stockholm T: 7, N: 7, D: 7.4.
(300 Meters)

			TOTAL PTS.
1.	SWE	(Mauritz Eriksson, C. Hugo Johansson, Erik Blomqvist, Carl Björkman, Bernhard Larsson, G. Adolf Jonsson)	5655
2.	NOR	(Gudbrand Skatteboe, Ole Saether, Östen Östensen, Albert Helgerud, Olaf Saether, Einar Liberg)	5605
3.	DEN	(Ole Olsen, Lars Jörgen Madsen, Niels Larsen, Lauritz Larsen, Niels Andersen, Jens Madsen Haislund)	5529
4.	FRA	(Paul Colas, Louis Percy, Léon Johnson, Pierre Gentil, Raoul de Boigne, Auguste Marion)	5471

5. FIN   (Voitto Kolho, Heikki Huttunen, Gustaf Richard   5323
          Nyman, Emil Holm, Huvi Tuiskunen, Vilho Vauh-
          konen)

6. SAF   (George Harvey, Robert Bodley, R. Patterson,   4897
          A.A. Smith, E.J. Keeley, G. Whelan)

7. RUS   (P. de Waldaine, Th. de Lebedeff, A. de Tillo, C.   4892
          de Kalinine, D. de Kouskoff, P. de Lesche)

1920 Antwerp T: 14, N: 14, D: 7.31.
(300 Meters)

			TOTAL PTS.
1.	USA	(Morris Fisher, Carl Osburn, Dennis Fenton, Lloyd Spooner, Willis Lee)	4876
2.	NOR	(Östen Östensen, Otto Olsen, Olaf Sletten, Harald Natvig, Ludvig Larsen)	4741
3.	SWI	(Fritz Kuchen, Albert Tröndle, Arnold Rösli, Caspar Widmer, Jakob Reich)	4698
4.	FIN	(Voitto Kolho, Kalle Lappalainen, Veli Nieminen, Magnus Wegelius, Vilho Vauhkonen)	4668
5.	DEN	(Niels Larsen, P. Geltzer, N. Laursen, Niels Andersen, Lars Jörgen Madsen)	4645
6.	SWE	(Mauritz Eriksson, C. Hugo Johansson, Erik Blomqvist, Viktor Knutsson, Leon Lagerlöf)	4591
7.	FRA		4485
8.	HOL		4381

1924 Paris T: 18, N: 18, D: 6.27.
(400 + 600 + 800 Meters)

			TOTAL PTS.
1.	USA	(Morris Fisher, Walter Stokes, Joseph Crockett, Chan Coulter, Sidney Hinds)	676
2.	FRA	(Emile Rumeau, Albert Courquin, Pierre Hardy, Georges Roes, Paul Colas)	646
3.	HAI	(Ludovic Augustin, Astrel Rolland, Ludovic Valborge, Destin Destine, Eloi Metullus)	646

4. SWI   (Jakob Reich, Arnold Rösli, Willy Schnyder, C.   635
          Stucheli, Albert Tröndle)

5. FIN   (A.J. Valkama, Vilho Nieminen, Voitto Kolho,   628
          Heikki Huttunen, Johannes Theslöf)

6. DEN   (Niels Larsen, Lars Jörgen Madsen, Anders   626
          Nielsen, Erik Saetter-Lassen, P. Geltzer)

7. SWE   (C. Hugo Johansson, Ivar Wester, Mauritz Eriksson, Olle Ericsson, Gustaf Anderson)   623

8. NOR   (I. Larsen, O. Johansson, W. Rogeberg, H. Angaard, Otto Olsen)   594

France defeated Haiti in the shoot-off for second place. Lieutenant Sidney Hinds shot a perfect 50 for the U.S. team, a performance that was all the more remarkable considering that he was accidentally shot in the foot in the middle of the competition, when the Belgian rifleman beside him knocked his rifle to the ground in the midst of an argument with an official.

FREE RIFLE, THREE POSITIONS

This event required 120 shots from 300 meters at a 39-inch target with a bull's-eye less than four inches in diameter. In other words, it was like shooting a bullet through an apple three football fields away.

1896 Athens C: 16, N: 2, D: 4.11.

		TOTAL PTS.
1. Georgios Orphanidis	GRE	1583
2. Ioannis Phrangoudis	GRE	1312
3. Viggo Jensen	DEN	1305
4. Anastasios Metaxas	GRE	1102

1900–1904 not held

1906 Athens C: 20, N: 4, D: 4.28. WR: 1004 (Charles Paumier de Verger)

		PRONE	KNEELING	STANDING	TOTAL PTS.
1. Gudbrand Skatteboe	NOR	339	310	324	973
2. Konrad Stäheli	SWI	328	340	278	946
3. Jean Reich	SWI	327	320	289	936
4. Louis Richardet	SWI	332	338	265	935
5. Léon Moreaux	FRA	322	317	293	932
6. Marcel Meyer de Stadelhofen	SWI	306	324	296	926
7. Julius Braathe	NOR	319	292	310	921
8. Maurice Lecoq	FRA	309	305	300	914

1908 London C: 51, N: 10, D: 7.11. WR: 1004 (Charles Paumier de Verger)

		PRONE	KNEELING	STANDING	TOTAL PTS.
1. Albert Helgerud	NOR	340	292	277	909
2. Harry Simon	USA	365	294	228	887
3. Ole Saether	NOR	327	284	272	883
4. Gustav Adolf Sjöberg	SWE	338	285	251	874
5. Janne Gustafsson	SWE	324	283	265	872
6. Julius Braathe	NOR	303	291	257	851
7. Axel Jansson	SWE	312	296	235	843
8. Léon Johnson	FRA	303	282	250	835

1912 Stockholm C: 84, N: 9, D: 7.2. WR: 1078 (Konrad Stäheli)

		PRONE	KNEELING	STANDING	TOTAL PTS.
1. Paul Colas	FRA	362	342	283	987
2. Lars Jörgen Madsen	DEN	330	333	318	981
3. Niels Larsen	DEN	355	334	318	962
4. C. Hugo Johansson	SWE	341	326	292	959
5. Gudbrand Skatteboe	NOR	343	308	305	956
6. Bernhard Larsson	SWE	341	339	274	954
7. Albert Helgerud	NOR	354	317	281	952
8. Tonnes Björkman	SWE	340	322	285	947

1920 Antwerp C: 70, N:14, D: 7.31. WR: 1078 (Konrad Stäheli)

		TOTAL PTS.
1. Morris Fisher	USA	997
2. Niels Larsen	DEN	985
3. Östen Östensen	NOR	980
4. Carl Osburn	USA	980
5. Gudbrand Skatteboe	NOR	975
6. Mauritz Eriksson	SWE	974

Sergeant Morris Fisher, who played the violin for relaxation, found himself too nervous to take the first shot in the standing position. After 20 minutes of standing at the firing line, aiming but not taking a shot, his coach ordered him to shoot even if he missed the target. Fisher shot wide but within the scoring rings, and then went on to win the match.

1924 Paris C: 73, N: 19, D: 6.27.
(600 Meters)

		TOTAL PTS.
1. Morris Fisher	USA	95
2. Carl Osburn	USA	95
3. Niels Larsen	DEN	93
4. Walter Stokes	USA	92
5. Ludovic Augustin	HAI	91
6. Albert Courquin	FRA	90
6. Ludovic Valborge	HAI	90
8. C. Hugo Johansson	SWE	88

Fisher earned two gold medals in 1924 to go with the three he had won in 1920.

1928–1936 not held

1948 London C: 46, N: 13, D: 8.6. WR: 1124 (E. Kivistik)

		PRONE	KNEELING	STANDING	TOTAL PTS.
1. Emil Grünig	SWI	390	375	355	1120
2. Pauli Janhonen	FIN	387	376	351	1114
3. Willy Rögeberg	NOR	382	373	357	1112
4. Kurt Johansson	SWE	383	374	347	1104
5. Kullervo Leskinen	FIN	389	368	346	1103
6. Olavi Elo	FIN	379	359	357	1095
7. H. Kongsjorden	NOR	384	373	336	1093
8. Holger Erbén	SWE	380	367	344	1091

1952 Helsinki C: 32, N: 18, D: 7.27. WR: 1124 (E. Kivistik)

		PRONE	KNEELING		STANDING	TOTAL PTS.	
1. Anatoly Bogdanov	SOV	388	376		359	1123	OR
2. Robert Bürchler	SWI	389	381	WR	350	1120	
3. Lev Vainshtein	SOV	378	376		355	1109	
4. August Hollenstein	SWI	384	370		354	1108	
5. Vilho Ylönen	FIN	379	377		351	1107	
6. Robert Sandager	USA	384	371		349	1104	
7. Holger Erbén	SWE	347	376		379	1102	
8. Walther Fröstell	SWE	335	375		389	1099	

1956 Melbourne C: 20, N: 14, D: 12.1. WR: 1143 (Anatoly Bogdanov)

		PRONE		KNEELING	STANDING	TOTAL PTS.	
1. Vassily Borissov	SOV	396	WR	383	359	1138	OR
2. Allan Erdman	SOV	392		385	360	1137	
3. Vilho Ylönen	FIN	387		382	359	1128	
4. Jorma Taitto	FIN	392		379	349	1120	
5. Constantin Antonescu	ROM	386		374	341	1101	
6. Nils Johan Sundberg	SWE	384		367	343	1094	
7. Anders Kvissberg	SWE	389		362	342	1093	
8. James Smith	USA	381		368	333	1082	

1960 Rome C: 39, N: 22, D: 9.5. WR: 1145 (Anatoly Bogdanov)

		PRONE	KNEELING	STANDING	TOTAL PTS.
1. Hubert Hammerer	AUT	390	379	360	1129
2. Hans Spillman	SWI	397	377	353	1127
3. Vassily Borissov	SOV	383	381	363	1127
4. Vilho Ylönen	FIN	389	381	356	1126
5. Moissey Itkis	SOV	380	379	365	1124
6. Vladimir Stiborik	CZE	383	380	360	1123
7. John Foster	USA	380	384	357	1121
8. Sandor Krebs	HUN	386	373	359	1118

1964 Tokyo C: 30, N: 18, D: 10.15. WR: 1150 (August Hollenstein)

		PRONE	KNEELING	STANDING	TOTAL PTS.	
1. Gary Anderson	USA	392	384	377	1153	WR
2. Shota Kveliashvili	SOV	389	389	366	1144	
3. Martin Gunnarsson	USA	389	380	367	1136	
4. Aleksandr Gerasimenok	SOV	396	376	363	1135	
5. August Hollenstein	SWI	382	381	372	1135	
6. Esa Kervinen	FIN	392	383	358	1133	
7. Kurt Müller	SWI	392	385	354	1121	
8. Harry Köcher	GDR	392	378	360	1130	

Gary Anderson was a theological student from Axtell, Nebraska.

1968 Mexico City C: 30, N: 16, D: 10.23. WR: 1156 (Gary Anderson)

		PRONE		KNEELING	STANDING	TOTAL PTS.	
1. Gary Anderson	USA	394		389	374	1157	WR
2. Vladimir Kornev	SOV	398	WR	384	369	1151	
3. Kurt Müller	SWI	395		379	374	1148	
4. Shota Kveliashvili	SOV	394		383	365	1142	
5. Erwin Vogt	SWI	398	WR	384	358	1140	
6. Hartmut Sommer	GER	389		384	358	1140	
7. John Foster	USA	386		386	368	1140	
8. Péter Sándor	HUN	394		376	368	1138	

Anderson, by now a 29-year-old army lieutenant and Presbyterian minister, told reporters that he intended to keep up his involvement in shooting "because I think it's important for a minister to be actively involved in what people are doing."

1972 Munich C: 33, N: 20, D: 9.2. WR: 1157 (Gary Anderson)

		PRONE	KNEELING	STANDING		TOTAL PTS.
1. Lones Wigger	USA	394	382	379	WR	1155
2. Boris Melnik	SOV	394	387	374		1155
3. Lajos Papp	HUN	394	391	364		1149
4. Uto Wunderlich	GDR	393	388	368		1149
5. Karel Bulan	CZE	394	382	370		1146
6. Jaakko Minkkinen	FIN	396	386	364		1146
7. Lanny Bassham	USA	389	387	368		1144
8. Valentin Kormev	SOV	391	387	365		1143

INDIVIDUAL MILITARY RIFLE

1900 Paris C: 30, N: 6, D: 8.5.
(300 Meters, Three Positions)

		PRONE	KNEELING	STANDING	TOTAL PTS.
1. Emil Kellenberger	SWI	324	314	292	930
2. Anders Peter Nielsen	DEN	330	314	277	921
3. Paul van Asbroeck	BEL	329	289	299	917
3. Ole Östmo	NOR	312	308	297	917
5. Lars Jörgen Madsen	DEN	301	299	305	905
6. Charles Paumier du Verger	BEL	302	297	298	897
7. Achille Paroche	FRA	332	287	268	887
8. Franz Böckli	SWI	289	300	294	883

(300 Meters, Standing)

		TOTAL PTS.
1. Lars Jörgen Madsen	DEN	305
2. Ole Östmo	NOR	299
3. Charles Paumier du Verger	BEL	298
4. Paul van Asbroeck	BEL	297
5. Franz Böckli	SWI	294
6. Emil Kellenberger	SWI	292
7. Jules Bury	BEL	282
7. Alfred Grütter	SWI	282

(300 Meters, Kneeling)

		TOTAL PTS.
1. Konrad Stäheli	SWI	324
2. Emil Kellenberger	SWI	314
2. Anders Peter Nielsen	DEN	314
4. Paul van Asbroeck	BEL	308
5. Maximilaan Ravenswaaij	HOL	306
6. Uilke Vuurman	HOL	303
7. Franz Böckli	SWI	300
8. Lars Jörgen Madsen	DEN	299

(300 Meters, Prone)

		TOTAL PTS.
1. Achille Paroche	FRA	332
2. Anders Peter Nielsen	DEN	330
3. Ole Östmo	NOR	329
4. Léon Moreaux	FRA	325
5. Emil Kellenberger	SWI	324
6. Henrik Sillem	HOL	317
7. Auguste Cavadini	FRA	316
8. Paul van Asbroeck	BEL	312
8. Uilke Vuurman	HOL	312

1904 not held

1906 Athens C: 31, N: 8, D: 4.24.
(200 Meters, Standing or Kneeling)

		PTS.
1. Léon Moreaux	FRA	187
2. Louis Richardet	SWI	187
3. Jean Reich	SWI	183
4. Johann Möller	NOR	175
5. Maurice Faure	FRA	173
6. Gerald Merlin	GBR	169
7. Sidney Merlin	GBR	166
8. Georgios Orphanidis	GRE	165

1906 Athens C: 46, N: 11, D: 4.23.
(300 Meters, Standing or Kneeling)

		PTS.
1. Louis Richardet	SWI	238
2. Jean Reich	SWI	234
3. Raoul de Boigne	FRA	232
4. Léon Moreaux	FRA	231
5. Maurice Lecoq	FRA	224
6. Julius Braathe	NOR	223
7. Marcel Meyer de Stadelhofen	SWI	222
8. Gudbrand Skatteboe	NOR	221

1908 not held

1912 Stockholm C: 91, N: 12, D: 7.1.
(300 Meters)

		PTS.
1. Sándor Prokopp	HUN	97
2. Carl Osburn	USA	95
3. Embret Skogen	NOR	95
4. Nicolaos Levidis	GRE	95
5. Nils Romander	SWE	94
6. Arthur Fulton	GBR	92
7. Rezsö Velez	HUN	92
8. Carl Flodström	SWE	91

1912 Stockholm C: 85, N: 12, D: 7.1.
(600 Meters, Any Position)

		PTS.
1. Paul Colas	FRA	94
2. Carl Osburn	USA	94
3. Joseph Jackson	USA	93
4. Allan Briggs	USA	93
5. Philip Plater	GBR	90
6. Verner Jernström	SWE	88
7. Harcourt Ommundsen	GBR	88
8. Charles Burdette	USA	87

1920 Antwerp T: 49, N: 12, D: 7.29.
(300 Meters, Prone)

		PTS.
1. Otto Olsen	NOR	60
2. Léon Johnson	FRA	59
3. Fritz Kuchen	SWI	59
4. Vilho Vauhkonen	FIN	59
5. Achille Paroche	FRA	59

1920 Antwerp C: 48, N: 12, D: 7.9.
(300 Meters, Standing)

		PTS.
1. Carl Osburn	USA	56
2. Lars Jörgen Madsen	DEN	55
3. Lawrence Nuesslein	USA	54
4. Erik Saetter-Lassen	DEN	54
5. Joseph Janssens	BEL	54
6. Ricardo Ticchi	ITA	54

1920 Antwerp C: 46, N: 11, D: 7.29.
(600 Meters, Prone)

		PTS.
1. C. Hugo Johansson	SWE	58
2. Mauritz Eriksson	SWE	56/6
3. Lloyd Spooner	USA	56/5
4. Ioannis Theophilakis	GRE	—
5. Olaf Sletten	NOR	—

MILITARY RIFLE TEAMS
1896 not held

1900 Paris T: 6, N: 6, D: 8.5.
(300 Meters)

			TOTAL PTS.
1.	SWI	(Emil Kellenberger, Franz Böckli, Konrad Stäheli, Louis Richardet, Alfred Grütter)	4399
2.	NOR	(Ole Östmo, Hellmer Hermandsen, Tom Seeberg, Ole Saether, Olaf Frydenlund)	4290
3.	FRA	(Achille Paroche, Léon Moreaux, Auguste Cavadini, Maurice Lecoq, René Thomas)	4278
4.	DEN	(Anders Peter Nielsen, Lars Jörgen Madsen, Viggo Jensen, Laurids Worslund Jensen-Kjaer, Axel Kristensen)	4265
5.	HOL	(Maximiliaan Ravenswaaij, Uilke Vuurman, Henrik Sillem, Antonius Bouwens, Solko van den Bergh)	4221
6.	BEL	(Paul van Asbroeck, Charles Paumier du Verger, Jules Bury, Edouard Myin, Joseph Baras)	4166

1904–1906 not held

1908 London T: 8, N: 8, D: 7.11.
(200 + 500 + 600+ 800 + 900 + 1000 Yards)

			TOTAL PTS.
1.	USA	(William Leushner, William Martin, C.B. Winder, Kellogg Kennon Casey, Albert Eastman, Charles Benedict)	2531
2.	GBR	(Harcourt Ommundsen, Fleetwood E. Varley, Arthur Fulton, Philip Richardson, W.G. Padgett, J.E. Martin)	2497
3.	CAN	(William Smith, Charles Crowe, B.M. Williams, D. McInnis, William Eastcott, S.H. Kerr)	2439
4.	FRA	(Raoul de Boigne, Albert Courquin, Eugène Balme, Daniel Merillon, Léon Hecht, André Parmentier)	2227
5.	SWE	(Claes Rundberg, O. Jörgensen, Janne Gustafsson, P. Olof Arvidsson, Axel Jansson, G. Adolf Jonsson)	2213
6.	NOR	(Ole Saether, Einar Liberg, Gudbrand Skatteboe, Albert Helgerud, M. Glomnes, Jörgen Bruu)	2192
7.	GRE	(Ioannis Theophilakis, Frangiskos Mavromatis, Alexandros Theophilakis, Georgios Orphanidis, M. Triantaphilades, D. Rediadis)	1999
8.	DEN	(Niels Andersen, Kristian Christensen, L.P.M. Jensen, N. Laursen, H. Jensen, Ole Olsen)	1909

The Russians had sent word that they were going to enter a team, but when they finally arrived the competition was long over. It turned out that Russia was still operating on the Julian calendar, whereas the rest of the world was using the Gregorian calendar; the two calendars were 12 days apart.

1912 Stockholm T: 10, N: 10, D: 6.29.
(200 + 400 + 500 + 600 Meters)

			TOTAL PTS.
1.	USA	(Charles Burdette, Allan Briggs, Harry Adams, Joseph Jackson, Carl Osburn, Warren Sprout)	1687
2.	GBR	(Harcourt Ommundsen, Henry Burr, Edward Skilton, James Reid, Edward Parnell, Arthur Fulton)	1602
3.	SWE	(Mauritz Eriksson, Verner Jernström, Carl Björkman, Tönnes Björkman, Bernhard Larsson, C. Hugo Johansson)	1570
4.	SAF	(George Harvey, Robert Bodley, A.A. Smith, E.J. Keeley, C.A. Jeffreys, R. Patterson)	1531
5.	FRA	(Louis Percy, Paul Colas, Raoul de Boigne, Pierre Gentil, Léon Johnson, Maxime Lardin)	1515
6.	NOR	(O. Christian Degnes, Arne Sunde, O.A. Jensen, Hans Nordvik, Olav Husby, M. Glomnes)	1473
7.	GRE	(Frangiskos Mavromatis, Alexandros Theophilakis, S. Theophilakis, Nicolaos Levidis, Iakovos Theophilas, S.D. Mostras)	1445
8.	DEN	(Niels Andersen, Lars Jörgen Madsen, R. Friis, H.K. Schultz, Niels Larsen, J.M. Haislund)	1419

1920 Antwerp T: 15, N: 15, D: 7.29.
(300 Meters, Standing)

			TOTAL PTS.
1.	DEN	(Lars Jörgen Madsen, Niels Larsen, Anders Petersen, Erik Saetter-Lassen, Anders Nielsen)	266
2.	USA	(Carl Osburn, Lawrence Nuesslein, Lloyd Spooner, Willis Lee, Thomas Brown)	255
3.	SWE	(Olle Ericsson, C. Hugo Johansson, Leon Lagerlöf, Walfried Hellman, Mauritz Eriksson)	255
4.	ITA	(Riccardo Ticchi, Camillo Isnardi, Luigi Favretti, Giancarlo Boriani, Sem De Ranieri)	251
5.	FRA	(Léon Johnson, Achille Paroche, Emile Rumeau, André Parmentier, Georges Roes)	249
6.	NOR	(Östen Östensen, Otto Olsen, Olaf Sletten, Albert Helgerud, Gudbrand Skatteboe)	242
7.	FIN		235
8.	SWI		234

1920 Antwerp T: 15, N: 15, D: 7.29.
(300 Meters, Prone)

			TOTAL PTS.
1.	USA	(Carl Osburn, Joseph Jackson, Lloyd Spooner, Morris Fisher, Willis Lee)	289
2.	FRA	(Léon Johnson, Achille Paroche, Emile Rumeau, André Parmentier, Georges Roes)	283
3.	FIN	(Voitto Kolho, Kalle Lappalainen, Veli Nieminen, Magnus Wegelius, Vilho Vauhkonen)	281
4.	SWI	(Fritz Kuchen, Albert Tröndle, Arnold Rösli, Walter Lienhard, Caspar Widmer)	281
5.	SWE	(Mauritz Eriksson, Erik Blomqvist, C. Hugo Johansson, Thure Holmberg, Verner Jernström)	281

6. NOR (Östen Östensen, Otto Olsen, Olaf Sletten, Albert   280
         Helgerud, Jacob Onsrud)
7. SPA   278
8. SAF   276

1920 Antwerp T: 70, N: 14, D: 7.29.
(600 Meters, Prone)

			TOTAL PTS.
1.	USA	(Dennis Fenton, Ollie Schriver, Willis Lee, Lloyd Spooner, Joseph Jackson)	287/283/284
2.	SAF	(David Smith, Robert Bodley, Ferdinand Buchanan, George Harvey, Frederick Morgan)	287/283/279
3.	SWE	(C. Hugo Johansson, Mauritz Eriksson, Erik Blomqvist, Erik Ohlsson, G. Adolf Jonsson)	287/275
4.	NOR	(Otto Olsen, Östen Östensen, Albert Helgerud, Olaf Sletten, Jacob Onsrud)	282
5.	FRA	(Léon Johnson, Achille Paroche, Emile Rumeau, André Parmentier)	280
6.	SWI	(Fritz Kuchen, Albert Tröndle, Arnold Rösli, Walter Lienhard, Caspar Widmer)	279
7.	GRE		270
8.	FIN		268

1920 Antwerp T: 70, N: 14, D: 7.29.
(300 + 600 Meters, Prone)

			TOTAL PTS.
1.	USA	(Joseph Jackson, Willis Lee, Ollie Schriver, Carl Osburn, Lloyd Spooner)	573
2.	NOR	(Otto Olsen, Albert Helgerud, Olaf Sletten, Östen Östensen, Jacob Onsrud)	565
3.	SWI	(Fritz Kuchen, Albert Tröndle, Arnold Rösli, Walter Lienhard, Caspar Widmer)	563
4.	FRA	(Léon Johnson, Achille Paroche, Emile Rumeau, André Parmentier, Georges Roes)	563
5.	SAF	(David Smith, Robert Bodley, Ferdinand Buchanan, George Harvey, Frederick Morgan)	560
6.	SWE	(Erik Blomqvist, C. Hugo Johansson, G. Adolf Jonsson, Mauritz Eriksson, B. Andreasson)	553
7.	GRE		553
8.	CZE		536

SMALL-BORE RIFLE

1896–1906 not held

1908 London C: 22, N: 5, D: 7.11.
(25 Yards, Moving Target)

			PTS.
1.	J.F. Fleming	GBR	24
2.	M.K. Matthews	GBR	24
3.	W.B. Marsden	GBR	24
4.	E.J.D. Newitt	GBR	24
5.	Philip Plater	GBR	22

6.	William Pimm	GBR	21
7.	William Milne	GBR	21
8.	Otto von Rosen	SWE	18

(25 Yards, Disappearing Target)

			PTS.
1.	William Styles	GBR	45
2.	H.I. Hawkins	GBR	45
3.	E.J. Amoore	GBR	45
4.	William Milne	GBR	45
5.	J.L. Milne	GBR	45
6	A.W. Wilde	GBR	45
7.	Wilhelm Carlberg	SWE	45
8.	Harry Humby	GBR	45

1912 Stockholm C: 36, N: 8, D: 7.5.
(25 Meters, Disappearing Target)

			PTS.
1.	Wilhelm Carlberg	SWE	242
2.	Johan Hübner von Holst	SWE	233
3.	Gustaf Ericsson	SWE	231
4.	Joseph Pepé	GBR	231
5.	Robert Cook Murray	GBR	228
6.	Axel Gyllenkrok	SWE	227
7.	William Pimm	GBR	225
8.	Frederick Hird	USA	221

MINIATURE RIFLE TEAMS

1896–1906 not held

1908 London T: 3, N: 3, D: 7.11.
(50 + 100 Yards)

			TOTAL PTS.
1.	GBR	(M.K. Matthews, Harry Humby, William Pimm, Edward Amoore)	771
2.	SWE	(Wilhelm Carlberg, Eric Carlberg, Johan Hübner von Holst, Frans Albert Schartau)	737
3.	FRA	(Paul Colas, André Regaud, Léon Lecuyer, Henri Bonnéfoy)	710

1912 Stockholm T: 4, N: 4, D: 7.5.
(25 Meters)

			TOTAL PTS.
1.	SWE	(Johan Hübner von Holst, Eric Carlberg, Wilhelm Carlberg, Gustaf Boivie)	925
2.	GBR	(William Pimm, Joseph Pepé, William Milne, William Styles)	917
3.	USA	(Frederick Hird, Warren Sprout, Neil McDonnell, William Leushner)	881
4.	GRE	(Ioannis Theophilakis, Frangiskos Mavromatis, Nicolaos Levidis, Iakovos Theophilas)	716

1912 Stockholm T: 6, N: 6, D: 7.3.
(50 Meters)

			TOTAL PTS.
1. GBR	(William Pimm, Edward Lessimore, Joseph Pepé, Robert Cook Murray)		762
2. SWE	(Arthur Nordenswan, Eric Carlberg, Ruben Örtegren, Wilhelm Carlberg)		748
3. USA	(Warren Sprout, William Leushner, Frederick Hird, Carl Osburn)		744
4. FRA	(Léon Johnson, Pierre Gentil, André Regaud, Maxime Lardin)		714
5. DEN	(Paul Gerlow, Lars Jörgen Madsen, Frants Nielsen, Hans Petter Denver)		708
5. GRE	(Ioannis Theophilakis, Iakovos Theophilas, Frangiskos Mavromatis, Nicolaos Levidis)		708

1920 Antwerp T: 10, N: 10, D: 8.2.
(50 Meters)

			TOTAL PTS.
1. USA	(Lawrence Nuesslein, Arthur Rothrock, Dennis Fenton, Willis Lee, Ollie Schriver)		1899
2. SWE	(Sigge Hultcrantz, Erik Ohlsson, Leon Lagerlöf, Ragnar Stare, Olle Ericsson)		1873
3. NOR	(Anton Olsen, Albert Helgerud, Sigvart Johansen, Olaf Sletten, Östen Östensen)		1865
4. DEN	(Lars Jörgen Madsen, Erik Saetter-Lassen, Anders Nielsen, O. Wegener, C. Möller)		1862
5. FRA	(Léon Johnson, Achille Paroche, Émile Rumeau, André Parmentier, Georges Roes)		1847
6. BEL	(Paul van Asbroeck, Norbert van Molle, Phillippe Cammaerts, Victor Robert, Louis Andrieu)		1785
7. ITA			1777
8. SAF			1755

RUNNING DEER SHOOTING, SINGLE SHOT

1896–1906 not held

1908 London C: 15, N: 4, D: 7.11.

			PTS.
1. Oscar Swahn		SWE	25
2. Ted Ranken		GBR	24
3. Alexander Rogers		GBR	24
4. Maurice Blood		GBR	23
5. Albert Joseph Kempster		GBR	22
6. W.R. Lane-Joynt		GBR	21
7. Walter Winans		USA	21
8. J.H. Cowan		GBR	21

In 1908, Oscar Swahn was already 60 years old when he won his *first* Olympic gold medal, taking a total of two gold and one bronze. In 1912 he won one gold and one bronze, and in Antwerp, in 1920, at the age of 72, he won his first silver medal as part of the Swedish double-shot running deer team. He died in 1927.

1912 Stockholm C: 34, N: 7, D: 7.1.

			PTS.
1. Alfred Swahn		SWE	41/20
2. Åke Lundeberg		SWE	41/17
3. Nestori Toivonen		FIN	41/11
4. Karl Larsson		SWE	39
5. Oscar Swahn		SWE	39
6. Sven Arvid Lindskog		SWE	39
7. Heinrich Elbogen		AUT	38
8. A.F. Ture Cederström		SWE	37

Although Oscar Swahn was able to finish only fifth in Stockholm, his 32-year-old son Alfred earned the gold medal after a three-way shoot-off. Alfred's Olympic career was even more successful than his father's. Between 1908 and 1924 he won nine medals—three gold, three silver, and three bronze.

1920 Antwerp C: 22, N: 4, D: 7.27.

		PTS.
1. Otto Olsen	NOR	43
2. Alfred Swahn	SWE	41
3. Harald Natvig	NOR	41

1924 Paris C: 32, N: 8, D: 7.3.

		PTS.
1. John Boles	USA	40
2. Cyril Mackworth-Praed	GBR	39
3. Otto Olsen	NOR	39
4. Otto Hultberg	SWE	39
5. Martti Liuttula	FIN	37
6. Alfred Swahn	SWE	37
7. Einar Liberg	NOR	36
8. Harold Natvig	NOR	36

TEAM RUNNING DEER SHOOTING, SINGLE-SHOT

1896–1906 not held

1908 London T: 2, N: 2, D: 7.11.

			TOTAL PTS.
1. SWE	(Alfred Swahn, Arvid Knöppel, Oscar Swahn, Ernst Rosell)		86
2. GBR	(C.J.A. Nix, W.R. Lane-Joynt, W. Ellicott, Ted Ranken)		85

1912 Stockholm T: 5, N: 5, D: 7.4.

			TOTAL PTS.
1. SWE	(Alfred Swahn, Oscar Swahn, Åke Lundeberg, P. Olof Arvidsson)		151
2. USA	(W. Neil McDonnell, Walter Winans, William Leushner, William Libbey)		132
3. FIN	(Axel Fredrik Londen, Nestori Toivonen, Toivo Väänänen, Ernst Rosenqvist)		123

4. AUT (Adolf Michel, Eberhard Steinböck, Peter Pater- 115
nelli, Heinrich Elbogen)

5. RUS (Harry Blau, Basil de Skrotsky, Dmitri de Barkov, 108
Aleksandr de Dobryansky)

1920 Antwerp T: 4, N: 4, D: 7.26.	TOTAL PTS.
1. NOR (Harald Natvig, Otto Olsen, Ole Adreas Lilloe-Ol-sen, Einar Liberg, Hans Nordvik)	178
2. FIN (Robert Tikkanen, Nestori Toivonen, Magnus Wegelius, K. Kalle Lappalainen, Yrjö Kolho)	159
3. USA (Thomas Brown, Lawrence Nuesslein, Lloyd Spooner, Carl Osburn, Willis Lee)	158
4. SWE (Per Kinde, Karl Larsson, Bengt Lagercrantz, Al-fred Swahn, Oscar Swahn)	153

1924 Paris T: 6, N: 6, D: 7.3.	TOTAL PTS.
1. NOR (Ole Andreas Lilloe-Olsen, Einar Liberg, Harald Natvig, Otto Olsen)	160
2. SWE (Alfred Swahn, Fredrik Landelius, Otto Hultberg, G. Mauritz Johansson)	154
3. USA (John Boles, Walter Stokes, Chan Coulter, Den-nis Fenton)	148
4. GBR (Cyril Mackworth-Praed, A.E. Rogers, J.C. Faunthorpe, J.J. O'Leary)	136
5. FIN (Magnus Wegelius, Martti Liuttula, Jalo Urho Au-tonen, Robert Tikkanen)	130
6. HUN (Gusztáv Szomjas, Rezsö Velez, Elemér Ta-kács, László Szomjas)	97

RUNNING DEER SHOOTING, DOUBLE-SHOT

1896–1906 not held

1908 London C: 15, T: 4, D: 7.11.		PTS.
1. Walter Winans	USA	46/44
2. Ted Ranken	GBR	46/41
3. Oscar Swahn	SWE	38
4. Maurice Blood	GBR	34
5. Albert Kempster	GBR	34
6. W. Ellicott	GBR	33
7. Alexander Rogers	GBR	33
8. Ernst Rosell	SWE	33

1912 Stockholm C: 20, N: 6, D: 7.3.		PTS.
1. Åke Lundeberg	SWE	79
2. Edvard Benedicks	SWE	74
3. Oscar Swahn	SWE	72

4. Alfred Swahn	SWE	68
5. P. Olof Arvidsson	SWE	68
6. Sven Arvid Lindskog	SWE	67
7. Erik Sökjer-Petersén	SWE	65
8. E.W. Lindewald	SWE	64

1920 Antwerp C: 23, N: 4, D: 7.27.		PTS.
1. Ole Andreas Lilloe-Olsen	NOR	82
2. Fredric Landelius	SWE	77
3. Einar Liberg	NOR	71

1924 Paris C: 31, N: 8, D: 7.3.		PTS.
1. Ole Andreas Lilloe-Olsen	NOR	76
2. Cyril Mackworth-Praed	GBR	72
3. Alfred Swahn	SWE	72
4. Fredric Landelius	SWE	70
5. Einar Liberg	NOR	70
6. Robert Tikkanen	FIN	69
7. John Boles	USA	64
8. Magnus Wegelius	FIN	64

TEAM RUNNING DEER SHOOTING, DOUBLE-SHOT

1896–1912 not held

1920 Antwerp T: 4, N: 4, D: 7.26.	TOTAL PTS.
1. NOR (Ole Andreas Lilloe-Olsen, Thorstein Johansen, Harald Natvig, Hans Nordvik, Einar Liberg)	343
2. SWE (Alfred Swahn, Oscar Swahn, Fredric Landelius, Bengt Lagercrantz, Edvard Benedicks)	336
3. FIN (Robert Tikkanen, Nestori Toivonen, Magnus Wegelius, Vilho Vauhkonen, Yrjö Kolho)	284
4. USA (Thomas Brown, Willis Lee, Lawrence Nuess-lein, Carl Osburn, Lloyd Spooner)	282

1924 Paris T: 6, N: 6, D: 7.3.	TOTAL PTS.
1. GBR (Cyril Mackworth-Praed, Allen Whitty, Herbert Perry, Philip Neame)	263
2. NOR (Ole Andreas Lilloe-Olsen, Otto Olsen, Harald Natvig, Einar Liberg)	262
3. SWE (Alfred Swahn, G. Mauritz Johansson, Fredric Landelius, Axel Ekblom)	250
4. FIN (Magnus Wegelius, Jalo Urho Autonen, Martti Liuttula, Robert Tikkanen)	239
5. USA (Chan Coulter, Walter Stokes, John Boles, Den-nis Fenton)	233
6. CZE (Miloslav Hlavác, Josef Sucharda, Rudolf Jelen, Josef Hosa)	204

RUNNING DEER SHOOTING, SINGLE- AND DOUBLE-SHOT

1896–1948 not held

1952 Helsinki T: 14, N: 7, D: 7.29. WR: 398 (Rolf Bergersen)

			PTS.	
1.	John Larsen	NOR	413	WR
2.	Per Olof Sköldberg	SWE	409	
3.	Tauno Mäki	FIN	407	
4.	Rolf Bergersen	NOR	399	
5.	B. Thorleif Kockgård	SWE	397	
6.	Yrjö Miettinen	FIN	392	
7.	Petr Nikolayev	SOV	385	
8.	Vladimir Sevryugin	SOV	383	

1956 Melbourne T: 11, N: 6, D: 12.4.

			PTS.	
1.	Vitaly Romanenko	SOV	441	OR
2.	Per Olof Sköldberg	SWE	432	
3.	Vladimir Sevryugin	SOV	429	
4.	Miklós Kovács	HUN	417	
5.	Miklós Kocsis	HUN	416	
6.	Rolf Bergersen	NOR	409	
7.	Benkt Austrin	SWE	405	
8.	John Larsen	NOR	390	

TRAP (CLAY PIGEON) SHOOTING TEAMS

1896–1906 not held

1908 London T: 4, N: 3, D: 7.11.

			TOTAL PTS.
1.	GBR	(Alexander Maunder, J.F. Pike, Charles Palmer, J.M. Postans, F.W. Moore, P. Easte)	407
2.	CAN	(Walter Ewing, George Beattie, A.W. Westover, Mylie Fletcher, George Vivian, D. McMackon)	405
3.	GBR	(George Whitaker, G.H. Skinner, John Butt, W.B. Morris, H.P. Creasey, R. Hutton)	372
4.	HOL	(J.W. Wilson, I. Von Voorst, C. Viroly, E. Von Voorst, De Pallandt, R. de Favauge)	174

1912 Stockholm T: 6, N: 6, D: 7.1.

			TOTAL PTS.
1.	USA	(Charles Billings, Ralph Spotts, John Hendrickson, James Graham, Edward Gleason, Frank Hall)	532
2.	GBR	(John Butt, William Grosvenor, Harry Robinson Humby, Alexander Maunder, Charles Palmer, George Whitaker)	511
3.	GER	(Erich Graf von Bernstorff, Freiherr von Zeidlitz und Leipe, Horst Goeldel-Bronikow, Albert Preuss, Erland Koch, Alfred Goeldel-Bronikowen)	510
4.	SWE	(Carl Wollert, Alfred Swahn, Johan Ekman, Hjalmar Frisell, Åke Lundeberg, Victor Wallenberg)	243

5.	FIN	(Edvard Bacher, Karl Fazer, Robert Huber, Gustaf Adolf Schnitt, Emil Johannes Collan, Axel Fredrik Londen)		233
6.	FRA	(Henri de Castex, Marquis de Crequi-Monfort, Edouard Creuzé de Lesser, André Fleury, Charles Jaubert, René Texier)		90

1920 Antwerp T: 8, N: 8, D: 7.22.

			TOTAL PTS.
1.	USA	(Mark Arie, Frank Troeh, Frank Wright, Frederick Plum, Horace Bonser, Forest McNeir)	547
2.	BEL	(Albert Bosquet, Joseph Cogels, Emile Dupont, Henri Quersin, Louis van Tilt, Edouard Fesinger)	503
3.	SWE	(Erik Lundqvist, Per Kinde, Fredric Landelius, Alfred Swahn, Karl Richter, Erik Sökjer-Petersén)	500
4.	GBR	(Harry Humby, William Grosvenor, W. Ellicot, George Whitaker, E. Pocock, Charles Palmer)	488
5.	CAN	(George Beattie, John Black, Samuel Vance, Ben McLaren, James Montogomery, J. "True" Oliver)	474
6.	HOL	(R. de Favauge, Gerard van der Vliet, Pieter Waller, Emile Jurgens, F. Jurgens, Eduardus Ludovicus van Voorst tot Voorst)	222
7.	FRA		210
7.	NOR		210

1924 Paris T: 12, N: 12, D: 7.7.

			TOTAL PTS.
1.	USA	(Frank Hughes, Samuel Sharman, William Silkworth, Fred Etchen)	363
2.	CAN	(George Beattie, James Montgomery, Samuel Vance, John Black, Samuel Newton, William Barnes)	360
3.	FIN	(Konrad Huber, Robert Huber, Werner Ekman, Robert Tikkanen)	360
4.	SWE	(Erik Ludqvist, Fredrik Landelius, Alfred Swahn, Magnus Hallman)	354
5.	BEL	(Albert Bosquet, Louis d'Heur, Emile Dupont, Jacques Mouton)	354
6.	AUT	(Heinrich Bartosch, August Baumgartner, Hans Schödl, Erich Zoigner)	347
7.	NOR	(Ole Andreas Lilloe-Olsen, O. Wessmann-Kjaer, E. Holmsen, M. Stenersen)	336
8.	GBR	(J.J. O'Leary, E. Jenkins, H.V. Larsen, Cyril Mackworth-Praed)	328

LIVE PIGEON SHOOTING

1900 Paris C:4, N:4, D: 6.27.

			BIRDS KILLED
1.	Léon de Lunden	BEL	21
2.	Maurice Faure	FRA	20
3.	Donald MacIntosh	AUS	18
3.	Crittenden Robinson	USA	18

This disgusting event marked the only time in Olympic history when animals were killed on purpose.

WOMEN

PISTOL MATCH

This event will be held for the first time in 1984.

STANDARD RIFLE

This event will be held for the first time in 1984.

AIR RIFLE

This event will be held for the first time in 1984.

SWIMMING

MEN

100-METER FREESTYLE

1896 Athens C: 13, N: 5, D: 4.11.

1. Alfréd Hajós	HUN	1:22.2 OR
2. Efstathios Choraphas	GRE	1:23.0
3. Otto Herschmann	AUT	—
4. Anninos	GRE	—
5. Gardner Williams	USA	—
6. Chrysaphos	GRE	—

The first Olympic swimming contests were held outdoors in open water, in and around the Bay of Zea at Phaleron, near Piraeus, and were watched by 40,000 people on the shore. The weather had turned unusually cold, and on the morning of the competition the temperature in the water dropped to 55 degrees Fahrenheit (13 degrees Centigrade). The eventual winner of two of the three races, the 100 meters and the 1200 meters, was Alfréd Hajós, an 18-year-old from Budapest. Hajós recalled the experience of climbing into the water from the boat that had carried the 13 swimmers to the starting point: "The icy water almost cut into our stomachs. Until 70 meters it was a neck-and-neck race, but then I got my second wind and won the competition. My time wasn't anything to brag about."

Hajós was 13 years old when he felt compelled to become a good swimmer after his father drowned in the Danube River. In 1895 he won the 100-meter title at the European championships in Vienna. In 1902 he was a member of the first Hungarian national football team. Hajós went on to become a successful architect, winning a prize in the architectural division of the Olympic Art Contest in 1924. He was born Alfréd Guttmann, but, following the fashion among wealthy Eastern Europeans of the time, he competed under a pseudonym. Later he legally changed his name to Hajós.

1900 not held

1904 St. Louis C: 8 or 9, N: 2, D: 9.5.
(100 yards)

1. Zoltán Halmay	HUN	1:02.8
2. Charles Daniels	USA	—
3. J. Scott Leary	USA	—
4. Francis Gailey	USA	—
5. David Hammond	USA	—
6. Leo Goodwin	USA	—

Including the Intercalated Games of 1906, in which he won one gold medal and one silver, Halmay earned a total of nine Olympic medals: three gold, five silver, and one bronze.

1906 Athens C: 9, N: 5, D: 4.24. WR: 1:05.8 (Zoltán Halmay)

1. Charles Daniels	USA	1:13.4 WR
2. Zoltán Halmay	HUN	1:14.2
3. Cecil Healy	AUS	—
4. Paul Radmilovic	GBR	—
5. John Derbyshire	GBR	—
6. Hjalmar Johansson	SWE	—

1908 London C: 34, N: 12, D: 7.20. WR: 1:05.8 (Zoltán Halmay)
1. Charles Daniels   USA   1:05.6   WR
2. Zoltán Halmay   HUN   1:06.2
3. Harald Julin   SWE   1:08.0
4. Leslie Rich   USA   —

In 1908, 24-year-old Charles Daniels of New York City closed out his Olympic career, having won five gold medals, one silver, and two bronze, including the Intercalated Games of 1906.

1912 Stockholm C: 34, N: 12, D: 7.10. WR: 1:02.4 (Kurt Bretting)
1. Duke Paoa Kahanamoku   USA   1:03.4
2. Cecil Healy   AUS   1:04.6
3. Kenneth Huszagh   USA   1:05.6
4. Kurt Bretting   GER   1:05.8
5. Walter Ramme   GER   1:06.4
DNS: William Longworth (AUS)

Kahanamoku was born on August 24, 1890, in the palace of Princess Ruth in Honolulu. At the time of his birth, Queen Victoria's son the Duke of Edinburgh was visiting Hawaii, so Kahanamoku's father named his own new son Duke in honor of the occasion. In Stockholm Kahanamoku impressed the European spectators with his powerful, smooth stroking, and quickly became one of the most popular figures at the Games. His first-round time of 1:02.6 was more than two seconds faster than any of the other swimmers. He won his second round heat in a leisurely 1:03.8, the fastest time of the round. Because of a misunderstanding, the three U.S. representatives, Kahanamoku, Kenneth Huszagh, and Perry McGillivray, failed to show up for the semifinals on Sunday evening July 7. Holding the final without them seemed absurd, so the three were allowed to take part in an extra heat on Tuesday, with the stipulation that to qualify for the final the winner would have to beat the time of William Longworth, who had finished third in the first heat in 1:06.2. If this happened, then the second-place finisher in the special heat would also advance to the final. Not wanting to take any chances, Duke Kahanamoku equaled Kurt Bretting's world record of 1:02.4, allowing Huszagh to qualify as well. In the final, the following day, Kahanamoku took the time to look back and survey the field at the halfway mark. Noting that he had a comfortable lead, he eased up a bit and still won by two yards.

1920 Antwerp C: 33, N: 15, D: 8.24/8.29. WR: 1:01.4 (Duke Paoa Kahanamoku)
First Final
1. Duke Paoa Kahanamoku   USA   1:00.4   WR
2. Pua Kela Kealoha   USA   1:02.2
3. William Harris   USA   1:03.2
4. Norman Ross   USA   1:03.8
5. William Herald   AUS   —
6. George Vernot   CAN   —

Second Final
1. Duke Paoa Kahanamoku   USA   1:01.4
2. Pua Kela Kealoha   USA   1:02.6
3. William Harris   USA   1:03.0
4. William Herald   AUS   1:03.8
5. George Vernot   CAN   —
DNS: Norman Ross (USA)

Kahanamoku equaled his own world record of 1:01.4 in the semifinals, and then set a new record of 1:00.4 in the final, to celebrate his 30th birthday. However, Herald claimed that he had been fouled by Ross, so the race was ordered reswum. The order of the finish was exactly the same the second time, except that Ross, who had won the 1500-meter championship the day after the first 100-meter final, didn't take part.

Kahanamoku eventually competed in four Olympics, winning three gold medals and two silver. Later he appeared in several Hollywood films, usually as a Hawaiian king. He also played a major role in introducing the sport of surfing around the world.

1924 Paris C: 30, N: 15, D: 7.20. WR: 57.4 (Johnny Weissmuller)
1. Johnny Weissmuller   USA   59.0   OR
2. Duke Paoa Kahanamoku   USA   1:01.4
3. Samuel Kahanamoku   USA   1:01.8
4. Arne Borg   SWE   1:02.0
5. Katsuo Takaishi   JAP   1:03.0
6. Orvar Trolle (SWE)

Johnny Weissmuller was born in Austria on June 2, 1904, and his family emigrated to the United States in 1908. His father worked as a coal miner before moving to Chicago, where he died of tuberculosis before his son had started on the path to fame and fortune. On July 9, 1922, Johnny made swimming history by becoming the first person to swim 100 meters in less than one minute. On February 17, 1924, he lowered his time from 58.6 to 57.4, establishing a world record that would last for ten years. At the start of the 100-meter final at the Paris Olympics, Weissmuller found himself with 34-year-old defending champion Duke Kahanamoku on one side of him and Duke's 19-year-old brother, Sam, on the other side. Weissmuller was worried that the two Hawaiians had planned to swim a team race against him, but as they stood above the water Duke turned to him and said, "Johnny, good luck. The most important thing in this race is to get the American flag up there three times. Let's do it." And they did, with Weissmuller starting quickly and winning easily. That day he also won a gold medal in the 4 × 200-meter relay and a bronze medal in water polo. Two days earlier he had won the 400-meter freestyle. Johnny Weissmuller was one of the most popular participants at the 1924 Olympics, delighting the tough Parisian crowd not only with his superb swimming, but also with a comedy diving act, which he put on several times between races with his partner, Stubby Kruger. After Weissmuller's 100 meters victory, the crowd of 7000 stood and called for him for two or three minutes, until it was announced that he would appear again later in the afternoon.

1928 Amsterdam C: 30, N: 17, D: 8.11. WR: 57.4 (Johnny Weissmuller)

1. Johnny Weissmuller	USA	58.6	OR
2. István Bárány	HUN	59.8	
3. Katsuo Takaishi	JAP	1:00.0	
4. George Kojac	USA	1:00.8	
5. Walter Laufer	USA	1:01.0	
6. Walter Spence	CAN	1:01.4	
7. Alberto Zorilla	ARG	1:01.6	

Coming out of the midrace turn in the 100 meters final at Amsterdam, Weissmuller inadvertently gulped a mouthful of water and almost blacked out. He lost two yards, but regained his composure and went on to win the fourth of his five Olympic gold medals. A couple of years later Weissmuller was training for the 1932 Olympics, when he got an offer of $500 a week to work for the BVD Underwear Company, advertising swimsuits. Out in Hollywood one of his BVD photos was noticed, and he was invited to try out for the part of Tarzan. Needless to say, he got the part, and in 1932 Weissmuller made his film debut in *Tarzan, the Ape Man*. The first of four Olympic medalists to play the part of Tarzan in the movies (the others being Buster Crabbe, Herman Brix, and Glen Morris), Weissmuller acted in 11 more Tarzan films in the next 16 years. Another activity he engaged in more than once was getting married, which he did five times.

In 1959 Johnny Weissmuller was taking part in a celebrity golf tournament in Havana during a period in which Fidel Castro's guerrilla troops were doing battle with the soldiers of the Batista government. Weissmuller was on his way to the golf course with some friends and a couple of bodyguards, when rebel soldiers suddenly appeared out of the bushes and surrounded their car. The guerrillas disarmed the guards and pointed their rifles at the decadent Yankee imperialists. But Weissmuller had the proper solution to an otherwise difficult situation. Slowly raising himself to his full height, he beat his chest with his fists and let out an enormous yell. After a moment of stunned silence, the revolutionaries broke into smiles of delight and began calling out, "Tarzan! Tarzan! *Bienvenido!* Welcome to Cuba!" Dropping their weapons, they crowded around Johnny, shaking his hand and asking for his autograph. After a few minutes Weissmuller and his party were not only not kidnapped, but they were actually given a rebel escort to the golf course.

1932 Los Angeles C: 22, N: 10, D: 8.7. WR: 57.4 (Johnny Weissmuller)

1. Yasuji Miyazaki	JAP	58.2
2. Tatsugo Kawaishi	JAP	58.6
3. Albert Schwartz	USA	58.8
4. Manuella Kalili	USA	59.2
5. Zenjiro Takahashi	JAP	59.2
6. Ramond Thompson	USA	59.5

The 1932 men's swimming contests were highlighted by the fantastic performances of the Japanese, who stunned the Americans by winning the relay and by taking first and second in four of the five individual events. The first of these victories was recorded by 15-year-old Yasuji Miyazaki, who brought his schoolbooks with him to Los Angeles so that he wouldn't fall too far behind in his studies. Miyazaki had set an Olympic record of 58.0 in the semifinals.

1936 Berlin C: 45, N: 23, D: 8.9. WR: 56.4 (Peter Fick)

1. Ferenc Csík	HUN	57.6
2. Masanori Yusa	JAP	57.9
3. Shigeo Arai	JAP	58.0
4. Masaharu Taguchi	JAP	58.1
5. Helmut Fischer	GER	59.3
6. Peter Fick	USA	59.7
7. Arthur Lindegren	USA	59.9

Between 1912 and 1944 there were only three world record holders for the 100-meter freestyle: Duke Kahanamoku (1912–1922), Johnny Weissmuller (1922–1934), and Peter Fick (1934–1944). After the first round it appeared that the final would be a contest between Fick and the three Japanese, Toguchi recording the fastest time of 57.5 (an Olympic record), followed by Fick's 57.6. The semifinals were won by Taguchi and Yusa in 57.9 and 57.5 respectively, with Fick looking unusually off form. However the final provided a major upset. While the Japanese and Americans raced against each other, a 22-year-old Hungarian medical student named Ferenc Csík sneaked up in the outside lane to win the race in his fastest time ever. Although there was no question of who had finished first, there was a good deal of controversy regarding the remaining places. Photos of the finish led observers to believe that the actual order was 2—Taguchi, 3—Yusa, 4—Fick, 5—Arai, 6—Fischer, 7—Lindegren.

Dr. Csík died in an air raid in 1945 while administering first aid to a wounded man.

1948 London C: 41, N: 20, D: 7.31. WR: 55.4 (Alan Ford)

1. Walter Ris	USA	57.3	OR
2. Alan Ford	USA	57.8	
3. Géza Kádas	HUN	58.1	
4. Keith Carter	USA	58.3	
5. Alexandre Jany	FRA	58.3	
6. Per-Olof Olsson	SWE	59.3	
7. Zoltán Szilárd	HUN	59.6	
8. Taha El Gamal	EGY	1:00.5	

Alex Jany led at the 50-meter turn, but he was passed in the next 25 meters by Ford, Kádas, and Ris. In the last ten meters Wally Ris of Iowa surged past the others to take first place.

1952 Helsinki C: 61, N: 33, D: 7.27. WR: 55.4 (Alan Ford)

1. Clarke Scholes	USA	57.4
2. Hiroshi Suzuki	JAP	57.4
3. Göran Larsson	SWE	58.2
4. Toru Goto	JAP	58.5
5. Géza Kádas	HUN	58.6
6. Rex Aubrey	AUS	58.7
7. Aldo Eminente	FRA	58.7
8. Ronald Gora	USA	58.8

Scholes set an Olympic record of 57.1 in his preliminary heat.

1956 Melbourne C: 34, N: 19, D: 11.30. WR: 54.8 (Richard Cleveland)

1. Jon Henricks	AUS	55.4	OR
2. John Devitt	AUS	55.8	
3. Gary Chapman	AUS	56.7	
4. Logan Reid Patterson	USA	57.2	
5. Richard Hanley	USA	57.6	
6. William Woolsey	USA	57.6	
7. Atsushi Tani	JAP	58.0	
8. Aldo Eminente	FRA	58.1	

Jon Henricks was the first favorite to win the 100-meter freestyle since Johnny Weissmuller. His victory in the final was his 56th straight win at that distance over a three-year period. When asked the secret of his success, Henricks, who was as feisty as his good friend and fellow Olympic champion Dawn Fraser, once replied, "You see that god-damn pool there—well, if you want to get to the top of it, dive in and start swimming. You do that for three, four or five years, and every time you stop swimming your coach bawls you out. . . . You get a crazy ear disease from these tropical waters, but you've still got to keep on swimming. You get your head shaved to make you look like a zombie so that you will cut down water resistance, and you shave your legs for the same reason. You get invitations to a party and you write back regretting you are unable to attend owing to a prior engagement. That's a lie, of course, the only prior engagement is at the pool, going up and down, up and down, then up and down again. You finish going up and down and it's time to do some weightlifting—or maybe go to sleep while your coach goes out playing golf or fishing."

1960 Rome C: 51, N: 34, D: 8.26. WR: 54.6 (John Devitt)

1. John Devitt	AUS	55.2	OR
2. Lance Larson	USA	55.2	OR
3. Manuel Dos Santos	BRA	55.4	
4. R. Bruce Hunter	USA	55.6	
5. Gyula Dobai	HUN	56.3	
6. Richard Pound	CAN	56.3	
7. Aubrey Burer	SAF	56.3	
8. Per-Ola Lindberg	SWE	57.1	

Two leading contenders were absent from the final. An appendectomy just prior to the U.S. trials prevented Jeff Far-rell from qualifying as one of the three American representatives, and defending champion Jon Henricks was eliminated in the semifinals as a result of intestinal problems developed on the way from Australia to Rome.

Dos Santos led the final at the turn, but Larson and Devitt passed him at 70 meters and finished in a near dead heat. Devitt congratulated Larson and left the pool in disappointment. Confusion developed, however, when the judges met to discuss their verdict. Of the three judges assigned to the task of determining who had finished first, two voted for Devitt and one for Larson. However the second-place judges also voted 2–1 for Devitt. In other words, of the six judges involved, three thought Devitt had won and three thought Larson had won. When the electronic timers were consulted, it turned out that Larson had registered 55.1 seconds and Devitt 55.2. The unofficial paper tapes at the end of the pool also showed Larson winning—by four inches. Despite this evidence, the chief judge, who did not have any say in the matter according to the official rules, ordered Larson's time changed to 55.2 and gave the decision to Devitt. Four years of protests failed to change the result.

1964 Tokyo C: 66, N: 33, D: 10.12. WR: 52.9 (Alain Gottvalles)

1. Donald Schollander	USA	53.4	OR
2. Robert McGregor	GBR	53.5	
3. Hans-Joachim Klein	GER	54.0	
4. Gary Ilman	USA	54.0	
5. Alain Gottvalles	FRA	54.2	
6. Michael Austin	USA	54.5	
7. Gyula Dobai	HUN	54.9	
8. Uwe Jacobsen	GER	56.1	

The fastest times of the qualifying rounds, 54.0 and 53.9, were recorded by Gary Ilman, with Don Schollander close behind at 54.3 and 54.0. In the final, however, Ilman ran into a wave just after the turn and momentarily lost his concentration. Schollander finished strongly, passed McGregor in the last five meters, and won by about six inches. Schollander, who was born in Charlotte, North Carolina, and raised in Lake Oswego, Oregon, was trained by George Haines in Santa Clara, California. Before the Tokyo Games were over, the 18-year-old Schollander had become the first swimmer to win four gold medals at one Olympics.

A minor controversy developed over the awarding of the bronze medal. The judges were split as to whether Ilman or Klein had finished third. Both were clocked in the same time. The Japanese had thoughtfully provided electronic timers for the swimming events and, even though they were not used officially, they were consulted by the judges. It turned out that Ilman and Klein had stopped the clock at the exact same hundredth of a second, but that Klein had finished one one-thousandth of a second sooner. After 35 minutes of consultation, the judges decided that even if the electronic timing was unofficial, it had provided sufficient cause to award third place to Klein.

1968 Mexico City C: 64, N: 35, D: 10.19. WR: 52.6 (Kenneth Walsh, Zachary Zorn)

1. Michael Wenden	AUS	52.2	WR
2. Kenneth Walsh	USA	52.8	
3. Mark Spitz	USA	53.0	
4. Robert McGregor	GBR	53.5	
5. Leonid Ilyichev	SOV	53.8	
6. Georgy Kulikov	SOV	53.8	
7. Luis Nicolao	ARG	53.9	
8. Zachary Zorn	USA	53.9	

Zac Zorn had equaled Ken Walsh's world record at the U.S. Olympic trials, and the Americans went to Mexico City as heavy favorites. But they hadn't counted on 18-year-old Michael Wenden of Liverpool, New South Wales. Wenden's heat time of 53.6 was seven-tenths of a second faster than anyone else's, and his semifinal time of 52.9 was a half-second better than the rest. In the final, Zac Zorn, weakened by a week-long illness, went all-out for the first 50 meters and reached the turn almost a full body length ahead of the other swimmers. But he had exhausted himself, and eventually faded to last place. Wenden, on the other hand, swam the race of his life to score the most decisive 100-meter victory in 40 years.

1972 Munich C: 48, N: 30, D: 9.3. WR: 51.47 (Mark Spitz)

1. Mark Spitz	USA	51.22	WR
2. Jerry Heidenreich	USA	51.65	
3. Vladimir Bure	SOV	51.77	
4. John Murphy	USA	52.08	
5. Michael Wenden	AUS	52.41	
6. Igor Grivennikov	SOV	52.44	
7. Michel Rousseau	FRA	52.90	
8. Klaus Steinbach	GER	52.92	

Mark Spitz had three goals at the Munich Games. The first was to prove himself better than Don Schollander by becoming the first swimmer to win five gold medals in one Olympics. The second was to become the first athlete in any sport to win six gold medals in one Olympics. The third goal was to go one better and win seven gold medals. It was this final goal that Mark Spitz was having doubts about on September 1. He had already won five gold medals. A sixth gold medal seemed assured, since the final race of the Olympics, the medley relay, looked to be a certain U.S. victory. But about the 100-meter freestyle, Spitz was not so certain. Jerry Heidenreich had been swimming very well lately and had to be considered a serious threat. Spitz's father, Arnold, had constantly stressed to his son from an early age the motto "Swimming isn't everything, winning is." For Mark Spitz, it would have been better to enter four events and win all four than to enter seven events and win only six.

When he heard rumors that Spitz was thinking of withdrawing from the 100 freestyle, Spitz's coach, Sherm Chavoor, who was in Munich as the coach of the U.S. women's team, rushed over to see his student. Chavoor successfully convinced Spitz that he would be perceived as "chicken" if he avoided a confrontation with Heidenreich. Finding this

an unacceptable option, Spitz decided against withdrawing.

The heats were swum on the morning of September 2, and the semifinals seven hours later. In both races Spitz held back and finished behind defending champion Michael Wenden and slower than Jerry Heidenreich. In the final the following night, Spitz surprised Heidenreich when he departed from his usual tactics by going out at full speed rather than saving his strength for the second lap, as he usually did. Spitz reached the turn with a clear lead. With 15 yards to go, Spitz suddenly lost his rhythm, but he pulled himself together and reached the wall a half-stroke ahead of the onrushing Heidenreich.

1976 Montreal C: 41, N: 28, D: 7.25. WR:50.59 (Jim Montgomery)

1. Jim Montgomery	USA	49.99	WR
2. Jack Babashoff	USA	50.81	
3. Peter Nocke	GER	51.31	
4. Klaus Steinbach	GER	51.68	
5. Marcello Guarducci	ITA	51.70	
6. Joe Bottom	USA	51.79	
7. Vladimir Bure	SOV	52.03	
8. Andrei Krylov	SOV	52.15	

Montgomery won his semifinal heat in 50.39 to break his own world record. In the final he not only set another record again, but he also became the first person to break the 50-second barrier for 100 meters. Three weeks later in Philadelphia, Jonty Skinner brought the record down to 49.49. Skinner was not allowed to compete in the Olympics because he was from South Africa. He later became a coach at the University of Alabama.

1980 Moscow C: 39, N: 27, D: 7.27. WR: 49.44 (Jonty Skinner)

1. Jörg Woithe	GDR	50.40
2. Per Holmertz	SWE	50.91
3. Per Johansson	SWE	51.29
4. Sergei Kopliakov	SOV	51.3
5. Raffaele Franceschi	ITA	51.69
6. Sergei Krasyuk	SOV	51.80
7. René Ecuyer	FRA	52.01
8. Graeme Brewer	AUS	52.22

Woithe recorded his best time ever, 50.21, in the semifinals. Three days after the boycotted Olympic final, the U.S. Outdoor National was won in 50.19 by Rowdy Gaines, who had twice clocked 49.61. Chris Cavanaugh was second in 50.26.

200-METER FREESTYLE

1896 not held

1900 Paris C: 26, N: 9, D: 8.12. WR(220 yards): 2:38.2 (Frederick Lane)

(220 Yards)

1. Frederick Lane	AUS	2:25.2 OR
2. Zoltán Halmay	HUN	2:31.4
3. Karl Ruberl	AUT	2:32.0

4. Richard Crawshaw   GBR   2:45.6
5. Maurice Hochepied   FRA   2:53.0
6. Stapleton   GBR   2:55.0

The unusually fast times were due to the fact that the 1900 swimming races were held in the River Seine and swum *with* the current.

1904 St. Louis C: 4, N: 2, D: 9.6. WR(220 yards): 2:28.6 (Frederick Lane)
(220 Yards)
1. Charles Daniels   USA   2:44.2
2. Francis Gailey   USA   2:46.0
3. Emil Rausch   GER   2:56.0
4. Edgar Adams   USA   —

1906–1964 not held

1968 Mexico City C: 57, N: 27, D: 10.24. WR: 1:54.3 (Donald Schollander)
1. Michael Wenden   AUS   1:55.2   OR
2. Donald Schollander   USA   1:55.8
3. John Nelson   USA   1:58.1
4. Ralph Hutton   CAN   1:58.6
5. Alain Mosconi   FRA   1:59.1
6. Robert Windle   AUS   2:00.9
7. Semyon Belits-Geiman   SOV   2:01.5
DNS: Stephen Rerych (USA)

Michael Wenden won his second gold medal, while Don Schollander added a silver to his five golds. Afterward Schollander announced his retirement, telling reporters, "I'm finished with water—in fact I may not take a bath or a shower for another two years."

1972 Munich C: 46, N: 31, D: 8.29. WR: 1:53.5 (Mark Spitz)
1. Mark Spitz   USA   1:52.78   WR
2. Steven Genter   USA   1:53.73
3. Werner Lampe   GER   1:53.99
4. Michael Wenden   AUS   1:54.40
5. Frederick Tyler   USA   1:54.96
6. Klaus Steinbach   GER   1:55.65
7. Vladimir Bure   SOV   1:57.24
8. Ralph Hutton   CAN   1:57.56

Spitz trailed Genter with 50 meters to go, but came from behind to win his third gold medal in two days. Genter's performance was remarkable for the fact that he underwent surgery in Munich for a partially collapsed lung and had been released from the hospital only the day before the race. On the victory platform Spitz waved his shoes at the crowd and the cameras. Called before an I.O.C. committee, he successfully convinced them that he had been motivated by exuberance rather than commercialism.

1976 Montreal C: 55, N: 33, D: 7.19. WR: 1:50.32 (Bruce Furniss)
1. Bruce Furniss   USA   1:50.29   WR
2. John Naber   USA   1:50.50
3. Jim Montgomery   USA   1:50.58

4. Andrei Krylov   SOV   1:50.73
5. Klaus Steinbach   GER   1:51.09
6. Peter Nocke   GER   1:51.71
7. Gordon Downie   GBR   1:52.78
8. Andrei Bogdanov   SOV   1:53.33

Furniss moved ahead in the last 50 meters to edge Naber, who had won the 100-meter backstroke an hour earlier.

1980 Moscow C: 42, N: 25, D: 7.21. WR: 1:49.16 (Ambrose "Rowdy" Gaines)
1. Sergei Kopliakov   SOV   1:49.81   OR
2. Andrei Krylov   SOV   1:50.76
3. Graeme Brewer   AUS   1:51.60
4. Jörg Woither   GDR   1:51.86
5. Ron McKeon   AUS   1:52.60
6. Paolo Revelli   ITA   1:52.76
7. Thomas Lejdström   SWE   1:52.94
8. Fabrizio Rampazzo   ITA   1:53.25

On August 1, the U.S. Outdoor National was won by Rowdy Gaines in 1:50.02.

400-METER FREESTYLE

1896 Athens C: 3, N: 2, D: 4.11.
(500 Meters)
1. Paul Neumann   AUT   8:12.6
2. Antonios Pepanos   GRE   —
3. Efstathios Choraphas   GRE   —

1900 not held

1904 St. Louis C: 4, N: 2, D: 9.7. WR(440 yards): 5:22.2
(440 Yards)
1. Charles Daniels   USA   6:16.2
2. Francis Gailey   USA   6:22.0
3. Otto Wahle   AUT   6:39.0
4. Leo Goodwin   USA   —

1906 Athens C: 12, N: 5, D: 4.26. WR(440 yards): 5:19.0
1. Otto Scheff   AUT   6:23.8
2. Henry Taylor   GBR   6:24.4
3. John Arthur Jarvis   GBR   6:27.2
4. Alajos Bruckner   HUN   —
5. Paul Radmilovic   GBR   —
6. Cecil Healy   AUS   —

1908 London C: 25, N: 10, D: 7.16. WR(440 yards): 5:19.0
1. Henry Taylor   GBR   5:36.8
2. Frank Beaurepaire   AUS   5:44.2
3. Otto Scheff   AUT   5:46.0
4. William Foster   GBR   —

Henry Taylor of Oldham, Lancashire, won the first of his three gold medals at the London Games. Including the Intercalated Games of 1906 and the Olympics of 1912 and 1920, Taylor earned a total of four gold medals, one silver, and three bronze. This race also marked the first appearance of Frank Beaurepaire, who won medals at four straight Olympics.

1912 Stockholm C: 26, N: 13, D: 7.14. WR: 5:23.0 (Frank Beaurepaire)

1. George Hodgson	CAN	5:24.4
2. John Hatfield	GBR	5:25.8
3. Harold Hardwick	AUS	5:31.2
4. Cecil Healy	AUS	5:37.8
5. Béla Las-Torres	HUN	5:42.0

Hodgson had won the 1500 meters four days earlier.

1920 Antwerp C: 20, N: 11, D: 8.28. WR: 5:14.6 (Norman Bass)

1. Norman Ross	USA	5:26.8
2. Ludy Langer	USA	5:29.0
3. George Vernot	CAN	5:29.6
4. Fred Kahele	USA	—

DNF: Frank Beaurepaire (AUS), William Harris (USA)

Twenty-four-year-old Norman Ross also won gold medals in the 1500-meter freestyle and in the 4×200-meter relay. He was also a member of the bronze-medal-winning U.S. water polo team. He later achieved success as a radio music announcer.

1924 Paris C: 23, N: 13, D: 7.18. WR: 4:54.7 (Arne Borg)

1. Johnny Weissmuller	USA	5:04.2	OR
2. Arne Borg	SWE	5:05.6	
3. Andrew "Boy" Charlton	AUS	5:06.6	
4. Åke Borg	SWE	5:26.0	
5. John Hatfield	GBR	5:32.0	
6. Lester Smith (USA)			

This was a thrilling race in which no more than five feet separated Weissmuller and Borg at any time. At 100 meters, Borg led by six inches. At the halfway mark, it was Weissmuller by nine inches, and at 300 meters, Borg touched first by three inches. Weissmuller finally drew away 20 meters from the finish and won by four feet.

Arne and Åke Borg were twin brothers.

1928 Amsterdam C: 26, N: 17, D: 8.9. WR: 4:50.3 (Arne Borg)

1. Alberto Zorilla	ARG	5:01.6	OR
2. Andrew "Boy" Charlton	AUS	5:03.6	
3. Arne Borg	SWE	5:04.6	
4. Clarence "Buster" Crabbe	USA	5:05.4	
5. Austin Clapp	USA	5:16.0	
6. Raymond Ruddy	USA	5:25.0	

Charlton and Borg were so intent on their personal duel that they failed to notice Zorilla creep up in the outside lane and move ahead in the last 50 meters.

1932 Los Angeles C: 19, N: 10, D: 8.10. WR: 4:47.0 (Jean Taris)

1. Clarence "Buster" Crabbe	USA	4:48.4	OR
2. Jean Taris	FRA	4:48.5	
3. Tsutomu Oyokota	JAP	4:52.3	
4. Takashi Yokoyama	JAP	4:52.5	
5. Noboru Sugimoto	JAP	4:56.1	
6. Andrew "Boy" Charlton	AUS	4:58.6	

Takashi Yokoyama set Olympic records of 4:53.2 and 4:51.4 in the opening round and the semifinals, but the fi-

nal turned out to be a duel between world record holder Jean Taris and local favorite Buster Crabbe. Taris sprinted to an early lead and reached the halfway mark two lengths ahead. By 300 meters, Crabbe had cut the gap to one length. He continued to edge closer, finally drawing even 25 meters from the finish. The excitement was so great that swimmers and ushers rushed over from all parts of the stadium, while Johnny Weissmuller, sitting in the front row, leaped a fence to get a closer view of the finish. Crabbe touched the wall inches ahead of Taris. "That one-tenth of a second changed my life," Crabbe later recalled. "It was then that [the Hollywood producers] discovered latent histrionic abilities in me." Crabbe went on to great fame as an actor; he was best known for his roles as Tarzan, Buck Rogers, and Flash Gordon. He died on April 23, 1983, at the age of 75.

1936 Berlin C: 34, N: 16, D: 8.12. WR: 4:38.7 (Jack Medica)

1. Jack Medica	USA	4:44.5	OR
2. Shumpei Uto	JAP	4:45.6	
3. Shozo Makino	JAP	4:48.1	
4. Ralph Flanagan	USA	4:52.7	
5. Hiroshi Negami	JAP	4:53.6	
6. Jean Taris	FRA	4:53.8	
7. Robert Leivers	GBR	5:00.9	

Jack Medica of Seattle staged a thrilling last-lap spurt to overtake Uto ten meters from the finish.

1948 London C: 41, N: 21, D: 8.4. WR: 4:35.2 (Alexandre Jany)

1. William Smith	USA	4:41.0	OR
2. James McLane	USA	4:43.4	
3. John Marshall	AUS	4:47.4	
4. Géza Kádas	HUN	4:49.4	
5. György Mitró	HUN	4:49.9	
6. Alexandre Jany	FRA	4:51.4	
7. Jack Hale	GBR	4:55.9	
8. Alfredo Yantorno	ARG	4:58.7	

Bill Smith had been stricken with typhoid when he was six years old, and took up swimming to build up his withered legs and body.

1952 Helsinki C: 51, N: 29, D: 7.30. WR: 4:26.9 (John Marshall)

1. Jean Boiteux	FRA	4:30.7	OR
2. Ford Konno	USA	4:31.3	
3. Per-Olof Östrand	SWE	4:35.2	
4. Peter Duncan	SAF	4:37.9	
5. John Wardrop	GBR	4:39.9	
6. Wayne Moore	USA	4:40.1	
7. James McLane	USA	4:40.3	
8. Hironashin Furuhashi	JAP	4:42.1	

Boiteux held off a late challenge from Ford Konno to win a surprise gold medal. As soon as he touched the wall, an older Frenchman in a beret rushed forward, leaped fully clothed into the water, and embraced the new champion. Reporters gathered around to find out who he was. "Coach?" "Manager?" they asked in various languages.

Beaming with pride and overcome with emotion, the man in the beret held his arms up and uttered one word: "Papa!"

1956 Melbourne C: 32, N: 19, D: 12.4. WR: 4:26.7 (Ford Konno)
1. Murray Rose   AUS   4:27.3   OR
2. Tsuyoshi Yamanaka JAP   4:30.4
3. George Breen   USA   4:32.5
4. Kevin O'Halloran   AUS   4:32.9
5. Hans Zierold   GDR   4:34.6
6. Garry Winram   AUS   4:34.9
7. Koji Nonoshita   JAP   4:38.2
8. Angelo Romani   ITA   4:41.7

Murray Rose was a 17-year-old vegetarian who became known as "The Seaweed Streak." Since his diet could not be provided for in the Olympic Village, Rose's parents moved him out and took care of his nutrition. His three gold medals at the Melbourne Games made a lot of Australians think twice about their diet.

1960 Rome C: 40, N: 25, D: 8.31. WR(440 yards): 4:15.9 (John Konrads)
1. Murray Rose   AUS   4:18.3   OR
2. Tsuyoshi Yamanaka JAP   4:21.4
3. John Konrads   AUS   4:21.8
4. Ian Black   GBR   4:21.8
5. Alan Somers   USA   4:22.0
6. Murray McLachlan   SAF   4:26.3
7. Eugene Lenz   USA   4:26.8
8. Makoto Fukui   JAP   4:29.6

By 1960, both Murray Rose and Tsuyoshi Yamanaka had moved to Los Angeles and become students at the University of Southern California. In Rome, Alan Somers set an Olympic record of 4:19.2 in the qualifying round, but was unable to reproduce his time in the final. Although four years had passed since the last Olympics, Rose and Yamanaka repeated their one-two finish, with the exact same distance separating them.

1964 Tokyo C: 49, N: 27, D: 10.15. WR: 4:12.7 (Donald Schollander)
1. Donald Schollander   USA   4:12.2   WR
2. Frank Wiegand   GDR   4:14.9
3. Allan Wood   AUS   4:15.1
4. Roy Saari   USA   4:16.7
5. John Nelson   USA   4:16.9
6. Tsuyoshi Yamanaka   JAP   4:19.1
7. Russell Phegan   AUS   4:20.2
8. Semyon Belits-Geiman   SOV   4:21.4

Schollander swam the last 100 meters in 1:01.7 to win his third gold medal.

1968 Mexico City C: 37, N: 20, D: 10.23. WR: 4:06.5 (Ralph Hutton)
1. Michael Burton   USA   4:09.0   OR
2. Ralph Hutton   CAN   4:11.7

3. Alain Mosconi   FRA   4:13.3
4. Gregory Brough   AUS   4:15.9
5. Graham White   AUS   4:16.7
6. John Nelson   USA   4:17.2
7. Hans-Joachim Fassnacht GER   4:18.1
8. Brent Berk   USA   4:26.0

The day before the qualifying heats, Mike Burton woke up feeling nauseated; later he fainted in an elevator in the Olympic Village. The next day he "took it easy" and qualified in 4:19.3. He took charge of the final before the halfway mark and won going away, covering the last 100 meters in 1:01.6.

1972 Munich C: 43, N: 28, D: 9.1. WR: 4:00.11 (Kurt Krumpholz)
— Rick DeMont   USA   4:00.26
1. Bradford Cooper   AUS   4:00.27   OR
2. Steven Genter   USA   4:01.94
3. Tom McBreen   USA   4:02.64
4. Graham Windeatt   AUS   4:02.93
5. Brian Brinkley   GBR   4:06.69
6. Bengt Gingsjö   SWE   4:06.75
7. Werner Lampe   GER   4:06.97

Rick DeMont was a 16-year-old from San Rafael, California. Allergic to wheat and fur, he had been taking medication for asthma since he was four years old. When DeMont qualified for the U.S. Olympic team, he was asked to fill out a standard medical form in which he listed all medications that he took. The team physicians of most other nations took this information from their athletes, found out the component parts of the various drugs from the *Physician's Desk Reference (PDR)* or similar works, and compared them to the list of banned drugs issued by the I.O.C. for the 1972 Olympics. If any forbidden drugs were being used, the physicians came up with acceptable substitutes for their athletes. Unfortunately the U.S. team physicians were not so well organized. Evidently they never even looked at the forms. Instead, they just told the athletes not to take any drugs within 48 hours of competing without first clearing it with a doctor.

The night before the 400 meters competition, Rick DeMont woke up wheezing between 1 a.m. and 2 a.m., and took a tablet of Marex, unaware that it contained the banned drug ephedrine. At 8 a.m. he took another tablet. He swam his heat at about noon and qualified easily. Since his prescription said to take one tablet every six hours, he might have taken one more dose of Marex later in the day. The final began at 6:40 p.m. DeMont started slowly, saving his strength. In last place after 100 meters and sixth after 200, he picked up speed in the second half of the race. Swimming the last 100 meters in 58.22 seconds, he defeated Cooper by one-hundredth of a second, the smallest margin possible. After the race, DeMont, along with the other two medalists, was taken away for dope testing. At the awards ceremony there was no indication of any problem.

Two days later, on Sunday, DeMont, who was the world record holder at 1500 meters, took part in the preliminary round of that event, qualifying without being pressed. The next morning, however, he was informed that he had failed the drug test after the 400 meters and therefore would not be allowed to take part in the final of the 1500 meters. A distraught DeMont watched from the stands.

Over the next couple of days, hearings were held, affidavits were filed, and confusion reigned. At one point, DeMont's pharmacist in California received a call from a U.S. doctor in Munich asking him, among other things, what Marex contained. Apparently, not one U.S. team physician had bothered to take a copy of the *PDR* to Germany. The I.O.C. ordered DeMont disqualified and issued a stern reprimand to the U.S. officials in charge. Put on the defensive, team physicians tried to blame the swimming coaches, DeMont's family doctor, even the teenager himself. Yet DeMont had made no attempt to hide the fact that he took Marex. He didn't even know it was forbidden. When team officials had entered his room at the Olympic Village on Sunday to confiscate his drugs, the bottle of Marex was sitting in plain view.

By 1976 U.S. swim officials had learned their lesson. Before the Montreal Olympics, the 51 members of the U.S. team were questioned carefully about their medications, and it was learned that 16 of them were unknowingly using banned drugs. Substitutes were found for those 16, but all of this was far too late to help Rick DeMont, who had become the first American since Jim Thorpe to be forced to return his gold medal.

1976 Montreal C: 47, N: 29, D: 7.22. WR: 3:53.08 (Brian Goodell)

1. Brian Goodell	USA	3:51.93	WR
2. Tim Shaw	USA	3:52.54	
3. Vladimir Raskatov	SOV	3:55.76	
4. Djan Madruga Garrido	BRA	3:57.18	
5. Stephen Holland	AUS	3:57.59	
6. Sándor Nagy	HUN	3:57.81	
7. Vladimir Mikheev	SOV	4:00.79	
8. Stephen Badger	CAN	4:02.83	

Brian Goodell had already won the 1500 meters gold medal two days earlier. United States dominance in the 400-meter freestyle was so great that Vladimir Raskatov's pre-Olympic European record of 3:58.02 would not have qualified him for the final at the U.S. trials.

1980 Moscow C: 28, N: 16, D: 7.24. WR: 3:50.49 (Peter Szmidt)

1. Vladimir Salnikov	SOV	3:51.31	OR
2. Andrei Krylov	SOV	3:53.24	
3. Ivar Stukolkin	SOV	3:53.95	
4. Djan Madruga Garrido	BRA	3:54.15	
5. Daniel Machek	CZE	3:55.66	
6. Sándor Nagy	HUN	3:56.83	
7. Max Metzker	AUS	3:56.87	
8. Ron McKeon	AUS	3:57.00	

Twenty-year-old Vladimir Salnikov of Leningrad was one of several Soviet swimmers who had been training in the United States when Jimmy Carter made his first speech threatening a boycott of the Moscow Olympics unless Soviet troops pulled out of Afghanistan. However, Soviet coach Sergei Vaitsekhovsky was quick to thank American swimmers and coaches for the subsequent Soviet successes at the Olympics. "The Americans," he explained, "surprised us by not keeping any of their training secrets from us, which means there must still be some decent people left in the world."

Peter Szmidt of Canada set a world record of 3:50.49 in the 400 meters just before the Moscow Games began. At the U.S. Outdoor National on July 31, Mike Bruner finished first in 3:52.19, followed by Brian Goodell in 3:52.99.

1500-METER FREESTYLE

1896 Athens C: 9, N: 4, D: 4.11.
(1200 Meters)

1. Alfréd Hajós	HUN	18:22.2	OR
2. Jean Andreou	GRE	21:03.4	
3. Efstathios Choraphas	GRE	—	
4. Gardner Williams	USA	—	

The competitors had to battle not only each other, but also horribly cold water and 12-foot waves. Alfréd Hajós, the eventual winner, gave the following graphic description of the race:

"Three small boats took us out to the open sea, which was quite rough. My body had been smeared with a half-inch-thick layer of grease, for I was more cunning after the 100 meters event, and tried to protect myself against the cold. We jumped into the water at the start of a pistol, and from that point on the boats left the competitors to the mercy of the waves, rushing back to the finish line, to inform the jury of the successful start.

"I must say that I shivered from the thought of what would happen if I got a cramp from the cold water. My will to live completely overcame my desire to win. I cut through the water with a powerful determination and only became calm when the boats came back in my direction, and began to fish out the numbed competitors who were giving up the struggle. At that time I was already at the mouth of the bay. The roar of the crowd increased . . . I won ahead of the others with a big lead."

1900 Paris C: 16, N: 6, D: 8.12.
(1000 Meters)

1. John Arthur Jarvis	GBR	13:40.2	
2. Otto Wahle	AUT	14:53.6	
3. Zoltán Halmay	HUN	15:16.4	
4. Max Hainle	GER	15:22.6	
5. Louis Martin	FRA	16:34.4	
6. Leuillieux	FRA	16:53.2	

1904 St. Louis C: 7, N: 4, D: 9.6. WR: 24:36.2
(1 Mile — 1609.34 Meters)

1. Emil Rausch	GER	27:18.2
2. Géza Kiss	HUN	28:28.2
3. Francis Gailey	USA	28:54.0
4. Otto Wahle	AUT	—

DNF: Edgar Adams (USA), Louis Handley (USA), John Meyers (USA)

1906 Athens C: 24, N: 10, D: 4.24.
(1 Mile — 1609.34 Meters)

1. Henry Taylor	GBR	28:28.0
2. John Arthur Jarvis	GBR	30:07.6
3. Otto Scheff	AUT	30:53.4
4. Max Pape	GER	32:34.6
5. Emil Rausch	GER	32:40.6
6. Ernst Bahnmeyer	GER	33:29.4
7. Oskar Schiele	GER	33:52.4
8. Leopold Mayer	AUT	34:41.0

1908 London C: 19, N: 8, D: 7.25.

1. Henry Taylor	GBR	22:48.4	WR
2. Thomas Battersby	GBR	22:51.2	
3. Frank Beaurepaire	AUS	22:56.2	

DNF: Otto Scheff (AUT)

Battersby led from the start and wasn't overtaken by Taylor until less than 200 meters remained. Taylor's time was the first internationally acknowledged world record for the 1500-meter freestyle. An English swimmer with the unusually appropriate name of L. Moist was eliminated in the semifinals.

1912 Stockholm C: 19, N: 11, D: 7.10. WR: 22:48.4 (Henry Taylor)

1. George Hodgson	CAN	22:00.0	WR
2. John Hatfield	GBR	22:39.0	
3. Harold Hardwick	AUS	23:15.4	

DNF: Malcolm Champion (NZE), Béla Las-Torres (HUN)

George Hodgson of Montreal is the only Canadian ever to have won an Olympic swimming championship. In the first round he set a world record of 22:23.0. He bettered this time in the final, setting a 1000-meter world record of 14:37.0 on the way. After completing 1500 meters, he continued on to swim the mile, setting three world records in one race. Four days later, he also won the 400-meter race. His 1500-meter record lasted for 11 years.

1920 Antwerp C: 24, N: 13, D: 8.25. WR: 22:00.0 (George Hodgson)

1. Norman Ross	USA	22:23.2
2. George Vernot	CAN	22:36.4
3. Frank Beaurepaire	AUS	23:04.0
4. Fred Kahele	USA	—
5. Eugene Bolden	USA	—
6. Harold Annison	GBR	—

1924 Paris C: 22, N: 12, D: 7.15. WR: 21:15.0 (Arne Borg)

1. Andrew "Boy" Charlton	AUS	20:06.6	WR
2. Arne Borg	SWE	20:41.4	
3. Frank Beaurepaire	AUS	21:48.4	
4. John Hatfield	GBR	21:55.6	
5. Katsuo Takaishi	JAP	22:10.4	
6. Åke Borg (SWE)			

Raised in the slums on the outskirts of Sydney, Boy Charlton was adopted by Tom Adrian, who also became his coach and trainer. At the age of 16, Charlton, along with Adrian, was on his way to the Paris Olympics on a steamer with the rest of the Australian team. Unfortunately, Adrian suffered a nervous breakdown and threw himself overboard. He was fished out safely, but he was never the same again, and there was great apprehension that Charlton's performance would be adversely affected. Instead, the teenager seemed more determined than ever, winning his preliminary heat in 21:20.8. Arne Borg, "The Swedish Sturgeon," came right back in the next heat to break his own world record in a time of 21:11.4. However, in the final, it was Charlton who prevailed, bettering Borg's two-day-old record by over a minute.

1928 Amsterdam C: 19, N: 13, D: 8.6. WR: 19:07.2 (Arne Borg)

1. Arne Borg	SWE	19:51.8	OR
2. Andrew "Boy" Charlton	AUS	20:02.6	
3. Clarence "Buster" Crabbe	USA	20:28.8	
4. Raymond Ruddy	USA	21:05.0	
5. Alberto Zorilla	ARG	21:23.8	
6. Garnet Ault	CAN	21:46.0	

Arne Borg led from start to finish to win his only Olympic gold medal. Borg was an extremely popular athlete in Sweden and abroad. Once he was called up for military service, but ignored the notice in order to take a tour of Spain. Imprisoned upon his return to Sweden, he received so many gifts of food and wine during his incarceration that he gained 17 pounds before he was finally released. Between 1921 and 1929, Borg set 32 world records at distances from 300 yards to one mile. His 1500 meters world record of 19:07.2, set in Bologna on September 2, 1927, remained unbroken for almost 11 years.

1932 Los Angeles C: 15, N: 8, D: 8.13. WR: 19:07.2 (Arne Borg)

1. Kusuo Kitamura	JAP	19:12.4	OR
2. Shozo Makino	JAP	19:14.1	
3. James Cristy	USA	19:39.5	
4. Noel Philip Ryan	AUS	19:45.1	
5. Clarence "Buster" Crabbe	USA	20:02.7	
6. Jean Taris	FRA	20:09.7	

Fourteen-year-old Kusuo Kitamura pulled away from his 17-year-old teammate, Shozo Makino, in the final 300 meters. Kitamura, the youngest male ever to win an Olympic swimming gold medal, grew up to become the Japanese representative to the International Labor Organization.

1936 Berlin C: 21, N: 10, D: 8.15. WR: 19:07.2 (Arne Borg)

1. Noboru Terada	JAP	19:13.7
2. Jack Medica	USA	19:34.0
3. Shumpei Uto	JAP	19:34.5
4. Sunao Ishiharada	JAP	19:48.5
5. Ralph Flanagan	USA	19:54.8
6. Robert Leivers	GBR	19:57.4
7. Heinz Arendt	GER	19:59.0

Terada took the lead at the gun and drew away slowly but steadily to win by 25 meters.

1948 London C: 39, N: 21, D: 8.7. WR: 18:58.8 (Tomikatsu Amano)

1. James McLane	USA	19:18.5
2. John Marshall	AUS	19:31.3
3. György Mitró	HUN	19:43.2
4. György Csordás	HUN	19:54.2
5. Marjan Stipetič	YUG	20:10.7
6. Forbes Norris	USA	20:18.8
7. Donald Bland	GBR	20:19.8
8. William Heusner	USA	20:45.4

1952 Helsinki C: 37, N: 22, D: 8.2. WR: 18:19.0 (Hironashin Furuhashi)

1. Ford Konno	USA	18:30.3	OR
2. Shiro Hashizume	JAP	18:41.4	
3. Tetsuo Okamoto	BRA	18:51.3	
4. James McLane	USA	18:51.5	
5. Joseph Bernardo	FRA	18:59.1	
6. Yasuo Kitamura	JAP	19:00.4	
7. Peter Duncan	SAF	19:12.1	
8. John Marshall	AUS	19:53.4	

Ford Konno of Hawaii caught up with Hashizume after 1200 meters and pulled away to a decisive victory, covering the last 100 meters in 1:11.7.

1956 Melbourne C: 20, N: 11, D: 12.7. WR: 17:59.5 (Murray Rose)

1. Murray Rose	AUS	17:58.9
2. Tsuyoshi Yamanaka	JAP	18:00.3
3. George Breen	USA	18:08.2
4. Murray Garretty	AUS	18:26.5
5. William Slater	CAN	18:38.1
6. Jean Boiteux	FRA	18:38.3
7. Yukiyoshi Aoki	JAP	18:38.3
8. Garry Winram	AUS	19:06.2

George Breen set a world record of 17:52.9 in the third heat of the qualifying round. After 800 meters in the final, he, Rose, and Yamanaka were neck and neck. Then Rose began to surge ahead. He had built up a six-meter lead with only 100 meters to go, when Yamanaka began to sprint. He drew to within a yard of Rose, while the Australian crowd screamed at their young hero until he was finally alerted to the danger behind him. One last push earned Rose his third gold medal.

1960 Rome C: 30, N: 19, D: 9.3. WR: 17:11.0 (John Konrads)

1. John Konrads	AUS	17:19.6	OR
2. Murray Rose	AUS	17:21.7	
3. George Breen	USA	17:30.6	
4. Tsuyoshi Yamanaka	JAP	17:34.7	
5. József Katona	HUN	17:43.7	
6. Murray McLachlan	SAF	17:44.9	
7. Alan Somers	USA	18:02.8	
8. Richard Campion	GBR	18:22.7	

Latvian-born John Konrads, a survivor of childhood polio, swam stroke for stroke with George Breen for 1050 meters before drawing away.

1964 Tokyo C: 31, N: 21, D: 10.17. WR: 16:58.7 (Roy Saari)

1. Robert Windle	AUS	17:01.7	OR
2. John Nelson	USA	17:03.0	
3. Allan Wood	AUS	17:07.7	
4. William Farley	USA	17:18.2	
5. Russell Phegan	AUS	17:22.4	
6. Sueaki Sasaki	JAP	17:25.3	
7. Roy Saari	USA	17:29.2	
8. József Katona	HUN	17:30.8	

Noticeably absent was Murray Rose, who had been refused a place on the Australian team because he wouldn't return home for the Australian National Championships in February, unaware that they also served as Olympic tryouts. Rose presented his own version of a tryout on August 2, when he set a world record of 17:01.8. This embarrassed the officials of the Australian Swimming Union, but they refused to make an exception to the rules they had laid down.

1968 Mexico City C: 21, N: 16, D: 10.26. WR: 16:08.5 (Michael Burton)

1. Michael Burton	USA	16:38.9	OR
2. John Kinsella	USA	16:57.3	
3. Gregory Brough	AUS	17:04.7	
4. Graham White	AUS	17:08.0	
5. Ralph Hutton	CAN	17:15.6	
6. Guillermo Echevarria	MEX	17:36.4	
7. Juan Alanis	MEX	17:46.6	
8. John Nelson	USA	18:05.1	

1972 Munich C: 42, N: 30, D: 9.4. WR: 15:52.91 (Rick DeMont)

1. Michael Burton	USA	15:52.58	WR
2. Graham Windeatt	AUS	15:58.48	
3. Douglas Northway	USA	16:09.25	
4. Bengt Gingsjö	SWE	16:16.01	
5. Graham White	AUS	16:17.22	
6. Mark Treffers	NZE	16:18.84	
7. Bradford Cooper	AUS	16:30.49	
8. Guillermo Garcia	MEX	16:36.03	

Burton led for the first 600 meters, then Windeatt took over. By the 1200-meter mark, Burton was back in the lead for good, and dipped just below Rick DeMont's world record to win the third gold medal of his career.

1976 Montreal C: 31, N: 20, D: 7.20. WR: 15:06.66 (Brian Goodell)

1. Brian Goodell	USA	15:02.40	WR
2. Bobby Hackett	USA	15:03.91	
3. Stephen Holland	AUS	15:04.66	
4. Djan Madruga Garrido	BRA	15:19.84	
5. Vladimir Salnikov	SOV	15:29.45	
6. Max Metzker	AUS	15:31.53	
7. Paul Hartloff	USA	15:32.08	
8. Zoltán Wladár	HUN	15:45.97	

The 1976 1500 meters final quickly resolved into a three-man race, with all three medalists ultimately breaking the world record. Bobby Hackett of Yonkers, New York, took the early lead and held it for 950 meters, at which point he was passed by Steve Holland. Holland was still in front after 1300 meters, but then Brian Goodell of Mission Viejo, California, stormed past both Hackett and Holland, taking the lead 150 meters from the finish and pulling away with a time of 57.73 seconds over the last 100 meters.

1980 Moscow C: 18, N: 11, D: 7.22. WR: 15:02.40 (Brian Goodell)

1. Vladimir Salnikov	SOV	14:58.27	WR
2. Aleksandr Chaev	SOV	15:14.30	
3. Max Metzker	AUS	15:14.49	
4. Rainer Strohbach	GDR	15:15.29	
5. Borut Petric	YUG	15:21.78	
6. Rafael Escalas	SPA	15:21.88	
7. Zoltán Wladár	HUN	15:26.70	
8. Eduard Petrov	SOV	15:28.24	

Vladimir Salnikov won three gold medals at the 1980 Olympics, but the big one was in the 1500 meters. In the final, on July 22, Salnikov became the first swimmer to break the 15-minute barrier, a feat that had been eagerly anticipated since Brian Goodell came within two and a half seconds at the previous Olympics.

100-METER BACKSTROKE

1896–1900 not held

1904 St. Louis C; 6, N: 2, D: 9.6.
(100 Yards)

1. Walter Brack	GER	1:16.8
2. Georg Hoffmann	GER	—
3. Georg Zacharias	GER	—
4. Charles Daniels	USA	—

AC: David Hammond (USA), Edwin Swatek (USA)

1906 not held

1908 London C: 21, N: 11, D: 7.17. WR: 1:25.0

1. Arno Bieberstein	GER	1:24.6	WR
2. Ludvig Dam	DEN	1:26.6	
3. Herbert Haresnape	GBR	1:27.0	
4. Gustav Aurisch	GER	—	

1912 Stockholm C: 18, N: 7, D: 7.14. WR: 1:15.6 (Otto Fahr)

1. Harry Hebner	USA	1:21.2
2. Otto Fahr	GER	1:22.4
3. Paul Kellner	GER	1:24.0
4. András Baronyi	HUN	1:25.2
5. Otto Gross	GER	1:25.8

Hebner set an Olympic record of 1:20.8 in the semifinals.

1920 Antwerp C: 12, N: 6, D: 8.23. WR: 1:15.6 (Otto Fahr)

1. Warren Paoa Kealoha	USA	1:15.2
2. Ray Kegeris	USA	1:16.2
3. Gérard Blitz	BEL	1:19.0
4. Percy McGillivray	USA	1:19.4
5. Harold Kruger	USA	—
6. Gaspard Lemaire	BEL	—

Seventeen-year-old Warren Kealoha set a world record of 1:14.8 in the preliminary round.

1924 Paris C: 20, N: 11, D: 7.8. WR: 1:12.4 (Warren Kealoha)

1. Warren Paoa Kealoha	USA	1:13.2	OR
2. Paul Wyatt	USA	1:15.4	
3. Károly Bartha	HUN	1:17.8	
4. Gérard Blitz	BEL	1:19.6	
5. Austin Rawlinson	GBR	1:20.0	
6. Giyo Saito (JAP)			

1928 Amsterdam C: 19, N: 12, D: 8.9. WR: 1:09.0 (George Kojac)

1. George Kojac	USA	1:08.2	WR
2. Walter Laufer	USA	1:10.0	
3. Paul Wyatt	USA	1:12.0	
4. Toshio Irie	JAP	1:13.6	
5. Ernst Küppers	GER	1:13.8	
6. John Besford	GBR	1:15.4	

1932 Los Angeles C: 16, N: 9, D: 8.12. WR: 1:08.2 (George Kojac)

1. Masaji Kiyokawa	JAP	1:08.6
2. Toshio Irie	JAP	1:09.8
3. Kentaro Kawatsu	JAP	1:10.0
4. Robert Zehr	USA	1:10.9
5. Ernst Küppers	GER	1:11.3
6. Robert Kerber	USA	1:12.8

1936 Berlin C: 30, N: 17, D: 8.14. WR: 1:04.8 (Adolf Kiefer)

1. Adolf Kiefer	USA	1:05.9	OR
2. Albert Vandeweghe	USA	1:07.7	
3. Masaji Kiyokawa	JAP	1:08.4	
4. Taylor Drysdale	USA	1:09.4	
5. Kiichi Yoshida	JAP	1:09.7	
6. Yasuhiko Kojima	JAP	1:10.4	
7. Percival Oliver	AUS	1:10.7	

1948 London C: 39, N: 24, D: 8.6. WR: 1:04.0 (Allen Stack)
1. Allen Stack   USA   1:06.4
2. Robert Cowell   USA   1:06.5
3. Georges Vallerey   FRA   1:07.8
4. Mario Chaves   ARG   1:09.0
5. Clemente Mejia Avila MEX 1:09.0
6. Johannes Wiid   SAF   1:09.1
7. John Brockway   GBR   1:09.2
8. Albert Kinnear   GBR   1:09.6

1952 Helsinki C: 38, N: 25, D: 8.1. WR: 1:03.6 (Allen Stack)
1. Yoshinobu Oyakawa USA   1:05.4 OR
2. Gilbert Bozon   FRA   1:06.2
3. Jack Taylor   USA   1:06.4
4. Allen Stack   USA   1:07.6
5. Pedro Galvao   ARG   1:07.7
6. Robert Wardrop   GBR   1:07.8
7. Boris Škanata   YUG   1:08.1
8. Nicolaas Meiring   SAF   1:08.3

1956 Melbourne C: 25, N: 14, D: 12.6. WR: 1:02.1 (Gilbert Bozon)
1. David Theile   AUS   1:02.2 OR
2. John Monckton   AUS   1:03.2
3. Frank McKinney   USA   1:04.5
4. Robert Christophe FRA   1:04.9
5. John Hayres   AUS   1:05.0
6. Graham Sykes   GBR   1:05.6
7. Albert Wiggins   USA   1:05.8
8. Yoshinobu Oyakawa USA   1:06.9

1960 Rome C: 37, N: 27, D: 8.31. WR(440 yards): 1:01.5 (John Monckton)
1. David Theile   AUS   1:01.9 OR
2. Frank McKinney   USA   1:02.1
3. Robert Bennett   USA   1:02.3
4. Robert Christophe FRA   1:03.2
5. Leonid Barbier   SOV   1:03.5
6. Wolfgang Wagner   GDR   1:03.5
7. John Monckton   AUS   1:04.1
8. Veiko Siymar   SOV   1:04.6

Between the 1956 and 1960 Olympics, David Theile of Brisbane had virtually retired from swimming so that he could concentrate on his medical studies. Yet he was able to come back better than ever to defend his championship.

1964 not held

1968 Mexico City C: 37, N: 26, D: 10.22. WR: 58.4 (Roland Matthes)
1. Roland Matthes   GDR   58.7   OR
2. Charles Hickcox   USA   1:00.2
3. Ronald Mills   USA   1:00.5
4. Larry Barbiere   USA   1:01.1
5. James Shaw   CAN   1:01.4
6. Bob Schoutsen   HOL   1:01.8
7. Reinhard Blechert GER   1:01.9
8. Franco Del Campo   ITA   1:02.0

Roland Matthes of Erfurt, Thuringia, was 16 years old when he set his first backstroke world record on September 11, 1967. In the next six years he would break records in the 100-meter and 200-meter backstroke 16 times. He also won four Olympic gold medals, two silver, and two bronze. In 1978 Matthes married Olympic champion Kornelia Ender. Their first child, Francesca, was born later that year, the product of parents who, between them, had earned eight gold medals, six silver medals, and two bronze.

1972 Munich C: 39, N: 27, D: 8.29. WR: 56.3 (Roland Matthes)
1. Roland Matthes   GDR   56.58 OR
2. Michael Stamm   USA   57.70
3. John Murphy   USA   58.35
4. Mitchell Ivey   USA   58.48
5. Igor Grivennikov   SOV   59.50
6. Lutz Wanja   GDR   59.80
7. Jürgen Krüger   GDR   59.93
8. Tadashi Honda   JAP   1:00.41

1976 Montreal C: 41, N: 29, D: 7.19. WR: 56.30 (Roland Matthes)
1. John Naber   USA   55.49 WR
2. Peter Rocca   USA   56.34
3. Roland Matthes   GDR   57.22
4. Carlos Berrocal   PUR   57.28
5. Lutz Wanja   GDR   57.49
6. Bob Jackson   USA   57.69
7. Mark Kerry   AUS   57.94
8. Mark Tonelli   AUS   58.42

When John Naber was 9 years old he visited Olympia, in Greece, and told his parents that someday he would become an Olympic champion. Eleven years later, now 6 feet 6 inches tall and 195 pounds, Naber fulfilled his vow. In 1974 he had ended Roland Matthes' seven-year winning streak. Matthes was still the holder of the world record, but an appendectomy six weeks before the 1976 Olympics hurt his chances for defending his title. Naber set a world record of 56.19 in the semifinals and then set another one 24 hours later to win the first of his four gold medals.

1980 Moscow C: 33, N: 23, D: 7.21. WR: 55.49 (John Naber)
1. Bengt Baron   SWE   56.33
2. Viktor Kuznetsov   SOV   56.99
3. Vladimir Dolgov   SOV   57.63
4. Miloslav Rolko   CZE   57.74
5. Sándor Wladár   HUN   57.84
6. Fred Eefting   HOL   57.95
7. Mark Tonelli   AUS   57.98
8. Gary Abraham   GBR   58.38

The victory of 18-year-old Bengt Baron of Finspang, Sweden, was so unexpected that even he was stunned. "I just can't understand how I did it," he told reporters afterward. His pre-Olympic best had been 57.77. Ten days later, the U.S. Outdoor National championship was won by Peter Rocca in a time of 56.64, with Bob Jackson second in 56.78.

200-METER BACKSTROKE

1896 not held

1900 Paris C: 36, N: 5, D: 8.12.
1. Ernst Hoppenberg	GER	2:47.0
2. Karl Ruberl	AUT	2:56.0
3. Johannes Drost	HOL	3:01.0
4. Johannes Bloemen	HOL	3:02.2
5. Thomas Burgess	FRA	3:12.6
6. de Romand	FRA	3:38.0

1904–1960 not held

1964 Tokyo C: 34, N: 21, D: 10.13. WR: 2:10.9 (Thomas Stock)
1. Jed Graef	USA	2:10.3	WR
2. Gary Dilley	USA	2:10.5	
3. Robert Bennett	USA	2:13.1	
4. Shigeo Fukushima	JAP	2:13.2	
5. Ernst-Joachim Küppers	GER	2:15.7	
6. Viktor Mazanov	SOV	2:15.9	
7. Ralph Hutton	CAN	2:15.9	
8. Peter Reynolds	AUS	2:16.6	

1968 Mexico City C: 30, N: 21, D: 10.25. WR: 2:07.5 (Roland Matthes)
1. Roland Matthes	GDR	2:09.6	OR
2. Mitchell Ivey	USA	2:10.6	
3. Jack Horsley	USA	2:10.9	
4. Gary Hall	USA	2:12.6	
5. Santiago Esteva	SPA	2:12.9	
6. Leonid Dobrosskokin	SOV	2:15.4	
7. Joachim Rother	GDR	2:15.8	
8. Franco Del Campo	ITA	2:16.5	

1972 Munich C: 36, N: 25, D: 9.2. WR: 2:02.8 (Roland Matthes)
1. Roland Matthes	GDR	2:02.82	EWR
2. Michael Stamm	USA	2:04.09	
3. Mitchell Ivey	USA	2:04.33	
4. Bradford Cooper	AUS	2:06.59	
5. Alexander "Tim" McKee	USA	2:07.29	
6. Lothar Noack	GDR	2:08.67	
7. Zoltán Verrasztó	HUN	2:10.09	
8. Jean-Paul Berjeaud	FRA	2:11.77	

1976 Montreal C: 33, N: 23, D: 7.24. WR: 2:00.64 (John Naber)
1. John Naber	USA	1:59.19	WR
2. Peter Rocca	USA	2:00.55	
3. Dan Harrigan	USA	2:01.35	
4. Mark Tonelli	AUS	2:03.17	
5. Mark Kerry	AUS	2:04.07	
6. Miloslav Rolko	CZE	2:05.81	
7. Robert Rudolf	HUN	2:07.30	
8. Zoltán Verrasztó	HUN	2:08.23	

With this race, John Naber won his fourth gold medal and became the first backstroker to break the two-minute barrier for 200 meters.

1980 Moscow C: 25, N: 16, D: 7.26. WR: 1:59.19 (John Naber)
1. Sándor Wladár	HUN	2:01.93
2. Zoltán Verrasztó	HUN	2:02.40
3. Mark Kerry	AUS	2:03.14
4. Vladimir Shemetov	SOV	2:03.48
5. Fred Eefting	HOL	2:03.92
6. Michael Söderlund	SWE	2:04.10
7. Douglas Campbell	GBR	2:04.23
8. Paul Moorfoot	AUS	2:06.15

Three days after the Moscow final, Steve Barnicoat won the U.S. Outdoor National in 2:01.06. Second place went to Peter Rocca in 2:01.34.

100-METER BREASTSTROKE

The most rigidly defined of swimming strokes, the breaststroke requires swimmers to follow several rules:

1. All leg and arm movements must be made simultaneously. Alternating movements are not allowed.

2. Both shoulders must be kept in line with the water.

3. The hands must be pushed forward together and from the breast, and must be brought back on or under the surface of the water.

4. Only the backward and out frog-leg kick is allowed.

5. At turns and at the finish, both hands must touch the wall simultaneously.

6. Except for the start and the first stroke and kick after each turn, a part of the head must be kept above the surface of the water.

The breaststroke has always been the most controversial stroke because of ongoing arguments as to what constitutes legal or illegal technique. In the early 1930s some U.S. swimmers discovered a "loophole" in the rules then in force and began bringing their arms back *above* the surface of the water, which saved precious time and energy. In 1952, this new technique, known as the butterfly, was officially recognized as the fourth Olympic swimming style and given its own set of competitions, separate from the breaststroke.

Classical breaststroke enthusiasts, rid at last of the upstart butterfly stroke, were not allowed even a moment to breathe a sigh of relief, thanks to the Japanese, who discovered another loophole—underwater swimming. Swimming *below* the surface of the water turned out to be faster than swimming on the surface, so in 1956 underwater swimming was banned from breaststroke competitions.

1896–1964 not held

1968 Mexico City C: 39, N: 24, D: 10.19. WR: 1:06.2 (Nikolai Pankin)

1. Donald McKenzie	USA	1:07.7	OR
2. Vladimir Kossinsky	SOV	1:08.0	
3. Nikolai Pankin	SOV	1:08.0	
4. José Sylvio Fiolo	BRA	1:08.1	
5. Yevgeny Mikhailov	SOV	1:08.4	
6. Ian O'Brien	AUS	1:08.6	
7. Alberto Forelli	ARG	1:08.7	
8. Egon Henninger	GDR	1:09.7	

1972 Munich C: 44, N: 31, D: 8.30. WR: 1:05.8 (Nikolai Pankin)

1. Nobutaka Taguchi	JAP	1:04.94	WR
2. Thomas Bruce	USA	1:05.43	
3. John Hencken	USA	1:05.61	
4. Mark Chatfield	USA	1:06.61	
5. Walter Kusch	GER	1:06.23	
6. José Sylvio Fiolo	BRA	1:06.24	
7. Nikolai Pankin	SOV	1:06.36	
8. David Wilkie	GBR	1:06.52	

In the first semifinal John Hencken set a world record of 1:05.68. Less than ten minutes later, Nobutaka Taguchi broke that record with a time of 1:05.13 in the second semifinal. The following evening, in the final, Taguchi overtook Tom Bruce in the last 25 meters and set yet another world record.

1976 Montreal C: 32, N: 22, D: 7.20. WR: 1:03.88 (John Hencken)

1. John Hencken	USA	1:03.11	WR
2. David Wilkie	GBR	1:03.43	
3. Arvidas Iuozaytis	SOV	1:04.23	
4. Graham Smith	CAN	1:04.26	
5. Giorgio Lalle	ITA	1:04.37	
6. Walter Kusch	GER	1:04.38	
7. Duncan Goodhew	GBR	1:04.66	
8. Chris Woo	USA	1:05.13	

John Hencken, a 22-year-old graduate of Stanford University with a degree in electrical engineering, equaled his own world record of 1:03.88 in the preliminary round, and broke it with a time of 1:03.62 in the semifinals. Hardpressed by David Wilkie in the final, he set another record of 1:03.11.

1980 Moscow C: 26, N: 20, D: 7.22. WR: 1:02.86 (Gerald Mörken)

1. Duncan Goodhew	GBR	1:03.34
2. Arsen Miskarov	SOV	1:03.82
3. Peter Evans	AUS	1:03.96
4. Aleksandr Fedorovsky	SOV	1:04.00
5. János Dzvonyár	HUN	1:04.67
6. Lindsay Spencer	AUS	1:05.04
7. Pablo Restrepo	COL	1:05.91
DISQ: Abán Vermes (HUN)		

Jeered at by his schoolmates as an adolescent because an accident had left him bald, and also because he was dyslexic, Duncan Goodhew vowed that he would become an Olympic champion. Although his stepfather, a retired air vice-marshal, refused to attend the Games because his government opposed British participation, Goodhew's mother was in the audience to watch her son's dream come true. Despite all the noise in the stadium, Goodhew "seemed to hear her voice above all the others."

At the U.S. Outdoor National a week later, Steve Lundquist clocked 1:02.88 and Bill Barrett 1:02.93. The world record of 1:02.86 had been set by Gerald Mörken of West Germany in 1977.

200-METER BREASTSTROKE
1896–1906 not held

1908 London C: 27, N: 10, D: 7.18.

1. Frederick Holman	GBR	3:09.2	WR
2. William Robinson	GBR	3:12.8	
3. Pontus Hanson	SWE	3:14.6	
4. Ödön Toldi	HUN	3:15.2	

Twenty-five meters from the finish, the 25-year-old Holman overtook Robinson, who was 38 years old.

1912 Stockholm C: 24, N: 11, D: 7.10. WR: 3:00.8 (Felicien Coubert)

1. Walter Bathe	GER	3:01.8	OR
2. Wilhelm Lützow	GER	3:05.0	
3. Kurt Mahlisch	GER	3:08.0	
4. Percy Courtman	GBR	3:08.8	
DNF: Thor Henning (SWE)			

1920 Antwerp C: 24, N: 12, D: 8.29. WR: 2:56.6 (Percy Courtman)

1. Håkan Malmroth	SWE	3:04.4
2. Thor Henning	SWE	3:09.2
3. Arvo Aaltonen	FIN	3:12.2
4. Jack Howell	USA	—
5. Ivan Stedman	AUS	—
DNF: Per Cederblom (SWE)		

1924 Paris C: 28, N: 16, D: 7.17. WR: 2:50.4 (Erich Rademacher)

1. Robert Skelton	USA	2:56.6
2. Joseph de Combe	BEL	2:59.2
3. William Kirschbaum	USA	3:01.0
4. Bengt Linders	SWE	3:02.2
5. Robert Wyss	SWI	3:05.6
6. Thor Henning (SWE)		

Skelton set an Olympic record of 2:56.0 in the opening round.

1928 Amsterdam C: 21, N: 13, D: 8.8. WR: 2:48.0 (Erich Rademacher)

1. Yoshiyuki Tsuruta	JAP	2:48.8	OR
2. Erich Rademacher	GER	2:50.6	
3 Teofilo Yldefonzo	PHI	2:56.4	
4. Erwin Sietas	GER	2:56.6	
5. Eric Harling	SWE	2:56.8	
6. Walter Spence	CAN	2:57.2	

1932 Los Angeles C: 18, N: 11, D: 8.13. WR: 2:44.0 (Leonard Spence)

1. Yoshiyuki Tsuruta   JAP   2:45.4
2. Reizo Koike   JAP   2:46.6
3. Teofilo Yldefonzo   PHI   2:47.1
4. Erwin Sietas   GER   2:48.0
5. Jikirum Adjaluddin   PHI   2:49.2
6. Shigeo Nakagawa   JAP   2:52.8

Koike defeated Tsuruta 2:44.9 to 2:45.4 in the first semifinal. The defending champion repeated his time exactly in the final, but this time it was good enough to win.

1936 Berlin C: 25, N: 11, D: 8.15. WR: 2:37.2 (Jack Kasley)

1. Tetsuo Hamuro   JAP   2:41.5   OR
2. Erwin Sietas   GER   2:42.9
3. Reizo Koike   JAP   2:44.2
4. John Herbert Higgins   USA   2:45.2
5. Saburo Ito   JAP   2:47.6
6. Joachim Balke   GER   2:47.8
7. Teofilo Yldefonzo   PHI   2:51.1

1948 London C: 32, N: 20, D: 8.7. WR: 2:30.0 (Joseph Verdeur)

1. Joseph Verdeur   USA   2:39.3   OR
2. Keith Carter   USA   2:40.2
3. Robert Sohl   USA   2:43.9
4. John Davies   AUS   2:43.7
5. Anton "Tone" Cerer   YUG   2:46.1
6. Willy Otto Jordan   BRA   2:46.4
7. A. Kandil   EGY   2:47.5
8. Bjorn Bonte   HOL   2:47.6

The first seven finishers all used the butterfly stroke. The judges awarded Bob Sohl the bronze medal even though his official time was slower than that of Davies.

1952 Helsinki C: 40, N: 27, D: 8.2. WR: 2:27.3 (Herbert Klein)

1. John Davies   AUS   2:34.4   OR
2. Bowen Stassforth   USA   2:34.7
3. Herbert Klein   GER   2:35.9
4. Nobuyasu Hirayama   JAP   2:37.4
5. Takayoshi Kajikawa   JAP   2:38.6
6. Jiro Nagasawa   JAP   2:39.1
7. Maurice Lusien   FRA   2:39.8
8. Ludevit Komadel   CZE   2:40.1

1956 Melbourne C: 21, N: 17, D: 12.6. WR: 2:31.0 (Masaru Furukawa)

1. Masaru Furukawa   JAP   2:34.7   OR
2. Masahiro Yoshimura   JAP   2:36.7
3. Charis Yunichev   SOV   2:36.8
4. Terry Gathercole   AUS   2:38.7
5. Igor Zasseda   SOV   2:39.0
6. Knud Gleie   DEN   2:40.0
7. Manuel Sanguily   CUB   2:42.0
DISQ: Hughes Broussard (FRA)

For the first time, the butterfly stroke and the breaststroke were separated into two different events. Differences in interpretation of what was a breaststroke and what wasn't led to six disqualifications. The most controversial was the ousting of Herbert Klein of Germany, who won the second heat. He was accused of using a scissors kick and of dipping his right shoulder. Furukawa was one of the least visible Olympic champions, since his unusual technique kept him underwater 75 percent of the time.

1960 Rome C: 42, N: 30, D: 8.30. WR: 2:36.5 (Terry Gathercole)

1. William Mulliken   USA   2:37.4
2. Yoshihiko Osaki   JAP   2:38.0
3. Wieger Mensonides   HOL   2:39.7
4. Egon Henninger   GDR   2:40.1
5. Roberto Lazzari   ITA   2:40.1
6. Terry Gathercole   AUS   2:40.2
7. Andrezj Klopotowski   POL   2:41.2
8. Paul Hait   USA   2:41.4

The slower times in 1960 were a result of the banning of underwater swimming in 1957, five months after Masaru Furukawa's Olympic victory. Bill Mulliken's win was considered a major upset, since his pre-Olympic best had been 2:40.9. In the semifinals he set an Olympic record of 2:37.2.

1964 Tokyo C: 33, N: 20, D: 10.15. WR: 2:28.2 (Chester Jastremski)

1. Ian O'Brien   AUS   2:27.8   WR
2. Georgy Prokopenko   SOV   2:28.2
3. Chester Jastremski   USA   2:29.6
4. Aleksandr Tutakayev   SOV   2:31.0
5. Egon Henninger   GDR   2:31.1
6. Osamu Tsurumine   JAP   2:33.6
7. Wayne Anderson   USA   2:35.0
8. Vladimir Kosinsky   SOV   2:38.1

Seventeen-year-old Ian O'Brien didn't catch Prokopenko until five meters from the finish.

1968 Mexico City C: 36, N: 23, D: 10.22. WR: 2:27.4 (Vladimir Kosinsky)

1. Felipe Muñoz   MEX   2:28.7
2. Vladimir Kossinsky   SOV   2:29.2
3. Brian Job   USA   2:29.9
4. Nikolai Pankin   SOV   2:30.3
5. Yevgeny Mikhailov   SOV   2:32.8
6. Egon Henninger   GDR   2:33.2
7. Philip Long   USA   2:33.6
8. Osamu Tsurumine   JAP   2:3..9

The 1968 Olympics was ten days old and the host country had yet to win a gold medal when 17-year-old Felipe "Pepe" Muñoz stood at the edge of the pool before the start of the final of the 200-meter breaststroke. He was also known as "Tibio" (lukewarm) because his father was from Aguascalientes (hot waters) and his mother from Rio Frio (cold river). Muñoz was not the favorite, that role falling to world record holder Vladimir Kosinsky, but there was hope that the Mexican would gain a medal, and since he *had* registered the fastest time of the heats (2:31.1), maybe, just maybe, a miracle might happen.

At the halfway mark Muñoz was in fourth place behind Kosinsky, Henninger, and Job. But then, in the most dramatic fashion possible, Muñoz began to gain on the leaders. Coming off the final turn, with 50 meters to go, he was only inches behind Kosinsky. The excitement in the stadium reached a fever pitch as 8000 cheering Mexicans voiced the hopes of the hundreds of thousands more who were watching on television. Twenty-five meters from the finish Muñoz caught Kosinsky, and in the last few meters he moved ahead, touching the wall a half-second ahead of the Soviet champion. At that moment absolute bedlam broke out; the scene resembled the Olympic stadium in Athens when Spiridon Louis won the 1896 marathon.

It was a good thing that the electronic timing and judging machines worked properly, because every Mexican official abandoned his post and ran forward to greet the conquering hero. Before he could make a move of his own, Muñoz was hoisted out of the pool and carried, dripping wet and in tears, around the arena. His American coach, Ron Johnson, was thrown into the pool despite the fact that his broken hand was encased in plaster. Mexican television announcers were too overcome to continue their commentary. Foreign journalists had never seen such scenes at a swimming meet, and they stood bewildered as they were hugged and kissed by their hosts and hostesses. All this was repeated at the victory ceremony, during which Muñoz wept uncontrollably at the playing of the Mexican national anthem.

1972 Munich C: 40, N: 27, D: 9.2. WR: 2:22.79 (John Hencken)

1. John Hencken	USA	2:21.55	WR
2. David Wilkie	GBR	2:23.67	
3. Nobutaka Taguchi	JAP	2:23.88	
4. Richard Colella	USA	2:24.28	
5. Felipe Muñoz	MEX	2:26.44	
6. Walter Kusch	GER	2:26.55	
7. Igor Cherdakov	SOV	2:27.15	
8. Klaus Katzur	GDR	2:27.44	

Hencken's superiority was never in doubt, as he led from start to finish.

1976 Montreal C: 26, N: 18, D: 7.24. WR: 2:18.21 (John Hencken)

1. David Wilkie	GBR	2:15.11	WR
2. John Hencken	USA	2:17.26	
3. Richard Colella	USA	2:19.20	
4. Graham Smith	CAN	2:19.42	
5. Charles Keating	USA	2:20.79	
6. Arvidas Iuozaytis	SOV	2:21.87	
7. Nikolai Pankin	SOV	2:22.21	
8. Walter Kusch	GER	2:22.36	

In 1976, 12 of the 13 men's swimming events were won by swimmers from the United States. The only exception was the 200-meter breaststroke. In that race, David Wilkie of Scotland gained the most decisive victory in the event since 1924. He was also the first British male to win an Olympic swimming title in 68 years.

1980 Moscow C: 19, N: 14, D: 7.26. WR: 2:15.11 (David Wilkie)

1. Robertas Zulpa	SOV	2:15.85
2. Abán Vermes	HUN	2:16.93
3. Arsen Miskarov	SOV	2:17.28
4. Gennady Utenkov	SOV	2:19.64
5. Lindsay Spencer	AUS	2:19.68
6. Duncan Goodhew	GBR	2:20.92
7. Peter Berggren	SWE	2:21.65
8. Jörg Walter	GDR	2:22.39

100-METER BUTTERFLY

As in the breaststroke, butterfly swimmers must keep their shoulders in line with the surface of the water, they must move their arms and legs simultaneously, and they must not swim underwater, except for the first stroke after the start and after each turn. Unlike the breaststroke, butterfly rules allow swimmers to bring back their arms over the water and to kick their legs and feet up and down.

1896–1964 not held

1968 Mexico City C: 47, N: 23, D: 10.21. WR: 55.6 (Mark Spitz)

1. Douglas Russell	USA	55.9	OR
2. Mark Spitz	USA	56.4	
3. Ross Wales	USA	57.2	
4. Vladimir Nemshilov	SOV	58.1	
5. Satoshi Maruya	JAP	58.6	
6. Yuri Suzdaltsev	SOV	58.8	
7. Lutz Stoklasa	GER	58.9	
8. Robert Cusack	AUS	59.8	

Mark Spitz and Doug Russell had raced against each other many times in the 100-meter butterfly, and the result was always the same: Russell would take the early lead and then Spitz would finish strongly to win. In Mexico City, though, the two Californians separately and secretly decided to reverse their tactics. This allowed Russell to come from behind and defeat Spitz for the first time.

1972 Munich C: 39, N: 26, D: 8.31. WR: 54.56 (Mark Spitz)

1. Mark Spitz	USA	54.27	WR
2. Bruce Robertson	CAN	55.56	
3. Jerry Heidenreich	USA	55.74	
4. Roland Matthes	GDR	55.87	
5. David Edgar	USA	56.11	
6. Byron MacDonald	CAN	57.27	
7. Hartmut Flöckner	GDR	57.40	
8. Neil Rogers	AUS	57.90	

Spitz won his fourth gold medal of the Munich Games.

1976 Montreal C: 43, N: 29, D: 7.21. WR: 54.27 (Mark Spitz)

1. Matt Vogel	USA	54.35
2. Joe Bottom	USA	54.50
3. Gary Hall	USA	54.65
4. Roger Pyttel	GDR	55.09
5. Roland Matthes	GDR	55.11
6. Clay Evans	CAN	55.81

7. Hideaki Hara	JAP	56.34
8. Neil Rogers	AUS	56.57

For 19-year-old Matt Vogel of Fort Wayne, Indiana, the instant celebrity that comes with being an Olympic champion was an unwanted surprise. He was unprepared for the public speeches, the interviews, the autograph seekers, the loss of anonymity. Vogel tried to go back to school and swimming at the University of Tennessee, but soon dropped out and returned home to Fort Wayne, where he got a job shelving groceries at a supermarket. By 1978 he was back on track again, swimming and pursuing teaching credentials.

1980 Moscow C: 34, N: 29, D: 7.23. WR: 54.15 (Par Arvidsson)

1. Pär Arvidsson	SWE	54.92
2. Roger Pyttel	GDR	54.94
3. David Lopez	SPA	55.13
4. Kees Vervoorn	HOL	55.25
5. Yevgeny Seredin	SOV	55.35
6. Gary Abraham	GBR	55.42
7. Xavier Savin	FRA	55.66
8. Alexei Markovsky	SOV	55.70

On August 2, William Paulus won the U.S. Outdoor National championship in 54.34. Second was Matt Gribble in 54.51.

200-METER BUTTERFLY

1896–1952 not held

1956 Melbourne C: 19, N: 14, D: 12.1. WR: 2:16.7 (William Yorzyk)

1. William Yorzyk	USA	2:19.3 OOR
2. Takashi Ishimoto	JAP	2:23.8
3. György Tumpek	HUN	2:23.9
4. Jack Nelson	USA	2:26.6
5. John Marshall	AUS	2:27.2
6. Eulalio Rios Aleman	MEX	2:27.3
7. Brian Wilkinson	AUS	2:29.7
8. Alexandru Popescu	ROM	2:31.0

1960 Rome C: 34, N: 23, D: 9.2. WR: 2:13.2 (Michael Troy)

1. Michael Troy	USA	2:12.8	WR
2. Neville Hayes	AUS	2:14.6	
3. J. David Gillanders	USA	2:15.3	
4. Federico Dennerlein	ITA	2:16.0	
5. Haruo Yoshimuta	JAP	2:18.3	
6. Kevin Berry	AUS	2:18.5	
7. Valentin Kuzmin	SOV	2:18.9	
8. Kenzo Izutsu	JAP	2:19.4	

1964 Tokyo C: 32, N: 19, D: 10.18. WR: 2:06.9 (Kevin Berry)

1. Kevin Berry	AUS	2:06.6	WR
2. Carl Robie	USA	2:07.5	
3. Fred Schmidt	USA	2:09.3	
4. Philip Riker	USA	2:11.0	
5. Valentin Kuzmin	SOV	2:11.3	

6. Yoshinori Kadonaga	JAP	2:12.6
7. Brett Hill	AUS	2:12.8
8. Daniel Sherry	CAN	2:14.6

1968 Mexico City C: 29, N: 18, D: 10.24. WR: 2:05.7 (Mark Spitz)

1. Carl Robie	USA	2:08.7
2. Martin Woodroffe	GBR	2:09.0
3. John Ferris	USA	2:09.3
4. Valentin Kuzmin	SOV	2:10.6
5. Peter Feil	SWE	2:10.9
6. Folkert Meeuw	GER	2:11.5
7. Victor Sharygin	SOV	2:11.9
8. Mark Spitz	USA	2:13.5

Having won five gold medals at the 1967 Pan-American Games, Mark Spitz brashly predicted that he would win six golds at the 1968 Olympics in Mexico City. Instead, he fell far short of his expectations. He did gain two gold medals, but they were in relays rather than individual events. After finishing third in the 100-meter freestyle, he placed second in his specialty, the 100-meter butterfly, thus losing his place on the medley relay team to the winner, Doug Russell. Spitz's last appearance of the 1968 Olympics was in the 200-meter butterfly, in which he was the world record holder. Along with John Ferris, Spitz managed to lead the qualifiers in 2:10.6. But in the final it was clear that his confidence had been shattered. Exhausted by a long week of races, he was never in contention and finished far back in last place.

Carl Robie, on the other hand, was in tip-top shape. Four years earlier he had been the favorite, but was upset by Kevin Berry. In Mexico City, with the attention on Spitz, Robie was able to relax and hold off a late challenge from Martin Woodroffe to gain the victory.

1972 Munich C: 29, N: 20, D: 8.28. WR: 2:01.53 (Mark Spitz)

1. Mark Spitz	USA	2:00.70	WR
2. Gary Hall	USA	2:02.86	
3. Robin Backhaus	USA	2:03.23	
4. Jorgé Delgado	ECU	2:04.60	
5. Hans Fassnacht	GER	2:04.69	
6. András Hargitay	HUN	2:04.69	
7. Hartmut Flöckner	GDR	2:05.34	
8. Folkert Meeuw	GER	2:05.57	

It seemed only fitting that Mark Spitz's first race of the 1972 Olympics should be the same one as his last race at the 1968 Games—the 200-meter butterfly. Here was a chance for Spitz to redeem himself immdediately for his disappointing performances four years earlier. Not surprisingly Spitz was more than a bit nervous as he stood on the starting block before the final, but once he was in the water his victory was never in doubt. Afterward he leaped out of the water with his arms held high. The four-year psychological burden had been lifted, and Mark Spitz was on his way to becoming the first person in history to win seven gold medals in one Olympics.

1976 Montreal C: 38, N: 25, D: 7.18. WR: 1:59.63 (Roger Pyttel)

1. Mike Bruner	USA	1:59.23	WR
2. Steven Gregg	USA	1:59.54	
3. Bill Forrester	USA	1:59.96	
4. Roger Pyttel	GDR	2:00.02	
5. Michael Kraus	GER	2:00.46	
6. Brian Brinkley	GBR	2:01.49	
7. Jorgé Delgado	ECU	2:01.95	
8. Aleksandr Manachinsky	SOV	2:04.61	

1980 Moscow C: 25, N: 19, D: 7.20. WR: 1:59.23 (Mike Bruner)

1. Sergei Fesenko	SOV	1:59.76
2. Philip Hubble	GBR	2:01.20
3. Roger Pyttel	GDR	2:01.39
4. Peter Morris	GBR	2:02.27
5. Mikhail Gorelik	SOV	2:02.44
6. Kees Vervoorn	HOL	2:02.52
7. Pär Arvidsson	SWE	2:02.61
8. Stephen Poulter	GBR	2:02.93

This was one event in which the boycotting Americans were sorely missed. In 1972 and 1976 U.S. swimmers had swept all three medals, and they probably would have done it again in 1980. At the U.S. Outdoor National on July 30, Craig Beardsley of Harrington, New Jersey, set a world record of 1:58.21 in his qualifying heat. He won the final in 1:58.46, followed by Mike Bruner in 1:59.13 and Bill Forrester in 1:59.40. Eighth-place finisher Steve Gregg clocked 2:00.98—faster than the silver medal winner in Moscow ten days earlier.

200-METER INDIVIDUAL MEDLEY

In individual medley races the order of strokes is butterfly, backstroke, breaststroke, and freestyle.

1896–1964 not held

1968 Mexico City C: 46, N: 27, D: 10.20. WR: 2:10.6 (Charles Hickcox)

1. Charles Hickcox	USA	2:12.0	OR
2. Gregory Buckingham	USA	2:13.0	
3. John Ferris	USA	2:13.3	
4. Juan Bello	PER	2:13.7	
5. George Smith	CAN	2:15.9	
6. John Gilchrist	CAN	2:16.6	
7. Michael Holthaus	GER	2:16.8	
8. Péter Lázár	HUN	2:18.3	

Hickcox won the first of his three gold medals.

1972 Munich C: 39, N: 26, D: 9.3. WR: 2:09.3 (Gunnar Larsson, Gary Hall)

1. Gunnar Larsson	SWE	2:07.17	WR
2. Alexander "Tim" McKee	USA	2:08.37	
3. Steven Furniss	USA	2:08.45	
4. Gary Hall	USA	2:08.49	

5. András Hargitay	HUN	2:09.66
6. Mikhail Suharev	SOV	2:11.78
7. Juan Bello	PER	2:11.87
8. Hans Ljungberg	SWE	2:13.56

Larsson and McKee duplicated their one-two finish in the 400-meter individual medley, as the first four finishers all broke the world record.

1976–1980 not held

This event will be reinstated at the 1984 Olympics.

400-METER INDIVIDUAL MEDLEY

1896–1960 not held

1964 Tokyo C: 30, N; 18, D: 10.14. WR: 4:48.6 (Richard Roth)

1. Richard Roth	USA	4:45.4	WR
2. Roy Saari	USA	4:47.1	
3. Gerhard Hetz	GER	4:51.0	
4. Carl Robie	USA	4:51.4	
5. John Gilchrist	CAN	4:57.6	
6. Johannes Jiskoot	HOL	5:01.9	
7. György Kosztolánczy	HUN	5:01.9	
8. Terry Buck	AUS	5:03.0	

Three days before the competition, world record holder Dick Roth was stricken with an acute attack of appendicitis. Japanese doctors recommended an immediate operation, but Roth refused. Since he also refused to take drugs, they packed him in ice instead. Willing the pain to subside temporarily, the 17-year-old Californian took the lead 70 meters from the finish and won the final in world record time.

1968 Mexico City C: 35, N: 22, D: 10.23. WR: 4:39.0 (Charles Hickcox)

1. Charles Hickcox	USA	4:48.4
2. Gary Hall	USA	4:48.7
3. Michael Holthaus	GER	4:51.4
4. Gregory Buckingham	USA	4:51.4
5. John Gilchrist	CAN	4:56.7
6. Reinhard Merkel	GER	4:59.8
7. Andrei Dunaev	SOV	5:00.3
8. Rafael Hernandez	MEX	5:04.3

Hickcox and Hall swam side by side, almost neck and neck for the entire race.

1972 Munich C: 32, N: 24, D: 8.30. WR: 4:30.81 (Gary Hall)

1. Gunnar Larsson	SWE	4:31.98	OR
2. Alexander "Tim" McKee	USA	4:31.98	OR
3. András Hargitay	HUN	4:32.70	
4. Steven Furniss	USA	4:35.44	
5. Gary Hall	USA	4:37.38	
6. Bengt Gingsjö	SWE	4:37.96	
7. Graham Windeatt	AUS	4:40.39	
8. Wolfram Sperling	GDR	4:40.66	

Both Larsson and McKee were credited with the Olympic record, but Larsson was declared the winner by two one-thousandths of a second, 4:31.981 to 4:31.983. Bronze medalist András Hargitay had almost drowned in the Danube River at the age of nine. "After that," he recalled, "my mother ordered me to learn how to swim, and this is what's come of it."

1976 Montreal C: 31, N: 22, D: 7.25. WR: 4:26.00 (Zóltan Verrasztó)

1. Rod Strachan	USA	4:23.68	WR
2. Alexander "Tim" McKee	USA	4:24.62	
3. Andrei Smirnov	SOV	4:26.90	
4. András Hargitay	HUN	4:27.13	
5. Graham Smith	CAN	4:28.64	
6. Steven Furniss	USA	4:29.23	
7. Andrew Ritchie	CAN	4:29.87	
8. Hans-Joachim Geisler	GER	4:34.95	

1980 Moscow C: 23, N: 17, D: 7.27. WR: 4:20.05 (Jesse Vassallo)

1. Aleksandr Sidorenko	SOV	4:22.89	OR
2. Sergei Fesenko	SOV	4:23.43	
3. Zoltán Verrasztó	HUN	4:24.24	
4. András Hargitay	HUN	4:24.48	
5. Djan Madruga Garrido	BRA	4:26.81	
6. Miloslav Rolko	CZE	4:26.99	
7. Leszek Górski	POL	4:28.89	
8. Daniel Machek	CZE	4:29.86	

Three days after the Olympic final, the U.S. Outdoor National was won by world record holder Jesse Vassallo in 4:21.51.

4×100-METER FREESTYLE RELAY
1896–1960 not held

1964 Tokyo T: 13, N: 13, D: 10.14. WR: 3:36.1 (USA—Clark, McDonough, Ilman, Townsend)

1. USA	(Stephen Clark, Michael Austin, Gary Ilman, Donald Schollander)	3:33.2	WR
2. GER/GDR	(Horst Loffler, Frank Wiegand, Uwe Jacobsen, Hans-Joachim Klein)	3:37.2	
3. AUS	(David Dickson, Peter Doak, John Ryan, Robert Windle)	3:39.1	
4. JAP	(Kunihiro Iwasaki, Tadaharu Goto, Tatsuo Fujimoto, Yukiaki Okabe)	3:40.5	
5. SWE	(Bengt-Olof Nordvall, E. Lester Eriksson, Jan Lundin, Per-Ola Lindberg)	3:40.7	
6. SOV	(Viktor Mazanov, Vladimir Schuvalov, Viktor Semchenkov, Yuri Sumtsov)	3:42.1	
7. GBR	(Robert Lord, John Martin Dye, Peter Kenfrew, Robert McGregor)	3:42.6	

DISQ: FRA (Alain Gottvalles, Gerard Gropaiz, Pierre Canavese, Jean Curtillet)

Steve Clark had failed to qualify for the U.S. team in any individual events, but he made up for it by winning three gold medals in the relays. His lead-off leg in the 4 × 100-meter freestyle relay equaled Alain Gottvalles' 100-meter world record of 52.9 seconds and also earned him the right to swim the freestyle leg of the medley relay.

1968 Mexico City T: 16, N: 16, D: 10.17. WR: 3:32.5 (USA—Zorn, Rerych, Walsh, Schollander)

1. USA	(Zachary Zorn, Stephen Rerych, Mark Spitz, Kenneth Walsh)	3:31.7	WR
2. SOV	(Semyon Belits-Geiman, Viktor Mazanov, Georgy Kulikov, Leonid Ilyichev)	3:34.2	
3. AUS	(Gregory/Rogers, Robert Windle, Robert Cusack, Michael Wenden)	3:34.7	
4. GBR	(Mike Turner, David Hembrow, Robert McGregor, Anthony Jarvis)	3:38.4	
5. GDR	(Frank Wiegand, Udo Poser, Horst-Günther Gregor, Lothar Gericke)	3:38.8	
6. GER	(Wolfgang Kremer, Olaf von Schilling, Peter Schorning, Hans Fassnacht)	3:39.0	
7. CAN	(Glen Finch, George Smith, Ralph Hutton, John Gilchrist)	3:39.2	
8. JAP	(Kunihiro Iwasaki, Masayuki Ohsawa, Satoru Nakano, Teruhiko Kitani)	3:41.5	

1972 Munich T: 13, N: 13, D: 8.28. WR: 3:28.8 (USA, Los Angeles Swim Club—Havens, Weston, Frawley, Heckll

1. USA	(David Edgar, John Murphy, Jerry Heidenreich, Mark Spitz)	3:26.42
2. SOV	(Vladimir Bure, Viktor Mazanov, Viktor Aboimov, Igor Grivennikov)	3:29.72
3. GDR	(Roland Matthes, Wilfried Hartung, Peter Bruch, Lutz Unger)	3:32.42
4. BRA	(Ruy Aquino Oliveira, Paulo Zanetti, Paulo Becskehazy, José Diaz-Aranha)	3:33.14
5. CAN	(Bruce Robertson, Brian Phillips, Timothy Bach, Robert Kasting)	3:33.20
6. GER	(Klaus Steinbach, Werner Lampe, Rainer Jacob, Hans Fassnacht)	3:33.90
7. FRA	(Gilles Vigne, Alain Mosconi, Alain Hermitte, Michel Rousseau)	3:34.13
8. SPA	(Jorge Comas, Antonio Culebras, Enrique Melo, José Pujol)	3:38.21

The U.S. "reserve" team of Dave Fairbank, Gary Conelly, Jerry Heidenreich, and Dave Edgar clocked 3:28.84 in the qualifying round to equal the world record. Six hours later, in the final, Fairbank and Conelly were replaced by John Murphy and Mark Spitz, and a new world record was set. It was Spitz's second gold medal of the evening.

1976–1980 not held

This event will be reinstated at the 1984 Olympics.

4×200-METER FREESTYLE RELAY

1896–1904 not held

1906 Athens T: 6, N: 6, D: 4.26.
(4×250 Meters)

1. HUN (József Ónody, Henrik Hajós, Geza Kiss, Zoltán   16:52.4
   Halmay)
2. GER (Ernst Bahnmeyer, Oskar Schiele, Emil Rausch,   17:16.2
   Max Pape)
3. GBR (William Henry, John Derbyshire, Henry Taylor,   —
   John Arthur Jarvis)
4. USA (Frank Bornamann, J.W. Spencer, Maquard   —
   Schwartz, Charles Daniels)
5. SWE (Harald Julin, Robert Andersson, Charles Nore-   —
   lius, Hjalmar Johansson)
DNF: AUT (Edmund Bernhardt, Leopold Mayer, Simon Orlik, Otto
   Scheff)

Forty-seven-year-old William Henry of the British team is
the oldest person ever to have won a swimming medal.

1908 London T: 6, N: 6, D: 7.24.

1. GBR (John Derbyshire, Paul Radmilovic,   10:55.6   WR
   William Foster, Henry Taylor)
2. HUN (József Munk, Imre Zachár, Béla   10:59.0
   Las-Torres, Zoltán Halmay)
3. USA (Harry Hebner, Leo Goodwin,   11:02.8
   Charles Daniels, Leslie Rich)
4. AUS/NZE (Frank Beaurepaire, F.W. Spring-   —
   field, R. L. Baker, Theodore Tarta-
   kover)

The Hungarians seemed to have the race well in hand,
when Halmay suddenly began to lose consciousness during
the last 50 meters. He struggled to the finish line, but had
to be hauled from the pool before he drowned.

1912 Stockholm T: 5, N: 5, D: 7.15.

1. AUS/NZE (Cecil Healy, Malcolm Champion,   10:11.6   WR
   Leslie Boardman, Harold Hardwick)
2. USA (Kenneth Huszagh, Harry Hebner,   10:20.0
   Perry McGillivray, Duke Paoa Kahanamoku)
3. GBR (William Foster, Thomas Battersby,   10:28.2
   John Hatfield, Henry Taylor)
4. GER (Oskar Schiele, George Kunisch,   10:37.0
   Curt Bretting, Max Ritter)

1920 Antwerp T: 7, N: 7, D: 8.29.

1. USA (Perry McGillivray, Pua Kela Kealoha,   10:04.4   WR
   Norman Ross, Duke Paoa Kahanamoku)
2. AUS (Henry Hay, William Herald, Ivan Sted-   10:25.4
   man, Frank Beaurepaire)
3. GBR (Leslie Savage, E. Percy Peter, Henry   10:37.2
   Taylor, Harold Annison)
4. SWE (Robert Andersson, Frans Moller, Orvar   —
   Trolle, Arne Borg)
5. ITA (Mario Massa, Agostino Frassinetti, Anto-   —
   nio Quarantotto, Gilio Bisagno)

1924 Paris T: 13, N: 13, D: 7.20.

1. USA (Wallace O'Connor, Harry Glancy, Ralph   9:53.4   WR
   Breyer, Johnny Weissmuller)
2. AUS (Maurice Christie, Ernest Henry, Frank   10:02.2
   Beaurepaire, Andrew "Boy" Charlton)
3. SWE (Georg Werner, Orvar Trolle, Åke Borg,   10:06.8
   Arne Borg)
4. JAP (Torahiko Miyahata, Katsuo Takaishi, Ka-   10:15.2
   zuo Noda, Kazuo Onoda)
5. GBR (J. Thomson, Albert Dicken, Harold Anni-   10:29.4
   son, E. Percy Peter)
6. FRA (Guy Middleton, Henri Padou, Edouard   —
   Vanzeveren, Emile Zeibig)

1928 Amsterdam T: 13, N: 13, D: 8.11.

1. USA (Austin Clapp, Walter Laufer, George Ko-   9:36.2   WR
   jac, Johnny Weissmuller)
2. JAP (Hiroshi Yoneyama, Nobuo Arai, Tokuhei   9:41.4
   Sada, Katsuo Takaishi)
3. CAN (F. Munro Bourne, James Thompson,   9:47.8
   Garnet Ault, Walter Spence)
4. HUN (András Wanié, Rezsö Wanié, Géza Szia-   9:57.0
   gritz-Tarródy, István Bárány)
5. SWE (Aulo Gustafsson, Sven Pettersson, Eskil   10:01.8
   Lundahl, Arne Borg)
6. GBR (Reginald Sutton, Joseph Whiteside, E.   10:15.8
   Percy Peter, Albert Dicken)
7. SPA (J. Gonzalez Espuglas, E. Artal Garriga,   —
   R. Artigas Rigual, F. Segala Torres)

Johnny Weissmuller completed his Olympic career by winning his fifth gold medal.

1932 Los Angeles T: 7, N: 7, D: 8.9. WR: 9:36.2 (USA—Clapp,
Laufer, Kojac, Weissmuller)

1. JAP (Yasuji Miyazaki, Masanori Yusa, Takashi   8:58.4   WR
   Yokoyama, Hisakichi Toyoda)
2. USA (Frank Booth, George Fissler, Marola Ka-   9:10.5
   lili, Manuella Kalili)
3. HUN (András Wanié, László Szabados, András   9:31.4
   Székely, István Bárány)
4. CAN (George Larson, George Burrows, Walter   9:36.3
   Spence, F. Munro Bourne)
5. GBR (Joseph Whiteside, Robert Leivers, Mos-   9:45.8
   tyn French-Williams, Reginald Sutton)
6. ARG (Carlos Kennedy, Leopoldo Tahier, Ro-   10:13.1
   berto Peper, Alfredo Rocca)
7. BRA (Manoel Lourenço Silva, Isaac Dos San-   10:36.5
   tos Moraes, Manoel Rocha Villar, Bene-
   venuto Martins Nunes)

1936 Berlin T: 18, N: 18, D: 8.11. WR:8:52.2 (JAP-Yusa, Makino,
Isharada, Negami)

1. JAP (Masanori Yusa, Shigeo Sugiura, Masa-   8:51.5   WR
   haru Taguchi, Shigeo Arai)
2. USA (Ralph Flanagan, John Macionis, Paul   9:03.0
   Wolf, Jack Medica)

3. HUN (Árpád Lengyel, Oszkár Abay-Nemes, 9:12.3
Ödön Gróf, Ferenc Csík)

4. FRA (Alfred Nakache, Chistian Talli, René Cava- 9:18.2
lero, Jean Taris)

5. GER (Werner Plath, Wolfgang Heimlich, Her- 9:19.0
mann Heibel, Helmut Fischer)

6. GBR (Mostyn French-Williams, Romana Gabriel- 9:21.5
son, Robert Leivers, Norman Wainwright)

7. CAN (F. Munro Bourne, Hamerton, Robert 9:27.5
Hooper, Robert Pirie)

8. SWE (Björn Borg, Sten Olov Bolldén, Sven Pet- 9:37.5
terson, Gunnar Werner)

1948 London T: 14, N: 14, D: 8.3. WR: 8:51.5 (JAP—Yusa,
Sugiura, Taguchi, Arai)

1. USA (Walter Ris, James McLane, Wallace Wolf, 8:46.0 WR
William Smith)

2. HUN (Elemér Szathmáry, György Mitró, Imre 8:48.4
Nyéki, Géza Kádas)

3. FRA (Joseph Bernardo, Henri Padou, Rene Cor- 9:08.0
nu, Alexandre Jany)

4. SWE (Martin Lundén, Per-Olof Östrand, Olle Jo- 9:09.1
hansson, Per-Olof Olsson)

5. YUG (Vanja Illič, Čiril Pelhan, Ivan Puhar, Branko 9:14.0
Vidovič)

6. ARG (Horatio White, José Duranona, Juan 9:19.2
Garay, Alfredo Yantorno)

7. MEX (R. Bravo Prieto, A. Maldonado Campos, 9:20.2
A. Diaz Castillo, Alberto Isaac Ahumada)

8. BRA (S. Alencar Rodrigues, W.O. Jordan, R. 9:31.0
Kestener Egon, Aram Boghossian)

1952 Helsinki T: 17, N: 17, D: 7.29. WR:8:29.4 (USA, Yale
University—Moore, McLane, Sheff, Thoman)

1. USA (Wayne Moore, William Woolsey, Ford 8:31.1 OR
Konno, James McLane)

2. JAP (Hiroshi Suzuki, Yoshihiro Hamaguchi, 8:33.5
Toru Goto, Teijiro Tanikawa)

3. FRA (Joseph Bernardo, Aldo Eminente, Alex- 8:45.9
andre Jany, Jean Boiteux)

4. SWE (Lars Svanteson, Göran Larsson, Per-Olof 8:46.8
Östrand, Olle Johansson)

5. HUN (László Gyöngyösi, György Csordás, Géza 8:52.6
Kádas, Imre Nyéki)

6. GBR (Frank Botham, Ronald Burns, Thomas 8:52.9
Welsh, John Wardrop)

7. SAF (Graham Johnston, Dennis Ford, John 8:55.1
Durr, Peter Duncan)

8. ARG (Federico Zwanck, Marcelo Trabucco, Pe- 8:56.9
dro Galvao, Severo Yantorno)

Knowing that they would lose under normal circumstances, the Japanese reversed the usual order of their
swimmers, putting the fastest man first and the slowest
last. They did build up a big lead, but Ford Konno closed
the gap and Jimmy McLane pulled away in the final 100
meters.

1956 Melbourne T: 11, N: 11, D: 12.3. WR: 8:24.5 (SOV—Nikitin,
Strushanov, Nikolayev, Sorokin)

1. AUS (Kevin O'Halloran, John Devitt, Mur- 8:23.6 WR
ray Rose, Jon Henricks)

2. USA (Richard Hanley, George Breen, Wil- 8:31.5
liam Woolsey, Ford Konno)

3. SOV (Vitaly Sorokin, Vladimir Strushanov, 8:34.7
Gennady Nikolayev, Boris Nikitin)

4. JAP (Manabu Koga, Atsushi Tani, Koji 8:36.6
Nonoshita, Tsuyoshi Yamanaka)

5. GER/GDR (Hans Köhler, Hans-Joachim Reich, 8:43.4
Hans Zierold, Horst Bleeker)

6. GBR (Kenneth Williams, Ronald Roberts, 8:45.2
Neil McKechnie, John Wardrop)

7. ITA (Frederico Dennerlein, Paolo Galletti, 8:46.2
Guido Elmi, Anthony Romani)

8. SAF (William Steuart, A. Briscoe, Dennis 8:49.5
Ford, Peter Duncan)

1960 Rome T: 15, N: 15, D: 9.1. WR(880 yards): 8:16.6 (AUS—
Henricks, Dickson, Konrads, Rose)

1. USA (George Harrison, Richard Blick, Mi- 8:10.2 WR
chael Troy, F. Jeffrey Farrell)

2. JAP (Makoto Fukui, Hiroshi Ishii, Tsuyoshi 8:13.2
Yamanaka, Tatsuo Fujimoto)

3. AUS (David Dickson, John Devitt, Murray 8:13.8
Rose, John Konrads)

4. GBR (Hamilton Milton, John Martin Dye, 8:28.1
Richard Campion, Ian Black)

5. FIN (Ilkka Suvanto, Kari Haavisto, Stig- 8:29.7
Olof Grenner, Harri Käyhko)

6. SWE (Sven-Göran Johansson, Lars-Erik 8:31.0
Bengtsson, Bengt Nordvall, Per-Ola
Lindberg)

7. GER/GDR (Frank Wiegand, Gerhard Hetz, Hans 8:31.8
Zierold, Hans Klein)

8. SOV (Igor Lushkovski, Gennady Nikola- 8:32.2
yev, Vitaly Sorokin, Boris Nikitin)

1964 Tokyo T; 15, N: 15, D: 10.18. WR: 8:01.8 (USA—Mettler,
Wall, Lyons, Schollander)

1. USA (Stephen Clark, Roy Saari, Gary Il- 7:52.1 WR
man, Donald Schollander)

2. GDR/GER (Horst-Günther Gregor, Gerhard 7:59.3
Hetz, Frank Wiegand, Hans-Joachim
Klein)

3. JAP (Makoto Fukui, Kunihiro Iwasaki, To- 8:03.8
shio Shoji, Yukiaki Okabe)

4. AUS (David Dickson, Allan Wood, Peter 8:05.5
Doak, Robert Windle)

5. SWE (Mats Svensson, E. Lester Eriksson, 8:08.0
Hans Rosendahl, Jan Lundin)

6. FRA (Jean-Pascal Curtillet, Pierre Cana- 8:08.7
vese, Francis Luyce, Alain Gottvalles)

7. SOV (Semynn Belits-Geiman, Vladimir 8:15.1
Berezin, Aleksandr Paramonov, Yevgeny Novikov)

8. ITA (Sergio De Gregorio, Bruno Bianchi, 8:18.1
Giovanni Orlando, Pietro Bascaini)

With this race Steve Clark earned his third gold medal, and Don Schollander became the first swimmer in Olympic history to win four gold medals in one Olympics.

1968 Mexico City T: 16, N: 16, D: 10.21 WR: 7:52.1 (USA—Clark, Saari, Ilman, Schollander; USA, Santa Clara Swim Club—Ilman, Spitz, Wall, Schollander)
1. USA (John Nelson, Stephen Rerych, Mark Spitz, 7:52.33 Donald Schollander)
2. AUS (Gregory Rogers, Graham White, Robert Windle, Michael Wenden) 7:53.77
3. SOV (Vladimir Bure, Semyon Belits-Geiman, Georgy Kulikov, Leonid Ilyichev) 8:01.66
4. CAN (George Smith, Ronald Jacks, John Gilchrist, Ralph Hutton) 8:03.22
5. FRA (Michel Rousseau, Gerard Letast, Francis Luyce, Alain Mosconi) 8:03.77
6. GER (Hans Fassnacht, Olaf von Schilling, Volkert Meeuw, Wolfgang Kremer) 8:04.33
7. GDR (Frank Wiegand, Horst-Günter Gregor, Alfred Müller, Jochen Herbst) 8:06.00
8. SWE (Hans Ljungberg, Karl Larson, Sven Ferm, Erik Eriksson) 8:12.11

1972 Munich T: 14, N: 14, D: 8.31. WR: 7:43.3 (USA—Spitz, Heidenreich, Tyler, McBreen)
1. USA (John Kinsella, Frederick Tyler, Steven Genter, Mark Spitz) 7:35.78 WR
2. GER (Klaus Steinbach, Werner Lampe, Hans-Günter Vosseler, Hans-Joachim Fassnacht) 7:41.69
3. SOV (Igor Grivennikov, Viktor Mazanov, Georgy Kulikov, Vladimir Bure) 7:45.76
4. SWE (Bengt Gingsjö, Hans Ljungberg, Anders Bellbring, Gunnar Larsson) 7:47.37
5. AUS (Michael Wenden, Graham Windeatt, Robert Nay, Bradford Cooper) 7:48.66
6. GDR (Wilfried Hartung, Peter Bruch, Udo Poser, Lutz Unger) 7:49.11
7. CAN (Bruce Robertson, Brian Phillips, Ian MacKenzie, Ralph Hutton) 7:53.61
8. GBR (Brian Brinkley, John Mills, Michael Bailey, Colin Cunningham) 7:55.59

One hour after winning the 100-meter butterfly, Mark Spitz was back in the water to swim the anchor leg for the 4 × 200-meter freestyle relay team. Steve Genter's third leg of 1:52.72 gave the U.S. a big lead. Spitz took over from there to gain his fifth gold medal and fifth world record in four days.

1976 Montreal T: 18, N: 18, D: 7.21. WR:7:30.54 (USA,Long Beach Swim Club—Favero, Shaw, S. Furniss, B. Furniss)
1. USA (Mike Bruner, Bruce Furniss, John Naber, Jim Montgomery) 7:23.22 WR

2. SOV (Vladimir Raskatov, Andrey Bogdanov, Sergei Kopliakov, Andrei Krylov) 7:27.97
3. GBR (Alan McClatchey, David Dunne, Gordon Downie, Brian Brinkley) 7:32.11
4. GER (Klaus Steinbach, Peter Nocke, Werner Lampe, Hans-Joachim Geisler) 7:32.27
5. GDR (Roger Pyttel, Wilfried Hartung, Rainer Strohback, Frank Pfütze) 7:38.92
6. HOL (Abdul Ressand, René van der Kuil, André In Het Veld, Henk Elzerman) 7:42.56
7. SWE (Pär Arvidsson, Peter Petterson, Anders Bellbring, Bengt Gingsjö) 7:42.84
8. ITA (Marcello Guarducci, Roberto Pangaro, Paolo Barelli, Paolo Rivelli) 7:43.39

The U.S. team of Doug Northway, Tim Shaw, Mike Bruner, and Bruce Furniss set a world record of 7:30.33 in the qualifying round. That night, Northway and Shaw were replaced by John Naber and Jim Montgomery, and another world record was set.

1980 Moscow T: 13, N: 13, D: 7.23. WR: 7:20.82 (USA—B. Furniss, Forrester, Hackett, Gaines)
1. SOV (Sergei Kopliakov, Vladimir Salnikov, Ivar Stukolkin, Andrei Krylov) 7:23.50
2. GDR (Frank Pfütze, Jörg Woithe, Detlev Grabs, Rainer Strohbach) 7:28.60
3. BRA (Jorge Lutz Fernandes, Marcus Laborne Mattioli, Cyro Marques, Djan Madruga Garrido) 7:29.30
4. SWE (Michael Söderlund, Pelle Wikström, Per-Alvar Magnusson, Thomas Lejdström) 7:30.10
5. ITA (Paolo Revelli, Raffaele Franceschi, Andrea Ceccarini, Fabrizio Rampazzo) 7:30.37
6. GBR (Douglas Campbell, Philip Hubble, Martin Smith, Andrew Astbury) 7:30.81
7. AUS (Graeme Brewer, Mark Tonelli, Mark Kerry, Ron McKeon) 7:30.82
8. FRA (Fabien Noel, Mark Lazzaro, Dominique Petit, Paskal Laget) 7:36.08

4×100-METER MEDLEY RELAY

In medley relays, the order of strokes is backstroke, breaststroke, butterfly, and freestyle.

1896–1956 not held

1960 Rome T: 18, N: 18, D: 9.1. WR: 4:09.2 (USA, Indianapolis Athletic Club—McKinney, Jastremski, Troy, Sintz)
1. USA (Frank McKinney, Paul Hait, Lance Larson, F. Jeffrey Farrell) 4:05.4 WR
2. AUS (David Theile, Terry Gathercole, Neville Hayes, Geoffrey Shipton) 4:12.0
3. JAP (Kazuo Tomita, Koichi Hirakida, Yoshihiko Osaki, Keigo Shimizu) 4:12.2
4. CAN (Robert Wheaton, Steve Rabinovitch, Cameron Grout, Richard Pound) 4:16.8

5. SOV (Leonid Barbier, Leonid Kolesnikov, Gri- 4:16.8
gory Kiselyov, Igor Lushkovski)

6. ITA (Guiseppe Avellone, Roberto Lazzari, Fe- 4:17.2
derico Dennerlein, Bruno Bianchi)

7. GBR (Graham Sykes, Christopher Walkden, Ian 4:17.6
Black, Stanley Clarke)

8. HOL (Johannes Jiskoot, Wieger Mensonides, 4:18.2
Gerrit Korteweg, Ronald Kroon)

The U.S. "reserve" team of Bob Bennett, Paul Hait, Dave
Gillanders, and Steve Clark set a world record of 4:08.2 in
the qualifying round. Only Hait also took part in the final,
in which a new U.S. team set another world record.

1964 Tokyo T: 14, N: 14, D: 10.16. WR: 4:00.1 (USA—McGeagh,
Craig, Richardson, Clark)

1. USA (Harold Thompson Mann, William 3:58.4 WR
Craig, Fred Schmidt, Stephen Clark)

2. GDR/GER (Ernst-Joachim Küppers, Egon Hen- 4:01.6
ninger, Horst-Günther Gregor, Hans-
Joachim Klein)

3. AUS (Peter Reynolds, Ian O'Brien, Kevin 4:02.3
Berry, David Dickson)

4. SOV (Viktor Mazanov, Georgy Proko- 4:04.2
penko, Valentin Kuzmin, Vladimir
Schuvalov)

5. JAP (Shigeo Fukushima, Kenji Ishikawa, 4:06.6
Isao Nakajima, Yukiaki Okabe)

6. HUN (József Csikány, Ferenc Lenkei, Jó- 4:08.5
sef Gurrich, Gyula Dobai)

7. ITA (Chiaffredo Rora, Gian Corrado 4:10.3
Gross, Giampiero Fossati, Pietro
Boscaini)

8. GBR (Geoffrey Thwaites, Neil Nicholson, 4:11.4
Brian Jenkins, Robert McGregor)

Backstroker Thompson Mann led off for the United States
with a world record of 59.6, the first time that the one minute barrier had ever been broken for the 100-meter backstroke. The German and Soviet teams caught up by the
halfway mark, but Fred Schmidt put the victory away for
the United States with a 56.8 butterfly, leg and Steve Clark
sealed it with a 52.4 anchor.

1968 Mexico City T: 18, N: 18, D: 10.26. WR: 3:56.5 (GDR—
Matthes, Henninger, Gregor, Wiegand)

1. USA (Charles Hickcox, Donald McKenzie, 3:54.9 WR
Douglas Russell, Kenneth Walsh)

2. GDR (Roland Matthes, Egon Henninger, Horst- 3:57.5
Günther Gregor, Frank Wiegand)

3. SOV (Yuri Gromak, Vladimir Kossinsky, Vladimir 4:00.7
Nemshilov, Leonid Ilyichev)

4. AUS (Karl Byrom, Ian O'Brien, Robert Cusack, 4:00.8
Michael Wenden)

5. JAP (Yasuo Tanaka, Nobutaka Taguchi, Satoshi 4:01.8
Maruya, Kunihiro Iwasaki)

6. GER (Reinhard Blechert, Gregor Betz, Lutz Stok- 4:05.4
lasa, Wolfgang Kremer)

7. CAN (James Shaw, William Mahony, Toomas 4:07.3
Arusoo, John Gilchrist)

8. SPA (Santiago Esteva, José Duran, Arturo Lang, 4:08.8
José Chicoy)

Roland Matthes opened with a backstroke world record of
58.0, but Doug Russell's butterfly leg put the United States
in the lead to stay.

1972 Munich T: 17, N: 17, D: 9.4. WR: 3:50.4 (USA—Campbell,
Dahlberg, Spitz, Heidenreich)

1. USA (Michael Stamm, Thomas Bruce, Mark 3:48.16 WR
Spitz, Jerry Heidenreich)

2. GDR (Roland Matthes, Klaus Katzur, Hartmut 3:52.12
Flöckner, Lutz Unger)

3. CAN (Eric Fish, William Mahony, Bruce Robert- 3:52.26
son, Robert Kasting)

4. SOV (Igor Grivennikov, Nikolai Pankin, Viktor 3:53.26
Sharygin, Vladimir Bure)

5. BRA (Romulo Duncan Arantes, José Sylvio 3:57.899
Fiolo, Sergio Waismann, José Roberto
Diñiz-Aranha)

6. JAP (Tadashi Honda, Nobutaka Taguchi, Ya- 3:58.233
suhiro Komazaki, Jiro Sasaki)

7. GBR (Colin Cunningham, David Wilkie, John 3:58.822
Mills, Malcolm Windeatt)

8. HUN (László Cseh, Sándor Szabó, István 3:59.077
Szentirmay, Attila Császári)

Once again, Roland Matthes opened with a world record
performance, but then the Americans took over, as Mark
Spitz, swimming the butterfly leg, won his seventh gold
medal.

1976 Montreal T: 14, N: 14, D: 7.22. WR: 3:48.16 (USA—Stamm,
Bruce, Spitz, Heidenreich)

1. USA (John Naber, John Hencken, Matt Vogel, 3:42.22 WR
Jim Montgomery)

2. CAN (Stephen Pickell, Graham Smith, Clay Ev- 3:45.94
ans, Gary MacDonald)

3. GER (Klaus Steinbach, Walter Kusch, Michael 3:47.29
Kraus, Peter Nocke)

4. GBR (James Carter, David Wilkie, John Mills, 3:49.56
Brian Brinkley)

5. SOV (Igor Omelchenko, Arvidas Iuozaytis, 3:49.90
Yevgeny Seredin, Andrei Krylov)

6. AUS (Mark Kerry, Paul Jarvie, Neil Rogers, Pe- 3:51.54
ter Coughlan)

7. ITA (Enrico Bisso, Giorgio Lalle, Paolo Barelli, 3:52.92
Marcello Guarducci)

8. JAP (Tadashi Honda, Nobutaka Taguchi, Hi- 3:54.74
deaki Hara, Tsuyoshi Yanagidate)

In the qualifying round, Americans Peter Rocca, Chris
Woo, Joe Bottom, and Jack Babashoff set a world record
of 3:47.28. The 1976 U.S. team was so strong that they
were able to field a completely different foursome in the final and set yet another world record.

1980 Moscow T: 11, N: 11, D: 7.24. WR: 3:42.22 (USA—Naber, Hencken, Vogel, Montgomery)

1.	AUS	(Mark Kerry, Peter Evans, Mark Tonelli, Neil Brooks)	3:45.70
2.	SOV	(Viktor Kuznetsov, Arsen Miskarov, Yevgeny Seredin, Sergei Kopliakov)	3:45.92
3.	GBR	(Gary Abraham, Duncan Goodhew, David Lowe, Martin Smith)	3:47.71
4.	GDR	(Dietmar Göhring, Jörg Walter, Roger Pyttel, Jörg Woithe)	3:48.25
5.	FRA	(Frédéric Delcourt, Olivier Borios, Xavier Savin, René Ecuyer)	3:49.19
6.	HUN	(Sándor Wladár, Janos Dzvonyar, Zoltán Verrasztó, Gábor Mészáros)	3:50.29
7.	HOL	(Fred Eefting, Albert Boonstra, Kees Vervoorn, Cees Jan Winkel)	3:51.81
8.	BRA	(Romulo Duncan Arantes, Sergio Pinto Ribeiro, Claudo Mamede Kestener, Jorge Luiz Fernandes)	3:53.23

Australian anchorman Neil Brooks swam a stirring 49.86 to overtake 200-meter freestyle gold medalist Sergei Kopliakov and give Australia an upset victory.

SPRINGBOARD DIVING

This event is performed from a springboard three meters (9 feet 10 inches) above the water. Since 1964 Olympic competitions have begun with a preliminary round of seven dives. The top twelve divers then advance to the final, which consists of 11 dives—five required and six voluntary. The judges' scores are multiplied by a coefficient that is determined by the degree of difficulty of the attempted dive.

1896–1906 not held

1908 London C: 23, N: 8, D: 7.18.

			PTS.
1.	Albert Zürner	GER	85.5
2.	Kurt Behrens	GER	85.3
3.	George Gaidzik	USA	80.8
3.	Gottlob Walz	GER	80.8

1912 Stockholm C: 18, N: 7, D: 7.9.

			PTS.
1.	Paul Günther	GER	79.23
2.	Hans Luber	GER	76.78
3.	Kurt Behrens	GER	73.73
4.	Albert Zürner	GER	73.33
5.	Robert Zimmerman	CAN	72.54
6.	Herbert Pott	GBR	71.45
7.	John Jansson	SWE	69.64
8.	George Gaidzik	USA	68.01

1920 Antwerp C: 14, N: 9, D: 8.27.

			PTS.
1.	Louis Kuehn	USA	675.4
2.	Clarence Pinkston	USA	655.3
3.	Louis Balbach	USA	649.5
4.	Gustaf Blomgren	SWE	587.5
5.	Gunnar Ekstrand	SWE	559.25
6.	John Jansson	SWE	544.75

1924 Paris C: 17, N: 9, D: 7.17.

			PTS.
1.	Albert White	USA	696.4
2.	Peter Desjardins	USA	693.2
3.	Clarence Pinkston	USA	653.0
4.	Edmund Lindmark	SWE	599.1
5.	Richmond Eve	AUS	564.3
6.	Adolf Hellqvist	SWE	544.9
7.	Kurt Sjöberg	SWE	538.3
8.	H. Hemsing	HOL	490.8

1928 Amsterdam C: 24, N: 15, D: 8.8.

			PTS.
1.	Peter Desjardins	USA	185.04
2.	Michael Galitzen (Mickey Reilly)	USA	174.06
3.	Farid Simaika	EGY	172.46
4.	Harold Smith	USA	168.96
5.	Arthur Mund	GER	154.72
6.	Ewald Riebschläger	GER	153.86
7.	Heinz Plumanns	GER	150.18
8.	Alfred Phillips	CAN	149.48

Born in Manitoba, Canada, and raised in Miami Beach, 5-foot 3-inch Pete Desjardins is the only male diver in Olympic history to win both the springboard and platform events. A graduate of Stanford University, he later turned professional and was billed as "The Little Bronze Statue From Florida."

1932 Los Angeles C: 13, N: 7, D: 8.8.

			PTS.
1.	Michael Galitzen (Mickey Reilly)	USA	161.38
2.	Harold Smith	USA	158.54
3.	Richard Degener	USA	151.82
4.	Alfred Phillips	CAN	134.64
5.	Leo Esser	GER	134.30
6.	Kazuo Kobayashi	JAP	133.76
7.	Emile Poussard	FRA	128.66
8.	Tetsutaro Namae	JAP	125.18

One month after the Los Angeles Games, Michael Galitzen married diver Georgia Coleman. Their Olympic records were exactly the same: a silver and bronze in 1928 and a gold and silver in 1932. Galitzen performed under the name Mickey Reilly.

1936 Berlin C: 24, N: 15, D: 8.11.

			PTS.
1.	Richard Degener	USA	163.57
2.	Marshall Wayne	USA	159.56

3. Albert Greene   USA   146.29
4. Tsuneo Shibahara   JAP   144.92
5. Erhard Weiss   GER   141.24
6. Leo Esser   GER   137.99
7. Winfried Marauhn   GER   134.61
8. Koyanagi   JAP   133.07

Degener's margin of victory was provided by an almost perfect full twist with a one and a half somersault. He was awarded a score of 19.55. Wayne attempted the same dive but earned only 15.54 points.

1948 London C: 26, N: 15, D: 8.3.

			PTS.
1.	Bruce Harlan	USA	163.64
2.	Miller Anderson	USA	157.29
3.	Samuel Lee	USA	145.52
4.	Joaquin Capilla Pérez	MEX	141.79
5.	Raymond Mulinghausen	FRA	126.55
6.	Svante Johansson	SWE	120.20
7.	Kamal Hassan	EGY	119.90
8.	Thomas Christiansen	DEN	114.59

1952 Helsinki C: 36, N: 20, D: 7.28.

			PTS.
1.	David Browning	USA	205.29
2.	Miller Anderson	USA	199.84
3.	Robert Clotworthy	USA	184.92
4.	Joaquin Capilla Pérez	MEX	178.33
5.	Roman Brener	SOV	165.63
6.	Milton Busin	BRA	155.91
7.	Tony Turner	GBR	151.90
8.	Aleksei Zigalov	SOV	151.31

The divers were somewhat distracted by the presence of too many people near the board, including a photographer in a frogman outfit who actually stationed himself *in* the pool.

1956 Melbourne C: 24, N: 19, D: 8.29.

			PTS.
1.	Robert Clotworthy	USA	159.56
2.	Donald Harper	USA	156.23
3.	Joaquin Capilla Pérez	MEX	150.69
4.	Glen Whitten	USA	148.55
5.	Gennady Udalov	SOV	140.64
6.	Roman Brener	SOV	139.14
7.	Gunther Mund	CHI	137.53
8.	József Gerlach	HUN	136.08

1960 Rome C: 32, N: 19, D: 8.29.

			PTS.
1.	Gary Tobian	USA	170.00
2.	Samuel Hall	USA	167.08
3.	Juan Botella	MEX	162.30
4.	Alvaro Gaxiola	MEX	150.42
5.	Ernest Meissner	CAN	144.07
6.	Lamberto Mari	ITA	143.97
7.	Toshio Yamano	JAP	140.46
8.	Hans-Dieter Pophal	GDR	133.95

After the preliminary round, one judge, a Soviet woman, was replaced for being overly nationalistic in her scoring.

1964 Tokyo C: 27, N: 16, D: 10.14.

			PTS.
1.	Kenneth Sitzberger	USA	159.90
2.	Francis Gorman	USA	157.63
3.	Larry Andreasen	USA	143.77
4.	Hans-Dieter Pophal	GDR	142.58
5.	Göran Lundqvist	SWE	138.65
6.	Boris Polulyakh	SOV	138.64
7.	Mikhail Safonov	SOV	134.00
8.	Vladimir Vasin	SOV	133.48

Navy Lieutenant Frank Gorman actually outscored Ken Sitzberger on nine of his ten dives. But he missed badly with his ninth round back two and a half somersault, tuck, and lost 11.20 points.

1968 Mexico City C: 28, N: 16, D: 10.20.

			PTS.
1.	Bernard Wrightson	USA	170.15
2.	Klaus Dibiasi	ITA	159.74
3.	James Henry	USA	158.09
4.	Luis Niño de Rivera	MEX	155.71
5.	Franco Giorgio Cagnotto	ITA	155.70
6.	Keith Russell	USA	151.75
7.	Tord Anderson	SWE	151.50
8.	Donald Wagstaff	AUS	150.18

Bernie Wrightson moved up from third place to first with his last three dives.

1972 Munich C: 32, N: 16, D: 8.30.

			PTS.
1.	Vladimir Vasin	SOV	594.09
2.	Franco Giorgio Cagnotto	ITA	591.63
3.	Craig Lincoln	USA	577.29
4.	Klaus Dibiasi	ITA	559.05
5.	Michael Finneran	USA	557.34
6.	Vyacheslav Strahov	SOV	556.20
7.	Falk Hoffmann	GDR	544.95
8.	Norbert Huda	GER	524.16

The U.S. string of eleven straight springboard victories was finally broken. The next to last dive was the decisive one. Cagnotto missed and was awarded only 48.72 points, while Vasin recorded 75.60 points, the highest score of the competition.

1976 Montreal C: 30, N: 16, D: 7.22.

			PTS.
1.	Philip Boggs	USA	619.05
2.	Franco Giorgio Cagnotto	ITA	570.48
3.	Aleksandr Kosenkov	SOV	567.24
4.	Falk Hoffmann	GDR	553.53
5.	Robert Cragg	USA	548.19
6.	Gregory Louganis	USA	528.96
7.	Carlos Giron	MEX	523.59
8.	Klaus Dibiasi	ITA	516.18

1980 Moscow C: 24, N: 16, D: 7.23.

		PTS.
1. Aleksandr Portnov	SOV	905.025
2. Carlos Giron	MEX	892.140
3. Franco Giorgio Cagnotto	ITA	871.500
4. Falk Hoffmann	GDR	858.510
5. Aleksandr Kosenkov	SOV	855.120
6. Christopher Snode	GBR	844.470
7. Vyacheslav Troshin	SOV	820.050
8. Ricardo Camacho	SPA	749.340

Aleksandr Portnov's victory was clouded by controversy. Distracted by the noise of the crowd watching the final of the men's 100-meter butterfly, Portnov turned a two and a half backward somersault into a belly flop. He immediately protested and was awarded a re-dive, which he hit beautifully. Giron, Cagnotto, and Hoffman objected, claiming that they had been subjected to similar distractions. Hoffman was particularly annoyed, since his later claim that one of his dives had been disrupted by a photographer's flash was denied. The medal ceremony was delayed for two days until a final decision was announced by the International Amateur Swimming Federation (F.I.N.A). In Mexico City demonstrations were held outside the Soviet embassy to protest the ruling.

PLATFORM DIVING

This event is staged from a rigid platform ten meters (30 foot 5 inches) above the water. The finalists perform four compulsory dives and six voluntary dives.

1896–1900 not held

1904 St. Louis C: 5, N: 2, D: 9.7.

		PTS.
1. George Sheldon	USA	12.66
2. Georg Hoffmann	GER	11.66
3. Frank Kehoe	USA	11.33
4. Alfred Braunschweiger	GER	11.33
5. Otto Hooff	GER	—

The German team protested Sheldon's victory, but their protest was rejected by James Sullivan, the U.S. official in charge. Kehoe and Braunschweiger tied, and a dive-off was ordered. Braunschweiger refused to take part, so Kehoe was awarded third place. Apparently the Americans and Germans disagreed as to what constituted a proper dive. The Americans felt that the manner in which a diver hit the water was important, while the Germans, who attempted more difficult dives but tended to land on their stomachs and chests, contended that landings didn't matter.

1906 Athens C: 24, N: 8, D: 4.26.

		PTS.
1. Gottlob Walz	GER	156.0
2. Goerg Hoffmann	GER	150.2
3. Otto Satzinger	AUT	147.4

4. Albert Zurner	GER	144.6
5. G. Melville Clark	GBR	144.0
6. Hjalmar Johansson	SWE	143.4
7. Robert Andersson	SWE	142.2
8. Fritz Nicolai	GER	138.0

1908 London C: 23, N: 6, D: 7.24.

		PTS.
1. Hjalmar Johansson	SWE	83.75
2. Karl Malmström	SWE	78.73
3. Arvid Spångberg	SWE	74.00
4. Robert Andersson	SWE	68.30
5. George Gaidzik	USA	56.30

1912 Stockholm D: 21, N: 6, D: 7.15.

		PTS.	ORDINALS
1. Erik Adlerz	SWE	73.94	7
2. Albert Zürner	GER	72.60	10
3. Gustaf Blomgren	SWE	69.56	16
4. Hjalmar Johansson	SWE	67.80	22
5. George Yvon	GBR	67.66	22
6. Harald Arbin	SWE	62.62	31
7. Albin Carlsson	SWE	63.16	32
8. Toivo Aro	FIN	57.05	40

1920 Antwerp C: 15, N: 7, D: 8.29.

		PTS.
1. Clarence Pinkston	USA	100.67
2. Erik Adlerz	SWE	99.08
3. Harry Prieste	USA	93.73
4. Gustaf Blomgren	SWE	90.78
5. Yngve Johnson	SWE	88.36
6. Louis Balbach	USA	84.80

1924 Paris C: 20, N: 10, D: 7.20.

		PTS.
1. Albert White	USA	97.46
2. David Fall	USA	97.30
3. Clarence Pinkston	USA	94.60
4. Erik Adlerz	SWE	93.78
5. Eugène Lenormand	FRA	87.54
6. Helge Öberg	SWE	85.80
7. S. Sorensen	DEN	80.92
8. Adolf Hellqvist	SWE	80.64

1928 Amsterdam C: 24, N: 12, D: 8.11.

		PTS.	ORDINALS
1. Peter Desjardins	USA	98.74	6
2. Farid Simaika	EGY	99.58	9
3. Michael Galitzen	USA	92.34	15
4. Walter Colbath	USA	87.78	21
5. Ewald Riebschläger	GER	82.44	27
6. Karl Schumm	GER	80.54	28
7. Alfred Phillips	CAN	77.26	35
8. A. Reginald Knight	GBR	72.22	41

Simaika was originally announced as the winner, and the Egyptian national anthem was played. Then it was declared that a mistake had been made, that ordinals (place-figures), not total points, determined the winner. Consequently, Desjardins was given his second gold medal.

1932 Los Angeles C: 8, N: 5, D: 8.13.

			PTS.
1.	Harold Smith	USA	124.80
2.	Michael Galitzen (Mickey Reilly)	USA	124.28
3.	Frank Kurtz	USA	121.98
4.	Josef Staudinger	AUT	103.44
5.	Carlos Curiel	MEX	83.82
6.	Jesús Flores Albo	MEX	77.94
7.	Alfred Phillips	CAN	77.10
8.	Hidekatsu Ishida	JAP	75.92

1936 Berlin C: 26, N: 15, D: 8.15.

			PTS.
1.	Marshall Wayne	USA	113.58
2.	Elbert Root	USA	110.60
3.	Hermann Stork	GER	110.31
4.	Erhard Weiss	GER	110.15
5.	Frank Kurtz	USA	108.61
6.	Tsuneo Shibahara	JAP	107.40
7.	Siegfried Viebahn	GER	105.00
8.	Koyanagi	JAP	94.54

1948 London C: 25, N: 15, D: 8.5.

			PTS.
1.	Samuel Lee	USA	130.05
2.	Bruce Harlan	USA	122.30
3.	Joaquin Capilla Pérez	MEX	113.52
4.	Lennart Brunnhage	SWE	108.62
5.	Peter Heatly	GBR	105.29
6.	Thomas Christiansen	DEN	105.22
7.	Raymond Mulinghausen	FRA	103.01
8.	George Athans	CAN	100.91

Sammy Lee was a 28-year-old Korean-American army doctor. For his last dive he chose a forward three and a half somersault. Once, when performing a similar dive, he had mistaken the sky for the water and pulled out too soon. Now with the Olympic title on the line, he was afraid he would repeat the mistake. "I dove, hit the water, felt numb and tingling and decided: 'I did a belly flop.'" When he popped out of the water he discovered that, far from belly-flopping, his dive had been rated almost perfect. "I just walked on water out of that pool," he later recalled.

1952 Helsinki C: 31, N: 17, D: 8.1.

			PTS.
1.	Samuel Lee	USA	156.28
2.	Joaquin Capilla Pérez	MEX	145.21
3.	Günther Haase	GER	141.31
4.	John McCormack	USA	138.74
5.	Alberto Capilla Pérez	MEX	136.44
6.	Rodolfo Perea	MEX	128.28
7.	Aleksandr Bakatin	SOV	126.86
8.	Roman Brener	SOV	126.31

Sammy Lee celebrated his 32nd birthday by winning his second gold medal.

1956 Melbourne C: 22, N: 10, D: 12.6.

			PTS.
1.	Joaquin Capilla Pérez	MEX	152.44
2.	Gary Tobian	USA	152.41
3.	Richard Connor	USA	149.79
4.	József Gerlach	HUN	149.25
5.	Roman Brener	SOV	142.95
6.	William Farrell	USA	139.12
7.	Ferenc Siák	HUN	138.83
8.	Mikhail Chachba	SOV	134.51

Third in 1948 and second in 1952, Capilla completed his set of platform diving medals by executing a superb forward one and a half somersault with a double twist on his final dive. The highest-scored dive of the competition, it gave Capilla a 0.03 point edge over Tobian. The U.S. team lodged a protest against the Soviet and Hungarian judges, but F.I.N.A. Secretary Bertil Sallfors rejected the complaint, explaining, "There can be no protests against the judges." Soviet judge Eva Bozd-Morskaya had given Gary Tobian an average score of 6.35, while his average overall score had been 7.3. On the other hand, she had scored Mikhail Chachba 7.38, while *his* overall average had been 6.37. This incident led to a change in the rules which allowed individual judges to be eliminated because of incompetence.

1960 Rome C: 28, N: 18, D: 9.2.

			PTS.
1.	Robert Webster	USA	165.56
2.	Gary Tobian	USA	165.25
3.	Brian Phelps	GBR	157.13
4.	Roberto Madrigal Garcia	MEX	152.86
5.	Rolf Sperling	GDR	151.83
6.	Gennady Galkin	SOV	141.69
7.	Fritz Enskat	GER	138.86
8.	Anatoly Sysoev	SOV	135.59

Webster moved from third place to first with his last three dives.

1964 Tokyo C: 30, N: 16, D: 10.18.

			PTS.
1.	Robert Webster	USA	148.58
2.	Klaus Dibiasi	ITA	147.54
3.	Thomas Gompf	USA	146.57
4.	Roberto Madrigal Garcia	MEX	144.27
5.	Viktor Palagin	SOV	143.77
6.	Brian Phelps	GBR	143.18
7.	Rolf Sperling	GDR	142.24
8.	Toshio Otsubo	JAP	142.05

This time Webster was only in sixth place with three dives to go, but still managed to withstand the pressure and successfully defend his championship.

1968 Mexico City C: 35, N: 17, D: 10.26.

		PTS.
1. Klaus Dibiasi	ITA	164.18
2. Alvaro Gaxiola	MEX	154.49
3. Edwin Young	USA	153.93
4. Keith Russell	USA	152.3
5. José Robinson	MEX	143.62
6. Lothar Matthes	GDR	141.75
7. Luis Niño de Rivera	MEX	141.16
8. Franco Giorgio Cagnotto	ITA	138.89

Coached by his father, Carlo, who had finished tenth in the 1936 Olympics, Klaus Dibiasi of Bolzano practiced between 130 and 150 dives a day, six days a week. In Mexico City, Dibiasi began his amazing Olympic winning streak by becoming the first Italian ever to win a gold medal in a swimming or diving event.

1972 Munich C; 35, N: 18, D: 9.4.

		PTS.
1. Klaus Dibiasi	ITA	504.12
2. Richard Rydze	USA	480.75
3. Franco Giorgio Cagnotto	ITA	475.83
4. Lothar Matthes	GDR	465.75
5. David Ambartsumyan	SOV	463.56
6. Richard Early	USA	462.45
7. Vladimir Kapirulin	SOV	459.21
8. Carlos Giron	MEX	442.41

1976 Montreal C: 25, N: 14, D: 7.27

		PTS.
1. Klaus Dibiasi	ITA	600.51
2. Gregory Louganis	USA	576.99
3. Vladimir Aleynik	SOV	548.61
4. Kent Vosler	USA	544.14
5. Patrick Moore	USA	538.17
6. Falk Hoffmann	GDR	531.60
7. David Ambartsumyan	SOV	516.21
8. Carlos Giron	MEX	513.93

Seventeen-year-old Soviet diver Sergei Nemtsanov finished a disappointing ninth, and then caused something of a sensation when he disappeared mysteriously from the Olympic Village. Soviet officials charged that he had been abducted. When he showed up again, the Western press claimed that Nemtsanov had left the Village voluntarily, but that the Soviets had tracked him down and hauled him back against his will.

1980 Moscow C: 23, N: 14, D: 7.28.

		PTS.
1. Falk Hoffmann	GDR	835.650
2. Vladimir Aleinik	SOV	819.705
3. David Ambartsumyan	SOV	817.440
4. Carlos Giron	MEX	809.805
5. Dieter Waskow	GDR	802.800
6. Thomas Knuths	GDR	783.975
7. Sergei Nemtsanov	SOV	775.860
8. Niki Sajkovic	AUT	725.145

WATER POLO

Water polo is played with seven men on a team. Since 1964, Olympic water polo matches have consisted of four five-minute quarters.

1896 not held

1900 Paris T: 4, N: 3, D: 8.12.

		W	L	PF	PA
1. GBR	(Osborne Swimming Club, Manchester—Arthur Robertson, Thomas Coe, Eric Robinson, Peter Kemp, George Wilkinson, John Henry Derbyshire, William Lister)	2	0	17	3
2. BEL	(Swimming et Water Polo Club, Brussels—Albert Michant, Fernand Feyaerts, Henri Cohen, Victor de Behr, Oscar Grégoire, Victor Sonnemans, Jean de Backer)	1	1	7	8
3. FRA	(Libellule de Paris—Henri Peslier, Thomas Burgess, Decuyper, Pesloy, Paul Vasseur, Devenot, Louis Laufray)	0	1	1	10
4. FRA	(Pupilles de Neptune de Lille—Louis Martin, Coulon, Fardelle, Favier, Leriche, Charles Treffel, Désiré Merchez)	0	1	1	5

Final: GBR 7–2 BEL

1904 St. Louis T: 3, N: 1, D: 9.6.

		W	L	PF	PA
1. USA	(New York Athletic Club—David Bratton, George Van Cleef, Leo Goodwin, Louis Handley, David Hesser, Joseph Ruddy, James Steen)	2	0	11	0
2. USA	(Chicago Athletic Club—Rex Breach, Jerome Steever, Edwin Swatek, Charles Healy, Frank Kehoe, David Hammond, William Tuttle)	0	1	0	6
3. USA	(Missouri Athletic Club—John Meyers, Manfred Toeppen, Gwynne Evans, Amadee Reyburn, Fred Schreiner, Agustus Goessling, William Orthwein)	0	1	0	5

The Missouri team refused to play for second place, so the Chicago team was awarded the silver medal by forfeit. Originally, a German team had also been entered, but when the Germans discovered that what the Americans called "water polo" was actually a strange sport called "softball water polo," they withdrew. The Americans used a deflated ball, and goals only counted if a player held the ball in the opposing goal.

1906 not held

1908 London T: 4, N: 4, D: 7.22.

			W	L	PF	PA
1.	GBR	(Charles Smith, George Nevinson, George Cornet, Thomas Thould, George Wilkinson, Paul Radmilovic, Charles Forsyth)	1	0	9	2
2.	BEL	(Albert Michant, Herman Meyboom, Victor Boin, Joseph Pletincx, Fernand Feyaerts, Oscar Grégoire, Herman Donners)	2	1	18	14
3.	SWE	(Torsten Kumfeldt, Axel Runström, Harald Julin, Pontus Hanson, Gunnar Wennerström, Robert Andersson, Erik Bergvall)	0	1	4	8
4.	HOL	(Johan Hendrik Rühl, Johan George Cortlever, Jan Frederik Hulswit, Eduard Meijer, Karel Meijer, Pieter Lodewijk Ooms, Bouke Benehga)	0	1	1	8

Final: GBR 9–2 BEL

Paul Radmilovic of the British team eventually took part in five Olympics as a swimmer and water polo player, and also competed in the 1906 Intercalated Games.

1912 Stockholm T: 6, N: 6, D: 7.22.

			W	L	PF	PA
1.	GBR	(Charles Smith, George Cornet, Charles Bugbee, Arthur Hill, George Wilkinson, Paul Radmilovic, Isaac Bentham)	3	0	21	8
2.	SWE	(Torsten Kumfeldt, Harald Julin, Max Gumpel, Pontus Hanson, Vilhelm Anderson, Robert Andersson, Erik Bergqvist)	3	1	22	11
3.	BEL	(Albert Durant, Herman Donners, Victor Boin, Joseph Pletincx, Oscar Grégoire, Herman Meyboom, Félicien Courbet, Jean Hoffman, Pierre Nijs)	3	2	22	21
4.	AUT	(Rudolf Buchfelder, Richard Manuel, Walter Schachtitz, Otto Scheff, Josef Wagner, Ernst Kovács, Hermann Buchfelder)	1	3	10	25
5.	HUN	(Sándor Ádám, László Beleznai, Tibor Fazekas, Jenö Hégner Tóth, Károly Rémi, János Wenk, Imre Zachár)	0	2	9	11
6.	FRA	(Gustave Prouvost, Gaston Vanlaere, Georges Rigal, Paul Louis Beulque, Jean Rodier, Jean Thorailler, Henri Decotu, Paul Vasseur)	0	2	3	11

Final: GBR 8—0 AUT

Great Britain's closest call was a 7–5 overtime victory over Belgium.

1920 Antwerp T: 11, N: 11, 8.28.

			W	L	PF	PA
1.	GBR/IRL	(Charles Smith, Noel Purcell, Christopher Jones, Charles Bugbee, William Dean, Paul Radmilovic, William Peacock)				

			W	L	PF	PA
2.	BEL	(Albert Durant, Paul Gailly, Pierre Nijs, Joseph Pletincx, Maurice Blitz, René Bauwens, Gérard Blitz, Pierre Dewin)	4	1	27	9
3.	SWE	(Theodor Nauman, Pontus Hanson, Max Gumpel, Vilhelm Anderson, Nils Backlund, Robert Andersson, Erik Andersson, Harald Julin, Erik Bergqvist)	4	1	35	9
4.	USA	(Preston Steiger, Sophus Jensen, Michael McDermott, Clement Browne, Herbert Vollmer, Harry Hebner, James Cardson, William Vosburgh, G. Albert Taylor, Duke Paoa Kahanamoku, Perry McGillivray, Norman Ross)	2	3	16	19
5.	HOL	(Karel Struys, Carl Kratz, Karel Meijer, Johan Cortlever, Piet Hein Plantinga, Gérard Bohlander, Jean van Silfhout)	1	2	12	11

Final: GBR 3—2 BEL

The victory of the team from the United Kingdom was not a popular one. After the final match Belgian spectators attacked the British and Irish players, who had to be taken away under the protection of armed guards.

1924 Paris T: 12, N: 12, D: 7.20.

			W	L	PF	PA
1.	FRA	(Paul Dujardin, Noël Delberghe, Georges Rigal, Henri Padou, Robert Desmettre, Albert Mayaud, Albert Delborgies)	4	0	16	6
2.	BEL	(Albert Durant, Joseph Pletincx, Pierre Dewin, Gerard Blitz, Joseph Cludts, Georges Fleurix, Paul Gailly, Jules Thiry, Pierre Vermetten, Joseph de Combe, Maurice Blitz)	5	1	20	11
3.	USA	(Frederick Lauer, Oliver Horn, Clarence Mitchell, George Schroth, Herbert Vollmer, Johnny Weissmuller, Arthur Austin, John Norton, Wallace O'Connor)	3	3	14	13
4.	SWE	(Theodor Nauman, Gösta Persson, Vilhelm Anderson, Martin Norberg, Erik Andersson, Nils Backlund, Cletus Anderson, Hilmer Wictorin)	3	3	27	12
5.	HUN	(István Barta, Tibor Fazekas, Márton Homonnai, Alajos Keserü, Lajos Homonnai, János Wenk, Ferenc Keserü, József Vértesy)	2	2	17	17
6.	CZE	(Václav Ankrt, František Franěk, František Kúrka, Hugo Klempfner, Josef Tomášek, Jiří Reitman, Béla Nemenyi, Jan Hora, František Vacin, Jaroslav Hummelhans)	2	2	11	15

Final: FRA 300 BEL

The French victory over Belgium came as a great surprise. The Parisian crowd was so excited that, after the playing of the "Marseillaise," they demanded that the Belgian national anthem be played as well. Belgium's loss dropped them into a playoff pool for second place. After defeating Sweden 4–2, they beat the United States, 2–1. However, the Americans lodged a protest, which was allowed. The match was replayed, and the Belgians won again, 2–1.

1928 Amsterdam T: 14, N: 14, D: 8.11.

		W	L	PF	PA
1. GER	(Erich Rademacher, Otto Cordes, Emil Benecke, Fritz Gunst, Joachim Rademacher, Karl Bähre, Max Amann, Johannes Blank)	3	0	18	10
2. HUN	(István Barta, Sándor Ivády, Alajos Keserü, Márton Homonnai, Ferenc Keserü, József Vértesy, Olivér Halassy)	3	1	26	8
3. FRA	(Paul Dujardin, Jules Keignaert, Henri Padou, Emile Bulteel, Achille Tribouillet, Henri Cuvelier, Albert Vandeplancke, Ernest Rogez, Albert Thévenon)	5	1	41	7
4. GBR	(E.H. Temme, Paul Radmilovic, E. Percy Peters, N.V. Beaman, J.E.C. Budd, L. Ablett, R. Hodgson, John Hatfield, W. Quick, W.G. Freeguard)	2	2	15	21

Final: GER 5—2 HUN

Germany defeated Hungary in overtime after the regulation periods ended in a 2–2 tie.

1932 Los Angeles T: 5, N: 5, D: 8.13.

		W	L	T	PF	PA
1. HUN	(György Bródy, Sándor Ivády, Márton Homonnai, Oliver Halassy, József Vértesy, Janös Németh, Ferenc Keserü, Alajos Keserü, István Barta, Miklós Sárkány)	3	0	0	30	2
2. GER	(Erich Rademacher, Fritz Gunst, Otto Cordes, Emil Benecke, Joachim Rademacher, Heiko Schwartz, Hans Schulze, Hans Eckstein)	2	1	1	23	13
3. USA	(Herbert Wildman, F. Calvert Strong, Charles Finn, Harold McAllister, Philip Daubenspeck, Austin Clapp, Wallace O'Connor)	2	1	1	20	12
4. JAP	(Takashige Matsumoto, Akira Fujita, Shuji Doi, Iwao Tokito, Yasutaro Sakagami, Takaji Takebayashi, Tosuke Sawami, Seibei Kimura)	0	3	0	0	37

The team from Brazil, having lost 7–3 to Germany, gave a cheer for their conquerors, climbed out of the pool, and physically attacked the Hungarian referee, Béla Komjadi. They didn't let up until the police arrived. Needless to say, the entire Brazilian team was suspended and their remaining games were forfeited.

1936 Berlin T: 16, N: 16, D: 8.15.

		W	L	T	PF	PA
1. HUN	(György Bródy, Kálmán Hazai, Márton Homonnai, Oliver Halassy, Jenö Brandi, Janös Németh, Mihály Bozsi, György Kutasi, Miklós Sárkány, Sándor Tarics, István Molnár)	8	0	1	57	5
2. GER	(Paul Klingenburg, Bernhard Baier, Gustav Schürger, Fritz Gunst, Josef Hauser, Hans Schneider, Hans Schulze, Fritz Stolze, Heinrich Krug, Alfred Kienzle, Helmuth Schwenn)	8	0	1	56	10
3. BEL	(Henri Disy, Joseph de Combe, Henri Stoelen, Fernand Isselé, Albert Castelyns, Gérard Blitz, Pierre Coppieters, Henri de Pauw, Edmond Michiels)	4	3	2	17	17
4. FRA	(Georges Delporte, Paul Lambert, Maurice Lefebvre, Henri Padou, Roger Vandecastelle, André Busch, René Joder)	4	5	0	21	37
5. HOL	(Johannes van Woerkom, Jean Marie van Oostrom Soede, Rudolf den Hamer, Gerard Regter, Hans Maier, Cornelius van Aelst, Alexander Franken, Herman Alex Veenstra, Jan van Heteren)	3	1	5	23	28
6. AUT	(Franz Wenninger, Karl Seitz, Karl Steinbach, Sebastian Ploner, Franz Schönfels, Alfred Lergetporer, Wilhelm Hawlik, Erwin Blasl, Otto Müller, Anton Kunz, Peter Reidl)	5	3	1	31	18
7. SWE	(Åke Nauman, Bertil Berg, Tore Ljungqvist, Gösta Persson, Erik Holm, Georg Svensson [Sollermark], Göte Andersson, Tore Lindzen, Runar Sandström)	3	6	0	29	18
8. GBR	(North, Grogan, George Matt Milton, Theodore Temme, Martin, Sutton, Mitchell, Ablett, David McGregor, Blake)	2	4	3	28	46

Hungary and Germany tied 2–2, but Hungary was awarded first place on the basis of a greater goal differential.

Oliver Halassy played on three Hungarian Olympic water polo teams, despite the fact that one of his legs had been amputated below the knee following an accident when he was 11. According to Hungarian sources, he died on September 10, 1946, at the age of 37, "under tragic circumstances."

1948 London T: 18, N: 18, D: 8.7.

		W	L	T	PF	PA
1. ITA	(Pasquale Buonocore, Emilio Bulgarelli, Cesare Rubini, Geminio Ognio, Ermenegildo Arena, Aldo Ghira, Gianfranco Pandolfini, Mario Maioni, Tullio Pandolfini)	8	0	2	47	24

			W	L	T	PF	PA
2.	HUN	(Endre Györffi, Miklós Holop, Dezsö Gyarmati, Károly Szittya, Oszkár Csuvik, István Szivós, Dezsö Lemhényi, László Jeney, Deszö Fábián, Jenö Brandi)	6	3	1	45	27
3.	HOL	(Johannes Rohner, Cornelis Korevaar, Cornelius Braasem, Hans Stam, Albert Ruimschotel, Rudolph van Feggelen, Fritz Smol, Pieter Salomons, Hendrikus Keetelaar)	6	1	3	65	23
4.	BEL	(Théo-Léo de Smet, Georges Leenheere, Emile d'Hooge, Paul Rigaumont, Fernand Isselé, Willy Simons, Alphonse Martin)	2	2	6	32	25
5.	SWE	(Rune Öberg, Erik Holm, Rolf Julin, Roland Spaongberg, Arne Jutner, Olle Johansson, Åke Julin, Folke Eriksson, Knut Gadd, Olle Ohlsson)	6	3	1	31	14
6.	FRA	(François Debonnet, Maurice Lefebvre, Robert Le Bras, Marco Diener, Robert Himgi, Roger Dewasch, Jacques Berthe, R. Massol, Jacques Viaene, Emile Bermyn, Marcel Spilliaert)	4	2	4	32	24
7.	EGY	(Ahmed Nessim, Taha El Gamal, M. Kadry, M. Haraga, H. Said, Abdel Aziz Mohammed Khalifa, S. Garbo, M. Hemmat)	1	4	5	26	35
8.	SPA	(J. Serra Liobet, J. Pujol Coma, C. Falp Mont, C. Marti Arenas, Francisco Castillo Caupana, Augustin Mestres Ribas, V. Sabate Mas, A. Sabata Figa)	2	8	0	26	33

1952 Helsinki T: 21, N: 21, D: 8.2.

			W	L	T	PF	PA
1.	HUN	(László Jeney, György Vízvári, Dezsö Gyarmati, Kálmán Markovits, Antal Bolvári, István Szivós, György Kárpáti, Róbert Antal, Dezsö Fábián, Károly Szittya, Dezsö Lemhényi, István Hasznos, Miklós Martin)	7	0	3	60	21
2.	YUG	(Zdravko Kovačić, Veljko Bakašun, Ivo Štakula, Ivo Kurtini, Boško Vuksanović, Zdravko Ježic, Lovro Radonjić, Marko Brainović, Vlado Ivković)	7	0	3	46	16
3.	ITA	(Raffaello Gambino, Vincenzo Polito, Cesare Rubini, Carlo Peretti, Ermenegildo Arena, Maurizio Mannelli, Renato De Sanzuane, Renato Traiola, Geminio Ognio, Salvatore Gionta, Lucio Ceccarini)	8	2	0	53	29
4.	USA	(Harry Bisbey, James Norris, Edward Jaworski, Norman Lake, William Kooistra, Peter Stange, Norman Dornblaser, John Spargo, Robert Hughes, Maroni Burns)	5	6	0	43	41

			W	L	T	PF	PA
5.	HOL	(Marcus van Gelder, Gerrit Bijsma, Cornelis Korevaar, Cornelius Braasem, Frits Smol, Rudolph van Geggelen, Johannes Cabout)	7	2	1	45	22
6.	BEL	(Théo-Léo de Smet, Alphonse Martin, Joseph Smits, André Laurent, Marcel Heyninck, Roland Sierens, Johan van den Steen, Francois Maesschalck, Georges Leenheere, Joseph Reynders)	6	3	1	37	35
7.	SOV	(Boris Goikhman, Yevgeny Semenov, Yuri Teplov, Lev Kokorin, Valentin Prokopov, Aleksandr Liferenko, Pyotr Mshvenieradze, Yuri Schlyapin, Vitaly Ushakov)	4	4	2	43	34
8.	SPA	(Leandro Ribera, Ricardo Conde, José Bazan, Roberto Queralt, Anthonio Subirana, Augustin Mestres Ribas, José Abellan, Francisco Castillo Caupano)	3	7	0	33	41

Holland defeated Yugoslavia 3–2 in a game of the semifinal round. However the Yugoslavs protested two decisions of the referee, and the match was ordered replayed. This time Yugoslavia won, 2–1, and advanced to the final round, in which they tied Hungary, 2–2, but lost because of a lower goal differential. One of the Hungarian players was Dezsö Gyarmati, who eventually won medals in five different Olympics (1948–1964.) His wife, Éva Székely, was a breaststroker who won a gold medal in 1952 and a silver in 1956.

1956 Melbourne T: 10, N: 10, D: 12.7.

			W	L	T	PF	PA
1.	HUN	(Ottó Boros, István Hevesi, Dezsö Gyarmati, Kálmán Markovits, Antal Bolvári, Mihály Mayer, György Kárpáti, László Jeney, István Szivós, Tivadar Kanizsa, Ervin Zádor)	7	0	0	32	6
2.	YUG	(Zdravko Kovačić, Ivo Cipci, Hrvoje Kačič, Marjan Žuzej, Zdravko Ježić, Lovro Radonjič, Tomislav Franjkovič, Vladimir Ivkovič)	6	1	1	28	13
3.	SOV	(Boris Goikhman, Viktor Ageyev, Yuri Schlyapin, Vyacheslav Kurennoi, Pyotr Breus, Pyotr Mshvenieradze, Nodar Gyakharia, Mikhail Ryschak, Valentin Prokopov, Boris Markarov)	5	3	0	23	20
4.	ITA	(Enzo Cavazzoni, Cesare Rubini, Angelo Marciani, Paolo Pucci, Federico Dennerlein, Giuseppe D'Altrui, Alfonso Buonocore, Cosimo Antonelli, Luigi Mannelli, Maurizio D'Achille)	4	3	0	21	16
5.	USA	(Robert Horn, William Ross, Robert Frojen, Wallace Wolf, Ronald Severa, James Gaughran, William	2	5	1	18	25

		W	L	T	PF	PA
	Kooistra, Kenneth Hahn, Robert Hughes, Sam Kooistra)					
6. GER	(Karl Neuse, Alfred Obschernikat, Wilfried Bode, Hans-Joachim Schneider, Wilhelm Sturm, Hans-Günther Hilker, Friedhelm Osselmann, Emil Bildstein, Erich Pennekamp, Hans Werner Seher)	1	5	1	18	25
7. GBR	(Arthur Grady, Gerald Worsell, John Shaw Jones, Peter Pass, Ronald Turner, Terence Miller, Edwin Spooner, John Ferguson, Robert Knights)	3	2	0	25	20
8. ROM	(Alexandru Marinescu, Zoltan Hospodar, Aurel Zahan, Gavril Nagy, Francisc Simon, Ivan Bordi, Alexandru Szabo, Alexandru Badita, Iosif Deutsch)	3	3	0	30	17

On November 4, 1956, 200,000 Soviet troops invaded Hungary to put down a major revolt against Communist rule. The bitter feelings between the Hungarians and Soviets carried over into the Olympics, which were held less than three weeks later. Hostilities culminated in the water polo match between the two countries on December 6. The game quickly turned into a brawl and was halted by the referee before completion, with Hungary leading 4–0. Hungary was credited with a victory; however the police had to be called in to prevent a riot, as the 5500 spectators wanted to punish the Soviets further.

1960 Rome T: 16, N: 16, D: 9.3.

		W	L	T	PF	PA
1. ITA	(Dante Rossi, Giuseppe D'Altrui, Eraldo Pizzo, Gianni Lonzi, Franco Lavoratori, Rosario Parmegiani, Danio Bardi, Brunello Spinelli, Salvatore Gionta, Amadeo Ambron, Giancarlo Guerrini)	8	0	1	37	15
2. SOV	(Leri Gogoladze, Givi Chikvanaya, Vyacheslav Kurennoi, Anatoly Kartashov, Yuri Grigorovsky, Pyotr Mshvenieradze, Vladimir Semyonov, Boris Goikhman, Yevgeny Salzyn, Viktor Ageyev, Vladimir Novikov)	6	2	1	35	26
3. HUN	(Ottó Boros, István Hevesi, Mihály Mayer, Dezsö Gyarmati, Tivadar Kanizsa, Zoltán Dömötör, László Felkai, László Jeney, András Katona, Kálmán Markovits, Péter Rusorán, György Kárpáti, János Konrád, András Bodnár)	5	2	2	45	22
4. YUG	(Milan Muškatirovič, Hrvoje Kačić, Zlatko Šimenc, Zdravko Ježić, Marijan Žužej, Ante Nardeli, Mirko Sandič, Božidar Staniŝić, Dragoljub Siljak)	7	2	0	31	15

		W	L	T	PF	PA
5. ROM	(Mircea Stefănescu, Alexandru Bădiță, Aurel Zahan, Gavrila Blajek, Alexandru Szabo, Anatol Grintescu, Stefan Kroner)	4	3	2	34	26
6. GER	(Hans Hoffmeister, Hans-Joachim Schneider, Hans Schepers, Bernd Strasser, Lajos Nagy, Friedhelm Osselmann, Dieter Seiz, Emil Bildstein, Jürgen Honig)	4	5	0	42	48
7. USA	(Robert Horn, Marvin Burns, Ronald Severa, Ronald Crawford, Fred Tisue, Wallace Wolf, Robert Volmer, Gordon Hall, Charles Bittick, Charles McIlroy)	4	5	0	42	48
8. HOL	(Lambertus Kniest, Harry Lamme, Frederik Van der Zwan, Harro Ran, C.W. Leenards Abraham, Henri Vriend, Alfred Van Dorp, Johannes Muller, Hendrik Hermsen)	1	7	1	32	38

1964 Tokyo T: 13, N: 13, D: 10.18.

		W	L	T	PF	PA
1. HUN	(Miklos Ambrus, László Felkai, János Konrád, Zoltán Dömötör, Tivadar Kanizsa, Péter Rusorán, György Kárpáti, Ottó Boros, Mihály Mayer, Dénes Pócsik, András Bodnár, Deszö Gyarmati)	6	0	2	43	17
2. YUG	(Milan Muškatirović, Ivo Trumbić, Vinko Rosić, Zlatko Šimenc, Bozidar Stanišić, Ante Nardeli, Zoran Janković, Mirko Sandić, Ozren Bonačič, Frane Nonkovič, Karlo Stipanić)	7	0	2	42	16
3. SOV	(Igor Grabovsky, Vladimir Kuznyetsov, Boris Grishin, Boris Popov, Nikolai Kalashnikov, Zenon Bortkevich, Nikolai Kuzynetsov, Viktor Ageyev, Leonid Osipov, Vladimir Semyonov, Eduard Yegorov)	5	2	1	20	13
4. ITA	(Dante Rossi, Giuseppe D'Altrui, Eraldo Pizzo, Gianni Lonzi, Franco Lavoratori, Rosario Parmegiani, Mario Cevasco, Eugenio Merello, Alberto Spinola, Danio Bardi, Giancarlo Guerrini, Federico Dennerlein)	4	4	0	17	19
5. ROM	(Mircea Ştefănescu, Anatol Grintescu, Alexandru Szabo, Ştefan Kroner, Nicolae Firoiu, Gruia Novac, Cornel Mărculescu, Emil Muresan, Aurel Zahan, Iosif Kulineac)	4	3	1	36	28
6. GDR	(Peter Schmidt, Hubert Höhne, Siegfried Ballerstedt, Edgar Thiele, Klaus Schulze, Jürgen Thiel', Klaus Schlenkrich, Heinz Mäder, Dieter Vohs, Jürgen Kluge, Heinz Wittig)	3	5	0	26	26
7. BEL	(Hendrik Hermsen, Abraham Leenards, Willem van Spingelen, Gerar-	2	6	0	28	43

dus Wormgoor, Alfred van Dorp, Henri Vriend, Nicolaas van der Voet, Willem Vriend, Johan Muller, Jan Bultman, Lambertus Kniest)

8. HOL (Bruno de Hesselle, Frank Dosterlinck, Roger de Wilde, Jacques Caufrier, Andre Laurent, Karel de Vis, Jose de Vis, Jose Dumont, Johan van den Steen, Leon Pickers, Joseph Stappers)   4 5 0 37 47

Thirty-seven-year-old Dezsö Gyarmati brought his medal total to three gold, one silver, and one bronze. The Hungarians' narrow victory was the result of a 4–4 tie with Yugoslavia, in which they scored their final goal with only 25 seconds to play. After that they won because of a greater goal differential in the final round. A minor controversy developed when Hungary and Italy complained that the shallow pool (5 feet 10 inches deep) allowed the taller Yugoslav players to stand with their heads above the water.

1968 Mexico City T: 15, N: 15, D: 10.26.

			W	L	T	PF	PA
1.	YUG	(Karlo Stipanić, Ivo Trumbić, Ozren Bonačić, Uroš Marović, Ronald Lopatny, Zoran Janković, Miroslav Poljak, Dejan Dabović, Djordje Perišić, Mirko Sandič, Zdravko Hebel)	7	1	1	86	35
2.	SOV	(Vadim Gulyayev, Givi Chikvanaya, Boris Grishin, Aleksandr Dolgushin, Aleksei Barkalov, Yuri Grigorovsky, Vladimir Semyonov, Aleksandr Shidlovsky, Vyacheslav Skok, Leonid Osipov, Oleg Bovin)	6	2	0	62	36
3.	HUN	Endre Molnár, Mihály Mayer, István Szivós, János Konrád, László Felkai, Ferenc Konrád, Dénes Pócsik, András Bodnár, Zoltán Dömötör, János Steinmetz)	6	2	0	54	26
4.	ITA	(Alberto Alberani Samaritani, Eraldo Pizzo, Mario Cevasco, Gianni Lonzi, Enzo Barlocco, Franco Lavoratori, Gianni De Magistris, Alessandro Ghibellini, Giancarlo Guerrini, Paolo Ferrando, Eugenio Merello)	6	2	1	57	38
5.	USA	(Anton Van Dorp, David Ashleigh, Russell Webb, Ronald Crawford, Stanley Cole, Bruce Bradlay, L. Dean Willeford, Barry Weitzenberg, Gary Sheerer, John Parker, Steven Barnett)	5	2	1	49	43
6.	GDR	(Hans-Georg Fehn, Klaus Schlenkrich, Jürgen Thiel, Siegfried Ballerstedt, Peter Rund, Jürgen Schüler, Jürgen Kluge, Veit Herrmanns, Manfred Herzog, Hans-Ulrich Lange, Peter Schmidt)	6	2	1	78	30

7. HOL (Feike de Vries, Hans Wouda, Louis Geutjes, Johannes Hoogveld, Alfred van Dorp, Hans Parrel, Nicolaas van der Voet, Ad Moolhuijzen, Bart Bonger, Andreas Hermsen, Evert Kroon)   5 3 1 53 39

8. CUB (Oscar Periche, Waldimiro Arcos, Miguel Garcia, Rolando Valdes, Ruben Junco, Guillermo Martinez, Ibrahim Rodriguez, Osvaldo Garcia, Roberto Rodriguez, Guillermo Canete, Jesús Perez)   3 4 1 38 51

In the final match, Yugoslavia defeated the U.S.S.R. 13–11 in overtime, despite seven goals by Aleksei Barkalov, including two in the last 35 seconds of regulation. Australia had been accepted as one of the 16 teams to take part in the tournament. However, the Australian Olympic Committee considered it a waste of money to send their team to Mexico City. The players paid their own way, but were not allowed to compete.

1972 Munich T: 16, N: 16, D: 9.4.

			W	L	T	PF	PA
1.	SOV	(Vadim Gulyaev, Anatoly Akimov, Aleksandr Dreval, Aleksandr Dolgushin, Vladimir Shmudski, Aleksandr Kabanov, Aleksei Barkalov, Aleksandr Shidlovsky, Nikolai Melnikov, Leonid Osipov, Vyacheslav Sobchenko)	7	0	2	52	25
2.	HUN	(Endre Molnár, András Bodnár, István Görgényi, Zoltán Kásás, Tamás Faragó, László Sárosi, István Szivós, István Magas, Dénes Pócsik, Ferenc Konrád, Tibor Cservenyák)	6	0	3	45	24
3.	USA	(James Slatton, Stanley Cole, Russell Webb, Barry Weitzenberg, Gary Sheerer, Bruce Bradley, Peter Asch, James Ferguson, Steven Barnett, John Parker, Eric Lindroth)	7	1	2	55	41
4.	GER	(Gerd Olbert, Hermann Haverkamp, Peter Teicher, Kurt Küpper, Günter Wolf, Ingulf Nossek, Ludger Weeke, Kurt Schuhmann, Jürgen Stiefel, Hans Georg Simon, Hans Hoffmeister)	2	2	5	36	31
5.	YUG	(Karlo Stipanić, Ratko Rudić, Ozren Bonačić, Uros Marović, Ronald Lopatni, Zoran Jankovic, Sinisa Belamarić, Dušan Antunović, Djordje Perišić, Mirko Sandić, Milos Marković)	5	4	1	55	48
6.	ITA	(Alberto Alberani Samaritani, Eraldo Pizzo, Roldano Simeoni, Mario Cevasco, Allessandro Ghibellini, Gianni De Magistris, Guglielmo Marsili, Silvio Baracchini,	3	4	2	48	42

		W	L	T	PF	PA
	Franco Lavoratori, Sante Marsili, Ferdinando Lignano)					
7. HOL	(Evert Kroon, Hans Wouda, Jan Evert Veer, Hans Hoogveld, Wim Hermsen, Hans Parrel, Ton Schmidt, Mart Bras, Tony Buunk, Gijs Stroboer, Wim van der Schilde)	6	1	2	43	31
8. ROM	(Serban Huber, Bogdan Mihailescu, Gheorghe Zamfirescu, Gruia Novac, Dinu Popescu, Claudiu Rusu, Iosif Kuliniac, Cornel Rusu, Viorel Rus, Radu Lazar, Corneliu Fratila)	5	4	1	62	45

The tournament included a bloody match between Yugoslavia and Cuba, and a contest between Hungary and Italy in which eight players were suspended within one 38-second span.

1976 Montreal T: 12, N: 12, D: 7.27.

		W	L	T	PF	PA
1. HUN	(Endre Molnár, István Szivós Jr., Tamás Faragó, László Sárosi, György Horkai, Gábor Csapó, Attila Sudár, György Kenéz, György Gerendás, Ferenc Konrád, Tibor Cservenyák)	7	0	1	45	32
2. ITA	(Alberto Alberani, Roldano Simeoni, Silvio Baracchini, Sante Marsili, Marcello Del Duca, Gianni De Magistris, Alessandro Ghibellini, Luigi Castagnola, Riccardo De Magistris, Vincenzo D'Angelo, Umberto Panerai)	4	1	3	47	33
3. HOL	(Evert Kroon, Nico Landeweerd, Jan Evert Veer, Hans van Zeeland, Ton Buunk, Piet de Zwarte, Hans Smits, Rik Toonen, Gyze Stroboer, Andy Hoepelman, Alex Boegschoten)	5	1	2	32	27
4. ROM	Florin Slavei, Corneliu Rusu, Gheorghe Zamfirescu, Adrian Nastasiu, Dinu Popescu, Claudiu Rusu, Ilie Slavei, Liviu Raducanu, Viorel Rus, Adrian Schervan, Doru Spinu)	2	2	4	44	39
5. YUG	(Milos Marković, Ozren Bonačić, Uros Marović, Predrag Manojlović, Djuro Savinović, Damir Polić, Sinisa Belamarić, Dušan Antunović, Dejan Dabović, Boško Loziča, Zoran Kačić)	1	2	5	46	34
6. GER	(Günter Kilian, Ludger Weeke, Hans-Georg Simon, Jürgen Stiefel, Roland Freund, Wolfgang Mechler, Martin Jellinghaus, Werner Obschernikat, Horst Kilian, Peter Röhle, Günter Wolf)	2	5	1	24	28

		W	L	T	PF	PA
7. CUB	(Oscar Periche, Osvaldo Garcia, Ramon Pena, Lazaro Costa, David Rodriguez, Nelson Dominguez, Jorge Rizo, Eugenio Almeneiro, Jesus Perez, Gerardo Rodriguez, Oriel Dominguez)	5	1	2	56	31
8. SOV	(Anatoly Klebanov, Sergei Kotenko, Aleksandr Dreval, Aleksandr Dolgushin, Vitaly Romanchuk, Aleksandr Kabanov, Aleksei Barkalov, Nikolai Melnikov, Nugzar Mshvenieradze, Vladimir Iselidze, Aleksandr Zakharov)	4	2	2	47	28

The Soviet team was so humiliated by their failure to qualify for the final round of six that they tried to withdraw from the losers' round for seventh to 12th places, claiming that five of their players were too ill to compete. After forfeiting one game against Cuba, F.I.N.A. officials convinced them to continue with the tournament.

1980 Moscow T: 12, N: 12, D: 7.29.

		W	L	T	PF	PA
1. SOV	(Yevgeny Sharonov, Sergei Kotenko, Vladimir Akimov, Yevgeny Grishin, Mait Riysman, Aleksandr Kabanov, Aleksei Barkalov, Erkin Shagaev, Georgy Mshvenieradze, Mikhail Ivanov, Vyacheslav Sobchenko)	8	0	0	58	31
2. YUG	(Luka Vezilic, Zoran Gopcevic, Damir Polić, Ratko Rudić, Zoran Mustur, Zoran Roje, Milivoj Bebic, Slobodan Trifunovic, Boško Loziča, Predrag Manojlović, Milorad Krivokapic)	5	1	2	58	42
3. HUN	(Endre Molnár, István Szivós Jr., Attila Sudár, György Gerendás, György Horkai, Gábor Csapó, István Kiss, István Udvardi, László Kuncz, Tamás Faragó, Károly Hauszler)	5	2	1	51	44
4. SPA	(Manuel Delgado, Gaspar Ventura, Antonio Esteller, Federico Sabria, Manuel Estiarte, Pedro Robert, Jorge Alonso, José Alcazar, Antonio Aguilar, Jorge Carmona, Salvador Franch)	4	4	0	43	42
5. CUB	(Oscar Periche Cordet, Orlando Cowley del Barrio, Barbaro Diaz Cervantes, Lazaro Costa Mendez, Pedro Rodriguez Rodriguez, Nelson Dominguez Avila, Jorge Rizo Perera, Arturo Ramos Hernandez, Carlos Benitez Suarez, Gerardo Rodriguez Peñalver, Oriel Dominguez Avila)	2	3	3	50	49
6. HOL	(Wouly de Bie, Nicolaas Landeweerd, Jan Evert Veer, Hans van	2	5	1	42	48

Zeeland, Ton Buunk, Erik Noorder-
graaf, Stan van Belkum, Adrianus
van Mil, Dick Nieuwenhuizen, Jan
Jaap Korevaar, Rudolf Misdorp)

7. AUS (Michael Turner, David Neesham,   5 2 1 45 39
Robert Bryant, Peter Montgomeri,
Julian Muspratt, Andrew Kerr, An-
thony Falson, Charles Turner, Mar-
tin Callaghan, Randall Goff, Andrew
Steward)

8. ITA (Alberto Alberani, Roldano Si- 4 3 1 40 35
meoni, Alfio Misaggi, Sante Marsili,
Massimo Fondelli, Gianni De Ma-
gistris, Antonello Steardo, Paolo
Ragosa, Romeo Collina, D'Angelo
Vincenzo, Umberto Panerai)

The U.S.S.R. clinched first place with a tension-packed
8–7 victory over Yugoslavia.

Discontinued Events

50-YARD FREESTYLE

1904 St. Louis C: 9, N: 2, D: 9.6.

			SWIM-OFF
1. Zoltán Halmay	HUN	28.2	28.0
2. J. Scott Leary	USA	28.2	28.6
3. Charles Daniels	USA	—	
4. David Gaul	USA	—	
5. Leo Goodwin	USA	—	
6. Raymond Thorne	USA	—	

Halmay defeated Leary by a foot. However, the U.S. judge
declared that Leary had won. A brawl broke out and went
on for some time. Finally it was decided to call the race a
dead heat and to have the two men swim again. After two
false starts, Halmay was off quickly and won easily.

100-METER FREESTYLE FOR SAILORS

1896 Athens C: 3, N: 1, D: 4.11.
1. Ioannis Matokinis   GRE   2:20.4
2. S. Chasapis   GRE   —
3. Dimitrios Drivas   GRE   —

This rather specialized event was limited to members of the
Greek navy.

880-YARD FREESTYLE

1904 St. Louis C: 6, N: 4, D: 9.7.
1. Emil Rausch   GER   13:11.4
2. Francis Gailey   USA   13:23.4
3. Géza Kiss   HUN   —
4. Edgar Adams   USA   —
AC: Jamison Handy (USA), Otto Wahle (AUT)

4000-METER FREESTYLE

1900 Paris C: 29, N: 7, D: 8.19.
1. John Arthur Jarvis   GBR   58:24.0
2. Zoltán Halmay   HUN   1:08:55.4
3. Louis Martin   FRA   1:13.08.4
4. Thomas Burgess   FRA   1:15:07.6
5. Eduard Meijer   HOL   1:16:37.2
6. Fabio Mainoni   ITA   1:18:25.4

400-METER BREASTSROKE

1904 St. Louis C: 4, N: 2, D: 9.7.
(440 Yards—402.33 Meters)
1. Georg Zacharias   GER   7:23.6
2. Walter Brack   GER   —
3. Jamison Handy   USA   —
4. Georg Hoffmann   GER   —

1906–1908 not held

1912 Stockholm C: 17, N: 10, D: 7.12.
1. Walter Bathe   GER   6:29.6   OR
2. Thor Henning   SWE   6:35.6
3. Percy Courtman   GBR   6:36.4
4. Kurt Malisch   GER   6:37.0
DNF: Willy Lützow (GER)

The appropriately named Walter Bathe won without being
seriously threatened.

1920 Antwerp C: 18, N: 10, D: 8.25.
1. Håkan Malmroth   SWE   6:31.8
2. Thor Henning   SWE   6:45.2
3. Arvo Aaltonen   FIN   6:48.0
4. Jack Howell   USA   6:51.0
5. Per Cederblom   SWE   —
6. Michael McDermott   USA   —

200-METER TEAM SWIMMING

1900 Paris T: 4, N: 2, D: 8.12.
1. GER (1—Ernst Hoppenberg 2:35.0, 2—Max Hainle   32
2:36.0, 4—Max Schöne, 6—Julius Frey, 19—Herbert
von Petersdorff)
2. FRA (Tritons Lillois—Maurice Hochepied, Verbecke, Ca- 51
det, Bertrand, Victor Hochepied)
3. FRA (Pupilles de Neptune, Lille—G. Leuillieux, Louis Mar- 61
tin, Houben, Tartara, Désiré Merchez)
4. FRA (Libellule de Paris—members unknown)   65

This was not a relay, but a team race in which 20 men were
entered. Each team was assigned points according to the
places in which its individual members finished. Von Petersdorff did not actually take part and so was awarded a
tie for last place. A British team had also been entered, but
was misinformed as to the starting time and arrived after
the race was over.

4×50-YARD FREESTYLE RELAY

1904 St. Louis T: 4, N: 1, D: 9.7.

1. USA (New York Athletic Club #1—Joseph Ruddy, 2:04.6
   Leo Goodwin, Louis Handle, Charles Daniels)
2. USA (Chicago Athletic Club—David Hammond, Wil- —
   liam Tuttle, Hugo Goetz, Raymond Thorne)
3. USA (Missouri Athletic Club—Amadee Reyburn, —
   Gwynne Evans, Marquard Schwartz, William
   Orthwein)
4. USA (New York Athletic Club #2—Edgar Adams, Da- —
   vid Bratton, George Van Cleaf, David Hesser)

A German team lined up to start the race, but the Americans objected, claiming that the race was for clubs only and that the German swimmers were not all from the same club. Not surprisingly, the U.S. officials in charge ruled in favor of the Americans.

OBSTACLE RACE

1900 Paris C: 12, N: 5, D: 8.12.

1. Frederick Lane	AUS	2:38.4
2. Otto Wahle	AUT	2:40.0
3. Peter Kemp	GBR	2:47.4
4. Karl Ruberl	AUT	2:51.2
5. Stapleton	GBR	2:55.0
6. William Henry	GBR	2:58.0

This quaint event required the participants to struggle past three sets of obstacles. First they had to climb over a pole, then they had to scramble over a row of boats, and finally they had to swim *under* another row of boats. Some sources state that the contestants swam through barrels rather than over and under boats. Frederick Lane was probably better known for his victory in the unimpeded 200-meter freestyle.

UNDERWATER SWIMMING

1900 Paris C: 10, N: 4, D; 8.12.

		M	TIME	PTS.
1. Charles de Vendeville	FRA	60	1:08.4	188.4
2. A. Six	FRA	60	1:05.4	185.4
3. Peder Lykkeberg	DEN	28.50	1:30.0	147.0
4. de Romand	FRA	47.50	50.2	145.0
5. Tisserand	FRA	30.75	48.0	109.5
6. Hans Aniol	GER	36.95	30.0	103.9

Two points were awarded for each meter swum and one point for each second that the swimmer was able to stay under water.

PLUNGE FOR DISTANCE

1904 St. Louis C: 5, N: 1, D: 9.5.

		M	FT.–IN.
1. William Dickey	USA	19.05	62–6
2. Edgar Adams	USA	17.53	57–6
3. Leo Goodwin	USA	17.37	57–0
4. Newman Samuels	USA	16.76	55–0
5. Charles Pyrah	USA	14.02	46–0

In the plunge for distance, the contestants began with a standing dive, then remained motionless for 60 seconds or until their heads broke the surface of the water, whichever came first. Then the length of their dives was measured. Charles Pyrah held the U.S. record at 63 feet, but was "completely out of form" according to the local newspapers. It was most unfortunate that the great British plungers John Arthur Jarvis and W. Taylor did not make the trip to St. Louis. Jarvis won the 1904 Amateur Swimming Association plunging championship with a plunge of 75 feet 4 inches, while Taylor was the national record holder at 78 feet 9 inches. In 1930 Arthur Beaumont plunged 85 feet 10 inches. The A.S.A. championship was discontinued after 1946.

PLAIN HIGH DIVING

The plain high dive was just that—nothing fancy, no twists or somersaults.

1912 Stockholm C: 30, N: 8, D: 7.11.

		POINTS	ORDINALS
1. Erik Adlerz	SWE	40.0	7
2. Hjalmar Johansson	SWE	39.3	12
3. John Janssen	SWE	39.1	12
4. Viktor Crondahl	SWE	37.1	22
5. Tovio Aro	FIN	36.5	26
6. Axel Runström	SWE	36.0	26
7. Ernst Brandsten	SWE	36.2	28

DNF: Paul Günther (GER)

1920 Antwerp C: 22, N: 11, D: 8.25.

		POINTS	ORDINALS
1. Arvid Wallman	SWE	183.5	7
2. Nils Skoglund	SWE	183.0	8
3. John Jansson	SWE	175.0	16
4. Erik Adlerz	SWE	173.0	19
5. Yrjö Valkama	FIN	167.5	23
6. Herold Jansson	DEN	159.0	27
7. F. Sauvage	BEL	—	34
8. A. Wellish	BRA	—	37

Silver medalist Nils Skoglund was 13 years old.

1924 Paris C: 25, N: 10, D: 7.15.

		TIME	ORDINALS
1. Richmond Eve	AUS	160.0	13.5
2. John Jansson	SWE	157.0	14.5
3. Harold Clarke	GBR	158.0	15.5
4. Ben Trash	USA	145.0	23.5
5. Raymond Vincent	FRA	144.0	26.5
6. Peter Desjardins	USA	141.0	28
7. A. Reginald Knight	GBR	137.0	31
8. Arvid Wallman	SWE	136.0	31

SWIMMING

123.

125.

123. Duke Kahanamoku, winner of the 1912 and 1920 100-meter freestyle. He also finished second in 1924 at the age of 33.

124. Johnny Weissmuller won five gold medals in 1924 and 1928 and then gained international fame as Tarzan.

125. Buster Crabbe came from behind to win the 1932 400-meter freestyle by one-tenth of a second, in a thrilling finish. He attracted the attention of Hollywood producers, who later cast him as Tarzan, Buck Rogers, and Flash Gordon.

SWIMMING

126. In 1964 Don Schollander became the first swimmer to earn four gold medals at one Olympics.

127. Jean Boiteux, winner of the 1952 400-meter freestyle, helps his proud father out of the pool after the latter leaped in to congratulate his son.

128. Alfréd Hajós survived 55-degree Fahrrenheit water and 12-foot waves to win the 1200-meter freestyle in 1896. He later recalled, "My will to live completely overcame my desire to win."

129. Mocked by his schoolmates because an accident left him bald and because he was dyslexic, Duncan Goodhew fought back by winning a gold medal in the 1980 100-meter breaststroke.

130. Klaus Dibiasi won an unprecedented three consecutive gold medals in the platform diving competitions of 1968, 1972, and 1976. He also earned a silver medal in 1964.

126.

128.

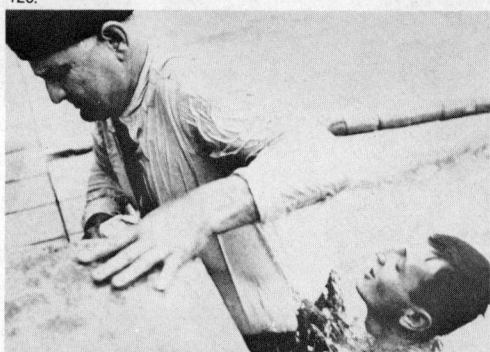
127.

130.

129.

131.

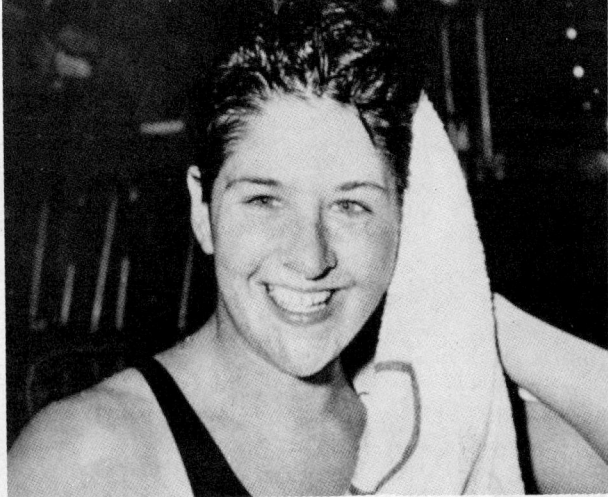

132.

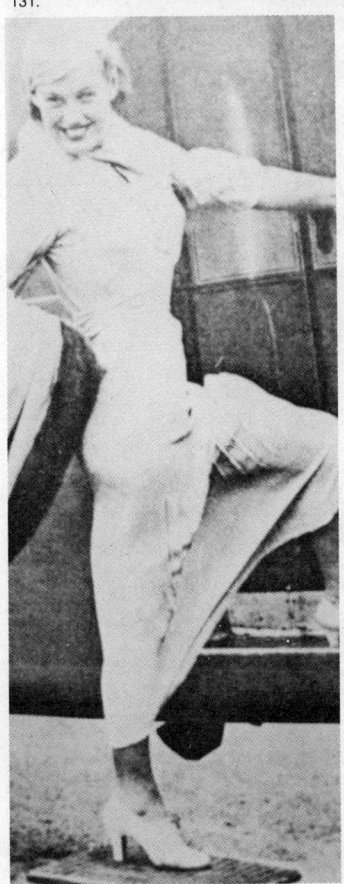

131. Little Francesca Matthes, with her parents, Kornelia Ender and Roland Matthes, who between them won 16 swimming medals in 1968, 1972, and 1976. 132. Controversial Dawn Fraser won a total of four gold medals and four silver medals in 1956, 1960, and 1964.

133. Eleanor Holm won the 100-meter backstroke in 1932 and was on her way to defend her title in Berlin in 1936 when she was derailed by a major scandal. 134. In 1952 and 1956 Pat Mc-Cormick swept both the springboard and platform diving competitions.

133.

134.

WEIGHTLIFTING

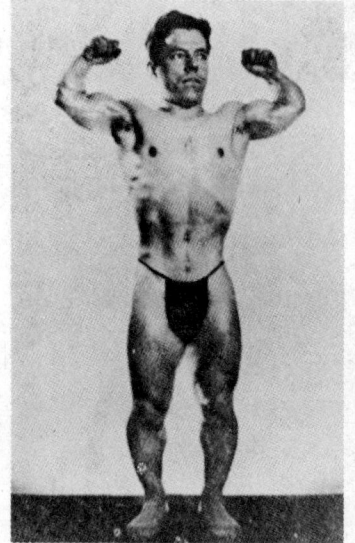

135.

136.

135. The arms of 4-foot 10-inch Joe Di Pietro were so short that he could barely raise the bar above his head. Yet he was still able to win the 1948 Bantamweight gold medal.

136. The 1936 Middleweight lifting champion, Khadr Sayed El Touni (center), lifted 15 pounds more than the Light Heavyweight winner.

137.

138.

137. Tommy Kono won three Olympic medals in three different weight categories in 1952, 1956, and 1960. His mental control led one rival to comment, "When Kono looks at me from the wings, he works on me like a python on a rabbit."

138. The 1948 Light Heavyweight silver medalist, Harold Sakata, gained greater fame as the evil Oddjob in the James Bond film Goldfinger.

WEIGHTLIFTING

139. Launceston Elliot, winner of the one-hand lift in 1896.

140. Vassily Alexeyev, Super Heavyweight weightlifting champion in 1972 and 1976, keeping in shape during the off-season.

WRESTLING

141. Thirty-nine-year-old Wilfried Dietrich (bottom) throwing 412-pound Chris Taylor during the 1972 Super Heavyweight freestyle wrestling tournament.

142. Anders Ahlgren and Ivar Böhling wrestled for nine hours in the final of the 1912 Greco-Roman Light Heavyweight division before officials declared a draw.

143. Carl Westergren won three Greco-Roman wrestling gold medals in three different weight divisions: Middleweight in 1920, Light Heavyweight in 1924, and Heavyweight in 1932 (at the age of 36).

DISCONTINUED SPORTS

145. The exotic sport of slalom, or white water, canoeing was included in the 1972 Olympics and dominated by the East Germans, who had constructed an exact copy of the West German course that was used for the Olympics.

144. George Lyon, winner of the 1904 golf event, keeping his ball on the eye.

144.

145.

TEAM SPORTS

146. An unusual play from the 1948 football (soccer) tournament. Henry Carlsson of Sweden scores a goal against Denmark which is caught by his teammate Gunnar Nordahl, who had dashed into the opposing goal to avoid an offside penalty.

146.

147.

148.

147. The famous 1964 Japanese women's volleyball team in action.

148. A typical scene from a team handball match.

SWIMMING

WOMEN

100-METER FREESTYLE

1896–1908 not held

1912 Stockholm C: 27, N: 8, D: 7.2. WR: 1:20.6 (Daisy Curwen)
1. Fanny Durack   AUS   1:22.2
2. Wilhelmina Wylie   AUS   1:25.4
3. Jennie Fletcher   GBR   1:27.0
4. Margarete "Grete" Rosenberg   GER   1.27.4
5. Annie Spiers   GBR   1:27.4
DNS: Daisy Curwen (GBR)

Fanny Durack's biggest struggle came before the Olympics. The men who were in charge of naming the Australian team thought it an absurd waste of time and money to send women to Stockholm. Fanny convinced them to give her a tryout, but the men were not impressed by what they saw. Eventually she built up enough support to allow her to go. In the fourth heat of the second round, Durack swam a 1:19.8 to break Daisy Curwen's world record. In the semifinals she defeated Curwen, who then went straight to the hospital for an emergency appendectomy. Durack led the final from start to finish and won easily. At one time Fanny Durack held every world record in women's swimming, from 50 yards to one mile.

1920 Antwerp C: 16, N: 8, D: 8.25. WR: 1:16.2 (Fanny Durack)
1. Ethelda Bleibtrey   USA   1:13.6   WR
2. Irene Guest   USA   1:17.0
3. Frances Schroth   USA   1:17.2
4. Constance Jeans   GBR   1:22.8
5. Violet Walrond   NZE   —
6. Jane Gylling   SWE   —
7. Charlotte Boyle   USA   —

Bleibtrey broke the world record in the third heat with a time of 1:14.4, then broke the record again in winning the final. Eventually she won all three swimming events for women at Antwerp.

1924 Paris C: 16, N: 7, D: 7.20. WR: 1:12.8 (Gertrude Ederle)
1. Ethel Lackie   USA   1:12.4
2. Mariechen Wehselau   USA   1:12.8
3. Gertrude Ederle   USA   1:14.2
4. Constance Jeans   GBR   1:15.4
5. Irene Tanner   GBR   1:20.8
6. Maria Vierdag (HOL)

The U.S. sweep was particularly impressive considering the absurd restrictions imposed on the female swimmers by the U.S. Olympic Committee. American officials, concerned about protecting their teenaged swimmers from the immoral temptations of Paris, housed the young ladies way outside the city and forced them to spend five to six hours a day traveling to and from the Olympic pool. In the first heat, Mariechen Wehselau of Honolulu set a world record of 1:12.2. Lackie and Ederle won the next two heats in 1:12.8 and 1:12.6. In the final race, Wehselau held a two-yard lead at the 50-meter turn, with Ederle second and Lackie third. But 17-year-old Ethel Lackie of Chicago put on a fantastic spurt in the last 25 meters to edge Wehselau for first place.

Two years later Gertrude Ederle, the 19-year-old daughter of a New York City butcher, carved herself a permanent place in the history books with a swimming feat that shocked the world. Just after seven a.m. on the morning of August 6, 1926, she set off from France in an attempt to become the first woman to swim the English Channel. That day, the London *Daily News* ran an editorial which haughtily announced, "Even the most uncompromising champion of the rights and capacities of women must admit that in contests of physical skill, speed and endurance they must remain forever the weaker sex." Such overblown male chauvinism was buried in an avalanche of feminist joy when Ederle reached the English coast at Kingsdown in a time of 14 hours 31 minutes—almost two hours faster than the *men's* record for the Channel swim.

Ederle returned home to a tickertape parade attended by an estimated 2,000,000 people. A slew of personal appearances followed, but this period involved a series of setbacks. By 1933 she had suffered a nervous breakdown, become deaf as a result of her Channel swim, and received a serious back injury that forced her to wear a cast for four and a half years. Not one to wallow in self-pity, Ederle went right ahead with her life and eventually began teaching swimming to deaf children.

1928 Amsterdam C: 24, N:11, D: 8.11. WR: 1:10.0 (Ethel Lackie)
1. Albina Osipowich   USA   1:11.0   OR
2. Eleanor Garatti   USA   1:11.4
3. Margaret Joyce Cooper   GBR   1:13.6
4. Jean McDowall   GBR   1:13.6
5. Susan Laird   USA   1:14.6
6. Charlotte Lehmann   GER   1:15.2

1932 Los Angeles C: 20, N: 10, D: 8.8. WR: 1:06.6 (Helene Madison)
1. Helene Madison   USA   1:06.8   OR
2. Willemijntje den Ouden   HOL   1:07.8
3. Eleanor Saville (Garatti) USA   1:09.3
4. Josephine McKim   USA   1:09.3
5. Neville Bult   AUS   1:09.9
6. Jennie Mckaal   SAF   1:10.8

If ever there was a sure bet for a gold medal, it was 5-foot 10½-inch, 154-pound Helene Madison, a 19-year-old from Seattle, Washington who was invariably referred to by the press as "shapely." During a 16½-month period in 1930–31, Madison broke all 16 world records for the distances between 100 yards and 1 mile. However, the results of the semifinals in Los Angeles raised serious doubts as to whether she could actually win the final. The first semifinal was won by 14-year-old Willy den Ouden in the surprisingly fast time of 1:07.6. In the second semi, Helene Madison went all out for the first 50 meters and then huffed home to win in 1:09.9, a time that would have placed her only fifth in the first semi. The American coaches advised Madison to change her tactics and save herself for the second half of the final race. This proved to be advice well worth taking, as Madison forged to a full-length lead between 50 and 75 meters before bumping into the lane divider. A final burst of speed provided her with a comfortable margin of victory.

Joyce Cooper of Great Britain was most unlucky to be drawn in the first semifinal. Her times of 1:09.0 and 1:09.2 would have been good enough for third place in the final.

After the Olympics it appeared that Helene Madison was headed for a very glamorous life, but things didn't work out that way. In 1933 she played a minor role in the

film *The Warrior's Husband*. Then she tried to earn a living as a nightclub entertainer, a swimming instructor, and a department store clerk. In 1935 she became a probationary nurse at a Seattle hospital, but she failed to earn a registered nurse's certificate. She was also frustrated in her personal life. Married and divorced three times, she was living alone with her Siamese cat when she died of cancer in 1970 at the age of 56.

1936 Berlin C: 33, N: 14, D: 8.10. WR: 1:04.6 (Willemijntje den Ouden)
1. Hendrika "Rie" Mastenbroek HOL   1:05.9   OR
2. Jeannette Campbell   ARG   1:06.4
3. Gisela Arendt   GER   1:06.6
4. Willemijntje den Ouden   HOL   1:07.6
5. Catherina Wagner   HOL   1:08.1
6. Olive McKean   USA   1:08.4
7. Katherine Rawls   USA   1:08.7

Six months before the Berlin Games, Willy den Ouden swam a phenomenal 1:04.6, setting a world record that would last for 20 years. But in the preliminary rounds of the Olympics, it was her 17-year-old teammate, Rie Mastenbroek, who recorded the fastest times. In the final Mastenbroek was fifth at the 50-meter turn and was still behind Arendt and Campbell (whose parents were Scottish) with only ten meters to go. But her furious finishing strokes gave her a dramatic victory. Over the next five days Mastenbroek won two more gold medals and one silver medal.

1948 London C: 34, N:14, D: 8.2. WR: 1:04.6 (Willemijntje den Ouden)
1. Greta Andersen   DEN   1:06.3
2. Ann Curtis   USA   1:06.5
3. Marie-Louise Vaessen   HOL   1:07.6
4. Karen-Margrete Harup   DEN   1:08.1
5. Ingegärd Fredin   SWE   1:08.4
6. Irma Schuhmacher   HOL   1:08.4
7. Elisabeth Ahlgren   SWE   1:08.8
8. Fritze Carstensen   DEN   1:09.1

Greta Andersen later became a professional and swam the English Channel six times, culminating in an England-to-France record of 13 hours 14 minutes, which she set in 1964 at the age of 36.

1952 Helsinki C: 41, N: 19, D: 7.28. WR: 1:04.6 (Willemijntje den Ouden)
1. Katalin Szöke   HUN   1:06.8
2. Johanna Termeulen   HOL   1:07.0
3. Judit Temes   HUN   1:07.1
4. Joan Harrison   SAF   1.07.1
5. Joan Alderson   USA   1:07.1
6. Irma Heijting-Schuhmacher HOL 1:07.3
7. Marilee Stepan   USA   1:08.6
8. Angela Barnwell   GBR   1:08.6

The 1952 100-meter freestyle race saw a thrilling finish, in which the lead changed hands three times in the last ten meters and the first six women finished within two feet of each other. Judit Temes, who had set an Olympic record of 1:05.5 in the first round, pushed to the front after 90 meters, but then Joan Harrison moved ahead. The South African swimmer had the unfortunate experience of finishing out of the medals despite the fact that she appeared to be in first place with only five meters to go. The eventual winner, 16-year-old Katalin Szöke, had been well-known in Hungary for quite some time. Her mother had introduced her to swimming when she was only six months old, and she became known as "Kati, the World's First Waterproof Baby." She was able to stay afloat unaided before she was two years old. Szöke's husband, Kalman Markovits, was a member of Hungary's gold medal water polo team in 1952 and 1956.

1956 Melbourne C: 35, N: 16, D: 12.1 WR: 1:02.4 (Lorraine Crapp)

1. Dawn Fraser	AUS	1:02.0	WR
2. Lorraine Crapp	AUS	1:02.3	
3. Faith Leech	AUS	1:05.1	
4. Joan Rosazza	USA	1:05.2	
5. Virginia Grant	CAN	1:05.4	
6. Shelley Mann	USA	1:05.6	
7. Marrion Roe	NZE	1:05.6	
8. Natalie Myburgh	SAF	1:05.8	

Dawn Fraser was the youngest of eight children born to working-class parents in Balmain, an industrial suburb of Sydney. On February 21, 1956, Fraser broke Willy den Ouden's 20-year-old world record and upset Lorraine Crapp to win the Australian championship in a time of 1:04.5. Dawn was not that impressed by her feat and told reporters that she could do a lot better. At the time some people may have considered Fraser to be excessively cocky, but it turned out that she was absolutely right. In fact, the quality of women's freestyle swimming was going through a period of rapid change. In the next eight months the 100 meters record was lowered five more times, twice by Cockie Gastelaars of the Netherlands, once more by Dawn Fraser, and, finally, twice in the month of October by Lorraine Crapp.

With Gastelaars out of the Games because of the Dutch Olympic boycott, there was no question that the battle for the gold medal would be between Crapp and Fraser. In the first heat of the first round, Crapp swam a 1:03.4 to lower the Olympic record by over two seconds. In the fifth heat Fraser lowered it further with a 1:02.4. The two Australian teenagers then won their semifinal races, Fraser in 1:03.0 and Crapp in 1:03.1. The day before the women's final, the Australian men had scored a sweep in the 100-meter freestyle, and with Faith Leech recording the third fastest time in each of the first two rounds, it looked as if the Australian women might match the accomplishments of their male counterparts.

The night before the race Dawn Fraser went to bed early, prayed for the strength to win, and then thought through the race, particularly the turn, before she finally dropped off to sleep. Before long she was stricken by a nightmare, which she later described quite graphically in her autobiography, *Below the Surface*. "The gun went off," she began, "but I had honey on my feet and it was hard to pull them away from the starting block. I finally fought free and dived high. . . . It seemed a long time before I hit the water, and the water wasn't water; it was spaghetti. I fought with it and kept going up and down in the one place, like a yo-yo. The spaghetti strands tangled and tied my feet, and I was swimming with my arms alone. Of course I fouled up the turn and took a few mouthfuls, and I woke up gasping and fighting in a sea of spaghetti."

She must have been somewhat relieved the next day to discover that the pool was in fact filled with water, although she was still incredibly nervous, since she had never before swum in an international meet. Fraser and Crapp pulled away from the others after only 25 meters. Fraser completed the turn first, but Crapp caught up with her with 25 meters to go; the two reached the finish without knowing which one had won. They were so far ahead of the others that they were able to turn around and watch their teammate, Faith Leech, win the battle for third place. After her victory was announced, Dawn Fraser borrowed a ladder from a TV crew and climbed into the stands to share tears of joy with her parents, and to savor a moment which they had all dedicated to Dawn's dead brother, Don, who had introduced her to swimming when she was a child. Starting with that day in Melbourne, Dawn Fraser was the world record holder at 100 meters for the next 15 years.

1960 Rome C: 32, N: 19, D: 8.29. WR(110 yards): 1:00.2 (Dawn Fraser)

1. Dawn Fraser	AUS	1:01.2	OR
2. S. Christine Von Saltza	USA	1:02.8	
3. Natalie Steward	GBR	1:03.1	
4. Carolyn Wood	USA	1:03.4	
5. Csilla Dobai-Madarász	HUN	1:03.6	
6. Erica Terpstra	HOL	1:04.3	
7. Cockie Gastelaars	HOL	1:04.7	
8. Marie Stewart	CAN	1:05.5	

Undefeated at 100 meters since the last Olympics, Dawn Fraser made news by becoming the first woman to defend an Olympic swimming title. But she made bigger news the following day with her defiance of Australian officials. Thinking she had the day off, she had stayed up late, celebrating. In the morning a routine meeting of the Australian women's swim team turned into a violent argument, which didn't end until Fraser had smacked teammate Jan Andrew in the face with a pillow. Fraser spent the rest of the morning shopping for a wedding dress (which she didn't use) and sightseeing in Rome. She returned to the Olympic Village in time for lunch and had just finished a big plate of spaghetti when Roger Pegram, the manager of the Australian swimming team, approached her and ordered her to get dressed so that she could swim the butterfly leg of the medley relay qualifying heat. Stating that she was stuffed and unprepared, Fraser refused to swim and returned to her room for a nap. Eventually Alva Colquhoun volunteered to take her place, but for the remainder of their stay in Rome, the Australian women punished Fraser by "sending her to Coventry." In other words, they refused to speak a single word to her or to each other as long as Fraser was in the room.

1964 Tokyo C: 44, N: 22, D: 10.13. WR: 58.9 (Dawn Fraser)
1. Dawn Fraser	AUS	59.5	OR
2. Sharon Stouder	USA	59.9	
3. Kathleen Ellis	USA	1:00.8	
4. Erica Terpstra	HOL	1:01.8	
5. Marion Lay	CAN	1:02.2	
6. Csilla Dobai-Madarász	HUN	1:02.4	
7. Ann Hagberg	SWE	1:02.5	
8. Lynette Bell	AUS	1:02.7	

On October 27, 1962, Dawn Fraser, swimming in Melbourne, became the first woman to break the one-minute barrier for 100 meters when she covered the longer distance of 110 yards in 59.9 seconds. By February 29, 1964, she had cut her time down to 58.9, and it was almost eight years before anyone would do better. But in March, tragedy struck. She was driving home from a football social with three passengers, her mother, her sister, and a friend, when her car skidded and crashed into a parked truck. Her mother was killed, her sister was knocked unconscious, and Dawn herself spent six weeks with her neck in plaster because of a chipped vertebra.

Seven months later Dawn Fraser was, remarkably, back in form for the Olympics. By this time she was 27 years old, an old-timer by swimming standards who was known to her teammates as "Granny." She had by no means lost her rebellious spirit, however. Ordered by team officials to skip the opening-day ceremonies, she sneaked in anyway and enjoyed the parade and festivities. She tied her own Olympic record of 1:00.6 (set in the 1960 relay) in the first round and then swam a 59.9 in the semifinals. Entering the final she was sure that her only serious challenger would be 15-year-old Sharon Stouder of Glendora, California. Fraser took the lead immediately, but Stouder swam a tremendous race and caught her at the 70-meter mark. Fraser was not to be denied, though, and she called on an extra reserve of strength to pull away once again. Stouder's time of 59.9 made her the first woman other than Dawn Fraser to break one minute. Later Fraser committed the final indiscretion of her career, when she led a middle-of-the-night raid to steal a "souvenir" flag from the Emperor's palace. This led to a ten-year suspension by the Australian Swimming Union, which was lifted after four years. The escapade in no way detracted from her status as a national heroine, since most Australians were less interested in her out-of-the-pool antics than they were by the fact that she had become the first Olympic swimmer of either sex to win the same event three times.

1968 Mexico City C: 57, N: 27, D: 10.19. WR: 58.9 (Dawn Fraser)
1. Jan Henne	USA	1:00.0
2. Susan Pedersen	USA	1:00.3
3. Linda Gustavson	USA	1:00.3
4. Marion Lay	CAN	1:00.5
5. Martina Grunert	GDR	1:01.0
6. Alexandra Jackson	GBR	1:01.0
7. Mirjana Segrt	YUG	1:01.5
8. Judit Turóczy	HUN	1:01.6

1972 Munich C: 46, N: 23, D: 8.29. WR: 58.5 (Shane Gould)
1. Sandra Neilson	USA	58.59	OR
2. Shirley Babashoff	USA	59.02	
3. Shane Gould	AUS	59.06	
4. Gabriele Wetzko	GDR	59.21	
5. Heidemarie Reineck	GER	59.73	
6. Andrea Eife	GDR	59.91	
7. Magdolna Patoh	HUN	1:00.02	
8. Enith Brigitha	HOL	1:00.09	

Following the Australian sweeps of 1956, the number of entrants per nation per event was reduced from three to two. This restriction was dropped after 1960, then reinstated after the U.S. sweeps of 1968. It was dropped again in 1976, but will be back once more in 1984 as a result of the East German sweeps of 1976 and 1980. In 1972 the Australian favorite, Shane Gould, lost her first freestyle race in two years when she was beaten by two Southern California high schoool students, Sandra Neilson and Shirley Babashoff. Neilson led all the way, but Babashoff had to come from seventh place at the turn to nip Gould for the silver. The one-two victory gave confidence to the U.S. swimmers, who had been wearing T-shirts that read, "All that glitters is not Gould."

1976 Montreal C: 45, N: 25, D: 7.19. WR: 55.73 (Kornelia Ender)
1. Kornelia Ender	GDR	55.65	WR
2. Petra Priemer	GDR	56.49	
3. Enith Brigitha	HOL	56.65	
4. Kim Peyton	USA	56.81	
5. Shirley Babashoff	USA	56.95	
6. Claudia Hempel	GDR	56.99	
7. Jill Sterkel	USA	57.06	
8. Jutta Weber	GER	57.26	

At Munich in 1972, the East German women swimmers failed to win a single gold medal, yet four years later in Montreal they were able to finish first in 11 of 13 events. This extraordinary transformation actually began at the 1973 world swimming championships in Belgrade, Yugoslavia, where the East German women appeared wearing the latest model of their skin-tight, semi-see-through Lycra suits. Some people began to raise a protest, until it was revealed that the suits had actually been invented and manufactured in *West* Germany. By 1976 the Americans in particular were also accusing the East German women of appearing too muscular and masculine, of being shot up with anabolic steroids, and of being "all work and no play" types, who would be unable ever to bear children.

The real reason for East Germany's success was the enormous emphasis that country placed on sports science. While U.S. and Soviet scientists were busy conquering space and designing weapons systems, the East Germans were studying athletes—taking blood tests and muscle biopsies, checking oxygen levels, and testing for nutritional needs. The scandalous "Belgrade suits" of 1973 soon became commonplace throughout the world. Likewise, the East Germans were years ahead in studies of such things as lactic acid buildup during training. When the East German coaches heard the accusations that their young swimmers were too muscular and that they were using steroids, the East Germans responded that the muscles were a result of a concentrated weightlifting program, and that if America's women swimmers didn't start lifting weights seriously, they would never catch up.

At the age of 13, Kornelia Ender of Bitterfeld won three silver medals at the 1972 Olympics. The following year, in East Berlin, she broke Shane Gould's world record in the 100-meter freestyle. In the three years preceding the 1976 Olympics, Ender broke the world record for that event nine times. Two months before the Montreal Games, the 5-foot 10-inch, 154-pound Ender announced her engagement to backstroker Roland Matthes. She set her tenth 100 meters world record in the Olympic final, her second gold medal of the Games. After the Olympics were over Kornelia Ender was reunited with her grandmother, who had left East Germany in 1961 and moved to Kansas.

1980 Moscow C: 30, N: 22, D: 7.21. WR: 55.41 (Barbara Krause)

1. Barbara Krause	GDR	54.79	WR
2. Caren Metschuck	GDR	55.16	
3. Ines Diers	GDR	55.65	
4. Olga Klevakina	SOV	57.40	
5. Conny Van Bentum	HOL	57.63	
6. Natalya Strunnikova	SOV	57.83	
7. Guylaine Berger	FRA	57.88	
8. Agneta Eriksson	SWE	57.90	

In 1980 the East German women duplicated their 1976 feat of winning 11 of 13 events. But this time, with the U.S. and Canada out of the Games, they were able to take 15 other medals as well, which meant that they *averaged* two out of three medals per event.

Like Kornelia Ender, Barbara Krause was introduced to swimming as therapy for orthopedic problems. One of East Germany's leading swimmers in 1976, she was forced to sit out the Montreal Games because of illness. As she followed the competition from her sickbed, she made the decision to continue swimming for four more years so that she could take part in the 1980 Olympics. With only 30 starters in the 100-meter freestyle, the smallest field since 1932, it was decided to skip the semifinals and simply allow the swimmers with the eight fastest times in the heats

to qualify directly for the final. Barbara Krause won the third heat in 54.98 to lower her own world record and to become the first woman to break the 55-second barrier. In the final she was hard-pressed by her East German teammates, but she led all the way and set yet another world record.

200-METER FREESTYLE
1896–1964 not held

1968 Mexico City C: 39, N: 23, D: 10.22. WR: 2:06.7 (Deborah Meyer)

1. Deborah Meyer	USA	2:10.5	OR
2. Jan Henne	USA	2:11.0	
3. Jane Barkman	USA	2:11.2	
4. Gabriele Wetzko	GDR	2:12.3	
5. Mirjana Segrt	YUG	2:13.3	
6. Claude Mandonnaud	FRA	2:14.9	
7. Lynette Bell	AUS	2:15.1	
8. Olga Kozicova	CZE	2:16.0	

This was Debbie Meyer's second gold medal of the 1968 Olympics.

1972 Munich C: 33, N: 17, D: 9.1. WR: 2:05.21 (Shirley Babashoff)

1. Shane Gould	AUS	2:03.56	WR
2. Shirley Babashoff	USA	2:04.33	
3. Keena Rothhammer	USA	2:04.92	
4. Ann Marshall	USA	2:05.45	
5. Andrea Eife	GDR	2:06.27	
6. Hansje Bunschoten	HOL	2:08.40	
7. Anke Rijnders	HOL	2:09.41	
8. Karin Tuelling	GDR	2:11.70	

Between July 1971 and January 1972, Shane Gould set world records in all five internationally recognized freestyle distances: the 100, 200, 400, 800, and 1500 meters. In the 1972 Olympics, the 15-year-old phenomenon swam 12 races in eight days, logging 4200 meters of competitive swimming. In the 200 meters final Gould built up a large lead in the first 100 meters. World record holder Shirley Babashoff almost cut the gap in half, but could get no further. Shane Gould closed out the Munich Olympics with three gold medals, one silver, and one bronze. A year later, tired of the sacrifices required of a champion swimmer, Gould announced her retirement at the age of 16.

1976 Montreal C: 40, N: 22, D: 7.22. WR: 1:59.78 (Kornelia Ender)

1. Kornelia Ender	GDR	1:59.26	WR
2. Shirley Babashoff	USA	2:01.22	
3. Enith Brigitha	HOL	2:01.40	
4. Annelies Maas	HOL	2:02.56	
5. Gail Amundrud	CAN	2:03.32	
6. Jennifer Hooker	USA	2:04.20	
7. Caludia Hempel	GDR	2:04.61	
8. Irina Vlasova	SOV	2:05.63	

Kornelia Ender had just broken Shirley Babashoff's world record to win the 100-meter butterfly when she faced Babashoff herself in the very next race, the 200-meter freestyle. Babashoff had defeated Ender in the 200 at the 1975 world championships, but Ender had chopped almost three seconds off her time in the following year. Babashoff took the early lead and held it for the first 100 meters, but Ender moved ahead over the next length of the pool and won going away to earn her second gold medal in 27 minutes. She thus became the first female swimmer to win four gold medals at one Olympics.

1980 Moscow C: 22, N: 14, D: 7.24. WR: 1.58.23 (Cynthia Woodhead)

1. Barbara Krause	GDR	1:58.33	OR
2. Ines Diers	GDR	1:59.64	
3. Carmela Schmidt	GDR	2:01.44	
4. Olga Klevakina	SOV	2:02.29	
5. Reggie De Jong	HOL	2:02.76	
6. June Croft	GBR	2:03.15	
7. Natalya Strunnikova	SOV	2:03.74	
8. Irina Aksyonova	SOV	2:04.00	

Krause staged a phenomenal comeback to win her second gold medal. Trailing Ines Diers by over a second after 150 meters, she swam the last 50 meters in 28.47 to win by a comfortable margin. Eight days later, world record holder Cynthia Woodhead won the U.S. Outdoor National championship in 1:59.44.

400-METER FREESTYLE

1896–1912 not held

1920 Antwerp C: 16, N: 7, D: 8.28. WR (300 meters): 4:43.6
(300 Meters)

1. Ethelda Bleibtrey	USA	4:34.0	WR
2. Margaret Woodbridge	USA	4:42.8	
3. Frances Schroth	USA	4:52.0	
4. Constance Jeans	GBR	4:52.4	
5. Eleanor Uhl	USA	—	
6. Jane Gylling	SWE	—	

1924 Paris C: 18, N: 8, D: 7.15. WR: 5:53.2 (Gertrude Ederle)

1. Martha Norelius	USA	6:02.2	OR
2. Helen Wainwright	USA	6:03.8	
3. Gertrude Ederle	USA	6:04.8	
4. Doris Molesworth	GBR	6:25.4	
DNF: Gwitha Shand (NZE)			
6. Irene Tanner (GBR)			

Fifteen-year-old, Stockholm-born Martha Norelius pulled away from Wainwright and Ederle in the final 15 meters. In the 1924 Olympics five swimmers took part in each final, while sixth place was awarded to the nonfinalist who recorded the fastest time in the semifinals.

1928 Amsterdam C: 14, N: 9, D: 8.6. WR: 5:49.6 (Martha Norelius)

1. Martha Norelius	USA	5:42.8	WR
2. Maria Braun	HOL	5:57.8	
3. Josephine McKim	USA	6:00.2	
4. Sarah Stewart	GBR	6:07.0	
5. Frederica van der Goes	SAF	6:07.2	
6. Irene Tanner	GBR	6:11.6	

Norelius swam a 5:45.4 opening heat to break her own world record and defended her title by winning the final easily, again in world record time. Norelius dominated women's swimming from 1922 to 1929, after which she turned professional. She later married Canada's 1928 double sculls silver medalist, Joe Wright.

1932 Los Angeles C: 14, N: 9, D: 8.13. WR: 5:31.0 (Helene Madison)

1. Helene Madison	USA	5:28.5	WR
2. Lenore Kight	USA	5:28.6	
3. Jennie Makaal	SAF	5:47.3	
4. Margaret Joyce Cooper	GBR	5:49.7	
5. Yvonne Godard	FRA	5:54.4	
6. Norene Forbes	USA	6:06.0	

Helene Madison and Lenore Kight pulled away from the others immediately and went through most of the race with Madison one foot ahead. Kight moved into the lead at 325 meters, but Madison drew even at the final turn. In the end, Madison was able to touch the last wall inches ahead of Kight and thus win her third gold medal.

1936 Berlin C: 20, N: 10, D: 8.15. WR: 5:16.0 (Willemijntjte den Ouden)

1. Hendrika "Rie" Mastenbroek	HOL	5:26.4	OR
2. Ragnhild Hveger	DEN	5:27.5	
3. Lenore Wingard (Kight)	USA	5:29.0	
4. Mary Lou Petty	USA	5:32.2	
5. Piedade Coutinho Azevedo	BRA	5:35.2	
6. Kazue Koijma	JAP	5:43.1	
7. Grete Frederiksen	DEN	5:45.0	
8. Catharine Wagner	HOL	5:46.0	

Fifteen-year-old Ragnhild Hveger led throughout the race, but Rie Mastenbroek fought back in the final 25 meters to gain a one-meter victory and win her third gold medal. Between 1936 and 1942 Hveger broke 42 individual world records. From 1938 until 1953 she was the official world record holder in the 200, 400, 800, and 1500 meters. She retired in 1945, but came back in 1952 to finish fifth in the 400 in the Helsinki Olympics at the age of 31. Rie Mastenbroek, who won three gold medals and one silver, had a most difficult post-Olympic life. After a disastrous first marriage ended, she worked 14 hours a day as a cleaning woman to support her children. In 1972 she told *Sports Illustrated,* "I am forgotten. No one remembers who I was. . . . Sometimes I think, 'Oh, dear, oh, dear, how good I must have been, how really *good*!' "

1948 London C: 19, N: 11, D: 8.7. WR: 5:00.1 (Ragnhild Hveger)

1. Ann Curtis	USA	5:17.8	OR
2. Karen-Margrete Harup	DEN	5:21.2	
3. Catherine Gibson	GBR	5:22.5	
4. Fernande Caroen	BEL	5:25.3	
5. Brenda Helser	USA	5:26.0	
6. Piedade Silva Tavares	BRA	5:29.4	
7. Fritze Carstensen	DEN	5:29.4	
8. Nancy Lees	USA	5:32.9	

1952 Helsinki C: 34, N: 17, D: 8.2. WR: 5:00.1 (Ragnhild Hveger)

1. Valéria Gyenge	HUN	5:12.1	OR
2. Éva Novák	HUN	5:13.7	
3. Evelyn Kawamoto	USA	5:14.6	
4. Carolyn Green	USA	5:16.5	
5. Ragnhild Andersen-Hveger	DEN	5:16.9	
6. Éva Székely	HUN	5:17.9	
7. Anna Maria Schultz	ARG	5:24.0	
8. Greta Andersen	DEN	5:27.0	

Ragnhild Hveger's 1940 world record was still in the books when, as Ragnhild Andersen-Hveger, she prepared for the start of the 1952 Olympic 400 meters final, the same event in which she had won a silver medal 16 years earlier. In Helsinki she led for the first 275 meters, but couldn't keep up the pace.

1956 Melbourne C: 26, N: 13, D: 12.7. WR: 4:47.2 (Lorraine Crapp)

1. Lorraine Crapp	AUS	4:54.6	OR
2. Dawn Fraser	AUS	5:02.5	
3. Sylvia Ruuska	USA	5:07.1	
4. Marley Shriver	USA	5:12.9	
5. Rypszima Székely	HUN	5:14.2	
6. Sandra Morgan	AUS	5:14.3	
7. Héda Frost	FRA	5:15.4	
8. Valéria Gyenge	HUN	5:21.0	

On August 25, 1956, 17-year-old Lorraine Crapp became the first woman to swim 400 meters in less than five minutes when she broke Ragnhild Hveger's 16-year-old world record with a time of 4:50.8. In that same race she also bettered the world records for 200 meters, 220 yards, and 440 yards. Two and a half months later at the Olympics, Dawn Fraser kept up with her teammate for 100 meters, but then Crapp drew clear to win by almost eight seconds.

1960 Rome C: 22, N: 13, D: 9.1. WR: 4:44.5 (S. Christine Von Saltza)

1. S. Christine Von Saltza	USA	4:50.6	OR
2. Jane Cederqvist	SWE	4:53.9	
3. Catharina Lagerberg	HOL	4:56.9	
4. Ilsa Konrads	AUS	4:57.9	
5. Dawn Fraser	AUS	4:58.5	
6. Nancy Rae	GBR	4:59.7	

7. Cornelia Schimmel	HOL	5:02.3
8. Bibbi Segerstrom	SWE	5:02.4

Sixteen-year-old Chris Von Saltza moved quickly into the lead, built up a five-second gap after 300 meters, and was too far ahead to be affected by the late surge of Jane Cederqvist. Von Saltza had won the first of her three gold medals. Third- and fourth-place finishers Lagerberg and Konrads were the world record holders at 800 meters and 1500 meters, respectively, neither of which was an Olympic distance at the time.

1964 Tokyo C: 30, N: 16, D: 10.18. WR: 4:39.5 (Marilyn Ramenofsky)

1. Virginia Duenkel	USA	4:43.3	OR
2. Marilyn Ramenofsky	USA	4:44.6	
3. Terri Stickles	USA	4:47.2	
4. Dawn Fraser	AUS	4:47.6	
5. Jane Hughes	CAN	4:50.9	
6. Elizabeth Long	GBR	4:52.0	
7. Kim Herford	AUS	4:52.9	
8. Gun Lilja	SWE	4:53.0	

Seventeen-year-old Ginny Duenkel of West Orange, New Jersey, also won a bronze medal in the 100-meter backstroke. In the 400-meter freestyle she took the lead after 175 meters and pulled away, slowly but steadily.

1968 Mexico City C: 30, N: 17, D: 10.20 WR: 4:24.5 (Debbie Meyer)

1. Debbie Meyer	USA	4:31.8	OR
2. Linda Gustavson	USA	4:35.5	
3. Karen Moras	AUS	4:37.0	
4. Pamela Kruse	USA	4:37.2	
5. Gabriele Wetzko	GDR	4:40.2	
6. Maria Teresa Ramirez	MEX	4:42.2	
7. Angela Coughlaw	CAN	4:51.9	
8. Ingrid Morris	SWE	4:53.8	

At the U.S. Olympic trials, 16-year-old Debbie Meyer set world records in the 200, 400, and 800. The rarefied air of Mexico City prevented her from duplicating that feat, but she did win all three races, starting with the 400 meters.

1972 Munich C: 29, N: 17, D: 8.30. WR: 4:21.2 (Shane Gould)

1. Shane Gould	AUS	4:19.44	WR
2. Novella Calligaris	ITA	4:22.44	
3. Gudrun Wagner	GDR	4:23.11	
4. Shirley Babashoff	USA	4:23.59	
5. Jenny Wylie	USA	4:24.07	
6. Keena Rothhammer	USA	4:24.22	
7. Hansje Bunschoten	HOL	4:29.70	
8. Anke Rijnders	HOL	4:31.51	

Shane Gould came back from her loss in the 100 meters the previous day to win her second gold medal.

1976 Montreal C: 34, N: 22, D: 7.20. WR: 4:11.69 (Barbara Krause)

1. Petra Thümer	GDR	4:09.89	WR
2. Shirley Babashoff	USA	4:10.46	
3. Shannon Smith	CAN	4:14.60	
4. Rebecca Perrott	NZE	4:14.76	
5. Kathy Heddy	USA	4:15.50	
6. Brenda Borgh	USA	4:17.43	
7. Annelies Maas	HOL	4:17.44	
8. Sabine Kahle	GDR	4:20.42	

On June 3, 1976, Barbara Krause broke Shirley Babashoff's world record by over three seconds. However, two weeks later she suffered an attack of angina and had to be dropped from the East German squad. Fifteen-year-old Petra Thümer, who had finished second to Krause in the East German championships, rose to the occasion at the Olympics. She built up most of her lead during the second 100 meters and then fought off Babashoff's attempts to close the gap. Thümer's time would have won her a silver medal in the 1968 *men's* 400-meter race and a gold in 1964.

1980 Moscow C: 19, N: 12, D: 7.22. WR: 4:06.28 (Tracey Wickham)

1. Ines Diers	GDR	4:08.76	OR
2. Petra Schneider	GDR	4:09.16	
3. Carmela Schmidt	GDR	4:10.86	
4. Michelle Ford	AUS	4:11.65	
5. Irina Aksyonova	SOV	4:14.40	
6. Annelies Maas	HOL	4:15.79	
7. Reggie de Jong	HOL	4;15.95	
8. Olga Klevakina	SOV	4:19.18	

This was one race that was definitely affected by the anti-Soviet boycott. Missing was world record holder Tracey Wickham of Australia as well as Kim Lineham and Cynthia Woodhead of the United States, who clocked 4:07.77 and 4:08.17, respectively, at the U.S. national championships on July 31. In their absence, the East Germans had a field day. Petra Schneider led for over 300 meters, but 16-year-old Ines Diers finished strongly to win. Before the Moscow Games were over Diers had won five medals: two gold, two silver and one bronze.

800-METER FREESTYLE
1896–1964 not held

1968 Mexico City C: 26, N: D: 10.24. WR: 9.10.4 (Deborah Meyer)

1. Deborah Meyer	USA	9:24.0	OR
2. Pamela Kruse	USA	9:35.7	
3. Maria Teresa Ramirez	MEX	9:38.5	
4. Karen Moras	AUS	9:38.6	
5. Patricia Caretto	USA	9:51.3	
6. Angela Coughlaw	CAN	9:56.4	
7. Denise Langford	AUS	9:56.7	
8. Laura Vaca	MEX	10:02.5	

Debbie Meyer was never really challenged as she became the first swimmer to win three individual gold medals in one Olympics. The only excitement of the race came when 15-year-old Maria Teresa Ramirez came from behind to nip Karen Moras for the bronze medal, bringing joy to the Mexican crowd.

1972 Munich C: 36, N: 19, D: 9.3. WR: 8:53.83 (Jo Harshbarger)

1. Keena Rothhammer	USA	8:53.68	WR
2. Shane Gould	AUS	8:56.39	
3. Novella Calligaris	ITA	8:57.46	
4. Ann Simmons	USA	8:57.62	
5. Gudrun Wegner	GDR	8:58.89	
6. Jo Harshbarger	USA	9:01.21	
7. Hansje Bunschoten	HOL	9:16.69	
8. Narelle Moras	AUS	9:19.06	

Calligaris led for 500 meters, but then Rothhammer, fourth at the halfway mark, took the lead and pulled away.

1976 Montreal C: 19, N: 11, D: 7.25. WR: 8:39.63 (Shirley Babashoff)

1. Petra Thümer	GDR	8:37.14	WR
2. Shirley Babashoff	USA	8:37.59	
3. Wendy Weinberg	USA	8:42.60	
4. Rosemary Milgate	AUS	8:47.21	
5. Nicole Kramer	USA	8:47.33	
6. Shannon Smith	CAN	8:48.15	
7. Regina Jäger	GDR	8:50.40	
8. Jennifer Turrall	AUS	8:52.88	

On June 4, 1976, Petra Thümer set a world record of 8:40.68, but 17 days later Shirley Babashoff bettered that time by a second. This was Babashoff's last chance for an individual gold medal so she withdrew from the 400-meter individual medley in order to save her strength for her long-distance showdown with Thümer, who had beaten her at 400 meters five days earlier. Shannon Smith led for 300 meters, but then Thümer took over. Babashoff trailed right behind her, but every time she drew closer, Thümer would draw away again. In the end Thümer had her second world record and Babashoff had her sixth Olympic silver medal.

1980 Moscow C: 14, N: 9, D: 7.27. WR: 8:24.62 (Tracey Wickham)

1. Michelle Ford	AUS	8:28.90	OR
2. Ines Diers	GDR	8:32.55	
3. Heike Dähne	GDR	8:33.48	
4. Irina Aksyonova	SOV	8:38.05	
5. Oxana Komissarova	SOV	8:42.04	
6. Pascale Verbauwen	BEL	8:44.84	
7. Ines Geissler	GDR	8:45.28	
8. Yelena Ivanova	SOV	8:46.45	

Eighteen-year-old Michelle Ford took the lead after 250 meters and pulled away to break the East German gold medal monopoly. Missing were world record holder Tracey Wickham of Australia and U.S. champion Kim Lineham, whose best time was 8:24.70 and who clocked an 8:27.86 two days after the Olympic final.

100-METER BACKSTROKE

1896–1920 not held

1924 Paris C: 10, N: 5, D: 7.20. WR: 1:22.4 (Sybil Bauer)
1. Sybil Bauer   USA   1:23.2   OR
2. Phyllis Harding   GBR   1:27.4
3. Aileen Riggin   USA   1:28.2
4. Florence Chambers   USA   1:30.8
5. Jarmila Müllerová   CZE   1:31.2
6. Ellen King (GBR)

Sybil Bauer of Chicago was the world record holder in all women's backstroke events when she completely outclassed her opposition at the Paris Olympics. She was still undefeated when she died of intestinal cancer on January 31, 1927, at the age of 23. Bronze medalist Aileen Riggin became the first person to win medals in both swimming and diving.

1928 Amsterdam C: 12, N: 7, D: 8.11 WR: 1:22.0 (Willy van den Turk)
1. Maria Braun   HOL   1:22.0
2. Ellen King   GBR   1:22.2
3. Margaret Joyce Cooper   GBR   1:22.8
4. Marion Gilman   USA   1:24.2
5. Eleanor Holm   USA   1:24.4
6. Lisa Lindstrom   USA   1:24.4
7. E.P. Stockley   NZE   1:25.8

Ellen King of Scotland equaled the world record in the first heat. In the second heat, 17-year-old local favorite Maria Braun broke the world record with a time of 1:21.6.

1932 Los Angeles C: 12, N: 7, D: 8.11. WR: 1:18.2 (Eleanor Holm)
1. Eleanor Holm   USA   1:19.4
2. Philomena "Bonny" Mealing   AUS   1:21.3
3. Elizabeth Valerie Davies   GBR   1:22.5
4. Phyllis Harding   GBR   1:22.6
5. Joan McSheehy   USA   1:23.2
6. Margaret Joyce Cooper   GBR   1:23.4
DNS: Maria Philipsen-Braun (HOL)

Eighteen-year-old Eleanor Holm, the daughter of a Brooklyn fire captain, inched ahead after 25 meters, held off the challenge of Bonny Mealing, and pulled away in the last 25 meters. Holm had set an Olympic record of 1:18.3 in her qualifying heat.

1936 Berlin C: 21, N: 12, D: 8.13. WR: 1:15.8 (Hendrika "Rie" Mastenbroek)
1. Dina "Nida" Senff   HOL   1:18.9
2. Hendrika "Rie" Mastenbroek   HOL   1:19.2
3. Alice Bridges   USA   1:19.4
4. Edith Motridge   USA   1:19.6
5. Tove Bruunström   DEN   1:20.4

6. Lorna Frampton   GBR   1:20.6
7. Phyllis Harding   GBR   1:21.5

Life had been very full for Eleanor Holm between Olympics. While in Hollywood she had met singer and orchestra leader Art Jarrett, who was a fellow alumnus of Erasmus Hall High School back in Brooklyn. Five months later, on September 2, 1933, they were married in Beverly Hills. For the next three years Holm led a very active social life and joined her husband singing in nightclubs. But she always kept in shape. In 1935 she set a world record for the 100-meter backstroke, and in 1936 she also broke the record for 200 meters. On February 27, 1936, her 100-meter record was broken by Rie Mastenbroek. However, when Eleanor Holm boarded the S.S. *Manhattan* on July 15 for the nine-day voyage to Germany, along with about 350 other members of the U.S. Olympic team, she was still the favorite to defend her championship, and there was little hint of the outrageous scandal that was about to bring an abrupt end to her amateur career.

Now on her way to her third Olympics, married and used to a flashy and independent life-style, Eleanor did not take too well to the third-class accommodations and strict regulations that had been arranged by the American Olympic Committee. She felt more comfortable in the first-class section, which happened to be where the American officials were staying, as well as the press. On Friday, July 17, Mr. Maybaum of the United States Lines, which owned the S.S. *Manhattan,* invited Eleanor to attend a party he was throwing that night in the A-deck bar and lounge. She was the only team member invited. Quick to accept, she stayed up until six a.m., matching drinks with the sportswriters. She had to be helped back to her cabin.

The next day there was much joking and wisecracking among the non-Olympic first-class passengers about the "training techniques" of the U.S. team. Embarrassed U.S. Olympic officials issued Holm a warning, but she was defiant and continued to drink in public off and on for the next few days. When advised by friends to moderate her behavior, she reminded them that she was "free, white, and 22."

On July 23, while the ship made a prolonged stopover in Cherbourg, France, with the passengers confined to ship, Holm attended an afternoon and evening champagne party. At about ten-thirty p.m. the official team chaperone, Ada Taylor Sackett, discovered Eleanor staggering along the deck, accompanied by a young man. After returning to her cabin, which she shared with two other swimmers, Holm stuck her head out the porthole and began shouting obscenities. Her roommates, Olive McKean and Mary Lou Petty, pulled her back inside and convinced her to go to sleep. At midnight Mrs. Sackett returned with the team doctor, J. Hubert Lawson, and the ship's doctor. Dr. Lawson found Holm "in a deep slumber which approached a state of coma." His diagnosis: "Acute alcoholism." The physical examination failed to awaken her. Members of the American Olympic Committee met to discuss the charges against Holm, which also included shooting craps. (She never denied the charges and later boasted that she had won "a couple hundred dollars" just before the final party.)

At six a.m. team manager Herbert Holm (no relation) woke Eleanor and informed her that the American Olympic Committee had voted to remove her from the team. She went to the stateroom of Avery Brundage, president of the A.O.C., and pleaded her case through a crack in the door. It was to no avail. More than half of the U.S. team members signed a petition asking for Eleanor's reinstatement and the press split was about the same.

The news of Eleanor Holm's expulsion caused a sensation when the S.S. *Manhattan* docked in Hamburg, particularly when word began to spread about the details of the case. When her final appeal was denied, Holm lashed back at the American officials, pointing out that they had held cocktail parties every night and that they had ignored the athletes. Joseph Goebbels' Nazi propaganda periodical, *Der Angriff*, took the side of the A.O.C., editorializing, "She probably didn't believe they could disqualify her, but she thought wrong. It wasn't herself who mattered. It was the others—and discipline. For that no sacrifice is too great, no matter how many tears are shed."

Eleanor Holm didn't get to participate in the 1936 Olympics, but that didn't prevent her from having a good time in Berlin. The Nazis quickly forgave her lack of discipline and entertained her as a special visitor. "I had such fun!" she told *Sports Illustrated* 36 years later. "I enjoyed the parties, the *Heil Hitlers,* the uniforms, the flags. . . . Goering was fun. He had a good personality. So did the one with the club foot [Goebbels]. Goering gave me a sterling-silver swastika. I had a mold made of it and I put a diamond Star of David in the middle." Holm issued a public challenge to whoever won the Olympic championship to face her in a swim-off, but when the day came for the final of the women's 100-meter backstroke, Eleanor Holm, who hadn't been beaten in seven years, was sitting in the stands instead of swimming in the pool.

As it happened, the competition, although it did not get as much press attention as all that had preceded it, was not without its own element of sensation. Sixteen-year-old Nida Senff surprised the experts by recording the fastest preliminary times, 1:16.6 and 1:17.1. In the final she was away quickly and had opened up a two-meter lead by the halfway mark. But she missed touching the wall and had to go back. This dropped her to sixth place out of seven, but she sped on, regained the lead with 20 meters to go, and won with a very little bit to spare. She might have lost anyway had not world record holder Rie Mastenbroek become entangled in the lane ropes. Of the four events which Mastenbroek entered in 1936, this was the only one she didn't win.

As for Eleanor Holm, she became more popular than ever. In 1938 she divorced Art Jarrett and also acted in her only film, co-starring as Jane in *Tarzan's Revenge* with 1936 decathlon champion Glenn Morris. The following

year she married impresario Billy Rose. The pair divorced in 1954 following a spicy case, which became known as "The War of the Roses" and which was filled with titillating accusations of sexual "misbehavior" on both sides. She later became an interior decorator and retired to Miami Beach.

1948 London C: 24, N: 16, D: 8.5. WR: 1:10.9 (Cor Kint)
1. Karen-Margrete Harup   DEN   1:14.4   OR
2. Suzanne Zimmerman   USA   1:16.0
3. Judith Davies   AUS   1:16.7
4. Ilona Novák   HUN   1:18.4
5. Hendrika van der Horst   HOL   1:18.8
6. Dirkje van Ekris   HOL   1:18.9
7. Muriel Mellon   USA   1:19.0
8. Greta Galliard   HOL   1:19.1

Eliminated in the semifinals was French swimmer and journalist Monique Berlioux who later became Director of the International Olympic Committee.

1952 Helsinki C: 20, N: 14, D: 7.31. WR: 1:10.9 (Cor Kint)
1. Joan Harrison   SAF   1:14.3
2. Geertje Wielema   HOL   1:14.5
3. Jean Stewart   NZE   1:15.8
4. Johanna de Korte   HOL   1:15.8
5. Barbara Stark   USA   1:16.2
6. Gertrud Herrbruck   GER   1:18.0
7. Margaret McDowall   GBR   1:18.4
DISQ: Hendrika van der Horst (HOL)

Joan Harrison's upset victory was so unexpected that Alex Bulley, the South African team manager, fainted from excitement when he realized she had won.

1956 Melbourne C: 23, N: 14, D: 12.5. WR: 1:10.9 (Cor Kint)
1. Judith Grinham   GBR   1:12.9   OR
2. Carin Cone   USA   1:12.9
3. Margaret Edwards   GBR   1:13.1
4. Helga Schmidt   GER   1:13.4
5. Maureen Murphy   USA   1:14.1
6. July Hoyle   GBR   1:14.3
7. Sara Barber   CAN   1:14.3
8. Gerganyia Beckitt   AUS   1:14.7

1960 Rome C: 30, N: 19, D: 9.3. WR: 1:09.2 (Lynn Burke)
1. Lynn Burke   USA   1:09.3   OR
2. Natalie Steward   GBR   1:10.8
3. Satoko Tanaka   JAP   1:11.4
4. Laura Ranwell   SAF   1:11.4
5. Rosy Piacentini   FRA   1:11.4
6. Sylvia Lewis   GBR   1:11.8
7. Maria van Velsen   HOL   1:12.1
8. Nadine Delache   FRA   1:12.4

1964 Tokyo C: 31, N: 17, D: 10.14. WR: 1:08.3 (Virginia Duenkel)
1. Cathy Ferguson   USA   1:07.7   WR
2. Christine Caron   FRA   1:07.9

3. Virginia Duenkel	USA	1:08.0
4. Satoko Tanaka	JAP	1:08.6
5. Nina Harmar	USA	1:09.4
6. Linda Ludgrove	GBR	1:09.5
7. Eilleen Weir	CAN	1:09.8
8. Jill Norfolk	GBR	1:11.2

The 1964 final matched six past and present world record holders at various backstroke distances: Caron, Duenkel, Tanaka, Ferguson, Ludgrove, and Norfolk. Sixteen-year-old Kiki Caron had set a 100 meters world record of 1:08.6 on June 14, but that was broken by Ginny Duenkel on September 28. In the Olympic final, however, it was 16-year-old 200 meters record holder Cathy Ferguson who edged ahead just before the finish to gain her second world record and her first gold medal.

1968 Mexico City C: 40, N: 23, D: 10.23. WR: 1:06.4 (Karen Muir)

1. Kaye Hall	USA	1:06.2	WR
2. Elaine Tanner	CAN	1:06.7	
3. Jane Swagerty	USA	1:08.1	
4. Kendis Moore	USA	1:08.3	
5. Andrea Gyarmati	HUN	1:09.1	
6. Lynette Watson	AUS	1:09.1	
7. Sylvie Canet	FRA	1:09.3	
8. Glenda Stirling	NZE	1:10.6	

Sixteen-year-old world record holder Karen Muir was excluded from Olympic competition because she was from South Africa, which has been banned from the Olympics since 1964 because of its government's racial policies. In Muir's absence, the favorite was 17-year-old Elaine Tanner of Vancouver, who had the fastest times of the qualifying rounds, setting Olympic records of 1:07.6 and 1:07.4 in the heats and semifinals. But as Canada's main gold medal hope, she carried a heavy burden. "Usually, before a race," she explained afterward, "you're concentrating on strategy, the other swimmers, the race. But at Mexico all I could think about was the twenty million people who were expecting me to win." Another finalist was 17-year-old Kaye Hall of Tacoma, Washington, who had been beaten by Tanner several times and as recently as the semifinals the previous day. Tanner and Hall swam neck and neck for 50 meters, but Hall surged ahead at the turn, and even though Tanner produced her best time ever, she couldn't catch the inspired American teenager.

1972 Munich C: 37, N: 21, D: 9.2. WR: 1:05.6 (Karen Muir)

1. Melissa Belote	USA	1:05.78	OR
2. Andrea Gyarmati	HUN	1:06:26	
3. Susie Atwood	USA	1:06.34	
4. Karen Moe	USA	1:06.69	
5. Wendy Cook	CAN	1:06.70	
6. Enith Brigitha	HOL	1:06.82	
7. Christine Herbst	GDR	1:07.27	
8. Silke Pielen	GER	1:07.36	

This was the first of Melissa Belote's three gold medals. She had originally turned to the backstroke because it was the only stroke that kept the chlorine out of her eyes. Belote attributed her fine performance in Munich to the fact that she felt relaxed and unpressured since she was not expected to win.

1976 Montreal C: 34, N: 21, D: 7.21. WR: 1:01.51 (Ulrike Richter)

1. Ulrike Richter	GDR	1:01.83	OR
2. Birgit Treiber	GDR	1:03.41	
3. Nancy Garapick	CAN	1:03.71	
4. Wendy Hogg-Cook	CAN	1:03.93	
5. Cheryl Gibson	CAN	1:05.16	
6. Nadejda Stavko	SOV	1:05.19	
7. Antje Stille	GDR	1:05.30	
8. Diane Edelijn	HOL	1:05.53	

The order of finish for the first four places was exactly the same as it had been a year earlier at the 1975 world championships in Cali, Colombia. Seventeen-year-old Ulrike Richter had broken the 100 meters world record nine times in the three years preceding the Montreal Olympics.

1980 Moscow C: 26, N: 18, D: 7.23. WR: 1:01.51 (Ulrike Richter)

1. Rica Reinisch	GDR	1:00.86	WR
2. Ina Kleber	GDR	1:02.07	
3. Petra Riedel	GDR	1:02.64	
4. Carmen Bunaciu	ROM	1:03.81	
5. Carine Verbauwen	BEL	1:03.82	
6. Larissa Gorchakova	SOV	1:03.87	
7. Monique Bosga	HOL	1:04.47	
8. Manuela Carosi	ITA	1:05.10	

Fifteen-year-old Rica Reinisch had quite a successful week at the Moscow Olympics. First she equaled Ulrike Richter's four-year-old 100-meter backstroke world record of 1:01.51 while swimming the opening leg for East Germany's victorious medley relay team. Two days later she broke Richter's record by clocking 1:01.50 in her elimination heat. In the final, 24 hours later, Reinisch took the lead early on the way to her third world record. Four days later, in the 200-meter backstroke final, she earned her third gold medal and her fourth world record.

200-METER BACKSTROKE

1896–1964 not held

1968 Mexico City C: 30, N: 19, D: 10.25. WR: 2:23.8 (Karen Muir)

1. Lillian "Pokey" Watson	USA	2:24.8	OR
2. Elaine Tanner	CAN	2:27.4	
3. Kaye Hall	USA	2:28.9	
4. Lynette Watson	AUS	2:29.5	
5. Wendy Burrell	GBR	2:32.3	
6. Zdenka Gasparac	YUG	2:33.5	
7. Maria Corominas	SPA	2:33.9	
8. Bendicte Duprez	FRA	2:36.6	

1972 Munich C: 37, N: 20, D: 9.4. WR: 2:20.64 (Melissa Belote)
1. Melissa Belote	USA	2:19.19	WR
2. Susie Atwood	USA	2:20.38	
3. Donna Gurr	CAN	2:23.22	
4. Annegret Kober	GER	2:23.35	
5. Christine Herbst	GDR	2:23.44	
6. Enith Brigitha	HOL	2:23.70	
7. Deborah Palmer	AUS	2:24.65	
8. Leslie Cliff	CAN	2:25.80	

Melissa Belote swam a 2:20.58 in the heats to break her own world record. She broke it again in the final eight hours later to win her third gold medal in three days.

1976 Montreal C: 31, N: 18, D: 7.25. WR: 2:12.47 (Birgit Treiber)
1. Ulrike Richter	GDR	2:13.43	OR
2. Birgit Treiber	GDR	2:14.97	
3. Nancy Garapick	CAN	2:15.60	
4. Nadejda Stavko	SOV	2:16.28	
5. Melissa Belote	USA	2:17.27	
6. Antje Stille	GDR	2:17.55	
7. Klavdia Studennikova	SOV	2:17.74	
8. Wendy Hogg-Cook	CAN	2:17.95	

The 200-meter backstroke had seen five different world record holders in the two and a half years prior to the Montreal Olympics: Belote, Richter, Garapick, Treiber, and Stille. All five started in the Olympic final. As it turned out, there was little drama; Ulrike Richter led from start to finish to gain her third gold medal.

1980 Moscow C: 21, N: 13, D: 7.27. WR: 2:11.95 (Linda Jezek)
1. Rica Reinisch	GDR	2:11.77	WR
2. Cornelia Polit	GDR	2:13.75	
3. Birgit Treiber	GDR	2:14.14	
4. Carmen Bunaciu	ROM	2:15.20	
5. Yolande van der Straeten	BEL	2:15.58	
6. Carine Verbauwen	BEL	2:16.66	
7. Lisa Forrest	AUS	2:16.75	
8. Larissa Gorchakova	SOV	2:17.72	

Reinisch improved her personal best from 2:15.59 in only eight weeks.

100-METER BREASTSTROKE

1896–1964 not held

1968 Mexico City C: 33, N: 20, D: 10.19. WR: 1:14.2 (Catie Ball)
1. Djurdjica Bjedov	YUG	1:15.8	OR
2. Galina Prozumenshikova	SOV	1:15.9	
3. Sharon Wichman	USA	1:16.1	
4. Uta Frommater	GER	1:16.2	
5. Catie Ball	USA	1:16.7	
6. Kyoe Nakagawa	JAP	1:17.0	
7. Svetlana Babanina	SOV	1:17.2	
8. Ana Norbis	URU	1:17.3	

Catie Ball of Jacksonville, Florida, set her fifth 100-meter breaststroke world record seven weeks before the opening of the 1968 Olympics. But in Mexico City she succumbed

to a viral infection and lost ten pounds. She competed anyway, but could finish only fifth. Twenty-one-year-old Djurdjica Bjedov is the only Yugoslav ever to have won an Olympic swimming championship. Previous to the Olympics her main claim to fame had been finishing third in a 200-meter heat at the 1966 European championships.

1972 Munich C: 40, N: 23, D: 9.2. WR: 1:14.2 (Catie Ball)
1. Catherine Carr	USA	1:13.58	WR
2. Galina Stepanova (Prozumenshikova)	SOV	1:14.99	
3. Beverley Whitfield	AUS	1:15.73	
4. Ágnes Kiss-Kaczander	HUN	1:16.26	
5. Judy Melick	USA	1:17.16	
6. Verena Eberle	GER	1:17.16	
7. Britt-Marie Smedh	SWE	1:17.19	
8. Dorothy Harrison	GBR	1:17.49	

1976 Montreal C: 38, D: 23, D: 7.24. WR: 1:11.93 (Carola Nitschke)
1. Hannelore Anke	GDR	1:11.16
2. Lyubov Rusanova	SOV	1:13.04
3. Marina Koshevaia	SOV	1:13.30
4. Carola Nitschke	GDR	1:13.33
5. Gabriele Askamp	GER	1:14.15
6. Marina Iurchenia	SOV	1:14.17
7. Margaret Kelly	GBR	1:14.20
8. Karla Linke	GDR	1:14.21

In the fifth heat of the opening round, 18-year-old Hannelore Anke of Aue set a new world record of 1:11.11. Nine hours later in the semifinals, she lowered the record to 1:10.86. In the final, two nights later, Anke's slowest performance of the Games was good enough for an easy gold medal.

1980 Moscow C: 25, N: 19, D: 7.26. WR: 1:10.20 (Ute Geweniger)
1. Ute Geweniger	GDR	1:10.22
2. Elvira Vasilkova	SOV	1:10.41
3. Susanne Nielsson	DEN	1:11.16
4. Margaret Kelly	GBR	1:11.48
5. Eva-Marie Håkansson	SWE	1:11.72
6. Susannah Brownsdon	GBR	1:12.11
7. Lina Kachushite	SOV	1:12.21
8. Monica Bonon	ITA	1:12.51

Sixteen-year-old Ute Geweniger clocked a 1:10.11 in the fourth heat to break her own world record. In the final she was only fifth at the turn. Three days later, Tracy Caulkins set a U.S. record of 1:10.40.

200-METER BREASTSTROKE

1896–1920 not held

1924 C: 15, N: 8, D: 7.18. WR: 3:20.4 (Irene Gilbert)
1. Lucy Morton	GBR	3:33.2	OR
2. Agnes Geraghty	USA	3:34.0	
3. Gladys Carson	GBR	3:35.4	

4. Vivan Pettersson   SWE 3:37.6
5. Irene Gilbert   GBR 3:38.0
6. Laury Koster   LUX 3:39.2
7. Hjördis Töpel   SWE 3:47.6

The first qualifying heat was won by Marie Baron of Holland in 3:22.6, with Agnes Geraghty second in 3:27.6. Baron was disqualified, however, for making a faulty turn. Geraghty led the final for 150 meters, but she couldn't withstand the surprising closing rush of 26-year-old Lucy Morton.

1928 Amsterdam C: 21, N: 12, D: 8.9. WR: 3:11.2 (Lotte Mühe)

1. Hildegard Schrader	GER	3:12.6
2. Mietje "Marie" Baron	HOL	3:15.2
3. Lotte Mühe	GER	3:17.6
4. Else Jacobsen	DEN	3:19.0
5. Margaret Hoffman	USA	3:19.2
6. Brita Hazelius	SWE	3:23.0

Lotte Mühe broke Marie Baron's world record on July 15, but three weeks later in Amsterdam it was her teammate, 18-year-old Hilde Schrader, who was in control. Her opening heat time of 3:11.6 bettered the Olympic record by 16 seconds. In the semifinals Schrader equaled Mühe's world record. The final was her slowest race, but she was still able to win comfortably.

1932 Los Angeles C: 11, N: 7, D: 8.9. WR: 3:03.4 (Else Jacobsen)

1. Clare Dennis	AUS	3:06.3	OR
2. Hideko Maehata	JAP	3:06.4	
3. Else Jacobsen	DEN	3:07.1	
4. Margery Hinton	GBR	3:11.7	
5. Margaret Hoffman	USA	3:11.8	
6. Anne Govednik	USA	3:16.0	
7. Jane Cadwell	USA	3:18.2	

Mere inches separated Dennis and Jacobsen for the first 175 meters. Jacobsen wilted slightly at the end, enabling the fast-finishing Maehata to beat her by a foot for second place.

1936 Berlin C: 23, N: 12, D: 8.11. WR: 3:00.4 (Hideko Maehata)

1. Hideko Maehata	JAP	3:03.6
2. Martha Geneger	GER	3:04.2
3. Inge Sörensen	DEN	3:07.8
4. Johanna "Hanni" Hölzner	GER	3:09.5
5. Johanna Waalberg	HOL	3:09.5
6. Doris Storey	GBR	3:09.7
7. K.H. Kastein	HOL	3:12.8

The year 1936 saw the first Olympic appearance of the controversial butterfly stroke, in which the swimmer recovers her arms above the water rather than under. The first woman to try the stroke in the Olympics was Lenk of Brazil who was eliminated in the semifinals. Silver medalist Martha Geneger was 14 years old, while bronze medalist Inge Sörensen was only 12 years and 24 days old. By contrast, Hideko Maehata, who set an Olympic record of 3:01.9 in her preliminary heat, was an elderly 22.

1948 London C: 22, N: 14, D: 8.3. WR: 2:49.2 (Petronella van Vliet)

1. Petronella van Vliet	HOL	2:57.2
2. Beatrice Lyons	AUS	2:57.7
3. Éva Novák	HUN	3:00.2
4. Éva Székely	HUN	3:02.5
5. Adriana de Groot	HOL	3:06.2
6. Elizabeth Church	GBR	3:06.1
7. A.J. Hom	HOL	3:07.5
8. Jytte Hansen	DEN	3:08.1

De Groot was awarded fifth place despite the fact that her official time was slower than that of Church.

1952 Helsinki C: 34, N: 19, D: 7.29. WR: 2:48.5 (Éva Novák)

1. Éva Székely	HUN	2:51.7	OR
2. Éva Novák	HUN	2:54.4	
3. Helen "Elenor" Gordon	GBR	2:57.6	
4. Klára Killermann	HUN	2:57.6	
5. Jytte Hansen	DEN	2:57.8	
6. Maria Gavrisch	SOV	2:58.9	
7. Ulla-Britt Eklund	SWE	3:01.8	
8. Petronella Garritsen	HOL	3:02.1	

Like 100-meter freestyle winner Katalin Szöke, 25-year-old Éva Székely was married to a member of the 1952 champion Hungarian water polo team. Husband Dezsö Gyarmati also won water polo gold medals in 1956 and 1964. Székely was the first female butterfly stroker to win a gold medal. Following the 1952 Olympics, the breaststroke and butterfly were separated into two different events.

1956 Melbourne C: 14, N: 10, D: 11.30. WR: 2:46.4 (Adelaide den Haan)

1. Ursula Happe	GER	2:53.1	OR
2. Éva Székely	HUN	2:54.8	
3. Eva-Maria ten Elsen	GDR	2:55.1	
4. Vinka Jeričevič	YUG	2:55.8	
5. Klára Killermann	HUN	2:56.1	
6. Helen "Elenor" Gordon	GBR	2:56.1	
7. Mary Sears	USA	2:57.2	
8. Christine Gosden	GBR	2:59.2	

World record holder Ada den Haan was unable to compete because the Netherlands withdrew from the 1956 Games to protest the Soviet invasion of Hungary.

1960 Rome C: 29, N: 19, D: 9.27. WR: 2:50.2 (Wiltrud Urselmann)

1. Anita Lonsbrough	GBR	2:49.5	WR
2. Wiltrud Urselmann	GER	2:50.0	
3. Barbara Göbel	GDR	2:53.6	
4. Adelaide den Haan	HOL	2:54.4	
5. Margareta Kok	HOL	2:54.6	
6. Anne Warner	USA	2:55.4	
7. Patty Kempner	USA	2:55.5	
8. Dorrit Kristensen	DEN	2:55.7	

In 1957 underwater stroking was banned from breaststroke competitions, which explains why the world record was slower in 1960 than it was in 1956. Nineteen-year-old Anita Lonsbrough, a clerk for the Huddersfield Corporation in Yorkshire, faced a problem not uncommon to amateur athletes in Great Britain. Far from being appreciative of the free publicity that her swimming exploits brought them, her employers actually docked her wages whenever she took time off for training. Her victory in Rome was the result of iron nerves and perfect tactics. She trailed Urselmann by two seconds at the halfway mark, then she gradually closed the gap, catching the tiring German with 25 meters to go. Urselmann surprised Lonsbrough with a final spurt, but Lonsbrough, who had calmly varnished her nails while waiting for the race to start, held on for the victory.

1964 Tokyo C: 26, N: 15, D: 10.12. WR: 2:45.4 (Galina Prozumenshikova)

1. Galina Prozumenshikova	SOV	2:46.4	OR
2. Claudia Kolb	USA	2:47.6	
3. Svetlana Babanina	SOV	2:48.6	
4. Stella Mitchell	GBR	2:49.0	
5. Jill Slattery	GBR	2:49.6	
6. Bärbel Grimmer	GDR	2:51.0	
7. Klena Bimoli	HOL	2:51.3	
8. Ursula Küper	GDR	2:53.9	

Prozumenshikova, a 15-year-old schoolgirl from Sevastopol, let Babanina set the pace for 100 meters and then surged ahead to win the U.S.S.R.'s first gold medal in swimming.

1968 Mexico City C: 31, N: 20, D: 10.23. WR: 2:38.5 (Catie Ball)

1. Sharon Wichman	USA	2:44.4	OR
2. Djurdjica Bjedov	YUG	2:46.4	
3. Galina Prozumenshikova	SOV	2:47.0	
4. Alla Grebennikova	SOV	2:47.1	
5. Cathy Jamison	USA	2:48.4	
6. Svetlana Babanina	SOV	2:48.4	
7. Chieno Shibata	JAP	2:51.5	
8. Ana Norbis	URU	2:51.9	

Prozumenshikova was leading after 175 meters when she suddenly ran out of energy and barely hung on for third place. She had to be administered oxygen as soon as the race was over. Sharon Wichman's victory meant that the gold medals in the first ten Olympic women's 200-meter breaststroke competitions had been won by swimmers from eight different nations.

1972 Munich C: 39, N: 22, D: 8.29. WR: 2:38.5 (Catie Ball)

1. Beverley Whitfield	AUS	2:41.71	OR
2. Dana Schoenfield	USA	2:42.05	
3. Galina Stepanova (Prozumenshikova)	SOV	2:42.36	
4. Claudia Clevenger	USA	2:42.88	
5. Petra Nows	GER	2:43.41	
6. Ágnes Kiss-Kaczander	HUN	2:43.41	
7. Lyudmila Porubaiko	SOV	2:44.48	
8. Éva Kiss	HUN	2:45.12	

As usual, Galina Prozumenshikova took the early lead and eventually opened a four-meter gap. But just as she had done four years earlier, the Soviet swimmer, now Galina Stepanova, "died" in the final 50 meters and faded to third place. Meanwhile, 18-year-old Beverley Whitfield, in last place afer 50 meters and fourth place after 150 meters, sprinted home to pass Stepanova and stave off a final challenge from Schoenfield. As she climbed out of the pool, Whitfield called out to her teammates, "For once I kept my cool. This is the greatest feeling in the world."

1976 Montreal C: 38, N: 21, D: 7.21. WR: 2:34.99 (Karla Linke)

1. Marina Koshevaia	SOV	2:33.35	WR
2. Marina Iurchenia	SOV	2:36.08	
3. Lyubov Rusanova	SOV	2:36.22	
4. Hannelore Anke	GDR	2:36.49	
5. Karla Linke	GDR	2:36.97	
6. Carola Nitschke	GDR	2:38.27	
7. Margaret Kelly	GBR	2:38.37	
8. Deborah Rudd	GBR	2:39.01	

Koshevaia moved up from fifth to first during the third 50 meters and then pulled away to the most decisive women's breaststroke victory in Olympic history.

1980 Moscow C: 25, N: 19, D: 7.23. WR: 2:28.36 (Lina Kačiušyté)

1. Lina Kačiušyté	SOV	2:29.54	OR
2. Svetlana Varganova	SOV	2:29.61	
3. Yulia Bogdanova	SOV	2:32.39	
4. Susanne Nielsson	DEN	2:32.75	
5. Irena Fleissnerová	CZE	2.33.23	
6. Ute Geweniger	GDR	2:34.34	
7. Bettina Löbel	GDR	2:34.51	
8. Sylvia Rinka	GDR	2:35.38	

Svetlana Varganova led for almost the entire race while Lithuanian Lina Kačiušyté improved from last place at 50 meters to fourth place at the halfway mark and second place, two and a half seconds behind Varganova, with 50 meters to go. An impressive finishing spurt earned 17-year-old Kačiušyté the gold medal.

100-METER BUTTERFLY

1896–1952 not held

1956 Melbourne C: 12, N: 8, D: 12.5. WR: 1:10.5 (Aartje Voorbij)

1. Shelly Mann	USA	1:11.0	OR
2. Nancy Ramey	USA	1:11.9	
3. Mary Sears	USA	1:14.4	
4. Mária Littomeritzky	HUN	1:14.9	
5. Beverly Bainbridge	AUS	1:15.2	
6. Jutta Langenau	GDR	1:17.4	
7. Elizabeth Whittall	CAN	1:17.9	
8. Sara Barber	CAN	1:18.4	

With world record holder Atie Voorbij absent because of the Dutch boycott, the inaugural women's butterfly event was swept by the Americans. Crippled by polio at the age of six, Shelly Mann began swimming to regain strength in her arms and legs.

1960 Rome C: 25, N: 16, D: 8.30. WR: 1:09.1 (Nancy Ramey)

1. Carolyn Schuler	USA	1:09.5	OR
2. Marianne Heemskerk	HOL	1:10.4	
3. Janice Andrew	AUS	1:12.2	
4. Sheila Watt	GBR	1:13.3	
5. Aartje Voorbij	HOL	1:13.3	
6. Zinaida Belovetskaya	SOV	1:13.3	
7. Kristina Larsson	SWE	1:13.6	

DNF: Carolyn Wood (USA)

Fourteen-year-old Carolyn Wood had beaten Carolyn Schuler at the U.S. trials. A close second after 70 meters of the Olympic final, Wood swallowed too much water, became confused, and stopped swimming.

1964 Tokyo C: 31, N: 16, D: 10.16 WR(110 yards): 1:05.1 (Ada Kok)

1. Sharon Stouder	USA	1:04.7	WR
2. Ada Kok	HOL	1:05.6	
3. Kathleen Ellis	USA	1:06.0	
4. Ella Pyrhönen	FIN	1:07.3	
5. Donna De Varona	USA	1:08.0	
6. Heike Hustede	GER	1:08.5	
7. Eiko Takahashi	JAP	1:09.1	
8. Mary Stewart	CAN	1:10.0	

1968 Mexico City C: 28, N: 21, D: 10.21. WR: 1:04.5 (Ada Kok)

1. Lynette McClements	AUS	1:05.5
2. Ellie Daniel	USA	1:05.8
3. Susan Shields	USA	1:06.2
4. Ada Kok	HOL	1:06.2
5. Andréa Gyarmati	HUN	1:06.8
6. Heike Hustede	GER	1:06.9
7. Toni Hewitt	USA	1:07.5
8. Helga Lindner	GDR	1:07.6

Lyn McClements, a 17-year-old typist from Perth, improved her pre-Olympic best time by 0.5 seconds.

1972 Munich C: 30, N: 21, D: 9.1. WR: 1:03.9 (Mayumi Aoki)

1. Mayumi Aoki	JAP	1:03.34	WR
2. Roswitha Beier	GDR	1:03.61	
3. Andréa Gyarmati	HUN	1:03.73	
4. Deena Deardurff	USA	1:03.95	
5. Dana Shrader	USA	1:03.98	
6. Ellie Daniel	USA	1:04.08	
7. Gudrun Beckmann	GER	1:04.15	
8. Noriko Asano	JAP	1:04.25	

Aoki was only in seventh place at the midrace turn. Bronze medalist Andréa Gyarmati was the daughter of 1952 breaststroke gold medalist Éva Székely and Dezsö Gyarmati, who won three gold medals in water polo.

1976 Montreal C: 39, N: 26, D: 7.22. WR: 1:00.13 (Kornelia Ender)

1. Kornelia Ender	GDR	1:00.13	EWR
2. Andrea Pollack	GDR	1:00.98	
3. Wendy Boglioli	USA	1:01.17	
4. Camille Wright	USA	1:01.41	
5. Rosemarie Gabriel (Kother)	GDR	1:01.56	
6. Wendy Quirk	CAN	1:01.75	
7. Lelei Fonoimoana	USA	1:01.95	
8. Tamara Shelofastova	SOV	1:02.74	

At 7:48 p.m. on July 22, 1976, Kornelia Ender won the 100-meter butterfly final in world record time. At 8:03 she descended from the victory platform and went to the dressing room. At 8:08 she returned to the pool for the final of the 200-meter freestyle. At 8:13 she was racing through the water again, and by 8:15 she had won her second gold medal in 27 minutes.

1980 Moscow C: 24, N: 18, D: 7.24. WR: 59.26 (Mary Meagher)

1. Caren Metschuck	GDR	1:00.42
2. Andrea Pollack	GDR	1:00.90
3. Christiane Knacke	GDR	1:01.44
4. Ann Osgerby	GBR	1:02.21
5. Lisa Curry	AUS	1:02.40
6. Agneta Mårtensson	SWE	1:02.61
7. Mariam Paris	COS	1:02.89
8. Janet Osgerby	GBR	1:02.90

The British representatives, Ann and Janet Osgerby, were 17-year-old twins from Chorley, Lancashire. Ann was 20 minutes older and 0.69 seconds faster. Missing from the competition due to the anti-Soviet boycott were world record holder Mary Meagher and Tracy Caulkins, who clocked 59.41 and 1:00.75, respectively, at the U.S. Outdoor National on August 2.

200-METER BUTTERFLY

1896–1964 not held

1968 Mexico City C: 21, N: 16, D: 10.24. WR(220 yards): 2:21.0 (Ada Kok)

1. Ada Kok	HOL	2:24.7	OR
2. Helga Lindner	GDR	2:24.8	
3. Ellie Daniel	USA	2:25.9	
4. Toni Hewitt	USA	2:26.2	
5. Heike Hustede	GER	2:27.9	
6. Diane Giebel	USA	2:31.7	
7. Margaret Auton	GBR	2:33.2	
8. Yasuko Fujii	JAP	2:34.3	

Six-foot, 183-pound Ada Kok, "The Gentle Giant," had experienced nothing but disappointment in the Olympics. Because of her world records and her general domination of international competitions, she had been expected to win gold medals, but in Tokyo she had to settle for two silver medals in the 100-meter butterfly and the medley relay. Four years later, in Mexico City, Kok was part of the Dutch medley relay team that finished seventh. Then, in the 100-meter butterfly, she finished a disappointing fourth. This left her one last chance for an Olympic victory—the 200-meter butterfly. Her chances seemed slim after her previous defeats, but she recorded the fastest time of the eliminations. In the final she was third at the turn behind Heike Hustede and Helga Lindner, but Kok's powerful finish gave her a popular and well-deserved victory.

1972 Munich C: 24, N: 17, D: 9.4. WR: 2:16.62 (Karen Moe)
1. Karen Moe   USA   2:15.57   WR
2. Lynn Colella   USA   2:16.34
3. Ellie Daniel   USA   2:16.74
4. Rosemarie Kother   GDR   2:17.11
5. Noriko Asano   JAP   2:19.50
6. Helga Lindner   GDR   2:20.47
7. Gail Neall   AUS   2:21.88
8. Mayumi Aoki   JAP   2:22.84

Karen Moe let Daniel and Kother set the pace for 150 meters and then took the lead after the final turn.

1976 Montreal C: 32, N: 19, D: 7.19. WR: 2:11.22 (Rosemarie Gabriel [Kother])
1. Andrea Pollack   GDR   2:11.41   OR
2. Ulrike Tauber   GDR   2:12.50
3. Rosemarie Gabriel (Kother) GDR   2:12.86
4. Karen Thorton (Moe)   USA   2:12.90
5. Wendy Quirk   CAN   2:13.68
6. Cheryl Gibson   CAN   2:13.91
7. Tamara Shelofastova   SOV   2:14.26
8. Natalia Popova   SOV   2:14.50

1980 Moscow C: 21, N: 14, D: 7.21. WR: 2:07.01 (Mary Meagher)
1. Ines Geissler   GDR   2:10.44   OR
2. Sybille Schönrock   GDR   2:10.45
3. Michelle Ford   AUS   2:11.66
4. Andrea Pollack   GDR   2:12.13
5. Dorota Brzozowska   POL   2:14.12
6. Ann Osgerby   GBR   2:14.83
7. Agneta Martensson   SWE   2:15.22
8. Alla Grishchenkova   SOV   2:15.70

Geissler led at 50 meters and 100 meters, while Schönrock was first to touch at 150. In the end, the 17-year-old Geissler reached the wall in time to win the closest of victories. However neither woman's time came close to the performance of 15-year-old Mary Meagher of Cincinnati, who set a world record of 2:06.37 at the U.S. Outdoor National nine days after the Olympic final.

200-METER INDIVIDUAL MEDLEY

In individual medley races the order of strokes is butterfly, backstroke, breaststroke, and freestyle.

1896–1964 not held

1968 Mexico City C: 39, N: 26, D: 10.20. WR: 2:23.5 (Claudia Kolb)
1. Claudia Kolb   USA   2:24.7   OR
2. Susan Pedersen   USA   2:28.8
3. Jan Henne   USA   2:31.4
4. Sabine Steinbach   GDR   2:31.4
5. Yoshimi Nishigawa   JAP   2:33.7
6. Marianne Seyedl   GDR   2:33.7
7. Larisa Zakharova   SOV   2:37.0
DISQ: Shelagh Ratcliffe (GBR)

When she was 14 years old, Claudia Kolb of Santa Clara, California earned a surprise silver medal in the 200-meter breaststroke. Four years later she overwhelmed her opposition to win both the 200-meter and 400-meter individual medleys.

1972 Munich C: 44, N: 26, D: 8.28. WR: 2:23.5 (Claudia Kolb)
1. Shane Gould   AUS   2:23.07   WR
2. Kornelia Ender   GDR   2:23.59
3. Lynn Vidali   USA   2:24.06
4. Jennifer Bartz   USA   2:24.55
5. Leslie Cliff   CAN   2:24.83
6. Evelyn Stolze   GDR   2:25.90
7. Yoshimi Nishigawa   JAP   2:26.35
8. Carolyn Woods   USA   2:27.42

Lynn Vidali led by over a second after 150 meters, but Shane Gould used her freestyle strength to catch her 20 meters later and win the first of her three gold medals. In second place was 13-year-old Kornelia Ender, who won the first of her eight Olympic medals.

1976–1980 not held

This event will be reinstated at the 1984 Olympics.

400-METER INDIVIDUAL MEDLEY

1896–1960 not held

1964 Tokyo C: 22, N: 12, D: 10.17. WR: 5:14.9 (Donna De Varona)
1. Donna De Varona   USA   5:18.7   OR
2. Sharon Finneran   USA   5:24.1
3. Martha Randall   USA   5:24.2
4. Veronika Holletz   GDR   5:25.6
5. Linda McGill   AUS   5:28.4
6. Elisabeth Heukels   HOL   5:30.3
7. Anita Lonsbrough   GBR   5:30.5
8. Márta Egerváry   HUN   5:38.4

Donna De Varona was a popular and much-photographed winner. She later became a television sports commentator as well as an activist for women in sports.

1968 Mexico City C: 28, N: 19, D: 10.25. WR: 5:04.7 (Claudia Kolb)

1. Claudia Kolb	USA	5:08.5	OR
2. Lynn Vidali	USA	5:22.2	
3. Sabine Steinbach	GDR	5:25.3	
4. Susan Pedersen	USA	5:25.8	
5. Shelagh Ratcliffe	GBR	5:30.5	
6. Marianne Seydel	GDR	5:32.0	
7. Tui Shipston	NZE	5:34.6	
8. Laura Vaca	MEX	5:35.7	

Claudia Kolb won by 20 meters, the most decisive women's swimming victory in 40 years.

1972 Munich C: 38, N: 26, D: 8.31. WR: 5:04.7 (Claudia Kolb)

1. Gail Neall	AUS	5:02.97	WR
2. Leslie Cliff	CAN	5:03.57	
3. Novella Calligaris	ITA	5:03.99	
4. Jennifer Bartz	USA	5:05.56	
5. Evelyn Stolze	GDR	5:06.80	
6. Mary Montgomery	USA	5:09.98	
7. Lynn Vidali	USA	5:13.06	
8. Nina Petrova	SOV	5:15.68	

Gail Neall, from the Sydney suburb of Gordon, led from start to finish and broke Claudia Kolb's four-year-old world record.

1976 Montreal C: 20, N: 11, D: 7.24. WR: 4:48.79 (Birgit Treiber)

1. Ulrike Tauber	GDR	4:42.77	WR
2. Cheryl Gibson	CAN	4:48.10	
3. Becky Smith	CAN	4:50.48	
4. Birgit Treiber	GDR	4:52.40	
5. Sabine Kahle	GDR	4:53.50	
6. Donnalee Wennerstrom	USA	4:55.34	
7. Joann Baker	CAN	5:00.19	
8. Monique Rodahl	NZE	5:00.21	

For the fourth straight time the 400-meter individual medley was led start to finish, as 18-year-old Ulrike Tauber of Karl-Marx Stadt bettered the world record by a phenomenal 6.02 seconds.

1980 Moscow C: 16, N: 11, D: 7.26. WR: 4:38.44 (Petra Schneider)

1. Petra Schneider	GDR	4:36.29	WR
2. Sharron Davies	GBR	4:46.83	
3. Agnieszka Czopek	POL	4:48.17	
4. Grit Slaby	GDR	4:48.54	
5. Ulrike Tauber	GDR	4:49.18	
6. Sonya Dingalakova	BUL	4:49.25	
7. Olga Klevakina	SOV	4:50.91	
8. Magdalena Bialas	POL	4:53.30	

Once again the 400-meter individual medley was completely dominated by one swimmer. This time it was an easy win and new world record for 17-year-old Petra Schneider, who had been trained in part by her older teammate Ulrike

Tauber. In the United States on July 30, Tracy Caulkins clocked 4:40.61 at the Outdoor National to bolster her position as second fastest female medley swimmer in the world.

4×100-METER FREESTYLE RELAY

1896–1908 not held

1912 Stockholm T: 4, N: 4, D: 7.15.

1. GBR	(Bella Moore, Jennie Fletcher, Annie Spiers, Irene Steer)	5:52.8	WR
2. GER	(Wally Dressel, Louise Otto, Hermine Stindt, Margarete Rosenberg)	6:04.6	
3. AUT	(Margarete Adler, Klara Milch, Josephine Sticker, Berta Zahourek)	6:17.0	
4. SWE	(Greta Johansson, Karin Lundgren, Sonja Johnsson, Vera Thulin)	—	

1920 Antwerp T: 3, N: 3, D: 8.29.

1. USA	(Margaret Woodbridge, Frances Schroth, Irene Guest, Ethelda Bleibtrey)	5:11.6	WR
2. GBR	(Hilda James, Constance Mabel Jeans, Charlotte Radcliffe, Grace McKenzie)	5:40.6	
3. SWE	(Aina Berg, Emy Machnow, Karin Nilsson, Jane Gylling)	5:43.6	

1924 Paris T: 6, N: 6, D: 7.18.

1. USA	(Gertrude Ederle, Euphrasia Donnelly, Ethel Lackie, Mariechen Wehselau)	4:58.8	WR
2. GBR	(Florence Barker, Grace McKenzie, Irene Vera Tanner, Constance Mabel Jeans)	5:17.0	
3. SWE	(Aina Berg, Wivan Pettersson, Gulli Everlund, Hjördis Töpel)	5:35.6	
4. DEN	(Vibeke Möller, Hedevig Rasmussen, Karen Maud Rasmussen, Agnete Olsen)	5:42.4	
5. FRA	(Ernestine Lebrun, Gilberte Mortier, Bibienne Pellegry, Marguerite Protin)	5:43.4	
6. HOL	(Mietje Baron, Alida Bolten, Geertruida Klapwijk, Maria Vierdag)	5:45.8	

1928 Amsterdam T: 7, N: 7, D: 8.9.

1. USA	(Adelaide Lambert, Eleanor Garatti, Albina Osipowich, Martha Norelius)	4:47.6	WR
2. GBR	(Margaret Joyce Cooper, Sarah Stewart, Irene Vera Tanner, Ellen King)	5:02.8	
3. SAF	(Kathleen Russell, Rhoda Rennie, Marie Bedford, Frederica van der Goes)	5:13.4	
4. GER	(Charlotte Lehmann, Reni Erkens-Küpper, Hertha Wunder, Irmintraut Schneider)	5:14.4	
5. FRA	(Bibienne Pellegry, A. Dupire, Marguerite Ledoux, Claire Horrent)	5:32.0	

DISQ: HOL (E.A.G. Smits, G.C. Baumeister, Maria Vierdag, Maria Braun)

1932 Los Angeles T: 5, N: 5, D: 8.12. WR: 4:47.6 (USA—Lambert, Garatti, Osipowich, Norelius)

1. USA (Josephine McKim, Helen Johns, Eleanor Saville [Garatti], Helene Madison) — 4:38.0 WR
2. HOL (Maria Vierdag, Maria Oversloot, Cornelia Laddé, Willemijntje den Ouden) — 4:47.5
3. GBR (Elizabeth Valerie Davies, Helen Varcoe, Margaret Joyce Cooper, Edna Hughes) — 4:52.4
4. CAN (Irene Pirie, Irene Mullen, Ruth Kerr, Betty Edwards) — 5:05.7
5. JAP (Kazue Kojima, Hatsuko Morioka, Misao Yokota, Yukie Arata) — 5:06.7

1936 Berlin T: 9, N: 9, D: 8.14. WR: 4:32.8 (HOL—Selbach, Mastenbroek, Wagner, den Ouden)

1. HOL (Johanna Selbach, Catherina Wagner, Willemijntje den Ouden, Hendrika "Rie" Mastenbroek) — 4:36.0 OR
2. GER (Ruth Halbsguth, Leni Lohmar, Ingeborg Schmitz, Gisela Arendt) — 4:36.8
3. USA (Katherine Rawls, Bernice Lapp, Mavis Freeman, Olive McKean) — 4:40.2
4. HUN (Ilona Ács, Ágnes Biró, Véra Harsányi, Magdolna Lenkei) — 4:48.0
4. CAN (Mary McConkey, Irene Milton-Pirie, Margaret Stone, Phyllis Dewar) — 4:48.0
6. GBR (Margaret Jeffery, Zilpha Grant, Edna Hughes, Olive Wadham) — 4:51.0
7. DEN (Ragnhild Hveger, Bruunstrom, Eva Svendsen, Eva Arendt) — 4:51.4

Germany led for 200 meters before den Ouden gave Holland the lead. The race was still in doubt with 20 meters to go, at which point Mastenbroek sprinted to victory.

1948 London T: 11, N: 11, D: 8.6. WR: 4:27.6 (DEN—Arndt, Kraft, Ove-Peterson, Hveger)

1. USA (Marie Corridon, Thelma Kalama, Brenda Helser, Ann Curtis) — 4:29.2 OR
2. DEN (Eva Riise, Karen-Margrete Harup, Greta Andersen, Fritze Carstensen) — 4:29.6
3. HOL (Irma Schuhmacher, Margot Marsman, Marie-Louise Vaessen, Johanna Termeulen) — 4:31.6
4. GBR (Patricia Nielsen, Margaret Wellington, Lillian Preece, Catherine Gibson) — 4:34.7
5. HUN (Mária Littomeritzky, Judit Temes, Ilona Novák, Éva Székely) — 4:44.8
6. BRA (Eleonora Schmitt, Maria Leão da Costa, Talita de Alencar Rodrigues, Piedade Silva Tavares) — 4:49.1
7. FRA (Josette Arene, Gisele Vallerey, Colette Thomas, Ginette Jany) — 4:49.8

DISQ: SWE (Gisela Thidholm, Elisabeth Ahlgren, Marianne Lundquist, Ingegard Fredin)

Ann Curtis swam a spectacular anchor leg to give the United States a come-from-behind victory over Denmark. She was timed in 1:04.4, which unofficially bettered Willy den Ouden's 12-year-old world record for the 100 meters.

However, marks set during relays do not qualify for world records unless they are accomplished on the first leg.

1952 Helsinki T: 13, N: 13, D: 8.1. WR: 4:27.2 (HUN—Littomeritzky, Novák, Székely, Szőke)

1. HUN (Ilona Novák, Judit Temes, Éva Novák, Katalin Szőke) — 4:24.4 WR
2. HOL (Marie-Louise Linssen [Vaessen], Koosje van Voorn, Johanna Termeulen, Irma Heijting-Schuhmacher) — 4:29.0
3. USA (Jacqueline La Vine, Marilee Stepan, Joan Alderson, Evelyn Kawamoto) — 4:30.1
4. DEN (Rita Larsen, Mette Ove-Peterson, Greta Andersen, Ragnhild Andersen-Hveger) — 4:36.2
5. GBR (Phyllis Linton, Jean Botham, Angela Barnwell, Lillian Preece) — 4:37.8
6. SWE (Marianne Lundquist, Anita Andersson, Maud Berglund, Ingegärd Fredin) — 4:39.0
7. GER (Elisabeth Rechlin, Vera Schäferkordt, Kati Jansen, Gisela Jacobs [Arendt]) — 4:40.3
8. FRA (Gaby Tanguy, Maryse Morandini, Ginette Jany, Josette Arene) — 4:44.1

Temes, Novák, and Szőke swam legs of 1:05.8, 1:05.1, and 1:05.7, respectively, each of which was a full second faster than Szőke's time when she won the 100-meter freestyle final four days earlier.

1956 Melbourne T: 10, N: 10, D: 12.6. WR: 4:19.7 (AUS—Crapp, Fraser, Leech, Gibson)

1. AUS (Dawn Fraser, Faith Leech, Sandra Morgan, Lorraine Crapp) — 4:17.1 WR
2. USA (Sylvia Ruuska, Shelly Mann, Nancy Simons, Joan Rosazza) — 4:19.2
3. SAF (Jeanette Myburgh, Susan Roberts, Natalie Myburgh, Moira Abernathy) — 4:25.7
4. GER (Ingrid Künzel, Hertha Haase, Käthi Jansen, Birgit Klomp) — 4:26.1
5. CAN (Helen Stewart, Gladys Priestley, Sara Narber, Virginia Grant) — 4:28.3
6. SWE (Anita Hellström, Birgitta Wängberg, Anna Larsson, Kate Jobson) — 4:30.0
7. HUN (Maria Littomeritzky, Katalin Szőke, Judit Temes, Valéria Gyenge) — 4:31.1
8. GBR (Frances Hogben, Judith Grinham, Margaret Girvan, Fearne Ewart) — 4:35.8

Lorraine Crapp's anchor leg of 1:03.1 sealed the victory.

1960 Rome T: 10, N: 12, D: 9.3. WR (440 yards): 4:16.2 (AUS—Fraser, Colquhoun, Konrads, Crapp)

1. USA (Joan Spillane, Shirley Stobs, Carolyn Wood, S. Christine Von Saltza) — 4:08.9 WR
2. AUS (Dawn Fraser, Ilsa Konrads, Lorraine Crapp, Alva Colquhoun) — 4:11.3
3. GDR/ GER (Christel Steffin, Heidi Pechstein, Gisela Weiss, Ursula Brunner) — 4:19.7
4. HUN (Anna Temesvári, Mária Frank, Kátalin Boros, Csilla Dobai-Madarász) — 4:21.2

5. GBR (Natalie Steward, Beryl Noakes, Judy   4:24.6
         Samuel, Christine Harris)
6. SWE (Inger Thorngren, Karin Larsson, Kristina   4:25.1
         Larsson, Birte Segerström)
7. ITA (Paola Saini, Annamaria Cecchi, Rosanna   4:26.8
         Contardo, Maria Christina Pacifici)
8. SOV (Irina Liakhovskaia, Ulvi Voog, Galina Sos-   4:29.0
         nova, Marina Shamal)

In 1956 Lorraine Crapp had been one of Austalia's hero-
ines, winning two gold medals and one silver. But in 1960
she had other things on her mind. The night before the
Australian team left for Rome she had secretly married
Bill Thurlow, one of the doctors associated with the Australian swimmers. Thurlow traveled to Rome on his own
and rented an apartment. After the lights were put out at
the Olympic Village, Crapp would sneak out and spend the
night with her husband. When Australian officials became
suspicious of her early morning absences, Crapp admitted
her deception. Unfortunately, the officials overreacted. Instead of simply giving her permission to sleep outside the
Village as many other married athletes did, they punished
her by restricting her movements and keeping watch on
her. Demoralized, Crapp swam a lackluster third leg in the
freestyle relay, losing a crucial five yards and 2.7 seconds
to Carolyn Wood.

1964 Tokyo T: 10, N: 10, D: 10.15. WR: 4:07.6 (USA—Allsup,
Stickles, Seidel, Bricker)
1. USA (Sharon Stouder, Donna De Varona, Lillian   4:03.8   WR
         ''Pokey'' Watson, Kathleen Ellis)
2. AUS (Robyn Thorn, Janice Murphy, Lynette Bell,   4:06.9
         Dawn Fraser)
3. HOL (Paulina van der Wildt, Catharina Beumer,   4:12.0
         Wilhelmina van Weerdenburg, Erica Terp-
         stra)
4. HUN (Judit Turóczy, Éva Erdélyi, Katalin Takács,   4:12.1
         Csilla Dobai-Madarász)
5. SWE (Ann-Charlott Lilja, Katrin Andersson, Ulla   4:14.0
         Jäfvert, Ann-Christine Hagberg)
6. GDR/ (Martina Grunert, Traudi Beierlein, Rita   4:15.0
   GER Schumacher, Heidi Pechstein)
7. CAN (Mary Stewart, Patricia Thompson, Helen   4:15.9
         Kennedy, Marion Lay)
8. ITA (Paola Saini, Maria Christina Pacifici, Mara   4:17.2
         Sacchi, Daniela Beneck)

1968 Mexico City T: 15, N: 15, D: 10.26. WR: 4:01.1 (USA,
Santa Clara Swim Club—Gustavson, Watson, Carpinelli, Henne)
1. USA (Jane Barkman, Linda Gustavson, Susan   4:02.5   OR
         Pedersen, Jan Henne)
2. GDR (Gabriele Wetzko, Roswitha Krause, Uta   4:05.7
         Schmuck, Martina Grunert)
3. CAN (Angela Coughlaw, Marilyn Corson, Elaine   4:07.2
         Tanner, Marion Lay)
4. AUS (Janet Steinbeck, Susan Eddy, Lynette   4:08.7
         Watson, Lynette Bell)
5. HUN (Edit Kovács, Magdolna Patoh, Andréa   4:11.0
         Gyarmati, Judit Turóczy)

6. JAP (Shigeko Kawanishi, Yoshimi Nishigawa,   4:13.6
         Yasuko Fujii, Miwako Kobayashi)
7. GBR (Shelagh Ratcliffe, Fiona Kellock, Susan   4:18.0
         Williams, Alexandra Jackson)
DISQ: FRA (Marie Kersaudy, Simone Hanner, Daniele Dorleans,
         Claude Mardonnaud)

1972 Munich T: 16, N: 16, D: 8.30. WR: 3:58.11 (USA—Peyton,
Neilson, Barkman, Babashoff)
1. USA (Sandra Neilson, Jennifer Kemp, Jane   3:55.19   WR
         Barkman, Shirley Babashoff)
2. GDR (Gabriele Wetzko, Andrea Eife, Elke Seh-   3:55.55
         misch, Kornelia Ender)
3. GER (Jutta Weber, Heidemarie Reineck, Gud-   3:57.93
         run Beckmann, Angela Steinbach)
4. HUN (Andréa Gyarmati, Judit Turóczy, Edit Ko-   4:00.39
         vács, Magdolna Patoh)
5. HOL (Enith Brigitha, Anke Rijnders, Hansje   4:01.49
         Bunschoten, Josien Elzerman)
6. SWE (Anita Zarnowiecki, Eva Andersson, Di-   4:02.69
         ana Olsson, Irwi Johansson)
7. CAN (Wendy Cook, Judy Wright, Mary-Beth   4:03.83
         Rondeau, Leslie Cliff)
8. AUS (Deborah Palmer, Leanne Francis, Shar-   4:04.82
         on Booth, Shane Gould)

Until August 18, 1972, no women's relay team had broken
the four-minute barrier. On that day Neilson, Barkman,
Babashoff, and Kim Peyton of the United States recorded
a time of 3:58.11. Twelve days later, in the qualifying heats
of the Olympics, the East Germans tied that mark. That
evening, in the final, the record took another battering.
Sandy Neilson took a quarter-second lead over Gabriele
Wetzko, and the remaining American swimmers held on
with great determination, withstanding a continuous challenge from the East Germans that lasted until the final
touch.

1976 Montreal T: 14, N: 14, D: 7.25. WR: 3:48.80 (GDR, Sports
Club Dynamo—Krause, Seltman, Gabriel, Pollack)
1. USA (Kim Peyton, Wendy Boglioli, Jill Sterkel,   3:44.82   WR
         Shirley Babashoff)
2. GDR (Kornelia Ender, Petra Priemer, Andrea   3:45.50
         Pollack, Claudia Hempel)
3. CAN (Gail Amundrud, Barbara Clark, Becky   3:48.81
         Smith, Anne Jardin)
4. HOL (Ineke Ran, Linda Faber, Annelies Maas,   3:51.67
         Enith Brigitha)
5. SOV (Lyubov Kobzova, Irina Vlasova, Marina   3:52.69
         Kliuchnikova, Larissa Tsareva)
6. FRA (Guylaine Berger, Sylvie Le Noach, Caro-   3:56.73
         line Carpentier, Chantal Schertz)
7. SWE (Pia Martensson, Ylva Persson, Diana   3:57.25
         Olsson, Ida Hansson)
8. GER (Jutta Weber, Marion Platten, Regina Nis-   3:58.33
         sen, Beate Jasch)

The freestyle relay was the last women's swimming event
of the Montreal Olympics. In the first 12 events, the East
Germans had won 11 gold medals, the Soviet Union had

won one, and the United States had won none. With 100-meter gold medalist Kornelia Ender swimming the first leg, East Germany took a 1.16-second lead. East Germany's second swimmer was 100-meter silver medalist Petra Priemer. But Wendy Boglioli swam a 55.81 leg to draw the United States 0.35 seconds closer. Jill Sterkel followed with a blistering 55.78, passing Andrea Pollack and giving the United States a lead of 0.40 seconds. Shirley Babashoff's 56.28 assured the United States of a gold medal at last. Babashoff finished her Olympic career with two gold medals, both in the freestyle relay, and six silver medals. On the victory stand she caused an unfortunate scene by refusing to accept the congratulations of the East German swimmers.

1980 Moscow T: 9, N: 9, D: 7.27. WR: 3:43.43 (USA—Caulkins, Elkins, Sterkel, Woodhead)

1. GDR (Barbara Krause, Caren Metschuck, Ines Diers, Sarina Hülsenbeck) 3:42.71 WR
2. SWE (Carina Ljungdahl, Tina Gustafsson, Agneta Mårtensson, Agneta Eriksson) 3:48.93
3. HOL (Conny van Bentum, Wilma van Velsen, Reggie de Jong, Annelies Maas) 3:49.51
4. GBR (Sharron Davies, Kaye Lovatt, Jacquelene Willmott, June Croft) 3:51.71
5. AUS (Lisa Curry, Karen van de Graaf, Rosemary Brown, Michelle Pearson) 3:54.16
6. MEX (Isabel Reuss, Dagmar Erdman, Teresa Rivera, Helen Plaschinski) 3:55.41
7. BUL (Dobrinka Mincheva, Roumiana Nikolova, Ani Kostova, Sonya Dingalakova) 3:56.34
8. SPA (Natalia Mas, Margarita Armengol, Laura Flaque, Gloria Casado) 3:58.73

Although there were only nine teams, two qualifying heats were held to determine which eight teams would advance to the final. In the second heat the Soviet Union was disqualified for an improper changeover, which made it much easier to decide who the finalists would be. The East Germans won easily. If the United States had entered a team they would have finished second, based on times from the same period.

4×100-METER MEDLEY RELAY

In medley relays the order of strokes is backstroke, breaststroke, butterfly, and freestyle.

1896–1956 not held

1960 Rome T: 13, N: 13, D: 9.2. WR: 4:44.6 (USA—Cone, Bancroft, Collins, Von Saltza)

1. USA (Lynn Burke, Patty Kempner, Carolyn Schuler, S. Christine Von Saltza) 4:41.1 WR
2. AUS (Marilyn Wilson, Rosemary Lassig, Janice Andrew, Dawn Fraser) 4:45.9
3. GDR/GER (Ingrid Schmidt, Ursula Küper, Bärbel Fuhrmann, Ursel Brunner) 4:47.6
4. HOL (Maria van Velsen, Adelaide den Haan, Marianne Heemskerk, Erica Terpstra) 4:47.6
5. GBR (Sylvia Lewis, Anita Lonsbrough, Sheila Watt, Natalie Steward) 4:47.6
6. HUN (Magdolna Dávid, Klara Bartos-Killermann, Márta Egerváry, Csilla Dobai-Madarász) 4:53.7
7. JAP (Satoko Tanaka, Yoshiko Takamatsu, Shizue Miyabe, Yoshiko Sato) 4:56.4
8. SOV (Larissa Viktorova, Lyudmila Korobova, Zinaida Belovezkaia, Marina Shamal) 4:58.1

U.S. leadoff swimmer Lynn Burke finished her leg in 1:09.0 to break the 100-meter backstroke world record for the fourth time in seven weeks. The race was no contest after that, with the United States winning by seven meters. Burke and Von Saltza were best friends who trained together and lived together in the home of Von Saltza's parents in Saratoga, California. They were both coached by George Haines. They dieted together, cut their hair the same way, and, in Rome, they won gold medals together. Von Saltza went home with three and Burke with two.

1964 Tokyo T: 9, N: 9, D: 10.18. WR: 4:34.6 (USA—Ferguson, Goyette, Ellis, Randall)

1. USA (Cathy Ferguson, Cynthia Goyette, Sharon Stouder, Kathleen Ellis) 4:33.9 WR
2. HOL (Kornelia Winkel, Klena Bimolt, Ada Kok, Erica Terpstra) 4:37.0
3. SOV (Tatyana Savelyeva, Svetlana Babanina, Tatyana Devyatova, Natalya Ustinova) 4:39.2
4. JAP (Satoko Tanaka, Noriko Yamamoto, Eiko Takahashi, Michiko Kihara) 4:42.0
5. GBR (Jill Norfolk, Stella Mitchell, Mary Anne Cotterill, Elizabeth Long) 4:45.8
6. CAN (Eillein Weir, Marion Lay, Mary Stewart, Helen Kennedy) 4:49.9

DISQ: GDR/GER (Ingrid Schmidt, Bärbel Grimmer, Heike Hustede, Martina Grunert), HUN (Mária Balla, Zsuzsa Kovacs, Márta Egerváry, Csilla Dobai-Madarász)

Cathy Ferguson gave the United States the lead after the first leg, but Svetlana Babanina, swimming two seconds faster than the official world record, touched first at 200 meters. Sharon Stouder then pulled away by a commanding margin, which Kathy Ellis added to. Stouder finished the Olympics with three gold medals and one silver, Ellis with two gold and two bronze.

1968 Mexico City T: 16, N: 16, D: 10.17. WR: 4:28.1 (USA—Hall, Ball, Daniel, Pedersen)

1. USA (Kaye Hall, Catie Ball, Ellie Daniel, Susan Pedersen) 4:28.3 OR
2. AUS (Lynette Watson, Lynette McClements, Judy Playfair, Janet Steinbeck) 4:30.0
3. GER (Angelika Kraus, Uta Frommater, Heike Hustede, Heidemarie Reineck) 4:36.4

4. SOV (Tinatin Lekveishvili, Alla Grebennikova, Ta- 4:37.0
tyana Devyatova, Lidia Grebets)

5. GDR (Martina Grunert, Eva Wittke, Helga 4:38.0
Lindner, Uta Schmuck)

6. GBR (Wendy Burrell, Dorothy Harrison, Margaret 4:38.3
Auton, Alexandra Jackson)

7. HOL (Jacobje Buter, Klena Bimolt, Ada Kok, Pe- 4:38.7
tronella Bos)

8. HUN (Mária Lantos, Edit Kovács, Andréa Gyar- 4:42.9
mati, Judit Turóczy)

The United States led Australia by 0.7 seconds at 100 meters, 0.3 at 200, and 0.5 at 300 before Susan Pedersen pulled away from Janet Steinbeck for the victory.

1972 Munich T: 16, N: 16, D: 8.30. WR: 4:25.34 (USA—Atwood, Vidali, Daniel, Barkman)

1. USA (Melissa Belote, Catherine Carr, Deena 4:20.75 WR
Deardurff, Sandra Neilson)

2. GDR (Christine Herbst, Renate Vogel, Roswitha 4:24.91
Beier, Kornelia Ender)

3. GER (Silke Pielen, Verena Eberle, Gudrun 4:26.46
Beckmann, Heidemarie Reineck)

4. SOV (Tinatin Ledveishvili, Galina Stepanova, 4:27.81
Irina Ustimenko, Tatyana Zolotnickaia)

5. HOL (Enith Brigitha, Alie te Riet, Anke Rijnders, 4:29.99
Hansje Bunschoten)

6. JAP (Suzuko Matsumura, Yoko Yamamoto, 4:31.56
Mayumi Aoki, Yoshimi Nishigawa)

7. CAN (Wendy Cook, Sylvia Dockerill, Marylin 4:31.56
Corson, Leslie Cliff)

8. SWE (Diana Olsson, Britt-Marie Smedh, Eva 4:32.61
Wikner, Anita Zarnowiecki)

1976 Montreal T: 17, N: 17, D: 7.18. WR: 4:13.41 (GDR, Sports Club Dynamo—Seltman, Nitschke, Pollack, Krause)

1. GDR (Ulrike Richter, Hannelore Anke, Andrea 4:07.95 WR
Pollack, Kornelia Ender)

2. USA (Linda Jezek, Lauri Siering, Camille 4:14.55
Wright, Shirley Babashoff)

3. CAN (Wendy Hogg, Robin Corsiglia, Susan 4:15.22
Sloan, Anne Jardin)

4. SOV (Nadezhda Stavko, Marina Iurchenia, Ta- 4:16.05
mara Shelofastova, Larissa Tsareva)

5. HOL (Diane Edelijn, Wijda Mazereeuw, Jose 4:19.03
Damen, Enith Brigitha)

6. GBR (Joy Beasley, Margaret Kelly, Susan Jen- 4:23.25
ner, Deborah Hill)

7. JAP (Yoshimi Nishigawa, Toshiko Haruoka, 4:23.47
Yasue Hatsuda, Sachiko Yamazaki)

8. AUS (Michelle Devries, Judith Hudson, Linda 4:25.91
Hanel, Jenny Tate)

The first women's swimming event to be decided in 1976, the medley relay was won with an awesome display by the East German swimmers. Richter, Anke, Pollack, and Ender each recorded the fastest time for her leg.

1980 Moscow T: 10, N: 10, D: 7.20. WR: 4:07.95 (GDR—Richter, Anke, Pollack, Ender)

1. GDR (Rica Reinisch, Ute Geweniger, Andrea 4:06.67 WR
Pollack, Caren Metschuck)

2. GBR (Helen Jameson, Margaret Kelly, Ann Os- 4:12.24
gerby, June Croft)

3. SOV (Yelena Kruglova, Elivira Vasilkova, Alla 4:13.61
Grishchenkova, Natalya Strunnikova)

4. SWE (Annika Uvehall, Eva-Marie Håkansson, 4:16.91
Agneta Mårtensson, Tina Gustafsson)

5. ITA (Laura Foralosso, Sabrina Seminatore, 4:19.05
Cinzia Savi Scarponi, Monica Vallarin)

6. AUS (Lisa Forrest, Lisa Curry, Karen Van De 4:19.90
Graaf, Rosemary Brown)

7. ROM (Carmen Bunaciu, Brigitte Press, Mariana 4:21.27
Parachiv, Irinel Panulescu)

8. BUL (Sonya Dingalakova, Tanya Bogomilova, 4:22.38
Ani Moneva, Dobrinka Mincheva)

Rica Reinisch opened with a world-record-equaling backstroke leg and Ute Geweniger followed with 100 meters of breaststroking that bettered the official world record. Pollack and Metschuck recorded the fastest times of their respective legs, and the East Germans were on their way again.

SYNCHRONIZED SWIMMING: DUETS

This event will be held for the first time in 1984.

SPRINGBOARD DIVING

This event is performed from a springboard three meters above the water. In women's competition each finalist makes five compulsory dives and five voluntary dives chosen from approved groups. Each type of dive is assigned a certain degree of difficulty, such as 1.8 or 2.5. Each judge's score is multiplied by the degree of difficulty to determine a total score.

1896–1912 not held

1920 Antwerp C: 4, N: 1, D: 8.29.

		PTS.	ORDINALS
1. Aileen Riggin	USA	539.9	9
2. Helen Wainwright	USA	534.8	9
3. Thelma Payne	USA	534.1	12
4. Aileen Allen	USA	489.9	20

Tiny Aileen Riggin of Newport, Rhode Island, was only 14 years old when she won her Olympic gold medal. In 1922 she was the subject of the first underwater and slow-motion swimming films. She returned to the Olympics in 1924 and won a silver medal for springboard diving and a bronze in the 100-meter backstroke. Later she turned professional, acted in movies, and starred in Billy Rose's first Aquacade.

1924 Paris C: 17, N: 7, D: 7.18.

		PTS.	ORDINALS
1. Elizabeth Becker	USA	474.5	8
2. Aileen Riggin	USA	460.4	12
3. Caroline Fletcher	USA	436.4	16
4. Eva Ollivier	SWE	412.6	20
5. Signe Johanson	SWE	412.6	21
6. Klara Bornett	AUT	370.2	28

1928 Amsterdam C: 10, N: 4, D: 8.9.

		PTS.	ORDINALS
1. Helen Meany	USA	78.62	6
2. Dorothy Poynton	USA	75.62	13
3. Georgia Coleman	USA	73.38	14
4. Ilse Meudtner	GER	67.42	22
5. Margret Borgs	GER	65.16	26
6. Lini Söhnchen	GER	63.28	34
7. G. Klapwijk	HOL	60.98	35
8. A.I.M. van Leewen	HOL	59.82	35

1932 Los Angeles C; 8, N: 6, D: 8.10.

		PTS.
1. Georgia Coleman	USA	87.52
2. Katherine Rawls	USA	82.56
3. Jane Fauntz	USA	82.12
4. Olga Jordan	GER	77.60
5. Doris Ogilvie	CAN	77.00
6. Magdalene Epply	AUT	63.70
7. Etsuo Kamakura	JAP	60.78
8. Ingrid Larsen	DEN	57.26

Georgia Coleman, the first woman to do a two and a half forward somersault, completed her Olympic career with four medals: one gold, two silver, and one bronze. She died in 1941 at the age of 29. In 1932 the system of ordinals (place-figures) was dropped and total points became the determining factor in deciding places.

1936 Berlin C: 16, N: 9, D: 8.12.

		PTS.
1. Marjorie Gestring	USA	89.27
2. Katherine Rawls	USA	88.35
3. Dorothy Poynton Hill	USA	82.36
4. Gerda Daumerlang	GER	78.27
5. Olga Jentsch-Jordan	GER	77.98
6. Masayo Osawa	JAP	73.94
7. Suse Heinze	GER	71.49
8. Fusako Kono	JAP	70.27

Gold medalist Marjorie Gestring of Los Angeles was only 13 years and 9 months old. Katherine Rawls repeated her silver medal and, two days later, added a bronze medal as a member of the U.S. freestyle relay team.

1948 London C: 16, N: 8, D: 8.3.

		PTS.
1. Victoria Draves	USA	108.74
2. Zoe Ann Olsen	USA	108.23
3. Patricia Elsener	USA	101.30

4. Nicole Pellissard	FRA	100.38
5. Gudrun Grömer	AUT	93.30
6. Edna Child	GBR	91.63
7. Madeleine Moreau	FRA	89.43
8. J. Heck	HOL	87.61

Vicki Draves had a Filipino father and an English mother, but she was born and raised in San Francisco. Silver medalist Zoe Ann Olsen married baseball star Jackie Jensen before the next Olympics.

1952 Helsinki C: 15, N: 7, D: 7.30.

		PTS.
1. Patricia McCormick	USA	147.30
2. Madeleine Moreau	FRA	139.34
3. Zoe Ann Jensen-Olsen	USA	127.57
4. Ninel Krutova	SOV	116.86
5. Charmian Welsh	GBR	116.38
6. Lyubov Shigalova	SOV	113.83
7. Nicole Pellissard	FRA	111.98
8. Phyllis Long	GBR	108.82

Pat McCormick of Long Beach, California, won the first of her four gold medals. Mady Moreau became the first non-American woman to win a springboard medal after six straight U.S. sweeps.

1956 Melbourne C: 17, N: 8, D: 12.4.

		PTS.
1. Patricia McCormick	USA	142.36
2. Jeanne Stunyo	USA	125.89
3. Irene McDonald	CAN	121.40
4. Barbara Gilders	USA	120.76
5. Valentina Chumicheva	SOV	118.50
6. Phyllis Long	GBR	107.61
7. Nicole Darrigrand (Pellissard)	FRA	106.32
8. Kanoko Tsutani	JAP	103.12

Eight months before the Melbourne Olympics, Pat McCormick gave birth to a baby boy. She had continued training throughout her pregnancy and swam a half-mile a day up until two days before childbirth. In 1956 she repeated her double gold medal performance of 1952.

1960 Rome C: 16, N: 10, D: 8.27.

		PTS.
1. Ingrid Krämer	GDR	155.81
2. Paula Jean Pope (Myers)	USA	141.24
3. Elizabeth Ferris	GBR	139.09
4. Mary "Patsy" Willard	USA	137.82
5. Ninel Krutova	SOV	136.11
6. Irene MacDonald	CAN	134.69
7. Phyllis Long	GBR	129.63
8. Dorothea DuPon	HOL	123.35

The U.S. string of eight consecutive springboard victories was finally broken by 17-year-old Ingrid Krämer of Dresden. The Rome Games were the fourth straight Olympics at which both diving events were won by the same woman.

1964 Tokyo C: 21, N: 9, D: 10.12.

		PTS.
1. Ingrid Engel-Krämer	GDR	145.00
2. Jeanne Collier	USA	138.36
3. Mary "Patsy" Willard	USA	138.18
4. Sue Gossick	USA	129.70
5. Tamara Fyedosova	SOV	126.33
6. Yelena Anokhina	SOV	125.60
7. Kanoko Mabuchi	JAP	125.28
8. Angelika Hilbert	GER	123.27

Ingrid Engel-Krämer took over the lead from Patsy Willard on her seventh dive and went on to win her third gold medal.

1968 Mexico City C: 22, N: 15, D: 10.18

		PTS.
1. Sue Gossick	USA	150.77
2. Tamara Pogoscheva (Fyedosova)	SOV	145.30
3. Keala O'Sullivan	USA	145.23
4. Maxine "Micki" King	USA	137.38
5. Ingrid Gulbin (Engel-Krämer)	GDR	135.82
6. Vyera Baklanova	SOV	132.31
7. Beverly Boys	CAN	130.31
8. Elena Anokhina	SOV	129.17

Twenty-year-old Sue Gossick of Tarzana, California, didn't move into the lead until the ninth round. Pogoscheva, leading after seven dives, missed her eighth dive badly, but earned the highest score of the competition with her final attempt, to jump back from fourth place to second. In fifth place was the one and only Ingrid Krämer, competing in her third Olympics, each under a different name.

1972 Munich C: 30, N: 18, D: 8.28.

		PTS.
1. Maxine "Micki" King	USA	450.03
2. Ulrika Knape	SWE	434.19
3. Marina Janicke	GDR	430.92
4. Janet Ely	USA	420.99
5. Beverly Boys	CAN	418.89
6. Agneta Henriksson	SWE	417.48
7. Cynthia Potter	USA	413.58
8. Elżbieta Wierniuk	POL	408.36

In Mexico City Micki King of Pontiac, Michigan, had been in first place after eight dives. But during her ninth dive, a reverse one and a half layout, she hit the board and broke her left forearm. She completed her final dive, but dropped to fourth place. Four years later in Munich, King, now a 28-year-old air force captain, took the lead from Ulrika Knape with her eighth dive and this time steered clear of the diving board to win the gold medal. Her final dive, a reverse one and a half somersault with one and a half twists, was the same dive she had attempted four years earlier with a broken arm. After her victory she had to submit to a drug test. However it took King two hours to produce a urine sample. By that time everyone but the doctors had gone home, so she returned alone to the Olympic Village and had a chocolate drink. Three Australian weightlifters told her "a gold medalist shouldn't be drinking chocolate" and shared with her a bottle of wine.

1976 Montreal C: 27, N: 15, D: 7.20.

		PTS.
1. Jennifer Chandler	USA	506.19
2. Christa Köhler	GDR	469.41
3. Cynthia Potter	USA	466.83
4. Heidi Ramlow	GDR	462.15
5. Karin Guthke	GDR	459.81
6. Olga Dmitrieva	SOV	432.24
7. Irina Kalinina	SOV	417.99
8. Barbara Nejman	USA	365.07

1980 Moscow C: 24, N: 13, D: 7.21.

		PTS.
1. Irina Kalinina	SOV	725.910
2. Martina Proeber	GDR	698.895
3. Karin Guthke	GDR	685.245
4. Zhanna Tsirulnikova	SOV	673.665
5. Martina Jäschke	GDR	668.115
6. Valerie McFarlane	AUS	651.045
7. Irina Sidorova	SOV	650.265
8. Lourdes Gonzalez	CUB	640.005

PLATFORM DIVING

This event is performed from a static board ten meters above the water. Each finalist attempts four compulsory dives and four voluntary dives.

1896–1908 not held

1912 Stockholm C: 14, N: 3, D: 7.13.

		PTS.	ORDINALS
1. Greta Johansson	SWE	39.9	5
2. Lisa Regnell	SWE	36.0	11
3. Isabelle White	GBR	34.0	17
4. Elsa Regnell	SWE	33.2	20
5. Ellen Eklund	SWE	31.9	22
6. Elsa Andersson	SWE	31.3	25
7. Selma Andersson	SWE	27.3	36
8. Thora Larsson	SWE	26.8	39

Seventeen-year-old Greta Johansson was the unanimous choice of the five judges.

1920 Antwerp C: 15, N: 7, D: 8.28.

		PTS.	ORDINALS
1. Stefani Fryland-Clausen	DEN	34.6	6
2. Eileen Armstrong	GBR	33.3	10
3. Eva Ollivier	SWE	33.3	11
4. Isabelle White	GBR	31.7	—
5. Aileen Riggin	USA	31.4	—
6. Betty Grimes	USA	26.7	—

1924 Paris C: 11, N: 6, D: 7.20.

		PTS.	ORDINALS
1. Caroline Smith	USA	33.2	10.5
2. Elizabeth Becker	USA	33.4	11
3. Hjördis Töpel	SWE	32.8	15.5
4. Edith Bechmann-Nielsen	DEN	31.6	17.5
5. Helen Meany	USA	29.6	22
6. Isabelle White	GBR	28.0	28.5

National prejudice reared its ugly head in the judging of the women's high dive. The Danish judge gave first place to Bechmann-Nielsen of Denmark. The Swedish judge voted for Töpel of Sweden, and the American judge registered a three-way tie for first among the three Americans. The British judge voted for Smith and the French judge for Becker.

1928 Amsterdam C: 17, N: 8, D: 8.11.

		PTS.	ORDINALS
1. Elizabeth Becker Pinkston	USA	31.6	9
2. Georgia Coleman	USA	30.6	10.5
3. Lala Sjöquist	SWE	29.2	13.5
4. Mietje Baron	HOL	27.2	21
5. Greta Onnela	FIN	26.0	25
6. Hanni Rehborn	GER	25.6	26

Elizabeth Becker Pinkston balanced her 1924 springboard gold with first place in the platform diving four years later. Between Olympics she had married Clarence Pinkston, whom she had met when both were members of the 1924 U.S. diving team in Paris.

1932 Los Angeles C: 7, N: 5, D: 8.12.

		PTS.
1. Dorothy Poynton	USA	40.26
2. Georgia Coleman	USA	35.56
3. Marion Roper	USA	35.22
4. Lala Sjöquist	SWE	34.52
5. Ingrid Larsen	DEN	31.96
6. Etsuko Kamakura	JAP	31.36
7. Magdalene Epply	AUS	26.76

1936 Berlin C: 22, N: 10, D: 8.13.

		PTS.
1. Dorothy Poynton Hill	USA	33.93
2. Velma Dunn	USA	33.63
3. Käthe Köhler	GER	33.43
4. Reiko Osawa	JAP	32.53
5. Cornelia Gilissen	USA	30.47
6. Fusako Kono	JAP	30.24
7. Jean Gilbert	GBR	30.16
8. Anne Ehseheidt	GBR	29.90

Stylish Dorothy Poynton Hill, competing in her third Olympics at the age of 21, gained her fourth medal. She won two gold medals in the platform and a silver and bronze in the springboard.

1948 London C: 15, N: 9, D: 8.6.

		PTS.
1. Victoria Draves	USA	68.87
2. Patricia Elsener	USA	66.28
3. Birte Chistoffersen	DEN	66.04
4. Ali Staudinger	AUT	64.59
5. Juno Stover	USA	62.63
6. Nicole Pellissard	FRA	61.07
7. Eva Petersen	SWE	59.86
8. I. Beeken-Gregersen	DEN	59.54

Vicki Draves became the first female diver to win two gold medals in one Olympics.

1952 Helsinki C: 15, N: 8, D: 8.2.

		PTS.
1. Patricia McCormick	USA	79.37
2. Paula Jean Myers	USA	71.63
3. Juno Irwin (Stover)	USA	70.49
4. Nicole Pellisard	FRA	66.89
5. Phyllis Long	GBR	63.19
6. Tatyana Vereina	SOV	61.09
7. Diana Spencer	GBR	60.76
8. Eugenia Bogdanovskaya	SOV	57.50

This was the second of Pat McCormick's four gold medals. Bronze medalist Juno Irwin was three and a half months' pregnant with her second child.

1956 Melbourne C: 18, N: 10, D: 12.7.

		PTS.
1. Patricia McCormick	USA	84.85
2. Juno Irwin (Stover)	USA	81.64
3. Paula Jean Myers	USA	81.58
4. Nicole Darrigrand (Pellissard)	FRA	78.80
5. Tatyana Karakashyants-Vereina	SOV	76.95
6. Lyubov Shigalova	SOV	76.40
7. Phyllis Long	GBR	76.15
8. Birte Hansson	SWE	75.21

Pat McCormick moved ahead of Juno Irwin after the sixth of seven dives to win her fourth gold medal. McCormick was a 26-year-old mother of one, Irwin a 28-year-old mother of three.

1960 Rome C: 18, N: 12, D: 8.30.

		PTS.
1. Ingrid Krämer	GDR	91.28
2. Paula Jean Pope (Myers)	USA	88.94
3. Ninel Krutova	SOV	86.99
4. Juno Irwin (Stover)	USA	83.59
5. Raisa Gorokhovskaya	SOV	83.03
6. Norma Thomas	GBR	82.21
7. Nicole Darrigrand (Pellissard)	FRA	81.18
8. Phyllis Long	GBR	80.98

Krämer clinched her diving double with a final one and a half forward somersault with a double twist that turned out to be the highest-scoring dive of the competition. Paula Jean Pope, a 25-year-old mother of two, won her third straight platform medal.

1964 Tokyo C: 24, N: 11, D: 10.15.

		PTS.
1. Lesley Bush	USA	99.80
2. Ingrid Engel-Krämer	GDR	98.45
3. Galina Alekseyeva	SOV	97.60
4. Linda Cooper	USA	96.30
5. Christine Lanzke	GDR	92.92
6. Ingeborg Pertmayr	AUT	92.70
7. Natalya Kuznetsova	SOV	90.91
8. Barbara Talmage	USA	89.60

Seventeen-year-old Lesley Bush of Princeton, New Jersey, took the lead after the first dive and was never headed. Asked afterward how she felt when she realized she was in first place and might upset Ingrid Krämer's attempt to match Pat McCormick's four gold medals, Bush replied, "It was sort of scary, but gee, gosh, it was great."

1968 Mexico City C: 24, N: 15, D: 10.23.

		PTS.
1. Milena Duchková	CZE	109.59
2. Natalya Lobanova (Kuznetsova)	SOV	105.14
3. Ann Peterson	USA	101.11
4. Beverly Boys	CAN	97.97
5. Boguslawa Pietkiewicz	POL	95.28
6. Regina Krause	GER	93.08
6. Keiko Ohsaki	JAP	93.08
8. Nancy Robertson	CAN	90.66

Duchková overcame Lobanova with her last two dives, much to the delight of the crowd, which favored the 16-year-old Czechoslovakian because she was small and because her nation was occupied by Soviet troops.

1972 Munich C: 27, N: 17, D: 9.2.

		PTS.
1. Ulrika Knape	SWE	390.00
2. Milena Duchková	CZE	370.92
3. Marina Janicke	GDR	360.54
4. Janet Ely	USA	352.68
5. Maxine "Micki" King	USA	346.38
6. Sylvia Fiedler	GDR	341.67
7. Nancy Robertson	CAN	334.02
8. Ingeborg Pertmayr	AUT	321.03

Knape took the lead from Duchková after the sixth of eight dives and then earned the gold medal with a final dive that received the highest score of the competition.

1976 Montreal C: 25, N: 12, D: 7.25.

		PTS.
1. Elena Vaytsekhovskaya	SOV	406.59
2. Ulrika Knape	SWE	402.60
3. Deborah Wilson	USA	401.00
4. Irina Kalinina	SOV	398.67
5. Cindy Shatto	CAN	389.50
6. Teri York	CAN	378.39
7. Melissa Briley	USA	376.86
8. Heidi Ramlow	GDR	365.64

Eighteen-year-old Ukrainian Elena Vaytsekhovskaya jumped from fifth place to first with her fifth dive, a superbly executed backward two and a half somersault, piked.

1980 Moscow C: 17, N: 11, D: 7.26.

		PTS.
1. Martina Jäschke	GDR	596.250
2. Servard Emirzyan	SOV	576.465
3. Liana Tsotadze	SOV	575.925
4. Ramona Wenzel	GDR	542.070
5. Yelena Matyushenko	SOV	540.180
6. Elsa Tenorio	MEX	539.445
7. Valerie McFarlane	AUS	499.785
8. Ildikó Kelemen	HUN	476.535

In fourth place after the preliminaries, Jäschke swept into first place on the fifth dive of the final round.

VOLLEYBALL

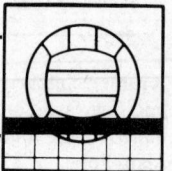

MEN

Volleyball matches are decided on the basis of the best three out five sets. A team wins a set when it scores 15 points, provided the margin is two or more points. Points can only be scored by the serving team. If the defensive team wins a rally, it gains the serve.

1896–1960 not held

1964 Tokyo T: 10, N: 10, D: 10.23.

		MATCHES		SETS			
		W	L	W	L	PF	PA
1. SOV	(Yvan Bugayenkov, Nikolai Burobin, Yuri Chesnokov, Vascha Kacharava, Valery Kalatschikhin, Vitaly Kovalenko, Stanislav Lyugaylo, Georgy Mondzolevsky, Yuri Poyarkov, Eduard Sibiryakov, Yuri Vengerovsky, Dmitri Voskoboynikov)	8	1	25	5	415	279
2. CZE	(Milan Čuda, Bohumil Golián, Zdenek Humhal, Petr Kop, Josef Labuda, Josef Musil, Karel Paulus, Boris Perušič, Pavel Schenk, Václav Šmidl, Josef Šorm, Ladislav Toman)	8	1	26	10	486	399
3. JAP	(Yutaka Demachi, Tsutomu Koyama, Sadatoshi Sugahara, Naohiro Ikeda, Yasutaka Sato, Toshiaki Kosedo, Tokihiko Higuchi, Masayuki Minami, Takeshi Tokutomi, Teruhisa Moriyama, Yuzo Nakamura, Katsutoshi Nekoda)	7	2	22	12	475	372
4. ROM	(Gheorghe Fieraru, Horatiu Nicolau, Aurel Drăgan, Iuliu Szőcs, William Schreiber, Mihai Grigorovici, Davila Plocon, Nicolae Bărbută, Eduard Derzsi, Mihai Chezan, Constantin Ganciu, Mihai Coste)	6	3	19	15	432	394
5. BUL	(Dimiter Karov, Yvan Gochev, Georgi Konstantinov, Petko Panteleev, Peter Kruchmarov, Simeon Srandev, Lachezar Stoyanov, Boris Gyuderov, Kiril Ivanov, Slavcho Slavov, Georgi Spasov, Angel Koritarov)	5	4	20	16	464	429
6. HUN	(Béla Czafik, Vilmos Iváncsó, Csaba Lantos, Gábor Bodò, István Molnár, Otto Prouza, Ferenc Tüske, Tibor Flórián, László Gálos, Antal Kangyerka, Mihály Tatár, Ferenc Jánosi)	4	5	18	18	449	474
7. BRA	(Joao Claudio Franca, Jose Schwart da Costa, H. Leao de Oliveira, Newdon Emanuel de Victor, Carlos Albano Feitosa, Marco Antonio Volpi, Carlos Arthur Nuzman, J. de Oliveira Ramalho, Decio Viotti de Azevedo, V.M. Barcellos Borges)	3	6	13	23	410	474
8. HOL	(Jacob Korsloot, Jurjaan Kodlen, Johannes Tinkhof, Jan Martinus Oosterbaan, Robert Groenhuijzen, Pieter Swieter, Johan Wilhelm van Wijnen, Jacques de Vink, Dingeman van der Stoep, Jacques Ewalds, Johannes van der Hoek, Franklin Constandsc)	2	7	11	24	378	482

The U.S.S.R. was awarded first place on the basis of a better ratio of points for and points against. The Soviets lost to Japan, but won their crucial match against Czechoslovakia, 15–9, 15–8, 5–15, 10–15, 15–7.

1968 Mexico City T: 10, N: 10, D: 10.26.

		MATCHES		SETS			
		W	L	W	L	PF	PA
1. SOV	(Eduard Sibiryakov, Valery Kravchenko, Vladimir Belyayev, Yevgeny Lapinsky, Oleg Antropov, Vasiliyus Matuschevas, Viktor Mikhalchuk, Vladimir Ivanov, Yvan Bugayenkov, Georgy Mondzolevsky)	8	1	26	8	464	326
2. JAP	(Masayuki Minami, Katsutoshi Nekoda, Mamoru Shiragami, Isao Koizumi, Yasuaki Mitsumori, Jungo Morita, Tadayoshi Yokota, Seiji Oko, Tetsuo Sato, Kenji Shimaoka, Kenji Kimura)	7	2	24	6	430	253
3. CZE	(Antonin Procházka, Jiři Svoboda, Lubomir Zajiček, Josef Musil, Josef Smolka, Vladimir Petlak, Petr Kop, František Sokol, Bohumil Golián, Zdenek Groessl, Pavel Schenk, Drahomir Koudelka)	7	2	22	15	454	412
4. GDR	(Horst Peter, Eckhardt Tielscher, Siegfried Schneider, Manfred Heine, Rainer Tscharke, Eckehard Pietzsch, Arnold Schulz, Rudi Schumann, Jürgen Kessel, Walter Toussaint, Jürgen Freiwald, Wolfgang Webner)	6	3	22	12	449	373
5. POL	(Stanislaw Zduńczyk, Aleksander Skiba, Jerzy Szymczyk, Edward Skorek, Zbigniew Jasiukiewicz, Tadeusz Siwek, Zdzislaw Ambroziak, Stanislaw Gościniak, Romuald Paszkiewicz, Hubert Wagner, Wojciech Rutkowski, Zbigniew Zarzycki)	6	3	18	11	370	280
6. BUL	(Alexander Trenev, Dimiter Zlatanov, Gramen Prinov, Peter Krutschmarov, Alexander Aleksandrov, Zdravko Simeonov, Milio Milev, Dim-	4	5	16	17	379	385

iter Karov, Kiril Slavov, Dinio Atanasov, Angel Koritarov, Stoyan Stoev)

7. USA	(Daniel Patterson, Pedro Velasco, John Henn, Robert May, Larry Rundle, David Bright, Smitty Duke, John Alstrom, Jon Stanley, Thomas Haine, Rudy Sumara, Winthrop Davenport)	4	5	15	18	382	414
8. BEL	(Jozef Mol, Pul Mesdagh, Fernand Walder, William Bossaerts, Bernard Vailant, Roger Maes, Ronald Vandewal, Hugo Huybrechts, Roger Vandergoten, Benno Saelens, Berto Poosen, Leo Dierckx)	2	7	6	24	239	417

The Soviet team was upset by the United States in their opening contest. Shaken out of their complacency, they went on to win the rest of their matches easily, with only a brief five-set scare from the East Germans. They beat Japan, 4–15, 15–13, 15–9, 15–13, in the decisive match.

1972 Munich T: 12, N: 12, D: 9.9.

		MATCHES		SETS			
		W	L	W	L	PF	PA
1. JAP	(Kenji Kimura, Yoshihide Fukao, Jungo Morita, Seiji Oko, Tadayoshi Yokota, Katsutoshi Nekoda, Yasuhiro Noguchi, Kenji Shimaoka, Yuzo Nakamura, Tetsuo Nishimoto, Masayuki Minami, Tetsuo Sato)	7	0	21	3	348	192
2. GDR	(Siegfried Schneider, Arnold Schulz, Wolfgang Webner, Eckehard Pietzsch, Rudi Schumann, Wolfgang Weise, Horst Hagen, Horst Peter, Wolfgang Löwe Rainer Tscharke, Wolfgang Maibohm, Jürgen Maune)	5	2	16	8	295	256
3. SOV	(Victor Borsch, Vyacheslav Domani, Vladimir Patkin, Leonid Zaiko, Yuri Starunski, Aleksandr Saprykine, Vladimir Kondra, Efim Chulak, Vladimir Poutiatov, Valery Kravchenko, Yevgeny Lapinsky, Yuri Poyarkov)	6	1	19	6	340	296
4. BUL	(Dimiter Karov, Brunko Iliev, Alexander Trenev, Ivan Ivanov, Dimiter Zla-	4	3	15	14	386	347

		MATCHES		SETS			
		W	L	W	L	PF	PA

tanov, Zdravko Simeonov, Tsano Tsanov, Kiril Slavov, Emil Vulchev, Emile Trenev, Luchezar Stoyanov, Ivan Dimitrov)

5. ROM	(Gabriel Udisteanu, Gyula Bartha, Corneliu Oros, Laurentju Dumănoiu, William Schreiber, Marian Stamate, Mircea Codoi, Romeo Enescu, Cristian Ion, Stelian Moculescu, Viorel Bălas)	4	3	9	15	300	286
6. CZE	(Drahomir Koudelka, Vladimir Petlak, Stefan Pipa, Pavel Schenk, Zdenek Groessl, Jaroslav Stanco, Miroslav Nekola, Milan Vapenka, Lubomir Zajiček, Jaroslav Penč, Milan Reznicek, Jaroslav Tomas)	4	3	15	9	321	274
7. KOR	(Jun-Tak Jin, Chung-Han Kim, Yong- Kwan Lee, Kun-Bong Kim, Sun-Koo Lee, Jong-Ok Choi, Kee-Won Park, Kyui-Hwan Kim, Dong-Kee Chung, Man-Soo Kang)	3	4	10	13	284	270
8. BRA	(Joao Ernesto Jens, Delano Couto Jorge Franco, Antonio Carlos Moreno, Luiz Eymard Zech Coelho, Jose Oswaldo Marcelino, Mario Marcos Procopio, Paulo Roberto de Freitas, Decio Cattaruzzi, Alexandre Abeid, Celso Alexandre Kalache)	2	5	12	16	316	373

Final: JAP—GDR 11–15, 15–2, 15–10, 15–10
3rd Place: SOV—BUL 15–11, 15–8, 15–13
5th Place: ROM—CZE 8–15, 15–7, 15–10, 16–14
7th Place: KOR—BRA 18–16, 15–7, 15–5

1976 Montreal T: 9, N: 9, D: 7.30.

		MATCHES		SETS			
		W	L	W	L	PF	PA
1. POL	(Wlodzimierz Stefański, Bronislaw Bebel, Lech Lasko, Edward Skorek, Tomasz Wójtowicz, Wieslaw Gawlowski, Mieczy-	6	0	18	9	377	293

slaw Rybaczewski, Zbigniew Lubiejewski, Ryszard Bosek, Wlodzimierz Sadalski, Zbigniew Zarzycki, Marek Karbarz)

2. SOV	(Anatoly Polishuk, Vyacheslav Zaitsev, Efim Chulak, Vladimir Dorohov, Aleksandr Ermilov, Pavel Selivanov, Oleg Moliboga, Vladimir Kondra, Yuri Starunski, Vladimir Chernyshev, Vladimir Ulanov, Aleksandr Savin, Yuri Chesnokov, Vladimir Patkin)	4	1	14	3	247	162
3. CUB	(Leonel Marshall, Victoriano Sarmientos, Ernesto Martinez, Victor Garcia, Carlosy Salas, Raul Virches, Jesus Savigne, Lorenzo Martinez, Diego Lapera, Antonio Rodriguez, Alfredo Figueredo, Jorge Perez)	4	2	14	7	280	212
4. JAP	(Takashi Maruyama, Katsutoshi Nekoda, Katsumi Oda, Tetsuo Nishimoto, Yasunori Yasuda, Yoshihide Fukao, Shoichi Yanagimoto, Mikiyasu Tanaka, Tadayoshi Yokota, Seiji Oko, Kenji Shimaoka, Tetsuo Sato)	2	3	8	8	157	204
5. CZE	(Miroslav Nekola, Jaroslav Penč, Stefan Pipa, Vladimir Petlak, Josef Mikunda, Jaroslav Stančo, Vlastimil Lenert, Milan Šlambor, Pavel Rerabek, Josef Vondrka, Drahomir Koudelka, Jaroslav Tomaš)	4	2	14	7	282	234
6. KOR	(Kon-Bong Kim, Jas-Back Cho, Yong-Kwan Lee, Ki-Won Park, Moon-Kyong Chong, Sun-Koo Lee, Choun-Pyo Lee, In Lee, Choong-Han Kim, Jong-Won Lee, Man-Soo Kang, Ho-Dam Lim)	2	4	10	14	245	295
7. BRA	(Paulo de Freitas, Sergio Danilas, Alexandre Abeid, Eloi Neto, Antonio Mereno, Berhard Rajzman, William da Silva, Celso Alexandre Kalache, Jose Guimaraes, Jean Luc	2	3	8	11	216	228

Rosat, Fernando de Avi-
la, Paulo Petterle)

		W	L	W	L	PF	PA
8. ITA	(Andrea Nannini, Paolo Montorsi, Stefano Sibani, Giorgio Goldoni, Francesco Dall Olio, Fabrizio Nassi, Rodolfo Giovenzana, Andrea Nencini, Mario Mattioli, Giovanni Lanfranco, Erasmo Salemme, Marco Negri)	0	5	2	15	125	148

Final: POL—SOV 11–15, 15–13
3rd Place: CUB—JAP 15–8, 15–9, 15–8
5th Place: CZE—KOR 15–9, 10–15, 15–2, 15–9
7th Place: BRA—ITA 15–8, 15–6, 15–8

The U.S.S.R. and Poland reached the final match by completely different routes. The Soviet team, whose members averaged 6 feet 4¼ inches, swept through its four preliminary matches without losing a single set. Poland, on the other hand, was extended to five sets in three of their five victories, including a tense 13–15, 10–15, 15–6, 15–9, 20–18 win over Cuba. The Poles, however, were well prepared for such marathons—their daily training regimen required each player to jump 392 times over a four-and-a-half-foot barrier while wearing 20- to 30-pound weights on his legs and body. The turning point in the two-and-a-half-hour final came in the fourth game, with the Soviet Union leading two games to one and 15–14—one point short of the gold medal. With the contest in the balance, 6-foot 7-inch Tomasz Wójtowicz smashed a long spike from behind the ten-foot line that saved the day. Eighteen serves later the Poles won the set, 19–17.

1980 Moscow T: 10, N: 10, D: 8.1.

		MATCHES		SETS			
		W	L	W	L	PF	PA
1. SOV	(Yuri Panchenko, Vyacheslav Zaitsev, Aleksandr Savin, Vladimir Dorokhov, Aleksandr Yermilov, Pavel Selivanov, Oleg Moliboga, Vladimir Kondra, Vladimir Chernyshev, Fyodor Lashchenov, Valery Krivov, Vilyar Loor)	6	0	18	2	297	190
2. BUL	(Stoyan Gounchev, Hristo Stoyanov, Dimiter Zlatanov, Dimitar Dimitrov, Petko Petkov, Mitko Todorov, Kaspar Simeonov, Emil Vulchev, Hristo Iliev, Yordan Angelov, Tsano Tsanov, Stefan Dimitrov)	4	2	13	8	263	241
3. ROM	(Corneliu Oros, Laurentiu Dumanoiu, Dan Girleanu, Nicu Stoian, Sorin Macavei, Constantin Sterea, Neculae Vasile Pop, Gunter Enescu, Valter-Korneliu Chifu, Marius Chata-Chitiga)						
4. POL	(Robert Malinowski, Maciej Jarosz Wieslaw Czaja, Lech Lasko, Tomasz Wójtowicz, Wieslaw Gawlowski, Wojciech Drzyzga, Boguslaw Kanicki, Ryszard Bosek, Wlodzimierz Nalazek, Leszek Molenda)	3	3	12	11	303	271
5. BRA	(Joao Alves Granjeiro, Mario Xando Oliveira Neto, Antonio Gueiros, Jose Montanaro, Antonio Carlos Moreno, Renan Dal Zotto, William Carvalho Silva, Amauri Ribeiro, Bernardo Rocha Rezende, Jean Luc Rosat, Deraldo Wanderley, Berhard Rajzman)	4	2	15	10	328	288
6. YUG	(Vladimir Bogoevski, Vladimir Trifunović, Aleksandar Tacevski, Ždravko Kuljić, Goran Srbinovski, Ivica Jelić, Boro Jović, Radovan Malević, Miodrag Mitić, Ljubomir Travica, Mladen Kasić, Slobodan Lozancić)	3	3	13	13	310	302
7. CUB	(Diego Lapera, Victor Garcia, Luis Oviedo, Ernesto Martinez, Ricardo Leyva, Jorge Garbey, Raul Vilches, Carlos Salas, Antonio Perez, Leonel Marshall, Carlos Ruiz, José David)	2	4	11	13	298	280
8. CZE	(Igor Prielozny, Pavel Valach, Vlado Sirvon, Jan Repak, Josef Novotny, Jaroslav Smid, Vlastimil Lenert, Nicu Stoian, Jan Cifra, Pavel Rerabek, Josef Pick, Cyril Krejci)	1	5	7	17	253	335

Final: SOV—BUL 15–7, 15–13, 14–16, 15–11
3rd Place: ROM—POL 15–10, 9–15, 15–13, 15–9
5th Place: BRA—YUG 14–16, 15–9, 8–15, 15–10, 15–8
7th Place: CUB—CZE 14–16, 15–7, 15–10, 15–6

The team from Libya had a particularly difficult tournament, losing all five matches and all 15 sets, and scoring only 30 points while giving up 225.

The ROM row shows: 4 2 13 9 290 230

WOMEN

1896–1960 not held

1964 Tokyo T: 6, N: 6, D: 10.23.

		MATCHES		SETS			
		W	L	W	L	PF	PA
1. JAP	(Masae Kasai, Emiko Miyamoto, Kinuko Tan-ida, Yuriko Handa, Yo-shiko Matsumura, Sata Isobe, Katsumi Matsu-mura, Yoko Shinozaki, Setsuko Sasaki, Yuko Fujimoto, Masako Kon-do, Ayano Shibuki)	5	0	15	1	238	93
2. SOV	(Nelly Abramova, Astra Biltauer, Lyudmila Bulda-kova, Lyudmila Gur-eyeva, Valentina Kamen-ek, Marita Katusheva, Ninel Lukanina, Valen-tina Mishak, Tatyana Roschina, Inna Ryzkal, Antonina Ryschova, Ta-mara Tikhonina)	4	1	12	3	212	97
3. POL	(Krystyna Czajkowska, Maria Golimowska, Krys-tyna Jakubowska, Dan-uta Kordaczuk-Wagner, Krystyna Krupa, Józefa Ledwig, Jadwiga Marko, Jadwiga Rutkowska, Ma-ria Śliwka, Zofia Szczęś-niewska)	3	2	10	6	180	162
4. ROM	(Ana Mocan, Cornelia Lăzeanu, Natalia Todor-ovschi, Doina Ivănescu, Doina Popescu, Sonia Colceru, Lia Vanea, Alexandrina Chezan, Ile-ana Enculescu, Elisabeta Goloşie, Marina Stanca, Doina Coste)	2	3	6	9	140	172
5. USA	(Jean Gaertner, Gail Pa-tricia O'Rourke, Linda Kathleen Murphy, Lou Sara Galloway, Verneda Estella Thomas, Mary Margaret Perry, Mary Joan Peppler, Nancy Owen, Patricia Ann Bright, Jane Lois Ward, Sharon Roberta Peter-son, Barbara Jean Har-werth)	1	4	3	12	98	213
6. KOR	(Choon-Kang Suh, Kyung-Sook Moon, Choon-Ja Ryoo, Kil-Ja Kim, Soon-Ok Oh, Jong-Uen Chung, Don-Hi Choi, Nam-Sun Hong, Chung-Ja Oh, Jung-Sook Yoon, Ryong-Ja Kwak, Keun-Soo Lee)	0	5	0	15	94	225

Ten of the 12 members of the Japanese team came from the Nichibo spinning mill in Kaizuku, near Osaka. Their coach, the notorious Hirofumi Daimatsu, was the manager of the office supplies procurement department at the mill. Daimatsu was famous for his draconian methods: hitting the young women on the head, kicking them on their hips, insulting them, goading them, making them practice a minimum of six hours a day, seven days a week, 51 weeks a year. He was the first coach to introduce the rolling re-ceive, in which a player dives to the ground, hits the ball, rolls over, and returns quickly to her feet.

Japanese sports fans looked forward with great anticipa-tion to the Olympic volleyball tournament. Their great hopes almost met with disaster when the North Korean team withdrew over a political dispute, leaving the compe-tition one team short of the six required to conduct an offi-cial tournament. The Japanese solved the problem by giving the South Korean Olympic Committee team 1,000,000 yen to send a team. The Japanese were never se-riously challenged. The only time they lost a set (15–13, to Poland) was because Daimatsu pulled some of his better players when he saw that the Soviet coach was watching. The final Japanese victory over the U.S.S.R. gained an 80 percent audience rating on Japanese television.

After the game, the team captain, 31-year-old Masae Kasai, was invited to the official residence of Japan's prime minister, Eisaku Sato. She confessed to Sato that she want-ed to marry, but that her rigorous training schedule had prevented her from meeting any men. Sato promised to help her and subsequently introduced Kasai to Kazuo Na-kamura, whom she later married. As for Daimatsu, he quit coaching and joined an advertising agency. In 1968 he was elected to the House of Councilors, the upper house of the Japanese parliament. He served until 1974 and died of a heart attack in 1978.

1968 Mexico City T: 8, N: 8, D: 10.26.

		MATCHES		SETS			
		W	L	W	L	PF	PA
1. SOV	(Lyudmila Buldakova, Ly-udmila Mikhailovskaya, Vera Lantratova, Vera Galushka, Tatyana Sary-cheva, Tatyana Ponya-yeva, Nina Smoleeva, In-na Ryskal, Galina Leon-tieva, Roza Salikhova, Valentina Vinogradova)	7	0	21	3	333	194
2. JAP	(Setsuko Yoshika, Suzue Takayama, Toyoko Iwa-	6	1	19	3	318	147

		W	L	W	L	PF	PA

hara, Yukiyo Kojima, Sa-
chiko Fukunaka, Kunie
Shishikura, Setsuko In-
oue, Sumie Oinuma,
Keiko Hama)

3. POL (Krystyna Czajkowska, Józefa Ledwig, Elżbieta Porzec, Wanda Wiecha, Zofia Szczęśniewska, Krystyna Jakubowska, Lidia Żmuda-Chmielnic-ka, Barbara Niemczyk, Halina Aszkielowicz, Krystyna Krupa, Jadwiga Marko-Książek, Krystyna Ostromęcka) — 5 2 15 11 324 304

4. PER (Esperanza Jimenez, Teresa Nuñez, Irma Cordero, Olga Asato, Aida Reyna, Alicia Sanchez, Luisa Fuentes, Ana Maria Ramirez, Norma Velarde) — 3 4 12 15 306 327

5. KOR (Kuyong-Sook Moon, Kum-Sook Park, Hee-Sook Suh, Eun-Ok Lee, Kyu-Ok Hwang, Hyang-Seem Lee, Jin-Soo Yang, Young-Ja Kim, Oe-Sun Kim, Kyoung-Ja An) — 3 4 11 14 276 305

6. CZE (Pavlina Šteffková, Elena Poláková, Karla Šašková, Jitka Senečká, Vera Strunčová, Vera Hrabáková, Julia Bendeová, Anna Mifková, Irena Tichá, Hana Vlašaková, Eva Siroká, Hilda Mazurová) — 3 4 11 15 307 307

7. MEX (Isabel Nogueira, Carolina Mendoza, Rogelia Romo, Yolanda Reynoso, Carmen Rodriguez, Gloria Inzua, Alicia Cardenas, Gloria Casales, Patricia Nava, Trinidad Macias, Blanca Garcia, Eloisa Cabada) — 1 6 7 18 215 228

8. USA (Jane Ward, Nancy Owen, Fanny Hopeau, Barbara Perry, Ninja Jorgensen, Miki McFadden, Sharon Peterson, Patti Bright, Laurie Lewis, Marilyn McReavy, Mary Perry, Kathryn Heck) — 0 7 4 21 196 353

The crucial match between the Japanese and the Soviets was won by the U.S.S.R., 15–10, 16–14, 3–15, 15–9. After his team had been booed during its game against Czechoslovakia, the Soviet coach was asked if his players had been affected by the crowd's hostility. He replied, "If my athletes cannot stand such distractions, they are not professionals and should be left home." Reminded that the Olympics were for amateurs only, the embarrassed coach claimed he had been misquoted.

1972 Munich T: 8, N: 8, D: 9.7.

		MATCHES		SETS			
		W	L	W	L	PF	PA
1. SOV	(Inna Ryskal, Vera Douiounova, Tatiana Tretiakova, Nina Smoleeva, Roza Salikhova, Lyudmila Buldakova, Tatiana Gonobobeleva, Lyubov Turina, Galina Leontieva, Tatyana Sarycheva)	5	0	15	5	270	206
2. JAP	(Sumie Oinuma, Noriko Yamashita, Seiko Shimakage, Makiko Furukawa, Takako Iida, Katsumi Matsumura, Michiko Shiokawa, Takako Shirai, Mariko Okamoto, Keiko Hama, Yaeko Yamazaki, Toyoko Iwahava)	4	1	14	3	244	131
3. PRK	(Chun-Ok Ri, Myong-Suk Kim, Zung-Bok Kim, Ok-Sun Kang, Yeun-Ja Kim, He-Suk Hwang, Ok-Rim Jang, Myong-Suk Paek, Chun-Ja Ryom, Su-Dae Kim, Ok-Jin Jong)	3	2	10	6	211	154
4. KOR	(Young-Ja Kim, In-Sook Lee, Soon-Bok Lee, Hea-Chung Jo, Kyung-Hwa Yu, Eun-Hee Kim, Jung-Ja Lee, Jung-Hyae Yu, Young-Nae Yoon)	2	3	7	9	169	189
5. HUN	(Éva Szalay Sebők, Judit Gerhard Kiss, Emerencia Király Siry, Ilona Buzek Maklári, Judit Hazsik Fekete, Ágnes Torma, Mária Gál, Katalin Schadek Eichler, Judit Blauman Schlégl, Emőke Énekes, Zsuzsanna Török Bokros)	3	2	10	10	256	252
6. CUB	(Mercedes Perez, Ana Diaz, Margarita Mayeta, Mercedes Pomares, Nurys Sebey, Claritza Herrera, Miriam Herrera, Mercedes Roca, Claudina Villaurrutia)	2	3	8	10	181	252

	MATCHES		SETS			
	W	L	W	L	PF	PA
7. CZE (Irena Svobodova, Ludmila Vinduskova, Jana Semecka, Dorota Jelinkova, Anna Mifkova, Marie Vapenkova, Elena Moskalova, Hilda Mazurova, Maria Malisova, Hana Vlasakova)	1	4	6	12	191	241
8. GER (Ingrid Lorenz, Annedore Richter, Ursel Westphal, Birgit Pörner, Margret Stender, Annette Ellerbracke, Rike Ruschenburg, Marianne Lepa, Traute Schäfer, Erika Heucke, Regina Pütz)	0	5	0	15	131	228

Final: SOV—JAP 15–11, 4–15, 15–11, 9–15, 15–11
3rd Place: PRK—KOR 15–7, 15–9, 15–9
5th Place: HUN—CUB 13–15, 16–14, 14–16, 15–5, 15–11
7th Place: CZE—GER 15–13, 15–4, 16–14

The final was so closely fought that at one point in the fourth set there were 24 service changes in a row without a single point being scored. During the tournament, a German woman named Ingeborg Schell filed a civil suit against the Japanese coach, Joji Kojima, for using "inhuman methods for making his team fit."

1976 Montreal T: 8, N: 8, D: 7.30.

	MATCHES		SETS			
	W	L	W	L	PF	PA
1. JAP (Takako Iida, Mariko Okamoto, Echiko Maeda, Noriko Matsuda, Takako Shirai, Kiyomi Kato, Yuko Arakida, Katsuko Kanesaka, Mariko Yoshida, Shoko Takayanagi, Hiromi Yano, Juri Yokoyama)	5	0	15	0	225	844
2. SOV (Anna Rostova, Lyudmila Shetinina, Lilia Osadchaya, Natalya Kushnir, Olga Kozakova, Nina Smoleeva, Lyubov Rudovskaya, Larisa Bergen, Inna Ryskal, Lyudmila Chernysheva, Zoya Iusova, Nina Muradian)	4	1	12	7	248	211
3. KOR (Soon-Bok Lee, Jung-Hye Yu, Kyung-Ja Byon, Soo-Nok Lee, Myung-Sun Baik, Hee-Sook Chang, Kum-Ja Ma, Young-Nae Yun, Kyung-Hwa Yu, Mi-Kum Park, Soo-Nok Jung, Hea-Jung Jo)	3	2	10	11	260	259
4. HUN (Zsuzsanna Szloboda, Gyöngyi Bardi, Éva Biszku, Zsuzsanna Biszku, Lucia Bánhegyi, Gabriella Feketé Csapó, Ágnes Hubai Gajdos, Judit Blauman Schlégl, Ágnes Torma, Katalin Schadek Eichler, Emerencia Király Siry, Eva Szalay Sebök)	2	3	7	11	192	234
5. CUB (Mercedes Perez Hernandez, Imilsis Tellez Quesada, Ana Diaz Martinez, Mercedes Pomares Primelles, Lucila Urgelles Savon, Mercedes Roca, Miriam Herrera, Claudina Villaurrutia, Melanea Tartabull, Nelly Barnet Wilson, Ana Maria Garcia Crespo, Evelina Borroto)	3	2	12	9	267	250
6. GDR (Karla Roffeis, Johanna Strotzer, Cornelia Rickert, Christine Walther, Ingrid Mierzwiak, Helga Offen, Barbara Czekalla, Jutta Balster, Anke Westendorf, Hannelore Meincke, Monika Meissner, Gudrun Gärtner)	1	4	8	14	237	286
7. PER (Mercedes Gonzales, Maria Cardenas, Teresa Nunez, Irma Cordero, Ana Cecilia Carrillo, Luisa Merea, Delia Cordova, Silvia Quevedo, Luisa Fuentes, Maria Del Risco, Maria Cervera, Maria Ostolaza)	2	3	9	12	239	250
8. CAN (Carole Bishop, Barbara Dalton, Kathy Girvan, Patty Olson, Regyna Armonas, Anne Ireland, Mary Dempster, Claire Lloyd, Betty Baxter, Connie Lebrun, Debbie Heeps, Audrey Vandervelden)	0	5	6	15	198	292

Final: JAP—SOV 15–7, 15–8, 15–2
3rd Place: KOR—HUN 12–15, 15–12, 15–10, 15–6
5th Place: CUB—GDR 15–12, 15–12, 15–8
7th Place: PER—CAN 15–9, 12–15, 15–4, 15–7

The Japanese team dominated the tournament so completely that only once did an opponent (South Korea) reach double figures in a single set.

1980 Moscow T: 8, N: 8, D: 7.29.

		MATCHES		SETS			
		W	L	W	L	PF	PA
1. SOV	(Nadezhda Radzevich, Natalya Razumova, Olga Solovova, Yelena Akhaminova, Larissa Pavlova, Yelena Andreyuk, Irina Makagonova, Lyubov Kozyreva, Svetlana Nikishina, Lyudmila Chernysheva, Svetlana Badulina, Lidiya Loginova)	5	0	15	3	254	172
2. GDR	(Ute Kostrzewa, Andrea Heim, Annette Schultz, Christine Mummhardt, Heike Lehmann, Barbara Czekalla, Karla Roffeis, Martina Schmidt, Anke Westendorf, Karin Püschel, Brigitte Fetzer, Katharina Bullin)	3	2	11	11	277	271
3. BUL	(Tania Dimitrova, Valentina Ilieva, Galina Stancheva, Silva Petrunova, Anka Hristolova, Verka Borisova, Margarita Gherasimova, Roumiana Kaicheva, Maya Georgieva, Tania Gogova, Tzvetana Bozhurina, Rossitza Dimitrova)	3	2	12	9	257	225
4. HUN	(Julianna Simon Szalonna, Éva Szalay Sebők, Gyöngyi Gerevich [Bardi], Ágnes Balajczá Juhász, Lucia Banhegyi Rado, Gabriella Feketé Csapó, Emöke Szegedi Varghá, Emerencia Királly Siry, Ágnes Torma, Erzsébet Vargá Palinkás, Gabriella Lengyel, Bernadett Köszegi)	2	3	10	12	234	279
5. CUB	(Mercedes Perez Hernandez, Imilsis Tellez Quesada, Ana Diaz Martinez, Mercedes Pomares Primelles, Mavis Guilarte Fernandez, Erenia Diaz Toca, Maura Alfonso Drake, Josefina Capote Travieso, Nelly Barnet Wilson, Ana Maria Garcia Crespo, Lucila Urgelles Savon)	3	2	10	7	219	166
6. PER	(Carmen Pimentel, Gaby Cardenas, Raquel Chumpitaz, Ana Cecilia Carrillo, Maria Del Risco, Cecilia Tait, Silvia Leon, Aurora Heredia, Gina Torrealva, Natalia Malaga)	1	4	7	12	189	257
7. BRA	(Denise Porto Mattioli, Ivonette das Neves, Lenice Peluso Oliveira, Regina Vilela Santos, Fernanda Emerick Silva, Paula Rodrigues Mello, Maria Isabel Alencar, Eliana Maria Aleixo, Maria Castanheira, Jacqueline Cruz Silva, Vera Helena Mossa, Rita Cassia Teixeira)	1	4	7	12	210	248
8. ROM	(Mariana Ionescu, Gabriela Coman, Dorina Savoiu, Victoria Georgescu, Ileana Dobroschi, Victoria Banciu, Irina Petculet, Orina Georgescu, Iuliana Enescu, Ioana Liteanu, Corina Crivat, Elena Piron)	2	3	7	13	221	243

Final: SOV—GDR 15–12, 11–15, 15–13, 15–7
3rd Place: BUL—HUN 15–5, 13–15, 6–15, 15–4, 15–8
5th Place: CUB—PER 15–9, 15–7, 12–15, 15–5
7th Place: BRA—ROM 15–8, 15–12, 15–12

WEIGHTLIFTING

Flyweight	Light Heavyweight
Bantamweight	Middle Heavyweight
Featherweight	100 Kg
Lightweight	Heavyweight
Middleweight	Super Heavyweight—Unlimited Weight

Each contestant is allowed three attempts at each type of lift. The *snatch* is performed by lifting the bar from the floor to overhead in one movement and holding it there for two seconds. The *clean and jerk*, or *jerk*, is a two-part lift. First the weight is brought up to the shoulders and then, using the combined strength of arms and legs, it is raised overhead.The *press*, which was discontinued following the 1972 Olympics, required the lifter to bring the bar to his shoulders, wait two seconds for the judges' approval, and then lift the bar overhead using only the arms. When a tie occurs, the man with the lower bodyweight is declared the winner. Often a champion will make a fourth attempt, which does not count as part of the competition but can count as a world record.

FLYWEIGHT
(52 kg—114.61 lbs)

1896–1968 not held

1972 Munich C: 17, N: 13, D: 8.31. WR: 342.5 kg (Sándor Holczreiter)

			PRESS		SNATCH		JERK		TOTAL KG
1.	Zygmunt Smalcerz	POL	112.5	OR	100.0		125.0		337.5
2.	Lajos Szücs	HUN	107.5		95.0		127.5		330.0
3.	Sándor Holczreiter	HUN	112.5		92.5		122.5		327.5
4.	Tetsuhide Sasaki	JAP	105.0		97.5		120.0		322.5
5.	Gyi Aung	BUR	95.0		105.0	WR	120.0		320.0
6.	Dong-Geun Pak	PRK	97.5		90.0		130.0	OR	317.5
7.	Chaiya Sukchinda	THA	100.0		92.5		120.0		312.5
8.	Ion Hortopan	ROM	97.5		95.0		117.5		310.0

Charlie Depthios of Indonesia took an extra lift at the end of the competition and set a world jerk record of 132.5 kg.

1976 Montreal C: 23, N: 18, D: 7.18. WR: 242.5 kg (Aleksandr Voronin)

			SNATCH	JERK	TOTAL KG	
1.	Aleksandr Voronin	SOV	105.0	137.5	242.5	EWR
2.	György Köszegi	HUN	107.5	130.0	237.5	
3.	Seresht Mohammad Nassiri	IRN	100.0	135.0	235.0	
4.	Masatomo Takeuchi	JAP	105.0	127.5	232.5	
5.	Francisco Casamayor	CUB	100.0	127.5	227.5	
6.	Stefan Leletko	POL	95.0	125.0	220.0	
7.	Boleslav Pachol	CZE	95.0	122.5	217.5	
8.	Daniel Nuñez Aguiar	CUB	92.5	122.5	215.0	

At 4 feet 8¾ inches, Voronin, an electrician from Kerekoo, was the shortest man in the competition. Taking an extra lift after winning the gold medal, he set a world jerk record of 141 kg.

1980 Moscow C: 18, N: 15, D: 7.20. WR: 247.5 kg (Aleksandr Voronin)

			SNATCH		JERK	TOTAL KG	
1.	Kanybek Osmanoliev	SOV	107.5		137.5	245.0	OR
2.	Bong-Choi Ho	PRK	110.0		135.0	245.0	
3.	Gyong-Si Han	PRK	110.0	OR	135.0	245.0	
4.	Béla Oláh	HUN	110.0		135.0	245.0	
5.	Stefan Leletko	POL	105.0		135.0	240.0	
6.	Ferenc Hornyák	HUN	107.5		130.0	237.5	
7.	Francisco Casamayor	CUB	102.5		130.0	232.5	
8.	Adjya Jugdernamjil	MON	97.5		117.5	215.0	

This unusually close contest was won by Osmanoliev as a result of his lower bodyweight. Han set a world snatch record of 113 kg on his fourth attempt.

BANTAMWEIGHT
(56 kg—123 lbs)

1896–1936 not held

1948 London C: 19, N: 14, D: 8.9. WR: 300 kg (Joseph Di Pietro)

			PRESS		SNATCH		JERK		TOTAL KG	
1.	Joseph Di Pietro	USA	105.0	OR	90.0		112.5		307.5	WR
2.	Julian Creus	GBR	82.5		95.0	OR	120.0		297.5	
3.	Richard Tom	USA	87.5		90.0		117.5		295.0	
4.	Kyu-Hyuk Lee	KOR	77.5		92.5		120.0		290.0	
5.	Mahmoud Namdjou	IRN	82.5		82.5		122.5	OR	287.5	
6.	Marcel Thévenet	FRA	90.0		80.0		110.0		280.0	
7.	Rosaire Smith	CAN	82.5		85.0		110.0		277.5	
8.	M. Crow	NZE	77.5		85.0		110.0		272.5	

Joe Di Pietro's height was variously reported as 4 foot 8 inches or 4 feet 10 inches. Whichever figure is correct, his arms were so short that he was barely able to raise the bar above his head.

1952 Helsinki C: 19, N: 18, D: 7.25. WR: 317.5 kg (Mahmoud Namdjou)

			PRESS	SNATCH		JERK		TOTAL KG	
1.	Ivan Udodov	SOV	90.0	97.5	OR	127.5	OR	315.0	OR
2.	Mahmoud Namdjou	IRN	90.0	95.0		122.5		307.5	
3.	Ali Mirzal	IRN	95.0	92.5		112.5		300.0	
4.	Hae-Nam Kim	KOR	80.0	95.0		120.0		295.0	
5.	Kamal Mahmoud Mahgoub	EGY	75.0	95.0		122.5		292.5	
6.	Pedro Landero	PHI	90.0	87.5		115.0		292.5	
7.	Maurice Megennis	GBR	82.5	85.0		112.5		280.0	
8.	Lon Mohamed Noor	SIN	77.5	85.0		112.5		275.0	

1956 Melbourne C: 16, N: 13, D: 11.23. WR: 335 kg (Vladimir Stogov)

			PRESS		SNATCH		JERK		TOTAL KG	
1.	Charles Vinci	USA	105.0	EOR	105.0	OR	132.5		342.5	WR
2.	Vladimir Stogov	SOV	105.0	EOR	105.0	OR	127.5		337.5	
3.	Mahmoud Namdjou	IRN	100.0		102.5		130.0		332.5	
4.	In-Ho Yu	KOR	90.0		95.0		135.0	OR	320.0	
5.	Hae-Nam Kim	KOR	85.0		95.0		127.5		307.5	
6.	Yoshio Nanbu	JAP	87.5		97.5		120.0		305.0	
7.	Reginald Gaffley	SAF	97.5		90.0		117.5		305.0	
8.	Yukio Furuyama	JAP	90.0		87.5		125.0		302.5	

As weigh-in time approached, the 4-foot 10-inch Vinci was one and a half pounds overweight. After an hour of running and sweating he was still seven ounces over the limit with 15 minutes to go. Fortunately, a severe last-minute haircut did the trick, and Vinci went on to win the gold medal.

1960 Rome C: 22, N: 18, D: 9.7. WR: 345 kg (Vladimir Stogov)

			PRESS		SNATCH		JERK		TOTAL KG	
1.	Charles Vinci	USA	105.0	EOR	107.5	EWR	132.5		345.0	EWR
2.	Yoshinobu Miyake	JAP	97.5		105.0		135.0	EOR	337.5	
3.	Esmail Elm Khan	IRN	97.5		100.0		132.5		330.0	
4.	Shigeo Kogure	JAP	90.0		102.5		130.0		322.5	
5.	Marian Jankowski	POL	92.5		100.0		130.0		322.5	
6.	Imre Földi	HUN	100.0		90.0		130.0		320.0	
7.	In-Ho Yu	KOR	90.0		95.0		130.0		315.0	
8.	Husain Hasan	IRQ	87.5		100.0		125.0		312.5	

1964 Tokyo C: 24, N: 18, D: 10.11. WR: 352.5 kg (Yoshinobu Miyake)

			PRESS		SNATCH		JERK		TOTAL KG	
1.	Aleksey Vakhonin	SOV	110.0		105.0		142.5	OR	357.5	WR
2.	Imre Földi	HUN	115.0	OR	102.5		137.5		355.0	
3.	Shiro Ichinoseki	JAP	100.0		110.0	OR	137.5		347.5	
4.	Henryk Trębicki	POL	105.0		102.5		135.0		342.5	
5.	Mu-Shin Yang	KOR	97.5		107.5		135.0		340.0	
6.	Yukio Furuyama	JAP	105.0		100.0		130.0		335.0	
7.	In-Ho Yu	KOR	97.5		100.0		137.5		335.0	
8.	Martin Dias	GUY	100.0		102.5		132.5		335.0	

Vakhonin, a 4-foot 10¾-inch, 29-year-old coal miner, set a world record in the jerk that was not allowed because he was, by then, overweight. The lift did count as an *Olympic* record, however. The same treatment was given to Ichinoseki's snatch record. Földi, who had sweated down from a featherweight, was handicapped in the snatch because one of his fingers was missing and another was paralyzed. Vakhonin disappeared from international competition prior to the 1968 Olympics after being accused of "conduct unbecoming a Master of Sport."

1968 Mexico City C: 20, N: 19, D: 10.13. WR: 367.5 kg
(Gennady Chetin)

		PRESS		SNATCH	JERK		TOTAL KG	
1. Seresht Mohammad Nassiri	IRN	112.5		105.0	150.0	WR	367.5	EWR
2. Imre Földi	HUN	122.5	OR	105.0	140.0		367.5	EWR
3. Henryk Trebicki	POL	115.0		107.5	135.0		357.5	
4. Gennady Chetin	SOV	110.0		102.5	140.0		352.5	
5. Shiro Ichinoseki	JAP	110.0		107.5	132.5		350.0	
6. Fernando Baez Cruz	PUR	120.0		92.5	132.5		345.0	
7. Atanas Kirov	BUL	105.0		100.0	130.0		335.0	
8. Chaiya Sukchinda	TAI	100.0		105.0	125.0		330.0	

Nassiri was awarded first place because his bodyweight was ten ounces less than Földi's.

1972 Munich C: 24, N: 20, D: 8.28. WR: 375 kg (Gennady Chetin)

		PRESS		SNATCH	JERK	TOTAL KG	
1. Imre Földi	HUN	127.5	OR	107.5	142.5	377.5	WR
2. Seresht Mohammad Nassiri	IRN	127.5	OR	100.0	142.5	370.0	
3. Gennady Chetin	SOV	120.0		107.5	140.0	367.5	
4. Henryk Trebicki	POL	122.5		107.5	135.0	365.0	
5. Atanas Kirov	BUL	117.5		105.0	140.0	362.5	
6. George Vasiliades	AUS	115.0		102.5	137.5	355.0	
7. Hiroshi Ono	JAP	115.0		105.0	135.0	355.0	
8. Georgi Todorov	BUL	110.0		100.0	140.0	350.0	

Tenth-place finisher Koji Miki of Japan set an Olympic snatch record of 112.5 kg and then broke the world record with an extra lift of 114 kg. Polish-born Zeev Friedman, who finished twelfth, was one of the 11 Israelis who were murdered at the Games by Palestinian terrorists.

1976 Montreal C: 27, N: 20, D: 7.19. WR: 260 kg (Atanas Kirov)

		SNATCH		JERK	TOTAL KG	
1. Norair Nurikian	BUL	117.5	OR	145.0	262.5	WR
2. Grzegorz Cziura	POL	115.0		137.5	252.5	
3. Kenkichi Ando	JAP	107.5		142.5	250.0	
4. Leszek Skorupa	POL	112.5		137.5	250.0	
5. Imre Földi	HUN	105.0		140.0	245.0	
6. Bernhard Bachfisch	GER	105.0		137.5	242.5	
7. Carlos Lastre	CUB	105.0		135.0	240.0	
8. Fazlolli Dehkhodah	IRN	105.0		135.0	240.0	

1980 Moscow C: 21, N: 17, D: 7.21. WR: 272.5 kg (Daniel Nuñez Aguiar)

		SNATCH		JERK		TOTAL KG	
1. Daniel Nuñez Aguiar	CUB	125.0	WR	150.0		275.0	WR
2. Yurik Sarkisian	SOV	112.5		157.5	WR	270.0	
3. Tadeusz Dembończyk	POL	120.0		145.0		265.0	
4. Andreas Letz	GDR	115.0		150.0		265.0	
5. Eui-Yong Yang	PRK	112.5		150.0		265.0	
6. Imre Stefanovics	HUN	115.0		145.0		260.0	
7. Gheorghe Maftei	ROM	105.0		142.5		247.5	
8. Pavel Petre	ROM	105.0		140.0		245.0	

FEATHERWEIGHT

(60 kg—132 lbs)

1896–1912 not held

1920 Antwerp C: 10, N: 8, D: 8.28.

		PRESS	SNATCH	JERK	TOTAL KG
1. Frans de Haes	BEL	60.0	65.0	95.0	220.0
2. Alfred Schmidt	EST	55.0	65.0	92.5	212.5
3. Eugène Ryther	SWI	55.0	65.0	90.0	210.0
4. Luigi Gatti	ITA	50.0	55.0	90.0	195.0
5. Ludvik Wágner	CZE	50.0	65.0	80.0	195.0
6. Gustav Eriksson	SWE	47.5	65.0	80.0	192.5

1924 Paris C: 21, N: 11, D: 7.21.

		ONE-HAND SNATCH		ONE-HAND JERK		PRESS		TWO-HAND SNATCH		TWO-HAND JERK		TOTAL KG
1. Pierino Gabetti	ITA	65.0	OR	77.5		72.5		82.5	OR	105.0	OR	402.5
2. Andreas Stadler	AUT	65.0	OR	75.0		65.0		75.0		105.0	OR	385.0
3. Arthur Reinmann	SWI	57.5		70.0		80.0	OR	75.0		100.0		382.5
4. Maurice Martin	FRA	60.0		62.5		75.0		82.5	OR	100.0		380.0
5. Wilhelm Rosinek	AUT	57.5		75.0		67.5		70.0		105.0	OR	375.0
6. Gustav Ernesaks	EST	60.0		80.0	OR	67.5		72.5		92.5		372.5
7. A. Baxter	GBR	55.0		65.0		70.0		75.0		105.0	OR	370.0
8. E. Juillerat	SWI	55.0		70.0		67.5		75.0		100.0		367.5

M.H. Djemal of Turkey, who finished 14th, was only 13 years old.

1928 Amsterdam C: 21, N: 13, D: 7.29.

		PRESS		SNATCH		JERK		TOTAL KG	
1. Franz Andrysek	AUT	77.5		90.0	OR	120.0	OR	287.5	OR
2. Pierino Gabetti	ITA	80.0		90.0	OR	112.5		282.5	
3. Hans Wölpert	GER	92.5	WR	82.5		107.5		282.5	
4. Giuseppe Conca	ITA	92.5	WR	80.0		105.0		277.5	
5. Arthur Reinmann	SWI	82.5		82.5		110.0		275.0	
6. Andreas Stadler	AUT	72.5		80.0		115.0		267.5	
7. H. Baudrand	FRA	77.5		80.0		107.5		265.0	
8. M.H. Djemal	TUR	85.0		75.0		102.5		262.5	
8. J. Vacek	CZE	80.0		82.5		100.0		262.5	

1932 Los Angeles C: 6, N: 4, D: 7.31.

		PRESS	SNATCH	JERK	TOTAL KG	
1. Raymond Suvigny	FRA	82.5	87.5	117.5	287.5	EOR
2. Hans Wölpert	GER	85.0	87.5	110.0	282.5	

3. Anthony Terlazzo	USA	82.5	85.0	112.5	280.0
4. Helmut Schäfer	GER	77.5	77.5	112.5	267.5
5. Attilio Bescapè	ITA	82.5	77.5	102.5	262.5
6. Richard Bachtell	USA	70.0	80.0	102.5	252.5

An eating binge on the way to Los Angeles forced Suvigny to lose ten pounds in one week in order to make the weight limit.

1936 Berlin C: 21, N: 13, D: 8.2. WR: 297.5 kg (Max Walther)

		PRESS		SNATCH		JERK		TOTAL KG	
1. Anthony Terlazzo	USA	92.5	EOR	97.5	OR	122.5		312.5	WR
2. Saleh Mohammed Soliman	EGY	85.0		95.0		125.0	OR	305.0	
3. Ibrahim Hassan Shams	EGY	80.0		95.0		125.0	OR	300.0	
4. Anton Richter	AUT	80.0		97.5	OR	120.0		297.5	
5. Georg Liebsch	GER	92.5	OR	90.0		107.5		290.0	
6. Attilio Bescapè	ITA	87.5		90.0		110.0		287.5	
7. John Terry	USA	75.0		92.5		120.0		287.5	
8. Max Walther	GER	75.0		90.0		115.0		280.0	

1948 London C: 23, N: 18, D: 8.9. WR: 320 kg (Arvid Anderson)

		PRESS		SNATCH		JERK		TOTAL KG	
1. Mahmoud Fayad	EGY	92.5		105.0	WR	135.0	WR	332.5	WR
2. Rodney Wilkes	TRI	97.5		97.5		122.5		317.5	
3. Jaffar Salmassi	IRN	100.0	OR	97.5		115.0		312.5	
4. Su-Il Nam	KOR	92.5		92.5		122.5		307.5	
5. Rodrigo Del Rosario	PHI	97.5		92.5		117.5		307.5	
6. Kotaro Ishikawa	USA	92.5		95.0		120.0		307.5	
7. Johan Runge	DEN	95.0		90.0		120.0		305.0	
8. Max Heral	FRA	85.0		95.0		120.0		300.0	

1952 Helsinki C: 22, N: 21, D: 7.25. WR: 332.5 kg (Mahmoud Fayad)

		PRESS		SNATCH		JERK		TOTAL KG	
1. Rafael Chimishkyan	SOV	97.5		105.0	EOR	135.0	EOR	337.5	WR
2. Nikolai Saksonov	SOV	95.0		105.0		132.5		332.5	
3. Rodney Wilkes	TRI	100.0		100.0		122.5		322.5	
4. Rodrigo Del Rosario	PHI	105.0	OR	92.5		120.0		317.5	
5. Said Khalifa Gouda	EGY	85.0		102.5		125.0		312.5	
6. Weng Yew Chay	SIN	87.5		97.5		127.5		312.5	
7. Balint Nagy	HUN	85.0		97.5		125.0		307.5	
8. Mohssai Tabatabai	IRN	90.0		97.5		120.0		307.5	

1956 Melbourne C: 21, N: 19, D: 11.23. WR: 350 kg (Rafael Chimishkyan)

		PRESS		SNATCH		JERK		TOTAL KG	
1. Isaac Berger	USA	107.5		107.5	OR	137.5	OR	352.5	WR
2. Yevgeny Minayev	SOV	115.0	WR	100.0		127.5		342.5	
3. Marian Zieliński	POL	105.0		102.5		127.5		335.0	
4. Rodney Wilkes	TRI	100.0		105.0		125.0		330.0	
5. Hiroyoshi Shiratori	JAP	97.5		100.0		127.5		325.0	
6. Georg Miske	GDR	100.0		95.0		125.0		320.0	
7. Ser-Cher Tan	SIN	92.5		92.5		130.0		315.0	
8. Kyung-Sob Lee	KOR	90.0		95.0		132.5		312.5	

Ike Berger was an Israeli-born teenager from Brooklyn.

1960 Rome C: 28, N: 25, D: 9.7. WR: 372.5 kg (Isaac Berger)

		PRESS		SNATCH		JERK		TOTAL KG	
1. Yevgeny Minayev	SOV	120.0	EWR	110.0	OR	142.5	OR	372.5	EWR
2. Isaac Berger	USA	117.5		105.0		140.0		362.5	
3. Sebastiano Mannironi	ITA	107.5		110.0		135.0		352.5	
4. Hae-Nam Kim	KOR	105.0		105.0		135.0		345.0	
5. Yukio Furuyama	JAP	107.5		102.5		135.0		345.0	
6. Hosny Abbas	UAR	102.5		95.0		140.0		337.5	
7. Kywe Tun	BUR	100.0		100.0		127.5		327.5	
8. Alberto Nogar	PHI	97.5		100.0		127.5		325.0	

The competition took ten hours and didn't end until four a.m., when Berger twice failed to jerk 152.5 kg. Minayev had lost to Berger six straight times prior to the Olympics. In Rome, he made all nine of his lifts.

1964 Tokyo C: 22, N: 20, D: 10.12. WR: 387.5 kg (Yoshinobu Miyake)

		PRESS		SNATCH		JERK		TOTAL KG	
1. Yoshinobu Miyake	JAP	122.5	OR	122.5	OR	152.5	WR	397.5	WR
2. Isaac Berger	USA	122.5	OR	107.5		152.5	WR	382.5	
3. Mieczyslaw Nowak	POL	112.5		115.0		150.0		377.5	
4. Hiroshi Fukuda	JAP	120.0		115.0		140.0		375.0	
5. Sebastiano Mannironi	ITA	112.5		112.5		145.0		370.0	
6. Hae-Nam Kim	KOR	115.0		112.5		140.0		367.5	
7. Rudolf Kozlowski	POL	110.0		107.5		140.0		357.5	
8. Hosny Abbas	UAR	105.0		100.0		137.5		342.5	

Yoshinobu Miyake, who had won the Bantamweight silver medal in 1960, was a 24-year-old lieutenant in the National Self-Defense Force. Only 5 feet tall, he came from a poor family in Miyagi prefecture in northern Japan. His parents sold some pigs to raise the money to see their son compete in the Olympics.

1968 Mexico City C: 28, N: 22, D: 10.14. WR: 397.5 kg (Yoshinobu Miyake)

		PRESS		SNATCH	JERK		TOTAL KG
1. Yoshinobu Miyake	JAP	122.5	EOR	117.5	152.5	EWR	392.5
2. Dito Shanidze	SOV	120.0		117.5	150.0		387.5
3. Yoshiyuki Miyake	JAP	122.5	EOR	115.0	147.5		385.0
4. Jan Wojnowski	POL	117.5		115.0	150.0		382.5
5. Mieczyslaw Nowak	POL	117.5		110.0	147.5		375.0
6. Nasrollah Dehnavi	IRN	117.5		107.5	140.0		365.0
7. Moo-Shin Young	KOR	110.0		115.0	140.0		356.0
8. Manuel Mateos	MEX	120.0		100.0	140.0		360.0

Yoshiyuki Miyake was six years younger than his brother Yoshinobu.

1972 Munich C: 13, N: 11, D: 8.29. WR: 402.5 kg (Dito Shanidze)

		PRESS		SNATCH	JERK		TOTAL KG	
1. Norair Nurikian	BUL	127.5	OR	117.5	157.5	WR	402.5	EWR
2. Dito Shanidze	SOV	127.5	OR	120.0	152.5		400.0	

3. János Benedek	HUN	125.0	120.0	145.0	390.0
4. Yoshinobu Miyake	JAP	120.0	120.0	145.0	385.0
5. Kurt Pittner	AUT	125.0	112.5	145.0	382.5
6. Rolando Chang	CUB	120.0	115.0	142.5	377.5
7. Mieczyslaw Nowak	POL	120.0	110.0	145.0	375.0
8. Peppino Tanti	ITA	120.0	107.5	140.0	367.5

This division saw the rare appearance of an athlete from Albania. Known only as Pampuri, he broke the Olympic record in the press and actually led the competition after the first round due to his lower bodyweight. However he could do no better than 12th and tenth in the snatch and jerk, respectively, and wound up in ninth place.

1976 Montreal C: 17, N: 13, D: 7.20. WR: 285 kg (Georgi Todorov)

		SNATCH		JERK		TOTAL KG	
1. Nikolai Kolesnikov	SOV	125.0	OR	160.0	OR	285.0	EWR
2. Georgi Todorov	BUL	122.5		157.5		280.0	
3. Kazumasa Hirai	JAP	125.0	OR	150.0		275.0	
4. Takashi Saito	JAP	110.0		152.5		262.5	
5. Edward Weitz	ISR	110.0		152.5		262.5	
6. Davoud Maleki	IRN	115.0		145.0		260.0	
7. Pedro Fuentes	CUB	112.5		145.0		257.5	
8. Jong-Guk Om	PRK	110.0		145.0		255.0	

1980 Moscow C: 16 N: 14, D: 7.22. WR: 297.5 kg (Viktor Mazin)

		SNATCH		JERK		TOTAL KG	
1. Viktor Mazin	SOV	130.0	OR	160.0	EOR	290.0	OR
2. Stefan Dimitrov	BUL	127.5		160.0	EOR	287.5	
3. Marek Seweryn	POL	127.5		155.0		275.0	
4. Antoni Pawlak	POL	120.0		150.0		275.0	
5. Julio Loscos	CUB	125.0		150.0		275.0	
6. František Nedved	CZE	122.5		150.0		272.5	
7. Victor Perez	CUB	117.5		152.5		270.0	
8. Gelu Radu	ROM	115.0		150.0		265.0	

LIGHTWEIGHT
(67.5 kg—148.75 lbs)
1896–1912 not held

1920 Antwerp C: 11, N: 9, D: 8.28.

		ONE-HAND SNATCH	ONE-HAND JERK	TWO-HAND JERK	TOTAL KG
1. Alfred Neuland	EST	72.5	75.0	110.0	257.5
2. Louis Williquet	BEL	60.0	75.0	105.0	240.0
3. Florimond Rooms	BEL	55.0	70.0	105.0	230.0
4. Giulio Monti	ITA	55.0	70.0	105.0	230.0
5. Martin Olofsson	SWE	55.0	70.0	95.0	220.0

1924 Paris C: 22, N: 12, D: 7.22.

		ONE-HAND SNATCH		ONE-HAND JERK		TWO-HAND PRESS	TWO-HAND SNATCH	TWO-HAND JERK		TOTAL KG
1. Edmond Décottignies	FRA	70.0		92.5		77.5	85.0	115.0	OR	440.0
2. Anton Zwerina	AUT	75.0	OR	80.0		77.5	82.5	112.5		427.5
3. Bohumil Durdis	CZE	70.0		82.5		72.5	90.0	110.0		425.0
4. Leopold Treffny	AUT	65.0		85.0		77.5	85.0	112.5		425.0
5. Joseph Jaquenoud	SWI	65.0		85.0		77.5	85.0	105.0		417.5
6. Eduard Vanaaseme	EST	65.0		77.5		85.0	80.0	107.5		415.0
7. August Scheffer	HOL	62.5		80.0		80.0	82.5	110.0		415.0
8. F. Bichsel	SWI	70.0		95.0	WR	65.0	75.0	105.0		410.0

1928 Amsterdam C: 16, N: 11, D: 7.29. WR: 325 kg (Kurt Helbig)

		PRESS		SNATCH		JERK		TOTAL KG
1. Hans Haas	GER	90.0	OR	97.5		135.0	OR	322.5
1. Kurt Helbig	AUT	85.0		102.5	OR	135.0	OR	322.5
3. Fernand Arnout	FRA	85.0		97.5		120.0		302.5
4. Albert Aeschmann	SWI	87.5		90.0		120.0		297.5
5. Willi Reinfrank	GER	85.0		90.0		120.0		295.0
6. Jules Meese	FRA	90.0	OR	87.5		115.0		292.5
7. Anton Hangel	AUT	77.5		90.0		120.0		287.5
8. Gastone Pierini	ITA	90.0	OR	82.5		110.0		282.5

1932 Los Angeles C: 6, N:4, D:7.31. WR: 325 kg (Kurt Helbig)

		PRESS		SNATCH		JERK	TOTAL KG	
1. René Duverger	FRA	97.5	OR	102.5	EOR	125.0	325.0	EWR
2. Hans Haas	AUT	82.5		100.0	EOR	125.0	307.5	
3. Gastone Pierini	ITA	92.5		90.0		120.0	302.5	
4. Pierino Gabetti	ITA	85.0		95.0		120.0	300.0	
5. Arnie Sundberg	USA	77.5		90.0		117.5	285.0	
6. Walter Zagurski	USA	82.5		90.0		112.5	285.0	

1936 Berlin C: 16, N: 12, D: 8.2. WR: 337.5 kg (Anwar Mohammed Mesbah)

		PRESS		SNATCH		JERK		TOTAL KG	
1. Robert Fein	AUT	105.0	OR	100.0		137.5		342.5	WR
1. Anwar Mohammed Mesbah	EGY	92.5		105.0	OR	145.0	OR	342.5	WR
3. Karl Jansen	GER	95.0		100.0		132.5		327.5	
4. Karl Schwitalle	GER	95.0		100.0		127.5		322.5	
5. John Terpak	USA	97.5		100.0		125.0		322.5	
6. Ibrahim Masoud El Sayed	EGY	90.0		100.0		132.5		322.5	
7. René Duverger	FRA	97.5		95.0		125.0		317.5	
8. Robert Mitchell	USA	85.0		97.5		130.0		312.5	

Originally Mesbah was awarded sole possession of first place because he had weighed three and a half ounces less than Fein at the precompetition weigh-in. The Austrians lodged a protest, which was upheld, and both men received gold medals.

1948 London C: 22, N: 17, D: 8.10. WR: 367.5 kg (Stanley Stanczyk)

		PRESS	SNATCH		JERK		TOTAL KG	
1. Ibrahim Hassan Shams	EGY	97.5	115.0	OR	147.5	OR	360.0	OR
2. Appia Hamouda	EGY	105.0	110.0		145.0		360.0	OR
3. James Halliday	GBR	90.0	110.0		140.0		340.0	
4. John Terpak	USA	102.5	102.5		135.0		340.0	
5. John Stuart	CAN	107.5	OR	100.0		125.0	332.5	
6. Suk-Young Kim	KOR	95.0	100.0		135.0		330.0	
7. See-Yun La	KOR	90.0	100.0		125.0		330.0	
8. Joseph Pittman	USA	100.0	95.0		127.5		322.5	

Shams won a dramatic confrontation with his teammate Hamouda. After Shams missed a jerk of 145 kg, Hamouda successfully lifted the same weight on his final attempt. This forced Shams, who had set the world jerk record nine years earlier, to add 2.5 kg to the bar if he hoped to tie Hamouda and win as a result of his lower bodyweight. With the audience in complete silence, Shams approached the bar twice and then turned away. The third time, he seized the bar quickly and, in a flash, had it up to his shoulders and over his head for the victory. Sham's 1939 snatch of 116.5 kg stood as a world record until the 1952 Olympics. His 153.5 kg jerk of the same year was still on the books in 1957.

1952 Helsinki C: 24, N: 22, D: 7.26. WR: 367.5 kg (Stanley Stanczyk)

		PRESS	SNATCH		JERK	TOTAL KG	
1. Tamio "Tommy" Kono	USA	105.0	117.5	WR	140.0	362.5	OR
2. Yevgeny Lopatin	SOV	100.0	107.5		142.5	350.0	
3. Verne Barberis	AUS	105.0	105.0		140.0	350.0	
4. Chang-Hee Kim	KOR	100.0	105.0		140.0	345.0	
5. Hassan Ferdows	IRN	102.5	107.5		135.0	345.0	
6. Abdel Khadr El Touni	EGY	105.0	107.5		130.0	342.5	
7. Johan Runge	DEN	105.0	97.5		127.5	330.0	
8. Ging Hwie Thio	INO	105.0	92.5		130.0	327.5	

Tommy Kono was a sickly child who suffered from asthma. His parents tried the usual traditional Japanese cures, such as bear kidneys, burned birds, and powdered snakes. "I used to wish with all my might for good health," he said. During World War II he and his family were forced to leave their home in Sacramento, California, and move to the Tule Lake detention camp for Japanese-Americans. It was there that 14-year-old Tommy was introduced to weightlifting. He caught on quickly and began what was to become an amazing career, which included two Olympic gold medals and one silver, and 21 world records set in four different divisions. His ability to move up and down in weight division without losing strength allowed him to fill in wherever the U.S. team needed him; thus each of his three Olympic medals was won in a different category. He accomplished this by following an unusual system of dieting. If he needed to add weight, he would eat six or seven meals a day. If he needed to shed a few pounds, he would restrict himself to "only" three meals a day. In 1954 Kono won the Mr. World contest, and in 1955 and 1957 he was chosen Mr. Universe. He balanced his muscle-man image by washing and ironing his own clothes and doing his own cooking and cleaning. Yet another talent of Tommy Kono was his mental control—always an important factor in weightlifting. One of his many victims was Fyodor Bogdanovsky who always lost to Kono, often performing well below his capabilities. Bogdanovsky once said, "When Kono looks at me from the wings, he works on me like a python on a rabbit."

1956 Melbourne C: 18, N: 17, D: 11.24. WR: 382.5 kg (Nicolai Kostilev)

		PRESS		SNATCH		JERK		TOTAL KG	
1. Igor Rybak	SOV	110.0		120.0	OR	150.0	OR	380.0	OR
2. Rafael Khabutdinov	SOV	125.0	OR	110.0		137.5		372.5	
3. Chang-Hee Kim	KOR	107.5		112.5		150.0	OR	370.0	
4. Kenji Onuma	JAP	110.0		110.0		147.5		367.5	
5. Henrik Tamraz	IRN	115.0		105.0		145.0		365.0	
6. Jan Czepulkowski	POL	120.0		105.0		135.0		360.0	
7. Ivam Abadzhiev	BUL	102.5		117.5		137.5		357.5	
8. Tun Maung	BUR	110.0		105.0		137.5		352.5	

1960 Rome C: 33, N: 29, D: 9.8. WR: 390 kg (Viktor Buschuyev)

		PRESS		SNATCH		JERK		TOTAL KG	
1. Viktor Buschuyev	SOV	125.0	EOR	122.5	OR	150.0		397.5	WR
2. Howe-Liang Tan	SIN	115.0		110.0		155.0	OR	380.0	
3. Abdul Wahid Aziz	IRQ	117.5		115.0		147.5		380.0	
4. Marian Zieliński	POL	115.0		110.0		150.0		375.0	
5. Waldemar Baszanowski	POL	105.0		117.5		147.5		380.0	
6. Mihály Huszka	HUN	110.0		107.5		147.5		365.0	
7. Werner Dittrich	GDR	107.5		115.0		140.0		362.5	
7. Zdenek Otahal	CZE	115.0		107.5		140.0		362.5	

Howe-Liang Tan is the only athlete from Singapore to have won an Olympic medal.

1964 Tokyo C: 20, N: 18, D:10.13. WR: 430 kg (Waldemar Baszanowski)

		PRESS		SNATCH	JERK		TOTAL KG	
1. Waldemar Baszanowski	POL	132.5		135.0	165.0	OR	432.5	WR
2. Vladimir Kaplunov	SOV	140.0	EWR	127.5	165.0		432.5	WR
3. Marian Zieliński	POL	140.0	EWR	120.0	160.0		420.0	
4. Anthony Garcy	USA	127.5		125.0	160.0		412.5	
5. Zdenek Otáhal	CZE	130.0		117.5	152.5		400.0	
6. Hiroshi Yamazaki	JAP	120.0		120.0	157.5		397.5	
7. Parviz Jalayer	IRN	120.0		120.0	155.0		395.0	
8. Alfred Kornprobst	GER	122.5		112.5	150.0		385.0	

One of the greatest weightlifters of all time, Waldemar Baszanowski defeated Vladimir Kaplunov because he was ten and a half ounces lighter than his rival. Nine months later, at the European championships in Sofia, Bulgaria, the men tied again, and again Baszanowski was awarded first place as a result of his lower bodyweight.

1968 Mexico City C: 20, N: 17, D: 10.15. WR: 440 kg (Waldemar Baszanowski)

			PRESS	SNATCH		JERK		TOTAL KG	
1.	Waldemar Baszanowski	POL	135.0	135.0	EOR	167.5	OR	437.5	OR
2.	Parviz Jalayer	IRN	125.0	132.5		165.0		422.5	
3.	Marian Zieliński	POL	135.0	125.0		160.0		420.0	
4.	Nobuyuki Hatta	JAP	135.0	127.5		155.0		417.5	
5.	Shin-Hee Won	KOR	127.5	125.0		162.5		415.0	
6.	Janós Bagócs	HUN	132.5	122.5		157.5		412.5	
7.	Takeo Kimura	JAP	125.0	120.0		160.0		405.0	
8.	Kostadin Tilev	BUL	132.5	115.0		150.0		397.5	

1972 Munich C: 22, N: 20, D: 8.30. WR: 450 kg (Waldemar Baszanowski)

			PRESS		SNATCH		JERK		TOTAL KG	
1.	Mukharbi Kirzhinov	SOV	147.5		135.0	EOR	177.5	WR	460.0	WR
2.	Mladen Kuchev	BUL	157.5	WR	125.0		167.5		450.0	
3.	Zbigniew Kaczmarek	POL	145.0		125.0		167.5		437.5	
4.	Waldemar Baszanowski	POL	142.5		130.0		162.5		435.0	
5.	Nasrollah Dehnavi	IRN	150.0		125.0		160.0		435.0	
6.	Jenö Ambrózi	HUN	142.5		120.0		165.0		427.5	
7.	Shin-Hee Won	KOR	132.5		130.0		165.0		427.5	
8.	Masao Kato	JAP	140.0		120.0		165.0		425.0	

1976 Montreal C: 23, N: 19, D: 7.21. WR: 312.5 kg (Mukharbi Kirzhinov)

			SNATCH		JERK	TOTAL KG	
–	Zbigniew Kaczmarek	POL	135.0	EOR	172.5	307.5	OR
1.	Piotr Korol	SOV	135.0	EOR	170.0	305.0	
2.	Daniel Senet	FRA	135.0	EOR	165.0	300.0	
3.	Kazimierz Czarnecki	POL	130.0		165.0	295.0	
4.	Gunter Ambrass	GDR	125.0		170.0	295.0	
5.	Yatsuo Shimaya	JAP	127.5		165.0	292.5	
6.	Roberto Urrutia	CUB	130.0		162.5	292.5	
7.	Werner Schraut	GER	127.5		162.5	290.0	
8.	Roland Chavigny	FRA	130.0		155.0	285.0	

Kaczmarek finished first but was subsequently disqualified after a test revealed that he had taken prohibited drugs.

1980 Moscow C: 20, N: 16, D: 7.23. WR: 337.5 kg (Yanko Roussev)

			SNATCH		JERK		TOTAL KG	
1.	Yanko Roussev	BUL	147.5	OR	195.0	WR	342.5	WR
2.	Joachim Kunz	GDR	145.0		190.0		335.0	
3.	Mincho Pachov	BUL	142.5		182.5		325.0	
4.	Daniel Senet	FRA	147.5	OR	175.0		322.5	
5.	Gunter Ambrass	GDR	140.0		180.0		320.0	
6.	Zbigniew Kaczmarek	POL	140.0		177.5		317.5	
7.	Raul Gonzalez	CUB	145.0		172.5		317.5	
8.	Virgel Dociu	ROM	140.0		170.0		310.0	

MIDDLEWEIGHT
(75 kg—165 lbs)

1896–1912 not held

1920 Antwerp C: 11, N: 8, D: 8.28.

		ONE-HAND SNATCH	ONE-HAND JERK	TWO-HAND JERK	TOTAL KG
1. Henri Gance	FRA	65.0	75.0	105.0	245.0
2. Pietro Bianchi	ITA	60.0	70.0	107.5	237.5
3. Albert Pettersson	SWE	55.0	75.0	107.5	237.5
4. Paul Ledran	FRA	55.0	65.0	100.0	220.0
5. M. Ringelberg	HOL	55.0	65.0	100.0	220.0

1924 Paris C: 25, N: 13, D: 7.22.

		ONE-HAND SNATCH	ONE-HAND JERK	TWO-HAND PRESS	TWO-HAND SNATCH	TWO-HAND JERK	TOTAL KG
1. Carlo Galimberti	ITA	77.5	95.0 OR	97.5 WR	95.0	127.5 WR	492.5
2. Alfred Neuland	EST	82.5 WR	90.0	77.5	90.0	115.0	455.0
3. Jaan Kikkas	EST	70.0	87.5	80.0	85.0	127.5 WR	450.0
4. Hamed Samy	EGY	72.5	77.5	97.5 WR	85.0	115.0	447.5
5. Albert Aeschmann	SWI	67.5	87.5	82.5	87.5	117.5	442.5
6. Roger François	FRA	72.0	80.0	87.5	87.5	117.5	442.5
7. R. Eidler	AUT	65.0	90.0	82.5	85.0	115.0	437.5
8. P. Vibert	FRA	72.5	75.0	80.0	85.0	115.0	432.5

1928 Amsterdam C: 23, N: 15, D: 7.29. WR: 320 kg (Carlo Galimberti)

		PRESS	SNATCH	JERK	TOTAL KG	
1. Roger François	FRA	102.5	102.5	130.0	335.0	WR
2. Carlo Galimberti	ITA	105.0 WR	97.5	130.0	332.5	
3. August Scheffer	HOL	97.5	105.0 OR	125.0	327.5	
4. Franz Zinner	GER	87.5	100.0	135.0 OR	322.5	
5. Gaston Le Pût	FRA	92.5	95.0	125.0	312.5	
6. Willy Hofmann	GER	90.0	95.0	120.0	305.0	
7. H. Mouktah	EGY	95.0	92.5	120.0	302.5	
8. J. van Rompey	BEL	92.5	85.0	115.0	292.5	

1932 Los Angeles C: 7, N: 6, D: 7.31. WR: 342.5 kg (Rudolf Ismayr)

		PRESS	SNATCH	JERK	TOTAL KG	
1. Rudolf Ismayr	GER	102.5	110.0 OR	132.5	345.0	WR
2. Carlo Galimberti	ITA	102.5	105.0	132.5	340.0	
3. Karl Hipfinger	AUT	90.0	107.5	140.0 OR	337.5	
4. Roger François	FRA	102.5	102.5	130.0	335.0	
5. Stanley Kratkowski	USA	82.5	102.5	120.0	305.0	
6. Julio Juaneda	ARG	75.0	90.0	120.0	285.0	

1936 Berlin C: 16, N: 12, D: 8.5. WR: 385 kg (Khadr Sayed El Touni)

		PRESS		SNATCH		JERK		TOTAL KG	
1. Khadr Sayed El Touni	EGY	117.5	WR	120.0	WR	150.0	OR	387.5	WR
2. Rudolf Ismayr	GER	107.5		102.5		142.5		352.5	
3. Adolf Wagner	GER	97.5		112.5		142.5		352.5	
4. Anton Hangel	AUT	95.0		110.0		137.5		342.5	
5. Stanley Kratkowski	USA	95.0		107.5		135.0		337.5	
6. Hans Valla	AUT	102.5		102.5		130.0		335.0	
7. Carlo Galimberti	ITA	100.0		102.5		130.0		332.5	
8. Pierre Alleene	FRA	90.0		105.0		135.0		330.0	

Twenty-one-year-old Khadr Sayed El Touni was one of the sensations of the 1936 Olympics. Not only did he outclass his opponents in the Middleweight division, but he actually lifted 15 pounds more than the winner of the Light Heavyweight division. El Touni died of electrocution in 1956 while making a home repair.

1948 London C: 24, N: 18, D: 8.10. WR: 405 kg (Stanley Stanczyk)

		PRESS		SNATCH		JERK		TOTAL KG	
1. Frank Spellman	USA	117.5		120.0		152.5		390.0	OR
2. Peter George	USA	105.0		122.5	OR	155.0	OR	382.5	
3. Sung-Jip Kim	KOR	122.5	OR	112.5		145.0		380.0	
4. Khadr Sayed El Touni	EGY	120.0		117.5		142.5		380.0	
5. Gérard Gratton	CAN	112.5		107.5		140.0		360.0	
6. Pierre Bouladoux	FRA	102.5		110.0		142.5		355.0	
7. O. Garrido Luloaga	CUB	112.5		107.5		135.0		355.0	
8. G. Watson	GBR	100.0		110.0		140.0		350.0	

Peter George's only chance to win the gold medal was to clean and jerk 165 kg—11 pounds more than Stanley Stanczyk's world record. After pacing back and forth for twelve tense minutes, the 19-year-old George rubbed his hands with a block of chalk. Suddenly he crushed the chalk to dust and approached the bar. With great deliberation and concentration, he took hold of the weight, prepared his body, and hoisted the bar to his shoulders. The audience burst into applause, but quieted down quickly as George prepared for the second part of the lift. He pushed the bar overhead, but staggered and dropped it and had to settle for second place.

1952 Helsinki C: 21, N: 20, D: 7.26. WR: 405 kg (Stanley Stanczyk)

		PRESS		SNATCH		JERK		TOTAL KG	
1. Peter George	USA	115.0		127.5	OR	157.5	OR	400.0	OR
2. Gérard Gratton	CAN	122.5	EOR	112.5		155.0		390.0	
3. Sung-Jip Kim	KOR	122.5	EOR	112.5		147.5		382.5	
4. Ismail Ragab	EGY	115.0		117.5		150.0		382.5	
5. Moustafa Laham	LEB	115.0		112.5		142.5		370.0	
6. Åke Hedberg	SWE	102.5		105.0		150.0		357.5	
7. Angel Sposato	ARG	107.5		110.0		140.0		357.5	
8. Djalal Mansouri	IRN	110.0		107.5		140.0		357.5	

1956 Melbourne C: 16, N: 15, D: 11.24. WR: 415 kg (Fyodor Bogdanovsky)

		PRESS		SNATCH		JERK		TOTAL KG	
1. Fyodor Bogdanovsky	SOV	132.5	OR	122.5		165.0	OR	420.0	WR
2. Peter George	USA	122.5		127.5	EOR	162.5		412.5	
3. Ermanno Pignatti	ITA	117.5		117.5		147.5		382.5	
4. Jan Bochenek	POL	120.0		112.5		150.0		382.5	
5. Sung-Jip Kim	KOR	125.0		110.0		145.0		380.0	
6. Krzysztof Beck	POL	122.5		112.5		145.0		380.0	
7. Ebrahim Payravi Reza Kolai	IRN	107.5		117.5		147.5		372.5	
8. Adrien Gilbert	CAN	112.5		115.0		142.5		370.0	

History repeated itself when defending champion Peter George, now a dentist in the U.S. Army, needed a world-record jerk to take first place. He attempted 170 kg, but couldn't make the weight. Nonetheless, his record of one gold and two silver medals is most impressive.

1960 Rome C: 27, N: 20, D: 9.8. WR: 430 kg (Tamio "Tommy" Kono)

		PRESS		SNATCH		JERK		TOTAL KG	
1. Aleksandr Kurynov	SOV	135.0		132.5	OR	170.0	WR	437.5	WR
2. Tamio "Tommy" Kono	USA	140.0	OR	127.5		160.0		427.5	
3. Gyözö Veres	HUN	130.0		120.0		155.0		405.0	
4. Marcel Paterni	FRA	127.5		120.0		152.5		400.0	
5. Krzysztof Beck	POL	135.0		117.5		147.5		400.0	
6. Mohammad Teherani Ami	IRN	117.5		120.0		155.0		392.5	
7. Yung-Chang Koh	KOR	115.0		120.0		150.0		385.0	
8. Lortz Roland	GER	115.0		112.5		155.0		382.5	

Tommy Kono, having already won gold medals as a Lightweight in 1952 and as a Light Heavyweight in 1956, decided to compete in the Middleweight division in 1960 because he had heard that Kurynov was "a very tough opponent." He heard right. The 26-year-old Soviet aviation engineer pulled off the victory and topped it with a world-record clean and jerk on his final attempt.

1964 Tokyo C: 19, N: 17, D: 10.14. WR: 445 kg (Viktor Kurentsov)

		PRESS	SNATCH		JERK		TOTAL KG	
1. Hans Zdražila	CZE	130.0	137.5	OR	177.5	WR	445.0	EWR
2. Viktor Kurentsov	SOV	135.0	130.0		175.0		440.0	
3. Masashi Ouchi	JAP	140.0	135.0		162.5		437.5	
4. Jong-Sup Lee	KOR	130.0	127.5		175.0		432.5	
5. Sadahiro Miwa	JAP	120.0	132.5		170.0		422.5	
6. Mihály Huszka	HUN	135.0	125.0		160.0		420.0	
7. Rolf Maier	FRA	130.0	122.5		165.0		417.5	
8. Veliko Konarov	BUL	130.0	130.0		155.0		415.0	

1968 Mexico City C: 20, N: 17, D: 10.16. WR: 482.5 kg (Viktor Kurentsov)

		PRESS		SNATCH		JERK		TOTAL KG	
1. Viktor Kurentsov	SOV	152.5	OR	135.0		187.5	WR	475.0	OR
2. Masashi Ouchi	JAP	140.0		140.0	OR	175.0		455.0	
3. Károly Bakos	HUN	137.5		132.5		170.0		440.0	

		PRESS	SNATCH		JERK	TOTAL KG	
4. Russell Knipp	USA	147.5	122.5		167.5	437.5	
5. Chun-Sik Lee	KOR	140.0	132.5		165.0	437.5	
6. Werner Dittrich	GDR	140.0	130.0		165.0	435.0	
7. Miroslav Kolarik	CZE	140.0	127.5		162.5	430.0	
8. Fred Lowe	USA	132.5	127.5		170.0	430.0	

In 1964 Kurentsov had entered the Olympics as the holder of the world record. However in Tokyo he suffered an attack of nervousness and completed only four of his nine lifts. Four years later, at the next Olympics, he was a new man. Between lifts he calmly laid on a bed backstage reading Tolstoi. His winning margin was the largest in the Middleweight division since El Touni's great performance in 1936.

1972 Munich C: 26, N: 22, D: 8.31. WR: 482.5 (Viktor Kurentsov)

		PRESS	SNATCH		JERK	TOTAL KG	
1. Yordan Bikov	BUL	160.0	140.0		185.0	485.0	WR
2. Mohamed Trabulsi	LEB	160.0	140.0		172.5	472.5	
3. Anselmo Silvino	ITA	155.0	140.0		175.0	470.0	
4. Ondrej Hekel	CZE	150.0	142.5	EOR	170.0	462.5	
5. Franklin Zielecke	GDR	150.0	140.0		170.0	460.0	
6. Gábor Szarvas	HUN	150.0	135.0		175.0	460.0	
7. András Stark	HUN	152.5	137.5		170.0	460.0	
8. Russell Knipp	USA	160.0	127.5		170.0	457.5	

Vladimir Kanygin of the U.S.S.R. set an Olympic record in the press of 165 kg, but he failed at all three attempts at the snatch and was disqualified.

1976 Montreal C:17, N: 14, D: 7.22. WR: 345 kg (Yordan Mitkov)

		SNATCH		JERK		TOTAL KG	
1. Yordan Mitkov	BUL	145.0	OR	190.0	OR	335.0	OR
2. Vartan Militosyan	SOV	145.0	OR	185.0		330.0	
3. Peter Wenzel	GDR	145.0	OR	182.5		327.5	
4. Wolfgang Hübner	GDR	142.5		177.5		320.0	
– Dragomir Ciorosian	ROM	142.5		177.5		320.0	
5. Arvo Ala-Pöntiö	FIN	137.5		177.5		315.0	
6. András Stark	HUN	140.0		175.0		315.0	
7. Ondrej Hekel	CZE	140.0		172.5		312.5	
8. Daniel Zayas	CUB	140.0		170.0		310.0	

Fifth-place finisher Ciorosian was disqualified for drug use.

1980 Moscow C:16, N: 14, D: 7.24. WR: 355 kg (Assen Zlatev)

		SNATCH		JERK		TOTAL KG	
1. Assen Zlatev	BUL	160.0	OR	200.0	OR	360.0	WR
2. Alexander Pervy	SOV	157.0		200.0	OR	357.5	
3. Nedelcho Kolev	BUL	157.5		187.5		345.0	
4. Julio Echenique Gonzalez	CUB	145.0		182.5		327.5	
5. Dragomir Ciorosian	ROM	140.0		182.5		322.5	
6. Tapio Kinnunen	FIN	142.5		177.5		320.0	
7. Bertil Sollevi	SWE	137.5		172.5		310.0	
8. Newton Burrowes	GBR	130.0		172.5		302.5	

After the formal competition was over, Zlatev jerked 205.5 kg for a new world record.

LIGHT HEAVYWEIGHT
(82.5 kg—181.5 lbs)
1896–1912 not held

1920 Antwerp C: 11, N: 8, D: 8.28.

		ONE-HAND SNATCH	ONE-HAND JERK	TWO-HAND JERK	TOTAL KG
1. Ernest Cadine	FRA	70.0	85.0	135.0	290.0
2. Fritz Hünenberger	SWE	75.0	85.0	115.0	275.0
3. Erik Pettersson	SWE	62.5	92.5	117.5	272.5
4. Erik Carlsson	SWE	67.5	75.0	120.0	262.5
5. Maurice Davéne	FRA	65.0	70.0	115.0	250.0

1924 Paris C: 20, N: 12, D: 7.23.

		ONE-HAND SNATCH	ONE-HAND JERK	TWO-HAND PRESS	TWO-HAND SNATCH	TWO-HAND JERK	TOTAL KG
1. Charles Rigoulot	FRA	87.5 OR	92.5	85.0	102.5	135.0	502.5
2. Fritz Hünenberger	SWI	80.0	107.5 WR	80.0	97.5	125.0	490.0
3. Leopold Friedrich	AUT	75.0	95.0	95.0	95.0	130.0	490.0
4. Karl Freiberger	AUT	75.0	95.0	92.5	95.0	130.0	487.5
5. Carlos Bergara	ARG	80.0	85.0	92.5	97.5	127.5	482.5
6. Mario Giambelli	ITA	77.5	95.0	82.5	95.0	130.0	480.0
7. A. Schaerer	SWI	75.0	85.0	100.0	95.0	120.0	475.0
8. Jaroslav Skobla	CZE	70.0	95.0	92.5	85.0	127.5	470.0

1928 Amsterdam C: 15, N: 10, D: 7.29. WR: 350 kg (Jakob Vogt)

		PRESS	SNATCH	JERK	TOTAL KG	
1. El Sayed Nosseir	EGY	100.0 EOR	112.5 OR	142.5 WR	355.0	WR
2. Louis Hostin	FRA	100.0 EOR	110.0	142.5 WR	352.5	
3. Johannes Verheijen	HOL	95.0	105.0	137.5	337.5	
4. Václav Pšenička	CZE	100.0 EOR	105.0	130.0	335.0	
4. Jakob Vogt	GER	100.0 EOR	105.0	130.0	335.0	
6. Karl Freiberger	AUT	95.0	95.0	132.5	322.5	
7. Karl Bierwirth	GER	95.0	95.0	125.0	315.0	
7. Josef Zemann	AUT	75.0	105.0	135.0	315.0	
7. P. Vibert	FRA	95.0	95.0	125.0	315.0	

El Sayed Nosseir caused quite a sensation due to his prelift ritual of raising his arms and head to the sky and calling out for Allah's assistance. A minor incident occurred during the award ceremony when the band struck up the Austrian national anthem by mistake instead of the French "Marseillaise." There were chuckles throughout the crowd, but the French were not amused.

1932 Los Angeles C: 4, N: 3, D: 7.31. WR: 365 kg (Jakob Vogt)

		PRESS	SNATCH	JERK	TOTAL KG	
1. Louis Hostin	FRA	102.5 OR	112.5 EOR	150.0 OR	365.0	EWR
2. Svend Olsen	DEN	102.5 OR	107.5	150.0 OR	360.0	
3. Henry Duey	USA	92.5	105.0	132.5	330.0	
4. William Good	USA	95.0	97.5	130.0	322.5	

Hostin was so confident of victory that he traded jokes with the referee while he was lifting.

1936 Berlin C: 14, N: 9, D: 8.3. WR: 375 kg (Fritz Haller)

		PRESS		SNATCH		JERK		TOTAL KG	
1. Louis Hostin	FRA	110.0	OR	117.5	OR	145.0		372.5	OR
2. Eugen Deutsch	GER	105.0		110.0		150.0	OR	365.0	
3. Ibrahim Wasif	EGY	100.0		110.0		150.0	OR	360.0	
4. Helmut Opschruf	GER	97.5		110.0		147.5		355.0	
5. Nicolas Scheitler	LUX	105.0		105.0		140.0		350.0	
6. Fritz Haller	AUT	97.5		110.0		142.5		350.0	
7. William Good	USA	100.0		105.0		145.0		350.0	
8. Ahmed Geissa	EGY	95.0		110.0		142.5		347.5	

Eugen Deutsch was originally disqualified for missing all three of his snatch attempts. An hour later the Jury of Appeal validated one of his snatches, giving him the silver medal and causing resentment among many non-German observers.

1948 London C: 16, N: 13, D: 8.11. WR: 425 kg (Grigory Novack)

		PRESS		SNATCH		JERK		TOTAL KG	
1. Stanley Stanczyk	USA	130.0	OR	130.0	OR	157.5	OR	417.5	OR
2. Harold Sakata	USA	110.0		117.5		152.5		380.0	
3. Gösta Magnusson	SWE	110.0		120.0		145.0		375.0	
4. Jean Debuf	FRA	107.5		112.5		150.0		370.0	
5. Osvaldo Forte	ARG	105.0		115.0		147.5		367.5	
6. James Varaleau	CAN	112.5		112.5		140.0		365.0	
7. Juhani Vellamo	FIN	100.0		115.0		140.0		355.0	
8. S. Raissi	IRN	110.0		110.0		135.0		355.0	

Stanczyk made a great impression on the audience, not only because of his superior lifting, but because of his outstanding sportsmanship. With his third snatch he attempted a new world record of 132.5 kg. He successfully hoisted the weight and the judges signaled a fair lift. However Stanczyk shook his head and tapped his leg to indicate that his knee had scraped the floor, thus invalidating his lift. Despite this miss, his eventual winning margin of 37.5 kg. was the largest in any division in Olympic history.

Stanley Stanczyk was a well-known figure in weightlifting circles, but the man who really achieved fame was silver medalist Harold Sakata. After completing a successful career as a professional wrestler (using the name Tosh Togo), Sakata became an actor. He eventually reached international stardom in the role of Oddjob in the James Bond film *Goldfinger*.

1952 Helsinki C: 22, N: 19, D: 7.27. WR: 425 kg (Grigory Novack)

		PRESS	SNATCH	JERK		TOTAL KG	
1. Trofim Lomakin	SOV	125.0	127.5	165.0	OR	417.5	EOR
2. Stanley Stanczyk	USA	127.5	127.5	160.0		415.0	
3. Arkady Vorobyev	SOV	120.0	127.5	160.0		407.5	
4. Mohamad Hassan Rahnavardi	IRN	120.0	122.5	160.0		402.5	
5. Jean Debuf	FRA	117.5	122.5	160.0		400.0	
6. Issy Bloomberg	SAF	127.5	115.0	150.0		392.5	
7. Osvaldo Forte	ARG	112.5	115.0	155.0		382.5	
8. Clyde Emrich	USA	120.0	115.0	145.0		380.0	

The 1952 Light Heavyweight competition was an excellent three-way contest which unfortunately got caught up in the Cold War. The United States fired the first salvo when they lodged a protest after American Clyde Emrich had a press of 120 kg disallowed. After much fussing and arguing by U.S. officials, Emrich went ahead and made the weight at his next attempt. Then Stanczyk was given credit for a press of 127.5 kg and the Soviets claimed that he had leaned back too far for a legal press. The judges voted 2–1 in Stanczyk's favor. When Vorobyev lost consciousness during his last press attempt, the Americans accused the Russians of drugging their lifters. At the end of the press, Stanczyk led Lomakin by 2.5 kg. Lomakin and Vorobyev both snatched 127.5 kg. at their first attempt, while Stanczyk achieved the weight only at his last try. However, both Soviet lifters failed twice at 132.5 kg. So, with only the jerk left, Stanczyk still led Lomakin by 2.5 kg. All three leaders successfully jerked 160 kg. Both Stanczyk and Lomakin missed at 165 kg, but Lomakin had one more attempt left to him. This time he made the weight and moved into first place.

Then came Vorobyev's turn. He decided to go for broke and called for 170 kg—a world record. Vorobyev approached the bar, took hold of it, raised it a couple inches and dropped it again. An argument immediately broke out as to whether his action should be counted as an official attempt. Vorobyev shut out the commotion and prepared himself for another try. When he turned again to the bar, silence returned. He heaved the weight onto his chest and thrust it into the air at arm's length. "Although my muscles strained to the very limit," Vorobyev later wrote, "my heart was singing. I had done it! I had won!" The audience roared with excitement. But then Vorobyev staggered and dropped the bar just as the referee called out, "Release." One judge ruled that it had been a valid lift, but the other two rejected it. Forty minutes of arguing ensued, until finally the results were announced: Lomakin first, Stanczyk second, Vorobyev third.

Vorobyev returned to the dressing room in a deep depression and began slowly to undress. Suddenly his coach burst into the room and told him that he had been awarded one more attempt. But Vorobyev was unprepared. He needed more time to compose himself and warm up, but the officials had already started the clock. Forced to hurry back to the platform, he was unable to handle the weight a second time and fell backward, with the bar pinning him to the floor. The Soviets continued to argue that Vorobyev had been forced to hold his previous lift for more than two seconds, but the results were allowed to stand.

1956 Melbourne C: 10, N: 9, D: 11.26. WR: 435 kg (Tamio "Tommy" Kono)

		PRESS		SNATCH		JERK		TOTAL KG	
1. Tamio "Tommy" Kono	USA	140.0	OR	132.5	OR	175.0	WR	447.5	WR
2. Vassily Stepanov	SOV	135.0		130.0		162.5		427.5	
3. James George	USA	120.0		130.0		167.5		417.5	
4. Mirjalal Ghafarzadeh Mansuri	IRN	132.5		122.5		162.5		417.5	
5. Philip Caira	GBR	127.5		122.5		155.0		405.0	
6. Václav Pšenička	CZE	125.0		120.0		155.0		400.0	
7. Marcel Paterni	FRA	132.5		115.0		147.5		395.0	
8. John Powell	AUS	120.0		117.5		145.0		382.5	

1960 Rome C: 25, N: 22, D: 9.9. WR: 457.5 kg (Rudolf Plukfelder)

		PRESS	SNATCH		JERK		TOTAL KG
1. Ireneusz Paliński	POL	130.0	132.5	EOR	180.0	WR	442.5
2. James George	USA	132.5	132.5	EOR	165.0		430.0
3. Jan Bochenek	POL	130.0	120.0		170.0		420.0
4. Géza Tóth	HUN	125.0	125.0		167.5		417.5
5. Jouni Kailajärvi	FIN	130.0	125.0		162.5		417.5
6. Peter Tachev	BUL	130.0	125.0		160.0		415.0
7. Minoru Kubota	JAP	125.0	120.0		155.0		400.0
8. Willy Claes	BEL	125.0	112.5		155.0		392.5

1964 Tokyo C: 24, N: 21, D: 10.16. WR: 477.5 kg (Győző Veres)

		PRESS		SNATCH		JERK		TOTAL KG	
1. Rudolf Plukfelder	SOV	150.0		142.5	OR	182.5		475.0	OR
2. Géza Tóth	HUN	145.0		137.5		185.0	OR	467.5	
3. Győző Veres	HUN	155.0	OR	135.0		177.5		467.5	
4. Jerzy Kaczkowski	POL	145.0		135.0		167.5		455.0	

5. Gary Cleveland	USA	152.5	135.0	167.5	455.0
6. Hyung-Woo Lee	KOR	145.0	132.5	175.0	452.5
7. Kaarlo Kangasniemi	FIN	150.0	135.0	165.0	450.0
8. Karl Arnold	GDR	140.0	132.5	167.5	435.0

1968 Mexico City C: 26, N: 22, D: 10.17. WR: 485 kg (Vladimir Belyayev)

		PRESS	SNATCH		JERK		TOTAL KG	
1. Boris Selitsky	SOV	150.0	147.5	OR	187.5	OR	485.0	EWR
2. Vladimir Belyayev	SOV	152.5	147.5	OR	185.0		485.0	EWR
3. Norbert Ozimek	POL	150.0	140.0		182.5		472.5	
4. Gyözö Veres	HUN	150.0	140.0		182.5		472.5	
5. Karl Arnold	GDR	155.0	137.5		175.0		467.5	
6. Hans Zdražila	CZE	135.0	147.5	OR	180.0		462.5	
7. Jouni Kailajärvi	FIN	140.0	130.0		175.0		445.0	
8. Jong-Sup Lee	KOR	135.0	130.0		175.0		440.0	

1972 Munich C: 24, N: 21, D: 9.2. WR: 527.5 kg (Valery Shary)

		PRESS		SNATCH		JERK		TOTAL KG	
1. Leif Jenssen	NOR	172.5	OR	150.0	OR	185.0		507.5	OR
2. Norbert Ozimek	POL	165.0		145.0		187.5		497.5	
3. György Horváth	HUN	160.0		142.5		192.5	OR	495.0	
4. Bernhard Radtke	GDR	162.5		145.0		185.0		492.5	
5. Christos Iakovou	GRE	170.0		137.5		182.5		490.0	
6. Kaarlo Kangasniemi	FIN	150.0		145.0		185.0		480.0	
7. Rolf Milser	GER	165.0		132.5		180.0		477.5	
8. Juhani Avellan	FIN	140.0		145.0		182.5		467.5	

The two Soviet representatives, world champion Boris Pavlov and world record holder Valery Shary, were so intent on beating each other that they started pressing at too high a weight. Both men missed all three attempts and were disqualified. Representing Israel was 28-year-old David Berger, originally of Shaker Heights, Ohio. The next day, Berger was one of the 11 Israelis who were killed by terrorists.

1976 Montreal C: 17, N: 14, D: 7.24. WR: 372.5 kg (Trendafil Stoichev)

		SNATCH		JERK		TOTAL KG	
1. Valery Shary	SOV	162.5	OR	202.5	OR	365.0	OR
– Blagoi Blagoev	BUL	162.5	OR	200.0		362.5	
2. Trendafil Stoichev	BUL	162.5	OR	197.5		360.0	
3. Péter Baczako	HUN	157.5		187.5		345.0	
4. Nicolaos Iliadis	GRE	150.0		190.0		340.0	
5. Juhani Avellan	FIN	145.0		185.0		330.0	
6. Stefan Jacobsson	SWE	147.5		170.0		317.5	
7. Sueo Fujishiro	JAP	140.0		175.0		315.0	
8. Gerd Kennel	GER	135.0		177.5		312.5	

Blagoev was disqualified for using prohibited drugs.

1980 Moscow C: 14, N: 12, D: 7.26. WR: 390 kg (Yurik Vardanyan)

		SNATCH		JERK		TOTAL KG	
1. Yurik Vardanyan	SOV	177.5	WR	222.5	WR	400.0	WR
2. Blagoi Blagoev	BUL	175.0		197.5		372.5	
3. Dušan Poliačik	CZE	160.0		207.5		367.5	
4. Jan Lisowski	POL	150.0		205.0		355.0	
5. Krassimir Drăndarov	BUL	155.0		200.0		355.0	
6. Pawel Rabczewski	POL	155.0		195.0		350.0	
7. Detlef Blasche	GDR	152.5		192.5		345.0	
8. Juhani Avellan	FIN	150.0		182.5		332.5	

MIDDLE HEAVYWEIGHT
(90 kg—198.25 lbs)
1896–1948 not held

1952 Helsinki C: 20, N: 20, D: 7.27. WR: 427.5 kg (Norbert Schemansky)

		PRESS		SNATCH		JERK		TOTAL KG	
1. Norbert Schemansky	USA	127.5		140.0	WR	177.5	WR	445.0	WR
2. Grigory Novak	SOV	140.0	OR	125.0		145.0		410.0	
3. Lennox Kilgour	TRI	125.0		120.0		157.5		402.5	
4. Mohammed Ibrahim Saleh	EGY	110.0		125.0		162.5		397.5	
5. Firouz Pojhan	IRN	112.5		120.0		155.0		387.5	
6. Kenneth McDonald	AUS	107.5		125.0		152.5		385.0	
7. Francisco Rensonnet	ARG	107.5		112.5		150.0		370.0	
8. Theunis Jonck	SAF	112.5		110.0		145.0		367.5	

The 5-foot 3½-inch, 195-pound Novak was hampered by a leg injury, but it is very doubtful that he could have beaten Detroit's Norbert Schemansky, who upped his own world record by 38½ pounds. Schemansky eventually won four Olympic medals in his career—more than any other weightlifter.

1956 Melbourne C: 15, N: 14, D: 11.26. WR: 460 kg (Arkady Vorobyov)

		PRESS		SNATCH	JERK		TOTAL KG	
1. Arkady Vorobyov	SOV	147.5	WR	137.5	177.5	EOR	462.5	WR
2. David Sheppard	USA	140.0		137.5	165.0		442.5	
3. Jean Debuf	FRA	130.0		127.5	167.5		425.0	
4. Mohamad Hassan Rahnavardi	IRN	140.0		127.5	157.5		425.0	
5. Ivan Veselinov	BUL	132.5		120.0	155.0		407.5	
6. Kim-Bee Tan	MAL	117.5		122.5	155.0		395.0	
7. Lennox Kilgour	TRI	127.5		117.5	145.0		390.0	
8. Leonard Treganowan	AUS	122.5		117.5	150.0		390.0	

A former deep-sea diver, Vorobyov made up for his disappointment in the controversial 1952 Light Heavyweight competition. He later became a doctor, wrote several textbooks on weightlifting, and served as coach of the Soviet team.

1960 Rome C: 20, N: 17, D: 9.9. WR: 470 kg (Arkady Vorobyov)

		PRESS		SNATCH		JERK		TOTAL KG	
1. Arkady Vorobyov	SOV	152.5		142.5	OR	177.5	EOR	472.5	WR
2. Trofim Lomakin	SOV	157.5	WR	130.0		170.0		457.5	
3. Louis Martin	GBR	137.5		137.5		170.0		445.0	
4. John Pulskamp	USA	140.0		125.0		167.5		432.5	
5. François Vincent	FRA	130.0		132.5		160.0		422.5	
6. Vladimir Savov	BUL	110.0		137.5		165.0		412.5	
7. Czeslaw Bialas	POL	130.0		122.5		157.5		410.0	
8. Leonardo Masu	ITA	135.0		117.5		155.0		407.5	

1964 Tokyo C: 19, N: 18, D: 10.17. WR: 480 kg (Louis Martin)

		PRESS		SNATCH		JERK		TOTAL KG	
1. Vladimir Golovanov	SOV	165.0	OR	142.5	EOR	180.0		487.5	WR
2. Louis Martin	GBR	155.0		140.0		180.0		475.0	
3. Ireneusz Paliński	POL	150.0		135.0		182.5	OR	467.5	
4. William March	USA	155.0		135.0		177.5		467.5	
5. Lazăr Baroga	ROM	145.0		135.0		180.0		460.0	
6. Árpád Nemessányi	HUN	140.0		142.5	EOR	177.5		460.0	
7. Jouni Kailajärvi	FIN	145.0		127.5		180.0		452.5	
8. Peter Tachev	BUL	145.0		130.0		170.0		445.0	

1968 Mexico City C: 29, N: 22, D: 10.18. WR: 522.5 kg (Kaarlo Kangasniemi)

		PRESS		SNATCH		JERK		TOTAL KG	
1. Kaarlo Kangasniemi	FIN	172.5	OR	157.5	WR	187.5		517.5	OR
2. Jan Taits	SOV	160.0		150.0		197.5	WR	507.5	
3. Marek Gołąb	POL	165.0		145.0		185.0		495.0	
4. Bo Johansson	SWE	165.0		145.0		182.5		492.5	
5. Jaako Kailajärvi	FIN	145.0		150.0		190.0		485.0	
6. Árpád Nemessányi	HUN	150.0		145.0		187.5		482.5	
7. Philip Grippaldi	USA	155.0		137.5		185.0		477.5	
8. Viteslav Orszag	CZE	157.5		130.0		175.0		462.5	

1972 Munich C: 23, N: 15, D: 9.3. WR: 562.5 kg (David Rigert)

		PRESS	SNATCH	JERK		TOTAL KG	
1. Andon Nikolov	BUL	180.0	155.0	190.0		525.0	OR
2. Atanas Shopov	BUL	180.0	145.0	192.5		517.5	
3. Hans Bettembourg	SWE	182.5	145.0	185.0		512.5	
4. Philip Grippaldi	USA	170.0	140.0	195.0		505.0	
5. Patrick Holbrook	USA	162.5	145.0	197.5	EOR	505.0	
6. Nicolo Ciancio	AUS	170.0	145.0	190.0		505.0	
7. Juan Curbelo	CUB	172.5	140.0	182.5		495.0	
8. Jaakko Kailajervi	FIN	150.0	150.0	187.5		487.5	

The clear favorite, world record holder David Rigert of Chatkhi, set an Olympic record in the press of 187.5 kg. However he failed at all three of his attempts to snatch 160 kg, despite the fact that he held the world record of 167.5 kg. Rigert was so upset that he literally pulled his hair out and banged his head against a wall. He was finally restrained by his colleagues, but the next day he threw another fit and had to be sent home. Gold-medal-winner Andon Nikolov was a former troublemaker who was introduced to weightlifting in reform school.

1976 Montreal C: 19, N: 16, D: 7.25. WR: 400 kg (David Rigert)

			SNATCH		JERK		TOTAL KG	
1.	David Rigert	SOV	170.0	OR	212.5	OR	382.5	OR
2.	Lee James	USA	165.0		197.5		362.5	
3.	Atanas Shopov	BUL	155.0		205.0		360.0	
–	Philip Grippaldi	USA	150.0		205.0		355.0	
4.	György Rehus	HUN	157.5		192.5		350.0	
5.	Peter Petzold	GDR	152.5		192.5		345.0	
6.	Alberto Blanco	CUB	152.5		192.5		345.0	
7.	Yvon Coussin	FRA	152.5		180.0		332.5	
8.	Gudmundur Sigurdsson	ICE	145.0		187.5		332.5	

Rigert, the heaviest man to snatch twice his bodyweight, had no reason to lose any hair this time in Montreal, as his excellent lifting gave him a comfortable victory. Fourth-place finisher Philip Grippaldi failed the urine test for drugs.

1980 Moscow C: 18, N: 16, D: 7.27. WR: 400 kg (David Rigert)

			SNATCH		JERK	TOTAL KG
1.	Péter Baczako	HUN	170.0	EOR	207.5	377.5
2.	Roumen Aleksandrov	BUL	170.0	EOR	205.0	375.0
3.	Frank Mantek	GDR	165.0		205.0	370.0
4.	Dalibor Rehak	CZE	165.0		200.0	365.0
5.	Witold Walo	POL	160.0		200.0	360.0
6.	Lubomír Sršeň	CZE	160.0		197.5	357.5
7.	Vasile Groapa	ROM	160.0		195.0	355.0
8.	Nicolaos Iliadis	GRE	150.0		195.0	345.0

David Rigert reverted to his form of eight years earlier when he started snatching at 170 kg, failed at all three attempts, and was eliminated.

100 KG
(220.25 lbs)
1896–1976 not held

1980 Moscow C: 17, N: 13, D: 7.28. WR: 402.5 kg (David Rigert)

			SNATCH		JERK		TOTAL KG	
1.	Ota Zaremba	CZE	180.0	OR	215.0		395.0	OR
2.	Igor Nikitin	SOV	177.5		215.0		392.5	
3.	Alberto Blanco Fernandez	CUB	172.5		212.5		385.0	
4.	Michael Hennig	GDR	165.0		217.5	OR	382.5	
5.	János Sólyomvári	HUN	175.0		205.0		380.0	
6.	Manfred Funke	GDR	170.0		207.0		377.5	
7.	Anton Baraniak	CZE	165.0		210.0		375.0	
8.	László Varga	HUN	172.5		195.0		367.5	

HEAVYWEIGHT

(110 kg—242.5 lbs)

1896–1968 not held

1972 Munich C: 26, N: 19, D: 9.22. WR: 590 kg (Valery Yakubovsky)

			PRESS		SNATCH	JERK	TOTAL KG	
1.	Yan Talts	SOV	210.0	OR	165.0	205.0	580.0	OR
2.	Alexander Kraichev	BUL	197.5		162.5	202.5	562.5	
3.	Stefan Grützner	GDR	185.0		162.5	207.5	555.0	
4.	Helmut Losch	GDR	190.0		152.5	205.0	547.5	
5.	Roberto Vezzani	ITA	192.5		147.5	205.0	545.0	
6.	János Hanzlik	HUN	190.0		157.5	195.0	542.5	
7.	Kauko Kangasniemi	FIN	175.0		165.0	197.5	537.5	
8.	Rainer Dörrzapf	GER	170.0		165.0	187.5	522.5	

1976 Montreal C: 22 N: 18, D: 7.26. WR: 417.5 kg (Valentin Hristov)

			SNATCH	JERK	TOTAL KG
—	Valentin Hristov	BUL	175.0	225.0	400.0
1.	Yuri Zaitsev	SOV	165.0	220.0	385.0
2.	Krustiu Semerdzhiev	BUL	170.0	215.0	385.0
3.	Tadeusz Rutkowski	POL	167.5	210.0	377.5
—	Mark Cameron	USA	162.5	212.5	375.0
4.	Pierre Gourrier	FRA	157.5	215.0	372.5
5.	Jürgen Ciezki	GDR	162.5	210.0	372.5
6.	Javier Gonzalez	CUB	160.0	205.0	365.0
7.	Leif Nilsson	SWE	157.5	207.5	365.0
8.	Rudolf Strejcek	CZE	162.5	200.0	362.5

Both Hristov and Cameron were disqualified as a result of positive drug tests.

1980 Moscow C: 13, N: 13, D: 7.29. WR: 420 kg (Leonid Taraneko)

			SNATCH		JERK		TOTAL KG	
1.	Leonid Taranenko	SOV	182.5		240.0	WR	422.5	WR
2.	Valentin Hristov	BUL	185.0	OR	220.0		405.0	
3.	György Szalai	HUN	172.5		217.5		390.0	
4.	Leif Nilsson	SWE	167.5		212.5		380.0	
5.	Vinzenz Hortnagl	AUT	170.0		202.5		372.5	
6.	Stefan Tasnadi	ROM	165.0		195.0		360.0	
7.	Donald Mitchell	AUS	162.5		190.0		352.5	
8.	Dimitrios Zarzavatsidis	GRE	155.0		192.5		347.5	

SUPER HEAVYWEIGHT—UNLIMITED WEIGHT

(Heavyweight 1896–1968)

1896 Athens C: 6, N: 5, D: 4.7.
One-Hand Lift

			KG
1.	Launceston Elliot	GBR	71.0
2.	Viggo Jensen	DEN	57.2
3.	Alexandros Nitolopoulos	GRE	57.2

Two-Hand Lift

		KG
1. Viggo Jensen	DEN	111.5
2. Launceston Elliot	GBR	111.5
3. Carl Schuhmann	GER	100.0
3. Sotirios Versis	GRE	100.0

The first instance of an Olympic judging controversy occurred in the two-handed lift. Jensen and Elliot tied at 111.5 kg, but the Dane was awarded first place as a result of his better style, Elliot having moved one foot while lifting. Jensen was quite a versatile athlete. In addition to winning the weightlifting competition, he also finished second in the free pistol, third in the military rifle, and fourth in the rope climb.

1900 Paris not held

1904 St. Louis C: 4, N: 2, D: 9.3.
Two-Hand Lift

		KG
1. Perikles Kakousis	GRE	111.70
2. Oscar Osthoff	USA	84.37
3. Frank Kungler	USA	79.61
4. Oscar Olson	USA	67.81

1904 St. Louis C: 3, N: 1, D: 9.3.
All-Around Dumbbell Contest

		KG
1. Oscar Osthoff	USA	48 points
2. Frederick Winters	USA	45 points
3. Frank Kungler	USA	10 points

The all-around dumbbell contest, won by Oscar Osthoff of Milwaukee, consisted of nine different types of lifts as well as an optional section.

1906 Athens C: 12, N: 7, D: 4.27.
One-Hand Lift

		KG
1. Josef Steinbach	AUT	76.55
2. Tullio Camilotti	ITA	73.75
3. Heinrich Schneidereit	GER	70.75
4. Carl Svensson	SWE	65.45
5. Alexandre Maspoli	FRA	65.45
6. I. Varanakis	GRE	60.40
6. M. Dubois	BEL	60.40
6. Heinrich Rondi	GER	60.40

1906 Athens C: 10, N: 6, D: 4.27.
Two-Hand Lift

		KG
1. Dimitrios Tofalos	GRE	142.5
2. Josef Steinbach	AUT	136.5
3. Alexandre Maspoli	FRA	129.5
3. Heinrich Rondi	GER	129.5
3. Heinrich Schneidereit	GER	129.5
6. Perikles Kakousis	GRE	121.5

Josef Steinbach caused a stir when he objected to the rules in the two-hand lift which required that the bar be raised straight to the shoulders before being brought overhead. Steinbach wanted to use the continental style, which allowed him to rest the weight at his waist before moving it to his shoulders. After Tofalos had won the competition and the jury had departed, Steinbach walked back to the bar and, using the forbidden style, lifted it easily over his head. The sportsmanlike Greek crowd, unaware of the rules, thought that Steinbach had been cheated of victory.

Tofalos, the son of a count, had been run over by a wagon as a young boy. His upper arm was crushed and doctors wanted to amputate it, but Tofalos' father wouldn't allow it. Dimitrios recovered the use of his arm even though it was two and a half inches shorter than his uninjured arm. After winning at the Olympics, Tofalas turned professional and eventually went to America, where he entered vaudeville and became a wrestler. In a match against world champion Frank Gotch, Tofalos got caught in one of Gotch's famous toe-holds, but refused to submit. His stubbornness cost him six months in the hospital with a dislocated hip. Tofalos became a U.S. citizen in 1921 and remained a popular figure in professional wrestling and physical culture circles for the rest of his life.

1908–1912 not held

1920 Antwerp C: 10, N: 8, D: 8.28.

		PRESS	SNATCH	JERK	TOTAL KG
1. Filippo Bottino	ITA	70.0	85.0	115.0	270.0
2. Joseph Alzin	LUX	65.0	80.0	110.0	255.0
3. Louis Bernot	FRA	65.0	75.0	110.0	250.0
4. Erik Jensen	DEN	60.0	75.0	115.0	250.0
5. Richard Brunn	SWE	60.0	80.0	110.0	250.0
6. Joseph Duchâteau	FRA	65.0	72.5	110.0	247.5

1924 Paris C: 19, N:12, D: 7.24.

		ONE-HAND SNATCH	ONE-HAND JERK		PRESS	TWO-HAND SNATCH	TWO-HAND JERK		TOTAL KG
1. Giuseppe Tonani	ITA	80.0	95.0		112.5	100.0	130.0		517.5
2. Franz Aigner	AUT	80.0	97.5	OR	112.5	95.0	130.0		515.0
3. Harold Tammer	EST	75.0	95.0		90.0	97.5	140.0	OR	497.5
4. Louis Dannoux	FRA	80.0	95.0		87.5	100.0	135.0		497.5
5. Karlis Leilands	LAT	77.5	87.5		100.0	100.0	132.5		497.5
6. Filippo Bottino	ITA	77.5	85.0		110.0	97.5	125.0		495.0
7. K. Raag	EST	80.0	92.5		90.0	97.5	130.0		490.0
8. C. Dutrieve	FRA	75.0	82.5		90.0	100.0	OR	120.0	467.5

1928 Amsterdam C: 17, N: 11, D: 7.29.

		PRESS		SNATCH		JERK		TOTAL KG	
1. Josef Strassberger	GER	122.5	OR	107.5		142.5		372.5	WR
2. Arnold Luhäär	EST	100.0		110.0	OR	150.0	OR	360.0	
3. Jaroslav Skobla	CZE	100.0		107.5		150.0	OR	357.5	
4. Karlis Leilands	LAT	110.0		105.0		140.0		355.0	
5. Josef Leppelt	AUT	105.0		110.0	OR	140.0		355.0	
6. Rudolf Schilberg	AUT	115.0		105.0		135.0		355.0	
7. Guiseppe Tonani	ITA	117.5		97.5		137.5		352.5	
8. Hermann Volz	GER	97.5		110.0		132.5		340.0	

1932 Los Angeles C: 6, N: 4, D: 7.30. WR: 400 kg (Mohamed Sayed Nosseir)

		PRESS		SNATCH		JERK		TOTAL KG	
1. Jaroslav Skobla	CZE	112.5		115.0		152.5	OR	380.0	OR
2. Václav Pšenička	CZE	112.5		117.5	OR	147.5		377.5	
3. Josef Strassberger	GER	125.0	OR	110.0		142.5		377.5	
4. Marcel Dumoulin	FRA	95.0		107.5		140.0		342.5	
5. Albert Manger	USA	100.0		92.5		122.5		315.0	
6. Howard Turbyfill	USA	77.5		95.0		132.5		305.0	

Twenty-four years later, Skobla's son Jiří won the bronze medal in the shot put at Melbourne.

1936 Berlin C: 13, N: 9, D: 8.5. WR: 407.5 kg (Vaclav Psenicka)

		PRESS		SNATCH		JERK		TOTAL KG	
1. Josef Manger	GER	132.5	OR	122.5		155.0		410.0	WR
2. Václav Pšenička	CZE	122.5		125.0		155.0		402.5	
3. Arnold Luhäär	EST	115.0		120.0		165.0	OR	400.0	
4. Ronald Walker	GBR	110.0		127.5	OR	160.0		397.5	
5. Hussein Mokhtar	EGY	112.5		122.5		160.0		395.0	
6. Josef Zemann	AUT	110.0		122.5		155.0		387.5	
7. Paul Wahl	GER	115.0		110.0		150.0		375.0	
8. Rudolf Shilberg	AUT	125.0		107.5		140.0		372.5	

1948 London C: 16, N: 14, D: 8.11. WR: 455 kg (John Davis)

		PRESS		SNATCH		JERK		TOTAL KG	
1. John Davis	USA	137.5	OR	137.5	OR	177.5	WR	452.5	OR
2. Norbert Schemansky	USA	122.5		132.5		170.0		425.0	
3. Abraham Charité	HOL	127.5		125.0		160.0		412.5	
4. Alfred Knight	GBR	117.5		117.5		155.0		390.0	
5. Hanafi Mustafa	EGY	120.0		115.0		150.0		385.0	
6. Niels Petersen	DEN	115.0		112.5		155.0		382.5	
7. Robert Allart	BEL	122.5		110.0		145.0		377.5	
8. P. Taljaard	SAF	117.5		112.5		145.0		375.0	

1952 Helsinki C: 13, N: 11, D: 7.27. WR: 482.5 kg (John Davis)

		PRESS		SNATCH		JERK	TOTAL KG	
1. John Davis	USA	150.0	OR	145.0	OR	165.0	460.0	OR
2. James Bradford	USA	140.0		132.5		165.0	437.5	
3. Humberto Selvetti	ARG	150.0	OR	120.0		162.5	432.5	
4. Heinz Schattner	GER	130.0		130.0		162.5	422.5	
5. William David Baillie	CAN	145.0		122.5		152.5	420.0	
6. Norberto Ferreira	ARG	140.0		115.0		155.0	410.0	
7. R. Harold Cleghorn	NZE	130.0		117.5		152.5	400.0	
8. Franz Hölbl	AUT	115.0		117.5		155.0	387.5	

John Davis of Brooklyn was never bested in Olympic competition in either the press, the snatch, or the jerk.

1956 Melbourne C: 9, N: 9, D: 11.26. WR: 519.5 kg (Paul Anderson)

		PRESS		SNATCH		JERK		TOTAL KG	
1. Paul Anderson	USA	167.5		145.0	EOR	187.5	OR	500.0	OR
2. Humberto Selvetti	ARG	175.0	OR	145.0	EOR	180.0		500.0	OR
3. Alberto Pigaiani	ITA	150.0		130.0		172.5		452.5	
4. Firouz Pojhan	IRN	147.5		132.5		170.0		450.0	
5. Eino Mäkinen	FIN	127.5		137.5		167.5		432.5	
6. William David Baillie	CAN	147.5		122.5		162.5		432.5	
7. Franz Hölbl	AUT	142.5		125.0		157.5		425.0	
8. Richard Jones	NZE	125.0		122.5		150.0		397.5	

What had been expected to be an easy victory for Paul Anderson of Toccoa, Georgia, developed instead into a dramatic showdown between Anderson and 1952's bronze medalist, Humberto Selvetti of Argentina. Selvetti surprised the audience by taking the lead in the press with a lift of 175 kg, after Anderson had missed twice at 172.5 kg. When it came time for the jerk, Selvetti was still ahead by 7.5 kg. Anderson watched as Selvetti successfully jerked 170 kg and 180 kg before missing at 185. Anderson, deciding to go straight for the victory, called for 187.5 kg for his first attempt. He failed. He tried it a second time, but missed again. Now he was down to one last lift that would determine if he would finish first or last. Straining heroically, Anderson balanced the weight above his head and finished the competition with a weight total of 500 kg, exactly the same as that of Humberto Selvetti. Paul Anderson was a huge man who weighed in at 303¼ pounds. (137.9 kg) after losing 60 pounds to get in shape for the Olympics. Ironically though, he won his gold medal because his bodyweight was actually *less* than that of Selvetti, who was a mammoth 316½ pounds. (143.5 kg). Anderson was a devout Christian who opened his home to delinquent and orphaned children.

1960 Rome C: 18, N: 15, D: 9.10. WR: 533 kg (Paul Anderson)

		PRESS		SNATCH		JERK		TOTAL KG	
1. Yury Vlassov	SOV	180.0	OR	155.0	OR	202.5	WR	537.5	WR
2. James Bradford	USA	180.0	OR	150.0		182.5		512.5	
3. Norbert Schemansky	USA	170.0		150.0		180.0		500.0	
4. Mohamed Mahmoud Ibrahim	UAR	140.0		137.5		177.5		455.0	
5. Eino Mäkinen	FIN	140.0		142.5		172.5		455.0	
6. William David Baillie	CAN	147.5		132.5		170.0		450.0	
7. Alberto Pigaiani	ITA	152.5		127.5		170.0		450.0	
8. Vaclav Syrovy	CZE	145.0		125.0		172.5		435.0	

Although Vlassov's main opponents were the two veterans Bradford and Schemansky, most of the audience was aware of a third, invisible opponent—Paul Anderson, who had turned professional, but whose world record was still on the books. Vlassov assured himself the gold medal and an Olympic record with his first jerk of 185 kg. He followed with a 195, then stunned the crowd by jerking 202.5 kg and setting two world records (jerk and total lifts) with one lift. After his Olympic victory, Vlassov quit lifting and turned to his great love—writing poetry. But he had trouble selling his work. He was also cast in the role of Pierre Bezukhov in the Soviet epic film *War and Peace*. However, at the last minute director Sergei Bondarchuk took the role for himself. Unable to support himself as a creative artist, Vlassov returned to weightlifting and began preparations for the Tokyo Olympics.

1964 Tokyo C: 21, N: 18, D: 10.18. WR: 580 kg (Yury Vlassov)

		PRESS		SNATCH		JERK		TOTAL KG	
1. Leonid Zhabotinsky	SOV	187.5		167.5	OR	217.5	WR	572.5	OR
2. Yury Vlassov	SOV	197.5	WR	162.5		210.0		570.0	
3. Norbert Schemansky	USA	180.0		165.0		192.5		537.5	
4. Gary Gubner	USA	175.0		150.0		187.5		512.5	
5. Károly Ecser	HUN	175.0		147.5		185.0		507.5	
6. Mohamed Mahmoud Ibrahim	UAR	162.5		145.0		187.5		495.0	
7. Ivan Veselinov	BUL	165.0		135.0		190.0		490.0	
8. Ho-Dong Hwang	KOR	162.5		135.0		185.0		482.5	

Zhabotinsky, a 341-pound Ukrainian, scored a major upset when he came from behind to defeat teammate Yury Vlassov by breaking Vlassov's world jerk record on his final attempt. A half hour earlier, Zhabotinsky had lulled Vlassov into a false sense of security by going up to him and conceding defeat. When Vlassov realized that he had been made the victim of a dishonest trick, he was furious. "I was choked with tears," he later wrote. "I flung the silver medal through the window. . . . I had always revered the purity, the impartiality of contests of strength. That night, I understood that there is a kind of strength that has nothing to do with justice."

1968 Mexico City C: 17, N: 14, D: 10.19. WR: 590 kg (Leonid Zhabotinsky)

		PRESS		SNATCH		JERK	TOTAL KG	
1. Leonid Zhabotinsky	SOV	200.0	OR	170.0	OR	202.5	572.5	EOR
2. Serge Reding	BEL	195.0		147.5		212.5	555.0	
3. Joseph Dube	USA	200.0	OR	145.0		210.0	555.0	
4. Manfred Rieger	GDR	175.0		155.0		202.5	532.5	
5. Rudolf Mang	GER	177.5		152.5		195.0	525.0	
6. Mauno Lindroos	FIN	157.5		145.0		192.5	495.0	
7. Kalevi Lahdenranta	FIN	160.0		147.5		185.0	492.5	
8. Donald Oliver	NZE	147.5		142.5		200.0	490.0	

Zhabotinsky, now up to 359 pounds, reveled in his role of "World's Strongest Man." At the opening ceremony in Mexico City he astonished the crowd by carrying the huge Soviet flag one-handed. In the competition, he was so sure of victory that he passed his last two attempts in the jerk, upsetting the audience, which had hoped to see him try for a world record.

1972 Munich C: 13, N: 11, D: 9.6. WR: 645kg (Vassily Alexeyev)

		PRESS		SNATCH		JERK		TOTAL KG	
1. Vassily Alexeyev	SOV	235.0	OR	175.0	OR	230.0	OR	640.0	OR
2. Rudolf Mang	GER	225.0		170.0		215.0		610.0	
3. Gerd Bonk	GDR	200.0		155.0		217.5		572.5	
4. Jouko Leppä	FIN	205.0		157.5		210.0		572.5	
5. Manfred Rieger	GDR	190.0		162.5		205.0		557.5	
6. Petr Pavlasek	CZE	192.5		165.0		200.0		557.5	
7. Kalevi Lahdenranta	FIN	190.0		165.0		200.0		555.0	
8. Fernando Bernal	CUB	190.0		147.5		207.5		545.0	

Vassily Alexeyev came to international attention on January 24, 1970, when he broke the world record for the press, the jerk, and the three-lift total. On March 18 of the same year, he became the first person to lift a combined total of 600 kg. Six months later, while competing in Columbus, Ohio, he broke the 500-pound barrier for the jerk. Since Alexeyev only operated on the metric system, he was somewhat confused when his successful lift brought in so much attention. At Munich, the 30-year-old champion checked in at 337 pounds. The competition was no competition as Alexeyev raked up a convincing 30 kg winning margin. Married in 1962 to a woman named Olympiada, Alexeyev was spotted in Munich having a breakfast of 26 fried eggs and a steak.

1976 Montreal C: 11, N: 8, D: 7.27. WR: 442.5 kg (Vassily Alexeyev)

		SNATCH		JERK		TOTAL KG
1. Vassily Alexeyev	SOV	185.0	OR	255.0	WR	440.0
2. Gerd Bonk	GDR	170.0		235.0		405.0
3. Helmut Losch	GDR	165.0		222.5		387.5
4. Jan Nagy	CZE	160.0		227.5		387.5
5. Bruce Wilhelm	USA	172.5		215.0		387.5
– Petř Pavlašek	CZE	172.5		215.0		387.5
6. Gerardo Fernandez	CUB	165.0		200.0		365.0
7. Robert Edmond	AUS	157.5		190.0		347.5
8. Jan-Olof Nolsjo	SWE	152.5		185.0		337.5

Once again, Alexeyev, now 34 years old and over 345 pounds, was unchallenged. Between 1970 and 1977 he set 80 world records, a number that is particularly significant when one considers that he allegedly received from the Soviet government a prize of $700 to $1500 every time he broke a world record. He was unbeaten from 1970 until 1978.

Sixth-place finisher Petř Pavlašek was disqualified when he registered a positive result on a urine test for drugs.

1980 Moscow C: 12, N: 8, D: 7.30. WR: 445kg (Vassily Alexeyev)

		SNATCH		JERK	TOTAL KG	
1. Sultan Rakhmanov	SOV	195.0	OR	245.0	440.0	EOR
2. Jürgen Heuser	GDR	182.5		227.5	410.0	
3. Tadeusz Rutkowski	POL	180.0		227.5	407.5	
4. Rudolf Strejček	CZE	182.5		220.0	402.5	
5. Bohuslav Braum	CZE	180.0		217.5	397.5	
6. Francisco Mendez Polo	CUB	175.0		220.0	395.0	

7. Robert Skolimowski	POL	175.0	210.0	385.0
8. Talal Najjar	SYR	157.5	205.0	362.5

Competing for the first time since he was injured during the 1978 world championship, Alexeyev failed three times to snatch 180 kg and was eliminated. Thirty-year-old Sultan Rakhmanov, whose mother was Ukrainian and whose father was an Uzbek, made six perfect lifts to score a decisive victory.

FREESTYLE WRESTLING

Light Flyweight	Welterweight
Flyweight	Middleweight
Bantamweight	Light Heavyweight
Featherweight	Heavyweight
Lightweight	Super Heavyweight—Unlimited Weight

International amateur wrestling follows a complicated system of scoring. Beginning in 1984, matches will consist of 2 three-minute rounds rather than 3 three-minute rounds. As a match progresses, contestants score points as a result of successful holds, positions of advantage, and near-throws. If the six-minute mark is reached without a fall, the wrestler with the most points is declared the winner. Each man is then assigned a certain number of penalty points or bad points for the match according to the following chart:

0	win by fall
0	win by 12 or more points
0	win by passivity—winner uncautioned
0.5	win by 8–11 points
1	win by less than 8 points
1	win by passivity—winner cautioned once
2	win by passivity—winner cautioned twice
3	lose by less than 8 points
3.5	lose by 8–11 points
4	lose by 12 or more points
4	withdraw due to injury
4	lose by passivity
4	lose by fall
4	lose by disqualification (the most common cause being passivity or lack of aggressiveness)

If a wrestler accumulates six or more bad points, he is eliminated from the tournament. The last two or three contestants then engage in a final round. If two finalists have already met in an earlier round, then the result of that match is counted in the final round. Ties in the final are decided by pre-round-robin bad marks, victories, and falls. If a round of bouts concludes with only one wrestler remaining with less than six points, then he is declared the winner without a final round.

Between 1936 and 1956 different systems of scoring were used, requiring only five penalty points for elimination.

LIGHT FLYWEIGHT
(48 kg—106 lbs)

1896–1900 not held

1904 St. Louis C: 4, N: 1, D: 10.15.
1. Robert Curry   USA
2. John Hein   USA
3. Gustav Thiefenthaler USA

Curry, of New York City, threw Thiefenthaler in 4:05 and Hein in 2:38.

1906–1968 not held

1972 Munich C: 14, N: 14, D: 8.31.

		ROUND ELIMINATED	BAD PTS.	FINAL ROUND
1. Roman Dmitriev	SOV	—	2	4
2. Ognyan Nikolov	BUL	—	5	4
3. Ebrahim Javadpour	IRN	—	3.5	4
4. Sefer Baygin	TUR	4	6.5	
5. Ion Arapu	ROM	4	7	
6. Masahiko Umeda	JAP	4	8	
7. Sergio Gonzalez	USA	3	6	
7. Jürgen Möbius	GDR	3	6	

1976 Montreal C: 18, N: 18, D: 7.31.

		ROUND ELIMINATED	BAD PTS.	FINAL ROUND
1. Hasan Isaev	BUL	—	4	3
2. Roman Dmitriev	SOV	—	1	5
3. Akira Kudo	JAP	—	0	8
4. Gombo Khishigbaatar	MON	5	6	
5. Hwa-Kyung Kim	KOR	5	6	
6. Yong-Nam Li	PRK	5	8	
7. Kuddusi Ozdemir	TUR	4	7	
8. Willi Heckmann	GER	4	8	

Dmitriev actually defeated two-time world champion Isaev, but lost four points as the result of a double disqualification against Kudo.

1980 Moscow C: 14, N: 14, D: 7.29.

		ROUND ELIMINATED	BAD PTS.	FINAL ROUND
1. Claudio Pollio	ITA	—	5.5	3
2. Se-Hong Jang	PRK	—	5	4
3. Sergei Kornilaev	SOV	—	1	5
4. Jan Falandys	POL	5	6.5	
5. Mahabir Singh	IND	5	9	
6. László Biró	HUN	4	9	
7. Roumen Yordanov	BUL	3	6	
8. Gheorghe Rasovan	ROM	3	7	

Pollio lost to Kornilaev, but won the gold medal anyway after the Soviet wrestler was thrown in the final match by Se-Hong Jang, who had been disqualified in his match against Pollio.

FLYWEIGHT
(52 kg—114½ lbs)
1896–1900 not held

1904 St. Louis C: 3, N: 1, D: 10.15.
(52.16 kg—115 lbs)
1. George Mehnert   USA
2. Gustav Bauer   USA
3. William Nelson   USA

1906–1936 not held

1948 London C: 11, N: 11, D: 7.31.

		ROUND ELIMINATED	BAD PTS.	FINAL ROUND
1. Lennart Viitala	FIN	—	2	2
2. Halit Balamir	TUR	—	4	2
3. Thure Johansson	SWE	—	5	6
4. Mohamad Rasul Raissi	IRN	4	6	
5. Pierre Baudric	FRA	4	7	
6. Kha-Shaba Jadav	IND	3	5	
7. William Jernigan	USA	3	7	

1952 Helsinki C: 16, N: 16, D: 7.23.

		ROUND ELIMINATED	BAD PTS.	FINAL ROUND
1. Hasan Gemici	TUR	—	4	3
2. Yushu Kitano	JAP	—	4	4
3. Mahmoud Mollaghassemi	IRN	—	3	4
4. Georgy Sayadov	SOV	5	6	
5. Heinrich Weber	GER	4	6	
6. Louis Baise	SAF	4	7	
7. Giordano Degiorgi	ITA	3	5	
7. Robert Peery	USA	3	5	

1956 Melbourne C: 11, N: 11, D: 12.1.

		ROUND ELIMINATED	BAD PTS.	FINAL ROUND
1. Mirian Tsalkalamanidze	SOV	—	5	3
2. Mohamad Ali Khojastehpour	IRN	—	3	3
3. Hüseyin Akbaş	TUR	—	2	4
4. Tadashi Asai	JAP	4	7	
5. Richard Delgado	USA	3	6	
5. André Zoete	FRA	3	6	
7. Abdul Aziz	PAK	3	7	
7. Baban Daware	IND	3	7	

Tsalkalamanidze gained the gold medal by throwing Khojastehpour after four minutes.

1960 Rome C: 17, N: 17, D: 9.6.

		ROUND ELIMINATED	BAD PTS.	FINAL ROUND
1. Ahmet Bilek	TUR	—	5	2
2. Masayuki Matsubara	JAP	—	4	4
3. Mohamad Saifpour Saidabadi	IRN	—	3	6
4. Paul Neff	GER	6	9	
5. Elliott Gray Simons	USA	5	8	
6. Ali Aliyev	SOV	5	8	
7. Nikola Dimitrov	BUL	4	7	
8. André Zoete	FRA	4	8	

1964 Tokyo C: 22, N: 22, D: 10.14.

		ROUND ELIMINATED	BAD PTS.	FINAL ROUND
1. Yoshikatsu Yoshida	JAP	—	2	1
2. Chang-Sun Chang	KOR	—	3	3
3. Said Aliakbar Haydari	IRN	5	6	
4. Ali Aliyev	SOV	5	7	
4. Cemal Yanilmaz	TUR	5	7	
4. André Zoete	FRA	5	7	
7. Elliott Gray Simons	USA	4	6	
8. Muhammed Niaz	PAK	4	7	

1968 Mexico City C: 23, N: 23, D: 10.20.

		ROUND ELIMINATED	BAD PTS.	FINAL ROUND
1. Shigeo Nakata	JAP	—	3.5	1
2. Richard Sanders	USA	—	0	4
3. Surenjav Sukhbaatar	MON	—	5	7
4. Nazar Albaryan	SOV	5	6.5	
5. Vincenzo Grassi	ITA	5	6.5	
6. Sudesh Kumar	IND	5	7.5	
7. Mohamad Ghorbani	IRN	5	8	
7. Paul Neff	GER	5	8	

1972 Munich C: 24, N: 24, D: 8.31.

		ROUND ELIMINATED	BAD PTS.	FINAL ROUND
1. Kiyomi Kato	JAP	—	1.5	2
2. Arsen Alkhverdiev	SOV	—	5.5	5
3. Gwong-Hyong Kim	PRK	—	5.5	5
4. Sudesh Sudeshkumar	IND	6	7	

5. Petru Ciarnău	ROM	6	7.5	
6. Gordon Bertie	CAN	5	7.5	
7. Henrik Gál	HUN	4	7	
7. John Kinsella	AUS	4	7	

1976 Montreal C: 19, N: 19, D: 7.31.

		ROUND ELIMINATED	BAD PTS.	FINAL ROUND
1. Yuji Takada	JAP	—	0	0.5
2. Aleksandr Ivanov	SOV	—	1.5	3.5
3. Hae-Sup Jeon	KOR	—	2	8
4. Henrik Gál	HUN	5	7	
5. Nermedin Selimov	BUL	5	8.5	
6. Wladyslaw Stecyk	POL	5	9	
7. Bong-Sun Li	PRK	4	7	
8. Eloy Abreu	CUB	4	9	

Two-time world champion Yuji Takada of Gunma overwhelmed the field, pinning six of his seven opponents, five of them in less than two minutes. He also outpointed Ivanov 20–11.

1980 Moscow C: 16, N: 16, D: 7.30.

		ROUND ELIMINATED	BAD PTS.	FINAL ROUND
1. Anatoly Beloglazov	SOV	—	1.5	0
2. Wladyslaw Stecyk	POL	—	4	5
3. Nermedin Selimov	BUL	—	4.5	7
4. Lajos Szabó	HUN	6	9	
5. Dok-Ryong Jang	PRK	4	6.5	
6. Nanzadying Burgedaa	MON	4	7	
7. Koce Efremov	YUG	4	8	
8. Hartmut Reich	GDR	3	6.5	

After winning his first two matches on decisions, Anatoly Beloglazov needed only 4:54 to dispose of his last four opponents. Twenty-four hours and 48 minutes after Beloglazov won the Flyweight gold medal, his twin brother, Sergei, won the Bantamweight tournament.

BANTAMWEIGHT
(57 kg—125½ lbs)
1896–1900 not held

1904 St. Louis C: 7, N: 1, D: 10.15.
(56.70 kg—125 lbs)
1. Isidor Niflot   USA
2. August Wester   USA
3. Z.B. Strebler   USA

Niflot won the championship by throwing Wester in 1:58.

1906 not held

1908 London C: 13, N: 3, D: 7.20.
(54 kg—119 lbs)
1. George Mehnert   USA
2. William Press   GBR
3. Aubert Côté   CAN
4. F. Tomkins   GBR
5. F. Davis (GBR), B. Sansom (GBR), G.J. Saunders (GBR)

Mehnert, a 26-year-old from Newark, New Jersey, had won the Flyweight championship in St. Louis four years earlier.

1912–1920 not held

1924 Paris C: 12, N: 8, D: 7.14.
(56 kg—123½ lbs)
1. Kustaa Pihlajamäki   FIN
2. Kaarlo Mäkinen   FIN
3. Bryant Hines   USA
4. Gaston Ducayla   FRA
5. Ragnar Larsson   SWE
5. H.E. Sansum   GBR

Pihlajamäki won the first of his three Olympic medals (two gold, one silver). His younger brother, Hermanni, also won a gold and a bronze in freestyle wrestling.

1928 Amsterdam C: 8, N: 8, D: 8.1.
(56 kg—123½ lbs)
1. Kaarlo Mäkinen   FIN
2. Edmond Spapen   BEL
3. James Trifunov   CAN
4. H.E. Sansum   GBR
5. Robert Hewitt   USA
6. A. Piguet   SWI

1932 Los Angeles C: 8, N: 8, D: 8.3.
(56 kg—123½ lbs)
1. Robert Pearce   USA
2. Ödön Zombori   HUN
3. Aatos Jaskari   FIN
4. Joseph Reid   GBR
5. Julien Depuichaffray   FRA
5. Georgios Zervinis   GRE

1936 Berlin C: 14, N: 14, D: 8.5.
(56 kg—123½ lbs)

		ROUND ELIMINATED	BAD PTS.	FINAL ROUND
1. Ödön Zombori	HUN	—	4	0
2. Ross Flood	USA	—	2	3
3. Johannes Herbert	GER	5	5	
4. Herman Tuvesson	SWE	5	6	
5. Aatos Jaskari	FIN	4	7	
6. Ahmet Çakiryildiz	TUR	4	7	
7. Nizzola	ITA	3	5	
8. Gaudard	SWI	3	6	
8. Laport	BEL	3	6	

1948 London C: 15, N: 15, D: 7.31.

		ROUND ELIMINATED	BAD PTS.	FINAL ROUND
1. Nasuh Akar	TUR	—	2	0
2. Gerald Leeman	USA	—	3	3
3. Charles Kouyos	FRA	5	7	
4. Joseph Trimpont	BEL	5	7	
5. Lajos Bencze	HUN	4	5	
5. Raymond Cazaux	GBR	4	5	
5. Sayad Hafez	EGY	4	5	
5. Erik Persson	SWE	4	5	

1952 Helsinki C: 20, N: 20, D: 7.23.

		ROUND ELIMINATED	BAD PTS.	FINAL ROUND
1. Shohachi Ishii	JAP	—	4	2
2. Rashid Mamedbekov	SOV	—	3	4
3. Kha-Shaba Jadav	IND	—	4	6
4. Edvin Westerby	SWE	5	7	
5. Cemil Saribacak	TUR	4	5	
6. Lajos Bencze	HUN	4	5	
7. Ferdinand Schmitz	GER	4	6	
8. Eigil Johansen	DEN	3	5	
8. Mohamad Yaghoubi	IRN	3	5	

A talented judoka, Ishii was forced to give up judo when U.S. occupation forces banned the sport after World War II. Ishii switched to wrestling and won Japan's first postwar gold medal.

1956 Melbourne C: 14, N: 14, D: 12.1.

		ROUND ELIMINATED	BAD PTS.	FINAL ROUND
1. Mustafa Dagistanli	TUR	—	4	1
2. Mohamad Yaghoubi	IRN	—	4	2
3. Mikhail Chakhov	SOV	5	6	
4. Sang-Kyoon Lee	KOR	5	7	
5. Minoru Iizuka	JAP	4	5	
6. Alfred Kämmerer	GDR	3	5	
7. Din Zahur	PAK	3	6	
8. Adolfo Diaz	ARG	3	7	
8. Tarakeshwar Pandey	IND	3	7	

1960 Rome C: 19, N: 19, D: 9.6.

		ROUND ELIMINATED	BAD PTS.	FINAL ROUND
1. Terrence McCann	USA	—	5	2
2. Nezhdet Zalev	BUL	—	2	4
3. Tadeusz Trojanowski	POL	—	4	6
4. Tadashi Asai	JAP	5	6	
5. Tauno Jaskari	FIN	5	7	
6. Mikhail Chakhov	SOV	5	8	
7. Mohamad Yaghoubi	IRN	4	6	
8. Luigi Chinazzo	ITA	4	8	

1964 Tokyo C: 20, N: 20, D: 10.14.

		ROUND ELIMINATED	BAD PTS.	FINAL ROUND
1. Yojiro Uetake	JAP	—	3	2
2. Hüseyin Akbaş	TUR	—	5	4
3. Aydyn Ibragimov	SOV	—	3	6
4. David Auble	USA	5	6	
5. Young-Kil Choi	KOR	5	7	
6. Bishamber Singh	IND	5	8	
7. János Varga	HUN	4	7	
8. Abdollah Khodabande	IRN	3	6	

1968 Mexico City C: 21, N: 21, D: 10.20.

		ROUND ELIMINATED	BAD PTS.
1. Yojiro Uetake	JAP	—	5.5
2. Donald Behm	USA	7	6.5
3. Abutaleb Gorgori	IRN	7	7.5
4. Ali Aliyev	SOV	7	8.5
5. Ivan Shavov	BUL	6	7.5
6. Zbigniew Żedzicki	POL	5	8
7. Bishamber Singh	IND	5	8.5
8. Sukhbaatar Bazaryn	MON	4	7

1972 Munich C: 28, N: 28, D: 8.31.

		ROUND ELIMINATED	BAD PTS.	FINAL ROUND
1. Hideaki Yanagida	JAP	—	4	1
2. Richard Sanders	USA	—	4	3
3. Lásló Klinga	HUN	7	8.5	
4. Prem Premnath	IND	7	9	
5. Ivan Shavov	BUL	6	7	
6. Horst Mayer	GDR	6	7.5	
7. Ramezan Kheder	IRN	6	8	
8. Jorge Ramos	CUB	5	6	

Silver medalist Richard Sanders, a bartender from Portland, Oregon, had long hair, a beard, and a mustache, and wore a bead necklace. Seven weeks after the Olympics, Sanders was killed in an automobile accident while touring in Europe. He was 23 years old.

1976 Montreal C: 21, N: 21, D: 7.31.

		ROUND ELIMINATED	BAD PTS.	FINAL ROUND
1. Vladimir Umin	SOV	—	7	2
2. Hans-Dieter Brüchert	GDR	—	3.5	4
3. Masao Arai	JAP	—	4.5	6
4. Miho Doukov	BUL	6	8	
5. Ramezan Kheder	IRN	6	8	
6. Migd Khoilogdorj	MON	6	8	
7. George Chatziioannidis	GRE	5	8.5	
8. Zbigniew Żedzicki	POL	4	6	

1980 Moscow C: 16, N: 16, D: 7.31.

		ROUND ELIMINATED	BAD PTS.	FINAL ROUND
1. Sergei Beloglazov	SOV	—	0	0
2. Ho-Pyong Li	PRK	—	6	5
3. Dugarsuren Ouinbold	MON	—	2	7
4. Ivan Tzochev	BUL	5	7	
5. Aurel Neagu	ROM	4	6	
6. Wieslaw Kończak	POL	4	7	
7. Karim Salman Muhsin	IRQ	4	8	
8. Sándor Németh	HUN	4	9	

Sergei Beloglazov, the twin brother of Flyweight winner Anatoly Beloglazov, threw five of his six opponents and defeated Ouinbold by disqualification, after leading in points 15–0. He outpointed his six victims 58–3.

FEATHERWEIGHT
(62 kg—136½ lbs)
1896–1900 not held

1904 St. Louis C: 9, N: 1, D: 10.15.
(61.23 kg—135 lbs)
1. Benjamin Bradshaw   USA
2. Theodore McLear   USA
3. Charles Clapper   USA

1906 not held

1908 London C: 12, N: 2, D: 7.22.
(60.3 kg—132½ lbs)
1. George Dole   USA
2. James Slim   GBR
3. William McKie   GBR
4. W. Tagg   GBR
5. A.J. Goddard (GBR), J.A. Webster (GBR), J.G. White (GBR)

Dole, a 5-foot 3½-inch student from Yale, was the only non-British wrestler in the Featherweight division.

1912 not held

1920 Antwerp C: 11, N: 6, D: 8.21.
(60 kg—132 lbs)
1. Charles Ackerly   USA
2. Samuel Gerson   USA
3. P.W. Bernard   GBR
4. Shindes   IND

Ackerly, former captain of the Cornell University team, and Gerson, former captain of the University of Pennsylvania team, had each defeated the other once in collegiate competition, but Ackerly won the tie-breaker across the seas in Antwerp. Thirty-two years later Gerson organized the U.S. Olympians, an alumni association for former members of U.S. Olympic teams.

1924 Paris C: 17, N: 12, D: 7.14.
(61 kg—134½ lbs)
1. Robin Reed   USA
2. Chester Newton   USA
3. Katsutoshi Naito   JAP
4. Sigfrid Hansson   SWE
5. Clifford Chilcott   CAN
6. Edvard Huupponen   FIN

Reed and Newton were longtime friends and rivals from Portland, Oregon.

1928 Amsterdam C: 9, N: 9, D: 8.1.
(61 kg—134½ lbs)
1. Allie Morrison   USA
2. Kustaa Pihlajamäki   FIN
3. Hans Minder   SWI
4. René Rottenfluc   FRA

1932 Los Angeles C: 10, N: 10, D: 8.3.
(61 kg—134½ lbs)
1. Hermanni Pihlajamäki   FIN
2. Edgar Nemir   USA
3. Einar Karlsson   SWE
4. Joseph Taylor   GBR
5. Ioannis Farmakidis   GRE
6. Jean Chasson   FRA

1936 Berlin C: 15, N: 15, D: 8.4.
(61 kg—134½ lbs)

		ROUND ELIMINATED	BAD PTS.
1. Kustaa Pihlajamäki	FIN	—	1
2. Francis Millard	USA	6	5
3. Gösta Jönsson	SWE	6	5
4. John Vernon Pettigrew	CAN	5	7
5. Ferenc Tóth	HUN	4	6
6. Mitsuzo Mizutani	JAP	4	7
7. Gavelli	ITA	3	5
8. Erkan (TUR), Hall (SAF), Morrell (GBR)		3	7

1948 London C: 17, N: 17, D: 7.31.
(63 kg—139 lbs)

		ROUND ELIMINATED	BAD PTS.	FINAL ROUND
1. Gazanfer Bilge	TUR	—	0	1
2. Ivar Sjölin	SWE	—	2	3
3. Adolf Müller	SWI	6	5	
4. Paavo Hietala	FIN	5	6	
4. Ferenc Tóth	HUN	5	6	
6. Harold "Hal" Moore	USA	4	5	
7. A. Raymackers	BEL	4	6	
8. I. Abdel Hamid	EGY	4	7	
8. A. Parsons	GBR	4	7	

Bilge was rewarded by the Turkish government with a house and 20,000 liras ($7,142). This made him ineligible for the 1952 Olympics, but he was able to parlay his rewards into a fortune as a bus mogul. In 1963 Bilge was imprisoned after he shot Adil Atan, a business rival who had won a bronze medal as a Light Heavyweight wrestler in 1952.

1952 Helsinki C: 21, N: 21, D: 7.23.
(63 kg—139 lbs)

		ROUND ELIMINATED	BAD PTS.	FINAL ROUND
1. Bayram Şit	TUR	—	2	1
2. Nasser Guivehtchi	IRN	—	4	4
3. Josiah Henson	USA	—	5	6
4. K.D. Mangave	IND	5	6	
5. Risaburo Tominaga	JAP	5	7	
6. Rauno Mäkinen	FIN	4	5	
7. Albert Bernard	CAN	4	6	
7. Abdel Essawi	EGY	4	6	

1956 Melbourne C: 13, N: 13, D: 12.1.
(63 kg—139 lbs)

		ROUND ELIMINATED	BAD PTS.	FINAL ROUND
1. Shozo Sasahara	JAP	—	4	1
2. Joseph Mewis	BEL	—	3	4
3. Erkki Penttilä	FIN	—	4	6
4. Myron Roderick	USA	4	5	
4. Bayram Şit	TUR	4	5	
6. Nasser Guivehtchi	IRN	4	7	
6. Linar Salimulin	SOV	4	7	
8. Ram Sarup	IND	3	6	

1960 Rome C: 25, N: 25, D: 9.6.
(63 kg—139 lbs)

		ROUND ELIMINATED	BAD PTS.	FINAL ROUND
1. Mustafa Dagistanli	TUR	—	4	1
2. Stancho Kolev	BUL	—	3	3
3. Vladimir Rubashvili	SOV	6	7	
4. Tamiji Sato	JAP	6	7	
5. Joseph Mewis	BEL	5	8	
6. Mohamed Akhtar	PAK	5	9	
7. Abraham Geldenhuys	SAF	4	6	
8. Azohadi Khaden	IRN	4	9	

1964 Tokyo C: 21, N: 21, D: 10.14.
(63 kg—139 lbs)

		ROUND ELIMINATED	BAD PTS.	FINAL ROUND
1. Osamu Watanabe	JAP	—	2	2
2. Stancho Kolev	BUL	—	5	5
3. Nodar Khokhashvili	SOV	—	5	5
4. Robert "Bobby" Douglas	USA	5	6	
5. Mohammed Ebrahimi	AFG	5	7	
6. Mohamad Saifpour Saidabadi	IRN	5	8	
7. Rainer Schilling	GER	4	6	
8. Mario Tovar Gonzalez	MEX	4	7	

Watanabe's 1–0 win over Khokhashvili was his 186th consecutive victory. He didn't give up a single point in any of his six Olympic matches. Kolev was awarded the silver medal because he weighed less than Khokhashvili.

1968 Mexico City C: 23, N: 23, D: 10.20.
(63 kg—139 lbs)

		ROUND ELIMINATED	BAD PTS.	FINAL ROUND
1. Masaaki Kaneko	JAP	—	1.5	3.5
2. Enyu Todorov	BUL	—	2	4.5
3. Shamseddin Seyed-Abassy	IRN	—	2.5	5
4. Nicolaos Karypidis	GRE	5	6.5	
5. Petre Coman	ROM	5	8	
6. Yeikan Tedeyev	SOV	4	6	
7. Vehbi Akdag	TUR	4	6.5	
7. Ismail Al Karaghouli	IRQ	4	6.5	

1972 Munich C: 26, N: 26, D: 8.31.

		ROUND ELIMINATED	BAD PTS.	FINAL ROUND
1. Zagalav Abdulbekov	SOV	—	3.5	2
2. Vehbi Akdag	TUR	—	5.5	5
3. Ivan Krustev	BUL	—	5	5
4. Kiyoshi Abe	JAP	6	6	
5. Shamseddin Seyed-Abassy	IRN	5	5.5	
6. Petre Coman	ROM	5	6	
7. Joseph Burge House	GUA	5	7	
8. Gerhard Weisenberg	GER	4	8	

1976 Montreal C: 17, N: 17, D: 7.31.

		ROUND ELIMINATED	BAD PTS.	FINAL ROUND
1. Jung-Mo Yang	KOR	—	1	3
2. Zeveg Oidov	MON	—	3	4
3. Gene Davis	USA	—	8	5
4. Mohamad Farahvashi-Fashandi	IRN	6	10	
5. Ivan Yankov	BUL	5	8	
6. Sergei Timofeev	SOV	4	7	
7. Kenkichi Maekawa	JAP	4	8	
8. Helmut Strumpf	GDR	4	9	

1980 Moscow C: 13, N: 13, D: 7.29.

		ROUND ELIMINATED	BAD PTS.	FINAL ROUND
1. Magomedgasan Abushev	SOV	—	2.5	1.5
2. Miho Doukov	BUL	—	5.5	3
3. Georges Hadjiioannidis	GRE	—	5	7.5
4. Raul Cascaret Fonseca	CUB	5	6.5	
5. Aurel Suteu	ROM	5	8.5	
6. Ulzibayar Nasanjargal	MON	4	6	
7. Brian Aspen	GBR	3	6.5	
8. Zoltán Szalontai	HUN	3	7.5	

LIGHTWEIGHT
(68 kg—149½ lbs)
1896–1900 not held

1904 St. Louis C: 10, N: 1, D: 10.15.
(65.77 kg—145 lbs)
1. Otto Roehm   USA
2. Rudolph Tesing   USA
3. Albert Zirkel   USA
4. William Hennessy   USA

1906 not held

1908 London C: 11, N: 2, D: 7.24.
(66.6 kg—147 lbs)
1. George de Relwyskow GBR
2. William Wood   GBR
3. Albert Gingell   GBR
4. George MacKenzie   GBR
5. J.H. Krug   USA

Relwyskow had already won a silver medal in the Middleweight division when he took first place against the lightweights.

1912 not held

1920 Antwerp C: 11, N: 6, D: 8.21.
(67.5 kg—149 lbs)
1. Kaarlo "Kalle" Anttila FIN
2. Gottfrid Svensson   SWE
3. Peter Wright   GBR
4. Auguste Thijs   BEL

1924 Paris C: 16, N: 10, D: 7.14.
(66 kg—145½ lbs)
1. Russell Vis   USA
2. Volmari Vikström   FIN
3. Arvo Haavisto   FIN
4. G. Gardiner   GBR
5. W. J. Montgomery   CAN
6. Emile Pouvroux   FRA

1928 Amsterdam C: 11, N: 11, D: 8.1.
(66 kg—145½ lbs)
1. Osvald Käpp   EST
2. Charles Pacôme   FRA
3. Eino Leino   FIN
4. Birger Nilsen   NOR
5. Carlo Tesdorf Jörgensen DEN
6. Clarence Berryman   USA

1932 Los Angeles C: 8, N: 8, D: 8.3.
(66 kg—145½ lbs)
1. Charles Pacôme   FRA
2. Károly Kárpáti   HUN
3. Gustaf Klarén   SWE
4. Melvin Clodfelter   USA
5. Kustaa Pihlajamäki FIN

In the 1928 final, Pacôme, a law student, had lost a controversial decision to Osvald Käpp. Four years later in Los Angeles, the two met again in the first round. This time Pacôme won on points. Three more victories later, he was awarded the gold medal.

1936 Berlin C: 17, N: 17, D: 8.4.
(66 kg—145½ lbs)

		ROUND ELIMINATED	BAD PTS.	FINAL ROUND
1. Károly Kárpáti	HUN	—	3	1
2. Wolfgang Ehrl	GER	—	4	2
3. Hermanni Pihlajamäki	FIN	—	4	6
4. Charles Delporte	FRA	5	6	
5. Harley De Witt Strong	USA	4	5	
6. Paride Romagnoli	ITA	4	7	
7. Kazama	JAP	4	5	
8. Toots	EST	4	7	

1948 London C: 18, N: 18, D: 7.31.
(67 kg—147½ lbs)

		ROUND ELIMINATED	BAD PTS.
1. Celal Atik	TUR	—	1
2. Gösta Frändfors	SWE	6	6
3. Hermann Baumann	SWI	6	8
4. Garibaldo Nizzola	ITA	6	10
5. William Koll	USA	4	6
6. Suk-Young Kim	KOR	4	7
6. Sulo Leppänen	FIN	4	7
8. László Bakos	HUN	3	5

Atik won five of his six bouts by falls and defeated Leppänen on points.

1952 Helsinki C: 23, N: 23, D: 7.23.
(67 kg—147½ lbs)

		ROUND ELIMINATED	BAD PTS.	FINAL ROUND
1. Olle Anderberg	SWE	—	1	2
2. Jay Thomas Evans	USA	—	2	4
3. Djahanbakte Tovfighe	IRN	—	4	6
4. Aram Yaltyryan	SOV	5	7	
5. Risto Talosela	FIN	5	7	
6. Heinrich Nettesheim	GER	4	6	
6. Takeo Shimotori	JAP	4	6	
8. Jan Cools	BEL	4	7	
8. Godfey Pienaar	SAF	4	7	

1956 Melbourne C: 19, N: 19, D: 12.1.
(67 kg—147½ lbs)

		ROUND ELIMINATED	BAD PTS.
1. Emamali Habibi	IRN	—	4
2. Shigeru Kasahara	JAP	5	6
3. Alimbeg Bestayev	SOV	6	6
4. Gyula Tóth	HUN	5	5
5. Jay Thomas Evans	USA	4	5
5. Garibaldo Nizzola	ITA	4	5
7. Mario Tovar González	MEX	4	7
8. Muhammad Ashraf	PAK	4	7

1960 Rome C: 24, N: 24, D: 9.6.
(67 kg—147½ lbs)

		ROUND ELIMINATED	BAD PTS.	FINAL ROUND
1. Shelby Wilson	USA	—	5	1
2. Vladimir Sinyavsky	SOV	—	5	3
3. Enyu Dimov	BUL	6	6	
4. Chang-Won Bong	KOR	6	8	
4. Moustafa Tajik	IRN	6	8	
6. Garibaldo Nizzola	ITA	5	7	
7. Martti Peltoniemi	FIN	5	8	
8. Kazuo Abe	JAP	4	8	
8. Raymond Lougheed	CAN	4	8	
8. Hayrullah Sahin	TUR	4	8	

Shelby Wilson was a 23-year-old preacher and student from Ponca City, Oklahoma. He won the gold medal without registering a single fall.

1964 Tokyo C: 22, N: 22, D: 10.14.
(70 kg—154½ lbs)

		ROUND ELIMINATED	BAD PTS.	FINAL ROUND
1. Enyu Vulchev (Dimov)	BUL	—	5	1
2. Klaus-Jürgen Rost	GER	—	5	3
3. Iwao Horiuchi	JAP	5	6	
4. Mahmut Atalay	TUR	5	6	
5. Abdollah Movahed Ardabili	IRN	5	7	
6. Zarbeg Beriashvili	SOV	4	6	
6. Dong-Goo Chung	KOR	4	6	
6. Gregory Ruth	USA	4	6	

1968 Mexico City C: 26, N: 26, D: 10.20.
(70 kg—154½ lbs)

		ROUND ELIMINATED	BAD PTS.	FINAL ROUND
1. Abdollah Movahed Ardabili	IRN	—	4	1
2. Enyu Vulchev (Dimov)	BUL	—	4	3
3. Sereeter Danzandarjaa	MON	6	7.5	
4. Wayne Wells	USA	6	8	
5. Zarbeg Beriashvili	SOV	5	6	
6. Udey Chand	IND	5	6	
7. Iwao Horivchi	JAP	5	8	
8. Klaus-Jürgen Rost	GER	5	9.5	

1972 Munich C: 25, N: 25, D: 8.31.

		ROUND ELIMINATED	BAD PTS.	FINAL ROUND
1. Dan Gable	USA	—	1.5	2
2. Kikuo Wada	JAP	—	4.5	3
3. Ruslan Ashuraliev	SOV	—	4.5	6
4. Tsedendamba Natsagdorj	MON	5	6	
5. Ali Sahin	TUR	5	6	
6. Udo Schröder	GDR	5	8	
7. Wlodzimierz Cieślak	POL	5	8.5	
8. József Rusznyák	HUN	4	7	

Twenty-three-year-old Dan Gable of Waterloo, Iowa, trained seven hours a day, every day, for three years prior to the Munich Olympics. He lost only one match in his entire career.

1976 Montreal C: 24, N: 24, D: 7.31.

		ROUND ELIMINATED	BAD PTS.	FINAL ROUND
1. Pavel Pinigin	SOV	—	6	3.5
2. Lloyd Keaser	USA	—	1	3.5
3. Yasaburo Sugawara	JAP	—	6	5
4. Doncho Zhekov	BUL	6	8.5	
5. José Ramos	CUB	5	7	
6. Tsedendamba Natsagdorj	MON	5	7	
7. Rami Miron	ISR	5	9	
8. Eberhard Probst	GDR	4	6.5	

Pinigin outpointed Keaser 12–1 in the final match.

1980 Moscow C: 18, N: 18, D: 7.29.

		ROUND ELIMINATED	BAD PTS.	FINAL ROUND
1. Saipulla Absaidov	SOV	—	1	1
2. Ivan Yankov	BUL	—	5	4
3. Saban Sejdi	YUG	—	2	7
4. Jagmander Singh	IND	5	6	
5. Eberhard Probst	GDR	5	7.5	
6. Octavian Dusa	ROM	4	7	
7. Ali Hussain Faris	IRQ	4	8	
8. Pekka Rauhala	FIN	4	9.5	

Absaidov outscored his five opponents 59–1, with only Yankov lasting the full nine minutes.

WELTERWEIGHT
(74 kg—163 lbs)
1896–1900 not held

1904 St. Louis C: 10, N: 1, D: 10.15.
(71.67 kg—158 lbs)
1. Charles Erickson   USA
2. William Beckmann   USA
3. Jerry Winholtz   USA
4. William Hennessy   USA
5. Otto Roehm   USA

Erickson was a member of the Norwegian Turnverein of Brooklyn.

1906–1920 not held

1924 Paris C: 13, N: 7, D: 7.14.
(72 kg—158½ lbs)
1. Hermann Gehri   SWI
2. Eino Leino   FIN
3. Otto Müller   SWI
4. Guy Lookabough   USA
5. William Johnson   USA

1928 Amsterdam C: 11, N: 11, D: 8.1.
(72 kg—158½ lbs)
1. Arvo Haavisto   FIN
2. Lloyd Appelton   USA
3. Maurice Letchford CAN
4. Jean Jourlin   FRA
5. T.H. Morris   AUS

1932 Los Angeles C: 9, N: 9, D: 8.3.
(72 kg—158½ lbs)
1. Jack Van Bebber   USA
2. Daniel MacDonald   CAN
3. Eino Leino   FIN
4. Jean Földeák   GER
5. Gyula Zombori   HUN

1936 Berlin C: 16, N: 16, D: 8.4.
(72 kg—158½ lbs)

		ROUND ELIMINATED	BAD PTS.	FINAL ROUND
1.	Frank Lewis	USA	—	3	3
2.	Ture Andersson	SWE	—	4	3
3.	Joseph Schleimer| CAN	—	3	6
4.	Jean Jourlin	FRA	5	5	
5.	Willy Angst	SWI	5	7	
6.	Josef Paar	GER	4	5	
7.	J. Beke	BEL	3	6	
7.	Erçetin	TUR	3	6	
7.	O'Hara	AUS	3	6	

Frank Lewis of Cushing, Oklahoma, was awarded first place even though he was thrown by Andersson in the fourth round.

1948 London C: 16, N: 16, D: 7.31.
(73 kg—161 lbs)

			ROUND ELIMINATED	BAD PTS.	FINAL ROUND
1.	Yaşar Dogu	TUR	—	0	1
2.	Richard Garrard	AUS	—	2	5
3.	Leland Merrill	USA	—	3	4
4.	Jean-Baptiste Leclerc	FRA	4	6	
5.	Kálmán Sóvári	HUN	4	7	
6.	Frans Westergren	SWE	3	5	

7. Willy Angst (SWI), H.F. Peace (CAN), Byung-Kwan Whang (KOR), Abbas Zandi (IRN)   3   6

1952 Helsinki C: 20, N: 20, D: 7.23.
(73 kg—161 lbs)

			ROUND ELIMINATED	BAD PTS.	FINAL ROUND
1.	William Smith	USA	—	2	4
2.	Per Berlin	SWE	—	3	4
3.	Abdullah Modjtabavi	IRN	—	4	4
4.	Alberto Longarela	ARG	4	5	
5.	Mohamed Hassan Moussa	EGY	4	6	
5.	Ladislav Sekal	CZE	4	6	
5.	Tsuguo Yamazaki	JAP	4	6	
8.	Aleksanteri Keisala	FIN	4	7	

Twenty-three-year-old Bill Smith of Cedar Falls, Iowa, was so surprised by his victory that at the medal ceremony he mounted the third-place stand instead of the winner's pedestal.

1956 Melbourne C: 15, N: 15, D: 12.1.
(73 kg—161 lbs)

			ROUND ELIMINATED	BAD PTS.	FINAL ROUND
1.	Mitsuo Ikeda	JAP	—	3	2
2.	Ibrahim Zengin	TUR	—	4	3
3.	Vakhtang Balavadze	SOV	—	4	6
4.	Per Berlin	SWE	4	5	
4.	Nabi Sorouri	IRN	4	5	
4.	Coenraad de Villiers	SAF	4	5	
7.	Mitious Petkov	BUL	4	6	
8.	Ernest Fischer	USA	3	7	
8.	Alfred Tischendorf	GDR	3	7	

1960 Rome C: 23, N: 23, D: 9.6.
(73 kg—161 lbs)

			ROUND ELIMINATED	BAD PTS.	FINAL ROUND
1.	Douglas Blubaugh	USA	—	0	1
2.	Ismail Ogan	TUR	—	4	4
3.	Muhammed Bashir	PAK	—	5	7
4.	Gaetano De Vescovi	ITA	5	7	
4.	Emam Goudarzi Habibi	IRN	5	7	
4.	Yutaka Kaneko	JAP	5	7	
7.	Coenraad de Villiers	SAF	4	7	
8.	Åxe Carlsson	SWE	4	8	

Doug Blubaugh of Ponca City, Oklahoma, qualified for the U.S. team by beating his former Oklahoma State teammate Phil Kinyon, after four scoreless draws. In fact, Blubaugh and Kinyon had drawn ten straight matches before Blubaugh finally won a decision. In Rome he tore through the opposition, winning five of his seven bouts by throws and one by default. Only Ogan lasted the full 12 minutes.

1964 Tokyo C: 22, N: 22, D: 10.14.
(78 kg—172 lbs)

		ROUND ELIMINATED	BAD PTS.	FINAL ROUND
1. Ismail Ogan	TUR	—	4	4
2. Guliko Sagaradze	SOV	—	4	4
3. Mohamad-Ali Sanatkaran	IRN	—	4	4
4. Petko Dermendzhiev	BUL	5	8	
5. Yasuo Watanabe	JAP	4	6	
6. Philip Oberlander	CAN	4	6	
7. Muhammad Afzal	PAK	4	7	
8. Madho Singh	IND	4	8	

Ogan was awarded first place because he weighed 2 kg (4.4 lbs) less than Sagaradze. Sanatkaran was relegated to third place because his two draws came in the final round.

1968 Mexico City C: 19, N: 19, D: 10.20.
(78 kg—172 lbs)

		ROUND ELIMINATED	BAD PTS.	FINAL ROUND
1. Mahmut Atalay	TUR	—	4.5	1
2. Daniel Robin	FRA	—	5	3
3. Dagvasuren Purev	MON	5	6	
4. Ali-Mohamad Momeni	IRN	5	6.5	
5. Tatsuo Sasaki	JAP	5	6.5	
6. Yuri Schakmuradov	SOV	5	8	
7. Stephen Combs	USA	5	8	
7. Angel Sotirov	BUL	5	8	

In 1968, Daniel Robin won silver medals in both the free-style and Greco-Roman competitions.

1972 Munich C: 25, N: 25, D: 8.31.

		ROUND ELIMINATED	BAD PTS.	FINAL ROUND
1. Wayne Wells	USA	—	2	2
2. Jan Karlsson	SWE	—	4	4
3. Adolf Seger	GER	—	5	6
4. Yancho Pavlov	BUL	6	7.5	
5. Mansour Barzegar	IRN	5	7	
5. Wolfgang Nitschke	GDR	5	7	
5. Daniel Robin	FRA	5	7	
8. Miklós Urbanovics	HUN	4	6.5	

Wells was a lawyer from Norman, Oklahoma.

1976 Montreal C: 21, N: 21, D: 7.31.

		ROUND ELIMINATED	BAD PTS.	FINAL ROUND
1. Jiichiro Date	JAP	—	0	1
2. Mansour Barzegar	IRN	—	2	5
3. Stanley Dziedzic	USA	—	2	6
4. Ruslan Ashuraliev	SOV	5	7.5	
5. Marin Pircalabu	ROM	5	9	
6. Fred Hempel	GDR	5	10	
7. Jarmo Overmark	FIN	4	7	
8. Kiro Ristov	YUG	4	8	

Date threw six of his seven opponents and outpointed Dziedzic 10–5.

1980 Moscow C: 18, N: 18, D: 7.30.

		ROUND ELIMINATED	BAD PTS.	FINAL ROUND
1. Valentin Angelov	BUL	—	2	2
2. Jamtsying Davaajav	MON	—	6	4
3. Dan Karabin	CZE	—	7.5	6
4. Pavel Pinigin	SOV	6	8.5	
5. Ryszard Ścigalski	POL	5	7	
6. Rajander Singh	IND	4	7	
7. István Fehér	HUN	4	9	
8. Riccardo Niccolini	ITA	4	9	

Angelov earned his gold medal by gaining five victories in one day. The big surprise was his win against Pinigin. Pinigin took Angelov to the mat twice in the first minute, but the Bulgarian came back to register a fall after 1:59. In the final match Angelov won on points, 6–5, over Davaajav.

MIDDLEWEIGHT
(82 kg—181 lbs)

1896–1906 not held

1908 London C: 12, N: 3, D: 7.21.
(73 kg—161 lbs)
1. Stanley Bacon   GBR
2. George de Relwyskow   GBR
3. Frederick Beck   GBR
4. Carl Georg Anderson   SWE
5. E.H. Bacon (GBR), A. Coleman(GBR)

1912 not held

1920 Antwerp C: 16, N: 9, D: 8.21.
(75 kg—165½ lbs)
1. Eino Leino   FIN
2. Väinö Penttala   FIN
3. Charles Johnson   USA
4. Angus Frantz   USA

1924 Paris C: 14, N: 9, D: 7.14.
(79 kg—174 lbs)
1. Fritz Hagmann   SWI
2. Pierre Ollivier   BEL
3. Vilho Pekkala   FIN
4. J. Pentillä   FIN
5. Robert Christoffersen DEN
6. Noel Rhys   GBR

1928 Amsterdam C: 9, N: 9, D: 8.1.
(79 kg—174 lbs)
1. Ernst Kyburz   SWI
2. Donald Stockton   CAN
3. Samuel Rabin   GBR
4. Ralph Hammond   USA
5. A. Praeg   SAF

1932 Los Angeles C: 7, N: 7, D: 8.3.
(79 kg—174 lbs)
1. Ivar Johansson   SWE
2. Kyösti Luukko   FIN
3. József Tunyogi   HUN
4. Robert Hess   USA
5. Sumiyuki Kotani   JAP
6. Emile Poilvé   FRA

This was the first of Johansson's three Olympic medals. Four days later he won the Greco-Roman Welterweight division and four *years* later, in Berlin, he was victorious as a Greco-Roman middleweight.

1936 Berlin C: 15, N: 15, D: 8.4.
(79 kg—174 lbs)

		ROUND ELIMINATED	BAD PTS.	FINAL ROUND
1. Emile Poilvé	FRA	—	1	0
2. Richard Voliva	USA	—	3	3
3. Ahmet Kireççi	TUR	5	6	
4. Ernst Krebs	SWI	5	7	
5. Jaroslav Sysel	CZE	4	6	
6. Kyösti Luukko	FIN	4	7	
7. Ercole Gallegati	ITA	3	5	
7. János Riheczky	HUN	3	5	

Poilvé registered five throws in six matches, as well as a second-round decision over Luukko.

1948 London C: 16, N: 16, D: 7.31.
(79 kg—174 lbs)

		ROUND ELIMINATED	BAD PTS.	FINAL ROUND
1. Glen Brand	USA	—	2	0
2. Adil Candemir	TUR	—	4	3
3. Erik Lindén	SWE	5	5	
4. Carel Reitz	SAF	4	5	
5. Paavo Sepponen	FIN	4	5	
6. André Brunaud	FRA	4	7	
7. M. Vachon	CAN	3	5	
8. R. Arthur	AUS	3	6	

Twenty-four-year-old Glen Brand of Clarion, Iowa, was awarded first place after he threw Candemir in the fourth round and then decisioned Linden in Round 5.

1952 Helsinki C: 17, N: 17, D: 7.23.
(79 kg—174 lbs)

		ROUND ELIMINATED	BAD PTS.	FINAL ROUND
1. David Tsimakuridze	SOV	—	4	2
2. Gholam Reza Takhti	IRN	—	2	3
3. György Gurics	HUN	—	5	6
4. Gustav Gocke	GER	5	6	
5. Haydar Zafer	TUR	4	5	
6. Leon Genuth	ARG	4	7	
6. Carel Reitz	SAF	4	7	
8. Bengt Lindblad	SWE	3	5	

1956 Melbourne C: 15, N: 15, D: 12.1.
(79 kg—174 lbs)

		ROUND ELIMINATED	BAD PTS.	FINAL ROUND
1. Nikola Stanchev	BUL	—	4	1
2. Daniel Hodge	USA	—	4	3
3. Georgy Skhirtladze	SOV	—	4	6
4. Ismet Atli	TUR	5	5	
5. Johann Sterr	GER	4	6	
5. Kazuo Katsuramoto	JAP	4	6	
7. Bengt Lindblad	SWE	3	7	
7. Abbas Zandi	IRN	3	7	

Stanchev was the first Bulgarian to win an Olympic gold medal.

1960 Rome C: 19, N: 19, D: 9.6.
(79 kg—174 lbs)

		ROUND ELIMINATED	BAD PTS.
1. Hasan Güngör	TUR	—	4
2. Georgy Skhirtladze	SOV	5	6
3. Hans Yngve Antonsson	SWE	5	6
4. Edward De Witt	USA	5	7
5. Prodan Gardzhev	BUL	4	6
5. Géza Hollósi	HUN	4	6
5. Madho Singh	IND	4	6
8. Takashi Nagai	JAP	4	7

1964 Tokyo C: 16, N: 16, D: 10.14.
(87 kg—192 lbs)

		ROUND ELIMINATED	BAD PTS.	FINAL ROUND
1. Prodan Gardzhev	BUL	—	5	2
2. Hasan Güngör	TUR	—	5	2
3. Daniel Brand	USA	5	6	
4. Mansour Mehdizadeh	IRN	5	6	
5. Géza Hollósi	HUN	4	6	
5. Tatsuo Sasaki	JAP	4	6	
7. Günther Bauch	GDR	4	9	
7. Faiz Muhammad	PAK	4	9	

Güngör was deprived of a second gold medal because he outweighed Gardzhev by 1 kg (2.2 lbs).

1968 Mexico City C: 22, N: 22, D: 10.20.
(87 kg—192 lbs)

		ROUND ELIMINATED	BAD PTS.
1. Boris Gurevitch	SOV	—	4.5
2. Munkbat Jigjid	MON	7	6.5
3. Prodan Gardzhev	BUL	7	7.5
4. Thomas Beckham	USA	7	8
5. Hüseyin Gürsoy	TUR	6	7
6. Peter Döring	GDR	4	6
7. Ronald Grimstead	GBR	4	8
8. Shigeru Endo	JAP	4	8.5

Gurevitch finished the tournament with draws against Jigjid and Gardzhev.

1972 Munich C: 24, N: 24, D: 8.31.

		ROUND ELIMINATED	BAD PTS.
1. Levan Tediashvili	SOV	—	4.5
2. John Peterson	USA	6	6
3. Vasile Iorga	ROM	6	7
4. Horst Stottmeister	GDR	6	7
5. Tatsuo Sasaki	JAP	5	6
6. Peter Neumair	GER	5	7
7. Kurt Elmgren	SWE	4	6
8. Jan Wypiórczyk	POL	4	7

1976 Montreal C: 18, N: 18, D: 7.31.

		ROUND ELIMINATED	BAD PTS.	FINAL ROUND
1. John Peterson	USA	—	2	0.5
2. Viktor Novoyilov	SOV	—	5.5	5
3. Adolf Seger	GER	—	6.5	6.5
4. Mehmet Uzun	TUR	6	7.5	
5. Ismail Abilov	BUL	5	7.5	
6. Henryk Mazur	POL	4	6	
7. István Kovács	HUN	4	6	
8. Masaru Motegi	JAP	4	8	

In 1972 John Peterson of Comstock, Wisconsin, won a silver medal, while his brother, Ben, a light heavyweight, won a gold. Four years later in Montreal they reversed medals.

1980 Moscow C: 14, N: 14, D: 7.31.

		ROUND ELIMINATED	BAD PTS.	FINAL ROUND
1. Ismail Abilov	BUL	—	1	1
2. Magomedhan Aratsilov	SOV	—	3	3
3. István Kovács	HUN	—	4	8
4. Henryk Mazur	POL	5	8.5	
5. Abdula Memedi	YUG	4	7	
6. Zevegying Duvchin	MON	4	8	
7. Gunter Busarello	AUT	3	7	
8. Mohammad Eloulabi	SYR	3	7.5	

Abilov outpointed his five opponents 50–5. Only Aratsilov lasted nine minutes, losing a fifth-round 8–4 decision to the 29-year-old Bulgarian champion.

LIGHT HEAVYWEIGHT
(90 kg—198½ lbs)
1896–1912 not held

1920 Antwerp C: 13, N: 8, D: 8.21.
80 kg—186½ lbs)

1. Anders Larsson   SWE
2. Charles Courant   SWI
3. Walter Maurer   USA
4. John Redman   USA

1924 Paris C: 16, N: 10, D: 7.14.
(87 kg—192 lbs)
1. John Spellman   USA
2. Rudolf Svensson   SWE
3. Charles Courant   SWI
4. Carl Westergren   SWE
5. W.G. Wilson   GBR
6. George Rumple   CAN

1928 Amsterdam C: 7, N: 7, D: 8.1.
(87 kg—192 lbs)
1. Thure Sjöstedt   SWE
2. Arnold Bögli   SWI
3. Henri Lefèbre   FRA
4. H.L. Edwards   USA
5. Jacques van Assche   BEL

1932 Los Angeles C: 4, N: 4, D: 8.3.
(87 kg—192 lbs)
1. Peter Mehringer   USA
2. Thure Sjöstedt   SWE
3. Eddie Scarf   AUS
4. H. Madison   CAN

1936 Berlin C: 12, N: 12, D: 8.4.
(87 kg—192 lbs)

		ROUND ELIMINATED	BAD PTS.	FINAL ROUND
1.	Knut Fridell	SWE	—	2	1
2.	August Neo	EST	—	5	4
3.	Erich Siebert	GER	—	5	6
4.	Paul Dätwyler	SWI	4	6	
5.	Ray Clemons	USA	4	7	
6.	Eddie Scarf	AUS	3	5	
7.	H. Prokop	CZE	3	7	
8.	Ede Virág-Ébner	HUN	3	7	

1948 London C: 15, N: 15, D: 7.31.
(87 kg—192 lbs)

		ROUND ELIMINATED	BAD PTS.	FINAL ROUND
1.	Henry Wittenberg	USA	—	1	2
2.	Fritz Stöckli	SWI	—	1	3
3.	Bengt Fahlkvist	SWE	—	2	4
4.	Muharrem Candaş	TUR	5	7	
4.	Fernand Payette	CAN	5	7	
6.	Patrick Morton	SAF	3	5	
7.	S. Defteraios (GRE), J. Sullivan (GBR), O. Verona (ITA)		3	6	

Each of the three matches of the final round was an epic struggle and each was decided by a split decision of the judges. Wittenberg was a 29-year-old New York policeman.

1952 Helsinki C: 13, N: 13, D: 7.23.
(87 kg—192 lbs)

		ROUND ELIMINATED	BAD PTS.	FINAL ROUND
1.	Wiking Palm	SWE	—	4	2
2.	Henry Wittenberg	USA	—	4	3
3.	Adil Atan	TUR	—	6	5
4.	Avgust Englas	SOV	5	7	
5.	Abass Zandi	IRN	4	5	
6.	Jacob Theron	SAF	3	5	
7.	Max Leichter	GER	3	7	

1956 Melbourne C: 12, N: 12, D: 12.1.
(87 kg—192 lbs)

		ROUND ELIMINATED	BAD PTS.	FINAL ROUND
1.	Gholam-Reza Takhti	IRN	—	0	2
2.	Boris Kulayev	SOV	—	2	4
3.	Peter Blair	USA	—	4	6
4.	Gerald Martina	IRL	4	6	
5.	Adil Atan	TUR	4	7	
5.	Kevin Coote	AUS	4	7	
7.	Mitsuhiro Ohira (JAP), Wiking Palm (SWE), Jacob Theron (SAF)		3	7	

1960 Rome C: 19, N: 19, D: 9.6.
(87 kg—192 lbs)

		ROUND ELIMINATED	BAD PTS.	FINAL ROUND
1.	Ismet Atli	TUR	—	5	1
2.	Gholam-Reza Takhti	IRN	—	0	3
3.	Anatoly Albul	SOV	5	6	
4.	Wiking Palm	SWE	5	6	
5.	Daniel Brand	USA	5	7	
6.	Hermanus van Zyl	SAF	5	9	
7.	Singh Sajjan	IND	4	8	
8.	Kazuo Abe	JAP	4	9	
8.	György Gurics	HUN	4	9	

Takhti pinned his first five opponents before losing on points to Atli. Albul was awarded the bronze medal over Palm on the basis of lower bodyweight.

1964 Tokyo C: 16, N: 16, D: 10.14.
(97 kg—214 lbs)

		ROUND ELIMINATED	BAD PTS.	FINAL ROUND
1.	Aleksandr Medved	SOV	—	3	2
2.	Ahmet Ayik	TUR	—	5	4
3.	Said Mustafov	BUL	—	5	6
4.	Gholam-Reza Takhti	IRN	5	6	
5.	Peter Jutzeler	SWI	5	9	
6.	Gerald Conine	USA	4	6	
7.	Heinz Kiehl	GER	4	7	
8.	Imre Vigh	HUN	3	6	

Medved secured the first of his three gold medals by pinning Mustafov in the final bout after only 39 seconds.

1968 Mexico City C: 16, N: 16, D: 10.20.
(97 kg—214 lbs)

			ROUND ELIMINATED	BAD PTS.	FINAL ROUND
1.	Ahmet Ayik	TUR	—	4	2
2.	Schota Lomidze	SOV	—	5	3
3.	József Csatári	HUN	—	5	7
4.	Said Mustafov	BUL	5	6.5	
5.	Khorloo Baianmunkh	MON	5	8.5	
6.	Jess Lewis	USA	4	7	
7.	Ryszard Dlugosz	POL	4	7	
8.	Gerd Bachmann	GDR	3	6	

1972 Munich C: 23, N: 23, D: 8.31.

			ROUND ELIMINATED	BAD PTS.	FINAL ROUND
1.	Benjamin Peterson	USA	—	4	2
2.	Gennady Strakhov	SOV	—	4	2
3.	Károly Bajkó	HUN	6	6.5	
4.	Rusi Petrov	BUL	6	8.5	
5.	Reza Hosainikhorami	IRN	5	7	
5.	Barbaro Morgan	CUB	5	7	
7.	Günter Spindler	GDR	5	8	
8.	Gueclue Mehmet	TUR	4	8	

Ben Peterson, whose brother, John, won a silver medal in the Middleweight division, picked up a surprise gold medal by pinning world champion Roussi Petrov after 2:41 of his final bout.

1976 Montreal C: 21, N: 21, D: 7.31.

			ROUND ELIMINATED	BAD PTS.	FINAL ROUND
1.	Levan Tediashvili	SOV	—	1	2
2.	Benjamin Peterson	USA	—	3.5	4
3.	Stelica Morcov	ROM	—	7	6
4.	Horst Stottmeister	GDR	6	7.5	
5.	Terry Paice	CAN	5	7	
6.	Pawel Kurczewski	POL	5	8.5	
7.	Frank Andersson	SWE	5	8.5	
8.	Barbaro Morgan	CUB	4	7.5	

One of the greatest amateur wrestlers of all time, Levan "Teddy" Tediashvili had not lost a match since 1971. At the Munich Olympics he had defeated John Peterson to win the Middleweight division. Four years later Tediashvili moved up to Light Heavyweight and outpointed John's brother, Ben, 11–5 for a second gold medal. Tediashvili, a law student and vineyard worker, was a brash performer who was known to wink at pretty women in the crowd just before pinning his opponents.

1980 Moscow C: 15, N: 15, D: 7.29.

			ROUND ELIMINATED	BAD PTS.	FINAL ROUND
1.	Sanasar Oganesyan	SOV	—	2	1.5
2.	Uwe Neupert	GDR	—	4.5	4
3.	Aleksander Cichoń	POL	—	0.5	6.5
4.	Ivan Ginov	BUL	5	7	
5.	Dashdorj Tserentogtokh	MON	5	8.5	
6.	Christophe Andanson	FRA	4	7	
7.	Ion Ivanov	ROM	4	7.5	
8.	Mick Pikos	AUS	4	8	

HEAVYWEIGHT
(100 kg—220 lbs)
1896–1968 not held

1972 Munich C: 17, N: 17, D: 8.31.

			ROUND ELIMINATED	BAD PTS.	FINAL ROUND
1.	Ivan Yarygin	SOV	—	0	0
2.	Khorloo Baianmunkh	MON	—	1	5
3.	József Csatári	HUN	—	2	7
4.	Vasil Todorov	BUL	5	7.5	
5.	Enache Panait	ROM	5	9	
6.	Ryszard Dlugosz	POL	4	7	
7.	Abolfazi Anvari	IRN	4	9	
8.	Julio Tamussin	ITA	3	6.5	

In an inspired performance, 23-year-old Ivan Yarygin pinned all seven of his opponents. Only Baianmunkh was able to last more than three minutes with the Soviet strongman. Yarygin spent a total of only 17 minutes and eight seconds on the mat in his seven matches.

1976 Montreal C: 15, N: 15, D: 7.31.

		ROUND ELIMINATED	BAD PTS.	FINAL ROUND
1. Ivan Yarygin	SOV	—	2	1.5
2. Russell Hellickson	USA	—	3.5	4
3. Dimo Kostov	BUL	—	4.5	6.5
4. Petr Drozda	CZE	5	8	
5. Khorloo Baianmunkh	MON	4	5.5	
6. Kazuo Shimizu	JAP	4	8	
7. Hans Stratz	GER	3	7	
8. Daniel Vernik	ARG	3	8	

In 1974 Yarygin was beaten in the European championships by Harald Büttner of East Germany. He was immediately removed from the Soviet team and replaced by veteran Vladimir Gulyutkin, who proceeded to win the 1974 world championship. But at the 1975 world championships, Büttner pinned Gulyutkin in 57 seconds and Yarygin was brought back after a year's absence from international competition. At the 1976 European championships, held in Leningrad three months before the Olympics, Yarygin was back to his old ways, overpowering each of his opponents. In Montreal, Yarygin faced Büttner in the very first round and defeated him 13–5. Yarygin's fifth and final victory was his most difficult, a 19–13 verdict over Russ Hellickson of Oregon, Wisconsin, who had moved up from Light Heavyweight to Heavyweight after losing five straight matches to Levan Tediashvili.

1980 Moscow C: 15, N: 15, D: 7.30.

		ROUND ELIMINATED	BAD PTS.	FINAL ROUND
1. Ilya Mate	SOV	—	2	1
2. Slavcho Chervenkov	BUL	—	3	3.5
3. Július Strnisko	CZE	—	4	7.5
4. Harald Büttner	GDR	5	6.5	
5. Tomasz Busse	POL	5	7	
6. Vasile Puscasu	ROM	4	6	
7. Barbaro Morgan	CUB	3	7.5	
8. Khorloo Baianmunkh	MON	3	8	

SUPER HEAVYWEIGHT—UNLIMITED WEIGHT

(Heavyweight 1904–1968)

1896–1900 not held

1904 St. Louis T: 5, N: 1, D: 10.15.
1. Bernhuff Hansen   USA
2. Frank Kungler   USA
3. Fred Warmbold   USA

Hansen, a representative of the Norwegian Turnverein of Brooklyn, needed only 7:30 to pin his three opponents. In

1904 anyone over 158 pounds was considered a heavyweight. Currently, a 158-pound wrestler would compete in the Welterweight division.

1906 not held

1908 London C: 11, N: 3, D: 7.23.
1. George Con O'Kelly   GBR/IRL
2. Jacob Gundersen   NOR
3. Edmond Barrett   GBR/IRL
4. E.E. Nixon   GBR
5. L. Bruce   GBR

Both O'Kelly and Barrett were from County Cork in Ireland. Shortly before the Olympic Games, Barrett had defeated O'Kelly for the British Heavyweight championship. But at the Olympics the 221-pound O'Kelly came up against Barrett in the third round and pinned him after 2:14. Gundersen put up a tougher battle, and it took O'Kelly 17:02 to keep him on the mat for the required two falls.

1912 not held

1920 Antwerp C: 8, N: 5, D: 8.21.
1. Robert Roth   SWI
2. Nathan Pendleton   USA
3. Frederick Meyer   USA
3. Ernst Nilsson   SWE

1924 Paris C: 12, N: 6, D: 7.14.
1. Harry Steel   USA
2. Henri Wernli   SWI
3. Andrew McDonald   GBR
4. Ernst Nilsson   SWE
5. Johan Richthoff   SWE
6. Edmond Dame   FRA

1928 Amsterdam C: 7, N: 7, D: 8.1.
1. Johan Richthoff   SWE
2. Aukusti Sihvola   FIN
3. Edmond Dame   FRA
4. Edward George   USA
5. Henri Wernli   SWI

Edward "Don" George later became a professional wrestling champion.

1932 Los Angeles C: 3, N: 3, D: 8.3.

		BAD PTS.
1. Johan Richthoff	SWE	2
2. John Riley	USA	3
3. Nikolaus Hirschl	AUT	6

Richthoff was 34 years old when he successfully defended his Olympic title.

1936 Berlin C: 11, N: 11, D: 8.4.

		ROUND ELIMINATED	BAD PTS.
1. Kristjan Palusalu	EST	—	2
2. Josef Klapuch	CZE	4	4
3. Hjalmar Nyström	FIN	5	5
4. Nils Åkerlindh	SWE	4	4
5. Robert Herland	FRA	4	6
6. Werner Bürki	SWI	4	7
7. Georg Gehring	GER	3	5
8. Chiga	CAN	3	6

The 27-year-old Palusalu, one of the quiet heroes of the Berlin Games, achieved a rare double by winning the Heavyweight title in both freestyle and Greco-Roman.

1948 London C: 9, N: 9, D: 7.31.

		ROUND ELIMINATED	BAD PTS.	FINAL ROUND
1. Gyula Bóbis	HUN	—	2	0
2. Bertil Antonsson	SWE	—	3	2
3. Joseph Armstrong	AUS	—	4	6
4. Sadik Esen	TUR	4	7	
5. Josef Ružička	CZE	3	5	
5. Abolghasem Sakhdari	IRN	3	5	
7. Richard Hutton	USA	3	6	

Bóbis began wrestling as a flyweight and kept moving up in division as he grew, until, at the age of 38, he won the Olympic gold medal as a heavyweight.

1952 Helsinki C: 13, N: 13, D: 7.23.

		ROUND ELIMINATED	BAD PTS.	FINAL ROUND
1. Arsen Mekokishvili	SOV	—	2	2
2. Bertil Antonsson	SWE	—	2	3
3. Kenneth Richmond	GBR	—	4	6
4. Irfan Atan	TUR	4	5	
5. William Kerslake	USA	4	6	
6. Taisto Kangasniemi	FIN	4	6	
7. Natale Vecchi	ITA	4	7	
7. Willi Waltner	GER	4	7	

When Ken Richmond entered the ring he was one of the most recognized men in the world, even though no one knew his name. Richmond's muscular body was famous because he was the one who struck the gong at the beginning of J. Arthur Rank films. Richmond almost pinned Mekokishvili in the second minute of their third-round bout, but the 256-pound Georgian broke loose and regained the offensive to win a split decision. The following day Mekokishvili won another split decision from Bertil Antonsson to secure the gold medal.

1956 Melbourne C: 11, N: 11, D: 12.1.

		ROUND ELIMINATED	BAD PTS.	FINAL ROUND
1. Hamit Kaplan	TUR	—	1	2
2. Yusein Mehmedov	BUL	—	3	3
3. Taisto Kangasniemi	FIN	—	3	6
4. Ray Mitchell	AUS	4	7	
4. Kenneth Richmond	GBR	4	7	
6. Ivan Vykhristyuk	SOV	3	5	
7. William Kerslake	USA	3	6	

1960 Rome C: 17, N: 17, D: 9.6.

		ROUND ELIMINATED	BAD PTS.	FINAL ROUND
1. Wilfried Dietrich	GER	—	1	2
2. Hamit Kaplan	TUR	—	5	4
3. Savkus Dzarassov	SOV	—	2	6
4. Pietro Marascalchi	ITA	5	8	
5. Lyutvi Ahmedov	BUL	4	6	
5. János Reznák	HUN	4	6	
7. Bertil Antonsson	SWE	4	7	
8. William Kerslake	USA	4	8	

Dietrich won Greco-Roman silver medals in 1956 and 1960, but his only gold came in freestyle wrestling, after he held defending champion Hamit Kaplan to a draw in the final match.

1964 Tokyo C: 13, N: 13, D: 10.14.

		ROUND ELIMINATED	BAD PTS.	FINAL ROUND AND 3RD PLACE
1. Aleksandr Ivanitsky	SOV	—	2	2
2. Lyutvi Ahmedov	BUL	—	3	2
3. Hamit Kaplan	TUR	4	7	2
4. Bohumil Kubat	CZE	4	7	2
5. Denis McNamara	GBR	4	7	8
6. Ştefan Ştîngu	ROM	4	8	
7. Wilfried Dietrich (GER), Larry Kristoff (USA), Masanori Saito (JAP)		3	6	

Thirty-one-year-old Hamit Kaplan of Amasya, Anatolia, completed his set of Olympic medals by winning the bronze.

1968 Mexico City C: 15, N: 15, D: 10.20.

		ROUND ELIMINATED	BAD PTS.	FINAL ROUND
1. Aleksandr Medved	SOV	—	1	1
2. Osman Duraliev	BUL	—	4	3
3. Wilfried Dietrich	GER	—	5	8
4. Ştefan Ştîngu	ROM	5	6	
5. Larry Kristoff	USA	4	6	
6. Abolfazi Anvari	IRN	4	9	
7. Erdeneotchir Elziisaihan	MON	4	9	
8. Raymond Uyttrheaeghe	FRA	3	9	

Dietrich won his fifth Olympic medal (one gold, two silver, two bronze) at the age of 35.

1972 Munich C: 13, N: 13, D: 8.31.

		ROUND ELIMINATED	BAD PTS.	FINAL ROUND
1. Aleksandr Medved	SOV	—	2	1
2. Osman Duraliev	BUL	—	4	3
3. Chris Taylor	USA	5	6	
4. Moslem Filabi	IRN	5	8.5	
5. Wilfried Dietrich	GER	4	6	
6. Peter Germer	GDR	4	8	
7. Ştefan Ştîngu	ROM	4	8.5	
8. Stanislaw Makowiecki	POL	3	7.5	

The biggest confrontation of the 1972 tournament came in the very first round, when two-time Olympic champion Aleksandr Medved of Minsk met 6-foot 5-inch, 412-pound Chris Taylor of Dowagiac, Michigan. Medved had beaten Taylor three times, but this time they fought to a standoff. The 231-pound Ukrainian was awarded a controversial decision when the Turkish referee, Umit Demirag, penalized Taylor for passivity. This evident injustice led to Demirag's dismissal as an Olympic referee, although the judgment against Taylor was allowed to stand. Both Medved and Taylor won the rest of their bouts. Medved became the only freestyle wrestler to win gold medals at three different Olympics.

A nasty incident took place in the third-round match between Giyasettin Yilmaz of Turkey and Bulgarian veteran Osman Duraliev. The two men collided in the third minute, and Yilmaz came away with a bleeding nose. Enraged, he refused to go to his corner and was disqualified. Then he went berserk, shouting at the referee, chasing Duraliev, and tearing apart his own dressing room. Yilmaz was finally subdued by 1968 Light Heavyweight gold medalist Ahmet Ayik.

1976 Montreal C: 15, N: 15, D: 7.31.

		ROUND ELIMINATED	BAD PTS.	FINAL ROUND
1. Soslan Andiev	SOV	—	2	1
2. József Balla	HUN	—	7	5
3. Ladislau Simon	ROM	—	6	6
4. Roland Gehrke	GDR	6	8	
5. Nikola Dinev	BUL	5	6	
6. Yorihide Isogai	JAP	4	7	
7. Eskandar Filabi	IRN	4	8	
8. Mamadou Sakho	SEN	4	8.5	

1980 Moscow C: 12, N: 12, D: 7.31.

		ROUND ELIMINATED	BAD PTS.	FINAL ROUND
1. Soslan Andiev	SOV	—	1	1
2. József Balla	HUN	—	5	5
3. Adam Sandurski	POL	—	0	6
4. Roland Gehrke	GDR	4	7	
5. Andrei Ianko	ROM	4	8	
6. Mamadou Sakho	SEN	4	8.5	
7. Petur Ivanov	BUL	3	7	
8. Arturo Diaz	CUB	3	8	

Seven-foot, 297-pound Adam Sandurski demolished his first four opponents in 9:50 but then lost on points, 6–3, to defending champion Soslan Andiev of Ordjenikidze, Georgia.

GRECO-ROMAN WRESTLING

Light Flyweight	Welterweight
Flyweight	Middleweight
Bantamweight	Light Heavyweight
Featherweight	Heavyweight
Lightweight	Super Heavyweight—Unlimited Weight

In Greco-Roman wrestling the use of the legs is prohibited, and no holds may be made below the hips. The system of scoring is the same as in freestyle wrestling.

LIGHT FLYWEIGHT

(48 kg—106 lbs)

1896–1968 not held

1972 Munich C: 20, N: 20, D: 9.10.

		ROUND ELIMINATED	BAD PTS.	FINAL ROUND
1. Gheorghe Berceanu	ROM	—	1	1
2. Rahim Aliabadi	IRN	—	5	3
3. Stefan Angelov	BUL	—	3.5	8
4. Raimo Hirvonen	FIN	5	6	
5. Kazuharu Ishida	JAP	5	7	
6. Lorenzo Calafiore	ITA	5	8	
7. Bernd Drechsel	GDR	4	7	
8. Günter Maas	GER	3	6.5	

1976 Montreal C: 15, N: 15, D: 7.24.

		ROUND ELIMINATED	BAD PTS.	FINAL ROUND
1. Alexei Shumakov	SOV	—	0	2
2. Gheorghe Berceanu	ROM	—	2	4
3. Stefan Angelov	BUL	—	3	6
4. Yoshite Moriwaki	JAP	5	8	
5. Dietmar Hinz	GDR	4	6	
6. Mitchell Kawasaki	CAN	4	7	
7. Salin Bora	TUR	4	7	
8. Michael Farina	USA	3	8	
8. Khalil Rashid	IRN	3	8	

In the final round Shumakov outpointed Angelov 5–4 and Berceanu 10–6.

1980 Moscow C: 10, N: 10, D: 7.22.

		ROUND ELIMINATED	BAD PTS.	FINAL ROUND
1. Zaksylik Ushkempirov	SOV	—	3.5	1.5
2. Constantin Alexandru	ROM	—	6	4
3. Ferenc Seres	HUN	—	7	6.5
4. Pavel Hristov	BUL	5	7.5	
5. Reijo Haaparanta	FIN	4	9	
6. Alfredo Olvera	MEX	3	7.5	

FLYWEIGHT

(52 kg—114½ lbs)

1896–1936 not held

1948 London C: 13, N: 13, D: 8.6.

		ROUND ELIMINATED	BAD PTS.	FINAL ROUND
1. Pietro Lombardi	ITA	—	3	1
2. Kenan Olcay	TUR	—	3	3
3. Reino Kangasmaki	FIN	5	6	
4. Malte Möller	SWE	5	6	
5. Gyula Szilágyi	HUN	5	5	
6. Fridtjof Clausen	NOR	4	7	
7. Mohamed Abd El Al	EGY	3	6	
7. M. Varela	ARG	3	6	

1952 Helsinki C: 17, N: 17, D: 7.27.

		ROUND ELIMINATED	BAD PTS.	FINAL ROUND
1. Boris Gurevitch	SOV	—	3	2
2. Ignazio Fabra	ITA	—	3	4
3. Leo Honkala	FIN	—	2	6
4. Heinrich Weber	GER	4	5	
5. Mahmoud Omar Fawzy	EGY	4	6	
5. Bengt Johansson	SWE	4	6	
7. Maurice Mewis	BEL	4	7	
7. Borivoje Vukov	YUG	4	7	

1956 Melbourne C: 11, N: 11, D: 12.6.

		ROUND ELIMINATED	BAD PTS.	FINAL ROUND
1. Nikolai Solovyov	SOV	—	4	3
2. Ignazio Fabra	ITA	—	4	4
3. Durum Ali Egribaş	TUR	—	4	4
4. Dumitru Pirvulescu	ROM	4	7	
5. István Baranya	HUN	3	5	
5. Borivoje Vukov	YUG	3	5	
7. Maurice Mewis	BEL	3	6	

1960 Rome C: 18, N: 18, D: 8.31.

		ROUND ELIMINATED	BAD PTS.
1. Dumitru Pirvulescu	ROM	—	5
2. Osman Sayed	UAR	5	6
3. Mohamed Paziraye	IRN	5	6
4. Takashi Hirata	JAP	5	7
5. Ignazio Fabra	ITA	5	8
5. Ivan Kochergin	SOV	5	8
7. Borivoje Vukov	YUG	4	6
8. Bengt Frandfors	SWE	4	7

1964 Tokyo C: 18, N: 18, D: 10.19.

		ROUND ELIMINATED	BAD PTS.	FINAL ROUND
1. Tsutomu Hanahara	JAP	—	3	1
2. Angel Kerezov	BUL	—	4	4
3. Dumitru Pirvulescu	ROM	—	2	7
4. Ignazio Fabra	ITA	4	6	
4. Rolf Lacour	GER	4	6	
4. Maurice Mewis	BEL	4	6	
4. J. Richard Wilson	USA	4	6	
8. Burhan Bozkurt (TUR), Vasilios Ganotis (GRE), Sang-Shik Shin (KOR)		3	6	

1968 Mexico City C: 24, N: 24, D: 10.26.

		ROUND ELIMINATED	BAD PTS.
1. Peter Kirov	BUL	—	5
2. Vladimir Bakulin	SOV	6	6
3. Miroslav Zeman	CZE	6	8
4. Imre Alker	HUN	6	8.5
5. Rolf Lacour	GER	5	6
6. Jussi Vesterinen	FIN	5	7.5
7. Enrique Jimenez	MEX	4	6
8. Metin Cikmaz	TUR	4	7
8. Sang-Shik Shin	KOR	4	7

1972 Munich C: 22, N: 22, D: 9.10.

		ROUND ELIMINATED	BAD PTS.	FINAL ROUND
1. Peter Kirov	BUL	—	2	4
2. Koichiro Hirayama	JAP	—	3	5
3. Giuseppe Bognanni	ITA	—	5	7
4. József Doncsecz	HUN	5	8	
4. Jan Michalik	POL	5	8	
4. Miroslav Zeman	CZE	5	8	
7. Vassilios Ganotis	GRE	4	6	
8. Jamsran Munkhotchir	MON	4	8	

1976 Montreal C: 17, N: 17, D: 7.24.

		ROUND ELIMINATED	BAD PTS.	FINAL ROUND
1. Vitaly Konstantinov	SOV	—	3	4
2. Nicu Ginga	ROM	—	5.5	5
3. Koichiro Hirayama	JAP	—	8	5
4. Rolf Krauss	GER	5	8.5	
5. Lajos Rácz	HUN	4	6	
6. Morad-Ali Shirani	IRN	4	7	
7. Antonino Caltabiano	ITA	4	7.5	
8. Seung-Hyun Baek	KOR	4	9	

1980 Moscow C: 10, N: 10, D: 7.23.

		ROUND ELIMINATED	BAD PTS.	FINAL ROUND
1. Vakhtang Blagidze	SOV	—	1	1
2. Lajos Rácz	HUN	—	4	5
3. Mladen Mladenov	BUL	—	5	6
4. Nicu Ginga	ROM	4	8	
5. Antonín Jelínek	CZE	4	8	
6. Stanisław Wróblewski	POL	3	7	

Blagidze defeated Racz, 19–1, in the final match.

BANTAMWEIGHT
(57 kg—125½ lbs)
1896–1920 not held

1924 Paris C: 25, N: 15, D: 7.10.
(58 kg—128 lbs)
1. Eduard Pütsep   EST
2. Anselm Ahlfors   FIN

3. Väinö Ikonen   FIN
4. Sigfrid Hansson   SWE
5. Adolf Herschmann AUT
6. R. Olsen   NOR
7. József Tasnádi   HUN
8. Armand Magyar   HUN

1928 Amsterdam C: 19, N: 19, D: 8.5.
(58 kg—128 lbs)
1. Kurt Leucht   GER
2. Jindrich Maudr   CZE
3. Giovanni Gozzi   ITA
4. Oscar Lindelöf   SWE
5. Ödön Zombori   HUN
6. Eduard Pütsep   EST
7. A. Andersen   DEN
8. Anselm Ahlfors   FIN

1932 Los Angeles C: 7, N: 7, D: 8.7.
(56 kg—123½ lbs)
1. Jakob Brendel   GER
2. Marcello Nizzola ITA
3. Louis François   FRA
4. Herman Tuvesson   SWE

1936 Berlin C: 18, N: 18, D: 8.9.
(56 kg—123½ lbs)

		ROUND ELIMINATED	BAD PTS.	FINAL ROUND
1. Márton Lőrincz	HUN	—	3	1
2. Egon Svensson	SWE	—	0	3
3. Jakob Brendel	GER	5	5	
4. Väinö Perttunen	FIN	5	5	
5. Iosef Tojar	ROM	5	6	
6. Evald Sikk	EST	4	5	
7. Voigt	DEN	4	7	
8. Bertoli	ITA	4	7	

1948 London C: 13, N: 13, D: 8.6.

		ROUND ELIMINATED	BAD PTS.	FINAL ROUND
1. Kurt Pettersén	SWE	—	4	1
2. Ali Mahmoud Hassan	EGY	—	2	3
3. Halil Kaya	TUR	5	6	
4. Taisto Lempinen	FIN	4	5	
5. Elvidio Flamini	ARG	4	6	
6. Lajos Bencze	HUN	3	5	
7. Reidar Maerlie	NOR	3	5	
8. N. Biris	GRE	3	6	

1952 Helsinki C: 17, N: 17, D: 7.27.

		ROUND ELIMINATED	BAD PTS.	FINAL ROUND
1. Imre Hódos	HUN	—	4	4
2. Zakaria Chihab	LEB	—	6	4
3. Artem Teryan	SOV	—	4	4
4. Hubert Persson	SWE	5	7	
5. Reidar Maerlie	NOR	4	5	

		ROUND ELIMINATED	BAD PTS.	FINAL ROUND
6. Ferdinand Schmitz	GER		4	6
7. Ion Popescu	ROM		4	7
8. Pietro Lombardi	ITA		3	5

1956 Melbourne C: 28, N: 28, D: 8.31.

		ROUND ELIMINATED	BAD PTS.	FINAL ROUND
1. Konstantin Vyrupayev	SOV	—	4	4
2. Edvin Westerby	SWE	—	1	4
3. Francisc Horvath	ROM	—	4	4
4. Imre Hódos	HUN	4	5	
5. Alfred Kämmerer	GER	4	5	
6. Dinko Petrov	BUL	3	5	
7. Adolfo Diaz	ARG	3	6	

1960 Rome C: 28, N: 28, D: 8.31.

		ROUND ELIMINATED	BAD PTS.	FINAL ROUND
1. Oleg Karavayev	SOV	—	2	1
2. Ion Cernea	ROM	—	5	3
3. Dinko Petrov	BUL	5	6	
4. Edvin Westerby	SWE	5	6	
5. Jiři Švec	CZE	5	7	
5. Yasar Yimaz	TUR	5	7	
7. Masamitsu Ichiguchi	JAP	5	8	
7. Bernard Knitter	POL	5	8	

1964 Tokyo C: 18, N: 18, D: 10.19.

		ROUND ELIMINATED	BAD PTS.
1. Masamitsu Ichiguchi	JAP	—	4
2. Vladlen Trostyansky	SOV	5	6
3. Ion Cernea	ROM	5	8
4. Jiři Švec	CZE	5	8
5. Kamal Ali	UAR	4	6
5. Tsviatko Pashkulev	BUL	4	6
5. Fritz Stange	GER	4	6
8. Unver Basergil	TUR	4	7

1968 Mexico City C: 24, N: 24, D: 10.26.

		ROUND ELIMINATED	BAD PTS.	FINAL ROUND
1. János Varga	HUN	—	6	—
2. Ion Baciu	ROM	6	7.5	4
3. Ivan Kochergin	SOV	6	7.5	6.5
4. Othon Moschidis	GRE	6	7.5	6.5
5. Koji Sakurama	JAP	5	6.5	
6. Elsayad Ibrahim	UAR	5	9	
6. Kaya Öczan	TUR	5	9	
8. Risto Björlin	FIN	4	6	

1972 Munich C: 30, N: 30, D: 9.10.

		ROUND ELIMINATED	BAD PTS.	FINAL ROUND
1. Rustem Kazakov	SOV	—	5	0
2. Hans-Jürgen Veil	GER	—	4	4
3. Risto Björlin	FIN	7	8	
4. János Varga	HUN	7	9	

		ROUND ELIMINATED	BAD PTS.	FINAL ROUND
5. Hristo Traikov	BUL		6	6
6. Ion Baciu	ROM		5	6
7. Ikuei Yamamoto	JAP		5	8.5
8. Józef Lipień	POL		4	8

World champion Rustem Kazakov pinned local favorite Hans-Jürgen Veil in 2:58 to win the gold medal.

1976 Montreal C: 17, N: 17, D: 7.24.

		ROUND ELIMINATED	BAD PTS.	FINAL ROUND
1. Pertti Ukkola	FIN	—	4.5	2
2. Ivan Frgić	YUG	—	6	3
3. Farhat Mustafin	SOV	—	4.5	7
4. Yoshima Suga	JAP	5	8	
5. Mihai Botila	ROM	5	8	
6. Krasimir Stefanov	BUL	4	6	
7. József Doncsecz	HUN	4	7.5	
8. Josef Krysta	CZE	4	8	

Ukkola earned his upset victory by barely outpointing Mustafin and Frgić with scores of 6–5 and 5–4.

1980 Moscow C: 13, N: 13, D: 7.24.

		ROUND ELIMINATED	BAD PTS.	FINAL ROUND
1. Shamil Serikov	SOV	—	1	1
2. Józef Lipień	POL	—	6	7
3. Benni Ljungbeck	SWE	—	5	8
4. Mihai Botila	ROM	5	11.5	
5. Antonino Caltabiano	ITA	4	7	
6. Josef Krysta	CZE	4	7	
7. Gyula Molnár	HUN	4	7	
8. Georgi Donev	BUL	3	7	

Serikov outpointed Lipień 11–4 in the final match.

FEATHERWEIGHT
(62 kg—136½ lbs)

1896–1908 not held

1912 Stockholm C: 38, N: 13, D: 7.12.
(60 kg—132½ lbs)

1. Kaarlo Koskelo   FIN
2. Georg Gerstäcker   GER
3. Otto Lasanen   FIN
4. Kaarlo Leivonen   FIN
5. Erik Öberg   SWE

1920 Antwerp C: 21, N: 10, D: 8.26.
(60 kg—132½ lbs)
1. Oskar Friman   FIN
2. Heikki Kähkönen   FIN
3. Fritiof Svensson   SWE
4. Alexandre Boumans BEL
5. Aage Tergersen   DEN
6. Josef Beranek   CZE

1924 Paris C: 27, N: 15, D: 7.10.
(60 kg—132½ lbs)

1. Kaarlo "Kalle" Anttila — FIN
2. Aleksanteri Toivola — FIN
3. Erik Malmberg — SWE
4. Arthur Nord — NOR
5. Fritiof Svensson — SWE
6. M. Capron — FRA
6. Ödön Radvány — HUN

Anttila was 36 years old when he won his second Olympic gold medal. In Antwerp in 1920 he had finished first in the freestyle Lightweight division.

1928 Amsterdam C: 20, N: 20, D: 8.5.
(60 kg—132½ lbs)

1. Voldemar Väli — EST
2. Erik Malmberg — SWE
3. Giacomo Quaglia — ITA
4. Károly Kárpáti — HUN
5. Ernst Steinig — GER
6. A.A. Meier (DEN), M. Saim (TUR), Aleksanteri Toivola (FIN)

1932 Los Angeles C: 8, N: 8, D: 8.7.
(61 kg—134½ lbs)

1. Giovanni Gozzi — ITA
2. Wolfgang Ehrl — GER
3. Lauri Koskela — FIN
4. Jindřich Maudr — CZE
5. Kiyoshi Kase — JAP

1936 Berlin C: 19, N: 19, D: 8.9.
(61 kg—134½ lbs)

		ROUND ELIMINATED	BAD PTS.
1. Yaşar Erkan	TUR	—	4
2. Aarne Reini	FIN	7	5
3. Einar Karlsson	SWE	7	5
4. Sebastian Hering	GER	5	5
5. Krishjanis Kundsinsh	LAT	5	6
6. Valentino Borgia	ITA	4	5
7. Henryk Ślązak	POL	4	6
8. Gyula Móri	HUN	4	6

1948 London C: 17, N: 17, D: 8.6.
(61 kg—134½ lbs)

		ROUND ELIMINATED	BAD PTS.	FINAL ROUND
1. Mehmet Oktav	TUR	—	3	0
2. Olle Anderberg	SWE	—	3	3
3. Ferenc Tóth	HUN	6	6	
4. Georg Weidner	AUT	5	5	
5. Luigi Campanella	ITA	5	6	
6. Sayed Kandil	EGY	4	7	
6. Egil Solsvik	NOR	4	7	
6. Safi Taha	LEB	4	7	
6. Erkki Talosela	FIN	4	7	

The decisive match took place in the third round, when Oktav threw Anderberg in 2:48.

1952 Helsinki C: 17, N: 17, D: 7.27.
(61 kg—134½ lbs)

		ROUND ELIMINATED	BAD PTS.	FINAL ROUND
1. Yakov Punkin	SOV	—	2	0
2. Imre Polyák	HUN	—	3	4
3. Abdel Rashed	EGY	—	5	6
4. Umberto Trippa	ITA	4	5	
5. Bartholomäus Brötzner	AUT	4	6	
6. Hasan Bozbey	TUR	4	7	
7. Safi Taha	LEB	3	3	
8. Ernest Gondzik	POL	3	5	
8. Erkki Talosela	FIN	3	5	

Punkin finished stongly, pinning Polyák in 1:26 and Rashed in 3:28.

1956 Melbourne C: 10, N: 10, D: 12.6.
(61 kg—134½ lbs)

		ROUND ELIMINATED	BAD PTS.	FINAL ROUND
1. Rauno Mäkinen	FIN	—	4	4
2. Imre Polyák	HUN	—	3	4
3. Roman Dzneladze	SOV	—	4	4
4. Müzahir Sille	TUR	4	6	
5. Gunnar Håkansson	SWE	3	5	
6. Umberto Trippa	ITA	3	7	
7. Ion Popescu	ROM	3	7	

Mäkinen was the son of 1928 freestyle Bantamweight winner Kaarlo Mäkinen.

1960 Rome C: 25, N: 25, D: 8.31.
(61 kg—134½ lbs)

		ROUND ELIMINATED	BAD PTS.	FINAL ROUND
1. Müzahir Sille	TUR	—	5	1
2. Imre Polyák	HUN	—	3	3
3. Konstantin Vyrupayev	SOV	6	6	
4. Umberto Trippa	ITA	6	6	
5. Mihai Schultz	ROM	6	8	
6. Said Ebrahimian	IRN	5	7	
6. Vojtech Toth	CZE	5	7	
8. Lee Allen	USA	4	7	

1964 Tokyo C: 27, N: 27, D: 10.19.
(63 kg—139 lbs)

		ROUND ELIMINATED	BAD PTS.	FINAL ROUND
1. Imre Polyák	HUN	—	1	2
2. Roman Rurua	SOV	—	4	2
3. Branislav Martinovič	YUG	5	4	
4. Ronald Finley	USA	5	6	
4. Mostafa Mansour	UAR	5	6	
6. Joseph Mewis	BEL	4	6	
6. Mohamad Mirmalek	IRN	4	6	
6. Koji Sakurama	JAP	4	6	

After finishing second three straight times, Polyák finally won an Olympic gold medal.

1968 Mexico City C: 23, N: 23, D: 10.26.
(63 kg—139 lbs)

		ROUND ELIMINATED	BAD PTS.	FINAL ROUND
1. Roman Rurua	SOV	—	2	2
2. Hideo Fujimoto	JAP	—	5	2
3. Simeon Popescu	ROM	6	6.5	
4. Dimiter Galinchev	BUL	6	8	
5. Hizir Alakoc	TUR	5	6	
6. Martti Laakso	FIN	4	6	
7. James Hazewinkel	USA	4	8.5	
8. Lothar Schneider	GDR	4	9	

1972 Munich C: 19, N: 19, D: 9.10.

		ROUND ELIMINATED	BAD PTS.
1. Georgi Markov	BUL	—	3
2. Heinz-Helmut Wehling	GDR	6	6.5
3. Kazimierz Lipień	POL	6	6.5
4. Hideo Fujimoto	JAP	6	7.5
5. Djemal Megrelishvili	SOV	6	8
6. Ion Păun	ROM	5	7.5
7. Martti Laakso	FIN	5	8
7. Stylianos Mygiakis	GRE	5	8

1976 Montreal C: 17, N: 17, D: 7.24.

		ROUND ELIMINATED	BAD PTS.	FINAL ROUND
1. Kazimierz Lipień	POL	—	3.5	3.5
2. Nelson Davidian	SOV	—	4	4
3. László Réczi	HUN	—	5.5	4.5
4. Teruhiko Miyahara	JAP	7	8	
5. Ion Păun	ROM	6	8	
6. Pekka Hjelt	FIN	4	7	
7. Stylianos Mygiakis	GRE	4	8.5	
8. Stoyan Lazarov	BUL	3	7	

Kazimierz Lipień won the world championship in 1973 and 1974, but in 1975 he lost a controversial decision to Nelson Davidian. The two met again in the sixth round of the Olympics in Montreal, with Davidian gaining another controversial victory, 10–6. In that match, Viktor Igumenov, the Soviet coach, was ordered to leave the competition area after he illegally shouted instructions to Davidian. Igumenov continued to yell orders, but from a greater distance. Lipień salvaged the gold medal anyway by outpointing Réczi 13–4, the nine-point margin reducing Lipień's bad marks for the bout from 1 to 0.5. Lipień's twin brother, Jozef, won a Bantamweight silver medal in 1980. At the 1975 world championships, the Poles were accused of substituting Jozef for Kazimierz in one match. Their accusers should have known better, since Jozef always parted his hair on the left side, while Kazimierz parted his on the right. At the post-tournament press conference in Montreal, Kazimierz, a 27-year-old plumber, advised aspiring wrestlers to abstain from smoking and drinking. "And no women," added bronze medalist László

Réczi. But Lipień disagreed. "That is taking sacrifices too far," he said, "women are good to wrestle with, too."

1980 Moscow C: 11, N: 11, D: 7.22.

		ROUND ELIMINATED	BAD PTS.	FINAL ROUND
1. Stylianos Mygiakis	GRE	—	6	2
2. István Tóth	HUN	—	3	4
3. Boris Kramorenko	SOV	5	7	
4. Ivan Frgić	YUG	5	7	
5. Panayot Kirov	BUL	4	9	
6. Kazimierz Lipień	POL	3	6	
7. Radwan Karout	SYR	3	8	
8. Michal Vejsada	CZE	3	8	

Mygiakis was the first "Greco" ever to win a Greco-Roman gold medal in the Olympics.

LIGHTWEIGHT
(68 kg—150 lbs)

1896–1904 not held

1906 Athens C: 12, N: 7, D: 5.1.
(75 kg—165½ lbs)
1. Rudolf Watzl   AUT
2. Karl Karlsen   DEN
3. Ferenc Holuban   HUN
4. R. Dobrinovitz   GRE
4. K. Halik   BOH
4. Al. Wentrinsky   AUT

1908 London C: 25, N: 10, D: 7.25.
(66.6 kg—147 lbs)
1. Enrico Porro   ITA
2. Nikolai Orlov   RUS
3. Arvid Lindén   FIN
4. Gunnar Persson   SWE
5. Gustaf Malmström (SWE), József Maróthy (HUN), A. C. Moller (DEN), Ödön Radvány (HUN)

Porro, a 23-year-old Milanese sailor, was unbeaten in international competition. He was awarded a decision over Orlov after 50 minutes of very little action.

1912 Stockholm C: 48, N: 13, D: 7.13.
(67.5 kg—149 lbs)
1. Eemil Wäre   FIN
2. Gustaf Malmström   SWE
3. Edvin Matiasson   SWE
4. Ödön Radvány   HUN
5. Johan Nilsson   SWE
5. Volmar Vikström   FIN

Wäre pinned all five of his opponents, completing his feat by defeating Malmström after an epic 60-minute struggle.

1920 Antwerp C: 22, N: 14, D: 8.26.
(67.5 kg—149 lbs)
1. Eemil Wäre   FIN
2. Taavi Tamminen   FIN
3. Frithjof Andersen   NOR
4. Frits Janssens   BEL
5. Lonets   FIN

1924 Paris C: 28, N: 18, D: 7.10.
(67.5 kg—149 lbs)
1. Oskar Friman   FIN
2. Lajos Keresztes   HUN
3. Kalle Westerlund   FIN
4. Albert Kusnets   EST
5. František Kratochvil   CZE
6. C. Frisenfeldt (DEN), A. Gaupseth (NOR), Mihály Matura (HUN)

In 1920 Friman won the Featherweight title. Four years later in Paris, at the age of 31, he gained his second gold medal.

1928 Amsterdam C: 19, N: 19, D: 8.5.
(67.5 kg—149 lbs)
1. Lajos Keresztes   HUN
2. Eduard Sperling   GER
3. Edvard Westerlund   FIN
4. Tayare Yalaz   TUR
5. Vladimir Vávra   CZE
6. Walter Massop   HOL
7. Ryszard Błażyca   POL
7. F. Janssens   BEL

Keresztes turned to wrestling on the advice of a doctor who prescribed the sport as a cure for "prolonged neurosis."

1932 Los Angeles C: 6, N: 6, D: 8.7.
(66 kg—145½ lbs)
1. Erik Malmberg   SWE
2. Abraham Kurland   DEN
3. Eduard Sperling   GER
4. Aarne Reini   FIN

With this victory the 35-year-old Malmberg completed his set of Olympic medals, having previously earned a Featherweight bronze in 1924 and silver in 1928.

1936 Berlin C: 18, N: 18, D: 8.9.
(66 kg—145½ lbs)

		ROUND ELIMINATED	BAD PTS.	FINAL ROUND
1. Lauri Koskela	FIN	—	2	2
2. Josef Herda	CZE	—	3	3
3. Voldemar Väli	EST	—	2	5
4. Herbert Olofsson	SWE	5	5	
5. Alberto Molfino	ITA	4	6	
6. Arild Dahl	NOR	4	7	
7. Zbigniew Szajewski	POL	4	7	
8. Borlovan	ROM	3	5	

1948 London C: 17, N: 17, D: 8.6.
(67 kg—147½ lbs)

		ROUND ELIMINATED	BAD PTS.	3RD PLACE
1. Gustav Freij	SWE	—	2	
2. Aage Eriksen	NOR	5	5	—
3. Károly Ferencz	HUN	5	6	1
4. Charif Damage	LEB	5	6	2
5. Johannes Munnikes	HOL	4	6	
6. Georgios Petmezas	GRE	4	7	
6. Ahmet Senol	TUR	4	7	
6. Eino Virtanen	FIN	4	7	

1952 Helsinki C: 19, N: 19, D: 7.27.
(67 kg—147½ lbs)

		ROUND ELIMINATED	BAD PTS.	FINAL ROUND
1. Schazam Safin	SOV	—	3	1
2. Gustav Freij	SWE	—	3	3
3. Mikuláš Athanasov	CZE	—	5	6
4. Gyula Tarr	HUN	5	6	
5. Franco Benedetti	ITA	4	7	
5. Dumitru Cuc	ROM	4	7	
5. Kalle Haapasalmi	FIN	4	7	
8. Kamel Hussein	EGY	3	5	
8. Erich Schmidt	SAA	3	5	

1956 Melbourne C: 10, N: 10, D: 12.6.
(67 kg—147½ lbs)

		ROUND ELIMINATED	BAD PTS.	FINAL ROUND
1. Kyösti Lehtonen	FIN	—	1	1
2. Riza Dogan	TUR	—	6	3
3. Gyula Tóth	HUN	—	2	6
4. Bartholomäus Brötzner	AUT	4	8	
4. Dimiter Yanchev	BUL	4	9	
6. Dumitru Gheorghe	ROM	3	7	

1960 Rome C: 23, N: 23, D: 8.31.
(67 kg—147½ lbs)

		ROUND ELIMINATED	BAD PTS.	FINAL ROUND
1. Avtandil Koridze	SOV	—	5	1
2. Branislav Martinovič	YUG	—	4	3
3. Gustav Freij	SWE	5	6	
4. Karel Matoušek	CZE	5	6	
— Dimitro Stoyanov (Dimiter Yanchev)	BUL	5	8	
5. Dumitru Gheorghe	ROM	4	7	
5. Ernest Gondzik	POL	4	7	
5. Adil Güngör	TUR	4	7	
5. Mitsuharu Kitamura	JAP	4	7	
5. Kyösti Lehtonen	FIN	4	7	
5. Jacques Pourtau	FRA	4	7	

Charges of "fix" were hurled following a fifth round bout between Koridze and Dimiter Yanchev of Bulgaria, then known as Dimitro Stoyanov. Koridze needed to score a fall to force a final showdown with Martinovič. Anything less—a draw or even a points victory—would give the gold medal to the Yugoslav. After 11 minutes of inactivity, with only one minute left before the end of the bout, Koridze spoke a few words to Stoyanov and then threw him to the ground and pinned him. The Yugoslavs immediately lodged a protest. Stoyanov, who had originally been awarded fifth place, was disqualified from the tournament, but Koridze was not punished and went on to defeat Martinovič and to win the gold medal.

1964 Tokyo C: 19, N: 19, D: 10.19.
(70 kg—154½ lbs)

		ROUND ELIMINATED	BAD PTS.	2ND PLACE
1. Kazim Ayvaz	TUR	—	5	—
2. Valeriu Bularcă	ROM	5	6	3
3. David Gvantseladze	SOV	5	6	4
4. Tokuaki Fujita	JAP	5	6	5
5. Stevan Horvat	YUG	5	7	
6. Eero Tapio	FIN	5	8	
7. Bror Jonsson	SWE	4	6	
8. Ivan Ivanov	BUL	4	7	

1968 Mexico City C: 26, N: 26, D: 10.26.
(70 kg—154½ lbs)

		ROUND ELIMINATED	BAD PTS.	FINAL ROUND
1. Munji Mumemura	JAP	—	5	3.5
2. Stevan Horvat	YUG	—	5	5
3. Petros Galaktopoulos	GRE	—	5	5.5
4. Klaus Rost	GER	6	8	
5. Eero Tapio	FIN	5	7.5	
6. Werner Holzer	USA	5	8	
6. Gennady Sapunov	SOV	5	8	
8. Antal Steer	HUN	4	6	

1972 Munich C: 23, N: 23, D: 9.10.

		ROUND ELIMINATED	BAD PTS.
1. Shamil Khisamutdinov	SOV	—	2.5
2. Stoyan Apostolov	BUL	6	5
3. Gian-Matteo Ranzi	ITA	6	6
4. Manfred Schöndorfer	GER	6	7.5
5. Takashi Tanoue	JAP	5	6
6. Seyit Hisirli	TUR	4	6
6. Antal Steer	HUN	4	6·
8. Sreten Damjanovic	YUG	4	7.5

1976 Munich C: 21, N: 21, D: 7.24.

		ROUND ELIMINATED	BAD PTS.	FINAL ROUND
1. Suren Nalbandyan	SOV	—	3	2
2. Ştefan Rusu	ROM	—	3	3
3. Heinz-Helmut Wehling	GDR	—	8	7
4. Lars-Erik Skiöld	SWE	6	9.5	
5. Andrzej Supron	POL	5	8	
6. Manfred Schöndorfer	GER	5	9	
7. Erol Mutlu	TUR	4	6	
8. Markku Yli-Isotalo	FIN	4	7	

The 20-year-old Nalbandyan gained a crucial 5–3 victory over Rusu in the fourth round and then outpointed Supron 7–4 and Wehling 12–9.

1980 Moscow C: 15, N: 15, D: 7.24.

		ROUND ELIMINATED	BAD PTS.	FINAL ROUND
1. Ştefan Rusu	ROM	—	4	2
2. Andrzej Supron	POL	—	1	3
3. Lars-Erik Skiöld	SWE	—	1	7
4. Suren Nalbandyan	SOV	5	8	
5. Buyandelger Bold	MON	5	9	
6. Ivan Atanassov	BUL	4	8	
7. Reinhard Hartmann	AUT	4	8	
8. Károly Gaál	HUN	3	7	

The cast of characters was almost the same as it was four years earlier. Nalbandyan was the first of the four favorites to be eliminated when he and Rusu were charged with a double disqualification after 7:09 of their fifth-round match. In the final round-robin Rusu outpointed Supron 3–2 and Skiöld 5–1.

WELTERWEIGHT

(74 kg—163 lbs)

1896–1928 not held

1932 Los Angeles C: 8, N: 8, D: 8.7.
(72 kg—159 lbs)

1. Ivar Johansson	SWE
2. Väinö Kajander-Kajukorpi	FIN
3. Ercole Gallegati	ITA
4. Osvald Käpp	EST
5. Börge Jensen	DEN

Ivar Johansson, a 29-year-old policeman from Norrköping, put on a remarkable performance from August 1 through August 7. First he won the freestyle Middleweight division with four bouts in three days. Then he spent the next 24 hours fasting and sweating in a sauna so that he could compete as a welterweight in the Greco-Roman competition. Eleven pounds lighter, he won four more matches and earned a second gold medal.

1936 Berlin C: 14, N: 14, D: 8.9.
(72 kg—159 lbs)

		ROUND ELIMINATED	BAD PTS.	FINAL ROUND
1. Rudolf Svedberg	SWE	—	2	2
2. Fritz Schäfer	GER	—	1	2
3. Eino Virtanen	FIN	—	4	6
4. Edgar Puusepp	EST	5	6	
5. Nurettin Boytorun	TUR	5	7	
5. Silvio Tozzi	ITA	5	7	
7. De Feu	BEL	4	6	
7. Rieder	SWI	4	6	

1948 London C: 16, N: 16, D: 8.6.
(73 kg—160 lbs)

		ROUND ELIMINATED	BAD PTS.	FINAL ROUND
1. Gösta Andersson	SWE	—	3	2
2. Miklós Szilvási	HUN	—	3	3
3. Henrik Hansen	DEN	—	4	6
4. René Chesneau	FRA	4	7	
4. Veikko Männikö	FIN	4	7	
4. Josef Schmidt	DEN	4	7	
7. B. Cook	NOR	3	5	
8. N. Felgen	LUX	3	6	
8. L. Rigamonti	ITA	3	6	

1952 Helsinki C: 18, N: 18, D: 7.27.
(73 kg—160 lbs)

		ROUND ELIMINATED	BAD PTS.	FINAL ROUND
1. Miklós Szilvási	HUN	—	1	1
2. Gösta Andersson	SWE	—	1	4
3. Khalil Taha	LEB	—	5	6
4. Semen Marushkin	SOV	4	6	
5. Marin Belusiça	ROM	3	5	
5. René Chesneau	FRA	3	5	
5. Osvaldo Riva	ITA	3	5	
5. Ahmet Şenol	TUR	3	5	

In 1946, while on duty as a policeman, Miklós Szilvási was accidentally shot in the left leg by a machine gun. His left foot was temporarily paralyzed. Through exercise and willpower, Szilvási regained the use of his foot and represented Hungary at the 1948 Olympics. He finished second, losing a decision to Gösta Andersson in the final match. Four years later the two met again for the championship, and this time Szilvási won a split decision.

1956 Melbourne C: 11, N: 11, D: 12.6.
(73 kg—160 lbs)

		ROUND ELIMINATED	BAD PTS.	FINAL ROUND
1. Mithat Bayrak	TUR	—	2	2
2. Vladimir Maneyev	SOV	—	2	4
3. Per Berlin	SWE	—	0	6
4. Veikko Rantanen	FIN	3	5	
5. James Holt	USA	3	6	
5. Siegfried Schäfer	GDR	3	6	
7. Miklós Szilvási	HUN	3	7	
8. Mitiou Petkov	ROM	3	7	

1960 Rome C: 27, N: 27, D: 8.31.
(73 kg—160 lbs)

		ROUND ELIMINATED	BAD PTS.	FINAL ROUND
1. Mithat Bayrak	TUR	—	5	1
2. Günter Maritschnigg	GER	—	5	5
3. René Schiermeyer	FRA	—	5	6
4. Stevan Horvat	YUG	6	6	
5. Grigory Gamarnik	SOV	6	7	
6. Matti Laakso	FIN	5	7	
7. Antal Rizmayer	HUN	5	8	
8. Hansjorg Hirschbuhl	SWI	4	9	

1964 Tokyo C: 19, N: 19, D: 10.19.
(78 kg—172 lbs)

		ROUND ELIMINATED	BAD PTS.	FINAL ROUND
1. Anatoly Kolesov	SOV	—	7	5
2. Kiril Petkov	BUL	—	7	6
3. Bertil Nyström	SWE	—	7	6
4. Boleslaw Dubicki	POL	—	7	7
5. Antal Rizmayer	HUN	4	6	
5. Ion Tăranu	ROM	4	6	
7. Russell Camilleri	USA	4	7	
7. Rene Schiermeyer	FRA	4	7	
7. Asghar Zoughian	IRN	4	7	

Five of the last six matches ended in draws, which meant that Kolesov's victory by decision over Dubicki was the tie-breaker.

1968 Mexico City C: 22, N: 22, D: 10.26.
(78 kg—172 lbs)

		ROUND ELIMINATED	BAD PTS.	FINAL ROUND
1. Rudolf Vesper	GDR	—	4.5	3.5
2. Daniel Robin	FRA	—	5	4
3. Károly Bajkó	HUN	—	5.5	5.5
4. Metodi Zarev	BUL	5	8	
5. Ion Tăranu	ROM	5	9.5	
6. Jan-Ivar Karström	SWE	4	6	
7. Harald Barlie	NOR	4	7	
7. Franz Berger	AUT	4	7	
7. Milovan Nenadic	YUG	4	7	

1972 Munich C: 21, N: 21, D: 9.10.

		ROUND ELIMINATED	BAD PTS.	FINAL ROUND
1. Vítězslav Mácha	CZE	—	5.5	1
2. Petros Galaktopoulos	GRE	—	3	3
3. Jan Karlsson	SWE	5	6	
4. Ivan Kolev	BUL	5	6.5	
5. Momir Kecman	YUG	5	7.5	
6. Daniel Robin	FRA	5	8	
7. Klaus-Jürgen Pohl	GDR	5	8	
8. Werner Schröter	GER	4	7.5	

Mácha lost his opening bout to Ivan Kolev, but then won five in a row to secure the gold medal. Married to Miss Bohemia of 1971, Mácha was technically a miner, although he actually spent six to seven hours a day training.

1976 Montreal C: 18, N: 18, D: 7.24.

		ROUND ELIMINATED	BAD PTS.	FINAL ROUND
1. Anatoly Bykov	SOV	—	1	1
2. Vítězslav Mácha	CZE	—	1.5	3
3. Karlheinz Helbing	GER	—	6	8
4. Mikko Huhtala	FIN	5	7.5	
5. Klaus-Dieter Göpfert	GDR	5	10	
6. Gheorghe Ciobotaru	ROM	4	7	
7. Jan Karlsson	SWE	4	8	
8. Petros Galaktopoulos	GRE	3	7	

Crucial matches took place in the fourth round when Bykov outpointed Ciobotaru 7–6 and Mácha edged Huhtala 4–3. In the fifth round Bykov was awarded a controversial victory by disqualification over Göpfert, with six seconds left and the score tied 5–5. Bykov's final win over Mácha was by a margin of 7–3.

1980 Moscow C: 14, N: 14, D: 7.23.

		ROUND ELIMINATED	BAD PTS.	FINAL ROUND
1. Ferenc Kocsis	HUN	—	1	2
2. Anatoly Bykov	SOV	—	4	5
3. Mikko Huhtala	FIN	—	5	7
4. Yanko Shopov	BUL	5	7	
5. Lennart Lundell	SWE	4	6	
6. Vítězslav Mácha	CZE	4	8	
7. Gheorghe Minea	ROM	4	8	
8. Jacques van Lancker	BEL	3	7	

The final bout between Kocsis and Bykov ended with Bykov disqualified for inactivity after 7:21.

MIDDLEWEIGHT

(82 kg—181 lbs)

1896–1904 not held

1906 Athens C: 16, N: 9, D: 5.1.
(85 kg—187½ lbs)
1. Verner Weckman   FIN
2. Rudolf Lindmayer   AUT

3. Robert Behrens   DEN
4. W. Goldbach   AUT
5. V. Hradecky (BOH), E. Pamburi (ITA), Sauveur (BEL), F. Solar (AUT)

1908 London C: 21, N: 9, D: 7.25.
(73 kg—161 lbs)
1. Frithiof Mårtensson   SWE
2. Mauritz Andersson   SWE
3. Anders Andersen   DEN
4. Jóhannes Jósefsson   DEN/ICE
5. J. Belmer (HOL), J. Eriksen (DEN), Axel Frank (SWE), A.A. Larson (DEN), Marcel du Bois (BEL)

The final between Mårtensson and Mauritz Andersson was postponed overnight due to a minor injury to Mårtensson. Jósefsson, an Icelandic nationalist forced to compete under the Danish flag, fractured his arm in the semifinals and had to forfeit the match for third place.

1912 Stockholm C: 38, N: 14, D: 7.13.
(75 kg—165½ lbs)
1. Claes Johanson   SWE
2. Martin Klein   RUS/EST
3. Alfred Asikainen   FIN
4. Karl Åberg   FIN
5. August Jokinen   FIN
6. Johannes Sint   HOL

The longest wrestling contest in Olympic history was the semifinal bout between Klein and Asikainen. The two men struggled on for hours under the hot sun, stopping every half hour for a brief refreshment break. Finally, after 11 hours, Klein, an Estonian competing for Czarist Russia, pinned his opponent. However he was so exhausted by his ordeal that he was unable to take part in the final. Johanson was awarded first place by default.

1920 Antwerp C: 22, N: 11, D: 8.26.
(75 kg—165½ lbs)
1. Carl Westergren   SWE
2. Artur Lindfors   FIN
3. Matti Perttilä   FIN
4. Johannes Eillebrecht   HOL

The phenomenal Carl Westergren won the first of his three Olympic gold medals, each in a different division.

1924 Paris C: 27, N: 19, D: 7.10.
(75 kg—165½ lbs)
1. Edvard Westerlund   FIN
2. Artur Lindfors   FIN
3. Roman Steinberg   EST
4. Giuseppe Gorletti   ITA
5. Viktor Fischer   AUT
6. Nikola Grbič   YUG
7. R. Christoffersen   DEN
7. Waclaw Okulicz-Kozaryn   POL

1928 Amsterdam C: 17, N: 17, D: 8.5.
(75 kg—165½ lbs)

1. Väinö Kokkinen   FIN
2. László Papp   HUN
3. Albert Kusnets   EST
4. Johannes Jacobsen   DEN
5. Jean Saenen   BEL
6. František Hála   CZE
7. E. Bonassin   ITA
7. Ch. Nouri   TUR

Kokkinen, a restaurant owner from Helsinki, pinned all five of his opponents.

1932 Los Angeles C: 4, N: 4, D: 8.7.
(79 kg—174 lbs)

1. Väinö Kokkinen   FIN
2. Jean Földeak   GER
3. Axel Cadier   SWE

1936 Berlin C: 16, N: 16, D: 8.9.
(79 kg—174 lbs)

		ROUND ELIMINATED	BAD PTS.	FINAL ROUND
1.	Ivar Johansson SWE	—	2	1
2.	Ludwig Schweikert GER	—	3	2
3.	József Palotás HUN	—	4	6
4.	Väinö Kokkinen FIN	5	6	
5.	Ibrahim Erabi EGY	4	6	
6.	Ercole Gallegati ITA	4	6	
7.	Cocos ROM	4	6	
8.	Kis (YUG), Pointner (AUT), Pribyl (CZE)	3	6	

1948 London C: 13, N: 13, D: 8.6.
(79 kg—174 lbs)

		ROUND ELIMINATED	BAD PTS.	FINAL ROUND
1.	Axel Grönberg SWE	—	2	1
2.	Muhlis Tayfur TUR	—	4	3
3.	Ercole Gallegati ITA	5	5	
4.	Jean-Baptiste Benoy BEL	5	6	
5.	Kaare Larsen NOR	5	7	
6.	Juho Kinnunen FIN	4	5	
7.	Gyula Németi HUN	4	5	
8.	A. Vogel AUT	3	6	

1952 Helsinki C: 11, N: 11, D: 7.27.
(79 kg—174 lbs)

		ROUND ELIMINATED	BAD PTS.	FINAL ROUND
1.	Axel Grönberg SWE	—	4	2
2.	Kalervo Rauhala FIN	—	3	4
3.	Nikolai Byelov SOV	—	3	6
4.	Gyula Németi HUN	4	5	
5.	Ali Özdemir TUR	3	5	
6.	Ercole Gallegati ITA	3	6	
7.	Gustav Gocke GER	3	7	

1956 Melbourne C: 10, N: 10, D: 12.6.
(79 kg—174 lbs)

		ROUND ELIMINATED	BAD PTS.	FINAL ROUND
1.	Givy Kartoziya SOV	—	3	2
2.	Dimiter Dobrev BUL	—	4	4
3.	Karl-Axel Rune Jansson SWE	—	5	6
4.	Johann Sterr GER	4	6	
5.	György Gurics HUN	3	5	
6.	Viljo Punkari FIN	3	6	
7.	James Peckham USA	3	7	

1960 Rome C: 24, N: 24, D: 8.31.
(79 kg—174 lbs)

		ROUND ELIMINATED	BAD PTS.
1.	Dimiter Dobrev BUL	—	4
2.	Lothar Metz GDR	6	6
3.	Ion Tăranu ROM	6	7
4.	Kazim Ayvaz TUR	6	7
5.	Boleslaw Dubicki POL	5	7
5.	Nikolai Chuchalov SOV	5	7
7.	Yacous Romanos LEB	4	7
8.	Russell Camilleri USA	4	7

1964 Tokyo C: 20, N; 20, D: 10.19.
(87 kg—192 lbs)

		ROUND ELIMINATED	BAD PTS.	2ND PLACE
1.	Branislav Simič YUG	—	4	—
2.	Jiři Kormanik CZE	5	6	1
3.	Lothar Metz GDR	5	6	3
4.	Géza Hollósi HUN	5	7	
4.	Valentin Olenik SOV	5	7	
6.	Kraliu Bimbalov BUL	5	8	
7.	Richard Wayne Baughman USA	4	7	
8.	Ismail Selekman TUR	4	7	

Simič, competing in his third Olympics, managed to take first place without having to face either Kormanik or Metz.

1968 Mexico City C: 19, N: 19, D: 10.26.
(87 kg—192 lbs)

		ROUND ELIMINATED	BAD PTS.
1. Lothar Metz	GDR	—	5
2. Valentin Olenik	SOV	6	6
3. Branislav Simić	YUG	6	6
4. Nicolae Neguţ	ROM	6	8.5
5. Richard Wayne Baughman	USA	5	8
5. Peter Krumov	BUL	5	8
7. Czeslaw Kwiciński	POL	4	7
8. Häkon Overby	NOR	4	7

1972 Munich C: 20, N: 20, D: 9.10.

		ROUND ELIMINATED	BAD PTS.	FINAL ROUND
1. Csaba Hegedüs	HUN	—	3	2
2. Anatoly Nazarenko	SOV	—	4	3
3. Milan Nenadič	YUG	—	4	7
4. Miroslav Janota	CZE	5	7	
5. Ion Gabor	ROM	5	9	
6. Frank Hartmann	GDR	4	6	
7. Ali Yagmur	TUR	4	7	
8. Kiril Dimitrov	BUL	4	7.5	

Nazarenko, the 1970 world champion, and Hegedüs, the 1971 world champion, met in the very first round, with Hegedüs winning a decision. Neither man lost another bout for the rest of the tournament.

1976 Montreal C: 17, N: 17, D: 7.24.

		ROUND ELIMINATED	BAD PTS.	FINAL ROUND
1. Momir Petković	YUG	—	4.5	2
2. Vladimir Cheboksarov	SOV	—	6	4
3. Ivan Kolev	BUL	—	7	6
4. Leif Andersson	SWE	6	8	
5. Miroslav Janota	CZE	5	8	
6. Kazuhiro Takanishi	JAP	5	8.5	
7. Ion Enache	ROM	4	7	
8. Adam Ostrowski	POL	4	7	

The crucial third-round contest between Petković and Cheboksarov ended in a 6–6 tie, but Petković was given the victory after complex tie-breaker rules were invoked.

1980 Moscow C: 12, N: 12, D: 7.24.

		ROUND ELIMINATED	BAD PTS.	FINAL ROUND
1. Gennady Korban	SOV	—	1	2
2. Jan Dolgowicz	POL	—	7	3
3. Pavel Pavlov	BUL	—	1	7
4. Leif Andersson	SWE	4	8	
5. Detlef Kühn	GDR	3	8	
6. Mihály Toma	HUN	3	8	
7. Mohammad Eloulabi	SYR	3	9	

Korban defeated Dolgowicz, 11–4, and Pavlov, 13–7.

LIGHT HEAVYWEIGHT

(90 kg—198½ lbs)

1896–1906 not held

1908 London C: 21, N: 9, D: 7.22.
(93 kg—205 lbs)
1. Verner Weckman   FIN
2. Yrjö Saarela   FIN
3. Carl Jensen   DEN
4. Hugó Payr   HUN
5. A. Banbrook (GBR), M. du Bois (BEL), Fritz Larsson (SWE), J. van Westerop (HOL)

In the final match, Weckman, who had won the Middleweight gold medal in 1906, scored the first fall in 4:22. But Saarela won the second one in 5:07. Weckman, a 25-year-old engineer, prevailed in the deciding confrontation, after 16:10. At the award ceremony the Finnish flag was not hoisted. In its place was a sign bearing the word "Finland." Rumors spread that the tyrannical Czarist Russian government had forbidden the use of the Finnish national flag. However the Finnish colors were raised up the flagpole later in the day.

1912 Stockholm C: 29, N: 11, D: 7.14.
(82.5 kg—182 lbs)
1. —
2. Anders Ahlgren   SWE
3. Ivar Böhling   FIN
3. Béla Varga   HUN
4. August Rajala   FIN

Ahlgren fought his way to the final match by pinning six opponents, each within 35 minutes. But in Böhling he met his equal—literally. Ahlgren and Böhling struggled hour after hour without either man giving in, until finally, after nine hours, officials called the contest a draw. The rules of the Olympic competition stated that it was necessary for a first-place winner actually to defeat his adversary, so the officials decided to declare Ahlgren and Böhling co-winners of the second prize.

1920 Antwerp C: 18, N: 10, D: 8.26.
(82.5 kg—182 lbs)
1. Claes Johanson   SWE
2. Edil Rosenqvist   FIN
3. Johannes Eriksen   DEN
4. Johannes Sint   HOL

1924 Paris C: 22, N: 15, D: 7.10.
(82.5 kg—182 lbs)
1. Carl Westergren   SWE
2. Rudolf Svensson   SWE
3. Onni Pellinen   FIN
4. Ibrahim Moustafa   EGY
5. Emil Weckstén   FIN
6. R. Loos (EST), A. Misset (HOL), Béla Varga (HUN)

Westergren had won the Middleweight title four years earlier in Antwerp.

1928 Amsterdam C: 17, N: 17, D: 8.5.
(82.5 kg—182 lbs)
1. Ibrahim Moustafa   EGY
2. Adolf Rieger   GER
3. Onni Pellinen   FIN
4. Nicolas Appels   BEL
5. Ejnar Hansen   DEN
6. Imre Szalay   HUN

1932 Los Angeles C: 3, N: 3, D: 8.7.
(87 kg—192 lbs)

		BAD PTS.
1. Rudolf Svensson	SWE	1
2. Onni Pellinen	FIN	3
3. Mario Gruppioni	ITA	6

1936 Berlin C: 13, N: 13, D: 8.9.
(87 kg—192 lbs)

		ROUND ELIMINATED	BAD PTS.	FINAL ROUND
1. Axel Cadier	SWE	—	2	1
2. Edwins Bietags	LAT	—	1	3
3. August Neo	EST	5	5	
4. Werner Seelenbinder	GER	5	6	
5. Umberto Silvestri	ITA	4	6	
6. Olaf Knutsen	NOR	4	6	
7. Foidl	AUT	4	6	
8. Avcioglu	TUR	3	5	

1948 London C: 14, N: 14, D: 8.6.
(87 kg—192 lbs)

		ROUND ELIMINATED	BAD PTS.	FINAL ROUND
1. Karl-Erik Nilsson	SWE	—	2	1
2. Kaelpo Gröndahl	FIN	—	1	3
3. Ibrahim Orabi	EGY	5	6	
4. Gyula Kovács	HUN	4	5	
5. Kenneth Richmond	GBR	4	6	
6. Erling Lauridsen	DEN	4	7	
7. P. Enzinger	AUT	3	6	
8. M. Cakmak	TUR	3	7	
8. K. Istaz	BEL	3	7	

An incident of sorts took place in the fifth round, when Nilsson threw Orabi over his head and the referee ruled it a fall. While the Egyptians protested, Orabi stretched out on the mat and refused to move. After 15 minutes Nilsson was called back from the dressing room and ordered to continue the match. Nilsson then scored another fall and the matter was settled.

1952 Helsinki C: 10, N: 10, D: 7.27.
(87 kg—192 lbs)

		ROUND ELIMINATED	BAD PTS.	FINAL ROUND
1. Kaelpo Gröndahl	FIN	—	2	2
2. Chalva Chikhladze	SOV	—	4	3
3. Karl-Erik Nilsson	SWE	—	5	6
4. Gyula Kovács	HUN	4	5	
5. Ismet Atli	TUR	3	6	
6. Umberto Silvestri	ITA	3	7	
6. Michel Skaff	LEB	3	7	

The final bout between Gröndahl and Chikhladze was a dull, cautious affair, which Gröndahl won on a split decision.

1956 Melbourne C: 10, N: 10, D: 12.6.
(87 kg—192 lbs)

		ROUND ELIMINATED	BAD PTS.	2ND PLACE
1. Valentin Nikolayev	SOV	—	4	
2. Petko Sirakov	BUL	4	5	1
3. Karl-Erik Nilsson	SWE	4	5	3
4. Robert Steckle	CAN	4	7	
5. Dale Thomas	USA	3	6	
5. Eugen Wiesberger	AUT	3	6	
7. Veikko Lahti	FIN	3	7	
8. Adil Atan	TUR	3	7	

1960 Rome C: 17, N: 17, D: 8.31.
(87 kg—192 lbs)

		ROUND ELIMINATED	BAD PTS.	FINAL ROUND
1. Tevfik Kis	TUR	—	6	2
2. Kralyu Bimbalov	BUL	—	6	2
3. Givy Kartozlya	SOV	6	8	
4. Péter Piti	HUN	6	8	
5. Antero Vanhanen	FIN	5	7	
6. José Panizo Rodriguez	SPA	4	7	
7. Gheorghe Popovici	ROM	4	8	
8. Eugen Wiesberger	AUT	4	8	

Kis was awarded first place because he weighed less than Bimbalov.

1964 Tokyo C: 18, N: 18, D: 10.19.
(97 kg—214 lbs)

		ROUND ELIMINATED	BAD PTS.
1. Boyan Radev	BUL	—	2
2. Per Svensson	SWE	5	6
3. Heinz Kiehl	GER	5	6
4. Nicolae Martinescu	ROM	5	8
5. Rostom Abashidze	SOV	4	6
5. Ferenc Kiss	HUN	4	6
5. Peter Jutzeler	SWI	4	6
8. Eugen Wiesberger	AUT	4	7

Radev breezed through the tournament, aided by the fact that he faced only one wrestler, Martinescu, who finished in the top eight.

1968 Mexico City C: 16, N: 16, D: 10.26.
(97 kg—214 lbs)

		ROUND ELIMINATED	BAD PTS.	FINAL ROUND
1. Boyan Radev	BUL	—	0.5	2.5
2. Nikolai Yakovenko	SOV	—	1	3.5
3. Nicolae Martinescu	ROM	—	4	7
4. Per Svensson	SWE	4	6	
5. Tore Hem	NOR	4	8	
6. Peter Jutzeier	SWI	3	6	
6. Cay Malmberg	FIN	3	6	
6. Waclaw Orlowski	POL	3	6	

Radev and Yakovenko tied, but Radev threw Martinescu in 4:58 to win the gold medal.

1972 Munich C: 14, N: 14, D: 9.10.

		ROUND ELIMINATED	BAD PTS.	FINAL ROUND
1. Valery Rezantsev	SOV	—	2	2
2. Josip Čorak	YUG	—	3	5
3. Czeslaw Kwieciński	POL	—	5	5
4. József Percsi	HUN	5	6.5	
5. Håkon Överbye	NOR	5	9	
6. Nicolae Neguţ	ROM	4	8	
7. Kimiichi Tani	JAP	4	9	
8. Günter Kowalewski	GER	3	8	

Rezantsev suffered a first-round draw with Neguţ and then won six straight bouts.

1976 Montreal C: 13, N: 13, D: 7.24.

		ROUND ELIMINATED	BAD PTS.	FINAL ROUND
1. Valery Rezantsev	SOV	—	2	2
2. Stoyan Ivanov	BUL	—	5	5
3. Czeslaw Kwieciński	POL	—	3	7
4. Darko Nisavić	YUG	5	9	
5. Frank Andersson	SWE	4	6	
6. István Séllyei	HUN	4	8	
7. James Johnson	USA	3	8	
7. Sadao Sato	JAP	3	8	

Valery Rezantsev dominated Light Heavyweight Greco-Roman wrestling in the 1970s. He went to Montreal as the defending Olympic champion and the five-time defending world champion. In his final bout he was held to a 6–6 tie by Ivanov, but a tie-breaker gave him the victory anyway.

1980 Moscow C: 15, N: 15, D: 7.22.

		ROUND ELIMINATED	BAD PTS.	FINAL ROUND
1. Norbert Növényi	HUN	—	1	2
2. Igor Kanygin	SOV	—	6.5	5
3. Petre Dicu	ROM	—	6	7
4. Frank Andersson	SWE	5	7	
5. Thomas Horschel	GDR	4	8	
6. José Poll Martinez	CUB	4	8.5	
7. Christophe Andanson	FRA	3	6.5	
8. Georges Pozidis	GRE	3	7	

Növényi scattered four opponents and then outpointed Kanygin 7–6 and Dicu 4–1.

HEAVYWEIGHT
(100 kg—220 lbs)
1896–1968 not held

1972 Munich C: 15, N: 15, D: 9.10.

		ROUND ELIMINATED	BAD PTS.	FINAL ROUND
1. Nicolae Martinescu	ROM	—	5.5	0
2. Nikolai Iakovenko	SOV	—	1	4
3. Ferenc Kiss	HUN	5	6.5	
4. Hristo Ignatov	BUL	5	9	
5. Fredi Albrecht	GDR	4	7	
6. Tore Hem	NOR	4	8	
7. Andrzej Skrzydlewski	POL	4	8.5	
8. Rudolf Luescher	SWI	2	6	

1976 Montreal C: 13, N: 13, D: 7.24.

		ROUND ELIMINATED	BAD PTS.	FINAL ROUND
1. Nikolai Balboshin	SOV	—	0	0
2. Kamen Goranov	BUL	—	4	5
3. Andrzej Skrzydlewski	POL	—	3	7
4. Brad Rheingans	USA	4	6	
5. Tore Hem	NOR	4	7	
6. Heinz Schäfer	GER	4	8	
7. József Farkas	HUN	3	8	
7. Nicolae Martinescu	ROM	3	8	

Balboshin needed only 16 minutes and 48 seconds to win his five matches.

1980 Moscow C: 9, N: 9, D: 7.23.

		ROUND ELIMINATED	BAD PTS.	FINAL ROUND
1. Georgi Raikov	BUL	—	1	2
2. Roman Bierla	POL	—	1	4
3. Vasile Andrei	ROM	4	7	
4. Refik Memisevic	YUG	4	7	
5. Georges Pikilidis	GRE	3	8	
6. Oldřich Dvorak	CZE	3	8	
7. Nikolai Balboshin	SOV	2	4	

Raikov defeated Bierla by disqualification after 7:52. Defending champion Nikolai Balboshin, injured during the second round, was forced to withdraw.

SUPER HEAVYWEIGHT— UNLIMITED WEIGHT

(Heavyweight 1896–1968)

1896 Athens C: 5, N: 4, D: 4.11.
1. Karl Schumann — GER
2. Georgios Tsitas — GRE
3. Stephanos Christopoulos — GRE
4. Launceston Elliott — GBR
5. Momcsilló Tapavicza — HUN

Schumann also won three first prizes in the gymnastics events.

1900–1904 not held

1906 Athens C: 10, N: 6, D: 5.1.
1. Soren Marius Jensen — DEN
2. Henri Baur — AUT
3. Marcel Dubois — BEL
4. Stephanos Christopoulos — GRE
5. D. Psaltopoulos — GRE

1908 London C: 7, N: 4, D: 7.24.
1. Richárd Weisz — HUN
2. Aleksandr Petrov — RUS
3. Soren Marius Jensen — DEN
4. Hugó Payr — HUN

1912 Stockholm C: 18, N: 9, D: 7.14.
1. Yrjö Saarela — FIN
2. Johan Olin — FIN
3. Sören Marius Jensen — DEN
4. Jakob Neser — GER
5. Emil Backenius — FIN
5. Kaarlo "Kalle" Wiljamaa — FIN

1920 Antwerp C: 22, N: 11, D: 8.26.
1. Adolf Lindfors — FIN
2. Poul Hansen — DEN
3. Martti Nieminen — FIN
4. Alexander Weyand — USA

1924 Paris C: 17, N: 10, D: 7.10.
1. Henri Deglane — FRA
2. Edil Rosenqvist — FIN
3. Rajmund Badó — HUN
4. Emil Larsen — DEN
5. Harry Nilsson (SWE), J. Polis (LAT), L. Pothier (BEL)

One of the many incidents which plagued the judgeable sports at the Paris Olympics occurred in the second round of the Greco-Roman Heavyweight tournament. Local favorite Henri Deglane, age 22, was pitted against 39-year-old Claes Johansson, who had won the Middleweight title in 1912 and the Light Heavyweight title in 1920. After 20 minutes of fighting, Johansson was declared the winner on points. The French team protested the decision, and the Jury of Appeal ordered the two men to wrestle for six more minutes, after which Deglane was declared the victor. Johansson was so disgusted that he withdrew from the competition. Deglane went on to win four more decisions and the gold medal.

1928 Amsterdam C: 15, N: 15, D: 8.5.
1. Rudolf Svensson — SWE
2. Hjalmar Eemil Nyström — FIN
3. Georg Gehring — GER
4. Eugen Wiesberger — AUT
5. Josef Urban — CZE
6. Rajmund Badó — HUN
7. Aleardo Donati — ITA
7. M. Mehmed — TUR

1932 Los Angeles C: 5, N: 5, D: 8.7.
1. Carl Westergren — SWE
2. Josef Urban — CZE
3. Nikolaus Hirschi — AUT
4. George Gehring — GER
5. Aleardo Donati — ITA

Westergren, a bus driver from Malmo, compiled an outstanding record at the Olympics. Following in the footsteps of Claes Johansson, he won the Middleweight title in 1920 and the Light Heavyweight title in 1924. In 1928, as a light heavyweight, he was pinned in the first round by Onni Pellinen. However he returned to the Olympics in 1932 as a 36-year-old heavyweight and won a third gold medal.

1936 Berlin C: 12, N: 12, D: 8.9.

		ROUND ELIMINATED	BAD PTS.	FINAL ROUND
1. Kristjan Palusalu	EST	—	3	1
2. John Nyman	SWE	—	3	3
3. Kurt Hornfischer	GER	5	5	
4. Mehmet Çoban	TUR	4	6	
5. Hjalmar Eemil Nyström	FIN	4	6	
6. Aleardo Donati	ITA	4	7	
7. Klapuch	CZE	3	6	
8. Swejnicks	LAT	3	6	

1948 London C: 9, N: 9, D: 8.6.

		ROUND ELIMINATED	BAD PTS.	FINAL ROUND
1. Ahmet Kirecci	TUR	—	1	1
2. Tor Nilsson	SWE	—	3	3
3. Guido Fantoni	ITA	—	1	6
4. Taisto Kangasniemi	FIN	3	5	
5. József Tarányi	HUN	3	6	
6. Moritz Inderbitzin	SWI	3	7	

Kirecci had received a bronze medal as a middleweight 12 years earlier in Berlin.

1952 Helsinki C: 10, N: 10, D: 7.27.

		ROUND ELIMINATED	BAD PTS.	FINAL ROUND
1. Johannes Kotkas	SOV	—	0	0
2. Josef Ružička	CZE	—	3	3
3. Tauno Kovanen	FIN	—	6	6
4. Willi Waltner	GER	4	7	
5. Alexandru Suli	ROM	3	5	
6. Bengt Fahlkvist	SWE	3	6	
6. Antoine Georgoulis	GRE	3	6	
8. Guido Fantoni	ITA	3	7	

Kotkas, a 37-year-old Estonian from Tartu, pinned his four opponents in an elapsed time of 13 minutes 36 seconds.

1956 Melbourne C: 10, N: 10, D: 12.6.

		ROUND ELIMINATED	BAD PTS.	FINAL ROUND
1. Anatoly Parfenov	SOV	—	4	2
2. Wilfried Dietrich	GER	—	5	4
3. Adelmo Bulgarelli	ITA	—	4	6
4. Hamit Kaplan	TUR	4	6	
5. Bertil Antonsson	SWE	4	7	
6. Taisto Kangasniemi	FIN	3	6	
7. Yusein Mehmedov	BUL	3	7	
7. Antoine Georgoulis	GRE	3	7	

Parfenov was one of the least overwhelming Olympic champions ever. He was originally declared the loser in his opening contest with Dietrich. However a protest by the Soviet team was upheld by the Jury of Appeal. In the second round Parfenov lost to Antonsson. Then he won a forfeit in the third round and received a bye in the fourth round. In the fifth round he gained his only undisputed victory, a decision over Bulgarelli. Fortunately for Parfenov, his two wins were enough to take first place.

1960 Rome C: 12, N: 12, D: 8.31.

		ROUND ELIMINATED	BAD PTS.	FINAL ROUND
1. Ivan Bogdan	SOV	—	4	4
2. Wilfried Dietrich	GER	—	5	4
3. Bohumil Kubát	CZE	—	5	4
4. István Kozma	HUN	4	6	
5. Lucjan Sosnowski	POL	4	6	

6. Radoslav Kasabov	BUL	4	8
7. Adelmo Bulgarelli	ITA	3	6
8. Sten Ragnar Svensson	SWE	3	9

Dietrich was awarded the silver medal because his bodyweight was less than that of Bohumil "Weeny" Kubat. In fact, it was 88 pounds less than Kubat's. Dietrich weighed 198 pounds, while Kubat weighed 286.

1964 Tokyo C: 11, N: 11, D: 10.19.

		ROUND ELIMINATED	BAD PTS.	FINAL ROUND
1. István Kozma	HUN	—	1	2
2. Anatoly Roshin	SOV	—	3	2
3. Wilfried Dietrich	GER	5	7	
4. Petr Kment	CZE	5	8	
5. Sten Ragnar Svensson	SWE	4	6	
6. Robert Pickens	USA	3	7	
7. Radoslav Kasabov	BUL	3	8	
8. Tsuneharu Sugiyama	JAP	3	8	

Kozma weighed in at 320 pounds.

1968 Mexico City C: 15, N: 15, D: 10.26.

		ROUND ELIMINATED	BAD PTS.	FINAL ROUND
1. István Kozma	HUN	—	2.5	2.5
2. Anatoly Roshin	SOV	—	3.5	2.5
3. Petr Kment	CZE	—	5	8
4. Sten Ragnar Svensson	SWE	5	7	
5. Constantin Buşiu	ROM	4	7	
6. Stefan Petrov	BUL	4	8	
7. Raymond Uytterheaeghe	FRA	4	9	
8. Edward Wojda	POL	4	9.5	

As in 1964, Kozma won the gold medal despite being held to a draw by Roshin. This time the huge Hungarian threw his other four opponents, two of them within 40 seconds. Kment was injured and forced to withdraw from his final two matches against Kozma and Roshin.

1972 Munich C: 13, N: 13, D: 9.10.

		ROUND ELIMINATED	BAD PTS.	FINAL ROUND
1. Anatoly Roshin	SOV	—	2	1
2. Alexander Tomov	BUL	—	3	5
3. Victor Dolîpschi	ROM	—	4	6
4. József Csatári	HUN	4	8	
4. Wilfried Dietrich	GER	4	8	
4. Istvan Semeredi	YUG	4	8	
7. Petr Kment	CZE	3	7	

Thirty-eight-year-old Wilfried Dietrich, attempting to win a medal in his fifth consecutive Olympics, was disqualified in his third-round match against Victor Dolîpschi. Dietrich was so upset by the decision that he withdrew from the competition even though he only had four bad points.

1976 Montreal C: 12, N: 12, D: 7.24.

		ROUND ELIMINATED	BAD PTS.	FINAL ROUND
1. Aleksandr Kolchinsky	SOV	—	0	1
2. Alexander Tomov	BUL	—	4	3
3. Roman Codreanu	ROM	—	2	8
4. Henryk Tomanek	POL	4	8	
5. William "Pete" Lee	USA	4	8	
6. János Rovnyai	HUN	3	8	
7. Einar Gundersen	NOR	3	8	
7. Richard Wolff	GER	3	8	

Three-time defending world champion Alexander Tomov had defeated Kolchinsky six straight times, culminating in the European championships three months before the Olympics. However in Montreal Tomov was upset in the first round when he was pinned in only 1:14 by 331-pound Pete Lee of Muncie, Indiana. Tomov recovered to win his next three matches and qualify for the final round-robin. In the meantime, Kolchinsky used up only six minutes and 38 seconds in finishing off his first four opponents. He followed this by outpointing Tomov 12–6 in his final bout.

1980 Moscow C: 10, N: 10, D: 7.24.

		ROUND ELIMINATED	BAD PTS.	FINAL ROUND
1. Aleksandr Kolchinsky	SOV	—	0	1
2. Alexander Tomov	BUL	—	0	3
3. Hassan Bchara	LEB	—	8	8
4. József Farkas	HUN	4	10	
5. Prvoslav Ilić	YUG	3	8	
6. Roman Codreanu	ROM	3	8	
6. Arturo Diaz Mora	CUB	3	8	

The superiority of Kolchinsky and Tomov was shown by the fact that the other eight wrestlers all reached eight penalty points before the two champions had even received their first bad mark. Kolchinsky, the lightest man in the tournament at 220 pounds, defeated 375-pound Roman Codreanu in 7:50 in his opening bout. Then he disposed of his next four opponents in an elapsed time of 11:27. In the final contest Kolchinsky outpointed Tomov 4–2 to win his second straight gold medal.

YACHTING

Finn
Boardsailing
Star
Flying Dutchman
Tornado
470
Soling
Discontinued Events

Each class in yachting runs seven races over a course usually marked by buoys. Since 1968 each yacht has been assessed minus points depending on its order of finish.

1st place: 0	5th place: 10
2nd place: 3	6th place: 11.7
3rd place: 5.7	7th place: 13
4th place: 8	add one point for each subsequent place

At the conclusion of the final race, each yacht is allowed to drop its worst score. The remaining minus points are added and the yacht with the lowest total wins.

FINN

The Finn class uses a centerboard dinghy and a one-man crew. Boats are assigned at random, although since 1976 a helmsman may provide his own sail and mast.

1896–1912 not held

1920 Antwerp T: 2, N: 1, D: 7.10.
12-Foot Dinghy
1. HOL (Johannes Hin, Franciscus Hin)
2. HOL (Arnoud Eugène van der Biesen, Petrus Beukers)

1920 Antwerp T: 1, N: 1, D: 7.10.
18-Foot Dinghy
1. GBR (Francis Richards, T. Hedberg)

1924 Paris C: 17, N: 17, D: 7.13.

		PTS.
1. Léon Huybrechts	BEL	2
2. Henrik Robert	NOR	7
3. Hans Dittmar	FIN	8
4. Santiago Amat Cansino	SPA	8
5. Johannes Joseph Hin	HOL	10
6. Clarence Hammar	SWE	11
7. G. Fowler	GBR	12
8. F. Guilherme-Burnay	POR	15

The Official Report of 1924 attributes to Huybrechts a sixth sense that allowed him to anticipate changes in wind direction. Second, third, and fourth places were decided by an extra race.

1928 Amsterdam C: 23, N: 20, D: 8.9.
1. Sven Thorell   SWE
2. Henrik Robert   NOR
3. Bertil Broman   FIN
4. Willem de Vries-Lentsch HOL
5. Egon Beyn   GER
6. Tito Nordio   ITA
7. J.J. Andersen   DEN
8. H.R. Gaydon, Gordon Fowler GBR

Thorell won four of eight races and also placed second twice.

1932 Los Angeles C: 11, N; 11, D: 8.12.

		PTS.
1. Jacques Lebrun	FRA	87
2. Adriaan Maas	HOL	85
3. Santiago Amat Cansino	SPA	76
4. Edgar Behr	GER	74
5. Reginald Dixon	CAN	72
6. Colin Ratsey	GBR	69
7. Charles Lyon	USA	66
8. Silvio Treleani	ITA	62

1936 Berlin–Kiel C: 25, N: 25, D: 8.12.

			PTS.
1. Daniel Kagchelland	HOL	163
2. Werner Krogmann	GER	150
3. Peter Scott	GBR	131
4. Erich Wichmann-Harbeck	CHI	130
5. Giuseppe Fago	ITA	115
6. Jacques Lebrun	FRA	109
7. Tibor Heinrich	HUN	102
8. Pieper	SWI	99

1948 London C: 21, N: 21, D: 8.12.

			PTS.
1. Paul Elvström	DEN	5543
2. Ralph Evans	USA	5408
3. Jacobus de Jong	HOL	5204
4. Richard Sarby	SWE	4603
5. Paul McLaughlin	CAN	4535
6. Felix Sienra Castellanos	URU	4079
7. Jean-Jacques Herbulot	FRA	4068
8. R. Van der Haeghen	BEL	3660

Twenty-year-old Paul Elvström began his Olympic career quietly, failing to finish the first day's race. After five races, the competition appeared to be a tight contest between Evans, McLaughlin, and Sarby. All the others were more than 800 points behind. Elvström was in eighth place. But on the sixth day the young Dane finished first, 23 seconds ahead of Herbulot, and the extra 301 points that he gained propelled Elvström into third place, 564 points behind Evans. This meant that Evans could clinch the gold medal by finishing third on the final day. However he landed in fifth place, three minutes away from his goal, while Elvström took first place again, three minutes and seven seconds ahead of de Jong; the 301-point bonus for winning provided the margin of victory in the final standings.

1952 Helsinki C: 28, N: 28, D: 7.28.

			PTS.
1. Paul Elvström	DEN	8209
2. Charles Currey	GBR	5449
3. Richard Sarby	SWE	5051
4. Jacobus de Jong	HOL	5033
5. Wolfgang Erndl	AUT	4273
6. Morits Skaugen	NOR	4073
7. Adelchi Pelaschiar	ITA	4068
8. Paul McLaughlin	CAN	4033

Elvström won three of the first four races and gained so many points that he had earned the gold medal without having to race the last day. He entered anyway and won again. His other placings were a fifth, a third, and a fourth.

1956 Melbourne C: 20, N: 20, D: 12.5.

			PTS.
1. Paul Elvström	DEN	7509
2. André Nelis	BEL	6254

3. John Marvin	USA	5953
4. Jürgen Vogler	GER	4199
5. Richard Sarby	SWE	3990
6. Eric Bongers	SAF	3912
7. Adelchi Pelaschiar	ITA	3409
8. Bruce Kirby	CAN	3213

Elvström finished first in the opening race, fell to eighth and 15th in the next two, and then won each of the last four races.

1960 Rome–Naples C: 35, N: 35, D: 9.7.

			PTS.
1. Paul Elvström	DEN	8171
2. Aleksandr Chuchelov	SOV	6520
3. André Nelis	BEL	5934
4. Ronald Jenyns	AUS	5758
5. Reinaldo Conrad	BRA	5176
6. Ralph Roberts	NZE	5140
7. Ian Bruce	CAN	5133
8. Kenneth Albury	BAH	5092

Elvström, now 32 years old, chalked up three firsts, one second, and two fifths to clinch his fourth gold medal without having to enter the final race. This time Elvström, who was not in perfect health, declined to start.

1964 Tokyo C: 33, N: 33, D: 10.21.

			PTS.
1. Wilhelm Kuhweide	GER	7638
2. Peter Barrett	USA	6373
3. Henning Wind	DEN	6190
4. Peter Mander	NZE	5684
5. Hubert Raudaschl	AUT	5405
6. Colin Ryrie	AUS	5273
7. Joerg Bruder	BRA	4956
8. Panagiotis Kouligas	GRE	4546

In 1964 East and West Germany entered a combined team. However a dispute developed as to which side should be represented in the Finn class. At the last moment the International Yacht Racing Union interceded and authorized the West German helmsman, Willi Kuhweide. Kuhweide sailed well throughout the regatta and won the gold medal by placing second, first, fourth, sixth, fifth, third, and first.

1968 Mexico City–Acapulco C: 36, N: 36, D: 10.21.

			PTS.
1. Valentin Mankin	SOV	11.7
2. Hubert Raudaschl	AUT	53.4
3. Fabio Albarelli	ITA	55.1
4. Ronald Jenyns	AUS	67.0
5. Panagiotis Kouligas	GRE	71.0
6. Jan Winquist	FIN	72.0
7. Arne Akerson	SWI	77.0
8. Philippe Soria	FRA	80.0

Mankin had a consistent series, placing third, fifth, first, first, second, second, and first.

1972 Munich–Kiel C: 35, N: 35, D: 9.8.

		PTS.
1. Serge Maury	FRA	58.0
2. Ilias Hatzipavlis	GRE	71.0
3. Victor Potapov	SOV	74.7
4. John Bertrand	AUS	76.7
5. Thomas Lundqvist	SWE	81.0
6. Kim Weber	FIN	85.7
7. Hans-Christian Schröder	GDR	91.0
8. György Fináczy	HUN	94.0

1976 Montreal–Kingston C: 28, N: 28, D: 7.27.

		PTS.
1. Jochen Schümann	GDR	35.4
2. Andrei Balashov	SOV	39.7
3. John Bertrand	AUS	46.4
4. Claudio Biekarck	BRA	54.7
5. Kent Carlson	SWE	66.4
6. Anastassios Boudouris	GRE	77.0
7. David Howlett	GBR	77.7
8. Sanford Riley	CAN	83.0

Schümann and Balashov entered the final race in a tie for first place. Schümann pulled away on the last day and finished 40 seconds ahead of his rival.

1980 Moscow–Tallinn C: 21, N: 21, D: 7.29.

		PTS.
1. Esko Rechardt	FIN	36.7
2. Wolfgang Mayrhofer	AUT	46.7
3. Andrei Balashov	SOV	47.4
4. Claudio Biekarck	BRA	53.0
5. Jochen Schümann	GDR	54.4
6. Kent Carlson	SWE	63.7
7. Ryszard Skarbiński	POL	71.1
8. Mark Neeleman	HOL	76.0

BOARDSAILING

This event will be held for the first time in 1984.

STAR

The Star class is a long shallow monotype of American origin, with a 281-square-foot sail. It has a two-man crew.

1896–1928 not held

1932 Los Angeles T: 7, N: 7, D: 8.12.

		PTS.
1. USA	(Gilbert Gray, Andrew Libano)	46
2. GBR	(Colin Ratsey, Peter Jaffe)	35
3. SWE	(Gunnar Asther, Daniel Sundén-Cullberg)	28
4. CAN	(Henry Wylie, Henry Simmonds)	27
5. FRA	(Jean-Jacques Herbulot, Jean Peytel)	26
6. HOL	(Jan Maas, Adriaan Maas)	14
7. SAF	(Arent Van Soelen, Cecil Goodricke)	7

The *Jupiter,* skippered by 30-year-old Gilbert Gray of New Orleans, won five of the seven races.

1936 Berlin–Kiel T: 12, N: 12, D: 8.10.

		PTS.
1. GER	(Peter Bischoff, Hans-Joachim Weise)	80
2. SWE	(Arvid Laurin, Uno Wallentin)	64
3. HOL	(Willem de Vries-Lentsch, Adriaan Maas)	63
4. GBR	(Keith Grogono, William Welply)	56
5. USA	(William Waterhouse, Woodbridge Metcalf)	51
6. NOR	(Öivind Christensen, Sigurd Herbern)	44
7. FRA	(Jean-Jacques Herbulot, de Montaut)	41
8. TUR	(Ulmann, Baydar)	38

Bischoff matched Gray's feat of winning five of seven races. The Germans had clinched the gold medals after the sixth race, but raced the next day anyway and won again.

1948 London T: 17, N: 17, D: 8.12.

		PTS.
1. USA	(Hilary Smart, Paul Smart)	5828
2. CUB	(Carlos De Cárdenas Culmell, Carlos De Cárdenas, Jr.)	4949
3. HOL	(Adriaan Maas, Edward Stutterheim)	4731
4. GBR	(Durward Knowles, Sloan Farringtn)	4372
5. ITA	(Agostino Straulino, Nicolo Rode)	4370
6. POR	(Joaquim De Mascarenhas Fiuza, Julio De Sousa Leite Gorinho)	4292
7. AUS	(Alexander Sturrock, L.A. Fenton)	3828
8. CAN	(Norman Gooderham, A. Fairhead)	2635

Paul Smart was a 56-year-old lawyer from New York. His 23-year-old son, Hilary, was a student at Harvard. Paul is the oldest American ever to have won an Olympic gold medal.

1952 Helsinki T: 21, N: 21, D: 7.28.

		PTS.
1. ITA	(Agostino Straulino, Nicolo Rode)	7635
2. USA	(John Reid, John Price)	7126
3. POR	(Joaquim De Mascarenhas Fiuza, Francisco Rebelo De Andrade)	4903
4. CUB	(Carlos De Cárdenas Culmell, Carlos De Cárdenas, Jr.)	4535
5. BAH	(Durward Knowles, Sloan Farrington)	4405
6. FRA	(Edouard Chabert, Jean-Louis Dauris)	3866
7. SWE	(Bengt Melin, Björn Carlsson)	3785
8. HOL	(Adrianus Maas, Edward Stutterheim)	3510

The Italians and the Americans engaged in a private battle, winning all seven races and generally leaving the others far behind. Straulino skippered the *Merope* to three firsts and four seconds. The U.S. pair placed first four times and third once, but also finished seventh in the second race and eighth on the final day.

1956 Melbourne T: 12, N: 12, D: 12.5.

			PTS.
1.	USA	(Herbert Williams, Lawrence Low)	5876
2.	ITA	(Agostino Straulino, Nicolo Rode)	5649
3.	BAH	(Durward Knowles, Sloan Farrington)	5223
4.	POR	(Duarte De Almeida Bello, José Bustorff Silva)	3825
5.	FRA	(Philippe Chancerel, Michel Parent)	3126
6.	CUB	(Carlos De Cárdenas Culmell, Jorge De Cárdenas)	2714
7.	GBR	(Bruce Banks, Stanley Potter)	2387
8.	SOV	(Timir Pinegin, Fyodor Shutkov)	1778

Skippered by 48-year-old Sussex-born Herbert Williams of Evanston, Illinois, the *Kathleen* placed first, fifth, second, first, second, second, second.

1960 Rome–Naples T: 26, N: 26, D: 9.7.

			PTS.
1.	SOV	(Timir Pinegin, Fyodor Shutkov)	7619
2.	POR	(José Quina, Mário Quina)	6665
3.	USA	(William Parks, Robert Halperin)	6269
4.	ITA	(Agostino Straulino, Carlo Rolandi)	6047
5.	SWI	(Hans Bryner, Ulrich Bucher)	5716
6.	BAH	(Durward Knowles, Sloan Farrington)	5282
7.	GER	(Bruno Splieth, Eckart Wagner)	4745
8.	YUG	(Mario Fafangel, Janko Kosmina)	3977

This was the first Soviet victory in Olympic yachting, a sport which had previously been considered the domain of capitalists. Oddly enough, the Soviet craft, the *Tornado,* had been built in Old Greenwich, Connecticut.

1964 Tokyo T: 17, N: 17, D: 10.21.

			PTS.
1.	BAH	(Durward Knowles, C. Cecil Cooke)	5664
2.	USA	(Richard Stearns, Lynn Williams)	5585
3.	SWE	(Pelle Pettersson, Holger Sundström)	5527
4.	FIN	(Peder Tallberg, Henrik Tallberg)	5402
5.	SOV	(Timir Pinegin, Fyodor Shutkov)	4305
6.	GER	(Bruno Splieth, Karsten Meyer)	4175
7.	CAN	(David Miller, William West)	3565
8.	POR	(Manuel Duarte, Pinto Fernando)	3330

Forty-six-year-old Durward Knowles was competing in his fifth Olympics. If Stearns and Williams had finished six seconds faster in the last race, they would have won the gold medal.

1968 Mexico City–Acapulco T: 20, N: 20, D: 10.21.

			PTS.
1.	USA	(Lowell North, Peter Barrett)	14.4
2.	NOR	(Peder Lunde, Per Olav Wiken)	43.7
3.	ITA	(Franco Cavallo, Camilo Gargano)	44.7
4.	DEN	(Paul Elvström, Poul Mik-Meyer)	50.4
5.	BAH	(Durward Knowles, Percival Knowles)	63.4
6.	AUS	(David Forbes, Richard Williamson)	68.7
7.	BRA	(Erik Schmidt, Axel Schmidt)	74.4
8.	SWI	(Edwin Bernet, Rolf Amrein)	75.0

North and Barrett secured first place after six races, but won the seventh race anyway.

1972 Munich–Kiel T: 18, N: 18, D: 9.8.

			PTS.
1.	AUS	(David Forbes, John Anderson)	28.1
2.	SWE	(Pelle Pettersson, Stellan Westerdahl)	44.0
3.	GER	(Wilhelm Kuhweide, Karsten Meyer)	44.4
4.	BRA	(Jorge Bruder, Jan Willem Aten)	52.7
5.	ITA	(Flavio Scala, Mauro Testa)	58.4
6.	POR	(Antonio Correia, Ulrich Anjos)	68.4
7.	GBR	(Stuart Jardine, John Wastall)	68.7
8.	HUN	(András Gosztonyi, György Holovits)	74.0

The Australians were assured of first place after the sixth race.

1976 not held

1980 Moscow–Tallinn T: 13, N: 13, D: 7.29.

			PTS.
1.	SOV	(Valentin Mankin, Aleksandr Muzychenko)	24.7
2.	AUT	(Hubert Raudaschl, Karl Ferstl)	31.7
3.	ITA	(Giorgio Gorla, Alfio Peraboni)	36.1
4.	SWE	(Peter Sundelin, Håkan Lindström)	44.7
5.	DEN	(Jens Håkon Christensen, Morten Nielsen)	45.7
6.	HOL	(Boudewijn Binkhorst, Jacob Vandenberg)	49.4
7.	SPA	(Antonio Gorostegui, José Maria Benavides)	72.7
8.	GDR	(Wolf-Eberhard Richter, Olaf Engelhardt)	83.7

Forty-one-year-old Valentin Mankin gained his third gold medal, having won the Finn class in 1968 and the Tempest in 1972. He also won a silver in the 1976 Tempest. The Austrians could have won with a fourth-place finish in the last race, but they could do no better than ninth. Most damaging to the Austrians was the third race, in which they were disqualified after finishing first.

FLYING DUTCHMAN

The Flying Dutchman class uses a centerboard dinghy and a crew of two, one of whom is attached to the boat by a rope and a trapeze. This allows him to lean far outside the craft without falling overboard.

1896–1956 not held

1960 Rome–Naples T: 31, N: 31, D: 9.7.

			PTS.
1.	NOR	(Peder Lunde, Jr., Björn Bergvall)	6774
2.	DEN	(Hans Fogh, Ole Erik Petersen)	5991
3.	GER	(Rolf Mulka, Ingo von Bredow, Achim Kadelbach)	5882
4.	ZIM	(David Butler, Christopher Bevan)	5792
5.	HOL	(Gijsbertus Verhagen, Gerardus Lautenschütz)	5452
6.	SOV	(Aleksandr Shelkovnikov, Viktor Pilchin)	5123
7.	GBR	(Slotty Dawes, James Ramus)	4954
8.	NZE	(Murray Rae, Ronald Watson)	4641

Eighteen-year-old Peder Lunde came from an illustrious sailing family. His grandfather Eugen won a gold medal in the six-meter class in 1924, and his father and uncle, Peder and Vibeke, won silver medals in the 5.5-meter class in 1952. Young Peder also gained a Star class silver medal in 1968.

1964 Tokyo T: 21, N: 21, D: 10.21.

			PTS.
1.	NZE	(Helmer Pedersen, Earle Wells)	6255
2.	GBR	(Franklyn Musto, Arthur Morgan)	5556
3.	USA	(Harry Melges, William Bentsen)	5158
4.	DEN	(Ole Petersen, Hans Fogh)	4500
5.	SOV	(Aleksandr Shelkovnikov, Viktor Pilchin)	4375
6.	HOL	(Gijsbertus Verhagen, Nicolaas de Jong)	4214
7.	FRA	(Marcel-André Buffet, Alain-François Lehoerff)	3864
8.	AUT	(Karl Geiger, Werner Fischer)	3706

Pedersen and Wells got off to a slow start, placing 16th the first day and failing to finish the second race. After that they picked up three firsts, a third, and a fourth.

1968 Mexico City–Acapulco T: 30, N: 30, D: 10.21.

			PTS.
1.	GBR	(Rodney Pattison, Iain Macdonald-Smith)	3.0
2.	GER	(Ullrich Libor, Peter Naumann)	43.7
3.	BRA	(Reinaldo Conrad, Burkhard Cordes)	48.4
4.	AUS	(Carl Ryves, James Sargeant)	49.1
5.	NOR	(Björn Lofteröd, Odd Lofteröd)	52.4
6.	FRA	(Bertrand Cheret, Bruno Trouble)	68.0
7.	CAN	(Roger Green, Stewart Green)	79.0
8.	NZE	(Geoffrey Smale, Ralph Roberts)	84.0

Submarine lieutenant Rod Pattison and solicitor's clerk Iain Macdonald-Smith finished first in the opening race, but were disqualified for interference. Undeterred by what they considered an unjust decision, the two men guided their boat *Superdocious* to five straight victories. Sailing cautiously on the final day, they still placed second to win the competition by a wide margin.

1972 Munich–Kiel T: 29, N: 29, D: 9.8.

			PTS.
1.	GBR	(Rodney Pattisson, Christopher Davies)	22.7
2.	FRA	(Yves Pajot, Marc Pajot)	40.7
3.	GER	(Ullrich Libor, Peter Naumann)	51.1
4.	BRA	(Reinaldo Conrad, Burkhard Cordes)	62.4
5.	YUG	(Anton Grego, Simo Nikolić)	63.7
6.	SOV	(Vladimir Leontiev, Valery Zoubanov)	67.7
7.	DEN	(Hans Fogh, Ulrik Brock)	74.4
8.	AUS	(Mark Bethwaite, Timothy Alexander)	75.7

Pattisson and Davies won four of the first six races and didn't bother to start on the final day.

1976 Montreal–Kingston T: 20, N: 20, D: 7.27.

			PTS.
1.	GER	(Jörg Diesch, Eckart Diesch)	34.7
2.	GBR	(Rodney Pattisson, Julian Brooke Houghton)	51.7
3.	BRA	(Reinaldo Conrad, Peter Ficker)	52.1
4.	CAN	(Hans Fogh, Evert Bastet)	57.1
5.	SOV	(Vladimir Leontiev, Valery Zubanov)	59.4
6.	USA	(Norman Freeman, John Mathias)	65.7
7.	SPA	(Alejandro Abascal, Jose Benavides)	66.0
8.	FRA	(Yves Pajot, Marc Pajot)	72.0

For the third straight time, Rod Pattison was first across the finishing line in the opening race. However he fell off badly in the last three races, placing 18th, 12th, and 11th. The Diesch brothers were ten points ahead after six races. On the way to the starting line for the final race they discovered that their centerboard was cracked. They returned to shore, obtained permission to replace the board, made the repair, and still arrived on time to compete. They placed fifth, good enough to take the gold medal.

1980 Moscow–Tallinn T: 15, N: 15, D: 7.29.

			PTS.
1.	SPA	(Alesandro Abascal, Miguel Noguer)	19.0
2.	IRL	(David Wilkins, James Wilkinson)	30.0
3.	HUN	(Szabolcs Detre, Zsolt Detre)	45.7
4.	GDR	(Wolfgang Haase, Wolfgang Wenzel)	51.4
5.	SOV	(Vladimir Leontyev, Valery Zubanov)	51.7
6.	DEN	(Jörgen Böjsen Möller, Jacob Böjsen Möller)	54.5
7.	HOL	(Jan Erik Vollebregt, Sjoerd Vollebregt)	54.7
8.	BRA	(Reinaldo Conrad, Manfred Kaufmann)	63.4

Helmsman Alesandro Abascal, a 28-year-old physicist, won without having to take part in the final race. He and medical student Miguel Noguer had three firsts, a second, and two fourths in the first six races.

TORNADO

The Tornado is a two-man catamaran, the fastest of all Olympic classes.

1896–1972 not held

1976 Montreal–Kingston C: 14, N: 14, D: 7.28.

			PTS.
1.	GBR	(Reginald White, John Osborn)	18.0
2.	USA	(David McFaull, Michael Rothwell)	36.0
3.	GER	(Jörg Spengler, Jörg Schmall)	37.7
4.	AUS	(Brian Lewis, Warren Rock)	44.4
5.	SWE	(Peter Kolni, Jörgen Kolni)	57.4
6.	SWI	(Walter Steiner, Albert Schiess)	63.4
7.	CAN	(Larry Woods, Michael de la Roche)	69.7
8.	ITA	(Franco Pivoli, Cesare Biagi)	71.7

Forty-year-old Reg White and his 30-year-old brother-in-law, John Osborn, won four of the first six races; they were able to sit out the final day.

1980 Moscow–Tallinn C: 11, N: 11, D: 7.29.

			PTS.
1.	BRA	(Alexandre Welter, Lars Sigurd Björkström)	21.4
2.	DEN	(Peter Due, Per Kjergard)	30.4
3.	SWE	(Göran Marström, Jörgen Ragnarsson)	33.7
4.	SOV	(Viktor Potapov, Aleksandr Zybin)	35.1
5.	HOL	(Willem Van Walt Meijer, Govert Brasser)	39.0
6.	FIN	(Pekka Narko, Juha Siira)	47.7
7.	AUT	(Hubert Porkert, Hermann Kupfner)	67.7
8.	GDR	(Uwe Steingross, Jörg Schramme)	82.0

470

The 470 is a two-man fiberglass craft that is 470 centimeters long. Like the Flying Dutchman, it uses a centerboard dinghy and a trapeze.

1896–1972 not held

1976 Montreal–Kingston C: 28, N: 28, D: 7.27.

			PTS.
1.	GER	(Frank Hübner, Harro Bode)	42.4
2.	SPA	(Antonio Gorostegui, Pedro Millet)	49.7
3.	AUS	(Ian Brown, Ian Ruff)	57.0
4.	SOV	(Viktor Potapov, Aleksandr Potapov)	57.0
5.	NZE	(Mark Paterson, Brett Bennett)	59.7
6.	GBR	(Philip Crebbin, Derek Clark)	69.4
7.	SWI	(Jean-Claude Vuithier, Laurent Quellet)	71.7
8.	FRA	(Marc Laurent, Roger Surmin)	79.4

1980 Moscow–Tallinn C: 14, N: 14, D: 7.29.

			PTS.
1.	BRA	(Marcos Rizzo Soares, Eduardo Penido)	36.4
2.	GDR	(Jörn Borowski, Egbert Swensson)	38.7
3.	FIN	(Jouko Lindgren, Georg Tallberg)	39.7
4.	HOL	(Henk Van Gent, Jan Van Den Hondel)	49.4
5.	POL	(Leon Wrobel, Tomasz Stocki)	53.0
6.	SPA	(Gustavo Doreste, Alfredo Rigau)	54.1
7.	ITA	(Ernesto Treves, Silvio Necchi)	57.7
8.	SWE	(Lars Bengtsson, Stefan Bengtsson)	60.0

Gold medal winners Soares and Penido, wind surfers from Rio de Janiero, were only 19 and 20 years old, respectively. Had Borowski and Swensson crossed the finish line two seconds sooner in the final race, they would have taken the championship away from the Brazilians. Borowski was the son of Paul Borowski, who won medals in the Dragon class in 1968 and 1972.

SOLING

The Soling is a three-man keelboat.

1896–1968 not held

1972 Munich–Kiel C: 26, N: 26, D: 9.8.

			PTS.
1.	USA	(Harry Melges, William Bentsen, William Allen)	8.7
2.	SWE	(Stig Wennerström, Lennart Roslund, Bo Knape, Stefan Krook)	31.7

3.	CAN	(David Miller, John Ekels, Paul Cote)	47.1
4.	FRA	(Jean-Marie le Guillou, Bernard Drubay, Jean-Yves Pellerin)	53.0
5.	GBR	(John Oakeley, Charles Reynolds, Barry Dunning)	54.7
6.	BRA	(Axel Schmidt-Preben, Patrick Matte Mascarenhas, Erik Schmidt-Preben)	64.7
7.	SOV	(Timir Pinegin, Valentin Zamotaikin, Rais Galimov)	65.0
8.	POL	(Zygfryd Perlicki, Józef Blaszczyk, Stanislaw Stefański)	75.0

The competition was limited to six races because of bad weather. Paul Elvström, attempting to become the first person in history to win gold medals at five different Olympics, packed up his boat and drove home in a huff after the fifth race, finishing 13th overall. Crown Prince Harald of Norway placed tenth. Less illustrious, but more successful, was helmsman Buddy Melges of Zelda, Wisconsin, who guided his boat to three firsts, a second, a third, and a fourth on his way to the gold medal.

1976 Montreal–Kingston C: 24, N: 24, D: 7.27.

			PTS.
1.	DEN	(Poul Jensen, Valdemar Bandolowski, Erik Hansen)	46.7
2.	USA	(John Kolius, Walter Glasgow, Richard Hoepfner)	47.4
3.	GDR	(Dieter Below, Michael Zachries, Olaf Engelhardt)	47.4
4.	SOV	(Boris Budnikov, Calentin Zamotaikin, Nikolai Poliakov)	48.7
5.	HOL	(Geert Bakker, Harald de Vlaming, Pieter Keijzer)	58.0
6.	GER	(Wilhelm Kuhweide, Karsten Meyer, Axel May)	60.7
7.	FRA	(Patrick Haegeli, Patrick Oeuvrard, Bruno Trouble)	64.0
8.	CAN	(Glen Dexter, Sandy Macmillan, Andreas Josenhans)	68.7

The 1976 Soling regatta was so close that the Danish team didn't know they had won until they returned to their berth and saw a large crowd waiting for them. Had they finished seven seconds slower in the final race they would have had to settle for bronze medals instead of gold. Instead, they swept past the French boat just before the finish line to place fifth, and the extra 1.7 points provided their margin of victory.

1980 Moscow–Tallinn C: 9, T: 9, D: 7.29.

			PTS.
1.	DEN	(Poul Jensen, Valdemar Bandolowski, Erik Hansen)	23.0
2.	SOV	(Boris Budnikov, Aleksandr Budnikov, Nikolay Polyakov)	30.4
3.	GRE	(Anastassios Boudouris, Anastassios Gavrilis, Aristidis Rapanakis)	31.1
4.	GDR	(Dieter Below, Bernd Klenke, Michael Zachries)	37.4
5.	HOL	(Geert Bakker, Steven Bakker, Dick Coster)	45.0
6.	BRA	(Vicente D'Avila Brun, Gastao D'Avila Brun, Roberto Luiz Souza)	47.1
7.	SWI	(Jean-François Corminboeuf, Roger-Claude Guignard, Robert Perret)	71.7
8.	SWE	(Jan Andersson, Göran Andersson, Bertil Larsson)	75.7

The three Danes defended their championship by winning the last two races, with the Soviet boat in second place both times.

Discontinued Events

.5 TON CLASS

1900 Paris–Meulan C: 7, N: 1, D: 5.24.

			PTS.	TIME
1.	Texier	FRA	18	20:40.38
2.	Pierre Gervais	FRA	18	20:56.12
3.	Henri Monnot	FRA	15	
4.	M. Monnot	FRA	13	
5.	G. Semichon	FRA	10	
6.	Jean d'Estournelles de Constant	FRA	6	

.5–1 TON CLASS

1900 Paris–Meulan T: 8, N: 3, D: 5.24.

			PTS.	TIME
1.	GBR	(Lorne Currie, John Gretton, Linton Hope)	17	6:42.01
2.	FRA	(Jacques Bandrier, Jean Lebret, Marcotte, R. William Martin, Jules Valton)	17	6:44.21
3.	FRA	(E. Michelet, F. Michelet)	17	6:49.37
4.	FRA	(J. de Chabannes la Palice)	13	

1–2 TON CLASS

1900 Paris–Meulan T: 5, N: 3, D: 5.24.

			PTS.
1.	SWI	(Hermann-Alexandre de Pourtalès)	19
2.	FRA	(F. Vilamitjana)	17
3.	FRA	(Jacques Baudrier)	15

2–3 TON CLASS

1900 Paris–Meulan T: 4, N: 3, D: 5.25.

			PTS.
1.	GBR	(William Exshaw)	20
2.	FRA	(Susse)	18
3.	FRA	(Auguste Donny)	15
4.	GER	(Ferdinand Schlatter)	15

3–10 TON CLASS

1900 Paris–Meulan T: 12, N: 3, D: 5.25.

			PTS.
1.	FRA	(E. Michelet, F. Michelet)	16
2.	FRA	(Maurice Gufflet)	16
3.	HOL	(H. Smulders)	15

10–20 TON CLASS

1900 Paris–Le Havre T: 6, N: 2, D: 8.6.

			PTS.
1.	FRA	(Emile Billard, P. Perquer)	29
2.	FRA	(Jean Decazes)	24
3.	GBR	(Edward Hore)	23
4.	FRA	(Cronier)	20
5.	GBR	(S.M. Mellor)	18
6.	FRA	(Jules Valton)	17

OPEN CLASS

1900 Paris–Meulan T: ?, N: ?, D: 5.20.

1.	GBR	(Lorne Currie, John Gretton, Linton Hope)	5:56:17
2.	GER	(Martin Wiesner, Heinrich Peters, Ottokar Weise, George Naue, Arthur Bloomfield, Karl Maria Binder, Futchtegott Baumann)	5:58:17
3.	FRA	(E. Michelet, F. Michelet)	6:12:12
4.	FRA	(Emile Sacre)	7:11:08
5.	FRA	(Jean d'Estournelles de Constant)	—
DISQ:	Texier (FRA), Louis-Auguste Dormeuil (FRA)		

5.5-METER

1952 Helsinki T: 16, N: 16, D: 7.28.

			PTS.
1.	USA	(Britton Chance, Sumner White, Edgar White, Michael Schoettle)	5751
2.	NOR	(Peder Lunde, Sr., Vibeke Lunde, Börre Falkum-Hansen)	5325
3.	SWE	(Folke Wassén, Magnus Wassén, Carl Erik Ohlson)	4554
4.	POR	(Duarte De Almeida Bello, Fernando Coelho Bello, Julio Sousa Leite Gorinho)	4450
5.	ARG	(Rodolfo Vollenweider, Tomas Galfrascoli, Ludovico Kempter)	3982
6.	GBR	(Robert Perry, John Dillon, Neil Cochran-Patrick)	3727
7.	SAF	(Leslie Horsfield, Joseph Ellis-Brown, Eric Benningfield)	3338
8.	FIN	(Hans Dittmar, Aarne Castrén, Johan Stadigh)	3292

1956 Melbourne T: 10, N: 10, D: 12.5.

			PTS.
1.	SWE	(Lars Thörn, Hjalmar Karlsson, Sture Stork)	5527
2.	GBR	(Robert Perry, Neil Cochran-Patrick, John Dillon, David Bowker)	4050
3.	AUS	(Alexander Sturrock, Deveraux Mytton, Douglas Buxton)	4022
4.	USA	(Ferdinand Schoettle, Victor Sheronas, John Bryant, Robert Stinson)	3971
5.	NOR	(Peder Lunde, Sr., Odd Harsheim, Halfdan Ditlev-Simonsen, Jr.)	3807
6.	FRA	(Albert Cadot, Jean-Jacques Herbulot, Dominque Perroud)	1779
7.	ITA	(Massimo Oberti, Antonio Carattino, Carlo Spirito, Antonio Cosentino)	1677
8.	SOV	(Konstantin Alexandrov, Konstantin Melgounov, Lev Alexeev)	1598

1960 Rome–Naples T: 19, N: 19, D: 9.7.

			PTS.
1.	USA	(George O'Day, James Hunt, David Smith)	6900
2.	DEN	(William Bernsten, Steen Christensen, Sören Hancke)	5678
3.	SWI	(Henri Copponex, Pierre Girard, Manfred Metzger)	5122
4.	ARG	(Roberto Sieburger, Enrique Sieburger, Carlos Sieburger)	4402
5.	SWE	(Bengt Sjösten, Claes Turitz, Göran Witting)	4277
6.	GBR	(Robin Aisher, George Nicholson, John Ruggles)	3807
7.	NOR	(Finn Ferner, Odd Harsheim, Knut Wang)	3765
8.	BAH	(Robert Symonette, Basil Kelly, George Roy Ramsey)	3024

1964 Tokyo T: 46, N: 15, D: 10.21.

			PTS.
1.	AUS	(William Northam, James Sargeant, Peter O'Donnell)	5981
2.	SWE	(Lars Thörn, Sture Stork, Ernst Arne Karlsson)	5284
3.	USA	(John McNamara, Francis Scully, Joseph Batchelder)	5106
4.	ITA	(Agostino Straulino, Bruno Petronio, Massimo Minervini)	4738
5.	GER	(Fritz Kopperschmidt, Herbert Reich, Eckart Wagner, Uwe Mares)	3057
6.	FIN	(Johann Gullichsen, K. Peter Fazer, Juhani Salovaara)	3039
7.	CAN	(S.A. McDonald, J.D. Woodward, G. Bernard Skinner)	2955
8.	NOR	(Crown Prince Harald, Eirik Johannessen, Stein Foyen)	2860

Former racing-car driver Bill Northam was 59 years old when he skippered the yacht *Barrenjoey* to a gold medal.

1968 Mexico City–Acapulco T: 14, N: 14, D: 10.21.

			PTS.
1.	SWE	(Ulf Sundelin, Jörgen Sundelin, Peter Sundelin)	8
2.	SWI	(Louis Noverraz, Bernhard Dunand, Marcel Stern)	32
3.	GBR	(Robin Aisher, Adrian Jardine, Paul Anderson)	39.8
4.	GER	(Rudolf Harmstorf, Karl-August Stolze, Harald Stein)	47.4
5.	ITA	(Giuseppe Zucchinetti, Antonio Carattino, Domenico Carattino)	51.1
6.	CAN	(Stanley Leibel, Ernest Weiss, Jack Hasen)	68
7.	AUS	(William Solomons, James Hardy, Gilbert Kaufman)	69.4
8.	USA	(Gardner Cox, Stephen Colgate, Stuart Walker)	74.7

The Sundelin brothers, from the small resort town of Ektorp, won five of the seven races, finishing fourth and fifth in the other two. Silver medalist Louis Noverraz was 66 years old.

6-METER

1908 London–Ryde T: 5, N: 4, D: 7.29.
1. GBR (Gilbert Laws, T.D. McMeekin, Charles Crichton)
2. BEL (Léon Huybrechts, Louis Huybrechts, Henri Weewauters)

3. FRA (Henri Arthus, Louis Potheau, P. Rabot)
4. GBR (J.W. Leuchars, W. Leuchars, F.R. Smith)
5. SWE (Karl Sjögren, Birger Gustafsson, Jonas Jonsson)

1912 Stockholm–Nynas T: 6, N: 5, D: 7.22.
1. FRA (Amédée Thubé, Gaston Thubé, Jacques Thubé)
2. DEN (Hans Meulengracht-Madsen, Steen Herschend, Sven Thomsen)
3. SWE (Harald Sandberg, Erik Sandberg, Otto Aust)
4. SWE (Olof Mark, Einar Hagberg, Jonas Jonsson)
5. FIN (Ernst Estlander, Torsten Sandelin, Ragnar Stenbäck)
5. NOR (Edvard Christansen, Hans Ferd. Christiansen, E. Kragh Christiansen)

1920 Antwerp T: 2, N: 2, D: 7.26.
1. NOR (Andreas Brecke, Paal Kaasen, Ingolf Röd)
2. BEL (Léon Huybrechts, John Klotz, Charles van den Bussche)

1924 Paris–Le Havre T: 9, N: 9, D: 7.26.

			PTS.
1.	NOR	(Eugen Lunde, Christopher Dahl, Anders Lundgren)	2
2.	DEN	(Wilhelm Vett, Knud Degn, Christian Nielsen)	5
3.	HOL	(Johan Carp, Johannes Guépin, Jan Vreede)	5
4.	SWE	(Nils Rinman, Olle Rinman, Magnus Hellström)	12
5.	BEL	(Léon Huybrechts, John Klotz, Léopold Standaert)	16
5.	FRA	(G. Herpin, H. Louit, Pierre Moussié)	16

1928 Amsterdam T: 13, N: 13, D: 8.9.
1. NOR (Crown Prince Olav, Johan Anker, Erik Anker, Haakon Bryhn)
2. DEN (Niels Otto Möller, Aage Höy-Petersen, Peter Schlütter, Svend Linck)
3. EST (Nikolai Wekshin, William von Wirén, Eberhard Vogdt, Andreas Fählmann, Georg Fählmann)
4. HOL (Hendrik Pluijgers, Carl Huisken, Willem Schouten, Hendrik Fokker)
5. BEL (Léon Huybrechts, Arthur Sneyers, Frits Mulder, Ludovic Franck, Willy van Rompaey)
6. USA (Herman Whiton, Conway Olmstead, Willets Outerbridge, James Thompson, Frederick Morris)
7. SWE (H. Hansson, G. Lindahl, Yngde Lindquist, Hakon Reuter)
8. FRA —

1932 Los Angeles T: 3, N: 3, D: 8.12.

			PTS.
1.	SWE	(Tore Holm, Martin Hindorff, Olle Åkerlund, Åke Bergqvist)	18
2.	USA	(Frederick Conant, Robert Carlson, Temple Ashbrook, Charles Smith, Donald Douglas, Emmett Davis)	12
3.	CAN	(Philip Rogers, Gerald Wilson, Gardner Boultbee, Kenneth Glass)	4

The Swedes won all six races.

1936 Berlin–Kiel T: 12, N: 12, D: 8.10.

		PTS.
1. GBR	(Charles Leaf, Christopher Boardman, Miles Belville, Russell Harmer, Leonard Martin)	67
2. NOR	(Magnus Konow, Karsten Konow, Fredrik Meyer, Vadjuv Nyquist, Alf Tveten)	66
3. SWE	(Sven Salén, Dagmar Salén, Lennart Ekdahl, Martin Hindorff, Torsten Lord)	62
4. ARG	(Julio Sieburger, Claudio Bincaz, Germán Frers, Edlef Hosmann, Jorge Linck)	52
5. ITA	(Renato Cosentino, Guiliano Oberti, Massimo Oberti, Giovanni Stampa, Giuseppe Volpi)	50
6. GER	(Hans Lubinus, Dietrich Christensen, Kurt Frey, Theodor Thomsen, Haimar Wedemeyer)	49
7. FIN	(Mattson, Pacius, Stenbaeck, H. Sumelius, Winqvist)	43
8. HOL	(Carp, Dokkum, Jonker, Looman, Moltzer)	42

1948 London T: 11, N: 11, D: 8.12.

		PTS.
1. USA	(Herman Whiton, Alfred Loomis, James Weekes, James Smith, Michael Mooney)	5472
2. ARG	(Enrique Sieburger, Emilio Homps, Rufino Rodriguez de la Torre, Rodolfo Rivademar, Julio Sieburger)	5120
3. SWE	(Tore Holm, Torsten Lord, Martin Hindorff, Karl Ameln, Gösta Salén)	4033
4. NOR	(Magnus Konow, Anders Evensen, Lars Musaeus, Håkon Solem, Ragnar Hargreaves)	3217
5. GBR	(J.H. Hume, J.D.H. Hume, B.G. Hardie, H.G. Hardie, H. Hunter)	2879
6. BEL	(Ludovic Franck, Emile Hayoit, Willy Huybrechts, Henri van Riel, Willy van Rompaey)	2752
7. SWI	(Henri Copponex, P. Bonnet, R. Fehlmann, André Firmenich, E. Lachapelle, Louis Noverraz, Charles Stern, Marcel Stern)	2594
8. ITA	(Giovanni Reggio, Giorgio Audizio, R. Costentino, A. Croce, G. deLuca, Luigi Poggi, Enrico Poggi)	2099

1952 Helsinki T: 11, N: 11, D: 7.28.

		PTS.
1. USA	(Herman Whiton, Eric Ridder, Julian Roosevelt, Everard Endt, Emelyn Whiton, John Morgan)	4870
2. NOR	(Finn Ferner, Johan Ferner, Erik Heiberg, Carl Mortensen, Tor Arneberg)	4648
3. FIN	(Ernst Westerlund, Paul Sjöberg, Ragnar Jansson, Adolf Konto, Rolf Turkka)	3944
4. SWE	(Sven Salén, Martin Hindorff, Torsten Lord, Jacob Lars Lundström, Karl Ameln)	3773
5. ARG	(Enrique Sieburger, Rufino Rodriguez de la Torre, Werner von Foerster, Horacio Monti, Hercules Morini)	3393
6. SWI	(Louis Noverraz, André Firmenich, Charles Stern, Marcel Stern, François Chapot)	3020
7. CAN	(Norman Gooderham, Kenneth Bradfield, William Copeland, William Macintosh, Donald Tytler)	3013
8. ITA	(Enrico Poggi, Antonio Cosentino, Pietro Reggio, Guisto Spigno, Andrea Ferrari)	2560

Herman Whiton and the *Llanoria* repeated their 1948 triumph, winning the final race by 81 seconds. Finland's bronze-medal-winning yacht, *Ralia,* was the same boat that Sweden had used four years earlier to gain the bronze medal in London. The Swedes had named it *Ali Baba.*

6-METER, 1907 RATING

1920 Antwerp T: 4, N: 2, D: 7.10.
1. BEL (Emile Cornellie, Florimond Cornellie, Fréderic-Albert Bruynseels)
2. NOR (Einar Torgersen, Leif Erichsen, Annan Knudsen)
3. NOR (Henrik Agersborg, Trygve Pedersen, Einar Bernsten)
4. BEL (Louis Depiere, Raymond Bauwens, Willy Valcke)

6.5-METER

1920 Antwerp T: 2, N: 2, D: 7.10.
1. HOL (Johan Carp, Petrus Wernink, Bernard Carp)
2. FRA (Albert Weil, Félix Picon, Robert Monier)

7-METER

1908 London–Ryde T: 1, N: 1, D: 7.29.
1. GBR (Charles Rivett-Carnac, Norman Bingley, Richard Dixon, Frances Clytie Rivett-Carnac)

1920 Antwerp T: 1, N: 1, D: 7.10.
1. GBR (Cyril Wright, Dorothy Wright, R.H. Coleman, W.J. Maddison)

8-METER

1908 London–Ryde T: 5, N: 3, D: 7.29.
1. GBR (Blair Cochrane, Arthur Wood, Hugh Sutton, John Rhodes, Charles Campbell)
2. SWE (Carl Hellström, Edmund Thormählen, Eric Wallerius, Erik Sandberg, Harald Wallin)
3. GBR (R. Himloke, Collingwood Hughes, Saint John Hughes, George Ratsey, William Ward)
4. NOR (Johan Anker, Einar Hvoslef, Christian Jensen, Magnus Konow, Eilert Falch Lund)
5. SWE (John Carlsson, Einar Hagberg, Hjalmar Lönnroth, Karl Ljungberg, August Olsson)

1912 Stockholm–Nynas T: 7, N: 4, D: 7.22.
1. NOR (Thoralf Glad, Thomas Valentin Aas, Andreas Brecke, Torleiv Corneliussen, Christian Jebe)
2. SWE (Bengt Heyman, Emil Henriques, Herbert Westermark, Nils Westermark, Alvar Thiel)
3. FIN (Bertil Tallberg, Gunnar Tallberg, Arthur Ahnger, Emil Lindh, Georg Westling)
4. FIN (Gustaf Estlander, Curt Andstén, Jarl Andstén, Carl Girsén, Bertil Juslén)
5. RUS (H. von Adlerberg, J. Färber, W. Yilevich, E. Kuhn, V. Kusmitschev)
5. SWE (Fritz Sjöqvist, Johan Sjöqvist, Ragnar Gripe, Theodor Grönfors, Erik Hagström)

1920 Antwerp T: 3, N: 2, D: 7.10.
1. NOR   (Magnus Konow, Reidar Marthiniussen, Ragnar Vig, Thorleif Christoffersen)
2. NOR   (Jens Salvesen, Lauritz Schmidt, Fin Schiander, Nils Thomas, Ralph Tschudi)
3. BEL   (Albert Grisar, Willy de l'Arbre, Georges Hellebuyck, Léopold Standaert, Henri Weewauters)

1924 Paris–Le Havre T: 5, N: 5, D: 7.26.

		PTS.
1. NOR	(August Ringvold, Sr., Rick Bockelie, Harald Hagen, Ingar Nielsen, August Ringvold, Jr.)	2
2. GBR	(E.E. Jacob, Thomas Riggs, Walter Riggs, Ernest Roney, Gordon Fowler)	5
3. FRA	(Louis Bréguet, Pierre Ganthier, R. Girardet, A. Guerrier, G. Mollard)	5
4. BEL	(Fernand Carlier, Maurice Passelecq, Emmanuel Pauwels, Victor Vandersleyen, Paul van Halteren)	8
5. ARG	(Louis Domingo Aguirre, C.J. Guerrico, J.C. Milberg, B. Milhas, M.R. Uriburu)	—

1928 Amsterdam T: 8, N: 8, D: 8.9.
1. FRA   (Donatien Bouché, André Lesauvage, Jean Lesieur, Virginie Hériot, Charles de la Sabliere, André Derrien)
2. HOL   (Lambertus Doedes, Maarten de Wit, Johannes van Hoolwerff, Gerardus de Vries Lentsch, Hendrik Kersken, Cornelis van Staveren)
3. SWE   (Johan Sandblom, Philip Sandblom, Carl Sandblom, Torè Holm, Clarence Hammar, Wilhelm Törsleff)
4. ITA   (Francesco Giovanelli, Guido Giovanelli, Marcantonio de Beaumont-Bonelli, Carlo Alberto d'Alberti, Edoardo Moscatelli, Mario Bruzzone)
4. NOR   (Jens Salvesen, Magnus Konow, W. Wilhelmsen, Bernhard Lund)
6. USA   (Owen Churchill, Benjamin Weston, Manfred Curry, Frank Hekma, Nicholas Barry Hekma)
7. GBR   (Kenneth Preston, Robert Steele, Joseph Compton, Beryl Preston, Francis Preston)
8. ARG   (Rodrigues de la Torre, Ortiz Sauze, Aguirre, Gil Elizalde, Iglesias, Peralta Ramos)

1932 Los Angeles T: 2, N: 2, D: 8.9.

		PTS.
1. USA	(Owen Churchill, John Biby, William Cooper, Carl Dorsey, Robert Sutton, Alan Morgan, Pierpont Davis, Alphonse Burnand, Thomas Webster, John Huettner, Richard Moore, Kenneth Carey)	8
2. CAN	(Ronald Maitland, Ernest Cribb, Harry Jones, Peter Gordon, Hubert Wallace, George Gyles)	4

1936 Berlin–Kiel T: 12, N: 10, D: 8.10.

		PTS.
1. ITA	(Giovanni Reggio, Bruno Bianchi, Luigi De Manincor, Domenico Mordini, Luigi Poggi, Enrico Poggi)	55
2. NOR	(Olav Ditlev-Simonsen, John Ditlev-Simonsen, Hans Struknaes, Lauritz Schmidt, Nordahl Wallem, Jacob Tullin Thams)	53

3. GER	(Hans Howaldt, Alfried Krupp von Bohlen und Halbach, Felix Scheder-Bieschin, Eduard Mohr, Otto Wachs, Fritz Bischoff)	53
4. SWE	(Marcus Wallenberg, Tore Holm, Wilhelm Moberg, Detlow von Braun, Per Gedda, Bo Westerberg)	51
5. FIN	(Gunnar Grönblom, Sven Grönblum, Hilding Silander, Oscar Sumelius, Olof Wallin, Walter Kjellberg)	37
6. GBR	(Kenneth Preston, Beryl Preston, Francis Preston, Robert Steele, Joseph Compton, John Eddy)	36
7. ARG	(Rodriguez de la Torre, Ortiz Sauze, Aguirre, Gil Elizalde, Iglesisas, Peralta Ramos)	25
8. DEN	(N.V. Hansen, Tholstrup, Danielsen, Berntsen, Kastrup, Schibbye)	22

The Germans led after six races, but finished only sixth on the final day. Norway was awarded second place after winning a sail-off against Germany two days later. Jacob Thams of the Norwegian crew had won the ski-jump in the first Winter Olympics at Chamonix in 1924.

8-METER, 1907 RATING
1920 Antwerp T: 2, N: 1, D: 7.10.
1. NOR   (August Ringvold, Sr., Thorleif Holbye, Tell Wagle, Kristoffer Olsen, A. Bruun Jacobsen)
2. NOR   (Niels Marius Nielsen, Johan Faye, Christian Dick, Sten Abel)

10-METER
1912 Stockholm T: 5, N: 3, D: 7.22.
1. SWE   (Carl Hellström, Erik Wallerius, Harald Wallerius, Humbert Lundén, Herman Nyberg, Harry Rosensvärd, Paul Isberg, Filip Ericsson)
2. FIN   (Harry Wahl, Waldemar Björkstén, Jacob Carl Björnström, Bror Benediktus Brennar, Allan Franck, Erik Lindh, Aarne Pekkalainen)
3. RUS   (Ester Beloselsky, Ernest Brasche, Pushnitsky, Aleksandr Rodionov, Jossif Schomaker, Filipp Strauch, Karl Lindblom)
4. SWE   (Björn Bothén, Bo Bothén, Wilhelm Forsberg, Einar Lindén, Karl Lindholm, Erik Waller)

10-METER, 1907 RATING
1920 Antwerp T: 1, N: 1, D: 7.10.
1. NOR   (Erik Herseth, Sigurd Holter, Ingar Nielsen, Ole Sörensen, Gunnar Jamvold, Petter Jamvold, Claus Juell)

10-METER 1919 RATING
1920 Antwerp T: 1, N: 1, D: 7.10.
1. NOR   (Archer Arentz, Willy Gilbert, Robert Gjertsen, Arne Sejersted, Halfdan Schjött, Trygve Schjött, Otto Falkenberg)

12-METER

1908 London–Firth of Clyde T: 2, N: 1, D: 8.12.
1. GBR (Thomas Glen-Coats, J.H. Downes, John Buchanan, J.C. Bunten, A.D. Downes, David Dunlop, John Mackenzie, Albert Martin, Gerald Tait, J.S. Aspin)
2. GBR (Charles Maclver, J.G. Kenion, James Baxter, W.P. Davidson, J.F. Jellico, T.A.R. Littledale, C. MacLeod Robertson, J.F.D. Spence, J.M. Adam, C.R. Maclver)

1912 Stockholm–Nynas T: 3, N: 3, D: 7.21.
1. NOR (Johan Anker, Alfred Larsen, Nils Bertelsen, Halfdan Hansen, Magnus Konow, Petter Larsen, Eilert Falch Lund, Fritz Staib, Arnfinn Heje, Gustav Thaulow)
2. SWE (Nils Persson, Hugo Clason, Richard Sällström, Nils Lamby, Kurt Bergström, Dick Bergström, Carl Lindqvist, Per Bergman, Sigurd Kander, Folke Johansson)
3. FIN (Ernst Krogius, Max Alfthan, Erik Hartvall, Jarl Hulldén, Sigurd Juslen, Eino Sandelin, John Silén)

12-METER, 1907 RATING

1920 Antwerp T: 1, N: 1, D: 7.10.
1. NOR (Henrik Östervold, Jan Östervold, Ole Östervold, Hans Naess, Lauritz Christiansen, Halvor Mögster, Rasmus Birkeland, Halvor Birkeland, Kristen Östervold)

12-METER, 1919 RATING

1920 Antwerp T: 1, N: 1, D: 7.10.
1. NOR (Johan Friele, Olav Örvig, Arthur Allers, Christen Wiese, Martin Borthen, Egil Reimers, Kaspar Hassel, Thor Örvig, Erik Örvig)

SHARPIE—12 SQUARE METERS

1956 Melbourne T: 13, N: 13, D: 12.5.

			PTS.
1.	NZE	(Peter Mander, John Cropp)	6086
2.	AUS	(Roland Tasker, John Scott)	6086
3.	GBR	(Jasper Blackall, Terrence Smith)	4859
4.	ITA	(Mario Capio, Emilio Massino)	3928
5.	SAF	(John Sully, Alfred Evans)	2917
6.	GER	(Rolf Mulka, Ingo von Bredow)	2840
7.	SOV	(Boris Iliine, Aleksandr Chumakov)	2479
8.	FRA	(Roger Tiriau, Claude Flahault)	2058

Tasker and Scott appeared to have won the final race and the gold medal, but a protest by the French led to their disqualification, leaving the Australians tied in points with New Zealand's Mander and Cropp. The New Zealand pair was awarded first place because they had won three races while the Australians had won only two.

30 SQUARE METERS

1920 Antwerp T: 1, N: 1, D: 7.10.
1. SWE (Gösta Lundqvist, Rolf Steffenburg, Gösta Bengtsson, Axel Calvert)

40 SQUARE METERS

1920 Antwerp T: 2, N: 1, D: 7.10.
1. SWE (Tore Holm, Yngve Holm, Axel Rydin, Georg Tengvall)
2. SWE (Gustav Svensson, Ragnar Svensson, Per Almstedt, Erick Mellbin)

SWALLOW

1948 London T: 14, N: 14, D: 8.12.

			PTS.
1.	GBR	(Stewart Morris, David Bond)	5625
2.	POR	(Duarte De Almeida Bello, Fernando Pinto Coelho Bello)	5579
3.	USA	(Lockwood Pirie, Owen Torry)	4352
4.	SWE	(Stig Hedberg, Lars Matton)	3342
5.	DEN	(Johan Rathje, Nolly Petersen)	2935
6.	ITA	(Dario Salata, Achille Roncoroni)	2893
7.	CAN	(John Robertson, R. Townsend)	2807
8.	NOR	(O. Christensen)	2768

The Swallow class was the same size as the Star, but with a smaller sail area (200 square feet rather than 281). Morris and Bond came within 15 seconds of losing the gold medal in the final race.

DRAGON

1948 London T: 12, N: 12, D: 8.12.

			PTS.
1.	NOR	(Thor Thorvaldsen, Sigve Lie, Håkon Barfod)	4746
2.	SWE	(Folke Bohlin, Hugo Jonsson, Gösta Brodin)	4621
3.	DEN	(William Berntsen, Ole Berntsen, Klaus Baess)	4223
4.	GBR	(W. Eric Strain, G.H. Brown, J. Wallace)	3943
5.	ITA	(Giuseppe Canessa, Bruno Bianchi, Luigi DeManincor)	3366
6.	FIN	(Rainer Packalen, Niilo Orama, Aatos Hirvisalo)	3057
7.	ARG	(Roberto Sieburger)	2843
8.	HOL	(C. Jonker)	2508

1952 Helsinki T: 17, N: 17, D: 7.28.

			PTS.
1.	NOR	(Thor Thorvaldsen, Sigve Lie, Håkon Barfod)	6130
2.	SWE	(Per Gedda, Sidney Boldt-Christmas, Erland Almkvist)	5556
3.	GER	(Theodor Thomsen, Erich Natusch, Georg Nowka)	5352
4.	ARG	(Roberto Sieburger, Jorge Del Rio Salas, Horacio Campi)	5339
5.	DEN	(Ole Bernsten, William Bernsten, Aage Birch)	4460
6.	HOL	(Willem van Duyl, Abraham Dudok van Heel, Michiel Dudok van Heel)	4041
7.	BRA	(Wolfgang Richter, Peter Mangels, Francisco Felici Italo Osoldi)	2884
8.	POR	(João Tito, Carlos Lourenco, Alberto Graca)	2782

1956 Melbourne T: 16, N: 16, D: 12.5.

		PTS.
1. SWE	(Folke Bohlin, Bengt Palmquist, Leif Wikström)	5723
2. DEN	(Ole Bernsten, Cyril Andresen, Christian von Bü-low)	5723
3. GBR	(Graham Mann, Ronald Backus, Jonathan Janson)	4547
4. ARG	(Jorge Salas Chaves, Arnoldo Pekelharing, Boris Belada)	4225
5. AUT	(Graham Drane, Brian Carolan, James Carolane)	3769
6. ITA	(Sergio Sorrentino, Piero Gorgatto, Adelchi Pelaschiar)	3404
7. NOR	(Thor Thorvaldsen, Carl Svae, Björn Gulbrandsen)	3253
8. CAN	(David Howard, Herald Howard, Donald Tytler)	3186

The Swedes came from behind to win the last two races and tie the Danes at 5723 points. Sweden was then awarded first place because they won three races to Denmark's one.

1960 Rome–Naples T: 27, N: 27, D: 9.7.

		PTS.
1. GRE	(Crown Prince Constantin, Odysseus Eskitzoglou, Georgios Zaimis)	6733
2. ARG	(Jorge Salas Chaves, Hector Calegaris, Jorge Del Rio)	5715
3. ITA	(Antonio Cosentino, Antonio Ciciliano, Giulio De Stefano)	5704
4. NOR	(Öivind Christensen, Arild Amundsen, Carl Otto Svae)	5403
5. CAN	(Samuel McDonald, Lynn Watters, Gordon Norton)	5177
6. DEN	(Aage Birch, Paul Jörgensen, Niels Markussen)	4715
7. GBR	(Graham Mann, Jonathan Janson, Ian Hannay)	4604
8. GER	(Hans Ravenborg, Günther Benecke, Peter Rebien)	4329

Twenty-year-old Crown Prince Constantin received the traditional victory dunking by being pushed into the water by his mother, Queen Frederika.

1964 Tokyo T: 23, N: 23, D: 10.21.

		PTS.
1. DEN	(Ole Berntsen, Christian von Bülow, Ole Poulsen)	5854
2. GDR	(Peter Ahrendt, Ulrich Mense, Wilfried Lorenz)	5826
3. USA	(Lowell North, Charles Rogers, Richard Deaver)	5523
4. GBR	(Edwin Parry, Jeremy Harris, Peter Reade)	5090
5. BER	(Edmund Cooper, Eugene Simmons, Conrad Soares)	5055
6. ITA	(Sergio Sorrentino, Sergio Furlan, Annibale Pelaschiar)	4636
7. BAH	(Godfrey Kelly, Basil Kelly, Robert Eardley)	4294
8. GRE	(Odysseus Eskitzoglou, Georgios Zaimis, Themistoklis Magoulas)	4188

The East Germans finished 16 seconds short of a gold medal in the final race.

1968 Mexico City–Acapulco T: 23, N: 23, D: 10.21.

		PTS.
1. USA	(George Friedrichs, Barton Jahncke, Gerald Schreck)	6.0
2. DEN	(Aage Birch, Poul Höj Jensen, Niels Markussen)	26.4
3. GDR	(Paul Borowski, Karl-Heinz Thun, Konrad Weichert)	32.7
4. CAN	(Stephen Tupper, David Miller, Timothy Irwin)	64.1
5. AUS	(John Cuneo, Thomas Anderson, John Ferguson)	65.0
6. SWE	(Gunnar Broberg, Lennart Eisner, Sven Hanson)	71.4
7. GER	(Klaus Oldendorff, Peter Stuicken, Axel May)	74.0
8. FRA	(Michel Briand, Michel Alexandre, Pierre Blanchard)	81.4

The U.S. crew won four of the seven races and also finished second twice and sixth once.

1972 Munich–Kiel T: 23, N: 23, D:9.8.

		PTS.
1. AUS	(John Cuneo, Thomas Anderson, John Shaw)	13.7
2. GDR	(Paul Borowski, Konrad Weichert, Karl Heinz Thun)	41.7
3. USA	(Donald Cohen, Charles Horter, John Marshall)	47.7
4. GER	(Franz Heilmeier, Richard Kuchler, Konrad Glas)	47.7
5. NZL	(Ronald Watson, Noel Everett, Fraser Beer)	51.0
6. SWE	(Jörgen Sundelin, Peter Sundelin, Ulf Sundelin)	67.4
7. DEN	(Poul Höj Jensen, Frank Höj Jensen, Gunnar Dahlgaard)	68.0
8. FIN	(Kurt Nyman, Göran Schauman, Aleksander Bielaczyc)	68.7

Skippered by 44-year-old optician John Cuneo, the Australian yacht won the first three races of a competition that was cut short after six races due to inclement weather.

TEMPEST

1972 Munich–Kiel T: 21, N: 21, D: 9.8.

		PTS.
1. SOV	(Valentin Mankin, Vitaly Dyrdyra)	28.1
2. GBR	(Alan Warren, David Hunt)	34.4
3. USA	(Glen Foster, Peter Dean)	47.7
4. SWE	(John Albrechtson, Ingvar Hansson)	57.4
5. HOL	(Bernard Staartjes, Kees Kuppershoek)	58.7
6. NOR	(Peder Lunde, Jr., Aksel Gresvig)	70.0
7. BRA	(Mario Buckup, Peter Ficker)	73.7
8. IRL	(David Wilkins, Sean Whitaker)	74.7

1976 Montreal–Kingston T: 16, N: 16, D: 7.27.

		PTS.
1. SWE	(John Albrechtson, Ingvar Hansson)	14.0
2. SOV	(Valentin Mankin, Vladislav Akimenko)	30.4
3. USA	(Dennis Conner, Conn Findlay)	32.7
4. GER	(Uwe Mares, Wolf Stadler)	42.1
5. ITA	(Giuseppe Milone, Roberto Mottola)	55.4
6. DEN	(Claes Thunbo Christensen, Finn Thunbo Christensen)	62.7
7. CAN	(Allan Leibel, Lorne Leibel)	65.1
8. HOL	(Ben Staartjes, Ab Ekels)	78.7

Funeral director Allen Warren and his partner, David Hunt, provided a light touch to the Kingston Regatta. Their six-year-old keelboat, *Gift 'Orse,* was damaged in transit and performed poorly at the Olympics. After the final race, Warren and Hunt took some acetone and a flare and set their boat on fire. "She went lame on us," said Warren, "so we decided the poor, old 'orse should be cremated." "My skipper has style," added Hunt, "but not that much. I tried to persuade him to burn with the ship, but he wouldn't agree."

Bronze medalist Conn Findlay also won two gold medals and one bronze medal in coxed pair rowing events of 1956–1964.

DISCONTINUED SPORTS

Cricket	Polo
Croquet	Rackets
Golf	Roque
Jeu De Paume	Rugby
Lacrosse	Tennis
Motor Boating	Tug Of War

CRICKET

1900 Paris T: 2, N: 2, D: 8.20.
1. GBR   (C.B.K. Beachcroft, John Symes, Frederick Cuming, Montagu Toller, Alfred Bowerman, Alfred Powlesland, William Donne, Frederick Christian, George Buckley, Francis Burchell, Harry Corner)
2. FRA   (T.H. Jordan, A.J. Schneidau, R. Horne, Henry Terry, F. Roques, W. Anderson, D. Robinson, W.T. Attrill, W. Browning, A. McEvoy, P.H. Tomalin, J. Braid)
   Final: GBR 262—104 FRA

CROQUET

1900 Paris C: 20, N: 1, D: 7.
Singles—1 Ball

		PTS.
1. Aumoitte	FRA	45
2. Johin	FRA	21

Singles—2 Balls
1. Waydelick	FRA
2. Vignerot	FRA
3. Sautereau	FRA

Doubles
1. FRA (Johin, Aumoitte)

GOLF

1900 Paris C: 30, N: 4, D:10.?, 10. 4.
Men

		SHOTS
1. Charles Sands	USA	167
2. Walter Rutherford	GBR	168
3. David Robertson	GBR	175
4. F.W. Taylor	USA	182
5. H.E. Daunt	FRA	184
6. G. Thorne	GBR	185

Women

		PTS.
1. Margaret Abbott	USA	47
2. Polly Whittier	SWI	49
3. Hager Pratt	USA	55
4. Froment-Meurice	FRA	56
5. Ridgeway	GBR	57
6. Fournier-Sarlovèze	FRA	58

Margaret Abbott was the first U.S. woman to win an Olympic gold medal. A 5-foot 11-inch, 22-year-old Chicago socialite, she traveled to Paris in 1899 with her mother, literary editor and novelist Mary Ives Abbott, so that she could study art. Ten women took part in the final nine-hole round of the ladies' golf competition. Abbott later told relatives that she won the tournament "because all the French girls apparently misunderstood the nature of the game scheduled for that day and turned up to play in high heels and tight skirts." Two years later Margaret Abbott, by then a resident of New York City, married political satirist Finley Peter Dunne.

1904 St. Louis C: 75, N: 2, D: 9.24.
Men

		SHOTS
1. George Lyon	CAN	3 and 2
2. H. Chandler Egan	USA	
3. Burt McKinnie	USA	
4. Francis Newton	USA	
5. Harry Allen (USA), Albert Lambert (USA), Mason Phelps (USA), Daniel Sawyer (USA)		

George Lyon was an eccentric athlete who didn't pick up a golf club until he was 38 years old. Before that he had competed successfully in baseball, tennis, and cricket. Once he even set a Canadian record in the pole vault. Lyon was 46 when he traveled down from Toronto to take part in the Olympics. He caused quite a stir when he played in St. Louis because of his unorthodox swing. He wielded the club more like a cricket bat, provoking some newspapers to criticize his "coal-heaver's swing." On the course he was an endless source of cheerful energy, singing, telling jokes and even doing handstands. A 36-hole qualifying round reduced the field from 75 to 32. The survivors then engaged in a match play elimination tournament. In the semifinals Lyon, the only golfer who wasn't from the United States, defeated Francis Newton, the Pacific Coast champion, on the last of 36 holes. His final match was a surprise victory over the 23-year-old U.S. champion, Chandler Egan. Lyon was awarded a $1500 sterling silver trophy, which he accepted after walking down the path to the ceremony on his hands. In 1908 George Lyon traveled to England to compete in the London Olympics. However an internal dispute among British golfers caused them to boycott the games, leaving Lyon as the only entrant. Offered the gold medal by default, he refused it. Lyon was still winning championships twenty years later and shot his age for 18 holes until he was 78 years old. He died the following year.

1904 St. Louis T: 3, N: 1, D: 9.17.
Teams

			SHOTS
1.	USA	(Western Golf Association—H. Chandler Egan, Robert Hunter, Kenneth Edwards, Clement Smoot, Walter Egan, Ned Sawyer, Edward "Ned" Cummins, Mason Phelps, Nathaniel Moore, Warren Wood)	1749
2.	USA	(Trans Mississippi Golf Association—Albert Lambert, Stewart Stickney, Bert McKinnie, William Stickney, Ralph McKittrick, Frederick Semple, Francis Newton, Harry Potter, John Cady, John Maxwell)	1770
3.	USA	(United States Golf Association—Douglas Cadwalader, Allan Lard, Jesse Carleton, Simeon Price, Harold Weber, John Rahm, Arthur Hussey, Orus Jones, Harold Fraser, George Oliver)	1839

JEU DE PAUME

Jeu de Paume was a form of tennis.

1908 London C: 11, N: 2, D: 5.28.

			SETS
1.	Jay Gould	USA	6–5, 6–4, 6–4
2.	Eustace Miles	GBR	
3.	Neville Lytton	GBR	6–2, 6–4, 6–4
4.	A. Page	GBR	

LACROSSE

1904 St. Louis T: 3, N: 2, D: 7.7.
1. CAN (Shamrock Lacrosse Team, Winnipeg, Manitoba—George Cloutier, George Cattanach, Benjamin Jamieson,

Jack Flett, George Bretz, Eli Blanchard, Hilliard Laidlaw, H. Lyle, W. Brennaugh, L.H. Pentland, Sandy Cowan, William Laurie Burns, William Orris)
2. USA (St. Louis Amateur Athletic Association, St. Louis, Missouri—Hunter, Patrick Grogan, Passmore, Lehman, Hess, J.W. Dowling, A.H. Venn, Sullivan, Murphy, Gibson, Woods, Partridge, Young, Ross)
3. CAN (Mohawk Indians, Brantford, Ontario—Black Hawk, Black Eagle, Almighty Voice, Flat Iron, Spotted Tail, Half Moon, Lightfoot, Snake Eater, Red Jacket, Night Hawk, Rain in Face, Man Afraid Soap)
   Final: Shamrock 6–1 St. Louis
   Shamrock 8–2 St. Louis

1908 London T: 2, N: 2, D: 10.24.
1. CAN (Frank Dixon, George "Doc" Campbell, Angus Dillion, Richard Louis Duckett, George Rennie, Clarence McKerrow, Alexander Turnbull, Henry Hoobin, Ernest Hamilton, John Broderick, Thomas Gorman, Patrick 'Paddy' Brennan)
2. GBR (C.H. Scott, G. Mason, H.W. Ramsay, E.O. Dutton, J. Parker-Smith, Wilfred Johnson, Norman Whitley, Gerald Buckland, S. Hayes, G. Alexander, R.G. Martin, E.P. Jones)
   Final: CAN 14—10 GBR

Good sportsmanship was the order of the day in the lacrosse competition. When Frank Dillon of Canada broke his stick, R.G. Martin of Great Britain offered to withdraw from the game until a new one could be found. The contest was tied at 9–9 when the Canadians scored five straight goals to clinch the victory.

MOTOR BOATING

1908 London C: 14, N: 2, D: 8.28–29.
Open Class, 40 Nautical Miles
1. Émile Thubron   FRA   2:26:53
8-Meter Class, 40 Nautical Miles
1. Thomas Thornycroft, Bernard Redwood   GBR   2:28:26
Under 60-Foot Class, 40 Nautical Miles
1. Thomas Thornycroft, Bernard Redwood   GBR   2:28:58

POLO

1900 Paris T: 4, N: 3, D: 6.2.
1. GBR/USA (Foxhunters Hurlingham—Alfred Rawlinson, Frank Mackey, Foxhall Keene, Dennis Daly, John George Beresford)
2. GBR/USA (Club Rugby—Walter McCreary, Frederick Freake, Walter Buckmaster, Joé de Madre)
3. FRA/GBR (Bagatelle Paris—Louis de Bisaccia, A. Fauquet Lemaitre, Jean Boussod, Maurice Raoul-Duval, Frederick Agnew Gill, Robert Fournier-Sarloveze, Edouard Alphonse de Rothschild)
4. USA/MEX (Guillermo Hayden Wright, Eustaquio de Escandón, Pablo de Escandón, Manuel de Escandón, Marquis de Villavieja)
   Final: Foxhunters 3—1 Club Rugby

1908 London T: 3, N: 1, D: 6.21.
1. GBR (Roehampton—Charles Miller, Patteson Nickalls, George Miller, Herbert Wilson)
2. GBR (Hurlingham—John Wodehouse, Walter Buckmaster, Frederick Freake, Walter Jones)
3. GBR (Ireland—Percy O'Reilly, Hardress Lloyd, John McCann, Anthony Rotherham)
   Scores: Roehampton 3—1 Hurlingham
   Roehampton 5—1 Ireland

1912 not held

1920 Antwerp T: 4, N: 4, D: 6.29.

		W	L	PF	PA
1. GBR	(Teignmouth Melville, Frederick Barrett, John Wodehouse, Vivian Lockett)	2	0	21	14
2. SPA	(Leopoldo de la Maza, Justo San Miguel, Alvaro de Figueroa, Hernando Fitz-James)	1	1	24	16
3. USA	(Arthur Harris, Terry Allen, John Montgormery, Nelson Margetts)	1	1	16	16
4. BEL	(Alfred Grisar, Maurice Lysen, Clément van der Straeten, Gaston Peers de Nieuwburg)	0	2	6	21

Final: GBR 13—11 SPA

1924 Paris T: 5, N: 5, D: 7.12.

		W	L	PF	PA
1. ARG	(Arturo Kenny, Juan Nelson, Enrique Padilla, Juan Miles, Guillermo Brooke Naylor)	4	0	46	14
2. USA	(Elmer Boeseke, Thomas Hitchcock, Frederick Roe, Rodney Wanamaker)	3	1	43	11
3. GBR	(Frederick Guest, Frederick Barrett, Denis Bingham, Percival Wise)	2	2	33	24
4. SPA	(Leopoldo de la Maza, Justo San Miguel, Luis de Figueroa, Alvaro de Figueroa, Rafael Henestrosa, Hernando Stuart)	1	3	22	42
5. FRA	(Charles Prince de Polignac, Pierre de Jumilhac, Jules Macaire, Hubert de Monbrison, Jean Pastra)	0	4	6	59

The decisive match was the one between Argentina and the United States. Juan Nelson was the hero of the game, scoring a goal in the closing seconds of the seventh-hand final chukker to give Argentina a surprise 6–5 victory.

1928–1932 not held

1936 Berlin T: 5, N: 5, D: 7.8.

		W	L	T	PF	PA
1. ARG	(Luis Duggan, Roberto Cavanagh, Andrés Gazzotti, Manuel Andrada)	2	0	0	26	5
2. GBR	(Bryan Fowler, W.N. Hinde, David Dawnay, Humphrey Guinness)	1	1	0	13	22
3. MEX	(Juan Gracia Zazueta, Antonio Nava Castillo, Julio Muller Luján, Aberto Ramos Sesma)	1	2	0	32	30
4. HUN	(Tivadar Dienes-Öhm, Imre Szentpály, Dezsö Kovács, István Bethlen, Kálmán Bartalis)	1	1	1	26	30
5. GER	(Heinrich Amsinck, Walter Bartram, Miles Reincke, Arthur Köser)	0	1	1	14	24

Final: ARG 11—0 GBR
3rd Place: MEX 16—2 HUN

Hungary and Germany were so outclassed that they weren't even included in the competition for first or second place. Instead, the tournament was arranged so that they played for the right to play for the bronze medal against the loser among the other three teams. Over 45,000 people watched Argentina's final victory over Great Britain.

RACKETS

Rackets was an early form of the sport now known as racquetball.

1908 London C: 7, N: 1, D: 4.27.
Men's Singles
1. GBR   Evan Noel
2. GBR   Henry Leaf
3. GBR   John Jacob Astor
3. GBR   Henry Brougham
   Final: Noel—Leaf WO

Leaf had to withdraw from the final because he had injured his hand in the doubles competition.

1908 London T: 3, N: 1, D: 4.27.
Men's Doubles
1. GBR   Vane Pennel/John Jacob Astor
2. GBR   Edward Bury/Cecil Browning
3. GBR   Evan Noel/Henry Leaf
   Final: Pennel/Astor—Bury/Browning, 6–15, 15–7, 16–15, 15–6, 15–7

ROQUE
1904 St. Louis C: 4, N: 1, D: 8.13.

		W	L	PF	PA
1. Charles Jacobus	USA	5	1	187	109
2. Smith Streeter	USA	4	2	156	142
3. Charles Brown	USA	2	4	(109?)	147
4. William Chalfant	USA	1	5	106	160

Roque is a variation of croquet, played on a hard-surfaced court with a raised border that can be used for bank shots. It is unknown how many points Brown scored in his loss to Chalfant.

RUGBY

1900 Paris T: 3, N:3, D: 10.28.

		W	L	PF	PA
1. FRA	(Alexandre Pharamond, Frantz Reichel, Jean Collas, Albert Henriquez, Auguste Giroux, André Rischmann, Jean Binoche, A. Albert, Charles Gondouin, Lefebvre-Hubert, Sarrade, Wladimir Aitoff, Joseph Olivier, G. Gautier, Victor Larchandat, J. Hervé, A. Roosevelt)	2	0	54	25
2. GER	(Hermann Kreuzer, Arnold Landvoigt, Heinrich Reitz, Jacob Herrmann, Erich Ludwig, Hugo Betting, August Schmierer, Fritz Müller, Adolf Stockhausen, Hans Latscha, Willy Hofmeister, Georg Wenderoth, Eduard Poppe, Richard Ludwig, Albert Arnheim)	0	1	17	27
3. GBR	(H.A. Loveitt, Raymond Whittindale, H.S. Nicol, Claudius Whittindale, L. Hood, J. Henry Birtles, J. Cantion, C.P. Deykin, J.G. Wallis, V. Smith, M.L. Logan, F.C. Bayliss, M.W. Talbot, Francis Wilson, Arthur Darby)	0	1	8	27

1908 London T: 2, N: 2, D: 10.19.
1. AUS (Phillip Carmichael, Charles Russell, Daniel Carroll, John Hickey, Francis Bede-Smith, Christopher McKivatt, Arthur McCabe, Thomas Griffen, Jumbo Barnett, Patrick McCue, Sydney Middleton, Thomas Richards, Mannie McArthur, Charles McMurtrie, Robert Craig)
2. GBR (Edward Jackett, J.C. "Barney" Solomon, Bert Solomon, L.F. Dean, J.T. Jose, Thomas Wedge, James Davey, Richard Jackett, E.J. Jones, Arthur Wilson, Nicholas Tregurtha, A. Lawry, C.R. Marshall, A. Willcocks, J. Trevaskis)
   Final: AUS 32–3 GBR

1912 not held

1920 Antwerp T: 2, N: 2, D: 9.5.
1. USA (Daniel Carroll, George Davis, Charles Doe, George Fish, Juner Fitzpatrick, Matt Hazeltine, Joseph Hunter, Morris Kirksey, Charles Meehan, John Muldoon, John O'Neil, John Patrick, Cornelius Righter, Colby Slater, Rudolph Scholz, Charles Tilden, Harold Von Schmidt, Davis Wallace, James Winston, Heaton Wrenn, Robert Templeton)
2. FRA (André Chilo, Grenet, François Bordes, René Crabos, Edouard Bader, Thiercelin, Curtet, Forestier, Raymond Berrurier, Eugène Soulié, Labeyrie, Alfred Eluère, Robert Lavasseur, Constant Lamaignière, Robert Thierry)
   Final: USA 8—0 FRA

The U.S. team included Morris Kirksey, who also won a silver medal in the 100-meter dash and a gold in the 4×100-meter relay, and Dink Templeton, who later became a famous track coach. Another American player was Daniel Carroll, who had been a member of the victorious Australian squad 12 years earlier.

1924 Paris T: 3, N: 3, D: 5.18.

		W	L	PF	PA
1. USA	(Philip Clark, Norman Cleveland, Hugh Cunningham, Dudley De Groot, Robert Devereaux, George Dixon, Charles Doe, Linn Farrish, Edward Graff, Richard Hyland, Caesar Manelli, John O'Neil, John Patrick, William Rogers, Rudolph Scholz, Colby Slater, Norman Slater, Edward Turkington, Alan Valentine, Alan Williams)	2	0	54	3
2. FRA	(René Araou, Jean Bayard, Louis Beguet, André Béhotéguy, Alexandre Bioussa, Etienne Bonnes, René Bousquet, Aime Cassayet, Clément Dupont, Albert Dupouy, Jean Etcheberry, Henri Galau, Gilbert Gerintes, Raoul Got, Adolphe Jauréguy, René Lasserre, Marcel-Frédéric Lubin-Lebrère, Etienne Piquirai, Jean Vaysse)	1	1	61	20
3. ROM	(Dumitru Armăsel, Eugen Sfetescu, Sorin Mihăilescu, Paul Nedelcovici, Teodor Marian, Mihail Vardala, Soare Sterian, Iosif Nemeş, Atanasie Tănăsescu, Dumitru Volvoreanu, Paul Vidraşcu, Nicolae Mărăscu, Mircea Sfetescu, Gheorghe Bentia, Teodor Florian, Ion Garlesteanu, Gheorge Sfetescu)	0	2	3	98

Over 30,000 French spectators watched in horror as their team was thrashed by the upstart Americans. After two French players were injured, the U.S. team was booed and hissed for the remainder of the game. Fighting broke out in the stands, and Gideon Nelson, an art student from De Kalb, Illinois, was knocked unconscious after being hit in the face with a walking stick. At the awards ceremony "The Star-Spangled Banner" was drowned out by the booing of the crowd, and the U.S. team had to be escorted from the field under police protection.

TENNIS

Men's Singles

1896 Athens C: 4, N: 4, D: 4.11.
1. John Pius Boland GBR/IRL
2. Demis Kasdaglis GRE
   Final: Boland—Kasdaglis, 7–5, 6–4, 6–1

Boland was a student at Oxford when he learned about the revival of the Olympic Games from a fellow student, S. Manaos of Greece. Boland traveled to Athens as a spectator, but Manaos, who was by then the secretary of the Organizing Committee, arranged to have Boland entered in the tennis competition. Later in life Boland became a renowned barrister, politician, author, and ardent proponent of Irish independence.

1900 Paris C: 4, N: 3, D: 7.9.
1. Hugh Doherty   GBR
2. Harold Mahony   GBR/IRL
3. Reginald Doherty   GBR
3. A.B.J. Norris   GBR
    Final: H. Doherty—Mahony, 6-4, 6-2, 6-3

The Doherty brothers were scheduled to play one another in the semifinals, but refused to do so in a "minor" tournament. Reginald stepped aside and agreed to let his younger brother advance to the final.

1904 St. Louis C: 27, N: 1, D: 9.3.
1. Beals Wright   USA
2. Robert LeRoy   USA
3. Alonzo Bell   USA
3. Edgar Leonard   USA
5. W.E. Blaterwick (USA), Charles Cresson (USA), John Neely (USA), Semp Russ (USA).
    Final: Wright—LeRoy, 6-4, 6-4

1906 Athens C: 18, N: 6, D: 4.23.
1. Max Decugis   FRA
2. Maurice Germot   FRA
3. Zdenek "Jánsky" Žemla   BOH
    Final: Decugis—Germot, 6-1, 7-9, 6-1, 6-1

1908 London C: 31, N: 9, D: 7.15.
1. Josiah Ritchie   GBR
2. Otto Froitzheim   GER
3. Wilberforce Vaughan Eaves   GBR
4. Ivie Richardson   SAF
5. C.R. Brown (CAN), George Caridia (GBR), Charles Dixon (GBR), Maurice Germot (FRA)
    Final: Ritchie—Froitzheim, 7-5, 6-3, 6-4
    3rd Place: Eaves—Richardson, 6-2, 6-2, 6-3

1908 London C: 7, N: 2, D: 5.14.
Indoor Courts
1. Arthur Gore   GBR
2. George Caridia   GBR
3. Josiah Ritchie   GBR
4. Wilberforce Vaughan Eaves   GBR
    Final: Gore—Caridia, 6-3, 7-5, 6-4

1912 Stockholm C: 49, N: 12, D: 7.5.
1. Charles Winslow   SAF
2. Harold Kitson   SAF
3. Oscar Kreuzer   GER
4. Ladislav "Rázny" Žemla BOH
5. Louis Heyden (GER), Otto von Müller (GER), L. Salm (AUT), A. Zborzil (AUT)
    Final: Winslow—Kitson, 7-5, 4-6, 10-8, 8-6
    3rd Place: Kreuzer—Žemla-Rázny, 6-2, 3-6, 6-3, 6-1

The level of competition at the 1912 Olympics was somewhat disappointing, due to the fact that the Swedish organizers scheduled the tournament at the same time as the Wimbledon championships.

1912 Stockholm C: 22, N: 6, D: 5.12.
Indoor Courts
1. André Gobert   FRA
2. Charles Dixon   GBR
3. Anthony Wilding   NZE
4. F. Gordon Lowe   GBR
5. George Caridia   GBR
5. Gunnar Setterwall   SWE
    Final: Gobert—Dixon, 8-6, 6-4, 6-4
    3rd Place: Wilding—Lowe, 4-6, 6-2, 7-5, 6-0

1920 Antwerp C: 41, N: 14, D: 8.23.
1. Louis Raymond   SAF
2. Ichiya Kumagae   JAP
3. Charles Winslow   SAF
4. O.G. Noel Turnball   GBR
    Final: Raymond—Kumagae, 5-7, 6-4, 7-5, 6-4
    3rd Place: Winslow—Turnball WO

The second round included one marathon match between Gordon Lowe of Great Britain and Zerlendi of Greece, which lasted for almost six hours over a two-day period. At one point, the ballboys, bored by the prolonged cautious rallying, left the court and went to lunch, forcing Lowe and Zerlindi to suspend play. Eventually Lowe won, 14-12, 6-8, 5-7, 6-4, 6-4. Lowe was subsequently eliminated in the fourth round after another five-set battle against Winslow. Raymond almost didn't make it into the final, having survived his semifinal match with Turnball 2-6, 1-6, 6-2, 6-2, 6-1.

1924 Paris C: 82, N: 27, D: 7.20.
1. Vincent Richards   USA
2. Henri Cochet   FRA
3. Umberto Luigi de Morpurgo   ITA
4. Jean Borotra   FRA
5. T. Harada (JAP), S. Jacob (IND), René Lacoste (FRA), R. Norris Williams (USA)
    Final: Richards—Cochet, 6-4, 6-4, 5-7, 4-6, 6-2
    3rd Place: de Morpurgo—Borotra, 1-6, 6-1, 8-6, 4-6, 7-5

Men's Doubles
1896 Athens T: 6, N: 4, D: 4.11.
1. IRL/GER   John Boland/Fritz Traun
2. GRE   Demis Kasdaglis/Demetrios Petrokokkinos
    Final: Boland/Traun—Kasdaglis/Petrokokkinos, 6-2, 6-4

Boland entered the tournament at the last minute, when Traun's partner fell ill. When the Union Jack was run up the pole to honor Boland's half of the victory, he objected vehemently, pointing out that the Irish had a flag of their own. The officials apologized and agreed to have an Irish flag prepared.

1900 Paris T: 8, N: 3, D: 7.9.
1. GBR   Reginald Doherty/Hugh Doherty
2. USA/FRA B. Spalding de Garmendia/Max Decugis
3. FRA   A. Prévost/G. de la Chapelle
3. IRL/GBR Harold Mahony/A.B.J. Norris
   Final: Doherty/Doherty—de Garmendia/Decugis, 6–1, 6–1, 6–0

1904 St. Louis T: 15, N: 2, D: 9.3.
1. USA   Edgar Leonard/Beals Wright
2. USA   Alonzo Bell/Robert LeRoy
3. USA   Joseph Wear/Allen West
3. USA   Clarence Gamble/Arthur Wear
5. Frank Wheaton/Hunter (USA), Charles Cresson/Semp Russ (USA), Ralph McKittrick/Dwight Davis (USA), Hugh McKittrick Jones/Harold Kauffman (USA)
   Final: Leonard/Wright—Bell/LeRoy, 6–4, 6–4, 6–2

1906 Athens T: 7, N: 5, D: 4.25.
1. FRA   Max Decugis/Maurice Germot
2. GRE   Xenophon Kasdaglis/Ioannis Ballis
3. BOH   Zdenek "Jánsky" Žemla/Ladislav "Rázny" Žemla
4. GRE   T. Simiriotis/N. Zariphis
   Final: Decugis/Germot—Kasdaglis/Ballis, 6–4, 6–2, 6–1
   3rd Place: Z. Žemla/L. Žemla—Simiriotis/Zariphis, 6–2, 6–3

1908 London T: 12, N: 7, D: 7.15.
1. GBR   George Hillyard/Reginald Doherty
2. GBR/IRL Josiah Ritchie/James Parke
3. GBR   Charles Cazalet/Charles Dixon
4. FRA   Max Decugis/Maurice Germot
5. GBR   W.C. Crawley/K. Powell
5. SAF   R. Gauntlett/Harald Kitson
   Final: Hillyard/Doherty—Ritchie/Parke, 9–7, 7–5, 9–7

Hillyard was 44 years old at the time of his Olympic victory.

1908 London T: 5, N: 2, D: 5.14.
Indoor Courts
1. GBR Arthur Gore/Herbert Roper Barrett
2. GBR George Simond/George Caridia
3. SWE Gunnar Setterwall/Wollmar Boström
4. GBR Josiah Ritchie/L.H. Escombe
   Final: Gore/Barrett—Simond/Caridia, 6–2, 2–6, 6–3, 6–3
   3rd Place: Setterwall/Boström—Ritchie/Escombe, 4–6, 6–3, 1–6, 6–0, 6–3

1912 Stockholm T: 21, N: 10, D: 7.4.
1. SAF Charles Winslow/Harold Kitson
2. AUT Felix Pipes/Arthur Zborzil
3. FRA Albert Canet/Marc Mény de Marangue
4. BOH Ladislav "Rázny" Žemla/Jiří Just
5. M. Soumarokoff/A. Alenitzyn (RUS), Wollmar Boström/Curt Benckert (SWE), Charles Wennergren/Carl Olof Nylén (SWE), Robert Spiess/Louis Heyden (GER)
   Final: Winslow/Kitson—Pipes/Zborzil, 4–6, 6–1, 6–2, 6–2
   3rd Place: Canet/Mény—L. Žemla/Just, 13–11, 6–3, 8–6

1912 Stockholm T: 8, N: 3, D: 5.12.
Indoor Courts
1. FRA André Gobert/Maurice Germot
2. SWE Gunnar Setterwall/Carl Kempe
3. GBR Charles Percy Dixon/Arthur Ernest Beamish
4. GBR Arthur Gore/Herbert Roper Barrett
   Final: Gobert/Germot—Setterwall/Kempe, 6–4, 12–14, 6–2, 6–4
   3rd Place: Dixon/Beamish—Gore/Barrett, 6–2, 0–6, 10–8, 2–6, 6–3

1920 Antwerp T: 22, N: 12, D: 8.23.
1. GBR O.G. Noel Turnball/Max Woosnam
2. JAP Ichiya Kumagae/Seiichiro Kashio
3. FRA Max Decugis/Pierre Albarran
4. FRA François Blanchy/Jacques Brugnon
5. Nielsen/Langaard (NOR), Norton/Louis Raymond (SAF), Dodd/Blackburn (SAF), Balbil/Colombo (ITA)
   Final: Turnball/Woosnam—Kamagae/Kashio, 6–2, 5–7, 7–5, 7–5
   3rd Place: Decugis/Albarran—Blanchy/Brugnon, WO

1924 Paris T: 39, N: 24, D: 7.21.
1. USA Vincent Richards/Frank Hunter
2. FRA Jacques Brugnon/Henri Cochet
3. FRA Jean Borotra/René Lacoste
4. SAF John Condon/Ivie John Richardson
5. Henning Müller/Charles Wennergren (SWE), R. Norris Williams/W. Washburn (USA), J. Alonso/M. Alonso-Areyzaga (SPA), S. Hadi/D. Rutnam (IND)
   Final: Richards/Hunter—Brugnon/Cochet, 4–6, 6–2, 6–3, 2–6, 6–3
   3rd Place: Borotra/Lacoste—Condon/Richardson, 6–3, 10–8, 6–3

Richards and Hunter, the reigning champions of Wimbledon, won an arduous five-set semifinal match against Borotra and Lacoste, 6–2, 6–3, 0–6, 5–7, 6–3. They won the final by taking four of the last five games.

Mixed Doubles
1900 Paris T: 6, N: 4, D: 7.9.
1. GBR   Charlotte Cooper/Reginald Doherty
2. FRA/IRL Hélène Prévost/Harold Mahony
3. BOH/GBR Hedwig Rosenbaum/Archibald Walden
3. USA/GBR Marion Jones/Hugh Doherty
   Final: Cooper/R. Doherty—Prévost/Mahony, 6–2, 6–4

1904 St. Louis not held

1906 Athens T: 4, N: 2, D: 4.26.
1. FRA Marie Decugis/Max Decugis
2. GRE Sophia Marinou/Georgios Simiriotis
3. GRE Aspasia Matsa/Xenophon Kasdaglis
   Final: Decugis/Decugis—Marinou/Simiriotis, 6–1, 6–2

1908 London not held

1912 Stockholm T: 6, N: 4, D: 7.5.
1. GER   Dora Köring/Heinrich Schomburgk
2. SWE   Sigrid Fick/Gunnar Setterwall
3. FRA   Marguerite Broquedis/Albert Canet
    Final: Koring/Schomburgk—Fick/Setterwall, 6–4, 6–0

Shortly after the final match began, Mrs. Fick inadvertently smashed her partner in the face rather severely. In the words of the Official Report for 1912: "This little accident seemed to put Setterwall off his game, for his play fell off tremendously. . . ."

1912 Stockholm T: 8, N: 3, D: 5.12.
Indoor Courts
1. GBR   Edith Hannam/Charles Percy Dixon
2. GBR   Helen Aitchison/Herbert Roper Barrett
3. SWE   Sigrid Fick/Gunnar Setterwall
4. SWE   Margareta Cederschiöld/Carl Kempe
    Final: Hannam/Dixon—Aitchison/Barrett, 4–6, 6–3, 6–2
    3rd Place: Fick/Setterwall—Cederschiöld/Kempe WO

1920 Antwerp T: 16, N: , D: 8.23.
1. FRA   Suzanne Lenglen/Max Decugis
2. GBR   Kathleen "Kitty" McKane/Max Woosnam
3. CZE   Milada Skrbková/Ladislav "Rázny" Žemla
4. DEN   Amory Folmer-Hansen/Erik Tegner
5. Chaudoir/Lammens (BEL), Marie Storms/Halot (BEL)
    Final: Lenglen/Decugis—McKane/Woosnam, 6–4, 6–2
    3rd Place: Skrbková/L. Žemla—Folmer-Hansen/Tegner, 8–6, 6–4

1924 Paris T: 21, N: 14, D: 7.21.
1. USA   Hazel Wightman/R. Norris Williams
2. USA   Marion Jessup/Vincent Richards
3. HOL   Cornelia Bouman/Hendrik Timmer
4. GBR   Kathleen "Kitty" McKane/J.B. Gilbert
5. P. Covell/Godfree (GBR), Sigrid Fick/Henning Müller (SWE), M. Wallis/E. McCrea (IRL)
    Final: Wightman/Williams—Jessup/Richards, 6–2, 6–3
    3rd Place: Bouman/Timmer—McKane/Gilbert, WO

Women's Singles
1900 Paris C: 6, N: 4, D: 7.9.
1. Charlotte Cooper   GBR
2. Hélène Prévost   FRA
3. Marion Jones   USA
4. Hedwig Rosenbaum   BOH
    Final: Cooper—Prévost, 6–1, 6–4

Charlotte Cooper had already won three of her five Wimbledon titles when she traveled to Paris for the Olympics.

1904 St. Louis not held

1906 Athens C: 5, N: 1, D: 4.24.
1. Esmee Simiriotou   GRE
2. Sophia Marinou   GRE
3. Euphrosine Paspati   GRE
    Final: Simiriotou—Marinou, 2–6, 6–3, 6–3

1908 London C: 5, N: 1, D: 7.15.
1. Dorothy Chambers   GBR
2. Dorothy Boothby   GBR
3. Joan Winch   GBR
    Final: Chambers—Boothby, 6–1, 7–5

Due to numerous withdrawals, only four matches were contested, and Chambers won three of them. Boothby advanced to the final without playing a single game.

1908 London C: 7, N: 2, D: 5.14.
Indoor Courts
1. Gwendoline Eastlake-Smith   GBR
2. Angela Greene   GBR
3. Märtha Adlerstråhle   SWE
4. Elsa Wallenberg   SWE
    Final: Eastlake-Smith—Greene, 6–2, 4–6, 6–0
    3rd Place: Adlerstråhle—Wallenberg, 1–6, 6–3, 6–2

1912 Stockholm C: 8, N: 4, D: 7.4.
1. Marguerite Broquedis   FRA
2. Dora Köring   GER
3. Molla Bjurstedt   NOR
4. Edit Arnheim   SWE
    Final: Broquedis—Köring, 4–6, 6–3, 6–4
    3rd Place: Bjurstedt—Arnheim, 6–2, 6–2

1912 Stockholm C: 8, N: 3, D: 5.11.
Indoor Courts
1. Edith Hannam   GBR
2. Thora Gerda Sophy Castenschiold   DEN
3. Mabel Parton   GBR
4. Sigrid Fick   SWE
    Final: Hannam—Castenschiold, 6–4, 6–3
    3rd Place: Parton—Fick, 6–3, 6–3

According to the Official Report of the 1912 Games, in the third-place match, "the difficult screws of [Mrs. Parton] were altogether too much for the Swedish representative."

1920 Antwerp C: 18, N: 7, D: 8.23.
1. Suzanne Lenglen   FRA
2. E. Dorothy Holman   GBR
3. Kathleen "Kitty" McKane   GBR
4. Sigrid Fick   SWE
5. Elisabeth Ayen (FRA), Lily von Essen (SWE)
    Final: Lenglen—Holman, 6–3, 6–0
    3rd Place: McKane—Fick, 6–2, 6–0

Defending Wimbledon champion Suzanne Lenglen was one of the greatest women tennis players of all time. In the ten sets that it took her to win the Olympic singles title, she lost only four games.

1924 Paris C: 31, N: 14, D: 7.20.
1. Helen Wills   USA
2. Julie Vlasto   FRA
3. Kathleen "Kitty" McKane   GBR
4. Germaine Golding   FRA
5. E. Alvarez (SPA), Marion Jessup (USA), Molla Bjurstedt-Mallory (NOR), Dorothy Shepherd-Barron (GBR)
    Final: Wills—Vlasto, 6–2, 6–2
    3rd Place: McKane—Golding, 5–7, 6–3, 6–0

In the semifinals McKane won her first set against Vlasto, 6–0, and was leading the second set 3–0 when a disruption occurred which turned the contest around. The match on the center court having just concluded, the Parisian crowd moved over to court number 3 to watch McKane and Vlasto. The umpire, Louis Raymond of South Africa, was calling the score in English and continued to do so, despite increasingly agitated requests from the audience that the score be announced in French. After things settled down, McKane had lost her touch and Vlasto was able to win 13 of the next 16 games to gain a 0–6, 7–5, 6–1 victory. However Vlasto was no match for the 18-year-old sensation Helen Wills, who succeeded Suzanne Lenglen as the queen of tennis.

Women's Doubles

1920 Antwerp T: 9, N: 5, D: 8.23.
1. GBR   Winifred Margaret McNair/Kathleen "Kitty" McKane
2. GBR   Geraldine Beamish/E. Dorothy Holman
3. FRA   Suzanne Lenglen/Elisabeth d'Ayen
4. BEL   Marie Storms/Fernande Arendt
    Final: McNair/McKane—Beamish/Holman, 8–6, 6–4
    3rd Place: Lenglen/d'Ayen—Storms/Arendt, WO

1924 Paris T: 11, N: 8, D: 7.19.
1. USA   Hazel Wightman/Helen Wills
2. GBR   P. Edith Covell/Kathleen "Kitty" McKane
3. GBR   Dorothy Shepherd-Barron/Evelyn Colyer
4. FRA   Marguerite Billout/Yvonne Bourgeois
5. SWE   Sigrid Fick/Lily von Essen
    Final: Wightman/Wills—Covell/McKane, 7–5, 8–6
    3rd Place: Shepherd-Barron/Colyer—Billout/Bourgeois, 6–1, 6–2

TUG OF WAR

In each contest, the first team to pull the other team six feet was declared the winner. If neither team succeeded in so doing in five minutes, the one which had pulled the furthest was given the victory.

1900 Paris T: 3, N: 4, D; 7.16.
1. SWE/DEN   (Gustaf Söderström, Karl Staaf, August Nilsson, Eugen Schmidt, Edgar Aabye, Charles Winckler)
2. USA   (Richard Sheldon, John Flanagan, Robert Garrett, Lewis Sheldon, Josiah McCracken, Thomas Truxton Hare)

3. FRA   (R. Basset, Jean Collas, Charles Gondouin, Joseph Roffo Farrade, Albert Henriquez de Zubiera)

1904 St. Louis T: 6, N: 3, D: 9.1.
1. USA   (Milwaukee Athletic Club—Oscar Olson, Sidney Johnson, Henry Seiling, Conrad Magnussen, Pat Flanagan)
2. USA   (St. Louis Southwest Turnverein #1—Max Braun, William Seiling, Orin Upshaw, Charles Rose, August Rodenberg)
3. USA   (St. Louis Southwest Turnverein #2—Charles Haberkorn, Frank Kungler, Charles Thias, Harry Jacobs, Oscar Friede)
4. USA   (New York Athletic Club—Charles Dieges, Samuel Jones, Leon Feuerbach, Charles Chadwick, James Mitchel)
5. GRE   (Pan-Hellenic Athletic Club—Nicolaos Georgantas, Perikles Kakousis, Demetri Demetracopoulos, Anastasios Georgopoulos, B. Metalos)
5. SAF   (Boer Team—C. Walker, P. Hillense, J. Schutte, P. Lombard, P. Visser)

1906 Athens T: 4, N: 4, D: 4.30.
1. GER   (Heinrich Schneidereit, Heinrich Rondi, Wilhelm Born, Willy Dörr, Karl Kaltenbach, Wilhelm Ritzenhof, Joseph Kramer, Julius Wagner)
2. GRE   (Spyros Vellas, Panagiotis Triboulidis, Vasilios Psachos, Georgios Psachos, Konstantinos Lazaris, Spyros Lazaris, Georgios Papachristou, Antonios Tsitas)
3. SWE   (Carl Svensson, Anton Gustafsson, Axel Norling, Claes Wersäll, Oswald Holmberg, Erik Granfeit, Gustaf Grönberger, Eric Lemming)
4. AUT   (Josef Steinbach, Rudolf Arnold, Henri Baur, Wenzel Goldbach, Rudolf Watzl, Rudolf Lindmayer, Leopold Lahner, Franz Solar)

1908 London T: 5, N: 3, D: 7.18.
1. GBR   (City Police—William Hirons, Frederick Goodfellow, Edmond Barrett, James Shephard, Frederick Humphreys, Edwin Mills, Albert Ireton, Frederick Merriman)
2. GBR   (Liverpool Police—Patrick Philbin, James Clark, Thomas Butler, Alexander Kidd, George Smith, Thomas Swindlehurst, Daniel McLowry, William Greggan)
3. GBR   (K. Division Metropolitan Police—Walter Tammas, Willy Slade, Alexander Munro, Ernest Ebbage, Thomas Homewood, Walter Chaffe, James Woodget, Joseph Dowler)

Surprising as it may seem, the friendly sport of tug of war touched off one of the biggest controversies of the 1908 Games. In the first round, the Liverpool Police pulled the U.S. team over the line in a matter of seconds. The Americans immediately protested that the Liverpudlians had used special illegal boots with steel cleats, spikes, and heels. The British maintained that they were wearing standard, run-of-the-mill police boots, and the protest was disallowed, whereupon the Americans withdrew from the remainder of the competition. After the tournament, the captain of the victorious London City Police team challenged the Americans to a pull in their stockinged feet, but there is no record of such a contest actually taking place.

1912 Stockholm T: 2, N: 2, D: 7.8.
1. SWE (Adolf Bergman, Arvid Andersson, Johan Edman, Erik Fredriksson, Carl Jonsson, Erik Larsson, August Gustafsson, Carl Lindström)
2. GBR (Alexander Munro, James Shepherd, John Sewell, Joseph Dowler, Edwin Mills, Frederick Humphreys, Mathias Hynes, Walter Chaffe)

1920 Antwerp T: 5, N: 5, D: 8.18.
1. GBR (George Canning, Frederick Holmes, Edwin Mills, James Shepherd, Harry Stiff, John Sewell, Frederick Humphreys, Ernest Thorn)
2. HOL (Wilhelmus Bekkers, Johannes Hengeveld, Sytse Jansma, Hendrikus Janssen, Antonius van Loon, Willem van Loon, Marinus van Rekum, Willem van Rekum)
3. BEL (Georges Bourguignon, Alphonse Ducatillon, R. Maertens, C. Piek, Henri Pintens, Charles van den Broeck, François van Hoorenbeeb, Désiré Wuyts)

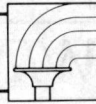

149.

149. *The 1932 U.S. four-man bobsled team: (left to right)* Jay O'Brien, Eddie Eagan, Clifford Gray, *and* Billy Fiske. *Eight years later, only Eagan was still alive.*

151.

150. *The 1980 U.S. ice hockey team celebrates its final victory over Finland.*
151. *Dick Button, men's figure skating champion of 1948 and 1952.*

152.

152. Sonja Henie was only 23 years old when she earned her third consecutive figure skating gold medal.

153. Peggy Fleming won an overwhelming victory in the 1968 women's figure skating competition.

154.

155.

154. Lyudmila Belousova and Oleg Protopopov, winners of the pairs skating in 1964 and 1968. "These pairs of brother and sister, how can they convey the emotion, the love, that exists between a man and a woman? That is what we try to show."

155. Irving Jaffee stumbles across the finish line of the 1932 10,000-meter speed skating race.

156. Eric Heiden had won only three gold medals when he posed for this photo; he borrowed the other two. Later he won two more of his own.

156.

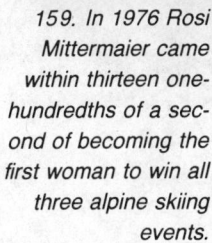

7.

158.

157. Lydia Skoblikova won six speed skating gold medals in 1960 and 1964, more than any other athlete in the history of the Winter Olympics.

158. The 1952 giant slalom champion, Stein Eriksen, was the inspiration for the stereotype of the suave and handsome ski instructor.

159. In 1976 Rosi Mittermaier came within thirteen one-hundredths of a second of becoming the first woman to win all three alpine skiing events.

159.

160.

161.

160. Winner of the 1980 slalom and giant slalom, Hanni Wenzel was the first-ever Olympic gold medalist from the tiny nation of Liechtenstein.

161. (Left to right) Seiji Aochi (bronze), Yukio Kasaya (gold), and Akitsugu Konno (silver), popular winners of the 1972 70-meter ski jump.

FOUR HAPPY WINNERS

162. Gaston Alibert,
1908 epée fencing.

162.

163.

163. F. Morgan Taylor,
1924 400-meter hurdles.

164. Chuhei Nambu,
1932 triple jump.

165. Jacques Lebrun,
1932 Finn class yachting.

164.

165.

THREE BIGGEST
GOLD MEDAL WINNERS

166. A rare photo of Paavo Nurmi smiling. Between 1920 and 1928 he won nine gold medals and three silver.
167. Between 1956 and 1964, gymnast Larissa Latynina won 18 medals (nine gold, five silver, and four bronze), more than any athlete in Olympic history.
168. In 1968 and 1972 Mark Spitz earned nine gold medals, one silver, and one bronze, including a record seven gold medals in 1972.

166.

167.

168.

CONTROVERSIES

169.

170.

171.

169. In 1964 Ewa Klobukowska won a bronze medal in the 100-meter dash and a gold in the 4 x 100-meter relay. Three years later she became the first athlete to fail a sex test.

170. Lance Larson, in Lane Four, appears to touch first at the finish of the 1960 100-meter freestyle. Yet John Devitt, in Lane Three, was awarded the gold medal.

171. Sixteen-year-old Rick DeMont (center) finished first in the 1972 400-meter freestyle, but was disqualified for taking an asthma drug he didn't know was on the prohibited list.

172. Lauri Lehtinen interfered with Ralph Hill during the homestretch of the 1932 5000-meter run. However, Hill declined to file a protest.

172.

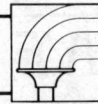

173.

173. The romance of U.S. hammer thrower Harold Connolly and Czechoslovakian discus thrower Olga Fikotová caused an international incident in 1956.

174. The Zátopeks, Dana and Emil, heroes of the 1952 Helsinki Olympics.

174.

FIVE HEROES OF LESSER-KNOWN SPORTS

175.

176.

177.

175. Gert Fredriksson won six canoeing gold medals between 1948 and 1960.
176. Dhyan Chand, star of the Indian field hockey team from 1928 to 1936, later became coach of the national team.
177. Lars Hall, the only repeat winner of the modern pentathlon (1952 and 1956).

178. Paul Elvström won four straight gold medals in the Finn class of the yachting competitions between 1948 and 1960.
179. Sixten Jernberg won nine medals (four gold, three silver, two bronze) in nordic skiing between 1956 and 1964.

178.

179.

WINTER
GAMES

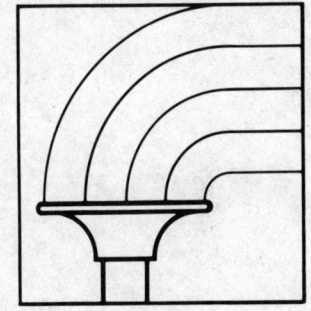

BIATHLON

10 Kilometers
20 Kilometers
4×7.5-Kilometer Relay

Biathlon is a combination of cross-country skiing and rifle shooting.

10 KILOMETERS

Each contestant stops twice during the course, once to shoot five shots prone and once to shoot five shots standing. Each missed target is punished by forcing the skiier to ski a 150-meter penalty loop.

1924–1976 not held

1980 Lake Placid C: 50, N: 17, D: 2.19.

		MISSED TARGETS	TIME
1. Frank Ullrich	GDR	2	32:10.69
2. Vladimir Alikin	SOV	0	32:53.10
3. Anatoli Aljabiev	SOV	1	33:09.16
4. Klaus Siebert	GDR	2	33:32.76
5. Kjell Sobak	NOR	1	33:34.64
6. Peter Zelinka	CZE	1	33:45.20
7. Odd Lirhus	NOR	2	34:10.39
8. Peter Angerer	GER	4	34:13.43

20 KILOMETERS

Each skiier stops four times—twice to take five shots prone and twice to take five shots standing. In 1960 and 1964 each missed target incurred a two-minute penalty. Since 1968 a missed *bull's-eye* equals a one-minute penalty, and only if a target is missed completely is a two-minute penalty assessed.

1924–1956 not held

1960 Squaw Valley C: 30, N: 9, D: 2.21.

		TIME	MISSED TARGETS	ADJUSTED TIME
1. Klas Lestander	SWE	1:33:21.6	0	1:33:21.6
2. Antti Tyrväinen	FIN	1:29:57.7	2	1:33:57.7
3. Aleksandr Privalov	SOV	1:28:54.2	3	1:34:54.2
4. Vladimir Melanin	SOV	1:27:42.4	4	1:35:42.4
5. Valentin Pshenitsin	SOV	1:30:45.8	3	1:36:45.8
6. Dmitri Sokolov	SOV	1:28:16.7	5	1:38:16.7
7. Ola Waerhaug	NOR	1:36:35.8	1	1:38:35.8
8. Martti Meinila	FIN	1:29:17.0	5	1:39:17.0

Lestander was only the 15th fastest skiier of 30, but he was also the only one to hit all 20 targets. The fastest man was Victor Arbez of France, who clocked in at 1:25:58.4. However he missed 18 of 20 targets and placed 25th. In fact, the entire four-man French team seemed ill-prepared for the shooting portion of the event: of 80 shots taken, they missed 68.

1964 Innsbruck–Seefeld C: 50, N: 14, D: 2.4.

		TIME	MISSED TARGETS	ADJUSTED TIME
1. Vladimir Melanin	SOV	1:20:26.8	0	1:20:26.8
2. Aleksandr Privalov	SOV	1:23:42.5	0	1:23:42.5
3. Olav Jordet	NOR	1:22:38.8	1	1:24:38.8
4. Ragnar Tveiten	NOR	1:19:52.5	3	1:25:52.5
5. Wilhelm György	ROM	1:22:18.0	2	1:26:18.0
6. József Rubiś	POL	1:22:31.6	2	1:26:31.6
7. Valentin Pshenitsin	SOV	1:22:59.0	2	1:26:59.0
8. Hannu Posti	FIN	1:25:16.5	1	1:27:16.5

1968 Grenoble–Autrans C: 60, N: 18, D: 2.12.

		TIME	MISSED TARGETS	ADJUSTED TIME
1. Magnar Solberg	NOR	1:13:45.9	0	1:13:45.9
2. Aleksandr Tikhonov	SOV	1:12:40.4	2	1:14:40.4
3. Vladimir Goundartsev	SOV	1:16:27.4	2	1:18:27.4
4. Stanislaw Szczepaniak	POL	1:17:56.8	1	1:18:56.8
5. Arve Kinnari	FIN	1:17:47.9	2	1:19:47.9
6. Nikolai Pousanov	SOV	1:17:14.5	3	1:20:14.5
7. Victor Mamatov	SOV	1:19:20.8	1	1:20:20.8
8. Stanislaw Lukaszczyk	POL	1:16:28.1	4	1:20:28.1

Magnar Solberg, a 31-year-old policeman, was practically unknown in the world of biathlon. He attained his victory by achieving a perfect shooting score—the first time he had ever accomplished such a feat. As photographers crowded around the surprised champion, he told them, "I am very happy, but too tired to smile."

1972 Sapporo–Makomanai C: 54, N: 14, D: 2.9.

			TIME	MISSED TARGETS	ADJUSTED TIME
1.	Magnar Solberg	NOR	1:13:55.50	2	1:15:55.50
2.	Hansjörg Knauthe	GDR	1:15:07.60	1	1:16:07.60
3.	Lars-Göran Arwidson	SWE	1:14:27.03	2	1:16:27.03
4.	Aleksandr Tikhonov	SOV	1:12:48.65	4	1:16:48.65
5.	Yrjö Salpakari	FIN	1:14:51.43	2	1:16:51.43
6.	Esko Saira	FIN	1:12:34.80	5	1:17:34.80
7.	Victor Mamatov	SOV	1:16:16.26	2	1:18:16.26
8.	Tor Svendsberget	NOR	1:15:26.54	3	1:18:26.54

1976 Innsbruck–Seefeld C: 51, N: 19, D: 2.6.

			TIME	MISSED TARGETS	ADJUSTED TIME
1.	Nikolai Kruglov	SOV	1:12:12.26	2	1:14:12.26
2.	Heikki Ikola	FIN	1:13:54.10	2	1:15:54.10
3.	Aleksandr Elizarov	SOV	1:13:05.57	3	1:16:05.57
4.	Willy Bertin	ITA	1:13:50.36	3	1:16:50.36
5.	Aleksandr Tikhonov	SOV	1:10:18.33	7	1:17:18.33
6.	Esko Saira	FIN	1:15:32.84	2	1:17:32.84
7.	Lino Jordan	ITA	1:15:49.83	2	1:17:49.83
8.	Sune Adolfsson	SWE	1:16:00.50	2	1:18:00.50

1980 Lake Placid C: 49, N: 18, D: 2.16.

			TIME	MISSED TARGETS	ADJUSTED TIME
1.	Anatoly Alyabiev	SOV	1.08.16.31	0	1.08.16.31
2.	Frank Ullrich	GDR	1.05.27.29	3	1.08.27.79
3.	Eberhard Rösch	GDR	1.09.11.73	2	1.11.11.73
4.	Svein Engen	NOR	1.08.30.25	3	1.11.30.25
5.	Erkki Antila	FIN	1.07.32.32	4	1.11.32.32
6.	Yvon Mougel	FRA	1.08.33.60	3	1.11.33.60
7.	Vladimir Barnashov	SOV	1.07.49.49	4	1.11.49.49
8.	Vladimir Alikin	SOV	1.06.05.30	6	1.12.05.30

4×7.5-KILOMETER RELAY

Each skiier shoots twice and has eight shots to make five hits. For each miss he has to ski a penalty loop of 150 meters. Unlike the individual events, in which the competitors race against the clock, one after another, in the biathlon relay all teams start at the same time.

1924–1964 not held

1968 Grenoble–Autrans T: 14, N: 14, D: 2.15.

		MISSED TARGETS	TIME
1. SOV	(Aleksandr Tikhonov, Nikolai Pousanov, Victor Mamatov, Vladimir Goundartsev)	2	2:13:02.4
2. NOR	(Ola Waerhavg, Olav Jordet, Magnar Solberg, Jon Istad)	5	2:14:50.2
3. SWE	(Lars-Göran Arwidson, Tore Eriksson, Olle Petrusson, Holmfrid Olsson)	0	2:17:26.3
4. POL	(Józef Rózak, Andrzej Fiedor, Stanislaw Lukaszczyk, Stanislaw Szczepaniak)	4	2:20:19.6
5. FIN	(Juhani Suutarinen, Heikki Floejt, Kalevi Vähäkylä, Arve Kinnari)	5	2:20:41.8
6. GDR	(Heinz Kluge, Hans-Gert Jahn, Horst Koschka, Dieter Speer)	4	2:21:54.5
7. ROM	(Gheorghe Cimpoia, Constant Carabela, Nicolae Barbarescu, Wilhelm Gyorgy)	4	2:25:39.8
8. USA	(Ralph Wakely, Edward Williams, William Spencer, John Ehrensbeck)	8	2:28:35.5

1972 Sapporo–Makomanai T: 13, N: 13, D: 2.11.

		MISSED TARGETS	TIME
1. SOV	(Aleksandr Tikhonov, Rinnat Safine, Ivan Biakov, Victor Mamatov)	3	1:51:44.92
2. FIN	(Esko Saira, Juhani Suutarinen, Heikki Ikola, Mauri Röppänen)	3	1:54:37.25
3. GDR	(Hansjörg Knauthe, Joachim Meischner, Dieter Speer, Horst Koschka)	4	1:54:57.67
4. NOR	(Tor Svendsberget, Kåre Hovda, Ivar Nordkild, Magnar Solberg)	7	1:56:24.41
5. SWE	(Lars-Göran Arwidson, Olle Petrusson, Torsten Wadman, Holmfrid Olsson)	6	1:56:57.40
6. USA	(Peter Karns, Dexter Morse, Dennis Donahue, William Bowerman)	1	1:57:24.32
7. POL	(Józef Rózak, Józef Stopka, Andrzej Rapacz, Aleksander Klima)	4	1:58:09.92
8. JAP	(Isao Ohno, Shozo Sasaki, Miki Shibuya, Kazuo Sasakubo)	5	1:59:09.48

1976 Innsbruck–Seefeld T: 15, N: 15, D: 2.13.

		MISSED TARGETS	TIME
1. SOV	(Aleksandr Elizarov, Ivan Biakov, Nikolai Kruglov, Aleksandr Tikhonov)	0	1:57.55.64
2. FIN	(Henrik Flöjt, Esko Saira, Juhani Suutarinen, Heikki Ikola)	2	2:01:45.58
3. GDR	(Karl-Heinz Menz, Frank Ullrich, Manfred Beer, Manfred Geyer)	5	2:04.08.61
4. GER	(Heinrich Mehringer, Gerd Winkler, Josef Keck, Claus Gehrke)	4	2:04:11.86
5. NOR	(Kjell Hovda, Terje Hanssen, Svein Engen, Tor Svendsberget)	6	2:05:10.28
6. ITA	(Lino Jordan, Pierantonio Clementi, Luigi Weiss, Willy Bertin)	3	2:06:16.55
7. FRA	(Rene Arpin, Yvon Mougel, Marius Falquy, Jean Claude Viry)	5	2:07:34.42
8. SWE	(Mats-Åke Lantz, Torsten Wadman, Sune Adolfsson, Lars-Göran Arwidson)	8	2:08:46.90

1980 Lake Placid T: 15, N: 15, D: 2.22.

		MISSED TARGETS	TIME
1. SOV	(Vladimir Alikin, Aleksandr Tikhonov, Vladimir Barnashov, Anatoly Alyabiev)	0	1:34:03.27
2. GDR	(Mathias Jung, Klaus Siebert, Frank Ullrich, Eberhard Rösch)	3	1:34:56.99
3. GER	(Franz Bernreiter, Hans Estner, Peter Angerer, Gerd Winkler)	2	1:37:30.26
4. NOR	(Svein Engen, Kjell Sobak, Odd Lirhus, Sigleif Johansen)	3	1:38:11.76
5. FRA	(Yvon Mougel, Denis Sandona, André Geourjon, Christian Poirot)	0	1:38:23.36
6. AUT	(Rudolf Horn, Franz-Josef Weber, Josef Koll, Alfred Eder)	4	1:38:32.02
7. FIN	(Keijo Kuntola, Erkki Antila, Kari Saarela, Raimo Seppanen)	6	1:38:50.84
8. USA	(Martin Hagen, Lyle Nelson, Donald Nielsen, Peter Hoag)	0	1:39:24.29

Thirty-three-year-old Aleksandr Tikhonov announced his retirement after winning his fourth straight biathlon relay gold medal.

BOBSLED

Two-Man
Four-Man

The final time is the combined total of four separate runs.

TWO-MAN

1924–1928 not held

1932 Lake Placid T: 12, N: 8, D: 2.10.
1. USA (J. Hubert Stevens, Curtis Stevens)   8:14.74
2. SWI (Reto Capadrutt, Oscar Geier)   8:16.28
3. USA (John Heaton, Robert Minton)   8:29.15
4. ROM (Alexandru Papana, Dumitru Hubert)   8:32.47
5. GER (Hanns Kilian, Sebastian Huber)   8:35.36
6. ITA (Teofilo Rossi di Montelera, Italo Casini)   8:36.33
7. GER (Werner Huth, Max Ludwig)   8:45.05
8. ITA (Agostini Lanfranchi, Gaetano Lanfranchi)   8:50.66

J. Hubert Stevens and his brother, Curtis, were local residents of Lake Placid. They trailed Capadrutt and Geier by 6.32 seconds after the first run, but registered the fastest times in each of the other three runs to overtake the Swiss team for the victory. The Stevens brothers, aged 41 and 33, attributed part of their success to the fact that they heated their runners with blowtorches for 25 minutes prior to hitting the snow, a tactic that is now highly illegal, but which was then considered unusual but acceptable.

1936 Garmisch-Partenkirchen T: 23, N: 13, D: 2.15.
1. USA (Ivan Brown, Alan Washbond)   5:29.29
2. SWI (Fritz Feierabend, Joseph Beerli)   5:30.64
3. USA (Gilbert Colgate, Richard Lawrence)   5:33.96
4. GBR (Frederick McEvoy, James Cardno)   5:40.25
5. GER (Hanns Kilian, Hermann von Valta)   5:42.01
6. GER (Fritz Grau, Albert Brehme)   5:44.71
7. SWI (Reto Capadrutt, Charles Bouvier)   5:46.23
8. BEL (Rene Lunden, Eric de Spoelberch)   5:46.28

Ivan Brown of Keene Valley, New York, was an especially superstitious competitor. One of his quirks was a need to find at least one hairpin on the ground every day. Fortunately he had been able to accomplish this feat for 24 consecutive days prior to the Olympics. Brown was also the only driver to compete without goggles; he claimed they dulled his eyesight and added wind resistance.

1948 St. Moritz T: 16, N: 9, D: 1.31.
1. SWI (Felix Endrich, Friedrich Waller)   5:29.2
2. SWI (Fritz Feierabend, Paul Hans Eberhard)   5:30.4
3. USA (Frederick Fortune, Schuyler Carron)   5:35.3
4. BEL (Max Houben, Jacques Mouvet)   5:37.5
5. GBR (W. Coles, G. Collings)   5:37.9
6. ITA (Mario Vitali, Dario Poggi)   5:39.0
7. NOR (Arne Holst, I. Johansen)   5:38.2
8. ITA (Nino Bibbia, Edilberto Campadese)   5:38.6

In 1953 Felix Endrich won the two-man bobsled world championship at Garmisch-Partenkirchen. Less than a week later he was leading a four-man bob down the same course when his sled hurtled over the wall at "dead man's curve" and crashed into a tree. The 31-year-old Endrich was killed almost instantly.

1952 Oslo T: 18, N: 9, D: 2.15.
1. GER (Andreas Ostler, Lorenz Nieberl)   5:24.54
2. USA (Stanley Benham, Patrick Martin)   5:26.89
3. SWI (Fritz Feierabend, Stephan Waser)   5:27.71
4. SWI (Felix Endrich, Werner Spring)   5:29.15
5. FRA (André Robin, Henri Rivière)   5:31.98
6. BEL (Marcel Leclef, Albert Casteleyns)   5:32.51
7. USA (Frederick Fortune, John Helmer)   5:33.82
8. SWE (Olle Axelsson, Jan de Man Lapidoth)   5:35.77

Ostler and Nieberl recorded the best time on each of the four runs despite the fact that they were using a 16-year-old bobsled.

1956 Cortina T: 25, N: 14, D: 1.28.
1. ITA (Lamberto Dalla Costa, Giacomo Conti)   5:30.14
2. ITA (Eugenio Monti, Renzo Alverà)   5:31.45
3. SWI (Max Angst, Harry Warburton)   5:37.46
4. SPA (Alfonso de Portago, Vicente Sartorius y
        Cabeza de Vaca)   5:37.60
5. USA (Waightman Washbond, Patrick Biesiadecki)   5:38.16
6. USA (Arthur Tyler, Edgar Seymour)   5:40.08
7. SWI (Franz Kapus, Heinrich Angst)   5:40.11
8. GER (Andreas Ostler, Hans Hohenester)   5:40.13

Dalla Costa and Monti finished first and second respectively on each of the four runs. Dalla Costa was a 35-year-old jet pilot who had never raced anywhere but Cortina.

1960 not held

1964 Innsbruck–Igls T: 19, N: 11 D: 2.1.

1.	GBR	(Anthony Nash, Robin Dixon)	4:21.90
2.	ITA	(Sergio Zardini, Romano Bonagura)	4:22.02
3.	ITA	(Eugenio Monti, Sergio Siorpaes)	4:22.63
4.	CAN	(Victor Emery, Peter Kirby)	4:23.49
5.	USA	(Lawrence McKillip, James Ernest Lamy)	4:24.60
6.	GER	(Franz Wörmann, Hubert Braun)	4:24.70
7.	USA	(Charles McDonald, Charles Pandolph)	4:25.00
8.	AUT	(Erwin Thaler, Josef Nairz)	4:25.51

The surprise victory of Nash and Dixon can be attributed to the great sportsmanship of eight-time world champion Eugenio Monti. As the British pair prepared for their second run, they noticed that an axle bolt had broken off their sled. Informed of the problem, Monti removed a bolt from his own sled and sent it over to Nash and Dixon. This good deed allowed them to complete the competition and prevented Monti from achieving his dream of winning an Olympic gold medal.

1968 Grenoble–Alpe d'Huez T: 22, N: 11, D:2.6.

1.	ITA	(Eugenio Monti, Luciano De Paolis)	4:41.54
2.	GER	(Horst Floth, Pepi Bader)	4:41.54
3.	ROM	(Ion Panţuru, Nicolae Neagoe)	4:44.46
4.	AUT	(Erwin Thaler, Reinhold Durnthaler)	4:45.13
5.	GBR	(Anthony Nash, Robin Dixon)	4:45.16
6.	USA	(Paul Lamey, Robert Huscher)	4:46.03
7.	GER	(Wolfgang Zimmerer, Peter Utzschneider)	4:46.40
8.	AUT	(Max Kaltenberger, Fritz Dinkhauser)	4:46.63

"Now I can retire a happy man," said Eugenio Monti after completing his 12-year quest for an Olympic gold medal. But his victory did not come easily. Trailing by one-tenth of a second after three runs, Monti drove his bob to a course record of 1:10.05, only to watch Floth race down in 1:10.15. This left the Italians and Germans in a tie for first place, and it was announced that both teams would be awarded gold medals. However the judges later reversed their decision, invoking world bobsled rules. Sole possession of first place was given to the team that recorded the fastest single heat time—and 40-year-old Eugenio Monti had finally won his Olympic gold medal.

1972 Sapporo–Teineyama T: 21, N: 11, D: 2.5.

1.	GER	(Wolfgang Zimmerer, Peter Utzschneider)	4:57.07
2.	GER	(Horst Floth, Pepi Bader)	4:58.84
3.	SWI	(Jean Wicki, Edy Hubacher)	4:59:33
4.	ITA	(Gianfranco Gaspari, Mario Armano)	5:00.45
5.	ROM	(Ion Panţuru, Ion Zangor)	5:00.53
6.	SWE	(Carl-Erik Eriksson, Jan Johansson)	5:01.40
7.	SWI	(Hans Candrian, Heinz Schenker)	5:01.44
8.	AUT	(Herbert Gruber, Josef Oberhauser)	5:01.60

1976 Innsbruck–Igls T: 24, N: 13, D: 2.6.

1.	GDR	(Meinhard Nehmer, Bernhard Germeshausen)	3:44.42
2.	GER	(Wolfgang Zimmerer, Manfred Schumann)	3:44.99
3.	SWI	(Erich Schärer, Josef Benz)	3:45.70
4.	AUT	(Fritz Sperling, Andreas Schwab)	3:45.74
5.	GER	(Georg Heibl, Fritz Ohlwärter)	3:46.13
6.	AUT	(Dieter Delle Karth, Franz Köfel)	3:46.37
7.	GDR	(Horst Schönau, Raimund Bethge)	3:46.97
8.	ITA	(Giorgio Alvera, Franco Perruquet)	3:47.30

Nehmer and Germeshausen together won four Olympic medals in 1976 and 1980, including three golds. A former javelin thrower, Nehmer was 35 years old when he earned his first medal.

1980 Lake Placid T: 20, N: 11, D: 2.16.

1.	SWI	(Erich Schärer, Josef Benz)	4:09.36
2.	GDR	(Bernhard Germeshausen, Hans Jürgen Gerhardt)	4:10.93
3.	GDR	(Meinhard Nehmer, Bogdan Musiol)	4:11.08
4.	SWI	(Hans Hiltebrand, Walter Rahm)	4:11.32
5.	USA	(Howard Silher, Dick Nalley)	4:11.73
6.	USA	(Brent Rushlaw, Joseph Tyler)	4:12.12
7.	AUT	(Fritz Sperling, Kurt Oberhöller)	4:13.58
8.	GER	(Peter Hell, Heinz Busche)	4:13.74

FOUR-MAN

1924 Chamonix T: 9, N: 5, D: 2.3.

1.	SWI	(Eduard Scherrer, Alfred Neveu, Alfred Schläppi, Heinrich Schläppi)	5:45.54
2.	GBR	(Ralph Broome, Thomas Arnold, Alexander Richardson, Rodney Soher)	5:48.83
3.	BEL	(Charles Mulder, René Mortiaux, Paul van den Broeck, Victor Verschueren, Henri Willems)	6:02.29
4.	FRA	(A. Berg, H. Aldebert, G. André, Jean de Suarez D'Aulan)	6:22.95
5.	GBR	(Gray Horton, A. Crabbe, Joe Fairlie, Cecil Pim)	6:40.71
6.	ITA	(Lodovico Obexer, Massimo Fink, Paolo Herbert, Giuseppe Steiner, Aloise Trenker)	7:15.41

1928 St. Moritz T: 23, N: 14, D: 3.19.

1.	USA	(William Fiske, Nion Tocker, Charles Mason, Clifford Gray, Richard Parke)	3:20.5
2.	USA	(Jennison Heaton, David Granger, Lyman Hine, Thomas Doe, Jay O'Brien)	3:21.0
3.	GER	(Hanns Kilian, Valentin Krempel, Hans Hess, Sebastian Huber, Hans Nägle)	3:21.9
4.	ARG	(Arturo Gramajo, R. Gonzales, M. de Maria, R. Iglesias, J. Nash)	3:22.6
5.	ARG	(Eduardo Hope, J. del Caril, H. Milberg, H. Iglesias, H. Gramajo)	3:22.9
6.	BEL	(Ernest Lambert, M. Sedille-Courbon, Léon Tom, Max Houben, Walter Ganshof van der Meersch)	3:24.5
7.	ROM	(G. Socolescu, J. Gavat, T. Nitescu, P. Ghitulescu, M. Socolescu)	3:24.6
8.	SWI	(C. Stoffel, R. Fonjallaz, H. Hohnes, E. Coppetti, L. Koch)	3:25.7

The competition was limited to two runs due to heavy thawing.

1932 Lake Placid, T: 7, N: 5, D: 2.15.

1. USA (William Fiske, Edward Eagan, Clifford Gray, 7:53.68
Jay O'Brien)
2. USA (Henry Homburger, Percy Bryant, F. Paul Ste- 7:55.70
vens, Edmund Horton)
3. GER (Hanns Kilian, Max Ludwig, Hans Melhorn, Se- 8:00.04
bastian Huber)
4. SWI (Reto Capadrutt, Hans Eisenhut, Charles Jenny, 8:12.18
Oscar Geier)
5. ITA (Teofilo Rossi Di Montelera, Agostino Lanfran- 8:24.21
chi, Gaetano Lanfranchi, Italo Casini)
6. ROM (Alexandru Papana, Alexandru Ionescu, Ulise 8:24.22
Petrescu, Dumitru Hubert)
7. GER (Walther von Mumm, Hasso von Bismarck, 8:25.45
Gerhard Hessert, Georg Gyssling)

Eddie Eagan is the only person to have won a gold medal in both the Summer and Winter Olympics. Eagan came from a poor family in Denver, but made his way through Yale, Harvard Law School, and Oxford, became a successful lawyer, and married an automobile heiress. He lived his life according to the precepts of Frank Merriwell, the fictional hero of dime novels. In 1932 he wrote, "To this day I have never used tobacco, because Frank didn't. My first glass of wine, which I do not care for, was taken under social compulsion in Europe. Frank never drank." Back in 1920, Eddie Eagan won the Light Heavyweight boxing championship at the Antwerp Olympics. Later he won the U.S. amateur Heavyweight title and became the first American to win the amateur championship of Great Britain. In 1932 he showed up as a member of the four-man bob team led by boy wonder Billy Fiske, who had driven a U.S. team to victory at the 1928 Olympics when he was only 16 years old. The other members of the 1932 squad were St. Moritz veterans 48-year-old Jay O'Brien, who happened to be the head of the U.S. Olympic Bobsled Committee, and 40-year-old Clifford "Tippy" Gray, a songwriter who was actually a citizen of Great Britain. Their main rivals were the team driven by civil engineer Henry Homburger, which was known as the Saranac Lake Red Devils.

The weather was so poor during the Olympics that the four-man bob had to be delayed until after the official closing ceremony. The officials in charge of the bobsled competitions ordered that all four heats be run on February 14. But after the second round, Paul Stevens of the Red Devils protested the poor racing conditions and stalked off. Most of the competitors followed him, and the officials were forced to reschedule runs 3 and 4 the next day. Fiske's team recorded the fastest time for each of the first three runs. The Red Devils picked up 2.31 seconds on their final run, but it wasn't enough.

Fiske and his partners never raced together again. In fact, three of them died within a one-year period starting in 1940. Jay O'Brien died of a heart attack at the age of 57. Billy Fiske was the first American to join the British Royal Air Force in 1939; wounded over Germany the following year, he died in England when he was only 29 years old.

Tippy Gray, whose 3000 songs included "Got a Date with an Angel" and "If You Were the Only Girl in the World," died in 1941. Gray was such a modest man that his children never even knew that he had won two Olympic gold medals until after he died.

1936 Garmisch-Partenkirchen T: 18, N: 10, D: 2.12.

1. SWI (Pierre Musy, Arnold Gartmann, Charles Bouvi- 5:19.85
er, Joseph Beerli)
2. SWI (Reto Capadrutt, Hans Aichele, Fritz Feiera- 5:22.73
bend, Hans Bütikofer)
3. GBR (Frederick McEvoy, James Cardno, Guy Dug- 5:23.41
dale, Charles Green)
4. USA (J. Hubert Stevens, Crawford Merkel, Robert 5:24.13
Martin, John Shene)
5. BEL (Max Houben, Martial van Schelle, Louis de 5:28.92
Ridder, Paul Graeffe)
6. USA (Francis Tyler, James Bickford, Richard Law- 5:29.00
rence, Max Bly)
7. GER (Hanns Kilian, Sebastian Huber, Fritz Schwarz, 5:29.07
Hermann von Valta)
8. BEL (Rene Lunden, Eric de Spoelberch, Philippe de 5:29.82
Pret Roose, Gaston Braun)

Again the bobsled competition was disrupted by bad weather—this time heavy rain. The first day's two runs were dangerous and unpredictable, but the next day the course was fast and smooth. Musy, a 25-year-old Swiss Army lieutenant, was the son of a former president of Switzerland.

1948 St. Moritz T: 15, N: 9, D: 2.7.

1. USA (Francis Tyler, Patrick Martin, Edward Rimkus, 5.20.1
William D'Amico)
2. BEL (Max Houben, Freddy Mansveld, Louis-Georges 5.21.3
Niels, Jacques Mouvet)
3. USA (James Bickford, Thomas Hicks, Donald Dupree, 5.21.5
William Dupree)
4. SWI (Fritz Feierabend, Friedrich Waller, Felix Endrich, 5.22.1
Heinrich Angst)
5. NOR (Arne Holst, I. Johansen, R.A. Berg, A. Large) 5.22.5
6. ITA (Nino Bibbia, Giancarlo Ronchetti, Edilberto 5.23.0
Campadese, Luigi Cavalieri)
7. GBR (E. Coles, J. McLean, W.P. Collings, C. Holliday) 5.23.9
8. SWI (Franz Kapus, W. Spring, B. Schilter, P. Eber- 5.25.4
hard)

The competition was halted in the middle of the second round when a water pipe burst, flooding the bob run. The winning team from Lake Placid, New York, weighed a total of 898 pounds.

1952 Oslo T: 15, N: 9, D: 2.22.

1. GER (Andreas Ostler, Friedrich Kuhn, Lorenz Nie- 5.07.84
berl, Franz Kemser)
2. USA (Stanley Benham, Patrick Martin, Howard Cros- 5.10.48
sett, James Atkinson)
3. SWI (Fritz Feierbend, Albert Madörin, André Filip- 5.11.70
pini, Stephan Waser)

4. SWI   (Felix Endrich, Fritz Stöckli, Franz Kapus, Werner Spring)   5.13.98

5. AUT   (Karl Wagner, Franz Eckhart, Hermann Palka, Paul Aste)   5.14.74

6. SWE   (Kjell Holmström, Felix Fernström, Nils Landgren, Jan de Man Lapidoth)   5.15.01

7. SWE   (Gunnar Åhs, Börje Ekedahl, Lennart Sandin, Gunnar Garpö)   5.17.86

8. ARG   (Carlos Tomasi, Roberto Bordeau, Hector Tomasi, Carlos Sareistian)   5.18.85

The four members of the winning Swiss team weighed in at 1041½ pounds. At a meeting held prior to the Olympics, the International Bobsled and Tobogganing Federation passed a rule limiting future teams from weighing more than 880 pounds.

1956 Cortina T: 21, N: 13, D: 2.4.

1. SWI   (Franz Kapus, Gottfried Diener, Robert Alt, Heinrich Angst)   5:10.44

2. ITA   (Eugenio Monti, Ulrico Girardi, Renzo Alverà, Renato Mocellini)   5:12.10

3. USA   (Arthur Tyler, William Dodge, Charles Butler, James Lamy)   5:12.39

4. SWI   (Max Angst, Albert Gartmann, Harry Warburton, Rolf Gerber)   5:14.27

5. ITA   (Dino DeMartin, Giovanni DeMartin, Giovanni Tabacchi, Carlo Da Pra)   5:14.66

6. GER   (Hans Rösch, Martin Pössinger, Lorenz Nieberl, Silvester Wackerle, Sr.)   5:18.02

7. AUT   (Loserth, Thurner, Schwarzböck, Dominik)   5:18.29

8. GER   (Franz Schelle, Jakob Nirschel, Hans Henn, Edmund Koller)   5:18.50

Franz Kapus was 46 years old when he drove the Swiss team to victory by scoring the fastest times in all but the first run.

1960 not held

1964 Innsbruck–Igls T: 18, N:11, D: 2.7.

1. CAN   (Victor Emery, Peter Kirby, Douglas Anakin, John Emery)   4:14.46

2. AUT   (Erwin Thaler, Adolf Koxeder, Josef Nairz, Reinhold Durnthaler)   4:15.48

3. ITA   (Eugenio Monti, Sergio Siorpaes, Benito Rigoni, Gildo Siorpaes)   4:15.60

4. ITA   (Sergio Zardini, Romano Bonagura, Sergio Mocellini, Ferruccio Dalla Torre)   4:15.89

5. GER   (Franz Schelle, Otto Göbl, Ludwig Siebert, Josef Sterff)   4:16.19

6. USA   (William Hickey, Charles Pandolph, Reginald Benham, William Dundon)   4:17.23

7. AUT   (Paul Aste, Hans Stoll, Herbert Gruber, Andreas Arnold)   4:17.73

8. SWI   (Herbert Kiesel, Oskar Lory, Bernhard Wild, Hansrudi Beuggar)   4:18.12

The winning Canadian team was made up of four bachelors from Montreal. Canada had never before entered an Olympic bobsled competition.

1968 Grenoble–Alpe d'Huez T: 19, N:11, D: 2.15.

1. ITA   (Eugenio Monti, Luciano De Paolis, Roberto Zandonella, Mario Armano)   2:17.39

2. AUT   (Erwin Thaler, Reinhold Durnthaler, Herbert Gruber, Eder Josef)   2:17.48

3. SWI   (Jean Wicki, Hans Candrian, Willi Hofmann, Walter Graf)   2:18.04

4. ROM   (Ion Panṭuru, Nicolae Neagoe, Petre Hristovici, Gheorghe Maftei)   2:18.14

5. GER   (Horst Floth, Pepi Bader, Willi Schäfer, Frank Lange)   2:18.33

6. ITA   (Gianfranco Gaspari, Leonardo Cavallini, Giuseppe Rescigno, Andrea Clemente)   2:18.36

7. FRA   (Francis Luiggi, Maurice Grether, Andre Patey, Gerard Monrazel)   2:18.84

8. GBR   (Anthony Nash, Robin Dixon, Guy Renwick, Robin Widdows)   2:18.84

The danger of a sudden thaw forced the officials to limit the contest to only two runs. Eugenio Monti won two silver medals in 1956, two bronze medals in 1964, and two gold medals in 1968.

1972 Sapporo–Teineyama T: 18, N:10, D: 2.11.

1. SWI   (Jean Wicki, Edy Hubacher, Hans Leutenegger, Werner Carmichel)   4:43.07

2. ITA   (Nevio De Zordo, Gianni Bonichon, Adriano Frassinelli, Corrado Dal Fabbro)   4:43.83

3. GER   (Wolfgang Zimmerer, Peter Utzschneider, Stefan Gaisreiter, Walter Steinbauer)   4:43.92

4. SWI   (Hans Candrian, Heinz Schenker, Erwin Juon, Gaudenz Beeli)   4:44.56

5. GER   (Horst Floth, Pepi Bader, Donat Ertel, Walter Gilik)   4:45.09

6. AUT   (Herbert Gruber, Josef Oberhauser, Utz Chwalla, Josef Eder)   4:45.77

7. AUT   (Werner Dellekarth, Fritz Sperling, Werner Moser, Walter Dellekarth)   4:46.66

8. ITA   (Gianfranco Gaspari, Luciano De Paolis, Roberto Zandonella, Mario Armano)   4:46.73

1976 Innsbruck–Igls T: 21, N: 12, D: 2.14.

1. GDR   (Meinhard Nehmer, Jochen Babock, Bernhard Germeshausen, Bernhard Lehmann)   3:40.43

2. SWI   (Erich Schärer, Ulrich Bächli, Rudolf Marti, Josef Benz)   3:40.89

3. GER   (Wolfgang Zimmerer, Peter Utzschneider, Bodo Bittner, Manfred Schumann)   3:41.37

4. GDR   (Horst Schönau, Horst Bernhard, Harald Seifert, Raimund Bethge)   3:42.44

5. GER   (Georg Heibl, Hans Morant, Siegfried Radant, Fritz Ohlwärter)   3:42.47

6. AUT   (Werner Delle Karth, Andreas Schwab, Otto Breg, Franz Köfel, Heinz Krenn)   3:43.21

7. AUT   (Fritz Sperling, Kurt Oberholler, Gerd Zaunschirm, Dieter Gehmacher)   3:43.79

8. ROM   (Dragos Panaitescu, Paul Neagu, Costel Ionescu, Gheorghe Lixandru)   3:43.91

1980 Lake Placid T: 17, N:10, D: 2.24.
1. GDR (Meinhard Nehmer, Bogdan Musiol, Bernhard   3.59.92
          Germeshausen, Hans-Jürgen Gerhardt)
2. SWI (Erich Schärer, Ulrich Bächli, Rudolf Marti, Jo-   4.00.87
          sef Benz)
3. GDR (Horst Schönau, Roland Wetzig, Detlef Richter,   4.00.97
          Andreas Kirchner)
4. AUT (Fritz Sperling, Heinrich Bergmüller, Franz Red-   4.02.62
          nak, Bernhard Purkrabek)
5. AUT (Walter Delle Karth, Franz Paulweber, Gerd   4.02.95
          Zaunschirm, Kurt Oberhöller)
6. SWI (Hans Hiltebrand, Ulrich Schindler, Walter   4.03.69
          Rahm, Armin Baumgartner)
7. GER (Peter Hell, Hans Wagner, Heinz Busche, Wal-   4.04.40
          ter Barfuss)
8. ROM (Drasos Panaitescu, Dorel Critudor, Sandu Mi-   4.04.68
          trofan, Gheorghe Lixandru)

Two members of the 12th-place U.S. team, Willie Davenport and Jeff Godley, were the first black Americans to take part in the Winter Olympics. Davenport had competed in the 100-meter high hurdles four times between 1964 and 1976, winning a gold medal in 1968 and a bronze in 1976.

ICE HOCKEY

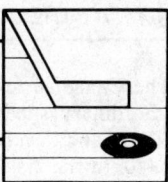

Ice hockey matches are divided into three 20-minute periods.

1920 Antwerp T: 7, N: 7, D: 4.30.

			W	L	PF	PA
1.	CAN	(Robert Benson, Wally Byron, Frank Fredrickson, Chris Fridfinnson, Michael Goodman, Haldor Halderson, Konrad Johannesson, Allan ''Huck'' Woodman)	3	0	29	1
2.	USA	(Raymond Booney, Anthony Conroy, Herbert Drury, J. Edward Fitzgerald, George Geran, Frank Goheen, Joseph McCormick, Lawrence McCormick, Frank Synott, Leon Parker Tuck, Cyril Weidenborner)	3	1	52	2
3.	CZE	(Adolf Dušek, Karel Hartman, Vilém Loos, Jan Peka, Karel Pešek, Josef Šroubek, Otakar Vindyš, Jan Palouš, Karel Wälver)	1	2	1	31
4.	SWE	(Vilhelm Arwe, Erik Burman, Seth Howander, Georg Johansson, Einar Lindqvist, Einar Lundell, Anton Mattsson, Nils Molander, Sven Säfwenberg, Einar Svensson)	3	3	17	19

Canada scored victories of 15–0 over Czechoslovakia, 2–0 over the United States, and 12–1 over Sweden. According to the rules of the tournament, the three teams that lost to Canada then played off for second place. The United States beat Sweden, 7–0, and Czechoslovakia, 16–0. Then Czechoslovakia defeated Sweden, 1–0, to win the bronze medal, even though the Czechs had been outscored 1 to 31 in their three matches. Canada was represented by the Winnipeg Falcons, who had just defeated the Universtiy of Toronto for the Canadian championship. The invitation to the Olympics came at such short notice that the Falcons didn't have time to return home to Winnipeg. Funds had to be raised to buy the players new clothes for the overseas journey.

1924 Chamonix T: 8, N: 8, D: 2.8.

			W	L	PF	PA
1.	CAN	(Jack Cameron, Ernest Collett, Albert McCaffery, Harold McMunn, Duncan Munro, W. Beattie Ramsay, Cyril Slater, Reginald Smith, Harry Watson)	5	0	110	3
2.	USA	(Clarence Abel, Herbert Drury, Alphonse Lacroix, John Langley, John Lyons, Justin McCarthy, Willard Rice, Irving Small, Frank Synott)	4	1	73	6
3.	GBR	(William Anderson, Lorne Carr-Harris, Colin Carruthers, Eric Carruthers, Guy Clarkson, Ross Cuthbert, George Holmes, Hamilton Jukes, Edward Pitblado, Blane Sexton)	3	2	40	38
4.	SWE	(Ruben Allinger, Vilhelm Arwe, Erik Burman, Birger Holmqvist, Gustaf Johansson, Hugo Johansson, Karl Josefson, Ernst Karlberg, Nils Molander, Einar Ohlsson)	2	3	21	49
5.	CZE	(W. Stransky, J. Rezac, Otakar Vindyš, Vilém Loos, Josef Šroubek, J. Jirkovsky, J. Malecek, J. Fleischmann, M. Fleischmann, Jan Palouš, J. Krasl)	1	2	14	41
5.	FRA	(B. Poule, P.E. Bouillon, L. Brasseur, A. Charlet, P. Charpentier, J. Chaudron, H. Couttet, R. Couvert, M. Del Valle, A. De Rauch, G.F. De Wilde, A. Hassler, C. Lavaivre, H. Levy-Grunwald, J. Nard, C. Payot, P. Payot, L. Quaglia, G. Simond)	1	2	9	42
7.	BEL	(Verschueren, P. Van den Broeck, Louette, F. Rudolph, Poplimont, G. Van Volxem, Franck, Ph. Van Volckxsom, Van den Driessche, de Ridder)	0	3	8	35
7.	SWI	(B. Leuzinger, W. deSiebenthal, D. Unger, E. Mottier, R. Savoie, M. Jaccard, F. Auckenthaler, E. Jacquet, P. Muller, A. Verdeil, E. Filiol)	0	3	2	53

The Canadian team, the Toronto Granites, displayed extraordinary superiority. After defeating Czechoslovakia, 30–0, and Sweden, 22–0, they outscored Switzerland, 18–0, in the first period alone and then breezed to a 33–0 victory, before crushing Great Britain, 19–2. Meanwhile the U.S. team had beaten Belgium 19–0, France 22–0, Great Britain 11–0, and Sweden 20–0. The final match between Canada and the United States was a rough battle that saw Canada's Harry Watson knocked cold after only 20 seconds of play. Watson recovered, however, and, with blood in his eyes, scored the first two goals of the game. Canada led 2–1 after the first period and 5–1 after the second. A single third-period goal accounted for the final score of 6–1.

1928 St. Moritz T: 11, N: 11, D: 2.19.

			W	L	T	PF	PA
1.	CAN	(Charles Delahay, Frank Fisher, Hudson Louis, Norbert Mueller, Herbert Plaxton, Hugh Plaxton, Roger Plaxton, John Porter, Frank Sullivan, Joseph Sullivan, Ross Taylor, David Trottier)	3	0	0	38	0
2.	SWE	(Carl Abrahamsson, Emil Bergman, Birger Holmqvist, Gustaf Johansson, Henry Johansson, Nils Johansson, Ernst Karlberg, Erik Larsson, Bertil Linde, Sigurd Öberg, Vilhelm Petersen, Kurt Sucksdorf)	3	1	1	12	14
3.	SWI	(Giannin Andreossi, Mezzi Andreossi, Robert Breiter, Louis Dufour, Charles Fasel, Albert Geromini, Fritz Kraatz, Arnold Martignoni, Heini Meng, Anton Morosani, Luzius Rüedi, Richard Torriani)	2	2	1	9	21
4.	GBR	(Blane Sexton, Eric Carruthers, Ross Cuthbert, F. Melland, U.H. Tait, C.F. Wylde, Colin Carruthers, W. Speechley, H. Greenwood, W.H. Brown, G. Rogers, B. Fawcett)	2	4	0	11	27

Canada was represented by the 1926 Toronto University team, which had stayed together and, renamed the Toronto Graduates, had won the Canadian championships. They arrived in Switzerland ten days before the opening of the Games. When Olympic officials saw the Canadians practice they realized that the rest of the teams would be completely outclassed. Consequently, they devised an unusual organization for the tournament. Canada was advanced straight to the final round, while the other ten nations were divided into three pools. The winners of the three pools then joined Canada in the final round. This odd system turned out to be well justified, as Canada obliterated Sweden 11–0, Great Britain 14–0, and Switzerland 13–0.

1932 Lake Placid T: 4, N: 4, D: 2.13.

			W	L	T	PF	PA
1.	CAN	(William Cockburn, Clifford Crowley, Albert Duncanson, George Garbutt, Roy Hinkel, Victor Lindquist, Norman Malloy, Walter Monson, Kenneth Moore, N. Romeo Rivers, Harold Simpson, Hugh Sutherland, W. Stanley Wagner, J. Aliston Wise)	5	0	1	32	4
2.	USA	(Osborn Anderson, John Bent, John Chase, John Cookman, Douglas Everett, Franklin Farrell, Joseph Fitzgerald, Edward Frazier, John Garrison, Gerard Hallock, Robert Livingston, Francis Nelson, Winthrop Palmer, Gordon Smith)	4	1	1	27	5
3.	GER	(Rudi Ball, Alfred Heinrich, Erich Herker, Gustav Jaenecke, Werner Korff, Walter Leinweber, Erich Römer, Marquardt Slevogt, Martin Schröttle, Georg Strobl)	2	4	0	7	26
4.	POL	(Adam Kowalski, Aleksander Kowalski, Wlodzimierz Krygier, Albert Maurer, Roman Sabiński, Kazimierz Sokolowski, Jósef Stogowski, Witalis Ludwiczak, Czeslaw Marchewczyk, Kazimierz Materski)	0	6	0	3	34

Because of the worldwide Depression, only four nations appeared for the Olympic hockey tournament. Consequently, it was decided that each team would play each other team twice. The Canadian team from Winnipeg won their first five matches, including a 2–1 victory over the United States. This meant that a win or a tie in the second match against the United States would assure Canada of first place. If the United States won, then a third match would be required. The United States took a 2–1 lead, but with 50 seconds to play, Rivers shot a bouncing puck into the net to tie the score. Three scoreless overtimes later, Canada was declared the tournament winner.

1936 Garmisch-Partenkirchen T: 15, N: 15, D: 2.16.

			W	L	T	PF	PA
1.	GBR	(Alexander Archer, James Borland, Edgar Brenchley, James Chappell, John Coward, Gordon Dailley, John Davey, Carl Erhardt, James Foster, John Kilpatrick, Archibald Stinchcombe, Robert Wyman)	5	0	2	17	3
2.	CAN	(Maxwell Deacon, Hugh Farquharson, Kenneth Farmer, James Haggarty, Walter Kitchen, Raymond Milton, Francis Moore, Herman Murray, Arthur Nash, David Neville, Ralph St. Germain, Alexander Sinclair, William Thomson)	7	1	0	54	7
3.	USA	(John Garrison, August Kammer, Philip LaBatte, John Lax, Thomas	5	2	1	10	4

Moone, Eldrige Ross, Paul Rowe, Francis Shaugnessy, Gordon Smith, Francis Spain, Frank Stubbs)

		W	L	T	PF	PA
4. CZE	(Josef Boháč, Alois Cetkovsky, Karel Hromádka, Drahos Jirotka, Zdenek Jirotka, Jan Košek, Oldřich Kučera, Josef Maleček, Jan Peka, Jaroslav Pusbauer, Jiři Tožička, Ladislav Troják, Walter Ullrich)	5	3	0	16	16
5. GER	(Wilhelm Egginger, Joachim Albrecht von Bethmann-Hollweg, Gustav Jaenecke, Phillip Schenk, Rudi Ball, Karl Kögel, Anton Wiedemann, Herbert Schibukat, Alois Kuhn, Werner George, Georg Strobl, Paul Trautmann)	3	2	1	10	9
5. SWE	(Herman Carlsson, Sven Bergquist, Bertil Lundell, Holger Engberg, Torsten Jöhncke, Yngve Liljeberg, Bertil Norberg, Vilhelm Petersen, Åke Ericson, Stig Andersson, Lennart Hellman, Vilhelm Larsson, Ruben Carlsson)	2	3	0	5	7
7. AUT	(Hermann Weiss, Hans Trauttenberg, Rudolf Vojta, Oskar Nowak, Friedrich Demmer, Franz Csöngei, Hans Tatzer, Willibald Stanek, Lambert Neumaier, Franz Schüssler, Emil Seidler, Josef Göbl)	2	4	0	12	11
7. HUN	(István Csak, Ferenc Monostori, Miklós Barcza, László Róna, Frigyes Helmeczi, Sándor Magyar, András Gergely, László Gergely, Béla Háray, Zoltán Jeney, Sándor Miklós, Ferenc Szamosi, Mátyás Farkas)	2	4	0	16	77

Germany's leading hockey player was Rudi Ball, a Jew who fled the country when the Nazis began their campaign of anti-Semitism. One month before the Games began, he returned to lead the German team after being invited back by the Nazi leadership. He was the only Jewish member of the German Winter Olympics team.

A major squabble developed over the eligibility of two British players, Alex Archer and goalie James Foster. Archer and Foster were Canadians who, along with 12 other players, had moved to England in 1935. The day before the Olympic tournament began, the International Ice Hockey Federation voted unanimously to ban the two players from competing in the Olympics. Two days later, however, Archer and Foster along with several other Canadian-born players, were on the ice playing in Great Britain's opening match against Sweden. Why they were allowed to play, and what happened in the interim, is still a subject of controversy. The British version is that the Canadians, proud to be members of the Commonwealth, graciously withdrew their objection to Foster and Archer playing for Great Britain. The American version is that the British simply ignored the rules and weren't punished. At any rate, Canada's Olympic undefeated streak was halted at 20 by Great Britain in the semifinal round, when Edgar Brenchley scored a goal in the 14th minute of the final period to give the British a 2–1 victory. Great Britain remained unbeaten by surviving a 0–0 triple overtime tie with the United States in their final match.

1948 St. Moritz T: 9, N: 9, D: 2.8.

		W	L	T	PF	PA
1. CAN	(Murray Dowey, Bernard Dunster, Jean Orval Gravelle, Patrick Guzzo, Walter Halder, Thomas Hibbert, Henri-André Laperrière, John Lecompte, George Mara, Albert Renaud, Reginald Schroeter, Irving Taylor)	7	0	1	69	5
2. CZE	(Vladimir Bouzek, Augustin Bubnik, Jaroslav Drobny, Přemysl Hajny, Zdenek Jarkovský, Stanislav Konopásek, Bohumil Modry, Miloslav Pokorny, Václav Rozinák, Miroslav Sláma, Karel Stibor, Vilibald Štovik, Ladislav Troják, Josef Trousilek, Oldřich Zábrodsky, Vladimir Zábrodský, Vladimir Kobranov)	7	0	1	80	18
3. SWI	(Hans Bänninger, Alfred Bieler, Heinrich Boller, Ferdinand Cattini, Hans Cattini, Hans Dürst, Walter Dürst, Emil Handschin, Heini Lohrer, Werner Lohrer, Reto Perl, Gebhard Poltera, Ulrich Poltera, Beat Rüedi, Otto Schubiger, Richard Torriani, Hans Trepp)	6	2	0	67	21
— USA	(Robert Baker, Ruben Bjorkman, Robert Boeser, Bruce Cunliffe, J. Garrity, D. Geary, G. Harding, V. H. Ingen, J. Kirrane, Bruce Mather, A. Opsahl, Fred Pearson, St. Priddy, Jack Riley, Ralph Warburton)	5	3	0	86	33
4. SWE	(Stig Andersson, Åke Andersson, Stig Carlsson, Åke Ericson, Rolf Ericson, Svante Granlund, Arne Johansson, Rune Johansson, Gunnar Landelius, Klas Lindström, Lars Ljungman, Holger Nurmela, Bror Pettersson, Rolf Pettersson, Kurt Svanberg, Sven Thunman)	4	4	0	55	28
5. GBR	(Leonhard Baker, Beryl Bailey, James Chappell, Gerry Davey, Fred Dunkelman, Arthur Green, Frank Green, Frank Jardine, John Murray, John Oxley, Stanley Simon, William Smith, Archibald Stinchecombe, Thomas Syme)	3	5	0	39	47

		W	L	T	PF	PA
6. POL	(Henryk Bromer, Mieczyslaw Burda, Stefan Csorich, Tadeusz Dolewski, Alfred Gansiniec, Thomas Jasiński, Mieczyslaw Kasprzycki, Boleslaw Kolasa, Adam Kowalski, Eugeniusz Lewacki, Jan Maciejko, Czeslaw Marchewczyk, Mieczyslaw Palus, Henryk Przeździecki, Hilary Skarżyński, Maksymilian Wiecek, Ernest Ziaja)	2	6	0	20	97
7. AUT	(A. Böhm, Franz Csöngei, Friedrich Demmer, E. Engel, W. Feistritzer, A. Gross, A. Hafner, A. Huber, J. Juhn, Oskar Nowack, H. Reichel, J. Schneider, Willibald Stanek, H. Ulrich, F. Walter, H. Winger, R. Wurmbrandt)	1	7	0	33	77
8. ITA	(C. Apollonio, G. Bassi, M. Bedogni, L. Bestagini, C. Bulgheroni, I. Dionisi, A. Fabris, V. Fardella, A. Federici, U. Gerli, D. Innocenti, C. Mangini, D. Menardi, O. Rauth, F. Rossi, G. Zopegni)	0	8	0	24	156

The controversy that engulfed the 1948 ice hockey tournament actually began a year earlier, when the International Ice Hockey Federation ruled that the Amateur Athletic Union was being replaced as the governing body for amateur ice hockey in the United States by the American Hockey Association (A.H.A.). Avery Brundage, chairman of the American Olympic Committee (A.O.C.), accused the A.H.A. of being under commercial sponsorship and refused to sanction its team. Consequently, two U.S. teams arrived in Switzerland prepared to play in the Olympic tournament. Two days before the opening ceremony, the executive committee of the International Olympic Committee (I.O.C.) voted to bar both U.S. teams from competition. However, the Swiss Olympic Committee, siding with the International Ice Hockey Federation, defied the International Olympic Committee and announced that the A.H.A. team would be allowed to play. The A.O.C. team got to take part in the opening-day parade, while the A.H.A. team watched from the stands. But after that, the A.O.C. team had nothing to do but enjoy their paid vacation.

Meanwhile, the A.H.A. players raked up a couple of amazing scores, beating Poland 23–4 and Italy 31–1. Their coach justified these thrashings because the rules stated that if two teams were tied at the end of the tournament, the one with the largest cumulative scoring margin would be declared the winner.

The I.O.C. disowned the ice hockey tournament, but later gave it official approval on the condition that the A.H.A. team not be included in the placings.

With one day left in the competition, three nations—Canada, Czechoslovakia, and Switzerland—all had a chance to finish in first place. In the morning Czechoslovakia defeated the United States, 4–3, which eliminated Switzerland's hopes of placing higher than second. The final match pitted Canada against the Swiss. Two days earlier the Czechs and the Canadians had played a 0–0 tie. Consequently, Canada needed to beat Switzerland by at least two goals to win the gold medal on the basis of the goal differential tie-breaker. About 5000 Swiss perched on mountain cliffs and watched the game, pelting officials with snowballs whenever they disagreed with a call. Their enthusiasm did little good, as the Canadian team tallied a goal in each period and won, 3–0. A final note about the Italian team: in addition to their 31–1 loss to the United States, they lost to Sweden 23–0, Canada 21–1, Czechoslovakia 22–3, and Switzerland 16–0.

1952 Oslo T: 9, N: 9, D: 2.24.

		W	L	T	PF	PA
1. CAN	(George Abel, John Davies, William Dawe, Robert Dickson, Donald Gauf, William Gibson, Ralph Hansch, Robert Meyers, David Miller, Eric Paterson, Thomas Pollock, Allan Purvis, Gordon Robertson, Louis Secco, Francis Sullivan, Robert Watt)	7	0	1	71	14
2. USA	(Ruben Bjorkman, Leonard Ceglarski, Joseph Czarnota, Richard Desmond, Andre Gambucci, Clifford Harrison, Gerald Kilmartin, John Mulhern, John Noah, Arnold Oss, Robert Rompre, James Sedin, Allen Van, Donald Whiston, Kenneth Yackel)	6	1	1	43	21
3. SWE	(Göte Almqvist, Hans Andersson, Stig "Tvilling" Andersson, Åke Andersson, Lars Björn, Göte Blomqvist, Thord Flodqvist, Erik Johansson, Gösta Johansson, Rune Johansson, Sven Johansson, Åke Lassas, Holger Nurmela, Hans Öberg, Lars Pettersson, Lars Svensson, Sven Thunman)	7	2	0	53	22
4. CZE	(Slavomir Barton, Miloslav Blažek, Václav Bubnik, Vlastimil Bubnik, Miloslav Charouzd, Bronislav Danda, Karel Gut, Vlastimil Hajšman, Jan Lidral, Miroslav Nový, Miloslav Ošmera, Zdenek Pýcha, Miroslav Rejman, Jan Richter, Oldrich Sedlak, Jiri Sekyra, Josef Záhorsky)	6	3	0	50	23
5. SWI	(Gian Bazzi, Hans Bänninger, François Blank, Bixio Celio, Reto Delnon, Walter Dürst, Emil Golaz, Emil Handschin, Paul Hofer, Willy Pfister, Gebhard Poltera, Ulrich Poltera, Otto Schläpfer, Otto Schubiger, Alfred Streun, Hans Trepp, Paul Wyss)	4	4	0	40	40

			W	L	T	PF	PA
6.	POL	(Michal Antuszewicz, Henryk Bromowicz, Kazimierz Chodakowski, Stefan Csorich, Rudolf Czech, Alfred Gansiniec, Jan Hampel, Marian Jeżak, Eugeniusz Lewacki, Roman Pęczek, Hilary Skarżyński, Konstanty Świcarz, Stanislaw Szlendak, Zdzislaw Trojanowski, Adolf Wróbel, Alfred Wróbel)	2	5	1	21	56
7.	FIN	(Yrjo Hakala, Aarne Honkavaara, Erkki Hytonen, Pentti Isotalo, Matti Karumaa, Ossi Kauppi, Keijo Kuusela, Kauko Makinen, Pekka Myllyla, Christian Rapp, Esko Rehoma, Matti Rintakoski, Eero Saari, Eero Salisma, Lauri Silvan, Unto Vitala, Jukka Vuolio)	2	6	0	21	60
8.	GER	(Karl Bierschel, Markus Egen, Karl Enzler, Georg Guggemos, Alfred Hoffmann, Engelbert Holderied, Walter Kremershof, Ludwig Kuhn, Dieter Niess, Hans Georg Pescher, Fritz Poitsch, Herbert Schibukat, Xaver Unsinn, Heinz Wackers, Karl Wild)	1	6	1	21	53

Canada, represented by the Edmonton Mercurys, won their first seven games. A final 3–3 tie with the United States gave them the championship. The Americans were just as thrilled by the outcome, since it meant they would finish second instead of fourth. The U.S. team was not popular with the spectators because of their rough style of play. In fact, three of the U.S. players, Czarnota, Yackel, and Gambucci, spent more time in the penalty box than the team totals of any of the other eight teams in the tournament.

Between 1920 and 1952, Canadian ice hockey teams compiled an extraordinary Olympic record of 37 wins, 1 loss, and 3 ties. In those 41 games they scored 403 goals while allowing only 34.

1956 Cortina T: 10, N: 10, D: 2.4.

			W	L	T	PF	PA
1.	SOV	(Yevgeny Babich, Usevolod Bobrov, Nikolai Chlystov, Aleksey Guryshev, Yuri Krylov, Alfred Kuchevsky, Valentin Kusin, Grigory Mkrtchan, Viktor Nikiforov, Yuri Pantyuchov, Nikolai Puchkov, Viktor Shuvalov, Genrich Sidorenkov, Nikolai Sologubov, Ivan Tregubov, Dmitri Ukolov, Aleksandr Uvarov)	7	0	0	40	9
2.	USA	(Wendell Anderson, Wellington Burnett, Eugene Campbell, Gordon Christian, William Cleary, Richard Dougherty, Willard Ikola, John Mat-	5	2	0	33	16
		chefts, John Mayasich, Daniel McKinnon, Richard Meredith, Weldon Olson, John Petroske, Kenneth Purpur, Donald Rigazio, Richard Rodenheiser, Edward Sampson)					
3.	CAN	(Denis Brodeur, Charles Brooker, William Colvin, Alfred Horne, Arthur Hurst, Byrle Klinck, Paul Knox, Kenneth Laufman, Howard Lee, James Logan Floyd Martin, Jack McKenzie, Donald Rope, Georges Scholes, Gérald Théberge, Robert White, Keith Woodall)	6	2	0	53	12
4.	SWE	(Lars Björn, Sigurd Bröms, Stig Carlsson, Yngve Casslind, Sven Johansson, Vilgot Larsson, Åke Lassas, Lars-Erik Lundvall, Ove Malmberg, Nils Nilsson, Holger Nurmela, Hans Öberg, Ronald Pettersson, Lars Svensson, Hans Tvilling [Andersson], Stig "Tvilling" Andersson, Bertz Zetterberg)	2	4	1	17	27
5.	CZE	(Stanislav Bacilek, Slavomir Barton, Václav Bubnik, Vlastimil Bubnik, Jaromir Bünter, Otto Čimrman, Bronislav Danda, Karel Gut, Jan Jendek, Jan Kasper, Miroslav Kluc, Ždenek Návrat, Václav Pantuček, Bohumil Prošek, František Vaněk, Jan Vodička, Vladimir Zábrodsky)	3	4	0	32	36
6.	GER	(Paul Ambros, Martin Beck, Toni Biersack, Karl Bierschel, Markus Egen, Arthur Endress, Bruno Guttowski, Alfred Hoffmann, Hans Huber, Ulrich Jansen, Günther Jochems, Rainer Kossmann, Rudolf Pittrich, Hans Rampf, Kurt Sepp, Ernst Trautwein, Martin Zach)	1	5	2	15	41
7.	ITA	(Carmine Tucci, Carlo Montemurro, Aldo Federici, Mario Bedogni, Bernardo Tomei, Giovanni Furlani, Giampiero Branduardi, Aldo Maniacco, Ernesto Crotti, Giancarlo Agazzi, Gianfranco Darin, Rino Alberton, Giulio Oberhammer, Francesco Macchietto)	3	1	2	26	14
8.	POL	(Janusz Zawadzki, Kazimierz Chodakowski, Stanislaw Olczyk, Mieczyslaw Chmura, Henryk Bromowicz, Józef Kurek, Zdzislaw Nowak, Szymon Janiczko, Adolf Wróbel, Kazimierz Bryniarski, Marian Herda, Hilary Skarżyński, Bronislaw Gosztyla, Rudolf Czech, Alfred Wróbel, Edward Koczab, Wladyslaw Pabisz)	2	3	0	15	22

The Soviet team made a great impression, not only with their excellent play, but with their good sportsmanship and clean style as well.

1960 Squaw Valley T: 9, N: 9, D: 2.28.

			W	L	T	PF	PA
1.	USA	(Roger Christian, William Christian, Robert Cleary, William Cleary, Eugene Grazia, Paul Johnson, John Kirrane, John Mayasich, Jack McCartan, Robert McVey, Richard Meredith, Weldon Olson, Edwyn Owen, Rodney Paavola, Lawrence Palmer, Richard Rodenheiser, Thomas Williams)	7	0	0	48	17
2.	CAN	(Robert Attersley, Maurice "Moe" Benoit, James Connelly, Jack Douglas, Fred Etcher, Robert Forhan, Donald Head, Harold Hurley, Kenneth Laufman, Floyd Martin, Robert McKnight, Clifford Pennington, Donald Rope, Robert Rousseau, George Samolenko, Harry Sinden, Darryl Sly)	6	1	0	55	15
3.	SOV	(Veniamin Aleksandrov, Aleksandr Alyimetov, Yuri Baulin, Mikhail Bychkov, Vladimir Grebennikov, Yevgeny Groshev, Viktor Yakushev, Yevgeny Yerkin, Nikolai Karpov, Alfred Kuchevsky, Konstantin Loktev, Stanislav Petuchov, Viktor Prjazhnikov, Nikolai Puchkov, Genrich Sidorenkov, Nikolai Sologubov, Yuri Tsitsinov)	4	2	1	40	23
4.	CZE	(Vlastimil Bubnik, Josef Černy, Bronislav Danda, Vladimir Dvořaček, Josef Golonka, Karel Gut, Jaroslav Jiřik, Jan Kasper, František Maslan, Vladimir Nadrchal, Vaclav Pantuček, Rudolf Potsch, Jan Starsi, František Tikal, František Vanek, Miroslav Vlach, Jaroslav Volf)	3	4	0	44	31
5.	SWE	(Anders Andersson, Lars Björn, Gert Blomé, Sigurd Bröms, Einar Granath, Sven Johansson, Bengt Lindqvist, Lars-Erik Lundvall, Nils Nilsson, Bert-Ola Nordlander, Carl-Göran Öberg, Ronald Pettersson, Ulf Sterner, Roland Stoltz, Hans Svedberg, Kjell Svensson, Sune Wretling)	2	4	1	40	24
6.	GER	(Paul Ambros, Georg Eberl, Markus Egen, Ernst Eggerbauer, Michael Hobelsberger, Hans Huber, Uli Jansen, Hans Rampf, Josef Reif, Otto Schneitberger, Siegfried Schubert, Horst Schuldes, Kurt Sepp, Ernst Trautwein, Xaver Unsinn, Leonhard Waitl, Horst Metzer)	1	6	0	9	54
7.	FIN	(Hakala, Kilpio, Kolso, Lampainen, Luostarinen, Niemi, Nieminen, Numminen, Pulli, Rassa, Rastio, Selstamo, Soini, Vainio, Wahlsten)	3	2	1	63	23
8.	JAP	(Akazawa, S. Honma, T. Honma, Inatsun, Inatsun, Irie, Iwaoka, Kakihara, Miyasaki, Murano, Ono, Segawa, Shimada, Takagi, Takeshima, Tenabu, Tomita, Yamada)	2	3	1	34	68

When they first started playing together, the U.S. squad hardly seemed to be the "Team of Destiny" that they were to become. Before leaving for Squaw Valley, they played an 18-game training tour and compiled an unimpressive record of ten wins, four losses, and four ties. Not only did they lose to Michigan Tech and Denver University, but less than three weeks before the Olympics began, the U.S. team actually lost, 7–5, to the Warroad Lakers of Warroad, Minnesota. However their first Olympic match set the tone for the rest of the tournament. Trailing Czechoslovakia 4–3 after two periods, they scored four straight goals in the final period and won, 7–5. This was followed by three convincing victories over Australia (12–1), Sweden (6–3), and Germany (9–1).

On February 25 they faced the cofavorite Canadian team. Bob Cleary of Westwood, Massachusetts, took a pass from John Mayasich and scored the first goal after 12 minutes and 47 seconds. Paul Johnson, formerly of the University of Minnesota, scored an unassisted goal in the second period, and the United States held on to win, 2–1. The real star of the game was goalie Jack McCartan, who turned back 39 shots, including 20 in the second period alone.

Two days later the United States went up against the defending champions from the U.S.S.R. The Americans drew first blood after 4:04 of the first period, when Bill Cleary scored after taking a pass from his brother Bob. However the Soviets tied the score a minute later on a goal by Aleksandrov. At the 9:37 mark Bychkov struck from 15 feet in front of the cage and the U.S.S.R. led 2–1. Their lead held for the rest of the first period and most of the second until Billy Christian, with an assist from *his* brother, Roger, fired a shot past Puchkov, the Soviet goalie, to make the score 2–2. The two teams fought on even terms for the next 24 minutes. Then, with five minutes to play, the Christian brothers teamed up for another goal. From there on McCartan took over and heroically protected the U.S. goal, while the partisan overflow crowd screamed with joy. It was the first time that the United States had beaten the U.S.S.R. at ice hockey.

All that stood between the U.S. team and the Olympic championship was an eight a.m. game the next day against the same Czechoslovakian team that they had beaten to open the tournament. But the Americans were so emotionally spent that they were unable to sleep, and they arrived at the arena exhausted and tense. The Czechs wasted no time, scoring their first goal after only eight seconds. After two periods, Czechoslovakia led 4–3. During the break between periods, Nikolai Sologubov, the captain of the U.S.S.R. team, entered the U.S. dressing room to give the Americans a piece of advice. Since he didn't speak English, Sologubov pantomined that the U.S. players should take some oxygen. A tank was obtained, and the revived Americans went back on the ice with visions of the gold medals that were almost within their grasp. After almost six scoreless minutes, the U.S. team went on a rampage, as the Clearys and Christians scored six straight goals to win 9–4. The very same team that had lost to the Warroad, Minnesota, Lakers had won the Olympic gold medal.

A few words about the 1960 Australian team: They lost all six of their matches, giving up 88 goals while scoring only ten. Even when things went right for the Australians they went wrong. Trailing in the first period of a consolation match against Finland, Cunningham scored Australia's only goal of the game. In his excited attempt to follow through of the shot, Australian center Ivor Vesley went straight into the net, smashed his head on the iron crossbar, and had to be taken to the hospital. Finland won, 14–1.

1964 Innsbruck T: 16, N: 16, D: 2.8.

		W	L	T	PF	PA
1.	SOV (Venianin Aleksandrov, Aleksandr Alyimetov, Vitaly Davidov, Anatoly Firsov, Eduard Ivanou, Viktor Konovalenko, Viktor Kuzkin, Konstantin Loktev, Boris Mayorov, Yevgeny Mairov, Stanislaus Petuchov, Aleksandr Ragulin, Vyacheslav Starshinov, Leonid Volkov, Victor Yakushev, Boris Zaitsev)	7	0	0	54	10
1.	SWE (Anders Andersson, Gert Blomé, Lennart Häggroth, Lennart Johansson, Nils Johansson, Sven "Tumba" Johansson, Lars Lundvall, Eilert Määttä, Hans Mild, Nils Nilsson, Bert Nordlander, Carl Öberg, Uno Öhrlund, Ronald Pettersson, Ulf Sterner, Roland Stoltz, Kjell Svensson)	5	2	0	47	16
3.	CZE (Vlastimil Bubnik, Josef Černý, Jiři Dolana, Vlado Dzurilla, Josef Golonka, František Gregor, Jiři Holik, Jaroslav Jiřik, Jan Klapáč, Vladimir Nadrchal, Rudolf Potsch, Stanislav Pryl, Ladislav Smid, Stanislav Sventek, František Tikal, Miroslav Vlach, Jaroslav Walter)	5	2	0	38	19
4.	CAN (Henry Akervall, Gary Begg, Roger Bourbonnais, Kenneth Broderick, Raymond Cadieux, Terrence Clancy, Brian Conacher, Paul Conlin, Gary Dineen, Robert Forhan, Larry Johnston, Seth Martin, John McKenzie, Terrence O'Malley, Rodney-Albert Seiling, George-Raymond Swarbrick)	5	2	0	32	17
5.	USA (David Brooks, Herbert Brooks, Roger Christian, William Christian, Paul Coppo, Daniel Dilworth, Dates Fryberger, Paul Johnson, Thomas Martin, James McCoy, Wayne Meredith, William Reichart, Donald Ross, Patrick Rupp, Gary Schmaltzbauer, James Westby, Thomas Yurkovich)	2	5	0	29	33
6.	FIN (Raimo Kilpiö, Juhani Lahtinen, Rauno Lehtiö, Esko Luostarinen, Ilka Mäsikämmen, Seppo Nikkilä, Kalevi Numminen, Lasse Oksanen, Jorma Peltonen, Heino Pulli, Matti Reunamäki, Jouni Seistamo, Jorma Suokko, Juhani Wahlsten, Jarmo Wasama)	2	5	0	10	31
7.	GER (Paul Ambros, Bernd Herzig, Michael Hobelsberger, Ernst Köpf, Albert Loibl, Josef Reif, Otto Schneitberger, Gerog Scholz, Sigfried Schubert, Dieter Schwimmbeck, Ernst Trautwein, Leonhard Waitl, Helmut Zanghellini)	2	5	0	13	49
8.	SWI (Franz Berry, Roger Chappot, Rolf Diethelm, Elvin Friedrich, Gaston Furrer, Oskar Jenny, René Kiener, Pio Parolini, Kurt Pfammatter, Gerald Rigolet, Max Rueegg, Walter Salzmann, Herold Truffer, Peter Wespi, Otto Wittwer)	0	7	0	9	57

The tournament was actually much closer than the standings make it appear. If Canada had been able to defeat the U.S.S.R. in their final match, they would have finished first instead of fourth. The Canadians did in fact take a 2–1 lead, but the well-balanced Soviet team tied the score with a goal by Starshinov at the end of the second period. The U.S.S.R. gained a 3–2 victory, thanks to an early third-period goal by Venianin Alekasndrov.

1968 Grenoble T: 14, N: 14, D: 2.17.

		W	L	T	PF	PA
1.	SOV (Viktor Konovalenko, Viktor Zinger, Viktor Blinov, Aleksandr Ragulin, Viktor Kuzkin, Oleg Zaitsev, Igor Romichevsky, Vitaly Davydov, Yevgeny Zymin, Vyacheslav Starshinov, Boris Mayorov, Viktor Polupanov, Anatoly Firsov, Yuri Moiseyev, Anatoly Ionov, Yevgeny Michakov, Veniamin Aleksandrov, Vladimir Vikulov)	6	1	0	48	10
2.	CZE (Vladimir Dzurilla, Vladimir Nadrchal, Josef Horešovský, Karel Masopust, Jan Suchý, František Pospišil, Jan Hrbatý, Jiři Kochta, Jan Klapáč, Jiři Holik, František Sevčik, Jaroslav Jiřik, Josef Černý, Jan Havel, Petr Hejma, Václav Nedomanský, Jozef Golonka, Oldřich Machač, Petr Hejma)	5	1	1	33	17

		W	L	T	PF	PA
3. CAN	(Wayne Stephenson, Kenneth Broderick, Terrence O'Malley, Paul Conlin, John Barry MacKenzie, Brian Glennie, Marshall Johnstone, Francis Huck, Morris Mott, Raymond Cadieux, Gerry Pinder, Stephen Monteith, Dan O'Shea, Roger Bourbonnais, William McMillan, Ted Hargreaves, Gary Dineen, Herbert Pinder)	5	2	0	28	15
4. SWE	(Leif Holmqvist, Hans Dahllöf, Lars-Erik Sjöberg, Arne Carlsson, Lennart Svedberg, Roland Stoltz, Nils Johansson, Björn Palmqvist, Folke Bengtsson, Carl-Göran Öberg, Håkan Wickberg, Tord Lundström, Henric Hedlund, Svante Granholm, Roger Olsson, Leif Henriksson, Lars-Göran Nilsson)	4	2	1	23	18
5. FIN	(Urpo Ylönen, Pentti Koskela, Paavo Tirkonen, Juha Rantasila, Ilpa Koskela, Pekka Kuusisto, Lalli Partinen, Seppo Lindström, Matti Reunamäki, Juhani Wahlsten, Matti Keinonen, Lasse Oksanen, Jorma Peltonen, Esa Peltonen, Karl Johanson, Veli-Pekka Ketola, Matti Harju, Pekka Leimu)	4	3	1	28	25
6. USA	(Herbert Brooks, John Cunniff, John Dale, Craig Falkman, Robert, Paul Hurley, Thomas Hurley, Leonard Lilyholm, James Logue, John Morrison, Louis Nanne, Robert Paradise, Lawrence Pleau, Bruce Riutta, Donald Ross, Patrick Rupp, Larry Stordahl, Douglas Volmar, Patrick Loyne)	2	4	1	23	28
7. GER	(Ernst Köpf, Bernd Kuhn, Lorenz Funk, Gustav Hanig, Horst Meindl, Heinz Weisenbach, Leonhard Waitl, Heinz Bader, Josef Schramm, Günther Knauss, Hans Schichtl, Josef Völk, Rudolf Thanner, Manfred Gmeiner, Peter Lax, Josef Reif, Alois Schloder)	2	6	0	20	39
8. GDR	(Ullrich Noack, Bernd Karrenbauer, Hartmut Nickel, Helmut Novy, Wolfgang Plotka, Wilfried Sock, Dieter Pürschel, Klaus Hirche, Dieter Kratzsch, Dieter Voigt, Manfred Buder, Lothar Fuchs, Peter Prusa, Joachim Ziesche, Bernd Poindl, Dietmar Peters, Bernd Hiller, Rüdiger Noack)	1	7	0	16	49

The final outcome of the 1968 competition was still in doubt with only two matches left to be played. The heavily favored Soviet team had received a shocking 5–4 defeat at the hands of Czechoslovakia, their first loss since 1963.

This meant that the championship hinged on the games between Czechoslovakia and Sweden and the U.S.S.R. and Canada, all of whom had records of five wins and one loss. A Czech win combined with a Soviet win would give the gold medal to Czechoslovakia. However the overcautious Czechoslovakian players, physically and emotionally exhausted by their upset victory over the U.S.S.R. in their previous game, fell behind the determined Swedes 2–1 late in the second period. They managed to score one goal to tie in the seventh minute of the final period, but that was all. The game ended in a 2–2 draw, which ended Czechoslovakia's chances for first place. This left the Canada–U.S.S.R. match to decide the winner. Firsov scored first for the Soviets after 14:51. Michakov made it 2–0 after 12:44 of the second period. Three more Soviet goals in the final period settled the issue, 5–0 for the U.S.S.R.

1972 Sapporo T: 11, N: 11, D: 2.13.

		W	L	T	PF	PA
1. SOV	(Vladislav Tretiak, Aleksandr Pachkov, Vitaly Davydov, Vladimir Lutchenko, Aleksandr Ragulin, Victor Kuzkin, Gennady Tsygankov, Valery Vasiliev, Valery Kharlamov, Yuri Blinov, Vladimir Petrov, Anatoly Firsov, Aleksandr Maltsev, Vladimir Chadrin, Boris Mikhailov, Vladimir Vikulov, Aleksandr Yakushev)	4	0	1	33	13
2. USA	(Michael Curran, Peter Sears, James McElmury, Thomas Mellor, Frank Sanders, Charles Brown, Richard McGlynn, Walter Olds, Kevin Ahearn, Stuart Irving, Mark Howe, Henry Boucha, Keith Christiansen, Robbie Ftorek, Ronald Naslund, Craig Sarner, Timothy Sheehy)	4	2	0	23	18
3. CZE	(Vladimir Dzurilla, Jiří Holeček, František Pospíšil, Karel Vohralik, Josef Horešovský, Oldřich Machač, Vladimir Bednář, Rudolf Tajcnár, Josef Černý, Jiří Holik, Bohuslav Šťastný, Richard Farda, Ivan Hlinka, Vacláv Nedomanský, Jiří Kochta, Vladimir Martinec, Eduard Novák, Jaroslav Holik)	4	2	0	34	15
4. SWE	(Leif Holmqvist, Christer Abrahamsson, Thomas Abrahamsson, Lars-Erik Sjöberg, Kjell-Rune Milton, Stig Östling, Bert-Ola Nordlander, Kenneth Ekman, Tord Lundstrom, Lars-Göran Nilsson, Håkan Pettersson, Håkan Wickberg, Mats Åhlberg, Björn Palmqvist, Hans Hansson, Inge Hammarström, Hans Lindberg, Thomas Bergman, Stig-Göran Johansson, Mats Lindh)	3	2	1	25	14
5. FIN	(Jorma Valtonen, Stig Wetzell, Ilpo Koskela, Seppo Lindström, Heikki	3	3	0	27	25

Riihiranta, Heikki Järn, Juha Ranta-
sila, Pekka Marjamäki, Jorma Veh-
manen, Jorma Peltonen, Veli-Pekka
Ketola, Matti Murto, Matti Keinonen,
Harri Linnonmaa, Juhani Tamminen, Lasse Oksanen, Esa Peltonen, Jorma Pettonen, Seppo
Repo, Lauri Mononen, Timo Tur-
unen)

6. POL   (Andrzej Tkacz, Walery Kosyl,   1 5 0 13 39
Ludwik Czachowski, Stanislaw
Fryźlewicz, Jerzy Potz, Marian
Feter, Adam Kopczyński, Andrzej
Szczepaniec, Feliks Góralczyk,
Tadeusz Kacik, Krzysztof Bialy-
nicki, Józef Slowakiewicz, Leszek
Tokarz, Wieslaw Tkacz, Józef
Batkiewicz, Tadeusz Oblój, Walenty
Ziętara, Robert Góralczyck, Stefan
Chowaniec)

7. GER   (Anton Kehle, Rainer Makatsch,   3 2 0 22 14
Otto Schneitberger, Josef Völk,
Werner Modes, Paul Langner, Ru-
dolf Thanner, Karl Egger, Rainer
Phillip, Bernd Kuhn, Reinhold
Bauer, Johann Eimannsberger, Lo-
renz Funk, Erich Kühnhackl, Alois
Schloder, Anton Hofherr, Hans
Rothkirch)

8. NOR   (Kare Ostensen, Tore Walberg, Oy-   3 2 0 17 27
vind Berg, Jan Kinder, Svein Han-
sen, Terje Steen, Birger Jansen,
Thor Martinsen, Tom Roymark,
Thom Kristensen, Steinar Bjolbakk,
Svein Hagensten, Roy Jansen,
Bjorn Johansen, Morten Sethereng,
Terje Thoen, Arne Mikkelsen)

Again the championship was decided by the final match—
this time between the U.S.S.R. and Czechoslovakia. The
winner-take-all game turned out to be an anticlimax, as the
Soviet team took a 4–0 lead in the second period and coasted to a 5–2 victory. The United States was awarded second
place because they had beaten Czechoslovakia, 5–1. For
the first time since the Winter Olympics began, Canada did
not take part in the ice hockey tournament. The Canadians
withdrew from international amateur competition in 1969
because they objected to facing the professional amateurs
of the U.S.S.R. and other Communist countries.

1976 Innsbruck T: 12, N: 12, D: 2.14.

			W	L	PF	PA
1.	SOV	(Vladislav Tretiak, Aleksandr Sidelni-kov, Boris Aleksandrov, Siergei Ba-binov, Aleksandr Gusiev, Valery Kharlamov, Aleksandr Yakushev, Vik-tor Zlukov, Siergei Kapustin, Vladimir Lutchenko, Yuri Lyapkin, Aleksandr Maltsev, Boris Mikhailov, Vladimir Pe-trov, Vladimir Chadrin, Viktor Szalimov, Gennady Tsygankov, Valery Vasiliev)	5	0	40	11
2.	CZE	(Jiří Holeček, Jiří Crha, Oldřich Ma-chač, Milan Chalupa, František Pospi-šil, Miroslav Dvořák, Milan Kajkl, Jiří Bubla, Milan Nový, Vladimir Martinec, Jiří Novák, Bohuslav Štastný, Jiri Holik, Ivan Hlinka, Eduard Novák, Jaroslav Pouzar, Bohuslav Ebermann, Josef Augusta)	2	2	17	10
3.	GER	(Erich Weishaupt, Anton Kehle, Rudolf Thanner, Josef Völk, Udo Kiessling, Stefan Metz, Klaus Auhuber, Ignaz Berndaner, Rainer Philipp, Lorenz Funk, Wolfgang Boos, Ernst Köpf, Fe-renc Vozar, Walter Köberle, Erich Kühnhackl, Alois Schloder, Martin Hin-terstocker, Franz Reindl)	2	3	21	24
4.	FIN	(Matti Hagman, Reijo Laksola, Antti Leppänan, Henry Leppä, Seppo Lind-ström, Pekka Marjamäki, Matti Murto, Timo Nummelin, Esa Peltonen, Timo Saari, Jorma Vehmanen, Urpo Ylönen, Hannu Haapalainen, Seppo Aho-kainen, Tapio Koskinen, Pertti Koivu-lahti, Hannu Kapanen, Matti Rautiainen)	2	3	19	18
5.	USA	(Steven Alley, Daniel Bolduc, Blane Comstock, Robert Dobek, Robert Har-ris, Jeffrey Hymanson, Paul Jensen, Steven Jensen, Richard Lamby, Robert Lundeen, Robert Miller, Douglas Ross, Gary Ross, William "Buzz" Schneider, Stephen Sertich, John Taft, Theodore Thorndike, James Wardén)	2	3	15	21
6.	POL	(Stefan Chowaniec, Andrzej Tkacz, Andrzej Iskrzycki, Marek Marcińczak, Josef Matiewicz, Tadeusz Oblój, Jerzy Potz, Andrzej Slowakiewicz, Andrzej Zabawa, Walenty Ziętara, Karol Żurek, Walery Kosyl, Robert Góralczyk, Kor-dian Jajszczok, Wieslaw Jobezyk, Les-nek Kokoszka, Henryk Pytel, Mieczyslaw Jaskierski, Marian Kaj-zerek)	0	4	9	37
7.	ROM	(Valerian Netedu, Vasile Morar, Elöd Antal, Sandor Gall, George Justinian, Ion Ionita, Desideriu Varga, Doru Moro-san, Doru Tureanu, Dumitru Axinte, Eduard Pana, Vasile Hutanu, Ion Gheorghiu, Tibri Miclos, Alexandru Ha-lauca, Marian Pisaru, Nicolae Visan)	4	1	23	15
8.	AUT	(Daniel Gritsch, Franz Schilcher, Walter Schneider, Gerhard Hausner, Johann Schuller, Michael Herzog, Günther Oberhuber, Othmar Russ, Max Moser, Rudolf Koenig, Josef Ruschnig, Franz Voves, Josef Schwitzer, Peter Cini, Jo-sef Kriechbaum, Alexander Sadjina, Herbert Poek, Herbert Moertl)	3	2	18	14

The tournament was thrown into confusion when Czechoslovakia's captain, František Pospišil, was chosen for a random drug test after a victory over Poland. The team trainer immediately admitted that Pospišil had been given codeine to combat a virus infection. The I.O.C. expelled Pospišil and ordered the game against Poland declared null and void. The final decision on the case was actually delayed, so as not to spoil the drama of the winner-take-all game between Czechoslovakia and the U.S.S.R. In that match, the Czechs led 3–2 in the final period. But with five minutes to play Aleksandr Yakushev tied the score. Twenty-four seconds later Valery Kharlamov knocked the disc into the net again to give the U.S.S.R. their fourth straight set of gold medals in ice hockey.

1980 Lake Placid T:12, N: 12, D: 2.24.

		W	L	T	PF	PA
1. USA	(James Craig, Kenneth Morrow, Michael Ramsey, William Baker, John O'Callahan, Bob Suter, David Silk, Neal Broten, Mark Johnson, Steven Christoff, Mark Wells, Mark Pavelich, Eric Strobel, Michael Eruzione, David Christian, Robert McClanahan, William ''Buzz'' Schneider, Philip Verchota, John Harrington)	6	0	1	33	15
2. SOV	(Vladimir Myshkin, Vladislav Tretiak, Vyacheslav Fetisov, Vasily Pervukhin, Valery Vasiliev, Aleksey Kasatonov, Sergei Starikov, Zinetulla Bilyaletdinov, Vladimir Krutov, Aleksandr Maltsev, Yuri Lebedev, Boris Mikhailov, Vladimir Petrov, Valery Kharlamov, Helmut Balderis, Viktor Zlukov, Aleksandr Golikov, Sergei Makarov, Vladimir Golikov, Aleksandr Skvortsov)	6	1	0	63	17
3. SWE	(Per-Eric ''Pelle'' Lindbergh, William Löfqvist, Tomas Jonsson, Sture Andersson, Ulf Weinstock, Jan Eriksson, Tommy Samuelsson, Mats Waltin, Thomas Eriksson, Per Lundqvist, Mats Åhlberg, Håkan Eriksson, Mats Näslund, Lennart Norberg, Bengt Lundholm, Leif Holmgren, Dan Söderström, Harald Lückner, Lars Mohlin, Bo Berglund)	4	1	2	31	19
4. FIN	(Antero Kivelä, Jorma Valtonen, Seppo Suoraniemi, Olli Saarinen, Hannu Haapalainen, Tapio Levo, Kari Eloranta, Lasse Litma, Esa Peltonen, Ismo Villa, Mikko Leinonen, Markku Kiimalainen, Jari Kurri, Jukka Koskilahti, Hannu Koskinen, Reijo Leppänen, Markku Hakulinen, Jukka Porvari, Jarmo Mäkitalo, Timo Susi)	3	3	1	31	25
5. CZE	(Jiři Kralik, Karel Lang, Jan Neliba, Vitezslav Duras, Milan Chalupa, Arnold Kadleč, Miroslav Dvořmak, František Kaberle, Jiři Bubla, Milan Nový, Jiři Novák, Miroslav Frycer, Marian Štastný, Anton Štastný, Vincent Lukač, Karel Holy, Jaroslav Pouzar, Bohuslav Ebermann, Peter Štastný)					
6. CAN	(Robert Dupuis, Paul Pageau, Warren Anderson, J. Bradley Pirie, Randall Gregg, Timothy Watters, D. Joseph Grant, Donald Spring, Terrence O'Malley, Ronald Davidson, Glenn Anderson, Kevin Maxwell, James Nill, John Devaney, Paul Maclean, Daniel D'Alvise, Ken Berry, David Hindmarch, Kevin Primeau, Stelio Zupancich)	3	3	0	29	18
7. POL	(Henryk Wojtynek, Pawel Lukaszka, Andrzej Ujwary, Henryk Janiszewski, Henryk Gruth, Andrzej Jańczy, Jerzy Potz, Ludwik Synowiec, Marek Marcińczak, Stefan Chowaniec, Wieslaw Jobczyk, Tadeusz Oblój, Dariusz Sikora, Leszek Kokoszka, Andrzej Zabawa, Henryk Pytel, Stanislaw Klocek, Leszek Jachna, Bogdan Dziubiński, Andrzej Malysiak)	2	3	0	15	23
7. ROM	(Valerian Netedu, Gheorghe Hutan, Mihail Popescu, Ion Berdila, Sandor Gall, Elöd Antal, Istvan Antal, Doru Morosan, George Justinian, Doru Tureanu, Dumitru Axinte, Marian Costea, Constantin Nistor, Alexandru Halauca, Laszlo Solyom, Bela Nagy, Traian Cazacu, Adrian Olenici, Marian Pisaru, Zoltan Nagy)	1	3	1	13	29

Just as Canada dominated Olympic ice hockey from 1920 through 1952, so the Soviet Union has been in control since then. Between 1956 and 1980 the U.S.S.R. played 45 games, tallying 39 victories, four defeats, and two ties. In those 45 games they scored 318 goals while giving up only 93. The only nation to break the Soviet monopoly has been the United States, which won the ice hockey tournament the two times during that period that the Winter Olympics were held in the United States—in 1960 and 1980. The 1960 and 1980 U.S. squads were remarkably similar. Both were patchwork teams whose success was completely unexpected. Both teams put together a series of upsets and come-from-behind wins, culminating in a come-from-behind victory over the favored Soviet team followed by one final come-from-behind performance against a lesser opponent, who almost spoiled the whole drama.

But there *were* two important differences. The first was television. In 1960 appreciation of the thrilling victories of the U.S. team was limited mostly to sports fans. In 1980 the excitement of the tournament reached into almost every U.S. household and united the country in a remarkable manner. The other difference was the mood of the country. In 1960 most Americans were feeling prosperous and proud. The victory of the Olympic ice hockey team was basically perceived as a pleasant surprise. In 1980 the United States was in the midst of an identity crisis. It is difficult for most people in the world to understand that Americans, as a nation, could ever feel persecuted and mistreated, but that was the case in 1980. With hostages in Iran, Russians in Afghanistan, and inflation on the rise, it seemed that nothing was going right. When President Jimmy Carter ordered a boycott of the Summer Olympics, Americans were left with the Winter Olympics as their only vehicle for regaining a sense of pride in the world arena. The problem was that speed skater Eric Heiden was the only likely prospect for a gold medal that the U.S. had. Then, with theatrically perfect timing, the 20 young men who comprised the U.S. ice hockey team showed up to offer the ideal tonic to cure the American malaise.

Nine of the U.S. players were from the University of Minnesota, as was the coach, two-time Olympian Herb Brooks. Known as "The Khomeini of Ice Hockey," Brooks was a fanatic disciplinarian who told his young team (average age, 22), "Gentlemen, you don't have enough talent to win on talent alone." Instead they played 63 exhibition games, including a final match, three days before the Olympics opened, against the same U.S.S.R. team that had beaten the National Hockey League All-Stars. The U.S. Olympic team was crushed by the Soviets, 10–3. When the tournament began, the United States was seeded seventh out of 12 teams.

The teams were split into two round-robin divisions. The first- and second-place teams in each division would then advance to a final round-robin of four teams. Favored to advance from the division in which the United States had been placed were Czechoslovakia and Sweden, who happened to be the Americans' first two opponents. In the opening game between the United States and Sweden, the Swedes scored first and led 2–1 as the contest entered its final minute. In desperation, Brooks pulled goalie Jim Craig and put in an extra skater. The gamble paid off as Bill Baker slammed in a shot from 55 feet with 27 seconds left in the game, allowing the United States to escape with a tie. Next came the powerful Czech team. Again the United States gave up the first goal, this time after only 2:23 of the first period. However the Americans had the game tied up 2–2 by the end of the period. Then, surprisingly, they forged ahead to a shocking 7–3 victory. By this time the U.S. ice hockey team had attracted the nation's attention. In their third game, they spotted Norway a 1–0 lead and then scored five goals in the last two periods to win 5–1. Their next match, against Romania, a 7–2 victory, was notable because it was the only one of seven games in which the Americans scored first. Against West Germany they fell behind 2–0 and then won 4–2.

This put the United States into the medal round along with Sweden, Finland, and the U.S.S.R. The 2–2 tie with

Sweden was carried over as part of the final round-robin, as was the Soviets' 4–2 victory over Finland. At five p.m. on Friday, February 22, the U.S. team went out onto the ice to face the best ice hockey team in the world, professional or amateur. That morning Coach Brooks had given his team an uncharacteristic pep talk. "You're born to be a player," he said. "You're meant to be here. This moment is yours. You're meant to be here at this time." Not surprisingly, the U.S.S.R. scored the first goal, as Vladimir Krutov cut off a slap shot by Aleksey Kasatonov and deflected it into the net. Buzz Schneider evened the score five minutes later, but three and a half minutes after that Sergei Makorov put the Soviets ahead again. It looked like the period would end with the score 2–1, but Mark Johnson knocked in a blocked shot with one second left, to bring the United States even once more.

When the second period began, Vladislav Tretiak, considered by many to be the best goalie in the world, had been replaced by Vladimir Myshkin. The U.S.S.R. quickly moved back into the lead on a power-play goal by Aleksandr Maltsev at 2:18, and the period ended with the Soviets ahead 3–2. Amazed to find themselves only one goal behind with 20 minutes to play, the U.S. players sensed their destiny. After 8:39 of the third period Mark Johnson picked up the puck as it slipped away from a Soviet defender and shoveled it past Myshkin from five feet out. The United States was tied again. Less than one and a half minutes later, at the ten-minute mark, team captain Mike Eruzione, using a Soviet defender as a screen, fired off a 30-foot shot that went through Myshkin and into the net. The partisan crowd burst into wild cheering that continued for the rest of the game. For the final 10 minutes goalie Jim Craig (who recorded 39 saves in the game) and the rest of the U.S. team fought off a seemingly endless barrage of attacks by the Soviets. When the last seconds had finally ticked off, the emotional excitement that filled the arena was so great that even many of the Soviet players had to smile as they congratulated their American counterparts. Back in the dressing room, the U.S. team sang "God Bless America," even though they couldn't remember all the words. Meanwhile, Coach Brooks had locked himself in the men's room with his emotions. "Finally I snuck out into the hall," he said, "and the state troopers were all standing there crying."

But there was still one more game to be played. In fact, if the United States lost to Finland on February 24, they would only finish in third place, and the U.S.S.R. would win the tournament anyway. And the Finns were not prepared to roll over and concede defeat. They scored first and led 2–1 after two periods. But the Americans had come too far to lose it all in the final match. Dave Christian, whose father and uncle had been members of the 1960 U.S. squad, sent a pass to Phil Verchota, who sped down the left side of the ice and tied the score with a 15-foot shot at 2:25. At 6:05 Rob McClanahan put the United States in the lead with a stuff shot, and at 16:25 Mark Johnson scored an insurance goal. When the game ended three and a half minutes later, the score was 4–2. American TV viewers were treated to two more emotional moments. While the rest of the team jumped for joy and hugged each other, Jim Craig skated around the rink until he found in the crowd the one person with whom he most wanted to share

this moment—his widowed father. Later, at the medal ceremony, Mike Eruzione took the stand as the captain of his team. But after the playing of "The Star-Spangled Banner," he called his teammates onto the platform to join him in accepting the cheers of the crowd.

LUGE (TOBOGGAN)

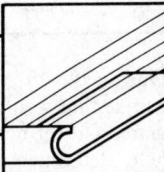

MEN	WOMEN
Single	Single
Two-Seater	
Discontinued Events	

MEN

SINGLE

Luge sleds are similar to toboggans. Participants, known as sliders, career down the course feet first, guiding the luge with their feet and with a hand-held strap connected to the front of one of the runners. Luge has the reputation of being one of the most dangerous sports in the Olympics, so it is not surprising that the rulemakers have seen fit to make it more dangerous by requiring that one of the four runs be done at night. The two-seater event is decided on the basis of two runs rather than four.

1924–1960 not held

1964 Innsbruck–Igls C: 36, N: 10, D: 2.1.
1. Thomas Köhler	GDR	3:26.77
2. Klaus Bonsack	GDR	3:27.04
3. Hans Plenk	GDR	3:30.15
4. Rolf Greger Ström	NOR	3:31.21
5. Josef Feistmantl	AUT	3:31.34
6. Mieczyslaw Pawelkiewicz	POL	3:33.02
7. Carlo Prinoth	ITA	3:33.49
8. Franz Tiefenbacher	AUT	3:33.86

Critics who had contended that luge was too dangerous a sport to be included in the Olympics gained sad support for their arguments when Polish-born British slider Kazimierz Kay-Skrzypeski was killed during a trial run on the Olympic course at Igls two weeks before the Games began. German sliders Josef Fleischmann and Josef Lenz were also severely injured in a separate accident.

1968 Grenoble–Alpe d'Huez C: 50, N: 15, D: 2.15.
1. Manfred Schmid	AUT	2:52.48
2. Thomas Köhler	GDR	2:52.66
3. Klaus Bonsack	GDR	2:53.33
4. Zbigniew Gawior	POL	2:53.51
5. Josef Feistmantl	AUT	2:53.57
6. Hans Plenk	GDR	2:53.67
7. Horst Hörnlein	GDR	2:54.10
8. Jerzy Wojnar	POL	2:54.62

After the East German women were disqualified for heating the runners on their sleds, the coaches of seven of the men's teams signed a petition saying they would all walk out if the East German men were allowed to continue in the contest, which still had one round to go. The International Luge Federation decided against suspending the East German men, but bad weather intervened and the competition was ended after three runs anyway.

1972 Sapporo–Teineyama C: 45, N: 13, D: 2.7.
1. Wolfgang Scheidel	GDR	3:27.58
2. Harald Ehrig	GDR	3:28.39
3. Wolfram Fiedler	GDR	3:28.73
4. Klaus Bonsack	GDR	3:29.16
5. Leonhard Nagenrauft	GER	3:29.67
6. Josef Fendt	GER	3:30.03
7. Manfred Schmid	AUT	3:30.05
8. Paul Hildgartner	ITA	3:30.55

1976 Innsbruck–Igls C: 43, N: 15, D: 2.7.
1. Dettlef Günther	GDR	3:27.688
2. Josef Fendt	GER	3:28.196
3. Hans Rinn	GDR	3:28.574
4. Hans-Heinrich Wickler	GDR	3:29.454
5. Manfred Schmid	AUT	3:29.511
6. Anton Winkler	GER	3:29.520
7. Reinhold Sulzbacher	AUT	3:30.398
8. Dainis Bremze	SOV	3:30.576

During the 1975 Olympic Test Competition on the same course that would be used for the Olympics, the East Germans had set up cameras and timers all along the run to help determine the fastest routes through each of the straightaways and curves.

1980 Lake Placid C: 30, N: 13, D: 2.16.
1. Bernhard Glass — GDR — 2:54.796
2. Paul Hildgartner — ITA — 2:55.372
3. Anton Winkler — GER — 2:56.545
4. Dettlef Günther — GDR — 2:57.163
5. Gerhard Sandbichler — AUT — 2:57.451
6. Franz Wilhelmer — AUT — 2:57.483
7. Gerd Böhmer — GER — 2:57.769
8. Anton Wembacher — GER — 2:58.012

After two runs Dettlef Günther seemed to be well on his way to a repeat victory. However he crashed near the end of his third run and, although he was able to climb back aboard and finish, the three seconds he had lost effectively removed him from the competition for first place. This left Italy's Ernst Haspinger in the lead, with one run to go. Unfortunately, he fell victim to the same turn as Günther and lost nine seconds, which dropped him to 21st place.

TWO-SEATER

1924–1960 not held

1964 Innsbruck–Igls T: 14, N: 8, D: 2.1.
1. AUT (Josef Feistmantl, Manfred Stengl) — 1:41.62
2. AUT (Reinhold Senn, Helmut Thaler) — 1:41.91
3. ITA (Walter Aussendorfer, Sigisfredo Mair) — 1:42.87
4. DEN (Walter Eggert, Helmut Vollprecht) — 1:43.08
5. ITA (Giampaolo Ambrosi, Giovanni Graber) — 1:43.77
5. POL (Lucjan Kudzia, Ryszard Pędrak) — 1:43.77
7. POL (Edward Fender, Mieczyslaw Pawelkiewicz) — 1:45.13
8. CZE (Jan Hamrik, Jiři Hujer) — 1:45.41

1968 Grenoble–Alpe d'Huez T: 14, N: 8, D: 2.18.
1. GDR (Klaus Bonsack, Thomas Köhler) — 1:35.85
2. AUT (Manfred Schmid, Ewald Walch) — 1:36.34
3. GER (Wolfgang Winkler, Fritz Nachmann) — 1:37.29
4. GER (Hans Plenk, Bernhard Aschauer) — 1:37.61
5. GDR (Horst Hörnlein, Reinhard Bredow) — 1:37.81
6. POL (Zbigniew Gawior, Ryszard Gawior) — 1:37.85
7. AUT (Josef Feistmantl, Wilhelm Biechl) — 1:38.11
8. ITA (Giovanni Graber, Enrico Graber) — 1:38.15

1972 Sapporo–Teineyama T: 20, N: 11, D: 2.10.
1. GDR (Horst Hörnlein, Reinhard Bredow) — 1:28.35
1. ITA (Paul Hildgartner, Walter Plaikner) — 1:28.35
3. GDR (Klaus Bonsack, Wolfram Fiedler) — 1:29.16
4. JAP (Satoru Arai, Masatoshi Kobayashi) — 1:29.63
5. GER (Hans Brandner, Balthasar Schwarm) — 1:29.66
5. POL (Miroslaw Więckowski, Wojciech Kubik) — 1:29.66
7. AUT (Manfred Schmid, Ewald Walch) — 1:29.75
8. ITA (Siegfried Mair, Ernst Mair) — 1:30.26

The results of the first run, which had been won by Hildgartner and Plaikner, were cancelled due to a malfunctioning starting gate. The Italians argued that the run should be counted, since all contestants had suffered equally. Their protest was denied. The tie which resulted from the two official runs caused a sticky problem. Finally the International Luge Federation, in consultation with I.O.C. president Avery Brundage, decided to award gold medals to both teams.

1976 Innsbruck–Igls T: 25, N: 15, D: 2.10.
1. GDR (Hans Rinn, Norbert Hahn) — 1:25.604
2. GER (Hans Brandner, Balthasar Schwarm) — 1:25.889
3. AUT (Rudolf Schmid, Franz Schachner) — 1:25.919
4. GER (Stefan Hölzlwimmer, Rudolf Grösswang) — 1:26.238
5. AUT (Manfred Schmid, Reinhold Sulzbacher) — 1:26.424
6. CZE (Jindřich Zeman, Vladimir Resl) — 1:26.826
7. ITA (Karl Feichter, Ernst Haspinger) — 1:27.171
8. SOV (Dainis Bremze, Aigars Krikis) — 1:27.407

1980 Lake Placid T: 19, N: 12, D: 2.19.
1. GDR (Hans Rinn, Norbert Hahn) — 1:19.331
2. ITA (Peter Gschnitzer, Karl Brunner) — 1:19.606
3. AUT (Georg Fluckinger, Karl Schrott) — 1:19.795
4. GDR (Bernd Hahn, Ulrich Hahn) — 1:19.914
5. ITA (Hansjörs Raffl, Alfred Silginer) — 1:19.976
6. GER (Anton Winkler, Anton Wembacher) — 1:20.012
7. GER (Hans Brandner, Balthasar Schwarm) — 1:20.063
8. CZE (Jindřich Zeman, Vladimir Resl) — 1:20.142

Hans Rinn and Norbert Hahn became the first repeat winners of an Olympic luge event. Norbert was no relation to Bernd and Ulrich Hahn, two brothers who finished fourth.

Discontinued Events
SKELETON (CRESTA RUN)

The skeleton is a heavy sled which is ridden head first in a prone position and steered by dragging one's feet and shifting one's weight. It is held only when the Olympics are in St. Moritz.

1928 St. Moritz C: 10, N: 6, D: 2.17.
1. Jennison Heaton — USA — 3:01.8
2. John Heaton — USA — 3:02.8
3. David Northesk — GBR — 3:05.1
4. Agostino Lanfranchi — ITA — 3:08.7
5. A. Berner — SWI — 3:08.8
6. Franz Unterlechner — AUT — 3:13.5
7. A. del Torso — ITA — 3:14.9
8. L. Hasenknopf — AUT — 3:36.7

The Heaton brothers recorded the two fastest times in each of the three runs.

1932–1936 not held

1948 St. Moritz C: 15, N: 6, D: 2.4.

1. Nino Bibbia	ITA	5:23.2
2. John Heaton	USA	5:24.6
3. John Crammond	GBR	5:25.1
4. William Martin	USA	5:28.0
5. Gottfried Kägi	SWI	5:29.9
6. Richard Bott	GBR	5:30.4
7. J. S. Coats	GBR	5:31.9
8. Fairchilds MacCarthy	USA	5:35.5

John Heaton of New Haven, Connecticut had the rare experience of winning consecutive silver medals in the same event—20 years apart. The first time he was 19, the second time 39.

WOMEN

SINGLE

1896–1960 not held

1964 Innsbruck–Igls C: 16, N: 6, D: 2.4.

1. Ortrun Enderlein	GDR	3:24.67
2. Ilse Geisler	GDR	3:27.42
3. Helene Thurner	AUT	3:29.06
4. Irena Pawelczyk	POL	3:30.52
5. Barbara Gorgón-Flont	POL	3:32.73
6. Oldřiska Tylová	CZE	3:32.76
7. Friederike Matejka	AUT	3.34.68
8. Helena Macher	POL	3.35.87

1968 Grenoble–Alpe d'Huez C: 26, N: 10, D: 2.15.

— Orthrun Enderlein	GDR	2:28.04
— Anna-Maria Müller	GDR	2:28.06
1. Erica Lechner	ITA	2:28.66
— Angela Knösel	GDR	2:28.93
2. Christa Schmuck	GER	2:29.37
3. Angelika Dünhaupt	GER	2:29.56
4. Helena Macher	POL	2:30.05
5. Jadwiga Damse	POL	2:30.15
6. Dana Beldová	CZE	2:30.35
7. Anna Mąka	POL	2:30.40
8. Ute Gaehler	GER	2:30.42

The weather-shortened competition ended with defending champion Ortrun Enderlein in first place and East German teammates Anna-Maria Müller and Angela Knösel in second and fourth. However the East German women aroused suspicion by consistently showing up at the last minute and then disappearing as soon as they finished a run. Their toboggans were examined, and it was discovered that their runners had been illegally heated. The three East Germans were disqualified by unanimous vote of the Jury of Appeal. The East German Olympic Committee made a pathetic attempt to blame the affair on a "capitalist revanchist plot," but they failed to address the fact that the problem had been discovered by the Polish president of the Jury, Lucian Swiderski.

1972 Sapporo–Teineyama C: 22, N: 8, D: 2.7.

1. Anna-Maria Müller	GDR	2:59.18
2. Ute Rührold	GDR	2:59.49
3. Margit Schumann	GDR	2:59.54
4. Elisabeth Demleitner	GER	3:00.80
5. Yuko Otaka	JAP	3:00.98
6. Halina Kanasz	POL	3:02.33
6. Wieslawa Martyka	POL	3:02.33
8. Sarah Felder	ITA	3:02.90

After the 1968 scandal, I.O.C. president Avery Brundage had spoken with the disqualified East German women and encouraged them to win the medals next time around. Anna-Maria Müller took this advice to heart and did exactly that, winning an especially close battle with her two teenage teammates. Asked why she enjoyed such a dangerous sport, Müller replied, "I love this sport because it provides a harmonious counterbalance to my work as a pharmacist."

1976 Innsbruck–Igls C: 26, N: 12, D: 2.7.

1. Margit Schumann	GDR	2:50.621
2. Ute Rührold	GDR	2:50.846
3. Elisabeth Demleitner	GER	2:51.056
4. Eva-Maria Wernicke	GDR	2:51.262
5. Antonia Mayr	AUT	2:51.360
6. Margit Graf	AUT	2:51.459
7. Monika Schefftschik	GER	2:51.540
8. Angelika Schafferer	AUT	2:52.322

Undefeated since the 1972 Olympics, Lieutenant Margit Schumann was only in fifth place after the first two runs, but recorded the best times on each of the last two runs to take the victory. The unusually attractive Ute Rührold won her second straight silver medal, even though she was only 21 years old.

1980 Lake Placid C: 18, N: 8, D: 2.16.

1. Vera Zozulia	SOV	2:36.537
2. Melitta Sollmann	GDR	2:37.657
3. Ingrida Amantova	SOV	2:37.817
4. Elisabeth Demleitner	GER	2:37.918
5. Ilona Brand	GDR	2:38.115
6. Margit Schumann	GDR	2:38.255
7. Angelika Schafferer	AUT	2:38.935
8. Astra Ribena	SOV	2:39.011

Zozulia recorded the fastest time in each of the four runs to upset two-time world champion Melitta Sollmann.

FIGURE SKATING

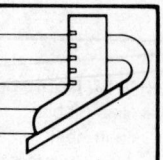

According to current figure skating rules for singles competitions, each skater appears three times, performing compulsory figures (30 percent of the total score), a two-minute short program with seven required moves (20 percent), and a freestyle long program (50 percent). In pairs competition, the compulsory figures are dropped, leaving the short program (25 percent) and the long program (75 percent). The nine judges assign each skater a score from 0 to 6 points, but more importantly, each judge ranks the skaters from best to worst. The numerical equivalents for each place (1 for first, 2 for second, etcetera) are called *ordinals*. If, at the end of the competition, one skater has received the first-place votes of a majority of the judges, then he is declared the winner. If no one has a majority, then the first-place votes are added to the second-place votes. If there is still no one with a majority of votes then the person with the lowest ordinal total is the winner. If a tie still exists, the skater with the most points is awarded the victory.

MEN

1908 London C: 9, N: 5, D: 10.29.

			ORDINALS	PTS.
1.	Ulrich Salchow	SWE	7	1886.5
2.	Richard Johansson	SWE	10	1826.0
3.	Per Thorén	SWE	14	1787.0
4.	John Keiller Greig	GBR	19	1554.5
5.	A. March	GBR	29	1160.0
6.	Irving Brokaw	USA	30	1201.0
7.	Henri Torrome	ARG	31	1144.5

Early in 1908 Salchow suffered his first defeat in six years, losing to Nicolai Panin (Kolomenkin) of Russia. At the

London Olympics, the two met again. Salchow was given three first-place votes for his compulsory figures to Panin's two. Panin withdrew in protest, claiming that the judging was stacked against him. Salchow was the originator of the jump which now bears his name. To perform a Salchow, a skater must take off from the back inside edge of one skate, make a complete turn in the air, and land on the back outside edge of the opposite skate.

1920 Antwerp C: 9, N: 9, D: 4.27.

			ORDINALS	PTS.
1.	Gillis Grafström	SWE	7	2838.50
2.	Andreas Krogh	NOR	18	2634.00
3.	Martin Stixrud	NOR	24.5	2561.50
4.	Ulrich Salchow	SWE	25.5	2572.50
5.	Sakari Ilmanen	FIN	30	2458.00
6.	Nathaniel Niles	USA	49	1976.25
7.	Basil Williams	GBR	49.5	—
8.	Alfred Megroz	SWI	52.5	—

All seven judges awarded first place to Grafström.

1924 Chamonix C: 11, N: 9, D: 1.30.

			ORDINALS	PTS.
1.	Gillis Grafström	SWE	10	367.89
2.	Willy Böckl	AUT	13	359.82
3.	Georges Gautschi	SWI	23	319.07
4.	Josef Sliva	CZE	28	310.77
5.	John Page	GBR	36	295.36
6.	Nathaniel Niles	USA	46	274.47
7.	Melville Rogers	CAN	51	269.82
8.	Pierre Brunet	FRA	54	268.61

The Czech judge ranked Sliva of Czechoslovakia first, the two Austrian judges voted for Böckl of Austria, and the other four judges, none of whom was Swedish, gave first place to Gillis Grafström.

1928 St. Moritz C: 17, N: 10, D: 2.17.

		ORDINALS	PTS.
1. Gillis Grafström	SWE	12	1630.75
2. Willy Böckl	AUT	13	1625.50
3. Robert von Zeebroeck	BEL	27	1542.75
4. Karl Schäfer	AUT	35	1463.75
5. Josef Sliva	CZE	36	1469.00
6. Marcus Nikkanen	FIN	46	1480.00
7. Pierre Brunet	FRA	50	1447.75
8. Ludwig Wrede	AUT	53	1368.75

The 34-year-old Grafström won his third straight gold medal despite suffering from a badly swollen knee. Grafström's smooth, orthodox, and perfectly executed routines appealed to the judges more than Böckl's more aggressive performance and von Zeebroeck's spectacular leaps and spins.

1932 Lake Placid C: 12, N: 8, D: 2.9.

		ORDINALS	PTS.
1. Karl Schäfer	AUT	9	2602.0
2. Gillis Grafström	SWE	13	2514.5
3. Montgomery Wilson	CAN	24	2448.3
4. Marcus Nikkanen	FIN	28	2420.1
5. Ernst Baier	GER	35	2334.8
6. Roger Turner	USA	40	2297.6
7. James Madden	USA	52	2049.6
8. Gail Borden II	USA	54	2110.8

This competition marked a changing of the guard, as 38-year-old three-time Olympic champion Gillis Grafström lost to 22-year-old, soon-to-be two-time Olympic champion Karl Schäfer. Grafström suffered a sudden mental lapse at the very beginning of his performance, evidently starting to trace a different figure than the one that was required. He recovered and skated smoothly thereafter, but he was penalized an average of almost eight points by each judge.

1936 Garmisch-Partenkirchen C: 25, N: 12, D: 2.14.

		ORDINALS	PTS.
1. Karl Schäfer	AUT	7	2959.0
2. Ernst Baier	GER	24	2805.3
3. Felix Kaspar	AUT	24	2801.0
4. Montgomery Wilson	CAN	30	2671.5
5. Henry Graham Sharp	GBR	34	2758.9
6. Jack Dunn	GBR	42	2714.0
7. Marcus Nikkanen	FIN	54	2664.7
8. Elemer Tardonfalvi	HUN	56	2652.3

Schäfer was the unanimous choice of the seven judges. An extreme example of national prejudice by a judge was committed by Judge von Orbán of Hungary, who placed the two Hungarian skaters, Dénes Pataky and Elemer Tardonfalvi, second and third, while none of the other judges ranked them higher than seventh and eighth.

1948 St. Moritz C: 16, N: 10, D: 2.5.

		ORDINALS	PTS.
1. Richard Button	USA	10	191.177
2. Hans Gerschwiler	SWI	23	181.122
3. Edi Rada	AUT	33	178.133
4. John Lettengarver	USA	36	176.400
5. Ede Király	HUN	42	174.400
6. James Grogan	USA	62	168.711
7. Henry Graham Sharp	GBR	67	167.044
8. Hellmut May	AUT	68	165.666

Two days before the free-skating portion of the competition, 18-year-old Dick Button, a Harvard freshman from Englewood, New Jersey, successfully completed a double axel for the first time. He was anxious to include this new move in his program but, as the leader going into the final round, he was hesitant to risk his position by trying a move with which he was not yet fully confident. In his book *Dick Button on Skates,* he recalled, "I disliked being so unprepared. But the cravenness of backing away from something because of the pressure of the Olympic games repulsed me and, once I had made up my mind, I could not divert the steps that culminated in the double axel." The jump went perfectly and Button was awarded first place by eight of the nine judges. Only the Swiss judge voted a first for Gerschwiler of Switzerland.

1952 Oslo C: 14, N: 11, D: 2.21.

		ORDINALS	PTS.
1. Richard Button	USA	9	1730.3
2. Helmut Seibt	AUT	23	1621.3
3. James Grogan	USA	24	1627.4
4. Hayes Alan Jenkins	USA	40	1571.3
5. Peter Firstbrook	CAN	43	1558.1
6. Carlo Fassi	ITA	50	1528.4
7. Alain Giletti	FRA	63	1469.1
8. Freimut Stein	GER	72	1403.6

By 1952 Dick Button was a Harvard senior working on a thesis entitled "International Socialism and the Schumann Plan." Once again he had a new move to unveil at the Olympics—the triple loop, which required him to make three complete revolutions in the air and then come down smoothly. He could have played it safe, skipped the triple loop, and probably won anyway, but he felt that this would have been a form of failure. Button was very anxious, and his parents were so nervous that they couldn't sit together. In his autobiography, Button describes the triple loop: "I forgot in momentary panic which shoulder should go forward and which back. I was extraordinarily conscious of the judges, who looked so immobile at rinkside. But this was it. . . . The wind cut my eyes, and the coldness caused tears to stream down my cheeks. Up! Up! Height was vital. Round and around again in a spin which took only a fraction of a second to complete before it landed on a clean steady back edge. I pulled away breathless, excited and overjoyed, as applause rolled from the faraway stands like the rumbling of a distant pounding sea."

All nine judges placed Button first, far ahead of the other skaters. Dick Button turned professional a few months later and toured with the Ice Capades. Later he became a lawyer, an actor, a TV sports commentator, and an entrepreneur. The seventh-place finisher in 1952, Alain Giletti, was only 12 years old.

1956 Cortina C: 16, N: 11, D: 2.1.

		ORDINALS	PTS.
1. Hayes Alan Jenkins	USA	13	166.43
2. Ronald Robertson	USA	16	165.79
3. David Jenkins	USA	27	162.82
4. Alain Giletti	FRA	37	159.63
5. Karol Divin	CZE	49.5	154.25
6. Michael Booker	GBR	53.5	154.26
7. Norbert Felsinger	AUT	71	150.55
8. Charles Snelling	CAN	67	150.42

The three Americans finished in the same order as they had in the 1955 world championships. Twenty-two-year-old Hayes Alan Jenkins of Colorado Springs, Colorado, had practiced 40 hours a week, 10 months a year, for nine years.

1960 Squaw Valley C: 19, N: 10, D: 2.26.

		ORDINALS	PTS.
1. David Jenkins	USA	10	1440.2
2. Karol Divin	CZE	22	1414.3
3. Donald Jackson	CAN	31	1401.0
4. Alain Giletti	FRA	31	1399.2
5. Timothy Brown	USA	43	1374.1
6. Alain Calmat	FRA	54	1340.3
7. Robert Brewer	USA	66	1320.3
8. Manfred Schnelldorfer	GER	75	1303.3

David Jenkins, the younger brother of 1956 champion Hayes Alan Jenkins, trailed Karol Divin after the compulsory figures. However his free-skating program won first-place votes from all nine judges, and he won eight of nine first places overall.

1964 Innsbruck C: 24, N:11, D: 2.6.

		ORDINALS	PTS.
1. Manfred Schnelldorfer	GER	13	1916.9
2. Alain Calmat	FRA	22	1876.5
3. Scott Allen	USA	26	1873.6
4. Karol Divin	CZE	32	1862.8
5. Emmerich Danzer	AUT	42	1824.0
6. Thomas Litz	USA	77	1764.7
7. Peter Jonas	AUT	79	1752.0
8. Nobuo Sato	JAP	88	1746.2

Manfred Schnelldorfer, a 20-year-old architecture student from Munich, was a former German roller skating champion. Two days shy of his 15th birthday, Scotty Allen of Smoke Rise, New Jersey, became the youngest person to win a medal in the Winter Olympics.

1968 Grenoble C: 28, N:15, D: 2.16.

		ORDINALS	PTS.
1. Wolfgang Schwarz	AUT	13	1904.1
2. Timothy Wood	USA	17	1891.6
3. Patrick Pera	FRA	31	1864.5
4. Emmerich Danzer	AUT	29	1873.0
5. Gary Visconti	USA	52	1810.2
6. John "Misha" Petkevich	USA	56	1806.2
7. Jay Humphry	CAN	63	1795.0
8. Ondrej Nepela	CZE	70	1772.8

Wolfgang Schwarz, who was famous for consistently finishing second behind fellow Austrian Emmerich Danzer, won the narrowest of victories over Tim Wood. If either the Canadian judge or the British judge had given one more point to Wood, he would have won. Instead, Schwarz earned five first-place votes, while Wood was awarded only four. World champion Danzer had the best scores of the free-skating portion of the competition, but he was only fourth in the compulsories. He lost out on a bronze medal because of the placement rule, five to four, despite the fact that he had more points and fewer ordinals than Patrick Pera.

1972 Sapporo C: 17, N: 10, D: 2.11.

		ORDINALS	PTS.
1. Ondrej Nepela	CZE	9	2739.1
2. Sergei Chetveroukhin	SOV	20	2672.4
3. Patrick Pera	FRA	28	2653.1
4. Kenneth Shelley	USA	43	2596.0
5. John "Misha" Petkevich	USA	47	2591.5
6. Jan Hoffmann	GDR	55	2567.6
7. Haig Oundjian	GBR	65	2538.8
8. Vladimir Kovalev	SOV	80	2521.6

Ondrej Nepela first competed in the Olympics in 1964, when he was 13 years old. That year he placed 22nd out of 24. In 1968 he moved up to eighth place, and in 1972, a seasoned veteran of 21, he was the unanimous choice of the judges, despite falling during a competition for the first time in four years. He had been attempting a triple-toe loop jump.

1976 Innsbruck C: 20, N: 13, D: 2.11.

		ORDINALS	PTS.
1. John Curry	GBR	11	192.74
2. Vladimir Kovalev	SOV	28	187.64
3. Toller Cranston	CAN	30	187.38
4. Jan Hoffman	GDR	34	187.34
5. Sergei Volkov	SOV	53	184.08
6. David Santee	USA	49	184.28
7. Terry Kubicka	USA	56	183.30
8. Yuri Ovchinnikov	SOV	75	180.04

Birmingham-born John Curry had two major obstacles to overcome on his way to a gold medal. The first was a lack of proper training facilities in England. This he solved by moving to Colorado in 1973. His second obstacle was the fact that the Soviet and Eastern European judges did not approve of his style of skating, which they considered too feminine. Actually Curry, who believed that figure skating was an art as well as a sport, felt that his style was in the tradition of three-time gold medalist Gillis Grafström. For the Olympics, however, Curry supplemented his natural elegance with enough "masculine" jumps, so that even the Communist judges could find no fault with his performance. The Soviet judge gave first place to Kovalev and the Canadian judge gave first place to Cranston, but even they placed Curry second.

1980 Lake Placid C: 17, N: 10, D: 2.21.

		ORDINALS	PTS.
1. Robin Cousins	GBR	13	189.48
2. Jan Hoffman	GDR	15	189.72
3. Charles Tickner	USA	28	187.06
4. David Santee	USA	34	185.52
5. Scott Hamilton	USA	45	181.78
6. Igor Bobrin	SOV	55	177.40
7. Jean-Christophe Simond	FRA	64	175.00
8. Mitsuru Matsumura	JAP	75	172.28

There were four favorites in the 1980 competition: world champion Vladimir Kovalev of the U.S.S.R., former world champions Charles Tickner and Jan Hoffman, and European champion Robin Cousins of Bristol, England. Hoffman was taking part in his fourth Olympics, having first competed in 1968 when he was 12 years old. Twenty-sixth in 1968, he moved up to sixth in 1972 and fourth in 1976. Cousins, like John Curry before him, trained in Colorado with Carlo and Christa Fassi, who had also coached Peggy Fleming and Dorothy Hamill. In Denver Cousins lived only a few blocks from Charles Tickner.

Kovalev dropped out after placing fifth in the compulsories. Hoffman was in first place, followed by Tickner, Santee, and Cousins. The next day Cousins skated a brilliant short program to move into second place. He made one slip at the beginning of his long program, but otherwise skated flawlessly. Six judges gave Cousins first place, while three voted for Hoffman. Actually Cousins' worst fall came at the awards ceremony, where, dazzled by the lights and the applause and the emotion, he stumbled while trying to negotiate the one and a half steps to the victory platform. In his book, *Skating for Gold,* Cousins recalls the raising of the British flag to honor his victory: "As it was slowly going up, I lost sight of [my parents] for a while. But when the Union Jack was finally above our heads, we were looking directly at each other. So I was able to know how they were feeling and they could see how I was feeling, but it is difficult to describe that to anyone else."

WOMEN

1908 London C: 5, N: 3, D: 10.29.

		ORDINALS	PTS.
1. Madge Syers	GBR	5	1262.5
2. Elsa Rendschmidt	GER	11	1055.0
3. Dorothy Greenhough-Smith	GBR	15	960.5
4. Elna Montgomery	SWE	21	851.5
5. Gwendolyn Lycett	GBR	23	820.0

Madge Syers, who came out of retirement to compete in the Olympics, was the unanimous choice of the five judges.

1920 Antwerp C: 6, N: 4, D: 4.25.

		ORDINALS	PTS.
1. Magda Julin	SWE	12	913.50
2. Svea Norén	SWE	12.5	887.75
3. Theresa Weld	USA	15.5	898.00
4. Phyllis Johnson	GBR	18.5	869.50
5. Margot Moe	NOR	22.5	859.75
6. Ingrid Gulbrandsen	NOR	24	847.50

Magda Julin won the closest of all Olympic figure skating contests despite the fact that she received no first-place votes. The British judge voted for Johnson, the Swedish judge for Norén, and the Norwegian judge placed Moe and Gulbrandsen first and second, even though the other judges put them last. The Belgian judge voted for Weld and the French judge declared a tie between Norén and Weld. Julin did receive three second-place votes and won according to the placings countback rule.

1924 Chamonix C: 8, N: 6, D: 1.29.

		ORDINALS	PTS.
1. Herma Planck-Szabó	AUT	7	299.17
2. Beatrix Loughran	USA	14	279.85
3. Ethel Muckelt	GBR	26	250.07
4. Theresa Blanchard-Weld	USA	27	249.53
5. Andrée Joly	FRA	38	231.92
6. Cecil Smith	CAN	44	230.75
7. Kathleen Shaw	GBR	46	221.00
8. Sonja Henie	NOR	50	203.82

In retrospect, the 1924 competition was most notable for the appearance of the last-place finisher, 11-year-old Sonja Henie, who was to become the most famous figure skater of all time. In Chamonix, however, it was Herma Planck-Szabó who received the first-place votes of all seven judges.

1928 St. Moritz C: 20, N: 8, D: 2.18.

		ORDINALS	PTS.
1. Sonja Henie	NOR	8	2452.25
2. Fritzi Burger	AUT	25	2248.50
3. Beatrix Loughran	USA	28	2254.50
4. Maribel Vinson	USA	32	2224.50
5. Cecil Smith	CAN	32	2213.75
6. Constance Wilson	CAN	35	2173.00
7. Melitta Brunner	AUT	48	2087.50
8. Ilse Hornung	AUT	54	2050.75

Sonja Henie was born in Oslo on April 8, 1912. Her father was a wealthy furrier, the owner of Norway's largest fur company, as well as the owner of Oslo's first automobile. Sonja gained valuable experience at the 1924 Olympics. Two years later she had improved enough to finish second at the world championships. In 1927 the world championships were held on Henie's home rink in Oslo. Henie won the title, but not without some controversy concerning the judging. There were five judges: one Austrian, one German, and three from Norway. The Austrian and the German both gave their first-place votes to Herma Planck-Szabó. However, all three Norwegian judges voted for Sonja Henie, giving her the championship. The ensuing uproar prompted the International Skating Union to institute a rule, still in existence, allowing only one judge per country in international meets. At the 1928 Olympics there was no such controversy, as Henie was awarded first place by six of the seven judges. Only the American judge voted for Beatrix Loughran, who had the unusual distinction of receiving one vote for each of the first seven places.

1932 Lake Placid C: 15, N: 7, D: 10.9.

		ORDINALS	PTS.
1. Sonja Henie	NOR	7	2302.5
2. Fritzi Burger	AUT	18	2167.1
3. Maribel Vinson	USA	23	2158.5
4. Constance Wilson-Samuel	CAN	28	2131.9
5. Vivi-Anne Hultén	SWE	29	2129.5
6. Yvonne de Ligne	BEL	45	1942.5
7. Megan Taylor	GBR	55	1911.8
8. Cecilia Colledge	GBR	64	1851.6

Sonja Henie was the unanimous choice of the seven judges. Already Sonja Henie imitators were springing up, wherever figure skating was appreciated. Two 11-year-olds from Great Britain, Megan Taylor and Cecilia Colledge, placed seventh and eighth at Lake Placid.

1936 Garmisch-Partenkirchen C: 26, N: 13, D: 2.15.

		ORDINALS	PTS.
1. Sonja Henie	NOR	7.5	425.5
2. Cecilia Colledge	GBR	13.5	418.1
3. Vivi-Anne Hultén	SWE	28	394.7
4. Liselotte Landbeck	BEL	32	393.3
5. Maribel Vinson	USA	39	388.7
6. Hedy Stenuf	AUT	40	387.6
7. Emmy Putzinger	AUT	49	381.8
8. Viktoria Lindpaintner	GER	51	381.4

By 1936 Sonja Henie was so popular that police had to be called out to control the crowds around her in places as far apart as New York City and Prague. She had announced that she would retire from competition following the 1936 world championships, to be held one week after the Olympics. She wanted to close out her amateur career with a third Olympic gold medal, so she felt great tension preceding the competition. When the scoring totals were posted for the compulsory figures, Henie was only 3.6 points

ahead of Colledge. When Henie was told the results she tore the offending sheet of paper off the announcements board and ripped it to shreds, stating that it was a misrepresentation. Fifteen-year-old Cecilia Colledge was the second skater to perform her free-skating program. As she glided onto the ice she gave the Nazi salute, which pleased the crowd. Just as she prepared to begin her routine, it was discovered that someone had put on the wrong music, and she was forced to endure a delay while the proper record was found. Not surprisingly, Colledge almost fell during the first minute of her performance. But she recovered sufficiently to earn an average score of 5.7. Sonja Henie, the last of the 26 skaters, appeared nervous, but skated with great vigor and precision. An average score of 5.8 assured her of her third gold medal. A week later she won her tenth straight world championship, a feat surpassed only by Ulrich Salchow, who won 11 consecutive world titles from 1901 through 1911.

During her competitive career, Sonja Henie accumulated 1473 cups, medals, and trophies. After she turned professional her parents convinced Twentieth Century-Fox to put her in the movies. Henie's first film, *One In a Million,* was a big success, and nine more films followed. In 1937 she earned over $200,000. Her father died that year, but Sonja definitely inherited his business acumen. She made enough money to allow her to engage in an occasional indulgence. The only person she trusted to sharpen her skates was Eddie Pec. One time while Sonja was performing in Chicago, she needed her skates sharpened. So she called Eddie Pec in New York. Pec took the next train to Chicago, arriving the following day. He spent a couple minutes sharpening Henie's skates, then turned around and took the next train back to New York.

Sonja Henie became a U.S. citizen in 1941. After divorcing two Americans, the 44-year-old Henie married her childhood sweetheart, Norwegian shipowner Neils Omstad. Sonja Henie died of leukemia at the age of 57, while on an ambulance airplane flying her from Paris to Oslo. She was worth over $47 million at the time of her death.

Another future actress who took part in the 1936 figure skating competition was Vera Hruba of Czechoslovakia, who placed 17th. As Vera Hruba Ralston, she starred in numerous B pictures, including *The Lady and the Monster, Hoodlum Empire,* and *I, Jane Doe.* Her specialties were Westerns and pioneer films.

1948 St. Moritz C: 25, N: 10, D: 2.6.

		ORDINALS	PTS.
1. Barbara Ann Scott	CAN	11	163.077
2. Eva Pawlik	AUT	24	157.588
3. Jeanette Altwegg	GBR	28	156.166
4. Jirina Nekolová	CZE	34	154.088
5. Alena Vrzánová	CZE	44	153.044
6. Yvonne Sherman	USA	62	149.833
7. Bridget Shirley Adams	GBR	69	148.644
8. Gretchen Merrill	USA	73	148.466

Barbara Ann Scott, the 19-year-old world champion from Ottawa, had put in 20,000 hours of practice prior to the Olympics. The day of the free-skating competition, the ice was badly chewed up by two hockey matches. Just before Scott went out to perform, one of the earlier skaters, Eileen Seigh of the United States, gave her a complete description of the location of all the ruts and clean spots all over the rink. Scott won seven of the nine first-place votes, with the Austrian judge voting for Pawlik and the British judge for Altwegg.

1952 Oslo C: 25, N: 12, D: 2.20.

			ORDINALS	PTS.
1.	Jeanette Altwegg	GBR	14	1455.8
2.	Tenley Albright	USA	22	1432.2
3.	Jacqueline du Bief	FRA	24	1422.0
4.	Sonya Klopfer	USA	36	1391.7
5.	Virginia Baxter	USA	50	1369.9
6.	Suzanne Morrow	CAN	56	1344.0
7.	Barbara Wyatt	GBR	63	1335.4
8.	Gundi Busch	GER	75	1316.6

Jeanette Altwegg placed only fourth in free-skating. However she had built up such a large lead during the compulsory figures that she won anyway.

1956 Cortina C: 21, N: 11, D: 2.2.

			ORDINALS	PTS.
1.	Tenley Albright	USA	12	169.67
2.	Carol Heiss	USA	21	168.02
3.	Ingrid Wendl	AUT	39	159.44
4.	Yvonne Sugden de Monfort	GBR	53	156.62
5.	Hanna Eigel	AUT	52	157.15
6.	Carole Jane Pachl	CAN	73	154.74
7.	Hannerl Walter	AUT	83.5	153.89
8.	Catherine Machado	USA	86.5	153.48

Tenley Albright, a surgeon's daughter from Newton Center, Massachusetts, had been stricken by nonparalytic polio at the age of 11. Less than two weeks before the Cortina Olympics, Tenley was practicing when she hit a rut. As she fell, her left skate hit her ankle joint, cut through three layers of her right boot, slashed a vein, and severely scraped the bone. Her father arrived two days later and patched her up. In the Olympic competition she skated well enough to earn the first-place votes of ten of the 11 judges. Back in the United States she entered Harvard Medical School and eventually became a surgeon herself.

1960 Squaw Valley C: 26, N: 13, D: 2.23.

			ORDINALS	PTS.
1.	Carol Heiss	USA	9	1490.1
2.	Sjoukje Dijkstra	HOL	20	1424.8
3.	Barbara Roles	USA	26	1414.9
4.	Jana Mrázková	CZE	53	1338.7
5.	Joan Haanappel	HOL	52	1331.9
6.	Laurence Owen	USA	57	1343.0
7.	Regine Heitzer	AUT	58	1327.9
8.	Anna Galmarini	ITA	79	1295.0

In 1956, 16-year-old Carol Heiss of Ozone Park, Queens, traveled to Cortina with her mother, who was dying of cancer. She gained a silver medal at the Olympics, but two weeks later, she defeated Tenley Albright for the first time to win the world championship in Garmisch-Partenkirchen. In October her mother died, but Carol Heiss took a vow to win an Olympic gold medal in her honor. This she did with extraordinary ease in 1960 , earning the first-place votes of all nine judges.

1964 Innsbruck C: 30, N: 14, D: 2.2.

			ORDINALS	PTS.
1.	Sjoukje Dijkstra	HOL	9	2018.5
2.	Regine Heitzer	AUT	22	1945.5
3.	Petra Burka	CAN	25	1940.0
4.	Nicole Hassler	FRA	38	1887.7
5.	Miwa Fukuhara	JAP	50	1845.1
6.	Peggy Fleming	USA	59	1819.6
7.	Christine Haigler	USA	74	1803.8
8.	Albertina Noyes	USA	73	1798.9

Two-time world champion Sjoukje Dijkstra was the unanimous first-place choice of the nine judges. She was the third straight silver medalist to win a gold medal four years later.

1968 Grenoble C: 32, N: 15, D: 2.11.

			ORDINALS	PTS.
1.	Peggy Fleming	USA	9	1970.5
2.	Gabriele Seyfert	GDR	18	1882.3
3.	Hana Mašková	CZE	31	1828.8
4.	Albertina Noyes	USA	40	1797.3
5.	Beatrix Schuba	AUT	51	1773.2
6.	Zsuzsa Almássy	HUN	57	1757.0
7.	Karen Magnussen	CAN	63	1759.4
8.	Kumiko Ohkawa	JAP	61	1763.6

Like Carol Heiss, Peggy Fleming came from a family which had sacrificed greatly to further her passion for figure skating. Peggy's father, who had moved the family from Cleveland to Pasadena, California, to Colorado Springs (and Carlo Fassi), died in 1966. Her mother designed and sewed all of Peggy's dresses. As a competition, the contest at Grenoble had little to offer. Fleming built up a huge lead after the compulsory figures and easily won all of the first-place votes. Likewise, Gaby Seyfert was awarded all of the second-place votes. Peggy Fleming was the only U.S. gold medal winner of the Grenoble Games.

1972 Sapporo C: 19, N: 14, D: 2.7.

			ORDINALS	PTS.
1.	Beatrix Schuba	AUT	9	2751.5
2.	Karen Magnussen	CAN	23	2673.2
3.	Janet Lynn	USA	27	2663.1
4.	Julie Holmes	USA	39	2627.0
5.	Zsuzsa Almássy	HUN	47	2592.4
6.	Sonja Morgenstern	GDR	53	2579.4
7.	Rita Trapanese	ITA	55	2574.8
8.	Christine Errath	GDR	78	2489.3

World champion Trixi Schuba built up a large lead with her compulsory figures and coasted to victory with a seventh place in free-skating.

1976 Innsbruck C: 21, N: 15, D: 2.13.

		ORDINALS	PTS.
1. Dorothy Hamill	USA	9	193.80
2. Dianne de Leeuw	HOL	20	190.24
3. Christine Errath	GDR	28	188.16
4. Anett Pötzsch	GDR	33	187.42
5. Isabel de Navarre	GER	59	182.42
6. Wendy Burge	USA	63	182.14
7. Susanna Driano	ITA	63	181.62
8. Linda Fratianne	USA	67	181.86

For the fifth straight time the women's figure skating was decided by unanimous decision. Hamill's victory was particularly exciting for her coach, Carlo Fassi, who achieved a unique double, having also coached the men's winner, John Curry.

1980 Lake Placid C: 22, N: 15, D: 2.23.

		ORDINALS	PTS.
1. Anett Pötzsch	GDR	11	189.00
2. Linda Fratianne	USA	16	188.30
3. Dagmar Lurz	GER	28	183.04
4. Denise Biellmann	SWI	43	180.06
5. Lisa-Marie Allen	USA	45	179.42
6. Emi Watanabe	JAP	48	179.04
7. Claudia Kristofics-Binder	AUT	60	176.88
8. Susanna Driand	ITA	77	172.82

The closest Olympic women's figure skating competition in 60 years showcased the friendly rivalry between Linda Fratianne of Los Angeles and Anett Pötzsch of Karl-Marx Stadt. In 1977 Fratianne had won the world championship, but in 1978 she was defeated by Pötzsch. The following year, Linda won back the title, but at the Olympics, the pendulum swung Anett's way. Both 19-year-olds tried to increase their chances of victory by altering their appearance. Linda had cosmetic surgery to her nose, while Anett lost ten pounds. Both tried to appear brighter, livelier, sexier. In the end, it turned out that glamour was unimportant, as Pötzsch gained a solid lead in the compulsory figures and Fratianne was unable to close the gap. Denise Biellmann ranked first in free-skating, but her 12th place in the compulsories kept her out of the medals.

PAIRS

1908 London T: 3, N: 2, D: 10.29.

		ORDINALS	PTS.
1. Anna Hübler Heinrich Burger	GER	5	56.0
2. Phyllis Johnson James Johnson	GBR	10	51.5
3. Madge Syers Edgar Syers	GBR	13	48.0

1920 Antwerp T: 8, N: 6, D: 4.26.

		ORDINALS	PTS.
1. Ludovika Jakobsson Walter Jakobsson	FIN	7	80.75
2. Alexia Bryn Yngvar Bryn	NOR	15.5	72.75
3. Phyllis Johnson Basil Williams	GBR	25	66.25
4. Theresa Weld Nathaniel Niles	USA	28.5	62.50
5. Ethel Muckelt Sydney Wallwork	GBR	34	61.25
6. Georgette Herbos Georges Wagemans	BEL	41.5	56.00
7. Simone Sabouret Charles Sabouret	FRA	45.5	—
8. Madeleine Macdonald Beaumont Kenneth Macdonald Beaumont	GBR	55	—

1924 Chamonix T: 9, N: 7, D: 1.31.

		ORDINALS	PTS.
1. Helene Engelmann Alfred Berger	AUT	9	10.64
2. Ludovika Jakobsson Walter Jakobsson	FIN	18.5	10.25
3. Andrée Joly Pierre Brunet	FRA	22	9.89
4. Ethel Muckelt John Page	GBR	30.5	9.93
5. Georgette Herbos Georges Wagemans	BEL	37	8.82
6. Theresa Blanchard-Weld Nathaniel Niles	USA	39	9.07
7. Cecil Smith Melville Rogers	CAN	41.5	9.11
8. Mildred Richardson Thomas Richardson	GBR	57	7.68

1928 St. Moritz T:13, N: 10, D: 2.19.

		ORDINALS	PTS.
1. Andrée Joly Pierre Brunet	FRA	14	100.50
2. Lilly Scholz Otto Kaiser	AUT	17	99.25
3. Melitta Brunner Ludwig Wrede	AUT	29	93.25
4. Beatrix Loughran Sherwin Badger	USA	43	87.50
5. Ludovika Jakobsson Walter Jakobsson	FIN	51	84.00
6. Josy van Leberghe Robert van Zeebroeck	BEL	54	83.00
7. Ethel Muckelt John Page	GBR	61.5	79.00
8. Ilse Kishauer Ernst Gaste	GER	63	75.75

1932 Lake Placid T: 7, N: 4, D: 2.12.

		ORDINALS	PTS.
1. Andrée Brunet (Joly) Pierre Brunet	FRA	12	76.7
2. Beatrix Loughran Sherwin Badger	USA	16	77.5
3. Emília Rotter László Szollás	HUN	20	76.4
4. Olga Orgonista Sándor Szalay	HUN	28	72.2
5. Constance Wilson-Samuel Montgomery Wilson	CAN	35	69.6
6. Frances Claudet Chauney Bangs	CAN	36	68.9
7. Gertrude Meredith Joseph Savage	USA	49	59.8

1936 Garmisch-Partenkirchen T: 18, N: 12, D: 2.13.

		ORDINALS	PTS.
1. Maxi Herber Ernst Baier	GER	11	11.5
2. Ilse Pausin Erik Pausin	AUT	19.5	11.4
3. Emília Rotter László Szollás	HUN	32.5	10.8
4. Piroska Szekrényessy Attila Szekrényessy	HUN	38.5	10.6
5. Maribel Vinson George Hill	USA	46.5	10.4
6. Louise Bertram Stewart Reburn	CAN	68.5	9.8
7. Violet Cliff Leslie Cliff	GBR	56.5	10.1
8. Eva Prawitz Otto Weiss	GER	74.5	9.5

Thirty-year-old Berlin architect Ernst Baier and his 15-year-old protégée, Maxi Herber, were early exponents of "shadow skating," in which both skaters perform the exact same moves without touching. The judges seemed to have trouble with the Canadian pair, Bertram and Reburn, who received a wide variety of scores, ranging from third and fourth place from the Swedish and Norwegian judges to 13th and 14th from the Austrian and German judges.

1948 St. Moritz T: 15, N: 11, D: 2.7.

		ORDINALS	PTS.
1. Micheline Lannoy Pierre Baugniet	BEL	17.5	11.227
2. Andrea Kékessy Ede Király	HUN	26	11.109
3. Suzanne Morrow Wallace Diestelmeyer	CAN	31	11.000
4. Yvonne Sherman Robert Swenning	USA	53	10.581
5. Winnifred Silverthorne Dennis Silverthorne	GBR	53	10.572
6. Karol Kennedy Michael Kennedy	USA	59.5	10.536

7. Marianna Nagy László Nagy	HUN	89	9.909
8. Jennifer Nicks John Nicks	GBR	98	9.700

1952 Oslo T: 13, N: 9, D: 2.22.

		ORDINALS	PTS.
1. Ria Falk Paul Falk	GER	11.5	102.6
2. Karol Kennedy Michael Kennedy	USA	17.5	100.6
3. Marianna Nagy László Nagy	HUN	31	97.4
4. Jennifer Nicks John Nicks	GBR	39	95.4
5. Frances Dafoe Norris Bowden	CAN	48	94.4
6. Janet Gerhauser John Nightingale	USA	54	92.6
7. Silvia Grandjean Michel Grandjean	SWI	53	92.7
8. Ingeborg Minor Hermann Braun	GER	73.5	81.8

1956 Cortina T: 11, N: 7, D: 2.3.

		ORDINALS	PTS.
1. Elisabeth Schwarz Kurt Oppelt	AUT	14	11.31
2. Frances Dafoe Norris Bowden	CAN	16	11.32
3. Marianna Nagy László Nagy	HUN	32	11.03
4. Marika Kilius Franz Ningel	GER	35.5	10.98
5. Carole Ormaca Robin Greiner	USA	56	10.71
6. Barbara Wagner Robert Paul	CAN	54.5	10.74
7. Lucille Ash Sully Kothmann	USA	59.5	10.63
8. Vera Suchanova Zdenek Dolezal	CZE	68.5	10.53

In this unusually close contest, both Schwarz and Oppelt and Dafoe and Bowden received four first-place votes, with the Hungarian judge voting for the Nagys. The Austrians won because they also received five second-place votes while the Canadians earned three seconds and two thirds. The decisive moment came when a tired Fran Dafoe lost her balance and faltered during a lift. The crowd, which had grumbled all along about the judging, became unruly when the popular German couple of 12-year-old Marika Kilius and 19-year-old Franz Ningel received scores only good enough for fourth place. Members of the audience pelted the judges and referee with oranges, and the ice had to be cleared three times before the competition could go on.

1960 Squaw Valley T: 13, N: 7, D: 2.19.

		ORDINALS	PTS.
1. Barbara Wagner Robert Paul	CAN	7	80.4
2. Marika Kilius Hans-Jürgen Bäumler	GER	19	76.8
3. Nancy Ludington Ronald Ludington	USA	27.5	76.2
4. Maria Jelinek Otto Jelinek	CAN	26	75.9
5. Margret Göbl Franz Ningel	GER	36	72.5
6. Nina Schuk Stanislav Zhuk	SOV	38	72.3
7. Rita Blumenberg Werner Mensching	GER	53	70.2
8. Diana Hinko Heinz Dopfl	AUT	54.5	69.8

Gold medal winner Bob Paul later gained further renown as a choreographer for Peggy Fleming, Dorothy Hamill, and Linda Fratianne, as well as for Donny and Marie Osmond.

1964 Innsbruck T: 17, N: 7, D: 1.29.

		ORDINALS	PTS.
1. Lyudmilla Belousova Oleg Protopopov	SOV	13	104.4
— Marika Kilius Hans-Jürgen Bäumler	GER	15	103.6
2. Debbi Wilkes Guy Revell	CAN	35.5	98.5
3. Vivian Joseph Ronald Joseph	USA	35.5	98.2
4. Tatiana Zhuk Aleksandr Gavrilov	SOV	45	96.6
5. Gerda Johner Rüdi Johner	SWI	56	95.4
6. Judianne Fotheringill Jerry Fotheringill	USA	69.5	94.7
7. Cynthia Kauffman Ronald Kauffman	USA	74.0	92.8
8. Agnesa Vlachovska Peter Bartosiewicz	CZE	84.0	91.8

Lyudmilla Belousova and her husband, Oleg Protopopov, were awarded five first-place votes to four for Kilius and Bäumler. The Leningrad couple had finished ninth in 1960. Kilius and Bäumler were later stripped of their medals for having taken part in a professional ice revue.

1968 Grenoble T: 18, N: 8, D: 2.14.

		ORDINALS	PTS.
1. Lyudmilla Belousova Oleg Protopopov	SOV	10	315.2
2. Tatiana Zhuk Aleksandr Gorelik	SOV	17	312.3
3. Margot Glockshuber Wolfgang Danne	GER	30	304.4
4. Heidemarie Steiner Heinz-Ulrich Walther	GDR	37	303.1

5. Tamara Moskvina Alexei Michine	SOV	44	300.3
6. Cynthia Kauffmann Ronald Kauffmann	USA	58	297.0
7. Sandi Sweitzer Roy Wagelein	USA	64.5	294.5
8. Gudrun Hauss Walter Häfner	GER	67	293.6

Belousova and Protopopov, now 32 and 35 years old, respectively, climaxed their spectacular amateur career with an elegant display that earned them a second Olympic championship. Protopopov told the press, "Art cannot be measured by points. We skate from the heart. To us it is spiritual beauty that matters.... These pairs of brother and sister, how can they convey the emotion, the love, that exists between a man and a woman? That is what we try to show."

1972 Sapporo T: 16, N: 9, D: 2.6.

		ORDINALS	PTS.
1. Irina Rodnina Aleksei Ulanov	SOV	12	420.4
2. Lyudmila Smirnova Andrei Suraikin	SOV	15	419.4
3. Manuela Gross Uwe Kagelmann	GDR	29	411.8
4. Alicia "Jojo" Starbuck Kenneth Shelley	USA	35	406.8
5. Almut Lehmann Herbert Wiesinger	GER	52	399.8
6. Irina Chernieva Vassily Blagov	SOV	52	399.1
7. Melissa Militani Mark Militano	USA	65.5	393.0
8. Annette Kansy Axel Salzmann	GDR	68.0	392.6

At the 1969 European championships, Belousova and Protopopov were dethroned by Irina Rodnina (19) and Aleksei Ulanov (21). The younger couple, knowing they couldn't compete on the same terms with the elegant and sophisticated Olympic champions, had developed a new style, full of dazzling and complex leaps and stunts. Rodnina and Ulanov thrilled the audience and the judges in 1969 and continued undefeated for the next three years. However, as the Sapporo Olympics approached, the Soviet team was in great turmoil. Ulanov, tired of being spurned and mocked by Rodnina, had became romantically involved with Lyudmila Smirnova of the number-two U.S.S.R. team. The harmonious interaction between the partners of the two pairs was severely disrupted. Nevertheless, they finished first and second, with Rodnina leaving the ice in tears.

1976 Innsbruck T: 14, N: 9, D: 2.7.

		ORDINALS	PTS.
1. Irina Rodnina Aleksandr Zaitsev	SOV	9	140.54

2. Romy Kermer Rolf Oesterreich	GDR	21	136.35
3. Manuela Gross Uwe Kagelmann	GDR	34	134.57
4. Irina Vorobieva Aleksandr Vlasov	SOV	35	134.52
5. Tai Babilonia Randy Gardner	USA	36	134.24
6. Kerstin Stolfig Veit Kempe	GDR	59	129.57
7. Karin Künzle Christian Künzle	SWI	64	128.97
8. Corinna Halke Eberhard Rausch	GER	72	127.37

Following the 1972 season, Aleksei Ulanov married Lyudmila Smirnova and a nationwide search was begun to find a new partner for Irina Rodnina. The winner was Aleksandr Zaitsev of Leningrad. Before long, the new pair had not only clicked as skaters, but they had also become wife and husband. Rodnina, still under the direction of the controversial Soviet trainer Stanislav Zhuk, continued her winning ways as if nothing had happened.

1980 Lake Placid T: 11, N: 7, D: 2.17.

		ORDINALS	PTS.
1. Irina Rodnina Aleksandr Zaitsev	SOV	9	147.26
2. Marina Cherkosova Sergei Shakrai	SOV	19	143.80
3. Manuela Mager Uwe Bewersdorff	GDR	33	140.52
4. Marina Pestova Stanislav Lednovich	SOV	31	141.14
5. Caitlin Carruthers Peter Carruthers	USA	46	137.38
6. Sabine Baess Tassilo Thierbach	GDR	53	136.00
7. Sheryl Franks Michael Botticelli	USA	64	133.84
8. Christina Riegel Andreas Nischwitz	GER	71	129.36

In 1978 Irina Rodnina won her tenth straight world championship. She took off the following year to have a baby and, in her absence, the world title was won by two young people from Los Angeles, Tai Babilonia and Randy Gardner. Tai and Randy had been skating together for over eight years, since they were 10 and 12. The stage was set for a dramatic confrontation as Rodnina and Zaitsev attempted a comeback, while Tai and Randy tried to end the Soviet domination of pairs skating. Unfortunately, Randy Gardner suffered a groin injury prior to his arrival in Lake Placid. With a shot of lidocaine to kill the pain, Randy went out on the ice to warm up before the Olympic short program. But he fell four times, and the disappointed pair were forced to withdraw. Rodnina and Zaitsev skated flawlessly and, for the second straight time, won the first-place votes of all nine judges. Thus Rodnina matched the accomplishments of Sonja Henie by winning ten world championships and three Olympic gold medals.

ICE DANCE

Ice dance competitions consist of three parts. First the skaters perform three compulsory dances, which represent 30 percent of their final score. Then comes the original set pattern dance (20 percent) and finally the four-minute free dance, which accounts for 50 percent of the total.

1924–1972 not held

1976 Innsbruck T: 18, N: 9, D: 2.9.

		ORDINALS	PTS.
1. Lyudmila Pakhomova Aleksandr Gorshkov	SOV	9	209.92
2. Irina Moiseeva Andrei Minenkov	SOV	20	204.88
3. Colleen O'Conner James Millns	USA	27	202.64
4. Natalia Linichuk Gennady Karponosov	SOV	35	199.10
5. Krisztina Regöczy András Sallay	HUN	48.5	195.92
6. Matilde Ciccia Lamberto Ceserani	ITA	58.5	191.46
7. Hilary Green Glyn Watts	GBR	57	191.40
8. Janet Thompson Warren Maxwell	GBR	78	186.80

Five-time world champions Lyudmila Pakhomova and Aleksandr Gorshkov sat out the 1979 world championships while Gorshkov underwent an operation. He was completely recovered for the Olympics, and the husband-wife team from Moscow had little trouble captivating the judges and garnering all nine first-place votes.

1980 Lake Placid T: 12, N: 8, D: 2.19.

		ORDINALS	PTS.
1. Natalia Linichuk Gennady Karponosov	SOV	13	205.48
2. Krisztina Regöczy András Sallay	HUN	14	204.52
3. Irina Moiseeva Andrei Minenkov	SOV	27	201.86
4. Liliana Rehakova Stanislav Drastich	CZE	39	198.02
5. Jayne Torvill Christopher Dean	GBR	42	197.12
6. Lorna Wighton John Dowding	CAN	54	193.80
7. Judy Blumberg Michael Seibert	USA	66	190.30
8. Natalia Bestemianova Andrei Bukin	SOV	75	188.38

The Soviet pair won a 5–4 decision over the Hungarians. The announcement of the results was greeted by catcalls and boos from the American audience, which preferred the lively, upbeat style of Regöczy and Sallay to the staid, traditional image of Linichuk and Karponosov.

Discontinued Events

SPECIAL FIGURES

1908 London C: 3, N: 2, D: 10.29.

		ORDINALS	PTS.
1. Nikolai Panin (Kolomenkin)	RUS	5	219
2. Arthur Cumming	GBR	10	164
3. George Hall-Say	GBR	15	104

The first Russian Olympic gold medal winner, 35-year-old Nikolai Kolomenkin, competed under a pseudonym, Nikolai Panin, a common practice among wealthy Russians for whom participation in sports was considered undignified. Four years later in Stockholm, Kolomenkin was a member of the Russian pistol team, which finished in fourth place.

SPEED SKATING

MEN

500 METERS

In speed skating, the competitors skate against the clock, although they race in pairs.

1924 Chamonix C: 27, N: 10, D: 1.26. WR: 43.4 (Oscar Mathisen)

1. Charles Jewtraw	USA	44.0
2. Oskar Olsen	NOR	44.2
3. Roald Larsen	NOR	44.8
3. A. Clas Thunberg	FIN	44.8
5. Asser Vallenius	FIN	45.0
6. Axel Blomqvist	SWE	45.2
7. Charles Gorman	CAN	45.4
8. Joseph Moore	USA	45.6
8. Harald Ström	NOR	45.6

This was the first event to be decided in the first Olympic Winter Games. Figure skating and ice hockey competitions held prior to 1924 were incorporated in the regular Summer Games.

1928 St. Moritz C: 33, N: 14, D: 2.13. WR: 43.1 (Roald Larsen)

1. Bernt Evensen	NOR	43.4	OR
1. A. Clas Thunberg	FIN	43.4	OR
3. John O'Neil Farrell	USA	43.6	
3. Jaako Friman	FIN	43.6	
3. Roald Larsen	NOR	43.6	
6. Håkon Pedersen	NOR	43.8	
7. Charles Gorman	CAN	43.9	
8. Bertel Backmann	FIN	44.4	

1932 Lake Placid C: 16, N: 4, D: 2.4. WR: 42.6 (A. Clas Thunberg)

1. John Shea	USA	43.4	EOR
2. Bernt Evensen	NOR	—	
3. Alexander Hurd	CAN	—	
4. Frank Stack	CAN	—	
5. William Logan	CAN	—	
6. John O'Neil Farrell	USA	—	

In 1932, for the only time in Olympic history, the speed skating competitions were held as actual races, with five or six men in a heat, rather than the usual way of two skaters at a time racing against the clock. This new method, known as the North American Rules, so outraged world record holder and five-time Olympic champion Clas Thunberg that he refused to participate. New York Governor Franklin D. Roosevelt officially opened the Third Olympic Winter Games on the morning of February 4. A local speed skater, 21-year-old Jack Shea, recited the Olympic oath on behalf of the 306 assembled athletes. A short time later the three qualifying heats were held for the 500 meters speed skating. Not surprisingly, five of the six qualifiers were North Americans. Following the heats, the first period of the Canada–U.S.A. ice hockey game was played. Then came the 500 meters final. Shea tore into the lead and finished five yards ahead of co-defending champion Bernt Evensen. Shea's victory was very popular, since he was a hometown boy from Lake Placid, as was 1924 winner Charles Jewtraw.

1936 Garmisch-Partenkirchen C: 36, N: 14, D: 2.11. WR: 42.4 (Allan Potts)

1. Ivar Ballangrud	NOR	43.4	EOR
2. Georg Krog	NOR	43.5	
3. Leo Freisinger	USA	44.0	
4. Shozo Ishihara	JAP	44.1	
5. Delbert Lamb	USA	44.2	
6. Karl Leban	AUT	44.8	
6. Allan Potts	USA	44.8	
8. Antero Ojala	FIN	44.9	
8. Jorma Ruissalo	FIN	44.9	
8. Birger Vasenius	FIN	44.9	

1948 St. Moritz C: 42, N: 15, D: 1.31. WR: 41.8 (Hans Engnestangen)

1. Finn Helgesen	NOR	43.1 OR
2. Kenneth Bartholomew	USA	43.2
2. Thomas Byberg	NOR	43.2
2. Robert Fitzgerald	USA	43.2
5. Kenneth Henry	USA	43.3
6. Sverre Farstad	NOR	43.6
6. Torodd Hauer	NOR	43.6
6. Delbert Lamb	USA	43.6
6. Frank Stack	CAN	43.6

1952 Oslo C: 41, N: 14, D: 2.16. WR: 41.2 (Yuri Sergeev)

1. Kenneth Henry	USA	43.2
2. Donald McDermott	USA	43.9
3. Gordon Audley	CAN	44.0
3. Arne Johansen	NOR	44.0
5. Finn Helgesen	NOR	44.0
6. Hroar Elvenes	NOR	44.1
6. Kiyotaka Takabayashi	JAP	44.1
8. Gerardus Maarse	HOL	44.2
8. Toivo Salonen	FIN	44.2

The Norwegian Skating Union chose as one of their four entrants in this race Finn Hodt, who had served a sentence for collaborating with the Nazis, and who had gone so far as to fight for the Germans on the Eastern Front. One month before the Oslo Games, the Norwegian Olympic committee overruled the Skating Union, voting 25–2 to ban Hodt and all other collaborators from representing Norway in the Oslo Olympics.

1956 Cortina C: 47, N: 17, D: 1.28. WR: 40.2 (Yevgeny Grishin)

1. Yevgeny Grishin	SOV	40.2 EWR
2. Rafael Gratch	SOV	40.8
3. Alv Gjestvang	NOR	41.0
4. Yuri Sergeev	SOV	41.1
5. Toivo Salonen	FIN	41.7
6. William Carow	USA	41.8
7. Malmsten Bengt	SWE	41.9
7. Colin Hickey	AUS	41.9

1960 Squaw Valley C: 46, N: 15, D: 2.24. WR: 40.2 (Yevgeny Grishin)

1. Yevgeny Grishin	SOV	40.2 EWR
2. William Disney	USA	40.3
3. Rafael Gratch	SOV	40.4
4. Hans Wilhelmsson	SWE	40.5
5. Gennady Voronin	SOV	40.7.
6. Alv Gjestvang	NOR	40.8
7. Richard "Terry" McDermott	USA	40.9
7. Toivo Salonen	FIN	40.9

Grishin's time was remarkable, considering that he stumbled and skidded in the homestretch, losing at least a second.

1964 Innsbruck C: 44, N: 19, D: 2.4. WR: 39.5 (Yevgeny Grishin)

1. Richard "Terry" McDermott	USA	40.1 OR
2. Alv Gjestvang	NOR	40.6
2. Yevgeny Grishin	SOV	40.6
2. Vladimir Orlov	SOV	40.6
5. Keiichi Suzuki	JAP	40.7
6. Edward Rudolph	USA	40.9
7. Heike Hedlund	FIN	41.0
8. William Disney	USA	41.1
8. Villy Haugen	NOR	41.1

Terry McDermott, a 23-year-old barber from Essexville, Michigan, stunned the skating world with his surprise victory, the only U.S. gold medal of the 1964 Winter Games. McDermott used skates that he had borrowed from the U.S. coach, Leo Freisinger. He also got some help from Mrs. Freisinger. When Lydia Skoblikova won four speed skating gold medals in 1964, she wore a good-luck pin that had been given to her by Mrs. Freisinger. McDermott heard about this story and asked the coach's wife if he too could have such a pin. Freisinger gave McDermott her last pin, and he put it to good use. In 1968 Dianne Holum also received a Freisinger pin, although she didn't win her gold medal until 1972.

1968 Grenoble C: 48, N: 17, D: 2.14. WR: 39.2 (Erhard Keller)

1. Erhard Keller	GER	40.3
2. Richard "Terry" McDermott	USA	40.5
2. Magne Thomassen	NOR	40.5
4. Yevgeny Grishin	SOV	40.6
5. Neil Blatchford	USA	40.7
5. Arne Herjuaunet	NOR	40.7
5. John Wurster	USA	40.7
8. Seppo Haenninen	FIN	40.8
8. Haakan Holmgren	SWE	40.8
8. Keiichi Suzuki	JAP	40.8

In 1968 McDermott had the misfortune of being drawn in the last of 24 pairs on ice that had been badly melted by the sun. Keller, a dental student from Munich, was a gracious winner. He said of McDermott, "What he did today was just sheer guts. If he had started in the earlier heats while the ice was still good, I'd have lost. It's as simple as that."

1972 Sapporo C: 37, N: 16, D: 2.5. WR: 38.0 (Leo Linkovesi)

1. Erhard Keller	GER	39.44 OR
2. Hasse Börjes	SWE	39.69
3. Valery Muratov	SOV	39.80
4. Per Björang	NOR	39.91
5. Seppo Hänninen	FIN	40.12
6. Leo Linkovesi	FIN	40.14
7. Ove Konig	SWE	40.25
8. Masaki Suzuki	JAP	40.35

This was the only one of the 1972 men's skating races that wasn't won by Ard Schenk, who fell after four steps and finished 34th.

1976 Innsbruck C: 29, N: 15, D: 2.10. WR: 37.00 (Yevgeny Kulikov)
1. Yevgeny Kulikov   SOV   39.17   OR
2. Valery Muratov   SOV   39.25
3. Daniel Immerfall   USA   39.54
4. Mats Wallberg   SWE   39.56
5. Peter Mueller   USA   39.57
6. Jan Bazen   HOL   39.78
6. Arnulf Sunde   NOR   39.78
8. Andrei Malikov   SOV   39.85

1980 Lake Placid C: 37, N: 18, D: 2.15. WR: 37.00 (Yevgeny Kulikov)
1. Eric Heiden   USA   38.03   OR
2. Yevgeny Kulikov   SOV   38.37
3. Lieuwe de Boer   HOL   38.48
4. Frode Rönning   NOR   38.66
5. Daniel Immerfall   USA   38.69
6. Jarle Pedersen   NOR   38.83
7. Anatoly Medennikov SOV   38.88
8. Gaetan Boucher   CAN   38.90

As a 17-year-old, Eric Heiden had competed in the 1976 Olympics in Innsbruck, finishing seventh in the 1500 and 19th in the 5000. Thus it came as quite a shock the following year when he seemingly appeared from nowhere to win the overall title at the 1977 world championships. His victory was so unexpected that even Heiden wondered if his performance might have been a fluke. It wasn't. He successfully defended his world title in 1978 and 1979, and became a national hero—not in his native country, the United States, but in Norway and the Netherlands, where speed skating is taken more seriously.

The 1980 Olympics began with Heiden the favorite in all five men's speed skating events. If there was one distance at which he was thought to be shaky, it was the 500. A week earlier Heiden had lost at 500 meters to teammate Tom Plant at the world speed skating sprint championship. At Lake Placid Heiden was paired against world record holder Yevgeny Kulikov. The two favorites were the first pair to skate. Kulikov was slightly ahead at 100 meters, but they raced neck and neck most of the way. Coming out of the last curve, Kulikov slipped slightly and Heiden, who had a 32-inch waist but 29-inch thighs, pulled ahead and won.

1000 METERS
1924–1972 not held

1976 Innsbruck C: 31, N: 16, 2.12. WR: 1:16.92 (Valery Muratov)
1. Peter Mueller   USA   1:19.32
2. Jörn Didriksen   NOR   1:20.45
3. Valery Muratov   SOV   1:20.57
4. Aleksandr Safronov SOV   1:20.84
5. Hans van Helden   HOL   1:20.85
6. Gaetan Boucher   CAN   1:21.23
7. Mats Wallberg   SWE   1:21.27
8. Pertti Niittylae   FIN   1:21.43

1980 Lake Placid C: 41, N: 19, D: 2.19. WR: 1:13.60 (Eric Heiden)
1. Eric Heiden   USA   1:15.18   OR
2. Gaetan Boucher   CAN   1:16.68
3. Vladimir Lobanov   SOV   1:16.91
4. Frode Rönning   NOR   1:16.91
5. Peter Mueller   USA   1:17.11
6. Bert de Jong   HOL   1:17.29
7. Andreas Dietel   GDR   1:17.71
8. Oloph Granath   SWE   1:17.74

Boucher had the good fortune to be skating first, paired against Eric Heiden. The silver medals in the three shortest races in 1980 were won by whoever was paired with Heiden.

1500 METERS
1924 Chamonix C: 22, N: 9, D: 1.27. WR: 2:17.4 (Oscar Mathisen)
1. A. Clas Thunberg   FIN   2:20.8
2. Roald Larsen   NOR   2:22.0
3. Sigurd Moen   NOR   2:25.6
4. Julius Skutnabb   FIN   2:26.6
5. Harald Ström   NOR   2:29.0
6. Oskar Olsen   NOR   2:29.2
7. Harry Kaskey   USA   2:29.8
8. Charles Jewtraw   USA   2:31.6
8. Joseph Moore   USA   2:31.6

In 1924 30-year-old A. Clas Thunberg won three gold medals, one silver, and one bronze. Four years later he followed up with two more gold medals.

1928 St. Moritz C: 30, N: 14, D: 2.14. WR: 2:17.4 (Oscar Mathisen)
1. A. Clas Thunberg   FIN   2:21.1
2. Bernt Evensen   NOR   2:21.9
3. Ivar Ballangrud   NOR   2:22.6
4. Roald Larsen   NOR   2:25.3
5. Edward Murphy   USA   2:25.9
6. Valentine Bialas   USA   2:26.3
7. Irving Jaffee   USA   2:26.7
8. John Farrell   USA   2:26.8

1932 Lake Placid C: 18, N: 6, D: 2.5. WR: 2:17.4 (Oscar Mathisen)
1. John Shea   USA   2:57.5
2. Alexander Hurd   CAN   —
3. William Logan   CAN   —
4. Frank Stack   CAN   —
5. Raymond Murray   USA   —
6. Herbert Taylor   USA   —

American officials, having already irritated the foreign teams with their strange mass starts, left them completely exasperated with a ruling in the second heat. In the middle of the race the judges suddenly stopped the contest, accused the skaters of "loafing," and ordered the race rerun. In the final Taylor was leading, but he lost his balance coming out of the last turn and tumbled across the track and into a snowbank. Shea found himself in first place and crossed the finish line eight yards ahead of Hurd.

1936 Garmisch-Partenkirchen C: 37, N: 15, D: 2.13. WR: 2:17.4
(Oscar Mathisen)

1. Charles Mathisen	NOR	2:19.2 OR
2. Ivar Ballangrud	NOR	2:20.2
3. Birger Wasenius	FIN	2:20.9
4. Leo Freisinger	USA	2:21.3
5. Max Stiepl	AUT	2:21.6
6. Karl Wazulek	AUT	2:22.2
7. Harry Haraldsen	NOR	2:22.4
8. Hans Engnestangen	NOR	2:23.0

A brief note about the world record: Oscar Mathisen of Norway first broke the world record for the 1500 meters in 1908. By January 11, 1914 he had lowered his time to 2:19.4. One week later, in Davos, Switzerland, he skated a 2:17.4. This time remained a world record for 23 years, until Michael Staksrud, also skating at Davos, recorded a 2:14.9. Mathisen's performance was only bettered twice in the 38 years between 1914 and 1952.

1948 St. Moritz C: 45, N: 14, D: 2.2. WR: 2:13.8 (Hans Engnestangen)

1. Sverre Farstad	NOR	2:17.6 OR
2. Åke Seyffarth	SWE	2:18.1
3. Odd Lundberg	NOR	2:18.9
4. Lauri Parkkinen	FIN	2:19.6
5. Gustav Harry Jansson	SWE	2:20.0
6. John Werket	USA	2:20.2
7. Kalevi Laitinen	FIN	2:20.3
8. Gothe Hedlund	SWE	2:20.7

Farstad was a 27-year-old cartoonist.

1952 Oslo C: 39, N: 13, D: 2.18. WR: 2:12.9 (Valentin Chaikin)

1. Hjalmar Andersen	NOR	2:20.4
2. Willem van der Voort	HOL	2:20.6
3. Roald Aas	NOR	2:21.6
4. Carl-Erik Asplund	SWE	2:22.6
5. Cornelis "Kees" Broekman	HOL	2:22.8
6. Lauri Parkkinen	FIN	2:23.0
7. Kauko Salomaa	FIN	2:23.3
8. Sigvard Ericsson	SWE	2:23.4

1956 Cortina C: 54, N: 18, D: 1.30. WR: 2:09.1 (Yuri Mikhailov)

1. Yevgeny Grishin	SOV	2:08.6 WR
1. Yuri Mikhailov	SOV	2:08.6 WR
3. Toivo Salonen	FIN	2:09.4
4. Juhani Järvinen	FIN	2:09.7
5. Robert Merkulov	SOV	2:10.3
6. Sigvard Ericsson	SWE	2:11.0
7. Hickey Colin	AUT	2:11.8
8. Boris Shilkov	SOV	2:11.9

1960 Squaw Valley C: 48, N: 16, D: 2.26. WR: 2:06.3 (Juhani Järvinen)

1. Roald Aas	NOR	2:10.4
1. Yevgeny Grishin	SOV	2:10.4
3. Boris Stenin	SOV	2:11.5
4. Jouko Jokinen	FIN	2:12.0

5. Per Olov Brogren	SWE	2:13.1
5. Juhani Järvinen	FIN	2:13.1
7. Toivo Salonen	FIN	2:13.2
8. André Kouprianoff	FRA	2:13.3

Grishin registered his second straight tie for first place at 1500 meters and collected his fourth Olympic gold medal. In 1952 he had also competed as a cyclist.

1964 Innsbruck C: 54, N: 21, D: 2.6. WR: 2:06.3 (Juhani Järvinen)

1. Ants Antson	SOV	2:10.3
2. Cornelis "Kees" Verkerk	HOL	2:10.6
3. Villy Haugen	NOR	2:11.2
4. Jouko Launonen	FIN	2:11.9
5. Lev Zaitsev	SOV	2:12.1
6. Ivar Eriksen	NOR	2:12.2
6. Edouard Matoussevitch	SOV	2:12.2
8. Juhani Järvinen	FIN	2:12.4

1968 Grenoble C: 53, N: 18, D: 2.16. WR: 2:02.5 (Magne Thomassen)

1. Cornelis "Kees" Verkerk	HOL	2:03.4 OR
2. Ivar Eriksen	NOR	2:05.0
2. Adrianus "Ard" Schenk	HOL	2:05.0
4. Magne Thomassen	NOR	2:05.1
5. Johnny Höglin	SWE	2:05.2
5. Björn Tveter	NOR	2:05.2
7. S. Erik Stiansen	NOR	2:05.5
8. Edouard Matoussevitch	SOV	2:06.1

Kees Verkerk was a 25-year-old bartender from the village of Putteshoak who also played the trumpet on a Dutch television show.

1972 Sapporo C: 39, N: 16, D: 2.6. WR: 1:58.7 (Adrianus "Ard" Schenk)

1. Adrianus "Ard" Schenk	HOL	2:02.96 OR
2. Roar Grönvold	NOR	2:04.26
3. Göran Claesson	SWE	2:05.89
3. Björn Tveter	NOR	2:05.94
5. Jan Bols	HOL	2:06.58
6. Valery Lavrouchkin	SOV	2:07.16
7. Daniel Carroll	USA	2:07.24
8. Cornelis "Kees" Verkerk	HOL	2:07.43

1976 Innsbruck C: 30, N: 19, D: 2.13. WR: 1:58.7 (Adrianus "Ard" Schenk)

1. Jan Egil Storholt	NOR	1:59.38 OR
2. Yuri Kondakov	SOV	1:59.97
3. Hans van Helden	HOL	2:00.87
4. Sergei Riabev	SOV	2:02.15
5. Daniel Carroll	USA	2:02.26
6. Piet Kleine	HOL	2:02.28
7. Eric Heiden	USA	2:02.40
8. Colin Coates	AUS	2:03.34

Storholt, an electrician from Trondheim, celebrated his 27th birthday the day he won the gold medal. He was paired against Kondakov, who ended up with the silver medal.

1980 Lake Placid C: 36, N: 16, D: 2.21. WR: 1:54.79 (Eric Heiden)
1. Eric Heiden   USA   1:55.44   OR
2. Kai Arne Stenshjemmet   NOR   1:56.81
3. Terje Andersen   NOR   1:56.92
4. Andreas Dietel   GDR   1:57.14
5. Yuri Kondakov   SOV   1:57.36
6. Jan Egil Storholt   NOR   1:57.95
7. Tomas Gustafson   SWE   1:58.18
8. Vladimir Lobanov   SOV   1:59.38

Midway through his race against Stenshjemmet, Heiden almost fell when he hit a rut in the ice. But he was able to steady himself before he had lost more than a few hundredths of a second, and he went on to win his fourth gold medal.

5000 METERS

1924 Chamonix C: 22, N: 10, D: 1.26. WR: 8:26.5 (Harald Ström)
1. A. Clas Thunberg   FIN   8:39.0
2. Julius Skutnabb   FIN   8:48.4
3. Roald Larsen   NOR   8:50.2
4. Sigurd Moen   NOR   8:51.0
5. Harald Ström   NOR   8:54.6
6. Valentine Bialas   USA   8:55.0
7. Edvin Paulsen   NOR   8:59.0
8. Richard Donovan   USA   9:05.3

Thunberg won the first of his five Olympic gold medals.

1928 St. Moritz C: 33, N: 14, D: 2.13. WR: 8:26.5 (Harald Ström)
1. Ivar Ballangrud   NOR   8:50.5
2. Julius Skutnabb   FIN   8:59.1
3. Bernt Evensen   NOR   9:01.1
4. Irving Jaffee   USA   9:01.3
5. Armand Carlsen   NOR   9:01.5
6. Valentine Bialas   USA   9:06.3
7. Michael Staksrud   NOR   9:07.3
8. Otto Polacsek   AUT   9:08.9

This was the first of Ballangrud's seven Olympic medals.

1932 Lake Placid C: 18, N: 6, D: 2.4. WR: 8:21.6 (Ivar Ballangrud)
1. Irving Jaffee   USA   9:40.8
2. Edward Murphy   USA   —
3. William Logan   CAN   —
4. Herbert Taylor   USA   —
5. Ivar Ballangrud   NOR   —
6. Bernt Evensen   NOR   —
7. Frank Stack   CAN   —
8. C. Harry Smyth   CAN   —

1936 Garmisch-Partenkirchen C: 37, N: 16, D: 2.12. WR: 8:17.2 (Ivar Ballangrud)
1. Ivar Ballangrud   NOR   8:19.6   OR
2. Birger Vasenius   FIN   8:23.3
3. Antero Ojala   FIN   8:30.1

4. Jan Langedijk   HOL   8:32.0
5. Max Stiepl   AUT   8:35.0
6. Ossi Blomqvist   FIN   8:36.6
7. Charles Mathisen   NOR   8:36.9
8. Karl Wazulek   AUT   8:38.4

1948 St. Moritz C: 40, N: 14, D: 2.1. WR: 8:13.7 (Åke Seyffarth)
1. Reidar Liaklev   NOR   8:29.4
2. Odd Lundberg   NOR   8:32.7
3. Göthe Hedlund   SWE   8:34.8
4. Gustav Jansson   SWE   8:34.9
5. Jan Langedijk   HOL   8:36.2
6. Cornelis "Kees" Broekman   HOL   8:37.3
7. Åke Seyffarth   SWE   8:37.9
8. Pentti Lammio   FIN   8:40.7

Åke Seyffarth, who had set the world record seven years earlier, lost precious seconds on the final lap when he brushed against a photographer who had jumped onto the ice to take a picture.

1952 Oslo C: 35, N: 13, D: 2.17. WR: 8:03.7 (Nikolai Mamonov)
1. Hjalmar Andersen   NOR   8:10.6   OR
2. Cornelis "Kees" Broekman HOL   8:21.6
3. Sverre Haugli   NOR   8:22.4
4. Anton Huiskes   HOL   8:28.5
5. Willem van der Voort   HOL   8:30.6
6. Carl-Erik Asplund   SWE   8:30.7
7. Pentti Lammio   FIN   8:31.9
8. Arthur Mannsbarth   AUT   8:36.2

Spurred on by a standing ovation from the crowd of 24,000, 28-year-old truck driver Hjalmar Andersen achieved the largest winning margin in the history of the 5000 meters.

1956 Cortina C: 46, N: 17, D: 1.29. WR: 7:45.6 (Boris Shilkov)
1. Boris Shilkov   SOV   7:48.7   OR
2. Sigvard Ericsson   SWE   7:56.7
3. Oleg Goncharenko   SOV   7:57.5
4. Willem de Graaf   HOL   8:00.2
4. Cornelis "Kees" Broekman HOL   8:00.2
6. Roald Aas   NOR   8:01.6
7. Olof Dahlberg   SWE   8:01.8
8. Knut Johannesen   NOR   8:02.3

1960 Squaw Valley C: 37, N: 15, D: 2.25. WR: 7:45.6 (Boris Shilkov)
1. Viktor Kosichkin   SOV   7:51.3
2. Knut Johannesen   NOR   8:00.8
3. Jan Pesman   HOL   8:05.1
4. Torstein Seiersten   NOR   8:05.3
5. Valery Kotov   SOV   8:05.4
6. Oleg Goncharenko   SOV   8:06.6
7. Ivar Nilsson   SWE   8:09.1
7. Keijo Tapiovaara   FIN   8:09.1

1964 Innsbruck C: 44, N: 19, D: 2.5. WR: 7:34.3 (Jonny Nilsson)
1. Knut Johannesen   NOR   7:38.4   OR
2. Per Ivar Moe   NOR   7:38.6
3. Fred Anton Maier   NOR   7:42.0
4. Victor Kosichkin   SOV   7:45.8
5. Herman Strutz   AUT   7:48.3
6. Jonny Nilsson   SWE   7:48.4
7. Ivar Nilsson   SWE   7:49.0
8. Rutgerus Liebrechts   HOL   7:50.9

Skating in the fifth pair, 19-year-old Per Ivar Moe recorded the second-fastest 5000 meters ever. Then he watched as Olympic veteran Knut Johannesen assaulted his time as part of the 14th pair. With five of 12½ laps to go, Johannesen was three seconds behind Moe's pace. But he caught up with two laps left and pushed for the finish with the crowd on its feet, rooting him on. Unfortunately, as he crossed the finish line, the clock stopped at 7:38.7—one-tenth of a second slower than Moe. But then the scoreboard was revised to match the official time—7:38.4—and Johannesen had won his second gold medal. Between 1956 and 1964 he won two gold, two silver, and one bronze.

1968 Grenoble C: 38, N: 17, D: 2.15. WR: 7:26.2. (Fred Anton Maier)
1. Fred Anton Maier   NOR   7:22.4   WR
2. Cornelis "Kees" Verkerk   HOL   7:23.2
3. Petrus Nottet   HOL   7:25.5
4. Per-Willy Guttormsen   NOR   7:27.8
5. Johnny Höglin   SWE   7:32.7
6. Örjan Sandler   SWE   7:32.8
7. Jonny Nilsson   SWE   7:32.9
8. Jan Bols   HOL   7:33.1

Verkerk broke Maier's world record by three seconds and then watched as the 29-year-old clerk won it back 20 minutes later.

1972 Sapporo C: 28, N: 14, D: 2.4. WR: 7:12.0 (Adrianus "Ard" Schenk)
1. Adrianus "Ard" Schenk   HOL   7:23.61
2. Roar Grönvold   NOR   7:28.18
3. Sten Stensen   NOR   7:33.39
4. Göran Claeson   SWE   7:36.17
5. Willy Olsen   NOR   7:36.47
6. Cornelis "Kees" Verkerk   HOL   7:39.17
7. Valery Lavrouchkin   SOV   7:39.26
8. Jan Bols   HOL   7:39.40

Schenk skated first, while it was snowing, but he still managed to outstrip the field.

1976 Innsbruck C: 31, N: 17, D: 2.11. WR: 7:07.82 (Hans van Helden)
1. Sten Stensen   NOR   7:24.48
2. Piet Kleine   HOL   7:26.47
3. Hans van Helden   HOL   7:26.54
4. Victor Varlamov   SOV   7:30.97

5. Klaus Wunderlich   GDR   7:33.82
6. Daniel Carroll   USA   7:36.46
7. Vladimir Ivanov   SOV   7:37.73
8. Örjan Sandler   SWE   7:39.69

1980 Lake Placid C: 29, N: 15, D: 2.16. WR: 6:56.9 (Kai Arne Stenshjemmet)
1. Eric Heiden   USA   7:02.29   OR
2. Kai Arne Stenshjemmet   NOR   7:03.28
3. Tom Erik Oxholm   NOR   7:05.59
4. Hilbert van der Duim   HOL   7:07.97
5. Öyvind Tveter   NOR   7:08.36
6. Piet Kleine   HOL   7:08.96
7. Michael Woods   USA   7:10.39
8. Ulf Ekstrand   SWE   7:13.13

Stenshjemmet, skating two pairs after Eric Heiden, stayed ahead of his pace for ten and a half laps, but began his arm swinging too early and couldn't keep it up. It was Heiden's second gold medal.

10,000 METERS

1924 Chamonix C: 16, N: 6, D: 1.27. WR: 17:22.6 (Oscar Mathisen)
1. Julius Skutnabb   FIN   18:04.8
2. A. Clas Thunberg   FIN   18:07.8
3. Roald Larsen   NOR   18:12.2
4. Fritjof Paulsen   NOR   18:13.0
5. Harald Ström   NOR   18:18.6
6. Sigurd Moen   NOR   18:19.0
7. Léon Quaglia   FRA   18:25.0
8. Valentine Bialas   USA   18:34.0

Skutnabb defeated Thunberg head-on, since they were paired together. This reversed the order of finish of the 5000, which had been held the previous day.

1928 St. Moritz C: 10, N: 6, D: 2.14. WR: 17:17.4 (Armand Carlsen)
1. Irving Jaffee   USA   18:36.5
2. Bernt Evensen   NOR   18.36.6
3. Otto Polacsek   AUT   20:00.9
4. Rudolf Riedl   AUT   20:21.5
5. Keistutis Bulota   LIT   20:22.2
6. Armand Carlsen   NOR   20:56.1
7. Valentine Bialas   USA   21:05.4

Officially, this race never took place. After seven of the ten entrants had completed their heats, the temperature rose suddenly, and the officials in charge ordered the day's times cancelled and the races rerun. By the time a final decision had been reached, the Norwegians, who had already made it clear that they considered Jaffe the champion, had gone home, so the contest was cancelled. As far as the skaters were concerned, the matter had been settled after the first heat, when Jaffe came from behind to nip Evensen just before the finish line. However sports historians generally consider the 1928 10,000 meters to have been a nonevent.

1932 Lake Placid C: 18, N: 6, D: 2.8. WR: 17:17.4 (Armand Carlsen)

1. Irving Jaffee	USA	19:13.6
2. Ivar Ballangrud	NOR	—
3. Frank Stack	CAN	—
4. Edwin Wedge	USA	—
5. Valentine Bialas	USA	—
6. Bernt Evensen	NOR	—
7. Alexander Hurd	CAN	—
8. Edward Schroeder	USA	—

The turmoil that marred the 1932 speed skating culminated in disputes that broke out during the heats of the 10,000 meters. For this contest the North Americans tacked on a rule which required each skater to do his share in setting the pace. After the first heat Alex Hurd, who won the race, as well as Edwin Wedge of the United States and Shozo Ishihara of Japan, were disqualified for not doing their share. In the second heat Frank Stack was disqualified for interference after a protest by Bernt Evensen. After much haggling and many threats it was decided to rerun the two races the following day. Ironically, the same eight men who had originally qualified for the final qualified again. The final race was slow and tactical, as all eight stayed in a bunch until the last lap. Jaffee won by five yards, but the finish was so close that only two yards separated Ballangrud in second place from Evensen in sixth. Bronze medalist Frank Stack was still competing in the Olympics in 1952 when, at the age of 46, he finished 12th in the 500 meters.

1936 Garmisch-Partenkirchen C: 30, N: 14, D: 2.14. WR: 17:17.4 (Armand Carlsen)

1. Ivar Ballangrud	NOR	17:24.3	OR
2. Birger Vasenius	FIN	17:28.2	
3. Max Stiepl	AUT	17:30.0	
4. Charles Mathisen	NOR	17:41.2	
5. Ossi Blomqvist	FIN	17:42.4	
6. Jan Langedijk	HOL	17:43.7	
7. Antero Ojala	FIN	17:46.6	
8. Edward Schroeder	GER	17:52.0	

Ballangrud and Vasenius, paired together, raced neck and neck for 4000 meters before the Norwegian began to pull away. Ballangrud completed his Olympic career with four gold medals, two silver, and one bronze.

1948 St. Moritz C: 27, N: 11, D: 2.3. WR: 17:01.5 (Charles Mathisen)

1. Åke Seyffarth	SWE	17:26.3
2. Lauri Parkkinen	FIN	17:36.0
3. Pentti Lammio	FIN	17:42.7
4. Kornel Pajor	HUN	17:45.6
5. Cornelis "Kees" Broekman	HOL	17:54.7
6. Jan Langedijk	HOL	17:55.3
7. Odd Lundberg	NOR	18:05.8
8. Harry Jansson	SWE	18:08.0

1952 Oslo C: 30, N: 12, D: 2.19. WR: 16:32.6 (Hjalmar Andersen)

1. Hjalmar Andersen	NOR	16:45.8	OR
2. Cornelis "Kees" Broekman	HOL	17:10.6	
3. Carl-Erik Asplund	SWE	17:16.6	
4. Pentti Lammio	FIN	17:20.5	
5. Anton Huiskes	HOL	17:25.5	
6. Sverre Haugli	NOR	17:30.2	
7. Kazuhiko Sugawara	JAP	17:34.0	
8. Lauri Parkkinen	FIN	17:36.8	

Hjalmar "Hjallis" Andersen's unusually large margin of victory, the most decisive in Olympic history, earned him his third gold medal in three days.

1956 Cortina C: 32, N: 15, D: 1.31. WR: 16:32.6 (Hjalmar Andersen)

1. Sigvard Ericsson	SWE	16:35.9	OR
2. Knut Johannesen	NOR	16:36.9	
3. Oleg Goncharenko	SOV	16:42.3	
4. Sverre Haugli	NOR	16:48.7	
5. Cornelis "Kees" Broekman	HOL	16:51.2	
6. Hjalmar Andersen	NOR	16:52.6	
7. Boris Yakimov	SOV	16:59.7	
8. Olof Dahlberg	SWE	17:01.3	

Skating three pairs after Johannesen, 25-year-old woodchopper Sigge Ericsson so exhausted himself keeping ahead of Johannesen's pace that he lost two seconds on the final lap. However he was able to hold on and win anyway.

1960 Squaw Valley C: 30, N: 15, D: 2.27. WR: 16:32.6 (Hjalmar Andersen)

1. Knut Johannesen	NOR	15:46.6	WR
2. Viktor Kosichkin	SOV	15:49.2	
3. Kjell Bäckman	SWE	16:14.2	
4. Ivar Nilsson	SWE	16:26.0	
5. Terence Monaghan	GBR	16:31.6	
6. Torstein Seiersten	NOR	16:33.4	
7. Olof Dahlberg	SWE	16:34.6	
8. Jouko Jarvinen	FIN	16:35.4	

Since February 10, 1952, the world record for 10,000 meters had been Hjallis Andersen's 16:32.6. But with the ice perfect and the weather sunny and calm, five different skaters bettered Andersen's mark. Skating in the second pair, Kjell Bäckman chopped over 18 seconds off the record with a 16:14.2. Two pairs later, Knut Johannesen, a 26-year-old carpenter, became the first person to break the 16-minute barrier with a phenomenal 15:46.6. Johannesen's world record lasted for three years, but it almost didn't survive the rest of the day. Two pairs after Johannesen came Viktor Kosichkin, who stayed ahead of Johannesen's pace for 6400 meters and was still even after 7600 meters. After that, though, Kosichkin began to tire and crossed the finish line 2.6 seconds too late. He did, however, have the rare experience of breaking the world record by more than 43 seconds and earning only a silver medal.

1964 Innsbruck C: 33, N: 19, D: 2.7. WR: 15:33.0 (Jonny Nilsson)

1. Jonny Nilsson	SWE	15:50.1
2. Fred Anton Maier	NOR	16:06.0
3. Knut Johannesen	NOR	16:06.3
4. Rutgerus Liebrechts	HOL	16:08.6
5. Ants Antson	SOV	16:08.7
6. Victor Kosichkin	SOV	16:19.3
7. Gerhard Zimmermann	GER	16:22.5
8. Alfred Malkin	GBR	16:35.2

1968 Grenoble C: 28, N: 13, D: 2.17. WR: 15:20.3 (Fred Anton Maier)

1. Johnny Höglin	SWE	15:23.6	OR
2. Fred Anton Maier	NOR	15:23.9	
3. Örjan Sandler	SWE	15:31.8	
4. Per-Willy Guttormsen	NOR	15:32.6	
5. Cornelis "Kees" Verkerk	HOL	15:33.9	
6. Jonny Nilsson	SWE	15:39.6	
7. Magne Thomassen	NOR	15:44.9	
8. Petrus Nottet	HOL	15:54.7	

Höglin, who had never before gone faster than 15:40, was one of the surprise winners of the 1968 Winter Games. Maier had the advantage of skating first, but Höglin, in the seventh pair, moved ahead of Maier's pace with three of 25 laps to go.

1972 Sapporo C: 24, N: 14, D: 2.7. WR: 14:55.9 (Adrianus "Ard" Schenk)

1. Adrianus "Ard" Schenk	HOL	15:01.35	OR
2. Cornelis "Kees" Verkerk	HOL	15:04.70	
3. Sten Stensen	NOR	15:07.08	
4. Jan Bols	HOL	15:17.99	
5. Valery Lavrouchkin	SOV	15:20.08	
6. Göran Claesson	SWE	15:30.19	
7. Kimmo Koskinen	FIN	15:38.87	
8. Gerhard Zimmermann	GER	15:43.92	

Handsome Ard Schenk won his third gold medal to match the single Olympics record of Ivar Ballangrud and Hjalmar "Hjallis" Andersen. Two weeks later in Norway, Schenk became the first person in 60 years to sweep all four events at the world championships. The last person to achieve the feat had been Oscar Mathisen in 1912.

1976 Innsbruck C: 20, N: 13, D: 2.14. WR: 14:50.31 (Sten Stensen)

1. Piet Kleine	HOL	14:50.59	OR
2. Sten Stensen	NOR	14:53.30	
3. Hans van Helden	HOL	15:02.02	
4. Victor Varlamov	SOV	15:06.06	
5. Örjan Sandler	SWE	15:16.21	
6. Colin Coates	AUS	15:16.80	
7. Daniel Carroll	USA	15:19.29	
8. Franz Krienbuhl	SWI	15:36.43	

Stenson had set a world record of 14:50.31 three weeks earlier. In Innsbruck, skating sixth, he was able to do only 14:53.30. Two pairs later, Piet Kleine, a 6-foot 5-inch 24-year-old unemployed carpenter, attacked Stenson's pace in steady fashion. He moved ahead at the halfway mark and stayed at least two seconds faster for the last eight laps.

1980 Lake Placid C: 25, N: 12, D: 2.23. WR: 14:34.33 (Viktor Leskin)

1. Eric Heiden	USA	14:28.13	WR
2. Piet Kleine	HOL	14:36.03	
3. T. Erik Oxholm	NOR	14:36.60	
4. Michael Woods	USA	14:39.53	
5. Öyvind Tveter	NOR	14:43.53	
6. Hilbert van der Duim	HOL	14:47.58	
7. Viktor Leskin	SOV	14:51.72	
8. Andreas Ehrig	GDR	14:51.94	

Having already become the first male speed skater to win four gold medals in one Olympics, Eric Heiden took the night off before his final race to attend the United States-U.S.S.R. ice hockey match. The U.S. team included two friends of Heiden's from Madison, Wisconsin, Mark Johnson and Bobby Suter. Heiden was so excited by the U.S. victory—more excited than by his own accomplishments—that he had trouble falling asleep and ended up oversleeping in the morning. Snatching a few pieces of bread for breakfast, he rushed to the track and, skating in the second pair, calmly broke the world record by over six seconds. He had become the first person in Olympic history to win five individual gold medals at one games (three of Mark Spitz's seven gold medals had been in relay events). Repelled by the instant celebrity that followed his feats, Eric Heiden announced that he would retire at the end of the season. "Maybe if things had stayed the way they were," he told the press, "and I could still be obscure in an obscure sport, I might want to keep skating. I really liked it best when I was a nobody."

Discontinued Events
FOUR RACES COMBINED EVENT
1924 Chamonix C: 22, N: 9, D: 1.27.

		PTS.
1. A. Clas Thunberg	FIN	5.5
2. Roald Larsen	NOR	9.5
3. Julius Skutnabb	FIN	11
4. Sigurd Moen	NOR	17
4. Harald Ström	NOR	17
6. Léon Quaglia	FRA	25
7. Alberts Rumba	LAT	27
8. Leon Jucewicz	POL	32

The concept of an all-around champion continued to be a matter of major importance in world championships, but was never included again in the Olympics.

SPEED SKATING

WOMEN

500 METERS

1924–1956 not held

1960 Squaw Valley C: 23, N: 10, D: 2.20. WR: 45.6 (Tamara Rylova)
1. Helga Haase	GDR	45.9
2. Natalia Donchenko	SOV	46.0
3. Jeanne Ashworth	USA	46.1
4. Tamara Rylova	SOV	46.2
5. Hatsue Takamizawa	JAP	46.6
6. Klara Guseva	SOV	46.8
6. Elwira Seroczyńska	POL	46.8
8. Fumie Hama	JAP	47.4

1964 Innsbruck C: 28, N: 14, D: 1.30. WR: 44.9 (Inga Voronina)
1. Lydia Skoblikova	SOV	45.0	OR
2. Irina Yegorova	SOV	45.4	
3. Tatiana Sidorova	SOV	45.5	
4. Jeanne Ashworth	USA	46.2	
4. Janice Smith	USA	46.2	
6. Gunilla Jacobsson	SWE	46.5	
7. Janice Lawler	USA	46.6	
8. Helga Haase	GDR	47.2	

On January 27, 1962, Inga Voronina of the U.S.S.R. set world records for the 500 meters and 1500 meters. The next day she broke the world record at 3000 meters. However, the following year it was another Soviet skater, Lydia Skoblikova, a teacher from Chelyabinsk, who won the gold medal for all four distances at the world championships in Karuizawa, Japan. Voronina, not fully recovered from a bad stomach ailment, failed to make the Soviet Olympic team in 1964. Skoblikova, on the other hand, entered the competition as the favorite in three of the four events. Only in the 500 meters, the first distance to be contested, was

she expected to have a tough time. Yegorova opened the day with a 45.4 This held up as the best time until Skoblikova, skating in the 13th of 14 pairs, zipped past the finish line in 45.0. Before the week was out she had duplicated her world championship feat by sweeping all four women's events.

1968 Grenoble C: 28, N: 11, D: 2.9. WR: 44.7 (Tatiana Sidorova)
1. Lyudmila Titova	SOV	46.1
2. Jennifer Fish	USA	46.3
2. Dianne Holum	USA	46.3
2. Mary Meyers	USA	46.3
5. Elisabeth van den Brom	HOL	46.6
6. Kaija Mustonen	FIN	46.7
6. Sigrid Sundby	NOR	46.7
8. Kirsti Biermann	NOR	46.8

On February 3, Tatiana Sidorova set a world record of 44.7, but six days later in Grenoble she could do no better than 46.9 and finished in a tie for ninth place. The unusual triple American tie for second place was accomplished by Mary Meyers of St. Paul, Minnesota (the day before her 22nd birthday), 16-year-old Dianne Holum of Northbrook, Illinois, and 18-year-old Jennifer Fish of Strongville, Ohio.

1972 Sapporo C: 29, N: 12, D: 2.10. WR: 42.5 (Anne Henning)
1. Anne Henning	USA	43.33	OR
2. Vera Krasnova	SOV	44.01	
3. Lyudmila Titova	SOV	44.45	
4. Sheila Young	USA	44.53	
5. Monika Pflug	GER	44.75	
6. Atje Keulen-Deelstra	HOL	44.89	
7. Kay Lunda	USA	44.95	
8. Alla Boutova	SOV	45.17	

Sixteen-year-old Anne Henning of Northbrook, Illinois, the world record holder and heavy favorite, was paired against Canada's Sylvia Burka, who had impaired vision in one eye. At the crossover Burka didn't see Henning and headed toward a collision. Rather than push her way past Burka, Henning stood up, let her pass, and then dug in faster than ever. Despite losing a full second because of the mishap (which caused Burka's disqualification), Henning still won the gold medal with a time of 43.70. The officials allowed her another run at the end of the competition and she improved to 43.33. Henning was undoubtedly aided by her superstitious mother, who watched the race while holding a clutch of good-luck charms, including a four-leaf clover, Japanese beads, a Christmas ornament, and two U.S. flags. Afterward Henning told reporters, "I just can't wait to be normal again. But, you know, I suppose people will never really let me be normal again, will they?"

1976 Innsbruck C: 27, N: 13, D: 2.6. WR: 40.91 (Sheila Young)
1. Sheila Young   USA   42.76   OR
2. Cathy Priestner   CAN   43.12
3. Tatiana Averina   SOV   43.17
4. Leah Poulos   USA   43.21
5. Vera Krasnova   SOV   43.23
6. Lyubov Sachikova   SOV   43.80
7. Makiko Nagaya   JAP   43.88
8. Paula Halonen   FIN   43.99

Sheila Young won a complete set of medals at the 1976 Games, the first U.S. athlete to win three medals at a single Winter Olympics.

1980 Lake Placid C: 31, N: 15, D: 2.15. WR: 40.68 (Sheila Young)
1. Karin Enke   GDR   41.78   OR
2. Leah Mueller (Poulos) USA   42.26
3. Natalia Petruseva   SOV   42.42
4. Ann-Sofie Järnström   SWE   42.47
5. Makiko Nagaya   JAP   42.70
6. Cornelia Jacob   GDR   42.98
7. Beth Heiden   USA   43.18
8. Tatiana Tarasova   SOV   43.26

Eighteen-year-old Karin Enke was practically unknown in speed skating circles until a week before the Olympics, when she won the world sprint championship in West Allis, Wisconsin, after qualifying for the East German team as an alternate. She showed that her victory was no fluke when she took the Olympic gold medal at Lake Placid.

1000 METERS

1924–1956 not held

1960 Squaw Valley C: 22, N: 10, D: 2.22. WR: 1:33.4 (Tamara Rylova)
1. Klara Guseva   SOV   1:34.1
2. Helga Haase   GDR   1:34.3
3. Tamara Rylova   SOV   1:34.8
4. Lydia Skoblikova   SOV   1:35.3
5. Helena Pilejczyk   POL   1:35.8
5. Hatsue Takamizawa   JAP   1:35.8
7. Fumie Hama   JAP   1:36.1
8. Jeanne Ashworth   USA   1:36.5

Elwira Seroczyńska of Poland had the fastest time going into the final curve, but with 100 meters to go, one of her skates hit the dividing line, and she fell.

1964 Innsbruck C: 28, N: 13, D: 2.1. WR: 1:31.8 (Lydia Skoblikova)
1. Lydia Skoblikova   SOV   1:33.2   OR
2. Irina Yegorova   SOV   1:34.3
3. Kaija Mustonen   FIN   1:34.8
4. Helga Haase   GDR   1:35.7
5. Valentina Stenina   SOV   1:36.0
6. Gunilla Jacobsson   SWE   1:36.5
7. Janice Smith   USA   1:36.7
8. Kaija-Lisa Keskivitikka   FIN   1:37.6

With this race Skoblikova became the first woman to win three gold medals at one Winter Olympics and the first person of either sex to win five Winter gold medals.

1968 Grenoble C: 29, N: 12, D: 2.11. WR: 1:31.8 (Lydia Skoblikova)
1. Carolina Geijssen   HOL   1:32.6   OR
2. Lyudmila Titova   SOV   1:32.9
3. Dianne Holum   USA   1:33.4
4. Kaija Mustonen   FIN   1:33.6
5. Irina Egorova   SOV   1:34.4
6. Sigrid Sundby   NOR   1:34.5
7. Jeanne Ashworth   USA   1:34.7
8. Kaija-Lisa Keskivitikka   FIN   1:34.8

Geijssen was a 21-year-old Amsterdam secretary who skated to work each day. She was the first Dutch skater to win an Olympic gold medal.

1972 Sapporo C: 33, N: 12, D: 2.11. WR: 1:27.3 (Anne Henning)
1. Monika Pflug   GER   1:31.40   OR
2. Atje Keulen-Deelstra   HOL   1:31.61
3. Anne Henning   USA   1:31.62
4. Lyudmila Titova   SOV   1:31.85
5. Nina Statkevitch   SOV   1:32.21
6. Dianne Holum   USA   1:32.41
7. Elly van den Brom   HOL   1:32.60
8. Sylvia Burka   CAN   1:32.95

Seventeen-year-old Monika Pflug was a surprise winner. A bookbinding apprentice from Munich, she false-started twice. Threatened with disqualification if she jumped the gun again, she started slowly, but was able to make up lost time after the first 200 meters.

1976 Innsbruck C: 27, N: 10, D: 2.7. WR: 1:23.46 (Tatiana Averina)
1. Tatiana Averina   SOV   1:28.43   OR
2. Leah Poulos   USA   1:28.57
3. Sheila Young   USA   1:29.14
4. Sylvia Burka   CAN   1:29.47
5. Monika Holzner (Pflug)   GER   1:29.54
6. Cathy Priestner   CAN   1:29.66
7. Lyudmila Titova   SOV   1:30.06
8. Heike Lange   GDR   1:30.55

1980 Lake Placid C: 37, N: 16 D: 2.17. WR: 1:23.46 (Tatiana Averina)

1. Natalia Petruseva — SOV 1:24.10 OR
2. Leah Mueller (Poulos) — USA 1:25.41
3. Silvia Albrecht — GDR 1:26.46
4. Karin Enke — GDR 1:26.66
5. Beth Heiden — USA 1:27.01
6. Annie Borckink — HOL 1:27.24
7. Sylvia Burka — CAN 1:27.50
8. Ann-Sofie Järnström — SWE 1:28.10

Petruseva and Mueller were the second pair to skate. Mueller was ahead at 200 meters, but Petruseva took the lead and eventually pulled away to win by 40 feet. For Mueller, it was her third Olympic silver medal. A couple of weeks earlier, Petruseva had won the world sprint championship in Norway, but then had taken seven hours to produce a urine sample, leading to rumors that she had taken illegal drugs. Suspicions seemed confirmed when she finished only eighth in the 1500 meters, the opening Olympic event. But after taking the bronze medal in the 500 meters, she won the 1000 meters and passed the urine test for drugs without any problems. Part of the Soviet success in speed skating has to be due to the fact that, as of 1980, there were 1202 Olympic-size speed skating rinks in the U.S.S.R., whereas in the United States, a nation of comparable population, there were only two.

1500 METERS

1924–1956 not held

1960 Squaw Valley C: 23, N: 10, D: 2.21. WR: 2:25.5 (Khalida Schegoleeva)

1. Lydia Skoblikova — SOV 2:25.2 WR
2. Elwira Seroczyńska — POL 2:25.7
3. Helena Pilejczyk — POL 2:27.1
4. Klara Guseva — SOV 2:28.7
5. Valentina Stenina — SOV 2:29.2
6. Iris Sihvonen — FIN 2:29.7
7. Christina Scherling — SWE 2:31.5
8. Helga Haase — GDR 2:31.7

This was the first of Skoblikova's six career gold medals.

1964 Innsbruck C: 30, N: 14, D: 1.31. WR: 2:19.0 (Inga Voronina)

1. Lydia Skoblikova — SOV 2:22.6 OR
2. Kaija Mustonen — FIN 2:25.5
3. Berta Kolokoltseva — SOV 2:27.1
4. Song-Soon Kim — PRK 2:27.7
5. Helga Haase — GDR 2:28.6
6. Christina Scherling — SWE 2:29.4
7. Valentina Stenina — SOV 2:29.9
8. Kaija-Lisa Keskivitikka — FIN 2:30.0

1968 Grenoble C: 30, N: 13, D: 2.10. WR: 2:19.0 (Inga Artamonova [Voronina])

1. Kaija Mustonen — FIN 2:22.4 OR
2. Carolina Geijssen — HOL 2:22.7
3. Christina Kaiser — HOL 2:24.5
4. Sigrid Sundby — NOR 2:25.2
5. Lasma Kaouniste — SOV 2:25.4
6. Kaija-Lisa Keskivitikka — FIN 2:25.8
7. Lyudmila Titova — SOV 2:26.8
8. Ruth Schleiermacher — GDR 2:27.1

Defending champion Lydia Skoblikova finished 11th, while future champion Dianne Holum was 13th.

1972 Sapporo C: 31, N: 12, D: 2.9. WR: 2:15.8 (Christina Baas-Kaiser)

1. Dianne Holum — USA 2:20.85 OR
2. Christina Baas-Kaiser — HOL 2:21.05
3. Atje Keulen-Deelstra — HOL 2:22.05
4. Elisabeth van den Brom — HOL 2:22.27
5. Rosemarie Taupadel — GDR 2:22.35
6. Nina Statkevitch — SOV 2:23.19
7. Connie Carpenter — USA 2:23.93
8. Sigrid Sundby — NOR 2:24.07

As a 16-year-old in 1968, Dianne Holum had won a silver medal in the 500 meters and a bronze in the 1000. In 1972 she added a gold in the 1500 meters and a silver in the 3000. The success of the Dutch system of training was shown not only by the fact that Dutch skaters finished second, third, and fourth, but by the fact that Dianne Holum used a Dutch coach as well. The following year she took on a young pupil of her own—14-year-old Eric Heiden—and coached him all the way to the 1976 and 1980 Olympics.

1976 Innsbruck C: 26, N: 12, D: 2.5. WR: 2:09.90 (Tatiana Averina)

1. Galina Stepanskaya — SOV 2:16.58 OR
2. Sheila Young — USA 2:17.06
3. Tatiana Averina — SOV 2:17.96
4. Lisbeth Korsmo — NOR 2:18.99
5. Karin Kessow — GDR 2:19.05
6. Leah Poulos — USA 2:19.11
7. Ines Bautzmann — GDR 2:19.63
8. Erwina Ryś — POL 2:19.69

1980 Lake Placid C: 31, N: 14, D: 2.14. WR: 2:07.18 (Halida Vorobieva)

1. Annie Borckink — HOL 2:10.95 OR
2. Ria Visser — HOL 2:12.35
3. Sabine Becker — GDR 2:12.38
4. Bjorg Eva Jensen — NOR 2:12.59
5. Sylvia Filipsson — SWE 2:12.84
6. Andrea Mitscherlich — GDR 2:13.05
7. Beth Heiden — USA 2:13.10
8. Natalia Petruseva — SOV 2:14.15

Borckink, a 28-year-old nursing student, had never before finished in the top three in an international meet.

3000 METERS

1924–1956 not held

1960 Squaw Valley C: 20, N: 10, D: 2.23. WR: 5:13.8 (Rimma Zukova)
1. Lydia Skoblikova   SOV   5:14.3
2. Valentina Stenina   SOV   5:16.9
3. Eevi Huttunen   FIN   5:21.0
4. Hatsue Takamizawa   JAP   5:21.4
5. Christina Scherling   SWE   5:25.5
6. Helena Pilejczyk   POL   5:26.2
7. Elwira Seroczyńska   POL   5:27.3
8. Jeanne Ashworth   USA   5:28.5

1964 Innsbruck C: 28, N: 13, D: 2.2. WR: 5:06.0 (Inga Voronina)
1. Lydia Skoblikova   SOV   5:14.9
2. Pil-Hwa Han   PRK   5:18.5
2. Valentina Stenina   SOV   5:18.5
4. Klara Nesterova (Guseva)   SOV   5:22.5
5. Kaija Mustonen   FIN   5:24.3
6. Hatsue Nagakubo   JAP   5:25.4
7. Song-Soon Kim   KOR   5:25.9
8. Doreen McCannel   CAN   5:26.4

With this race Lydia Skoblikova became the first person to win four gold medals in a single Winter Olympics and the first to win six gold medals all together. Further excitement was caused by the last skater, tiny Pil-Hwa Han, a previously unknown North Korean who kept up Skoblikova's pace for four of the seven laps before falling back to a tie for second place.

1968 Grenoble C: 26, N: 12, D: 2.12. WR: 4:54.6 (Christina Kaiser)
1. Johanna Schut   HOL   4:56.2   OR
2. Kaija Mustonen   FIN   5:01.0
3. Christina Kaiser   HOL   5:01.3
4. Kaija-Lisa Keskivitikka   FIN   5:03.9
5. Wilhelmina Burgmeijer   HOL   5:05.1
6. Lydia Skoblikova   SOV   5:08.0
7. Christina Lindblom   SWE   5:09.8
8. Anna Sablina   SOV   5:12.5

1972 Sapporo C: 22, N: 10, D: 2.12. WR: 4:46.5 (Christina Baas-Kaiser)
1. Christina Baas-Kaiser   HOL   4:52.14   OR
2. Dianne Holum   USA   4:58.67
3. Atje Keulen-Deelstra   HOL   4:59.91
4. Sippie Tigelaar   HOL   5:01.67
5. Nina Statkevitch   SOV   5:01.79
6. Kapitolina Sereguina   SOV   5:01.88
7. Tuula Vilkas   FIN   5:05.92
8. Lyudmila Savroulina   SOV   5:06.61

After the race, the two Dutch medalists, both of whom were 33 years old, were asked by a reporter if they were planning to retire. Baas-Kaiser replied, "What's the matter, don't we skate fast enough?"

1976 Innsbruck C: 26, N: 12, D: 2.8. WR: 4:44.69 (Tamara Kuznyetsova)
1. Tatiana Averina   SOV   4:45.19   OR
2. Andrea Mitscherlich   GDR   4:45.23
3. Lisbeth Korsmo   NOR   4:45.24
4. Karin Kessow   GDR   4:45.60
5. Ines Bautzmann   GDR   4:46.67
6. Sylvia Filipsson   SWE   4:48.15
7. Nancy Swider   USA   4:48.46
8. Sylvia Burka   CAN   4:49.04

If the top three skaters had actually been on the ice at the same time, only 16 inches would have separated them at the finish.

1980 Lake Placid C: 29, N: 14, D: 2.20. WR: 4:31.00 (Galina Stepanskaya)
1. Bjorg Eva Jensen   NOR   4:32.13   OR
2. Sabine Becker   GDR   4:32.79
3. Beth Heiden   USA   4:33.77
4. Andrea Mitscherlich   GDR   4:37.69
5. Erwina Ryś-Ferens   POL   4:37.89
6. Mary Docter   USA   4:39.29
7. Sylvia Filipsson   SWE   4:40.22
8. Natalia Petruseva   SOV   4:42.59

ALPINE SKIING

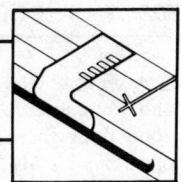

MEN
DOWNHILL

The first downhill race was held in Montana, Switzerland, in 1911. It was organized by an Englishman, Arnold Lunn, who also invented the modern slalom in 1922 and was the main force in obtaining Olympic recognition for alpine skiing in 1936.

Of the 27 medals which have been awarded in the men's downhill race, 26 have gone to Western Europeans; of these, ten went to Austria, six to France, and five to Switzerland.

1924–1932 not held

1948 St. Moritz C: 112, N: 25, D: 2.2.
1. Henri Oreiller   FRA   2:55.0
2. Franz Gabl   AUT   2:59.1
3. Karl Molitor   SWI   3:00.3
3. Rolf Olinger   SWI   3:00.3
5. Egon Schöpf   AUT   3:01.2
6. Silvio Alverà   ITA   3:02.4
6. Carlo Gartner   ITA   3:02.4
8. Fernand Grosjean   SWI   3:03.1

A member of the French underground during World War II, Henri Oreiller was a cocky, clowning fellow who warned the other skiers he was so confident of victory that they needn't bother racing against him. He careened down the two-mile course like an acrobat, flying over bumps without caution and then regaining his balance in midair.

1952 Oslo–Norefjell C: 81, N: 27, D: 2.16.
1. Zeno Colò   ITA   2:30.8
2. Othmar Schneider   AUT   2:32.0
3. Christian Pravda   AUT   2:32.4
4. Fredy Rubi   SWI   2:32.5
5. William Beck   USA   2:33.3
6. Stein Eriksen   NOR   2:33.8
7. Gunnar Hjeltnes   NOR   2:35.9
8. Carlo Gartner   ITA   2:36.5

Zeno Colò was a colorful 31-year-old restaurant owner from Tuscany, whose form on the slopes was almost as unorthodox as that of Oreiller.

1956 Cortina C: 75, N: 27, D: 2.3.
1. Anton Sailer   AUT   2:52.2
2. Raymond Fellay   SWI   2:55.7
3. Andreas Molterer   AUT   2:56.2
4. Roger Staub   SWI   2:57.1
5. Hans-Peter Lanig   GER   2:59.8
6. Gino Burrini   ITA   3:00.2
7. Kurt Hennrich   CZE   3:01.5
8. Charles Bozon   FRA   3:01.9

Toni Sailer had already won the giant slalom and the slalom and was confident of completing his alpine sweep, since he held the course record of 2:46.2 for the downhill. However, as he tightened the straps that tied his boots to his skis, one of the straps broke. "That had never happened to me before," he later wrote. "I had not even thought it possible that such straps could break and had therefore not taken along a spare." It was almost his turn to race. If he couldn't find a strap, he would have to withdraw. Unfortunately, the problem was so rare that none of the other skiers had brought along spare straps either. Then Hansl Senger, the trainer of the Italian team, walked by and noticed the Austrians in panic. Senger immediately took the straps from his own bindings and handed them to Sailer. Strong winds and a glassy course prevented 28 of the 75 starters from reaching the finish line, and sent eight men to the hospital. But Sailer was able to survive one near spill and complete the course three and a half seconds faster than anyone else.

After the victory ceremony, Sailer joined his parents and, holding his three gold medals in his hand, said, "It's a good thing there are three medals. One for you, Father, one for you, Mother. Then there is a third one for me." Sailer later became an actor and singer, and then went into business as a hotel owner and an investor in a textile company.

1960 Squaw Valley C: 63, N: 21, D: 2.22.

1.	Jean Vuarnet	FRA	2:06.0
2.	Hans-Peter Lanig	GER	2:06.5
3.	Guy Périllat	FRA	2:06.9
4.	Willy Forrer	SWI	2:07.8
5.	Roger Staub	SWI	2:08.9
6.	Bruno Alberti	ITA	2:09.1
7.	Karl Schranz	AUT	2:09.2
8.	Charles Bozon	FRA	2:09.6

In 1960 the downhill race was postponed for three days because of heavy snow. Vuarnet was the first Olympic gold medalist to use metal skis and no wax.

1964 Innsbruck C: 84, N: 27, D: 1.30.

1.	Egon Zimmermann	AUT	2:18.16
2.	Leo Lacroix	FRA	2:18.90
3.	Wolfgang Bartels	GER	2:19.48
4.	Joos Minsch	SWI	2:19.54
5.	Ludwig Leitner	GER	2:19.67
6.	Guy Périllat	FRA	2:19.79
7.	Gerhard Nenning	AUT	2:19.98
8.	Willi Favre	SWI	2:20.23

The downhill competition was held under a cloud of gloom following the death of 19-year-old Ross Milne of Australia, who was killed during a practice run on January 25 when he flew off the course and smashed into a tree. Twenty-four-year-old Egon Zimmermann was the third alpine gold medalist to come from Lech, a hamlet of less than 200 people which had been converted to a ski resort following World War II. Also from Lech were Othmar Schneider, the 1952 slalom winner, and Trude Beiser, who won the women's downhill the same year.

1968 Grenoble–Chamrousse C: 86, N: 29, D: 2.9.

1.	Jean-Claude Killy	FRA	1:59.85
2.	Guy Périllat	FRA	1:59.93
3.	John-Daniel Dätwyler	SWI	2:00.32
4.	Heinrich Messner	AUT	2:01.03
5.	Karl Schranz	AUT	2:01.89
6.	Ivo Mahlknecht	ITA	2:02.00
7.	Gerhard Prinzing	GER	2:02.10
8.	Bernard Orcel	FRA	2:02.22

Jean-Claude Killy grew up in the resort village of Val d'Isère in the French Savoy Alps. His love of danger worried his parents, but his father encouraged his sporting endeavors anyway. Killy dropped out of school at the age of 16 in order to join the French ski team, and soon became known for his fun-loving attitude. Once he entered a ski-jump competition in Wengen, Switzerland, and caused a sensation by dropping his pants after takeoff and finishing his jump in longjohns. Apparently he dropped his pants in other places as well, since he also contracted VD in Sun Valley and was named in a paternity suit in Austria. He was declared innocent. While serving with the French Army in Algeria, Killy contracted amoebic parasitosis, but he regained his health sufficiently to qualify for the 1964 French Olympic team in all three alpine events. At Innsbruck he placed fifth in the giant slalom, but failed to finish the downhill and slalom. Killy started to pick up speed after the 1964 Olympics, however, and by 1967 he was on top of the world. During the 1966–67 season he won 12 of 16 World Cup meets, and the following summer he won a sports car race in Sicily. Despite some troubles at the start of the 1967–68 season, Killy went to the 1968 Olympics confident of victory.

There was certainly a lot of pressure on Killy to win in Grenoble. French fans were anxious for him to duplicate the 1952 triple-gold performance of Austria's Toni Sailer. In addition, a huge Jean-Claude Killy industry was waiting to spring into production if Killy won three gold medals. Ski-makers, boot-makers, binding-makers, glove-makers, and others were ready with fat contracts for Killy's product endorsements, which he had already been giving out as readily as he could within the restrictions set up by the International Ski Federation. But these restrictions weren't good enough for I.O.C. President Avery Brundage. Shortly before the games, Killy signed a contract with an Italian ski pole manufacturer. The International Ski Federation informed Killy that the contract violated the rules of amateurism, so Killy backed off, whereupon the ski pole manufacturer threatened to sue him. The French Ski Federation and the French Sports Ministry undertook hasty negotiations with the Italian ski pole manufacturer in an attempt to settle the issue before the Olympics. "Payments for damages"—sums never revealed—satisfied the Italians.

Brundage demanded that all trade names and trademarks be removed from the skis used by competitiors in the 1968 Olympics. The International Ski Federation, the team managers, and the skiers themselves rejected the ban, claiming that the entire sport of alpine skiing was dependent on the financial support of ski-makers. On the eve of the Games an awkward compromise was reached whereby the skiers would be allowed to keep the trade names and trademarks on their skis, but their skis would be taken away from them before they could be photographed. The policemen in charge of this unpleasant task were particularly on edge when Jean-Claude Killy, the favorite, shot down the slopes as the 14th contestant in the opening alpine race—the downhill. Killy slashed across the finish line eight one-hundredths of a second faster than his teammate, yoga practitioner Guy Périllat. Immediately, Michel Arpin, Killy's friend and adviser, rushed out and embraced Killy, making sure that the photographers got a good view of the pouch on his back, which was emblazoned with the word "Dynamic," the brand of skis that Killy used, and his gloves, which bore the Dynamic trademark—two yellow bars. When a policeman, surrounded by a horde of photographers, confiscated Killy's skis, Michel Arpin took one of his own skis and planted it in the snow so that the two yellow bars on the tip were right next to Killy's head.

Eventually Killy gave up competitive skiing and traveled to the United States, where he signed commercial contracts with Chevrolet, United Air Lines, Bristol-Myers, *Ladies' Home Journal*, Head Skis, Lange boots, Mighty Mac sportswear, Wolverine gloves and after-ski boots, and numerous other companies.

1972 Sapporo–Eniwadake C: 55, N: 20, D: 2.7.

1. Bernhard Russi	SWI	1:51.43
2. Roland Collombin	SWE	1:52.07
3. Heinrich Messner	AUT	1:52.40
4. Andreas Sprecher	SWI	1:53.11
5. Erik Håker	NOR	1:53.16
6. Walter Tresch	SWI	1:53.19
7. Karl Cordin	AUT	1:53.32
8. Robert Cochran	USA	1:53.39

Most people in the sports world breathed a sigh of relief when Avery Brundage announced that he would retire after the completion of the 1972 Olympics. But the 84-year-old Brundage decided to go out with a bang by staging one final attack against commercialism in alpine skiing. Although he considered at least 30 or 40 skiers to be in violation of the rules of amateurism, Brundage chose to concentrate his attack on Austrian hero Karl Schranz, who was reputedly earning at least $40,000 to $50,000 a year as a "tester and designer" for various ski product manufacturers. Schranz was not alone in receiving such income, but he had also committed the crime of being outspoken in his criticism of Brundage.

Karl Schranz was the son of a poor railway worker in St. Anton in the Arlberg Mountains. His father died of work-related tuberculosis at an early age. In 1962 Schranz won the world downhill and combined championships and in 1964 he earned a silver medal in the Olympic giant slalom. In 1968 he appeared to have won the Olympic slalom until his disqualification for missing a gate was announced. By 1972 he had won every honor that is offered in international alpine skiing—except an Olympic gold medal. The 33-year-old Schranz delayed his retirement in the hope of achieving that final goal. But three days before the opening of the Sapporo Games, Avery Brundage got his way, and the I.O.C. voted 28–14 to ban Schranz from participating in the Olympics. Austrian Olympic officials announced that their ski team would withdraw from the games, but the Austrian skiers decided to compete anyway. While Brundage accused the alpine skiers of being "trained seals of the merchandisers," Schranz told the press, "If Mr. Brundage had been poor, as I was, and as were many other athletes, I wonder if he wouldn't have a different attitude. . . . If we followed Mr. Brundage's recommendations to their true end, then the Olympics would be a competi-

tion only for the very rich. No man of ordinary means could ever afford to excel in his sport."

When Schranz returned to Vienna he was met by 100,000 Austrian supporters and treated to a tickertape parade. It was the largest demonstration in Austria since World War II. Because Brundage was an American (he was known in Austria as "the senile millionaire from Chicago"), the U.S. embassy in Vienna was subjected to bomb threats and protests. The hypocrisy of the I.O.C.'s decision against Schranz was shown by the fact that the eventual downhill gold medalist, Bernhard Russi, had allowed his photo and name to be used on matchboxes, car stickers, and newspaper advertisements as part of a large-scale pre-Olympic publicity campaign for a Swiss insurance company. Karl Schranz announced his retirement from competitive skiing as soon as the 1972 Olympics had ended.

1976 Innsbruck C: 74, N: 27, D: 2.5.

1. Franz Klammer	AUT	1:45.73
2. Bernhard Russi	SWI	1:46.06
3. Herbert Plank	ITA	1:46.59
4. Philippe Roux	SWI	1:46.69
5. Ken Read	CAN	1:46.83
6. Andy Mill	USA	1:47.06
7. Walter Tresch	SWI	1:47.29
8. David Irwin	CAN	1:47.41

In 1975 Franz Klammer of Mooswald in Carinthia won eight of nine World Cup downhill races. When the Olympics came to Innsbruck the following year there was great pressure on the 22-year-old Klammer as an Austrian favorite competing in Austria. Further pressure was exerted by defending champion Bernhard Russi, who sped down the 3145-meter (1.95 miles) Olympic hill in 1:46.06. The 15th starter of the day, Klammer fell one-fifth of a second off Russi's pace, but fought back wildly in the last 1000 meters to nip Russi by one-third second. Flushed with excitement, Klammer told repeorters, "I thought I was going to crash all the way. . . . Now I've got everything. I don't need anything else."

1980 Lake Placid C: 47, N: 22, D: 2.14.

1. Leonhard Stock	AUT	1:45.50
2. Peter Wirnsberger	AUT	1:46.12
3. Steve Podborski	CAN	1:46.62
4. Peter Müller	SWI	1:46.75
5. Pete Patterson	USA	1:47.04
6. Herbert Plank	ITA	1:47.13
7. Werner Grissmann	AUT	1:47.21
8. Valery Tsyganov	SOV	1:47.34

The Austrian alpine team was so strong that they had seven men ranked in the top 20 in the world. When it was decided to leave Franz Klammer behind, team manager Karl "Downhill Charlie" Kahr had to explain the decision on national television. Leonhard Stock, who had broken a collarbone in December, was chosen to go to Lake Placid as an alternate. But when he recorded the fastest times in two of the three pre-Olympic trial runs, Austrian alpine officials changed their minds and declared that Stock was now a starter, along with Harti Weirather, but that the other three Austrians—Wirnsberger, Grissman, and Sepp Walcher—would have to have a race-off for the final two spots. Walcher lost out. The four remaining Austrians all placed in the top nine, as Leonhard Stock went from being an alternate who had never won a World Cup downhill to being an Olympic champion in less than 30 hours.

SLALOM

Whereas the downhill requires pure speed, the slalom (or "special slalom") is more a test of control. Each skier is required to weave in and out of blue- and red-flagged double poles, or "gates." There are two runs on different courses. Times for the two runs are added to determine final places.

1924–1936 not held

1948 St. Moritz C: 76, N: 22, D: 2.5.
1. Edi Reinalter   SWI   2:10.3
2. James Couttet   FRA   2:10.8
3. Henri Oreiller   FRA   2:12.8
4. Silvio Alverà   ITA   2:13.2
5. Olle Dahlman   SWE   2:13.6
6. Egon Schöpf   AUT   2:14.2
7. Jack Reddish   USA   2:15.5
8. Karl Molitor   SWI   2:16.2

Alverà led after the first run, followed by Couttet, Reinalter, and Oreiller. Reinalter's second run of 1:02.6 was a half second faster than the next best skier, Egon Schöpf.

1952 Oslo C: 86, N: 27, D: 2.19.
1. Othmar Schneider   AUT   2:00.0
2. Stein Eriksen   NOR   2:01.2
3. Guttorm Berge   NOR   2:01.7
4. Zeno Colò   ITA   2:01.8
5. Stig Sollander   SWE   2:02.6
6. James Couttet   FRA   2:02.8
7. Fredy Rubi   SWI   2:03.3
8. Per Rollum   NOR   2:04.5

The fastest time of the first run, 59.2, was first posted by Stein Eriksen, who had won the giant slalom four days earlier, and then equaled by Hans Senger of Austria. Downhill silver medalist Othmar Schneider was third in 59.5. The second run saw Senger fall, while Schneider's 1:00.5 was beaten only by Fredy Rubi's 59.7. Antoin Miliordos of Greece, disgusted by the fact that he fell 18 times, sat down and crossed the finish line backward. His time for one run was 26.9 seconds slower than Schneider's time for two runs.

1956 Cortina C: 89, N: 29, D: 1.31.
1. Anton Sailer   AUT   3:14.7
2. Chiharu Igaya   JAP   3:18.7
3. Stig Sollander   SWE   3:20.2
4. Joseph Brooks Dodge   USA   3:21.8
5. Georges Schneider   SWI   3:22.6
6. Gérard Pasquier   FRA   3:24.6
7. Charles Bozon   FRA   3:26.2
8. Bernard Perret   FRA   3:26.3

Sailer recorded the fastest times in both runs and won his second gold medal.

1960 Squaw Valley C: 63, N: 21, D: 2.24.
1. Ernst Hinterseer   AUT   2:08.9
2. Matthias Leitner   AUT   2:10.3
3. Charles Bozon   FRA   2:10.4
4. Ludwig Leitner   GER   2:10.5
5. Josef "Pepi" Stiegler AUT   2:11.1
6. Guy Périllat   FRA   2:11.8
7. Hans-Peter Lanig   GER   2:14.3
8. Paride Milianti   ITA   2:14.4

Eighteen-year-old Willy Bogner of Germany, whose father was the first designer of stretch pants, had the fastest time of the first run, 1:08.8. Hinterseer and Leitner, fifth and ninth after the first run, led the way on the second course in 58.2 and 59.2. Bogner, meanwhile, had fallen and was disqualified.

1964 Innsbruck C: 96, N: 28, D: 2.8.
1. Josef "Pepi" Stiegler AUT   2:11.13
2. William Kidd   USA   2:11.27
3. James Heuga   USA   2:11.52
4. Michel Arpin   FRA   2:12.91
5. Ludwig Leitner   GER   2:12.94
6. Adolf Mathis   SWI   2:12.99
7. Gerhard Nenning   AUT   2:13.20
8. Wallace "Bud" Werner   USA   2:13.46

Pepi Stiegler, a 26-year-old photographer, had twice been removed from the Austrian team and replaced by Egon Zimmermann. Both times he was reinstated after public pressure. After the first run, Stiegler led by a second over Karl Schranz, who was followed by Huega, Nenning, Mathis, and Kidd. Stiegler skied cautiously the second time around, registering the 8th best time, but his first-round performance turned out to be good enough to edge the Americans.

1968 Grenoble–Chamrousse C: 100, N: 33, D: 2.17.
1. Jean-Claude Killy   FRA   1:39.73
2. Herbert Huber   AUT   1:39.82
3. Alfred Matt   AUT   1:40.09
4. Dumeng Giovanoli   SWE   1:40.22
5. Vladimir Sabich   USA   1:40.49
6. Andrzej Bachleda   POL   1:40.61
7. James Heuga   USA   1:40.97
8. Alain Penz   FRA   1:41.14

With two gold medals down and one to go for Jean-Claude Killy, the slalom was held in bad weather, with fog, mist, and shadows prevailing. The skiers pleaded that the contest be postponed, but the officials in charge refused. Appropriately, the sun shown through only once—during Killy's first run, which was good enough to put him in first place. Killy was the first skier of the second round, so he was forced to wait anxiously as the others came down the hill. Häkon Mjön of Norway bettered Killy's time, but was disqualified for missing two gates. Then came the turn of Karl Schranz, the biggest threat to Killy's goal of a triple crown. But something curious happened as Schranz sped through the fog, something that has never been fully explained. As Schranz approached the 22nd gate, a mysterious figure in black crossed the course. Schranz skidded to a halt and, with three witnesses in tow, walked back to the starting point to ask for a rerun. Colonel Robert Readhead, the British referee, granted Schranz's request. This time Schranz achieved an almost perfect run, beat Killy's time, and was declared the unofficial winner. Schranz was allowed to enjoy the postrace press conference, while Killy sulked in the corner. But two hours later it was announced that Schranz had been disqualified for missing two gates just prior to his encounter with the mysterious interloper.

The Austrians were outraged. Schranz claimed that if he did miss a gate or two it was because he had already been distracted by the sight of someone on the course. His supporters contended that the mystery man had been a French policeman or soldier who had purposely interfered with Schranz in order to insure Killy's victory. The French, on the other hand, hinted that Schranz had made up the whole story after he had missed a gate. A final five-hour meeting of the Jury of Appeal ended with a 3–2 vote against Schranz, with two Frenchmen and a Swiss voting to give the gold medal to Killy, while Colonel Readhead and a Norwegian supported Schranz. Because of this incident, the 1968 Winter Olympics ended in a rather ugly mood, but back home in Val d'Isère Killy had no trouble putting it out of his mind. "The party went on for two and a half days," he later recalled, "and the whole time I never saw the sun once."

1972 Sapporo–Teineyama C: 72, N: 31, D: 2.13.

1. Francisco Fernandez Ochoa	SPA	1:49.27
2. Gustav Thöni	ITA	1:50.28
3. Roland Thöni	ITA	1:50.30
4. Henri Duvillard	FRA	1:50.45
5. Jean-Noël Augert	FRA	1:50.51
6. Eberhard Schmalzl	ITA	1:50.83
7. David Zwilling	AUT	1:51.97
8. Edmund Bruggmann	SWI	1:52.03

The biggest surprise of the 1972 Winter Games was the sensational victory of 21-year-old Paquito Ochoa of Spain, who had never before finished higher than sixth in an international meet. Not only was Ochoa's gold medal the

first ever won by Spain in the Winter Olympics, but it was the first Spanish victory of any kind since the equestrian team jumping competition of 1928. Ochoa was so overcome by emotion that he was unable to speak to reporters except to say, "I can't believe it. It can't be true." An hour later, referring to Spain's leading matador, he said, "El Cordobés is a little man compared with me. I am the champion."

1976 Innsbruck C: 94, N: 31, D: 2.14.

1. Piero Gros	ITA	2:03.29
2. Gustav Thöni	ITA	2:03.73
3. Willy Frommelt	LIE	2:04.28
4. Walter Tresch	SWI	2:05.26
5. Christian Neureuther	GER	2:06.56
6. Wolfgang Junginger	GER	2:07.08
7. Alois Morgenstern	AUT	2:07.18
8. Peter Luscher	SWI	2:08.10

Fifth after the first run, Gros was "as sure as I could be that I could never beat Thöni. In my opinion at that time Gustavo had the gold medal in his pocket." But a superb second run, over a second faster than that of Thöni, his teammate and mentor, gave Gros the victory.

1980 Lake Placid C: 79, N: 28, D: 2.22.

1. Ingemar Stenmark	SWE	1:44.26
2. Phillip Mahre	USA	1:44.76
3. Jacques Lüthy	SWI	1:45.06
4. Hans Enn	AUT	1:45.12
5. Christian Neureuther	GER	1:45.14
6. Peter Popangelov	BUL	1:45.40
7. Anton Steiner	AUT	1:45.41
8. Gustav Thöni	ITA	1:45.99

Skiing with a three-inch metal plate and four screws in his left ankle joint, the result of a bad fall 11 months earlier, Phil Mahre of White Pass, Washington, whizzed down the first run in 53.31. Because he was the first skier to compete, there was no way to judge if this was a good time or a bad time. But by the time the 13th skier, favorite Ingemar Stenmark, had completed the course over a half second slower than Mahre, it was clear that the 22-year-old American would enter the second round in first place. However Stenmark, in fourth place, had come from behind three days earlier to win the giant slalom, and he was known for his lightning second runs. Sure enough, he tore down the course in 50.37, a time that no one could beat. Three skiers later, Phil Mahre, needing a 50.94 to win the gold medal, never gained his rhythm and could only manage 51.45. Ingemar Stenmark, the Silent Swede, had completed his slalom double, but was not impressed by his accomplishment. "History is not important," he said. "The important thing is that I am satisfied with myself." As for Phil Mahre, he was back on the slopes the next day—filming an American Express commercial.

GIANT SLALOM

The giant slalom is similar to the slalom except the course is longer, the gates are farther apart, and the corners are not so sharp.

1924–1948 not held

1952 Oslo–Norefjell C: 83, N: 26, D: 2.15.
1. Stein Eriksen	NOR	2:25.0
2. Christian Pravda	AUT	2:26.9
3. Toni Spiss	AUT	2:28.8
4. Zeno Colò	ITA	2:29.1
5. Georges Schneider	SWI	2:31.2
6. Joseph Brooks Dodge	USA	2:32.6
6. Stig Sollander	SWE	2:32.6
8. Bernhard Perren	SWI	2:33.1

Stein Eriksen was the first of only three skiers from outside of the Alps to win an Olympic men's alpine gold medal. He was also the first skiing superstar. He was handsome, stylish, and glamorous. At the Oslo Games he proved to be a modest winner, declaring, "I had a great advantage over most of the others because I knew the course by heart." In 1954 Eriksen won the world combined alpine championship. Immediately afterward, he became a ski school director at Boyne Mt., Michigan. He moved on to Heavenly Valley, California, in 1957, Aspen Highlands, Colorado, in 1959, Sugarbush, Vermont, in 1965, Snowmass, Colorado, in 1969, and Park City, Utah, in 1973. Everywhere he went Stein Eriksen became the inspiration for the stereotypical ski instructor of the 1950s and 1960s—rich, good-looking, an outdoorsman who made women melt, and, above all, an Olympic champion.

1956 Cortina C: 95, N: 29, D: 1.29.
1. Anton Sailer	AUT	3:00.1
2. Andreas Molterer	AUT	3:06.3
3. Walter Schuster	AUT	3:07.2
4. Adrien Duvillard	FRA	3:07.2
5. Charles Bozon	FRA	3:08.4
6. Ernst Hinterseer	AUT	3:08.5
7. Hans-Peter Lanig	GER	3:08.6
8. Sepp Behr	GER	3:11.4

The 1956 giant slalom was held on the "Ilio Colli" course at Cortina. Ilio Colli was a local skier who had crashed into a tree at 50 m.p.h. during a race. He broke his skull and died instantly. Each participant in the giant slalom was handed a souvenir picture of Colli. In his book *My Way to the Triple Olympic Victory,* Toni Sailer wrote, "It is a beautiful thought to name such a famous course . . . after a dead racer, even if it is not exactly encouraging for those starting to be handed such a death notice." When the sixth skier, Andreas "Anderl" Molterer, came down in 3:06.3, he was mobbed and congratulated. But Molterer waved everyone away, telling them, "Toni hasn't come yet." When Toni did come, he came really fast—in 3:00.1, over six sec-

onds better than any of the other 94 skiers. In the next five days Sailer also won the slalom and the downhill.

1960 Squaw Valley C: 65, N: 21, D: 2.21.
1. Roger Staub	SWI	1:48.3
2. Josef "Pepi" Stiegler	AUT	1:48.7
3. Ernst Hinterseer	AUT	1:49.1
4. Thomas Corcoran	USA	1:49.7
5. Bruno Alberti	ITA	1:50.1
6. Guy Périllat	FRA	1:50.7
7. Karl Schranz	AUT	1:50.8
8. Paride Milianti	ITA	1:50.9

1964 Innsbruck C: 96, N: 29, D: 2.2.
1. François Bonlieu	FRA	1:46.71
2. Karl Schranz	AUT	1:47.09
3. Josef "Pepi" Stiegler	AUT	1:48.05
4. Willy Favre	SWI	1:48.69
5. Jean-Claude Killy	FRA	1:48.92
6. Gerhard Nenning	AUT	1:49.68
7. William Kidd	USA	1:49.97
8. Ludwig Leitner	GER	1:50.04

Mountain guide François Bonlieu engaged in a running battle with the French coaches and officials and refused to listen to their advice. His rebelliousness turned out to be wisdom, as he upset the Austrians on their own course.

1968 Grenoble–Chamrousse C: 99, N: 36, D: 2.12.
1. Jean-Claude Killy	FRA	3:29.28
2. Willy Favre	SWI	3:31.50
3. Heinrich Messner	AUT	3:31.83
4. Guy Périllat	FRA	3:32.06
5. William Kidd	USA	3:32.37
6. Karl Schranz	AUT	3:33.08
7. Dumeng Giovanoli	SWI	3:33.55
8. Gerhard Nenning	AUT	3:33.61

For the first time the giant slalom was decided by a combination of two runs on separate days, rather than by a single run. This was the second of Killy's three gold medals. He had the fastest time of the first run and extended his winning margin over the second run.

1972 Sapporo–Teineyama C: 73, N: 27, D: 2.10.
1. Gustav Thöni	ITA	3:09.62
2. Edmund Bruggmann	SWI	3:10.75
3. Werner Mattle	SWE	3:10.99
4. Alfred Hagn	GER	3:11.16
5. Jean-Noël Augert	FRA	3:11.84
6. Max Rieger	GER	3:11.96
7. David Zwilling	AUT	3:12.32
8. Reinhard Tritscher	AUT	3:12.42

Erik Håker of Norway had the fastest time of the first run, followed by Alfred Hagn and Gustav Thöni. When Håker opened the second run by falling and Hagn skied too cautiously, the way was open for the 20-year-old Thöni to become the first Italian to win an alpine gold medal since Zeno Colò won the downhill in 1952.

1976 Innsbruck C: 97, N: 32, N: 2.9.

1. Heini Hemmi — SWI — 3:26.97
2. Ernst Good — SWI — 3:27.17
3. Ingemar Stenmark — SWE — 3:27.41
4. Gustav Thöni — ITA — 3:27.67
5. Phillip Mahre — USA — 3:28.20
6. Engelhard Pargätzi — SWI — 3:28.76
7. Fausto Radici — ITA — 3:30.09
8. Franco Bieler — ITA — 3:30.24

Neither Hemmi nor Good had ever won a World Cup race. They had been placed third and second after the first run, behind Gustav Thöni. However Thöni's second run was only the eighth best of the day, while Hemmi's and Good's were second and third best. Ingemar Stenmark, ninth after the first run, stormed back with the fastest second-round time to take the bronze medal and establish a pattern that was to make him extremely famous in the years to come.

1980 Lake Placid C: 78, N: 28, D: 2.19.

1. Ingemar Stenmark — SWE — 2:40.74
2. Andreas Wenzel — LIE — 2:41.49
3. Hans Enn — AUT — 2:42.51
4. Bojan Krizaj — YUG — 2:42.53
5. Jacques Lüthy — SWI — 2:42.75
6. Bruno Nöckler — ITA — 2:42.95
7. Joel Gaspoz — SWI — 2:43.05
8. Boris Strel — YUG — 2:43.24

Born in the small village of Tarnaby in Swedish Lapland, about 100 miles south of the Arctic Circle, Ingemar Stenmark learned to ski at an early age because, "It was a thing I could do alone." On September 14, 1979, Stenmark, then 23 years old, was practicing his downhill technique in the Italian Alps when he lost control and tumbled violently down the hill for 200 meters. Lying unconscious on the snow, he began foaming at the mouth and experiencing spasms. He had suffered a major concussion. But five months later he was in top shape again for the Olympics, although he did skip the downhill race. As usual, Stenmark skied somewhat cautiously on his first run of the giant slalom, placing third behind Andreas Wenzel and Bojan Krizaj. But on the second day Stenmark roared down the course almost a full second faster than anyone else. "I'm not disappointed," said silver medalist Wenzel. "I had an idea this would happen."

Discontinued Events

ALPINE COMBINED

1924–1932 not held

1936 Garmisch-Partenkirchen C: 66, N: 21, D: 2.9.

		PTS.
1. Franz Pfnür	GER	99.25
2. Gustav Lantschner	GER	96.26
3. Emile Allais	FRA	94.69
4. Birger Ruud	NOR	93.38
5. Roman Wörndle	GER	91.16
6. Rudolf Cranz	GER	91.03
7. Giacinto Sertorelli	ITA	90.39
8. Alf Konningen	NOR	90.06

This event combined one long downhill run and, two days later, two slalom runs. Franz Pfnür, a 27-year-old woodcarver and cabinetmaker from Bavaria, was second to Birger Ruud in the downhill and first in both runs of the slalom. Silver medalist Gustav "Guzzi" Lantschner was described by Albion Ross of *The New York Times* as "a violent Nazi." Born and raised in Innsbruck, Austria, Lantschner moved to Germany and became a cameraman for the Nazi party. He was killed during World War II. Resat Erces of Turkey showed great patience when he completed the downhill course in 22:44.4—18 minutes slower than Birger Ruud.

1948 St. Moritz C: 78, N: 24, D: 2.4.

		PTS.
1. Henri Oreiller	FRA	3.27
2. Karl Molitor	SWI	6.44
3. James Couttet	FRA	6.95
4. Edi Mall	AUT	8.54
5. Silvio Alverà	ITA	8.71
6. Hans Hansson	SWE	9.31
7. Vittorio Chierroni	ITA	9.69
8. Hans Nogler	AUT	9.96

ALPINE SKIING

WOMEN
Downhill
Slalom
Giant Slalom
Discontinued Events

WOMEN
DOWNHILL
1924–1936 not held

1948 St. Moritz C: 37, N: 11, D: 2.2.
1. Hedy Schlunegger   SWI   2:28.3
2. Trude Beiser   AUT   2:29.1
3. Resi Hammer   AUT   2:30.2
4. Celina Seghi   ITA   2:31.1
5. Lina Mittner   SWI   2:31.2
6. Suzanne Thiollière   FRA   2:31.4
7. Françoise Gignoux   FRA   2:32.4
7. Laila Schou-Nilsen   NOR   2:32.4

1952 Oslo–Norefjell C: 42, N: 13, D: 2.17.
1. Trude Jochum-Beiser   AUT   1:47.1
2. Annemarie Buchner   GER   1:48.0
3. Giuliana Minuzzo   ITA   1:49.0
4. Erika Mahringer   AUT   1:49.5
5. Dagmar Rom   AUT   1:49.8
6. Madeleine Berthod   SWI   1:50.7
7. Margit Hvammen   NOR   1:50.9
8. Joanne Hewson   CAN   1:51.3

1956 Cortina C: 47, N: 16, D: 2.1.
1. Madeleine Berthod   SWI   1:40.7
2. Frieda Dänzer   SWI   1:45.4
3. Lucile Wheeler   CAN   1:45.9
4. Giuliana Chenal-Minuzzo   ITA   1:47.3
4. Hilde Hofherr   AUT   1:47.3
6. Carla Marchelli   ITA   1:47.7
7. Dorothea Hochleitner   AUT   1:47.9
8. Neivier Josette   FRA   1:49.2

Madeleine Berthod, the favorite in the event, celebrated her 25th birthday the day she won the downhill gold med-

al. Her margin of victory was four times larger than any other winner's in this event.

1960 Squaw Valley C: 42, N: 14, D: 2.20.
1. Heidi Biebl   GER   1:37.6
2. Penelope Pitou   USA   1:38.6
3. Traudl Hecher   AUT   1:38.9
4. Pia Riva   ITA   1:39.9
5. Jerta Schir   ITA   1:40.5
6. Anneliese Meggl   GER   1:40.8
7. Sonja Peril   GER   1:41.0
8. Erika Netzer   AUT   1:41.1

As a first-year student in high school, Penny Pitou made the boys' varsity ski team and finished fifth in the New Hampshire state slalom championship before being banned from further competition by the local school board. At the age of 15 she qualified for the U.S. Olympic team, finishing 31st, 34th, and 34th. Four years later she was the favorite at Squaw Valley, but the pressure on her was great. "The predictions that I'm going to win make me nervous," she said. "America is putting its hopes on me and it's a terrible feeling. . . . I'd be much happier being a normal girl, sitting at home or going to school." A near-fall three gates from the finish cost her about two seconds and the gold medal. Later she was married for a few years to Austrian downhill gold medalist Egon Zimmermann. And later still she became New Hampshire's first female bank director.

1964 Innsbruck C: 43, N: 15, D: 2.6.
1. Christl Haas   AUT   1:55.39
2. Edith Zimmermann   AUT   1:56.42
3. Traudl Hecher   AUT   1:56.66
4. Heidi Biebl   GER   1:57.87
5. Barbara Henneberger   GER   1:58.03
6. Madeleine Bochatay   FRA   1:59.11
7. Nancy Greene   CAN   1:59.23
8. Christine Terraillon   FRA   1:59.66

When she was three years old, Christl Haas told her parents that she wanted to become a ski racer. Seventeen years later the 5-foot 10-inch Haas, skiing in the 13th position, had no trouble living up to her role of an Austrian favorite competing in Austria.

1968 Grenoble–Chamrousse C: 39, N: 14, D: 2.10.
1. Olga Pall   AUT   1:40.87
2. Isabelle Mir   FRA   1:41.33
3. Christl Haas   AUT   1:41.41
4. Brigitte Seiwald   AUT   1:41.82
5. Annie Famose   FRA   1:42.15
6. Felicity Field   GBR   1:42.79
7. Fernande Bochatay   SWI   1:42.87
8. Marielle Goitschel   FRA   1:42.95

1972 Sapporo–Eniwadake C: 41, N: 13, D: 2.5.
1. Marie-Theres Nadig   SWI   1:36.68
2. Annemarie Pröll   AUT   1:37.00
3. Susan Corrock   USA   1:37.68
4. Isabelle Mir   FRA   1:38.62
5. Rosi Speiser   GER   1:39.10
6. Rosi Mittermaier   GER   1:39.32
7. Bernadette Zurbriggen   SWI   1:39.49
8. Annie Famose   FRA   1:39.70

The first noteworthy time was 1:38.62, registered by the eighth skier, Isabelle Mir. Next on the course was French heroine Annie Famose, who was having an exhausting time defending her eligibility from accusations of "commercialism" by the International Ski Federation. Famose finished in ninth place. The tenth skier, unheralded Susan Corrock of Ketchum, Idaho, surprised the experts by taking the lead in 1:37.68. Three skiers later came an even bigger surprise. Seventeen-year-old Marie-Theres Nadig of Flums, Switzerland, who had never won a World Cup race, beat Corrock's time by exactly one second. The 15th skier was the pre-Olympic favorite, 18-year-old Annemarie Pröll. The previous year she had become the youngest-ever overall winner of the World Cup. Pröll skied an excellent race, but finished one third of a second slower than Nadig. Disappointed and angry, she refused to attend the postrace press conference.

According to *Ski* magazine, after her victory Marie-Theres Nadig told the following story to her coach: "I was on the last flat stretch that leads into the steep wall before the finish, when I thought suddenly of a film I had seen last summer. It was about a funny little car that dreamed of racing in the Grand Prix. The little car was called Herbie. In each race it would start ahead of the other champions who would chase it. Suddenly I saw myself in the role of Herbie. I was being chased by hordes of other racers. A voice inside me said, 'Go, Herbie, go, go, go.' At each 'go,' I would lower my body still further to cut the wind resistance. In my whole life I never skied in such a low crouch. I could easily have fallen. But inside me, I always heard the voice crying out, 'Go, Herbie, go.' "

1976 Innsbruck C: 38, N: 15, D: 2.8.
1. Rosi Mittermaier   GER   1:46.16
2. Brigitte Totschnigg   AUT   1:46:68
3. Cynthia Nelson   USA   1:47.50
4. Nicola-Andrea Spiess   AUT   1:47.71
5. Danielle Debernard   FRA   1:48.48
6. Jacqueline Rouvier   FRA   1:48.58
7. Bernadette Zurbriggen SWI   1:48.62
8. Marlies Oberholzer   SWI   1:48.68

Rosi Mittermaier had never before won a major downhill race, even though she was competing in her tenth World Cup season and her third Olympics.

1980 Lake Placid C: 28, N: 13, D: 2.17.
1. Annemarie Moser-Pröll   AUT   1:37.52
2. Hanni Wenzel   LIE   1:38.22
3. Marie-Theres Nadig   SWI   1:38.36
4. Heidi Preuss   USA   1:39.51
5. Kathy Kreiner   CAN   1:39.53
6. Ingrid Eberle   AUT   1:39.63
7. Torill Fjeldstad   NOR   1:39.69
8. Cindy Nelson   USA   1:39.69

Winning two Olympic silver medals would probably be a dream come true for most skiers, but when Annemarie Pröll won two silvers at Sapporo in 1972, losing both times to Marie-Theres Nadig, she considered it a failure and a humiliation. She was back to her winning ways before long, but in March 1975, after marrying ski salesman Herbert Moser, she retired from competitive skiing and bypassed the 1976 Olympics. After her father died later that year, Annemarie Pröll returned to the circuit. By 1979 she had won six of the last nine annual World Cups and finished second twice. However the 1980 season had seen her win only one downhill race to Nadig's six. Motivated by the only achievement that had eluded her, Moser-Pröll, the sixth skier, sped down the course on Whiteface Mountain in 1:37.52. Her time withstood the onslaughts of Nadig and Wenzel and earned her the final jewel in her champion's crown.

SLALOM
1924–1936 not held

1948 St. Moritz C: 28, N: 10, D: 2.5.
1. Gretchen Fraser   USA   1:57.2
2. Antoinette Meyer   SWI   1:57.7
3. Erika Mahringer   AUT   1:58.0
4. Georgette Miller-Thiollière FRA   1:58.8
5. Renée Clerc   SWI   2:05.8
6. Anneliese Schuh-Proxauf   AUT   2:06.7
7. Rese Hammerer   AUT   2:08.6
8. Andrea Mead   USA   2:08.8

Gretchen Fraser of Vancouver, Washington, had qualified for the U.S. team for the 1940 Olympics that were never held. Eight years later she was considered an unknown quantity. Skiing in the first position she clocked the fastest time of the first run—59.7. Erika Mahringer was one-tenth of a second behind her. As Fraser prepared to lead off the second round, a problem suddenly developed in the telephone timing system between the top and the bottom of the hill. Despite a 17-minute delay at such a critical time, Fraser finished the second run in 57.5, a time beaten only by Antoinette Meyer (57.0.)

1952 Oslo C: 40, N: 14, D: 2.20.

1. Andrea Mead Lawrence	USA	2:10.6
2. Ossi Reichert	GER	2:11.4
3. Annemarie Buchner	GER	2:13.3
4. Celina Seghi	ITA	2:13.8
5. Imogene Anna Opton	USA	2:14.1
6. Madeleine Berthod	SWI	2:14.9
7. Agnel Marysette	FRA	2:15.6
8. Trude Jochum-Beiser	AUT	2:15.9
8. Giuliana Minuzzo	ITA	2:15.9

Nineteen-year-old Andrea Mead Lawrence of Rutland, Vermont, fell early in her first run, but got up, and showed her superiority by finishing the course with the fourth best time. She overhauled the leaders with a second run that was two seconds faster than anyone else's. Lawrence became the first American skier to win two gold medals. By the time of the opening of the 1956 Games, she had given birth to three children.

1956 Cortina C: 48, N: 16, D: 1.30.

1. Renée Colliard	SWI	1:52.3
2. Regina Schöpf	AUT	1:55.4
3. Yevgenia Sidorova	SOV	1:56.7
4. Giuliana Chenal-Minuzzo	ITA	1:56.8
5. Josefine Frandl	AUT	1:57.9
6. Inger Björnbakken	NOR	1:58.0
6. Astrid Sandvik	NOR	1:58.0
8. Josette Neviere	FRA	1:58.3

Renée Colliard, a pharmacy student from Geneva, was making her first appearance as a member of the Swiss team. Racing in the number-one position, she registered the fastest time in each run.

1960 Squaw Valley C: 43, N: 14, D: 2.26.

1. Anne Heggtveit	CAN	1:49.6
2. Betsy Snite	USA	1:52.9
3. Barbara Henneberger	GER	1:56.6
4. Thérèse Leduc	FRA	1:57.4
5. Hilde Hofherr	AUT	1:58.0
5. Liselotte Michel	SWI	1:58.0
7. Stalian Korzukhina	SOV	1:58.4
8. Sonja Sperl	GER	1:58.8

1964 Innsbruck C: 48, N: 16, D: 2.1.

1. Christine Goitschel	FRA	1:29.86
2. Marielle Goitschel	FRA	1:30.77
3. Jean Saubert	USA	1:31.36
4. Heidi Biebl	GER	1:34:04
5. Edith Zimmermann	AUT	1:34.27

6. Christl Haas	AUT	1:35.11
7. Liv Jagge	NOR	1:36.38
8. Patricia du Roy de Blicquy	BEL	1:37.01

Christine and Marielle Goitschel, teenaged sisters from Val d'Isère, the home of Jean-Claude Killy, were the stars of the 1964 ski contests. Marielle, the favorite, had the fastest time of the first run, 43.09, with her older sister, Christine, in second place at 43.85. Christine prevailed in the second round, giving the Goitschels a one-two finish. That same day, back in France, their younger sister, Patricia, won a National Junior title.

1968 Grenoble–Chamrousse C: 49, N: 18, D: 2.13.

1. Marielle Goitschel	FRA	1:25.86
2. Nancy Greene	CAN	1:26.15
3. Annie Famose	FRA	1:27.89
4. Gina Hathorn	GBR	1:27.92
5. Isabelle Mir	FRA	1:28.22
6. Burgl Färbinger	GER	1:28.90
7. Glorianda Cipolla	ITA	1:29.74
8. Bernadette Rauter	AUT	1:30.44

Sixteen-year-old Judy Nagel of Enumclaw, Washington, was the surprise leader of the first run, but she fell at the beginning of her second run and, although she finished the course, was disqualified for missing a gate.

1972 Sapporo–Teineyama C: 42, N: 13, D: 2.11.

1. Barbara Cochran	USA	1:31.24
2. Danièlle Debernard	FRA	1:31.26
3. Florence Steurer	FRA	1:32.69
4. Judy Crawford	CAN	1:33.95
5. Annemarie Pröll	AUT	1:34.03
6. Pamela Behr	GER	1:34.27
7. Monika Kaserer	AUT	1:34.36
8. Patricia Boydstun	USA	1:35.59

Back home in Richmond, Vermont, Barbara Cochran's father had taught his talented children how to save a tenth of a second by setting their bodies in motion before pushing open the starting wand that sets off the timing mechanism. That one-tenth second turned out to be the difference between gold and silver for Barbara Cochran. Her time for the first run was three one-hundredths of a second faster than Danièlle Debernard. In the final run Debernard was able to pick up only one of the three-hundredths of a second. Only 19 of 42 starters made it through both runs without falling or missing a gate.

1976 Innsbruck C: 42, N: 14, D: 2.11.

1. Rosi Mittermaier	GER	1:30.54
2. Claudia Giordani	ITA	1:30.87
3. Hanni Wenzel	LIE	1:32.20
4. Danièlle Debernard	FRA	1:32.24
5. Pamela Behr	GER	1:32.31
6. Linda Cochran	USA	1:33.24
7. Christa Zechmeister	GER	1:33.72
8. Wanda Bieter	ITA	1:35.66

For the second straight time, 42 women started the Olympic slalom, but only 19 finished both courses without missing a gate. Rosi Mittermaier recorded the fastest time of the second run after trailing teammate Pamela Behr by nine-hundredths of a second after the first run. Mittermaier had already won the downhill race three days earlier.

1980 Lake Placid C: 47, N: 21, D: 2.23.

1.	Hanni Wenzel	LIE	1:25.09
2.	Christa Kinshofer	GER	1:26.50
3.	Erika Hess	SWI	1:27.89
4.	Mariarosa Quario	ITA	1:27.92
5.	Claudia Giordani	ITA	1:29.12
6.	Nadezhda Patrakeeva	SOV	1:29.20
7.	Daniela Zini	ITA	1:29.22
8.	Christin Cooper	USA	1:29.28

German-born Hanni Wenzel moved to tiny Liechtenstein (population 25,000) when she was one year old. She was granted Liechtenstein citizenship after winning the slalom at the 1974 world championships in St. Moritz. Having already finished second in the downhill and first in the giant slalom at the 1980 Olympics, Wenzel breezed through the slalom, registering the best time in both the first and second runs. By earning two gold medals and one silver in one Olympics, she matched the 1976 feat of Rosi Mittermaier. Hanni's brother, Andreas, won the silver medal in the downhill, to give Liechtenstein four medals at the Lake Placid Games, one for every 6250 people. If the U.S. had won the same number of medals per capita it would have won 36,000 medals. Actually there were only 114 medals awarded.

GIANT SLALOM

1924–1948 not held

1952 Oslo–Norefjell C: 45, N: 15, D: 2.14.

1.	Andrea Mead Lawrence	USA	2:06.8
2.	Dagmar Rom	AUT	2:09.0
3.	Annemarie Buchner	GER	2:10.0
4.	Trude Klecker	AUT	2:11.4
5.	Katy Rodolph	USA	2:11.7
6.	Borghild Niskin	NOR	2:11.9
7.	Celina Seghi	ITA	2:12.5
8.	Ossi Reichert	GER	2:13.2

Silver medalist Dagmar Rom was a well-known Austrian film actress.

1956 Cortina C: 49, N: 16, D: 1.27.

1.	Ossi Reichert	GER	1:56.5
2.	Josefine Frandl	AUT	1:57.8
3.	Dorothea Hochleitner	AUT	1:58.2
4.	Madeleine Berthod	SWI	1:58.3
4.	Andrea Mead Lawrence	USA	1:58.3
6.	Lucile Wheeler	CAN	1:58.6
7.	Borghild Niskin	NOR	1:59.0
8.	Marysette Agnel	FRA	1:59.4

1960 Squaw Valley C: 44, N: 14, D: 2.23.

1.	Yvonne Rüegg	SWI	1:39.9
2.	Penelope Pitou	USA	1:40.0
3.	Giuliana Chenal-Minuzzo	ITA	1:40.2
4.	Betsy Snite	USA	1:40.4
5.	Carla Marchelli	ITA	1:40.7
5.	Anneliese Meggl	GER	1:40.7
7.	Thérèse Leduc	FRA	1:40.8
8.	Anne-Marie Leduc	FRA	1:41.5

1964 Innsbruck C: 46, N: 15, D: 2.3.

1.	Marielle Goitschel	FRA	1:52.24
2.	Christine Goitschel	FRA	1:53.11
2.	Jean Saubert	USA	1:53.11
4.	Christl Haas	AUT	1:53.86
5.	Annie Famose	FRA	1:53.89
6.	Edith Zimmermann	AUT	1:54.21
7.	Barbara Henneberger	GER	1:54.26
8.	Traudl Hecher	AUT	1:54.55

On February 1, Christine Goitschel had won the slalom with her younger sister, Marielle, second and Jean Saubert third. Christine was the first of the three to go down the course of the giant slalom two days later. Her time of 1:53.11 looked good. Three skiers later Jean Saubert clocked the exact same time despite the introduction of timing to the hundredth of a second. When Marielle Goitschel, the 14th skier, heard that Saubert had equaled her sister's time, she attacked the course with extra determination and earned herself the gold medal.

After her victory, 18-year-old Marielle announced to the press that she had just become engaged to a 20-year-old French skier by the name of Jean-Claude Killy, who had finished fifth in the giant slalom the day before. "I am happy and I am in love," she enthused. While the more gullible reporters scurried away to spread the exciting news around the world, Marielle and Christine sat back and enjoyed their little hoax. When the press caught up with Killy, he smiled and spilled out the truth. "The joke of a tomboy," he said. "Marielle talks too much." It says a lot about the fully justified self-confidence of the Goitschel sisters that they had actually planned their practical joke the night before the race, on the assumption that one of them would win the gold medal.

1968 Grenoble–Chamrousse C: 47, N: 18, D: 2.15.

1.	Nancy Greene	CAN	1:51.97
2.	Annie Famose	FRA	1:54.61
3.	Fernande Bochatay	SWI	1:54.74
4.	Florence Steurer	FRA	1:54.75
5.	Olga Pall	AUT	1:55.61
6.	Isabelle Mir	FRA	1:56.07
7.	Marielle Goitschel	FRA	1:56.09
8.	Divina Galica	GBR	1:56.58

In 1967 Nancy Greene of Rossland, British Columbia, won the inaugural World Cup despite missing three of the nine meets. The following year she participated in her third Olympics, finally winning a well-deserved gold medal.

1972 Sapporo–Teineyama C: 42, N: 13, D: 2.8.
1. Marie-Theres Nadig   SWI   1:29.90
2. Annemarie Pröll   AUT   1:30.75
3. Wiltrud Drexel   AUT   1:32.35
4. Laurie Kreiner   CAN   1:32.48
5. Rosi Speiser   GER   1:32.56
6. Florence Steurer   FRA   1:32.59
7. Divina Galica   GBR   1:32.72
8. Britt Lafforgue   FRA   1:32.80

Hoping to avenge her upset defeat at the hands of Marie-Theres Nadig in the downhill, Annemarie Pröll, the second skier, skimmed down the course in 1:30.75. Her time held up until Nadig, in the tenth spot, clocked 1:29.90. Pröll, bearing the burden of being the favorite, was bitterly disappointed. "Two silver medals don't equal one gold medal," she said. Nadig attributed her victory to the fact that she was relaxed while Pröll had been under enormous pressure. After the Olympics, however, Nadig learned first hand what her rival had had to endure. "After Sapporo," Nadig later said, "people expected everything from me. They expected me to win all the time, and after a while I didn't know where I was."

1976 Innsbruck C: 45, N: 17, D: 2.13.
1. Kathy Kreiner   CAN   1:29.13
2. Rosi Mittermaier   GER   1:29.25
3. Danièlle Debernard   FRA   1:29.95
4. Lise-Marie Morerod   SWI   1:30.40
5. Marie-Theres Nadig   SWI   1:30.44
6. Monika Kaserer   AUT   1:30.49
7. Wilma Gatta   ITA   1:30.51
8. Evi Mittermaier   GER   1:30.64

There was great excitement before the running of the giant slalom because everyone wanted to know if Rosi Mittermaier would become the first woman to sweep the three alpine races. They didn't have to wait long to find out. The first skier on the course, 18-year-old Kathy Kreiner of Timmins, Ontario, had an excellent run and flashed across the finish line in 1:29.13. Three skiers later it was Rosi Mittermaier's turn. A half-second ahead of Kreiner's pace at the halfway mark, Mittermaier lost precious fractions of a second when she approached one of the lower gates too directly. Her final time was one-eighth of a second slower that Kreiner's.

1980 Lake Placid C: 46, N: 21, D: 2.21.
1. Hanni Wenzel   LIE   2:41.66
2. Irene Epple   GER   2:42.12
3. Perrine Pelen   FRA   2:42.41
4. Fabienne Serrat   FRA   2:42.42
5. Christa Kinshoffer   GER   2:42.63
6. Annemarie Moser-Pröll   AUT   2:43.19
7. Christin Cooper   USA   2:44.71
8. Maria Epple   GER   2:45.56

For the first time, the women's giant slalom was held as a two-run competition. Wenzel had the fastest time of the first run and the third fastest of the second. She was Liechtenstein's first Olympic gold medal winner.

Discontinued Events
ALPINE COMBINED
1924–1932 not held

1936 Garmisch-Partenkirchen C: 37, N: 13, D: 2.8.
            PTS.
1. Christl Cranz   GER   97.06
2. Käthe Grasegger   GER   95.26
3. Laila Schou Nilsen   NOR   93.48
4. Erna Steuri   SWI   92.36
5. Hadi Pfeiffer   GER   91.85
6. Lisa Resch   GER   88.74
7. Johanne Dybwad   NOR   85.90
8. Jeanette Kessler   GBR   83.97

Christl Cranz was only sixth in the downhill, but her times in the two slalom runs were so superior that she won anyway. Her first run was four seconds faster than her closest competitor and her second run was 7.2 seconds better than any of her rivals. Diana Gordon-Lennox, representing Canada, received an ovation because she skied both the downhill and slalom with one arm in a cast and using only one pole. She also wore a monocle while competing. Gordon-Lennox finished 29th.

1948 St. Moritz C: 28, N: 10, D: 2.4.
            PTS.
1. Trude Beiser   AUT   6.58
2. Gretchen Fraser   USA   6.95
3. Erika Mahringer   AUT   7.04
4. Celina Seghi   ITA   7.46
5. Françoise Gignoux   FRA   8.14
6. Rosmarie Bleuer   SWI   8.80
7. Anneliese Schuh-Proxauf   AUT   9.76
8. Hedy Schlunegger   SWI   10.20

NORDIC SKIING

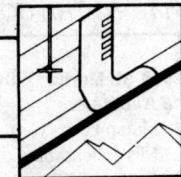

MEN

Cross-country, or *langlauf* races are run against the clock with the skiers leaving the starting line at 30-second intervals. The only exception is the 4×10-kilometer relay, in which the first runners for each team start together.

15 KILOMETERS

The 18- and 15-kilometer cross-country race has been thoroughly dominated by four nations: Norway, Sweden, Finland, and the U.S.S.R. These four nations have won all 39 medals, and only four other countries have managed to finish in the top eight.

1924 Chamonix C: 41, N: 12, D: 2.2.
18 Kilometers

1.	Thorleif Haug	NOR	1:14:31.0
2.	Johan Gröttumsbråten	NOR	1:15:51.0
3.	Tapani Niku	FIN	1:16:26.0
4.	Jon Maardalen	NOR	1:16:56.0
5.	Einar Landvik	NOR	1:17:27.0
6.	Per Erik Hedlund	SWE	1:17:49.0
7.	Matti Raivio	FIN	1:19:10.0
8.	Elis Sandin	SWE	1:19:24.0

Thorleif Haug won the second of his three gold medals, having won the 50-kilometer race three days earlier. The Scandinavians took the first 11 places.

1928 St. Moritz C: 49, N: 15, D: 2.17.
18 Kilometers

1.	Johan Gröttumsbråten	NOR	1:37:01.0
2.	Ole Hegge	NOR	1:39:01.0
3.	Reidar Ödegaard	NOR	1:40:11.0
4.	Veli Saarinen	FIN	1:40:57.0
5.	Hagbart Haakonsen	NOR	1:41:29.0
6.	Per Erik Hedlund	SWE	1:41:51.0
7.	Lars Theodor Johnsson	SWE	1:41:59.0
7.	Martti Lappalainen	FIN	1:41:59.0

1932 Lake Placid C: 42, N: 11, D: 2.10.
18 Kilometers

1.	Sven Utterström	SWE	1:23:07.0
2.	Axel Wikström	SWE	1:25:07.0
3.	Veli Saarinen	FIN	1:25:24.0
4.	Martti Lappalainen	FIN	1:26:31.0
5.	Arne Rustadstuen	NOR	1:27:06.0
6.	Johan Gröttumsbråten	NOR	1:27:15.0
7.	Valmari Toikka	FIN	1:27:51.0
8.	Ole Stenen	NOR	1:28:05.0

Once again, Scandinavians took the first 11 places.

1936 Garmish-Partenkirchen C: 75, N: 22, D: 2.12.
18 Kilometers

1.	Erik-August Larsson	SWE	1:14:38.0
2.	Oddbjörn Hagen	NOR	1:15:33.0
3.	Pekka Niemi	FIN	1:16:59.0
4.	Martin Matsbo	SWE	1:17:02.0
5.	Olaf Hoffsbakken	NOR	1:17:37.0
6.	Arne Rustadstuen	NOR	1:18:13.0
7.	Sulo Nurmela	FIN	1:18:20.0
8.	Artur Häggblad	SWE	1:18:55.0

1948 St. Moritz C: 84, N: 15, D: 1.31.
18 Kilometers
1. Martin Lundström   SWE   1:13:50.0
2. Nils Östensson   SWE   1:14:22.0
3. Gunnar Eriksson   SWE   1:16:06.0
4. Heikki Hasu   FIN   1:16:43.0
5. Nils Karlsson   SWE   1:16:54.0
6. Sauli Rytky   FIN   1:18:10.0
7. August Kiuru   FIN   1:18:25.0
8. Teuvo Laukkanen   FIN   1:18:51.0

1952 Oslo C: 80, N: 18, D: 2.18.
18 Kilometers
1. Hallgeir Brenden   NOR   1:01:34.0
2. Tapio Mäkelä   FIN   1:02:09.0
3. Paavo Lonkila   FIN   1:02:20.0
4. Heikki Hasu   FIN   1:02:24.0
5. Nils Karlsson   SWE   1:02:56.0
6. Martin Stokken   NOR   1:03:00.0
7. Nils Täpp   SWE   1:03:35.0
8. Tauno Sipila   FIN   1:03.40.0

In an amazing display of regional dominance, Finland, Norway, and Sweden claimed the first 17 places. Hallgeir Brenden, a 23-year-old lumberjack and farmer from the small town of Tyrsil, was also Norway's national steeplechase champion.

1956 Cortina C: 62, N: 20, D: 1.30.
1. Hallgeir Brenden   NOR   49:39.0
2. Sixten Jernberg   SWE   50:14.0
3. Pavel Kolchin   SOV   50:17.0
4. Veikko Hakulinen   FIN   50:31.0
5. Håkon Brusveen   NOR   50:36.0
6. Martin Stokken   NOR   50:45.0
7. Nikolai Anikin   SOV   50:58.0
8. Lennart Larsson   SWE   51.03.0

Kolchin and Anikin were the first non-Scandinavians to crack the top eight in this event. This was also the first time that the race was conducted at 15 kilometers rather than 18.

1960 Squaw Valley C: 54, N: 19, D: 2.23.
1. Håkon Brusveen   NOR   51:55.5
2. Sixten Jernberg   SWE   51:58.6
3. Veikko Hakulinen   FIN   52:03.0
4. Einar Östby   NOR   52:18.0
4. Gennady Vaganov   SOV   52:18.0
6. Eero Mäntyranta   FIN   52:40.6
7. Janne Stefansson   SWE   52:41.0
8. Rolf Rämgård   SWE   52:47.3

1964 Innsbruck–Seefeld C: 71, N: 24, D: 2.2.
1. Eero Mäntyranta   FIN   50:54.1
2. Harald Grönningen   NOR   51:34.8
3. Sixten Jernberg   SWE   51:42.2
4. Väinö Huhtala   FIN   51:45.4
5. Janne Stefansson   SWE   51:46.4
6. Pavel Kolchin   SOV   51:52.0

7. Igor Voronchikin   SOV   51:53.9
8. Magnar Lundemo   NOR   51:55.2

Mäntyranta and Grönningen took the same places they had taken in the 30-kilometer race three days earlier. Mäntyranta made his living on skis as a border patrol officer, a common vocation for state-supported skiers.

1968 Grenoble–Autrans C: 75, N: 24, D: 2.10.
1. Harald Grönningen   NOR   47:54.2
2. Eero Mäntyranta   FIN   47:56.1
3. Gunnar Larsson   SWE   48:33.7
4. Kalevi Laurila   FIN   48:37.6
5. Jan Halvarsson   SWE   48:39.1
6. Bjarne Andersson   SWE   48:41.1
7. Pål Tyldum   NOR   48:42.0
8. Odd Martinsen   NOR   48:59.3

A three-time silver medalist, Grönningen finally beat his friend and rival Mäntyranta.

1972 Sapporo–Makomanai C: 62, N: 19, D: 2.7.
1. Sven-Ake Lundbäck   SWE   45:28.24
2. Fedor Simashov   SOV   46:00.84
3. Ivar Formo   NOR   46:02.68
4. Juha Mieto   FIN   46:02.74
5. Yuri Skobov   SOV   46:04.59
6. Axel Lesser   GDR   46:17.01
7. Walter Demel   GER   46:17.36
8. Gunnar Larsson   SWE   46:23.29

1976 Innsbruck–Seefeld C: 80, N: 25, D: 2.8.
1. Nikolai Bazhukov   SOV   43:58.47
2. Yevgeny Beliaev   SOV   44:01.10
3. Arto Koivisto   FIN   44:19.25
4. Ivan Garanin   SOV   44:41.98
5. Ivar Formo   NOR   45:29.11
6. William Koch   USA   45:32.22
7. Georg Zipfel   GER   45:38.10
8. Odd Martinsen   NOR   45:41.33

1980 Lake Placid C: 63, N: 22, D: 2.17.
1. Thomas Wassberg   SWE   41:57.63
2. Juha Mieto   FIN   41:57.64
3. Ove Aunli   NOR   42:28.62
4. Nikolai Zimyatov   SOV   42:33.96
5. Yevgeny Beliaev   SOV   42:46.02
6. Józef Luszczek   POL   42:59.03
7. Aleksandr Zavyalov   SOV   43:00.81
8. Harri Kirvesniemi   FIN   43:02.01

Six-foot 5-inch Juha Mieto could be forgiven if he cursed the invention of electronic timing. In 1972 he missed winning a bronze medal because a clock registered his time as six one-hundredths of a second slower than that of Ivar Formo. Eight years later in Lake Placid, Mieto was the 54th skier to start and he finished 36 seconds faster than any of the other 53. But then he watched anxiously as Thomas Wassberg strained toward the finish line and crossed in 41 minutes and 57.63 seconds—one one-hundredth of a second faster than Juha Mieto. This incident led the rulemakers to decree that henceforth all times in cross-country races would be rounded to the nearest full second.

30 KILOMETERS

1924–1952 not held

1956 Cortina C: 54, N: 18, D: 1.27.
1. Veikko Hakulinen   FIN   1:44:06.0
2. Sixten Jernberg   SWE   1:44:30.0
3. Pavel Kolchin   SOV   1:45:45.0
4. Anatoly Shelyukin   SOV   1:45:46.0
5. Vladimir Kuzin   SOV   1:46:09.0
6. Fedor Terentyev   SOV   1:46:43.0
7. Per-Erik Larsson   SWE   1:46:51.0
8. Lennart Larsson   SWE   1:46:56.0

1960 Squaw Valley C: 48, N: 17, D: 2.19.
1. Sixten Jernberg   SWE   1:51:03.9
2. Rolf Rämgård   SWE   1:51:16.9
3. Nikolai Anikin   SOV   1:52:28.2
4. Gennady Vaganov   SOV   1:52:49.2
5. Lennart Larsson   SWE   1:53:53.2
6. Veikko Hakulinen   FIN   1:54:02.0
7. Toimo Alatalo   FIN   1:54:06.5
8. Aleksei Kuznyetsov   SOV   1:54:23.9

1964 Innsbruck–Seefeld C: 69, N: 22, D: 1.30.
1. Eero Mäntyranta   FIN   1:30:50.7
2. Harald Grönningen   NOR   1:32:02.3
3. Igor Voronchikin   SOV   1:32:15.8
4. Janne Stefansson   SWE   1:32:34.8
5. Sixten Jernberg   SOV   1:32:39.6
6. Kalevi Laurila   FIN   1:32:41.4
7. Assar Rönnlund   SWE   1:32:43.6
8. Einar Östby   NOR   1:32:54.6

1968 Grenoble–Autrans C: 66, N: 22, D: 2.6.
1. Franco Nones   ITA   1:35:39:2
2. Odd Martinsen   NOR   1:36:28:9
3. Eero Mäntyranta   FIN   1:36:55:3
4. Vladimir Voronkov   SOV   1:37:10:8
5. Giulio De Florian   ITA   1:37:12:9
6. Kalevi Laurila   FIN   1:37:29:8
7. Kalevi Oikarainen   FIN   1:37:34:4
8. Gunnar Larsson   SWE   1:37:48:1

Of the 43 cross-country events that have been held in the Olympics, 42 of them have been won by Sweden (13), Norway (11), Finland (10), and the U.S.S.R. (8). The only gold medalist from a non-nordic nation has been Franco Nones, a 27-year-old customs officer from the village of Catella di Fiemma in the Dolomite Mountains. It is true that Nones was trained in northern Sweden by a Swedish coach, but his victory was nonetheless a major surprise, particularly

coming as it did in the first event of the 1968 Winter Games. It is also worth noting that of the 129 medals that have been awarded in cross-country skiing the Scandinavians and Soviets have won 123 of them.

1972 Sapporo–Makomanai C: 59, N: 19, D: 2.4.
1. Vyacheslav Vedenine   SOV   1:36:31.15
2. Pål Tyldum   NOR   1:37:25.30
3. Johs Harviken   NOR   1:37:32.44
4. Gunnar Larsson   SWE   1:37:33.72
5. Walter Demel   GER   1:37:45.33
6. Fedor Simachev   SOV   1:38:22.50
7. Alois Kälin   SWI   1:38:40.72
8. Gert-Dietmar Klause   GDR   1:39:15.54

The 5-foot 4¾-inch Vedenine was the first Soviet skier to win an individual Olympic gold medal.

1976 Innsbruck–Seefeld C: 69, N: 21, D: 2.5.
1. Sergei Saveliev   SOV   1:30:29.38
2. William Koch   USA   1:30:57.84
3. Ivan Garanin   SOV   1:31:09.29
4. Juha Mieto   FIN   1:31:20.39
5. Nikolai Bazhukov   SOV   1:31:33.14
6. Gert-Dietmar Klause   GDR   1:32:00.91
7. Albert Giger   SWI   1:32:17.71
8. Arto Koivisto   FIN   1:32:23.11

The only American ever to have won an Olympic nordic skiing medal, Bill Koch of Guilford, Vermont, responded to his sudden celebrity in a typically Vermont manner. When a reporter asked, "Have you lived in Vermont all your life?" Koch replied, "Not yet."

1980 Lake Placid C: 57, N: 20, D: 2.14.
1. Nikolai Zimyatov   SOV   1:27:02.80
2. Vassily Rochev   SOV   1:27:34.22
3. Ivan Lebanov   BUL   1:28:03.87
4. Thomas Wassberg   SWE   1:28:40.35
5. Józef Luszczek   POL   1:29:03.64
6. Matti Pitkänen   FIN   1:29:35.03
7. Juha Mieto   FIN   1:29:45.08
8. Ove Aunli   NOR   1:29:54.02

Zimyatov won the first of his three gold medals. Lebanov was the first Bulgarian to win a medal in the Winter Olympics.

50 KILOMETERS

1924 Chamonix C: 33, N: 11, D: 1.30.
1. Thorleif Haug   NOR   3:44:32.0
2. Thoralf Strömstad   NOR   3:46:23.0
3. Johan Gröttumsbråten   NOR   3:47:46.0
4. Jon Maardalen   NOR   3:49:48.0
5. Torkel Persson   SWE   4:05:59.0
6. Ernst Alm   SWE   4:06:31.0
7. Matti Raivio   FIN   4:06.50.0
8. Oscar Lindberg   SWE   4:07.44.0

1928 St. Moritz C: 41, N: 11, D: 2.14.

1. Per Erik Hedlund	SWE	4:52:03.0
2. Gustaf Jonsson	SWE	5:05:30.0
3. Volger Andersson	SWE	5:05.46.0
4. Olav Kjelbotn	NOR	5:14:22.0
5. Ole Hegge	NOR	5:17:58.0
6. Tauno Lappalainen	FIN	5:18:33.0
7. Anders Strom	SWE	5:21:54.0
8. J. Stoa	NOR	5:25:30.0

Hedlund's phenomenal margin of victory is unequaled in Olympic history.

1932 Lake Placid C: 32, N: 9, D: 2.13.

1. Veli Saarinen	FIN	4:28:00.0
2. Väinö Liikkanen	FIN	4:28:20.0
3. Arne Rustadstuen	NOR	4:31:53.0
4. Ole Hegge	NOR	4:32:04.0
5. Sigurd Vestad	NOR	4:32:40.0
6. Sven Utterström	SWE	4:33:25.0
7. Tauno Lappalainen	FIN	4:45:02.0
8. Karl Lindberg	SWE	4:47.22.0

The 1932 race was held in a raging blizzard. The start was delayed three hours while contestants and officials argued about the course.

1936 Garmisch-Partenkirchen C: 36, N: 11, D: 2.15.

1. Elis Wiklund	SWE	3:30:11.0
2. Axel Wikström	SWE	3:33:20.0
3. Nils-Joel Englund	SWE	3:34:10.0
4. Hjalmar Bergström	SWE	3:35:50.0
5. Klaes Karppinen	FIN	3:39:33.0
6. Arne Tuft	NOR	3:41:18.0
7. Frans Heikkinen	FIN	3:42:44.0
8. Pekka Niemi	FIN	3:44:14.0

1948 St. Moritz C: 28, N: 9, D: 2.6.

1. Nils Karlsson	SWE	3:47:48.0
2. Harald Eriksson	SWE	3:52:20.0
3. Benjamin Vanninen	FIN	3:57:28.0
4. Pekka Vanninen	FIN	3:57:58.0
5. Anders Törnkvist	SWE	3:58:20.0
6. Edi Schild	SWI	4:05:37.0
7. Pekka Kuvaja	FIN	4:10:02.0
8. Jaroslav Cardal	CZE	4:14:34.0

1952 Oslo C: 36, N: 13, D: 2.20.

1. Veikko Hakulinen	FIN	3:33:33.0
2. Eero Kolehmainen	FIN	3:38:11.0
3. Magnar Estenstad	NOR	3:38:28.0
4. Olav Ökern	NOR	3:38:45.0
5. Kalevi Mononen	FIN	3:39:21.0
6. Nils Karlsson	SWE	3:39:30.0
7. Edvin Landsem	NOR	3:40:43.0
8. Harald Maartmann	NOR	3:43:43.0

This was the first of woodchopper Veikko Hakulinen's seven Olympic medals.

1956 Cortina C: 33, N: 13, D: 2.2.

1. Sixten Jernberg	SWE	2:50:27.0
2. Veikko Hakulinen	FIN	2:51:45.0
3. Fedor Terentyev	SOV	2:53:32.0
4. Eero Kolehmainen	FIN	2:56:17.0
5. Anatoly Shelyukin	SOV	2:56:40.0
6. Pavel Kolchin	SOV	2:58:00.0
7. Victor Baranov	SOV	3:03:55.0
8. Antti Sivonen	FIN	3:04:16.0

1960 Squaw Valley C: 31, N: 10, D: 2.27.

1. Kalevi Hämäläinen	FIN	2:59:06.3
2. Veikko Hakulinen	FIN	2:59:26.7
3. Rolf Rämgård	SWE	3:02:46.7
4. Lennart Larsson	SWE	3:03:27.9
5. Sixten Jernberg	SWE	3:05:18.0
6. Pentti Pelkonen	FIN	3:05:24.5
7. Gennady Vaganov	SOV	3:05:27.6
8. Veikko Rasanen	FIN	3:06:04.4

Finland, Norway, Sweden, and the U.S.S.R. took the first 15 places.

1964 Innsbruck–Seefeld C: 41, N: 14, D: 2.5.

1. Sixten Jernberg	SWE	2:43:52.6
2. Assar Rönnlund	SWE	2:44:58.2
3. Arto Tiainen	FIN	2:45:30.4
4. Janne Stefansson	SWE	2:45:36.6
5. Sverre Steinsheim	NOR	2:45:47.2
6. Harald Grönningen	NOR	2:47:03.6
7. Einar Östby	NOR	2:47:20.6
8. Ole Ellefsaeter	NOR	2:47:45.8

In 1956 Sixten Jernberg had predicted that whoever started the course last in the 50-kilometer race would win. Instead Jernberg, who started next to last, was the winner. At Innsbruck in 1964 he was the next to last starter again, and again he finished in first place. Three days later he earned another gold medal by skiing the second leg on Finland's relay team. He closed out his Olympic career two days after his 35th birthday, having won nine medals: four gold, three silver, and two bronze.

1968 Grenoble–Autrans C: 51, N: 17, D: 2.15.

1. Ole Ellefsaeter	NOR	2:28:45:8
2. Vyacheslav Vedenine	SOV	2:29:02:5
3. Josef Haas	SWI	2:29:14:8
4. Pål Tyldum	NOR	2:29:26:7
5. Melcher Risberg	SWE	2:29:37:0
6. Gunnar Larsson	SWI	2:29:37:2
7. Jan Halvarsson	SWE	2:30:05:9
8. Reidar Hjermstad	NOR	2:31:01:8

Ole Ellefsaeter, a forestry technician and pop singer, celebrated his 29th birthday by winning the 50-kilometer gold medal.

1972 Sapporo–Makomanai C: 40, N: 13, D: 2.10.

1. Pål Tyldum	NOR	2:43:14.75
2. Magne Myrmo	NOR	2:43:29.45

3. Vyacheslav Vedenine   SOV   2:44:00.19
4. Reidar Hjermstad   NOR   2:44:14.51
5. Walter Demel   GER   2:44:32.67
6. Werner Geeser   SWI   2:44:34.13
7. Lars-Arne Bolling   SWE   2:45:06.80
8. Fedor Simachev   SOV   2:45:08.93

Tyldum, the next to last starter, was only placed 18th after 15 kilometers, 78½ seconds behind the leader, Werner Geeser. By the 25-kilometer mark he had moved up to tenth place, but he was now 103½ seconds slower than Geeser. At 40 kilometers Geeser was still in first, but fading, while Tyldum had moved up to third, less than 26 seconds off Geeser's pace. While Geeser and Simachev tired dramatically in the last 10 kilometers, Tyldum plowed on to win the closest ever Olympic 50-kilometer race.

1976 Innsbruck–Seefeld C: 59, N: 15, D: 2.14.
1. Ivar Formo   NOR   2:37:30.05
2. Gert-Dietmar Klause   GDR   2:38:13.21
3. Benny Södergren   SWE   2:39:39.21
4. Ivan Garanin   SOV   2:40:38.94
5. Gerhard Grimmer   GDR   2:41:15.46
6. Per Knut Aaland   NOR   2:41:18.06
7. Pål Tyldum   NOR   2:42:21.86
8. Tommy Limby   SWE   2:42:43.58

1980 Lake Placid C: 51, N: 14, D: 2.23.
1. Nikolai Zimyatov   SOV   2:27:24.60
2. Juha Mieto   FIN   2:30:20.52
3. Alexandre Zavyalov   SOV   2:30:51.52
4. Lars Erik Eriksen   NOR   2:30:53.00
5. Sergei Saveliev   SOV   2:31:15.82
6. Yevgeny Beliaev   SOV   2:31:21.19
7. Oddvar Brå   NOR   2:31:46.83
8. Sven-Åke Lundbäck   SWE   2:31:59.65

Zimyatov won his third gold medal in nine days, having skied a total of 95 kilometers.

4×10-KILOMETER RELAY
1924–1932 not held

1936 Garmisch-Partenkirchen T: 16, N: 16, D: 2.10.
1. FIN   (Sulo Nurmela, Klaes Karppinen, Matti Lähde, Kalle Jalkanen)   2:41:33.0
2. NOR   (Oddbjörn Hagen, Olaf Hoffsbakken, Sverre Brodahl, Bjarne Iversen)   2:41:39.0
3. SWE   (John Berger, Erik Larsson, Arthur Häggblad, Martin Matsbo)   2:43:03.0
4. ITA   (Giulio Gerardi, Severino Menardi, Vincenzo Demetz, Giovanni Kasebacher)   2:50:05.0
5. CZE   (Cyril Musil, Gustav Berauer, Lukas Mihalak, František Simunek)   2:51:56.0
6. GER   (Friedel Däuber, Willi Bogner, Herbert Leupold, Anton Zeller)   2:54:54.0
7. POL   (Michal Górski, Marian Woyna-Orlewicz, Stanislaw Karpiel, Bronislaw Czech)   2:58:50.0
8. AUT   (Alfred Robner, Harald Bosio, Erich Gallwitz, Hans Baumann)   3:02:48.0

Kalle Jalkanen, the last Finnish skier, staged a spectacular come-from-behind victory. Trailing Bjarne Iversen of Norway by 82 seconds when he took over the baton, he caught him as they entered the ski stadium and won by only 20 yards.

1948 St. Moritz T: 11, N: 11, D: 2.3.
1. SWE   (Nils Östensson, Nils Täpp, Gunnar Eriksson, Martin Lunström)   2:32:08.0
2. FIN   (Lauri Silvennoinen, Teuvo Laukkanen, Sauli Rytky, August Kiuru)   2:41:06.0
3. NOR   (Erling Evensen, Olaf Ökern, Reidar Nyborg, Olav Hagen)   2:44:33.0
4. AUT   (Josl Gstrein, Josef Deutschmann, Engelbert Hundertpfund, Karl Rafreider)   2:47:18.0
5. SWI   (Niklaus Stump, Robert Zurbriggen, Max Müller, Edi Schild)   2:48:07.0
6. ITA   (Vincenzo Perruchon, Silvio Confortola, Rizzieri Rodighiero, Severino Compagnoni)   2:51:00.0
7. FRA   (Rene Jeandel, Gerard Perrier, Marius Mora, Benoit Carrara)   2:51:53.0
8. CZE   (Stefan Kovalcik, Frantisek Balvin, Jaroslav Zejicek, Jaroslav Cardal)   2:54:56.0

1952 Oslo T: 13, N: 13, D: 2.23.
1. FIN   (Heikki Hasu, Paavo Lonkila, Urpo Korhonen, Tapio Mäkelä)   2:20:16.0
2. NOR   (Magnar Estenstad, Mikal Kirkholt, Martin Stokken, Hallgeir Brenden)   2:23:13.0
3. SWE   (Nils Täpp, Sigurd Andersson, Enar Josefsson, Martin Lundström)   2:24:13.0
4. FRA   (Gerard Perrier, Benoit Carrara, Jean Mermet, René Mandrillon)   2:31:11.0
5. AUT   (Hans Eder, Friedrich Krischan, Karl Rafreider, Josef Schneeberger)   2:34:36.0
6. ITA   (Arrigo Delladio, Nino Anderlini, Frederico de Florian, Vincenzo Perruchon)   2:35:33.0
7. GER   (Hubert Egger, Albert Mohr, Heinz Hauser, Rudi Kopp)   2:36:37.0
8. CZE   (Vladimir Simunek, Stefan Kovalcik, Vlastimil Melich, Jaroslav Cardal)   2:37:12.0

1956 Cortina T: 14, N: 14, D: 2.4.
1. SOV   (Fedor Terentyev, Pavel Kolchin, Nikolai Anikin, Vladimir Kuzin)   2:15:30.0
2. FIN   (August Kiuru, Jormo Kortalainen, Arvo Viitanen, Veikko Hakulinen)   2:16:31.0
3. SWE   (Lennart Larsson, Gunnar Samuelsson, Per-Erik Larsson, Sixten Jernberg)   2:17:42.0
4. NOR   (Håkon Brusveen, Per Olsen, Marten Stokken, Hallgeir Brenden)   2:21:16.0
5. ITA   (Pompeo Fattor, Ottavio Compagnoni, Innocenzo Chatrian, Federico De Florian)   2:23:28.0
6. FRA   (Victor Arbez, René Mandrillon, Benoit Carrara, Jean Mermet)   2:24:06.0
7. SWI   (Werner Zwingli, Victor Kronig, Fritz Kocher, Marcel Huguenin)   2:24:30.0
8. CZE   (Emil Okuliar, Vlastimil Melich, Josef Prokes, Ilja Matous)   2:24:54.0

The first two Soviet skiers, Terentyev and Kolchin, built up an insurmountable lead of two and three-quarter minutes.

1960 Squaw Valley T: 11, N: 11, D: 2.25.
1. FIN (Toimi Alatalo, Eero Mäntyranta, Väinö Huh- 2:18:45.6
        tala, Veikko Hakulinen)
2. NOR (Harald Grönningen, Hallgeir Brenden, Einar 2:18:46.4
        Östby, Håkon Brusveen)
3. SOV (Anatoly Shelyukin, Gennady Vaganov, Alek- 2:21:21.6
        sei Kuznetsov, Nikolai Anikin)
4. SWE (Lars Olsson, Janne Stefansson, Lennart 2:21:31.8
        Larsson, Sixten Jernberg)
5. ITA (Giulio De Florian, Giuseppe Steiner, Pompeo 2:22:32.5
        Fattor, Marcello De Dorigo)
6. POL (Andrzej Mateja, Józef Rysula, Józef Gut-Mis- 2:26:25.3
        iaga, Kazimierz Zelek)
7. FRA (Victor Arbez, René Mandrillon, Benoit Carra- 2:26:30.8
        ra, Jean Mermet)
8. SWI (Fritz Kocher, Marcel Huguenin, Lorenz 2:29:36.8
        Possa, Alphonse Baume)

Since the relay is the only skiing event in which the participants actually race against each other, it is also the only event which has the potential for a truly exciting finish. Such a finish occurred in 1960. Lars Olsson gave Sweden a seven-second lead at the end of the first leg, but the second Swedish skier, Janne Stefansson, was quickly overtaken by Brenden and Mäntyranta. At the halfway mark, Norway and Finland were tied. Then Norway's Einar Östby pulled away to a 20-second lead. Håkon Brusveen, winner of the 15-kilometer race two days earlier, took over the last leg for Norway, followed by six-time Olympic medalist, 35-year-old Veikko Hakulinen. After eight kilometers Hakulinen overhauled Brusveen, but the Norwegian pulled back into the lead. With 100 meters to go, Hakulinen began to pass Brusveen again. Edging ahead in the final strides, the great Finnish veteran managed to win by three feet. It was a fitting ending to Hakulinen's marvelous Olympic career, during which he earned three gold medals, each in a different event and each in a different Olympics, as well as three silver medals and one bronze.

1964 Innsbruck–Seefeld T: 15, N: 15, D: 2.8.
1. SWE (Karl-Åke Asph, Sixten Jernberg, Janne Ste- 2:18:34.6
        fansson, Assar Rönnlund)
2. FIN (Väinö Huhtala, Arto Tiainen, Kalevi Laurila, 2:18:42.4
        Eero Mäntyranta)
3. SOV (Ivan Utrobin, Gennady Vaganov, Igor Voron- 2:18:46.9
        chikin, Pavel Kolchin)
4. NOR (Magnar Lundemo, Erling Steineidet, Einar 2:19:11.9
        Östby, Harald Grönningen)
5. ITA (Giuseppe Steiner, Marcello De Dorigo, Giulio 2:21:16.8
        De Florian, Franco Nones)
6. FRA (Victor Arbez, Felix Mathieu, Roger Pires, 2:26:31.4
        Paul Romand)
7. GDR/ (Heinz Seidel, Helmut Weidlich, Enno Röder, 2:26:34.4
   GER Walter Demel)

8. POL (Józef Gut-Misiaga, Tadeusz Jankowski, Ed- 2:27:27.0
        ward Budny, Józef Rysula)

Another thrilling finish, in which Väinö Huhtala gave Finland a 5.9-second lead after the first lap with the U.S.S.R. in second, Norway third, and Sweden fourth. By the halfway mark, Vaganov of the Soviet Union had moved into a 11.6-second lead over second-place Norway, with Italy in third, followed by Sweden and Finland. Pavel Kolchin took over the last leg for the Soviet Union, followed 13.4 seconds later by Grönningen of Norway, 31.5 seconds later by Assar Rönnlund of Sweden, and 32.3 seconds later by Eero Mäntyranta. Grönningen passed Kolchin to take the lead, but he exhausted himself by his effort and was passed shortly afterward by Mäntyranta, Rönnlund, and Kolchin. A few hundred meters short of the finish line Rönnlund summoned an extra reserve of energy, pushed ahead of Mäntyranta, and won by 7.8 seconds.

1968 Grenoble–Autrans T: 15, N: 15, D: 2.14.
1. NOR (Odd Martinsen, Pål Tyldum, Harald Grönnin- 2:08:33.5
        gen, Ole Ellefsaeter)
2. SWE (Jan Halvarsson, Bjarne Andersson, Gunnar 2:10:13.2
        Larsson, Assar Rönnlund)
3. FIN (Kalevi Oikarainen, Hannu Taipale, Kalevi 2:10:56.7
        Laurila, Eero Mäntyranta)
4. SOV (Vladimir Voronkov, Anatoly Akentiev, Valery 2:10:57.2
        Tarakanov, Vyacheslav Vedenine)
5. SWI (Konrad Hischier, Josef Haas, Florian Koch, 2:15:32.4
        Alois Kälin)
6. ITA (Giulio De Florian, Franco Nones, Palmiro 2:16:32.2
        Serafini, Aldo Stella)
7. GDR (Gerhard Grimmer, Axel Lesser, Peter Thiel, 2:19:22.8
        Gert-Dietmar Klause)
8. GER (Helmut Gerlach, Walter Demel, Herbert 2:19:37.6
        Steinbeisser, Karl Buhl)

Eero Mäntyranta made up over 26 seconds on the final leg to nip Vedenine at the finish line for the bronze medal. This gave Mäntyranta an Olympic medal total of three gold, two silver, and two bronze.

1972 Sapporo–Makomanai T: 14, N: 14, D: 2.13.
1. SOV (Vladimir Voronkov, Yuri Skobov, Fedor Si- 2:04:47.94
        machev, Vyacheslav Vedenine)
2. NOR (Oddvar Brå, Pål Tyldum, Ivar Formo, Johs 2:04:57.06
        Harviken)
3. SWI (Alfred Kälin, Albert Giger, Alois Kälin, 2:07:00.06
        Eduard Hauser)
4. SWE (Thomas Magnusson, Lars-Göran Åslund, 2:07:03.60
        Gunnar Larsson, Sven-Åke Lundbäck)
5. FIN (Hannu Taipale, Juha Mieto, Juhani Repo, 2:07:50.19
        Osmo Karjalainen)
6. GDR (Gerd Hessler, Axel Lesser, Gerhard Grim- 2:10:03.73
        mer, Gert-Dietmar Klause)
7. GER (Franz Betz, Urban Hettich, Hartmut Dopp, 2:10:42.85
        Walter Demel)
8. CZE (Stanislav Henych, Jan Fajstavr, Jan Mi- 2:11:27.55
        chalko, Jan Ilavsky)

Vedenine began the final leg 61½ seconds behind Johs Harviken, but he overtook the Norwegian one kilometer from the finish and won by over nine seconds.

1976 Innsbruck–Seefeld T: 16, N: 16, D: 2.12.

1.	FIN	(Matti Pitkänen, Juha Mieto, Pertti Teurajärvi, Arto Koivisto)	2:07:59.72
2.	NOR	(Pål Tyldum, Einar Sagstuen, Ivar Formo, Odd Martinsen)	2:09:58.36
3.	SOV	(Yevgeny Beliaev, Nikolai Bazhukov, Sergei Saveliev, Ivan Garanin)	2:10:51.46
4.	SWE	(Benny Södergren, Christer Johansson, Thomas Wassberg, Sven-Åke Lundbäck)	2:11:16.88
5.	SWI	(Franz Renggli, Edi Hauser, Heinz Gähler, Alfred Kälin)	2:11:28.53
6.	USA	(Douglas Peterson, Timothy Caldwell, William Koch, Ronny Yaeger)	2:11:41.35
7.	ITA	(Renzo Chiocchetti, Tonio Biondini, Ulrico Kostner, Giulio Capitanio)	2:12:07.12
8.	AUT	(Rudolf Horn, Reinhold Feichter, Werner Vogel, Herbert Wachter)	2:12:22.80

East Germany was in second place when their second skier, Axel Lesser, ran into a spectator, injured his knee, and had to abandon the race.

1980 Lake Placid T: 10, N: 10, D: 2.20.

1.	SOV	(Vassily Rochev, Nikolai Bazhukov, Yevgeny Beliaev, Nikolai Zimyatov)	1:57:03.46
2.	NOR	(Lars Erik Eriksen, Per Knut Aaland, Ove Aunli, Oddvar Brå)	1:58:45.77
3.	FIN	(Harri Kirvesniemi, Pertti Teurajärvi, Matti Pitkänen, Juha Mieto)	2:00:00.18
4.	GER	(Peter Zipfel, Wolfgang Müller, Dieter Notz, Jochem Behle)	2:00:22.74
5.	SWE	(Sven-Åke Lundbäck, Thomas Eriksson, Benny Kohlberg, Thomas Wassberg)	2:00:42.71
6.	ITA	(Maurillo De Zolt, Benedetto Carrara, Giulio Capitanio, Giorgio Vanzetta)	2:01:09.93
7.	SWI	(Hansüli, Konrad Hallenbarter, Edi Hauser, Gaudenz Ambühl)	2:03:36.57
8.	USA	(William Koch, Timothy Caldwell, James Galanes, Stanley Dunklee)	2:04:12.17

SKI JUMP, 70-METER HILL

The first ski-jumping contest was held in Trysil, Norway, in 1862. Jumps are scored according to two criteria: distance and style. Style points are determined by five judges. The highest and lowest scores are dropped and the points awarded by the remaining three judges are added together. Each contestant takes two jumps. In 1964 the ski jump was split into two events: the small hill, or 70-meter jump, and the big hill, or 90-meter jump.

1924–1960 not held

1964 Innsbruck–Seefeld C: 53, N: 15, D: 1.31.

			FIRST JUMP (M)	SECOND JUMP (M)	TOTAL PTS.
1.	Veikko Kankkonen	FIN	80.0	79.0	229.9
2.	Toralf Engan	NOR	78.5	79.0	226.3
3.	Targeir Brandtzaeg	NOR	79.0	78.0	222.9
4.	Josef Matous	CZE	77.0	76.5	218.2
5.	Dieter Neuendorf	GDR	77.0	75.0	214.7
6.	Helmut Recknagel	GDR	77.0	75.0	210.4
7.	Kurt Elima	SWE	75.0	75.0	208.9
8.	Hans Olav Sorensen	NOR	73.5	74.5	208.6

In 1964 the competitors were allowed to use the best two of three jumps. This rule saved Kankkonen, whose mediocre first jump landed him in 29th place. However his second and third leaps were masterpieces.

1968 Grenoble–Autrans C: 58, N: 18, D: 2.11.

			FIRST JUMP (M)	SECOND JUMP (M)	TOTAL PTS.
1.	Jiri Raška	CZE	79.0	72.5	216.5
2.	Reinhold Bachler	AUT	77.5	76.0	214.2
3.	Baldur Preiml	AUT	80.0	72.5	212.6
4.	Björn Wirkola	NOR	76.5	72.5	212.0
5.	Topi Mattila	FIN	78.0	72.5	211.9
6.	Anatoly Zheglanov	SOV	79.5	74.5	211.5
7.	Dieter Neuendorf	GDR	76.5	73.0	211.3
8.	Vladimir Beloussov	SOV	73.5	73.0	207.5

1972 Sapporo–Miyanomori C: 56, N: 16, D: 2.6.

			FIRST JUMP (M)	SECOND JUMP (M)	TOTAL PTS.
1.	Yukio Kasaya	JAP	84.0	79.0	244.2
2.	Akitsugu Konno	JAP	82.5	79.0	234.8
3.	Seiji Aochi	JAP	83.5	77.5	229.5
4.	Ingolf Mork	NOR	78.0	78.0	225.5
5.	Jiri Raška	CZE	78.5	78.0	224.8
6.	Wojciech Fortuna	POL	82.0	76.5	222.0
7.	Karel Kodejska	CZE	80.0	75.5	220.2
7.	Gari Napalkov	SOV	79.5	76.0	220.2

Before 1972 Japan had won a total of one medal in the Winter Olympics. Consequently, when 28-year-old Yukio Kasaya won three straight meets in Europe one month before the Sapporo Games, Japan's hopes for a gold medal at the first Winter Olympics to be held in Asia were concentrated on Kasaya. The excitement was particularly great because Kasaya was a hometown boy from Japan's northernmost island of Hokkaido, where the games were being held. Kasaya's teammates, Akitsugu Konno and Seiji Aochi, were also from Hokkaido. Scattered among the 100,000 people at the bottom of the jumping hill were old schoolmates of Kasaya's waving the flag of Yoichimachi High School, Kasaya's alma mater. Despite the enormous pressure, Kasaya produced the best jump of each round. While the nation rejoiced over the stunning Japanese sweep, Kasaya, who had made 10,000 jumps since he was 11 years old, reminded the press of his personal motto, "Challenge not your rivals, but yourself."

1976 Innsbruck–Seefeld C: 55, N: 15, D: 2.7.

		FIRST JUMP (M)	SECOND JUMP (M)	TOTAL PTS.
1. Hans-Georg Aschenbach	GDR	84.5	82.0	252.0
2. Jochen Danneberg	GDR	83.5	82.5	246.2
3. Karl Schnabl	AUT	82.5	81.5	242.0
4. Jaroslav Balcar	CZE	81.0	81.5	239.6
5. Ernst von Grüningen	SWI	80.5	80.5	238.7
6. Reinhold Bachler	AUT	80.5	80.5	237.2
7. Anton Innauer	AUT	80.5	81.5	233.5
7. Rudolf Wanner	AUT	79.5	79.5	233.5

1980 Lake Placid C: 48, N: 16, D: 2.17.

		FIRST JUMP (M)	SECOND JUMP (M)	TOTAL PTS.
1. Anton Innauer	AUT	87.2	87.7	266.3
2. Manfred Deckert	GDR	88.2	88.2	249.2
2. Hirokazu Yagi	JAP	87.2	87.1	249.2
4. Masahiro Akimoto	JAP	87.2	87.7	248.5
5. Pentti Kokkonen	FIN	87.7	88.2	247.6
6. Hubert Neuper	AUT	88.1	87.6	245.5
7. Alfred Groyer	AUT	87.7	88.1	245.3
8. Jouko Tormanen	FIN	87.5	88.0	243.5

Toni Innauer, a 21-year-old vegetarian, used his superb form to achieve the largest winning margin in Olympic jumping history.

SKI JUMP, 90-METER HILL
(1924–1956: Various Lengths)

1924 Chamonix C: 27, N: 9, D: 2.4.

		FIRST JUMP (M)	SECOND JUMP (M)	TOTAL PTS.
1. Jacob Tullin Thams	NOR	49.0	49.0	18.960
2. Narve Bonna	NOR	47.5	49.0	18.689
3. Anders Haugen	USA	49.0	50.0	17.916
4. Thorleif Haug	NOR	44.0	44.5	17.821
5. Einar Landvik	NOR	42.0	44.5	17.521
6. Axel Nilsson	SWE	42.5	44.0	17.146
7. Menotti Jacobsen	SWE	43.0	42.0	17.083
8. Alexander Girardbille	SWI	40.5	41.5	16.794

The final results of this event were not decided until 50 years after it took place. In 1924 it appeared that the great Thorleif Haug had finished third, thus winning two medals at one time: a bronze in the ski jump and a gold in the nordic combined, to go with the two gold medals he had already won in the 50-kilometer and 15-kilometer races. However, in 1974 Toralf Strömstad, who had earned a sil-

ver medal in the 1924 nordic combined, discovered an error in the computation of the scores. Haug, who had been dead for 40 years, was demoted to fourth place, while Norwegian-born Anders Haugen was moved up to third. Haugen, the only American ever to place in the top four in ski-jumping, was awarded his medal in a special ceremony in Oslo. He was 83 years old.

1928 St. Moritz C: 38, N: 13, D: 2.18.

		FIRST JUMP (M)	SECOND JUMP (M)	TOTAL PTS.
1. Alf Andersen	NOR	60.0	64.0	19.208
2. Sigmund Ruud	NOR	57.5	62.5	18.542
3. Rudolf Burkert	CZE	57.0	59.5	17.937
4. Axel Nilsson	SWE	53.5	60.0	16.937
5. Sven Lundgren	SWE	48.0	59.0	16.708
6. Rolf Monsen	USA	53.0	59.5	16.687
7. Sepp Muhlbauer	SWI	52.0	58.0	16.541
8. E. Feuz	SWI	52.5	58.5	16.458

The longest jump of the day was recorded by defending champion Jacob Tullin Thams, who stretched out to 73 meters but fell badly when he reached the ground. The consequent loss in style points dropped him to 28th place.

1932 Lake Placid C: 3,, N: 10, D: 2.12.

		FIRST JUMP (M)	SECOND JUMP (M)	TOTAL PTS.
1. Birger Ruud	NOR	66.5	69.0	228.1
2. Hans Beck	NOR	71.5	63.5	227.0
3. Kaare Wahlberg	NOR	62.5	64.0	219.5
4. Sven Eriksson	SWE	65.5	64.0	218.9
5. Caspar Oimen	USA	63.0	67.5	216.7
6. Fritz Kaufmann	SWI	63.5	65.5	215.8
7. Sigmond Ruud	NOR	63.0	62.5	215.1
8. Goro Adachi	JAP	60.0	66.0	210.7

Hans Beck and the Ruud brothers were brought up together in the mining town of Kongsberg. Confusion concerning the scoring computations caused a four-hour delay in the announcement of the placings, and even then it was originally stated that Beck had won.

1936 Garmisch-Partenkirchen C: 48, N: 14, D: 2.16.

		FIRST JUMP (M)	SECOND JUMP (M)	TOTAL PTS.
1. Birger Ruud	NOR	75.0	74.5	232.0
2. Sven Eriksson	SWE	76.0	76.0	230.5
3. Reidar Andersen	NOR	74.0	75.0	228.9
4. Kaare Wahlberg	NOR	73.5	72.0	227.0
5. Stanislaw Marusarz	POL	73.0	75.5	221.6
6. Lauri Valonen	FIN	73.5	67.0	219.4
7. Masaji Iguro	JAP	74.5	72.5	218.2
8. Arnold Kongsgaard	NOR	74.5	72.5	217.7

1948 St. Moritz C: 49, N: 14, D: 2.7.

		FIRST JUMP (M)	SECOND JUMP (M)	TOTAL PTS.
1. Petter Hugsted	NOR	65.0	70.0	228.1
2. Birger Ruud	NOR	64.0	67.0	226.6
3. Thorleif Schjelderup	NOR	64.0	67.0	225.1
4. Matti Pietikainen	FIN	69.5	69.0	224.6
5. Gordon Wren	USA	68.0	68.5	222.8
6. Leo Laakso	FIN	66.0	69.5	221.7
7. Asbjorn Ruud	NOR	58.0	67.5	220.2
8. Aatto Pietikainen	FIN	69.0	68.0	215.4

Two-time gold medalist Birger Ruud, now 36 years old, went to St. Moritz as a coach. But when he saw the poor weather the night before the competition, he decided to compete in place of the less experienced George Thrane. Ruud's confidence in himself paid off with a silver medal.

1952 Oslo C: 44, N: 13, D: 2.24.

		FIRST JUMP (M)	SECOND JUMP (M)	TOTAL PTS.
1. Arnfinn Bergmann	NOR	67.5	68.0	226.0
2. Torbjörn Falkanger	NOR	68.0	64.0	221.5
3. Karl Holmström	SWE	67.0	65.5	219.5
4. Toni Brutscher	GER	66.5	62.5	216.5
4. Halvor Naes	NOR	63.5	64.5	216.5
6. Arne Hoel	NOR	66.5	63.5	215.5
7. Antti Hyvärinen	FIN	66.5	61.5	213.5
8. Sepp Weiler	GER	67.0	63.0	213.0

Between 1924 and 1952 Norway won 14 of the 18 medals awarded in the ski jumps. Since 1952, the Norwegians have earned only five of the 36 medals.

1956 Cortina C: 51, N: 16, D: 2.5.

		FIRST JUMP (M)	SECOND JUMP (M)	TOTAL PTS.
1. Antti Hyvärinen	FIN	81.0	84.0	227.0
2. Aulis Kallakorpi	FIN	83.5	80.5	225.0
3. Harry Glass	GDR	83.5	80.5	224.5
4. Max Bolkart	GER	80.0	81.5	222.5
5. Sven Pettersson	SWE	81.0	81.5	220.0
6. Andreas Däscher	SWI	82.0	82.0	219.5
7. Eino Kirjonen	FIN	78.0	81.0	219.0
8. Werner Lesser	GDR	77.5	77.5	210.0

1960 Squaw Valley C: 45, N: 15, D: 2.28.
80 Meters

		FIRST JUMP (M)	SECOND JUMP (M)	TOTAL PTS.
1. Helmut Recknagel	GDR	93.5	84.5	227.2
2. Niilo Halonen	FIN	92.5	83.5	222.6
3. Otto Leodolter	AUT	88.5	83.5	219.4
4. Nikolai Kamensky	SOV	90.5	79.0	216.9
5. Thorbjörn Yggeseth	NOR	88.5	82.5	216.1
6. Max Bolkart	GER	87.5	81.0	212.6
7. Ansten Samuelstuen	USA	90.0	79.0	211.5
8. Juhani Karkinen	FIN	87.5	82.0	211.4

1964 Innsbruck C: 52, N: 15, D: 2.9.
80 Meters

		FIRST JUMP (M)	SECOND JUMP (M)	TOTAL PTS.
1. Toralf Engan	NOR	90.5	73.0	230.7
2. Veikko Kankkonen	FIN	90.5	88.0	228.9
3. Torgeir Brandtzaeg	NOR	90.0	87.0	227.2
4. Dieter Bokeloh	GDR	83.0	83.5	214.6
5. Kjell Sjöberg	SWE	82.0	85.0	214.4
6. Aleksandr Ivannikov	SOV	81.5	83.5	213.3
7. Helmut Recknagel	GDR	86.5	78.0	212.8
8. Dieter Neuendorf	GDR	84.5	83.0	212.6

A second ski jump event was added in 1964 in order to give more competitors a chance to win medals in a sport where a sudden gust of wind or a split-second mistake can send the best jumper down to defeat. As it turned out, however, the same three men took the medals in both events.

1968 Grenoble–St. Nizier C: 58, N: 17, D: 2.18.

		FIRST JUMP (M)	SECOND JUMP (M)	TOTAL PTS.
1. Vladimir Beloussov	SOV	101.5	98.5	231.3
2. Jiři Raška	CZE	101.0	98.0	229.4
3. Lars Grini	NOR	99.0	93.5	214.3
4. Manfred Queck	GDR	96.5	98.5	212.8
5. Bent Tomtum	NOR	98.5	95.0	212.2
6. Reinhold Bachler	AUT	98.5	95.0	210.7
7. Wolfgang Stöhr	GDR	96.5	92.5	205.9
8. Anatoly Zheglanov	SOV	99.0	92.0	205.7

1972 Sapporo–Okurayama C: 52, N: 15, D: 2.11.

		FIRST JUMP (M)	SECOND JUMP (M)	TOTAL PTS.
1. Wojciech Fortuna	POL	111.0	87.5	219.9
2. Walter Steiner	SWI	94.0	103.0	219.8
3. Rainer Schmidt	GDR	98.5	101.0	219.3
4. Tauno Käyhkö	FIN	95.0	100.5	219.2
5. Manfred Wolf	GDR	107.0	89.5	215.1
6. Garii Napalkov	SOV	99.5	92.0	210.1
7. Yukio Kasaya	JAP	106.0	85.0	209.4
8. Danilo Pudgar	YUG	92.5	97.5	206.0

Fortuna's first jump was so spectacular that he was able to win the gold medal even though his second jump was only the 22nd best of the round.

1976 Innsbruck C: 54, N: 15, D: 2.15.

		FIRST JUMP (M)	SECOND JUMP (M)	TOTAL PTS.
1. Karl Schnabl	AUT	97.5	97.0	234.8
2. Anton Innauer	AUT	102.5	91.0	232.9
3. Henry Glass	GDR	91.0	97.0	221.7
4. Jochen Danneberg	GDR	102.0	89.5	221.6
5. Reinhold Bachler	AUT	95.0	91.0	217.4
6. Hans Wallner	AUT	93.5	92.5	216.9
7. Bernd Eckstein	GDR	94.0	91.5	216.2
8. Hans-Georg Aschenbach	GDR	92.5	89.0	212.1

1980 Lake Placid C: 50, N: 16, D: 2.23.

		FIRST JUMP (M)	SECOND JUMP (M)	TOTAL PTS.
1. Jouko Törmänen	FIN	96.7	96.4	271.0
2. Hubert Neuper	AUT	97.1	97.0	262.4
3. Jari Puikkonen	FIN	96.5	96.5	248.5
4. Anton Innauer	AUT	96.2	96.2	245.7
5. Armin Kogler	AUT	97.3	97.2	245.6
6. Roger Ruud	NOR	96.8	97.3	243.0
7. Hansjoers Sumi	SWI	96.5	96.6	242.7
8. James Denney	USA	96.6	96.6	239.1

NORDIC COMBINED

1924 Chamonix C: 30, N: 9, D: 2.4.

		18 KM	SKI JUMP	TOTAL PTS.
1. Thorleif Haug	NOR	1:14:31.0	17.821	18.906
2. Thoralf Strömstad	NOR	1:17:03.0	17.687	18.219
3. Johan Gröttumsbråten	NOR	1:15:51.0	16.333	17.854
4. Harald Ökern	NOR	1:20:30.0	17.395	17.260
5. Axel Nilsson	SWE	1:25:29.0	16.500	14.063
6. Josef Adolf	CZE	1:31:17.0	12.833	13.729
7. Vincenz Buchberger	CZE	1:32:32.0	16.250	13.625
8. Menotti Jacobsson	SWE	1:37:10.0	16.896	12.823

1928 St. Moritz C: 35, N: 14, D: 2.18.

		18 KM	SKI JUMP	TOTAL PTS.
1. Johan Gröttumsbråten	NOR	1:37:01.0	15.667	17.833
2. Hans Vinjarengen	NOR	1:41:44.0	12.856	15.303
3. John Snersrud	NOR	1:50:51.0	16.917	15.021
4. Paavo Nuotio	FIN	1:48:46.0	15.729	14.927
5. Esko Järvinen	FIN	1:46:33.0	14.286	14.810
6. Sven Eriksson	SWE	1:52:20.0	16.312	14.593
7. Ludwig Böck	GER	1:48:56.0	11.812	13.260
8. Ole Kolterrud	NOR	1:50:17.0	13.500	13.146

1932 Lake Placid C: 33, N: 10, D: 2.11.

		18 KM	SKI JUMP	TOTAL PTS.
1. Johan Gröttumsbråten	NOR	1:27:15.0	206.0	446.00
2. Ole Stenen	NOR	1:28:05.0	200.3	436.05

3. Hans Vinjarengen	NOR	1:32:40.0	221.6	434.60
4. Sverre Kolterud	NOR	1:34:36.0	214.7	418.70
5. Sven Eriksson	SWE	1:39:32.0	220.8	402.30
6. Antonin Barton	CZE	1:33:39.0	188.6	397.10
7. Bronislaw Czech	POL	1:36:37.0	197.0	392.00
8. František Simunek	CZE	1:39:58.0	196.8	375.30

Gröttumsbråten closed out his Olympic career with three gold medals, one silver, and two bronze.

1936 Garmisch-Partenkirchen C: 51, N: 16, D: 2.13.

		18 KM	SKI JUMP	TOTAL PTS.
1. Oddbjörn Hagen	NOR	1:15:33.0	190.3	430.3
2. Olaf Hoffsbakken	NOR	1:17:37.0	192.0	419.8
3. Sverre Brodahl	NOR	1:18:01.0	182.6	408.1
4. Lauri Valonen	FIN	1:26:34.0	222.6	401.2
5. František Simunek	CZE	1:19:09.0	175.3	394.3
6. Bernt Osterklöft	NOR	1:21:37.0	188.7	393.8
7. Stanislaw Marusarz	POL	1:25:27.0	208.9	393.3
7. Timo Murama	FIN	1:24:52.0	205.8	393.3

1948 St. Moritz C: 39, N: 13, D: 2.1.

		18 KM	SKI JUMP	TOTAL PTS.
1. Heikki Hasu	FIN	1:16:43.0	208.8	448.80
2. Martti Huhtala	FIN	1:19:28.0	209.5	433.65
3. Sven Israelsson	SWE	1:21:35.0	221.9	433.40
4. Niklaus Stump	SWI	1:21:44.0	213.0	421.50
5. Olavi Sihvonen	FIN	1:21:50.0	209.2	416.20
6. Eilert Dahl	NOR	1:22:12.0	208.8	414.30
7. Pauli Salonen	FIN	1:22:15.0	206.3	413.30
8. Olav Dufseth	NOR	1:22:26.0	201.1	412.60

1952 Oslo C: 25, N: 11, D: 2.18.

		SKI JUMP	18 KM	TOTAL PTS.
1. Simon Slåttvik	NOR	223.5	1:05:40.0	451.621
2. Heikki Hasu	FIN	207.5	1:02:24.0	447.500
3. Sverre Stenersen	NOR	223.0	1:09:44.0	436.335
4. Paavo Korhonen	FIN	206.0	1:05:30.0	434.727
5. Per Gjelten	NOR	212.0	1:07:40.0	432.848
6. Ottar Gjermundshaug	NOR	206.0	1:06:13.0	432.121
7. Aulis Sipponen	FIN	198.5	1:06:03.0	425.227
8. Eeti Nieminen	FIN	206.0	1:08:24.0	424.181

February 18, 1952, was a great day in the history of Norwegian sports. Hjallis Andersen won the 1500-meter skating event, Hallgeir Brenden won the 18-kilometer cross-country race, and Simon Slåttvik won the nordic combined. People all over Oslo left their jobs and spilled into the streets to celebrate. *The New York Times* reported, with some annoyance, that at the Hotel Viking, where the press was staying, half of the waiters walked out, and "It took more than an hour to order food and another two hours to get it." The year 1952 was the first time that the jumping half of the nordic combined was held before the skiing.

1956 Cortina C: 36, N: 12, D: 1.31.

			SKI JUMP	15 KM	TOTAL PTS.
1.	Sverre Stenersen	NOR	215.0	56:18.0	455.000
2.	Bengt Eriksson	SWE	214.0	1:00:36.0	437.400
3.	Franciszek Gasienica-Groń	POL	203.0	57:55.0	436.800
4.	Paavo Korhonen	FIN	196.5	56:32.0	435.597
5.	Arne Barhaugen	NOR	199.0	57:11.0	435.581
6.	Tormod Knutsen	NOR	203.0	58:22.0	435.000
7.	Nikolai Gusakov	SOV	200.0	58:17.0	432.300
8.	Alfredo Prucker	ITA	201.0	58:52.0	431.100

1960 Squaw Valley C: 33, N: 13, D: 2.22.

			SKI JUMP	15 KM	TOTAL PTS.
1.	Georg Thoma	GER	221.5	59:23.8	457.952
2.	Tormod Knutsen	NOR	217.0	59:31.0	453.000
3.	Nikolay Gusakov	SOV	212.0	58:29.4	452.000
4.	Pekka Ristola	FIN	214.0	59:32.8	449.871
5.	Dmitri Kochkin	SOV	219.5	1:01:32.1	444.694
6.	Arne Larsen	NOR	215.0	1:01:10.1	444.613
7.	Sverre Stenersen	NOR	205.5	1:00:24.0	438.081
8.	Lars Dahlqvist	SWE	201.5	59:46.0	436.532

1964 Innsbruck–Seefeld C: 32, N: 11, D: 2.3.

			SKI JUMP (70 M)	15 KM	TOTAL PTS.
1.	Tormod Knutsen	NOR	238.9	50:58.6	469.28
2.	Nikolai Kiselev	SOV	233.0	51:49.1	453.04
3.	Georg Thoma	GDR	241.1	52:31.2	452.88
4.	Nikolai Gusakov	SOV	223.4	51:19.8	449.36
5.	Arne Larsen	NOR	198.3	50:49.6	430.63
6.	Arne Barhaugen	NOR	191.3	50:40.4	425.63
7.	Vyacheslav Driagin	SOV	216.2	52:58.3	422.75
8.	Ezio Damolin	ITA	198.1	51:42.3	419.54

1968 Grenoble–Autrans C: 41, N: 13, D: 2.11.

			SKI JUMP (70 M)	15 KM	TOTAL PTS.
1.	Franz Keller	GER	240.1	50:45.2	449.04
2.	Alois Kälin	SWI	193.2	47:21.5	447.99
3.	Andreas Kunz	GDR	216.9	49:19.8	444.10
4.	Tomáš Kučera	CZE	217.4	50;07.7	434.14
5.	Ezio Damolin	ITA	206.0	49;36.2	429.54
6.	Jósef Gąsienica	POL	217.7	50:34.5	428.78
7.	Robert Makara	SOV	222.8	51:09.3	426.92
8.	Vyacheslav Driagin	SOV	222.8	51:22.0	424.38

Had **Kälin** been able to finish the cross-country race 2.3 seconds sooner, he would have won the gold medal.

1972 Sapporo–Miyanomori/Makomanai C: 39, N: 14, D: 2.5.

		SKI JUMP (70 M)	15 KM	TOTAL PTS.
1. Ulrich Wehling	GDR	200.9	49:15.3	413.340
2. Rauno Miettinen	FIN	210.0	51:08.2	405.505
3. Karl-Heinz Luck	GDR	178.8	48:24.9	398.800
4. Erkki Kilpinen	FIN	185.0	49:52.6	391.845
5. Yuji Katsuro	JAP	195.1	51:10.9	390.200
6. Tomáš Kučera	CZE	191.8	51:04.0	387.935
7. Aleksandr Nossov	SOV	201.3	52:08.7	387.730
8. Kaare Olavberg	NOR	180.4	50:08.9	384.800

Hideki Nakano of Japan had the unusual distinction of finishing first among the competitors in the nordic combined in the ski jump, but last in the 15-kilometer race. This left him in 13th place overall.

1976 Innsbruck–Seefeld C: 34, N: 14, D: 2.8.

		SKI JUMP (70 M)	15 KM	TOTAL PTS.
1. Ulrich Wehling	GDR	225.5	50:28.95	423.39
2. Urban Hettich	GER	198.9	48:01.55	418.90

3. Konrad Winkler	GDR	213.9	49:51.11	417.47
4. Rauno Miettinen	FIN	219.9	51:12.21	411.30
5. Claus Tuchscherer	GDR	218.7	51:16.12	409.51
6. Nikolai Nagovitzin	SOV	196.1	49:05.97	406.44
7. Valery Kapayev	SOV	202.9	49:53.26	406.14
8. Tom Sandberg	NOR	195.7	49:09.34	405.53

1980 Lake Placid C: 31, N: 9, D: 2.18.

		SKI JUMP (70 M)	15 KM	TOTAL PTS.
1. Ulrich Wehling	GDR	227.2	49:24.5	432.200
2. Jouko Karjalainen	FIN	209.5	47:44.5	429.500
3. Konrad Winkler	GDR	214.5	48:45.7	425.320
4. Tom Sandberg	NOR	203.7	48:19.4	418.465
5. Uwe Dotzauer	GDR	217.6	49:52.4	412.210
6. Karl Lustenberger	SWI	212.7	50:01.1	412.210
7. Aleksandr Maiorov	SOV	194.4	48:19.6	409.135
8. Gunter Schmieder	GDR	201.7	49:42.0	404.075

The 27-year-old Wehling became the first man to win three consecutive gold medals in the same individual Winter event.

NORDIC SKIING

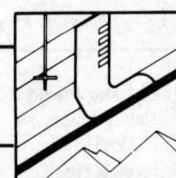

WOMEN

In the individual events, participants start at 30-second intervals and race against the clock. In the relay all teams start at the same time.

5 KILOMETERS

1924–1960 not held

1964 Innsbruck–Seefeld C: 32, N: 14, D: 2.5.
1. Claudia Boyarskikh   SOV   17:50.5
2. Mirja Lehtonen   FIN   17:52.9
3. Alevtina Kolchina   SOV   18:08.4
4. Eudokia Mekshilo   SOV   18:16.7
5. Toini Pöysti   FIN   18:25.5
6. Toini Gustaffson   SWE   18:25.7
7. Barbro Martinsson   SWE   18:26.4
8. Eeva Ruoppa   FIN   18:29.8

In 1964 Claudia Boyarskikh, a 24-year-old teacher from Siberia, swept all three women's nordic events.

1968 Grenoble–Autrans C: 34, N: 12, D: 2.13.
1. Toini Gustafsson   SWE   16:45.2
2. Galina Kulakova   SOV   16:48.4
3. Alevtina Kolchina   SOV   16:51.6
4. Barbro Martinsson   SWE   16:52.9
5. Marjatta Kajosmaa   FIN   16:54.6
6. Rita Achkina   SOV   16:55.1
7. Inger Aufles   NOR   16:58.1
8. Senja Pusula   FIN   17:00.3

Toini Gustafsson was the last skier to leave the starting line. Kept informed of Kulakova's time at each kilometer, she knew exactly what time she had to beat. Four seconds off Kulakova's pace with only one kilometer to go, Gustafsson poured it on to win with three seconds to spare. A 26-year-old physical education teacher, Gustafsson also won the 10-kilometer contest and gained a silver medal in the relay after recording the fastest leg of the race.

1972 Sapporo–Makomanai C: 43, N: 12, D: 2.9.
1. Galina Kulakova   SOV   17:00.50
2. Marjatta Kajosmaa   FIN   17:05.50
3. Helena Šikolová   CZE   17:07.32
4. Alevtina Olunina   SOV   17:07.40
5. Hilkka Kuntola   FIN   17:11.67
6. Lyubov Moukhatcheva   SOV   17:12.08
7. Berit Mördre-Lammedal   NOR   17:16.79
8. Aslaug Dahl   NOR   17:17.49

Kulakova, a 29-year-old physical education teacher from Izhevsk, matched Claudia Boyarskikh's feat of capturing all three women's nordic gold medals.

1976 Innsbruck–Seefeld C: 44, N: 14, D: 2.9.
1. Helena Takalo   FIN   15:48.69
2. Raisa Smetanina   SOV   15:49.73
— Galina Kulakova   SOV   16:07.36
3. Nina Baldycheva   SOV   16:12.82
4. Hilkka Kuntola   FIN   16:17.74
5. Eva Olsson   SWE   16:27.15
6. Zinaida Amosova   SOV   16:33.78
7. Monika Debertshäuser   GDR   16:34.94
8. Grete Kummen   NOR   16:35.43

Defending champion Kulakova finished third, but was disqualified for having used a nasal spray which contained the banned drug ephedrine. She was, however, allowed to compete in the 10-kilometer race and the relay.

1980 Lake Placid C: 38, N: 12, D: 2.15.

1. Raisa Smetanina	SOV	15:06.92
2. Hilkka Riihivuori (Kuntola)	FIN	15:11.96
3. Kvetoslava Jeriova	CZE	15:23.44
4. Barbara Petzold	GDR	15:23.62
5. Nina Baldycheva	SOV	15:29.03
6. Galina Kulakova	SOV	15:29.58
7. Veronika Hesse	GDR	15:31.83
8. Helena Takalo	FIN	15:32.12

10 KILOMETERS

1924–1948 not held

1952 Oslo C: 20, N: 8, D: 2.23.

1. Lydia Wideman	FIN	41:40.0
2. Mirja Hietamies	FIN	42:39.0
3. Siira Rantanen	FIN	42:50.0
4. Märta Norberg	SWE	42:53.0
5. Sirkka Polkunen	FIN	43:07.0
6. Rakel Wahl	NOR	44:54.0
7. Marit Oiseth	NOR	45:04.0
8. Margit Albrechtsson	SWE	45:05.0

1956 Cortina C: 40, N: 11, D: 1.28.

1. Lyubov Kosyreva	SOV	38:11.0
2. Radya Eroshina	SOV	38:16.0
3. Sonja Edström	SWE	3::23.0
4. Alevtina Kolchina	SOV	38:46.0
5. Siira Rantanen	FIN	39:40.0
6. Mirja Hietamies	FIN	40:18.0
7. Irma Johansson	SWE	40:20.0
8. Sirkka Polkunen	FIN	40:25.0

1960 Squaw Valley C: 24, N: 7, D: 2.20.

1. Maria Gusakova	SOV	39:46.6
2. Lyubov Baranova (Kosyreva)	SOV	40:04.2
3. Radya Eroshina	SOV	40:06.0
4. Alevtina Kolchina	SOV	40:12.6
5. Sonja Ruthström (Edström)	SWE	40:35.5
6. Toini Pöysti	FIN	40:41.9
7. Barbro Martinsson	SWE	41:06.2
8. Irma Johansson	SWE	41:08.3

1964 Innsbruck–Seefeld C: 35, N: 13, D: 2.1.

1. Claudia Boyarskikh	SOV	40:24.3
2. Eudokia Mekshilo	SOV	40:26.6
3. Maria Gusakova	SOV	40:46.6
4. Britt Strandberg	SWE	40:54.0
5. Toini Pöysti	FIN	41:17.4
6. Senja Pusula	FIN	41:17.8
7. Alevtina Kolchina	SOV	41:26.2
8. Toini Gustafsson	SWE	41:41.1

1968 Grenoble–Autrans C: 34, N: 11, D: 2.9.

1. Toini Gustafsson	SWE	36:46.5
2. Berit Mördre	NOR	37:54.6
3. Inger Aufles	NOR	37:59.9
4. Barbro Martinsson	SWE	38:07.1
5. Marjatta Kajosmaa	FIN	38:09.0
6. Galina Kulakova	SOV	38:26.7
7. Alevtina Kolchina	SOV	38:52.9
8. Babben Damon-Enger	NOR	38:54.4

1972 Sapporo–Makomanai C: 42, N: 11, D: 2.6.

1. Galina Kulakova	SOV	34:17.82
2. Alevtina Olunina	SOV	34:54.11
3. Marjatta Kajosmaa	FIN	34:56.45
4. Lyubov Moukhatcheva	SOV	34:58.56
5. Helena Takalo	FIN	35:06.34
6. Aslaug Dahl	NOR	35:18.84
7. Helena Šikolová	CZE	35:29.33
8. Hilkka Kuntola	FIN	35:36.71

1976 Innsbruck–Seefeld C: 44, N: 15, D: 2.10.

1. Raisa Smetanina	SOV	30:13.41
2. Helena Takalo	FIN	30:14.28
3. Galina Kulakova	SOV	30:38.61
4. Nina Baldycheva	SOV	30:52.58
5. Eva Olsson	SWE	31:08.72
6. Zinaida Amosova	SOV	31:11.23
7. Barbara Petzold	GDR	31:12.20
8. Veronika Schmidt	GDR	31:12.33

1980 Lake Placid C: 38, N: 12, D: 2.18.

1. Barbara Petzold	GDR	30:31.54
2. Hilkka Riihivuori (Kuntola)	FIN	30:35.05
3. Helena Takalo	FIN	30:45.25
4. Raisa Smetanina	SOV	30:54.48
5. Galina Kulakova	SOV	30:58.46
6. Nina Balycheva	SOV	31:22.93
7. Marlies Rostock	GDR	31:28.79
8. Veronika Hesse (Schmidt)	GDR	31:29.14

The East German propaganda apparatus broke down somewhat in the case of Barbara Petzold, who was described in half the press releases as a medical student and in the other half as a law student. Either way, she told the press that training and competing left her little time for her studies.

20 KILOMETERS

This event will be held for the first time in 1984.

4×5-KILOMETER RELAY

1924–1952 not held

1956 Cortina T: 10, N: 10, D: 2.1.

3×5-Kilometer

1. FIN (Sirkka Polkunen, Mirja Hietamies, Siira Rantanen)   1:09:01.0

2. SOV (Lyubov Kozyreva, Alevtina Kolchina, Radya 1:09:28.0
        Eroshina)

3. SWE (Irma Johansson, Anna-Lisa Eriksson, Sonja 1:09.48.0
        Edström)

4. NOR (Kjellfrig Brusveen, Gina Regland, Rakel 1:10.50.0
        Wahl)

5. POL (Maria Gąsienica-Bukowa, Józefa Pęksa, Zo- 1:13.20.0
        fia Krzeptowska)

6. CZE (Eva Benešová, Libuse Patocková, Eva 1:14.19.0
        Lauermanová)

7. GDR/ (Elfriede Uhlig, Else Ammann, Sonnhilde 1:15.33.0
   GER Hausschild)

8. ITA (Fides Romanin, Rita Bottero, Ildegarda Taf- 1:16.11.0
        fra)

Rantanen of Finland took off six seconds behind Eroshina, passed her, lost the lead, then passed her again to win by 100 yards.

1960 Squaw Valley T: 5, N: 5, D: 2.26.
3x5-Kilometer

1. SWE (Irma Johansson, Britt Strandberg, Sonja 1:04:21.4
        Ruthström)

2. SOV (Radya Eroshina, Maria Gusakova, Lyubov 1:05:02.6
        Baranova [Kosyreva])

3. FIN (Siira Rantanen, Eeva Ruoppa, Toini Pöysti) 1:06:27.5

4. POL (Stefania Biegun, Helena Gąsienica-Daniel, 1:07:24.6
        Józefa Pęksa-Czerniawska)

5. GDR/ (Rita Czech-Blasl, Renate Borges, Sonnhilde 1:09:25.7
   GER Kallus)

On the first leg, Radya Eroshina fell and broke one of her skis. She picked up a replacement, but lost over a minute, a delay which cost the U.S.S.R. the gold medal. The Soviets lodged a protest, claiming that Irma Johansson of Sweden had cut in front of Eroshina and caused her to fall. After viewing films of the race, the U.S.S.R. withdrew their protest.

1964 Innsbruck–Seefeld T: 8, N: 8, D: 2.7.
3x5-Kilometer

1. SOV (Alevtina Kolchina, Edokia Mekshilo, Claudia 59:20.2
        Boyarskikh)

2. SWE (Barbro Martinsson, Britt Strandberg, Toini 1:01:27.0
        Gustafsson)

3. FIN (Senja Pusula, Toini Pöysti, Mirja Lehtonen) 1:02:45.1

4. GER (Christine Nestler, Rita Czech-Blasl, Renate 1:04:29.9
        Dannhauser)

5. BUL (Rosa Dimova, Nadezhda Vasileva, Krastana 1:06:40.4
        Stoeva)

6. CZE (Jarmila Skodová, Eva Brizová, Eva Paulu- 1:08.42.8
        sová)

7. POL (Teresa Trzebunia, Czeslawa Stopka, Ste- 1:08.55.4
        fania Biegun)

8. HUN (Éva Blazs, Mária Tarnai, Ference Hemrik) 1:10:16.3

1968 Grenoble–Autrans T: 8, N: 8, D: 2.16.
3x5-Kilometer

1. NOR (Inger Aufles, Babben Damon-Enger, Berit 57:30.0
        Mördre)

2. SWE (Britt Strandberg, Toini Gustafsson, Barbro 57:51.0
        Martinsson)

3. SOV (Alevtina Kolchina, Rita Achkina, Galina Kula- 58:13.6
        kova)

4. FIN (Senja Pusula, Marjatta Olkkonen, Marjatta 58:45.1
        Kajosmaa)

5. POL (Weronika Budny, Józefa Pęksa-Czerniaw- 59:04.7
        ska, Stefania Biegun)

6. GDR (Renate Köhler, Gudrun Schmidt, Christine 59:33.9
        Nestler)

7. GER (Michaela Endler, Barbara Barthel, Monika 1:01:49.3
        Mrklas)

8. BUL (Pandeva Velitska, Nadezhda Vasileva, Szve- 1:05:35.7
        tana Sotirova)

1972 Sapporo–Makomanai T: 11, N: 11, D: 2.12.
3x5-Kilometer

1. SOV (Lyubov Moukhatcheva, Alevtina Olunina, Ga- 48:46.15
        lina Kulakova)

2. FIN (Helena Takalo, Hilkka Kuntola, Marjatta Ka- 49:19.37
        josmaa)

3. NOR (Inger Aufles, Aslaug Dahl, Berit Mördre-Lam- 49:51.49
        medal)

4. GER (Monika Mrklas, Ingrid Rothfuss, Michaela 50:25.61
        Enler)

5. GDR (Gabriele Haupt, Renate Fischer, Anni Unger) 50:28.45

6. CZE (Alena Bartušová, Helena Šikolová, Milena 51:16.16
        Cillerová)

7. POL (Anna Duraj, Józefa Chromik, Weronika 51:49.13
        Budny)

8. SWE (Meeri Bodelid, Eva Ohlsson, Birgitta Lindq- 51:51.84
        vist)

1976 Innsbruck–Seefeld T: 9, N: 9, D: 2.12.

1. SOV (Nina Baldycheva, Zinaida Amosova, Raisa 1:07:49.75
        Smetanina, Galina Kulakova)

2. FIN (Liisa Suihkonen, Marjatta Kajosmaa, Hilkka 1:08:36.57
        Kuntola, Helena Takalo)

3. GDR (Monika Debertshäuser, Sigrun Krause, Bar- 1:09:57.95
        bara Petzold, Veronika Schmidt)

4. SWE (Lena Carlzon, Görel Partapuoli, Marie Jo- 1:10:14.68
        hansson, Eva Olsson)

5. NOR (Berit Kvello, Marit Myrmael, Berit Jo- 1:11:09.08
        hannessen, Grete Kummen)

6. CZE (Hana Pasiárová, Gabriela Sekajová, Alena 1:11:27.83
        Bartosová, Blanka Paulu)

7. CAN (Shirley Firth, Joan Groothuysen, Susan 1:14:02.72
        Holloway, Sharon Firth)

8. POL (Anna Pawlusiak, Anna Gębala-Duraj, Maria 1:14:13.40
        Trebunia, Wladyslawa Majerczyk)

1980 Lake Placid T: 8, N: 8, D: 2.21.

1. GDR (Marlies Rostock, Carola Anding, Veronika 1:02:11.10
   Hesse [Schmidt], Barbara Petzold)
2. SOV (Nina Baldycheva, Nina Rocheva, Galina 1:03:18.3
   Kulakova, Raisa Smetanina)
3. NOR (Brit Pettersen, Anette Böe, Marit Myrmael, 1:04:13.50
   Berit Aunli)
4. CZE (Dagmar Paleckova, Gabriela Svobodova, 1:04:31.39
   Blanka Paulu, Kvetoslava Jeriova)
5. FIN (Marja Auroma, Marja-Liis Hämäläinen, Hel- 1:04:41.28
   ena Takalo, Hilkka Riihivuori [Kuntola])
6. SWE (Marie Johansson, Karin Lamberg, Eva Ols- 1:05:16.32
   son, Lena Carlzon-Lundbäck)
7. USA (Alison Owen-Spencer, Beth Paxson, Leslie 1:06:55.41
   Bancroft, Margaret Spencer)
8. CAN (Angela Schmidt, Shirley Firth, Esther Miller, 1:07:45.75
   Joan Groothuysen)

The U.S.S.R.'s second-place finish gave Kulakova her eighth Olympic medal—four gold, two silver, and two bronze. Smetanina brought her total to five—three gold and two silver.